P9-CQU-095

PAGE 52 ON THE ROAD

YOUR COMPLETE DESTINATION GUIDE
In-depth reviews, detailed listings
and insider tips

Kaua'i
p462

Ni'ihau
p460

O'ahu
p54

Moloka'i
p428

Lana'i
p412

Maui
p304

Kaho'olawe
p410

Hawai'i
the Big
Island
p165

PAGE 627 SURVIVAL GUIDE

VITAL PRACTICAL INFORMATION TO
HELP YOU HAVE A SMOOTH TRIP

Directory A–Z 628
Transportation 637
Health 642
Glossary 644
Index 649
Map Legend 662

Transportation

THIS EDITION WRITTEN AND RESEARCHED BY

Sara Benson,

Amy C Balfour, Glenda Bendure, E Clark Carroll, Ned Friary, Conner Gorry,

Ryan Ver Berkmoes, Luci Yamamoto

❯ Hawaii

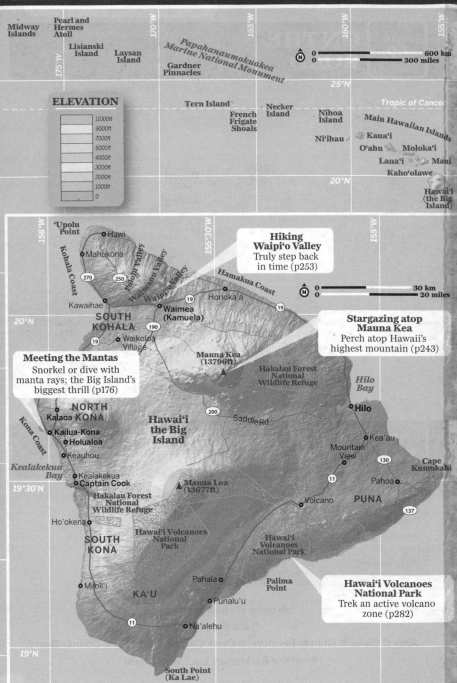

ELEVATION

11000ft
9000ft
7000ft
5000ft
4000ft
3000ft
2000ft
1000ft
0

Midway Islands

Pearl and Hermes Atoll

Lisianski Island

Laysan Island

Papahanaumokuakea Marine National Monument

Gardner Pinnacles

0 — 600 km
0 — 300 miles

25°N

Tern Island

French Frigate Shoals

Necker Island

Nihoa Island

Tropic of Cancer

Main Hawaiian Islands

Ni'ihau

Kaua'i

O'ahu   Moloka'i

Lana'i   Maui

Kaho'olawe

20°N

Hawai'i (the Big Island)

'Upolu Point

Hawi

Mahukona

Kohala Coast

270   250

Pololu Valley

Waimanu Valley

Waipi'o Valley

Hamakua Coast

Honoka'a

Kawaihae

19

Waimea (Kamuela)

Hiking Waipi'o Valley
Truly step back in time (p253)

0 — 30 km
0 — 20 miles

SOUTH KOHALA

190

Waikoloa Village

19

Mauna Kea (13796ft)

Hakalau Forest National Wildlife Refuge

Stargazing atop Mauna Kea
Perch atop Hawaii's highest mountain (p243)

Hilo Bay

Meeting the Mantas
Snorkel or dive with manta rays; the Big Island's biggest thrill (p176)

NORTH KONA

Kalaoa

Kailua-Kona

Holualoa

Keauhou

Kona Coast

Hawai'i the Big Island

200

Saddle Rd

Hilo

Kea'au

Mountain View

130

Cape Kumukahi

Kealakekua Bay

Kealakekua

Captain Cook

19°30'N

Hakalau Forest National Wildlife Refuge

Ho'okena

Mauna Loa (13677ft)

11

Pahoa

PUNA

Volcano

137

SOUTH KONA

Hawai'i Volcanoes National Park

Hawai'i Volcanoes National Park

Palima Point

Hawai'i Volcanoes National Park
Trek an active volcano zone (p282)

Miloli'i

KA'U

Pahala

Punalu'u

11

Na'alehu

19°N

South Point (Ka Lae)

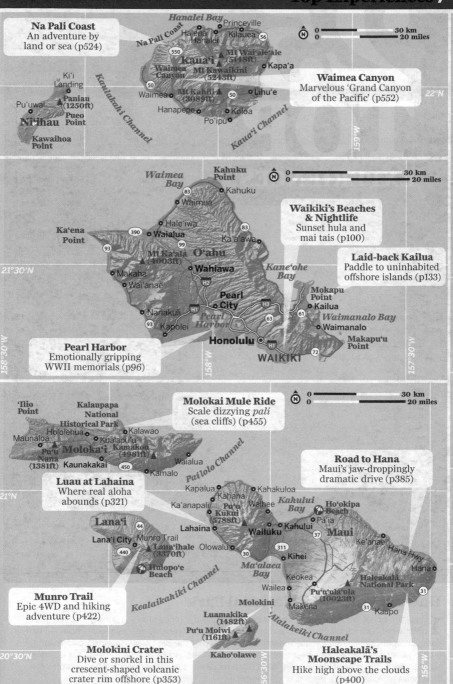

Na Pali Coast
An adventure by
land or sea (p524)

Waimea Canyon
Marvelous 'Grand Canyon
of the Pacific' (p552)

**Waikiki's Beaches
& Nightlife**
Sunset hula and
mai tais (p100)

Laid-back Kailua
Paddle to uninhabited
offshore islands (p133)

Pearl Harbor
Emotionally gripping
WWII memorials (p96)

Molokai Mule Ride
Scale dizzying *pali*
(sea cliffs) (p455)

Road to Hana
Maui's jaw-droppingly
dramatic drive (p385)

Luau at Lahaina
Where real aloha
abounds (p321)

Munro Trail
Epic 4WD and hiking
adventure (p422)

Molokini Crater
Dive or snorkel in this
crescent-shaped volcanic
crater rim offshore (p353)

**Haleakalā's
Moonscape Trails**
Hike high above the clouds
(p400)

25 TOP EXPERIENCES

Hawai'i Volcanoes National Park

1 Pack the boots, friends – you'll want them to explore the miles of trails running through this unique national park (p282). Crossing lava flows, old and new, while steam vents huff and native honeycreepers sing in rain forested oases, it's obvious why the Big Island is a world-class hiking destination. Day hikes, lava-tube adventures and backcountry treks (including to the summit of mighty Mauna Loa, p291) are hallmarks here. What the park doesn't usually offer is live lava action – for that, head to Puna (p292). Halema'uma'u Crater

Kaua'i's Na Pali Coast

2 The Na Pali Coast (p524), which can be experienced by land, sea or air, should head everyone's Kaua'i to-do list. Make a gentle oceanic journey by boat, with motors or sails or, for true sea adventure, pit your paddle and kayak against the elements: wind, swell, and sunshine. For hikers, Ke'e Beach is the entry point for the rugged 11-mile long Kalalau Trail. This trek will transport you to a place distant and distinct from all others, with verdant cliffs soaring above a sloping valley abundant with fruit trees, bearded hippies and solace seekers.

Waikiki's Beaches & Nightlife

3 Waikiki (p99) is back, baby! Hawaii's most famous beach resort may still be a haven for tacky plastic lei, coconut-shell bikini tops and motorized hip-shaking hula dolls, but real aloha has returned to this prototypical paradise. By day beachboys surf the legendary waves. At sunset tiki torches are lit and the conch shell blown at Kuhio Beach Park (p101), where hula dancers sway to ancient and modern rhythms nightly at beachfront resort hotels, bars and even shopping malls and famous island musicians strum slack-key guitars and ukuleles.

Road to Hana

4 Ready for an adventure? Of all the jaw-droppingly dramatic drives in Hawaii, this is the Big Kahuna. A roller coaster of a ride, the Hana Hwy (p385) winds down into jungly valleys and back up towering cliffs, curling around 600 twists and turns along the way. Fifty-four one-lane bridges cross nearly as many waterfalls – some eye-popping torrents, others so gentle they beg a dip. But the ride's only half the thrill. Get out and swim in a Zen -like pool, hike a ginger-scented trail and explore the wonders along the way. Three Bears Falls

Haleakalā's Moonscape Trails

5 You might think you're walking on the moon as you wind down into the belly of Haleakalā (p403). First thing you notice is how eerily quiet everything is; the only sound is the crunching of loose volcanic cinders beneath your feet. The path descends gently into an unearthly world, a landscape of stark lava and ever-changing clouds. Russet-colored cinder cones rise from the crater floor. Looking back toward the summit, eyes focused on the steep crater walls, it's impossible not to be awed by the raw beauty. Sliding Sands Trail

JOHN ELK III / LONELY PLANET IMAGES ©

ANN CECIL / LONELY PLANET IMAGES ©

Laid-back Kailua

6 If Waikiki's impersonal, high-rise condoville scene isn't for you, hop over the *pali* (mountains) from Honolulu to O'ahu's Windward Coast. Kailua Bay (p134) has awesome scenery, with offshore islands that practically beg you to jump in the ocean or launch your kayak and paddle over for a little sunbathing and snorkeling. Kailua's beaches also offer wicked windsurfing and kitesurfing. And at the end of the day, you can retreat to your own little beachfront cottage. Now that's bliss.

CLAY M. ROGERS / ALAMY

Surfing

7 Even if you never set foot on a board, there's no denying the influence of surfing on all aspects of island life, from fashion to slang. When giant rollers come crashing in, head to the North Shore for a glimpse of Hawaii's rock stars of the ocean (p146). Forget having to pull out a camera lens larger then a howitzer – you can practically look the surfers in the eye as they paddle into monster surf here. Or experience the adrenaline rush for yourself by learning to ride da kine (the best kind of) waves. Hang loose, brah!

Pearl Harbor

8 Hawaii's active US military bases, particularly on O'ahu, evidence its continued strategic importance in the Pacific. For the most dramatic reminder of why, visit the USS Arizona Memorial (p96), a somber site commemorating the Pearl Harbor attack and its tragic cost in human lives. Nearby, military history buffs can clamber inside a WWII submarine, tour the historic hangars of the ever-expanding Pacific Aviation Museum, and stand proudly on the decks of the 'Mighty Mo' battleship, where imperial Japan surrendered in 1945. USS Arizona Memorial

ANN CECIL / LONELY PLANET IMAGES ©

REINHARD DIRSCHERL / ALAMY

Molokini Crater

9 Hawaiian legend says that Molokini (p353) was a beautiful woman turned to stone by a jealous Pele, goddess of fire and volcanoes. Today Molokini is the stuff of legends among divers and snorkelers. The crescent-shaped rock, about three miles from the South Maui coast, is the rim of a volcanic crater. The shallow waters cradled within are a hospitable spot for coral and a calling card for more than 250 fish species. For an iconic Hawaii dive, this is the place.

Hawaii's Cuisine

10 Forget about pineapple upside-down cake and tiki drinks. Hawaii provides a multicultural taste explosion, influenced by the Pacific Rim but rooted in the islands' natural bounty. The first Polynesians brought nourishing staples, such as *kalo* (taro), *ko* (sugarcane) and *niu* (coconut). Plantation immigrants from East and West added global flavors to the mix – Japanese rice, Chinese noodles, Portuguese sweet bread. Over time all of these flavors fused to become simply 'local' (p592). So, be brave and eat everything in sight. It's all *'ono grinds* (good eats).

HAWAII TOURISM AUTHORITY

GREG ELMS / LONELY PLANET IMAGES ©

Ho'okipa Beach & Pa'ia

11 If you're on the pro -windsurfing circuit, meet your buddies at Ho'okipa Beach Park (p371). The rest of us can grab a voyeur's seat on the adjacent hillside and watch the death-defying action. Want the ultimate North Shore experience? Follow Ho'okipa's windsurfing theatrics by immersing yourself in the funky vibe of nearby Pa'ia. Maui's hippest burg, hang-loose Pa'ia will woo you with artsy shops, cool surfer haunts and the island's hottest dinner scene. Ah, the choices – perhaps fresh catch at Maui's top fish-house or savory duck crepes in a jazzy cafe.

Kealakekua Bay

12 Whether you hike down, kayak across, or slide from a catamaran into this blue gem, the underwater wonder-world of Kealakekua Bay (p204) is worth the trip. In depths akin to your average kiddie pool, tangs, Moorish Idols, unicornfish and triggerfish teem around the historic shores where Captain Cook met his demise. Playful spinner dolphins also habitually rest in this bay, eliciting gasps of delight from visitors, but groans of dread from wildlife conservationists as increased traffic and use threatens their habitat. New kayak-landing regulations are now in effect (p205).

Hiking Waipi'o Valley

13 A fertile, emerald valley, threaded with waterfalls and framed by a black-sand beach: they don't call Waipi'o (p252) the Valley of Kings for nothing. Sure you can linger at the lookout with the rest of the drive-by tourists, but head on down into the valley itself for the real deal: crashing surf, pounding waterfalls and some of the state's most Hawaiian vibe. With a bit of planning (and good weather), you can be among the few hiking into magical Waimanu (p254), the next valley over.

Sunset & Sunrise

14 Just as the sun, wind, moon and stars once guided ancient Polynesian wayfarers, the rhythms of nature still govern island life today. Even if you've just recently stepped off a plane, ignore the jet lag and wake up early to catch sunrise breaking over the beach. At day's end, stick your toes in the sand once again as the sun rebounds back into the sea. For an extra thrill, capture these panoramas from atop an ancient volcanic peak, such as Maui's Haleakalā (p404), aka House of the Sun. Lana'i from atop Mt Haleakalā

Molokai Mule Ride

15 Your sure-footed steed may seem mulish, but that's just genetic. On the Molokai Mule Ride (p455), from a lofty perch more than 1600ft above Moloka'i's Kalaupapa Peninsula, you'll ride down a steep trail with a dizzying number of switchbacks; the views of the Kalaupapa National Historical Park below are spectacular. At the bottom you'll learn the dramatic tales of Hawaii's former colony for people with leprosy. It's eerie and isolated, but you'll take heart from the tales of people who lived here, including Father Damien, America's first saint. Then your mule will haul you back up to the top.

PETER HENDRIE / LONELY PLANET IMAGES ©

Halawa Valley

16 Moloka'i's Halawa Valley (p446) seems to be from another time. Enjoying end-of-the-road isolation, which Moloka'i residents guard jealously, and stunningly gorgeous scenery, this important settlement in pre-contact Moloka'i had a population of more than 1000 and a complex irrigation system watering over 700 taro patches. It's uninhabited and almost untouched today; you can hike with a guide through dense tropical forest, where waterfalls and wildflowers vie for your attention. Explore a lost part of a Hawaii you probably didn't think still existed.

Farmers Markets

17 Want to meet the locals? Just find the nearest farmers market (p600). Besides being places to pick up the islands' very freshest papaya, pineapples, macadamia nuts, homegrown honey and more, Hawaii's farmers markets are also celebrations of community. You might meet a traditional *kahuna lapa'au* (healer) extolling the virtues of the noni (Indian mulberry) plant; tipple a coconut cup full of a mildly intoxicating brew made from 'awa (kava); or find a genuine *lauhala* (pandanus leaf) woven hat. If you're craving island-style fun and cultural authenticity, start here.

GREG ELMS / LONELY PLANET IMAGES ©

The Munro Trail

18 The Munro Trail (p422), an exhilarating 12-mile adventure, follows a surviving forest across the hills above Lana'i's one and only town. Passing through eucalyptus groves and otherworldly Norfolk Island pines, the trail was once a Hawaiian footpath and a place of taro farms, which drew on the frequent rainfall. On a clear day along the route you can see all of the inhabited Hawaii islands except for distant Kaua'i and Ni'ihau. Just listening to the myriad birdcalls will have you singing your own song.

KARL LEHMANN / LONELY PLANET IMAGES ©

Feeling the Aloha

19 Real aloha (spirit of loving kindness) is a philosophy of life in these islands. You'll be immersed in it from the moment you step off the plane and don a lei at the airport. From your hotel's front-desk staff asking you at check-in if you'd like to borrow an umbrella and head straight to the beach, to driving the islands' highways, where local drivers rarely honk, preferring to wave the friendly shaka sign and let each other pass instead – such genuine friendliness is contagious.

CHRIS MELLOR / LONELY PLANET IMAGES ©

ANN CECIL / LONELY PLANET IMAGES ©

Waimea Canyon

20 Formed by millions of years of erosion and the collapse of the volcano that formed Kaua'i, the Grand Canyon of the Pacific (p552) stretches 10 miles long, 1 mile wide and more than 3600ft deep. Waimea Canyon Lookout (p553) provides panoramic views of rugged cliffs, crested buttes and deep valley gorges. While the lookout is easily accessible from Waimea Canyon Dr, hiking trails allow the adventurous a chance to delve to the canyon floor and survey its interior, satisfying all curiosities – or creating even more.

Hulopo'e Beach

21 The free public park (p423) at the main beach on company-run Lana'i is maintained by the same gardeners who manicure the Four Seasons resorts. So, predictably, it's lovely. The postcard-perfect crescent of curving white-sand is enjoyed by all, from locals taking the kids for a swim, to tourists on day trips from Maui; many a visitor has ended up losing track of time here. Be sure to take a break from lounging on the sand and take advantage of the amazing snorkeling and walks to ancient Hawaiian sites.

Hanalei Bay

22 Voted nicest beach in the USA, many times over, this crescent-shaped bay (p513) will suit both passive and active beach-goers. Surfers can charge a slew of waves while onlookers lounge on or amble along the 2 miles of glorious sandy shore. Surf lessons are available near the pier, and most afternoons see locals and visitors alike firing up the BBQ, cracking open a brew and humbly watching the daylight fade.

Luau at Lahaina

23 They had us at aloha, but who are we to refuse the cold mai tai and sweet-smelling lei that follow? At Maui's most authentic luau (p321), Hawaiian history, culture and culinary prowess are the focus, presented like a gift from the most hospitable of hosts. Highlights? The unearthing of the imu-cooked pig, the dancing of the hula kahiko and, of course, the savoring of the feast – a table-topping spread of hearty salads, fresh fish and grilled and roasted meats. But it's the sense of shared community that will linger longest in your memory.

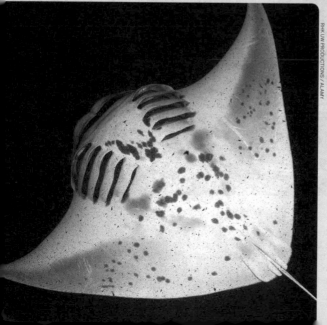

Meeting the Mantas

24 Anyone who has hovered over a giant ray, its 13ft span blocking out the dive lights and its sandpaper belly nearly brushing against yours, can tell you this is one of the number-one experiences of any Hawaii trip. Jumping off the boat in the dark of night (p229) is phenomenal enough, but once below the surface the experience is downright transcendental. Don't worry if you don't dive – the underwater tango is an even closer encounter for snorkelers. Bring your own (powerful) dive light and underwater camera – your boat mates will thank you.

25 Star light, star bright, the first star I see tonight...whoops, scratch that. Up here, where the night skies are brighter than almost anywhere on Earth, stars – even galaxies – sear the night white, and choosing the first is near impossible. Not to worry though: with the telescopes (free!) set up each night for visitors to browse the night skies in all their celestial glory (p245), you don't have to choose just one. Get up here by sunset for a heavenly double feature. Real mavericks opt for sunrise. Are you up for it?!

welcome to Hawaii

Bountiful Beauty

The natural beauty of these scattered islands in the cobalt blue Pacific Ocean is heavenly, without the need for any tourist-brochure embellishment. And, as tropical getaways go, Hawaii couldn't be easier or more worth the trip. Visiting these Polynesian islands is not always cheap, and they're certainly a long way from anywhere, but whether you're after an urban jungle or a cloud forest, a snowy mountain or a nude beach, you can find what you're looking for here. Sunrises and sunsets are so spectacular that they're cause for celebration all by themselves, while after-dark stargazing from Hawaii's volcano summits is unparalleled.

Play Outdoors

Just like in days of old, life in Hawaii is lived outdoors. Whether it's surfing, swimming, fishing or picnicking with the entire *'ohana* (family), encounters with nature are infused with the Hawaiian sensibilities of *aloha 'aina* and *malama 'aina* – love and care for the land. For *malihini* (newcomers, visitors), to appreciate Hawaii's infinitely varied landscapes and seascapes is to experience their ancient *mana* (spiritual power).

Start by hiking across ancient lava flows, up craggy volcanic peaks and down fluted *pali* (sea cliffs). Learn to surf, the ancient Hawaiian sport of 'wave sliding,' then snorkel or dive with rainbow-colored schools of

It's easy to see why Hawaii has become synonymous with paradise. Just look around at the sugary beaches, Technicolor coral reefs and volcanoes ready for adventure and cherished by local traditions.

(below) Hula skirts at T&L Muumuu Factory, Honolulu (p94)
(left) Kahanamoku Beach, Waikiki (p100)

tropical fish, giant manta rays and endangered sea turtles. You can even kayak to your own deserted offshore island, or hop aboard a whale-watching cruise in winter. Thirsty for even more adventures? Back on land, crawl through lava tubes, gallop along *paniolo* (Hawaiian cowboy) ranch trails and zipline through forest canopies.

Kaleidoscopic Culture

Floating all by itself in the middle of the Pacific Ocean, Hawaii maintains its own sense of self apart from the US mainland. Spam, shave ice, surfing, ukulele, hula, pidgin, rubbah slippah – these are just some of the touchstones of everyday life in the islands. Everything here is easygoing, low-key and casual, bursting with genuine aloha and fun. You'll feel equally welcome whether you're a surf bum, solo backpacker or a big family with rambunctious kids tagging along.

Like O'ahu-born President Barack Obama, Hawaii is proud of its multicultural heritage; descendents of Native Hawaiians, European and Asian plantation immigrants and US missionary families mix and mingle. What's most remarkable about contemporary island society is that multiculturalism is the rule, not the exception. Boisterous year-round arts and cultural festivals keep the islands' diverse traditions alive, from ancient sacred hula and outrigger canoe races to Japanese *taiko* drumming and modern-day surf championships.

need to know

When to Go

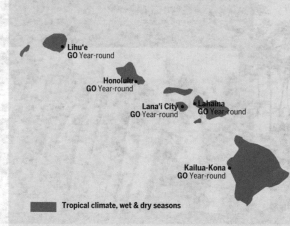

Lihu'e
GO Year-round

Honolulu
GO Year-round

Lana'i City
GO Year-round

Lahaina
GO Year-round

Kailua-Kona
GO Year-round

Tropical climate, wet & dry seasons

High Season
(Dec–Apr & Jun–Aug)

» Accommodation prices up 50–100%

» Christmas to New Year's, and Easter are more expensive and busier

» Winter is slightly wetter (prime time for whale watching); summer is hotter

Shoulder
(May & Sep)

» Crowds and prices drop slightly between schools' spring break and summer vacation

» Temperatures remain mild, with mostly sunny cloudless days, some scattered showers

Low Season
(Oct–Nov)

» Fewest crowds, accommodation rates drop statewide (except possibly Waikiki)

» Weather is dry, hot and extremely humid

Your Daily Budget

Budget less than

$100

» Dorm beds: $20–30

» Farmers markets and plate lunches for cheap eats

» Hit the beaches and use public transportation instead of renting a car

Midrange

$100– $250

» Double room in a midrange hotel or B&B: $120–200

» Rental car from $35/150 per day/week, excluding insurance and gas

Top End over

$250

» Resort hotel room or one-bedroom condo rental: over $200

» Three-course meal with a cocktail in top restaurant: $75

Money

» ATMs widely available. Credit cards widely accepted; required for reservations (eg hotels, car rentals). Traveler's checks (US dollars) sometimes accepted. Tipping customary.

Visas

» Generally not required for citizens of Visa Waiver Program (VWP) countries with ESTA approval (apply online at least 72 hours in advance); see p634.

Cell Phones

» Cell-phone coverage can be spotty in non-urban areas. The only foreign phones that will work are GSM multiband models; buy prepaid SIM cards locally.

Driving

» Drive on the right; steering wheel is on the left side of the car; seatbelts required. Avoid weekday rush hours (usually 7am to 9:30am and 3:30pm to 6:30pm).

Websites

» **Hawaii Visitors and Convention Bureau** (www.gohawaii.com) Official tourist site; multilingual planning guides.

» **Honolulu Star-Advertiser** (www .staradvertiser.com) State's biggest daily newspaper.

» **Lonely Planet** (www .lonelyplanet.com/ hawaii) Destination info, hotel bookings, travelers' forums and more.

» **Hawaii on TV** (http://hawaiiontv .com) Award-winning travel videos.

» **Hawaii Magazine** (www.hawaiimagazine .com) All-islands news, fun features, travel tips and deals.

Exchange Rates

Australia	A$1	$0.99
Canada	C$1	$1.02
China	Y10	$1.52
Euro zone	€1	$1.40
Japan	¥100	$1.23
New Zealand	NZ$1	$0.73
UK	£1	$1.61

For current exchange rates see www.xe.com.

Important Numbers

Hawaii has only one area code: ☑808, which is not used when making local calls, but must be used when calling between islands. For toll-free numbers all 10 digits must be dialled; dial ☑1 before any long-distance or toll-free call.

Country code	1
International dialing code	011
Operator	0
Emergency(ambulance, fire & police)	911
Directory assistance	411

Arriving in Hawaii

» **Honolulu International Airport** (HNL; see p58)

Car 25 to 45 minutes' drive to Waikiki via Nimitz Hwy or H-1 Fwy

Taxis Metered, usually $35 to $45 to Waikiki (more during rush hour), plus 35¢ per bag

Door-to-door shuttles $9/15 one way/round-trip to Waikiki hotels; operate 24 hours (every 20 to 60 minutes)

Buses TheBus 19 or 20 to Waikiki ($2.50) every 20 minutes from 6am to 11pm daily (large baggage prohibited)

Local Transportation

The majority of interisland travel is by plane, although a limited number of boats connect Maui with Lana'i and Moloka'i. Renting a car is usually necessary if you want the freedom to really explore; on Hawai'i the Big Island and Lana'i, a 4WD vehicle may come in handy for off-the-beaten-path adventures.

Public buses run around the four largest main islands: O'ahu, Maui, the Big Island and Kaua'i, but often infrequent bus schedules and routes are designed to serve commuters, not tourists. You'll find it time-consuming and difficult to get around relying only on public transportation, except on O'ahu, where TheBus route network is extensive. For more transportation tips, see p638.

if you like...

Beaches

Think of Hawaii, and you're instantly dreaming about golden sands backed by giant surf, bronzed surfer bods and palm trees blowing in tropical breezes, right? The quintessential island lifestyle is all about the beach, it's true. With six main islands and hundreds of miles of coastline, you'll be spoiled for choice in Hawaii, whether you want to surf, go whale watching or just lie around on the sand.

Waikiki Learn to surf, jump aboard a sunset 'booze cruise' and catch a hula show under the stars on O'ahu (p100)

Ho'okipa Beach Near Pa'ia on Maui, this is a mecca for pro windsurfers and surfers – and awed spectators, too (p371)

Kauna'oa Bay Aka Mauna Kea Beach is the Big Island's Hollywood-worthy crescent of white sand (p225)

Hulopo'e Beach By Lana'i's Manele Bay, it's a sun-kissed playground for snorkelers (p423)

Hanalei Bay Arguably Kaua'i's most postcard-perfect beaches, it offers something for everyone (p513)

Waterfalls & Swimming Holes

Ready to wade through the mud, step over slippery tree roots and tread trails paved with roly-poly kukui nuts, all to swim in a crystal-clear pool of water under a rainforest cascade? We thought so. Just be careful of falling rocks and flash floods (see p633).

Oheo Gulch In Haleakalā National Park, Maui's best-known series of waterfalls and natural pools tumble down into the sea (p408)

Wailua Falls You might recognize Kaua'i's famous twin cascades from the opening scenes of TV's *Fantasy Island* (p470)

Manoa Falls A short family-friendly hike in O'ahu's shady Ko'olau Range above downtown Honolulu – no swimming, sorry! (p77)

Rainbow Falls Outside Hilo on the Big Island, visit these misty falls in the early morning to catch their namesake (p263)

Waipi'o & Waimanu Valleys Earn Hawai'i's most epic waterfall views after some rugged hiking (p252)

Hiking & Backpacking

You're not a pro surfer or PADI-certified scuba diver? No worries, brah. Hawaii's islands have as many adventures to offer landlubbers as water babies. Hikers and backpackers can choose among scores of foot trails, from easy waterfall and botanical garden strolls to multiday volcano treks.

Haleakalā National Park Cloud forest walks and volcano summit trails through Maui's high-altitude wilderness, where cozy 1930s cabins can be rented (p403)

Kalalau Trail Hawaii's best-known backpacking route traces the fluted cliffs and stream-cut valleys of Kaua'i's jewel-like Na Pali Coast (p525)

Hawai'i Volcanoes National Park For thrills, nothing beats trekking through the wonderland ruled by Pele, goddess of fire and volcanoes (p288)

Kalaupapa Peninsula Rating sky-high for scenery, snake down the cliffs to Moloka'i's historic leprosy settlement, now a national historic park (p453)

Makiki Forest Recreation Area Walk into Honolulu's windblown Ko'olau Range (p76)

» Road to Hana (p385), Maui.

Scenic Drives

Are you ready to roll? The Hawaii Islands may be small, but they possess a surprising number of scenic drives: up volcano summits, into rain forests, over high *pali* (cliffs) and through pastoral *paniolo* (cowboy) country.

Road to Hana Curving down Maui's lushest coast, this roller-coaster route passes dozens of waterfalls and crosses 54 stone bridges (p385)

Haleakalā Crater Rd A drive up Maui's biggest volcano measures 37 miles from sea to summit, boasting the steepest elevation gain of any road in the world (p408)

Oʻahu's Windward Coast Leave behind the urban jungles of Honolulu and Waikiki and get lost on the island's rural, wilder side (p129)

Chain of Craters Rd Drop almost 4000ft through the Big Island's active volcano zone where lava may still be flowing into the sea (p285)

Munro Trail Rent a jeep (or grab a mountain bike) to challenge Lanaʻi's epic red-dirt 4WD route (p422)

Small Towns

For a real taste of everyday life in Hawaii, forget big-name beach resorts and spend a day (or a week) immersing yourself in off-the-beaten-path places where the pace of life is slower, the smiles are more genuinely friendly and the aloha overflows.

Hana When you're ready to un-plug and truly get away from it all, Maui's most remote hamlet beckons (p392)

Hilo Not even a tsunami could keep this old-school Big Island bayside town down for long (p260)

Haleʻiwa Surf culture meets laid-back rural life in Oʻahu's North Shore hub (p152)

Holualoa A Hawaiʻi heritage village that time has passed by, tucked among Kona's mountain-side coffee fields (p192)

Hanapepe Calling itself Kauaʻi's 'biggest little town,' this valley has been revitalized as an arts center (p543)

Kaunakakai A Native Hawaiian stronghold on Molokaʻi, this dusty, old-fashioned village has real heart (p435)

History

From Polynesian wayfar-ers and Native Hawaiian *aliʻi* (royalty) through early Christian missionaries, 19th-century sugar barons and plantation immigrants to the US military from WWII onward, Hawaii's story is often written on the land – if you know where to look.

USS Arizona Memorial Pay your respects to those who died in the Japanese attack on Oʻahu's Pearl Harbor of Decem-ber 8, 1941 (p96)

Puʻuhonua o Honaunau National Historical Park Gaze into the eyes of *kiʻi* (carved deity statues) at an ancient Hawaiian place of refuge on the Big Island (p207)

Lahaina Once a rowdy 19th-century whaling port and Christian mission, this West Maui harbor town still gives glimpses of its historic past (p310)

Moʻokini Luakini Heiau Visit a windswept Hawaiian temple, once used for human sacri-fices, and the birthplace of King Kamehameha I (p230)

Bishop Museum Learn about ancient and modern Hawaiian ways in Honolulu (p73)

GREG ELMS / LONELY PLANET IMAGES ©

» Making a braided lei (p610) of 'ohi'a lehua on Hawai'i the Big Island.

Festivals

There's always a party going on somewhere in the islands. From outrigger canoe races and ancient hula performed on the rim of an active volcano to film festivals and pro-surfing competitions, you definitely won't run out of excuses to extend your trip to Hawaii just a little bit longer.

Aloha Festivals September brings colorful celebrations of Hawaiian arts and culture on all the main islands, especially O'ahu (p25)

Merrie Monarch Festival On Easter Sunday, 'the Olympics of hula' happens in Hilo on the Big Island (p268)

Triple Crown of Surfing Gnarly waves, rip curls and giant swells bring out the pro action – and thousands of spectators – on O'ahu's North Shore (p153)

Kona Coffee Cultural Festival For anyone addicted to Hawai'i's richest, most potent brews (p180)

Lei Day May Day (May 1) sets the scene for fun-filled floral festivities statewide (p24)

Food & Drink

We dare you to not gain 10lb during your Hawaii vacation. Seriously, there are so many 'ono grinds (good eats) dished up around the islands that you might find yourself eating more than three times a day – and that's even before *pau hana* (happy hour) rolls around!

Mixed-plate lunches Asian and European immigrant cuisines mix with the indigenous flavors of the islands, traditionally served with macaroni salad and two-scoop rice

Loco moco The breakfast of champions: rice, fried egg and a hamburger patty doused in gravy

Crack seed Got a sweet tooth? Maybe a salty, sour and/ or spicy craving? Hawaii's Chinese-influenced dried-fruit candy snacks will satisfy

Poke Hawaii's version of a marinated sashimi salad

'Awa A traditional Polynesian brew made from the kava plant that's mildly intoxicating

Shave ice Nothing tastes better after a hot day at the beach

Arts & Crafts

Some Hawaiian art stretches back to the early days when the first Polynesian canoes washed up on these shores. Beginning in the 1970s, a Hawaiian cultural renaissance has made ancient arts and crafts flower once again, along with encouraging new contemporary expressions of island cultures.

Lei making Hawaii's most delicate art form is one that everyone can appreciate. Stop by Waikiki's Na Lima Hulu No'eau workshop to see gorgeous feather lei being handcrafted (p119)

Lauhala weaving Only a few artisans nowadays carry out this painstaking work by hand, such as at Kimura Lauhala Shop on the Big Island (p193)

Visual arts Every island has its bohemian gathering spots for artists, but the epicenter for the state's arts scene is Honolulu, with its museums and nouveau Chinatown gallery scene (p71)

month by month

1 **Aloha Festivals**, September

2 **Triple Crown of Surfing**, November

3 **Merrie Monarch Festival**, April

4 **Ironman World Championship**, October

5 **Hawaii International Film Festival**, October

January

Typically Hawaii's wettest month, January is nevertheless when peak tourist season gets into full swing, with snowbirds escaping winter elsewhere. The Martin Luther King Jr holiday, on the third Monday of the month, is particularly busy.

 Chinese New Year

On the second new moon after the winter solstice, usually between mid-January and mid-February, look for lion dances, firecrackers, street fairs and parades. Honolulu's celebration is the biggest, but Lahaina's (Maui) and Hilo's (Big Island) are notable, too.

February

Peak tourist season continues, with weekends around Valentine's Day (February 14) and President's Day (third Monday of February) usually booked solid at resorts. Winter storms bring more rainfall.

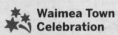 Waimea Town Celebration

For two action-packed days in mid-February, Waimea (Kaua'i) hosts more than 10,000 folks for the island's biggest festival (p547), celebrated with canoe and foot races, a rodeo, lei and ukulele contests, live music and much more.

Whale Day

Throughout the winter Maui celebrates its most famous visitors – migratory humpback whales – with a family-oriented slate of events, including a winter whale count and live entertainment and kids' activities on Whale Day (p357) in mid-February.

Waimea 'Ukulele & Slack Key Guitar Institute

On the Big Island, rural Waimea town hosts two nights of concerts (p237) with ukulele and slack key guitar legends, who also teach beginners' workshops and master classes over a long weekend in mid-February.

March

Another busy month to visit Hawaii, despite lingering rainfall. College students take a one- or two-week 'spring break' around Easter, in March or April.

Honolulu Festival

For three days in mid-March, this festival (p80) celebrates the harmony of Pacific Rim cultures. It's a unique blend of East Asia, Polynesia and more, with live music and dance performances and a craft fair, culminating in a grand parade followed by a fireworks show.

Prince Kuhio Day

All islands honor the March 26 birthday of Prince Kuhio Kalaniana'ole, the man who would've become king if Queen Lili'uokalani hadn't been overthrown and the kingdom annexed by the USA. Kaua'i holds a weeklong arts and cultural festival (p535) centered on Kuhio's birthplace.

April

As peak tourist season ends, Hawaii's resorts start to slow down after Easter and college students finish their 'spring break.' Rainstorms lessen, too.

☆ Merrie Monarch Festival

The Big Island's most famous festival (p268) starts on Easter Sunday in Hilo. A week-long celebration of Hawaiian arts and culture revolves around the Olympics of hula competitions, which draws top troupes from all islands, the US mainland and abroad.

✕ East Maui Taro Festival

On Maui, the rural town of Hana throws its biggest party (p394) for two weekend days in late April, with poi (fermented taro) making, a local arts-and-crafts fair, Hawaiian hula dancing and lots of island music.

✕ Waikiki Spam Jam

How much does Hawaii love Spam? Apparently, residents consume seven million cans a year. Waikiki's wacky one-day street festival (p108) in late April probably accounts for 10,000 all by itself, prepared hundreds of ways – that's *'ono grinds*!

May

Crowds thin and prices drop slightly in the shoulder season between spring break and summer vacation. Temperatures remain mild, with mostly sunny and cloudless days.

Hotels sell out for the Memorial Day holiday weekend.

✕ Maui Onion Festival

For a weekend in late April or early May, Maui's famously sweet onions inspire delicious events, appealing to gourmet and gourmand alike. Live music and pan-Polynesian hula shows happen at Ka'anapali's Whalers Village (p328).

★ Lei Day

Across Hawaii the ancient, beautiful tradition of lei making gets its own holiday on May 1. O'ahu crowns a lei queen Waikiki's Kap'iolani Park. On Kaua'i, Lihu'e holds a lei-making competition, while Hilo on the Big Island hosts lei demonstrations, hula dancing and more.

☆ Moloka'i Ka Hula Piko

According to Hawaiian oral history, Moloka'i is the birthplace of hula. On the third weekend in May, this three-day hula festival (p434) draws huge crowds to its sacred, traditional hula performances and Native Hawaiian *ho'olaule'a* (celebration).

June

Before summer vacation really gets going, visitors in early June can take advantage of warm, dry weather and discounts on accommodations and flights.

★ Pan-Pacific Festival

In Honolulu, this three-day weekend festival (p80) in early June combines family-friendly celebrations of Japanese, Hawaiian and South Pacific cultures, with hula dancing, *taiko* drumming, Hawaiian music, folk-art workshops, and a huge parade and block party in Waikiki.

★ King Kamehameha Day

On June 11, this state holiday is celebrated on all islands. Downtown Honolulu's statue of Kamehameha the Great is ceremoniously draped with lei, after which a parade and live music follows. The capital city's weekend King Kamehameha Hula Competition (p80) is one of Hawaii's biggest contests.

✕ Kapalua Wine & Food Festival

Hawaii's longest-running culinary extravaganza (p336) makes things festive for four days in late June at the Ritz-Carlton resort in West Maui. Show up for cooking demonstrations by Hawaii's hottest chefs and wine tastings with master sommeliers.

July

Temperatures rise, rain is scarce. School summer vacations and the July 4 holiday make this one of the busiest travel months. Book early and expect high prices.

★ Independence Day

Across the islands, Fourth of July celebrations inspire fireworks and fairs, but the most fun is had at the July 4 rodeos held in the *paniolo* (cowboy)-friendly towns of

Waimea (Kamuela; p237) on the Big Island and Makawao (p378) on Maui.

Pineapple Festival

In early July this festival (p417) celebrating Lana'i's special relationship with the pineapple is the island's main bash, featuring kid-friendly activities, live music and food. (Never mind that Lana'i no longer grows any of its own pineapples!)

Prince Lot Hula Festival

On the third Saturday in July, one of O'ahu's premier Hawaiian cultural festivals (p82) features noncompetitive hula performances in a garden setting at a former royal retreat, giving it a particularly graceful, traditional feeling.

Koloa Plantation Days Celebration

On Kauai's south shore, this nine-day festival (p528) in late July is a huge celebration of sugar-plantation heritage and island life. It's like a state fair, Hawaii-style, including a parade, rodeo, canoe race, live entertainment, historical walks and much more.

August

Families taking summer vacations keep things busy all around the islands. Sunny weather continues nearly everywhere, especially on the islands' leeward sides. Statehood Day is celebrated on the third Friday of the month.

Hawaiian International Billfish Tournament

Kailua-Kona, on the Big Island, is the epicenter of big-game fishing – particularly for Pacific blue marlin – and for more than 50 years this has been Hawaii's grand tournament (p180). It's accompanied by a week of festive entertainment in late July or early August.

September

After Labor Day weekend in early September, crowds melt away as beach resorts as students go back to school. Temperatures dip slightly as trade winds blow.

Aloha Festivals

Begun in 1946, Aloha Festivals is the state's premier Hawaiian cultural festival, an almost nonstop, multiweek series of events across the islands, mostly held during September. On O'ahu the signature events are a Hawaiian royal court procession and Waikiki's block party and floral parade. For a listing of events, visit www.alohafestivals.com.

Queen Lili'uokalani Canoe Race

Hawaiian outrigger canoeing is alive and well, and fall is the big season for long-distance events. Everything kicks off over Labor Day weekend with these much-watched outrigger canoe races along the Big Island's Kona Coast.

Kaua'i Mokihana Festival

In mid-September Kaua'i's week-long contemporary arts and cultural festival includes an exceptional three-day hula competition in Po'ipu (p536), and the Kaua'i Composers Contest & Concert (p474) in Lihu'e. The finale is a royal court procession.

Na Wahine O Ke Kai

Held in late September, this is the powerful all-women sister event (p434) of the all-male Moloka'i Hoe in early October. Both are legendary long-distance outrigger canoe races that traverse the 41-mile Ka'iwi Channel between Moloka'i and O'ahu.

October

The slowest month for visiting Hawaii, October brings travel bargains on both accommodations and flights. Weather is reliably sunny, but very humid as trade winds depart.

Coconut Festival

You can't call yourself a Coconut Festival (p493) and not get a little nutty. In fact, Kapa'a on Kaua'i gets downright silly, with two days of pie-eating contests, coconut crafts, cook-offs and live entertainment in early October.

Eo e Emalani I Alaka'i

On Kaua'i, Koke'e State Park re-enacts Queen Emma's historic 1871 journey to Alaka'i Swamp, with a powerfully moving one-day festival (p557) in early October, full of authentic hula and live Hawaiian music performances and traditional crafts.

Ironman Triathlon World Championship

This legendary triathlon (p180) on the Big Island is the ultimate endurance contest, combining a 2.4-mile ocean swim, 112-mile bike race and 26.2-mile marathon. Watch 1800 athletes wear themselves to the nub in early October.

Maui 'Ukulele Festival

Herald Hawaii's favorite stringed musical instrument (p343) outdoors at the Maui Arts & Cultural Center on a Sunday in mid-October, with guest appearances by stars like Jake Shimabukuro and Kelly Boy De Lima.

Hawaii International Film Festival

In late October this highly regarded celebration of Pacific Rim cinema screens some 200 Asian, Polynesian and Hawaii-made films in a dozen venues statewide, with the main action in Honolulu (for full schedules, see www.hiff.org).

Halloween

Lahaina's (Maui) Halloween celebration (p317) was once so huge it was dubbed the Mardi Gras of the Pacific. It has been scaled back since then, but it's still a great street party. Other islands also get festive on October 31.

November

Toward the end of the month vacationing crowds and scattered rainfall start returning. Around Thanksgiving (fourth Thursday in November) is a busy time to visit.

Moku O Keawe

In early November, this four-day international hula festival (p218) on the Big Island draws top hula troupes from Hawaii, Japan and the US mainland for workshops and competitions. Traditional craftspeople gather for a marketplace fair.

Kona Coffee Cultural Festival

For 10 days during the harvest season in early November, the Big Island celebrates (p180) its Kona brews with parades, concerts, a cupping competition, a coffee-picking race, coffee farm tours, a lantern parade and multicultural festivities.

Triple Crown of Surfing

O'ahu's North Shore – specifically Hale'iwa, Sunset Beach and Pipeline – hosts three of surfing's ultimate contests, known as the Triple Crown of Surfing (p153). Competitions run from mid-November through mid-December, depending on when the surf's up.

December

As winter rainstorms return and temperatures cool slightly, peak tourist season begins in mid-December, with the Christmas to New Year's holiday period extremely busy – and expensive.

Honolulu Marathon

Held on the second Sunday in December, the Honolulu Marathon (p82) is without a doubt Hawaii's biggest and most popular marathon. It attracts more than 25,000 runners every year (more than half hailing from Japan), making it one of the world's top 10 largest marathons.

Christmas

Hawaii hosts Christmas celebrations all month long. Honolulu City Lights starts in early December with a parade and concert and greets the New Year with fireworks. Other towns, notably Holualoa on the Big Island and Lahaina on Maui, have tree-lighting festivals.

itineraries

Whether you've got six days or 60, these itineraries provide a starting point for the trip of a lifetime. Want more inspiration? Head online to lonelyplanet .com/thorntree to chat with other travelers.

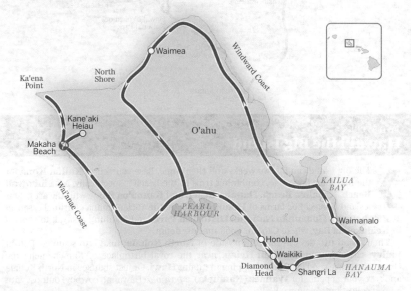

One Week
O'ahu

> Immerse yourself in the skyscrapers and kaleidoscopic streets of **Honolulu** and **Waikiki**'s oceanfront resorts for four days. Between sessions at Waikiki's beaches, eat your heart out in the capital, tour **Chinatown**, visit the **Bishop Museum** and **'Iolani Palace**, explore WWII history at **Pearl Harbor**, enjoy live Hawaiian music and hula at sunset, hike up **Diamond Head** and tour Doris Duke's incomparable **Shangri La**.

Now relax. Heading east: spend a day snorkeling at **Hanauma Bay**. Then swim off the white-sand beaches of **Waimanalo** and surf, kayak or windsurf at **Kailua Bay**. Wind your way along the rural **Windward Coast**, saving a day or two to savor the **North Shore** and the famous beaches around **Waimea**. In winter, watch big-wave surfers carve; in summer, snorkel with sea turtles.

If the clock's run out, drive along the scenic Kamehameha Hwy through **central O'ahu** and hit the airport; otherwise, veer west on H1 and explore the **Wai'anae Coast**. Hike to **Ka'ena Point**, watch (or join) the surfers at **Makaha Beach** and get in touch with Hawaii's sacred side at Makaha Valley's **Kane'aki Heiau**.

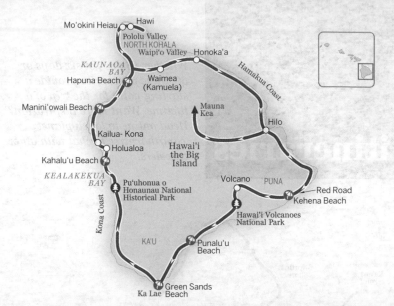

Two Weeks
Hawai'i the Big Island

The Big Island can fill two weeks and then some. Base yourself in **Kailua-Kona** for the first four days or so, combining trips to the beach – specifically, **Manini'owali Beach**, **Kahalu'u Beach**, **Hapuna Beach** and **Kauna'oa Bay** – with the art galleries and Kona coffee farms of **Holualoa**, feeling the ancient mana (spiritual essence) at **Pu'uhonua o Honaunau National Historical Park**, and paddling a kayak to snorkel in **Kealakekua Bay**, where Captain Cook met his doom.

Then spend two days in the countryside of **North Kohala**: hike into sculpted **Pololu Valley**; circle around **Mo'okini Heiau**, near the royal birthplace of Kamehameha the Great; and graze good eats after shopping in quaint **Hawi**. Or just sightsee in North Kohala and save your appetite for **Waimea (Kamuela)**, a *paniolo* (Hawaiian cowboy) outpost with a posh collection of country B&Bs.

Is that a week already? Well, keep going. Take a leisurely drive along the **Hamakua Coast**, making sure to at least peek into **Waipi'o Valley**, if not to hike down to the wild beach. Wander the antique and artisan shops of quaint **Honoka'a**, an ex-sugar-plantation town. Spend two days in **Hilo**, exploring its historic downtown architecture, the farmers market and excellent museums, particularly the **'Imiloa Astronomy Center of Hawai'i** and **Pacific Tsunami Museum**.

If you have extra time, detour either up to **Mauna Kea** for an evening of stargazing or venture down into **Puna**, lingering along **Red Road** and perhaps getting nekkid at **Kehena Beach**. But leave at least two days for **Hawai'i Volcanoes National Park**: hike the other-worldly **Kilauea Iki Trail**, drive along the **Chain of Craters Road** and hopefully trek to see some hot lava. While adventuring, stay in one of the lovely rainforest cottage B&Bs in nearby **Volcano**.

We understand that some have a plane to catch, but with another day or two for **Ka'u**, you can admire sea turtles at black-sand **Punalu'u Beach**, get in a last hike to **Green Sands Beach** and wave good-bye to the island from windswept **Ka Lae**, the southernmost geographical point in the USA.

» (above) **Kahalu'u Beach Park** (p187), on the Big Island, fronts Kahalu'u Bay's easy-access snorkeling and is a favorite surf spot.

» (left) **Saddle Rd** (p247) will take you to the Mauna Kea Access Rd and several exceptional hikes.

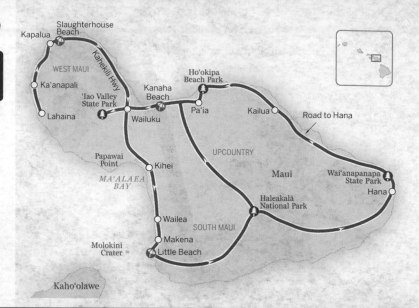

10 Days
Maui

> You're on your honeymoon, right? Well, we're not waiting around for lazy bums – there are too many mind-blowing experiences on Maui. Just try to keep up, OK?

Start off in the old whaling town of **Lahaina** and explore its pirates' treasure chest of **historical sites**, perhaps celebrating 'getting Maui'd' at the superb **Old Lahaina Luau**. In winter, spot whales breaching offshore, particularly at **Papawai Point**, and take a whale-watching boat tour.

Then head north into **West Maui**. Naturally, at a time like this, money is no object, so book a lavish suite at a resort in **Ka'anapali** or even more romantic **Kapalua**, and enjoy West Maui's excellent beaches. Spend two days (three if you're really in love), but then let's go! Drive north around the peninsula, stopping to snorkel with spinner dolphins at **Slaughterhouse Beach**, then get on the scenic, narrow cliffside **Kahekili Highway**.

As you cruise into Central Maui, stop to admire the legendary jungle spire at **'Iao Valley State Park** and amble the antiques shops of **Wailuku**. Then keep going to **south Maui**: book a snorkel cruise to **Molokini Crater**, check out more whales at **Kihei**, and snorkel around **Makena** or perhaps sunbathe au naturel at **Little Beach**. Rejuvenate at a spa resort in **Wailea**, or just take an unbeatable sunset oceanfront stroll.

Oh my, look at the time – only a few days left? Make sure you get to **Haleakalā National Park** before you go. Spend a day hiking around this awesome volcano and catching sunrise from the summit. Then drive the cliff-hugging **Road to Hana**, stopping frequently to gape in wonder at the windward coastal scenery and to follow muddy paths to waterfall swimming holes. Kick back on a black-sand beach at **Wai'anapanapa State Park** or drive further for a bamboo rain forest hike and to take a dip in the cascading waterfall pools of the Haleakalā national park's **'Oheo Gulch**.

If you don't overnight in rural **Hana**, drive back to civilization and hang loose in **Pa'ia**, enjoying *ono grinds* (delicious food) downtown and admiring the daredevil windsurfers at **Ho'okipa Beach Park**. Or follow the remote **Pi'ilani Highway** around Haleakalā's back side, ending your trip among the cowboy ranches of Maui's **Upcountry**.

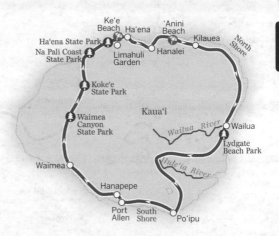

10 Days
Kaua'i

Kaua'i is Hollywood's ready-made set whenever it needs a 'tropical paradise.' These soul-inspiring canyons, cliffs, waterfalls, rivers, bays and beaches are more than just pretty backdrops, however.

If you've chosen Kaua'i, you're looking for heart-stopping adventure, but let's start off nice and easy in **Po'ipu**. Nap off your jet lag for a day or two on the sunny beaches of the **South Shore**. Head to **Port Allen** for a **Na Pali Coast snorkeling tour**; scuba divers can take this chance to tour the waters around offshore **Ni'ihau**.

Now, lace up your hiking boots and spend the next couple days in **Waimea Canyon State Park** and **Koke'e State Park**: trek the bogs of the **Alaka'i Swamp**, traverse knife-edge 2000ft cliffs on the **Awa'awapuhi Trail** and wear yourself out on the **Kukui Trail**, which descends into the 'Grand Canyon of the Pacific.' If you aren't camping, then stay in the old sugar-plantation town of **Waimea** and eat and shop in revitalized **Hanapepe** – if it's Friday night, join the festive art-gallery walk.

Well rested, head east: hit **Wailua** and kayak the **Wailua River** or the less crowded **Hule'ia River** inside a national wildlife refuge. Get a glimpse of misty Mt Wai'ale'ale while hiking the rolling **Kuilau Ridge and Moalepe Trails**. If you have kids, don't miss **Lydgate Beach Park**. The Eastside's most charming small town, **Kapa'a** is worth a wander for its artisan shops and organic, locavarian restaurants and cafes. Bed down at a B&B cottage here or further north in peaceful **Kilauea**.

Giddy-up to the **North Shore**, which deserves a few days. Get in some swimming, snorkeling and windsurfing at **'Anini Beach**, and check out the beach-bum town of **Hanalei** after surfing, outrigger canoeing or kayaking around **Hanalei Bay**. Scenic drives hardly get more scenic than driving to the end of the North Shore's road in **Ha'ena State Park**; mix in snorkeling at **Ke'e Beach** with a visit to beautiful **Limahuli Garden**.

OK, ready? **Na Pali Coast State Park** is what's left: in summer, kayak the 17 miles along the coast; otherwise, backpack the **Kalalau Trail**. Either way, you've saved the best for last. Now you'll have an epic Hawaii story to impress your buddies back home.

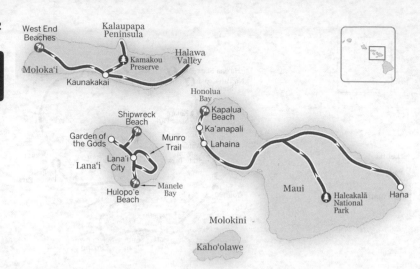

Two Weeks
Island Hopping: Maui, Lana'i & Moloka'i

You've got time, you've got money and you want culture, outdoor adventure and peaceful relaxation in equal measure. Combine Maui, Moloka'i and Lana'i – half the time, you won't even need to drive. This trip is for lovers, culture vultures and anyone happy to spend a little more for plush lodgings and gourmet eats. But you've also got to be willing to rough it once in a while, when the rewards – hidden waterfalls, epic sea cliffs – make it worthwhile.

First, spend five or six days on **Maui**. Make it easy on yourself: get a resort hotel room or a condo for the duration of your stay at **Ka'anapali** or **Kapalua**. Immerse yourself in Lahaina's whaling history and browse Ka'anapali's **Whalers Village Museum**, enjoy some old-school aloha at the **Old Lahaina Luau**, take a whale-watching cruise, and for a thrill, try ziplining. As for beach time, some of Hawaii's most seductive strands await nearby, like **Kapalua Beach** or **Honolua Bay**. Take one full day to hike **Haleakalā National Park**'s summit moonscapes and another to lazily drive down the **Road to Hana**, stopping off for waterfall hikes and to buy fresh coconuts.

Next, hop over to **Lana'i** and take your pick of world-class resorts located in Lana'i City and at Manele Bay, staying three or four nights. Things have been a little hectic so far, so play a round of golf, snorkel at **Hulopo'e Beach** or take in the vistas from the **Munro Trail**. To really get away from it all, rent a 4WD and head for the **Garden of the Gods** and **Shipwreck Beach**.

Finally, spend four or five days on **Moloka'i**. Stay in a condo or B&B in or nearby small-town **Kaunakakai**. Day one: explore **East Moloka'i**, checking out **Halawa Valley** and perhaps a waterfall or two. Day two: trek to the **Kalaupapa Peninsula** and munch macadamia nuts at Purdy's farm. Day three: head out to the remote beaches of the island's **West End** or penetrate the dense forests of the **Kamakou Preserve**.

See the individual island chapters later in this guide for details on island hopping by air and/or boat.

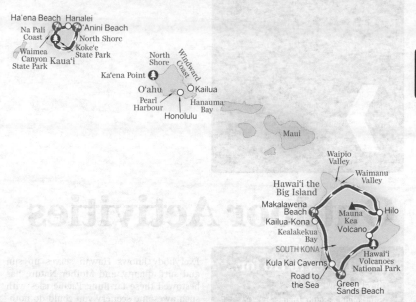

Island Hopping: O'ahu, the Big Island & Kaua'i

> If you want to live in the scenery (not just admire it), consider combining O'ahu, the Big Island and Kaua'i, all of which together offer the hiking and backcountry adventures of a lifetime plus plenty of traditional and contemporary Hawaiian culture, not to mention tasty treats for your tummy.

Start on the capital island of **O'ahu**, basing yourself in **Waikiki** or **Kailua** for a week. Among the major cultural sights around **Honolulu**, don't miss the **Bishop Museum**, **'Iolani Palace**, the **Honolulu Academy of Arts** and **Pearl Harbor**. Along with time spent on Waikiki's beaches, snorkel at **Hanauma Bay** and hike to **Manoa Falls** after visiting the **Lyon Arboretum**. End each day exploring Honolulu's cuisine scene and enjoying heavenly Hawaiian music and hula with sunset cocktails by the ocean. Drive up the **Windward Coast** to the **North Shore** for surfing, stand up paddle boarding and windy walks out to **Ka'ena Point**.

Mosey over to **Hawai'i the Big Island** and book a B&B in **South Kona** for a few nights. For ocean adventures, hike to secluded **Makalawena Beach**, kayak and snorkel at **Kealakekua Bay** and snorkel or dive at night with manta rays around **Kailua-Kona**. In **Ka'u**, go caving at **Kula Kai Caverns**, hike to **Green Sands Beach** and follow the rugged **Road to the Sea**. Next, **Hawai'i Volcanoes National Park** offers spectacular hiking and, if you're lucky, a chance to watch live lava flow into the sea. Afterward, bed down in a rainforest cottage in **Volcano**. Spend a night or two in **Hilo**, taking time to day-hike on **Mauna Kea** or to drive partway up the mountain for stargazing after dark. Last, explore **Waipi'o Valley**; if you've got the time, consider backpacking to **Waimanu Valley**.

With another week or more, head to **Kaua'i**. Spend a couple of nights camping and hiking at **Koke'e State Park** and **Waimea Canyon State Park**, then boogie up to the **North Shore**, mixing some camping at **'Anini Beach** or **Ha'ena Beach** with lodgings in **Hanalei**. Swim, snorkel and surf, but don't leave without tackling the Na Pali Coast's *amazing* **Kalalau Trail**.

Outdoor Activities

Best Times to Go for...

Kayaking May–Sep

Snorkeling & Scuba Diving Apr–Oct

Surfing Nov–Apr

Swimming Year-round

Whale Watching Dec–Mar

Windsurfing & Kitesurfing Jun–Aug

Hiking Apr–Sep

Top Adrenaline-Fueled Experiences

Surf the giant waves of Pipeline (off Oʻahu; p149)

Kayak the Na Pali Coast (Kauaʻi; p528)

Night dive with manta rays (Hawaiʻi the Big Island; p229)

Hike and backpack in Haleakalā's volcano summit area (Maui; p403)

Ride a mule down to the Kalaupapa Peninsula (Molokaʻi; p453)

4WD the Munro Trail (Lanaʻi; p422)

Everybody knows Hawaii serves up sun and surf aplenty, and Mother Nature has bestowed these far-flung Pacific isles with such awesome scenery you could do nothing but lie on your beach towel and still go home with stories to tell.

But we feel certain you didn't come all this way merely to rest on your elbows. If you're also after the outdoor adventures of a lifetime, the real question is – how much time have you got?

After this chapter whets your appetite, turn to the individual island chapters for full details of the unforgettable outdoor experiences that await, both on land and at sea. Remember: take nothing but photos, and leave nothing but footprints (for more ecotourism tips, see p625).

At Sea

The Pacific Ocean. You probably noticed it on the flight over – here are almost all the ways you can play in it.

Beaches & Swimming

When it comes to swimming beaches, you're spoiled for choice in Hawaii. Coastal strands come in a rainbow of hues and an infinite variety of textures – with sand that's white, tan, black, charcoal, green or orange, or sea-glass, pebbled, rocky or cratered with lava-rock tide pools.

Never turn your back on the ocean. Waves and water conditions can change abruptly, so pay attention and never swim alone. Drowning is the leading cause of accidental death for tourists.

Rogue waves All waves are not the same. They often come in sets: some bigger; some smaller. And sometimes one really big 'rogue wave' sweeps in and literally catches sunbathers napping.

Shorebreaks Waves breaking close to shore are called shorebreaks. Smaller ones are great for bodysurfing. Large shorebreaks, though, can slam down hard enough to knock you out.

Undertows Particularly on sloped beaches, undertows occur when large waves wash back directly into incoming surf. If one pulls you under the water, don't panic. Go with the current until you get beyond the wave.

Rip currents These fast-flowing ocean currents can drag swimmers out into deeper water. Anyone caught in a rip should either go with the flow until it loses power or swim parallel to shore to slip out of it.

Tsunami See p633.

Best Swimming Spots & Seasons

Water temperatures are idyllic here, ranging from 72°F to 80°F year-round. It's almost always possible to find somewhere to swim, no matter what time of year you visit: when it's rough or rainy on one side of any given island, it will usually be calm and clear on another. The only island where swimming isn't great is Moloka'i, where incessant winds often make ocean waters too rough year-round.

Each island has four distinct coastal areas – the north shore, south shore, leeward (west) coast and windward (east) coast – each with its own peculiar weather and water conditions. As a rule, the best places to swim in the winter are along the south shores; and the best places to swim in summer, along the north shores.

Bodysurfing & Bodyboarding

Sure, you might not be able to bodysurf like a ballet dancer – like the locals do – but anybody can give it a go and have some fun with it. And bodyboarding is even easier – giving you a slice of foam to hang on to. Best of all, except in the gnarliest or calmest surf, you can do both on almost any beach. If you're new to it, don't underestimate small-looking waves – they can roll you just like the five-footers.

Best Beaches for Bodysurfing & Bodyboarding

O'ahu	Sandy Beach (p128)
	Makapu'u Beach (p129)
	Kapahulu Groin (p101)
Hawai'i the Big Island	White Sands Beach (p172)
	Hapuna Beach (p225)
Maui	Kapalua Beach (p334)
	Keawakapu Beach (p354)
Kaua'i	Brennecke's Beach (p526)

Diving

Hawaii's underwater scenery is every bit the equal of what's on land: you can dive shipwrecks and lava tubes, listen to whale-song and go nose-to-nose with sharks and manta rays. For coral-reef etiquette, see p625.

If you don't already know how to dive, Hawaii is a great place to learn. Most dive companies offer both 'intro' dives for beginners and reasonably priced open-water certification courses. Experienced divers just need to bring their certification card.

Dive costs range widely depending on gear, dive length, location and so on, but in general, one-/two-tank dives run from $110 to $160, and **PADI** (Professional Association of Divers; www.padi.com) certification courses cost from $450 to $650.

» (above) **Shark's Cove** (p150), has super snorkeling and O'ahu's most popular cavern dive.

» (left) **Kailua Beach** (p38) is the launching point for some of O'ahu's best kayaking, to offshore islands.

CLOSE ENCOUNTERS: DOLPHIN SWIMS

Signing up for a 'dolphin encounter' in the Hawaiian Islands, especially on O'ahu, de-serves careful consideration. Although many programs claim to be ecofriendly and educational, the effects, for dolphins, of interaction with humans can be far more complex, and some tourist-oriented businesses commonly flaunt federal guidelines designed to protect these intelligent animals. Some widely reported concerns:

» In the wild, acrobatic spinner dolphins are nocturnal feeders that come into sheltered bays during the day to rest; they are sensitive to human disturbance, and federal guidelines recommend that swimmers don't approach within 50yd. Some tour boats allow swimmers to approach the dolphins much closer than this.

» According to many marine biologists, encountering humans can tire dolphins out, leaving them without enough critical energy to feed or defend themselves later. Repeated encounters with humans have driven some dolphins out of their natural habitats to seek less-safe resting places.

» In captivity, dolphins are trained to perform for humans using a variety of tech-niques, ranging from positive behavioral training to food deprivation; they can also be exposed to human-borne illnesses and bacteria.

» Some captive dolphins have had to undergo surgery to repair damaged fins after participating in programs that allow dolphin rides by hanging on to their dorsal fins.

» The US National Marine Fisheries Service has reported that programs in which people touch dolphins tend to make captive animals act more aggressively, espe-cially if the human participants are nervous. Injuries to human participants, such as broken arms and ribs, have occurred.

The 2008 Oscar-winning documentary *The Cove*, featuring an ex–dolphin trainer turned activist, looks at the 'dolphinarium' biz and the global industry of dolphin captivity. Find out more at www.thecovemovie.com.

Best Scuba-Diving Spots

O'ahu	Hanauma Bay (p124)
	Three Tables (p149)
	Shark's Cove (p149)
Hawai'i the Big Island	off the Kona Coast (p176)
	Kealakekua Bay (p205)
	nighttime sojourns with manta rays (p229)
Maui	offshore Molokini Crater (p353)
Lana'i	Hulopo'e Bay (p423)
Moloka'i	Pala'au barrier reef (p432)
Kaua'i	off Po'ipu (p533)
	neighboring Ni'ihau (p534)
Northwestern Islands	Midway Islands (p560)

For more on Hawaii dive spots, pick up Lone-ly Planet's *Diving & Snorkeling Hawaii*.

Safety Tips

» Ensure your travel medical kit contains treatment for coral cuts and tropical ear infections, as well as the standard problems.

» Have a dive medical before you leave your home country – your dive operator may not always ask about medical conditions that are incompatible with diving.

» Check that your travel and/or health insurance covers decompression illness – or get specialized dive insurance through **Divers Alert Network** (DAN; www.diversalertnetwork.org).

Fishing

The sea has always been Hawaii's bread-basket. You will see locals everywhere casting from shore, and no fishing license is required to join them (only freshwater fishing requires a license). However, byz-antine regulations govern exactly what you can catch and when; for details, consult the **Division of Aquatic Resources website** (http://hawaii.gov/dlnr/dar).

Most visiting anglers are more interested in deep-sea sportfishing charters for such legendary quarry as ahi (yellowfin tuna), swordfish, spearfish, mahimahi (dolphinfish) and, most famous of all, Pacific blue marlin, which can reach 1000lb ('granders'). Hawaii has some of the world's best sportfishing, chiefly off the Big Island's Kona Coast (p188) and Moloka'i (p431) and Kaua'i (p473).

Kayaking

Only Kaua'i offers river kayaking, but kayakers will find heavenly bits of coastline reserved for them on every island. Indeed, there are many beaches, bays and valleys that can be reached in no other way but from the sea. For outrigger canoeing, see the boxed text, p40.

Best Places to Kayak

O'ahu	from Kailua Beach (p135) to offshore islands (p135)
Hawai'i the Big Island	Kealakekua Bay (p205)
	Puako Bay (p225)
Maui	Makena (p369)
	Honolua Bay (p334)
Moloka'i	Halawa Beach (p447)
	Pali Coast (p447)
Kaua'i	Na Pali Coast (p528)
	Wailua River (p484)

Kitesurfing

Kitesurfing, also called kiteboarding, is a little like strapping on a snowboard, grabbing a parachute and sailing over the water. It's an impressive feat to watch, and if you already know how to windsurf, surf or wakeboard, there's a good chance you'll master it quickly. Any place that's good for windsurfing (see p40) is also good for kitesurfing.

Maui should dominate the attention of kitesurfers, aspiring or otherwise. At Kite Beach (p341) you can find instruction and rentals. O'ahu's Kailua Bay (p135) is another great place to learn. On Kaua'i, Kawailoa Bay (see the boxed text, p516) is popular, while windy Moloka'i calls to pros (p431).

Sailing

The most common sailing excursion is a two-fer: a catamaran cruise that doubles as a snorkel, dive or whale-watching tour. Sometimes nonsnorkeling and nondiving passengers can pay a reduced fare to ride along. But if your sole desire is to feel the sails luff with wind as you tack into the open ocean, then seek out each island's small boat harbor and start talking to captains.

Best Island Boat Harbors

O'ahu	Waikiki (p107)
Hawai'i the Big Island	Honokohau Harbor (p194)
Maui	Lahaina (p315)
	Ka'anapali (p327)
	Ma'alaea (p352)
Kaua'i	Port Allen (p542)
	Waimea (p547)

Snorkeling

Coming to Hawaii and not snorkeling is like climbing the Eiffel Tower and closing your eyes – the most bright and beautiful underwater city in the world lies at your feet, and all you need is some molded plastic and antifog gel to see it. If you can swim, Hawaii's magnificent coral reefs are yours. In addition to over 500 species of sometimes neon-colored tropical fish, sea turtles are increasingly common, and you may see manta rays, spinner dolphins, jacks, sharks and other impressive predators.

Every island has fantastic shoreline snorkeling spots, in addition to snorkeling cruises that get you places you can't swim to.

Best Places to Snorkel

O'ahu	Hanauma Bay (p124)
	Pupukea Beach (p149)
Hawai'i the Big Island	Kealakekua Bay (p204)
	Kapoho (p279)
	Two-Step (p208)
	nighttime snorkeling with manta rays off the Kona coast (p178)
Maui	Molokini Crater (p353)

	Malu'aka Beach (p368)
	'Ahihi-Kina'u Natural Area Reserve (p370)
	Black Rock (p326)
Lana'i	Hulopo'e Beach (p423)
Moloka'i	Dixie Maru Beach (p457)
	Twenty Mile Beach (p445)
Kaua'i	Makua (Tunnels) Beach (p499)
	Po'ipu Beach (p530)

Rental & Safety Tips

» Gear rental – including snorkel, mask, fins and usually a bag to carry them in – costs around $10 a day or $25 per week, depending on the quality of the gear.

» It may be a worthwhile investment to buy your own high-quality mask.

» As a rule, snorkel early – morning conditions are often best, and if everyone else is sleeping, they won't be crowding the water.

» Snorkelers often forget – whoops! – about the waves. Review our ocean safety advice on p35.

» For coral-reef etiquette, see the boxed text, p625.

Helpful Resources

There are myriad marine life and snorkel guides to Hawaii, but photographer John Hoover publishes some great ones: snorkelers and divers should pick up *Hawaii's Fishes* or the waterproof pocket guide *Reef Fish Hawaii*, while tide-pool enthusiasts might grab *Hawaii's Sea Creatures*. His *Ultimate Guide to Hawaiian Reef Fishes, Sea Turtles, Dolphins, Whales and Seals* covers everything.

Surfing & Stand Up Paddle (SUP) Boarding

Native Hawaiians invented surfing, and in Hawaii today surfing is both its own intense subculture as well as a casual part of everyday island life. Hawaii's biggest waves roll in to the north shores of the islands from November through February. Summer swells, which break along the south shores, aren't as frequent or as large as their winter counterparts.

The latest trend in surfing is stand up paddle (SUP) boarding – which, as the name implies, means standing on the surfboard and using a paddle to propel yourself into waves. It's great for less-limber folks, since you don't need to pop up into a stance. It takes coordination to learn, but isn't any harder than regular surfing.

Surf lessons and board rentals are available at just about every tourist beach that has rideable waves. To buy or trade used gear, look for surfboard swap meets around the islands.

With its excellent variety of surf spots, O'ahu is where all the major surfing competitions happen; its epic North Shore is home to surfing's 'Triple Crown' (p153). All the other main islands have good, even great surfing, but more laid-back scenes. Every island chapter in this guide features a boxed text describing that island's local surf scene and famous breaks and beaches.

Surf Respect and Etiquette

As a tourist in Hawaii, there are some places you go, and some places you don't. For many locals, beach parks are places where generations gather to celebrate life under the sun. They're tied to these places by a sense of community and culture. Residents are usually willing to share surf spots that have become popular tourist destinations, but they reserve the right to protect other 'secret' and sacred surf grounds. As a responsible traveler it's important to respect this.

In the water, basic surf etiquette is vital. The person 'deepest,' or furthest outside, has the right of way. When somebody is already up and riding, don't take off on the wave in front of them. Also, as a visitor in the lineup, don't expect to get every wave that comes your way. There's a definite pecking order and, frankly, tourists are at the bottom. That being said, usually if you give a wave, you'll get a wave in return. In general, be generous in the water, understand your place and surf with a smile, and you should be fine. In well-known spots where surfers can be ferociously territorial, ask a local for an introduction first.

Best Surf Beaches & Breaks

» O'ahu (p61)

» Hawai'i the Big Island (p173)

» Maui (p310)

» Lana'i (p416)

» Moloka'i (p438)

» Kaua'i (p466)

PADDLING POLYNESIAN-STYLE

Hawaii was settled by Polynesians who paddled outrigger canoes across more than 2000 miles of open ocean, so you could say canoeing was Hawaii's original sport. Europeans, who marveled at so much when they first arrived, were awestruck at the skill Hawaiians displayed in their canoes near shore – timing launches and landings perfectly, and paddling among the waves like dolphins.

Today dozens of outrigger canoe clubs throughout the islands are keeping the state's official sport alive and well, primarily through racing in single, double and six-person canoes. The main racing season runs from January to May. Major canoe racing organizations:

Kanaka Ikaika (www.kanakaikaika.com) On O'ahu.

Hawaii Island Paddlesports Association (www.hawaiipaddling.com) On the Big Island.

Maui Canoe & Kayak Club (http://mauicanoeandkayak.org)

Garden Island Canoe Racing Association (www.gicra.com) On Kaua'i.

The most impressive long-distance events, though, happen in the fall. In early September, the Queen Lili'uokalani Canoe Race (p25) sprints for 18 miles along the Big Island's Kona Coast. Then in late September and early October men and women compete separately in a 41-mile race across the channel from Moloka'i to O'ahu (p101).

To dip a paddle yourself, outrigger canoe trips are offered at Waikiki's Kuhio Beach (p101); on Kaua'i's Wailua River (p481) and Hanalei Bay (p516); at Kihei (p355) and Wailea (p365) on Maui; and at the Big Island's Kamakahonu Beach (p178).

Helpful Resources

Surf News Network (www.surfnewsnetwork .com) Comprehensive island weather-and-wave reports online.

Surfer's Guide to Hawaii (rev 2006; published by Bess Press) Greg Ambrose helps you find the best waves.

Surfrider Foundation (www.surfrider.org) Nonprofit organization with chapters on O'ahu, the Big Island, Maui and Kaua'i that help protect oceans and beaches.

Whale Watching

Each winter, mainly from January through March, about 10,000 North Pacific humpback whales (see p617) migrate to the shallow coastal waters off the Hawaiian Islands for breeding, calving and nursing. Five main areas are protected as the **Hawaiian Islands Humpback Whale National Marine Sanctuary** (http://hawaiihumpbackwhale .noaa.gov). Visiting the sanctuary waters at this time is a hot-ticket item. The western coastline of Maui (see boxed text, p358), the eastern shore of Lana'i and Moloka'i's south coast are the whales' chief birthing and nursing grounds. But the Big Island's west coast also sees lots of activity, including the acrobatic breaching displays for which humpbacks are famous. All islands offer whale-watching tours and have areas where you can spot whales from shore, including from the sanctuary's headquarters visitor center in Kihei (p354) on Maui.

Windsurfing

With warm waters and steady winds, Hawaii ranks as one of the world's premier spots for windsurfing. Generally, the best winds blow from June through September, but Pacific trade winds will keep windsurfers – somewhere, at least – happy all year.

As O'ahu's North Shore is to surfing, so Maui's Ho'okipa Beach (p371) is to windsurfing: it is the sport's Everest, its Olympics – a dangerous, fast arena where the top international windsurfing competitions sort out who's best. The other islands have windsurfing, but they don't reach the pinnacle of Maui. Only Moloka'i, bracketed by wind-whipped ocean channels, provides an equivalent challenge for experts.

Mere mortals might prefer windsurfing Maui's Kanaha Beach Park (p341) or Ma'alaea Bay (p352). If you're looking to learn, O'ahu's Kailua Beach (p135) is consistently good year-round and home to top-notch schools. Other windsurfing spots on O'ahu include Waikiki's Fort DeRussy Beach (p101), Diamond Head (p121) and the North Shore's Backyards (p149).

Kaua'i has only one prime spot for windsurfers: 'Anini Beach (p506), which has lessons and rentals. On the Big Island, conditions are consistent at 'Anaeho'omalu Bay (p215), where windsurfing rentals and lessons may be available.

On Land

As Hawaii's volcanic mountains rise above the waterline, they evolve into one of the planet's richest and most varied ecosystems – or what's also been called paradise.

Caving

Funny thing, lava. As the top of a flow cools and hardens, the molten rock beneath keeps moving. Then when the eruption stops and the lava drains, what's left behind is an underground maze of tunnels like some colossal ant farm. For more information, visit the **Cave Conservancy of Hawai'i website** (www.hawaiicaves.org).

Being the youngest and still volcanically active, the Hawai'i the Big Island is a caving hot spot, with six of the world's 10 longest lava tubes. Many of the islands' lava tubes are cultural as well as ecological wonders, since ancient Hawaiians used them as burial chambers, water caches, temporary housing and more. Check out Ka'u's Kanohina cave system (p302), with 20 miles of complex tunnels, and Puna's Kazumura Cave (p274). Also reserve a ranger-led cave tour in Hawai'i Volcanoes National Park (see the boxed text, p290).

Other islands have fewer caving opportunities, but along Maui's Road to Hana (p391) is a tube system once used as a slaughterhouse!

Cycling & Mountain Biking

Quality trumps quantity when it comes to cycling and mountain biking in Hawaii. Cyclists will find the friendliest roads and the most organizational support on O'ahu and the Big Island, but all islands have rentals, trails and 4WD roads that double as two-wheel, pedal-powered adventures.

For more about road rules, rentals and transporting bicycles on planes and public buses, see p638.

Best Places to Ride & Race

O'ahu	Ka'ena Point (p163)
	'Aiea Loop Trail (p98)
	Maunawili Trail (p132)
Hawai'i the Big Island	Ironman Triathlon World Championship (p180)
	Hawai'i Volcanoes National Park (p288)
	Pine Trees (p210)
	Puna (p279)
Maui	Haleakalā's Skyline Trail (p406)
	Polipoli Spring State Recreation Area (p383)
Lana'i	Munro Trail (p422)
Moloka'i	Moloka'i Forest Reserve (p431)
Kaua'i	Ke Ala Hele Makalae (see the boxed text, p494)
	Waimea Canyon (p554)
	Powerline Trail (p483)

Helpful Resources

» *Mountain Biking the Hawaiian Islands* by John Alford is a good mountain-bike trail guide covering all the islands. The author runs guided rides and multisport adventure tours on O'ahu (see www.bikehawaii.com).

» **Hawaii Bicycling League website** (www.hawaiibicyclingleague.org) provides advice and can help you find island bicycle shops and group rides.

Golf

Golfing is as popular with locals as with the PGA Tour, which always finds some excuse – any excuse – to visit Hawaii. Island resorts host some of the world's most lauded, challenging and beautiful courses. While playing on one of these elite, professionally designed courses can cost upwards of $200 a round, Hawaii also offers well-loved, affordable municipal courses (typically $10 to $50) boasting scenery you probably can't get back home. Playing in the afternoon is usually discounted.

For a statewide overview, visit **Tee Times Hawaii** (www.teetimeshawaii.com).

GREG ELMS / LONELY PLANET IMAGES ©

» (above) **Sliding Sands (Keonehe'ehe'e) Trail** (p404) winds down to the floor of Haleakalā Crater.

» (left) **Skyline Eco-Adventures** (p382) offers ziplining on the slopes of Haleakalā.

Never let it be said that ancient Hawaiians didn't know how to play. Every ruler had to prove his prowess in sports – to demonstrate his chiefly mana (spiritual essence) – and the greater the danger, the better. *He'e nalu* (wave sliding, or surfing) was integral to society; when the surf was up, *ali'i* (royalty) raced to grab the biggest waves. In boxing matches, combatants didn't dodge the blows. Kamehameha the Great is said to have once demonstrated his skill by having six spears thrown at him at once – he caught two and deflected the rest.

No chiefly contest topped the *holua* – an ancient sled that averaged 6in wide and 12ft long. That's right, it was just a little wider than this book, and it raced down a mountain at speeds of up to 50mph. The longest known course, near Keauhou on the Big Island, descended more than a mile before plunging into the sea. Losing your balance could mean death – but greatness isn't proved without risk, right?

Not every sport was potentially deadly, though many involved gambling – like foot and canoe racing, wrestling, cockfighting and *'ulu maika* (stone bowling). As for the gods, no athlete topped Lono, who could kill sharks with stones. Another legend tells of a young chief who casually dismissed a frail old woman's challenge to a *holua* race. She then transformed into a very angry Pele who, with thunder under her feet and lightning in her hair, surfed a crested wave of lava down the mountain, killing all who'd laughed at her.

Hang Gliding & Paragliding

Remove the engine, and flying becomes a wonderfully ecofriendly adrenaline rush.

» On O'ahu, glider rides (and skydiving) are offered at the North Shore's Dillingham Airfield (p157).

» On Maui, take tandem paraglider rides near Polipoli Spring State Recreation Area (p157) or tandem pilot an ultralight (powered hang glider) outside Hana (p382).

» On Kaua'i, book a ride in an ultralight in Hanapepe (p544).

Helicopter & Airplane Tours

Far and away the most popular places to visit by air are Kaua'i's remote Na Pali Coast (p473) and the Big Island's active volcano zones (see the boxed text, p179). Visiting these areas by air provides unforgettable vantages and experiences you simply can't get any other way. Helicopter tours are also popular ways to see Maui (p343), where some air tours include a jaunt over to Moloka'i's towering Pali Coast.

That said, helicopter and airplane tours negatively impact Hawaii's environment, both in noise generated and fuel burned. For an overview of the ecotourism issues involved, see the boxed text, p545.

Hiking & Backpacking

Hikers will find that, mile for mile, these tiny islands cannot be topped for heart-stopping vistas and soulful beauty. And being small, even the most rugged spots are usually accessible as day hikes. Backpacking is rarely common, though when it is the rewards so outstrip the effort it's almost ludicrous. Begin exploring Hawaii's trails by visiting **Na Ala Hele** (Hawaii Trail & Access System; http://hawaiitrails.ehawaii.gov). For an overview of Hawaii's parks and preserves, see p619.

Best Islands for Hiking

For variety, **Hawai'i the Big Island** wins by a nose. Hawai'i Volcanoes National Park contains an erupting volcano, plus steaming craters, lava deserts and native rain forests. Then there are the two nearly 14,000ft mountains to scale – Mauna Loa and Mauna Kea.

Maui's volcano may be dormant, but Haleakalā National Park provides awe-inspiring descents across the summit's eroded moonscape. The Road to Hana offers many short excursions to waterfalls and through rain forest.

Kaua'i's legendary Kalalau Trail on the Na Pali Coast edges spectacularly fluted sea cliffs, while an abundance of paths crisscross Koke'e State Park and cavernous Waimea Canyon.

On **O'ahu**, you can escape Honolulu in a hurry along the forests of the Manoa and Makiki Valleys around Mt Tantalus or lose the crowds entirely out at Ka'ena Point.

Best Day Hikes with Views

Sliding Sands and Halemau'u Trails, Haleakalā National Park, Maui (p403)

'Awa'awapuhi and Nu'alolo Cliffs Trails, Koke'e State Park, Kaua'i (p352)

Kilauea Iki Trail, Hawai'i Volcanoes National Park, Hawai'i the Big Island (p289)

Kalaupapa Trail, Kalaupapa Peninsula, Moloka'i (p455)

Ka'ena Point Trail, Ka'ena Point State Park, O'ahu (p164)

Best Backcountry Hikes & Backpacking Treks

Kalalau Trail, Na Pali Coast, Kaua'i (p553)

Muliwai Trail, Hawai'i the Big Island (p254)

Kaupo Trail, Haleakalā National Park, Maui (p405)

Mauna Loa Trail, Hawai'i the Big Island (p291)

Pepe'opae Trail, Kamakou Preserve, Moloka'i (p449)

Safety Tips

» A hat, sunscreen and lots of water are always mandatory; coastal trails can bake you to a crisp, especially when walking across sun-reflective lava.

» If you're looking to spend hours (or days) on the trail, bring hiking boots and rain gear – weather is changeable, and trails can be rocky, uneven and muddy.

» If you'll be tackling a mountain summit, carry a fleece jacket (even in summer).

» Always bring a flashlight: in the middle of the ocean it gets dark fast after sunset.

» All freshwater – whether flowing or from a pond – must be treated before drinking. Avoid giardiasis (p642) and leptospirosis (p642).

» Depending on the hike, potential hazards range from vog (p643), flash floods (p633) and crumbling cliffs to heatstroke and heat exhaustion (p643).

Horseback Riding

All the islands have ranch country for memorable horseback rides. But the Big Island (p255 and p235) and Maui (p309) have the richest living *paniolo* (Hawaiian cowboy) culture and offer the most extensive riding opportunities. Or take a mule ride down to the Kalaupapa Peninsula (p455) on Moloka'i.

Running

Hawaii's scenery enhances almost any sport, and running is no exception. Marathons are quite popular, and each of the biggest islands has its own signature races.

Best Marathons & Fun Runs

Honolulu Marathon (p82) On O'ahu in December.

Volcano Art Center Rain Forest Runs (p293) On the Big Island in August.

Maui Marathon (http://mauimarathonhawaii .com) In September.

Kaua'i Marathon (www.thekauaimarathon .com) In September.

Best Triathlons

Ironman World Championship (p180) On the Big Island's Kona coast in October; star athletes swim 2.4 miles, cycle 112 miles and run 26.2 miles. One of sport's ultimate endurance contests.

Ironman 70.3 Hawaii (www.ironman703ha waii.com) Half an Ironman; run in June on the Big Island's Kohala coast.

Tinman Triathlon (www.tinmanhawaii.com) In Honolulu in July.

Xterra World Championship (www.xterra planet.com/maui) Maui's off-road event, in October.

Tennis

If you bring your own racket and balls, free public tennis courts are available in just about every town of any size. However, as with golf courses, upscale resorts really pull out the stops, and at many of these you'll find immaculate tennis courts of professional-level quality, sometimes along with pro shops, round-robin tournaments and partner-matching. Resorts and hotels often reserve courts for guests only, but some also allow nonguests to rent court time and tennis equipment.

Yoga, Spas & Massage

Yoga studios thrive across the islands, allowing you to keep up with your practice while on holiday, and full-on retreats turn meditation into your vacation. Meanwhile, spas often highlight traditional Hawaiian healing arts, like *lomilomi* and hot-stone massage, and herbal treatments. Spas reach their pinnacle at luxury resorts.

STARGAZING

Astronomers are drawn to Hawaii's night sky the way surfers are drawn to Hawaii's big waves. The view from Mauna Kea volcano on the Big Island is unmatched in clarity, and it has more astronomical observatories than any mountain on earth. On Mauna Kea's summit road, the Onizuka Visitor Information Station hosts free public stargazing programs (p245). Also on the Big Island, Hilo has the excellent 'Imiloa Astronomy Center of Hawai'i (p261).

Astronomical observatories on Maui's towering Haleakalā volcano study the sun, not the stars. Nevertheless, Haleakalā National Park rangers lead free stargazing programs (p403), usually on summer weekends. Across the state, especially on the Big Island and Maui, top-end resort hotels occasionally offer their guests stargazing programs using high-quality telescopes.

On **O'ahu**, Waikiki resort hotels are famous for their spas (p109), while Kailua has a vibrant collection of yoga studios and massage therapists (p136).

On **Hawai'i the Big Island**, yoga studios abound in Kailua-Kona (p179), Hilo (p265) and also smaller towns, while Puna (p281) is the main destination for all-encompassing yoga retreats.

Kaua'i and **Maui** each have fewer yoga studios, but still plenty to keep you limber. Even tiny **Moloka'i** offers a private back-to-nature yoga retreat (p443).

Ziplining

Another fad that's growing in Hawaii is ziplining – a thrilling ride among the treetops that was first developed as a tourist adventure in the rain-forest canopy of Costa Rica and is infiltrating jungles everywhere. The only skill required is the ability to hang on (to your lunch). Currently Kaua'i (p471), Maui (p309) and the Big Island (p170) all offer ziplining thrills.

Travel with Children

Best Islands for Kids

Oʻahu

Waikiki Beach is stuffed full of family-friendly accommodations. Everything else on the island is less than a half-day's drive away, from hiking Diamond Head to snorkeling at Hanauma Bay.

Hawaiʻi the Big Island

Horseback riding like a *paniolo* (Hawaiian cowboy), ziplining through forests and hopping on a boat to see live lava flow are just a few of Hawaiʻi's unforgettable experiences for *na keiki* (children).

Maui

Rent a family-sized condo and relax on Maui's sunny leeward shores. Kids' eyes will pop on a winter whale-watching cruise, while swimming in waterfalls off the Road to Hana or when catching sunrise high atop Haleakalā volcano.

Kauaʻi

Calm beaches and rivers are perfect places for the pint-sized set to get wet. Older kids can even learn to surf in Hanalei. Don't forget to peer into the 'Grand Canyon of the Pacific,' either! Then go for adventurous hikes in Kokeʻe State Park.

With its phenomenal natural beauty, Hawaii always appeals to honeymooners and adventurers. But it's also perfect for families, especially active, outdoorsy ones. Instead of hanging out in shopping malls, kids can enjoy sand beaches galore, snorkel amid tropical fish, zipline in forest canopies and maybe even watch live lava flow. Add to their deeper appreciation of these islands by visiting museums, aquariums and historical attractions, from WWII-era battleships to ancient Hawaiian temples. And don't think a luau dinner show is too hokey – they'll leave most kids spellbound!

Hawaii for Kids

There's not too much to worry about when traveling in Hawaii with your kids, as long as you keep them covered in sunblock. Here, coastal temperatures rarely drop below 65°F, driving distances are relatively short and everyone speaks English, of course.

Still, proper planning (see p48) will ease the complexities of traveling with children. Depending on your kids' ages, interests and energy levels, you can either tone down or ramp up any of our recommended island itineraries (see p27). Just don't try to do or see too much, especially not if it's your first trip to Hawaii. Slow down, hang loose and just enjoy your family's time away.

Although you can't hike the steepest trails or go scuba diving if you're traveling with a

To learn to surf Kids who are part fish (and can swim comfortably in the ocean) are candidates for lessons. Teens can usually join group lessons, although younger kids may be required to take private lessons.

To take a snorkel cruise Depending on the outfit and type of boat (catamaran, raft), tours sometimes set minimum ages, usually from five to eight years. Larger boats might allow tots as young as two to ride along.

To ride in a helicopter Most tour companies set minimum ages (eg two to five) and some also set minimum body weights (eg 35lb). Toddlers must be strapped into their own seat and pay the full fare.

To go ziplining Minimum age requirements range from eight to 12 years, depending on the company. And participants must also meet weight minimums (usually 60lb to 80lb).

To ride a horse For trail rides the minimum age ranges from seven to 10, depending on the outfitter. It helps if your child already has some riding experience. Short pony rides may be available for younger kids.

toddler, parents will find equally enjoyable substitutes for outdoor family fun on all of the islands. Some activities require that children be of a certain age, height or weight to participate (see the boxed text, above); always ask about restrictions when making reservations to avoid disappointment – and tears.

Each island chapter in this guide includes specific advice for the best kid-friendly things to see and do there; see the following:

» O'ahu (p83)

» Hawai'i the Big Island (p192)

» Maui (p381)

» Lana'i (p423)

» Moloka'i (p445)

» Kaua'i (p490)

Eating Out & Entertainment

Hawaii is a family-oriented and unfussy place, so most restaurants welcome children; notable exceptions are some high-end resort dining rooms. Children's menus and high chairs are usually available everywhere – but if a high chair is a necessity at every meal, bring a collapsible seat.

If restaurant dining is inconvenient, no problem! Eating outdoors at a beach park is among the simplest and best island pleasures. Pack finger foods for a picnic, pick up fruit from farmers markets, stop for smoothies at roadside stands and order plate lunches at drive-in counters.

The food itself should pose little trouble, as grocery and convenience stores stock mainstream national brands. A kid who eats nothing but Honey Nut Cheerios will not go hungry here. But the local diet, with its variety of cuisines and plethora of sweet treats, such as crack seed (p592), will probably tempt kids away from mainland habits.

At resort hotel luau, kids receive a discount (and sometimes free admission when accompanied by a paying adult). Commercial luau might seem like cheesy Vegas dinner shows to adults, but many kids love the flashy dances and fire tricks.

If parents need a night out to themselves, the easiest and most reliable way to find babysitters is to ask a hotel concierge.

Children's Highlights
Beaches

Kuhio Beach Sand, surf and outrigger canoe rides at Waikiki

Ko Olina Lagoons Artificial pools for splashing around on O'ahu

'Anaeho'omalu Beach Sunsets on the Big Island's Kohala coast

Wailea Beach South Maui's gentlest crescent-shaped strand

Baby Beach Kaua'i's shallow Westside waters beckon

Water Adventures

Hanauma Bay Snorkel in a giant outdoor fishbowl on O'ahu

Kealakekua Bay Snorkeling cruises off the Big Island's Kona coast

HELPFUL WEBSITES & BOOKS

Travel with Children (Lonely Planet) is loaded with valuable tips and amusing tales, especially for first-time parents.

Lonelyplanet.com (www.lonelyplanet.com) Ask questions and get advice from other travelers in the Thorn Tree's online 'Kids to Go' and 'Hawaii' forums.

GoHawaii.com (www.gohawaii.com) The state's official tourism site lists family-friendly activities, special events and more – just search the site using terms like 'kids' or 'family'.

Family Travel Files (www.thefamilytravelfiles.com/locations/hawaiianislands) Info-packed family-vacation-planning articles and travel deals for all of Hawaii's main islands.

Parents Connect (www.parentsconnect.com/family-travel) Encyclopedia of everything first-time family travelers need to know, plus additional tips for O'ahu.

Whale-watching cruises Winter sailing with Maui's Pacific Whale Foundation

Hulopo'e Beach Snorkeling and sailing in Lana'i's Manele Bay

Inner-tube rides Family-friendly aquatic trips from Lihu'e on Kaua'i

Hiking

Makapu'u Point Climb to an O'ahu lighthouse with whale spotting in winter

Pololu Valley Walk deep into an ancient valley on the Big Island

Sliding Sands Trail Trek in Maui's volcanic moonscape above the clouds

Waihe'e Valley Trail Ramble over swinging bridges to a hidden waterfall on Maui

Iliau Nature Loop Canyon walls, waterfalls and native flora await on Kaua'i's Westside

Land Adventures

Kualoa Ranch Movie and TV set tours, trail rides and hula lessons on O'ahu's Windward Coast

Dahana Ranch Roughriders Genuine *paniolo* (Hawaiian cowboy) ranch trails on the Big Island

Ziplining on Maui Hawaii's original zipline adventure on the slopes of Haleakalā volcano

Kalaupapa Mule Ride Navigate mile-high *pali* (sea cliffs) on Moloka'i

Cultural Activities

Waimea Valley Botanical gardens and archeological sites on O'ahu's North shore, with poi-pounding, lei-making and hula-dancing lessons, too

Na Mea Hawai'i Hula Kahiko Traditional and sacred hula dancing and chanting inside Hawai'i Volcanoes National Park

Old Lahaina Luau Hawaii's most authentic, aloha-filled luau comes with music, dancing and an *imu*-cooked whole roasted pig, on Maui

Kamokila Hawaiian Village Outrigger canoe rides, tropical fruit trees and replicas of ancient Hawaiian houses, on Kaua'i

Museums

Bishop Museum Polynesian war clubs, feathered masks, an exploding faux-volcano and eye-opening planetarium sky shows in Honolulu

Hawaii Children's Discovery Center Best rainy-day indoor playground for tots and schoolchildren, not far from Waikiki

'Imiloa Astronomy Center of Hawai'i Hands-on multimedia astronomy museum and 3D planetarium, plus Native Hawaiian mythology, near Hilo on the Big Island

Whalers Village Museum In West Maui, let kids imagine themselves aboard a 19th-century whaling ship, complete with harpoons and scrimshaw carvings

Aquariums & Zoos

Maui Ocean Center USA's largest tropical aquarium has special kid-sized viewing ports

Waikiki Aquarium University aquarium at O'ahu's most popular beach

Ocean Rider Seahorse Farm Unique family-friendly tour spot on the Big Island

Pana'ewa Rainforest Zoo & Gardens Free kiddie zoo with walking trails, outside Hilo on the Big Island

Planning

To get the most out of traveling with your children in Hawaii, plan ahead. For tips on the best times to go and setting your trip budget, see p18. For a calendar of Hawaii's biggest annual events, many of which are family-friendly, turn to p23.

What to Pack

Hawaii's small-town vibe means that almost no place – apart from top-chef's restaurants and five-star resorts – is formal, whether in attitude or attire. There's no need to pack your kids' designer jeans or collector's kicks. Wearing T-shirts, shorts and rubbah slip-pahs (flip-flops) will help you blend in.

Hawaii's main islands have convenience and tourist shops, such as the ubiquitous ABC Store and Costco, where you can buy or rent inexpensive water-sports equipment (eg floaties, snorkel sets, boogie boards), so there's no need to lug them from home, unless your kids have some super-specialized gear.

Baby supplies, such as disposable diapers and infant formula, are sold everywhere, but try shopping in major towns for the best selection and prices. Facilities for diaper-changing and breast-feeding are scarce; chances are you'll need to improvise in the back seat of the car. Be discreet.

If you do forget some critical piece of equipment, **Baby's Away** (✍on Oʻahu 800-496-6386, on the Big Island 800-996-9030, on Maui 800-942-9030; www.babysaway.com) rents cribs, strollers, car seats, high chairs, backpacks, beach equipment and more. Major car-rental companies are required to provide infant and child-safety seats, but only if you reserve them in advance (see p640). If you bring your own instead, you'll avoid any mix-ups, as well as the added rental expense (typically $10 per day, maximum $50 per rental).

Where to Stay

When setting up a home base, choose accommodations based on your family's activity and sightseeing priorities. Resorts offer spectacular swimming pools and other distractions, along with kids' activity day camps and on-call babysitting services. But parents might prefer the convenience and cost savings of having a full kitchen and washer/dryer, which many condominiums and vacation rental cottages and beach houses offer.

Always ask about policies and bedding before booking any accommodations. Children under 17 or 18 often stay free when sharing a hotel or resort room with their parents, but only if they use existing bedding. Cots and roll-away beds may be available (usually for an additional fee). Condo and vacation-rental rates may apply only for double occupancy; kids above a certain age might count as extra guests and entail an additional nightly surcharge.

Kids and even babies are welcome at some B&Bs, but not all. For advice about Hawaii's camping and wilderness cabins, see p629.

regions at a glance

Ready for some island hopping? Wherever you travel around the Hawaii Islands, fantastic beaches, friendly faces and *ono grinds* (good eats) are practically guaranteed. Be swept up by the kinetic energy of the capital island, O'ahu. Hang loose on Maui, which offers a little something for everyone, but especially for beach bums. Be awed by towering sea cliffs on ancient Kaua'i, then gape at new land being birthed by volcanoes on the Big Island, Hawaii's youngest isle. Escape to total resort luxury on Lana'i or learn to live life off the land on rural Moloka'i, where Native Hawaiian traditions run strong. Whatever paradise you're seeking, the Aloha State has it – all you have to do is open your eyes.

O'ahu

Beaches ✓✓✓
Food ✓✓✓
Museums ✓✓✓

Multicultural Modernism
O'ahu will give you the measure of multiracial Hawaii, which confounds the categories of census-takers. East and West merge as ancient Hawaii greets the 21st century.

Big City, Small Island
Three-quarters of state residents call 'the Gathering Place' home. It's crowded – everyone rubs elbows on the bus and the city sidewalks. Yet miles of beaches are just a short drive from Honolulu's galleries, museums and monuments.

Endless Feast
If you do nothing else on O'ahu, eat. Japanese *izakaya*, island-style food trucks, high-wire fusion menus by Hawaii's top chefs – it's all here, waiting to be tasted.

p54

Hawai'i the Big Island

Hiking ✓✓✓
Culture ✓✓✓
Wildlife ✓✓

Trail Junkies Unite!
Kilauea, earth's most active volcano, conjures up a dreamscape for hikers: emerald valleys, icy waterfall pools, lava flows (active and ancient) crashing against rain forest and some of the loftiest summits your boots will ever struggle to top.

Cultural Border Crossing
On the Big Island culture is participatory – absorbed, rather than simply observed. You're invited to create a lei, dance a hula, beware the night marchers and watch as giant *ulua* (trevally) are caught the old Hawai'i way.

Wildlife
Spinner dolphins leap, sea turtles glide and endangered nene cross the road regularly. In winter humpback whales steal the show.

p165

Maui

Beaches ✓✓✓
Hiking ✓✓✓
Food ✓✓✓

Sun & Surf
Justifiably famed for its glorious strands, Maui's got a beach for every mood – kiteboarding meccas, snorkeling coves, hidden gems and some of the biggest surfable waves on the planet.

Trails Galore
Maui's trails go to the most amazing places: bamboo forests, towering ridge-tops, cascading waterfalls and a cindery volcanic national park. Choose from easy strolls to hardy backcountry treks.

Locavore Heaven
Grass-fed beef from Upcountry pastures, day-boat fish and bountiful organic gardens ensure Maui's chef-driven restaurants always have the raw ingredients to whip up their famed Hawaii Regional creations.

p304

Lana'i

Beaches ✓✓
Remoteness ✓✓
History ✓✓

'South Pacific'
Ignoring the great views of other islands, Lana'i feels like an isolated bit of subtropical pleasure far from the rest of the world. There aren't many people, the landscape is stark and exploring its unvisited corners is easy adventure.

Pineapples
Nearly the entire island was planted with pineapples, which were exported around the world, for much of the 20th century. The crops are gone but the vintage plantation town of Lana'i City still beguiles.

Hulopo'e Beach
Lana'i's one main beach is a beaut: a long crescent of sand on a bay good for snorkeling, backed by a tidy, uncrowded park.

p412

Moloka'i

Culture ✓✓✓
History ✓✓
Activities ✓✓

Most Hawaiian
More than 50% of Moloka'i's people have indigenous heritage. Locals favor preservation of land and culture over schemes promoting tourism. Yet there is aloha spirit everywhere and visitors find a genuine – rather than a paid-for – welcome.

Saint Damien
A young priest who traveled to Moloka'i's remote Kalaupapa Peninsula in 1873 to care for leprosy patients is America's first saint. Today the spectacular peninsula is a national park offering one of Hawaii's top adventures.

Wild Adventure
The world's tallest sea cliffs, misty rain forests, hidden waterfalls and deserted beaches are just some of the wild natural features that beckon.

p428

Kaua'i

Beaches ✓✓✓
Trekking ✓✓✓
Food ✓✓

Northern Bubble
With the closest traffic light 20 miles away, the North Shore is home to many who came to check in and stayed to tune out. Surfing, hiking and a contagious (if not invasive) laid-back vibe perpetuate the North Shore life.

Sunny Po'ipu
The most consistently sunny area on the island, Po'ipu is like a tropical version of sleep-away camp. Smiles abound on the South Shore as most days offer activities galore.

Canyons & Cliffs
The rugged terrain on the Garden Island ranges from gaping chasms to dramatic coastal cliffs, balanced out by copious verdant flora. It is exemplary of Mother Earth's highest potential for land creation.

p462

Look out for these icons:

 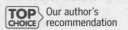 **TOP CHOICE** Our author's recommendation

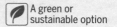 A green or sustainable option

 FREE No payment required

O'AHU..............54

HONOLULU.............. 61
PEARL HARBOR..........96
WAIKIKI..................99
SOUTHEAST COAST..... 121
Diamond Head & Kahala..................121
Hawai'i Kai...............123
Hanauma Bay Nature Preserve................124
Koko Head Regional Park....................128
Makapu'u Point.........129
WINDWARD COAST......129
Waimanalo...............130
Kailua...................133
Kane'ohe................139
Waiahole................140
Kualoa..................141
Ka'a'awa................142
Kahana Valley...........142
Punalu'u................143
La'ie....................144
Malaekahana State Recreation Area.........145
Kahuku..................146
NORTH SHORE..........146
Kawela (Turtle) Bay......147
Waimea.................148
Hale'iwa................152
Waialua.................155
Mokule'ia to Ka'ena Point...................156
CENTRAL O'AHU........ 157
Wahiawa.................158
Kolekole Pass...........158
WAI'ANAE COAST (LEEWARD O'AHU)......159
Ko Olina Resort.........160

Kahe Point.............160
Wai'anae 161
Makaha 162
Makua Valley............162
Ka'ena Point State Park....................163

HAWAI'I THE BIG ISLAND..........165

KAILUA-KONA........... 172
AROUND KAILUA-KONA................... 187
Keauhou Resort Area..... 187
Holualoa.................192
Honokohau Harbor & Around..................194
SOUTH KONA COAST 196
Kealakekua..............197
Captain Cook 201
Kealakekua Bay State Historical Park 203
Honaunau................206
Pu'uhonua o Honaunau National Historical Park 207
Miloli'i..................209
NORTH KONA COAST 210
Kaloko-Honokohau National Historical Park....................210
Keahole Point............210
Kekaha Kai State Park..................... 211
Ka'upulehu.............213
Kiholo Bay.............214
SOUTH KOHALA........ 215
Waikoloa Resort Area....215
Mauna Lani Resort Area.. 222
Mauna Kea Resort Area . 225
Kawaihae & Around..... 226

NORTH KOHALA........229
Akoni Pule Highway (Hwy 270).............. 229
Hawi 230
Kapa'au 232
Pololu Valley 234
WAIMEA (KAMUELA).....235
MAUNA KEA & SADDLE ROAD 240
HAMAKUA COAST 248
Honoka'a & Around 248
Waipi'o Valley 252
Hakalau & Around 257
Onomea Bay & Around 259
HILO 260
PUNA 274
Pahoa...................275
Red Road (Hwy 137) ...278
HAWAI'I VOLCANOES NATIONAL PARK........282
KA'U 297

MAUI............ 304

LAHAINA 310
WEST MAUI.............322
Ka'anapali 326
Honokowai...............331
Kahana..................331
Napili 332
Kapalua & Around 333
Kahekili Highway 338
'IAO VALLEY & CENTRAL MAUI 340
Kahului..................340
Wailuku 346
'Iao Valley State Park ... 350
Pu'unene 350

On the Road

Kealia Pond National
Wildlife Refuge 351
Ma'alaea 351
Molokini Crater........ 353
KIHEI & SOUTH MAUI 353
Kihei 353
Wailea.................. 364
Makena................. 368

NORTH SHORE &
UPCOUNTRY............ 371
Pa'ia 371
Makawao 377
Ha'iku 380
Pukalani & Around...... 381
Kula..................... 381
Polipoli Spring State
Recreation Area 383
Keokea 384
'Ulupalakua Ranch...... 385
THE ROAD TO HANA 385
Huelo 386
Ko'olau Forest Reserve .. 386
Ke'anae 388
Wailua................. 389
'Ula'ino Road........... 390
Wai'anapanapa State
Park 391
HANA & EAST MAUI...... 392
Hana.................... 392
Kipahulu............... 397
Pi'ilani Highway 398
HALEAKALĀ NATIONAL
PARK................... 400

KAHO'OLAWE 410

LANA'I 412
Lana'i City 416
Munro Trail............ 422

Hulopo'e & Manele
Bays 422
Keomuku Road......... 424
Road to Garden
of the Gods 425
Kaumalapa'u Highway.... 426

MOLOKA'I 428
KAUNAKAKAI 435
EAST MOLOKA'I 442
'Ualapu'e 443
Puko'o 444
Waialua................ 445
Halawa Valley 446
Pali Coast.............. 447
CENTRAL MOLOKA'I..... 448
Kamakou Area 448
Kualapu'u 449
Kala'e 450
Pala'au State Park 450
Ho'olehua.............. 451
Mo'omomi Beach....... 452
KALAUPAPA NATIONAL
HISTORICAL PARK....... 453
WEST END.............. 456
Maunaloa.............. 457
Kaluakoi Resort Area.... 457
West End Beaches 458

NI'IHAU 460

KAUA'I 462
LIHU'E 468
KAPA'A & THE
EASTSIDE 479
Wailua................. 479
Waipouli............... 489
Kapa'a 491

Anahola 497
Ko'olau Road........... 498
HANALEI BAY &
THE NORTH SHORE 499
Kilauea................. 499
Kalihiwai............... 506
'Anini 506
Princeville 507
Hanalei Valley 513
Hanalei................. 513
Ha'ena 522
Ha'ena State Park 524
Na Pali Coast State
Park 524
THE SOUTH SHORE......526
Koloa 526
Po'ipu 530
Kalaheo 540
WAIMEA CANYON &
THE WESTSIDE.......... 541
Port Allen.............. 542
Hanapepe 543
Waimea 546
Kekaha................. 551
Waimea Canyon
State Park 552
Koke'e State Park 554

PAPAHANAUMOKUAKEA
MARINE NATIONAL
MONUMENT........560
Nihoa &
Mokumanamana 560
French Frigate
Shoals 560
Laysan Island 561
Midway Islands......... 561

O'ahu

Includes »

Honolulu 61

Pearl Harbor 96

Waikiki 99

Diamond Head &
Southeast Coast 121

Windward Coast &
Kailua 129

North Shore &
Hale'iwa 146

Central O'ahu 157

Wai'anae Coast
(Leeward O'ahu) 159

Best Places to Eat

» Morimoto Waikiki (p112)

» Roy's Waikiki Beach (p113)

» Ted's Bakery (p152)

» Leonard's (p114)

» Halili's Hawaiian Foods (p114)

Best Places to Stay

» Halekulani (p108)

» Royal Hawaiian (p109)

» Waikiki Edition (p109)

» Malaekahana State Recreation Area (p145)

Why Go?

Nicknamed 'The Gathering Place,' O'ahu is home to nearly three-quarters of Hawaii's residents. Landing at Honolulu's airport plunges you into the urban jungle, but relax – this is still Polynesia. Even among the high-rises of downtown Honolulu, you'll find power brokers in breezy aloha shirts.

The jangling nerve center of the archipelago brings you face-to-face with contemporary Hawaii as it really is, not just a postcard fantasy. O'ahu has the most complex, multi-ethnic society in the islands, and through it all pulses the lifeblood of Hawaiian traditions, including at ancient heiau (stone temples).

O'ahu is not just a transit point en route to the Neighbor Islands. It's the thrill-of-a-lifetime adventure. Here you can surf the North Shore's giant waves, hike atop knife-edged *pali* (cliffs), dive into Hanauma Bay's outdoor fishbowl, go windsurfing or kayak to uninhabited islands off Kailua and still be back in Waikiki for sunset drinks. No worries, brah.

When to Go
Honolulu

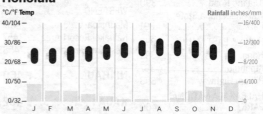

Apr Sunnier skies; peak crowds depart after Easter and spring break; Waikiki's Spam Jam.

Sept Room rates drop after summer vacation; arts and cultural festivals in Honolulu and Waikiki.

Mid-Nov–mid-Dec Triple Crown of Surfing champs invade the North Shore just before high season.

History

Around AD 1350, Ma'ilikukahi, the ancient *mo'i* (king) of O'ahu, moved his capital to Waikiki, a coastal wetland known for its fertile farmlands and abundant fishing, as well as being a place of recreation and healing. O'ahu's fall to Kamehameha the Great in 1795 signaled the beginning of a united Hawaiian kingdom. Kamehameha later moved his royal court to Honolulu ('Sheltered Bay').

In 1793 the English frigate *Butterworth* became the first foreign ship to sail into what is now Honolulu Harbor. In the 1820s, Honolulu's first bars and brothels opened to international whaling crews. Protestant missionaries began arriving around the same time. Honolulu replaced Lahaina as the capital of the kingdom of Hawai'i in 1845. Today Hawaii's first church is just a stone's throw from 'Iolani Palace.

In the 1830s, sugar became king of O'ahu's industry. Plantation workers from across Asia and Europe were brought to fill the island's labor shortage. The names of some of Honolulu's richest and most powerful plantation families – Alexander, Baldwin, Cooke and Dole – read like rosters from the first mission ships. The 19th century ended with the Hawaiian monarchy violently overthrown in Honolulu, creating a short-lived independent republic dominated by sugar barons and ultimately annexed by the USA in 1898.

During WWII after the bombing of Pearl Harbor, O'ahu was placed under martial law. As civil rights were suspended, a detention center for Japanese Americans and resident aliens was established on Honolulu's Sand Island, and later an internment camp was established in the Honouliuli area of Kunia Rd in central O'ahu. The federal government didn't apologize for these injustices until 1988.

After WWII, modern jet-age travel and baby-boom prosperity provided O'ahu with a thriving tourism business to replace its declining shipping industry. In the 1960s and '70s, the Hawaiian renaissance flowered, especially on the University of Hawai'i's Manoa campus and after the successful voyage of the *Hokule'a* (p571) to Tahiti, first launched from O'ahu's Windward Coast.

By the 1980s, rampant tourist development had overbuilt Waikiki and turned some of O'ahu's agricultural land into water-thirsty golf courses and sprawling resorts. The island's last sugar mills closed in the 1990s, leaving O'ahu more heavily dependent on tourism than ever. Debates about economic diversification, sustainable tourism and the continuing US military presence continue today.

National, State & County Parks

Even though O'ahu is Hawaii's most populous island, nature sits right outside of Waikiki's high-rise hotels. About 25% of the island is protected natural areas. The entire coastline is dotted with beaches, while the lush mountainous interior is carved by hiking trails, including in forest reserves just above Honolulu's steel skyscrapers.

O'AHU IN...

Two Days

Got only a weekend in the sun? Then it's all about you and **Waikiki**, baby. Laze on the beach, learn to surf, and enjoy the sunset torch lighting and hula. The next day get up early to snorkel at **Hanauma Bay**, then hike up **Diamond Head** or out to the lighthouse at **Makapu'u Point** in the afternoon. Reward yourself with a few sunset mai tais on a **catamaran cruise** or at the Halekulani's **House Without a Key**.

Four Days

With two extra days, rent a car or hop on a bus to the **North Shore** and **Windward Coast**. Stop off wherever golden beaches catch your eye – especially, say, around **Waimea** or **Kailua Bays**. Spend at least a full morning or afternoon exploring the capital city of **Honolulu**, with its impressive museums, historical sites, revitalized Chinatown arts scene and nightlife, or visit the WWII memorials at **Pearl Harbor**.

One Week

Switch over to island time; take everything a little more slowly. Complete your circle-island tour by cruising past the nearly empty beaches of the **Wai'anae Coast** out to **Ka'ena Point**.

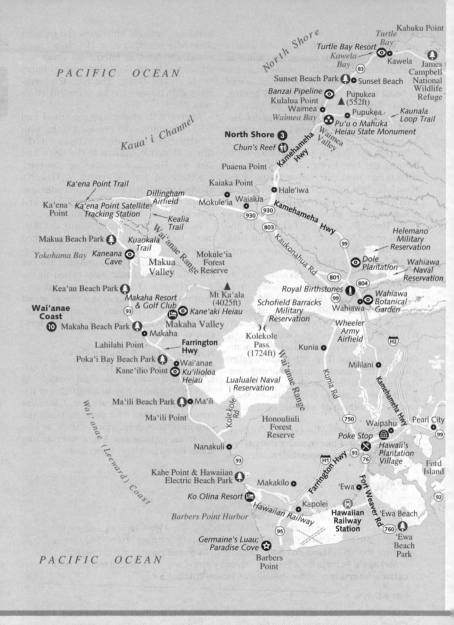

O'ahu Highlights

1 Swizzle sunset mai tais while slack key guitars play at **Waikiki** (p117)

2 Be moved by WWII-era history at **Pearl Harbor** (p96)

3 Surf giant winter waves on the **North Shore** (p146)

4 Snorkel and dive with marine wildlife at **Hanauma Bay** (p124)

5 Kayak to deserted offshore islands from **Kailua Beach** (p135)

6 Go art gallery-hopping, vintage shopping and

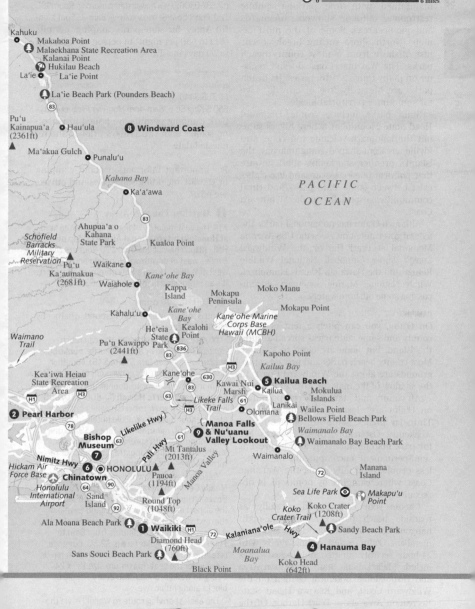

0 — 10 km
0 — 6 miles

Kahuku
Makahoa Point
Malaekhana State Recreation Area
Kalanai Point
Hukilau Beach
La'ie
La'ie Point
La'ie Beach Park (Pounders Beach)
83

Pu'u
Kainapua'a
(2361ft)
Hau'ula
8 Windward Coast

Ma'akua Gulch
Punalu'u

Kahana Bay
Ka'a'awa

83

*PACIFIC
OCEAN*

Schofield
Barracks
Military
Reservation
Pu'u
Ka'aumakua
(2681ft)
Waikane
Waiahole

Ahupua'a o
Kahana
State Park
Kualoa Point

Kane'ohe Bay
Kappa
Island
Moko Manu

Mokapu
Peninsula
Mokapu Point

Kahalu'u
*Kane'ohe
Bay*
Kealohi
Point
Kane'ohe Marine
Corps Base
Hawaii (MCBH)

Waimano
Trail
Pu'u Kawippo
(2441ft)
He'eia
State
Park
836

Kapoho Point

Kailua Bay

Kea'iwa Heiau
State Recreation
Area
H3
83
Kane'ohe
630
83
Kawai Nui
Marsh
5 Kailua Beach
Kailua
Mokulua
Islands
H1
63
H3
*Likeke Falls
Trail*
Olomana
Lanikai
Wailea Point
Bellows Field Beach Park

2 Pearl Harbor
78
Likelike Hwy
61
**Manoa Falls
& Nu'uanu
Valley Lookout**
9
Waimanalo Bay
Waimanalo Bay Beach Park

Bishop
Museum
63
7
Mt Tantalus
(2013ft)
Waimanalo

Nimitz Hwy
6 HONOLULU
72
Manana
Island

Hickam Air
Force Base
Chinatown
Pauoa
(1194ft)
Manoa Valley

Honolulu
International
Airport
64
90
Sand
Island
92
Round Top
(1048ft)
Sea Life Park
Koko
Crater Trail
Makapu'u
Point
Koko Crater
(1208ft)

Ala Moana Beach Park
1 Waikiki
H1
72
Kalaniana'ole Hwy
Sandy Beach Park

Diamond Head
(760ft)
4 Hanauma Bay

Sans Souci Beach Park
*Moanalua
Bay*
Koko Head
(642ft)
Black Point

nightclubbing in Honolulu's hip
Chinatown (p71)

7 Inspect royal feathered
capes and ancient temple
carvings at the **Bishop
Museum** (p73)

8 Cruise past rural valleys,
ranches, wild beaches and
roadside shrimp trucks on the
Windward Coast (p129)

9 Hike into Honolulu's green
belt to **Manoa Falls & Nu'uanu
Valley Lookout** (p77)

10 Get lost on the
untrammeled beaches of the
Wai'anae Coast (p159)

Most county beach parks are well-maintained with free parking, public restrooms, outdoor showers, lifeguards and picnic areas. Some of the most famous North Shore surfing breaks occur just offshore from modest county beach parks. The Wai'anae Coast doesn't register on many tourists' itineraries; its beach parks are blessedly free of crowds, save for sometimes territorial locals.

State parks include iconic Diamond Head State Monument, where hikers summit the landmark volcanic tuff cone, and idyllic, crescent-shaped Hanauma Bay, the island's premier snorkeling spot. Beware that political tensions over land-use rights exist between some state parks and rural communities, especially on the Windward Coast.

Although O'ahu has no national parks, the federal government oversees the USS Arizona Memorial at Pearl Harbor, the Windward Coast's James Campbell National Wildlife Refuge and the Hawaiian Islands Humpback Whale National Marine Sanctuary, encompassing some offshore waters.

CAMPING

On O'ahu, you can pitch a tent at many county and some state parks spread around the island, but none are close to Waikiki. Most county beach parks and private campgrounds are along the Windward Coast, in the shadow of the majestic Ko'olau Range.

All county and state park campgrounds on O'ahu are closed on Wednesday and Thursday nights; some are open only on weekends. Ostensibly, these closures are for park maintenance, but also to prevent semi-permanent encampments by homeless people, especially along the Wai'anae Coast, where camping by nonlocals is not recommended.

Choose your campground carefully, as roadside beach parks can be late-night hangouts for drunks, drug dealers and gang members. O'ahu's safest campgrounds with 24-hour security guards and locked gates include Malaekahana State Recreation Area and Ho'omaluhia Botanical Garden on the Windward Coast, and Kea'iwa Heiau State Recreation Area above Pearl Harbor. Of the 15 county parks that allow camping on O'ahu, the most protected is at Bellows Field Beach Park on the Windward Coast.

You must get camping permits in advance from one of the following:

Division of State Parks CAMPING PERMITS
(587-0300; www.hawaiistateparks.org; Room 131, 1151 Punchbowl St, Honolulu; 8am-3:15pm Mon-Fri) Apply for state-park camping permits ($12 to $30 per night) in person or online up to 30 days in advance.

Department of Parks & Recreation CAMPING PERMITS
(768-3440; ground fl, Frank F Fasi Municipal Bldg, 650 S King St; 8am-4pm Mon-Fri) Free county-park camping permits are issued in person no sooner than two Fridays prior to the requested date.

For important information about camping in Hawaii, including safety tips and advice, see p629.

❶ Getting There & Away

AIR The vast majority of flights into Hawaii land at **Honolulu International Airport** (Map p63; HNL; http://hawaii.gov/hnl; 300 Rodgers Blvd), 6 miles west of downtown Honolulu and 9 miles west of Waikiki. O'ahu's only commercial airport, it's an interisland flight hub (see p638).

❶ Getting Around

O'ahu is an easy island to get around, whether by public bus or rental car.

TO/FROM THE AIRPORT You can reach Honolulu or Waikiki by airport shuttle, public bus or taxi (average cab fare $35 to $45). For other points around O'ahu, it's convenient to rent a car.

Among several door-to-door airport shuttle companies, **Roberts Hawaii** (808-441-7800, 800-831-5541; www.robertshawaii.com) operates 24-hour buses to Waikiki hotels, departing every 20 to 60 minutes. The fare is $9/15 one way/round-trip with surcharges for bicycles, surfboards, strollers or extra baggage. For return trips, reserve at least 48 hours ahead.

You can travel to downtown Honolulu, Ala Moana Center and Waikiki via TheBus 19 or 20. Buses fill up, so catch them at the first stop at the airport in front of the interisland terminal; the next stop is outside the main terminal Lobby 4. Buses run every 20 minutes from 6am to 11pm daily; the regular fare is $2.50. Luggage is restricted to what you can hold on your lap or stow under the seat (maximum size 18" x 24" x 12"). In Waikiki, buses stop every couple of blocks along Kuhio Ave.

The easiest driving route to Waikiki is via the Nimitz Hwy (92), which becomes Ala Moana Blvd. Although this route hits local traffic, it's hard to get lost. For the fast lane, take the H-1 Fwy eastbound, then follow signs 'To Waikiki.' On the return trip to the airport, beware of the poorly marked interchange where H-1 and Hwy

ACTIVITY	DESTINATION
Bird-watching	James Campbell National Wildlife Refuge p147
Bodyboarding & bodysurfing	Kapahulu Groin (Waikiki; p101) Sandy Beach (Southeast Coast; p128) Makapu'u Beach (Southeast Coast; p129) Waimea Bay (North Shore; p150)
Golf	Olomana Golf Links (Windward Coast; p132) Ko'olau Golf Club (Windward Coast; p140) Turtle Bay Resort (North Shore; p147) Ko Olina Golf Club (Leeward O'ahu; p160)
Hang gliding & sky diving	Dillingham Airfield (North Shore; p157)
Hiking	Manoa Falls & Nu'uanu Valley Lookout (Honolulu; p77) Wa'ahila Ridge Trail (Honolulu; p79) 'Aiea Loop Trail (Pearl Harbor; p98) Diamond Head Crater (Southeast Coast; p122) Ka'ena Point (Wai'anae Coast; p163)
Horseback riding	Kualoa Ranch (Windward Coast; p142) Turtle Bay Resort (North Shore; p147)
Kayaking	Kailua Beach (Windward Coast; p135)
Kitesurfing	Kailua Beach (Windward Coast; p135)
Mountain biking	'Aiea Loop Trail (Pearl Harbor; p98) Maunawili Trail (Windward Coast; p132) Ka'ena Point (Wai'anae Coast; p163)
Scuba diving & snorkeling	Hanauma Bay (Southeast Coast; p124) Shark's Cove (North Shore; p150) Three Tables (North Shore; p150) Kawela Bay (North Shore; p147)
Spas	Waikiki p109
Surfing	Waikiki p61 North Shore p61 Wai'anae Coast p61
Swimming	Ala Moana Beach Park p62 Waikiki p100 Waimanalo (Windward Coast; p130) Kailua (Windward Coast; p141) Kualoa (Windward Coast; p141) Malaekahana State Recreation Area p145
Windsurfing	Kailua Beach (Windward Coast; p135) Backyards (North Shore; p149) Fort DeRussy Beach (Waikiki; p101)

78 split; if you're not in the right-hand lane at that point, you could easily end up on Hwy 78.

BICYCLE It's possible to cycle around O'ahu, but consider taking TheBus to get beyond Honolulu metro-area traffic. Hawaii's **Department of Transportation** (http://hawaii.gov/dot/high ways/Bike) publishes a free *Bike O'ahu* route map, available at Honolulu's Bike Shop (p79), which offers top-quality rentals.

BUS O'ahu's public bus system, **TheBus** (☑848-5555; www.thebus.org), is extensive but hiking trails and some of the best viewpoints are beyond its reach.

Ala Moana Center (Map p72) is Honolulu's central bus transfer point. Each bus route can have a few different destinations and buses generally keep the same number inbound and outbound.

All buses are wheelchair-accessible and have front-loading racks accommodating two bicycles at no extra charge (let the driver know first). Air-conditioning is arctic.

USEFUL O'AHU BUS ROUTES

ROUTE NO	DESTINATION
A City Express!	UH Manoa, Ala Moana Center, Downtown Honolulu, Chinatown, Aloha Stadium
B City Express!	Waikiki, Honolulu Academy of Arts, Downtown Honolulu, Chinatown, Bishop Museum
E Country Express!	Waikiki, Ala Moana Center, Restaurant Row, Aloha Tower, Downtown Honolulu
2 & 13	Waikiki, Honolulu Convention Center, Honolulu Academy of Arts, Downtown Honolulu, Chinatown; also Waikiki Aquarium and Bishop Museum (No 2) and Kapahulu Ave (No 13)
4	Waikiki, Honolulu Zoo, UH Manoa, Downtown Honolulu, 'Iolani Palace, Foster Botanical Garden, Queen Emma Summer Palace
6	UH Manoa, Ala Moana Center, Downtown Honolulu
8	Waikiki, Ala Moana Center
19 & 20	Waikiki, Ala Moana Center, Ward Centers, Restaurant Row, Aloha Tower, Downtown Honolulu, Chinatown, Honolulu International Airport
22	'Beach Bus': Waikiki, Diamond Head, Koko Marina, Sandy Beach, Hanauma Bay (no service Tuesday)
23	Ala Moana, Waikiki, Diamond Head, Hawai'i Kai (inland), Sea Life Park
42	Waikiki, Ala Moana, Downtown Honolulu, Chinatown, USS Arizona Memorial (limited hours)
52 & 55	'Circle Isle' buses: Ala Moana Center, North Shore, Windward Coast
57	Ala Moana, Kailua, Waimanalo, Sea Life Park

FARES & PASSES The one-way adult fare is $2.50 (children aged six to 17 $1). Use coins or $1 bills; bus drivers don't give change. One free transfer (two-hour time limit) is available per paid fare.

A $25 visitor pass valid for unlimited rides over four consecutive days is sold at Waikiki's ubiquitous ABC Stores and **TheBus Pass Office** (☑848-4444; 811 Middle St; ☷7:30am-4pm Mon-Fri).

A monthly bus pass ($60), valid for unlimited rides during a calendar month (not just any 30-day period), is sold at TheBus Pass Office, 7-Eleven convenience stores and Foodland and Times supermarkets.

Seniors (65 years and older) and anyone with a physical disability can buy a $10 discount ID card at TheBus Pass Office entitling them to pay $1 per one-way fare or $5/30 for a pass valid for unlimited rides during one calendar month/year.

CAR, MOTORCYCLE & MOPED For more about driving in Hawaii, including road rules and car rental rates and reservations, see p639.

Most major car-rental agencies have multiple branch locations in Waikiki, usually in the lobbies of larger hotels. Although the best rental rates are usually offered at Honolulu's airport, Waikiki branches can be less hassle if you're only renting a car for a day or two.

Independent car-rental agencies in Waikiki may offer much lower rates, especially for one-day rentals and 4WD vehicles like Jeeps. They're also more likely to rent to drivers under 25. Many independent agencies also rent mopeds and motorcycles (see p641).

Hawaii Campers (☑222-2547; www .hawaiicampers.net) rents pop-top VW camper vans equipped with kitchens, memory-foam mattresses and more (from $125 per day). But you'll also need to pay for campsites and reserve camping permits in advance (see p58).

ℹ **AIRPORT CAR RENTALS**

Avis, Budget, Dollar, Enterprise, National and Hertz have rental cars at Honolulu International Airport. Alamo and Thrifty operate about a mile outside the airport off Nimitz Hwy (free airport courtesy shuttles). All things being equal, try to rent from a company with its lot inside the airport. On the drive back to the airport, all highway signs lead to on-site airport car returns. Looking for a lot outside the airport when you're trying to catch a flight can be stressful.

'The Gathering Place' has become a hub for Hawaii's surf economy. With some of the most diverse surf breaks in all of the islands, boarders of all skill levels can find what they're looking for on O'ahu.

In Waikiki, slow and mellow combers provide the perfect training ground for beginners. Board rentals abound on Waikiki Beach and local beachboys are always on hand for lessons at spots like mellow **Queens**, mushy left- and right-handed **Canoes**, gentle but often crowded **Populars** and ever-popular **Publics**. In Honolulu proper, **Ala Moana** offers a heavy tubing wave. Waves in this area are best during summer, when south swells arrive from New Zealand and Tahiti.

Reckon yourself a serious surfer? A pilgrimage to the famed North Shore is mandatory. In winter, when the waves can reach heights of more than 30ft, spots like **Waimea Bay**, **Pipeline** and **Sunset Beach** beckon to the planet's best professional surfers. Watch out for turf-protective locals, some organized into surfer gangs.

While home to some great waves, O'ahu's Wai'anae Coast has even more turf issues; the locals who live and surf here cherish this area and are trying to hold onto their Hawaiian culture and community. In the winter, large west swells can make for big surf at places like **Makaha Beach**, but tread lightly: locals know each other, so there will be no question that you're from out of town.

If you're looking for a multipurpose wave, **Diamond Head Beach** is friendly to short-boarders, longboarders, windsurfers and kitesurfers. For an adrenaline-fueled day of bodysurfing, **Sandy Beach** and **Makapu'u Beach** on the island's southeast shore are ideal. If you go out here, do so with caution: the pounding waves and shallow bottom have caused serious neck and back injuries.

Surf News Network (☎596-7873; www.surfnewsnetwork.com) runs a recorded surf-conditions phone line that reports winds, wave heights and tide information.

Times vary depending upon traffic , but here are typical driving times and distances from Waikiki:

DESTINATION	MILES	TIME
Diamond Head	2	10min
Hale'iwa	37	60min
Hanauma Bay	11	25min
Honolulu International Airport	9	25min
Ka'ena Point State Park	47	70min
Kailua	17	35min
Makaha Beach	41	1hr
Makapu'u Point	15	30min
Nu'uanu Pali Lookout	10	25min
Sunset Beach	43	65min
USS Arizona Memorial	15	30min

TAXI Taxis are readily available at the airport, resort hotels and shopping centers. Otherwise, you'll probably have to call for one. Taxis have meters and charge $3.25 at flag-fall, plus $3 per mile and 35¢ per suitcase or backpack.

TOURS Prices usually include Waikiki hotel pickups; ask when booking.

Roberts Hawaii (☎954-8652, 866-898-2519; www.robertshawaii.com) Conventional bus and van sightseeing tours of O'ahu, including marathon full-day 'Circle Island' trips (adult/child from $51/28) and eclectic options like an evening 'Honolulu Haunts' walking tour (adult/child $29/22).

E Noa Tours (☎591-2561, 800 824 8804; www.enoa.com) O'ahu-based tour company utilizes smaller buses and knowledgeable guides certified in Hawaiiana. Standard tours circle the island (adult/child from $80/66) and visit Pearl Harbor (adult/child from $24/22).

Earth Bound Tours (☎776-1771; http://earthboundtours.com) Small-group agritourism van tours visit organic farms, small-scale chocolate and coffee plantations, and sustainable aquaculture enterprises.

HONOLULU

POP 377,360

You can't claim to have really gotten to know O'ahu if you never even leave Waikiki. Venture downtown not just for its unmatched collection of historical sites, museums and gardens, but also to eat your way through the island's intoxicating blend of ethnic cultures, from the pan-Asian alleyways of Chinatown where 19th-century whalers once brawled, to hole-in-the-wall diners where local kids slurp saimin (local-style noodle soup), to bistros dishing up the freshest bounty from land and sea.

Then escape the concrete jungle for a hike up into the lush valleys nestled beneath the jagged Ko'olau Mountains, especially in the forest reserves around Mt Tantalus, traditionally called Pu'u 'Ohi'a. At sunset, cool off with a breezy walk along Honolulu's historic harborfront or splash into the Pacific at Ala Moana Beach Park, a rare beauty in the middle of the city. After dark, migrate over to Chinatown's edgy nightlife scene. You won't even miss Waikiki, we promise.

Beaches

Ala Moana Beach Park　　　　BEACH
(Map p72; 1201 Ala Moana Blvd; P) Opposite Ala Moana Center shopping mall, this city fave is fronted by a broad, golden-sand beach, nearly a mile long and buffered from passing traffic noise by statuesque shade trees. For distance swimmers, at low tide the deep channel that runs the length of the beach can be a hazard – it drops off suddenly to overhead depths.

Ala Moana is hugely popular, yet big enough that it never feels too crowded. Honolulu residents come here to go running after work, play volleyball and enjoy weekend picnics. The park has full facilities, including ball fields, lighted tennis courts, picnic tables, restrooms, showers, drinking water and free parking.

The peninsula jutting from the east side of the park is 'Aina Moana State Recreation Area, aka Magic Island. High-school outrigger-canoe teams practice here in the late afternoon when school's in session. In summer it's a hot surfing spot. Year-round, there's an idyllic walk around the peninsu-

WARNING!

When visiting O'ahu's beach parks, hiking trails or 'secret' spots off the side of the highway, take all valuables with you. Don't leave anything visible inside your car or stowed in the trunk. Car break-ins – and on O'ahu, that means not just rental cars but also locals' vehicles – are common all over the island and can happen within a matter of minutes. Some locals leave their cars unlocked to avoid the hassles of broken windows or jimmied door locks.

la's perimeter. It's especially picturesque at sunset, with sailboats pulling in and out of adjoining Ala Wai Yacht Harbor.

◉ Sights

Honolulu's compact downtown set the stage for the rise and fall of the 19th-century Hawaiian monarchy, all just a lei's throw from the harborfront. Nearby, the buzzing streets of Chinatown are packed with open-air markets, antiques shops, art galleries and bars. East of downtown and not far from Waikiki, Ala Moana is Honolulu's beach. The University of Hawai'i area is a gateway to Manoa Valley and the Mt Tantalus green belt. A few outlying sights, including the Bishop Museum, are worth a detour, too.

DOWNTOWN

'Iolani Palace　　　HISTORICAL BUILDING
(Map p64; ☑info 538-1471, tour reservations 522-0832/0823; www.iolanipalace.org; 364 S King St; grounds admission free, basement galleries adult/child 5-12yr $6/3, tours adult/child 5-12yr self-guided audio $12/5, guided $20/5; ⊙9am-4pm Mon-Sat) Perhaps no other place evokes a more poignant sense of Hawaii's history than this royal palace where plots and counterplots simmered.

The regal palace was built by King David Kalakaua in 1882. At that time, the Hawaiian monarchy observed many of the diplomatic protocols of the Victorian world. The king traveled abroad meeting with leaders around the globe and received foreign emissaries at 'Iolani Palace. Although the palace was modern and opulent for its time, it did little to assert Hawaii's sovereignty over powerful US-influenced business interests, who overthrew the kingdom in 1893.

Two years after the coup, the former queen, Lili'uokalani, who had succeeded her brother David to the throne, was convicted of treason and spent nine months imprisoned in her former home. Later the palace served as the capitol of the republic, then the territory and later the state of Hawaii. In 1969 the government finally moved into the current state capitol, leaving 'Iolani Palace a shambles. The palace has since been painstakingly restored to its former glory, although many original royal artifacts were lost or stolen over the years.

The only way to see the palace's handsome interior is to take a guided group or self-guided audio tour (children under five not allowed). Guided tours are offered between

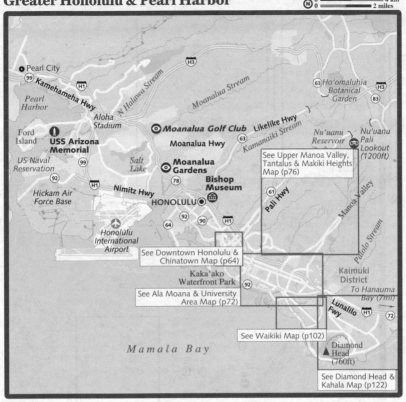

Pearl City
99
Kamehameha Hwy
H1
Pearl
Harbor
N Halawa Stream
Moanalua Stream
H3
Moanalua Stream
Ho'omaluhia
63 Botanical
Garden
H3
83
Aloha
Stadium
Moanalua Golf Club
Likelike Hwy
Nu'uanu
Reservoir
Nu'uanu
Pali
Lookout
(1200ft)
Ford
Island
USS Arizona
Memorial
Moanalua Hwy
Kamanaiki Stream
US Naval
Reservation
99
Salt
Lake
Moanalua
Gardens
See Upper Manoa Valley,
Tantalus & Makiki Heights
Map (p76)
92
H1
78
Bishop
Museum
61
Pali Hwy
Manoa Valley
Hickam Air
Force Base
Nimitz Hwy
HONOLULU
92
90
H1
Honolulu
International
Airport
64
Pulolo Stream
See Downtown Honolulu &
Chinatown Map (p64)
Kaka'ako
Waterfront Park
92
Kaimuki
District
To Hanauma
Bay (7mi)
See Ala Moana & University
Area Map (p72)
Lunalilo
Fwy
H1
72
See Waikiki Map (p102)
Mamala Bay
Diamond
Head
(760ft)
See Diamond Head &
Kahala Map (p122)

9am and 10am Tuesday and Thursday, and 9am and 11:15am Wednesday, Friday and Saturday; you can take a self-guided tour from 9am Monday, 10:30am Tuesday or Thursday, or noon Wednesday, Friday or Saturday. Sometimes you can join a guided tour on the spot, but it's advisable to call ahead for reservations and to double-check schedules, especially during peak periods. If you're short on time, browse the museum exhibits in the basement, which include royal regalia, historical photographs and reconstructions of the palace kitchen and chamberlain's office.

Outside on the palace grounds, the former Royal Household Guards barracks is now the ticket booth. The domed pavilion was originally built for the coronation of King Kalakaua, underneath a huge banyan tree thought to have been planted by Queen Kapi'olani. The Royal Hawaiian Band gives free concerts here from noon to 1pm most Fridays.

FREE Hawai'i State Art Museum   MUSEUM
(Map p64; ☎586-0900; www.hawaii.gov/sfca; 2nd fl, No 1 Capitol District Bldg, 250 S Hotel St; ☉10am-4pm Tue-Sat, 5-9pm 1st Fri of each month) With its vibrant, thought-provoking collections, this eclectic art museum showcases traditional and contemporary art from Hawaii's multiethnic communities. The museum inhabits a grand 1928 Spanish Mission-style building, formerly a YMCA. Upstairs revolving exhibits of paintings, sculptures, fiber art, photography and mixed media reveal a blending of Western, Asian and Polynesian art forms and traditions that have shaped a unique aesthetic that captures the soul of the islands and the hearts of the people. Drop by at noon on the last Tuesday of the month for free 'Art Lunch' lectures or from 11am to 3pm on the second Saturday for hands-on educational family activities.

Downtown Honolulu & Chinatown

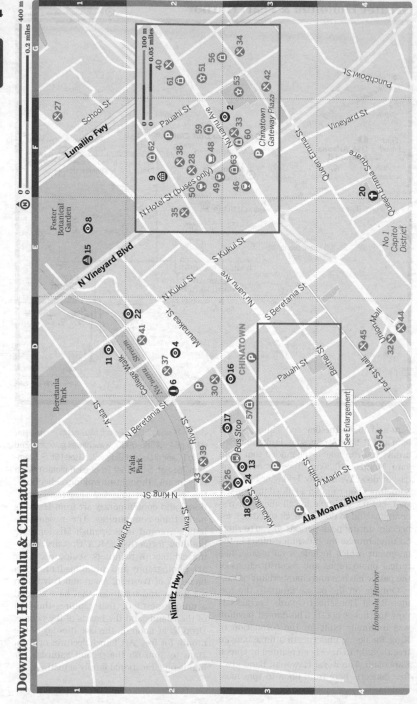

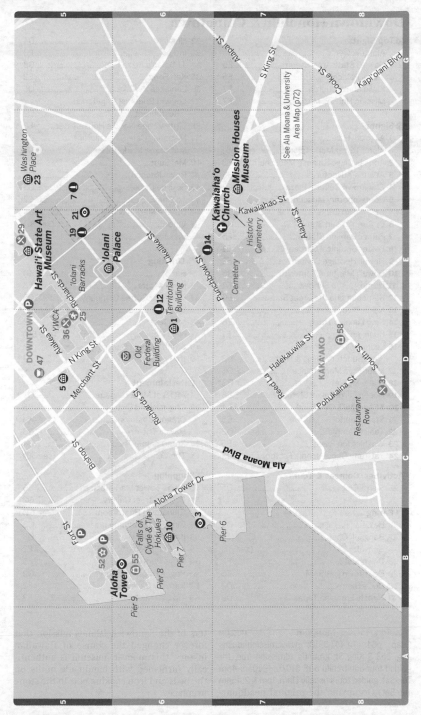

See Ala Moana & University Area Map (p72)

Washington Place 23

Hawai'i State Art Museum

29

7 21 19

'Iolani Palace

'Iolani Barracks

Richards St

N King St

Merchant St

Likelike St

Punchbowl St

Territorial Building

12 1

Old Federal Building

Kawaiaha'o Church

Mission Houses Museum

Kawaiahao St

Historic Cemetery

Cemetery

Alapai St

Halekauwila St

Reed La

KAKA'AKO

Pohukaina St

Restaurant Row

South St

58

31

DOWNTOWN P

47

5

36

25

YWCA

Alakea St

Bishop St

Fort St

Richards St

Ala Moana Blvd

Aloha Tower Dr

Falls of Clyde & The Hokule'a

10

3

Pier 6

Pier 7

Pier 8

Pier 9

Aloha Tower

52

55

Alapai St

S King St

Cooke St

Kapi'olani Blvd

Downtown Honolulu & Chinatown

◎ Top Sights

Aloha Tower	B6
Hawai'i State Art Museum	E5
'Iolani Palace	E5
Kawaiaha'o Church	E7
Mission Houses Museum	F7

◎ Sights

1	Ali'iolani Hale	D6
	Aloha Tower Marketplace	(see 55)
2	Anna Li Clinic Chinese Medicine	F3
3	Atlantis Adventures	B6
4	Chinatown Cultural Plaza	D2
5	Contemporary Museum at First Hawaiian Center	D5
6	Dr Sun Yat-sen Statue	D2
7	Father Damien Statue	F5
8	Foster Botanical Garden	E1
9	Hawaii Heritage Center	F2
10	Hawai'i Maritime Center	B6
11	Izumo Taisha Shrine	D1
12	Kamehameha the Great Statue	E6
13	Kekaulike Market	C3
14	King Lunalilo Tomb	E6
15	Kuan Yin Temple	E1
16	Leanne Chee Chinese Acupuncture Clinic & Herbs	D3
17	Maunakea Marketplace	C3
18	O'ahu Market	B3
19	Queen Lili'uokalani Statue	E5
20	St Andrew's Cathedral	F4
21	State Capitol	E5
22	Taoist Temple	D2
23	Washington Place	F5
24	Yat Tung Chow Noodle Factory	C3

Activities, Courses & Tours

25	Sierra Club	D5

⊗ Eating

26	Ba Le	C3
27	Bangkok Chef	F1
	Bonsai	(see 31)
28	Downbeat	F2
29	Downtown @HISAM	E5
30	Duc's Bistro	D2
31	Hiroshi Eurasian Tapas	D8

32	Hukilau	D4
33	Indigo	F3
34	JJ Dolan's Pizza Pub	G3
35	Ken Fong	E2
36	Laniakea YWCA	D5
37	Legend Buddhist Vegetarian Restaurant	D2
38	Little Village Noodle House	F2
39	Mabuhay Cafe & Restaurant	C2
	Maunakea Marketplace	(see 17)
40	Mei Sum	G2
41	Royal Kitchen	D2
42	Soul de Cuba	G3
43	To Chau	C2
44	Umeke Market & Deli	D4
	Vino	(see 31)
45	Vita Juice	D4

◎⊙ Drinking

	Bar 35	(see 50)
46	Hank's Cafe	F3
47	Honolulu Coffee Company	D5
	Indigo Lounge	(see 33)
48	Manifest	F2
	Next Door	(see 50)
49	Smith's Union Bar	F2
50	thirtyninehotel	F2

◎ Entertainment

51	ARTS at Marks Garage	G2
52	Chai's Island Bistro	B5
	Dragon Upstairs	(see 46)
53	Hawaii Theatre	G3
54	Kumu Kahua Theatre	C4
	The Venue	(see 56)

◎ Shopping

55	Aloha Tower Marketplace	B6
56	Bethel Street Gallery	G2
	Chinatown Boardroom	(see 61)
57	Cindy's Lei Shoppe	C3
58	Kamaka Hawaii	D8
59	Lai Fong Department Store	F2
60	Louis Pohl Gallery	F3
61	Pegge Hopper Gallery	G2
62	Ramsay Galleries	F2
63	Tin Can Mailman	F3

Mission Houses Museum   MUSEUM
(Map p64; ☑447-3910; www.missionhouses.org; 553 S King St; grounds admission free, 1hr guided tour adult/child 6-18 $10/6; ⊙10am-4pm Tue-Sat, guided tours usually 11am, 1pm & 2:45pm Tue-Sat) Occupying the original headquarters of the Sandwich Islands mission that forever changed the course of Hawaiian history, this modest museum is authentically furnished with handmade quilts on the beds and iron cooking pots in the stone fireplaces.

The Protestant missionaries packed more than their bags when they left Boston; they also brought a prefabricated wooden house, now called the Frame House, with them around the Horn. Designed to withstand cold New England winter winds, the small windows instead block out Honolulu's cooling tradewinds, keeping the two-story house hot and stuffy. Erected in 1821, it's the oldest wooden structure in Hawaii.

The coral-block Chamberlain House was the early mission's storeroom, a necessity because Honolulu had few shops in those days. Upstairs are hoop barrels, wooden crates packed with dishes, and the desk and quill pen of Levi Chamberlain. He was appointed by the mission to buy, store and dole out supplies to missionary families, who survived on a meager allowance – as the account books on his desk testify.

Nearby, the Printing Office houses a lead-type press used to print the first Bible in Hawaiian.

FREE Kawaiaha'o Church   HISTORICAL BUILDING
(Map p64; www.kawaihao.org; 957 Punchbowl St; ⊘8am-4pm Mon-Fri, worship service 9am Sun) O'ahu's oldest Christian church stands on the site where the first Protestant missionaries built a grass-thatch church shortly after their arrival in 1820. The original structure seated 300 Hawaiians on *lauhala* mats, woven from *hala* (screwpine) leaves.

This 1842 New England Gothic–style church is made of 14,000 coral slabs, which divers chiseled out of O'ahu's underwater reefs – a task that took four years. The clock tower was donated by Kamehameha III, and the old clock, installed in 1850, still keeps accurate time. The rear seats of the church, marked by *kahili* (feather staffs) and velvet padding, were reserved for royalty.

The tomb of King Lunalilo, the short-lived successor to Kamehameha V, stands near the main entrance to the church grounds. The cemetery at the rear of the church is almost like a who's who of colonial history. Early missionaries are buried alongside other important figures of the day, including infamous Sanford Dole, who became the first Hawai'i's first territorial governor after Queen Lili'uokalani was overthrown.

Aloha Tower   LANDMARK
(Map p64; www.alohatower.com; 1 Aloha Tower Dr; admission free; ⊘9am-5pm; P) Built in 1926, this 10-story landmark was once the city's tallest building. In the golden days when all

tourists to Hawaii arrived by ship, this pre-WWII waterfront icon greeted every visitor; cruise ships still disembark at the terminal beneath the tower today. Take the elevator to the top-floor tower observation deck for sweeping 360-degree views, then peek through the cruise-ship terminal windows back below on ground level to see colorful murals depicting bygone Honolulu.

Hawai'i Maritime Center   MUSEUM
(Map p64; ☑523-6151; www.bishopmuseum.org; Pier 7, Honolulu Harbor; ⊘closed temporarily; ⊕) As this book went to press, this museum was temporarily closed to the public, so call ahead before you visit. A great place to get a sense of Hawaii's history, this educational museum covers everything from the arrival of Captain Cook and 19th-century whaling ships to modern-day windsurfing. Displays on early tourism include a reproduction of a Matson liner stateroom and historical photos of Waikiki from the early 20th century.

The museum's centerpiece is *Hokule'a,* a traditional double-hulled sailing canoe that has repeatedly sailed from Hawaii to the South Pacific and back, retracing the routes of the islands' original Polynesian settlers using only ancient methods of wayfaring (navigation that relies on the sun, stars and wind and wave patterns).

Outside, climb aboard the *Falls of Clyde,* the world's last four-masted, four-rigged ship. Built in 1878 in Glasgow, the ship once carried sugar and passengers between Hilo on the Big Island of Hawai'i and San Francisco, then oil, before finally being stripped down to a barge. Today it's a floating National Historic Landmark.

FREE Contemporary Museum
at First Hawaiian Center   ART GALLERY
(Map p64; www.tcmhi.org; 999 Bishop St; ⊘8:30am-4pm Mon-Thu, to 6pm Fri) Inside the high-rise headquarters of the First Hawaiian Bank, this downtown art gallery livens up the briefcase district with changing exhibits of modern and contemporary art. Even the building itself features a four-story-high art-glass wall incorporating 185 prisms.

FREE Ali'iolani Hale   HISTORICAL BUILDING
(Map p64; 417 S King St; ⊘9am-4pm Mon-Fri) The first major government building constructed by the Hawaiian monarchy in 1874, the 'House of Heavenly Kings' was designed by Australian architect Thomas Rowe to be a royal palace, although it was never used as

such. It was on these steps in January 1893 that Sanford Dole proclaimed the end of the Hawaiian monarchy. Today this dignified Italianate structure houses the Hawaii Supreme Court. Step inside for historical displays about Hawaii's judicial history.

Outside, a statue of Kamehameha the Great faces 'Iolani Palace. The statue was cast in 1880 in Florence, Italy, by American sculptor Thomas Gould. The current statue is actually a recast, as the first statue was lost at sea near the Falkland Islands. The original statue, which was later recovered from the ocean floor, now stands in Kapa'au on the Big Island of Hawai'i, where Kamehameha was born.

FREE **State Capitol** NOTABLE BUILDING
(Map p64; 415 S Beretania St) Built in the architecturally interesting 1960s, Hawaii's state capitol is not your standard gold dome. It's a poster-child of conceptual postmodernism: the two cone-shaped legislative chambers represent volcanoes; the supporting columns symbolize palm trees; and a large pool encircling the rotunda represents the Pacific Ocean surrounding the Hawaiian Islands.

In front of the capitol stands a highly stylized statue of Father Damien, the Belgian priest who lived and worked among patients with Hansen's Disease (formerly called leprosy) forcibly exiled to the island of Moloka'i in the 19th century, before dying of the disease himself.

Symbolically positioned between the palace and the state capitol is a bronze statue of Queen Lili'uokalani, Hawaii's last reigning monarch. Lili'uokalani holds the constitution that she wrote in 1893 in a failed attempt to strengthen Hawaiian rule; 'Aloha 'Oe,' a popular song she composed; and *Kumulipo*, the Native Hawaiian chant of creation.

Washington Place HISTORICAL BUILDING
(Map p64; 586-0240; tours by appointment only) Surrounded by stately trees, this large colonial-style mansion was erected in 1846 by US sea captain John Dominis. The captain's son, also named John, became the governor of O'ahu and married the Hawaiian princess who became Queen Lili'uokalani. After the queen was released from house arrest at 'Iolani Palace in 1896, she lived at Washington Place until her death in 1917. A plaque near the sidewalk is inscribed with the words to 'Aloha 'Oe,' the farewell song Liliu'okalani composed. For tour reservations, call in advance.

St Andrew's Cathedral CHURCH
(Map p64; 524-2822; www.saintandrewscathedral.net; 229 Queen Emma Sq; tours usually 11:15am Sun;) This French Gothic cathedral was King Kamehameha IV's personal homage to the architecture and faith of the Church of England. The king and his consort, Queen Emma, founded the Anglican Church in Hawaii in 1861. Historical tours usually meet by the pulpit after the 10am Sunday worship service, but call ahead to confirm. For a free concert, the largest pipe organ in the Pacific is sonorously played every Wednesday starting at 12:15pm.

CHINATOWN

The location of this mercantile district is no accident. Between Honolulu's port and what was once the countryside, enterprises selling goods to city folks and visiting ship crews alike sprang up. In the late 19th century, many of these shops were established by Chinese laborers who had completed their sugarcane plantation contracts. The most successful entrepreneurs have long since moved out of this low-rent district into the suburbs, however, making room for newer waves of Southeast Asian immigrants.

The scent of burning incense still wafts through Chinatown's buzzing markets, fire-breathing dragons spiral up the columns of buildings and steaming dim sum awakens even the sleepiest of appetites. Take time to explore: browse cutting-edge art galleries and vintage antiques stores, rub shoulders with locals over a bowl of noodles, consult with an herbalist, buy a flower lei and take a meditative botanical garden stroll. For a self-guided historical walking tour, see p81.

Drug dealing and gang activity are prevalent on the north side of Chinatown, particularly along Nu'uanu Stream and the River St pedestrian mall, which should be avoided after dark. Chinatown's skid rows include blocks of Hotel St.

Chinatown Markets MARKET
The commercial heart of Chinatown revolves around the markets and food shops on Kekaulike and Maunakea Sts. Noodle factories, pastry shops and produce stalls line the streets crowded with feisty grandmothers and errand-running families.

The 1904 O'ahu Market (Map p64; 145 N King St) sells everything a Chinese cook needs: ginger root, fresh octopus, quail eggs, slabs of tuna, jasmine rice, long beans and salted jellyfish. You owe yourself a bubble tea if you spot a pig's head among the stalls.

A block away is **Yat Tung Chow Noodle Factory** (Map p64; 150 N King St), one of the neighborhood's half-a-dozen family-run noodle factories. Stop by in the early morning when a cloud of flour seemingly covers every surface.

Pedestrian-only Maunakea St is bookended by the vibrant **Kekaulike Market** (Map p64; Kekaulike St, btwn N King & Hotel Sts) and **Maunakea Marketplace** (Map p64; 1120 Maunakea S), with its bustling food court.

Foster Botanical Garden   GARDEN
(Map p64; www.co.honolulu.hi.us/parks/hbg/fbg.htm; 50 N Vineyard Blvd; adult/child 6-12yr $5/1; ⊙9am-4pm, guided tours usually 1pm Mon-Sat; P) Tropical plants you've only ever read about can be spotted in all their glory at this botanical garden, which took root here in 1850. Among its rarest specimens are the Hawaiian *loulu* palm and the East African *Gigasiphon macrosiphon,* both thought to be extinct in the wild. Several of the garden's towering trees are the largest of their kind in the USA. Oddities include the cannonball tree, the sausage tree and the double coconut palm capable of producing a 50lb nut – watch your head! Follow your nose past fragrant vanilla vines and cinnamon trees in the spice and herb gardens, then pick your way among the poisonous and dye plants. Don't miss the blooming orchid gardens. All of the species are labeled, and a free self-guided tour booklet is available at the garden entrance.

FREE **Kuan Yin Temple**   TEMPLE
(Map p64; 170 N Vineyard Blvd; ⊙hours vary) With its green ceramic-tile roof and bright red columns, this ornate Chinese Buddhist temple is Honolulu's oldest. The richly carved interior is filled with the sweet, pervasive smell of burning incense. The temple is dedicated to Kuan Yin, goddess of mercy, whose statue is the largest in the interior prayer hall. Devotees burn paper 'money' for prosperity and good luck, while offerings of fresh flowers and fruit are placed at the altar. The large citrus fruit stacked pyramid-style is pomelo, a symbol of fertility because of its many seeds.

FREE **Izumo Taisha**   TEMPLE
(Map p64; 215 N Kukui St; ⊙usually 9am-4pm) Across the river, this shintō shrine was built by Japanese immigrants in 1906. During

WWII the property was confiscated by the city; it wasn't returned to the community until the early 1960s. The 100lb sacks of rice near the altar symbolize good health. Ringing the bell at the shrine entrance is considered an act of purification for those who come to pray and seek blessings, especially on January 1, when the temple heaves with celebrants from all around O'ahu.

Taoist Temple   TEMPLE
(Map p64; 1315 River St; ⊙usually 8:30am-2pm) Founded in 1889, the Lum Sai Ho Tong Society was one of more than 100 societies started by Chinese immigrants in Hawaii to help preserve their cultural identity. The society's Taoist temple with its ornate altar honors the goddess Tin Hau, a Lum child who rescued her father from drowning and was later deified – the devout may claim to see her apparition when traveling by boat.

Hawai'i Heritage Center   MUSEUM
(Map p64; 1040 Smith St; admission $1; ⊙9am-2pm Mon-Sat) Local volunteers with family ties to the community run this gallery, which offers changing exhibitions on O'ahu's Chinese and other ethnic communities.

ALA MOANA

Meaning 'Path to the Sea,' Ala Moana is the nickname of the neighborhood west of Waikiki, which includes Honolulu's largest beach park and Hawaii's largest shopping mall.

TOP
CHOICE **Honolulu Academy of Arts**   MUSEUM
(Map p72; ☎532-8700; www.honoluluacademy.org; 900 S Beretania St; adult/child $10/free, all free 1st Wed & 3rd Sun of each month; ⊙10am-4:30pm

---

FLOWER POWER

Chinatown herbalists are both physicians and pharmacists, with walls full of small wooden drawers, each filled with a different herb. They'll size you up, feel your pulse and listen to you describe your ailments before deciding which drawers to open, mixing herbs and flowers and wrapping them for you to take home and boil together. Find traditional herbalists at **Chinatown Cultural Plaza** (Map p64), **Anna Li Clinic of Chinese Medicine** (Map p64; ☎537-1133; 1121 Nu'uanu Ave) or **Leanne Chee Chinese Herbs & Acupuncture** (Map p64; ☎533-2498; 1159 Maunakea St).

Tue-Sat, 1-5pm Sun, also 6-9pm last Fri of each month; P⏳) This exceptional museum may be the biggest surprise of your trip to O'ahu. It covers the artistic traditions of almost every continent, playing a leading role in the area of Asian art. Here you can also see masterpieces by Monet, Matisse and O'Keefe; galleries of Greek and Roman antiquities and Italian Renaissance paintings; major works of American modern art; ancient Japanese woodblock prints by Hiroshige and Hokusai; Ming dynasty Chinese calligraphy and painted scrolls; Indian temple carvings; war clubs and masks from Papua New Guinea – and so much more.

The museum was founded in 1927 by Anna Rice Cooke, an heiress who wanted to create an art collection that would reflect the diversity of the island's local population. She wanted this to be a place where children born in Hawaii could come and examine their own cultural roots – and perhaps just as importantly, discover something about their neighbors – all through the window of works of art.

Plan on spending a couple of hours here, perhaps having lunch at the Pavilion Café and joining a tour out to Shangri La, Doris Duke's enchanting estate near Diamond Head. Check the museum website for special events, including gallery tours, family-friendly Sundays, films and chamber music at the Doris Duke Theatre, and hip Art After Dark (www.artafterdark.org) parties with food, drinks and live entertainment.

Four-hour validated parking at the Art Center lot, just southeast of the museum, costs $3. From Waikiki, take TheBus 2 or 13 or B City Express.

UNIVERSITY AREA

In the foothills of Manoa Valley, the walkable university area has a youthful collection of cool cafes, ethnic restaurants and boutique shops.

University of Hawai'i at Manoa   UNIVERSITY, MUSEUM
(UH; Map p72; ☎956-8111; www.uhm.hawaii.edu; cnr University Ave & Dole St; P) Born too late for the tweedy academic architecture of the mainland, University of Hawai'i at Manoa is the central campus of the statewide university system. Filled with shade trees and well-bronzed students from around Polynesia, UH Manoa has strong academic programs in astronomy, geophysics, marine sciences, and Hawaiian and Pacific studies.

The UH Information & Visitor Center (Map p72; Room 212, Campus Center; ◷8:30am-4:30pm Mon-Fri) offers free one-hour walking tours of campus, emphasizing history and architecture. Tours usually leave at 2pm on Monday, Wednesday and Friday; to join a tour, no reservations are necessary; just check in 10 minutes beforehand. A Campus Art brochure, also available at the information center, outlines a self-guided walking tour of outdoor sculptures and other works by distinguished Hawaii artists.

A short walk downhill from Campus Center, the John Young Museum of Art (Map p72; www.outreach.hawaii.edu/JYMuseum; Krauss Hall, 2500 Dole St; admission free; ◷11am-2pm Mon-Fri, 1-4pm Sun) houses a 20th-century Hawaii painter's eclectic collection of artifacts from around the Pacific, Africa and Asia, including ceramics, pottery and sculpture. Although it only fills a couple of rooms, it's worth a quick look.

On the east side of campus, the East-West Center (; ☎944-7111; www.eastwestcenter.org; 1601 East-West Rd) aims to promote mutual understanding among the peoples of Asia, the Pacific and the USA. Changing exhibitions of art and culture are displayed in the center's EWC Gallery (Burns Hall; admission free; ◷usually 8am-5pm Mon-Fri, noon-4pm Sun). The center also hosts multicultural programs, including lectures, films, concerts and dance performances.

On-campus parking costs $4 before 4pm on weekdays; otherwise it's $5.

UPPER MANOA VALLEY & MAKIKI HEIGHTS

Welcome to Honolulu's green belt. The verdant Manoa Valley climbs beyond the UH Manoa campus, passing through exclusive residential neighborhoods and into forest reserve land above downtown.

Lyon Arboretum   GARDEN
(Map p76; ☎988-0456; www.hawaii.edu/lyonarboretum; 3860 Manoa Rd; admission by donation, guided tour $5; ◷8am-4pm Mon-Fri, 9am-3pm Sat; P⏳) Beautifully unkempt walking trails wind through this highly regarded 200-acre arboretum, founded in 1918 and managed by the University of Hawai'i. This is not your typical overly manicured tropical flower garden, but a mature and largely wooded arboretum, where related species cluster in a seminatural state. Guided tours are available at 10am on weekdays (reservations required).

CHINATOWN ART AFTER DARK

Chinatown's somewhat seedy Nuʻuanu Ave and Hotel St are surprisingly cool places for a hip dose of art and culture, socializing, live music and bar-hopping during the First Friday Honolulu Gallery Walk (www.firstfridayhawaii.com), held from 5pm to 9pm on the first Friday of each month. Pick up a free map from any of Chinatown's two dozen art galleries; most are within a two-block radius of the Hawaii Theatre (p92).

All of these well-established galleries stay open later during First Friday events:

» **ARTS at Marks Garage** (Map p64; 1159 Nuʻuanu Ave; ⊙11am-6pm Tue-Sat) Eclectic works by up-and-coming island artists in all types of media.

» **Bethel St Gallery** (Map p64; www.bethelstreetgallery.com; 1140 Bethel St; ⊙11am-4pm Tue-Fri, 11am-3pm Sun) Artist-owned cooperative exhibits a mixed plate of island artworks, from blown-glass sculptures to abstract paintings.

» **Chinatown Boardroom** (Map p64; www.chinatownboardroom.com; 1160 Nuʻuanu Ave; ⊙11am-4pm Tue-Sat) For ubercool 'lowbrow' art and one-of-a-kind customized surfboards.

» **Louis Pohl Gallery** (Map p64; www.louispohlgallery.com; 1111 Nuʻuanu Ave; ⊙11am-6pm Tue-Sat) Paintings by contemporary island artists and a former 'living treasure' of Hawaii.

» **Pegge Hopper Gallery** (Map p64; www.peggehopper.com; 1164 Nuʻuanu Ave; ⊙11am-4pm Tue-Fri) Represents the namesake artist's distinctive prints and paintings depicting voluptuous island women.

» **Ramsay Galleries** (Map p64; www.theramasymuseum.org; 1128 Smith St; ⊙9am-5pm Tue-Fri) Detailed pen-and-ink drawings and other works by well-known Hawaii artists like Dietrich Varez.

Take a break from the culture vultures at Hank's Cafe (p91), a dive bar that serves thirsty locals, while jazz cats play at the Dragon Upstairs (p92). Or grab dinner at a neighborhood restaurant before hitting Chinatown's nightclub, lounge and live music scene that cranks up later in the evening.

Among the plants in the Hawaiian ethnobotanical garden are ʻulu (breadfruit), kalo (taro) and ko (sugarcane) brought by early Polynesian settlers; kukui, once harvested to produce lantern oil; and ti, which was used for medicinal purposes during ancient times and for making moonshine after Westerners arrived. If you walk uphill for about a mile along a dirt jeep road, a narrow, tree-root-entangled footpath leads to seasonal ʻAihualama Falls, a lacy cliffside cascade (no swimming).

From Ala Moana Center, catch TheBus 5 to Manoa Valley and get off at the last stop, then walk 0.6 miles uphill to the end of Manoa Rd. Limited free parking.

Contemporary Museum MUSEUM
(TCM; Map p76; ☑526-1322; www.tcmhi.org; 2411 Makiki Heights Dr; adult/child under 13yr $6/free, all free 3rd Thu of each month; ⊙10am-4pm Tue-Sat, noon-4pm Sun, tours usually 1:30pm; ℗) Inside an estate house with meditative sculpture and flowering gardens, this small art museum features changing exhibits of paint-

ings, sculpture and other artwork dating from the 1940s onward by Hawaii-born, mainland and international artists. A lawn pavilion holds the museum's most prized piece, an environmental installation by David Hockney based on sets for L'Enfant et les Sortilèges, Ravel's 1925 opera. Downstairs, the modest **Contemporary Café** serves drinks and light lunches, including romantic picnic baskets for two (reserve ahead).

From Waikiki, take either TheBus 2 or B City Express! toward downtown Honolulu and get off at Beretania and Alapaʻi Sts. Walk one block toward the ocean along Alapaʻi St to King St and transfer to TheBus 15, which stops at the museum.

Manoa Heritage Center HEIAU (TEMPLE)
(☑988-1287; www.manoaheritagecenter.org; adult/child $7/free; ⊙tours by appointment only 9:30am-3:30pm Wed-Sat; ℗) Hidden on a private family's estate in the lush valley above UH Manoa, Manoa Heritage Center is a unique Hawaiian heritage site. The centerpiece is a stone-walled agricultural heiau

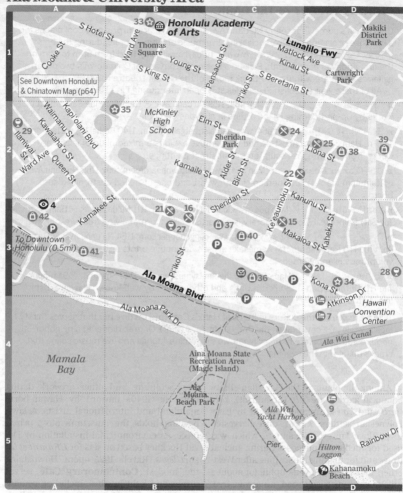

(temple) surrounded by Hawaiian ethnobotanical gardens, which include rare native and Polynesian-introduced plants. Take a turn at the *konane* board (a Hawaiian version of checkers), then follow the path downhill to learn how taro was traditionally farmed. Walking tours are led by knowledgeable volunteers and staff eager to share island lore and Hawaiian traditions. Try to call at least a week in advance for tour reservations and to get directions (no walk-ins can be accommodated, due to the need to protect both the site and the resident family's privacy).

Tantalus–Round Top Scenic Drive
SCENIC DRIVE

Starting just 2 miles above downtown Honolulu, a narrow switchback road cuts its way up into the Makiki Valley's forest reserves. Rewarding drivers with skyline views, it climbs almost to the top of Mt Tantalus (2013ft), aka Pu'u 'Ohi'a. Bamboo, ginger, elephant-eared taro and eucalyptus trees make up a profusion of tropical plants along the way, as vines climb to the tops of telephone poles and twist their way across the wires. This 8.5-mile circuit is a two-way

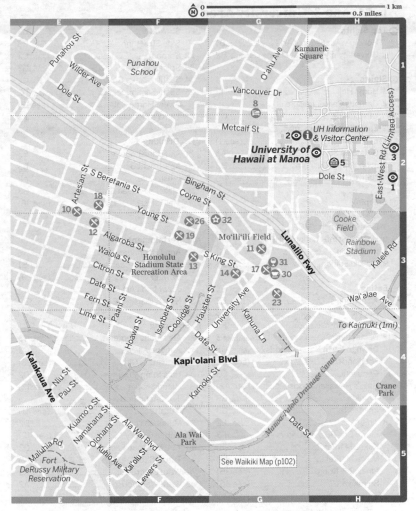

loop called Tantalus Dr on its western side, Round Top Dr to the east.

Pu'u 'Ualaka'a State Wayside
(Map p76; ☺7am-6:45pm Apr-early Sep, to 6:45pm early Sep-Mar) For the most remarkable panoramas, stop at Pu'u 'Ualaka'a State Wayside. About 2.5 miles up Round Top Dr from Makiki Heights is the park entrance, from where it's another half-mile to the lookout (bear left at the fork). Sweeping views extend from Diamond Head on the far left, across Waikiki and downtown Honolulu, to the Wai'anae Range on the right. South-

east sprawls the University of Hawai'i, easily recognized by its sports stadium. Looking southwest you can see into the green mound of Punchbowl crater. The airport is visible on the coast and Pearl Harbor beyond that.

GREATER HONOLULU

Bishop Museum
MUSEUM
(Map p63; ☎847-3511; www.bishopmuseum.org; 1525 Bernice St; adult/child 4-12 $18/15; ☺9am-5pm Wed-Mon; ℙ👶) Like Hawaii's version of the Smithsonian Institute in Washington, DC, this museum showcases a remarkable array of cultural and natural history and science

◉ **Top Sights**
   Honolulu Academy of Arts B1
   University of Hawaii at Manoa H2

◉ **Sights**
1 Burns Hall H2
2 Campus Center Leisure
   Programs G2
3 East-West Center H2
   EWC Gallery .... (see 1)
4 Girls Who Surf A3
5 John Young Museum...........................H2
   Native Books/Nā Mea Hawaii ..... (see 42)

🛏 **Sleeping**
6 Ala Moana Hotel.......................D4
7 Central Branch YMCA D4
8 Hostelling International (HI)
   Honolulu................................G1
9 Waikiki Edition............................D5

🍴 **Eating**
10 Alan Wong's...................................E2
11 Bubbies G3
12 Chef Mavro.....................................E3
13 Da Kitchen F3
14 Down to Earth Natural Foods...............G3
   Foodland .... (see 36)
15 Gomaichi...C3
   Halili's Hawaiian Foods .... (see 42)
16 Ichiriki..B3
17 Imanas Tei G3
18 Jimbo...E2
19 Kiawe Grill BBQ & Burgers F3
   Kokua Market...............................(see 23)
   Makai Market................................ (see 36)
   Pineapple Room...........................(see 36)
   Shirokiya .... (see 36)

20 Shokudo..................................D3
21 Side Street Inn.......................B3
22 Sorabol C2
23 Spices G3
24 Sushi Izakaya Gaku................................C2
25 Sushi Sasabune.....................D2
   Sweet Home Café........................(see 19)
26 Yama's Fish Market.............................F3

🍷 **Drinking**
27 Aku Bone Lounge B3
28 Apartment 3...........................D3
29 Fresh Cafe A2
30 Glazer's Artisan Coffee..........................G3
   Mai Tai Bar..................................(see 36)
31 Varsity......................................G3

🎭 **Entertainment**
32 Anna Bannanas...................................G3
33 Doris Duke Theatre B1
   HawaiiSlam..................................(see 29)
34 Jazz Minds Art & Cafe....................D3
35 Neal S Blaisdell Center B2

🛍 **Shopping**
36 Ala Moana Center.........................C3
37 Antique Alley C3
   Cinnamon Girl.............................(see 36)
38 Hula Supply Center D2
   Island Slipper ....(see 42)
   Jeff Chang Pottery & Fine
   Crafts ....(see 41)
39 Manuheali'i D2
   Nohea Gallery ....(see 42)
40 T&L Muumuu Factory...........................C3
   Tutuvi Sitoa.................................(see 17)
41 Ward Centre..............................A3
42 Ward Warehouse.....................................A3

exhibits. It's often ranked as the world's finest Polynesian anthropological museum. Founded in 1889 in honor of Princess Bernice Pauahi Bishop, a descendant of the Kamehameha dynasty, it originally housed only Hawaiian and royal artifacts.

The recently renovated main gallery, the **Hawaiian Hall**, resides inside a dignified three-story Victorian building. Displays covering the cultural history of Hawaii include a *pili*-grass thatched house, carved *ki'i akua* (temple images), *kahili* (feathered staffs used at royal funerals and coronations), shark-toothed war clubs and traditional *tapa* cloth made by pounding the

bark of the paper mulberry tree. Don't miss the feathered cloak once worn by Kamehameha the Great, created entirely from the yellow feathers of the now-extinct *mamo* – some 80,000 birds were caught and plucked to create this single adornment. Upper-floor exhibits delve further into *ali'i* (royal) history and the relationship between Native Hawaiians and the natural world.

The two-story exhibits inside the adjacent **Polynesian Hall** cover the myriad cultures of Polynesia, Micronesia and Melanesia. You could spend hours gazing at astounding and rare ritual artifacts, from elaborate dance masks and ceremonial costumes to carved canoes and tools of warfare. Next door, the museum's more modern wing, the **Castle Memorial Building**, has changing traveling exhibitions.

Across the Great Lawn, the state-of-the-art, family-oriented **Science Adventure Center** uses interactive multimedia exhibits and demonstrations to explain Hawaii's natural environment, letting kids walk through an erupting volcano or take a mini-sub dive. The museum is also home to O'ahu's only planetarium (☑848-4136), which highlights traditional Polynesian methods of wayfaring (navigation), along with astronomy and the telescope observatories atop Mauna Kea. Shows are usually held at 11:30am, 1:30pm and 3:30pm, and are included in the museum admission price.

A **gift shop** off the main lobby sells books on the Pacific not easily found elsewhere, as well as some high-quality Hawaiian crafts and souvenirs. Check the museum website for special events, including the popular 'Moonlight Mele' summer concert series under the stars, family-friendly Hawaiian cultural festivities and after-dark planetarium shows (buy tickets or make reservations in advance).

From Waikiki or downtown Honolulu, take TheBus 2 to School St/Middle St or B City Express! to the intersection of School St and Kapalama Ave; walk one block *makai* (seaward) on Kapalama Ave, then turn right on Bernice St. By car, take eastbound H-1 Fwy exit 20, turn right on Houghtailing St, then left on Bernice St; free parking.

FREE National Memorial
Cemetery of the Pacific   HISTORICAL SITE
(2177 Puowaina Dr; ☺8am-5:30pm Sep 30-Mar 1, 8am-6:30pm Mar 2-Sep 29, 7am-7pm Memorial Day; ℗) A mile northeast of downtown Honolulu surrounded by freeways and residential neighborhoods is a bowl-shaped crater, nicknamed the Punchbowl, formed by a long-extinct volcano. Early Hawaiians called the crater Puowaina ('hill of human sacrifices'). It's believed that at an ancient heiau here the slain bodies of *kapu* (taboo) breakers were ceremonially cremated upon an altar.

Today ancient Hawaiians sacrificed to appease the gods share the crater floor with the buried remains of almost 50,000 US soldiers, many of whom were killed in the Pacific during WWII. The remains of Ernie Pyle, the distinguished war correspondent

who covered both world wars and was hit by machine-gun fire on Ie-shima during the final days of WWII, lie in section D, grave 109. Five stones to the left, at grave D-1, is the marker for Ellison Onizuka, the Big Island astronaut who perished in the 1986 *Challenger* space-shuttle disaster.

For plum views of the city and Diamond Head, head up to the lookout by bearing left after passing through the main cemetery gates. Special events held at the cemetery include Memorial Day ceremonies to honor military veterans and a traditional Easter sunrise church service.

From Waikiki, take TheBus 2 toward downtown Honolulu and get off at Beretania and Alapa'i Sts, walk one block *makai* (seaward) along Alapa'i St and transfer to TheBus 15. From the closest bus stop, it's about a 15-minute uphill walk to the cemetery entrance. If you're driving, there's a marked exit as you start up the Pali Hwy – watch closely, because it comes up quickly! Then carefully follow the signs through twisting, narrow residential streets.

Queen Emma Summer
Palace   HISTORICAL BUILDING
(Map p76; ☑595-3167; www.daughtersofhawaii.org; 2931 Pali Hwy; adult/child $6/1; ☺9am-4pm; ℗) In the heat and humidity of summer, Queen Emma, the royal consort of Kamehameha IV, used to slip away to this genteel hillside retreat, now a historical museum. The exterior somewhat resembles an old Southern plantation house, with its columned porch, high ceilings and louvered windows catching the breezes.

Forgotten after Queen Emma's death in 1885, this stately home was slated to be razed and the estate turned into a public park. The Daughters of Hawai'i, whose members are all descendants of early missionary families, rescued it. The interior now looks much as it did in Queen Emma's day, decorated with period furniture, including a koa-wood cabinet displaying a set of china from England's Queen Victoria and elaborate feather cloaks and capes once worn by Hawaiian royalty.

To get here, take TheBus 4 from Waikiki or downtown Honolulu, or bus 56 or 57A from the Ala Moana Center. Be sure to let the bus driver know where you're going, so you don't miss the stop. If you're driving, look for the entrance near the 2-mile marker on the northbound Pali Hwy (Hwy 61).

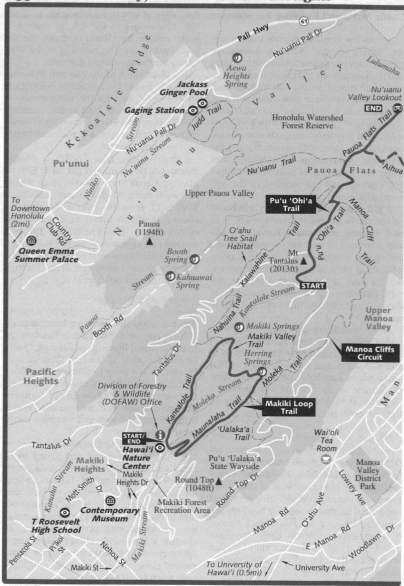

Activities

UH Manoa's **Campus Center Leisure Programs** (Map p72; ☎956-6468; www.hawaii.edu/cclp; Room 101, Hemenway Hall, 2445 Campus Center Rd) runs a healthy variety of public classes and outdoors trips, from half-day hikes ($10) or kayaking excursions ($30) to introductory bodyboarding ($20) or sailing classes ($130).

Hiking

You could spend days enjoying the solitude of the forests around the city. Some of O'ahu's most popular trails lead into the

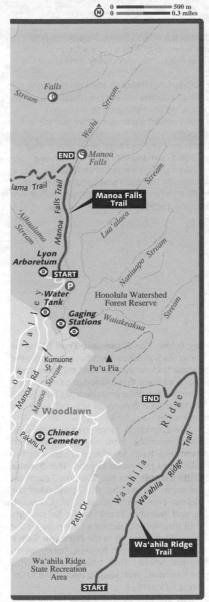

lush, windy Koʻolau Range just above downtown. For more trails beyond those we've described here, visit the government-sponsored Na Ala Hele Trail & Access System website (http://hawaiitrails.ehawaii.gov). To join group hikes, check the calendar in the free *Honolulu Weekly* or check with the following organizations:

Hawaiʻi Nature Center   OUTDOOR ACTIVITIES
(Map p76; ☎955-0100; www.hawaiinaturecenter .org; 2131 Makiki Heights Dr) Low-cost family-oriented hikes and environmental programs; reservations usually required.

Hawaiian Trail & Mountain Club   HIKING
(http://htmclub.org; hike donation per adult $3) Volunteer-run community organization arranges group hikes and offers extensive online resources.

Sierra Club   HIKING
(Map p64; ☎538-6616; www.hi.sierraclub.org/ oahu; 1040 Richards St) Leads weekend hikes and other outings around Oʻahu, including volunteer opportunities to rebuild trails and restore native plants.

Manoa Falls & Nuʻuanu Valley Lookout   HIKING
Perhaps Honolulu's most rewarding short hike, the 1.6-mile round-trip **Manoa Falls Trail** (Map p76) runs above a rocky streambed through lush vegetation. Tall tree trunks lining the often muddy and slippery path include *Eucalyptus robusta*, with soft, spongy, reddish bark; flowering orange African tulip trees; and other arboreals that creak like wooden doors in old houses. Wild orchids and red ginger grow near the falls, which drop about 100ft into a small, shallow pool. Falling rocks and leptospirosis (see p642) make swimming inadvisable, unfortunately.

Just before reaching Manoa Falls, the inconspicuous **ʻAihualama Trail** branches off west of a chain-link fence, offering broad views of Manoa Valley starting just a short way up the path. After a five-minute walk, you'll enter a bamboo forest with some massive old banyan trees, which contours around the ridge, then switchbacks up. You can hike the trail as a side spur from the Manoa Falls trail or orchestrate a 5.5-mile round-trip hike by connecting with the **Pauoa Flats Trail**, which leads up to the **Nuʻuanu Valley Lookout**, from where it's possible to peer through a gap in the steep *pali* (cliffs) over to the Windward Coast.

By car, follow University Ave north of the UH Manoa campus. Continue on Oʻahu Ave, taking the right fork when the road splits and follow Manoa Rd up to the trailhead parking lot ($5). From Ala Moana Center, take TheBus 5 Manoa Valley to the end of the line (25 minutes, hourly), from where it's

MR OBAMA'S NEIGHBORHOOD

During the 2008 race to elect the 44th President of the United States, Republican vice-presidential candidate Sarah Palin kept asking the country, 'Who is Barack Obama?' It was Obama's wife, Michelle, who had an answer ready: 'You can't really understand Barack until you understand Hawaii.'

Obama, who grew up in Makiki Heights, has written that 'Hawaii's spirit of tolerance... became an integral part of my world view, and a basis for the values I hold most dear.' The local media and many *kama'aina* (those who were born and grew up in Hawaii) agree that Hawaii's diverse multiethnic social fabric helped shape the leader who created a rainbow coalition during the 2008 US election.

Obama has also said Hawaii is a place for him to rest and recharge, as he does during annual family vacations while in office. Back in 1999, Obama wrote, 'When I'm heading out to a hard day of meetings and negotiations, I let my mind wander back to Sandy Beach, or Manoa Falls... It helps me, somehow, knowing that such wonderful places exist and [that]...I'll always be able to return to them.'

If you want to walk in Obama's footsteps on O'ahu, here are a few of his favorite places:

» Manoa Falls (p77)
» Rainbow Drive-In (p115)
» Kapi'olani Beach Park (p101)
» Hanauma Bay (p124)
» Sandy Beach (p128)
» Olomana Golf Links (p132)

a 0.5-mile uphill walk to the trailhead. Limited free street parking is available downhill from the bus stop, but pay attention to all posted restrictions.

Makiki Valley Loop & Manoa Cliffs Circuit

HIKING

A favorite workout for city dwellers, the 2.5-mile **Makiki Valley Loop** (Map p76) links three Tantalus area trails. These trails are usually muddy, so wear shoes with traction and pick up a walking stick. The loop cuts through a lush and varied tropical forest, mainly composed of nonnative species introduced to reforest an area denuded by the 19th-century *'iliahi* (sandalwood) trade. Keep watch for the tumbled-down remains of ancient Hawaiian stone walls and a historic coffee plantation.

Starting past the Hawaii Nature Center, the **Maunalaha Trail** crosses a small stream, passes taro patches and climbs up the eastern ridge of Makiki Valley, passing Norfolk pine, banyans, bamboo and some clear views. After 0.7 miles, you'll reach a four-way junction. Continue uphill on the 1.1-mile **Makiki Valley Trail**, which traverses small gulches and across gentle streams bordered by patches of ginger and guava trees while offering glimpses of the city below. The **Kanealole Trail** begins as you cross Kanealole Stream, then follows the stream back to the baseyard, 0.7 miles away. This trail leads down through a field of Job's tears; the beadlike psuedocarps ('false fruit') of the female flowers of this tall grass are sometimes used for lei.

Alternatively, a more strenuous 6.2-mile hike beginning from the same trailhead eventually leads to sweeping views of the valley and the ocean beyond. This **Manoa Cliffs Circuit**, aka the 'Big Loop,' starts on the same Maunalaha Trail, then takes the Moleka Trail to the Manoa Cliff, Kalawahine and Nahuina Trails. At the Kalawahine Trail intersection, detour to the right on the Pauoa Flats Trail up to the **Nu'uanu Valley Lookout**. From the lookout, backtrack to the Kalawahine Trail, which connects with the Kanealole Trail leading back down to the forest baseyard.

The starting point for both hiking loops is the Makiki Forest Recreation Area baseyard, less than 0.5 miles up Makiki Heights Dr from Makiki St. The forest baseyard turnoff is a little lane at a sharp bend in the main road. Park along the shoulder before reaching the Hawaii Nature Center and the Division of Forestry & Wildlife (DOFAW)

office (Map p76; ☎973-9778; http://hawaii.gov/
dlnr/dofaw; 2135 Makiki Heights Dr; ⊙7:45am-
4:30pm Mon-Fri), which distributes free trail
maps.

From downtown, take TheBus 15, which
runs into Pacific Heights. Get off near the
intersection of Mott-Smith Dr and Makiki
Heights Dr, then walk about 0.4 miles along
Makiki Heights Dr to the baseyard. From
Waikiki, take TheBus 4 Nu'uanu to the corner of Wilder Ave and Makiki St, then walk
approximately 0.7 miles up Makiki St.

Pu'u 'Ohi'a (Mt Tantalus) Trail   HIKING
Along the Tantalus–Round Top scenic drive
(p72), a network of hiking trails littered with
fragrant *liliko'i* (passion fruit) encircles Mt
Tantalus, offering contemplative forest hikes
combined with city views. The hardy **Pu'u
'Ohi'a Trail** (Map p76), in conjunction with
the Pauoa Flats Trail, leads up to **Nu'uanu
Valley Lookout**, traveling almost 2 miles
each way. The trailhead hides at the very
top of Tantalus Dr, about 3.6 miles up from
Makiki Heights Dr. There's a parking turnoff
opposite the trailhead, on the *makai* (seaward) side of the road.

The trail begins with reinforced log
steps, leading past fragrant ginger, musical bamboo groves and lots of eucalyptus,
a fast-growing tree planted to protect the
watershed. After 0.5 miles, the trail summits
Mt Tantalus (2013ft), aka Pu'u 'Ohi'a, then
leads back onto a service road ending at a
telephone relay station. Behind that building, the trail continues until it reaches the
Manoa Cliff Trail, where you'll go turn left.
At the next intersection, turn right onto the
muddy **Pauoa Flats Trail**, which leads up
to the **Nu'uanu Valley Lookout**, high in
the Ko'olau Range.

You'll pass two trailheads before reaching the lookout. The first is the **Nu'uanu
Trail**, on the left, which runs 0.75 miles
along the western side of the upper Pauoa
Valley, offering broad views of Honolulu
and the Wai'anae Range. The second is the
'Aihualama Trail, a bit further along on
the right, which heads 1.3 miles through
tranquil bamboo groves and past huge old
banyan trees to Manoa Falls.

Wa'ahila Ridge Trail   HIKING
Popular with families, the boulder-strewn
Wa'ahila Ridge Trail (Map p76) offers
a cool retreat amid Norfolk pines and endemic plants, with ridgetop views of Honolulu and Waikiki. The 4.8-mile trail covers

a variety of terrain in a short time, making
an enjoyable afternoon's walk for novice
hikers. Look for the Na Ala Hele trailhead
sign just past the picnic tables deep inside
Wa'ahila Ridge State Recreation Area
(www.hawaiistateparks.org; ⊙sunrise to sunset), at
the back of the St Louis Heights subdivision,
east of Manoa Valley.

By car, follow Wai'alae Ave east of the
university area into the Kaimuki neighborhood (Map p72), turning left at the stop-
light onto St Louis Dr. As you drive uphill,
veer left onto Bertram St, turn left onto Peter St, then left again onto Ruth Pl, which
runs west into the park. From Waikiki, The-
Bus 14 St Louis Heights stops hourly at the
intersection of Peter and Ruth Sts, about
0.4 miles from the trailhead.

Cycling
Road cyclists looking for an athletic workout
head up the scenic Tantalus–Round Top loop
road. Honolulu's Bike Shop (☎596-0588;
www.bikeshophawaii.com; 1149 S King St; rentals per
day $20-85, car rack $5; ⊙9am-7pm Mon-Fri, 9am-
5pm Sat, 10am-5pm Sun) rents top-quality road
bikes and can provide maps of suggested cycling routes.

Surfing
You'll find beginner and intermediate-level
surf breaks at Ala Moana Beach Park,
while those off Kaka'ako Waterfront Park
(Map p63) are for advanced boarders only.
You can rent surfboards and arrange lessons
in Waikiki (see p107).

Golf
Moanalua Golf Club   GOLF
(☎839-2411; 1250 Ala Aolani St; greens fee $20-
30; ⊙by appointment only) Built in 1898 by a
missionary family, Hawaii's oldest golf club
is a fairly quick course with an elevated
green, straight fairways and nine holes
that can be played twice around from different tees.

 Courses

Campus Center Leisure
Programs   ARTS, FITNESS
(Map p72; ☎956-6468; www.hawaii.edu/cclp;
Room 101, Hemenway Hall, 2445 Campus Center Rd; classes $10-65) UH Manoa offers
a variety of short-term courses open to
the public. Some classes, including hula,
Tahitian dance, yoga and ukulele, meet
once or twice weekly during a month-
long session.

Native Books/Nā Mea Hawaii ARTS, CULTURE
(Map p72; ☑596-8885; www.nativebookshawaii
.com; Ward Warehouse, 1050 Ala Moana Blvd)
This independent bookstore hosts free
classes, workshops and demonstrations in
hula dancing, Hawaiian language, traditional feather lei-making and *lauhala*
weaving, ukulele playing and more.

Aloha Tower Marketplace ARTS, CULTURE
(Map p64; ☑566-2337; www.alohatowermarket
place.com; 1 Aloha Tower Dr) This harborfront
mall offers casual introductory drop-in
classes in hula dancing and ukulele playing (nominal fee may apply).

Honolulu for Children

For endless sand and a children's playground, take your *keiki* to Ala Moana Beach
Park (p62), where local families hang out.
For more of O'ahu's great outdoors, head up
into the Manoa Valley to Lyon Arboretum
(p70), then hike to pretty Manoa Falls (p77).

Indoors, the Bishop Museum (p73) is
entertaining for kids of all ages. There's an
interactive family art center in the basement
of the Honolulu Academy of Arts (p69).

For the best islandwide activities for kids,
see p83.

Hawaii Children's Discovery Center MUSEUM
(☑524-5437; www.discoverycenterhawaii.org; 111
'Ohe St; adult/child 1-17yr $10/10; ⊗9am-1pm
Tue-Fri, 10am-3pm Sat & Sun; P♿) On a rainy
day when you can't go to the beach, take
your tots to this hands-on, family-oriented
museum. Occupying a 38,000-sq-ft waterfront site, this was once the city's garbage
incinerator, as evidenced by the surviving
smokestack.

Interactive exhibits are geared toward
elementary school-aged children and pre-
schoolers. The **Fantastic You!** exhibit
explores the human body, allowing kids
to walk through a mock human stomach.
More traditional displays are found in the
Your Town section, where kids can drive a
play fire engine or conduct a TV interview.
Two other interesting sections, **Hawaiian
Rainbows** and **Your Rainbow World**,
introduce children to Hawaii's multicultural
heritage.

From Waikiki, take TheBus 19 or 20; it is
a five-minute walk *makai* (seaward) to the
center from the nearest bus stop on Ala Moana Blvd at Kolua St. There is also limited
free on-site parking.

Tours

For a self-guided historical walking tour of
Chinatown, see p81. For island sightseeing
bus and van tours, see p58.

Atlantis Adventures BOAT TOURS
(Map p64; ☑800-548-6262; www.atlantis
adventures.com; Pier 6, 1 Aloha Tower Dr; 2hr tour
adult/child from $49/25; ♿) Usually from late
December through March, Atlantis offers naturalist-led whale-watching cruises
aboard a high-tech catamaran designed
to minimize rolling. Tours include a light
breakfast or a lunch buffet; reservations
essential.

Hawaii Food Tours VAN TOURS
(☑926-3663; www.hawaiifoodtours.com; tours incl
transportation from $99) Designed by a for-
mer chef and restaurant critic, this four-
hour lunchtime tour samples Chinatown's
hole-in-the-walls, island plate lunches,
famous bakeries, crack-seed candy shops
and more.

O'ahu Ghost Tours WALKING TOURS
(☑877-597-7325; www.oahughosttours.com; tours
incl transportation adult/child from $34/29)
Hear spooky stories from local guides
and go hunting for paranormal orbs on
hokey, but amusing guided walking tours
of Honolulu's haunted places. No skeptics
allowed.

✿ Festivals & Events

Year-round, festivals and events take place
all over the city, including in Waikiki (p108).

Chinese New Year CULTURE
(www.chinatownhi.com) Between late January
and mid-February, Chinatown festivities
include a parade, block party, lion dances
and firecrackers.

Honolulu Festival ARTS, CULTURE
(www.honolulufestival.com) Three days of
Asian-Pacific cultural exchange with
music, dance and drama performances, an
arts-and-crafts fair, a parade and fireworks
in mid-March.

Pan-Pacific Festival ARTS, CULTURE
(www.pan-pacific-festival.com) Three days of
Japanese, Hawaiian and South Pacific
entertainment in early June, with music,
dancing and *taiko* drumming at Ala
Moana Center.

King Kamehameha Hula
Competition HULA
(www.hulacomp.com) One of Hawaii's biggest
hula contests, with hundreds of dancers

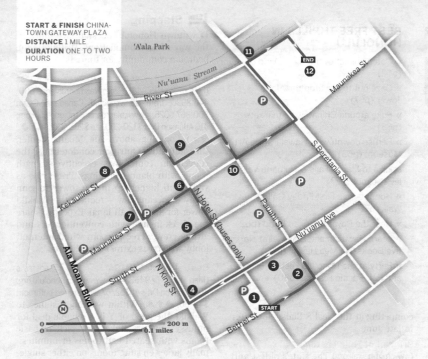

'A'ala Park

Nu'uanu Stream

River St

Maunakea St

S Beretania St

N Hotel St (buses only)

Pauahi St

Nu'uanu Ave

Kekaulike St

Maunakea St

Ala Moana Blvd

Smith St

N King St

Bethel St

END

START

0 ___ 200 m
0 ___ 0.1 miles

Walking Tour
Historical Chinatown

❯ Honolulu's most foot-trafficked neighborhood, Chinatown, is also its most historic.
Start at ❶ **Chinatown Gateway Plaza**, where
stone lions mark the neighborhood's official
entrance. Walk northeast to the neoclassical 1922 ❷ **Hawaii Theatre**, nicknamed the
'Pride of the Pacific,' then continue around the
corner onto Pauahi St, heading northwest.

Turn left onto Nu'uanu Ave, where the now-
abandoned ❸ **Pantheon Bar** was a favorite of
sailors in days past. The avenue's granite-block
sidewalks are themselves relics, built with the
discarded ballasts of 19th-century trading
ships that brought tea from China in exchange
for 'iliahi (sandalwood). At the corner of King
St, peek into the ❹ **First Hawaiian Bank**, with
its antique wooden teller cages.

Turn right onto King St, then right on Smith
St. Poke your head into the ❺ **Hawai'i Heritage Center**. Soon you'll intersect seedy Hotel St,
undergoing a transformation
from a red-light district into a row of nightclubs, hip lounges and coffeehouses. Turn
left onto Hotel St and walk to the corner of

Maunakea St, where the ornate facade of the
❻ **Wo Fat Building** resembles a Chinese
temple. Turn left and walk down Maunakea St,
then right onto King St.

Continue past the red pillars coiled with
dragons outside the ❼ **Bank of Hawaii**
to the corner of Kekaulike St and the bustling ❽ **O'ahu Market**. Walk north up the
Maunakea St pedestrian mall and into the
❾ **Maunakea Marketplace**, turning right as
you emerge back onto Pauahi St. Soon you'll
pass ❿ **lei shops** where skilled artisans string
and braid blossom after blossom, filling the air
with the scents of pikake and ginger.

Turn left onto Maunakea St, then left again
onto Beretania St. Down by the riverside, the
⓫ **statue of Dr Sun Yat-sen**, a Chinese revolutionary, stands guard as senior citizens play
checkers and mahjong outdoors. Inside the
courtyard of utilitarian modern ⓬ **Chinatown
Cultural Plaza**, acupuncturists and callig-
raphers work with elderly Chinese who also
come to light incense before a statue of Kuan
Yin, goddess of mercy.

BEST FREE THRILLS IN HONOLULU

» Catch sunset over Magic Island (p62)

» Gaze out to sea atop the Aloha Tower (p67)

» Poke around Chinatown's markets (p68)

» Peruse downtown's Hawai'i State Art Museum (p63)

» Hike to Manoa Falls & Nu'uanu Valley Lookout (p77)

» Hobnob on a First Friday Gallery Walk (p71)

» Hear the Royal Hawaiian Band (p62)

» Learn Hawaiian and make lei at Native Books/Nā Mea Hawaii (p80)

» Party at the Honolulu Festival (p80) and Pan-Pacific Festival (p80)

competing at the Neal S Blaisdell Center in late June.

Prince Lot Hula Festival HULA
(www.mgf-hawaii.org) The state's oldest and largest noncompetitive hula event at the Moanalua Gardens on the third Saturday in July.

Hawaii Dragon Boat Festival SPORTS, MUSIC
Colorful dragon boats race to the beat of island drummers at Ala Moana Beach Park in late June.

Talk Story Festival STORYTELLING
(www.co.honolulu.hi.us/parks/programs; [小]) Storytellers gather at Ala Moana Beach Park in mid-October; Friday is usually spooky stories.

Hawaii International Film Festival MOVIES
(www.hiff.org) A celluloid celebration of Pacific Rim and homegrown films in late October.

King Kalakaua's Birthday MUSIC, CULTURE
Victorian-era decorations and a concert of traditional monarchy-era music by the Royal Hawaiian Band at 'Iolani Palace on November 16.

Honolulu Marathon SPORTS
(www.honolulumarathon.org) One of the world's 10 largest marathon races from downtown to Diamond Head on the second Sunday of December.

🛏 Sleeping

Downtown Honolulu doesn't have much in the way of accommodations. Waikiki is the bedroom community for tourists.

Ala Moana Hotel HOTEL $$
(Map p72; ☑955-4811, from Neighbor Islands 800-446-8990, from US mainland, Canada & Guam 800-367-6025; www.alamoanahotelhonolulu.com; 410 Atkinson Dr; r $120-200, ste $260-310; P✸@🛜🏊) Looming above Ala Moana Center, this multistory Outrigger condotel near the convention center has executive-strength rooms with bland trimmings. Prices rise as you climb higher up in the tower to gain a city or ocean view – request the Waikiki Tower for an open-air lanai. Expect to share the check-in line with conventioneers and airline crews. Free in-room wired internet; lobby wi-fi costs extra. Parking $20.

Central Branch YMCA HOSTEL $
(Map p72; ☑941-3344; www.ymcahonolulu.org; 401 Atkinson Dr; s/d $52/67, with shared bathroom $42/60; @🛜🏊) Within walking distance to Waikiki, the good ol' Y is a reliable deal for unfussy travelers. Take your pick of basic rooms with shared bathrooms or infinitesimally larger en suite rooms on either single-sex or co-ed floors. Bonus perks include an Olympic-sized swimming pool and a modern, fully equipped gym.

Hostelling International (HI) Honolulu HOSTEL $
(Map p72; ☑946-0591; www.hostelsaloha.com; 2323-A Seaview Ave; dm $20-23, r $50-56; ⏱reception 8am-noon & 4pm-midnight; P@🛜) Tidy little house is tucked away in a residential neighborhood near UH Manoa, just a short bus ride from Waikiki. Sex-segregated dorms are sunny and breezy. Some students crash here while looking for apartments, so it's often full. There's a kitchen, laundry room, lockers and limited free parking.

For overnight layovers near the airport and complimentary 24-hour airport shuttles:

Ohana Honolulu Airport Hotel HOTEL $$
(☑836-0661, 866-968-8744; www.ohana hotels.com; 3401 N Nimitz Hwy; r from $110; P✸@🛜🏊) Best pick among airport-area hotels, with free lobby wi-fi and wired in-room internet; parking $20.

Best Western Plaza Hotel HOTEL $$
(☑836-3636, 800-800-4683; www.bestwestern hawaii.com; 3253 N Nimitz Hwy; r $130-170; P✸@🏊) Noisier rooms front the highway. Free in-room wired internet; parking $20.

Eating

You might sleep and play in Waikiki, but you should definitely eat in Honolulu. In fact, if O'ahu weren't so far away from the US mainland, you'd definitely hear a lot more buzz about this multiethnic chowhound capital. During **Restaurant Week Hawaii** (www.restaurantweekhawaii.com), usually in mid-November, many local restaurants offer dining-out discounts, including prix-fixe dinner menus.

DOWNTOWN

Many eateries are only open during lunch on weekdays for the downtown office crowd. Aloha Tower Marketplace is great for sunset drinks and *pupu* (appetizers), but not full meals. After dark, Restaurant Row has a few hot spots that often come and go.

Hiroshi Eurasian Tapas   FUSION $$
(Map p64; ☎533-4476; www.hiroshihawaii.com; Restaurant Row, 500 Ala Moana Blvd; shared plates $11-17, mains $25-28; ☺5:30-9:30pm) Chef Hiroshi Fukui puts a Japanese twist on Pacific Rim fusion styles, from crab cannelloni swirled with miso sauce to smoked *hamachi* (yellowtail) spiced with habanero peppers and a garlic kicker. Order foamy tropical martinis and fresh-fruit sodas at the bar, or duck next door to vivacious Vino (a wine bar and Italian tapas joint) or mod Bonsai (a sushi, sake and shochu bar).

Downtown @HiSAM   ISLAND CONTEMPORARY $$
(Map p64; www.slowdowntown.com; 1st fl, 250 S Hotel St; mains $10-16; ☺11am-2pm Mon-Fri, 5:30-9:30pm 1st Fri of each month) At the Hawai'i State Art Museum, this arty cafe is an outpost of Kaimuki's trendy bistro Town. Market-fresh salads, soups, sandwiches and creative plate lunches break culinary barriers – witness the lotus-root chips, ahi club sandwiches and guava chiffon cake.

Hukilau   ISLAND CONTEMPORARY $$
(Map p64; ☎523-3460; www.dahukilau.com/honolulu; 1088 Bishop St; mains lunch $11-17, dinner $12-20; ☺11am-2pm Mon-Fri, 4-9pm Mon-Fri) Friendly tiki-themed sports bar and grill lies underground at downtown's highest high-rise hotel. Huge salads, sandwiches and burgers aren't as tempting as the only-in-Hawaii specialties like miso butterfish, kalua pig spring rolls, ahi *poke* and other tasty happy-hour *pupus*.

People's Open Market FARMERS MARKET $
(POM; off Map p64; City Hall parking lot deck, cnr Alapa'i & Beretania Sts; ☺11:45am-12:30pm Mon; 🐾) Sells fresh island bounty from the land and sea.

'Umeke Market & Deli   SUPERMARKET $
(Map p64; www.umekemarket.com; 1001 Bishop St; mains $4-10; ☺7am-4pm Mon-Fri; 🐾) Organic produce, natural-foods groceries and a vegetarian-friendly takeout deli and cafe.

Laniakea YWCA   CAFE $
(Map p64; 1040 Richards St; mains $8-12; ☺usually 11am-2:30pm Mon-Fri) Inside the historic Julia Morgan-designed YWCA, a daily-changing menu of light lunches is committed to locally grown, often organic ingredients.

Vita Juice   HEALTHY, TAKEOUT $
(Map p64; 1111-C Fort St Mall; items $3-6; ☺7am-5pm Mon-Fri; 🐾) Exotic smoothie bar mixes up 'brain food' and sells homemade cookies.

O'AHU FOR CHILDREN

» Outrigger canoe rides, swimming and a sunset torch lighting and hula show at Waikiki's Kuhio Beach (p101)

» Touch tanks at Waikiki Aquarium (p105)

» Planetarium shows and exploding faux volcanoes at Honolulu's Bishop Museum (p73)

» Hiking to Manoa Falls (p77) or up Diamond Head (p122)

» Snorkeling at Hanauma Bay (p124)

» Wading into Ko Olina Lagoons (p160)

» Steam-train rides and a giant maze at Dole Plantation (p158)

» Movie and TV filming tours at Kualoa Ranch (p142)

» Rainy-day indoor fun at Hawaii Children's Discovery Center (p80)

1. Royal Hawaiian, Waikiki (p106)
Once the playground of A-list celebrities, including the Rockefellers and Groucho Marx.

2. Diamond Head & Waikiki (p121)
A massive backdrop to Waikiki, Diamond Head is O'ahu's best-known landmark.

3. Shave Ice (p156)
Stop for a shave ice, the most spectacular snow cone on earth, at Matsumoto's or Aoki's.

4. Laysan Albatross, Ka'ena Point (p163)
Also known as *moli*, Laysan Albatross can be found nesting at Ka'ena Point during winter.

This historic downtown neighborhood is packed with open-air markets, hole-in-the-wall noodle kitchens, dim-sum palaces, pan-Asian kitchens and trendy fusion eateries.

Royal Kitchen
CHINESE, BAKERY $

(Map p64; http://royalkitchenhawaii.com; Chinatown Cultural Plaza, 100 N Beretania St; bakery items $1-2; ☺5:30am-4:30pm Mon-Fri, 6:30am-4:30pm Sat, 6:30am-2:30pm Sun) This humble takeout shop is worth fighting Chinatown's snarled traffic just for its famous *manapua* with sweet and savory fillings such as *char siu* (Chinese barbecue pork), chicken curry, sweet potato, *kalua* pig or black sugar.

Little Village Noodle House
CHINESE $$

(Map p64; ☎545-3008; www.littlevillagehawaii.com; 1113 Smith St; mains $10-22; ☺10:30am-10:30pm Sun-Thu, to midnight Fri & Sat) Forget about chop suey. If you live for anything fishy in black-bean sauce, this is Honolulu's gold standard. On the eclectic pan-Chinese menu, regional dishes are served garlicky, fiery or with just the right dose of saltiness. Bonuses: air-con and free parking out back. Reservations recommended.

Duc's Bistro
EURASIAN $$

(Map p64; ☎531-6325; www.ducsbistro.com; 1188 Maunakea St; mains $12-26; ☺11am-2pm Mon-Fri, 5-10pm daily) This swank French-Vietnamese bistro is an escape from the seediness just outside. Flat-iron steaks, buttery escargots, fire-roasted eggplant with lime dressing, green papaya salad and pan-fried fish with mango relish round out a haute fusion menu. A small jazz combo serenades some evenings. Reservations recommended.

To Chau
VIETNAMESE $

(Map p64; 1007 River St; mains $6-9; ☺8am-2:30pm) Always packed, this Vietnamese restaurant holds fast to its reputation for serving Honolulu's best *pho* (Vietnamese noodle soup). Beef, broth and vegetables – the dish is a complete meal in itself, but the menu includes other Vietnamese standards, too. Just 16 tables inside equals long lines.

Soul de Cuba
CUBAN $$

(Map p64; ☎545-2822; www.souldecuba.com; 1121 Bethel St; mains $8-22; ☺11:30am-10pm Mon-Thu, to 11pm Fri & Sat, to 8:30pm Sun) Sate your craving for Afro-Cuban food and out-of-this-world *mojitos* inside this fashionable resto-lounge near Chinatown's art galleries, often with live music at night. Stick with family-recipe classics like *ropa vieja* (shredded beef in tomato sauce) and black-bean soup.

Bangkok Chef
THAI $

(Map p64; www.bangkokchefexpress.com; 1627 Nu'uanu Ave; mains $6-9; ☺10:30am-9pm Mon-Sat, noon-8pm Sun) Open-air kitchen feels strangely like eating out of someone's garage. But who cares when the Thai curries, noodles dishes and savory salads taste exactly like from a Bangkok street cart? Dessert is mango ice cream over warm sticky rice topped with salty peanuts. Also at 2955 E Manoa Rd, north of UH Manoa.

Indigo
FUSION $$

(Map p64; ☎521-2900; www.indigo-hawaii.com; 1121 Nu'uanu Ave; lunch buffet $16, dinner mains $18-30; ☺11:30am-2pm Tue-Fri, 6-9:30pm Tue-Sat) Once a standard-bearer for a revitalized Chinatown, this still-busy eatery has let its lunch slide to a buffet level. Creative dim-sum appetizers include ahi tempura rolls and goat-cheese wontons. Dinner features Pacific Rim and Asian fusion fare such as cocoa-bean seafood curry and little-known classics like Malaysian beef *rendang*.

Ken Fong
CHINESE $

(Map p64; 1030 Smith St; mains $5-12; ☺10:30am-3pm & 5-9pm Mon-Sat) You can forget about the hipsters' Chinatown art scene at this homestyle storefront. Feast on savory roast duck or ginger chicken atop a mountain of jasmine rice or tuck into a spicy lamb hot-pot casserole. The family who cooks here, eats here – now that's a real vote of confidence.

Mei Sum
CHINESE $

(Map p64; 1170 Nu'uanu Ave; dim-sum dishes $2-4, mains $6-12; ☺7am-8:45pm) Where else are you gonna go to satisfy that crazy craving for dim sum after noon? This no-nonsense spot cranks out cheap, delectable little plates all day long. They've also got a full spread of Chinese mains; order the secret garlic eggplant not on the menu.

Mabuhay Cafe & Restaurant
FILIPINO $$

(Map p64; 1049 River St; mains $6-12; ☺10am-10pm) Red-and-white checked tablecloths, well-worn counter stools and jukebox should clue you in that this is a mom-and-pop joint. In fact, they've been cooking up pots full of succulent, garlic-laden pork adobo and *kare-kare* (oxtail stew) on this same corner by the river since the 1960s.

Ba Le
VIETNAMESE, DELI $

(Map p64; www.ba-le.com; 150 N King St; mains $3-9; ⊙6am-5pm Mon-Sat, to 3pm Sat) Its name is a corruption of the word 'Paris,' this fluorescent-lit bakery-cafe is an island-born chain, best known for its chewy baguette sandwiches and equally chewy cups of coffee served either hot or iced, loaded with sugar and milk. Also at 1154 Fort St Mall.

JJ Dolan's Pizza Pub
PUB GRUB $

(Map p64; www.jjdolans.com; 1147 Bethel St; pizzas from $15; ⊙11am-2am Mon-Sat) Two guys running a sociable Irish pub in Chinatown, baking NYC-style pizza and pouring cold beer. What's not to like?

Downbeat
DINER $

(Map p64; www.downbeatdiner.com; 42 N Hotel St; mains $6-9; ⊙11am-3am Mon-Thu, to 4am Fri & Sat; ✍) This shiny late-night diner posts a vegetarian/vegan-friendly menu of burgers, sandwiches and island breakfasts like *loco moco*. Otto's cheesecake is addictive.

Maunakea Marketplace
PAN-ASIAN, TAKEOUT $

(Map p64; 1120 Maunakea St; mains $4-8; ⊙7am-5:30pm) Hidden in a food court, mom-and-pop vendors dish out home-style Chinese, Filipino, Thai, Vietnamese, Korean and Japanese fare. Cash only.

Legend Buddhist Vegetarian Restaurant
CHINESE, VEGETARIAN $

(Map p64; Chinatown Cultural Plaza, 100 N Beretania St; mains $8-13; ⊙10:30am-2pm Thu-Tue; ✍) This lunch-only spot is 100% vegetarian with an extensive, if somewhat bland, menu of fake seafood and meat dishes.

ALA MOANA
A bevy of local restaurants inhabit the side streets around Ala Moana Center mall.

TOP CHOICE Alan Wong's
HAWAII REGIONAL $$$

(Map p72; ☎949-2526; www.alanwongs.com; 1857 S King St; mains $27-52; ⊙5-10pm) One of O'ahu's big-gun chefs, Alan Wong offers his creative interpretations of island cuisine inside an office building with, sadly, no view. Extra emphasis goes to fresh seafood and local produce, especially at the chef's bimonthly 'farmers series' dinners. Skip the daily tasting menus, however. Instead rely on signature dishes like ginger-crusted *onaga* (red snapper) and twice-cooked *kalbi* short ribs. Reservations essential. Valet parking.

Side Street Inn
ISLAND CONTEMPORARY $$

(Map p72; ☎591-0253; www.sidestreeetinn.com; 1225 Hopaka St; shared plates $9-21; ⊙2pm-2am) The outside looks like hell, and the sports-bar atmosphere wouldn't rate on a Zagat's survey, but this late-night mecca is where you'll find some of Honolulu's top chefs hanging out in the Naugahyde booths up front after work. Divinely tender *kalbi* short ribs and pork chops are the most famous dishes. Bring a big, hungry group. Reservations advised. Also at 614 Kapahulu Ave in Waikiki.

Sushi Izakaya Gaku
JAPANESE $$$

(Map p72; ☎589-1329; 1329 S King St; most shared plates $6-28; ⊙5-11pm Mon-Sat) Popularized by word-of-mouth, this *izakaya* (Japanese gastropub) beats the competition with adherence to tradition and supremely fresh sushi and sashimi. A spread of savory and sweet hot and cold dishes includes hard-to-find specialties like *chazuke* (tea-soaked rice porridge) and *natto* (fermented soybeans). Reservations recommended.

Chef Mavro
EURASIAN $$$

(Map p72; ☎944-4714; www.chefmavro.com; 1969 S King St; 3-course dinner without/with wine pairings from $75/123; ⊙6:30-9:30pm Tue-Sun) At Honolulu's most avant-garde restaurant, maverick chef George Mavrothalassitis creates conceptual dishes like kabocha coconut custard and bigeye ahi with olive tapenade, each paired with Old and New World wines. Unfortunately the cutting-edge experimental cuisine, like the half-empty atmosphere, often falls flat. Reservations essential.

Pineapple Room
HAWAII REGIONAL $$

(Map p72; ☎945-6573; www.alanwongs.com; 3rd fl, Macy's, Ala Moana Center, 1450 Ala Moana Blvd; mains breakfast & lunch $12-22, dinner $19-35; ⊙11am-8:30pm Mon-Fri, 8-10:30am & 11am-8:30pm Sat, 9-10:30am & 11am-3pm Sun) At this dressed-down department store cafe, acclaimed island chef Alan Wong's classics are made in an exhibition kitchen, including island-style comfort food like *kalua* pig BLT sandwiches, *loco moco* specials and killer desserts. Reservations advised.

Gomaichi
JAPANESE, TAIWANESE $$

(Map p72; www.rikautsumi.com/demo/gomaichi; 631 Ke'eaumoku St; mains $7-10; ⊙11am-2pm & 5:30-9pm Mon-Sat) Squeaky-clean ramen shop's name roughly translates as 'No 1 Sesame' and die-hard fans agree. Gomaichi's *tantan* menu of noodle soup in sesame broth reigns supreme, especially if you get an extra order of falling-apart *char siu* pork. Or try a spicy *sung hong* Chinese-style hot-and-sour noodle soup instead.

Shokudo
JAPANESE **$$**
(Map p72; ☑941-3701; www.shokudojapanese .com; 1585 Kapi'olani Blvd; most shared plates $5-25; ☺11:30am-1am Sun-Thu, to 2am Fri & Sat, last orders 1hr before closing) Knock back sake-tinis at this modern dance hall-sized dining room that's always filled to the rafters. A mixed traditional Japanese and fusion menu lists dizzying dozens of small plates, from *mochi* cheese gratin to lobster dynamite rolls, more traditional noodle and sushi, and silky homemade tofu. Reservations recommended.

Jimbo
JAPANESE **$**
(Map p72; 1936 S King St; mains $10-15; ☺11am-2:30pm daily, 5-9:30pm Sun-Thu, to 10:30pm Fri & Sat) Drop by for handmade soba and thick udon noodles, always fresh and flavorful. Order 'em cooked in hot broth on rainy days or chilled on a summer's afternoon, then slurp your way to happiness.

Makai Market
FOOD COURT **$**
(Map p72; 1st fl, Ala Moana Center, 1450 Ala Moana Blvd; mains $6-12; ☺9:30am-9pm Mon-Sat, 10am-7pm Sun; 🖼) Would you rather die than be caught eating inside a mall? Let your preconceptions fly out the window at this Asian-fusion marketplace. Tasty spots include Japanese CoCo Ichibanya Curry House and Donburiya Dondon, and Hawaii-flavored Lahaina Chicken and Ala Moana Poi Bowl.

Sushi Sasabune
JAPANESE **$$**
(Map p72; ☑947-3800; 1417 King St; most dishes $15-31; ☺12:30-2pm Mon-Fri, 5:30pm-10pm Mon-Sat) Honolulu's top-shelf choice for sushi purists, but locals say beware the 'sushi nazi' chef behind the counter. Reservations recommended.

Ichiriki
JAPANESE **$$**
(☑589-2299; http://ichirikinabe.com; 510 Pi'ikoi St; set meals lunch $11-23, dinner $22-60; ☺11am-2pm daily, 5pm-11pm Mon-Thu, to midnight Fri & Sat, to 10pm Sun) Authentic Japanese *nabemono, shabu-shabu* and *sukiyaki* hot-pot restaurant utilizes fresh, island-grown ingredients. Reservations recommended.

Halili's Hawaiian Foods
HAWAIIAN, TAKEOUT **$**
(http://mybackyardluau.ning.com; Ward Warehouse, 1050 Ala Moana Blvd; plate lunches $6-10;

☺11am-3pm Mon-Fri) A branch of Waikiki's family fave, this lunch-wagon truck parks under the hala tree in the outdoor lot.

Shirokiya
FOOD COURT **$**
(Map p72; Ala Moana Center, 1450 Ala Moana Blvd; most items $2-12; ☺9:30am-8pm Mon-Sat, to 6pm Sun) Japanese department store's upper-level marketplace is a gold mine of takeout hot and cold dishes.

Sorabol
KOREAN **$$**
(Map p72; www.sorabolhawaii.com; 805 Ke'eaumoku St; set meals $15-38; ☺24hr) Korean BBQ house that serves lunching ladies by day and bleary-headed clubbers at dawn.

Foodland
SUPERMARKET **$**
(Map p72; Ala Moana Center, 1450 Ala Moana Blvd; ☺5am-10pm Mon-Sat, 6am-8pm Sun) A full-service supermarket at Hawaii's biggest mall.

UNIVERSITY AREA
Internationally flavored restaurants that'll go easy on your wallet cluster south of the UH Manoa campus, just a short bus ride from Waikiki.

⭐TOP CHOICE Imanas Tei
JAPANESE **$$$**
(Map p72; ☑941-2626; 2626 S King St; most shared dishes $5-30; ☺5-11:30pm Mon-Sat) Staff will shout a chorus of '*Irrashaimase!*' as you walk in the door of this *izakaya* (Japanese gastropub) with polished wooden tables and tatami-mat booths. Sushi and sake fans can booze it up as they graze their way through a seemingly endless menu of epicurean and country-style Japanese fare, including crowd-pleasing *nabemono* (clay-pot meat and vegetable soups). Reserve days, if not weeks in advance.

Spices
SOUTHEAST ASIAN **$$**
(Map p72; ☑949-2679; www.spiceshawaii.com; 2671 S King St; mains $13-16; ☺11:30am-2pm Tue-Fri, 5:30-9:30pm Tue-Sat, 5-9pm Sun; ☑) Setting a neighborhood-friendly table free of suffocating kitsch, this modern Southeast Asian kitchen charges more than the competition, but its variety of homemade Thai curries, Lao soups and Burmese noodles is worth it. Look for wild flavors of homemade ice cream like durian, chili pepper-lemongrass, pineapple-basil, banana-cinnamon or Okinawan sweet potato.

Sweet Home Café
TAIWANESE **$**
(Map p72; ☑947-3707; 2334 S King St; mains $6-14; ☺4-11pm) You won't believe the lines snaking

BEST JAPANESE BITES

Tired of Pacific Rim fusion? Take heart: for authentic tastes of the Land of the Rising Sun, Honolulu and Waikiki can't be beat.

Imanas Tei (p88) Traditional *izakaya* (gastropub) with endless sake

Sushi Izakaya Gaku (p87) Cult chef's word-of-mouth *izakaya*

Ichiriki (p88) Every kind of *nabemono* hot pot imaginable

Sushi Sasabune (p88) Only die-hard sushi aficionados allowed

Menchanko-tei (p113) Hakata-style ramen and *tonkotsu* pork chops

Ramen Nakamura (p113) Busy as a Tokyo subway station

Chibo (p113) Sleek *okonomiyaki* and *teppanyaki* grill

Shirokiya (p88) Department store's indoor food festival

Iyasume Musubi-ya (p114) Tiny *musubi* and *bentō* box kitchen

Gomaichi (p87) Sesame-flavored ramen is No 1!

Jimbo (p88) Soul-soothing homemade soba and udon noodles

Gyū-kaku (p113) DIY Japanese BBQ grill house

outside this strip-mall eatery's door. On 10 long wooden family-style tables squat heavily laden, steaming hot pots filled with stewed lemongrass beef, sour cabbage, mixed tofu or Asian pumpkin squash, plus spicy dipping sauces and extra lamb, chicken or tender beef tongue as side dishes. Make reservations or risk waiting an hour or more outside.

Kiawe Grill BBQ & Burgers   KOREAN, BBQ **$**
(Map p72; www.kiawegrill.com; 2334 S King St; meals $8-14; ☻10am-9pm Mon-Sat, to 8pm Sun) Formica tables heave with plastic plates of exotic venison, ostrich, buffalo and Kobe beef burgers piled high with steak fries and spicy Korean vegetables. Warning: you'll smell like BBQ smoke for the rest of the day.

Da Kitchen   HAWAIIAN, LOCAL **$**
(Map p72; www.da-kitchen.com; 925 Isenberg St; meals $7-12; ☻11am-9pm Mon-Sat) Crowded neighborhood storefront is home base for an

enterprising family whose Hawaiian food is just so dang *'ono* that they've even cooked at the White House for O'ahu-born President Obama.

For takeout meals and snacks:

Kokua Market   SUPERMARKET **$**
(Map p72; http://kokuamarket.ning.com; 2643 S King St; ☻8am-9pm;) Hawaii's only natural-foods co-op offers an organic salad bar and vegan-friendly deli.

Down to Earth Natural Foods   SUPERMARKET **$**
(Map p72; www.downtoearth.org; 2525 S King St; ☻7:30am-10pm;) Natural-foods supermarket and deli with a vegetarian-friendly salad bar.

Yama's Fish Market   HAWAIIAN, SEAFOOD **$**
(Map p72; www.yamasfishmarket.com; 2332 Young St; meals $5-10; ☻9am-7pm Mon-Sat, 9am-5pm Sun) Hawaiian plate lunches (eg kalua pig, lau lau, lomilomi salmon), plus freshly mixed *poke* by the pound.

Bubbies   DESSERT **$**
(Map p72; Varsity Center, 1010 University Ave; items $2-6; ☻noon-midnight Mon-Thu, to 1am Fri & Sat, to 11:30pm Sun;) Homemade tropical ice cream, including bite-sized frozen *mochi* treats.

GREATER HONOLULU

In the low-key Kaimuki neighborhood east of the university, Wai'alae Ave is Honolulu's homegrown 'restaurant row'. More off-the-beaten path eateries are scattered around the metro area.

Town   ISLAND CONTEMPORARY **$$**
(735-5900; www.townkaimuki.com; 3435 Wai'alae Ave; mains breakfast & lunch $5-16, dinner $16-26; ☻7am-2:30pm daily, 5:30-9:30pm Mon-Thu, to 10pm Fri & Sat) The motto at this buzzing Kaimuki bistro with urban coffee shop decor is 'local first, organic whenever possible, with aloha always.' On the daily-changing menu of boldly flavored cooking are burgers and steaks made from North Shore free-range cattle and salads that taste as if the ingredients were just plucked from a backyard garden.

Soul   SOUTHERN **$$**
(735-7685; http://pacificsoulhawaii.com; 3040 Wai'alae Ave; mains $8-20; ☻11am-9pm Tue-Thu, 11am-10pm Fri, 9am-10pm Sat, 10:30am-8pm Sun) Authentic, rib-sticking Southern soul food with a Motown soundtrack in Honolulu?

Chef Sean is all smiles as he delivers island-grown cabbage coleslaw, buttermilk fried chicken, BBQ spare ribs and sassy vegetarian chili to your table. Gumbo, grits and Carolina pulled pork adobo are also on the menu. Wednesday's special chicken-and-waffles usually sell out fast.

Helena's Hawaiian Food HAWAIIAN $$
(1240 N School St; dishes $1-10, meals $9-18; ⊙10:30am-7:30pm Tue-Fri) This humble Honolulu institution dates back to 1946. The menu is mostly à la carte dishes, some smoky and salty, others sweet or spicy. Start with *poi* (fermented taro), then add some *pipi kaula* (beef jerky), *kalua* pig, fried butterfish or squid cooked in coconut milk, and you've got a mini-luau.

Nico's at Pier 38 SEAFOOD, LOCAL $
(www.nicospier38.com; 1133 N Nimitz Hwy; meals $5-10; ⊙6:30am-5pm Mon-Fri, to 2:30pm Sat) French chef Nico cranks up island culinary traditions with fresh seafood from Honolulu's nearby fish auction. Local faves include furikake-crusted ahi with ginger-garlic sauce, fried calamari on Nalo greens, chicken katsu and hoisin BBQ chicken. Casual outdoor tables are within spitting distance of the sea.

Also recommended:

Liliha Bakery BAKERY, DINER $
(www.lilihabakeryhawaii.com; 515 N Kuakini, cnr Liliha St; items from $2, mains $6-10; ⊙nonstop 6am Tue-8pm Sun) This all-night diner and bakery has been causing traffic jams for its coco puff pastries (chocolate and green tea are classic flavors) since the 1950s.

Kaimuki Crack Seed CANDY SHOP $
(1156 Koko Head Ave; ⊙9am-6:30pm Mon-Sat; ⊛) Mom-and-pop candy store with overflowing glass jars of crack seed, plus sugary frozen slushies spiked with li hing mui.

Whole Foods SUPERMARKET $$
(4211 Wai'alae Ave; ⊙7am-10pm; ⊘) Near Kaimuki, this organic and natural-foods grocery store has a vegetarian-friendly takeout deli and hot-and-cold salad bar.

Drinking & Entertainment

For up-to-date listings of live-music gigs, DJ clubs, movies, theater and cultural events, check the *Honolulu Star-Advertiser*'s TGIF section, which comes out on Friday, and the free tabloid *Honolulu Weekly,* published every Wednesday.

Cafes

Manifest CAFE
(Map p64; http://manifesthawaii.com; 32 N Hotel St; ⊙10am-midnight Mon-Sat; ⊛) Right smack in the middle of Chinatown's art scene, this lofty apartment-like space with provocative photos and paintings on the walls is a serene coffee shop by day and a cocktail bar by night, with hipster events like movie and trivia nights and DJs spinning (no cover).

Fresh Cafe CAFE
(Map p72; www.freshcafehi.com; 831 Queen St; ⊙7am-1am Mon-Thu, 7am-1:30am Fri & Sat, noon-7pm Sun; ⊛) Alternative coffeehouse for artists, bohemians and hipster hangers-on in an Ala Moana industrial area. Sip a Vietnamese coffee, pikake iced tea or a haupia-flavored or Thai latte, or nosh on healthy soups, sandwiches and vegan cupcakes.

Honolulu Coffee Company CAFE
(Map p64; www.honolulucoffee.com; 1001 Bishop St; ⊙6am-5:30pm Mon-Fri, 7am-noon Sat; ⊛) Overlooking Bishop Sq with city skyline views, take a break for a java jolt brewed from handpicked, hand-roasted 100% Kona estate-grown beans. Free wi-fi. Also at Ala Moana Center.

Glazer's Artisan Coffee CAFE
(Map p72; www.glazerscoffee.com; 2700 S King St; ⊙6:30am-11pm Mon-Thu, 6:30am-9pm Fri, 9am-11pm Sat & Sun; ⊛) They're serious about brewing perfect espresso drinks and fresh roasted coffee at this university-student hangout, with comfy sofas and jazzy artwork. Free wi-fi.

Lion Coffee CAFE $
(1555 Kalani St; ⊙6am-5pm Mon-Fri, 9am-3pm Sat; ⊛) The out-of-the-way warehouse of this discount Hawaii coffee giant blends flavors from strong (100% Kona 24-Karat and Diamond Head espresso blend) to outlandishly wacky (chocolate macadamia-nut, toasted coconut). Ask the coffee-bar brewers for a free taste. Free wi-fi.

Waioli Tea Room CAFE $
(Map p76; ⎗888-340-8917; www.thewaioliteroom.net; 2950 Manoa Rd; ⊙10:30am-3:30pm) If 19th-century author Robert Louis Stevenson was still hanging around Honolulu today, this is where you'd find him. Set in the verdant Manoa Valley, this open-air cafe overlooks lush gardens. The real event is afternoon high tea (reservations required).

Bars, Lounges & Clubs

Wherever you go in Honolulu, any self-respecting bar or lounge has a *pupu* menu to complement the liquid sustenance, and some bars are as famous for their appetizers as their good-times atmosphere. A key term to know is *pau hana* (literally 'stop work'), Hawaiian pidgin for 'happy hour.' Chinatown's hip nightlife scene revolves around Nu'uanu Ave and N Hotel St, once the city's notorious red-light district.

thirtyninehotel   NIGHTCLUB, LOUNGE
(Map p64; http://thirtyninehotel.com; 39 N Hotel St; ⏰4pm-2am Tue-Sat) More arty than club-by, this multimedia space is a gallery by day, club by night. DJs don aloha wear for weekend spins, while rock bands test the acoustics some weeknights. Next-door Bar 35 stocks over 100 bottled beers to choose from, plus more DJs and live bands.

Next Door   NIGHTCLUB, LOUNGE
(Map p64; www.nextdoorhnl.com; 43 N Hotel St; ⏰8pm-2am Wed-Sat) Situated on the same seedy stretch of Hotel St, where dive bars are the order of the day, this svelte lounge is a red-brick walled retreat with lipstick-red couches and flickering candles. DJs spin mostly house and hip hop; live local bands play just about anything.

Hank's Cafe   DIVE BAR
(Map p64; www.hankscafehonolulu.com; 1038 Nu'uanu St; ⏰1pm-2am Mon-Sat, 1pm-midnight Sun) You can't get more legit than this neighborhood bar on the edge of Chinatown. Owner Hank Taufaasau is a jack-of-all-trades when it comes to the barfly business: the walls are decorated with Polynesian-themed art, all kinds of live music rolls in nightly and regulars call it home.

TOP CHOICE La Mariana Sailing Club   TIKI BAR
(http://lamarianasailingclub.squarespace.com; 50 Sand Island Access Rd; ⏰11am-9pm) Who says all the great tiki bars have gone to the dogs? Irreverent and kitschy, this 1950s joint by the lagoon is filled with yachties and long-suffering locals. Classic mai tais are as good as the other signature tropical potions, complete with tiki-head swizzle sticks. Grab a waterfront table and dream of sailing to Tahiti.

Indigo Lounge   BAR, LOUNGE
(Map p64; www.indigo-hawaii.com; 1121 Nu'uanu Ave; ⏰5pm-midnight Tue, to 1:30am Wed-Sat) Indigo restaurant mixes tropical fruit-flavored martinis during happy hour in the lounge. Live jazz is sometimes heard during the week, with old-school and electronica DJs slotted in for the weekend.

Apartment 3   LOUNGE
(Map p72; www.apartmentthree.com; 1750 Kalakaua Ave; ⏰6pm-2am Mon-Sat) This under-the-radar petite cocktail lounge is the kind of place Johnny Depp likes to drink when he's in town. Order up the classic Honolulu No 2 cocktail. Tuesdays are all-night happy hour, live music usually happens on Thursdays and DJs spin all weekend long.

Mai Tai Bar   BAR
(Map p72; www.maitaibar.com; Ho'okipa Tce, 3rd fl, Ala Moana Center; ⏰11am-1am; ☎) A happening bar in a shopping mall? We don't make the trends, we just report 'em. During Friday happy hours, this suburban-style bar is packed with a see-and-flirt crowd. There's live island-style music nightly, or join the cougar-ish dance divas at nearby Pearl nightclub.

Aku Bone Lounge   DIVE BAR
(Map p72; 1201 Kona St; ⏰5pm-2am) This down-home dive bar brings a tasty *pupu* menu and an older rubbah slippah crowd that believes in 'keeping Old Hawaii alive, one beer at a time.' Karaoke and live Hawaiian music take over some nights.

Smith's Union Bar   DIVE BAR
(Map p64; 19 N Hotel St; ⏰6pm-midnight) Only dive-bar aficionados will appreciate Smith's Union, dating from 1935 when this section of Chinatown was a red-light district and playground for merchant seamen. For wage-slave hipsters, it's a cheap front-loading PBR hangout before clubbing.

Varsity   COLLEGE BAR
(Map p72; 1019 University Ave; ⏰11am-2am) Formerly Magoo's, this UH student-friendly bar has open-air sidewalk tables and plenty of microbrews from Hawaii and the US mainland on tap. Weekday happy-hour specials bring in the co-ed crowds.

Sam Choy's Big Aloha Brewery   BREWPUB
(580 N Nimitz Hwy; ⏰10:30am-9pm Sun-Thu, to 10pm Fri & Sat) At the back of Sam Choy's Breakfast, Lunch & Crab restaurant, sip Kaka'ako Cream Ale and Kiawe Honey Porter next to shiny brewing vats and sports TVs.

Live Music

If traditional and contemporary Hawaiian music is what you want, look no further than Waikiki. But if it's jazz, alt-rock and punk sounds you're after, then venture outside the tourist zone into Honolulu's other neighborhoods.

TOP CHOICE **Chai's Island Bistro**   LIVE MUSIC
(Map p64; 585-0011; www.chaisislandbistro.com; Aloha Tower Marketplace, 1 Aloha Tower Dr; live music from 7pm nightly) When the sun sets over Honolulu Harbor, you'll find some of Hawaii's top contemporary musicians performing here, including the Brothers Cazimero and Jerry Santos. Come for the drinks and the music, not the food.

The Venue   LIVE MUSIC
(Map p64; 528-1144; 1146 Bethel St; schedule varies) At the edge of Chinatown's new-wave arts district, the Venue is a come-as-you-are multipurpose stage for everyone from indie singer-songwriter acts to contemporary Hawaiian musicians to old-school and hip-hop DJs. Look for alt-cultural events, like poetry slams or goth beauty pageants, too.

Dragon Upstairs   LIVE MUSIC
(Map p64; 526-1411; www.thedragonupstairs .com; 2nd fl, 1038 Nu'uanu Ave; schedule varies, usually Mon-Sat) This hideaway above Hank's Cafe has a soothing vibe, funky artwork and lots of mirrors. An intimate space, it hosts a rotating line-up of local jazz cats, from experimental bands to bop trios to piano and vocal soloists.

Jazz Minds Art & Café   LIVE MUSIC
(Map p72; 945-0800; www.honolulujazzclub .com; 1661 Kapi'olani Blvd; cover charge $5, plus 2-drink minimum; 9pm-2am Mon-Sat) Don't let the nearby strip clubs necessarily turn you off. This tattered dive somehow pulls in Honolulu's top jazz talent – big band, bebop, salsa and minimalist sounds.

Anna Bannanas   LIVE MUSIC
(Map p72; 946-5190; 2440 S Beretania St; usually until 2am daily) A college dive bar, part roadhouse and part art-house, Anna Bananas goes beyond its retro-1960s 'Summer of Love' atmosphere to put local reggae, alt-rock, punk and metal bands on stage.

Ward's Rafters   LIVE MUSIC
(735-8012; by donation; schedules varies) Make your way to a family affair in Kaimuki, where Jackie Ward opens up her

home to O'ahu's tight-knit jazz community. It's a word-of-mouth place that informs regulars of gigs via an email list. You can call with questions, to ask for directions and to get on the guest list. BYOB.

Performing Arts

Hawaii's capital city is home to a symphony orchestra, an opera company, ballet troupes, chamber orchestras and over a dozen diverse community theater groups.

Hawaii Theatre   PERFORMING ARTS
(Map p64; 528-0506; www.hawaiitheatre.com; 1130 Bethel St) In a beautifully restored historic building in Chinatown, this is a major venue for dance, music and theater. Performances range from local live music and international touring acts to modern dance, contemporary plays and film festivals. The theater also hosts the Ka Himeni 'Ana competition in which famous musicians play in traditional Hawaiian styles. Guided theater tours are usually given at 11am on the first Tuesday of the month (reservations required).

Neal S Blaisdell Center   PERFORMING ARTS
(Map p72; 591-2211; www.blaisdellcenter.com; 777 Ward Ave) A cultural lynchpin, this performing-arts center stages symphonic and chamber-music concerts, opera performances and ballet recitals, prestigious hula competitions, Broadway shows, arts-and-crafts fairs, farmers markets and more. Occasionally big-name pop and rock touring acts play here instead of Aloha Stadium (Map p63).

ARTS at Marks Garage   PERFORMING ARTS
(Map p64; 521-2903; www.artsatmarks.com; 1159 Nu'uanu Ave) On the cutting edge of Chinatown's arts scene, this community gallery and performance space puts on a variety of live shows, from conversations with island-born artists to live jazz and Hawaiian music.

Kumu Kahua Theatre   PLAYS
(Map p64; 536-4441; www.kumukahua.org; 46 Merchant St) In the Kamehameha V Post Office building, this little 100-seat treasure is dedicated to premiering works by multicultural contemporary playwrights, often peppered richly with Hawaiian pidgin.

HawaiiSlam   SPOKEN WORD
(Map p72; 387-9664; www.hawaiislam.com; Fresh Cafe, 813 Queen St; admission $3-5; 8:30pm 1st Thu of month) One of the USA's biggest poetry slams, here international wordsmiths,

artists, musicians, MCs and DJs share the stage. Sign-up for aspiring poetry-slam stars starts at 7:30pm.

Cinemas

Doris Duke Theatre   CINEMA
(Map p72; ☑532-8768; www.honoluluacademy .org; Honolulu Academy of Arts, 900 S Beretania St; admission $5-9) Inside an art museum, this intimate movie house showcases homegrown and imported independent cinema, foreign films and avant-garde and experimental shorts. Look for screenings of ground-breaking Hawaii and Pacific Rim documentaries here. Buy tickets online.

Movie Museum   CINEMA
(☑735-8771; www.kaimukihawaii.com; 3566 Harding Ave; admission $5; ⊙usually 12:30-10:30pm Thu-Mon) This Kaimuki neighborhood spot is a sociable place to watch classic oldies, foreign flicks and indie films (including Hawaii premieres) in a theater equipped with digital sound and just 20 comfy Barcalounger chairs. Reservations recommended.

🔒 Shopping

Although not a shopping powerhouse like Waikiki, Honolulu's unique shops offer plenty of local flavor, from traditional flower lei and ukulele makers to antiques stores and island-style clothing boutiques.

Ala Moana Center   SHOPPING MALL
(Map p72; www.alamoanacenter.com; 1450 Ala Moana Blvd; ⊙9am-9pm Mon-Sat, 10am-7pm Sun; 🚹) Holy fashion! This open-air shopping mall and its department stores could compete on an international runway with some of Asia's most famous malls. A favorite stop for local color is the Crack Seed Center, where you can scoop from jars full of pickled mangoes, dried plums, candied ginger and dozens more exotic tropical flavors.

TOP CHOICE Ward Warehouse   SHOPPING MALL
(Map p72; www.victoriaward.com; 1050 Ala Moana Blvd; ⊙10am-9pm Mon-Sat, to 6pm Sun) Across the street from Ala Moana Beach Park, this mini-mall is home to more one-of-a-kind island shops, including Native Books/Nā Mea Hawaii, which sells gourmet foodstuffs, wooden koa bowls, hand-carved fishhook jewelry, authentic Hawaiian quilts and oodles of books, CDs and DVDs.

Aloha Tower Marketplace   SHOPPING MALL
(Map p64; www.alohatower.com; 1 Aloha Tower Dr; ⊙9am-9pm Mon-Sat, to 6pm Sun) Beside the landmark Aloha Tower, this harborfront shopping center has dozens of shops varying in quality from kitschy to high-end, with barely an off-island chain among them. Hula dancers often welcome arriving cruise ships on the nearby pier.

Art & Hawaiian Crafts

For Chinatown's art galleries, see the boxed text, p71.

Cindy's Lei Shoppe   CRAFTS, SOUVENIRS
(Map p64; www.cindysleishoppe.com; 1034 Maunakea St; ⊙6am-7:30pm Mon-Sat, 6am-6pm Sun) This friendly, inviting little place sells leis made of *maile* (a native twining plant), lantern *ilima* (a native ground cover) and Micronesian ginger, as well as more common orchids and plumeria. If you don't see something you like, there are a half dozen or more lei shops on nearby streets, so have a wander.

Kamaka Hawaii   MUSIC
(Map p64; www.kamakahawaii.com; 550 South St; ⊙8am-4pm Mon-Fri) Skip right by those shops selling cheap plastic and wooden ukuleles. Kamaka specializes in handcrafted ukuleles made on Oʻahu since 1916, with prices starting at around $500. Their signature is an oval-shaped 'pineapple' ukulele that has a more mellow sound. Call ahead to ask about 30-minute factory tours, usually given at 10:30am Tuesdays to Fridays.

Hula Supply Center   SOUVENIRS
(Map p72; www.hulasupplycenter.com; 1481 S King St; ⊙9am-5:30pm Mon-Fri, to 5pm Sat) For over 60 years, Hawaiian musicians and dancers have come here to get their *kukui* (candlenut) leis, calabash drum gourds, Tahitian grass skirts, nose flutes and the like. If you're not a dancer yet, they've also got aloha shirts, Hawaiiana books, CDs and DVDs. Also at Waikiki Beach Walk.

Jeff Chang Pottery & Fine Crafts   ART, CRAFTS
(Map p72; ☑591-1440; www.wardcentre.com; Ward Centre, 1200 Ala Moana Blvd; ⊙10am-5pm Mon-Fri) Not everything at this mall art gallery is island-made, but it's all handcrafted. Striking *raku* pottery molded by Chang himself sits beside hand-turned bowls of tropical hardwoods, art jewelry and blown glass by some of Hawaii's finest artisans. On some Sundays between 11am and 4pm, Chang demonstrates wheel-throwing and *raku*-firing techniques ($20 for an interactive class, including a take-home piece).

Nohea Gallery ART, CRAFTS

(Map p72; www.noheagallery.com; Ward Warehouse, 1050 Ala Moana Blvd; ⏲10am-9pm Mon-Sat, to 6pm Sun) A meditative space amid the mall madness, this high-end gallery sells handcrafted jewelry, glassware, pottery and woodwork, the majority of it made in Hawaii. Island artisans occasionally give demonstrations of their crafts right on the sidewalk outside.

Clothing & Shoes

Manuheali'i CLOTHING

(Map p72; www.manuhealii.com; 930 Punahou St; ⏲9:30am-6pm Mon-Fri, 9am-4pm Sat, 10am-3pm Sun) Look to this island-born shop for original and modern designs. Hawaiian musicians often sport Manuheali'i's bold-print silk aloha shirts. Flowing rayon dresses take inspiration from the traditional muumuu, but are transformed into sprightly contemporary looks. Also in Kailua.

Tutuvi Sitoa CLOTHING

(Map p72; www.tutuvi.com 2636 King St; ⏲10am-5pm Tue-Sat) Near the UH Manoa campus, designer Colleen Kimura's tiki-esque storefront floats racks of T-shirts, dresses, *pa'u* skirts, beach wraps, aloha shirts and natural-fiber sandals, all handmade from fabrics screen-printed with designs drawn from nature, like banana leaves, hibiscus and forest ferns.

Montsuki CLOTHING

(☑734-3457; 1132 Koko Head Ave; ⏲8:30am-6pm Tue-Sat) In the low-key Kaimuki neighborhood east of UH Manoa and Waikiki, the mother-daughter design team of Janet and Patty Yamasaki refashions classic kimono and *obi* designs into modern attire. East–

West wedding dresses, formal wear or sleek day fashions can all be custom-crafted. Try to call ahead before dropping by.

Cinnamon Girl CLOTHING

(Map p72; http://cinnamongirl.com; Ala Moana Center, 1450 Ala Moana Blvd; ⏲9am-9pm Mon-Sat, 10am-7pm Sun) With whimsy by O'ahu fashionista Jonelle Fujita, flirty rayon dresses that are cool, contemporary and island-made hang on the racks, while feminine sandals, bejeweled necklaces and sweet floppy sun hats line the shelves. Also at Ward Warehouse.

Island Slipper SHOES

(Map p72; www.islandslipper.com; Ward Warehouse, 1050 Ala Moana Blvd; ⏲10am-9pm Mon-Sat, to 6pm Sun) There are scores of stores selling flip-flops (aka 'rubbah slippah') across Honolulu, but nobody carries such ultracomfy suede and leather styles – some made right here in the islands – let alone such giant sizes.

Lily Lotus CLOTHING

(http://lilylotus.com; 1127 11th Ave; ⏲10am-5pm) In the uptown Kaimuki neighborhood, this boutique storefront is run by Honolulu-born Momi Chee, who has made a name for herself designing eco-friendly yoga and fitness wear for women. Staff can help you connect with the local yoga scene.

T&L Muumuu Factory CLOTHING

(Map p72; www.muumuufactory.com; 1423 Kapi'olani Blvd; ⏲9am-6pm Mon-Sat, 10am-4pm Sun) So much flammable aloha wear in one space! This is a shop for *tutu* (grandmothers), to whom polyester represents progress. Bold-print muumuus run in sizes from supermodel skinny to queen, and *pa'u* skirts are just funky enough to wedge into an urban outfit.

Antiques & Vintage

Tin Can Mailman ANTIQUES, BOOKS

(Map p64; http://tincanmailman.net; 1026 Nu'uanu Ave; ⏲11am-5pm Mon-Sat, 11am-4pm Sun) If you're a big fan of vintage tiki wares and 20th-century books about the Hawaiian Islands, you'll fall in love with this little Chinatown antiques shop. Thoughtfully collected treasures include 20th-century jewelry and ukuleles, silk aloha shirts, tropical-wood furnishings, vinyl records, and rare prints and tourist brochures from the post-WWII tourism boom.

HAWAIIANA SHOPS IN HONOLULU & WAIKIKI

» Bishop Museum (p73)

» Native Books/Nā Mea Hawai'i (p80)

» Cindy's Lei Shop (p93)

» Bailey's Antiques & Aloha Shirts (p119)

» Na Lima Mili Hulu No'eau (p119)

» Manuheali'i (p94)

» Tin Can Mailman (p94)

» Kamaka Hawaii (p93)

» Hula Supply Center (p93)

» Hawai'i State Art Museum (p63)

Antique Alley ANTIQUES
(Map p72; www.portaloha.com/antiquealley; 1347 Kapi'olani Blvd; ◎11am-5pm) Delightfully crammed full of rare collectibles and other cast-off memorabilia from Hawaii through the decades, this shop that cameoed on *Antiques Roadshow* sells everything from poi pounders to vintage hula dolls and Matson cruise liner artifacts.

Lai Fong Department Store ANTIQUES
(Map p64; 1118 Nu'uanu Ave; ◎usually 9am-6:30pm Mon-Sat) This family-owned shop sells a hodgepodge of antiques and knickknacks in all price ranges, from Chinese silk and brocade clothing to vintage postcards of Hawaii from the early 20th century.

❶ Information

Emergency

Police, Fire & Ambulance (☏911) For emergencies.
Police (☏529-3111) For nonemergencies.

Internet Access

Cheaper fly-by-night cybercafés near the UH Manoa campus stay open late.

FedEx Office (www.fedex.com; per hr $12) Ala Moana (1500 Kapi'olani Blvd; ◎7:30am-9pm Mon-Thu, 10am-6pm Sat, noon-6pm Sun); Downtown (590 Queen St; ◎7am-11pm Mon-Fri, 9am-9pm Sat & Sun); University Area (2575 S King St; ◎24hr; @☎) Self-serve, pay-as-you-go computer terminals and wi-fi, plus digital-photo printing and CD-burning stations.

Hawaii State Library (☏586-3500; www.librarieshawaii.org; 478 S King St; ◎10am-5pm Mon & Wed, 9am-5pm Tue, Fri & Sat, 9am-8pm Thu; @☎) The main branch of the state system; there are also 23 neighborhood library branches around O'ahu. All provide free reservable internet terminals (see p631); some offer free wi-fi.

Media

NEWSPAPERS & MAGAZINES Honolulu Magazine (www.honolulumagazine.com) Glossy monthly magazine covers arts, culture, fashion, lifestyle and cuisine.

Honolulu Star-Advertiser (www.staradvertiser.com, http://tgif.staradvertiser) Honolulu's daily newspaper; look for TGIF, Friday's events and entertainment pull-out section.

Honolulu Weekly (www.honoluluweekly.com) Free weekly tabloid with an events calendar featuring arts and entertainment, classes, volunteering and outdoor activities.

RADIO & TV KDNN (89.5FM) Island-style music and Hawaiian reggae.

KHET (cable channel 10) Hawaii public TV (PBS).

KHPR (88.1FM) Hawaii Public Radio; classical music.

KIKU (cable channel 9) Multicultural TV programming.

KINE (105.1FM) Classic and contemporary Hawaiian music.

KIPO (89.3FM) Hawaii Public Radio; jazz and world music.

KTUH (90.3FM) University of Hawai'i student-run radio.

Medical Services

Hyperbaric Treatment Center (☏851-7030, 851-7032; www.hyperbaricmedicinecenter.com; 275 Pu'uhale Rd) For scuba divers with the bends.

Longs Drugs (☏949-4781; www.cvs.com/longs; 2220 S King St; ◎24hr) Convenient 24-hour pharmacy near UH Manoa.

Queen's Medical Center (☏538-9011; www.queensmedicalcenter.net; 1301 Punchbowl St; ◎24hr) O'ahu's biggest, best-equipped hospital has a 24-hour emergency room.

Straub Clinic & Hospital (☏522-4000; www.straubhealth.org; 888 S King St; ◎24hr) Operates a 24-hour emergency room.

Money

Banks with convenient branches and ATMs around the island:

Bank of Hawaii (☏888-643-3888; www.boh.com)

First Hawaiian Bank (☏844-4444; www.fhb.com)

Post

Ala Moana post office (www.usps.com; ground fl, Ala Moana Center, 1450 Ala Moana Blvd; ◎8:30am-5pm Mon-Fri, to 4:15pm Sat)

Downtown post office (www.usps.com; Old Federal Bldg, 335 Merchant St; ◎9am-4:30pm Mon-Fri)

Main post office (☏423-6029; www.usps.com; Honolulu International Airport, 3600 Aolele St, Honolulu, HI 96820; ◎8am-8pm Mon-Fri, 8am-4pm Sat) General-delivery (poste-restante) mail normally held for 10 days (international mail up to 30 days).

❶ Getting There & Around

To/From the Airport

For transportation to/from Honolulu International Airport, see p58.

Bus

The Ala Moana Center mall, just northwest of Waikiki, is O'ahu's central transfer point for

TheBus. For more information about TheBus, including routes, schedules, fares and passes, see p58.

Car

Downtown Honolulu and Chinatown are full of one-way streets, traffic is thick and parking can be tight, so consider taking TheBus instead of driving.

Honolulu traffic jams up during rush hours, from 7am to 9am and 3pm to 6pm on weekdays. Expect heavy traffic in both directions on the H-1 Fwy during this time, as well as on the Pali and Likelike Hwys headed into Honolulu in the morning and away from the city in the late afternoon.

PARKING Hourly parking is available at several municipal parking lots and garages around downtown. On-street metered parking is hard to find on weekdays, but easier on weekends. Bring lots of quarters. Major shopping centers offer free parking for customers. The Aloha Tower Marketplace offers validated paid parking with purchase: on weekdays after 4pm and all day on weekends and holidays, a $2 flat-rate applies; otherwise, it's $2 for the first three hours, then $3 per 30 minutes.

Taxi

You'll probably have to call for a taxi (for metered rates, see p58):

Charley's (📞233-3333, from payphones 📞877-531-1333; www.charleystaxi.com)

City Taxi (📞524-2121; www.citytaxihonolulu.com)

TheCab (📞422-2222; www.thecabhawaii.com)

PEARL HARBOR

The WWII-era rallying cry 'Remember Pearl Harbor!' that once mobilized an entire nation dramatically resonates on O'ahu. It was here that the surprise Japanese attack on December 7, 1941 hurtled the US into war in the Pacific. Every year 1.5 million tourists visit Pearl Harbor's unique collection of war memorials and museums, all clustered around a quiet bay where oysters were once farmed west of Honolulu.

Today Pearl Harbor is still home to an active and mind-bogglingly enormous US naval base. Anyone looking for a little soul-soothing peace and quiet, especially after a solemn visit to the USS Arizona Memorial, can head up into the misty Ko'olau Mountains above the harbor, where an ancient Hawaiian medicinal temple and forested hiking trails await.

◉ Sights & Activities

The offshore shrine at the sunken USS Arizona is Hawaii's most-visited tourist attraction. Nearby are two other floating historical sites: the USS *Bowfin* submarine, aka the 'Pearl Harbor Avenger,' and the battleship USS *Missouri,* where General Douglas MacArthur accepted the Japanese surrender at the end of WWII. Together, for the US, these military sites represent the beginning, middle and end of the war. To visit all three, as well as the Pacific Aviation Museum, dedicate at least a half-day, preferably on a weekday morning when it's less crowded. All of Pearl Harbor's attractions are wheelchair-accessible and closed on Thanksgiving, Christmas and New Year's Day.

TOP CHOICE **USS Arizona Memorial**   MUSEUM, MEMORIAL

(📞422-3300; www.nps.gov/valr; 1 Arizona Memorial Dr, 'Aiea; admission free; ⊘visitor center & museum 7am-5pm, boat tour departures 8am-3pm) One of the USA's most significant WWII sites, this somber memorial narrates the history of the Pearl Harbor attack and commemorates its fallen service members. Run by the National Park Service (NPS), the memorial comprises a visitor center and offshore shrine. On land inside the newly rebuilt visitor center, a modern multimedia museum presents rare WWII memorabilia, a model of the battleship and shrine, as well as historical photos and oral history.

The offshore shrine was built over the midsection of the sunken USS *Arizona,* with deliberate geometry to represent initial defeat, ultimate victory and eternal serenity. In the farthest of three chambers inside the shrine, the names of crewmen killed in the attack are engraved onto a marble wall. In the central room are cutaway well sections that allow visitors to see the skeletal remains of the ship, which even now oozes about a quart of oil each day into the ocean. In its rush to recover from the attack and prepare for war, the US Navy exercised its option to leave the servicemen inside the sunken ship. They remain entombed in its hull, buried at sea. Visitors are asked to maintain respectful silence at all times, although unfortunately some tour groups and their guides don't comply.

Boat trips to the shrine depart from the visitor center every 15 minutes from 8am until 3pm on a first-come, first-served basis (weather permitting). At the visitor center, you'll be given a ticket stating exactly when your 75-minute tour program, which includes a 23-minute documentary film on the

December 7, 1941 – 'a date which will live in infamy,' President Franklin D Roosevelt later said – began at 7:55am with a wave of over 350 Japanese planes swooping over the Ko'olau Range headed toward the unsuspecting US Pacific Fleet in Pearl Harbor.

The battleship USS *Arizona* took a direct hit and sank in less than nine minutes, trapping its crew beneath the surface. The average age of the 1177 enlisted men who died on the ship was just 19 years. It wasn't until 15 minutes after the bombing started that American anti-aircraft guns began to shoot back at the Japanese warplanes. Twenty other US military ships were sunk or seriously damaged and 347 airplanes were destroyed during the two-hour attack.

In hindsight, there were two significant warnings prior to the attack that were disastrously dismissed or misinterpreted. Over an hour before Japanese planes arrived, USS *Ward* spotted a submarine conning tower approaching the entrance of Pearl Harbor. The *Ward* immediately attacked with depth charges and sank what turned out to be one of five midget Japanese submarines launched to penetrate the harbor. At 7:02am a radar station on the north shore of O'ahu reported planes approaching. Even though they were coming from the west rather than the east, it was assumed that the planes were from the US mainland.

For more about Hawaii's WWII-era history, see p581.

attack, will begin. In the afternoon, waits of a couple hours are not uncommon. In peak summer months, 4500 people take the tour daily, and the day's allotment of tickets is often gone by noon.

USS Bowfin Submarine Museum & Park   MUSEUM

(☎423-1341; www.bowfin.org; 11 Arizona Memorial Dr, 'Aiea; park admission free, museum & self-guided submarine audio tour adult/child $10/4; ⊙7am-5pm, last entry 4:30pm) If you have to wait an hour or two for your USS Arizona Memorial tour to begin, this adjacent site harbors the moored WWII-era submarine USS *Bowfin* and a niche museum that traces the development of submarines from their origins to the nuclear age, including footage from wartime submarine patrols.

Undoubtedly the highlight of the park is clambering aboard the historic submarine. Launched on December 7, 1942, one year after the Pearl Harbor attack, the USS *Bowfin* completed nine war patrols and sank 44 enemy ships in the Pacific by the end of WWII. A self-guided audio tour explores the life of the crew – watch your head below deck! Children under age four are not allowed on board.

As you stroll around the surrounding waterfront park, peer through periscopes and inspect a Japanese *kaiten* (suicide torpedo), the marine equivalent of a kamikaze pilot's plane, developed as a last-ditch effort by the Japanese military near the end of WWII.

Battleship Missouri Memorial   MUSEUM, MEMORIAL

(☎455-1600, 877-644-4896; www.ussmissouri .com; 63 Cowpens St, Ford Island; admission incl tour adult/child 4-12yr from $20/10; ⊙8am-4pm) The last battleship built at the end of WWII, the USS *Missouri* provides a unique historical 'bookend' to the US campaign in the Pacific during WWII. Nicknamed the 'Mighty Mo' (it's bigger than the RMS *Titanic*), this decommissioned battleship saw action during the decisive WWII battles of Iwo Jima and Okinawa.

The USS *Missouri* is now docked on Ford Island, just a few hundred yards from the sunken remains of the USS *Arizona*. On a self-guided audio tour, you can poke about the officers' quarters, browse exhibits on the ship's history and walk the deck where General Douglas MacArthur accepted the Japanese surrender on September 2, 1945. More expensive guided battle-station tours are sometimes led by knowledgeable military veterans.

To visit the memorial, you must first buy tickets at Bowfin Park, then board the mandatory visitor shuttle bus to Ford Island.

Pacific Aviation Museum   MUSEUM

(☎441-1000; www.pacificaviationmuseum.org; 319 Lexington Blvd, Ford Island; adult/child 4-12yr $20/10, incl guided tour $30/20, with flight simulator add $10; ⊙9am-5pm, guided tours 10am-3pm, last entry 4pm) Still a work-in-progress, this military aircraft museum covers the period from WWII through the US conflicts in Korea and Vietnam. The first aircraft hangar has been outfitted with exhibits on the Pearl Harbor attack, the Doolittle Raid on mainland Japan in 1942 and the pivotal Battle of Midway, when the tides of WWII in the Pacific turned in favor of the Allies. Authentically restored planes on display here include a Japanese Zero and a Dauntless navy dive bomber. Guided tours currently explore the MiG Alley Korean War exhibit and peek behind the scenes at restoration work in historic WWII-era Hangar 79.

To visit the museum, you must first buy tickets at Bowfin Park, then board the mandatory visitor shuttle bus to Ford Island.

FREE **Kea'iwa Heiau State**
Recreation Area PARK
(off 'Aiea Heights Dr, 'Aiea; ☺7am-7:45pm April-early Sep, 7am-6:45pm early Sep-Mar) In the hills above Pearl Harbor, this park protects **Kea'iwa Heiau**, an ancient Hawaiian stone temple used by *kahuna lapa'au* (herbalist healers). The kahuna used hundreds of medicinal plants and grew many on the grounds surrounding the heiau. Among those still found here are *noni* (Indian mulberry), whose pungent yellow fruit was used to treat heart disease; *kukui* (candlenuts), a laxative; and *ti* leaves, which were wrapped around a sick person to break a fever. Not only did these herbs have medicinal value, but the heiau itself was believed to possess life-giving energy that could be channeled by the kahuna.

For hikers and mountain bikers, the park's scenic 4.5-mile **'Aiea Loop Trail** starts from the top of the paved driving loop road and ends at the campground, about 0.3 miles below the trailhead. Along the way you'll get sweeping vistas of Pearl Harbor, Diamond Head and the Ko'olau Range. About two-thirds of the way along, the wreckage of a C-47 cargo plane that crashed in 1943 can be spotted through the foliage on the east ridge.

The park's few campsites are maintained well, but there's not a lot of privacy. In winter bring waterproof gear, as it rains frequently at this elevation. The park has covered picnic pavilions with BBQ grills, restrooms, showers, drinking water and a payphone. There's a resident caretaker by the front gate, which is locked at night for security. Camping is not permitted on Wednesday

and Thursday nights; advance permits are required (see p58).

From Honolulu or Waikiki, drive west on the H-1 Fwy, then merge onto Hwy 78 and take the exit 13A 'Aiea turnoff onto Moanalua Rd. Turn right onto 'Aiea Heights Dr at the third traffic light. The road winds up through a residential area for over 2.5 miles to the park. From downtown Honolulu, TheBus 11 'Aiea Heights stops about 1.3 miles downhill from the park entrance (35 minutes, hourly).

☞ Tours

Widely advertised in Waikiki, Pearl Harbor tours range from shuttle buses to excursions in WWII-era amphibious armored vehicles ('ducks'). These tours don't add much, if anything, to the experience of visiting the memorials and museums, however. Besides, tourist boats aren't allowed to disembark at the USS Arizona Memorial.

✖ Eating

Next to the visitor center, Bowfin Park has concession stands. On Ford Island, the Battleship Missouri Memorial and Pacific Aviation Museum both offer fast-food cafes. Down-home local island eateries are flung further east along the Kamehameha Hwy (Hwy 99) near Pearlridge Center mall.

Poke Stop SEAFOOD, TAKEOUT $
(Map p56; www.poke-stop.com; Waipahu Town Center, 94-050 Farrington Hwy, Waipahu; dishes $4-10, meals $8-14; ☺8am-7pm Mon-Sat, 9am-4pm Sun) It's a longish detour west of Pearl Harbor, but we'd drive all the way across the island just to bite into these spicy eggplant fries, deconstructed sushi bowls, gourmet plate lunches and over 20 kinds of *poke* – the *furikake* salmon and 'Da Works' *'o'io* (bonefish) will leave you salivating for more.

Chun Wah Kam Noodle Factory PAN-ASIAN $$
(www.chunwahkam.com; Waimalu Shopping Center, 98-040 Kamehameha Hwy, 'Aiea; items $1-8, meals $7-10; ☺7:30am-6:30pm Mon-Fri, 8:30am-6:30pm Sat, 8:30am-4pm Sun) Fanatics line up for *manapua* stuffed with anything from *char siu* pork or *kalua* pig to black sugar and taro. Generous mix-and-match plate lunches could easily feed two people. This mini-mall is chockablock with more Asian takeout joints, too, such as Shiro's Saimin and Egoziku Ramen.

Kuru Kuru Sushi JAPANESE $$
(Pearl Kai Shopping Center, 98-199 Kamehameha Hwy; items $2-8; ☺11am-9pm Sun-Thu, to 10pm

Fri & Sat) This island sushi-bar chain runs its *nigiri* sushi, *kalbi* short-rib rolls, vegetable croquettes and fruit-jelly desserts around a conveyor belt.

Forty Niner Restaurant
LOCAL $

(98-110 Honomanu St, 'Aiea; mains $3-8; ⊙7am-2pm daily, 4-8pm Mon-Thu, to 9pm Fri & Sat) This little 1940s noodle shop and soda fountain may look abandoned, but its old-fashioned saimin (local-style noodle soup) is made with a secret-recipe broth.

Elena's House of Finest Fillipino Foods
FILIPINO $

(www.elenasrestaurant.com; Tropicana Sq, 94-866 Moloalo St, Waipahu; mains $6-12; ⊙6am-9pm) Elena's home-style kitchen has been crankin' out pork *adobo* fried-rice omelettes, *pansit* (noodles), *sari-sari* stew and other Filipino classics since 1974.

ℹ Information

Strict security measures are in place at Pearl Harbor's memorials, museums and visitor centers. You are not allowed to bring in any items that allow concealment (eg purses, camera bags, fanny packs, backpacks, diaper bags). Personal-sized cameras and camcorders are allowed. Don't lock valuables in your car. Instead use the **storage facility** (per item $3; ⊙6:30am-5:30pm) to the right outside Bowfin Park.

ℹ Getting There & Away

BUS From Waikiki, TheBus 42 'Ewa Beach is the most direct route, stopping outside the USS Arizona Memorial visitor center between 7:30am and 3pm daily, taking just over an hour each way. TheBus 20 Airport-Pearlridge detours to the airport, taking about 15 minutes longer. Both routes run at least twice hourly.

CAR The USS Arizona Memorial visitor center and Bowfin Park are off Kamehameha Hwy (Hwy 99) southwest of Aloha Stadium. Coming from Honolulu or Waikiki (30 minutes without traffic), take the H-1 Fwy west to exit 15A (Arizona Memorial/Stadium), then follow the signs for the USS Arizona Memorial, not Pearl Harbor; the latter lead onto the military base. There's ample free parking.

Civilians are not allowed to drive onto Ford Island, an active military base. Instead, a frequent visitor shuttle bus picks up ticketholders outside Bowfin Park, stopping at the Battleship Missouri Memorial, then the Pacific Aviation Museum.

WAIKIKI

POP 27,510

Waikiki – just the name alone will have you thinking of boundless horizons, Pacific sunsets and hula dancers gently swaying to the beat of island rhythms. Once the playground of Hawaiian royalty, this remains O'ahu's quintessential beach.

After emerging from the long shadow of WWII, Waikiki recaptured the popular imagination as an idyllic tropical island vacation complete with flower leis, aloha shirts and romance. Celebrities like Elvis sang about it and strummed ukuleles, while bronzed beachboys walked on water thanks to their long wooden surfboards.

Today Waikiki has reinvented itself. Although tacky tiki drinks and resort luaus featuring all-you-can-eat buffets and Samoan fire-dancing are still a fixture on the scene, Hawaii's most-visited beach is moving beyond plasticky mass tourism, with its stylish boutique hotels and sophisticated restaurants and cocktail lounges.

BE YOUR OWN TOUR GUIDE

Unlike on many other Hawaiian Islands, you won't need to rent a car or take a tour to explore O'ahu. You can travel at your own pace, and save money – not to mention the environment – by circling the island on O'ahu's public transit system, TheBus.

Starting from the Ala Moana Center near Waikiki, TheBus 52 Wahiawa Circle Isle bus goes clockwise up Hwy 99 to Hale'iwa and along the North Shore. At Turtle Bay Resort, on the island's northern tip, it switches signs to 55 and comes down the Windward Coast to Kane'ohe and back over the Pali Hwy to Ala Moana. The 55 Kane'ohe Circle Isle bus does the same route in reverse. These buses operate every 30 minutes from 6:30am to around 10pm daily. If you ride the circle-island route nonstop, it takes four hours.

For a shorter excursion from Waikiki, make a scenic loop around southeast O'ahu by taking the 'Beach Bus' 22 (no service on Tuesday) to Sea Life Park, then transfer to the 57 bound for Kailua and back over the Pali Hwy to Ala Moana Center. Ask the driver for a free transfer upon boarding. With fast connections, this loop takes about 2½ hours.

A lazy day of lying on the white sand here is only the beginning of the fun. Take a surfing lesson, sip a fruity mai tai as the sun drops into the sea, listen to slack key guitars and ukuleles, and just enjoy life. It's for good reason that everyone's here.

History

Fed by mountain streams from Manoa Valley, Waikiki ('Spouting Water') was once a fertile wetland of *kalo lo'i* (taro fields) and fishponds. In 1795 when Kamehameha the Great conquered O'ahu, he built his royal court here. For almost the next century, Waikiki became a privileged royal retreat. But by the 1880s, Honolulu's wealthier citizens started building gingerbread-style cottages along the narrow beachfront.

Tourism started booming in 1901, when the Moana opened its doors as Waikiki's first luxury hotel, built on a former royal compound. A tram line connected Waikiki with downtown Honolulu, and city folk crowded aboard for weekend beach outings. Tiring quickly of the pesky mosquitoes that thrived in Waikiki's wetlands, beachgoers petitioned to have the 'swamps' brought under control. In 1922 the Ala Wai Canal was dug to divert streams and dry out the wetlands.

Old Hawaii lost out: local farmers had the water drained out from under them and Waikiki's water buffaloes were quickly replaced by tourists. In 1927 the Royal Hawaiian Hotel opened to serve passengers arriving on luxury ocean liners from San Francisco. During WWII, this 'Pink Palace' was turned into an R&R playground for US Navy sailors on shore leave.

As late as 1950, surfers could still drive their cars right up onto Waikiki Beach and park on the sand. But by then passenger jets had already started making regularly scheduled flights to Hawaii, as mainland tourism boomed again after WWII. Only a lack of available land finally halted Waikiki's expansion in the late 1980s. The only place left to go was up, and that's why so many high-rises cluster here today.

Dangers & Annoyances

Day or night, you won't be able to walk down Kalakaua Ave without encountering timeshare salespeople, often sitting behind the desk of a so-called 'activity center' advertising free luau, sunset cruises or $10-per-day car rentals. Caveat emptor.

It can be risky to stroll along the beach or the Ala Wai Canal after dark, whether alone or in groups. At night, especially along Kuhio Ave, prostitutes aggressively solicit male tourists.

Beaches

The 2-mile stretch of white sand commonly referred to as Waikiki Beach runs from the Hilton Hawaiian Village down to Kapi'olani Park. Along the way, the beach changes names and personalities. In the early morning, quiet seaside paths belong to walkers and joggers. By midmorning it looks like a resort beach – water-sports concessionaires and lots of tourist bodies. At noon it's challenging to walk along the packed beach without stepping on anyone.

Offshore Waikiki is good for swimming, bodyboarding, surfing, sailing and other water sports most of the year, and there are lifeguards and outdoor showers scattered along the beachfront. Between May and September, summer swells make the water rougher for swimming, but great for surfing. For snorkeling, head to Sans Souci Beach or Queen's Surf Beach. For windsurfing, go to Fort DeRussy Beach.

After tourism took off in the 1950s, Waikiki's beachfront inevitably became more developed. Private landowners haphazardly constructed seawalls and offshore barriers (called groins) to protect their properties. In doing so, they blocked the natural forces of sand accretion, which has made erosion a serious problem. Today, some of Waikiki's legendary white sands have actually had to be barged in from Papohaku Beach on the neighbor island of Moloka'i.

The following beaches are listed from northwest to southeast.

Kahanamoku Beach   BEACH

Fronting Hilton Hawaiian Village, Kahanamoku Beach is protected by a breakwater wall at one end and a pier at the other, with a coral reef running between the two. It's a calm swimming area with a gently sloping, somewhat rocky bottom. The beach is named for Duke Kahanamoku (1890–1968), the legendary Waikiki beachboy, champion surfer and Olympic gold medal-winning swimmer whose family once owned this land.

Fort DeRussy Beach   BEACH

Seldom crowded, this overlooked beauty extends along the shore of a military reservation.

Like all beaches in Hawaii, it's public; the only area off-limits to civvies is the military-owned Hale Koa Hotel. The water is usually calm and good for swimming, but shallow at low tide. When conditions are right, windsurfers, bodyboarders and board surfers play here.

There are two beach huts, both open daily, which rent windsurfing equipment, bodyboards, kayaks and snorkel sets. In addition to lifeguards and outdoor showers, you'll find a grassy lawn with palm trees offering some sparse shade, an alternative to frying on the sand. Pay parking is available in front of the Hawai'i Army Museum.

Gray's Beach — BEACH
Near the Halekulani Hotel, Gray's Beach has suffered some of the Waikiki strip's worst erosion. Because the seawall in front of the Halekulani hotel is so close to the waterline, the beach sand fronting the hotel is often totally submerged by surf, but offshore waters are usually shallow and calm, offering decent swimming.

Central Waikiki Beach — BEACH
Between the Royal Hawaiian Hotel and the Moana Surfrider, Waikiki's busiest section of sand and surf is great for sunbathing, swimming and people-watching.

Most of the beach has a shallow bottom with a gradual slope. The only drawback for swimmers is the beach's popularity with beginner surfers and the occasional catamaran landing. **Queens** and **Canoes**, Waikiki's best-known surf breaks, are just offshore, and sometimes there are scores of surfers lined up on the horizon waiting to catch a wave. Paddle further offshore to **Populars** (aka 'Pops'), favored by longboarders.

You'll find restrooms, showers, a snack bar, surfboard lockers and beach-gear concessionaire rental stands at **Waikiki Beach Center**.

Kuhio Beach Park — BEACH
(2453 Kalakaua Ave; 🚻) This beach is for everything from protected swimming to outrigger canoe rides. It's marked on its eastern end by **Kapahulu Groin**, a walled storm drain with a walkway on top that juts out into the ocean. A low stone breakwater, called **The Wall**, runs out from Kapahulu Groin, parallel to the beach. It was built to control sand erosion and, in the process, two nearly enclosed swimming pools were formed.

Local kids walk out on the Wall, but it can be dangerous, due to its slippery surface and the breaking surf. The pool closest to Kapa-

» Waikiki (p100) – Hawaii's always-busy oceanfront carnival

» Hanauma Bay (p124) – snorkeling even kiddies can enjoy

» Waimanalo (p130) – O'ahu's longest, calmest golden strand

» Kailua (p141) – swimming, kayaking, stand up paddle boarding, windsurfing and kitesurfing

» Malaekahana State Recreation Area (p145) – wild, untamed windward O'ahu beach

» Pipeline (p149) – North Shore's epic surfing break

» Pupukea (p149) – superb summertime snorkeling and diving

» Makaha (p163) – Wai'anae Coast's favorite big-wave beach

hulu Groin is best for swimming, with the water near the breakwater reaching overhead depths. However, because circulation is limited, the water gets murky, with a noticeable film of suntan oil. The 'Watch Out Deep Holes' sign refers to holes in the pool's sandy bottom created by swirling currents, so waders should be cautious in the deeper part of the pool.

Kapahulu Groin is one of Waikiki's hottest bodyboarding spots. If the surf's right, you can find a few dozen bodyboarders, mostly teenagers, riding the waves. These experienced local kids ride straight for the groin's cement wall and then veer away at the last moment, thrilling tourists watching them from the little pier above.

Kapi'olani Beach Park — BEACH
South of Kapahulu Groin to the Natatorium, this peaceful stretch of beach is backed by banyan trees and grassy lawns. Here you'll find far less of the hubbub than in front of Waikiki's beachfront hotels. It's a popular weekend picnicking spot for families, who unload the kids to splash in the water while they fire up the BBQ grills.

Queen's Surf Beach is the nickname for the widest section of Kapi'olani Beach. The stretch in front of the pavilion, which has restrooms and showers, is popular with the gay community, and its sandy bottom offers decent swimming. The beach between

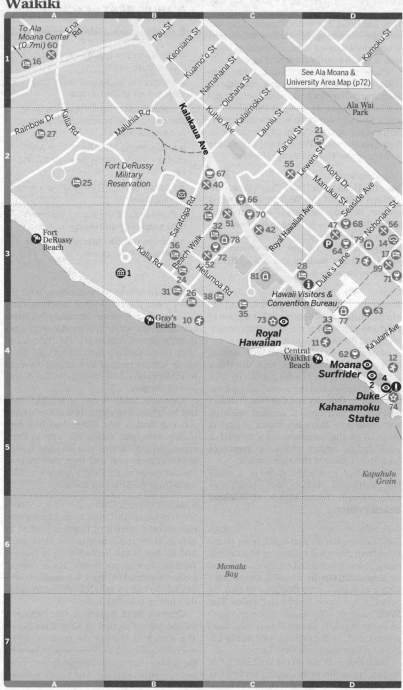

O'AHU WAIKIKI

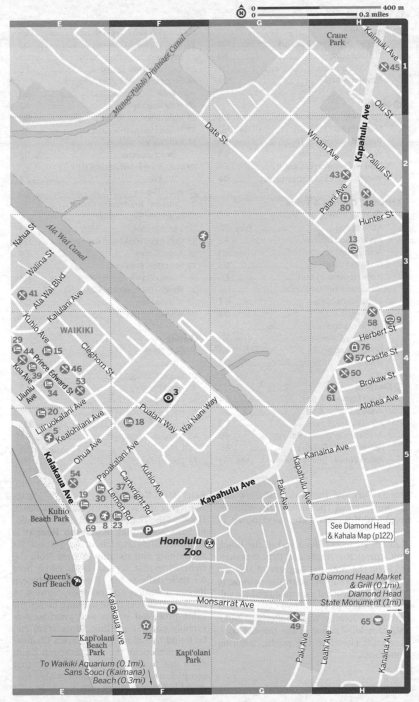

◎ **Top Sights**
Duke Kahanamoku Statue................D4
Honolulu Zoo...............................F6
Moana Surfrider...........................D4
Royal Hawaiian............................C4

◎ **Sights**
1 Hawai'i Army Museum.................B3
Mana Hawai'i............................(see 78)
Royal Hawaiian Center................(see 81)
2 Waikiki Beach Center..................D4
3 Waikiki Community Center...........F4
4 Wizard Stones of Kapaemahu........D4

Activities, Courses & Tours
5 24-Hour Fitness........................E5
Abhasa Spa.............................(see 73)
6 Ala Wai Golf Course...................F3
Aquazone...............................(see 31)
7 Go Nuts Hawaii.........................D3
8 Hans Hedemann Surf..................E6
9 Hawaiian Fire Surf School............H4
10 Maita'i Catamaran......................B4
11 Na Hoku II..............................D4
12 Na Ho'ola Spa...........................D4
Outrigger Catamaran...................(see 31)
13 Snorkel Bob's...........................H3
14 Waikiki Diving Center.................D3

◎ **Sleeping**
15 Aqua Bamboo & Spa...................E4
16 Aqua Bamboo & Spa...................A1
17 Aqua Waikiki Pearl.....................D3
18 Aston at the Waikiki Banyan.........F5
19 Aston Waikiki Beach Hotel...........E5
Aston Waikiki Beach Tower........(see 20)

20 Aston Waikiki Circle Hotel...........E5
21 Best Western Coconut Waikiki.......D2
22 Breakers................................C3
23 Castle Waikiki Grand..................F6
24 Embassy Suites Waikiki Beach
Walk...................................B3
25 Hale Koa................................A2
26 Halekulani.............................B3
27 Hilton Hawaiian Village..............A2
28 Holiday Inn Waikiki
Beachcomber..........................C3
29 Hostelling International (HI)
Waikiki................................E4
30 Hotel Renew...........................E5
31 Outrigger Reef on the Beach.........B3
32 Outrigger Regency on
Beachwalk.............................C3
33 Outrigger Waikiki on the Beach.....D4
34 Royal Grove............................E4
35 Sheraton Waikiki......................C4
36 Trump Waikiki Beach Walk...........B3
37 Waikiki Beachside Hostel.............F5
38 Waikiki Parc............................C3
39 Waikiki Prince..........................E4

⊗ **Eating**
BLT Steak...............................(see 36)
Chibo...................................(see 81)
40 Eggs 'n' Things.........................C2
41 Food Pantry............................E3
42 Gyū-kaku...............................C3
43 Halili's Hawaiian Foods...............H2
Hula Grill...............................(see 33)
44 Iyasume Musubi-ya....................E4
La Mer..................................(see 26)
45 Leonard's...............................H1

Queen's Surf and the Wall is shallow and has broken coral. The surfing area offshore, called **Publics**, gets some good waves in winter.

At the Diamond Head end of the beach park, the 1920s **Natorium** (http://natorium. org) is on the National Register of Historic Places. This 100m-long saltwater swimming pool was constructed as a memorial for soldiers who died in WWI. Two Olympic gold medalists – Johnny Weissmuller and Duke Kahanamoku – swam in the tide-fed pool. It remains closed to the public, awaiting renovations.

Sans Souci Beach Park   BEACH
Bordering the New Otani Kaimana Beach Hotel, at the Diamond Head edge of Waikiki Sans Souci (aka **Kaimana Beach**) is a prime sandy stretch of oceanfront for sunbathing and swimming away from the frenzied tourist scene. Locals come here for their daily swims. Facilities include a lifeguard station and outdoor showers. A shallow coral reef close to shore makes for calm, protected waters and provides reasonably good snorkeling. More coral can be found by following the Kapua Channel as it cuts through the reef, although if you swim out, beware of strong currents that can pick up. Check conditions with a lifeguard before venturing out.

46 Me BBQ E4
47 Menchanko-tei D3
  Nobu Waikiki................................. (see 38)
48 Ono Seafood....................................H2
49 People's Open Market.......................G7
50 Rainbow Drive-In..............................H4
51 Ramen Nakamura.............................C3
52 Roy's Waikiki Beach...........................C3
53 Ruffage Natural Foods.......................E4
54 Sansei Seafood Restaurant
  & Sushi Bar....................................E5
55 Siam Square....................................C2
56 Tapa's Restaurant & Lanai
  Bar...D3
57 Tokkuri Tei......................................H4
58 Uncle Bo's.......................................H4
59 Veggie Star Natural Foods D3
  Waikiki Farmers Market..................(see 3)
60 Waliana Coffee House........................A1
61 ZenShu...H4

◐◑ Drinking
62 Banyan Court Beach Bar.....................D4
63 Coconut Willy's D4
64 Da Big Kahuna.................................D3
65 Diamond Head Cove Health
  Bar...H7
  Duke's Waikiki...........................(see 33)
  Fusion Waikiki ....(see 68)
  House Without a Key...................(see 26)
  Hula's Bar & Lei Stand ....(see 23)
66 In-Between C2
67 Kimo Bean C2
  Lewers Lounge .... (see 26)
68 Lo Jax Waikiki..................................D3
69 Lulu's Surf Club................................E6

Mai Tai Bar ....(see 73)
Moana Terrace..............................(see 54)
70 Moose McGillicuddy's.........................C3
71 Nashville Waikiki...............................D3
  Rumfire ....(see 35)
  Tapa Bar ....(see 27)
  The Shack...................................(see 47)
  Tiki's Grill & Bar ....(see 19)
  Top of Waikiki.............................(see 28)
  Wang Chung's.............................(see 44)
72 Yard House......................................C3

⊙ Entertainment
73 'Aha 'Aina.......................................C4
74 Kuhio Beach Hula Show D4
  Pacific Swing..............................(see 54)
75 Royal Hawaiian Band.........................F7
  Royal Hawaiian Center.................(see 81)
  Waikiki Starlight Luau...................(see 27)

⊙ Shopping
  80% Straight ....(see 23)
76 Bailey's Antiques & Aloha
  Shirts H4
  Bob's Ukulele..............................(see 54)
77 International Market Place..................D4
  Island Treasures Antiques...........(see 64)
  Little Hawaiian Craft Shop ....(see 81)
78 Mana Hawai'i C3
79 Muse..D3
80 Na Lima Mili Hulu No'eau....................H2
  Newt at the Royal........................(see 73)
  Reyn Spooner..............................(see 35)
81 Royal Hawaiian Center.......................C3

⊙ Sights

Let's be honest: you're probably just here for the beach. But Waikiki's other diversions include historical hotels, spas, a popular golf course and an eco-friendly aquarium.

Waikiki Aquarium   AQUARIUM
(☎923-9741; www.waquarium.org; 2777 Kalakaua Ave; adult/child $9/2; ☺9am-5pm, last entry 4:30pm; 🚼) Next to a living reef on Waikiki's shoreline, this modern university-managed, child-friendly aquarium features a jaw-dropping shark gallery and dozens of tanks that re-create different Pacific Ocean reef habitats. It's a great place to identify the colorful coral and fish you've already seen while snorkeling.

There are rare fish species from the Northwestern Hawaiian Islands, as well as hypnotic moon jellies and flashlight fish that host bioluminescent bacteria. Especially hypnotizing are the Paluan chambered nautiluses with their unique spiral shells – this is the world's first aquarium to breed these endangered creatures in captivity. An outdoor tank is home to a pair of rare and endangered Hawaiian monk seals.

Check the website or call to make reservations for special family-friendly events and fun educational programs for kids like 'Aquarium After Dark.'

WAIKIKI'S SORCERERS & SURFERS

On the Diamond Head side of Waikiki's police substation, look for four boulders, known as the Wizard Stones of Kapaemahu. They're said to contain the secrets and healing powers of four sorcerers who visited Hawaii from Tahiti during the 16th century.

Just east of the stones is a bronze statue of Duke Kahanamoku standing with one of his longboards, often with fresh flower lei draped around his neck. Considered the father of modern surfing, Duke made his home in Waikiki and gave surfing demonstrations around the world, from Sydney to New York. Many local surfers have taken issue with the placement of the statue – Duke is standing with his back to the sea, a position they say he never would've taken in real life.

Moana Surfrider   HISTORICAL BUILDING
(☎922-3111; www.moana-surfrider.com; 2365 Kalakaua Ave; ⊗free tours usually 11am Mon, Wed & Fri) Christened the Moana Hotel when it opened in 1901, this hotel is built in the beaux-arts style of a plantation inn. The Moana joined what was then an exclusive neighborhood for Hawaiian royalty and business tycoons. Early guests included aristocrats, princes and Hollywood movie stars. If you don't join a tour, at least visit the mezzanine **museum**, which displays period photographs and hotel memorabilia, including scripts from the famed *Hawaii Calls* radio show that was broadcast from the banyan courtyard between 1935 and 1975.

Royal Hawaiian   HISTORICAL BUILDING
(☎923-7311; www.royal-hawaiian.com; 2259 Kalakaua Ave; ⊗free tours usually 2pm Tue, Thu & Sat) With its Moorish-style turrets and archways, this beautifully restored 1927 art deco hotel is a landmark. During the days of luxury ocean liners, the hotel practically became an extension of the cruise ships run by Matson Navigation. Dubbed the 'Pink Palace,' its guest list once read like a who's who of A-list celebrities, from royalty to Rockefellers, plus pop-culture stars like Charlie Chaplin and Babe Ruth. Today, historic tours explore the architecture and lore of this grand dame, including the gardens where Queen Ka'ahumanu's summer palace once stood.

FREE Hawai'i Army Museum   MUSEUM
(www.hiarmymuseumsoc.org; 2161 Kalia Rd; donations welcome, audio tour $5; ⊗9am-5pm Tue-Sun; P) At Fort DeRussy, this museum showcases an almost mind-numbing array of military paraphernalia as it relates to Hawaii's history, starting with shark-tooth clubs that Kamehameha the Great used to win control of the island over two centuries ago. Concentrating on the US military presence in Hawaii, extensive exhibits include displays on the 442nd, the Japanese American regiment that became the most decorated regiment in WWII, as well as a Cobra helicopter and military tanks and machinery. Free validated parking.

Kapi'olani Park   PARK
In its early days, horse racing and band concerts were the biggest attractions at Waikiki's favorite green space. Although the racetrack is long gone, this park named after a Hawaiian queen is still a favorite venue for live music and local community gathering, from farmers markets to arts-and-crafts fairs. The tree-shaded Kap'iolani Bandstand is also the perfect venue for the time-honored **Royal Hawaiian Band**, which performs classics from the monarchy era here on many Sunday afternoons.

Honolulu Zoo   ZOO
(☎971-7171; www.honoluluzoo.org; adult/child 4-12yr $6/3; ⊗9am-4:30pm; P♿) Badly in need of renovations, this zoo on the north side of Kapi'olani Park features some 300 species spread across over 40 acres of tropical greenery. In the aviary near the entrance you'll spot native birds, including the *ae'o* (Hawaiian black-necked stilt), *nene* (Hawaiian goose) and *'apapane,* a bright red Hawaiian honeycreeper. Check the online calendar of family-friendly twilight tours, overnight campouts and 'breakfast with a keeper' events (reservations recommended). The zoo parking lot costs $1 per hour. There's free parking on Monsarrat Ave by the Waikiki Shell.

🏃 Activities

In the mornings, runners pound the pavement next to Ala Wai Canal, while in the late afternoon outrigger canoe teams ply the canal's waters en route to Ala Wai Yacht Harbor. Kapi'olani Park has tennis courts and sports fields for soccer and softball, even cricket. For an indoor workout, 24-Hour Fitness (☎923-9090; www.24hourfitness.com; 2490 Kalakaua Ave; daily/weekly pass $25/69; ☺24hr) has a small, fully equipped gym and group exercise classes.

Surfing

Waikiki has good surfing year-round, but gentler winter breaks are best suited for beginners. For surfing lessons (two-hour group classes from around $100) and surfboard and stand up paddle boarding (SUP) rentals ($20 to $45 per day), try one of the following:

TOP CHOICE Hawaiian Fire Surf School LESSONS
(☎737-3743, 888-955-7873; www.hawaiianfire.com; 3318 Campbell Ave; 2hr group/private lesson from $109/189) With lessons taught by real-life firefighters, this safety-conscious surf school offers free pick-ups near Waikiki and transportation to/from a quiet beach near Barbers Point in Leeward O'ahu.

Hans Hedemann Surf RENTALS, LESSONS
(☎924-7778; www.hhsurf.com; Park Shore Waikiki, 2586 Kapahulu Ave; ☺8am-5pm) Local pro surfer's well-established school, conveniently opposite the beach.

Girls Who Surf RENTALS, LESSONS
(Map p72; ☎772-4583; www.girlswhosurf.com; 1020 Auahi St; ☺8am-6pm) Surf lessons in Waikiki and at Ko Olina, with free hotel pick-ups. For surfboard rentals, delivery to the beach costs an extra $10.

Go Nuts Hawaii RENTALS, LESSONS
(☎926-3367; www.gonuts-hawaii.com; 2301 Kuhio Ave; ☺8am-9pm) Japanese-speaking instructors are available at this group-friendly surfing school and outfitter.

Scuba Diving & Snorkeling

To really see the gorgeous stuff – coral gardens, manta rays and exotic tropical fish – head out on a boat dive. For snorkel set and scuba-diving equipment rentals, PADI certification courses (from $350) and boat trips (from $110), try one of the following:

AquaZone RENTALS, LESSONS
(☎866-923-3483; www.scubaoahu.com; Outrigger Waikiki on the Beach, 2335 Kalakaua Ave; ☺8am-5pm Mon-Sat) This dive shop and tour outfitter has a second beachside location in front of the Waikiki Beach Marriott Resort.

Waikiki Diving Center LESSONS, TOURS
(☎922-2121; www.waikikidiving.com; 424 Nahua St; ☺7am-5pm) This full-service dive shop offers small-group boat dives.

Snorkel Bob's RENTALS
(☎735-7944; www.snorkelbob.com; 700 Kapahulu Ave; ☺8am-5pm) Rates vary here depending on the quality of the snorkeling gear and accessories packages.

O'ahu Diving LESSONS, TOURS
(☎721-4210; www.oahudiving.com; ☺8am-9pm) Specializes in first-time experiences for beginning divers without PADI certification.

Golf

Ala Wai Golf Course GOLF
(☎733-7387, reservations 296-2000; www1.honolulu.gov/des/golf/alawai.htm; 404 Kapahulu Ave; greens fee $23-46, cart rental $20) With views of Diamond Head, this flat 18-hole, par-70 layout has bagged a Guinness World Record for being the world's busiest golf course. Make tee-time reservations as far in advance as possible. Otherwise, if you get there early in the day and get on the waiting list, you'll probably get a tee time later that day, as long as your entire party waits at the course. Club rentals available.

LET'S SAIL AWAY

Several catamaran cruises leave right from Waikiki Beach – just walk down onto the sand, step into the surf and hop aboard. A 90-minute, all-you-can-drink 'booze cruise' costs $25 to $40 per adult.

Maita'i Catamaran
(☎922-5665, 800-462-7975; www.leahi.com; 📵) Offers the biggest variety of boat trips, including reef snorkeling, moonlight cruises and a sunset mai tai sail (kids allowed); call ahead for schedules and reservations.

Na Hoku II
(☎554-5990; www.nahokuii.com) With its yellow-and-red-striped sails, this frat-boy-friendly, hard-drinkin' catamaran departs five times daily between 9:30am and 5:30pm; the sunset sail usually sells out, so book ahead.

Outrigger Catamaran
(☎922-2210; www.outriggercatamaranhawaii.com) Family-friendly snorkeling trips, daytime sailings and yes, a sunset booze cruise; reservations required.

🍃 Courses

Mana Hawai'i   HAWAIIANA
(☎923-2220; www.waikikibeachwalk.com; 226
Lewers St) This Hawaiiana shop offers
free weekly drop-in classes in Hawaiian
language, lei making, hula dancing and
ukulele playing, including just for *keiki*.

Royal Hawaiian Center   HAWAIIANA
(☎922-2299; www.royalhawaiiancenter.com; 2201
Kalakaua Ave) A mega-mall that offers free
Hawaiian cultural classes and demonstrations in arts and crafts, including quilts,
leis, *kapa* (pounded-bark cloth), coconut-
leaf weaving, hula and ukulele playing.

Waikiki Community Center   HAWAIIANA
(☎923-1802; www.waikikicommunitycenter.org;
310 Pa'oakalani Ave; lesson $3-15) Try your hand
at mah-jongg, the ukulele, hula or other
island arts and crafts. Instructors at this
homespun community center are brim-
ming with aloha. Most classes are held on
weekdays; call or go online for schedules
(pre-registration may be required).

✨ Festivals & Events

Waikiki loves to party. Every Friday night at
7:30pm from October to March (8pm from
April to September), the Hilton Hawaiian
Village shoots off a big ol' fireworks display,
visible from the beach. For more festivals
and events around Honolulu, see also p80.

Duke Kahanamoku
Challenge   CULTURE, SPORTS
(www.waikikicommunitycenter.com) Outrigger
canoe and stand up paddle races, local food,
traditional Hawaiian games, arts-and-crafts
vendors and live entertainment in January.

Honolulu Festival   ARTS, CULTURE
(www.honolulufestival.com) Cultural performances at Waikiki Beach Walk and
Waikiki Shopping Plaza and a festive
parade along Kalakaua Ave followed by a
fireworks show in mid-March.

Waikiki Spam Jam   FOOD, MUSIC
(www.spamjamhawaii.com) Late April sees a
street festival devoted to Hawaii's favorite
canned meat product: Spam.

Pan-Pacific Festival   ARTS, CULTURE
(www.pan-pacific-festival.com) Hula dancing,
Japanese *taiko* drumming, an arts-and-
crafts fair and a huge *ho'olaule'a* (block
party) in early June.

Na Hula Festival   ARTS, CULTURE
(www1.honolulu.gov/parks/programs) Local hula
halau (schools) gather for a full day of

music and dance celebrations at Kapi'olani
Park in early August.

Hawaiian Slack Key Guitar Festival MUSIC
(www.slackkeyfestival.com) Traditional Hawaiian guitar and ukulele music at Kapi'olani
Park in mid-August.

Aloha Festivals   ARTS, CULTURE
(www.alohafestivals.com) During a statewide
cultural festival, Waikiki is famous for its
royal court ceremonies and *ho'olaule'a* in
September.

🛏 Sleeping

Wherever you stay in Waikiki, reserve
rooms as far in advance as possible. Overnight parking costs $10 to $30, whether
for valet or self-parking. Increasingly, hotels are also charging mandatory 'resort
fees,' which tack another $5 to $25 per day
onto your final bill. Resort fees may cover
internet connections, local and toll-free
phone calls and fitness room access, or
no extra perks at all, but regardless, you'll
have to pay.

Be aware that 'ocean view' and its cous-
ins 'ocean front' and 'partial ocean view'
are all liberally used and may require a
periscope to spot the waves. 'City', 'garden'
or 'mountain' views may be euphemisms
for overlooking the parking lot. When
making hotel or condo reservations, check
property maps online or call a reservations
agent directly to ask.

For an island chain with mod style, look
into Aqua Hotels & Resorts (www.aquare
sorts.com), the best of which offer free high-speed
internet, complimentary continental breakfast,
tiny pools and small workout rooms. Designed
for both business and leisure travelers, Aqua
properties are also gay-friendly.

Resorts

Waikiki's main beachfront strip, Kalakaua
Ave, is lined with high-end resort hotels.

TOP
CHOICE Halekulani   RESORT $$$
(☎923-2311, 800-367-2343; www.halekulani.com;
2199 Kalia Rd; r $435-690; 🅿❄@📶♨) With
modern sophistication, this resort hotel lives
up to its name, which means 'House Befitting
Heaven.' It's an all-encompassing experience
of gracious living, not merely a place to crash.
Peaceful rooms are equipped with modern
gadgets, such as high-tech entertainment
centers, along with deep soaking tubs and
expansive lanai. Eclectic luxury suites include
one personally designed by Vera Wang. Find

SPA ME, BABY

What's a beach vacation without a little pampering? Especially with Hawaii's traditions of *lomilomi* ('loving touch') and *pohaku* (hot-stone) massage, coupled with gentle aloha spirit. Call ahead for appointments, including at these top-notch spas:

Abhasa Spa
(☎922-8200; www.abhasa.com; Royal Hawaiian Hotel, 2259 Kalakaua Ave) Hawaiian massage and Kona coffee-oil skin toning treatments in cabanas set amid tropical gardens.

Na Hoʻola Spa
(☎923-1234; http://waikiki.hyatt.com; Hyatt Regency Waikiki Beach Resort & Spa, 2424 Kalakaua Ave) Traditional seaweed, mud and *ti*-leaf wraps, plus macadamia-nut exfoliation and coconut moisturizers.

AquaSPA
(☎924-2782, 866-971-2782; www.aqua resorts.com/aqua-spa; various locations) Intimate boutique-hotel cabana massages, often at discounted rates, plus tropical fruit scrubs; same-day reservations often available.

The **Halekulani** and **Moana Surfrider** resort hotels have top-notch spas too.

ultimate relaxation in the Halekulani's pampering spa.

Royal Hawaiian　　　　　RESORT **$$$**
(☎923-7311, 866-716-8110; www.royal-hawaiian .com; 2259 Kalakaua Ave; r $295-505; P✳@ 🛜🏊🐾) The aristocratic Royal Hawaiian was Waikiki's first true luxury hotel. Now the Spanish Moorish-style 'Pink Palace' looks better than ever, thanks to multimillion-dollar renovations. It's all about ambience, with airy walkways, soaring ceilings and an indulgent spa. Rooms in the historic section maintain classic appeal, though many guests prefer the modern high-rise tower's ocean views. In-room wired internet and limited common-area wi-fi cost extra.

Moana Surfrider　　　　RESORT **$$$**
(☎922-3111, 866-716-8109; www.moana-surfrider .com; 2365 Kalakaua Ave; r $250-525; P✳@🛜🏊) Waikiki's most historic hotel retains most of its colonial character in the common areas, with high plantation-style ceilings, Hawaiian artwork on the walls and koa-wood rocking chairs beckoning on the front veranda. Compact rooms have been upgraded with 21st-century amenities. Expect to be dodging wedding parties in the lobby and corridors during your stay. In-room wired internet and lobby and poolside wi-fi cost extra. Self-parking offsite.

Outrigger Reef on the Beach　　RESORT **$$$**
(☎923-3111, 866-956-4262; www.outriggerreef .com; 2169 Kalia Rd; r $189-389; P✳@🛜🏊🐾) Forget the hoity-toity attitudes of the Outrigger's higher-priced beachfront neighbors. Here the Hawaiiana flows from the handmade outrigger canoe in the Polynesian-style lobby through hula and lei-making classes and guided historical walking tours of Waikiki. Rooms are modern and functional enough for the mostly suburban crowd. Free in-room wired internet and lobby and poolside wi-fi.

Sheraton Waikiki　　　　RESORT **$$$**
(☎922-4422, 866-716-8109; www.sheratonwaikiki .com; 2255 Kalakaua Ave; r $235-390; P✳@ 🛜🏊🐾) Looming over the historic Royal Hawaiian, this chain megahotel boasts modern amenities. It's ginormous enough to accommodate package-tour groups and conferences. Facing the beach, a 'superpool' amphibious playground keeps the kiddos entertained with a 70ft-long waterslide, while adults retreat to the oceanview infinity pool. In-room wired internet and common-area wi-fi cost extra.

Hilton Hawaiian Village　　RESORT **$$$**
(☎949-4321, 800-445-8667; www.hawaiianvillage .hilton.com; 2005 Kalia Rd; r $210-425; P✳@ 🛜🏊🐾) On the Fort DeRussy side of Waikiki, the Hilton is Waikiki's largest hotel – practically a self-sufficient tourist fortress of towers, restaurants, bars and shops. It's geared almost entirely for families and package tourists. Expect check-in lines to move as slowly as TSA airport-security checkpoints.

Boutique Hotels
Waves of chic boutique hotels are just starting to come ashore in Waikiki.

TOP CHOICE **Waikiki Edition**　　BOUTIQUE HOTEL **$$**
(☎943-5800, 800-466-9695; www.editionhotels .com; 1775 Ala Moana Blvd; r $345-525; P✳@ 🛜🏊) Whimsical postmodernity is hotelier Ian Schrager's signature, from the revolving

bookcase that hides the lobby bar to an outdoor movie theater showing indie flicks and contemporary video art. Terraced oceanview rooms and suites are crisp, chic and elemental, showing off teak doors, Frette linens and marble baths. A lanai deck pool overlooks Ala Wai Yacht Harbor, as does epicurean eatery Morimoto Waikiki. Your bod isn't quite ready for the beach? Enroll in surf-and-bikini boot camp, customized by a celebrity nutritionist, yogis and pro surfers.

Hotel Renew   BOUTIQUE HOTEL **$$**
(☑687-7700, 888-485-7639; www.hotelrenew .com; 129 Pa'oakalani Ave; r incl breakfast $150-215; P❋@☎) Just a half-block from the beach, this eco-conscious boutique hotel has attentive concierge staff who can be counted on to provide all of the little niceties, from chilled drinks upon arrival to beach mats and bodyboards to borrow. Design-savvy accommodations come with platform beds, projection-screen TVs, spa robes, earth-toned furnishings and *shōji* sliding screens. It's romantic enough for honeymooners, and also gay-friendly. No swimming pool, though.

Waikiki Parc   BOUTIQUE HOTEL **$$$**
(☑921-7272, 800-422-0450; www.waikikiparc .com; 2233 Helumoa Rd; r $285-415; P❋@☎) Epitomizing new-wave Waikiki, the Parc is an affordably hip hangout that oddly mixes nostalgic touches like plantation-shuttered windows with minimalist contemporary furnishings. Although the staff pampers, guest rooms are not nearly as chic as the Parc's upmarket sister resort, the Halekulani, or Nobu sushi bar downstairs. In-room wired internet and lobby wi-fi complimentary.

Aqua Bamboo & Spa   BOUTIQUE HOTEL **$$**
(☑922-7777, 866-971-2782; www.aquabamboo .com; 2425 Kuhio Ave; r $129-159, 1 bedroom $199-239, all incl breakfast; P❋@☎❄) Looking for a meditative retreat from Waikiki's urban jungle? An intimate boutique hotel with a cabana spa, the Bamboo also has a small saltwater pool, should you tire of the ocean. Stylishly minimalist rooms include suites with kitchenettes or full kitchens. Free in-room wired internet and lobby and poolside wi-fi.

New Otani Kaimana Beach   BOUTIQUE HOTEL **$$$**
(☑923-1555, 800-356-8264; www.kaimana.com; 2863 Kalakaua Ave; r $170-505; P❋@☎) Just half a mile from the throbbing hub of Waikiki, this low-key hotel sits oceanside in front of Sans Souci Beach. Book early, because repeat guests also crave the seclusion and idyllic beach access. Outdated rooms are small, but the views are large and all have private lanai. Japanese spoken.

Chain Hotels & Condos

If you don't mind walking a few minutes to the beach, hotels along Kuhio Ave and the Ala Wai Canal may have rooms for half the price of beachfront properties. But the latter may be in renovated apartment buildings or aging 1960s and '70s high-rises.

Trump Waikiki Beach Walk   HOTEL **$$$**
(☑683-7777, 877-683-7401; www.trumpwaikiki hotel.com; 223 Saratoga Rd; studio $329-699, 1br $449-1279; P❋@☎❄✋) The pinnacle of condo luxury, Trump's high-rise hotel tower boasts an infinity pool and apartment-style suites with panoramic windows, marble baths, full kitchens and 24-hour room service. Welcome goodies for children include a stuffed animal, books, games, movies, milk and cookies, and pint-sized robes and slippers.

Aston Waikiki Beach Tower   HOTEL **$$$**
(☑926-6400, 877-997-6667; www.astonhotels.com; 2470 Kalakaua Ave; 2br $455-710; P❋@☎❄✋) A full-service apartment-style hotel in the heart of Waikiki that's perfectly poised for family reunions. Each contemporary condominium measures over 1000 sq ft and has a full kitchen, washer/dryer and a private lanai with at least a partial ocean view. Free in-room wired internet and common-area wi-fi. Complimentary valet parking.

Embassy Suites Waikiki Beach Walk   HOTEL **$$$**
(☑921-2345, 800-362-2779; www.embassysuites waikiki.com; 201 Beach Walk; 1 bedroom $235-369, 2 bedroom $499-620, all incl breakfast; P❋@☎❄✋) Enviably near the beach, restaurants and nightlife, this newer chain property has no-nonsense, tropically inspired suites big enough for families, each with a microwave, mini-fridge and flat-screen TV. There's also a 24-hour fitness room. Free in-room wired internet and common-area wi-fi.

Outrigger Regency on Beachwalk   HOTEL **$$$**
(☑922-3871, 866-956-4262; www.outrigger.com; 255 Beach Walk; 1 bedroom $189-345, 2 bedroom $289-469; P❋@✋) This sleek modern high-rise is designed with earth- and jewel-toned furnishings, marble baths and bold artwork.

Spacious condo suites all have full kitchens; some have lanai with partial ocean views. Step outside the lobby downstairs, and you're right on buzzing Waikiki Beach Walk. Free in-room wired internet. Offsite swimming pool.

TOP CHOICE Best Western Coconut Waikiki
HOTEL $$

(☎923-8828, 866-971-2782; www.coconutwaikiki hotel.com; 450 Lewers St; r incl breakfast $115-210; P❋@🛜🏊) Don't let the chain-gang name fool you: this Aqua-managed property has hip, edgy decor: atomic starburst mirrors in the hallways, and cool mint green rooms, each with private lanai. Designed with business travelers in mind, rooms have ergonomic work desks, microwaves and mini-fridges. A small exercise room is well-equipped, but the pool is barely big enough to dip your toes in.

Aston Waikiki Beach Hotel
HOTEL $$$

(☎922-2511, 800-877-7666; www.astonhotels .com; 2570 Kalakaua Ave; r incl breakfast $175-300; P❋@🛜🏊🍴) With cheery surf-themed decor and a rooftop bar lit by tiki torches, this contemporary number opposite the beach is frequently sold out. If you get an online-booking discount, you too will be a devotee. Free souvenir soft-sided cooler bags can be filled with breakfast goodies to take to the beach. In-room wired internet and lobby and poolside wi-fi costs extra.

Aston at the Waikiki Banyan
HOTEL $$

(☎922-0555, 877-977-6667; www.astonhotels.com; 201 Ohua Ave; 1 bedroom $130-235; P❋@🛜🏊🍴) This family-friendly, all-suites high-rise hotel is a short walk from the aquarium, the zoo and, of course, the beach. Roomy, if sometimes beat-up suites have a handy sofabed in the living room. Kids get a free souvenir sand pail full of cool, fun stuff at check-in, and the pool deck has a playground, tennis and basketball courts, and a putting green. In-room wired internet costs extra.

Aqua Waikiki Pearl
HOTEL $$

(☎922-1616, 866-971-2782; www.aquaresorts .com; 415 Nahua St; r $110-135, 1/2/3 bedroom $200/230/335; P❋@🛜🏊) This centrally located, dog-friendly hotel with a downstairs sports bar can be a bargain. Although kinda bland, shoebox-sized contemporary rooms each have a microwave, mini-fridge and coffeemaker, while some spacious suites

have full kitchens. Free in-room wired internet and lobby and poolside wi-fi.

Aston Waikiki Circle
HOTEL $$

(☎923-1571, 877-997-6667; www.astonhotels.com; 2464 Kalakaua Ave; r $105-210; P❋) Tired of square boxes? This circular building must have been *très chic* back in the playful era of postmodernism. Today this survivor is all about value, not fashion. About half of the rooms, all with lanai, enjoy a full ocean view. The drawback? They aren't big enough to practice your hula dancing in. In-room wired internet costs extra.

Aqua Palms & Spa
HOTEL $$

(☎947-7256, 866-971-2782; www.aquapalms.com; 1850 Ala Moana Blvd; r incl breakfast $99-200, 1 bedroom $250; P❋@🛜🏊) A short walk from Ala Moana Center, this high-rise hotel feels more functional than fun, but still delivers bang for your buck. Tiny rooms lack tropical panache but you can't fault those plush beds or fluffy robes. There's a postage stamp–sized swimming pool and workout room. Free in-room wired internet and lobby wi-fi.

Holiday Inn Waikiki Beachcomber
HOTEL $$

(☎922-4646, 888-465-4329; www.holidayinn .com; 2300 Kalakaua Ave; r $160-235; P❋@ 🛜🏊🍴) On Waikiki's main strip, this contemporary nonsmoking hotel is remarkable for its prime location and sub-prime rates. Free in-room wired internet and poolside wi-fi.

Castle Waikiki Grand
HOTEL $$

(☎923-1814, 800-367-5004; www.waikikigrand. com; 134 Kapahulu Ave; r $85-450; P❋@🛜) Gay-friendly condotel that rents individually owned studios (some with kitchenettes) that vary from horrifying to heavenly, so view online photos with skepticism. Free in-room wired internet. Ask about weekly discounts.

Independent Hotels

Breakers
HOTEL $$

(☎923-3181, 800-426-0494; www.breakers-hawaii .com; 250 Beach Walk; r $120-185; P❋🏊) You'll either love it or hate it: this older, Polynesian-style hotel is a throwback to earlier times, with a petite garden and floor-to-ceiling louvered windows. Very old, creaky rooms all have kitchenettes; those on the second-floor also have Japanese-style *shōji* (translucent paper-covered wooden sliding doors). Free poolside and lobby wi-fi. Extremely limited self-parking. Japanese spoken.

BEST FAMILY-FRIENDLY HOTELS IN WAIKIKI

» Royal Hawaiian (p109)

» Hilton Hawaiian Village (p109)

» Sheraton Waikiki (p109)

» Outrigger Reef on the Beach (p109)

» Trump Waikiki Beach Walk (p110)

» Aston Waikiki Beach Tower (p110)

» Aston at the Waikiki Banyan (p111)

» Aston Waikiki Beach Hotel (p111)

» Embassy Suites Waikiki Beach Walk (p110)

» Outrigger Regency on Beachwalk (p110)

Royal Grove   HOTEL $
(☎923-7691; www.royalgrovehotel.com; 151 Uluniu Ave; r with kitchenette $55-125; ❄@☀) No frills but plenty of aloha characterize this garishly pink low-rise courtyard spot, a favorite of 'snowbird' retirees who return each winter to this home-away-from-home complete with a pet bird and a piano in the lobby. Economy rooms in the older Mauka Wing have no air-con and suffer heavy traffic noise. Low-season weekly rates.

Waikiki Prince   HOTEL $
(☎922-1544; www.waikikiprince.com; 2431 Prince Edward St; r $55-80; P❄☀) What ocean views? Never mind the cramped check-in office either. This 1970s apartment complex on an anonymous side street is a standout budget option, as some of the two dozen compact, cheerful rooms have kitchenettes. Free lobby wi-fi during office hours only. Weekly rates available year-round.

Hale Koa   HOTEL $$
(☎955-0555, 800-367-6027; www.halekoa.com; 2055 Kalia Rd; r $90-290; P❄@☀❄🍴) This high-rise hotel fronting Fort DeRussy Beach is reserved for active and retired US military personnel. Ask for more recently renovated Ilima Tower rooms. In-room wired internet and common-area wi-fi costs extra.

Hostels

Lemon Rd, an alley set back from the Diamond Head end of the beach, is filled with backpacker hostels catering to twentysomething global nomads.

Hostelling International (HI) Waikiki   HOSTEL $
(☎926-8313; www.hostelsaloha.com; 2417 Prince Edward St; dm $25-28, d $58-64; ☀reception 7am-3am; P@) Occupying a converted low-rise, bright-aqua apartment building, this tidy hostel has simple single-sex dormitories, a common kitchen and bodyboards to borrow. There's no curfew or daytime dormitory lockout. No smoking or alcohol allowed. Reservations strongly recommended. Limited parking ($5).

Waikiki Beachside Hostel   HOSTEL $
(☎923-9566, 866-478-3888; www.waikikibeachsidehostel.com; 2556 Lemon Rd; dm $15-35, semi-private r $75; P@☀) Security and cleanliness can be lax here, but an on-site cybercafe and discounts on surfboards, bodyboards, snorkel sets and moped rentals are perks for the international backpacker party crowd. Each dormitory (co-ed or women-only) is equipped with a full kitchen and a telephone. Covered parking ($7).

✖ Eating

Warning: many of Waikiki's middle-of-the-road restaurants are overpriced and not worth eating at, no matter how enticing the ocean views. Along Kalakaua Ave, suburban chains like the Cheesecake Factory overflow with hungry tourists, while a few stellar beachfront hotel restaurants are run by top chefs. A block further inland, Kuhio Ave is filled with cheap grazing, especially multiethnic takeout joints. On the outskirts of Waikiki, you'll find stand-out neighborhood eateries, drive-ins and bakeries around Kapahulu Ave.

Kalakaua & Kuhio Aves

TOP CHOICE Morimoto Waikiki   JAPANESE, FUSION $$$
(☎943-5900; www.morimotowaikiki.com; Edition Waikiki, 1775 Ala Moana Blvd; breakfast mains $16-30, lunch & dinner mains $22-50; ☀6:30am-10am & 11am-2:30pm daily, 5-10pm Sun-Thu, to 11pm Fri & Sat) Hidden upstairs inside the chic Waikiki Edition hotel, Iron Chef Morimoto's ocean-front dining room immediately seduces with coconut cocktails and Ala Wai Yacht Harbor views from a sun-drenched poolside patio. Sink back against a mod sea-green pillowed banquette and fork into ahi *poke*, ginger-soy braised black cod and curried whole roasted lobster – even breakfast gets an upgrade with *wagyū* beef *loco moco*. Every dish gets presented with the same artistic whimsy

you've seen on TV. Complimentary valet parking with restaurant validation.

TOP CHOICE Roy's Waikiki Beach HAWAII REGIONAL $$$
(☑923-7697; www.roysrestaurant.com; 226 Lewers St; mains $28-40; ◎11am-10pm) This ocean-front incarnation of Roy Yamaguchi's island-born chain is perfect for a flirty date or just celebrating the good life with friends. The ground-breaking Hawaii Regional chef doesn't actually cook in the kitchen here, but his signature *misoyaki* butterfish, blackened ahi, macadamia nut-encrusted mahimahi and deconstructed sushi rolls are always on the menu. Molten-chocolate souf-flé for dessert is a must.

La Mer   EURASIAN, SEAFOOD $$$
(☑923-2311; Halekulani, 2199 Kalia Rd; 2-/3-/4-course dinner from $95/125/145, 9-course tasting menu $165; ◎6-10pm) Inside the posh Halekulani resort, La Mer boasts a spectacu-lar view of Diamond Head through swaying palms. A neoclassical French menu puts the emphasis on Provençal cuisine and adds fresh Hawaii-grown ingredients (vegetar-ian options available). Wines are perfectly paired. Formal is the byword: men must wear a jacket or collared long-sleeved shirt.

Sansei Seafood Restaurant & Sushi Bar   JAPANESE, FUSION $$
(☑931-6286; www.sanseihawaii.com; 3rd fl, Waikiki Beach Marriott Resort, 2552 Kalakaua Ave; mains $16-35; ◎5:30-10pm Sun-Thu, to 1am Fri & Sat) From the mind of one of Hawaii's hottest chefs, DK Kodama, this Pacific Rim fusion menu rolls out everything from traditional sashimi to Dungeness crab ramen with black-truffle butter sauce. Tables on the torchlit veranda enjoy prime sunset views. Queue for early-bird specials, available from 5:15pm to 6pm on Sunday and Monday, or enjoy 50% off all food after 10pm on Thurs-day through Saturday nights.

Nobu Waikiki   JAPANESE, FUSION $$$
(☑237-6999; www.noburestaurants.com/waikiki; Waikiki Parc, 2233 Helumoa Rd; shared dishes $2-32, mains $32-40; ◎5:30-10pm Sun-Wed, to 11pm Thu-Sat, lounge 5pm-midnight daily) Iron Chef Mat-suhisa's original Japanese fusion restaurant and sushi bar in Waikiki made a big splash when it opened, and his modern dishes still seem right at home inside the Waikiki Parc hotel. Broiled black cod with miso sauce, Japanese-Peruvian *tiradito* (ceviche) and seafood tartar with caviar are among Nobu's

signature tastes. A low-lit cocktail lounge serves appetizing small bites and 'sake-tinis.'

BLT Steak   STEAK, SEAFOOD $$$
(☑683-7440; www.bltsteak.com; Waikiki Beach Walk, 223 Saratoga Rd; mains $26-52; ◎5:30-10pm Sun-Thu, to 11pm Fri & Sat) A trendy NYC im-port, chef Laurent Tourondel's steakhouse has some fine chops broiled at 1700°F and finished off with herb butter and your pick of no fewer than nine sauces. The daily blackboard of specials lists fresh Pacific sea-food, including Hawaiian lobster and a raw bar of oysters flown in from the mainland. With walnut floors, chocolate leather chairs and a breezy outdoor patio, the atmosphere is date-worthy.

Gyū-kaku   JAPANESE $$
(☑926-2989; www.gyu-kaku.com; 307 Lewers St; shared dishes $4-24; ◎11:30am-12am) Who doesn't love a grill-it-yourself Japanese BBQ joint? Settle in with your entourage for Kobe rib-eye steak, *kalbi* short ribs, garlic shrimp and enoki mushrooms, all served with sweet and spicy marinades and dips. Show up for afternoon happy-hour specials or all-you-can-eat lunch deals (from $25).

Menchanko-tei   JAPANESE $$
(Waikiki Trade Center, 2255 Kuhio Ave; mains $6-12; ◎11am-11pm) Japanese expats head to this unassuming kitchen for their fix of Hakata-style ramen soup with freshly made noodles, citrus pepper and a creamy broth. Mechanko-tei also makes a mean *tonkatsu* (deep-fried pork cutlet), *gyōza* and Nagasa-ki-style *sara-udon* (stir-fried noodles with veggies).

Ramen Nakamura   JAPANESE $$
(2141 Kalakaua Ave; mains $9-14; ◎11am-11:30pm) You'll have to strategically elbow aside Japanese tourists toting Gucci and Chanel bags just to sit down. Then you're free to dig into hearty bowls of oxtail or tonkotsu kimchi ramen soup with crunchy fried garlic slices on top. It's almost always worth the wait.

Chibo   JAPANESE $$
(☑922-9722; www.chibohawaii.com; 3rd fl, Royal Hawaiian Center, 2201 Kalakaua Ave; lunch mains $11-25, set dinners $30-75; ◎11:30am-2am & 5-10pm) This high-end Japanese *teppan-yaki* grill is a standout for its chef-made *okonomiyaki* (savory cabbage pancakes). Go traditional and order one made with *buta* (pork) or *ika* (squid), or splurge on

steak, scallops and prawns. Lunch is a better deal.

Iyasume Musubi-ya   JAPANESE, LOCAL $

(2410 Koa Ave; meals $4-8; ☺6am-4pm) Hole-in-the-wall that keeps busy making fresh *onigiri* (rice balls) stuffed with seaweed, salmon roe, sour plums and even Spam. Other specialties include *donburi* rice bowls, hearty *udon* noodle soup, Japanese curry and island-style *mochiko* fried chicken. In a hurry? Grab a *bentō* boxed lunch to go.

Me BBQ   LOCAL, TAKEOUT $

(151 Uluniu Ave; meals $4-11; ☺7am-8:45pm Mon-Sat; ⊞) This streetside takeout counter has zero atmosphere, but you can chow down at plastic picnic tables. Succulent *kalbi* short ribs and spicy kimchi are house specialties, but the wall-sized picture menu also includes local plate-lunch combos with chicken katsu, shrimp tempura and more.

Siam Square   THAI $$

(www.siamsquaredining.com; 2nd fl, 408 Lewers St; mains $11-16; ☺11am-12am Mon-Sat, to 10pm Sun; ◢) It's Waikiki's most authentic Thai restaurant, although that's not saying a lot. You want it spicy? Good, because that's the best way to order larb pork salad or fried fish with chili sauce here. Service is smiley, but standoffish.

Ruffage Natural Foods   VEGETARIAN, TAKEOUT $

(2443 Kuhio Ave; items $4-8; ☺9am-6pm; ◢) This pint-sized health-food store whips up taro burgers, veggie burritos, vegan chili and real-fruit smoothies that to revitalize your whole bod. At night, the shop shares space with a tiny, backpacker-friendly sushi bar run by a Japanese chef.

Hau Tree Lanai   PACIFIC RIM $$$

(☎921-7066; New Otani Kaimana Beach Hotel, 2863 Kalakaua Ave; breakfast & lunch $12-17, dinner $30-52; ☺breakfast 7-10:45am, lunch 11:45am-2pm Mon-Sat & noon-2pm Sun, dinner 5:30-9pm) Under an arbor of hau trees is where you'll find this open-air hideaway with pink tablecloths on Sans Souci Beach. Breakfast and lunch menus abound in local flavor from poi pancakes to furikake ahi burgers. Surf-and-turf dinners are more mediocre.

Eggs 'n' Things   BREAKFAST $

(www.eggsnthings.com; 343 Saratoga Rd; mains $6-12; ☺6am-2pm & 5-10pm; ⊞◢) Never empty, this diner dishes up banana macadamia nut pancakes topped with your choice of honey,

guava or coconut syrup, and fluffy omelets with Portuguese sausage for jetlagged tourists from the US mainland and Japan. Kids' menu available.

Hula Grill   ISLAND CONTEMPORARY $$

(☎923-4852; www.hulagrillwaikiki.com; 2nd fl, Outrigger Waikiki on the Beach, 2335 Kalakaua Ave; breakfast dishes $4-9, dinner mains $17-33; ☺6:30am-10:30am Mon-Sat, 9am-2pm Sun, 5-10pm daily; ℗) Come early to score a table on a wraparound lanai and watch sunset over the beach. Reward yourself with 'wrong island' ice teas and island-style *pupu* like mango-barbecued ribs. Validated parking $5.

Wailana Coffee House   DINER $

(1860 Ala Moana Blvd; mains $5-15; ☺24hr, except 12am-6am Wed) This classic all-night coffee shop is stuck in the 1970s with its Naugahyde booths and counter stools and serves heaping portions of greasy-spoon fare and tropical fruity drinks. Waitstaff all know the regulars by name. Locals sing karaoke in the cocktail lounge.

Kapahulu Ave & Around

TOP CHOICE Leonard's   BAKERY $

(933 Kapahulu Ave; pastries 75¢-$2; ☺5:30am-9pm Sun-Thu, to 10pm Fri & Sat; ⊞) With an eye-catching vintage 1950s neon sign that makes it almost impossible to drive by without stopping in, this Portuguese bakery is famous all over O'ahu for its *malasadas* (sweet, fried dough rolled in sugar), served oven-fresh and warm in a cotton-candy pink bakery box. Try the *haupia* (coconut-cream) or *liliko'i* (passion fruit) filling, and you'll be hooked for life. Pick up a souvenir 'got malasadas?' T-shirt, too.

Halili's Hawaiian Foods   HAWAIIAN $$

(http://mybackyardluau.ning.com; 760 Palani Ave; meals $10-15; ☺10am-3pm Mon, 10am-7pm Tue-Thu, 10am-8pm Fri & Sat, 11am-3pm Sun) Halili's has been cooking up homegrown Hawaiian fare since the 1950s. Locals shoehorn themselves into cheery booths and tables with heaping plates of *kalua* pig, *lomilomi* salmon and *laulau* (meat wrapped in *ti* leaves and steamed) served with poi or rice, plus grilled ahi plate lunches, bowls of tripe stew and fat tortilla wraps. Also near Ala Moana Center.

Uncle Bo's   ASIAN FUSION $$

(☎735-8311; www.unclebosrestaurant.com; 559 Kapahulu Ave; small plates $7-14, mains $16-27;

⏰5pm-2am) Inside a simple storefront, boisterous groups of friends devour an endless list of *pupu* crafted with island flair, like Thai street-style grilled chicken or *kalua* pig nachos with wonton chips. For dinner, feast on market-fresh seafood like baked *opah* (moonfish) with parmesan-panko crust or Chinese-style steamed *opakapaka* (pink snapper). Reservations recommended.

ZenShu
JAPANESE, KOREAN $$
(☎739-7017; 477 Kapahulu Ave; shared plates $4-20; ⏰11am-1:30pm Tue-Sat, 5pm-10pm Mon-Thu, to midnight Fri & Sat) Is it a brick-walled sports pub? A sushi and sake bar? A friendly Japanese *izakaya* with Korean spice? Yes, yes and yes! Order the kimchi caesar salad, lemongrass pork chops, *okonomiyaki* fries and if you're brave, *natto* (fermented soybean) shooters. Look for happy-hour discounts and late-night specials on weekends. Reservations recommended for dinner.

Diamond Head Market & Grill
LOCAL, TAKEOUT $
(www.diamondheadmarket.com; 3158 Monsarrat Ave; meals $5-15; ⏰market 6:30am-9pm, grill 7am-10:30am & 11am-9pm) This drive-in and market with a bakery and gourmet deli feeds neighborhood families who don't want to heat up their kitchens at home. Chow down on *char siu* pork plate lunches, portobello-mushroom burgers, kimchi fried rice or tropical-fruit pancakes at picnic tables outside.

Tokkuri Tei
JAPANESE $$
(☎732-6480; 449 Kapahulu Ave; small plates $3-15; ⏰11am-2pm Mon-Fri, 5:30pm-midnight Mon-Sat, 5-10pm Sun) This upbeat neighborhood *izakaya* offers contemporary versions of Japanese standards, while shelves behind the bar store customers' private bottles of sake and *shōchū* (potato liquor). Try the house spider *poke* with fish roe or the *hamachi kama* (yellowtail cheek) sushi. Call ahead for reservations, or be prepared to wait. Valet parking $5.

Rainbow Drive-In
LOCAL, TAKEOUT $
(www.rainbowdrivein.com; 3308 Kanaina Ave; meals $4-8; ⏰7am-9pm; 🅿) Started by an island-born US Army cook after WWII, this classic Hawaii drive-in wrapped in rainbow-colored neon is a throwback to another era. From the takeout counter, construction workers and gangly surfers order all the local favorites: *loco moco*, teriyaki burgers, mixed-plate lunches, Portuguese sweet-bread French toast and more.

BEST ISLAND SWEETS

» Leonard's (p114) – hot-out-of-the-oven, sugar-dusted malasadas

» Liliha Bakery (p90) – coco-puff pastries that cause traffic jams

» Bubbies (p89 & p124) – mochi ice cream in a rainbow of flavors

» Lanikai Juice (p137) – O'ahu's best fresh-fruit smoothies

» Ching's General Store (p143) – melt-in-your-mouth butter mochi bars

» Matsumoto's (p156) – North Shore's classic shave-ice stand

» Dole Plantation (p158) – cones of frozen pineapple soft-serve whip

» Pa'ala'a Kai Bakery (p156) – country home of the chocolate-cream 'snow puffy'

Self-Catering

Food Pantry
GROCERIES $
(2370 Kuhio Ave; ⏰6am-1am) More expensive than chain supermarkets (all outside Waikiki), but cheaper than convenience stores.

Veggie Star Natural Foods
GROCERIES $
(417 Nahua St; ⏰9am-9pm Mon-Sat; 🌱) Organic, all-natural and healthy groceries, plus smoothies and veggie burritos, burgers, sandwiches and salads.

Ono Seafood
SEAFOOD $
(747 Kapahulu Ave; items $3.50-14; ⏰9am-6pm Mon-Sat, 10am-3pm Sun) Addictive, made-to-order *poke* shop – get there early before they run out.

Gina's Barbecue
KOREAN $
(Market City Shopping Center, 2919 Kapi'olani Blvd; mains $6-10; ⏰10am-10pm Mon-Fri, 10am-11pm Sat & Sun) Unfussy strip-mall Korean kitchen's BBQ ribs plate lunch is huge.

🍴 People's Open Market
FARMERS MARKET $
(cnr Monsarrat & Paki Aves, Kapi'olani Park; ⏰10-11am Wed; 🌱) For fresh island bounty from the land and the sea.

🍴 Waikiki Farmers Market
FARMERS MARKET $
(Waikiki Community Center, 310 Pa'oakalani Ave; ⏰7am-1pm Tue & Fri; 🌱) Fresh produce stands set up in the parking lot.

ISLAND SOUNDS

You might be surprised to learn that some of Hawaii's leading local musicians play regular gigs at Waikiki's resort hotels and bars. Here are some stars to watch out for.

» **Jake Shimabukuro** The 'Jimi Hendrix of the uke' has been lured away from the islands by record companies, but sometimes plays live shows in his hometown, Honolulu.

» **Henry Kapono** This Kapahulu-born singer-songwriter is O'ahu's renaissance man, putting out innovative Hawaiian rock albums since the 1970s.

» **Brothers Cazimero** The O'ahu-born, Hawaiian heritage–conscious duo (12-string guitar and bass) played in Peter Moon's legendary Sunday Manoa band in the early '70s.

» **Kapena** The group Kapena may not have won O'ahu's high-school battle of the bands back in the day, but founding member Kelly Boy De Lima is a ukulele star.

» **Jerry Santos and Olomana** Traditional and contemporary ukulele and falsetto performers from Windward O'ahu have been performing for decades.

» **Martin Pahinui** The son of late slack key master Gabby Pahinui is a gifted vocalist and often performs with guitarist George Kuo and former Royal Hawaiian Band leader Aaron Mahi.

» **Keawe 'Ohana** Some say the granddaughter of the late great *ha'i* (high falsetto) singer Genoa Keawe sounds just like Genoa in her younger days.

» **Sam Kapu III** Part of a musical dynasty, Sam Kapu performs traditional ukulele music and contemporary three-part harmonies with his trio.

» **Po'okela** A contemporary trio fronted by Honolulu-born slack key artist Greg Sardinha, who studied with the late great steel-guitar player Jerry Byrd.

» **Makana** An O'ahu-born singer-songwriter who studied guitar with Sonny Chillingworth and is a leading proponent of slack key fusion rock.

» **Natural Vibrations** A standout among O'ahu's 'Jawaiian' island reggae groups.

🍷 Drinking & Entertainment

Waikiki is tourist central with all the telltale signs, including weak alcoholic fruity umbrella drinks and coconut bikini bras. But underneath all of the commoditized cheesiness, authentic Hawaiian music and hula dancing have made a joyful comeback.

For spring-break party spots and dive bars, hit Kuhio Ave after dark. For sunset 'booze cruises,' see p107.

Cafes, Bars & Lounges

Kimo Bean   COFFEEHOUSE
(http://kimobean.com; 2113 Kalakaua Ave; 7am-6pm; 📶) With multiple branches in Waikiki, this Hawaii coffee roaster is your best bet for a rich, fresh-brewed cup of hand-picked Kona peaberry, Maui Moka and Ka'aui estate reserve coffee. Fruit smoothies, banana waffles and Bubbie's *mochi* ice cream round out the menu.

Also at the Hyatt Regency and Ohana East hotels.

Duke's Waikiki   BAR
(Outrigger Waikiki, 2335 Kalakaua Ave; 4pm-midnight) It's a raucous, surf-themed party scene mostly for baby boomers, with lots of drunken souvenir photo-taking and vacationland camaraderie. Weekend afternoon concerts by big names like Henry Kapono (usually 4pm to 6pm Sunday) can't help but spill out onto the sand.

Lewers Lounge   LOUNGE
(Halekulani, 2199 Kalia Rd; 7:30pm-1am, live music usually 8:30pm-midnight Wed & Thu, 8:30pm-12:30am Fri & Sat) Waikiki as an aristocratic playground is kept alive at the Halekulani hotel. Cocktails are made from scratch using fresh (not canned) juices, including tropical lychee and ginger. Smooth-jazz combos serenade some nights.

The Shack
BAR

(Waikiki Trade Center, 2255 Kuhio Ave; cover for live shows usually $10; ⊙11am-4am) If you're wondering where Waikiki's hotel bartenders hang out after their shifts, check out this tiki-esque sports bar with huge TVs, a waterfall and live music most nights (except Sunday), often 'Jawaiian' island reggae, rock or hip-hop acts.

Diamond Head Cove Health Bar
CAFE, BAR

(www.diamondheadcovehealthbar.com; 3045 Monsarrat Ave; ⊙10am-8pm Fri, 10am-11pm Sat-Thu) Why rot your guts with the devil's brew when you can chill-out with a coconut-husk bowl of 'awa (kava), Polynesia's spicy, mildly intoxicating elixir made from the *Piper methysticum* plant? Local musicians jam some nights.

Tiki's Grill & Bar
BAR

(Aston Waikiki Beach Hotel, 2570 Kalakaua Ave; ⊙10:30am-midnight, sometimes later on weekends) Tacky and touristy, yes. But also an upper-story oceanview patio and local bands jamming almost every night (except Wednesday open-mic).

Yard House
BAR

(226 Lewers St; ⊙11am-1am) Waikiki Beach Walk's busiest bar is this raucous mainland chain with big-screen sports TVs, gigantic glasses of microbrewed draft beer and a classic-rock soundtrack that never dies.

Lulu's Surf Club
BAR

(2586 Kalakaua Ave; ⊙7am-2am) Across from the beach, live local bands play for a revved-up beach-party crowd, usually after 10pm on weekends and 8pm some weeknights.

Da Big Kahuna
BAR

(2299 Kuhio Ave; ⊙7am-4am) This frat-boy tiki bar serves fruity, Kool-Aid-colored drinks with names like 'Da Fish Bowl' in ceramic mugs carved with the faces of Polynesian gods. Pool tables and pub grub until 3am.

Top of Waikiki
BAR

(www.topofwaikiki.com; 18th fl, Waikiki Business Plaza, 2270 Kalakaua Ave; ⊙5-11pm) Spinning around just once an hour, this slow-mo revolving restaurant's cocktail lounge hosts twice-nightly happy hours.

Hawaiian Music & Hula

Performances are free, unless otherwise noted. All schedules are subject to change. (For more island sounds, head to waterfront Chai's Island Bistro (p92) in Honolulu.)

TOP CHOICE Kuhio Beach Hula Show
MUSIC, HULA

(www.honolulu.gov/moca; Kuhio Beach Park; ⊙usually 6:30-7:30pm Tue, Thu, Sat & Sun, weather permitting; ⬛) Some of O'ahu's top hula troupes perform at the hula mound near the Duke Kahanamoku Statue on the Waikiki strip. It starts off with a traditional torch lighting and conch shell ceremony after sunset. Then lay back on the grass or sand and enjoy the authentic Hawaiian music and dance show. It's full of aloha, and afterward the performers often hang around the stage to chat with visitors.

House Without a Key
MUSIC, HULA

(Halekulani Hotel, 2199 Kalia Rd; ⊙7am-9pm, live music usually 5:30-8:30pm) Named after a 1925 Charlie Chan novel set in Honolulu, this genteel open-air oceanfront bar sprawled beneath a century-old kiawe tree simply has no doors to lock. A well-heeled crowd gathers here for Waikiki's best sunset cocktails, panoramic ocean views, live music and solo hula dancing by former Miss Hawaii pageant winners.

Mai Tai Bar
LIVE MUSIC

(Royal Hawaiian Hotel, 2259 Kalakaua Ave; ⊙10am-11pm, live music usually 6-10pm Tue-Sun) At the Royal Hawaiian's low-key bar (no preppy resort wear required), you can catch some great island musical duos and trios. Even if you don't dig who's playing that night, the signature Royal Mai Tai still packs a punch and romantic views of the breaking surf extend all the way down to Diamond Head.

Royal Hawaiian Center
MUSIC, HULA

(☎922-2299; 2201 Kalakaua Ave; ⊙schedule varies) This shopping mall may lack oceanfront views, but you can still enjoy Hawaiian music and hula performances by top island talent here almost every evening, as well as twice-weekly lunchtime shows by Polynesian Cultural Center performers.

Royal Hawaiian Band
LIVE MUSIC

(☎922-5331; www1.honolulu.gov/rhb; Kapi'olani Park; ⊙usually 2-3pm Sun) Performing classical music from the 19th-century monarchy era, Hawaii's 'official' band takes over the Kapi'olani Bandstand on most Sunday afternoons. It's a quintessential island scene that caps off with the audience joining hands and singing Queen Lili'uokalani's 'Aloha 'Oe.' Other concerts around O'ahu take place at 'Iolani Palace.

Waikiki's LGBT community is tightly knit, but still full of aloha for visitors. Free monthly magazine Odyssey (www.odysseyhawaii.com) covers the scene; it's available at the convenience shop 80% Straight (www.80percentstraight.com; Castle Waikiki Grand, 134 Kapahulu Ave; ⏰10am-11pm Mon-Thu, 10am-midnight Fri & Sat, noon-11pm Sun), which sells books, magazines, videos, beachwear and novelty toys.

Upstairs from 80% Straight, the friendly, open-air Hula's Bar & Lei Stand (www .hulas.com; 2nd fl, Castle Waikiki Grand, 134 Kapahulu Ave; ⏰10am-2am; @🛜) has a great ocean view of Diamond Head. Stop by for drinks and to meet a variety of new faces, play pool and boogie, or even do yoga by the beach. For nonstop karaoke, head to sidestreet Wang Chung's (www.wangchungs.com; 2410 Koa Ave; ⏰2pm-2am).

Tapa's Restaurant & Lanai Bar (www.tapaswaikiki.com; 407 Seaside Ave; ⏰9am-2am) is another popular chill-out spot with talkative bartenders, pool tables, a jukebox and karaoke nights. Nearby Lo Jax Waikiki (www.lojaxwaikiki.com; 2256 Kuhio Ave; ⏰noon-2am Mon-Sat, 6am-2am Sun; 🛜) is a gay sports bar with pool tournaments, all-male revues and weekend DJs. Next door Fusion Waikiki (www.fusionwaikiki.com; 2nd fl, 2260 Kuhio Ave; ⏰10pm-4am Sun-Thu, 8pm-4am Fri & Sat) is a high-energy nightclub with weekend drag shows. Further northwest, In-Between (2155 Lau'ula St; ⏰4pm-2am Mon-Thu, noon-2am Fri & Sat, 2pm-2am Sun), a laid-back neighborhood bar, attracts an older crowd for 'the happiest of happy hours.'

By day, you can have fun in the sun at Queen's Surf Beach and (illegally clothing-optional) Diamond Head Beach. At night, check into the gay-friendly Castle Waikiki Grand, Hotel Renew or just about any Aqua Hotels & Resorts property.

More beach hotel bars with live Hawaiian music:

Banyan Court Beach Bar LIVE MUSIC
(Moana Surfrider, 2365 Kalakaua Ave; ⏰10:30am-midnight, live music usually 6-9pm Wed-Sat) Soak up the sounds of contemporary Hawaiian music beneath the old banyan tree where *Hawaii Calls* broadcast its nationwide radio show over four decades beginning in 1935.

Rumfire LIVE MUSIC
(Sheraton Waikiki, 255 Kalakaua Ave; ⏰11am-midnight, live music usually 5-8pm Sun-Fri, 5pm-close Sat) Cabinets full of vintage rum, flirty beachfront fire pits with ocean views and live contemporary Hawaiian (or jazz) musicians, usually soloists.

Moana Terrace LIVE MUSIC
(2nd fl, Waikiki Marriott Beach Resort, 2552 Kalakaua Ave; ⏰11am-11pm, live music usually 6:30-9:30pm) Local Hawaiian slack key guitarists, ukulele players and *ha'i* falsetto singers play to a family-friendly crowd at this open-air poolside bar.

Tapa Bar LIVE MUSIC
(Tapa Tower, Hilton Hawaiian Village, 2005 Kalia Rd; ⏰3-11pm, live music schedule varies) On Friday fireworks show nights, head to the Hilton Hawaiian Village resort where Jerry Santos and Olomana usually play a few sets.

Nightclubs

If you don't feel like making the trek out to Ala Moana or Chinatown after dark, there are still a few dance floors in Waikiki for getting your ya-yas out.

Coconut Willy's NIGHTCLUB, BAR
(Waikiki Beach Walk, 227 Lewers St; ⏰10pm-4am, bar open from 5pm Mon-Thu, 11am Fri-Sun) Hard-core binge drinkin', beer pong and wild spring-break dancing to 1980s, '90s and '00s DJs who think they're comedians.

Nashville Waikiki NIGHTCLUB, BAR
(2330 Kuhio Ave; ⏰4pm-4am) This country-and-western bar and grill can get as rowdy as a West Texas brawl. Show up for sports TVs, billiards, darts, pool tournaments and free line-dancing lessons.

Moose McGillycuddy's NIGHTCLUB, BAR
(310 Lewers St; ⏰4pm-4am) A total tourist cliché, this nightspot upstairs from a restaurant has pool tables and hip hop, rock and mash-up DJs usually after 10pm.

Luau & Dinner Shows

If your Hawaii vacation just won't be complete without taking in a touristy luau, you can choose a resort-hotel production right by the beach or a big bash outside town.

'Aha 'Aina
LUAU

(☎921-4600; www.royal-hawaiian.com/dining/ahaaina; Royal Hawaiian, 2259 Kalakaua Ave; adult/child 5-12yr from $155/83; ⏰usually 5:30-9pm Mon) Graciously set on the manicured oceanfront lawns of the historic Royal Hawaiian hotel, this sit-down dinner show is like a three-act musical play narrating the history of Hawaiian *mele* (songs) and hula dancing, starting from ancient times. Tickets are high-priced, but the food is top-notch and there's an open bar.

Pacific Swing
DINNER SHOW

(☎800-453-8020; www.pacificswinghawaii.com; Waikiki Beach Marriott Resort, 2552 Kalakaua Ave; adult/child under 12yr from $87/67; ⏰usually 7pm Tue-Thu) Starring Nathan Osmond (Donny and Marie's nephew) as the MC, this 1940s-style big band show is a nostalgic, fun-loving romp through Hawaii's WWII days. Stick around after the show when the dance floor opens and do some jitterbugging with your sweetie. Free validated hotel valet or self-parking.

Waikiki Starlight Luau
LUAU

(☎949-4321; www.hiltonhawaiianvillage.com; Hilton Hawaiian Village, 2005 Kalia Rd; adult/child 4-11yr from $98/49; ⏰5:30-8pm Sun-Thu, weather permitting) Rooftop luau features a buffet-style dinner and just two complimentary mai tais. The enthusiastic, if not exactly authentic Polynesian show, with fire dancing and a fashion show, is a crowd-pleaser for families. Free validated self-parking.

Commercial luau outside Waikiki (tickets include shuttle transportation to/from Kapolei, taking about an hour each way):

Germaine's Luau
LUAU

(Map p56; ☎949-6626, 800-367-5655; www.germainesluau.com; 91-119 Olai St, Kapolei; adult/child 6-13yr $72/52; ⏰6-9pm) Nightly dinner buffet and Polynesian-style show on the beach.

Paradise Cove
LUAU

(Map p56; ☎842-5911, 800-775-2683; www.paradisecove.com; 92-1089 Ali'inui Dr, Kapolei; adult/child 4-12yr $82/62; ⏰5-9pm; ♿) Like Germaine's, but also includes demonstrations of Hawaiian games and crafts.

🔒 Shopping

Catwalk designer boutiques hover around DFS Galleria at the north end of Kalakaua Ave, while a handful of only-in-Hawaii stores line Waikiki Beach Walk. Ubiquitous ABC Stores are the place to pick up beach mats, sunblock, snacks and sundries, 'I got lei'd in Hawaii' T-shirts and motorized grass-skirted hula girls for the dashboard of your car back home.

TOP CHOICE ⟩ Bailey's Antiques & Aloha Shirts
CLOTHING, ANTIQUES

(www.alohashirts.com; 517 Kapahulu Ave; ⏰10am-6pm) There's no place like Bailey's, which has without a doubt the finest aloha shirt collection on O'ahu. Racks are crammed with thousands of collector-worthy vintage aloha shirts in every conceivable color and style, from 1920s kimono-silk classics to 1970s polyester specials. Of the new generation of shirts, Bailey's only carries Hawaii-made labels, including Mamo and RJC. Prices vary from five bucks up to several hundred dollars.

🖉 Na Lima Mili Hulu No'eau
LEI

(☎732-0865; 762 Kapahulu Ave; ⏰usually 9am-5pm Mon-Sat) Aunty Mary Louise Kaleonahenahe Kekuewa's daughter Paulette keeps alive the ancient craft of feather lei-making at this humble storefront, the name of which means 'the skilled hands that touch the feathers.' The mother-daughter duo created the book *Feather Lei as an Art* to encourage a revival of this indigenous art. It can take days to produce a single lei, prized by collectors.

Mana Hawai'i
ART, CRAFTS

(www.manahawaiiinwaikiki.com; 2nd fl, Waikiki Beach Walk, 226 Lewers St; ⏰10am-10pm) Unlike many other shops on Waikiki Beach Walk, this airy space displays authentic Hawaii-made products such as island woodcarvings, fine-art photography and Hawaiiana books and CDs by everyone from Bruddah Iz to Jake Shimabukuro. The shop also hosts free Hawaiian cultural classes.

Reyn Spooner
CLOTHING

(www.reynspooner.com; Sheraton Waikiki, 2259 Kalakaua Ave; ⏰8am-10:30pm) Since 1956, Reyn Spooner's subtle reverse-print preppy aloha shirts have been the standard for Honolulu's power brokers and social movers-and-shakers. The new Waikiki flagship is a bright, mod and clean-lined store, carrying men's shirts and board shorts. Ask about downtown Reyn's Rack for discounts on factory seconds.

Muse
CLOTHING

(www.musebyrimo.com; 2310 Kuhio Ave; ⏰10am-11pm) Blowsy, breezy feminine fashions are what's sewn by this mainland designer from LA, whose Waikiki Beach locations appeals to jet-setters from Tokyo. Take your pick of cotton-candy tissue tanks, lighter-than-air sundresses, floppy hats and sparkly belts and jewelry. Also in Kailua.

Newt at the Royal
CLOTHING
(www.newtattheroyal.com; Royal Hawaiian Hotel, 2259 Kalakaua Ave; ☉9am-9pm) With stylish flair and panache, Newt specializes in Montecristi Panama hats – classic men's fedoras, plantation-style hats and women's fino – and fine reproductions of aloha shirts using 1940s and '50s designs. Everything's tropical, neat as a pin and top-drawer quality.

Royal Hawaiian Center
SHOPPING MALL
(www.royalhawaiiancenter.com; 2201 Kalakaua Ave; ☉10am-10pm) Waikiki's biggest shopping center has mostly name-brand international chains, but also some Hawaii-born labels like Crazy Shirts and Honolua Surf Co. The Little Hawaiian Craft Shop displays cheap Hawaiiana trinkets next to high-quality koa bowls, Ni'ihau shell-lei necklaces and other pan-Polynesian artisan crafts.

Bob's Ukulele
MUSIC
(www.bobsukulele.com; Waikiki Beach Marriott Resort, 2552 Kalakaua Ave; ☉9am-noon & 5-9pm) Avoid those cheap, flimsy imported ukuleles sold at so many Waikiki shopping malls. Instead let the knowledgeable staff here teach you about island-made ukes handcrafted from native woods, including by Kamaka (p93).

International Market Place
SOUVENIRS
(www.internationalmarketplacewaikiki.com; 2330 Kalakaua Ave; ☉10am-9pm) At this kitschy market set under a sprawling banyan tree, more than 100 touristy stalls sell everything from seashell necklaces to sarongs and hibiscus-print handbags, with live Hawaiian music and Polynesian dancing almost nightly.

❶ Information

Emergency
Police, Fire & Ambulance (☎911)
Waikiki Police Substation (www.honolulupd.org; 2405 Kalakaua Ave; ☉24hr) If you need help, or just friendly directions, at Kuhio Beach.

Internet Access
Cybercafes along Kuhio Ave and inside backpacker hostels on Lemon Rd rarely offer wi-fi. Many hotels offer wired high-speed connections in guest rooms, but only limited wi-fi in lobby or poolside areas; daily surcharges of $10 or more may apply.

Hula's Bar & Lei Stand (2nd fl, Castle Waikiki Grand, 134 Kapahulu Ave; ☉10am-2am) Free wi-fi and two internet terminals inside the bar.

Waikiki-Kapahulu Public Library (☎733-8488; www.librarieshawaii.org; 400 Kapahulu Ave; ☉10am-5pm Mon-Tue & Thu-Fri, 1-8pm Wed) Free wi-fi and reservable internet terminals.

Medical Services
Straub Doctors on Call (www.straubhealth.org) North Waikiki (☎973-5250; 2nd fl, Rainbow Bazaar, Hilton Hawaiian Village, 2005 Kalia Rd; ☉8am-4:30pm Mon-Fri); South Waikiki (☎971-6000; Sheraton Princess Kaiulani, 120 Ka'iulani Ave; ☉24hr) Call for all-night pharmacies and hospitals with 24-hour emergency rooms in downtown Honolulu. Nonemergency walk-in clinics accept some travel health insurance policies.

Money
There are 24-hour ATMs all over Waikiki, including at these full-service banks:

Bank of Hawaii (www.boh.com; 2155 Kalakaua Ave; ☉8:30am-4pm Mon-Thu, 8:30am-6pm Fri, 9am-1pm Sat)

First Hawaiian Bank (www.fhb.com; 2181 Kalakaua Ave; ☉8:30am-4pm Mon-Thu, 8:30am-6pm Fri) Lobby displays Hawaii history murals by French artist Jean Charlot.

Post
Post office (www.usps.com; 330 Saratoga Rd; ☉9am-4:30pm Mon-Fri, 9am-1pm Sat)

Tourist Information
Freebie tourist magazines containing discount coupons like *This Week O'ahu* and *101 Things to Do* can be found on street corners, in hotel lobbies and at the airport.

Hawaii Visitors & Convention Bureau (HVCB; ☎923-1811, 800-464-2924; www.gohawaii.com; Suite 801, Waikiki Business Plaza, 2270 Kalakaua Ave; ☉8am-4:30pm Mon-Fri) Visitor information office offering free maps and brochures.

❶ Getting There & Around

To/From the Airport
For transportation to/from Honolulu International Airport, see p58.

Bicycle
Several shops rent beach cruisers or commuter bikes for about $20 per day, with discounts for multiday or weekly rentals. For top-quality road and mountain-bike rentals, head to Honolulu's Bike Shop (p79).

Bus

TheBus runs frequent routes through Waikiki, with most stops along Kuhio Ave. Outside Waikiki, the Ala Moana Center is O'ahu's central bus terminal and transfer point to other lines across Honolulu and around the island. For more information about TheBus, including routes, schedules, fares and passes, see p58.

Car

Several Waikiki car-rental offices are affiliated with international agencies, but rates are usually higher than at the airport (see p58).

Most hotels charge $20 to $30 per night for valet or self-parking. The **Waikiki Trade Center Parking Garage** (2255 Kuhio Ave, enter off Seaside Ave) and next-door **Waikiki Parking Garage** (333 Seaside Ave) usually offer Waikiki's cheapest flat-rate day, evening and overnight rates. At the far southeast end of Waikiki, there's a free parking lot along Monsarrat Ave beside Kapi'olani Park with no time limit. Waikiki's cheapest metered lot (25¢ per hour, four-hour limit) is along Kapahulu Ave next to the zoo. But neither of these lots is a particularly safe spot for rental cars.

Moped

Mopeds may seem like a great way of getting around Waikiki, but they can actually be more expensive to rent than a car. They're best suited to those who already have experience riding in city traffic. For more moped and motorcycle information, including rental rates and road rules, see p641.

Taxi

Metered taxis wait at resort hotels and shopping malls (see p58).

Trolley

The motorized **Waikiki Trolley** (593-2822; www.waikikitrolley.com; adult/child $52/20, 7-day pass $58/22) runs three color-coded lines that connect Waikiki with the Ala Moana Center and downtown Honolulu. These services don't offer much in the way of value, however, compared with TheBus. Purchase passes at the **DFS Galleria Waikiki** (330 Royal Hawaiian Ave) or **Royal Hawaiian Center** (2201 Kalakaua Ave), or buy them online at a discount.

DIAMOND HEAD & SOUTHEAST COAST

Be the star of your own movie, livin' large in a tropical paradise on O'ahu's most glam stretch of coastline. Cruise past the mansion-filled suburbs of Kahala and Hawai'i Kai along the Kalaniana'ole Hwy (Hwy 72), a slow-and-go coastal drive that swells and

dips like the sea itself as it rounds ancient volcanic Koko Head. The snorkeling hot spot of Hanauma Bay, hiking trails to the top of Diamond Head and the windy lighthouse at Makapu'u Point, and O'ahu's most famous bodysurfing beaches are just a short bus ride or drive from Waikiki. Save time for more hidden delights, too, such as billionaire Doris Duke's former mansion, with its trove of Islamic art.

Diamond Head & Kahala

A massive backdrop to Waikiki and the wealthy Kahala neighborhood, Diamond Head is O'ahu's best-known landmark. It's a tuff cone and crater formed by a violent steam explosion long after most of the island's other volcanic activity had stopped. Ancient Hawaiians called it Le'ahi and at its summit they built a *luakini* heiau, a temple dedicated to the war god Ku and used for human sacrifices.

Ever since 1825, when British sailors found calcite crystals sparkling in the sun and mistakenly thought they'd struck it rich, it's been called Diamond Head. In the early 1900s the US Army began building Fort Ruger at the edge of the crater. They constructed a network of tunnels and topped the rim with cannon emplacements, bunkers and observation posts. Reinforced during WWII, the fort is a silent sentinel whose guns have never been fired.

Beaches

From Waikiki, TheBus 14 runs by these beaches once or twice hourly.

Diamond Head Beach Park   BEACH
(3300 Diamond Head Rd) Southwest of the lighthouse, this beach draws surfers, snorkelers and tide-poolers, plus a few picnickers. The narrow strand north of the lighthouse is popular with gay men, who park off Diamond Head Rd on dead-end Beach Rd, then walk along the shore to find a little seclusion and (illegally) sunbathe au naturel.

Kuilei Cliffs Beach Park   BEACH
(3450 Diamond Head Rd) This beach draws experienced windsurfers when the tradewinds are blowing. Surfers take over the waves when the swell is up. This little beach park has drinking water and outdoor showers, but no other facilities. Park in the public lot off Diamond Head Rd

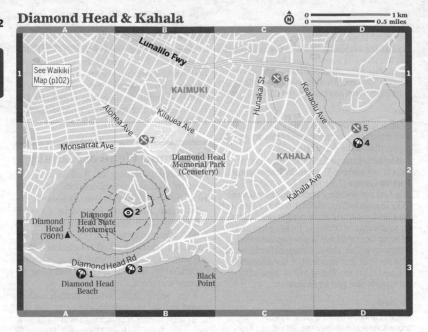

Diamond Head & Kahala

◎ Sights
1 Diamond Head Beach Park.................A3
2 Diamond Head State
   Monument.......................................B2
3 Kuilei Cliffs Beach Park....................B3
4 Wai'alae Beach Park.........................D2

✖ Eating
5 Hoku's...D2
6 Olive Tree Cafe................................C1
7 Saturday Farmers Market at
   KCC..B2
   Whole Foods...............................(see 6)

just south of the lighthouse, then take the paved trail down to the beach.

Wai'alae Beach Park   BEACH
In between Kahala's multimillion-dollar mansions, a half-dozen shoreline access points provide public rights-of-way to the beach, but the swimming ain't grand – it's mostly shallow, with sparse pockets of sand. One picturesque exception is this beach near Kahala's resort. Here you'll find a sandy strand where Wai'alae Stream flows into the sea and a shallow offshore

reef. Surfers challenge Razors, a break off the west side of the channel.

◎ Sights & Activities

Diamond Head State Monument   HIKING
(www.hawaiistateparks.org; off Diamond Head Rd btwn Makapu'u & 18th Aves; admission per pedestrian/vehicle $1/5; ⊙hiking 6am-6pm, last trail entry 4:30pm; 🚗) The historic trail to the summit of Diamond Head was built in 1908 to service military observation stations along the crater rim. Although it's a fairly steep 0.8-mile hike to the top, the trail is fully paved and plenty of people of all ages make it. The return trip takes about an hour. The trail, which passes through several tunnels and up dizzying staircases, is mostly open and hot, so bring plenty of water and wear a hat and sunscreen. The windy summit affords fantastic 360-degree views of the southeast coast to Koko Head and west to the Wai'anae Range. A lighthouse, coral reefs and surfers waiting to catch a wave are visible below.

From Waikiki, take TheBus 22 or 23, which run twice hourly. From the closest bus stop, it's a 20-minute walk to the trailhead. By car, take Monsarrat Ave to Diamond Head Rd and turn right past

Kapi'olani Community College into the parking lot.

Shangri La
HISTORICAL BUILDING

(☑866-385-3849; www.shangrilahawaii.org; 2½hr tour incl transportation $25; ☉tours usually 8:30am, 11am & 1:30pm Wed-Sat Oct-Aug) Once called 'the richest little girl in the world,' heiress Doris Duke (1912–93) had a lifelong passion for Islamic art and architecture that was first inspired by a visit to the Taj Mahal during her honeymoon voyage to India in 1935. During her honeymoon, she also stopped on O'ahu, fell in love with the island and decided to build Shangri La, a private seasonal residence on Black Point. Over the next six decades, she traveled the globe from Indonesia to Istanbul, collecting priceless art en route.

Doris made Shangri La into an intimate sanctuary rather than an ostentatious mansion. One of the true beauties of the place is its harmony with the natural environment. Finely crafted interiors open to embrace gardens and fountain courtyards. Collections blend with the architecture to represent a theme or region, for instance in the Damascus Room, the restored interior of an 18th-century Syrian merchant's house. Duke's extensive collections included gemstone-studded enamels, glazed ceramic paintings and silk *suzanis* (intricate needlework tapestries).

You can only visit Shangri La on a guided tour, departing from downtown's Honolulu Academy of Arts. Tours aren't recommended for children under 12 years old. Advance reservations are essential.

🛏 Sleeping & Eating

There's a luxury hotel by the beach, and more restaurants around the Kahala Mall.

📷 Saturday Farmers Market at KCC
FARMERS MARKET $

(www.hfbf.org; Parking Lot C, Kapi'olani Community College, off Diamond Head Rd; ☉7:30am-11am Sat; ☑) At O'ahu's premier gathering of farmers and their fans, everything sold is local and has a loyal following, from 'Nalo greens to Kahuku shrimp and corn. Different restaurants each week are invited to sell tasty takeout meals.

Hoku's
PACIFIC RIM $$$

(☑739-8780; www.kahalaresort.com; 5000 Kahala Ave; dinner mains $30-65, Sun brunch adult/child 4-12yr $58/29; ☉10:30am-2pm Sun, 5:30-10pm daily) Nestled on a private beach, this dated resort is an intimate haven for rich-and-famous folks who crave seclusion above all. Hotel rooms are overpriced, but Hoku's restaurant is revered for its East–West fusion, like Kurobata pork loin with apple-miso sauce or truffle-crusted Maine lobster with seaweed salad. Make reservations; inquire about the dress code.

Olive Tree Cafe
MEDITERRANEAN $

(☑737-0303; 4614 Kilauea Ave, cnr Pahoa Ave; mains $6-13; ☉5-10pm) Hidden on the east side of Kahala Mall, this always-packed Mediterranean restaurant swears by the motto: 'Mostly Greek, not so fast food.' Try the succulent chicken souvlaki and *dolmadakia* (stuffed grape leaves). Expect long waits. Cash only. The next-door Greek deli has a cache of imported wines for BYOB.

Hawai'i Kai

POP 29,875

With its marina and picturesque canals surrounded by mountains, bays and beach parks, this meticulously planned suburb designed by the late steel tycoon Henry J Kaiser (he's the Kai in Hawai'i Kai) is a nouveau-riche scene. Everything revolves around mega-shopping centers off Kalaniana'ole Hwy (Hwy 72). If you're driving around Southeast O'ahu, it's a convenient stop for a bite to eat or sunset drinks.

🏃 Activities

The marina is flush with tour operators and water-sports outfitters that can hook you up with jet skis, banana and bumper boats, parasailing trips, wakeboarding, scuba dives, speed sailing – whatever will get your adrenaline pumping. Just take a look around and talk to the staff (some are professionals, others aren't so helpful).

Hawai'i Kai Golf Course
GOLF

(☑395-2358; www.hawaiikaigolf.com; 8902 Kalaniana'ole Hwy; greens fee incl cart rental $40-110) About 4 miles east of town, Hawai'i Kai Golf Course features a challenging par-72 championship course with Koko Head views, and a smaller par-54 executive course designed by Robert Trent Jones Sr in the 1960s. Call ahead for tee-time reservations; club rentals available.

Hiking

In the mountains of the Ko'olau Range that make a cinematic backdrop for Hawai'i

Kai, you'll find often-overlooked local hiking trails to try. Just west of Hawai'i Kai, the 5-mile round-trip **Kuli'ou'ou Ridge Trail** is open to hikers and mountain bikers. It winds up forested switchbacks, then makes a stiff but satisfying ascent along a ridgeline to a windy summit for heart-stopping 360-degree views of Koko Head, Makapu'u Point, the Windward Coast, Diamond Head and Honolulu. The trail, which may be partly overgrown with vegetation, starts from the Na Ala Hele (www .hawaiitrails.org) trailhead sign at the end of Kala'au Pl, which branches right off Kuli'ou'ou Rd a mile *mauka* (inland) from Kalaniana'ole Hwy (Hwy 72).

✖ Eating & Drinking

BluWater Grill   SEAFOOD $$
(☎395-6224; Hawai'i Kai Shopping Center, 377 Keahole St; mains lunch $10-16, dinner $13-29; ☺11am-11pm Mon-Thu, 11am-midnight Fri & Sat, 10am-1pm Sun) Perfect for chilling out with a cocktail, this breezy open-air restaurant overlooks the waterfront and dishes up decent kiawe-grilled fare such as seafood kebabs and chicken with papaya-ginger glaze. Sunday brunch features spicy ahi eggs Benedict, haute *loco moco* and a tropical pancake bar. Request an outside patio table.

Kona Brewing Company   BREWPUB $$
(☎394-5662; www.konabewingco.com; Koko Marina Center, 7192 Kalaniana'ole Hwy; mains $11-28; ☺11am-10pm) This Big Island import is known for its microbrews, such as Longboard Lager and Castaway IPA, and live Hawaiian music on weekends, including by big-name musicians like slack key guitar and ukulele master Ledward Ka'apana. The pub's island-style *pupu*, wood-fired pizzas, burgers and salads are just so-so. Kids' menu available.

For snacks and beach picnics:

🍴 Kale's Natural Foods   SUPERMARKET $
(www.kalesnaturalfoods.com; Hawai' Kai Shopping Center, 377 Keahole St; mains $8-11; ☺8am-8pm Mon-Fri, to 5pm Sat & Sun; 🖋) Near a Safeway supermarket, this health-minded grocery store has a takeout deli, cafe and smoothie bar.

Bubbie's   DESSERT $
(Koko Marina Center, 7192 Kalaniana'ole Hwy; items $2-6; ☺10am-11pm Sun-Thu, to midnight Fri & Sat; 🖋) Tropically flavored and *mochi* ice cream; a Foodland supermarket is nearby.

Hanauma Bay Nature Preserve

A stunning palette of sapphire and turquoise hues all mix together in modern-art abstractions in this bowl-shaped bay, ringed by the remnants of an eroded volcano. Just below the sparkling surface are coral reefs, some of which may be 7000 years old. These craggy and ancient underwater formations are a city for fish, providing food, shelter and an interspecies 'pick-up' scene. You'll see schools of glittering silver fish, bright blue flashes of parrotfish and perhaps sea turtles so used to snorkelers that they'll go eyeball to face mask with you. Despite its protected status as a marine-life conservation district since 1967, this beloved bay is still a threatened ecosystem, constantly in danger of being loved to death by the huge number of annual visitors – an average of 3000 people hit the beach each day.

Past the ticket booth at the entrance to the park is an award-winning educational center run by the University of Hawai'i. Here interactive, family-friendly displays teach visitors about the unique geology and ecology of the bay. Everyone should watch the 12-minute video, intended to stagger the crowds and inform you about environmental precautions before snorkeling. Down below at beach level you'll find snorkel-gear rental concessions, lockers, lifeguards and restrooms.

🏃 Activities

The bay is well protected from the vast ocean by various reefs and the inlet's natural curve, making conditions favorable for snorkeling year-round. The fringing reef closest to shore has a large, sandy opening known as the **Keyhole Lagoon**, which is the best place for novice snorkelers. The deepest water is 10ft, though it's very shallow over the coral. The Keyhole is well protected and usually very calm. Because most visitors are beginners, this is also the most crowded part of the bay later in the day and visibility can be poor from swimming. Be careful not to step on the coral or to accidentally knock it with your fins. Feeding the fish is strictly prohibited.

For confident snorkelers and strong swimmers, it's better on the outside of the reef, where there are large coral heads, bigger fish and fewer people; to get there follow the directions on the signboard or ask the lifeguard at the southern end of the beach. There are two channels on either side of the

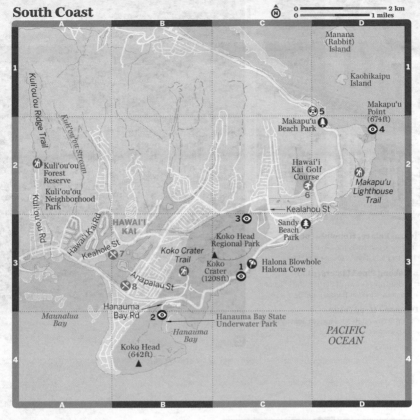

bay that experience very strong currents. Don't attempt to swim outside the reef when the water is rough or choppy.

Scuba divers have the whole bay to play in, with crystal-clear water, coral gardens and sea turtles. Beware of currents when the surf's up, especially those surges near the shark-infested Witches' Brew, on the bay's right-hand side, and the amusingly named Moloka'i Express, a treacherous current on the left-hand side of the bay's mouth.

ℹ️ Information

Hanauma Bay is both a county beach park and a state underwater **park** (☎396-4229; www .honolulu.gov/parks/facility/hanaumabay, www .soest.hawaii.edu/seagrant/education/Hanauma; adult/child under 13yr $7.50/free; ⊗6am-6pm Wed-Mon Nov-Mar, to 7pm Wed-Mon Apr-Oct; ♿). To beat the crowds, especially during peak summer season, arrive right when the park opens, and avoid Mondays and Wednesdays. All built park facilities are wheelchair-accessible.

South Coast

◎ Sights

1	Fishing Shrine	C3
2	Hanauma Bay Nature Preserve	B4
3	Koko Crater Botanical Garden	C3
4	Makapu'u Point Lighthouse	D2
5	Sea Life Park	D1

Activities, Courses & Tours
| 6 | Hawai'i Kai Golf Course | C2 |

⊗ Eating
7	BluWater Grill	B3
	Bubbie's	(see 8)
8	Kona Brewing Company	B3

ℹ️ Getting There & Away

Hanauma Bay is about 10 miles east of Waikiki along the Kalaniana'ole Hwy (Hwy 72). The parking lot sometimes fills by mid-morning, after which drivers will be turned away, so the earlier you get there the better. Parking costs $1.

1. 'Iolani Palace, Honolulu (p62)
'Iolani Palace served as the capitol of the republic, the territory and, finally, the state of Hawaii.

2. Billabong Pipe Masters (p153)
Part of the Triple Crown of Surfing, the Billabong Pipe Masters is held at Banzai Pipeline.

3. Diamond Head (p122)
Hiking up Diamond Head is a great activity if you have kids in tow on O'ahu.

FUMIS KAHUKU SHRIMP

OPEN

LIVE SHRIMP F...
COOKED 活エビ料

4. Makapuʻu Beach Park (p129)

Makapuʻu Beach Park is one of the top winter spots for experienced bodysurfers.

5. Fumi's Shrimp Truck, Kahuku (p146)

Colorful shrimp trucks are thick along the highway through Kahuku.

CHRISTINA LEASE / LONELY PLANET IMAGES ©

From Waikiki, TheBus 22 (nicknamed the 'Beach Bus') runs hourly to Hanauma Bay, except on Tuesday, when the park is closed anyway; the one-way trip takes about 50 minutes. Buses leave Waikiki between 8am and 4pm (till 4:45pm on Saturday and Sunday); the corner of Kuhio Ave and Namahana St is the first stop, and buses often fill up shortly thereafter. Buses back to Waikiki leave Hanauma Bay between 10:35am and 5:15pm (5:45pm on weekends).

Koko Head Regional Park

With mountains on one side and a sea full of bays and beaches on the other, the drive along this coast rates among O'ahu's best. The highway rises and falls as it winds its way round the tip of the Ko'olau Range, looking down on stratified rocks, lava sea cliffs and other fascinating geological formations. At last, you've left the city behind.

Less than a mile east of Hanauma Bay, the roadside **Lana'i Lookout** offers a panorama on clear days of several Hawaiian islands: Lana'i to the right, Maui in the middle and Moloka'i to the left. About 0.5 miles further east, at the highest point on a sea cliff known as Bamboo Ridge, look for a **fishing shrine**. This temple-like mound of rocks surrounds Jizō, a Japanese Buddhist deity and guardian of fishers. The statue is often decked in colorful lei and surrounded by sake cups.

🏖 Beaches

Halona Blowhole & Cove   BEACH
Follow all of the tour buses to find the Halona Blowhole. Here the water surges through a submerged tunnel in the rock and spouts up through a hole in the ledge. It's preceded by a gushing sound, created by the air that's being forced out by the rushing water. The action depends on water conditions – sometimes it's barely discernible, while at other times it's a showstopper. Ignore the temptation to ignore the warning signs and walk down toward the blowhole, as several people have been fatally swept off the ledge by rogue waves.

Down to the right of the lookout parking lot is Halona Cove, the gem-like beach where the steamy love scene with Burt Lancaster and Deborah Kerr in *From Here to Eternity* (1953) was filmed. There's no lifeguard on duty, and when the surf's up, this beach really earns its nickname 'Pounders' – never turn your back on the sea.

Sandy Beach Park   BEACH
(8800 Kalaniana'ole Hwy) Here the ocean heaves and thrashes like a furious beast. This is one of O'ahu's most dangerous beaches, with a punishing shorebreak, powerful backwash and strong rip currents. Expert bodysurfers spend hours trying to mount the skull-crushing waves, as crowds gather to watch the daredevils being tossed around. When the swells are big, bodyboarders hit the beach's multiple breaks.

Sandy Beach is wide, very long and, yes, sandy, but this is no place to frolic. Dozens of people are injured every year, some with just broken arms and dislocated shoulders, but others with serious spinal injuries. Red flags flown on the beach indicate hazardous water conditions. Even if you don't see flags, always check with the lifeguards before entering the water.

Not all the action is in the water. The grassy strip on the inland side of the parking lot is used by people looking skyward for their thrills – it's both a hang-glider landing site and a popular place for flying kites. On weekends, you can usually find a food truck selling plate lunches in the parking lot. The beach park has picnic tables, restrooms, outdoor showers and sparse shade trees.

From Waikiki, TheBus 22 stops here approximately hourly (no service Tuesday); the trip takes about an hour.

◉ Sights & Activities

Koko Crater   GARDEN
According to Hawaiian legend, Koko Crater is the imprint left by the magical flying vagina (yes, really) of Kapo sent from the Big Island to lure the pig-god Kamapua'a away from her sister Pele, goddess of fire and volcanoes.

One of O'ahu's tallest and best-preserved tuff cones, Koko Crater now embraces a 60-acre county-run botanical garden (end of Kokonani St; admission free; ⊙sunrise-sunset), planted with aloes, cacti and other exotic and native dryland species. You'll probably have the garden's interconnecting loop trails to yourself.

To get here, turn inland off the Kalaniana'ole Hwy (Hwy 72) onto Kealahou St, opposite the north end of Sandy Beach. After 0.5 miles, turn left onto Kokonani St. From Waikiki, TheBus 23 stops approximately hourly near the corner of Kealahou St and Kalohelani St, about 0.4 miles from the garden entrance; the trip takes about an hour.

Makapu'u Point

The coastal **lighthouse** at the tip of Makapu'u Point marks O'ahu's easternmost point. The mile-long service road is closed to private vehicles, but hikers can park off the highway in the lot and walk in. Although not a difficult hike, it's a steady uphill walk and conditions can be hot and very windy. The path and the lighthouse lookout provide spectacular coastal views. In winter, you may spot migratory whales offshore.

A little further along the highway, on the north side of the point, a scenic **roadside lookout** gazes down at aqua waters outlined by white sand and black lava beds – an even more spectacular sight when hang-gliders take off from the cliffs. Offshore is **Manana Island**. This aging volcanic crater is populated by feral rabbits and wedge-tailed shearwaters The island even looks vaguely like the head of a rabbit, ears folded back. In front of it is smaller, flat **Kaohikaipu Island**. Both are seabird sanctuaries.

Opposite Sea Life Park and just within view of the lighthouse, **Makapu'u Beach Park** (41-095 Kalaniana'ole Hwy) is one of the island's top winter bodysurfing spots, with waves reaching 12ft and higher. It also has the island's best shorebreak. As with Sandy Beach, Makapu'u is strictly the domain of experienced bodysurfers, who can handle rough water and dangerous currents. Even for them, the risk of injury is always present, especially during winter. Even if you don't see flags on the beach (which indicate hazardous conditions), check with the lifeguards before entering the water. Board surfing is prohibited. In summer, when the wave action disappears, calmer waters may afford good swimming. The beach park has restrooms, outdoor showers, drinking water and lifeguards.

Sea Life Park

More like a circus than an aquarium, Hawaii's only **marine park** (www.sealifepark hawaii.com; 41-202 Kalaniana'ole Hwy; adult/child 3-11yr $30/20; ◷10:30am-5pm; ♿) offers a mixed bag of run-down, decaying attractions that, frankly, aren't worth your time. The theme-park entertainment includes choreographed shows and pool encounters with imported Atlantic bottlenose dolphins, a controversial activity (see the boxed text, p37).

The park's 300,000-gallon aquarium is filled mostly with marine animals not found in Hawaiian waters, including rays and sharks. There's also a penguin habitat, a turtle lagoon and a seabird 'sanctuary' with native '*iwa*. The park works to rehabilitate some injured seabirds and also maintains a breeding colony of green sea turtles, releasing young hatchlings back into their natural habitat each year. But if you really want to learn about Hawaii's marine life, visit the educational, eco-conscious Waikiki Aquarium (p105) instead.

Parking in the main lot costs $5, but if you continue past the ticket booth to an area marked 'additional parking,' there's typically no fee. TheBus 22 (Beach Bus), 23 (Hawai'i Kai-Sea Life Park) and 57 (Kailua Sea Life Park) all stop here.

WINDWARD COAST & KAILUA

In the dramatic Ko'olau Range, *pali* (cliffs) are shrouded in mist as often as they are bathed in glorious sunshine. Tropical rain showers guarantee that everything shares a hundred different shades of green, which is even more dazzling when set against the Windward Coast's turquoise bays and white-sand beaches. Repeat visitors to O'ahu often make this side of the island their adventure base camp, whether they've come to kayak, windsurf, snorkel, dive or just laze on the sand.

Although some enticing beaches are found here, especially around Waimanalo and Kailua, keep in mind that many spots further north along the coast are too silted to be much more than a snapshot. Once you've left behind the affluent suburbs of Kailua and Kane'ohe, the rest of the Windward Coast is surprisingly rural, dotted with small farms and taro patches. Kamehameha Hwy becomes a modest two-lane road that runs the length of the entire coast, doubling as Main St for small towns along the way.

Pali Highway

Slicing through the emerald Ko'olau Range, the Pali Hwy (Hwy 61) soars between Honolulu and Kailua. If it has been raining heavily recently, every fold and crevice in the jagged *pali* (cliffs) will have a fairyland waterfall streaming down it.

An ancient footpath once wound its way perilously over these cliffs. In 1845 the path

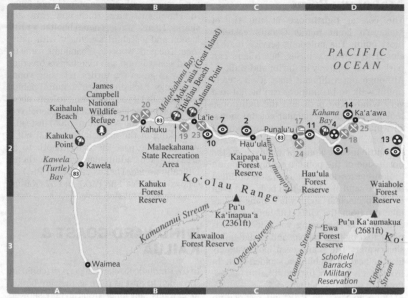

was widened into a horse trail and, later again, into a cobblestone road that would allow carriage traffic. You can still drive a scenic stretch of the Old Pali Hwy, called Nu'uanu Pali Dr (Map p76), by turning east off the modern Pali Hwy (Hwy 61) a half-mile north of the Queen Emma Summer Palace. The drive takes you through a cathedral of trees including banyans draped with hanging aerial roots, bamboo groves and Cup of Gold, a tall climbing vine with showy golden flowers.

This short detour returns you to the Pali Hwy just in time to exit at the **Nu'uanu Pali Lookout** (Map p130) with its sweeping view of the Windward Coast from a height of 1200ft. Standing at this popular lookout, Kane'ohe lies below straight ahead, Kailua to the right, and Mokoli'i Island and the coastal fishpond at Kualoa Point to the far left. The winds that funnel through the *pali* here are so strong you can sometimes lean against them, and it's usually so cool, you'll want a jacket.

A pedestrian-only section of the Old Pali Hwy winds down from the right of the lookout, ending abruptly at a barrier near the current highway about a mile away. Few people realize the road is here, let alone venture down it. It's worth walking just five minutes down the paved path for a photo op with magnificent views looking back up at the snaggle-toothed Ko'olau Range and out across the broad valley.

As you get back on the highway, it's easy to miss the sign leading you out of the parking lot, and instinct could send you in the wrong direction. Exiting the parking lot, go left toward Kailua or right toward Honolulu. Several TheBus routes travel the Pali Hwy, but none stop at the lookout.

Waimanalo

POP 3740

Nestled in a breadbasket of small family farms, the proudly Hawaiian community of Waimanalo sprawls alongside O'ahu's longest beach, where white sands stretch for miles to Makapu'u Point. What could be just another palm-fringed beach is prettily punctuated by offshore islands and a coral reef that keeps breaking surf waves at a reasonable distance.

🏖 Beaches

As elsewhere at O'ahu's beaches, don't leave any valuables in your car since break-ins and theft are common.

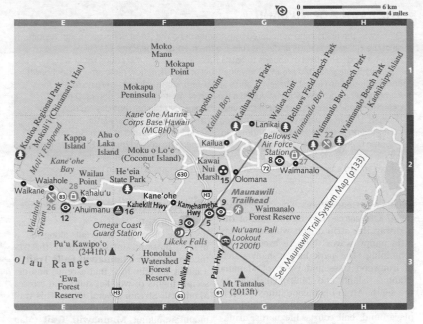

Windward Coast

⊙ Sights

1 Ahupua'a o Kahana State Park	D2
Crouching Lion	(see 18)
2 Hau'ula Beach Park	C2
3 Ho'omaluhia Botanical Garden	F3
4 Huilua Fishpond	D2
5 Ko'olau Golf Club	F2
6 Kualoa Ranch	D2
7 La'ie Beach Park (Pounders)	C2
8 Olomana Golf Links	G2
9 Pali Golf Course	G2
10 Polynesian Cultural Center	C2
11 Punalu'u Beach Park	D2
12 Senator Fong's Plantation & Gardens	E2
13 Sugar Mill Ruins	D2
14 Swanzy Beach Park	D2
15 Ulupo Heiau	G2
16 Valley of the Temples & Byōdō-In	F2

⊜ Sleeping

Ho'omaluhia Botanical Garden	(see 3)

17 Pat's at Punalu'u	C2

⊗ Eating

Angel's Ice Cream	(see 23)
Aunty Pat's Cafe	(see 6)
Ching's General Store	(see 24)
18 Crouching Lion Inn Bar & Grill	D2
Fiji Market	(see 20)
Foodland	(see 23)
19 Hukilau Cafe	B2
20 Kahuku Grill	B2
21 Kahuku Shrimp Trucks	B2
22 Keneke's	H2
23 La'ie Chop Suey	B2
24 Shrimp Shack	C2
Sweet Home Waimanalo	(see 27)
25 Uncle Bobo's	D2
26 Waiahole Poi Factory	E2

⊡ Shopping

27 Naturally Hawaiian Gallery	G2
28 Sunshine Arts Gallery	E2

THE BATTLE OF NU'UANU

O'ahu was the final island conquered by Kamehameha the Great in his campaign to unite all of the Hawaiian Islands under his rule. On the then-rural beaches of Waikiki, Kamehameha landed his fleet of canoes to battle Kalanikupule, the *mo'i* (king) of O'ahu.

Heavy fighting started around Puowaina ('Hill of Sacrifice,' now nicknamed Punchbowl), and continued up Nu'uanu Valley. O'ahu's spear-and-stone warriors were no match for Kamehameha's troops, which included a handful of Western sharpshooters. O'ahu's defenders made their last stand at the narrow ledge near the current-day Nu'uanu Pali Lookout. Hundreds were driven over the top to their deaths. A century later, during the construction of the Old Pali Hwy, more than 500 skulls were found at the base of the cliffs.

Some O'ahu warriors, including their king, escaped into upland forests. But when Kalanikupule surfaced a few months later, he was sacrificed by Kamehameha to the war god, Ku. Kamehameha's taking of O'ahu was the last battle ever fought between Hawaiian warriors.

Waimanalo Beach Park BEACH
(41-147 Kalaniana'ole Hwy) By the side of the highway, this strip of soft white sand has little puppy waves that are excellent for swimming. The park has a shady patch of ironwood trees and views of Manana (Rabbit) Island and Makapu'u Point to the south. An in-town community park, it also has a grassy picnic area, a children's playground, ball courts, lifeguards, drinking water, restrooms and outdoor showers. Camping is allowed in an open area near the road, but it's uninviting.

Waimanalo Bay Beach Park BEACH
(41-043 Aloiloi St) Just over a mile north of Waimanalo Beach Park, Waimanalo Bay's biggest waves break onshore here, drawing dedicated board surfers and bodysurfers. Through a wide forest of ironwoods, you'll find a thick mane of blond sand for long walks and ocean ogling. There are lifeguards, a picnic area with BBQ grills, restrooms, outdoor showers and fewer than a dozen just-OK campsites.

Bellows Field Beach Park BEACH
(41-043 Kalaniana'ole Hwy) Fronting Bellows Air Force Station, this is a long beach with fine sand and a natural setting backed by ironwood trees. The small shorebreak waves are good for beginner bodysurfers and board surfers. The beach is open to civilians only on national holidays and weekends, usually from noon Friday until 8am Monday. There are lifeguards, showers, restrooms, drinking water and 60 campsites nestled among trees and by the beach. Buses stop in front of the park entrance road, just north of Waimanalo Bay Beach Park; from the bus stop, it's a 1.5-mile walk in.

⚡ Activities

Maunawili Falls HIKING
Reaching a small waterfall alongside a muddy, mosquito-infested stream, the 2.5-mile round-trip **Maunawili Falls Trail** is a family-friendly hike that ascends and descends flights of wooden stairs and crosses Maunawili Stream several times. This trail also connects with the 10-mile hiking and mountain-biking **Maunawili Trail** (Map opposite), which gently contours around a series of *pali* lookouts in the Ko'olau Range, between the Pali Hwy and Waimanalo town.

To reach the main Maunawili Falls trailhead, drive north on the Pali Hwy from Honolulu, then take the *second* right-hand exit onto A'uloa Rd. At the first fork veer left onto Maunawili Rd, which ends in a residential subdivision; look for a gated trailhead-access road on the left. Note that this road is accessible only by pedestrians (and by residents' vehicles); nonresidents may not drive or park along this road. Instead, park along nearby residential streets that aren't gated. Respect residents by not loitering or being noisy while walking along the road.

Olomana Golf Links GOLF
(📞259-7926; www.olomanagolflinks.com; 41-1801 Kalaniana'ole Hwy; greens fee incl cart rental from $80, club rental $35) With the dramatic backdrop of the Ko'olau Range, this is where LPGA star Michelle Wie got her start and President Obama swings his clubs during trips back to O'ahu. Two challenging nine-hole courses are played together as a regulation 18-hole, par-72 course.

🛏 Sleeping & Eating

All three of Waimanalo's public beach parks allow camping with an advance permit (see p58).

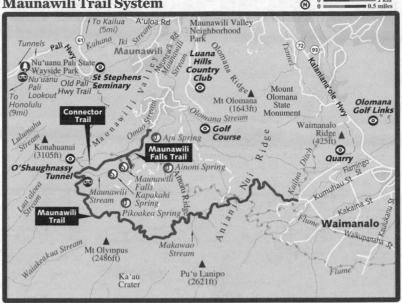

Sweet Home Waimanalo LOCAL, TAKEOUT
(259-5737; http://sweethomewaimanalo.com; 41-1025 Kalaniana'ole Hwy; mains $6-12; 9:30am-7pm)
Taste Waimanalo's back-to-the-earth farm goodness at this family kitchen, where tri-tip steak gets sauced with guava and chipotle, and wraps roll up BBQ chicken with bok-choy slaw. Slurp tropical fruit smoothies and chow down at picnic tables with umbrellas out front next to the highway. The attached market sells fresh fruit and veggies, too.

Keneke's LOCAL, TAKEOUT
(259-9811; www.kenekes.net; 41-857 Kalaniana'ole Hwy; items $3-7; 9:30am-5:30pm;) Just north of Waimanalo Beach Park, this red-and-white checkered drive-in cooks up island-style barbecue, triple-decker *loco moco*, plate lunches (*laulau* and *mochiko* chicken) and rainbow shave ice. Christian scripture is written on the walls, but cleanliness isn't necessarily next to godliness here.

🛍 Shopping

Naturally Hawaiian Gallery ART, SOUVENIRS
(www.naturallyhawaiian.com; 41-1025 Kalaniana'ole Hwy; 10am-6pm) Inside a converted gas station, browse handmade works by O'ahu artists, including wooden koa bowls, carved bone fishhook pendants and other jewelry. Owner Patrick Ching

sells his own naturalist paintings, prints and illustrated books here.

ℹ Getting There & Away

TheBus route 57 between Honolulu's Ala Moana Center and Waimanalo (one hour) via Kailua runs once or twice hourly, making stops along the Kalania'ole Hwy (Hwy 72) through town. Some buses continue to Sea Life Park.

Kailua

POP 36,510

Suburban Kailua is the Windward Coast's largest town, a fairly easy title to win. A long graceful bay protected by a coral reef is Kailua's claim to fame, and many repeat visitors to O'ahu leapfrog over touristy Waikiki to hang out here in laid-back surf style.

The sunny weather and wave conditions are just about perfect for swimming, kayaking, windsurfing and kitesurfing. Retro beach cottages, mostly cooled by tradewinds and not air-conditioning, crowd into little neighborly lanes. Further south along the shore, the exclusive enclave of Lanikai is where you'll find million-dollar views – and mansions easily valued at least twice that much.

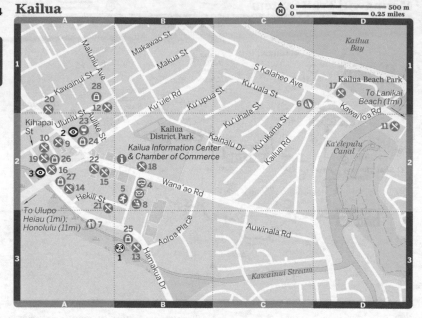

In ancient times Kailua (meaning 'two seas') was a place of legends and home to Hawaiian chiefs, including briefly Kamehameha the Great after he conquered O'ahu. Rich in stream-fed agricultural land, fertile fishing grounds and protected canoe landings, Kailua supported at least three temples, one of which you can still visit.

🏖 Beaches & Sights

Kailua Beach Park   BEACH
(526 Kawailoa Rd;) A wide arc of white sand drapes around the jewel-colored waters of Kailua Bay, with formidable volcanic headlands pinning either side. Sea turtles poke their heads above the gentle waves, while residents swap gossip during daily dog walks along the sand.

The beach has a gently sloping sandy bottom with usually calm waters, good for swimming year-round, especially in the morning. In the afternoons, winds transform the bay into a windsurfing and kitesurfing rink.

The beach park is the primary access point for visitors and has the usual public facilities, including lifeguard towers, drinking water, restrooms and outdoor showers.

Lanikai Beach   BEACH
Southeast of Kailua Beach Park, Lanikai is fronted by what was once one of Hawaii's prettiest stretches of powdery white sand. Today the beach is shrinking, as nearly half of the sand has washed away as a result of retaining walls built to protect the neighborhood's multimillion-dollar mansions. Still, it's a rare beauty, at its best during full-moon phases.

Beyond Kailua Beach Park, the coastal road turns into one-way A'alapapa Dr, which loops back around as Mokulua Dr, passing almost a dozen narrow public-access walkways to the beach. The most luxurious stretches of sand are the furthest southeast toward Wailea Point.

Kalama Beach Park   BEACH
(248 N Kalaheo Ave;) On the northern side of Kailua Bay, this beach has the roughest shorebreak, making it popular with experienced bodyboarders. Surfers usually head for the northernmost tip of Kailua Bay at Kapoho Point. When waters are calm, you'll find families with kids sunning themselves and splashing around here, while locals jog along the soft sands. The park has restrooms, but no showers or drinking water.

Kailua

◎ Sights
1 Hamakua Marsh Wildlife
   Sanctuary B3
2 Hawaiian Healing Arts College............A2
3 Kailua Movement Studio A2

Activities, Courses & Tours
4 Aaron's Dive Shop B2
5 Hawaiian Watersports.........................B2
6 Kailua Sailboards & Kayaks.................C1
7 Naish Hawaii A3
8 Twogood Kayaks Hawaii.....................B2

◉ Eating
9 Agnes Bake Shop................................A2
10 Boston's North End Pizza
   Bakery A2
11 Buzz's..D2
12 Cinnamon's Restaurant.......................A1
13 Down to Earth Natural Foods.............B3
14 Foodland..A2
15 Kailua Farmers Market........................A2
16 Kalapawai Café & Wine Bar.................A2
17 Kalapawai Market...............................D1
18 Lanikai Juice......................................B2
19 Lemongrass..A2
20 Rai Rai Ramen A1
   Sweet Paradise Chocolatier..... (see 19)
21 Uahi Island Grill.................................A2
22 Whole Foods......................................A2

◎ Drinking
23 Kailua Town Pub A2
   Morning Brew............................ (see 18)
   Ohana Karaoke........................... (see 21)

◉ Shopping
24 Coconut Grove Music..........................A2
25 Island Glassworks...............................B3
26 Maunaheali'i A2
27 Mu'umu'u Heaven................................A2
28 Muse Room...A1

Ulupo Heiau State Monument HEIAU (TEMPLE)
(Map p130; www.hawaiistateparks.org; admission
free; ◎sunrise-sunset) Construction of this imposing platform temple was traditionally attributed to *menehune,* the 'little people' who
legends say created much of Hawaii's stonework, finishing each project in one night.
Fittingly, Ulupo means 'night inspiration.' In
front of the temple, thought to have been a
luakini used for human sacrifice, is an artist's rendition of the site as it probably looked
in the 18th century.

The temple is a mile southwest of downtown Kailua, behind the YMCA at 1200
Kailua Rd. Coming over the Pali Hwy from
Honolulu, take Uluoa St, the first left after
passing the Hwy 72 junction, then turn
right on Manu Aloha St and right again on
Manu O'o St.

✈ Activities

Kayaking & Surfing

Three of Kailua's pretty little offshore islands are seabird sanctuaries, accessible
only by kayak. Landings are allowed on
Popoi'a (Flat) Island, off the south end
of Kailua Beach Park. Twin **Mokulua Islands**, Moku Nui and Moku Iki, sit directly off Lanikai. It's possible to kayak
from Kailua Beach Park to Moku Nui, but
landings are prohibited on **Moku Iki**, the
smaller of the two islands. Landings are
allowed on **Moku Nui**, which has a beautiful beach for sunbathing and snorkeling.

A few kayaking, windsurfing, kitesurfing
and stand up paddle (SUP) boarding outfitters have rental-gear concession stands by
the beach and at in-town shops, where you
can arrange for private or group lessons
and guided tours.

Kailua Sailboards & Kayaks, Inc   RENTALS
(☑262-2555, 888-457-5737; www.kailuasailboards
.com; Kailua Beach Center, 130 Kailua Rd; kayak
rentals per day $50-70; ◎8:30am-5pm) A short
walk from the beach.

Twogood Kayaks Hawaii   RENTALS
(☑262-5656; www.twogoodkayaks.com; 345
Hahani St; kayak rentals per day $55-65; ◎9am-
6pm Mon-Fri, 8am-6pm Sat & Sun) Free delivery next to Kailua Beach Park.

Naish Hawaii   RENTALS
(☑262-6068, 800-767-6068; www.naish.com; 155
Hamakua Dr; windsurfing rig rentals per day $45-
55; ◎9am-5:30pm) Owned by windsurfing
champion Robby Naish.

Hawaiian Watersports   RENTALS
(☑262-5483; www.hawaiianwatersports.com;
354 Hahani St; kayak rentals per day $40-80;
◎9am-5pm) Gives discounts for online
bookings.

Scuba Diving

Aaron's Dive Shop   DIVING
(☑262-2333, 888-847-2822; www.hawaii-scuba
.com; 307 Hahani St; 2-tank boat dive $115-125;
◎7am-7pm Mon-Fri, to 6pm Sat, to 5pm Sun) Sea
caves, lava tubes, coral gardens and WWII

shipwrecks can all be explored courtesy of this five-star PADI operation. Discounts available for booking ahead online.

Bird-watching

FREE Kawai Nui Marsh   PARK
(Map p130; www.kawainuimarsh.com; ☉sunrise-sunset) One of Hawaii's largest freshwater marshes, Kawai Nui provides flood protection for the town. The inland water catchment is also one of the largest remaining fishponds used by ancient Hawaiians. Legend says the edible mud of the fishpond was once home to a *mo'o* (lizard spirit). Park at the end of Kaha St, off Oneawa St, just over a mile northwest of Kailua Rd. A wheelchair-accessible recreational path leads around the marsh.

FREE Hamakua Marsh Wildlife Sanctuary   PARK
(http://hamakuamarsh.com; ☉sunrise-sunset) Downstream from Kawai Nui, this smaller marsh also provides habitat for rare endemic waterbirds, including the *koloa maoli* (Hawaiian duck), *ae'o* (Hawaiian black-necked stilt), *'alae ke'oke'o* (Hawaiian coot) and *'alae 'ula* (Hawaiian moorhen). Birders flock here after heavy rains. Free parking off Hamakua Dr, behind Down to Earth Natural Foods supermarket.

Yoga & Massage

Kailua has a vibrant yoga scene. As a drop-in visitor, expect to pay about $12 to $18 for a group class. **Kailua Movement Studio** (262-1933; www.kailuamovementstudio.com; 776 Kailua Rd) offers lessons for all skill levels in yoga, pilates, belly dancing, capoeira and African and Latin dance.

To let someone else stretch your muscles instead, make an appointment with the **Hawaiian Healing Arts College** (266-2648; www.hhacdirect.com; 407 Uluniu St; 1hr massage $30-60 plus tip; ☉by appointment only) or **Windward Community Massage** (853-0491; http://windwardmassage.com; 22 Oneawa St; 1hr massage from $60 plus tip; ☉by appointment only).

🛏 Sleeping

Kailua has no hotels but suburban home B&Bs and vacation rentals abound, many just a short walk from the beach. Most are nonsmoking, don't accept credit cards, require an advance deposit and multiple-night stays, charge cleaning fees and are legally prohibited from displaying signs or offering a hot breakfast. Call ahead (not just from the airport or the Pali Hwy!), ideally a few months in advance, for reservations.

Kailua Guesthouse   B&B $$
(261-2637, 888-249-5848; www.kailuaguesthouse.com; tr $129-159; 🕸) Not far from downtown, this contemporary home rents out two blissfully quiet apartment-style suites with king-size or twin beds that open onto lanai overhanging with plumeria blossoms. Modern amenities include flat-screen TVs with DVD players, digital in-room safes and shared washer/dryer access. Japanese spoken.

Tee's at Kailua   B&B $$
(261-0771; www.teesinn.com; 771 Wana'ao Rd; d incl breakfast $200; ❄🕸) This suburban home rents out just one deluxe guest room, decorated with tropical hardwood furnishings, a king-size sleigh bed and Aveda products in the bathroom. Breakfast includes homegrown organic teas from the garden. Japanese spoken.

Manu Mele Bed & Breakfast   B&B $$
(262-0016; www.manumele.net; 153 Kailuana Pl; d $100-120; ❄🕸) A little out of the way but still just steps from the beach, these simple guest rooms in the contemporary home of English-born host Carol Isaacs appeal. Each has a private entrance, heavenly seven-layer bed with a Hawaiian quilt, cable TV, a mini-fridge, microwave and coffeemaker.

Hula Breeze   B&B $$
(469-7623; www.vrbo.com/242098; 172 Ku'umele Pl; d $135; 🕸) A 15-minute walk from Kailua Beach Park, this contemporary home splashes tropical colors throughout its chic studio bedroom, which has high thread-count sheets and its own kitchenette. Guests enjoy access to a shared washer/dryer and an outdoor shower, swimming pool and BBQ grill in the garden.

Sheffield House   B&B $$
(262-0721; www.hawaiisheffieldhouse.com; 131 Ku'ulei Rd; d $120-145; 🕸) Around the corner from Kailua Beach, this kid-friendly house has tasteful kitchenette units. The smaller guest room has a wheelchair-accessible bathroom and built-in bookshelves full of beach reading, while the suite has a foldout futon and a peaceful garden lanai.

Papaya Paradise Bed & Breakfast   B&B **$$**
(☑261-0316; www.kailuaoahuhawaii.com; 395
Auwinala Rd; d incl breakfast from $100; ☜☲)
About a mile inland from the beach, this
suburban home run by a retired couple has
a big outdoor sitting area with backyard
views of Mt Olomana, a shared fridge and
microwave, and quiet lodgings best suited
to more mature audiences.

Paradise Palms Bed & Breakfast   B&B **$$**
(☑254-4234;   www.paradisepalmshawaii.com;
804 Mokapu Rd; d $110-120; ✲) You'll feel
like you're visiting newfound relatives at
this tidy suburban home. Beds claim most
of the limited room, although efficiency
studios with private entrances also sport
kitchenettes.

Beach Lane B&B   B&B **$$**
(☑262-8286; www.beachlane.com; d $95-135; ☜)
A short walk from the beach, this breezy
contemporary home offers airy floral stu-
dios with kitchenettes and a private two-
bedroom cottage with full kitchen. Beach
gear is free to borrow. German, Danish,
Norwegian and Swedish spoken.

✖ Eating

Kailua has dozens of places to eat, from fast-
food joints to upscale restaurants, but most
are mediocre. We've reviewed some stand-
out exceptions here.

⬛Lanikai Juice   HEALTHY, TAKEOUT **$**
(www.lanikaijuice.com; Kailua Shopping Center,
600 Kailua Rd; items $4-8; ☾6am-8pm Mon-Fri,
7am-7pm Sat & Sun) With fresh fruit grown
by local farmers blended into biodegrad-
able cups, this addictive juice bar adver-
tises yogi-worthy smoothies with names
like Ginger 'Ono and Coco Champ. In the
morning, devour overflowing bowls of
granola topped with *açai* berries, apple
bananas and grated coconut at sunny side-
walk tables.

Kalapawai Market   DELI, TAKEOUT **$**
(306 S Kalaheo Ave; items $2-10; ☾6am-9pm, deli
6:30am-8pm) En route to the beach, every-
one stops at this 1930s landmark to stock
their picnic basket with made-to-order
sandwiches and market-fresh salads. Ear-
ly-morning regulars often toast their own
bagels while helping themselves to fresh
coffee. The market's in-town cafe and wine
bar serves haute bistro dinners.

⬛Uahi Island Grill   ISLAND CONTEMPORARY **$$**
(☑266-4646; www.uahiislandgrill.com; 131 Hekili
St; mains $7-20; ☾10:30am-8:30pm Mon-Thu,
10:30am-9:30pm Fri & 11:30am-9:30pm Sat) Get
your fresh, flavorful and healthy plate-lunch
fix – *furikake*-crusted grilled tofu, red seafood curry and garlicky chicken with brown
rice – until 5pm daily. Or make reservations
for sophisticated dinners like seared steak
with Maui onions, lemongrass lamb or vegan
tempeh with Japanese pumpkin. Tables are
tightly packed inside a sleek dining room.

Cinnamon's Restaurant   BREAKFAST, CAFE **$**
(www.cinnamonsrestaurant.com;   315   Uluniu
St; mains $6-13; ☾7am-2pm Mon-Sat; ☲) Lo-
cals pack this family cafe decorated like
Gramma's house for the airy chiffon pancakes drowning in guava syrup, Portuguese

sweetbread French toast, eggs Benedict mahimahi, curried chicken-and-papaya salad, and frittatas with sun-dried-tomato pesto and artichoke hearts.

Rai Rai Ramen   JAPANESE $
(124 Oneawa St; mains $7-10; ⊘11am-8:30pm Wed-Mon) Look for the red-and-white banner written in kanji outside this brightly lit noodle shop, where the straightforward menu of ramen styles ranges from Sapporo south to Hakata, all with rich broth and topped with tender pork, if you like. *Gyōza* are grilled or steamed bundles of heaven.

Lemongrass   SOUTHEAST ASIAN $$
(20 Kainehe St; mains $8-15; ⊘11am-3pm Mon-Fri, 5-9pm Sun-Thu, 5-10pm Fri & Sat) This Thai-Vietnamese joint will sooth your soul, with its earth-toned decor, an avocado-colored bar and tropical flower prints on the wall. The *pho* and Thai noodle and curry dishes may be a tad too sweet rather than spicy, but it's all fresh and served with a smile.

Buzz's   STEAKHOUSE $$$
(☏261-4661; www.buzzssteakhouse.com; 413 Kawailoa Rd; mains lunch $9-15, dinner $15-36; ⊘11am-3pm & 4:30-9:30pm) By the canal across the road from Kailua Beach park, this old-school hangout has a tiki-lit lanai and often disappointing menu of charbroiled fish and burgers at lunch, and kiawe-grilled surf-and-turf at dinner. Waits are long, service only so-so.

For more quick bites and self-catered meals:

🍴 Kailua Farmers Market FARMERS MARKET $
(http://hfbf.org; parking garage behind Longs Drugs, 609 Kailua Rd; ⊘5-7:30pm Thu; 🖉) Artisan breads, organic fruit and veggies and island-style plate meals.

🍴 Down to Earth Natural Foods   SUPERMARKET $
(www.downtoearth.org; 201 Hamakua Dr; ⊘8am-10pm; 🖉) Natural-foods store with a delish takeout deli and hot-and-cold salad bar.

🍴 Whole Foods   SUPERMARKET $
(www.wholefoodsmarket.com; 70 Ka'ahumanu Ave; ⊘8am-9pm; 🖉) Organic supermarket chain also has a takeout deli and salad bar.

Foodland   SUPERMARKET $
(www.foodland.com; 108 Hekili St; ⊘24hr) Look for an R Field Wine Co gourmet food specialty shop inside this chain grocery store.

Agnes Bake Shop   BAKERY, TAKEOUT $
(☏262-5367; http://agnesbakeshop.com; 46 Ho'olai St; items from $1; ⊘6am-6pm Tue-Sat, to 2pm Sun) Chocolate-macadamia nut log pastries and hot *malasadas* (allow 15 minutes or call ahead to pre-order).

Boston's North End Pizza Bakery   PIZZERIA, TAKEOUT $
(31 Ho'olai St; slices $4-6; ⊘11am-8pm Sun-Thu, to 9pm Fri & Sat; ⊕) Supersized slices of pie with thick, chewy crust.

Sweet Paradise Chocolatier   DESSERT $
(www.sweetparadisechocolate.com; 20 Kainehe St; items from $3; ⊘11am-6pm Tue-Sat) Haute handmade artisan chocolates and truffles with tropical flavors.

🍷 Drinking & Entertainment

Though it's not a party spot like Waikiki, Kailua has a few bars.

Morning Brew   COFFEEHOUSE
(http://morningbrewhawaii.com; Kailua Shopping Center, 600 Kailua Rd; ⊘6am-9pm Sun-Thu, to 10pm Fri & Sat; ⊕🛜) Bustling espresso bar with local attitude. Thai iced tea or a 'Funky Monkey' mocha, anyone?

Kailua Town Pub   PUB
(26 Ho'olai St; ⊘10am-2am Mon-Sat, 7am-2am Sun) Faux-Irish bar with tasty from-scratch Bloody Marys; skip the pub grub, though.

Ohana Karaoke   BAR
(131 Hekili St; ⊘5pm-2am) Island-style *pupus* and howlin' karaoke late-night.

🔒 Shopping

Downtown is blessed with antique stores, island-born art galleries and whimsical clothing boutiques.

Mu'umu'u Heaven   CLOTHING
(www.muumuuheaven.com; 767 Kailua Rd; ⊘10am-6pm Mon-Sat, 11am-4pm Sun) Hidden behind the fine-arts Nohea Gallery, this chic contemporary boutique vends flowing tropical-print dresses, skirts and feminine tops all handmade from vintage muumuus, as glimpsed in fashion mags like *Lucky*.

Island Glassworks   ART, CRAFTS
(☏261-1705; www.islandglassworks.com; 171-A Hamakua Dr; ⊘usually 9am-4pm Mon-Wed & Fri, 10am-4pm Sat) Part glassblowing workshop, part art gallery, here you can peruse one-of-a-kind pieces like calabash-shaped vases and bowls with elemental color palettes. Call ahead to check hours or sign up for classes.

Coconut Grove Music
MUSIC

(418 Ku'ulei Rd; ⊙10am-6pm Mon-Sat) This island guitar shop carries name-brand ukuleles – including Kamaka, handmade in Honolulu – and vintage 20th-century ukes. Next-door Hungry Ear Records stocks new, used and collectible Hawaiian music CDs and vinyl.

Manuheali'i
CLOTHING

(5 Ho'olai St; ⊙9:30am-6pm Mon-Fri, 9am-4pm Sat, 10am-3pm Sun) Branch of the famous, aloha-filled Honolulu designer.

Muse Room
CLOTHING

(332 Uluniu St; ⊙10am-5pm) Beachy, dreamy and grown-up girly styles inspired by LA and Waikiki.

ℹ Information

Kailua Information Center & Chamber of Commerce (☑261-2727; www.kailuachamber.com; Kailua Shopping Center, 600 Kailua Rd; ⊙10am-4pm Mon-Fri) Free local maps and brochures.

Kailua Post Office (335 Hahani St; ⊙8:30am-5pm Mon-Fri, 9am-4pm Sat)

Kailua Public Library (☑266-9911; www.librarieshawaii.org; 239 Ku'ulei Rd; ⊙10am-5pm Mon, Wed, Fri & Sat, 1-8pm Tue & Thu) Free reservable internet terminals with a temporary nonresident library card ($10).

Morning Brew (http://morningbrewhawaii.com; Kailua Shopping Center, 600 Kailua Rd; per hr $6; ⊙6am-9pm Sun-Thu, to 10pm Fri & Sat) Fee-based internet terminals; free wi-fi with purchase.

ℹ Getting There & Away

From Honolulu's Ala Moana Center, TheBus routes 56 and 57 run over the *pali* to downtown Kailua (45 to 60 minutes, every 15 minutes). To reach Kailua Beach Park or Lanikai, get off in downtown Kailua at the corner of Kailua Rd and Oneawa St, then transfer to TheBus 70, which runs every 60 to 90 minutes.

BICYCLE Avoid parking headaches and traffic jams by renting a bike.

Bike Shop (☑261-1553; www.bikeshophawaii.com; 270 Ku'ulei Rd; rentals per day/week from $20/100; ⊙10am-7pm Mon-Fri, 9am-5pm Sat, 10am-5pm Sun) Top-quality rentals, repairs and cycling gear.

Kailua Sailboards & Kayaks (☑262-2555, 888-457-5737; www.kailuasailboards.com; Kailua Beach Center, 130 Kailua Rd; per half-day/full day/week $20/25/85; ⊙8:30am-5pm) Rents single-speed beach cruisers.

Kane'ohe
POP 35,915

Although Kane'ohe is blessed with Hawaii's biggest reef-sheltered bay, its largely silty waters are not good for swimming. Neighboring the Marine Corps Base Hawaii, this workaday town doesn't receive nearly as many tourists as the surf-and-sun village of Kailua, but it does have a few attractions worth stopping briefly for.

Two highways run north–south through Kane'ohe. The coastal Kamehameha Hwy (Hwy 836) is slower, but more scenic. The inland Kahekili Hwy (Hwy 83) intersects the Likelike Hwy (Hwy 63) and continues north past Valley of the Temples. Both highways merge into the Kamehameha Hwy (Hwy 83) a few miles north of town.

◉ Sights

Valley of the Temples
CEMETERY

The Valley of the Temples is an interdenominational cemetery that is famously home to the Byōdō-In (www.byodo-in.com; 47-200 Kahekili Hwy; adult/child under 13yr $3/1; ⊙9am-5pm), a replica of a 900-year-old temple in Uji, Japan. The temple's symmetry is a classic example of Japanese Heian architecture, with rich vermilion walls set against the verdant fluted cliffs of the Ko'olau Range.

In the main hall, a 9ft-tall Amida Buddha, covered in gold leaf, is positioned to catch the first rays of morning sunlight. Outside, wild peacocks roam beside a koi pond and a garden designed to symbolize the Pure Land of Amitabha Buddhism. The three-ton brass bell is said to bring peace and good fortune to anyone who rings it – and so, of course, everyone does.

From Honolulu's Ala Moana Center, TheBus 65 stops near the cemetery entrance on Kahekili Hwy, from where it's a winding 0.7-mile walk uphill to the temple.

FREE **Ho'omaluhia Botanical Garden** GARDEN
(☑233-7323; www.co.honolulu.hi.us/parks/hbg; 45-680 Luluku Rd; ⊙9am-4pm) Set against a dramatic backdrop of *pali* at the foot of the Ko'olau Range, O'ahu's biggest botanical garden is planted with 400 acres of trees and shrubs from the world's tropical regions.

This peaceful nature preserve is networked by sporadically marked, soft grassy and often muddy trails winding around an artificial reservoir (no swimming). A small visitor center features displays on the park's history, flora and fauna, and Hawaiian ethnobotany. Call ahead to register for two-hour guided nature hikes, usually offered at 10am Saturday and 1pm Sunday. Camping is allowed (see p143).

The park is at the end of Luluku Rd, over a mile *mauka* (inland) from Kamehameha Hwy. TheBus 55 stops behind the Windward City Shopping Center, opposite the start of Luluku Rd, from where the visitor center is a 2-mile uphill walk.

Senator Fong's Plantation & Gardens   GARDEN
(☑239-6775; www.fonggarden.net; 47-285 Pulama Rd; adult/child 5-12yr $14.50/9; ⊙10am-2pm, tours usually 10:30am & 1pm) A labor of love by Hiram Fong (1907–2004), the first Asian American elected to the US Senate, these flowering gardens aim to preserve Hawaii's plant life for future generations. The Fong family offers informal lei-making classes ($6.50) and one-hour, 1-mile guided tours that wind past tropical flowers, sandalwood and palm trees, and other endemic plants.

The gardens are 0.8 miles *mauka* (inland) from the Kamehameha Hwy – watch for the signed turnoff around a half-mile north of **Sunshine Arts Gallery** (www.sunshinearts .net; 47-653 Kamehameha Hwy; ⊙9am-5:30pm), also worth a stop to browse works by island-born potters, painters, printmakers and photographers.

FREE He'eia State Park   PARK
(46-465 Kamehameha Hwy; ⊙7am-6:45pm early Sep-Mar, to 7:45pm Apr-early Sep) Despite looking abandoned, this park offers picturesque views of **He'eia Fishpond**, an impressive survivor from the days when stone-walled ponds used for raising fish for royalty were common on Hawaiian shores. It remains largely intact despite invasive mangrove plants.

Just offshore to the southeast, **Moku o Lo'e** was a royal playground. Its nickname 'Coconut Island' comes from the trees planted there by Princess Bernice Pauahi Bishop in the mid-19th century. During WWII, the US military used it for R&R. Today the Hawai'i Institute of Marine Biology occupies much of the island, which you might recognize from the opening scenes of the *Gilligan's Island* TV series.

Near the park entrance, there's a traditional Hawaiian canoe shed and workshop.

🏃 Activities

Golf
Club and handcart rentals are available at these popular golf courses (reserve tee times in advance):

Ko'olau Golf Club   GOLF
(☑247-7088; www.koolaugolfclub.com; 45-550 Kionaole Rd; greens fee $60-150) O'ahu's toughest championship course, scenically nestled beneath the Ko'olau Range.

Pali Golf Course   GOLF
(☑266-7612, reservations ☑296-2000; www1 .honolulu.gov/des/golf; 45-050 Kamehameha Hwy; greens fee $23-46) Municipal 18-hole hillside course that also has stunning mountain views, stretching across to Kane'ohe Bay.

🛏 Sleeping & Eating
The nearby beach town of Kailua has more places to bed down and fuel up.

Ho'omaluhia Botanical Garden CAMPGROUND $
(☑233-7323; www.co.honolulu.hi.us/parks/hbg; 45-680 Luluku Rd; campsites free; ⊙visitor center 9am-4pm) This county-run garden allows camping from 9am Friday until 4pm Monday. With an overnight guard and gates that open after-hours only for pre-registered campers, it's among O'ahu's safest places to camp. Get a permit inside the visitor center, but call first to confirm that space is available. No alcohol allowed.

❶ Getting There & Away
TheBus 55 departs Honolulu's Ala Moana Center every 30 minutes, taking about an hour to reach Kane'ohe. TheBus 56 runs once or twice hourly from Kailua to Kane'ohe. Onward from Kane'ohe, TheBus 55 trundles north along the Kamehameha Hwy to Turtle Bay Resort, taking an hour to reach La'ie; it runs every 30 minutes during the day, hourly during the evening.

Waiahole

Driving north along the Kamehameha Hwy, you'll cross the bridge beside Kahulu'u's Hygienic Store. There you'll make a physical and cultural departure from the gravitational pull of Honolulu. Now you've officially crossed into 'the country,' where the highway becomes a two-laner and the ocean shares the shoulder. You'll cruise through sun-dappled valleys inhabited by small towns and farms. A roadside landmark, the **Waiahole Poi Factory** (☑239-5117; 48-140 Kamehameha Hwy;

LIKEKE FALLS

Ready for a hidden waterfall, and maybe even being lucky enough to have it to yourself? The family-friendly **Likeke Falls Trail** winds through a forest of native and exotic trees into the lush Koʻolau Range.

The trail starts from the upper end of the Koʻolau Golf Club parking lot. Enter off Kionaole Rd, just west of Kamehameha Hwy (Hwy 83) near the H-3 Fwy junction. Walk through the chain-link gate and uphill along a paved maintenance road. Before reaching the water tank, veer left onto a well-used trail that ascends a set of wooden steps alternating with moss-covered rocks and gnarled tree roots.

This shady forest path eventually emerges onto a cobblestone road that continues climbing. Keep a sharp eye out for the (often muddy) side trail leading off to the right toward the waterfall, a lacy 20ft-high cascade, where usually the only sounds are of tumbling water and tropical bird song. The water is too shallow to take a dip, but you can get your feet wet.

Do not attempt this hike if any rain is forecast or dark clouds are in the sky, due to the danger of flash floods along the stream. The 2-mile round-trip hike takes about an hour.

Be aware that this trail accesses an informal right-of-way on private land. While there were no 'Kapu' or 'No Trespassing' signs posted at the time of research, these could appear at any time. If so, then consider this trail closed to the public. It is illegal (not to mention unsafe) to trespass in Hawaii.

⊙usually 10am-2pm Fri & Sat) sell *'ono* Hawaiian plate lunches.

Kualoa

Although there's not a lot to see nowadays, in ancient times Kualoa was one of the most sacred places on Oʻahu. When a chief stood on Kualoa Point, passing canoes lowered their sails in respect. The children of *aliʻi* (royalty) were brought here to be educated, and it may have been a place of refuge where *kapu* (taboo) breakers and fallen warriors could seek reprieve.

In 1850 Kamehameha III leased over 600 acres of this land to Gerrit Judd, a missionary doctor who was one of the king's advisers. Judd planted the land with sugarcane, built flumes to transport it and imported Chinese laborers to work the fields. Drought spelled the end of Oʻahu's first sugar plantation in 1870. Today you can still see the ruins of the mill's stone stack, and a bit of the crumbling walls, about a half-mile north of the beach park, past the main entrance to Kualoa Ranch.

🐟 Beaches

Kualoa Regional Park   BEACH
(49-479 Kamehameha Hwy) Offering an expansive vista of offshore islands, this park is backed by magnificent mountain scenery. Palm trees shade a narrow white-sand beach that offers safe swimming, but watch out for jellyfish in summer. There are picnic areas, restrooms, drinking water, outdoor showers and sometimes a lifeguard.

During low tide, you'll see fishers wade out toward Mokoliʻi. If you go, avoid walking on the fragile island itself or disturbing its burrowing seabirds. Birders will want to stroll south along the beach to **ʻApua Pond**, a 3-acre brackish salt marsh on Kualoa Point, and a nesting area for the endangered *aeʻo* (Hawaiian black-necked stilt). Further down the beach, the rock walls of **Moliʻi Fishpond** are covered with mangrove.

That eye-catching peaked volcanic islet you see offshore is **Mokoliʻi** ('little lizard'). According to legend, it's the tail of a *moʻo* (lizard spirit) slain by the goddess Hiʻiaka and thrown into the ocean. Following the immigration of Chinese laborers to Hawaii, this cone-shaped island also came to be called 'Chinaman's Hat,' a nickname that persists today, regardless of political correctness.

Roadside camping is allowed at this county park, although it's often a hangout for drinking and carousing at night. For advance permits (required), see p58.

WHOSE LAND IS IT?

Not everything in these parts is as peaceful as the *lo'i kalo* (taro fields) alongside the Kamehameha Hwy. Large tracts of the Waikane Valley were taken over by the US military during WWII for training and target practice, which continued into the 1970s. The military once claimed that the land has so much live ordnance it couldn't be returned to the mostly Hawaiian families it was leased from, a bone of contention with locals. After decades of pressure from locals, clean-up by the military is slowly getting under way. Not surprisingly, you'll encounter quite a few Hawaiian sovereignty activists here. Anti-development signs, Hawaiian flags hanging upside down (the sign of distress) and bumper stickers with slogans like 'Keep the Country Country' are everywhere you look along the roadside.

◉ Sights & Activities

Kualoa Ranch TOURS
(☎237-7321, 800-231-7321; www.kualoa.com; 49-560 Kamehameha Hwy; 1hr movie tour, catamaran cruise or hula lesson adult/child 3-12yr from $23/15; ⊛) With an almost irresistibly scenic location, you may recognize this tourbus destination from various movies and TV shows. If you want to see where Hurley built his *Lost* golf course, where Godzilla left his footprints or where the *Jurassic Park* kids hid from dinosaurs, take a jeep or ATV tour of the movie-set sites (try to book a few days in advance to avoid disappointment, although walk-ups are entirely welcome on a space-available basis). The ranch's horseback trail rides lack much giddy-up.

✖ Eating

Aunty Pat's Café CAFE
(www.kualoa.com; 49-560 Kamehameha Hwy; most items $2-10, lunch buffet $16; ⊙7:30am-3pm, buffet 10:30am-1:30pm; ⊛) Inside Kualoa Ranch's visitor center, this cafeteria-style dining hall lays out a decent supersized buffet featuring island-style BBQ. Banana breakfast pancakes and grass-fed ranch beef burgers for lunch are cooked à la carte.

Ka'a'awa

Here the road really hugs the coast and the *pali* move right on in, with barely enough space to squeeze a few houses between the base of the cliffs and the road. Swanzy Beach Park (51-369 Kamehameha Hwy), a narrow neighborhood beach used mainly by fisherfolk, is fronted by a shore wall. You'll see kids splashing around here and families picnicking on weekends.

Across the road from the beach is a convenience store, gas station and hole-in-the-wall post office – pretty much the center of town, such as it is. Uncle Bobo's (www.uncle bobos.com; 51-480 Kamehameha Hwy; mains $7-12; ⊙10:30am-7pm Tue-Sun) drive-in fills beach-goers up with smoked BBQ combo plates, chili-cheese fries, chocolate-macadamia nut cookies and shave ice.

The Crouching Lion is a rock formation just north of the 27-mile marker on the Kamehameha Hwy. The Hawaiian version of the legend goes like so: a demigod from Tahiti sent to O'ahu as a watchdog became cemented to the mountain when he attempted to leave his post and follow the sweet-singing goddess Hi'iaka. As he struggled to free himself, he was turned to stone. To find him, stand at the restaurant sign with your back to the ocean and look straight up to the left of the coconut tree at the cliff above.

Sharing real estate with its namesake landmark, Crouching Lion Inn Bar & Grill (☎237-8981; www.crocuhinglionhawaii.com; 51-666 Kamehameha Hwy; mains $12-27; ⊙11am-10pm) has country roosters parading around the parking lot. During the day, busloads of day-trippers stop in for a light lunch of predictably bland salads and sandwiches. In the evening, tiki torches are lit for forgettable surf-and-turf dinners and cocktails on a sunset-view lanai.

Kahana Valley

In ancient Hawaii, all of the islands were divided into *ahupua'a* – pie-shaped land divisions that ran from the mountains to the sea – providing everything Hawaiians needed for subsistence. Modern subdivisions and town boundaries have erased this traditional organization almost everywhere except here, O'ahu's last publicly owned *ahupua'a*.

Before Westerners arrived, the Kahana Valley was planted with wetland taro, which thrived in the rainy valley. Archaeologists have identified the remnants of over 120 agricultural terraces and irrigation canals, as well as the remains of a heiau, fishing shrines and numerous *hale* (house) sites.

In the early 20th century the lower valley was planted with sugarcane, which was hauled north to Kahuku via a small railroad. During WWII the upper valley was taken over by the US military and used to train soldiers in jungle warfare. It remains undeveloped today, used mostly by locals who come to hunt feral pigs on weekends.

🏖 Beaches & Sights

Kahana Bay   BEACH

While many archaeological sites are hidden inaccessibly deep in the valley, Kahana's most impressive site, **Huilua Fishpond**, is readily visible from the main road and can be visited simply by walking down to the beach. Part of Ahupua'a o Kahana State Park, the beach is a locals' hangout that offers mostly safe swimming with a gently sloping sandy bottom. Watch out for the riptide near the reef break on the south end of the bay. The state park provides restrooms, outdoor showers, picnic tables and usually drinking water. The 10 roadside campsites don't offer much privacy, and they're mostly used by local families. For advance camping permits (required), see p58.

🏃 Activities

Ahupua'a o Kahana State Park   PARK

(www.hawaiistateparks.org; 52-222 Kamehameha Hwy; ⊙sunrise-sunset) In spite of over 40 years of political controversy, this park is currently still open to visitors, although wandering around may feel like intruding on someone's private home. And actually, it kind of is. When the state purchased Kahana Valley, it acquired tenants, mostly Hawaiian families who had lived in the valley for a long time. What the future holds is anybody's guess, especially after the state's moratorium on tenant evictions is lifted.

The signposted park entrance is about a mile north of Crouching Lion Inn. Starting from an unstaffed orientation center, the gentle, 1.2-mile **Kapa'ele'ele Trail** runs along a former railbed and visits both a fishing shrine and a bay-view lookout, then follows the highway back to the park entrance. Starting further up the rough, unpaved valley road, the less well-maintained **Nakoa Trail** is a 2.5-mile forest loop that confusingly crisscrosses Kahana Stream, passing by a swimming hole next to an artificial dam. Both trails can be very slippery and muddy when wet. Avoid the Nakoa Trail if any rain is forecast or if any dark clouds are threatening in the sky, because flash floods are a dangerous possibility.

Punalu'u

POP 905

This inconspicuous seaside community is just another string of houses along the highway that most visitors drive by en route to the North Shore. It's only about an hour from O'ahu's major surf scene, and offers some affordable accommodations.

🏖 Beaches

Punalu'u Beach Park   BEACH

(53-509 Kamehameha Hwy) This long, narrow swimming beach has an offshore reef that protects the shallow waters in all but stormy weather. Be cautious of strong currents near the mouth of the stream and in the channel leading out from it, especially during high surf. The park has restrooms, outdoor showers and picnic tables.

🛏 Sleeping

Pat's at Punalu'u   CONDO $$

(☑255-9840; 53-567 Kamehameha Hwy; ⊛) Largely residential and looking a bit neglected from the outside, this oceanfront condominium houses privately owned units that are spacious, if well worn. It's best for repeat island visitors, or those who truly want to get away from it all. There's no front desk; rental arrangements are handled by local real-estate agents and private owners, including through **Vacation Rentals by Owner** (www.vrbo.com).

Paul Comeau Condo Rentals   CONDO $$

(☑293-2624, 800-467-6215; www.paulspunaluu condos.com; studio/1 bedroom from $100/125, plus cleaning fee $50; ⊛) Some units have air-con and high-speed internet.

Oceanfront Condo & Our Getaway   CONDO $$

(☑261-0316, 262-1008; http://kailuaoahuhawaii .com; d from $125, plus cleaning fee $75; ⊛) Kailua B&B owners rent two studios at Pat's.

🍴 Eating

Shrimp Shack   SEAFOOD, TAKEOUT $$

(http://shrimpshackoahu.com; 53-352 Kamehameha Hwy; snacks $2-4, main plates $11-18; ⊙10am-5pm)

Bite into deep-fried coconut shrimp imported from Kaua'i or seafood plate lunches with snow-crab legs or mussels, all made to order and served hot out of this sunny yellow food truck. For dessert, step inside Ching's general store next door to sample the addictive butter *mochi* (pounded-rice cakes).

 ## Shopping

Kim Taylor Reece Gallery ART
(www.kimtaylorreecegallery.com; 53-866 Kamehameha Hwy; ☺noon-5pm Thu-Sat) Reece's sepia-toned photographs of traditional Hawaiian *hula kahiko* dancers in motion are widely recognized, but it's his images of Kalaupapa, a place of exile on Moloka'i, that haunt. Look for the airy, light-filled two-story white house on the *mauka* (inland) side of the highway.

Hau'ula

POP 3750

Aside from a couple of gas pumps, a general store and a 7-Eleven store, just about the only point of interest in this small coastal town is shallow, rocky-bottomed **Hau'ula Beach Park** (54-135 Kamehameha Hwy). Roadside camping is allowed, though it's mostly the domain of locals, some living out of their cars; for advance permits (required), see p58.

Behind Hau'ula's commercial strip is a scenic backdrop of hills and majestic Norfolk pines, with secluded hiking trails that head into the Ko'olau Range. One signposted trailhead appears at a sharp bend in Hau'ula Homestead Rd above the Kamehameha Hwy, north of Hau'ula Beach Park. Follow the paved access road inland, past the hunter check-in station that marks the start of the forest reserve.

The tranquil **Hau'ula Loop Trail**, which clambers through Waipilopilo Gulch and onto a ridge over Kaipapa'u Valley, rewards hikers with views of the lush interior with native flora all along the way, including sweet-smelling guava and octopus trees with their spreading tentacle-like branches of reddish-pink flowers. This moderate 2.5-mile lollipop loop hike takes about 1½ hours. Wear bright safety colors.

La'ie

POP 4585

Feeling almost like a big city compared to its rural neighbors, life in La'ie revolves around Brigham Young University-Hawaii (BYUH), where scholarship programs recruit students from islands throughout the Pacific. Some students help pay for expenses by working as guides at the Polynesian Cultural Center (PCC), a tourist mega complex that draws nearly a million visitors each year.

La'ie is thought to have been the site of an ancient Hawaiian *pu'uhonua* – a place where *kapu* (taboo) breakers could escape being put to death. Today, La'ie is the center of the Mormon community in Hawaii. After an attempt to establish a 'City of Joseph' on the island of Lana'i failed amid a land scandal in the mid-1860s, Hawaii's Mormon missionaries moved to O'ahu's Windward Coast.

 ## Beaches

La'ie's beaches are more attractive than those to the immediate south, but they're not as impressive as at Malaekahana State Recreation Area, just north of town.

Lai'e Beach Park BEACH
A half-mile south of the PCC's main entrance, this is an excellent bodysurfing beach, but the shorebreak can be brutal, thus its nickname **Pounders Beach**. Summer swimming is generally good, but watch out for strong winter currents. The area around the old landing is usually the calmest.

Hukilau Beach BEACH
Just over a half-mile north of Lai'e Shopping Center, this tucked-away pocket of white sand is a leisurely place for swimming in summer when waters are calm. In winter, beware of strong currents and stay out of the water anytime the surf's up.

The beach is named for the traditional Hawaiian method of fishing with drag nets. This community celebration was revived for tourists by the Mormon church as a local fundraiser for two decades until the PCC opened its doors in 1963.

 ## Sights & Activities

Polynesian Cultural Center THEME PARK
(PCC; ☎293-3333, 800-367-7060; www.polynesia
.com; 55-370 Kamehameha Hwy; park adult/child 5-11yr $50/40, incl evening show from $70/55; ☺11:45am-9pm Mon-Sat, villages noon-5pm or 5:30pm only; ⊕) A nonprofit theme park showcasing the cultures of Polynesia, this center owned by the Mormon Church is one of O'ahu's biggest attractions, second only to the USS Arizona Memorial at Pearl Harbor.

Continually overrun by tour-bus crowds, the park revolves around eight Polynesian-themed 'villages' representing Hawaii, Rapa Nui (Easter Island), Samoa, Aotearoa (New Zealand), Fiji, Tahiti, Tonga and other South Pacific islands. The villages contain authentic-looking huts and ceremonial houses, many elaborately built with twisted ropes and hand-carved posts. BYUH students dressed in native garb gamely demonstrate poi pounding, coconut-frond weaving, handicrafts and games.

Although steep, the basic admission price also includes a canoe parade show in the afternoon. You'll have to pay extra to attend the evening Polynesian song-and-dance revue that's partly authentic, partly Bollywood-style with creative sets and costumes, and BYUH college students animatedly performing on stage.

Lai'e Point State Wayside PARK

Crashing surf, a lava arch and a slice of Hawaiian folk history await at La'ie Point. The tiny offshore islands are said to be the surviving pieces of a *mo'o* (lizard spirit) slain by a legendary warrior. The islet to the left with the hole in it is Kukuiho'olua (Puka Rock). To get here from the highway, head seaward on Anemoku St, opposite La'ie Shopping Center, then turn right on Naupaka St, which dead ends at the ocean.

Lai'e Temple TEMPLE

(www.ldschurchtemples.com/laie; 55-600 Naniloa Loop) In 1919 Mormons constructed a smaller, but still showy version of their Salt Lake City, Utah temple here at the foot of the Ko'olau Range. It was the first Mormon temple built outside continental US, and today this dazzlingly white edifice may be the Windward Coast's most incongruous sight. There's a visitor center where volunteers will tell you about their faith, but nonbelievers are not allowed inside the temple itself.

✕ Eating

Restaurants, shops and services cluster in Lai'e Shopping Center, about a half-mile north of the PCC.

Hukilau Cafe LOCAL $

(55-662 Wahinepe'e St; mains $4-9; ⊙7am-2pm Tue-Fri, 7am-11:30am Sat) On the north side of town, this hole-in-the-wall is the kind of place locals would rather keep to themselves. Island-sized breakfasts and lunches, including Portuguese sweetbread French toast, *loco moco* and teriyaki burgers, are mostly right on.

La'ie Chop Suey CHINESE, AMERICAN $

(La'ie Shopping Center, 55-510 Kamehameha Hwy; mains $6-12; ⊙10am-8:45pm Mon-Sat) No place in town gets more packed than this family-owned Chinese kitchen, with its long menu of Americanized and island-flavored dishes, ranging from lemon chicken to pot-roast pork.

Foodland SUPERMARKET $

(La'ie Shopping Center, 55-510 Kamehameha Hwy; ⊙5am-midnight Mon-Sat) Grocery store, bakery, deli and pharmacy, but no alcohol sold and it's closed Sunday (this is Mormon country).

Angel's Ice Cream DESSERT, SMOOTHIES $

(La'ie Shopping Center, 55-510 Kamehameha Hwy; items $3-6; ⊙9am-9pm Mon-Fri, to 11pm Sat; ♿) Cool off with an 'Angel's Halo' shave ice or a real-fruit smoothie.

Malaekahana State Recreation Area

You'll feel all sorts of intrepid pride when you discover this wild and rugged beach, just north of town. A long, narrow strip of sand stretches between Makahoa Point to the north and Kalanai Point to the south, with a thick inland barrier of ironwoods.

Swimming is generally good year-round, although strong currents occur in winter. This popular family beach is also good for many other water sports, including bodysurfing, board surfing and windsurfing. Kalanai Point, the main section of the park, is less than a mile north of La'ie and has picnic tables, BBQ grills, camping, restrooms, drinking water and outdoor showers, but no lifeguards.

Moku'auia (Goat Island), a state bird sanctuary about 400yds offshore from Malaekahana Beach, has a small sandy cove with good swimming and snorkeling. Don't approach or disturb the nesting and burrowing seabirds. It's possible to wade over to the islet when the tide is low and the water's calm. Be careful of the shallow coral (sharp) and sea urchins (sharper). When the water is deeper, strong swimmers can make it across, but only at low tide – watch out for rip currents!

🛌 Sleeping

Malaekahana has the Windward Coast's safest, most sheltered public campgrounds. Camping at Kalanai Point requires getting a state-park permit in advance (see p58).

As with all public campgrounds on O'ahu, camping is not permitted on Wednesday and Thursday nights.

You can also let the surf be your lullaby at Makahoa Point, about 0.7 miles north of the park's main entrance. **Friends of Malaeka-hana** (☎293-1736; www.malaekahana.net; 56-335 Kamehameha Hwy; tent site per person $8.50, cabins/yurts from $80/130) maintains this end of the park, offering tent sites, very rustic 'little grass shacks,' duplex cabins and eco-yurts, plus 24-hour security and outdoor hot showers. Reservations are strongly recommended; there's usually a two-night minimum stay. Gates are locked after 7pm.

Kahuku

POP 2155

Kahuku is a former sugar-plantation town, its roads lined with wooden ex-workers' houses. Most of the old sugar mill that operated here until 1996 has been knocked down, but the remnants of the smokestack and the old iron gears can be seen behind the post office. The rest of the former mill grounds have been turned into a small shopping center containing the town's bank, gas station and cafes.

✗ Eating

Even though Kahuku's sugar mill has long since closed, locals are once again looking to the land for their livelihoods. Roadside stands sell Kahuku corn on the cob, a famously sweet variety of corn that gets name-brand billing on Honolulu menus. Shrimp ponds on the north side of town also supply O'ahu's top restaurants, while colorful lunch trucks that cook up the crustaceans – in sweet-and-spicy sauce, for example, or fried with butter and garlic – are thick along the highway.

Always popular with circle-island tour groups and road trippers, Kahuku's shrimp trucks are usually open from 10am to 6pm daily (later in summer), depending upon supply and demand. But not all of these trucks serve shrimp and prawns actually raised in Kahuku; some trucks import the crustacean critters from elsewhere in Hawaii, or even overseas.

Expect to pay $13 or more for a plate of a dozen shrimp or prawns with two-scoop rice. You'll usually encounter long waits at the most-famous Kahuku shrimp trucks (listed from south to north).

Giovanni's   SHRIMP TRUCK $$
(56-505 Kamehameha Hwy) Giovanni's graffiti-covered truck is the original, and still a classic. Next-door trucks serve smoothies, shave ice and BBQ, too.

Famous Kahuku Shrimp   SHRIMP TRUCK $$
(56-580 Kamehameha Hwy) Offers some more unusual menu choices like Japanese-style tempura shrimp and hot 'n' spicy squid.

Fumi's   SHRIMP TRUCK $$
(www.fumiskahukushrimp.com; 56-777 Kamehameha Hwy) Sit down by the live-shrimp tank and dig into a coconut shrimp plate lunch.

Romy's   SHRIMP TRUCK $$
(www.romyskahukuprawns.org; 56-781 Kamehameha Hwy) Just north of town, picnic tables overlook an aquaculture farm. *Pani popo* (Samoan coconut buns) for dessert!

Kahuku Grill   BURGERS, SEAFOOD $
(55-565 Kamehameha Hwy; mains $6-12; ⊙11am-9pm Mon-Sat; 🖘) On the old mill grounds in the middle of town, this tidy farmhouse-like kitchen has aloha spirit. The handmade beef burgers are juicy and the coconut-encrusted shrimp delicately fried – yum.

Fiji Market   POLYNESIAN, TAKEOUT $
(55-565 Kamehameha Hwy; mains $7-11; ⊙9am-9pm Mon-Sat) Farther back inside the old mill shopping complex, this Polynesian mini-mart serves up South Pacific curry plate lunches with fresh, hot roti rounds or imported New Zealand meat pies.

NORTH SHORE & HALE'IWA

You don't have to know much about the world of surfing to know a few things about the North Shore. Iconic breaks such as Pipeline, Sunset and Waimea are known all over the globe. In winter the big swells come in and the wave heights reach gigantic proportions. The ocean rears its head in profound beauty or utter terror – depending on your point of view.

To say that the North Shore is just about big waves is misleading – the beaches are amazing by anyone's standards, and the sleepy rural lifestyle sits in harmony with its bohemian underpinnings. In summer the waves peter out and surf tribes migrate to the next big break – in their wake all that is left is calm water, perfect for snorkeling, and those same stunning beaches.

Before the surfing revolution of the 1950s, the North Shore was little more than a collection of fishing villages, sugarcane plantations and dilapidated houses. The rebirth of board riding saw the arrival of surfers, surf competitions and eventually those eager to cash in on the trend. The North Shore is far from a sellout though – there is a strong current within the local community to 'Keep the North Shore Country'. Development is frowned upon and conservation is the coolest concept in town.

Kawela (Turtle) Bay

Hoisted upon the crown of northeastern O'ahu, the defining coves and lava beds of Kawela Bay are a handy marker between the island's Windward Coast and the North Shore. The Turtle Bay Resort hulks over this landscape with a view-perfect hotel, golf course, condo village and public access to the nearby beaches. There are rumors of expansion afoot – while the resort is keen, most locals are opposed. Only time will tell if the development goes through after a state supreme court–ordered environmental impact statement, or if tough economic times are enough to sway locals' opinions.

🏖 Beaches

Kuilima Cove BEACH
Kuilima Cove, with a beautiful little strand known as **Bayview Beach**, is a stunner. It has something for everyone, and there is plenty of sand to stretch out on, which should keep the placid placated. On the right-hand side of the bay is an outer reef that not only knocks down the waves but facilitates some great snorkeling in summer – and, in winter, some moderate surf.

On the main beach, the Turtle Bay Resort's Sand Bar (◷usually 9am-5pm) rents snorkel sets, boogie boards and beach volleyball equipment. Public-access beach parking on the resort grounds costs $5 per day.

Kaihalulu Beach BEACH
Just a mile east of Kuilima Cove is Kaihalulu Beach, a beautiful, curved, white-sand beach backed by ironwoods. The rocky bottom makes for poor swimming, but the shoreline attracts morning beachcombers. Walk another mile east to reach scenic Kahuku

IT'S FOR THE BIRDS

Minimally signposted less than 2 miles north of Kahuku, **James Campbell National Wildlife Refuge** (☑637-6330; www.fws.gov/jamescampbell) encompasses freshwater wetland habitat for four of Hawaii's six species of endangered waterbirds: the *'alae ke'oke'o* (Hawaiian coot), *ae'o* (Hawaiian blacknecked stilt), *koloa maoli* (Hawaiian duck) and *'alae 'ula* (Hawaiian moorhen). During stilt nesting season, normally from mid-February to mid-October, the refuge is off-limits to visitors. The rest of the year, free bird-watching tours are usually given by volunteers on Thursday afternoon and either Saturday morning or afternoon. Reservations are required, although sometimes if you just show up at pre-scheduled tour time, you can tag along. Finding the refuge is tricky, so call for driving directions and to check current tour schedules.

Point, where local fishers cast throw-nets and pole fish from the rocks.

Kawela Bay BEACH
For excellent swimming and snorkeling, hike about 1.5 miles west of Kuilima Cove on a shoreline trail that runs from the resort all the way to Kawela Bay. In winter you might spy whales cavorting offshore. After walking for just about 15 minutes, you'll first reach the western point of Turtle Bay, known as **Protection Point** for its WWII bunker. Once you've walked around the point, voila! You've found Kawela Bay. The best conditions for swimming and snorkeling are smack in the middle of the bay.

🏃 Activities

The **Turtle Bay Resort** (☑293-6000; www.turtlebayresort.com; 57-091 Kamehameha Hwy, Kahuku) has two top-rated 18-hole championship **golf courses** (☑293-8574; greens fee $100-175; ◷tee times by reservation only), one designed by George Fazio and the other by Arnold Palmer, with a pro shop providing instruction and club rentals; a **tennis center** (court fees per hr $10, rental racquet & balls $16), which is highly rated by *Tennis* magazine, and offers group clinics and mixers; and **horseback rides** (per

North Shore

person $65-125) on gentle forest and ocean-front trails. For guests, the resort can also arrange sea-kayaking tours and surfing lessons.

🛏 Sleeping

Turtle Bay Resort   RESORT $$$
(Map p130; ☎293-6000, 800-203-3650; www
.turtlebayresort.com; 57-091 Kamehameha Hwy, Ka-
huku; hotel d $215-560; ❉@🛜🏊🐾) Out of sync
with the North Shore's beatnik reputation,
Turtle Bay offers all the modern convenienc-
es of family-friendly resort life. Dated and in
dire need of renovations, every hotel room
has a private lanai with a breathtaking ocean
view. More romantic options nearby the
multistory hotel are beach-chic cottages and
resort villas with high ceilings, deep soaking
tubs and the beach right outside your door. A
four-night minimum stay may apply.

The resort's Turtle Bay Resort condos
are individually owned, which means you
may get a slice of vacation-rental paradise
or a taste of timeshare hell. Choose your
unit carefully by searching for reviews and
photos online. Quoted rates don't include a
one-time cleaning fee ($50 to $200); a multi-
night minimum stay may apply. Condo
bookings are handled by the following:

Turtle Bay Condos (☎293-2800, 888-266-
3690; www.turtlebaycondos.com; studio from
$110, 1/2/3 bedroom from $135/190/240)

Estates at Turtle Bay (☎293-0600, 888-
200-4202; www.turtlebay-rentals.com; studio from
$90, 1/2/3 bedroom from $125/175/200)

Team Real Estate (☎637-3507, 800-982-
8602; www.teamrealestate.com; 1/2 bedroom
from $100/150) Based in Hale'iwa.

🍴 Eating & Drinking

Ola   ISLAND CONTEMPORARY $$$
(☎293-0801; Turtle Bay Resort, 57-091 Kame-
hameha Hwy; www.olaislife.com; mains lunch $11-
24, dinner $20-60; ☉11am-10pm) With table
legs and tiki torches sticking out of the
sand, this high-ceilinged cabana stakes out
an unparalleled position right on the beach.
When it's sunny, Ola is an irresistible spot
for lunch, although the food is far from outstanding. Service is so laid-back, you might
find yourself staying straight through happy
hour for tastier *pupus* like kalua pork nachos and ahi *poke*.

21 Degrees North   PACIFIC RIM $$$
(☎293-8811; Turtle Bay Resort, 57-091 Kame-
hameha Hwy; mains $27-50, 5-course tasting menu
$75; ☉6-10pm Tue-Sat) Panoramic windows
with ocean views are the hallmark of this
chef's white-tablecloth dining room. Expect
perfectly prepared seafood with local flavor
like braised Kona lobster or pepper-crusted
ahi with Kahuku corn fritters on an all-
organic menu. Discerning global wine list.

Waimea

POP 2450

This tiny community is little more than a
collection of a few ramshackle shops and
houses, across the road from one of the best
surf breaks on the planet. Revered the world
over for its monster winter waves, Waimea
is a sort of loose gathering point for the
world's best surfers, ardent fans and enthu-
siastic wannabes. Beyond the beach, which

shouldn't be ignored, lie pockets of lush green beauty.

Even if you don't surf, the river valley and hillsides are flush with native tropical forests and archeological treasures. In ancient Hawaii, Waimea Valley was heavily settled, with the lowlands terraced in taro, the valley walls dotted with houses and the ridges topped with heiau sites. Waimea River, now blocked at the ocean by a sandbar, was a passage for canoes traveling to villages upstream.

🐟 Beaches

Sunset Beach Park   BEACH
(59-104 Kamehameha Hwy) Like many North Shore beaches, this one has a seasonally split personality. In winter the big swells come in and the sand is pounded into submission by spectacularly large waves. It's a hot spot for pro wave riders and the posse of followers these rock stars of the sea attract.

In summer the waves calm down and the beach increases in size, thanks to a lack of pounding. Though the water is more inviting then, be aware there are still some nasty currents about. The beach park has restrooms, outdoor showers and a lifeguard tower. If the beachside parking lot is full, you'll find more parking across the street.

Backyards
A smokin' surf break off Sunset Point at the northern end of the beach, Backyards draws top windsurfers. There's a shallow reef and strong currents to contend with, but also the island's biggest waves for sailing. Turn *makai* (seaward) off Kamehameha Hwy onto O'opuola St, near Ted's Bakery.

'Ehukai Beach Park   BEACH
(59-337 Ke Nui Rd) 'Ehukai Beach, aka Banzai Pipeline, aka Pipeline, aka Pipe – call it what you want, but if it's big surf you seek, this is *the* place. Pipeline is known the world over as one of the biggest, heaviest and closest-to-perfect barrels in all of wave riding. When the strong westerly swells kick up in winter the waves jack up to monster size, often reaching over 15ft before breaking on the ultrashallow reef below. For those who know what they're doing (and no, a day of surfing lessons at Waikiki doesn't count) this could very well be the holy grail of surfing.

For the non-world-class surfer this is a great venue to watch the best do their thing – the waves break only a few yards offshore, so spectators are front-row and center. In the summer months everything is calm and there is even some decent snorkeling off this beach – oh, how the seasons change!

The entrance to 'Ehukai Beach Park is opposite Sunset Beach Neighborhood Park. At the beach, there's a lifeguard tower, outdoor showers, restrooms and drinking water.

Pupukea Beach Park   BEACH
(59-727 Kamehameha Hwy) Pupukea Beach Park is a long beach further southwest along the highway that includes Three Tables to the south, Shark's Cove to the north and Old Quarry in between. Pupukea, meaning 'white shell,' is an unusually scenic beach, with deep blue waters, a varied coastline and a mix of lava and white sand. The waters off Pupukea Beach are protected as a marine-life conservation district.

The large boulders standing at the end of Kulalua Point, which marks the northernmost end of Pupukea Beach, are said to be followers of Pele, the Hawaiian goddess of fire and volcanoes. To acknowledge their loyalty (or in alternative tellings of the legend, to punish their nosiness for observing the goddess' passage from onshore), Pele made her followers immortal by turning them to stone.

There are outdoor showers, drinking water and restrooms in front of Old Quarry.

Shark's Cove

Shark's Cove is beautiful both above and below the water's surface. Don't worry too much about the cove's name – the white-tipped reef sharks here aren't usually aggressive unless you disturb or otherwise provoke them. Keep your distance and just don't approach.

In summer, when the seas are calm, Shark's Cove has super snorkeling conditions, as well as O'ahu's most popular cavern dive. A fair number of beginner divers take lessons here, while the underwater caves will thrill advanced divers.

To get to the caves, swim out of the cove and around to the right. Some of the caves are very deep and labyrinthine, and there have been a number of drownings, so divers should only venture into them with a local expert.

Old Quarry

The beach's natural rock features are jagged, sculpted and look as if they were cut by human hands, but rest assured that these features are natural. Coastal tide pools are interesting micro-habitats for marine creatures, best explored at low tide. Be careful, especially if you have kiddos in tow, because the rocks are razor sharp.

Three Tables

Three Tables gets its name from the flat ledges rising above the water. In summer when the waters are calm, Three Tables is good for snorkeling and diving. It's possible to see some action by snorkeling around the tables, but the best coral and fish, as well as some small caves, lava tubes and arches, are in deeper water further out. This is a summer-only spot! In winter dangerous rip currents flow between the beach and the tables. Watch for sharp rocks and coral, too – and, as always, don't touch the fragile reef.

Waimea Bay Beach Park   BEACH
(61-031 Kamehameha Hwy) It may be a beauty but it's certainly a moody one. Waimea Bay changes dramatically with the seasons: it can be tranquil and flat as a lake in summer, then savage in winter, with incredible surf waves the island's meanest rip currents.

Winter is prime time for surfers. On the calmer days bodyboarders are out in force, but even then sets come in hard and people get pounded. Winter water activities at this beach are *not* for novices. Typically the only days calm enough for swimming and snorkeling are between June and September.

This is the North Shore's most popular beach, so parking is often tight. Don't park along the highway, even if you see others doing so; police may tow away dozens of cars at once, particularly when surf competitions are happening. Beach facilities include restrooms, outdoor showers and drinking water. A lifeguard is on duty daily.

◉ Sights & Activities

Based in nearby Hale'iwa, Deep Ecology (p153) leads scuba diving trips around Waimea, including at Shark's Cove and Three Tables.

Waimea Valley   GARDEN
(📞638-7766; www.waimeavalley.net; 59-864 Kamehameha Hwy; adult/child 4-12 $13/6; ⊙9am-5pm; 🚼) Craving more jungle than beach? This 1800-acre Hawaiian cultural and nature park, just inland from Waimea Bay, is a sanctuary of tropical tranquility. Wander among the botanical gardens alongside Kamananui Stream or even take a dip at the base of 45ft-high Waimea Falls. Among the foliage you'll find up to 5000 native and exotic plant species.

Equally interesting are the replicas of buildings ancient Hawaiians dwelled in and a restored heiau (temple) dedicated to Lono, the traditional god of fertility and agriculture. Daily cultural activities like pounding poi, lei-making and hula lessons are aimed at the tour-bus crowd. Guided botanical walking tours are worth making time for; call ahead to check schedules.

Pu'u o Mahuka Heiau State Monument   HEIAU (TEMPLE)
A stellar view of the coast and a stroll around the grounds of O'ahu's largest temple reward those who venture up to this national historic landmark, perched on a bluff above Waimea.

Eddie Aikau was a legendary waterman and Waimea lifeguard. You only have to see Waimea on a stormy winter day to know the courage it takes to wade into the water to save a swimmer in trouble. But it was another act of heroism that spawned the slogan 'Eddie Would Go' you'll still see on bumper stickers around the islands.

In 1978 Eddie joined an expedition to re-create the Polynesian journey to Hawaii by sailing a replica double-hulled canoe from O'ahu to Tahiti and back. Soon after the craft left the shore it got into trouble and capsized in rough water. Eddie decided to go for help – he grabbed his surfboard and set off to paddle the almost 20 miles to shore to raise the alarm. Eddie was never seen again. His companions survived, but the legendary waterman was gone.

Named in memory of the late Eddie Aikau, an annual big-wave surfing event at Waimea Bay is perhaps the most prestigious and spiritual surf contest anywhere. It's invitation-only and only runs when waves are giant enough (ie 30ft minimum), meaning the bay picks the day. It doesn't happen every year and you can't predict the waves – but that's somehow fitting. People like Eddie are one in a million, and waves that honor his memory are worth the wait.

The temple's stacked stone construction is attributed to the legendary *menehune* (the 'little people' who, according to legend, built many of Hawaii's fishponds, heiau and other stonework), who are said to have completed their work in just one night. Pu'u O Mahuka means 'hill of escape' – but this was a *luakini* heiau, where human sacrifices took place.

Likely dating from the 16th century, the terraced stone walls are a few feet high of lava rocks. Collectively, the three adjoining enclosures that form the main body of the heiau are more than 550ft in length. It's a dramatic site for a temple, and worth the drive for the commanding view, especially at sunset.

Do not walk around inside the site, to avoid damaging it. To find it, turn *mauka* (inland) up Pupukea Rd at Foodland supermarket; the heiau turnoff is half a mile up, from where it's a roughshod 0.7 miles to the site.

Kaunala Loop Trail   HIKING, MOUNTAIN BIKING
Sitting quietly above Waimea Valley, the little-known Kaunala Loop Trail mixes an easy walk with a moderately steep ridge climb. After seeing the beauty of the bay from viewpoints high atop this trail, it's easy to see why Hawaiian royalty considered it sacred.

The 4.5-mile hike averages about two hours. This trail is officially open to the public only on weekends and state holidays. Hunting is allowed in the area, so hikers should wear bright colors and avoid wandering off the trail, which is also open to mountain bikers.

To get to the trailhead, turn *mauka* (inland) up Pupukea Rd at Foodland supermarket and continue for 2.5 miles until the road ends at a Boy Scout camp. Park in the lot and follow the Na Ala Hele signs to the trailhead.

Sleeping

Like on much of the North Shore, accommodations are thin on the ground here. The bulletin board at Pupukea's Foodland supermarket has notices of roommates wanted and occasional vacation-rental listings. Several vacation-home owners rely on word-of-mouth advertising and local real-estate agencies, for example, in nearby Hale'iwa (see p154).

Ke Iki Beach Bungalows   VACATION RENTALS **$$**
(☑638-8229, 866-638-8229; www.keikibeach.com; 59-579 Ke Iki Rd; 1 bedroom $155-215, 2 bedroom $175-230; ❄) Just north of Pupukea Beach Park, these hideaway retreats are furnished with tropical flair in floral prints and rattan chairs that fit the beachfront setting like a glove. Each of almost a dozen units has a full kitchen, TV and phone, and all guests have access to a BBQ, picnic tables and hammocks strung between coconut trees. The location is idyllic – oceanfront units are right on the sand, while others are just a minute's walk from the water.

Backpackers Vacation Inn & Plantation Village   HOSTEL, CABINS **$**
(☑638-7838; http://backpackers-hawaii.com; 59-788 Kamehameha Hwy; dm/d/studio/cabin from $30/72/130/175; @) The only budget option

in town, this scruffy backpacker-style village is a groovy place to stay. In keeping with the local vibe, digs are modest to the point of ramshackle. If you don't mind peeling paint and thrown-together decor, you'll feel right at home. The location can't be beat.

✕ Eating

TOP CHOICE Ted's Bakery   LOCAL, TAKEOUT $
(www.tedsbakery.com; 59-024 Kamehameha Hwy; dishes $1-8; ☺7am-6pm Mon & Tue, 7am-8pm Wed-Sun; ⊛) You can't get more North Shore than this quintessential drive-in joint. Famous island-wide, Ted's is the place for a quick bite or a huge mixed-plate lunch (think chicken katsu, teriyaki beef, BBQ pork, mahi mahi) that will feed two hungry surfers. The chocolate-haupia pie is legendary, but picky eaters have more than a dozen more flavors to choose from, including macadamia-nut cream and lilikoi-cheesecake.

Tacos Vicente   MEXICAN, TAKEOUT $
(Kamehameha Hwy; items $3-6, meals $8-12; ☺usually 11-4pm Thu & Sat) Spot this red-and-green truck parked on the *makai* (seaward) side of the highway near Sunset Beach. Rock up to the takeout window for a platter of tacos al pastor or a burrito stuffed with grilled meat or veggies, beans, cheese and rice, all washed down with a cinnamon-spiked *horchata* (rice drink). Check the website for current hours and locations.

Shark's Cove Grill   LOCAL, TAKEOUT $
(www.sharkscovegrill.com; 59-712 Kamehameha Hwy; dishes $7-15; ☺8:30am-8:30pm) This little roadside aquamarine-colored shack cranks out just-OK taro-bun breakfast sandwiches, fruit smoothies, and steak and seafood skewers on paper plates.

Foodland   SUPERMARKET $
(59-720 Kamehameha Hwy; ☺6am-11pm) Opposite Pupukea Beach Park, it has everything you need for a beach picnic, quick snack or more elaborate DIY meals.

Hale'iwa

POP 2285

The best way to know if the surf's up is by how busy Hale'iwa is. If the town is alive with activity, hustle and bustle, then chances are the surf is flat. If you arrive into town and find it eerily quiet, check the beach – odds are the waves are pumping. It's that sort of town: it's all about the surf and everyone knows it.

Despite being quite a touristy hub, there's a laid-back ambience to Hale'iwa that's in perfect concert with the rest of the North Shore. The biggest town around, this is the place to find a decent meal, to pick up a new T-shirt, to rent a longboard for the day and then hang around after sunset, wishing you could stay just a little bit longer.

⛱ Beaches

Hale'iwa has a picturesque boat harbor bounded on both sides by beach parks. The wave action attracts annual international surf competitions and lots of local attention, especially in winter.

Hale'iwa Ali'i Beach Park   BEACH
(66-167 Hale'iwa Rd) It's home to some of the best surf on the North Shore and as a result is a popular spot for surf contests. In late November the Triple Crown of Surfing gets underway on this break, bringing in the best surfers in the world. The waves here can be huge, with double or triple overhead tubes not uncommon.

When it's flat, the local kids rip it up with their bodyboards and mere mortals test their skills on the waves with stand up paddle boards (SUP). The shallow areas on the southern side of the beach are generally the calmest places to swim. The beach park has restrooms and lifeguards (trivia factoid: scenes from *Baywatch* were filmed here).

Hale'iwa Beach Park   BEACH
(62-449 Kamehameha Hwy) On the northern side of Waialua Bay, the park is protected by a shallow shoal and breakwater so the water is usually calm, and a good choice for swimming. There's little wave action, except for the occasional north swells that ripple into the bay.

Although the beach isn't as pretty as Hale'iwa's other strands, this community park has basketball and volleyball courts, a softball field, a children's playground, restrooms and outdoor showers. It also offers good views of Ka'ena Point far to the west.

Kaiaka Bay Beach Park   BEACH
(66-449 Hale'iwa Rd) Those wanting to get away from Hale'iwa can head less than a mile southwest of town. There are a few more trees here, so it's a good option when the mercury climbs and shade is necessary. Swimming is better at other local beaches,

however, so look elsewhere if you're looking to get wet. The park has restrooms, outdoor showers, picnic tables and campsites.

◉ Sights

In 1832 John and Ursula Emerson, the first missionaries to come to the North Shore, built Hale'iwa – meaning house (*hale*) of the great frigate bird *'iwa* – a grass house and missionary school on the banks of the Anahlu River that flows out of the harbor.

**North Shore Surf & Cultural
Museum**   MUSEUM
(☑637-8888; www.northshoresurfmuseum.com; North Shore Marketplace, 66-250 Kamehameha Hwy; admission by donation; ⊙usually noon-6pm Tue-Sun) It's impossible to separate surfing from the culture of the North Shore – the best place to see how deep that connection runs is hidden inside a shopping plaza. The little museum is packed with vintage boards, fading photographs and some great stories. Cool vintage memorabilia is for sale too. It's definitely worth a wander.

🏃 Activities

Surfing & Snorkeling

If you're a beginner board rider, the North Shore has a few tame breaks like Puaena Point, just north of Hale'iwa Beach Park, and Chun's Reef, north of town. Even if you've ridden a few waves in Waikiki, it's smart to take a lesson with one of the many freelancing surfers to get an introduction to local underwater hazards. Ask around for recommendations, or just turn up at the beach, where surf school vans rent gear and offer same-day instruction, including for stand up paddle boarding (SUP). Expect to pay from $75 for a two-hour group surfing lesson, or $30 to $45 to rent a board for the day (with paddle $60). Popular local surf schools and all-around water-sports outfitters include the following:

Surf 'n' Sea   RENTALS, LESSONS
(www.surfnsea.com; 62-595 Kamehameha Hwy; ⊙9am-7pm) Rents surfboards, paddles, wetsuits, car racks, snorkel sets, kayaks, beach umbrellas and chairs.

North Shore Surf Girls   LESSONS
(☑637-2977; www.northshoresurfgirls.com; 66-031 Kamehameha Hwy; ⊙by reservation) Board and paddle surfing lessons and camps with multilingual instructors.

Rainbow Watersports   LESSONS
(☑372-9304, 800-470-4964; www.rainbowwatersports.com; Hale'iwa Beach Park; ⊙by reserva-

TRIPLE CROWN OF SURFING

During the world's premier surfing event, the North Shore's **Triple Crown of Surfing** (www.triplecrownofsurfing .com), top pros compete for pride – and $1 million in prizes. For men, the kick-off leg is the Reef Hawaiian Pro held at Hale'iwa Ali'i Beach Park in mid-November. The second leg of the competition, the O'Neill World Cup of Surfing (late November to early December), rides at Sunset Beach. The final leg, the Billabong Pipe Masters, is in early to mid-December at Banzai Pipeline. Parallel events for world-class pro women surfers, who triple-crown their own queen, take place alongside the men's battles.

tion) Specializes in SUP, with lessons along flat-water rivers or beaches.

Sunset Surratt Surf Academy   LESSONS
(☑783-8657; http://sunsetsurattsurfschool.com) Learn to surf with pro coach Uncle Bryan, born and raised on the North Shore.

Deep Ecology   RENTALS
(☑637-7946; www.oahuscubadive.com; 66-456 Kamehameha Hwy; ⊙8am-5pm) Ecoconscious dive shop rents boogie boards and snorkel sets.

Scuba Diving & Whale Watching

Deep Ecology   RENTALS, TOURS
(☑637-7946, 800-578-3992; www.oahuscubadive .com; 66-456 Kamehameha Hwy; shore/boat dive from $109/139, whale-watching tour $80; ⊙8am-5pm) If you'd rather get under the waves as opposed to on top of them, the folks at Deep Ecology can sort you out. With a strong ecological bent, these divers are conscious about the ocean and lead dive trips with that in mind. Summer shore dives explore Shark's Cove and Three Tables in nearby Waimea, while offshore lava tubes, coral reefs, arches and cathedrals await boat divers. Rental scuba gear also available. Between January and April, tour boats head out for migratory whale watching, too.

🛏 Sleeping

Vacation rentals are the most common lodging in Hale'iwa, although there are a few B&Bs and fly-by-night hostels. Locals occasionally rent out rooms in their homes –

search Vacation Rentals By Owner (www.vrbo.com) online or check the bulletin boards at Malama Market and Celestial Natural Foods. For more sleeping options in nearby Waimea. There are no hotels or condos on the North Shore, except at Turtle Bay Resort (p148).

Hale'iwa's only campground is at Kaiaka Bay Beach Park, where the county allows camping except on Wednesday and Thursday nights. For advance permits (required), see p58.

Team Real Estate   VACATION RENTAL $$
(☏637-3507, 800-982-8602; www.teamrealestate.com; North Shore Marketplace; 66-250 Kamehameha Hwy; 1/2/3 bedroom from $100/150/200) This real-estate agency handles a couple dozen vacation rentals on the North Shore, running the gamut from duplex studio apartments and condos to multibedroom beachfront luxury homes. Most budgets can be accommodated, but book early, especially for the busy winter season.

✖ Eating & Drinking

Most of Hale'iwa's restaurants are along the Kamehameha Hwy, the main street.

Luibueno's   MEXICAN, SEAFOOD $$
(☏637-7717; www.luibueno.com; Hale'iwa Town Center, 66-165 Kamehameha Hwy; mains $7-25; ⏱11am-midnight) Solid Mexican food is what attracts crowds of locals and tourists alike to this sunset-colored faux-adobe hacienda. If you've never tried a beer-battered mahi taco or a big ol' grilled ahi burrito, here's your chance. Luibueno's also serves decent upmarket seafood and steaks. An après-surf crowd hogs the bar while knocking back margaritas during twice-daily '*bueno*' happy hours.

Kua 'Aina   BURGERS $
(www.kua-aina.com; 66-160 Kamehameha Hwy; mains $7-10; ⏱11am-8pm; ⊙) Want some of the best burgers in all of O'ahu? Look no further then this North Shore classic. Kua 'Aina has a list of monster-sized burgers and sandwiches a mile long: take your pick of grilled ahi or mahimahi with Ortega cheese, teriyaki chicken, peppery eggplant or pineapple-topped North Shore grass-fed beef patties with homemade fries.

Café Hale'iwa   BREAKFAST, BRUNCH $
(66-460 Kamehameha Hwy; mains $5-10; ⏱7am-12:30pm Mon-Sat, 7am-2pm Sun; ⊙) This laid-back surf-style diner been hanging around

a corner in Hale'iwa since the 1980s. Before a day out paddling the waves, fuel up at a table on the sunny patio with an 'off the wall' omelette or 'breakfast in a barrel' (ie a Mexican burrito splashed with green salsa). The joint's kid-friendly, too.

Grass Skirt Grill   LOCAL, TAKEOUT $
(66-214 Kamehameha Hwy; mains $7-13; ⏱11am-6pm) It's Hale'iwa's micro-tiki room, with retro surf decor on the walls that fits right in with the local fare of island-style mixed plates, seafood specialties (try the juicy ahi steak) and luau salads. Popular with locals, it's great for a takeout meal when you're bound for the beach.

Banzai Sushi   JAPANESE $$
(North Shore Marketplace, 66-246 Kamehameha Hwy; mains $10-20; ⏱noon-9:30pm) It's all about atmosphere at the North Shore's only sushi bar, where surf videos scroll on the walls and live bands jam on weekends. Classic nigiri and nouveau fusion rolls are just okay, and service can be slooooww. Happy hour rocks.

Hale'iwa Joe's   SEAFOOD, STEAK $$
(☏637-8005; www.haleiwajoes.com; 66-011 Kamehameha Hwy; mains lunch $9-20, dinner $17-30; ⏱11:30am-9:30pm Sun-Thu, to 10pm Fri & Sat) Scenically overlooking the marina, Hale'iwa Joe's is frankly overrated. Freshness is the goal, with some seafood coming from the boats seen out the windows, but the execution just doesn't live up to this place's reputation. Stick with cocktails and creative *pu-pus* instead.

Hale'iwa Farmers Market   FARMERS MARKET $
(www.haleiwafarmersmarket.com; junction Kamehameha Hwy & Joseph Leong Hwy; ⏱9am-1pm Sun; ⊘) At the north end of town, where the bypass road splits, 40 vendors sell organic, seasonal edibles and artisan crafts.

Storto's Deli   DELI, TAKEOUT $
(66-215 Kamehameha Hwy; sandwiches $5-8; ⏱10am-6pm) Made-to-order hoagie sandwich shop is da bomb. Just don't feed those aggro chickens outside!

Waialua Bakery   BAKERY, TAKEOUT $
(66-200 Kamehameha Hwy; items $2-8; ⊘) Hidden off a parking lot, drop by for home-baked goodies, deli sandwiches, açai fruit bowls and fresh smoothies.

Celestial Natural Foods   GROCERIES $
(66-443 Kamehameha Hwy; ⏱9am-6pm Mon-Sat, 10am-6pm Sun; ⊘) Hole-in-the-wall

that stocks good-karma organic produce and groceries, plus there's a tiny vegan-friendly cafe.

Malama Market   SUPERMARKET $
(66-190 Kamehameha Hwy; ⊙7am-9pm) Grab a quick bite from the deli and stock up on picnic fixin's at this modern supermarket.

🛍 Shopping

Hale'iwa is the best place on the North Shore to undertake some retail therapy. From trendy to quirky, most of the town's shops and galleries are either in or nearby **North Shore Marketplace** (66-250 Kamehameha Hwy).

Turtles & More   ART, SOUVENIRS
(66-218 Kamehameha Hwy; ⊙10:30am-5:30pm) If your digital snaps just don't measure up, photos from this gallery will surely impress the gang back home. Browse stunning underwater images of sea life with some killer surfing shots thrown in.

Oceans in Glass   CRAFTS, SOUVENIRS
(North Shore Marketplace, 66-250 Kamehameha Hwy; ⊙10am-6pm) Who says glass baubles are just for Gramma? Handmade fish, turtles and dolphins are made before your very eyes and, even better, replaced for free if you break 'em on the way home.

Barnfield's Raging Isle Surf   CLOTHING, OUTDOORS
(www.ragingisle.com; North Shore Marketplace, 66-250 Kamehameha Hwy; ⊙10am-6:30pm) Packed full of beachwear, surfboards, skateboards and anything else you might need for life on the North Shore.

Guava   CLOTHING
(http://guavahawaii.com; 66-165 Kamehameha Hwy; ⊙10am-6pm) Chic, beachy boutique for women's apparel like kimono-patterned sundresses, sexy bikinis, hip denim and strappy sandals.

North Shore Swimwear   CLOTHING
(www.northshoreswimwear.com; North Shore Marketplace, 66-250 Kamehameha Hwy; ⊙10am-6pm) Ground zero for fashionable women's wet-and-wild styles, all free to mix and match. Custom orders are handmade in Hawaii.

Growing Keiki   CLOTHING, TOYS
(66-051 Kamehameha Hwy; ⊙usually 10am-6pm; 🐾) This kids' shop has gear for junior surf grommets and budding beach bun-

MOBILE MEALS

On the south side of Hale'iwa town, between the bridge and the round-about, pull over for a **food truck lot** where takeout meals and plate lunches go for around $6 to $12 each. Locals hotly debate which trucks grills the best shrimp, but almost everyone agrees that **Opal** is tops for Thai food, while **Holy Smokes** is the BBQ champ. Back in the center of town, **Roy's Kiawe Broiled Chicken** is another smokin' hot pick-up food truck.

nies, including mini aloha shirts, trunks and toys.

Global Creations & Interiors   SOUVENIRS
(www.globalcreationscart.com; 66-079 Kamehameha Hwy; ⊙10am-6pm) Funky, floral and colorful island-themed shop for clothing, jewelry, housewares, art, music and more.

Hale'iwa Art Gallery   ART, SOUVENIRS
(www.haleiwaartgallery.com; North Shore Marketplace, 66-252 Kamehameha Hwy; ⊙10am-6pm) Featuring works by 20-plus local and regional painters, photographs, sculptors and mixed-media artists, from the kitschy to the dramatic.

ℹ Information

Coffee Gallery (☑637-5355; North Shore Marketplace, 66-250 Kamehameha Hwy; per 30min $3; ⊙6:30am-8pm; @🛜) Pay-as-you-go internet terminals; free wi-fi.

First Hawaiian Bank (Hale'iwa Town Center, 66-135 Kamehameha Hwy; ⊙8:30am-4pm Mon-Thu, to 6pm Fri) With a 24-hour ATM.

Longs Drugs (☑637-9393; Hale'iwa Shopping Plaza, 66-197 Kamehameha Hwy; ⊙8am-8pm Mon-Sat, 8am-7pm Sun) Pharmacy and convenience store.

Post office (66-437 Kamehameha Hwy; ⊙8am-4pm Mon-Fri, 9am-noon Sat) At the south end of town.

Waialua

POP 3860

If you find the relatively slow pace of life on the North Shore just too hectic, head over to Waialua. This sugar-mill town ground to a halt in 1996, when the mill shut for good. Since then, creative locals have trans-

SHAVE ICE

O'ahu's classic circle-island drive just isn't complete without stopping for shave ice at **Matsumoto's** (www .matsumotoshaveice.com; 66-087 Kamehameha Hwy; ⊙9am-6pm; 🚻) tin-roofed 1950s general store. Some families drive from Honolulu to the North Shore with one goal only in mind: to stand in line here and walk out with a delicious shave ice cone, drenched with island flavors, such as *liliko'i* (passion fruit), banana, mango and pineapple.

Tourists flock to Matsumoto's, but some locals prefer **Aoki's** (www.aokis shaveice.com; 66-117 Kamehameha Hwy; ⊙11am-6:30pm), which does have much shorter lines. But the souvenir T-shirts aren't nearly as cool as at Matsumoto's.

formed the old mill into a crafty, island-born shopping complex.

Yet the area remains economically depressed, with many of the surrounding fields overgrown with feral sugarcane. Other sections are newly planted with coffee trees – a labor-intensive crop that holds promise for job creation. You can see the coffee trees, planted in neat rows, as you come down the slopes into Waialua.

The **Waialua Farmers Market** (⊙8:30am-2pm Sat, 4:30-7:30pm Wed) sets up nearby the sugar mill. Some former sugar-plantation workers now farm small plots of land leased from Dole Food Company, an agreement reached to help displaced workers after the mill's closure. Surfboard makers and artisan craft vendors also keep this market lively.

✗ Eating

Nui's Thai   THAI, TAKEOUT **$**
(www.nuisthaifood.com; 67-196 Goodale Ave; ⊙10:30am-6:30pm) A Bangkok-born cook oversees the kitchen squeezed inside this roadside lunch truck, with a few picnic tables out front. Flavors tend toward the tame (ask for extra-spicy), but the big plates of traditional curries, stir-fried noodles and savory salads are still satisfying.

Pa'ala'a Kai Bakery & Market   BAKERY, TAKEOUT **$**
(www.pkbsweets.com; 66-945 Kaukonahua Rd; ⊙5:30am-8pm) Take a detour down a coun-

try road to find this family-run bakery, a pilgrimage for anyone craving a 'snow puffy' (flaky chocolate cream puff dusted with powdered sugar).

🛍 Shopping

Waialua Sugar Mill (www.sugarmillhawaii.com) has been redeveloped into an ever-changing hub for locally owned shops and businesses.

North Shore Soap Factory CRAFTS, SOUVENIRS (Old Sugar Mill, 67-106 Kealohanui St; ⊙9am-6pm Mon-Sat, 10am-5pm Sun) Peek through the glass and watch the soapmakers craft their bars, all made with local ingredients such as *kukui* (candlenut tree) nuts and coconut cream.

Island X Hawaii   SOUVENIRS (Old Sugar Mill, 67-106 Kealohanui St; ⊙9am-5pm Mon-Fri, 8:30am-5pm Sat, 10am-5pm Sun) Rambling warehouse that stocks everything from cheap aloha shirts to original and vintage art pieces, plus Waialua coffee, chocolate and soda.

Mokule'ia to Ka'ena Point

Hello? Is there anybody out there? These empty stretches show the last few signs of human habitation before the island terminates in the deep and fearsome ocean. Farrington Hwy (Hwy 930) runs west from Thompson's Corner toward Ka'ena. The road along the Wai'anae Coast is also called Farrington Hwy, but these roads don't connect – each side reaches a dead end about 2½ miles short of Ka'ena Point.

🏖 Beaches

Mokule'ia Beach Park   BEACH (68-919 Farrington Hwy) Keen windsurfers often congregate on this stretch of shore, taking advantage of the consistent winds. The beach park sports a large grassy area with picnic tables, restrooms and outdoor showers. The beach itself is a nice sandy stretch, but the rocky seabed makes for poor swimming. When waters are calm and flat in summer, snorkelers swim out along the shallow reef. During winter, the currents pick up and entering the water isn't advisable. No lifeguards.

Mokule'ia Army Beach   BEACH Opposite the western end of Dillingham Airfield, this is the widest stretch of sand on the Mokule'ia shore. Once reserved for military personnel, the beach is now open to the public, although it's no longer maintained and there are no facilities. The beach is also unprotected and has very strong rip currents, especially during high winter surf.

Ka'ena Point
BEACH

From Mokulei'a Army Beach you can drive another 1.6 miles down the road, passing still more white-sand beaches with aqua blue waters. The terrain is scrubland reaching up to the base of the Wai'anae Range, while the shoreline is wild and windswept. The area is not only desolate, but can also be a bit trashed. Graffiti, empty liquor bottles and car break-ins are all commonplace.

Farrington Hwy ends at the beginning of a dirt footpath leading out to Ka'ena Point, which connects to the Wai'anae Coast. You can hike or mountain-bike around the point, but to get to the other side by car, you'll need to backtrack through Central O'ahu and up the Wai'anae Coast, about a 50-mile trip that takes over an hour.

⚔ Activities

Skydiving & Glider Rides
All operations are headquartered at Dillingham Airfield.

Honolulu Soaring Club
GLIDER RIDES

(☑637-0207; www.honolulusoaring.com; 69-132 Farrington Hwy; ⊙10am-5:30pm) The trade winds that visit O'ahu create perfect conditions for sailplanes to glide over the North Shore. Prices start at $80 for 10 minutes, rising to $305 for an aerobatic one-hour flight with a hands-on mini lesson. Call ahead, as flights are weather-dependent.

Pacific Skydiving Center
SKYDIVING

(☑637-7472; www.pacific-skydiving.com; 68-760 Farrington Hwy; jumps per person $180-320; ⊙8am-3pm) Wanna get tossed out of a perfectly good airplane, preferably with a parachute attached? Novices can take a tandem jump attached to an instructor for the stomach-turning 14,000ft freefall, followed by a 15-minute glide back to earth. No scuba diving allowed for 24 hours prior to jumping. Japanese spoken.

Hiking
Ascending from Dillingham Airfield, the **Kealia Trail** (Map p56) switchbacks its way up the cliffs, offering ocean views along the way, through a forest of ironwoods and *kukui* trees. The Kealia Trail is great for anyone wishing to avoid the hassle of securing a permit and driving up the Wai'anae (Leeward) Coast just to hike

the **Kuaokala Trail**, which reaches a justly celebrated viewpoint over Makua Valley and the Wai'anae Range.

The Kealia Trail starts at the back of Dillingham Airfield. Enter via the West Gate and just before the airfield ends, take the road marked Gate D and follow it inland about 0.4 miles. Park in the air control tower parking lot, then walk 0.3 miles down the access road on the right and look for a brown-and-yellow Na Ala Hele trailhead marker. Give yourself three hours to walk the 5-mile round-trip Kealia Trail, plus 2½ more hours if you add the Kuaokala Loop.

If all that walking sounds like too much work, all of these trails are also open to mountain bikes. Whether you're on foot or bicycle, watch out for rockfalls.

🛏 Sleeping

Camp Mokule'ia
CAMPGROUND $

(☑637-6241; www.visitcampmokuleia.com; 68-729 Farrington Hwy; campsites per person $15; ⊙office 8:30am-5pm Mon-Fri, 10am-5pm Sat) Those wanting to really escape from the tourist scene may find solace here. Opposite Dillingham Airfield, this church-run camp is open to travelers as long as there isn't a prebooked group on the site. Amenities are ultrabasic, with outdoor showers and chemical toilets. Give the well-worn lodge rooms, cabins and beach cottage a miss. Open by reservation only.

CENTRAL O'AHU

Central O'ahu is the island's forgotten backwater. Squeezed between giant military reservations and the hip, laid-back North Shore, it's more of a thoroughfare then a destination unto itself. Three routes head north from Honolulu to Wahiawa, the region's central

---

NOT LOST AFTER ALL

Does Mokulei'a Army Beach look familiar? It appeared in the pilot of the hit TV drama *Lost*. When *Lost* first started filming here, tourists driving along the highway would see the smokin' wreckage of a crashed plane sitting on the beach. Needless to say a burned-out 747 is an alarming site, and many called emergency services to mistakenly report an emergency.

town. The H-2 Fwy is the fastest route. Kunia Rd (750), the furthest west, is the most scenic. The least interesting of the options, Farrington Hwy (Hwy 93), catches local traffic. Onward from Wahiawa, two routes – rural Kaukonahua Rd (Hwy 803) and busy Kamehameha Hwy (Hwy 99) – lead through pineapple plantation country to the North Shore.

Wahiawa

POP 16,590

This town itself isn't the sort of destination that most travelers seek out. That is, of course, unless you're looking for a new tattoo, a military buzz cut or shiny rims for your lowrider.

◎ Sights & Activities

FREE **Dole Plantation** THEME PARK
(☑621-8408; 64-1550 Kamehameha Hwy (Hwy 99); ◎9:30am-5:30pm; ▮) Less than 3 miles north of town, this busy tourist complex has a split personality. Outdoors the mega-sized maze and miniature train are great fun for kids. Inside the gift shop is overflowing with pineapple-themed tacky tourist kitsch. It's a sickly sweet overdose of everything pineapple – the final touch being pineapples for sale for 20% more than at the grocery store in town.

After you've devoured a cone of frozen pineapple whip, get hopelessly lost in the 'world's largest' maze (adult/child 4-12yr $6/4), as verified by Guinness World Records in 2008. It's truly a gigantic undertaking, with over 2.5 miles of pathways. The goal is to find eight secret stations before making your way out. You'd better be quick if you want to beat the current record of six minutes – most people take 30 minutes, and the geographically challenged can take *hours*.

A vintage-style steam train (adult/child $8/6) chugs around the plantation, taking budding engineers and conductors for a 2-mile, 20-minute ride. Or take a self-guided audio walking tour (adult/child $5/4.25) of the plantation's bountiful gardens for an up-close look at pineapple, banana, mango, papaya, coffee, cacao and other imported exotic and native Polynesian plants.

FREE **Wahiawa Botanical Garden** GARDEN
(1396 California Ave; ◎9am-4pm) While much of Wahiawa is drab, grey and bordering on ugly, this botanical garden just over a mile east of Kamehameha Hwy (Hwy 83) is a slice of arboreal heaven. Nature lovers and gardeners will delight in the rollicking grounds that stretch for 27 acres.

Started in the 1920s as an experiment by local sugarcane farmers, the garden is a mix of the manicured, with beautiful lawns and pruned ornamental plants, and the wild, through a gully of towering hardwoods, tropical ferns and bamboo groves. Several paths weave their way through the garden, about half of which are wheelchair-friendly. Enthusiastic volunteers will answer questions and point you in the right direction.

✕ Eating

Maui Mike's BBQ, TAKEOUT $
(96 S Kamehameha Hwy; meals $5-9; ◎11am-8:30pm) At this island fast-food joint, you have your choice of chicken, chicken or chicken, all fire-roasted and so fresh it was clucking when you woke up this morning. Grab some BBQ dipping sauce and Cajun-spiced fries, too.

Sunny Side LOCAL, DINER $
(1017 Kilani Ave; meals $4-8; ◎7am-2pm) Down a side street, the parking lot looks like a motocross track and the last renovations were done a half century ago: think plastic furniture and faded photographs. All is forgotten when the homestyle cooking arrives – save room for wickedly delicious pie.

Da Pokeman SEAFOOD, TAKEOUT $
(36 N Kamehameha Hwy; plate lunch $7-10; ◎10:30am-6pm Mon-Sat) Take your pick of fresh *poke* (kimchi or spicy tuna, anyone?) at the front of this hole-in-the-wall market. Keep it local with a pork laulau or butterfish plate lunch.

Kolekole Pass

The rural landscape of plantation fields unfolds along Kunia Rd (Hwy 750) until you pass by Schofield Barracks Military Reservation. This massive army base is the largest on O'ahu and is a hive of activity – it's not uncommon to be passed on the highway by camo-painted Humvees while a Black Hawk chopper hovers overhead.

At 1724ft, Kolekole Pass occupies the gap in the Wai'anae Range that WWII Japanese fighter planes only appeared to have flown through on their way to bomb Pearl Harbor. Film buffs may recognize the landscape, as the historic flight was re-created here three decades later for the classic war film *Tora! Tora! Tora!*

Kolekole Pass, on military property above Schofield Barracks, can be visited as long as the base isn't on military alert. Bring photo ID and your rental-car contract or proof of vehicle insurance. Access is granted by the security guards at Lyman Gate off Hwy 750, under a mile south of Hwy 750's intersection with Hwy 99. Follow Lyman Rd over 5 miles, passing a military infantry battle course, to reach the pass. Park on the left side of the road before reaching a security gate (without military ID, you can't keep driving over to the coast).

From a dirt parking pull-off, a short, steep hiking path with wooden steps leads for 10 minutes up to a viewpoint. En route you'll pass a large, ribbed stone allegedly used by ancient Hawaiians for ritual sacrifices of fallen warrior *ali'i* (chiefs). In Hawaiian mythology, the stone is also believed to be the embodiment of a woman named Kolekole, who took this form in order to become the perpetual guardian of the pass. If you touch the stone, bad luck may follow, locals say.

Honouliuli Forest Reserve

Honouliuli Forest Reserve is home to nearly 70 rare and endangered plant and animal species. The land once belonged to Hawaiian royalty and was named Honouliuli ('dark harbor') for the dark, fertile *ahupua'a* (an ancient land division) that stretched from the waters of Pearl Harbor to the summit of the Wai'anae Range.

At press time, public access to the forest reserve's hiking trails on the slopes of the Wai'anae Range was temporarily suspended. Check the Na Ala Hele website (http://hawaiitrails.ehawaii.gov) to see if any trails have since reopened and for current volunteer opportunities to combat invasive species and help maintain trails.

Hawaii's Plantation Village

The lives of the people who came to Hawaii to work on the sugarcane plantations are examined at Hawaii's Plantation Village (☑677-0110; www.hawaiiplantationvillage.org; 94-695 Waipahu St, Waipahu; adult/child 4-11yr $13/5; ⊙90min tours start on the hour 10am-2pm Mon-Sat). Waipahu was one of O'ahu's last planta-

TASTY TIDBITS

» In 1901 James Dole planted O'ahu's first pineapple patch in Wahiawa.

» Today, each acre of a pineapple field can support around 30,000 plants.

» The commercial variety of pineapple grown in Hawaii is smooth cayenne.

» It takes nearly two years for a pineapple plant to reach maturity.

» Each plant usually produces just two pineapples, one in its second year and one in its third year, after which it's knocked down.

» Pineapples are harvested year-round, but the long, sunny days of summer produce the sweetest fruit.

» Pineapples are unusual among fruits in that they don't continue to ripen after they're picked.

tion towns, and its rusty sugar mill, which operated for almost a century until being shut down in 1995, still looms on a knoll directly above this site.

This dusty, spread-out educational center is aimed primarily at schoolchildren's tours. It encompasses two dozen buildings typical of an early-20th-century plantation village, including a community bathhouse, a Japanese Shintō shrine and authentically replicated homes of the ethnic groups – Hawaiian, Japanese, Chinese, Korean, Portuguese, Puerto Rican and Filipino – who labored on the plantations.

To get to the village by car from Honolulu, take the H1 to exit 7, turn left onto Paiwa St, then right onto Waipahu St, continue past the sugar mill and turn left into the complex. Otherwise, take TheBus 42 from Waikiki, which stops about a half-mile downhill.

WAI'ANAE COAST (LEEWARD O'AHU)

O'ahu's lost coast is full of contradictions. There is a collective feeling of the forgotten here, with the wealthy of Honolulu sweeping what they don't want in their backyard under the Wai'anae rug. You'll find the garbage dump, the power plant and the economically disadvantaged all living here.

While you might imagine this as depressing, it's quite the contrary. The Wai'anae (Leeward) Coast is in some ways the heart and soul of O'ahu. You'll find more Native Hawaiians here than anyplace else, and cultural pride is alive. The land may be dry, with mountains that seem to push you into the sea, but the beaches are wide, untouched by tourism, and the community spirit of aloha is authentic.

Farrington Hwy (Hwy 93) runs the length of the Wai'anae Coast, scooting past working-class neighborhoods and strip malls on one side with gorgeous white-sand beaches on the other. Further up the coast habitation yields to the velvet-tufted mountains and rocky coastal ledges leading to the sacred tip of the island at Ka'ena Point.

Ko Olina Resort

No beach? No problem. All it takes is a little bit of lateral thinking and a couple of thousand tons of imported sand. When this resort was still on the drawing board it lacked the signature feature that is key for all Hawaiian resorts – a beach. In exchange for public access, investors were allowed to carve out four kidney-shaped lagoons and line them with soft white sand.

Today these artificial beaches are worth a visit – the calm waters are perfect for kids, although the current picks up near the opening to the ocean. To peer at the rainbow-colored tropical fish circling underwater, rent snorkel sets at the biggest lagoon, furthest north. A wide, paved recreational path connects all four lagoons, inviting a lazy stroll. Limited free public beach-access parking can be found at each lagoon, off Aliinui Dr inside the resort area. From Honolulu airport, it's about a 30-minute drive via the Farrington Hwy (Hwy 93), or longer in rush-hour traffic.

For the energetic, the resort also features the touring pro–worthy **Ko Olina Golf Club** (☑676-5300; 92-1220 Aliinui Dr, Kapolei; www.koolinagolf.com; greens fee $110-170, rental clubs $50, round-trip transportation from Waikiki $10; ⊗tee times by reservation only). Book the decadent **Ihilani Spa** (☑679-3321; www.ihilanispa.com; JW Marriott Ihilai Resort, 92-1001 Olina St, Kapolei; 50min massage from $140; ⊗by appointment only 7am-7pm daily) if you're in need of a little pampering instead.

🛌 Sleeping & Eating

JW Marriott Ihilani Resort RESORT $$$
(☑679-0079, 800-626-4446; www.ihilani.com; 92-1001 Olina St, Kapolei; r $290-795; ❋@🛜🏊⛱🐾) Right on the beach, but extremely isolated from the rest of the island, this resort hotel is palatial and architecturally soothing. Given its remoteness and sky-high room rates, it's still inexplicably popular with first-time visitors, families with kids, and anyone avoiding the Waikiki scene who still wants all the trappings of mainstream luxury. Hollywood has checked in here – the Ihilani is where the surfer girls worked in the movie *Blue Crush*. For high-end Hawaii regional cuisine, book a table for dinner at the hotel's Azul restaurant or Roy's Ko Olina at the golf club.

Ko Olina Hawaiian Bar-b-que LOCAL, TAKEOUT $
(92-1047 Olina St, Kapolei; meals $8-15; ⊗9am-9pm; 🐾) Escape Ko Olina's high-dollar resort dining rooms for full-on plate lunches of mochiko fried chicken, BBQ short ribs, teriyaki beef, pork katsu and much more, all served with brown rice and green salad options. It's hidden in a strip mall on the resort grounds, nearby an ABC Store selling snacks, drinks and everything else for a day at the beach.

Pho & Co VIETNAMESE $
(890 Kamokila Blvd, Kapolei; meals $6-10; ⊗10am-9pm Mon-Fri, 11am-9pm Sat, 11am-7pm Sun) Locals say you can't miss the *pho* (beef noodle soup) at this strip-mall storefront also serving spring rolls, rice plates, crunchy sandwiches and bubble tea.

Marketplace at Kapolei INTERNATIONAL, TAKEOUT $
(http://themarketplaceatkapolei.com; 590 Farrington Hwy, Kapolei; meals $6-10; 🐾) This down-to-earth strip mall is stuffed with pan-Asian noodle joints, island BBQ, East Coast–style pizza, a pancake house and a Safeway supermarket with a deli.

Kahe Point

A hulking power plant complete with towering smokestacks isn't the best neighbor to a beach. At **Kahe Point Beach Park** (92-301 Farrington Hwy), there isn't actually a beach, just a rocky point that's popular with fishers and snorkelers who are good swimmers and can handle strong currents. There are great panoramas looking north, as well as picnic tables, restrooms and outdoor showers, but no lifeguards.

Further north of Kahe Point lies Hawaiian Electric Beach. Locals have nicknamed this stretch of sand **Tracks** after the train that once transported beachgoers here from Honolulu prior to WWII. The sandy shores are good for swimming in summer and great for surfing in winter.

Nanakuli

Nanakuli, the biggest town on the Wai'anae Coast, is the site of a Hawaiian Homesteads settlement with one of the largest Native Hawaiian populations on O'ahu. But all you'll likely see from the highway is a strip of fast-food joints.

Nanakuli Beach Park (89-269 Farrington Hwy) fronts a broad, sandy beach that lines the town, offering swimming, snorkeling and diving during the calmer summer season. In winter high surf can create rip currents and dangerous shore-breaks. As an in-town community park, there's also a playground, sports fields, picnic tables and full beach facilities. To get to here, turn *makai* (seaward) at the traffic lights on Nanakuli Ave.

Ma'ili

Ma'ili has a long, grassy roadside park with a seemingly endless stretch of white beach. Like other places on this coast, ocean conditions at Ma'ili Beach Park are often treacherous in winter (which pleases local surfers), but calm enough for swimming in summer. There's a lifeguard station and run-down beach facilities. Coconut palms provide scant shade.

Wai'anae

POP 10,790

Wai'anae is the leeward coast's hub for everyday services, from grocery stores to the commercial boat harbor and a well-used beach park.

🏝 Beaches & Sights

Poka'i Bay Beach Park   BEACH
(85-037 Wai'anae Valley Rd) Protected by Kane'ilio Point and a long breakwater, this beach features the Wai'anae Coast's calmest year-round swimming. Waves seldom break inside the bay, and the sandy

sea floor slopes gently, making the beach a popular spot for families. Snorkeling is fair near the breakwater, where fish gather around the rocks. You can watch local canoe clubs rowing in the late afternoon and lots of family luau on weekends. There are restrooms, outdoor showers, drinking water and picnic tables, and a lifeguard on duty daily.

Ku'ilioloa Heiau   HISTORICAL SITE
Kane'ilio Point, along the south side of the bay, is the site of this stone temple, partly destroyed by the army during WWII and later reconstructed by local conservationists. To get here, turn *makai* (seaward) onto Lualualei Homestead Rd from Farrington Hwy and park in the public beach lot, then walk toward the sea. At the foot of the heiau, if the waves aren't crashing strongly, you'll find little tidepools harboring marine life, too.

🍴 Eating

At strip malls alongside Farrington Hwy, it's all local grinds, all the time.

Kahumana Cafe   HEALTH FOOD $$
(☎696-8844; http://kahumanafarms.org; 86-660 Lualualei Homestead Rd; meals $8-13; ⊗11:30am-2:30pm & 6-7:30pm Tue-Sat; ☑) Off the beaten track, this organic farm's nonprofit cafe inhabits a cool, tranquil hardwood-floored dining room with green field views. Fork into fresh daily specials, bountiful salads, macadamia-nut pesto pasta, international veggie stir-fries and wraps, and homemade lilikoi and mango cheesecake. Call ahead to check if they're open. The farm is about 2 miles *mauka* (inland) from Farrington Hwy via Ma'ili'ili Rd.

Ono Polynesian Market POLYNESIAN, TAKEOUT $
(85-998 Farrington Hwy; meals $6-10; ⊗7am-9pm) Ready for a true taste of the South Seas? This ramshackle little market across the street from the beach dishes up takeout treats like Samoan *palusami* (corned beef wrapped in taro leaves and slow-cooked in coconut milk) and pan-Polynesian curries.

Barbeque Kai   LOCAL, TAKEOUT $
(85-973 Farrington Hwy; mains $4-8; ⊗8am-8pm) On sunny days, the tables out front at this classic drive-in are overflowing with local crews. Island-style mixed plates, burgers and other *'ono grinds* populate the signboard menu.

Tacos & More   MEXICAN $

(85-993 Farrington Hwy; mains $7-12; ☺11am-8pm Sun-Thu, 11am-9pm Fri & Sat) Owned by a family who started out in Mexico City, this ever-expanding Mexican cantina (vegetarian options available) is a local favorite showing plenty of aloha.

Makaha

POP 7695

Free of the gawking tourists of the North Shore, Makaha is where big-wave surfing got its start in the 1950s. Makaha means 'ferocious,' and while in days past the valley was notorious for the bandits who waited along the cliffs to ambush passing travelers, the word could just as easily describe the rugged landscape. Today Makaha offers year-round world-class surfing, a fine beach and O'ahu's best-restored heiau (temple).

Beaches & Sights

Makaha Beach Park   BEACH

(84-369 Kamehameha Hwy) With a history of big-wave surfing that ranks among the richest on the island, Makaha is a beautiful arcing beach with a soft stretch of sand that invites you to spread out your towel and spend the day. The beach has showers and restrooms, and lifeguards are on duty.

Makaha Beach hosted Hawaii's first international surfing competition in 1954, and the long point break here produced the waves that inspired the first generation of big-wave surfers. It's still possible to rekindle that pioneering feeling, as you're likely to have the place virtually to yourself.

Winter months bring big swells that preclude swimming much of the time – the golden sand, however, is a permanent feature. In summer when the water is calmer, you can snorkel with sea turtles or take a dive trip to offshore Makaha Caverns.

Kane'aki Heiau   HEIAU (TEMPLE)

(☏695-8174; admission free; ☺10am-2pm Tue-Sun) Hidden within the Makaha Valley, this quietly impressive temple is one of O'ahu's best-restored sacred sites. Originally an agricultural temple dedicated to Lono, the Hawaiian god of agriculture and fertility, the site was later used as a *luakini*, a type of temple dedicated to the war god Ku and a place for human sacrifices. Kamehameha the Great worshipped here and it remained in use until the time of his death in 1819.

Restoration, undertaken by the Bishop Museum and completed in 1970, added two prayer towers, a *kapu* (taboo) house, drum house, altar and god images. The heiau was reconstructed using traditional ohia tree logs and *pili* (a type of Hawaiian grass used for thatching buildings) from the Big Island. The immediate setting surrounding the heiau remains undisturbed, though it's in the midst of a residential estate.

To get here, turn *mauka* (inland) off Farrington Hwy onto Makaha Valley Rd. After just over a mile, follow Huipu Dr as it briefly curves left, then right. Turn right again onto Mauna Olu St, which leads into Mauna Olu Estates. Half a mile ahead, the security guard allows nonresidents to visit the heiau, which is just a short drive past the gatehouse. Public access can be inconsistent, so call in advance, especially during (and immediately after) wet weather.

Sleeping

Out-of-the-way local accommodations include beachside condos and an inland hotel.

Makaha Resort & Golf Club   HOTEL $$

(☏695-9544; www.makaharesort.net; 84-626 Makaha Valley Rd; r from $100; ✿@☎☀) Straight from the 1970s, this decidedly retro establishment at least offers panoramic views of the valley and the ocean far below. Generic rooms are outdated, but with a golf course and tennis courts right out the door, sporty types or anyone looking for a quiet getaway might not mind too much. Wi-fi in lobby and poolside.

Hawaii Hatfield Realty   CONDO RENTALS $$

(☏696-4499; www.hawaiiwest.com; Suite 201, 85-833 Farrington Hwy, Wai'anae; studio/1 bedroom from $75/100) Handles vacation-rental condos and long-term rentals.

Makua Valley

Wide and grassy, backed by a fan of sharply fluted mountains, this scenic valley is the controversial location of the Makua Military Reservation's infantry and artillery range. A seaside road opposite the southern end of the reservation leads to a little graveyard that's shaded by yellow-flowered trees. This site is all that remains of the Makua Valley community, which was forced to evacuate during WWII when the US military took over the entire valley for bombing practice.

War games still take place in the valley, which is fenced off with barbed wire and signs that warn of stray explosives. A citizens' coalition led by Earthjustice legal defense fund has filed a suit against the US Army for allegedly failing to properly assess environmental impacts, including on Native Hawaiian archaeological sites.

🐚 Beaches

Makua Beach
BEACH

This beach has an interesting history – in ancient Hawaii, it was a canoe landing site for interisland travelers. In the late 1960s it was used as the backdrop for the movie *Hawaii*, starring Julie Andrews and Max von Sydow. These days there is little here beyond a nice stretch of sand opposite Makua Military Reservation.

Locals crawl out from their nine-to-five lives on holiday weekends to absorb the sun and spirit of the beach. The powerful shorebreaks are popular with bodyboarders, and high surf waves appear in winter and spring, when the sand practically disappears. In summer, give the wild spinner dolphins plenty of room to rest – do not approach or try to swim with them.

There are two parking lots on either side of the beach, but no facilities. A local homeless population sometimes sets up camp along the coast here.

⊙ Sights & Activities

Kaneana Cave
HISTORICAL SITE

The waves that created this giant stone amphiteater receded long ago, and now Farrington Hwy sits between the seashore and the cave, located about 2 miles north of Keaʻau Beach. *Kahuna* (priests) once performed rituals inside the cave's inner chamber, which according to legend was the abode of a vicious shark-man, a shapeshifter who lured human victims into the cave before devouring them. Some Hawaiians consider it a sacred place and won't enter the cave for fear that it's haunted by the spirits of deceased chiefs. Judging by the collection of broken beer bottles and graffiti inside, not everyone shares their sentiments.

Kaʻena Point Satellite Tracking Station
HIKING

The US Air Force operates a satellite tracking station high on the ridge of Oʻahu's northwesternmost tip. It was originally built in the 1950s for use in the USA's first reconnaissance satellite program, but now those giant white golf balls

perched on the hillsides support weather, early-warning, navigation and communications systems.

The station is not open to the public but the surrounding acreage is managed by Hawaii's **Division of Forestry & Wildlife** (DOFAW; ⌨587-0166), which issues advance hiking permits for public access to the trail system that connects to the North Shore. Part of the land is also open to hunting, so hikers should wear bright, safety-colored clothing. The dusty 2.5-mile **Kuaokala Trail** (Map p56) follows a high ridge into Mokuleʻia Forest Reserve, although you'll need a 4WD vehicle to reach the trailhead. On a clear day hikers can see Mt Kaʻala (4025ft), Oʻahu's highest peak and part of the Waiʻanae Range. This route connects to the **Kealia Trail**, which starts at the North Shore's Dillingham Airfield, and requires neither hiking permits nor 4WD to access.

Kaʻena Point State Park

You don't have to be well versed in Hawaiian legends to know that something mystical occurs at this dramatic convergence of land and sea at the far northwestern tip of the island. Powerful ocean currents altered by Oʻahu's landmass have been battling against each other for millennia here. The watery blows crash onto the long lava bed fingers, sending frothy explosions skyward. All along this untamed coastal slice, nature is at its most furious and beautiful.

Running along both sides of the westernmost point of Oʻahu, Kaʻena Point State Park today is a totally undeveloped coastal strip. Until 1947 the Oʻahu Railway ran up here from Honolulu and continued around the point, carrying passengers on to

SOULS' LEAP

Ancient Hawaiians believed that when people went into a deep sleep or lost consciousness, their souls would wander. Souls that wandered too far were drawn west to Kaʻena Point. If they were lucky, they were met here by their ʻaumakua (guardian spirit), who led their souls back to their bodies. If unattended, their souls would be forced to leap from Kaʻena Point into the endless night, never to return.

HOMELESS IN PARADISE

On O'ahu, especially the Wai'anae Coast, some city- and county-managed beach parks have become almost permanent homeless encampments. But the profile of the average homeless person here may be different than on the US mainland. Many beach tenters are low-income families who were pushed out by the island's previous housing boom, while others lost their jobs and then their housing in the recent US recession.

The county doesn't have an accurate figure of how many people are living at the beaches, but recent estimates put the number of homeless people on O'ahu at around 5800. When Hawaii's economy was strong and housing prices were soaring, many rental properties were sold, thus diminishing the available rental accommodations and driving up rents. Many low-income families – some with service-industry or construction jobs, others receiving some form of government assistance – simply couldn't afford the increase.

Another aggravating factor is Hawaii's stagnant stock of public housing, with waiting lists of up to 10,000 people statewide. In late 2010 voters on O'ahu approved new public-housing funds, but the island's homeless crisis continues, as do evictions of squatters from beaches on the Wai'anae Coast. But without enough jobs or affordable housing, where are all of these struggling families supposed to go?

Hale'iwa on the North Shore. The gorgeous, mile-long sandy beach on the southern side of Ka'ena Point is called Yokohama Bay after the Japanese fishers who used to come here during the railroad days.

Don't leave anything valuable in your car at Ka'ena Point State Park. Telltale mounds of shattered windshield glass litter the road's-end parking area used by most hikers. Instead, park closer to the lifeguard station and restrooms, and consider leaving your doors unlocked and windows rolled down, to decrease the odds of having your car damaged by a break-in.

🏖 Beaches

Yokohama Bay   BEACH

Some say this is the best sunset spot on the island. It certainly has the right west-facing orientation and a blissfully scenic mile-long sandy beach. Winter brings huge pounding waves, making Yokohama a popular seasonal surfing and bodysurfing spot best left to the experts because of the submerged rocks, strong rips and dangerous shorebreak.

Swimming is limited to the summer and then only when calm. When the water's flat, it's possible to snorkel. The best spot with the easiest access is on the south side of the bay. You'll find restrooms, showers and a lifeguard station at the park's southern end. Occasionally, a food truck rolls up here, but you're better off bringing plenty of snacks and drinks with you.

🏃 Activities

Ka'ena Point Trail   HIKING, MOUNTAIN BIKING

An extremely windy, but mostly level 2.5-mile (one-way) coastal trail runs from Yokohama Bay to Ka'ena Point, then more than two more miles around the point to the North Shore, utilizing the old railroad bed. Most hikers take the trail, which begins from the end of the paved road at Yokohama Bay, as far as the point then return the same way, taking two or three hours round-trip. Watch out for mountain bikers, who share trail access.

This family-friendly hike offers fine views the entire way, with the ocean on one side and the Wai'anae Range's craggy cliffs on the other. Along the trail are tidepools, sea arches and lazy blowholes that occasionally come to life on high-surf days. As well as myriad native and migratory seabirds, you might spot Hawaiian monk seals hauled out on the sand – be careful not to not approach or otherwise disturb these endangered creatures.

The trail is extremely exposed and lacks shade, so take sunscreen and plenty of water. Be cautious near the shoreline, as there are strong currents, and rogue waves can reach extreme heights. In fact, winter waves at Ka'ena Point are Hawaii's highest, sometimes towering in excess of 50ft!

Hawai'i the Big Island

Includes »

Kailua-Kona......... 172

Around Kailua-Kona...187

Kona Coast 196

Kohala 215

Waimea (Kamuela) ..235

Mauna Kea 240

Hamakua Coast 248

Hilo 260

Puna................274

Hawai'i Volcanoes National Park & Around 282

Ka'u 297

Why Go?

Our boat captain summed it up neatly as we rocked in 4ft waves watching live lava pour into the sea: very few have set eyes on new earth being created in such a fiery display of raw power. Sunrise rainbows and romping dolphins aside, it's all about the lava here – from palm-fringed black-sand beaches to lava tide pools teeming with Technicolor life.

But it's the people, as much as the land, that keeps legends like Pele the volcano goddess pulsing on the Big Island. Ancient chants accompanied by sacred hula are still performed here, fish are netted in an old-fashioned *hukilau*, and the Big Island work day ends in *pau hana* (happy hour).

Hawai'i is so big (twice as big as the other islands combined), it's the only island where you feel you're on a road trip.

Best Places to Eat

» Annie's Island Fresh Burgers (p197)

» Hilo Bay Cafe (p269)

» Sansei Seafood Restaurant & Sushi Bar (p218)

» Holuakoa Gardens & Café (p193)

Best Places to Stay

» Mauna Lani Bay Hotel & Bungalows (p223)

» Holualoa Inn (p192)

» Volcano Rainforest Retreat (p295)

When to Go
Kailua-Kona

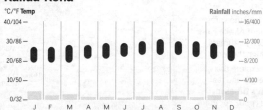

Jan Surf's up and summits are snow-capped during the Big Island 'winter.'

Late Mar-early Apr Catch the world's greatest hula at Hilo's Merrie Monarch Festival.

Oct Tenacious triathletes compete in the legendary swim-bike-run race born in Kailua-Kona.

Big Island Highlights

1 Hike the smoking craters and lava terrain of **Hawai'i Volcanoes National Park** (p288)

2 Watch the sun set and the stars blaze from **Mauna Kea** (p243)

3 Snorkel in **Kealakekua Bay** (p204), the state's top underwater spot

4 Lounge with wild horses and surfers on a black-sand beach in **Waipi'o Valley** (p252)

5 Brush bellies, almost, with **Pacific manta rays** (p178), while snorkeling

6 Enjoy fun in the sun (and surf) at **Hapuna Beach** (p225), one of the island's all-round top beaches

7 Be transported by traditional hula expertly executed at the **Merrie Monarch Festival** (p268)

8 Commune with the ancients at **Pu'uhonua o Honaunau National Historical Park** (p207), and snorkel at stellar **Two-Step** (p208)

9 Feel the spray as giant **Akaka Falls** (p258) plummets through the forest

10 Explore the underground realm of **lava tubes** in Ka'u (p302) or Puna (p274)

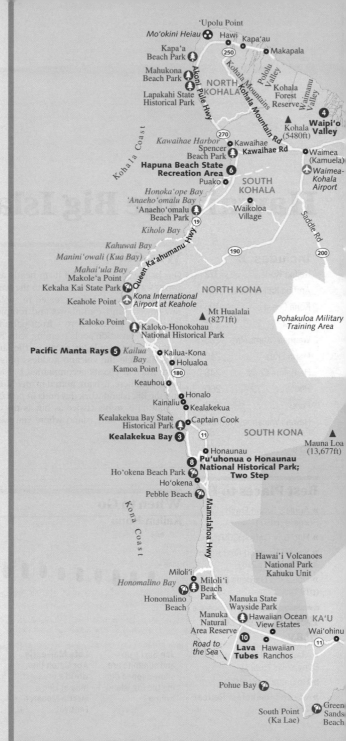

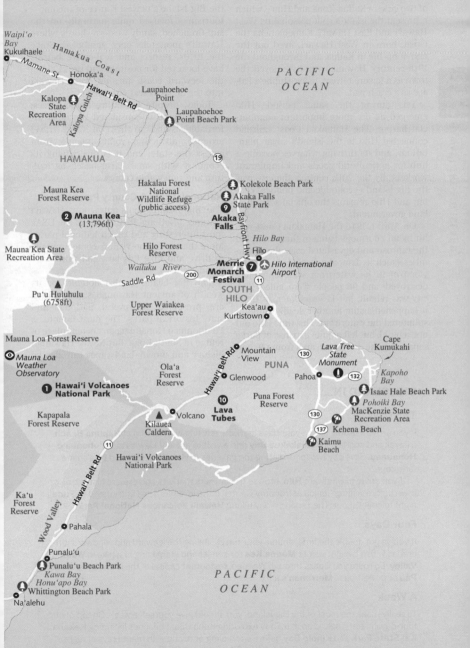

History

The modern history of the Big Island is a tale of two cities – Kailua-Kona and Hilo – which represent the island's split personality: West Hawai'i and East Hawai'i. Kamehameha the Great, born in West Hawai'i, lived out the end of his life in Kailua, and throughout the 19th century, Hawaiian royalty enjoyed the town as a leisure retreat, using Hulihe'e Palace as a crash pad.

Yet, during the same period, Hilo emerged as the more important commercial harbor. The Hamakua Coast railroad connected Hilo to the island's sugar plantations, and its thriving wharves became a hub for agricultural goods and immigrant workers. By the 20th century the city was the Big Island's economic and political center, and Hilo remains the official seat of island government.

On April 1, 1946 the Hamakua Coast was hit by an enormous tsunami that crumpled the railroad and devastated coastal communities (such as Laupahoehoe). Hilo got the worst of it: its waterfront was completely destroyed, and 96 people were killed. The city was rebuilt, but 14 years later, in 1960, it happened again: another deadly tsunami splintered the waterfront. This time Hilo did not rebuild, but left a quiet expanse of parks separating the downtown area from the bay.

After that the sugar industry steadily declined (sputtering out in the 1990s), and the Big Island's newest source of income – tourism – focused quite naturally on the sun-drenched, sandy western shores where Hawaii's monarchs once gamboled. Since the 1970s, resorts and real-estate barons have jockeyed for position and profit along the leeward coast, turning West Hawai'i into the de facto seat of power.

Today, despite escalating home prices, the Big Island is considered the most affordable island to live on (and travel around), attracting young people from across the state; and it is diversifying its economy with small farm–based agriculture and renewable energy.

National, State & County Parks

The Big Island's main attraction, Hawai'i Volcanoes National Park, is one of the USA's most interesting and varied national parks. More than a million visitors come annually to drive and hike this lava and rain-forest wonderland.

The Big Island is also notable for its wealth of ancient Hawaiian sights, which are preserved in several national and state historical parks. The most famous is Pu'uhonua o Honaunau, an ancient place of refuge in South Kona. But Native Hawaiian history and moody landscapes can also be

BIG ISLAND IN...

Two Days

If you arrive in **Kona**, spend your days leeward, starting with a swim at **Hapuna Beach**, a kayak and snorkel at **Kealakekua Bay** and a visit to ancient Hawai'i at **Pu'uhonua o Honaunau**. Save day two for exploring the galleries in **Holualoa**, followed by a coffee farm tour.

If you arrive in windward **Hilo**, browse the farmers markets and explore historic downtown before visiting 'Imiloa Astronomy Center. If the lava has a sea entry, head to **Puna** at night to check it out. Then spend a day hiking **Hawai'i Volcanoes National Park**.

Four Days

If you've got double the time, double your fun by linking the leeward and windward itineraries with a twilight visit to **Mauna Kea** for sunset and stargazing or a hike in **Waipi'o Valley**. En route you'll pass through Waimea, restaurant capital of the island: give casual **Pau** or powerhouse **Merriman's** a try.

A Week

To really make the most of the Big Island, you should give yourself a week. On top of our four-day itinerary, spend an extra day exploring Kona Coast beaches including **Kekaha Kai State Park** and **Kiholo Bay** before snorkeling or diving with manta rays at night. Bookend these experiences with a visit north to quaint **Hawi** and hiking the **Pololu Valley**. Close out your adventures with a trip to **South Point** and **Green Sands Beach**.

found at remote Mo'okini Heiau in North Kohala; snorkeling mecca Kealakekua Bay, where Captain Cook met his demise; the restored fishponds of Kaloko-Honokohau near Kailua-Kona; and the imposingly majestic Pu'ukohola Heiau just south of Kawaihae.

Many of the Big Island's finest beaches lie within parkland, such as the world-renowned Hapuna Beach. The beaches within Kekaha Kai State Park are also idyllic, though only Manini'owali is accessible by paved road.

Other parks worth seeking out on the Windward Coast are Kalopa State Recreation Area, preserving a native forest; Laupahoehoe, site of a tsunami disaster; and Akaka Falls, the prettiest 'drive-up' waterfalls in Hawai'i. Though not a designated park, Waipi'o Valley shouldn't be missed.

CAMPING

Hawai'i has enough good campgrounds that you can enjoyably circumnavigate the island in a tent; plus there are several highly memorable backcountry camping opportunities. Some parks also offer simple cabins and DIYers can rent camper vans (see the boxed text, p270). For detailed recommendations, see specific parks.

Hawai'i Volcanoes National Park has free camping at its two drive-up campgrounds and its great backcountry sites (at the time of writing, the cabins were closed for renovation), and only backcountry sites require permits (available at the visitor center).

State parks require camping permits for tent sites ($12/18 residents/non-residents) and cabins. The easiest way to make a reservation and obtain a permit for state park cabins and campgrounds (plus those in Waimanu Valley) is via the online reservation system for the State of Hawaii Department of Land and Resources (https://camping.ehawaii.gov); reservations must be made seven days prior to check in. The maximum length of stay per permit is five consecutive nights.

County Park facilities and upkeep range from good to minimal, with the exception of renovated Isaac Hale, which is sparkling. Some parks are isolated, raising concerns about personal safety.

Camping permits are required for county parks, and can be obtained (up to a year in advance) online from the Department of Parks & Recreation (www.ehawaii.gov/Hawaii_County/camping/exe/campre.cgi). Daily camping fees are $6/2/1 for adults/teens/children 12 years and under. Details about facilities at each county park are available at http://co.hawaii.hi.us/parks/parks.htm.

Apart from those specified (Backcountry), all of the campsites listed here are drive-up.

NAME	FEATURES
Hawai'i Volcanoes National Park	
'Apua Point	Backcountry; no water; shelter
Halape Shelter	Backcountry; closes during drought; turtle nesting site
Ka'aha Shelter	Backcountry; shelter
Keauhou Shelter	Backcountry; shelter
Kulanaokuaiki Campground	No water; views
Namakanipaio Campground & Cabins	Full facilities
Napau Crater	Backcountry; no water
State Parks	
Hapuna Beach State Recreation Area	Cabins only
Kalopa State Recreation Area	Full facilities; cabins
MacKenzie State Recreation Area	Full facilities
Manuka State Wayside Park	No water
County Parks	
Ho'okena Beach Park	Full facilities
Isaac Hale Beach Park	Full facilities; surfing
Kapa'a Beach Park	No water
Kolekole Beach Park	Full facilities; surfing
Laupahoehoe Point Beach Park	Full facilities
Mahukona Beach Park	No water
Miloli'i Beach Park	No water
Punalu'u Beach Park	Full facilities; turtles
Spencer Beach Park	Full facilities
Whittington Beach Park	Full facilities

ACTIVITY	PLACE
Caving	Kazumura cave (p274)
	Lava tubes in Hawai'i Volcanoes National Park (p285)
	Kula Kai Caverns (p302)
Diving	Kealakekua Bay (p205)
	Manta rays at night (p178)
	Two-Step (p208)
Fishing	Kailua-Kona (p177)
	kayak fishing (p188)
Golf	Mauna Kea & Hapuna (p225)
	Mauna Lani (p222)
	Hilo Municipal (p265)
Hiking	Hawai'i Volcanoes National Park (p288)
	Waimanu Valley (p254)
	Mauna Kea (p288)
Kayaking	Kealakekua Bay (p205)
	Puako (p224)
	Pebble Beach (p209)
Snorkeling	Kahalu'u Beach Park (p187)
	Kapoho Tide Pools (p279)
	Kealakekua Bay (p204)
	Two-Step (p208)
Stand Up Paddle Boarding	Kailua-Kona (p178)
	Kealakekua Bay (p203)
	Kahalu'u Beach (p187)
Ziplining	Hawi (p230)
	Hakalau & Around (p257)

🛈 Getting There & Away

Most interisland and domestic US flights arrive in Kona. Continental is the only carrier serving the mainland to Hilo; many flights route through Honolulu first.

Hilo International Airport (ITO; ☎961-9321; http://hawaii.gov/ito) Off Hwy 11, just under a mile south of the intersection of Hwys 11 and 19.

Kona International Airport at Keahole (KOA; ☎327-9520; http://hawaii.gov/koa) On Hwy 19, 7 miles north of Kailua-Kona. For directions to/from the airport, see p186.

There are two major interisland carriers: **Hawaiian Airlines** (HA; ☎800-367-5320; www. hawaiianair.com) and **go!** (YV; ☎888-435-9462; www.iflygo.com). Both have multiple interisland flights daily, though go! has more direct flights, while many of Hawaiian's require a stopover in Honolulu. Fares range from $70 to $90 one way, though advance-purchase fare wars can slash prices by nearly half.

Another option is **Island Air** (WP; ☎800-652-6541; www.islandair.com), with one daily flight between Kona and Maui, and direct flights daily from Kona to Honolulu and Kaua'i. Fares are typically $90 to $100 one way.

See p638 for more on interisland flights.

🛈 Getting Around

The Big Island is divided into six districts: Kona, Kohala, Waimea, Hilo, Puna and Ka'u. The Hawai'i Belt Rd circles the island, connecting the main towns and sights. It's possible but neither efficient nor convenient to get around by bus. If you really want to explore, you'll need a car.

The best foldout map is the Hawaii Street Guide *Big Island Manini Map*. The colorful Franko's *Hawai'i (Big Island) Guide Map* features watersports and is sold at dive shops. For longer visits, consider getting the Ready Mapbook series' encyclopedic books covering East and West Hawai'i.

To/From the Airports

CAR Most visitors rent cars at the airport; car-hire booths for the major agencies line the road outside the arrivals area at both airports.

SHUTTLE Shuttle-bus services typically cost as much as taxis. **Speedi Shuttle** (☑329-5433, 877-242-5777; www.speedishuttle.com) will get you to destinations up and down the Kona Coast, plus Waimea, Honoka'a and Hawai'i Volcanoes National Park (although that will cost $165-plus). Book in advance.

TAXI Taxis are curbside.

» The approximate fare from Hilo airport to downtown is $20.

» The approximate fare from Kona airport to Kailua-Kona is $30, and to Waikoloa is $55.

Bicycle

As your primary transportation, cycling around the Big Island is easiest with the support of a tour. Though doable on one's own, it's a challenge, particularly if the weather doesn't co-operate. However, Kona – the hub for the Ironman Triathlon – has top-notch bike shops that sell and repair high-caliber equipment.

Bus

The island-wide **Hele-On Bus** (☑961-8744; www.heleonbus.org) will get you (most) places on the Big Island, but Sunday service is limited. Fares are between 50¢ and $1 per ride; always check the website for current routes and schedules. Most buses originate from Mo'oheau terminal in Hilo. You cannot board with a surfboard or bodyboard, while luggage, backpacks and bicycles are charged $1 apiece.

Car & Motorcycle

See p640 for companies with car-hire booths at Kona and Hilo airports. Local companies:

Harper Car & Truck Rentals (☑969-1478, 800-852-9993; www.harpershawaii.com; 456 Kalaniana'ole Ave, Hilo) No restrictions on driving its 4WDs up Mauna Kea, but driving into Waipi'o Valley and to Green Sands Beach is prohibited. Damage to a vehicle entails a high deductible; rates are generally steeper than at major agencies.

Big Island Harley-Davidson (☑635-0542; www.hawaiiharleyrental.com) Choose from a fleet of 19 new, well-maintained motorcycles. Rates start at $139/day.

» Reserve well in advance for decent rental rates.

» During nonpeak periods weekly rates fall to $130 for compact and $160 for full-size cars; taxes and fees add 16% to 30% to the base estimate.

» Rates rise precipitously (to between $300 and $400 per week, plus taxes and fees), for peak-season and last-minute bookings.

» Rates for 4WD vehicles range from $60 to $100 per day, but only Harper Car & Truck Rentals allows driving to the Mauna Kea summit.

DRIVING DISTANCES & TIMES

To circumnavigate the island on the 230-mile Hawai'i Belt Rd (Hwys 19 and 11), you'll need about six hours.

FROM HILO

DESTINATION	MILES	TIME
Hawai'i Volcanoes National Park	28	½hr
Hawi	86	2¼hr
Honoka'a	40	1hr
Kailua-Kona	92	2½hr
Na'alehu	64	1¾hr
Pahoa	16	½hr
Waikoloa	80	2¼hr
Waimea	54	1½hr
Waipi'o Lookout	50	1¼hr

FROM KAILUA-KONA

DESTINATION	MILES	TIME
Hawai'i Volcanoes National Park	98	2½hr
Hawi	51	1¼hr
Hilo	92	2½hr
Honoka'a	61	1½hr
Na'alehu	60	1½hr
Pahoa	108	3hr
Waikoloa	18	¾hr
Waimea	43	1hr
Waipi'o Lookout	70	1¾hr

Taxi

It's easy to find a cab at either airport, but cabs don't run all night or cruise for passengers, so in town call ahead. The standard flag-down fee is $2, plus $2 per mile thereafter.

Tours

Activity tours (eg snorkeling cruises, helicopter rides and farm visits) are reviewed in regional sections. Group tours typically involve superficial 'stop and click' sightseeing tours by **Jack's Tours** (www.jackshawaii.com), **Roberts Hawaii** (www.robertshawaii.com) and **Polynesian Adventure Tours** (www.polyad.com).

Recommended tour providers:

Road Scholar (☎800-454-5768; www.road scholar.org) Offers tours (including accommodations, meals and lectures) for the 55 and older crowd. Most of the themed trips are multi-island and focus on Hawaiian history, culture and geography.

Earth Bound Tours (http://earthboundtours .com) Excellent way to tour a variety of boutique farms, many of which are otherwise inaccessible to the public. Founder Jim Reddekopp is also a farmer and the owner of Hawaiian Vanilla Company.

Orchid Isle Bicycling (☎800-219-2324; www .orchidislebicycling.com) Kona outfit with bike tours through the Kohala Mountains, to South Point and more.

KAILUA-KONA

POP 11,465

In 1866 Mark Twain described Kailua-Kona as 'a little collection of native grass houses reposing under tall coconut trees – the sleepiest, quietest, Sundayest looking place you can imagine.' My, how things have changed.

Known as 'Kona town' to locals, you'll also hear this town referred to as Kailua, Kailua-Kona or just plain Kona. It was officially renamed Kailua-Kona to distinguish it from Kailua on O'ahu.

BIG ISLAND'S BEST BEACHES

Hapuna Beach (p225) Tops most 'best' lists.

Mauna Kea Beach (p225) Picture perfect; provides opportunities for exploration.

Beach 69 (p224) Gay- and family-friendly.

Waipi'o Valley (p253) Black-sand beauty.

Manini'owali Beach (p213) Drive up, roll out towel.

Makalawena Beach (p211) Beautifully remote.

Kailua now has the worst traffic, the most hotels and condos, the most tourists, the most souvenirs per square foot, and is the most likely place on the island to find businesses open on Sunday. Along shoreline Ali'i Dr, Kailua works hard to evoke the nonchalance of a sun-drenched tropical getaway, but in an injection-molded, bargain-priced way.

Which isn't to say Kailua isn't fun. Most Big Island visitors pass through at some point, and Kailua can make an affordable, pleasant base from which to enjoy the Kona Coast's nearby beaches, fantastic snorkeling and watersports, and preeminent ancient Hawaiian sites. Besides, Kailua has the best nightlife. Amid the town's forgettable dross, there are some delicious restaurants and cool shops and, of course, plenty of chances to share your adventures with fellow travelers over a coconutful of kava or an umbrella-shaded cocktail.

🏖 Beaches

White Sands Beach Park   BEACH
(off Map p174) This small but gorgeous beach (also called La'aloa Beach) has crystal-clear turquoise waters and tall palms (but little shade). During high winter surf the beach can lose its sand literally overnight, earning it nicknames like Magic Sands and Disappearing Sands. When its rocks and coral are exposed, the beach becomes too treacherous for most swimmers. Gradually the sand returns, transforming the shore back into its former beachy self. White Sands is always packed and is an extremely popular bodyboarding and bodysurfing spot. Facilities include rest rooms, showers, picnic tables and a volleyball court; a lifeguard is on duty. The park is about 4 miles south of the center.

Old Kona Airport State Recreation Area   BEACH
(off Map p174) Maybe it's the name, but visitors often overlook this quiet, 217-acre park a mile from downtown. The old airport runway skirts a long, sandy beach laced with thick strips of black lava rock. Granted, this doesn't make for good swimming, but low tide reveals countless aquariumlike **tide pools**. Bring a picnic, meander through the pools and enjoy a little solitude. Just inside the southern entrance gate, one pool is large and sandy enough to be the perfect *keiki* (child) pool. The waters offshore are a marine-life conservation district.

Because Hawai'i is the youngest island and its coastline is still quite rugged, it's often assumed there isn't much in the way of surfable waves. As a result places like O'ahu and Kaua'i have stolen the surf spotlight, but archaeologists and researchers believe that **Kealakekua Bay** is probably where ancient Polynesians started riding waves. Today a fun little left-hander called Ke'ei breaks near the bay.

Unlike its neighboring islands, whose north and south shores are the primary center of swell activity, the east and west shores are the Big Island's focal points. Because swells are shadowed by the other islands, as a general rule the surf doesn't get as big here. The Kona Coast (see Map p212) offers the best opportunities, with north and south swell exposures, as well as offshore trade winds. **Kawaihae Harbor** is surrounded by several fun, introductory reefs near the breakwall, while further south, near **Kekaha Kai State Park**, is a considerably more advanced break that challenges even the most seasoned surfers. If you have a 4WD vehicle or don't mind an hour-long hike, be sure to check out heavy reef breaks like Mahai'ula and Makalawena. They break best on northwest swells, making the later winter months the prime season. A hike or 4WD is also necessary to reach **Pine Trees** at Keahole Point.

On East Hawai'i, just outside of Hilo (see Map p259), are several good intermediate waves. **Richardson Ocean Park** is a slow-moving reef break that's great for learning, and just west of town is **Honoli'i**, a fast left and right peak breaking into a river mouth. Further up the Hamakua Coast is **Waipi'o Bay**; while access to the beach requires a long walk or a 4WD vehicle, the waves and scenery are worth the effort. Puna's **Pohoiki Bay**, meanwhile, with three breaks (the most challenging of which can serve up waves '15 feet Hawaiian') offers the island's best surfing, according to many. In Ka'u, locals brace a rough paddle out to catch long rides on the nearly perfect left break at **Kawa Bay**. Newbies take lessons and test the waves at **Kahalu'u Beach Park**.

Top bodyboarding and bodysurfing spots include **Hapuna Beach**, **White Sands Beach** (surfers favor **Banyans**, marked by a tree of the same name here), near Kailua-Kona, and the beaches at **Kekaha Kai State Park**.

A few breaks in the lava allow entry into the water, but **fishing** is the main activity. Scuba divers and confident snorkelers can make for Garden Eel Cove, a short walk from the north end of the beach. The reef fish are large and plentiful, and a steep coral wall in deeper waters harbors moray eels and small caves. When the surf's up, local surfers flock to an offshore break here.

Facilities include rest rooms, showers and covered picnic tables on a lawn dotted with beach heliotrope and short coconut palms. Runners enjoy a mile-long **jogging track**.

To get here, follow Kuakini Hwy to its end.

◉ Sights

Kailua is a breezy waterfront tourist town. Its main attraction is watersports in the sparkling Pacific Ocean. There are a few historic buildings well worth seeing, but it's only crowded because of its proximity to sunny beaches, cruise ships disgorging the masses, and watersports north and south.

Hulihe'e Palace   HISTORICAL BUILDING
(Map p174; ☑329-1877; www.daughtersofhawaii .org; 75-5718 Ali'i Dr; adult/senior/under 18 $6/4/1; ◷10am-3pm Wed-Sat) Hawai'i's second governor, 'John Adams' Kuakini, built this simple two-story, lava-rock house as his private residence in 1838. After Kuakini's death in 1844, it became the favorite vacation getaway for Hawaiian monarchs. In the mid-1880s Hulihe'e Palace was thoroughly renovated by the globe-trotting King David Kalakaua, who felt it needed more polish. He stuccoed the lava rock outside, plastered it inside, and added decorative ceilings, gold-leaf picture moldings and crystal chandeliers.

Hard times befell the monarchy in the early 20th century, and the house was sold and the furnishings and artifacts auctioned

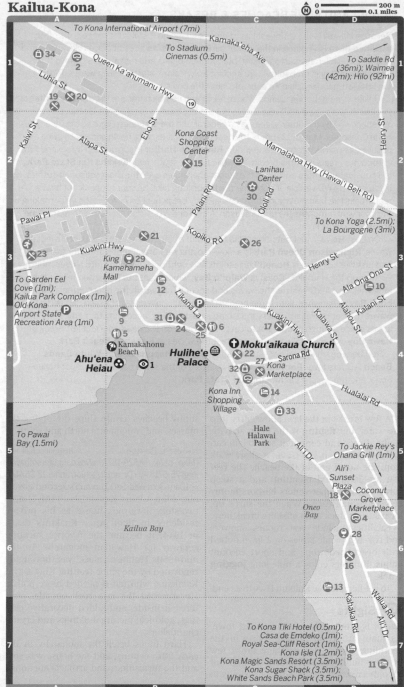

0   200 m
0   0.1 miles

To Kona International Airport (7mi)

Kamaka'eha Ave

To Stadium
Cinemas (0.5mi)

To Saddle Rd
(36mi); Waimea
(42mi); Hilo (92mi)

34

2

19   20

Luhia St

Queen Ka'ahumanu Hwy

Kaiwi St

Alapa St

Eho St

Mamalahoa Hwy (Hawai'i Belt Rd)

Kona Coast
Shopping
Center

15

Lanihau
Center

30

To Kona Yoga (2.5mi);
La Bourgogne (3mi)

Pawai Pl

3

23

Kuakini Hwy

21

Kopiko Rd

26

Henry St

Ala Ona Ona St

10

King
Kamehameha
Mall

29

To Garden Eel
Cove (1mi);
Kailua Park Complex (1mi);
Old Kona
Airport State
Recreation Area (1mi)

12

Likana La

Kalani St

9

31   24   25   6

17

Kuakini Hwy

Kalawa St

5

Kamakahonu
Beach

**Ahu'ena
Heiau**

1

**Huliheʻe
Palace**

Mokuʻaikaua Church

22

27   Kona
Marketplace

32

Sarona Rd

7

14

Hualalai Rd

Kona Inn
Shopping
Village

33

To Jackie Rey's
Ohana Grill (1mi)

To Pawai
Bay (1.5mi)

Hale
Halawai
Park

Ali'i Dr

Ali'i
Sunset
Plaza

18

Coconut
Grove
Marketplace

4

*Oneo
Bay*

28

Kailua Bay

16

13

Kanakai Rd

Ali'i Dr

Wallia Rd

To Kona Tiki Hotel (0.5mi);
Casa de Emdeko (1mi);
Royal Sea-Cliff Resort (1mi);
Kona Isle (1.2mi);
Kona Magic Sands Resort (3.5mi);
Kona Sugar Shack (3.5mi);
White Sands Beach Park (3.5mi)

8

11

◉ **Top Sights**

Ahu'ena Heiau..........................B4
Hulihe'e Palace..........................C4
Moku'aikaua Church..........................C4

◉ **Sights**

1 Kailua Pier..........................B4
   Kona Brewing Company..............(see 21)

Activities, Courses & Tours

2 Big Island Divers..........................A1
3 Bikram Yoga Kona..........................A3
4 Jack's Diving Locker..........................D6
5 Kona Boys Beach Shack..........................B4
6 Pacific Vibrations..........................C4
7 Sandwich Isle Divers..........................C4
   Snorkel Bob's..........................(see 16)

🛏 **Sleeping**

8 Hale Kona Kai..........................D7
9 King Kamehameha's Kona
   Beach Hotel..........................B4
10 Koa Wood Hale
   Inn/Patey's Place..........................D3
11 Kona Reef..........................D7
12 Kona Seaside Hotel..........................B3
13 Royal Kona Resort..........................D6
14 Uncle Billy's Kona Bay
   Hotel..........................C4

🍴 **Eating**

15 Ba-Le Kona..........................B2
16 Basik Acai..........................D6
17 Big Island Grill..........................C4
18 Island Lava Java..........................D5

19 Island Naturals..........................A1
   Kanaka Kava..........................(see 4)
20 Killer Tacos..........................A1
21 Kona Brewing Company..........................B3
22 Kope Lani..........................C4
   KTA Super Store..........................(see 15)
23 Orchid Thai..........................A3
24 Rapanui Island Café..........................B4
25 Scandinavian Shaved Ice
   Internet Café..........................B4
   Sushi Shiono..........................(see 18)
26 Tex Drive-In..........................C3
27 You Make the Roll..........................C4

🍸 **Drinking**

Don's Mai Tai Bar..........................(see 13)
28 Huggo's on the Rocks..........................D6
   Humpy's Big Island Alehouse........(see 4)
   Java on the Rocks..........................(see 28)
29 Mixx..........................B3
   Okolemaluna Tiki Bar..........................(see 18)

🎭 **Entertainment**

Journeys of the South Pacific.......(see 13)
30 KBXtreme..........................C2
   King Kamehameha's Kona Beach
   Hotel Luau..........................(see 9)

🛍 **Shopping**

31 Big Island Jewelers..........................B4
32 Conscious Riddims Records..........................C4
   Crazy Shirts..........................(see 32)
33 Kailua Village Farmers Market..........................C5
34 Kona International Market..........................A1
   Na Makana..........................(see 6)

off by Prince Kuhio. Luckily his wife and other royalty meticulously numbered each piece and recorded the names of bidders. In 1925 the Territory of Hawaii purchased the house to be a museum run by the Daughters of Hawai'i, a women's group dedicated to the preservation of Hawaiian culture and language. This group tracked down the furnishings and royal memorabilia, such as a table inlaid with 25 kinds of native woods and several of Kamehameha the Great's war spears.

You'll learn these and other stories on 40-minute **guided tours**. The free **concert series**, held at 4pm on the 3rd Sunday of each month, here is a treat, with Hawaiian music and hula performed on the grass facing sparkling Kailua Bay.

Ahu'ena Heiau   HEIAU (TEMPLE)
(Map p174) After uniting the Hawaiian islands, Kamehameha the Great established his kingdom's royal court in Lahaina on Maui, but he continued to use Ahu'ena Heiau as his personal retreat and temple. This is where he died in May 1819, and where his body was prepared for burial, though in keeping with tradition his bones were secreted elsewhere, hidden so securely no one has ever found them.

Reconstructed with palm-leaf shacks and carved wooden *ki'i* (statues), the small, dramatically positioned heiau (closed to the public) sits next to Kailua Pier, and the adjacent King Kamehameha Beach Hotel uses it as a backdrop for its luau. The heiau's tiny cove doubles as a placid saltwater pool where locals fish, children swim and seniors lounge on its comma of sand, **Kamakahonu Beach**.

Moku'aikaua Church CHURCH

(Map p174; www.mokuaikaua.org; 75-5713 Ali'i Dr; ☉dawn-dusk) On April 4, 1820, the first Christian missionaries to the Hawaiian Islands sailed into Kailua Bay. When they landed they were unaware that Hawai'i's old religion had been abolished on that very spot just a few months before. King Liholiho gave them this site, just a few minutes' walk from Kamehameha's Ahu'ena Heiau, to establish Hawai'i's first Christian church.

Completed in 1836, the church is a handsome building with walls of lava rock held together by sand and coral-lime mortar. The posts and beams, hewn with stone adzes and smoothed with chunks of coral, are made from ohia, and the pews and pulpit are made of koa, the most prized native hardwood. The steeple tops out at 112ft, making this the tallest structure in Kailua. The church is popular for weddings, and inside is a dusty model of the missionaries' ship, *Thaddeus,* and a history of their arrival.

Contemporary **services** are held at 9am on Sundays, with traditional services following at 11am. The latter features the Ohana Choir and is followed by a short lecture on the history of the church.

Kailua Pier LANDMARK

(Map p174) The town's pier, built in 1915, was once a major cattle-shipping point. Cattle driven down from hillside ranches were stampeded into the water and forced to swim out to waiting steamers, where they were hoisted aboard by sling and shipped to Honolulu slaughterhouses.

Today Kailua Pier is where locals get wet on their lunch hour, the Ironman Triathlon starts and finishes, and the official weigh-ins happen at the annual Hawaiian International Billfish Tournament.

Kona Brewing Company MICROBREWERY

(Map p174; ☏334-2739; www.konabrewingco.com; North Kona Shopping Center, 75-5629 Kuakini Hwy; admission free; ☉tours 10:30am & 3pm Mon-Fri) Founded in 1994, the Big Island's first microbrewery now ships its handcrafted brews throughout the islands and beyond. Tours of this family-run Kona icon are free, and include sampling.

🏃 Activities

Most of Kailua's activities focus on the sea. Coconut Grove on Ali'i Dr has a sandy volleyball court (BYO volleyball or join a pickup game). To rent a bicycle, see p186.

Kailua Park Complex RECREATIONAL CENTER

(off Map p174; ☏327-3553; ☉6:30am-7:30pm Mon-Fri, 8:30am-5:30pm Sat & Sun) Adjacent to the Old Kona Airport State Recreation Area, the county's Kailua Park Complex's extensive facilities include a toddler playground, an attractive Olympic-size lap pool and kids' pool (get your swim in here), soccer and softball fields, four night-lit tennis courts and a gym.

Diving

The area's snorkeling and diving tours are gathered here, so you can see the range of options on offer.

Near the shore, divers can see steep drop-offs with lava tubes, caves and diverse marine life. In deeper waters there are 40 popular boat-dive areas, including an airplane wreck off Keahole Point. Visibility is typically 100ft, with the best conditions prevailing April through August.

One well-known dive spot is **Red Hill** (Map p198), an underwater cinder cone about 10 miles south of Kailua. It has beautiful lava formations (including ledges and lots of honeycombed lava tubes) as well as coral pinnacles and brightly colored nudibranchs (mollusks).

Two-tank dives range from $100 to $140. One-tank night dives and manta-ray dives are similarly priced. The larger five-star PADI operations offer certification courses for between $500 and $600.

Also see the list of snorkel outfits (p178), as some accommodate divers, too; conversely, some dive companies accommodate snorkelers.

For a truly amazing experience, do a **night snorkel or dive with Pacific manta rays**. The ocean at night is spooky enough, but to see these graceful, gentle creatures (with 8ft to 14ft wing spans) glide out of the darkness and spin cartwheels as they feed is unforgettable. There are two main dive locations: the original site in front of the Sheraton Keauhou Bay Resort (Map p198) and a more northerly site near Garden Eel Cove (p172). The Sheraton site is usually choppier and the ocean floor (where divers are required to park themselves during the 'show') rockier, making it slightly more challenging than the north-

THREE RING RANCH

Dr Ann Goody doesn't just talk to the animals, she also fixes their broken bones and psyches. When she can, she then sets them free, but if they can't cut it in the wild they become residents of the **Three Ring Ranch Exotic Animal Sanctuary** (www.threering ranch.org) on five lovely acres in upland Kona.

Licensed by the US Department of Agriculture and accredited by the American Association of Sanctuaries, Three Ring currently hosts South African crowned cranes, lesser flamingos, David and Goliath (a pair of gigantic African spur-thigh tortoises) and much more, including native endangered species such as the Hawaiian owl. Amid all this wonderful wildlife, zebra Zoe is something special: rescued from the failed Moloka'i Ranch Safari Park, Zoe has amelanosis, meaning her stripes are the color of Hapuna Beach sand and her eyes the color of the water.

Dr Goody – who has been struck by lightning, tossed by a shark and is a breast cancer survivor – is as good with people as she is with animals. This has led to enormously successful educational initiatives, including an after-school program, a resident-intern program and a residency placement program for pre-veterinarian students. Since the sanctuary's primary commitment is to the animals, it leads two-hour **tours** (⊙11am; suggested donation $35) by prior arrangement only. See the website for details.

ern site. Most manta night excursions are two-tank dives exploring one mediocre site during sunset before heading to the manta grounds. Most operators offer manta dive and snorkel excursions.

TOP CHOICE **Jack's Diving Locker** DIVING
(Map p174; ✆329-7585, 800-345-4807; www .jacksdivinglocker.com; Coconut Grove Marketplace, 75-5813 Ali'i Dr) One of the best outfits for introductory dives and courses, with extensive programs for kids. Housed at a 5000ft facility, with a store, classrooms, a tank room and a 12ft-deep dive pool, it offers boat and shore dives, as well as night manta-ray dives; snorkelers are welcome on many trips. Its five boats (from 23ft to 46ft) handle groups of six to 18 divers. Jack's has a reputation for environmental preservation and establishing ecofriendly moorings.

Big Island Divers DIVING
(Map p174; ✆329-6068; www.bigislanddivers.com; 74-5467 Kaiwi St) This outfit has personable staff and an expansive shop offering tours and certification courses; all boat dives are open to snorkelers. It also specializes in night and manta dives, including black night dives.

Sandwich Isle Divers DIVING
(Map p174; ✆329-9188, 888-743-3483; www.sand wichisledivers.com; Kona Marketplace, 5729 Ali'i Dr) This smaller outfit run by a husband-and-wife team runs trips that feel person-alized due to a six-person maximum and the captain's marine biology degree. These folks have decades of experience in Kona waters.

Fishing

Kona is the world's number-one spot for catching Pacific blue marlin (June to August is peak season) and is also home to ahi (yellowfin tuna), *aku* (bonito or skipjack tuna), swordfish, spearfish and mahimahi (white-fleshed fish called 'dolphin'). Most of the world records for catches of such fish belong to Kona fishermen.

Not surprisingly, hundreds of charter fishing boats ply these waters; many are listed in the *Fishing* freebie available around town and online at *Hawaii Fishing News* (www .hawaiifishingnews.com). The standard cost to join an existing party starts at $80 per person for a four-hour (half-day) trip. Otherwise, a charter for up to six people costs between $450 and $600 for a half-day, and $750 and $3500 for a full day, depending on the boat. Prices include equipment and license.

Next to the weigh station at Honoko-hau Marina, the **Charter Desk** (Map p212; ✆326-1800, 888-566-2487; www.charterdesk.com; ⊙6am-6pm) is the main booking service. Another option is **Charter Services Hawaii** (✆800-567-2650; www.konazone.com).

For tournament schedules, check the **Hawaii Big Game Fishing Club** (www.hbgfc.org).

For **kayak fishing** see p188.

Outrigger Canoeing

Kona Boys Beach Shack   OUTRIGGER CANOEING
(Map p174; ☎329-2345; www.konaboys.com; Kamakahonu Beach; adult/child $50/25; ☺8am-5pm) Visitors can finally try their hand at traditional outrigger canoeing thanks to the friendly folks at the Kona Boys Beach Shack at Kamakahonu Beach. With celebrated Hawaiian paddler Uncle Jesse as your guide, experience what original Polynesian settlers must have felt with the water rushing under their hull as they approached the volcanic shores of the Big Island. Prices quoted above are per person for a minimum of two people. Also rents kayaks, stand up paddleboards and surfboards, as well as doing lessons.

Snorkeling

Some of the island's best, most accessible snorkeling is an easy drive from Kailua: to the south check out Kahalu'u Beach Park, Two-Step and Kealakekua Bay; to the north try lovely Makalawena Beach. Shops all along Ali'i Dr rent gear for between $7 and $10 per day or $15 and $45 per week; a good choice is Snorkel Bob's (Map p174; ☎329-0770; www .snorkelbob.com; 75-5831 Kahakai Rd; ☺8am-5pm), with Rx masks, baby reef shoes and more.

Boat cruises (aka 'dolphin cruises'), including snorkeling, are plentiful around Kailua. A four-hour cruise offers snorkeling in otherwise inaccessible places, the chance to spot whales and dolphins, and knowledgeable guides. When choosing, always opt for morning departures, when conditions are best.

Ultimately the captain decides the best destination for the day's conditions, but by far the most common (and crowded) snorkeling spot is Kealakekua Bay. However, the coast south of Kailua has beautiful lava cliffs and caves, while the northern coast is a flat lava shelf with great snorkeling aplenty.

Cruises come in two main types: small Zodiac rafts, which can zip into sea caves but (usually) lack shade or toilets; and large catamarans, which have a smoother, comfier ride but aren't as nimble around small coves. Cruise prices usually include snorkeling gear, beverages and snacks. Most offer internet discounts.

Captain Zodiac   ZODIAC CRUISE
(Map p212; ☎329-3199; www.captainzodiac .com; Honokohau Harbor; half-day cruise adult/ child 4-12yr $100/84) In business since 1974, Captain Zodiac makes daily trips to Kealakekua Bay in 24ft rigid-hull inflatable Zo- diacs with up to 16 passengers and a jaunty pirate theme.

Sea Quest   ZODIAC CRUISE
(Map p198; ☎329-7238, 888-732-2283; www.sea questhawaii.com; Keauhou Bay; 1-snorkel cruise adult/child $72/62, 2-snorkel cruise $92/75, whale watching cruise $72/62) Sea Quest has four rigid-hull inflatable rafts that take up to six or 14 passengers. On offer are one and two-stop snorkel adventures, plus **whale watching** cruises. All snorkel cruises visit Kealakekua Bay, with Honaunau Bay (Two-Step) serving as the second stop.

⬛TOP CHOICE   Sea Paradise   CATAMARAN CRUISE
(Map p198; ☎322-2500, 800-322-5662; www .seaparadise.com; Keauhou Bay; snorkel cruise incl 2 meals adult/child $99/59, manta snorkel $89/59, 2-tank dive $145, manta dive $110) Sea Paradise offers morning snorkel cruises to Kealakekua Bay, dive trips and a sunset dinner sail on a classy 50ft catamaran with a fun and professional crew. The **manta night cruises** include experts from the Manta Network and guarantee sightings (or you repeat for free).

Fair Wind   CATAMARAN CRUISE
(Map p198; ☎345-0268, 800-677-9461; www.fair -wind.com; Keauhou Bay; morning snorkel adult/ child $125/75, afternoon snorkel $109/69) The *Fair Wind II* is a 100-passenger catamaran with two kickin' 15ft slides and a BBQ, sailing daily to Kealakekua Bay. You'll have 2½ hours snorkel time and a meal included. Cruises on the luxury Hydrofoil catamaran *Hula Kai* (per person including a meal $155) are longer and motor to the most crowd-free spots. The *Hula Kai* also does a **night manta trip** (snorkel $99; dive $130 to $145). Divers are also accommodated and they guarantee sightings or you repeat the cruise free. Book in advance.

Kamanu Charters   CATAMARAN CRUISE
(Map p212; ☎329-2021, 800-348-3091; www .kamanu.com; Honokohau Harbor; adult/child $90/50) Snorkel without crowds at Pawai Bay, just north of the protected waters of the Old Kona Airport State Park. The 36ft catamaran, which motors down and sails back, takes a maximum of 24 people. Has a **night manta snorkel** ($80), and the boat can be privately chartered.

Stand Up Paddling (SUP)

Two huge trends have taken the Big Island by storm in recent years: Zumba and stand up paddling (with kayak fishing close behind). Both get you moving, but only SUP delivers a core workout accompanied by dolphins, turtles and tropical fish. And the best part is anyone can do this easy and fun activity. Lessons and rentals are available at the Kona Boys Beach Shack (p178; 90-minute lesson $75, one-hour rental $25), right on Kamakahonu Beach.

Surfing

What little surf there is on the Leeward Coast is not in Kailua-Kona but a short drive north at Banyans and Pine Trees or south at Kahaluʻu Beach (equipment and lessons available). See the boxed text, p173, for more information.

Right in Kailua, family-run **Pacific Vibrations** (Map p174; ☑329-4140; 75-5702 Likana Lane; board per day $15-20; ◷10am-5:30pm Mon-Fri, to 3:30pm Sat) has board rentals, clothes and tips. Surfboards can also be rented at Kona Boys Beach Shack, where you can also be hooked up with lessons.

Whale Watching

The season for humpback whales starts around January and runs to March or April.

Dan McSweeney's Whale Watch

WHALE WATCHING

(☑322-0028, 888-942-5376; www.ilovewhales.com; 3hr cruise adult/child $80/70; ◷Jul, Aug & Nov–Apr) While many maritime tour operators add whale-watching trips in season, we recommend marine mammal biologist Dan McSweeney. An active researcher, he leads educational excursions where observing whales is always the main focus. Several other types of whales, and five species of dolphin, can also be seen in Kona waters year-round. Hydrophones allow passengers to hear whale songs. Trips leave from Honokohau Harbor.

Yoga

Kona Yoga

(off Map p174; ☑331-1310; www.konayoga.com; Sunset Shopping Plaza, 77-6425 Hwy 11, D202; drop-in class $15) A local favorite, no-frills studio with a limited schedule where owner

HELICOPTER & AIR TOURS

Gazing, from the air, upon the world's most active volcano, live lava and gushing waterfalls is an excellent way for travelers (including those with disabilities) to experience Hawaiʻi's grandeur. Although helicopter tours are hyped, fixed-wing planes offer a smoother, quieter ride and are less expensive.

Standard helicopter volcano–waterfall tours last 45 minutes ($160 to $200); circle-island tours go for two hours ($400). There are also 'doors off' and 'valley landing' options. Questions to ask before booking: what can I expect to see; do all passengers have a 360-degree view; do valley tours enter valleys; and are noise-cancelling headsets provided? For the best views and smoothest riding, sit up front.

Helicopter tours fly if it's cloudy, but not if it's raining; wait for a sparkling clear day if you can – more likely in the summer. Another hot planning tip is to arrange a tour towards the end of your trip so you can contextualize what you're seeing. Most outfits offer online discounts, and free tourist magazines often contain coupons. (For an overview of the environmental impacts of helicopter tours, see the boxed text, p545.)

Blue Hawaiian Helicopters
(☑961-5600, 800-786-2583; www.bluehawaiian.com) Reliable, dependable and high volume. Departures from Waikoloa and Hilo.

Iolani Air Tour Company
(☑329-0018, 800-538-7590; www.iolaniair.com) Cheaper 50-minute 'flightseeing tours' by small prop plane. Discounts for children.

Paradise Helicopters
(☑969-7392, 866-876-7422; http://paradisecopters.com) A good reputation for more personal tours.

Safari Helicopters
(☑969-1259, 800-326-3356; www.safarihelicopters.com)

Tropical Helicopters
(☑866-961-6810; www.tropicalhelicopters.com) Also does custom charters.

Barbara Uechi teaches Iyengar-inspired classes with lots of care and humor.

Bikram Yoga Kona

(Map p174; ☎443-9990; www.bikramkona.com; Kuakini Center, 74-5563 Kaiwi St; drop-in class $16) The island's only Bikram studio.

☞ Tours

TOP CHOICE Body Glove Historical Sunset Dinner Cruise
CRUISE

(☎800-551-8911; www.bodyglovehawaii.com; adult/child $94/58; ☉historical cruise 4pm Tue, Thu & Sat, cocktail cruise 5:30pm Wed & Fri) This popular historical cruise along the Kona coast lasts three hours and includes dinner, kickin' live music and engaging historical narration. The **sunset 'booze' cruise** is two hours and features an open bar. The boat is wheelchair accessible.

Kona Historical Society
WALKING TOUR

(☎323-3222; www.konahistorical.org; 90min tour $15) This worthwhile and informational walking tour covers historical sites in downtown Kailua-Kona, and includes a booklet. Ten-person minimum and a cruise-ship maximum. Tours by appointment.

Atlantis Submarines
SUBMARINE

(☎329-6626, 800-548-6262; www.atlantisadven tures.com; adult/child $99/45; ☉rides 10am, 11:30am & 1pm) The underwater portion lasts 35 minutes. It descends 100ft into a coral crevice in front of the Royal Kona Resort and explores a couple of nearby shipwrecks. The battery-powered sub has 26 portholes and carries 48 passengers.

Kailua Bay Charter Company
GLASS-BOTTOM BOAT

(☎324-1749; www.konaglassbottomboat.com; 50min tour adult/child $40/20; ☉tours hourly from 10:30am) See Kailua's coastline and underwater reef and sea life from a 36ft glass-bottom boat with a pleasant crew and onboard naturalist. Easy boarding for mobility impaired passengers.

✯ Festivals & Events

TOP CHOICE Kona Brewers Festival
BEER & FOOD

(☎331-3033, 334-1884; www.konabrewersfestival .com; admission $50) Held in mid-March, this 'just folks' festival features samples from over 30 craft breweries and gourmet eats from scores of local restaurants. Proceeds benefit local environmental and cultural organizations. Get your tickets early or you'll miss out.

Hawaiian International Billfish Tournament
FISHING

(www.hibtfishing.com) 'The grandfather of all big-game fishing tournaments' is also Kona's most prestigious. It's accompanied, in late July to August, by a week of festive entertainment; 2009 marked its 50th anniversary.

Ironman Triathlon World Championship
TRIATHLON

(http://ironman.com) This legendary event, held in early October, combines a 2.4-mile ocean swim, 112-mile bike race and 26.2-mile marathon – the ultimate race, which has to be completed in 17 hours. Around 1800 competitors flood into Kona each year to give it their all.

Kona Coffee Cultural Festival
COFFEE

(www.konacoffeefest.com) For 10 days during harvest season in November the community celebrates Kona coffee pioneers and their gourmet brew. Events include a cupping competition (like a wine tasting), art exhibits, farm tours, parades, concerts and a coffee-picking race.

🛏 Sleeping

The quality of hotels and condos along Ali'i Dr in the walkable center of Kailua-Kona is only fair to middling. More attractive offerings are just outside town (in all directions, including 'upcountry'). Reservations for all Kailua properties are recommended in high season.

Condos tend to be cheaper than hotels for longer stays, and they offer more independence for DIY types (and families). Condo vacation rentals are handled directly by owners or by property management agencies. Vacation rentals are another family-friendly option; check listings on **Alternative Hawaii** (www.alternative-hawaii.com) and **Vacation Rentals by Owner** (www.vrbo.com).

ATR Properties

(☎329-6020, 888-311-6020; www.konacondo.com)

Kona Hawaii Vacation Rentals

(☎329-3333, 800-244-4752; www.konahawaii .com)

Knutson & Associates

(☎329-6311, 800-800-6202; www.konahawaii rentals.com)

SunQuest Vacations & Property Management Hawaii

(☎329-6438, 800-367-5168; www.sunquest -hawaii.com)

Kona Tiki Hotel
TOP CHOICE   HOTEL **$**

(off Map p174; ☑329-1425; www.konatiki.com; 75-5968 Ali'i Dr; r $85-113; P🛜🏊) The nothing-special rooms (with refrigerator, but no TV or phone) in this older three-story building would be forgettable if the intimate hush of crashing waves didn't tuck you in every night. Snug on a restless cove, the Kona Tiki is acceptably well kept and friendly; that it is also surprisingly romantic is all about the setting. The more expensive rooms have kitchenettes – perfect for DIY types. No credit cards.

Plumeria House
TOP CHOICE   INN **$$**

(Map p212; ☑326-9255; www.plumeriahouse.com; Kilohana St; 1 bedroom $80-120; 🅰️) Shh, this immaculate 800-sq-ft one-bedroom deal is a downright steal for longer stays (four-night minimum). Located in an upland residential neighborhood, the unit features many convenient touches: full kitchen, filtered water, patio tables and use of washer–dryer. Wheelchair accessible; $50 cleaning fee.

Hale Kona Kai
TOP CHOICE   CONDO **$$**

(Map p174; ☑329-6402, 800-421-3696; www.halekonakai-hkk.com; 75-5870 Kahakai Rd; 1 bedroom $140-185; P🅰️🛜🏊) Quietly positioned on a hidden lane just walkable to downtown, this three-story block of frequently upgraded units is a satisfying choice. All face the ocean and have lanai.

Royal Sea-Cliff Resort
TOP CHOICE   CONDO **$$**

(off Map p174; ☑329-8021, 800-688-7444; www.outrigger.com; 75-6040 Ali'i Dr; studios $130, 1 bedroom $150-195, 2 bedroom $165-200; P🅰️@🏊) Outrigger runs the condo side of this seven-floor time-share complex like an upscale hotel, giving you the best of both worlds. Immaculate units are generous-sized and uniformly appointed with pretty furniture and lots of amenities – well-stocked kitchens, washers and dryers, sauna and two oceanfront pools. You can't go wrong.

Kona Sugar Shack
TOP CHOICE   INN **$$**

(off Map p174; ☑895-2203, 877-324-6444; www.konasugarshack.com; 77-6483 Ali'i Dr; r $140-500; P🅰️🛜🏊) Your friendly, artistic hosts have created an attractively funky yet homey three-room inn, mostly solar powered, with shared outdoor kitchen, a miniscule pool, eclectic furnishings and lots of amenities. Also, they love kids. What will you say when you see the location (and views) almost directly across from White Sands Beach? Sweet. Three-night minimum stay required; the entire house, sleeping 15, is available for rent as well.

Casa de Emdeko
CONDO **$$**

(off Map p174; ☑329-2160; www.casadeemdeko.org; 75-6082 Ali'i Dr, 1 & 2 bedroom from $95; 🅰️🏊) With Spanish-tile roofs, white stucco, immaculate gardens and two pools, this vacation rental complex is stylish and restful. Units are overall up-to-date, well cared for, and nicely priced. The off-highway location means no noise except wind, surf and the tinkling of chimes.

Koa Wood Hale Inn/Patey's Place
HOSTEL **$**

(Map p174; ☑329-9663; www.alternative-hawaii.com/affordable/kona.htm; 75-184 Ala Ona Ona St; dm/s/d from $25/55/65; @🛜) This well-managed hostel is Kona's best budget deal, offering basic, quiet and clean dorms and private rooms (all with shared baths, kitchens and living rooms) on a residential street that's walking distance to Ali'i Dr. A fully equipped, two-bedroom apartment is also available for $130 per night. Hostel travelers young and old create a friendly, low-key vibe. No drugs, alcohol or shoes indoors.

Kona Magic Sands Resort
CONDO **$$**

(off Map p174; ☑329-3333, 800-244-4752; www.konahawaii.com/ms.htm; 77-6452 Ali'i Dr; studio units $125-160; P🅰️🏊) This three-story building is an ugly cinderblock shoebox, but the compact studios are surprisingly cool and quiet. Each has a full kitchen and an oceanfront lanai. White Sands Beach next door is an important plus.

King Kamehameha's Kona Beach Hotel
HOTEL **$$**

(Map p174; ☑329-2911, reservations 800-367-2111; www.konabeachhotel.com; 75-5660 Palani Rd; r $170-230; P🅰️🛜🏊) Location and spiffy renovation are the watchwords for the historic 'King Kam' anchoring Ali'i Dr. Chic room decor, a brand-new Herb Kawainui Kane exhibit in the lobby (open to nonguests) and free in-room wi-fi are all draws here. Walk to some of our favorite restaurants or hop over to the Kona Boys Beach Shack to try stand up paddling or sea kayaking.

Royal Kona Resort
RESORT **$$$**

(Map p174; ☑329-3111, reservations 800-222-5642; www.royalkona.com; 75-5852 Ali'i Dr; r $180-265, ste $210-330; P🅰️@🏊) You can't miss the Royal Kona, thrusting like a ship's prow, whose '70s

Polynesian kitsch is so potent you half expect the Brady Bunch to come tumbling out of the elevator – making this Kailua's most enjoyable big hotel. The good-sized, freshly renovated rooms are attractive, with nice touches such as wood-shutter closet doors; corner-room lanai have tremendous views, but others lack privacy. Check out the extensive services at the Lotus Center Spa (www.konaspa.com) here.

If you're desperate to stay close to downtown, you might consider these functional standbys. Look online for discounts.

Kona Reef CONDOS $$$
(Map p174; 329-2959, 800-367-5004; www.kona-reef.com; 75-5888 Ali'i Dr; 1br $260-350, 2br $425-520; P✸@≋) Spacious, well-kept, condos in a nondescript complex; a better deal with internet discount.

Kona Seaside Hotel HOTEL $$
(Map p174; 329-2455, 800-560-5558; http://seasidehotelshawaii.com; 75-5646 Palani Rd; r $110-130; P✸≋) The Garden Wing is quietest; rooms with a view aren't worth the extra cash.

Uncle Billy's Kona Bay Hotel HOTEL $
(Map p174; 329-1393, 800-367-5102; www.unclebilly.com; 75-5744 Ali'i Dr; r $95-120; P✸🄪≋) Looks retro-cool outside, but badly designed inside; too much street noise.

Kona Isle CONDO $$
(off Map p174; 329-6311, 800-800-6202; www.konaislacondos.com; 75-6100 Ali'i Dr; 1 bedroom $95-155; P✸≋) Inoffensively plain but clean home base for exploring. Saltwater pool.

✗ Eating

You don't have to spend a lot in Kailua-Kona to dine on *'ono grinds* – you just to need to know where to go.

TOP CHOICE Kanaka Kava HAWAIIAN $
(Map p174; www.kanakakava.com; Coconut Grove Marketplace, 75-5803 Ali'i Dr; à la carte $4-6, mains $14-16; ⊙10am-10pm Sun-Wed, to 11pm Thu-Sat) This tiny, cafe is the perfect place to try kava (the juice of the *'awa* plant), grown by owner–chef Zachary Gibson. Granted, kava tastes like dirt, but give it a chance and its legendary relaxing qualities become evident. Gibson's delicious organic salads are topped with fish, shellfish, chicken, tofu or *poke* (cubed raw fish marinated in soy sauce, oil and chili pepper). The *kalua* (traditional method of cooking) pork is phenomenal. Cash only.

TOP CHOICE Big Island Grill DINER $$
(Map p174; 75-5702 Kuakini Hwy; plate lunches $10, mains $10-19; ⊙7:30am-9pm Mon-Sat) Everyone loves this spot, which serves Hawaii's comfort foods – aka plate lunches and *loco moco* – as fresh and flavorful as home cooking. Choose from fried chicken katsu (deep-fried fillets), fried mahimahi, shrimp tempura, beef teriyaki, *kalua* pork and more; all come with two scoops of rice, potato-mac salad and rich gravy. It's always packed, but swift service is warm with aloha.

Rapanui Island Café ISLAND CONTEMPORARY $$
(Map p174; Banyan Court mall, 75-5695 Ali'i Dr; lunch $6-10, dinner mains $10-16; ⊙lunch & dinner Mon-Fri, dinner Sat) This cafe's New Zealand owners know curry, which they prepare with a delicious tongue-tingly warmth. Choose from various satays, spiced pork, seafood and salads. Order the house coconut rice; and wash it down with lemongrass ginger tea or a New Zealand wine.

Jackie Rey's Ohana Grill ISLAND CONTEMPORARY $$
(www.jackiereys.com; Pottery Terrace, 75-5995 Kuakini Hwy; mains lunch $11-15, dinner $14-28; ⊙lunch 11am-5pm Mon-Fri, dinner 5-9pm daily) This casual, family-owned grill has Polynesian flair and a fun retro Hawaii vibe. Yummy fare, including glazed short ribs, wasabi-seared ahi and killer fresh fish tacos, is served with aloha, making this place a local favorite. Kids are king here, getting their own menu, crayons for creating on the 'tablecloths' and tours of the walk-in freezer to ogle the giant fish hanging about. Locals come in droves for half-priced pupu from 2pm to 5pm, Monday to Friday.

Island Lava Java CAFE $$
(Map p174; www.islandlavajavakona.com; Ali'i Sunset Plaza, 75-5799 Ali'i Dr; meals $9-18; ⊙6:30am-9:30pm; @🄪) This cafe is a favorite gathering spot for sunny breakfasts (and Sunday brunch) with almost-oceanside dining on the outdoor patio. The food aims for upscale diner; if it sometimes hits closer to greasy spoon, no one minds – especially since the coffee is 100% Kona, and the beef and chicken are Big Island–raised. Portions are huge and baked goods sinful.

La Bourgogne FRENCH $$$
(off Map p174; 329-6711; Kuakini Plaza, 77-6400 Nalani St, at Hwy 11; mains $28-38; ⊙6-10pm Tue-Sat) Kona's best choice for special-occasion fine dining is this classic French restaurant,

PAUL STREITER, RESTAURATEUR

Streiter, a transplanted New Yorker and dedicated dad, runs a restaurant (named after his young daughter) with his wife.

Best Activity for Kids

The Fair Wind snorkel cruise (p178) to Kealakekua Bay is great. The crew is fun and kids love jumping off the upper deck or riding the slide into the bay. They always have fun sea toys that make you feel safe while snorkeling.

Romantic Dining

Seaside at the Beach Tree (p214). It's completely renovated and they have an awesome Mediterranean menu crafted by their hot new young chef. Holuakoa Gardens & Café (p193) is also very romantic.

The Fish Lowdown

The Big Island has amazing fishing grounds right off the coast – it tops all Hawaiian islands for fresh fish. The KTA Super Store (p273) has the best fish counter. Top quality, nothing is ever frozen – this is the real deal. Try the *poke*.

Ironman Tips

Watch the swim portion from Kailua Pier and then come up to Jackie Rey's Ohana Grill (p182) to watch the cycling leg – we set up lawn chairs in the parking lot. They go up at 25mph and then whiz back down at 45mph. Cyclists can feel like an Ironman for a day by renting a top-end road bike and peddling the official Kailua-Kona to Hawi route.

where the cuisine and the presentation exude skill and refinement. Expect baked brie in puff pastry, roast duck, rabbit in white wine, foie gras and Kona's best wine list. The dining room is Parisian-intimate, and the service is good, if not always up to the food. Reservations are a must.

Kona Brewing Company AMERICAN $$
(Map p174; ☎334-2739; www.konabrewingco.com; 75-5629 Kuakini Hwy; sandwiches & salads $11-16, pizzas $15-26; ☺11am-9pm Sun-Thu, to 10pm Fri & Sat) Good beer, green stewardship and lots of aloha: the Big Island's first microbrewery serves up one of Kona's liveliest scenes. A Certified Green Restaurant, Kona Brewing Company's latest concoctions include Oceanic Organic Saison (a singular certified-organic brew) and Suncharged Pale Ale, made using solar power. Either at the bright bar (closes an hour after the kitchen) or on the torch-lit patio, diners enjoy meal-sized salads, juicy burgers and thin-crust pizzas from a stone oven. Make reservations.

Orchid Thai THAI $$
(Map p174; Kuakini Center, 74-5555 Kaiwi St; lunch specials $10, dinner $10-16; ☺11:30am-3pm, 5-9pm Mon-Sat; ☑) Orchid Thai is the neighborhood stalwart locals seek out when they need a curry fix. The classic preparations are handled well and without fuss. Strip mall location, but fake brick and eggplant-colored curtains warm up the interior. Bring your own alcohol.

You Make the Roll SUSHI $
(Map p174; Kona Marketplace, 75-5725 Ali'i Dr; sushi rolls $5-7; ☺11am-7pm Mon-Fri, to 4pm Sat) This high-concept hole-in-the-wall presents 20 sushi ingredients you can combine however you like. Fat loose rolls, low prices, lots of fun and a hidden location: it's a budgeter's dream.

Ba-Le Kona VIETNAMESE $
(Map p174; Kona Coast Shopping Center, 74-5588 Palani Rd; sandwiches $4-7, soups & plates $9-13; ☺10am-9pm Mon-Sat, 11am-7pm Sun; ☑) Don't let the fluorescent-lit dining room and polystyrene plates fool you: Ba-Le serves up raveworthy Vietnamese fare. Flavors are simple, refreshing and bright, from the green-papaya salad to traditional *pho* (Vietnamese noodle soup) and saimin (local-style noodle soup), and rice plates of spicy lemongrass chicken, tofu, beef or roast pork.

Killer Tacos MEXICAN $
(Map p174; 74-5483 Kaiwi St; mains $3-8; ☺10am-8pm Mon-Fri, to 6pm Sat; ☎) If you've been wondering where locals and surfers chow down

after a long, hot day of work and play, look no further. The burritos are a better bang for your buck than the tacos, but everything here is made tasty to order. Ask about additional hot sauces – the salsa is anemic.

Scandinavian Shaved Ice
Internet Café   SHAVE ICE $
(Map p174; www.scandinavianshaveice.com; 75-5699 Ali'i Dr; shave ice $3.50-7.25; ⊘11am-7pm) Shave ice is served here in huge, psychedelic-colored mounds that are as big as your head. There is an orgy of syrup choices. At night folks sometimes break out board games.

Other recommended places downtown:

Sushi Shiono   SUSHI $
(Map p174; www.sushishiono.com; Ali'i Sunset Plaza, 75-5799 Ali'i Dr; sushi & rolls $4-12; ⊘lunch Mon-Fri, dinner daily) Awesomely fresh fish and nice sake list.

Basik Acai   ACAI BOWLS $
(Map p174; www.basikacai.com; 75-5831 Kahakai Rd; bowls $6-11; ⊘8am-4pm Mon-Sat; 🛜🅿) Healthy, wholesome bowls bursting with goodness (granola, tropical fruit, nuts) are blended with acai for added punch. Nice ocean views from up here.

Tex Drive-In   DRIVE-IN $
(Map p174; Kopiko Plaza; 🅿) Sinful *malasadas* now available at this new outpost of the famous Honoka'a drive in (p251), plus (wait for it!) vegetarian *loco moco*.

Kope Lani   CAFE $
(Map p174; www.kopelani.com; 75-5719 Ali'i Dr; ⊘7am-9pm) Potent coffee drinks, ice cream and sandwiches.

KTA Super Store (Map p174; www.ktasuperstores.com; Kona Coast Shopping Center, 74-5594 Palani Rd; ⊘5am-11pm) and Island Naturals (Map p174; www.islandnaturals.com; 74-5487 Kaiwi St; ⊘7:30am-8pm Mon-Sat, 9am-7pm Sun; 🅿) should have everything you need in the way of groceries. Each has a deli, and at KTA you'll find sushi, some of the island's best *poke*, kimchi (seasoned vegetable pickle) and other local specialties.

🍺 Drinking

The Big Island has no nightlife scene comparable to Waikiki or Maui. For sheer number of bars, Kailua-Kona is as good as it gets, but most are fairly touristy. Don't forget the Kona Brewing Company (p183).

Humpy's Big Island Alehouse   PUB
(Map p174; www.humpyshawaii.com; Coconut Grove Marketplace, 75-5815 Ali'i Dr; ⊘9am-1am) Smack on the strip overlooking the Bay, Humpy's would probably survive in touristy Kailua-Kona even if it didn't have more than three dozen beers on tap. But fresh, foamy brews bring in the locals, giving the upstairs balcony – with its sea breeze and views – special cachet. Drop in for happy hour, 3pm to 6pm Monday to Friday.

Mixx   BAR
(Map p174; www.mixxbistro.com; King Kamehameha Mall, 75-5626 Kuakini Hwy; pupu $6-15; ⊘5pm-late Tue-Sat) Mixx is a small spot that's tucked away in a shopping mall and attracts a local crowd; often it's a quiet place for wine and *pupu* (snacks), but if there's a DJ or salsa it gets lively. And those $5 martinis: wow.

Huggo's on the Rocks   BAR
(Map p174; www.huggos.com/all/rocksdefault.htm; 75-5828 Kahakai Rd; ⊘11:30am-midnight) Right on the water, with a thatched-roof bar and live music nightly, Huggo's is an ideal sunset spot. Whether it's worth staying longer depends on who's playing and who shows up. In the mornings, this place reverts to Java on the Rocks (⊘6-11am), with terrific coffee drinks and inventive breakfasts.

Don's Mai Tai Bar   BAR
(Map p174; www.royalkona.com; 75-5852 Ali'i Dr; ⊘10am-10pm) For pure kitsch, nothing beats the shameless lounge-lizard fantasy of Don's, in the Royal Kona. Behold killer ocean views, with one of 10 different mai tais. Real fans roll in for the annual **Mai Tai Festival** held here each August.

Okolemaluna Tiki Bar   BAR
(Map p174; www.okolemalunalounge.com; Ali'i Sunset Plaza, 75-5799 Ali'i Dr; ⊘3-11pm Mon-Fri, to midnight Sat & Sun) A nearly seaside new bar to the Kailua-Kona cocktail scene, specializing in all manner of tropical umbrella drinks. Fruit juice mixers are freshly squeezed.

☆ Entertainment

Kailua-Kona's two hokey, cruise-ship friendly luau include a ceremony, a buffet dinner with Hawaiian specialties, an open bar and a Polynesian dinner show featuring a cast of flamboyant dancers and fire twirlers.

Journeys of the South Pacific   LUAU
(Map p174; 🎵329-3111; www.konaluau.com; Royal Kona Resort; adult/child 6-11yr $60/24; ⊘6pm

Mon, Wed & Fri) One child under six years admitted free with each paying adult.

King Kamehameha's Kona Beach Hotel
LUAU

(Map p174; ☑329-4969; www.islandbreezeluau.com; adult/child 5-12yr $74/37; ⊙5pm Tue, Thu & Sun)

If the rain or vog is bringing you down head to **Stadium Cinemas** (off Map p174; ☑327-0444; Makalapua Shopping Center; 74-5469 Kamaka'eha Ave) for the latest Hollywood flicks; or to **KBXtreme** (☑326-2695; www.kbxtreme.com;75-5591 Palani Rd; per hr $29, shoe rental $3; ⊙9am-midnight, bar to 2am) for some bowling fun – weekdays from 1pm to 4pm are deeply discounted and weekend nights feature 'cosmic bowling' followed by a DJ and dancing.

🛍 Shopping

Kailua-Kona is swamped with run-of-the-mill, dubious-quality Hawaiiana, but there's good stuff, too. You never know when you'll find that perfectly sublime kitschy tacky something.

TOP CHOICE Big Island Jewelers
JEWELRY

(Map p174; ☑329-8571; www.bigislandjewelers.com; 75-5695 Ali'i Dr) Family owned and operated for nearly four decades, with master jeweler Flint Carpenter at the wheel, this jewelry store offers authentic Big Island keepsakes (or rings if you need to pop the question!). The keshi natural pearl line is especially gorgeous.

Na Makana
SOUVENIRS

(Map p174; ☑938-8577; 75-5722 Likana Lane; ⊙9am-5pm) This odds-and-ends shop is a rarity in Kailua – offering authentic Hawaii-made gifts, books and collectibles, with unusual finds such as Japanese glass fishing floats. Opening hours vary according to the owner's schedule.

Kailua Village Farmers Market
SOUVENIRS

(Map p174; www.konafarmersmarket.com; Ali'i Dr; ⊙7am-4pm Wed-Sun) First, wander through this market where craft stalls outnumber produce stands two to one. Then purchase your coconut purses, cheap kids wear and koa wood Harleys. Do like the locals and get your fresh lei ($5) here.

Kona International Market
SOUVENIRS

(Map p174; www.konainternationalmarket.com; 74-5533 Luhia St; ⊙9am-5pm) Five large ware-house buildings make up this expansive, attractive complex, where individual stalls sell everything imaginable: beach gear, fresh fish, boutique clothing, music, gifts and crafts galore. Has a food court and ample parking.

Crazy Shirts
CLOTHING

(Map p174; www.crazyshirts.com; Kona Market-place, 75-5719 Ali'i Dr; ⊙9am-9pm) The iconic T-shirt company, founded in 1964, offers unique island designs on heavyweight cotton. The quality shows and, just for fun, shirts are dyed in coffee, beer, tea, volcanic ash and more.

Conscious Riddims Records
MUSIC

(Map p174; ☑326-7685; www.consciousriddims.org; Kona Marketplace, Ali'i Dr; ⊙10am-6pm Sun-Fri) A wide selection of reggae and Jawaiian music, plus clothing and *pakalolo* (marijuana) activism.

ℹ Information

Bookstores

Kona Bay Books (www.konabaybooks.com; 74-5487 Kaiwi St; ⊙10am-6pm) The island's best used-book store, with a nice selection of Hawaiian titles, plus used CDs.

Internet Access

Island Lava Java (☑327-2161; Ali'i Sunset Plaza, 75-5799 Ali'i Dr; per 20min $4; ⊙6am-10pm) Wireless, plus two computer terminals.

Kona Business Center (☑329-0006; www.konacopy.com; Suite B-1A, Kona International Market, 74-5533 Luhia St; per 30min $5.25, per hour $10; ⊙8:30am-5:30pm Mon-Fri) Complete business services; internet and wi-fi.

Scandinavian Shaved Ice Internet Café (☑331-1626; 75-5699 Ali'i Dr; per hour $8; ⊙10am-7pm) Six computers, all connected to printers.

Internet Resources

Big Island Visitors Bureau (www.bigisland.org) Basic info geared to the mainstream; handy calendar of events.

Kona Web (www.konaweb.com) This wonderfully helpful site has been collecting reviews from locals and visitors about the entire Big Island since 1995.

Media

NEWSPAPERS Hawaii Tribune-Herald (www.hawaiitribune-herald.com) The Big Island's main daily newspaper.

West Hawaii Today (www.westhawaiitoday.com) Kona Coast's daily newspaper.

RADIO A station guide is available at http://hawaiiradiotv.com/BigIsleRadio.html.

GETTING ROUND TOWN

The highways and major roads in the Kona district parallel the coastline, so you're unlikely to get lost. Kailua-Kona is south of the airport on Hwy 19 (Queen Ka'ahumanu Hwy), which becomes Hwy 11 (Mamalahoa Hwy) at Palani Rd. What makes navigation a bit tricky is when Queen Ka'ahumana (Hwy 19) confusingly becomes Kuakini Hwy (Hwy 11) at the intersection with Palani Rd, then connects with the historic Kuakini Hwy toward the ocean. In other words, there are two Kuakini Hwys for a stretch!

From the highway, Kaiwi St, Palani Rd and Henry St are the primary routes into town. Ali'i Dr is Kailua's main drag; the first mile, from Palani Rd to Kahakai Rd, is a pedestrian-friendly ramble lined with shops, restaurants and hotels. Ali'i Dr then continues another 4 miles along the coast to Keauhou, and is cheek-by-jowl condo complexes, vacation rentals, B&Bs, hotels and private homes.

To beat commuter traffic in and out of town, check out the new Haleki'i Bypass Rd connecting Kealakekua with Keauhou (see p200).

KAGB 99.1 FM (www.kaparadio.com) The Kona-side home of effervescent KAPA – Hawaii and island music.

KKUA 90.7 FM (www.hawaiipublicradio.org) Hawaii Public Radio; classical music, talk and news.

KLUA 93.9 FM Native FM plays island and reggae tunes.

KMWB 93.1 Classic rock.

Medical Services

Kona Community Hospital (322-9311; www.kch.hhsc.org; 79-1019 Haukapila St, Kealakekua) Located about 10 miles south of Kailua-Kona.

Longs Drugs (Lanihau Center, 75-5595 Palani Rd; ⊗8am-9pm Mon-Sat, to 6pm Sun) Centrally located drugstore and pharmacy.

Money

The following have 24-hour ATMs:

Bank of Hawaii (Lanihau Center, 75-5595 Palani Rd)

First Hawaiian Bank (Lanihau Center, 74-5593 Palani Rd)

Post

Post office (Lanihau Center 74-5577 Palani Rd; ⊗8:30am-4:30pm Mon-Fri, 9:30am-1:30pm Sat)

Getting There & Away

AIR The island's primary airport is **Kona International Airport at Keahole** (KOA; ⟨☑⟩327-9520; http://hawaii.gov/koa; Hwy 19), located 7 miles north of Kailua-Kona. When booking, keep in mind that late afternoon weekday traffic is brutal on southbound Hwy 19.

BUS The **Hele-On Bus** (www.heleonbus.org) runs from Kailua-Kona to Captain Cook (1½ hours) multiple times daily except Sunday. Twice daily except Sunday, it runs to Pahala (two hours), Hilo (3½ hours) and Waimea (1½

hours). The South Kohala resorts, meanwhile, are serviced three times a day except Sunday (1½ hours).

Another option between Kailua-Kona and Keauhou is the Honu Express (p192), a $1 shuttle that runs daily between Kailua Pier and Keauhou Shopping Center.

CAR The trip from Hilo to Kailua-Kona is 92 miles and takes 2½ hours via Waimea, a bit longer via Volcano; for other driving times and distances, see p171.

To avoid snarly traffic during rush hour try the Haleki'i Bypass Road (see p200).

ⓘ Getting Around

TO/FROM THE AIRPORT If you're not picking up a rental car, taxis can be found curbside; the fare averages $30 to Kailua-Kona and $55 to Waikoloa. **Speedi Shuttle** (☑329-5433, 877-242-5777; www.speedishuttle.com) charges about the same, and only a couple of dollars for each additional person. Book in advance.

If you've got a rental car, a right out of the airport takes you south 7 miles to Kailua-Kona; left takes you up the coast to North Kona.

BICYCLE Bicycle is an ideal way to get around Kailua.

Hawaiian Pedals (☑329-2294; www.hawaiian pedals.com; Kona Inn Shopping Village, 75-5744 Ali'i Dr; per day $20; ⊗9:30am-8pm) Rents well-used hybrid bikes for cruising.

Bike Works (☑326-2453; www.bikeworkskona .com; Hale Hana Center, 74-5583 Luhia St; per day $40-60; ⊗9am-6pm Mon-Sat, 10am-4pm Sun) Rents high-quality mountain and touring bikes for the serious cyclist; offers multiday discounts. Rentals include helmet, lock, pump and patch kit.

BUS The **Hele-On Bus** (www.heleonbus.org) and the **Honu Express** (see p192) both make stops within Kailua-Kona.

CAR Ali'i Dr, in downtown Kailua-Kona, gets very congested in the late afternoon and evening. Free public parking is available in a lot between Likana Lane and Kuakini Hwy. Shopping centers along Ali'i Dr usually provide free parking for patrons behind their center.

MOPED & MOTORCYCLE Scooter Brothers (☑327-1080; www.scooterbrothers.com; King Kamehameha Mall, 75-5626 Kuakini Hwy; per 6hr/day/week $20/60/266; ⊙10am-6pm) Get around town like a local, on a moped. The official riding area is from Waikoloa up north to Captain Cook down south.

Big Island Harley Davidson (☑635-0542; www.hawaiiharleyrental.com; 75-5633 Palani Rd; per day/week $179/763)

TAXI Call ahead for pickups from the following companies:

Laura's Taxi (☑326-5466; www.luanalimo .com; ⊙5am-10pm)

D&E Taxi (☑329-4279; ⊙6am-9pm)

AROUND KAILUA-KONA

Immediately south of Kailua-Kona is the upscale Keauhou resort area, while in the mountains to the southeast is the dropped-in-amber town of Holualoa, now an intriguing artists' community. Just north of Kailua-Kona is Honokohau Harbor (setting off point for the lion's share of maritime tours). Inland and upslope from the harbor are some excellent places to stay and eat.

Keauhou Resort Area

Keauhou has no town center, unless you count the shopping mall. Rather, it is a collection of destinations: Keauhou Harbor for boat tours, Kahalu'u Beach for snorkeling and surfing, resorts and condos for sleeping, a farmers market and good restaurants, and a significant ancient Hawaiian settlement.

🏝 Beaches

Kahalu'u Beach Park   BEACH
(Map p198) One of the island's most thrilling and easy-access snorkeling spots, Kahalu'u Bay is a giant natural aquarium loaded with colorful marine life. It's the classic medley of rainbow parrotfish, silver needlefish, brilliant yellow tangs and Moorish idols, plus green sea turtles often swim in to feed and rest on the beach. An ancient breakwater, which according to legend was built by the *menehune* (Hawaii's mythical race of little people), is on the reef and protects the bay.

This is a favorite surf spot that, when conditions are mellow, is ideal for beginners and for learning to stand up paddle (SUP); when surf is high, strong rip currents make it challenging. Across the road from Kahalu'u Bay, **Kona Surf School** (Map p198; ☑217-5329; www.konasurfschool.com; 78-6685 Ali'i Dr; board rental per day/week $25/99, surf lessons $100-150; ⊙8:30am-5pm) offers board rentals and lessons daily (reservations required), including SUP surfing ($75).

One thing not to come here for is peace and quiet. The tiny salt-and-pepper beach is hemmed in on all sides: by the busy highway, by the adjacent resort, by the covered pavilion with picnicking families, and by the throngs of snorkelers constantly paddling in and out of the water. Come early; the parking lot can fill up by 10am. Facilities include showers, rest rooms, picnic tables, grills, and snorkel and locker rentals. A lifeguard is on duty.

⊙ Sights & Activities

St Peter's Church   CHURCH
(Map p198) The 'Little Blue Church' is one of Hawaii's most photographed, and a favorite for weddings. The striking sea-green and white building sits almost in Kahalu'u Bay.

Built in the 1880s, St Peter's was moved from White Sands Beach to this site in 1912. It now sits on an ancient Hawaiian religious site, Ku'emanu Heiau. Hawaiian royalty, who surfed Kahalu'u Bay, prayed for good surf at this temple before hitting the waves.

Heiau & Historical Sites   HISTORICAL SITE
(Map p198) Kahalu'u Bay is adjacent to the Outrigger Keauhou Beach Resort, which sits where a major ancient Hawaiian settlement once existed. An easy path leads from the beach into and around the protected sites – the front desk has displays and a map brochure. Guided tours are also offered by the Outrigger (8am Tuesday).

At the north end are the ruins of Kapuanoni, a fishing heiau, and a replica of the summer beach house of King Kalakaua next to a spring-fed pond, once either a fishpond or a royal bath. To the south are two major heiau. The first, Hapaiali'i Heiau, was built 600 years ago and in 2007 was completely restored by dry-stack masonry experts into a 15,000-sq-ft platform; the speculation is that the heiau was used as a sun calendar to mark the solstice and equinox. Next to Hapaiali'i is the even larger Ke'eku Heiau, also recently restored. Legends say

KAYAK FISHING

The Big Island is big on the newest watersport adventure: kayak fishing. Imagine landing a 25lb ahi or 35lb *ono* from a kayak – but not without a fight! A couple of professional, licensed outfitters can hook you up to do exactly that (okay, yours might be a wee bit smaller...). No experience is necessary, and due to the nature of the sport, tours are usually just you and your guide.

For fully guided tours and all gear:

Lucky Gecko Kayak Fishing (☑557-9827; www.luckygeckokayakfishing.com; 5hr tour $125) Leaves from Keauhou Bay.

Kayak Fishing Hawai'i (☑936-4400; www.kayakfishinghawaii.com; 6hr tour $250) This outfitter is based in Kawaihae but travels islandwide.

that Ke'eku was a *luakini* (temple of human sacrifice); most famously, a Maui chief who tried to invade the Big Island was sacrificed here, and his grieving dogs guard the site still. Nearby petroglyphs, visible only at low tide, tell this story.

FREE **Keauhou Kahalu'u Heritage Center** (☉10am-5pm), an unstaffed, well-lit space in the Keauhou Shopping Center, will teach you more about the restoration of Keauhou's heiau; it's near KTA Super Store. Displays and videos also describe *holua,* the ancient Hawaiian sport of sledding.

Keauhou Bay   PARK
This bay, with a small boat harbor and launch ramp, is one of the most protected on the west coast. There's no real reason to come unless you've booked, or want to book, a tour (see p178). However, there's a small grassy area with picnic tables, showers and rest rooms, a sand volleyball court, and the headquarters of the local outrigger canoe club. To get to the bay, turn *makai* (seaward) off Ali'i Dr onto Kamehameha III Rd.

TOP CHOICE **Keauhou Farmers Market**   MARKET
(www.keahoufarmersmarket.com; ☉8am-noon Sat) One of the Big Island's best farmers markets is at the Keauhou Shopping Center. Though not large, it focuses almost solely on high-quality organic produce and products from local small farms. The warm community feeling is enhanced by live Hawaiian music and presentations by local chefs. Grab a coffee and come early!

Original Hawaiian Chocolate Factory   CHOCOLATE FACTORY
(☑322-2626, 888-447-2626; www.ohcf.us; adult/child under 12yr $10/free; ☉9am Wed, 9:30am Fri) A must for chocolate fans, these exclusive one-hour tours detail how the *only* Hawai-

ian chocolate is grown, harvested, processed and packaged. Samples and sales available at tour's end. By appointment only.

👉 Tours & Courses

Outrigger Keauhou Beach Resort Cultural Program   ARTS , CULTURE
(☑324-2540; www.keauhoubeachresort.com, click on the Dining/Activities tab; ☉classes 8am-3pm weekdays) Intriguing Hawaiian language, hula and lei-making classes are held on the grounds of the Outrigger as part of its cultural program. Ukulele and chant classes are also on offer. Guided **daytime tours** (adult/child 8-12yr incl lunch $60/30) of the resort's historical and cultural sites are available, while **evening tours** (adult/child 8-12yr incl dinner $85/45) highlight traditional navigating known as wayfaring.

Outrigger also conducts free, one-hour **cultural tours** (☉8am Tue) of its grounds, including the restored heiau.

Keauhou Shopping Center   MUSIC, DANCE
(www.keauhoushoppingcenter.com) Free **ukulele jams** (BYO uke) are held from 6pm to 8pm Wednesday, as well as **Polynesian dance shows** at 6pm Friday. Check the website for other classes and activities.

🎉 Festivals & Events

The **Kona Chocolate Festival** (☑987-8722; www.konachocolatefestival.com; Sheraton Keauhou Bay Resort; advance booking/day of event $40/50; ☉late Mar/early Apr) is a three-day celebration of (surprise!) all things chocolate. It includes a 'chocolate symposium' of workshops and culminates in a gala evening celebration, with live music and a chocolate cook-off among island chefs. The 2011 festival was postponed due to damage at the host site caused by the tsunami generated by the 2011 earthquake in Japan. Check the website for updates.

Sleeping

For a list of property management agencies, see p180.

Outrigger Kanaloa at Kona
CONDO $$$

(Map p198; ☎322-9625, reservations 866-733-0361; www.outriggerkanaloaatkonacondo.com; 78-261 Manukai St; 1 bedroom $295-365, 2 bedroom $325-499; P✳@◎⊛⊠) These tropical townhouse-style condominiums are simply splendid. Large, immaculate and fully stocked, units are gathered in small, well-designed clusters that afford privacy. One-bedroom units easily fit a family of four, and you'll want to rip the kitchen out to take home. A daily maid service is included; two-night minimum stay required.

Outrigger Keauhou Beach Resort
RESORT $$

(Map p198; ☎322-3441, reservations 866-326-6803; www.keauhoubeachresort.com; 78-6740 Ali'i Dr; r $140-230; P✳@◎⊛⊠) This gated, townhouse-style condo feels exclusive, safe and private, sitting on an oceanfront lava ledge. Units are huge (one-bedrooms average 1200 sq ft to 1300 sq ft); two-bedroom units include two full bathrooms. With three pools, night-lit tennis courts and an adjacent golf course, you can practically stay put. Of the 166 units, Outrigger manages 84.

Sheraton Keauhou Bay Resort
RESORT $$$

(Map p198; ☎930-4900, 866-716-8109; www.sheratonkeauhou.com; 78-128 'Ehukai St; r $350-460; ✳@◎⊛⊠) The only bona fide resort in the Kailua-Kona area, the Sheraton boasts a sleekly modern design, over 500 rooms, upscale spa, fine dining and massive pool (with spiral slide) threading through the canyon-like atrium, but no beach. The theatrical atmosphere is topped off by the manta rays, which gather offshore nightly. Sheraton will hit you with a $16 per night mandatory resort fee (for parking, wi-fi and other amenities). Check online for deep discounts.

Eating

TOP CHOICE Kenichi Pacific
JAPANESE $$

(☎322-6400; www.restauranteur.com/kenichi; Keauhou Shopping Center; sushi $5.50-10, mains $26-33; ⊙11:30am-1:30pm Tue-Fri, dinner from 5pm daily) Kenichi prepares well-executed and beautifully presented Pacific fusion cuisine. Highlights include scallops in red curry over soba noodles, grilled ono with a ponzu glaze and sweet potatoes, and sautéed shiitake mushrooms over spaghettini.

The sushi and sashimi here are extraordinarily fresh. While the mall setting doesn't affect the sleek, stylish dining room, it kills the outdoor terrace. Don't miss happy hour (4:30pm to 6:30pm), with half-price sushi rolls and drink specials.

Peaberry & Galette
CAFE $

(www.peaberryandgalette.com; Keauhou Shopping Center; crepes $8-14; ⊙7am-7pm Mon-Thu, to 8pm Fri & Sat, 8am-6pm Sun) For a dose of European hipness, order a sweet or savory crepe here. The quality of the salads and quiches is above average and the espresso machine hisses constantly, of course. Tea drinkers can get a quality fix here, too.

Kama'aina Terrace
HAWAII REGIONAL $$

(Map p198; ☎322-3441; Outrigger Keauhou Beach Resort; ⊙6:30-10:30am & 5:30-9pm) Breakfast or *pupu* just go down better when you can see, smell and hear the ocean, like you can here at the Outrigger's ocean-front restaurant. The Aloha all-you-can-eat **buffet** (adult/child 6-12yr $26/13; ⊙11am-1pm), hosted every third Sunday, is an extravaganza of traditional Hawaiian dishes accompanied by fine Hawaiian music.

For quick, economical groceries and takeout:

KTA Super Store
GROCERY

(Keauhou Shopping Center; ⊙7am-10pm)

Habaneros
MEXICAN

(☎324-4688; Keauhou Shopping Center; à la carte $3-7, plates $7-8; ⊙9am-9pm Mon-Sat). Passable Mexican food.

Drinking & Entertainment

Verandah Lounge
BAR

(Map p198; ☎322-3441; Outrigger Keauhou Beach Resort; ⊙11am-9pm Sun-Thu, to 10pm Fri & Sat) Waves crashing just below greatly enhance the atmosphere of this wraparound bar. Live Hawaiian music sets the tone from 6:30pm to 9:30pm Friday and Saturday.

Firenesia
LUAU

(Map p198; ☎326-4969; www.firenesia.com; Sheraton Keauhou Bay Resort; adult/child 5-12 $80/50; ⊙4:30pm Mon) The Sheraton luau (another Island Breeze production) is a fiery hero narrative weaving together several Polynesian tales and themes.

Regal Cinemas Keauhou
CINEMA

(☎324-0172; Keauhou Shopping Center) Hollywood flicks fill seven screens. Matinee and Tuesday discounts.

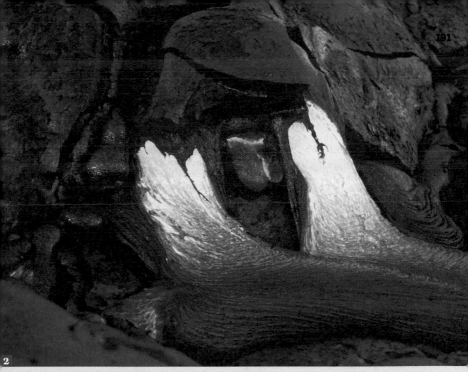

1. Hawai'i Volcanoes National Park (p282)
Sea arches are formed by crashing surf constantly pounding and eroding lava cliffs.

2. Live Lava (p292)
Check http://hawaiianlavadaily.blogspot.com to find out where live lava is flowing when you arrive.

3. Akaka Falls State Park (p258)
Features include banyan trees, orchids, gigantic bamboo groves and the 420ft Akaka Falls.

4. Pu'uhonua o Honaunau (p207)
Carved wooden *ki'i* (deity images) front a heiau (temple) in Pu'uhonua o Honaunau.

THE BIG ISLAND FOR CHILDREN

» Explore Hawai'i's underwater wonderland on a snorkel tour (p178)

» Learn to stand up paddle or surf at Kahalu'u Beach Park (p187)

» Behold as chocolate is transformed from bean to bar on a tour of the Original Hawaiian Chocolate Factory (p188)

» Hop and swim among lava pools filled with tropical fish at Kapoho Tide Pools (p279) and Puako (p224)

» Fly over rainforest and waterfalls on a Kohala zipline adventure (p230)

» Watch molten lava pouring into the sea on a spectacular lava boat tour (p275)

» Picnic and swim at Lili'uokalani Park (p261)

» Ride the range on a horseback tour (p236)

❶ Information

The following are all in the **Keauhou Shopping Center** (www.keauhoushoppingcenter.com; cnr Ali'i Dr & Kamehameha III Rd):

Bank of Hawaii (⊘9am-6pm Mon-Fri, to 2pm Sat & Sun) Has a 24-hour ATM.

Keauhou Urgent Care Center (☏322-2544; ⊘9am-7pm) Treatment for minor emergencies and illness. Walk-ins OK.

Kona Stories (www.konastories.com; ⊘10am-7pm Mon-Fri, to 8pm Sat, to 5pm Sun) Good independent bookstore with fun events for kids and adults.

Longs Drugs (⊘8am-9pm Mon-Sat, to 6pm Sun)

Post office (⊘9am-4pm Mon-Fri, 10am-3pm Sat)

❶ Getting Around

The **Honu Express** (⊘9am-8pm; one-way ticket $1) runs between Keauhou Shopping Center and Kailua Pier in Kailua-Kona, stopping at the Keauhou resorts, White Sand Beach and elsewhere. It makes half a dozen trips into downtown Kailua-Kona. Schedules are available at the shopping center, www.keauhoushoppingcenter.com or any Keauhou hotel.

Holualoa

POP 7093

Holualoa, at 1400ft on the lush slopes of Mt Hualalai above Kailua-Kona, has come a long way from its days as a tiny, one-donkey coffee village. Today this friendly outpost is one of West Hawai'i's prime addresses, and the town's ramshackle buildings hold a stunning collection of sophisticated artist-owned galleries. Head here for a look at a unique and quirky historic town.

Most businesses close on Sunday and Monday. During November's Kona Coffee Cultural Festival (p180), Holualoa hosts a popular day-long block party called the **Coffee & Art Stroll**. The **Summer Farmfest & 'Ukulele Jam** each June is a bounty of local produce and music, and December's **Music & Light Festival** is a wonderful Christmas celebration. For more information see www.holualoahawaii.com.

⊙ Sights & Activities

FREE **Donkey Mill Art Center**   ART GALLERY
(www.donkeymillartcenter.org; 78-6670 Hwy 180; ⊘10am-4pm Tue-Sat) The Holualoa Foundation for Arts & Culture created this community-minded art center in 2002. There are free exhibits, plus lectures and workshops – taught by recognized national and international artists – open to visitors. The center's building, built in 1953, was once a coffee mill with a donkey painted on its roof, hence the name. It's 3 miles south of the village center.

Malama I'ka Ola Holistic Health Center   HEALTH CENTER
(☏324-6644; 76-5914 Hwy 180) Taking care of mind, body and spirit is easy at this center offering yoga and pilates classes, plus massage, acupuncture and other alternative skin and healthcare treatments.

⌂ Sleeping

TOP CHOICE **Holualoa Inn**   B&B $$$
(☏324-1121, 800-392-1812; www.holualoainn.com; 76-5932 Hwy 180; r $260-350, ste $280-375; ℙ❷❸❹) The Holualoa Inn is one of the island's classiest, most romantic properties. From the gleaming eucalyptus floors to the unwoven *lauhala* (hala leaf) walls and river-rock showers, serene beauty and comfort shines in every detail; several gorgeous public rooms graced with tasteful Asian art and exquisite carved furniture segue seamlessly into the outdoor gardens and pool, while the rooftop gazebo surveys the world. The six rooms don't disappoint, making this a peaceful, intimate retreat that you'll long remember. No TVs, phones or children under

13. There's a kitchenette for guest use. Rates listed include breakfast.

Lilikoi Inn (⌨333-5539; www.lilikoiinn.com; incl breakfast $110-135; 🖥) You're going to love the four rooms here, each with a private entrance, and access to hot tub, guest laundry, kitchen and lanai. Breakfasts are restaurant-worthy.

The Orchid Inn (⌨324-0252; www.theorchidinn.com; 76-5893A Old Government Rd; d $169; @🖥) One African-exotic suite with a handsome bed angled for a stupendous ocean view.

Kona Hotel HOTEL $ (⌨324-1155; Hwy 180; s $30, d $35-40) Although attractive from the outside, this shockingly pink historic boarding house (c 1926) is one of those 'only if necessary' properties. It's cheap and you get what you pay for: surly service, dirty communal bathrooms (for all rooms) and some territorial long-term residents sharing them with you.

Eating

Holuakoa Gardens & Café ISLAND CONTEMPORARY $$ (⌨322-2233; Hwy 180; brunch $11-15, dinner $22-32; ⏱restaurant 10am-2:30pm & 5:30-8:30pm Tue-Fri, from 9am Sat, 9am-2:30pm Sun, cafe 6:30am-3pm Mon-Fri, from 8am Sat & Sun) The storefront cafe here serves espressos and sandwiches, while the organic, slow-food restaurant in the garden dishes up sophisticated yet casual bistro-style cuisine. The creative, seasonal menu may include homemade gnocchi with morels, leeks and edamame (boiled soybeans), or grilled ahi with roasted fig and ginger fried rice. This is one of Hawai'i's most dedicated establishments for supporting local farmers and fishermen. Book ahead for dinner. You can get your own local organic produce and products at the **Saturday Farmers' Market** (⏱9am-noon) hosted here.

🔒 Shopping

Ipu Hale Gallery GALLERY (www.ipuguy.com; Hwy 180; ⏱10am-4pm Tue-Sat) This gallery sells *ipu* (gourds) decoratively carved with Hawaiian imagery using an ancient method unique to the Hawaiian island of Ni'ihau (see p460). Lost after the introduction of Western crockery, the art form was revived by a Big Island scholar just 15 years ago, and is now practiced by Michael Harburg, artist and co-owner of the gallery.

UPCOUNTRY COFFEE TASTING

Gourmet coffee has long gone mainstream, and many farms have established visitor centers, where they give free tours and samples. See www.konacoffeefest.com/driving-tour for a list.

Mountain Thunder Coffee Plantation (Map p198; ⌨325-2136, 888-414-5662; www.mountainthunder.com; 73-1944 Hao St; ⏱9am-4pm Mon-Sat) Established in 1998, this award-winning organic farm is located in lush Kaloko Mauka, about 15 minutes from Kailua-Kona. Free 20-minute tours are detailed (and wheelchair accessible), but for a real in-depth look at Kona coffee, try the VIP Tours ($65 to $135 per person, reserve ahead, lunch extra) or become Roast Master for a Day ($199 per person) and roast 5lb of your own beans.

Holualoa Kona Coffee Company (⌨877-322-9937, 800-334-0348; www.konalea.com; 77-6261 Mamalahoa Hwy; ⏱8am-4pm Mon-Fri) The Kona Le'a Plantation in Holualoa does not use pesticides or herbicides on its beautiful organic farm; the tours are excellent.

Hula Daddy Kona Coffee (⌨327-9744, www.huladaddy.com; 74-4944 Hwy 180; ⏱10am-4pm) The attractive tasting room of this multiple-award winner is the place for cupping seminars. See the website for directions to its upland Honokohau location.

Kona Blue Sky Coffee (⌨877-322-1700; www.konablueskycoffee.com; 76-973A Hualalai Rd; ⏱9am-3:30pm Mon-Sat) In Holualoa village, this estate's tour includes the traditional open-air drying racks and a video; it has a nice gift shop.

Holualoa Ukulele Gallery MUSIC

(☎324-4100; www.konaweb.com/ukegallery/index.html; Hwy 180; ⏱11am-4:30pm Tue-Sat) In the super-cool historic Holualoa post office building, Sam Rosen sells his handcrafted ukuleles, and those of other luthiers. Sam is happy to talk story all day and show you his workshop. Drop by Wednesday nights (6pm to 8:30pm) for a ukelele jam or, if you have two weeks, take a class and build your own.

Kimura Lauhala Shop ACCESORIES

(☎324-0053; cnr Hualalai Rd & Hwy 180; ⏱9am-5pm Mon-Fri, to 4pm Sat) Three generations of Kimuras weave *lauhala* products here, as they have since the 1930s. Originally they purchased *lauhala* products from Hawaiian weavers to sell. When demand increased they took on the production themselves, assisted by local farming wives, who do piecework at home outside of coffee season. Don't fall prey to cheap imports – the *lauhala* hats, placemats, baskets and floor mats sold here are the real deal.

Studio 7 Gallery ART GALLERY

(☎324-1335; ⏱11am-5pm Tue-Sat) Artist Hiroki Morinoue led Holualoa's artistic renaissance in the 1980s. Japanese woodblocks and sophisticated art in all media are displayed in his serene gallery.

Dovetail ART GALLERY

(☎322-4046; www.dovetailgallery.net) Funky and cool Asian and Hawaiian-style art.

Holualoa Gallery ART GALLERY

(☎322-8484; www.lovein.com; ⏱10am-5pm Tue-Sat) Matt and Mary Lovein specialize in whimsical, oversized paintings and raku pottery.

❶ Getting There & Away

From Kailua-Kona, turn *mauka* (inland) on Hualalai Rd off Hwy 11, and wind 3 miles up to Hwy 180; turn left for most sights. If coming from North Kona, Hina Lani St and Palani St are straighter shots to Hwy 180 than Hualalai Rd, though they are a little indirect. From South Kona, head up Hwy 180 immediately north of Honalo.

Honokohau Harbor & Around

Almost all of Kona's catch comes in at this harbor 2 miles north of Kailua-Kona, including the 'granders' – fish weighing over 1000lb. To witness the sometimes dramatic **weigh-ins**, head to the far side of the harbor, near the gas station, at 11am or 3:30pm; the weigh-in station is behind Bite Me Bar & Grill.

The majority of snorkeling/diving tours, whale-watching tours and fishing charters (p177) leave from here. To reach the harbor, turn *makai* (seaward) on Kealakehe Rd, just north of the 98-mile marker.

🏖 Beaches

Honokohau Beach BEACH

(Map p212) Just minutes from the bustle of Kailua-Kona is this beautiful hook-shaped beach with a mix of black lava, white coral and wave-tossed shells. Bring your reef shoes – you'll need them for the rocky bottom here. The water is usually too cloudy for snorkeling, but just standing on shore you'll see green turtles. Look for more feeding around the 'Ai'opio fishtrap, bordered by an ancient heiau at the south end of the beach. Snorkeling and swimming is permitted here and it's perfect for *na keiki* (kids). Just don't climb on the rocks or disturb the turtles.

To get here, turn right into the first harbor parking lot (look for the small public coastal access sign). Near the end of the road is the signposted trailhead; a five-minute walk on a well-beaten path leads to the beach. You can also reach Honokohau Beach along the easy Ala Hele Ike Trail starting from Kaloko-Honokohau National Historical Park (p210).

🏃 Activities

Snorkeling & Diving

The area south of Honokohau Harbor all the way to Kailua Bay is a marine-life conservation district (accessible by boat); diving here is better than snorkeling, though nearby 'Ai'opio fishtrap is a good snorkel alternative.

Turtle Pinnacle DIVING

(Map p212) Straight out from Honokohau Harbor, this is a premier dive site for spotting turtles, which congregate here to let small fish feed off the algae and parasites on their shells.

Kaiwi Point DIVING

(Map p212) Off this point south of Honokohau Harbor, sea turtles, large fish and huge eagle rays swim around some respectable drop-offs.

Suck 'Em Up DIVING

(Map p212) The swell pulls divers through a couple of lava tubes like an amusement-park ride, near Kaiwi Point.

Kayaking

Not just for paddling anymore, kayaks now come ready to sail, surf, snorkel, even fish.

Plenty Pupule
KAYAKING

(Map p212; ☑880-1400; www.plentypupule.com; Kaloko Industrial Park, Suite 102, 73-4976 Kamanu St; ⊙9am-5pm Mon-Fri; s/d kayak rental per day $20/28). One of the island's top outfitters for adventure kayaking, these folks can recommend good put-in and snorkeling spots beyond Kealakekua Bay, customize tours, teach you to kayak surf or take you kayak sailing (½-day tour $195) – particularly memorable during whale watching season.

Surfing

There are a few decent breaks within striking distance of the harbor.

Ocean Eco Tours

(Map p212; ☑324-7873; www.oceanecotours.com; Honokohau Harbor; group/private surf lessons $95/150) For lessons and equipment; the only operator permitted to surf within the boundaries of Kaloko-Honokohau National Historical Park.

Hiking

To explore the lush upper slopes of Mt Hualalai (largely private land), your only choices are Hawaii Forest & Trail or Hawaiian Walkways (☑800-457-7759; www.hawaiianwalkways.com). See their websites for prices and descriptions of tours.

TOP CHOICE Hawaii Forest & Trail

(Map p212; ☑331-8505, 800-464-1993; www.hawaii-forest.com; 74-5035B Queen Ka'ahumanu Hwy) This multi-award winning outfit is a top choice for those wishing to delve into the island's greenest depths. From its super popular **Mauna Kea stargazing** tour to its exclusive hikes into the Hakalau Forest

National Wildlife Refuge, you won't regret an adventure with these experts and green stewards. The **retail store** here sells high-quality outdoor gear, clothing, topo maps and camping equipment.

🛏 Sleeping

One of the best-kept secrets along this stretch of coast directly north of Kailua-Kona are the B&Bs tucked into the cool cloud forest on the slopes of Mt Hualalai.

Honu Kai B&B
B&B $$

(Map p212; ☑329-8676; www.honukaibnb.com; 74-1529 Hao Kuni St; d incl breakfast $150-195; @🛜) This attractive, get-away-from-it-all B&B sparkles with four plush, upscale rooms done up with rich fabrics, carved bed frames and Asian and Hawaiian decor. Tip: book the Lani or Mahina suites and access the roof deck. A separate cottage has full kitchen, and the well-tended gardens afford privacy and seclusion, whether lounging on the huge porch or in the Jacuzzi. Your hostess, to her chagrin, is a former Dallas Cowboys cheerleader.

Nancy's Hideaway
B&B $$

(Map p212; ☑325-3132, 866-325-3132; www.nancyshideaway.com; 73-1530 Uanani Pl; studio/cottage incl breakfast $130/150; 🛜) If you're looking for peace, quiet and privacy, the independent cottage or studio in this well-located residential neighborhood is ideal. The decor is functional and both units have kitchenettes, lanai with views, and king-sized beds. Either place is perfect for a couple. Call for directions.

Mango Sunset B&B
B&B $$

(Map p212; ☑325-0909; www.mangosunset.com; 73-4261 Mamalahoa Hwy; r $100-120; @🛜) Tightly bunched accommodation on an

---

WORTH A TRIP

KONA CLOUD FOREST SANCTUARY

Above 3000ft on the slopes of Mt Hualalai, the Kaloko Mauka subdivision contains this spectacular 70-acre forest sanctuary (Map p212; www.konacloudlforest.com) protecting an unusual 'cloud forest' ecosystem, creating a lush haven for native plants and birds. The sanctuary also contains demonstration gardens of non-native species, including more than 100 varieties of bamboo, which horticulture expert Norm Bezona is studying for their viability for use on the Big Island. Sustainable agriculture types and horticulturists won't want to miss a visit to this well-kept Kona secret most locals don't even know about!

Hawaiian Walkways (☑800-457-7759; www.hawaiianwalkways.com; adult/child $95/75; ⊙8:30am-1pm), leads a daily morning tour to the sanctuary, including a stop at adjacent Mountain Thunder Coffee (p193).

organic coffee farm with sweeping views from the shared lanai; choose room wisely as not all have views.

✗ Eating & Drinking

✐ Ceviche Dave's   CEVICHE $

(Map p212; Suite 100, 73-4976 Kaloko Industrial Park, Kamanu St; ceviche $8; ⊙11am-7pm Tue-Sat, to 3pm Sun & Mon) Dave is a surfer, world traveler, ecoconscious business guy and ceviche phenom. Pull up one of the four stools for the island-inspired Kohanaiki (cilantro, mac nuts, bell pepper and *liliko'i* juice) or the Tahitian-style Ta'apuna, featuring coconut milk. Everything is made with fish 'caught yesterday at South Point' or equally fresh. Thatched lanai, sparkling conversation and loads of aloha give Dave's the warmth of a true beach-shack *cevicheria*.

[TOP CHOICE] Kailua Candy Company   CANDY $$

(Map p212; ☑329-2522, 800-622-2462; www.kailua-candy.com; Kaloko Industrial Park, cnr Kamanu & Kauhola Sts; per pound from $25; ⊙closed Sun) A detour to this chocolate shop is mandatory for every sweet tooth. Try the handmade chocolate-covered macadamia-nut *honu* (turtles), Kona coffee swirls, *liliko'i* truffles or dark-chocolate-covered crystallized ginger. The cheesecake is the tastiest ever to pass our lips. They give good samples. Turn *mauka* (inland) on Hina Lani St off Hwy 19 and right on Kamanu St.

Bite Me Bar & Grill   SEAFOOD $$

(Map p212; www.bitemefishmarket.com; Honokohau Harbor complex; seafood bar & mains $9-23; ⊙6am-9pm; 🔊🚻) Steps from the harbor boat ramp, this casual place makes a logical stop for some mahimahi tacos or Longboard Lager after a day fishing or night dive with manta rays. With a *keiki* menu and shady picnic tables on a patio overlooking boat traffic, it also makes a good family spot. The **fish market** here stocks more than a dozen types of local fresh fish daily.

Harbor House Restaurant   SEAFOOD $$

(Map p212; Honokohau Harbor complex; mains $8-20; ⊙11am-7pm Mon-Sat, to 6pm Sun) After fishing, the place to spin your tale is at a wharfside table here chowing on a burger or excellent fish and chips. Happy hour runs from 4pm to 6pm Monday to Saturday and to 5:15pm Sunday and features 18oz 'schooners' for $2.50. Service is good.

Kona Coffee & Tea Company   CAFE $$

(www.konacoffeeandtea.com; Suite 5A, 73-5053 Hwy 19; ⊙7am-5:30pm Mon-Fri, 8am-5pm Sat, from 11am Sun; 🔊) Life is too short for bad coffee: head here for award-winning 100% Kona. Free tastings include Peaberry, which mitigates the parking lot location.

SOUTH KONA COAST

Heading south from Kailua-Kona, Hwy 11 climbs steadily, slipping back in time as you gain elevation. In South Kona, past and present coexist dreamily on the steep mountainsides, where ominous gray clouds daily threaten the impossibly verdant slopes, while nary a drop of rain falls on the blazing coast.

This is the acclaimed Kona Coffee Belt, consisting of 22 miles patchworked with more than 600 small coffee farms. That there is no cost-efficient way to industrialize the hand-picking and processing of the beans contributes to the time-warp quality of local life. But the reasons are also cultural: at the turn of the 20th century, thousands of Japanese immigrants arrived to labor as independent coffee farmers, and their influence – along with that of Chinese, Filipino and Portuguese workers – remains richly felt in Buddhist temples, fabric stores and restaurant menus.

Meanwhile, traditional Hawaiian lifestyles are jealously guarded in coastal villages such as Miloli'i, and ancient Hawaiian sites resonate with peculiar force – such as when snorkeling in the shadow of Pu'uhonua o Honaunau, and kayaking in the bay where Captain Cook met his grisly demise.

Honalo

POP 2300

At a bend in the road past the intersection of Hwys 11 and 180, little Honalo is your first sign that mere miles separate you from touristy Kailua. The first building you see is the **Daifukuji Soto Mission** (Map p198; www.daifukuji.org; 79-7241 Hwy 11; ⊙8am-4pm Mon-Sat), a humble-looking Buddhist temple. Slip off your shoes and admire the two ornate, lovingly tended altars. Everyone is welcome to join **Zen meditation** sessions at 6am Wednesday, and **taiko** (Japanese drum) groups practice at 6:30pm on Tuesday and 6pm on Saturday.

If you have young kids, return north a mile or so and enjoy shady **Higashihara Park** (Map p198; ☉7am-8pm). Its unique Hawaii-themed wooden play structure is both attractive and endlessly climbable. It is on the *makai* (seaward) side, between mile marker 114 and 115.

For a real window into local life, grab a table at **Teshima Restaurant** (Map p198; Hwy 11; mains $13-23; ☉6:30am-1:45pm & 5-9pm; ⊞), which has dished up delicious Japanese comfort food since the 1940s. Served in an old school, diner-like atmosphere, the unpretentious country cooking is usually spot on – order *donburi* (bowl of rice and main dish), ahi sashimi, butterfish and teriyaki, or better yet, sample a bit of everything with a *teishoku* (set meal). Four generations of Teshimas keep guests happy, but the star is Grandma Teshima, the delightful centenarian owner who still clears tables when regulars aren't insisting she sit and talk story. Cash only.

Kainaliu

Packed with quaint shops and good places to eat, Kainaliu is a prime lunch and linger spot – which is handy if you get caught in the 'Kainaliu Krawl' traffic nightmare. Check out fine Hawaiian fabrics at the longstanding **Kimura Store** (Map p198; 79-7408 Mamalahoa Hwy; ☉9am-6pm Mon-Sat, noon-4:30pm Sun) and then pop in to **Just Ukes** (Map p198; ☑323-0808; 79-7412 #A Mamalahoa Hwy; ☉noon-5pm Mon & Wed-Fri, to 6:30pm Tue, to 4pm Sat) for some instruments, plus photos by the talented Kim Taylor Reece. Across the street, **Yoganics Hawaii Limited** (Map p198; www.yoganicshawaii.com; 79-7401 Mamalahoa Hwy; ☉10am-5pm Mon-Sat) features all natural clothing; an attached studio has **yoga** and **belly dancing classes** (drop-in $15).

For a night on the town, grab a toothsome meal (or *liliko'i* mojito) at the **Aloha Theatre Café** (Map p198; ☑322-3383; www.alohathetrecafe.com; 79-7384 Mamalahoa Hwy; breakfast & lunch $7-15, dinner $14-22; ☉7:30am-2:30pm, dinner on show nights) and seats at the handsome **Aloha Theatre** (Map p198; 79-7384 Mamalahoa Hwy; ☑322-2323; www.apachawaii.org; tickets $10-25). Quality theater, indie films and live music are the program here. Budget tip: buy in advance to save $5.

TOP CHOICE Roadhouse Café (Map p198; 79-7399 Mamalahoa Hwy; sandwiches $5; ☉11am-5pm Mon-Fri) is one of the island's best-value institutions, with bodacious submarine sandwiches and inventive phyllo parcels. Everything here – down to the sandwich bread – is homemade. Try the award-winning carrot cake or cheesecake.

Annie's Island Fresh Burgers (Map p198; www.anniesislandfreshburgers; Mango Court, 79-7460 Hwy 11; burgers $9-14; ☉11am-8pm; ⊞) On its way to superstardom is this outfit where local veggies and grass-fed Big Island beef make Hawai'i's best burgers. Vegetarian? No worries – dig into a portobello mushroom stuffed with parmesan cheese and bulgur while enjoying the views from the back lanai.

Kealakekua

POP 1900

With the lion's share of essential services – banks, a post office, the hospital and so on – Kealakekua is more utilitarian than titillating. However, it contains a few standout places to experience the region's 'living history.' Its name means Path of the Gods, to recognize a chain of 40 heiau (temples) that once ran from Kealakekua Bay to Kailua-Kona.

Heading north towards Kailua-Kona, you can pick up the handy Haleki'i bypass road between the 111- and 112-mile markers.

◉ Sights

Kona Coffee Living History Farm FARM (Map p198; ☑323-2006; www.konahistorical.org; adult/child 5-12yr $20/5; ☉tours on the hour 10am-2pm Mon-Thu) Many free coffee-farm tours are a perfunctory 15 minutes. To really understand coffee farming, and for an evocative look at rural Japanese-immigrant life, visit the Kona Historical Society's 5.5-acre, working coffee farm. The Uchida family lived here till 1994, but the farm has been returned to the era of the 1920s to 1940s. Several docents grew up on similar farms, so they speak from experience as they present the orchards, processing mill, drying roofs and main house. On these two-hour tours you'll learn how to pick cherry, heat a bathhouse and prepare a traditional *bentō* (Japanese-style box lunch). It's worth the high ticket price. Call ahead, as time slots can fill up.

Greenwell Farms HISTORICAL SITE (Map p198; 888-592-5662; www.greenwellfarms.com; Hwy 11; ☉8am-5pm) This 150-acre family farm established in 1850 is run by 4th-generation Greenwells and is one of Kona's

South Kona Coast

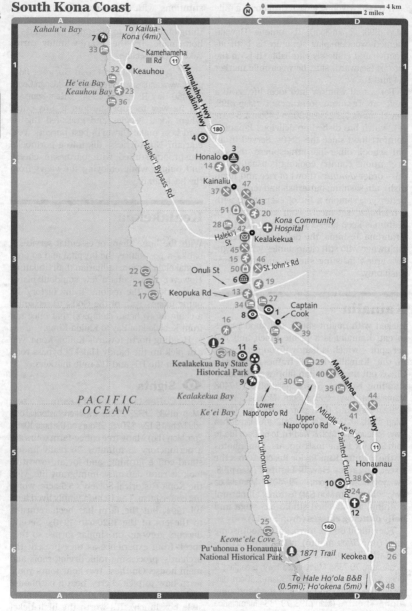

oldest and best-known coffee plantations. It currently roasts coffee cherry from more than 200 local growers. Take a **free tour** and sample coffee and fruit at a shady picnic table. You can also purchase Kona Red (www.konared.com) here, an intriguing new superfood made from cherry pulp. The farm is between the 110- and 111-mile markers.

HN Greenwell Store Museum MUSEUM
(Map p198; Hwy 11; adult/child $7/3; ⊙10am-2pm Mon-Thu) Next door to Greenwell Farms,

⊚ **Sights**

1	Amy BH Greenwell Ethnobotanical Garden	C4
2	Captain Cook Monument	C4
3	Daifukuji Soto Mission	C2
	Greenwell Farms	(see 6)
	Heiau & Historical Sites	(see 33)
4	Higashihara Park	B2
5	Hiki'au Heiau	C4
6	HN Greenwell Store Museum	C3
7	Kahalu'u Beach Park	A1
8	Kona Coffee Living History Farm	C4
	Kona Potter's Guild	(see 24)
9	Manini Beach	C4
10	Paleaku Gardens Peace Sanctuary	D5
11	Pali Kapu o Keoua	C4
12	St Benedict's Painted Church	D6
	St Peter's Church	(see 7)

Activities, Courses & Tours

13	Adventures in Paradise	C3
14	Aloha Kayak Company	C2
15	Big Island Yoga Centre	C3
16	Captain Cook Monument Trail	C4
17	Driftwood	B3
	Fair Wind	(see 23)
18	Ka'awaloa Cove	C4
19	Kings' Trail Rides	C3
20	Kona Boys	C3
	Kona Surf School	(see 7)
21	Long Lava Tube	B3
22	Red Hill	B3
23	Sea Paradise	B1
	Sea Quest	(see 23)
24	SKEA	D5
25	Two-Step	C6

💤 **Sleeping**

26	Aloha Guest House	D6
27	Areca Palms Estate B&B	C3
28	Banana Patch	C3
29	Ka'awaloa Plantation & Guesthouse	D4
30	Luana Inn	C4
31	Manago Hotel	C4
32	Outrigger Kanaloa at Kona	B1
33	Outrigger Keauhou Beach Resort	A1
34	Pineapple Park	C3
35	Pomaika'i 'Lucky' Farm B&B	D4
36	Sheraton Keauhou Bay Resort	B1

🍴 **Eating**

	Adriana's	(see 39)
37	Aloha Theatre Café	C2
	Annie's Island Fresh Burgers	(see 42)
	Big Jake's Island BBQ	(see 44)
38	Bong Brothers & Sistahs	D5
39	ChoiceMart	C4
40	Coffee Shack	D4
41	Coffees 'n' Epicurea	D5
42	Island Naturals	C3
	Kama'aina Terrace	(see 33)
43	Ke'ei Café	C2
	Kona Cold Lobsters	(see 27)
44	Kona Seafood	D4
	Manago Hotel	(see 31)
	Mi's Italian Bistro	(see 27)
45	Orchid Isle Café	C3
46	Patz Pies	C3
47	Roadhouse Café	C2
48	South Kona Fruit Stand	D6
	South Kona Green Market	(see 39)
49	Teshima Restaurant	C2

Drinking

	Verandah Lounge	(see 33)

Entertainment

	Aloha Theatre	(see 37)
	Firenesia	(see 36)

🛍 **Shopping**

50	Discovery Antiques	C3
51	Just Ukes	C2
	Kimura Store	(see 51)
	Re-Psychles	(see 27)
	Yoganics Hawaii Limited	(see 47)

the Kona Historical Society has turned the 1890 stone-and-mortar Greenwell General Store into a very clever museum. Shelves and walls are meticulously stocked with brand-new or re-created dry goods and farm equipment authentic to the period. Inside, docents hand you a shopping list and a character profile (based on actual custom-ers from Henry Greenwell's journals) from Kona's multi-ethnic, farming and ranching community of the 1890s. Then you shop, learning as you do. Out back, the **Portuguese bread oven** turns out fresh-baked bread from 11am on Thursdays. The museum is located between the 110- and 111-mile markers.

BYPASS THE TRAFFIC

The long-awaited bypass road between Keauhou and Kealakekua is now open. This cut-through allows savvy drivers to avoid the worst of commuter traffic in and out of Kailua-Kona. The road connects Haleki'i Rd in Kealakekua (between the 111- and 112-mile markers) to Kamehameha III Rd in Keauhou and Ali'i Dr and Hwy 11 beyond. It's open in both directions from 6:30am to 6:30pm, seven days a week.

Amy BH Greenwell Ethnobotanical Garden
GARDEN

(Map p198; www.bishopmuseum.org/greenwell; suggested entry donation $4, tours $5; ⊙8:30am-5pm Mon-Sat, guided tours 1pm Wed & Fri) Without pottery or metals, ancient Hawaiians fashioned most of what they needed from plants. This ethnobotanical garden preserves Hawaii's original native and Polynesian-introduced plants in a typical *ahupua'a*, the ancient land division system that ensured all Hawaiians had access to everything they needed. Plaques are informative, but guided tours are helpful to appreciate the humble grounds. A free guided tour is offered at 10am on the 2nd Saturday of the month. Bring insect repellant. The garden is just south of the 110-mile marker.

Activities

TOP CHOICE Mamalahoa Hot Tubs & Massage
HOT TUBS

(Map p198; ☑323-2288; www.mamalahoa-hottubs .com; hot tub per hour for 2 people $30; ⊙by appointment noon-9pm Wed-Sat) Soak away your blisters or blues in one of two jarrah-wood tubs set in a lush garden at this mini-oasis. The tubs, sheltered by thatched roofs, are open yet private. Hawaiian hot stone, *lomi-lomi* (traditional Hawaiian), Swedish, deep tissue and couples' massage are offered. A half-hour tub and one-hour massage package costs $95. Bottled water, towels and bathing facilities provided.

Big Island Yoga Center
YOGA

(Map p198; ☑329-9642; www.bigislandyoga.com; 81-6623 Hwy 11; drop-in class adult $14) For Iyengar yoga, Big Island Yoga Center is the place. The bright studio occupies the 2nd floor of a beautiful old house, and is stocked with mats and props. There's a free class at 10:30am on the first Sunday of every month.

Sleeping

Areca Palms Estate B&B
B&B $$

(Map p198; ☑800-545-4390, 323-2276; www.ko nabedandbreakfast.com; Mamalahoa Hwy; r incl breakfast $110-145; @) Country comfort and aloha combine seamlessly in this spotless, wooden home. The airy rooms are meticulously outfitted (lots of pillows and closet space, plus lush robes) and your hosts share their local knowledge freely. Kick back in the family room or watch the sun set in the Jacuzzi. You'll eat like royalty here, with fresh, unique breakfasts daily. It's between the 110- and 111-mile markers.

Banana Patch
COTTAGE $$

(Map p198; ☑322-8888, 800-988-2246; www.ba nanabanana.com; Mamao St; studio $115, 1-/2-bed-room cottages $125/150; @) Let it all hang out in one of these comfortable, clothing-optional cottages secluded amid tropical foliage. Clean and tasteful, these units are terrific for DIYers, with full kitchen, lanai, gardens and Jacuzzi.

Pineapple Park
HOSTEL $

(Map p198; ☑323-2224, 877-800-3800; www .pineapple-park.com; 81-6363 Mamalahoa Hwy; dm $25, r with/without bathroom $85/65; ⊙office 7am-8pm; @🛜) South Kona's only hostel is a basic backpacker dive. Choose from cramped dorms (No 10 is best) or fresher, more comfortable (but overpriced) private rooms. Bathrooms are shared. It's between the 110- and 111-mile markers; look for the kayaks (singles/doubles $38/58).

Eating

Mi's Italian Bistro
ITALIAN $$

(Map p198; ☑323-3880; www.misitalianbistro.com; 81-6372 Hwy 11; mains $15-30; ⊙4:30-8:30 Tue-Sun) This intimate eatery run by husband-and-wife team Morgan Starr and Ingrid Chan features homemade pasta, organic veggies and a laid-back, classy vibe. Combine a wickedly good seafood corn chowder with a thin-crust pizza or Italian sausage *rigate*. The lasagna is lackluster, however, and the wine can be a short pour, so bring your own ($15 corkage).

Patz Pies
PIZZA $

(Map p198; ☑323-8100; 86-6596 Hwy 11; slices/ pies $2.50/17 ⊙10am-8pm) Thin crust, zesty sauce and a nice price: claims to dishing good NY-style pizza are not exaggerated here. Not surprisingly, Pat's a native NYer.

Orchid Isle Café
CAFE $

(Map p198; ☑323-2700; 81-6637 Hwy 11; snacks $5-9; ☺6am-5pm Mon-Fri, 7am-2pm Sat & Sun; @☎) Hang out on the lanai, surf the internet ($10 per hour), and refuel with coffee and quiche at this relaxed coffeehouse.

Ke'ei Café
BRAZILIAN BISTRO $$

(Map p198; ☑322-9992; 79-7511 Hwy 11; mains $15-23; ☺11am-2pm & 5-9pm Tue-Fri, 5-9pm Sat) Once a foodie standby, food and service here can be great or not so much at this long-standing upscale eatery. Try for a balcony table.

Kona Cold Lobsters
SEAFOOD $

(Map p198; ☑854-1881; 81-6372 Hwy 11) Get to Re-psychles (below) early on Friday to snag one of these fresh Maine lobsters.

🛍 Shopping

TOP CHOICE Re-psychles
THRIFT STORE

(Map p198; www.repsychles.com; 81-6372 Hwy 11; ☺10am-5pm Mon, Tue, Thu & Fri, from noon Sat & Sun) If you're a sucker for quality second-hand vintage and designer fashion (think Manolo Blahniks, Coach and Ann Taylor), this is a compulsory stop while wending your way along the Kona Coast. Aloha shirts, collectible housewares and fun accessories shine here. **Kona Cold Lobsters** are sold here for $10 per pound at 10am on Friday.

Discovery Antiques
ANTIQUES

(Map p198; Hwy 11; ☺10am-5pm Mon-Sat, 11am-4pm Sun) Tin toys and aloha shirts, bric-a-brac and boxing gloves – who knows what you'll find at this secondhand antiques and curiosities shop.

ℹ Information

A **post office** (cnr Hwy 11 & Haleki'i St), several banks with ATMs, and the primary hospital serving the leeward side, **Kona Community Hospital** (☑322-9311; www.kch.hhsc.org; 79-1019 Haukapila St), are all in close proximity.

Captain Cook

POP 3700

As Hwy 11 winds southward, the greenery thickens and the ocean views become more compelling and it can be hard to tell where towns start and stop. Captain Cook is signaled by the historic Manago Hotel, which began in 1917 as a restaurant cater-

ing to salesmen on the then-lengthy journey between Hilo and Kona. The stout building remains a regional touchstone for travelers and residents alike.

Captain Cook is also where you access Kealakekua Bay, and the area offers a great selection of B&Bs and down-home cooking. Sinewy Napo'opo'o Rd is a pretty place to meander without an agenda; don't miss the fresh lei stand on the road's lower portion, just after the junction with Middle Ke'ei Rd, where $3 lei are sold on the honor system.

🛏 Sleeping

TOP CHOICE Ka'awaloa Plantation & Guesthouse
B&B $$

(Map p198; ☑323-2686; www.kaawaloaplantation .com; 82-5990 Upper Napo'opo'o Rd; r incl breakfast $125-145, cottage/ste $150/195; @☎) This rambling plantation home, set in more than 5 acres of lush jungle gardens abloom with tropical fruit, is one of South Kona's most romantic stays. Perhaps it's the dramatic four-poster beds, or the living-room fireplace, or the tasteful art and fine linens, or the divine outdoor shower, or the hot tub and Hawaiian steam box. It certainly has to do with the hosts' aloha and attention to detail. Watching the sunset from the wraparound lanai, with the coast unfolding below, doesn't hurt. The suite has the only full bath (it's a doozy); a separate cottage has a kitchenette but no views.

Luana Inn
B&B $$

(Map p198; ☑328-2612; www.luanainn.com; 82-5856 Lower Napo'opo'o Rd; r incl breakfast $180-200; ✸@☎☎) Some people (and properties) are perfectly suited to hosting in comfort and style. Welcome to spotless, aloha-filled Luana Inn. Each spacious, uncluttered and tastefully understated room has a private entrance and equipped kitchenette – two open right onto the pool and Jacuzzi with jaw-dropping bay views; two others are cozy private digs perfect for a couple or family. Pick your hosts' brains over a lavish breakfast for the best of the Big Island – they've been around.

Manago Hotel
HOTEL $

(Map p198; ☑323-2642; www.managohotel.com; Hwy 11; s $33-61, d $36-62, Japanese-style s/d $75/78) The Manago is a classic Hawai'i experience. The shared-bath boarding-house rooms are the same today as they were over 80 years ago – that is, plain, no frills and well kept. A more modern block of motel-style

THE CAPTAIN COOK STORY

On January 17, 1779, Captain Cook sailed into Kealakekua Bay (see p572), touching off one of the most controversial months in Hawaii's history.

Cook's visit coincided with the annual *makahiki*, a four-month period when all warfare and heavy work was suspended to pay homage to Lono – the god of agriculture and peace. *Makahiki* was marked by an islandwide procession to collect the chief's annual tribute, which set off celebrations, sexual freedom and games.

Cook's welcome in Kealakekua Bay was spectacular: over 1000 canoes surrounded his ships and 9000 people hailed him from shore. Once landed, Cook was treated with supreme deference – feted as any ruling chief would be, with huge celebrations and overwhelming offerings. The Hawaiians also bartered for goods – particularly for metals, which they'd never seen before. Though Cook tried to keep his sailors from fraternizing with Hawaiian women, he failed utterly and ultimately gave up: Hawaiian women flocked to the boats, having sex freely and frequently in exchange for nails.

On February 4, restocked and ready to go, Cook departed Kealakekua Bay. But only a short way north he encountered a huge storm, and the *Resolution* broke a foremast. Unable to continue, Cook returned to the safety of Kealakekua Bay on February 11.

This time, no canoes rowed out in greeting. Chief Kalaniopu'u instead seemed to indicate Cook had worn out his welcome. For one, captain and crew had already depleted the Hawaiians supplies of food, plus the *makahiki* season had ended; the party was over.

As Hawaiian generosity decreased, petty thefts increased; insults and suspicion replaced politeness on both sides. After a rowboat was stolen, Cook ordered a blockade of Kealakekua Bay and took chief Kalaniopu'u hostage until the boat was returned, a tactic that had netted results on other islands.

Cook convinced Kalaniopu'u to come to the *Resolution* to resolve their disputes. But as they walked to shore, Kalaniopu'u learned that sailors had killed a lower chief attempting to exit the bay in his canoe. At this, Kalaniopu'u apparently sat and refused to continue, and a large angry crowd gathered.

Thinking to frighten the Hawaiians, Cook fired his pistol, killing one of the chief's bodyguards. Incensed, the Hawaiians attacked. In the deadly melee, Captain Cook was stabbed with a dagger and clubbed to death.

Cook's death stunned both sides and ended the battle. In the days afterward, the Hawaiians took Cook's body and dismembered it in the custom reserved for high chiefs. The Englishmen demanded Cook's body back, and in a spasm of gruesome violence torched homes and slaughtered Hawaiians – women and children included. Eventually the Hawaiians returned some bits and pieces – a partial skull, hands and feet – which the Englishmen buried at sea, as per naval tradition. However, the Hawaiians kept the bones that held the most mana (spiritual essence), such as his femurs.

rooms sits behind the historic building; the 2nd and 3rd floors are the hotel's quietest and enjoy ocean views, while 1st floor digs are for smokers. Consider packing earplugs for the highway drone and early-morning rooster revelry. Reserve far in advance. It's between the 109- and 110-mile markers.

Pomaika'i 'Lucky' Farm B&B $ B&B
(Map p198; ☎328-2112, 800-325-6427; www .luckyfarm.com; 83-5465 Mamalahoa Hwy; d incl breakfast $80-140; ☎☞) Tropical abundance abounds at this mac nut and fruit farm with a variety of cozy accommodations. Two simple rooms share the main house, while attached are two airy 'Greenhouse' rooms with queen beds and screened

windows. Separate and hidden by banana plants, the Barn is a charmingly unadorned shack with screened, half-open walls and an outdoor shower – a budget traveler's jungle fantasy. Families are particularly welcome, and breakfast is a social occasion. Two-night minimum stay.

 Eating

TOP CHOICE **Manago Hotel** ECLECTIC $
(Map p198; ☎323-2642; Hwy 11; breakfast $4-6, dinner mains $8-14; ☺7-9am, 11am-2pm & 5-7:30pm Tue-Sun; ☞) Don't be put off by the bingo parlor ambience at this historic traveler's stopover where locals and visitors devour Manago's famous pork chops. The liver and

onions is a house specialty, or try the fried whole '*opelu* (mackerel scad). For breakfast there's a complete egg, meat, toast, juice and coffee combo for $5.50 – one of South Kona's best deals.

Coffees 'n' Epicurea
COFFEE SHOP $
(Map p198; www.coffeeepicurea.com; 83-5315 Hwy 11; ⊘6:30am-6pm) A coffee-tasting room/tea bar is an unlikely place for this sublime patisserie with flaky pastries, delicate éclairs and gorgeous pies. (The baker defected from the Kohala Coast resorts.) There's also a gift shop. It's on the *makai* (seaward) side at the 106-mile marker.

Coffee Shack
CAFE $$
(Map p198; ☑328-9555; www.coffeeshack.com; 83-5799 Hwy 11; meals $9-14; ⊘7:30am-3pm) Perched precariously next to the highway, the Shack is famous for the insane views of Kealakekua Bay from its open-air deck; you may never have a cup of coffee with a better vista. However, the service and the food (omelettes, pizza and salads) can be inconsistent, and the prices high. It is definitely worth stopping, but save your real appetite. It's between the 108- and 109-mile markers.

Other places around here worth a stop include the following:

Big Jake's Island BBQ
BBQ $
(Map p198; Mamalahoa Hwy; meals $10-16; ⊘11am-6pm Sat-Thu, to 7pm Fri) Features flavorful BBQ'd delicacies cooked in the fat barrel smoker parked at the 106-mile marker.

Kona Seafood
SEAFOOD $$
(Map p198; 83-5308 Hwy 11; ⊘10am-6:30pm Mon-Fri, to 5:30pm Sat & Sun) For all your fresh fish needs.

Adrianna's
MEXICAN $
(Map p198; Kealakekua Ranch Center, Mamalahoa Hwy; meals $5-11; ⊘10am-5pm Mon-Fri; 🛜) Serves solid Mexican food with typical upbeat Latino flair.

South Kona Green Market
FARMERS MARKET $
(Map p198; www.skgm.org; ⊘9am-2pm Sun) Behind the ChoiceMart, this farmers market epitomizes South Kona's diversity, with organic produce, musical performances and funky crafts.

ChoiceMart
GROCERY $
(Map p198; Kealakekua Ranch Center, Hwy 11; ⊘6am-9pm Mon-Sat, to 8:30pm Sun) South Kona's largest grocery store.

Kealakekua Bay State Historical Park

Kealakekua Bay is a wide, calm bay shouldered by a low lava point to the north, tall reddish *pali* (cliffs) in the center and miles of green mountain slopes to the south. The bay is both a state park and a marine-life conservation district, and is famous for its rich variety of sea life, including spinner dolphins. This entire area is considered sacred, and deserves your respect.

Napoʻopoʻo Rd, off Hwy 11, winds 4.5 miles down to the bay, leaving behind the lush foliage of the rainier uplands for the perpetually sunny coast; never assume that rain on the highway means rain in the bay. The road ends at the parking lot for Napoʻopoʻo Beach and Wharf, the kayak launch (p205).

🏝 Beaches

Manini Beach
BEACH
(Map p198) On its southern shoreline, Kealakekua Bay is rocky and exposed to regular northwest swells, making for poor swimming and snorkeling conditions. However, Manini Beach makes a highly scenic, shady picnic spot, and confident swimmers use a small break in the lava (to the right) to access the water. Surfers head to the point just south of Manini Beach. The park has portable toilets and picnic tables. From Napoʻopoʻo Rd, turn left on Puʻuhonua Rd, then right on Kahauloa Rd; after 0.25 mile, turn right on Manini Beach Rd and park at the blue house.

Keʻei Bay
BEACH
Continuing south on Puʻuhonua Rd, you'll come across attractive Keʻei Bay. While popular with surfers and kayakers, it's rough for swimming. To get there, take the ragged dirt road past the turnoff for Manini Beach (if you reach Keʻei Transfer Station, you've gone too far). If you don't have a high-clearance vehicle, park along the dirt road and walk in. At the bay, there's a beach, a small canoe launch and a few shacks, but no facilities – be respectful of residents here; you're essentially in their front yard.

Puʻuhonua Rd continues for several miles south through scrub brush to Puʻuhonua o Honaunau National Historical Park.

RED HOT GREEN ISSUES

Understanding issues that impassion locals – invasive species, resort developments, renewable energy, sovereignty – provides insight into what makes this island tick. You'll see placards, squatters, DIY projects and graffiti addressing all these in your travels. Also see the boxed text, p278.

10% Kona coffee blends These cheaper blends using foreign beans threaten local farmers who are currently fighting for recognition of Kona coffee as a Product of Designated Origin. This would protect the name and origin of Kona coffee à la Napa Valley Wines and Parmigiano-Reggiano cheese.

Coffee berry borer This destructive beetle, which had infected over 20 Kona farms by early 2011, resulted in a quarantine of Hawai'i's $30 million crop. Eradication solutions are being sought, but the bug is causing high anxiety among Kona coffee farmers.

Solar power In 2010 the Hawaiian Electric Company (HECO) sought to ban new solar-power systems, saying the excess energy they feed to the electric grid could be destabilizing. While ultimately rejected by state regulators, HECO continues to push back against smaller, distributed solar generation. The debate rages.

Thirty meter telescope Mauna Kea – Hawai'i's most sacred spot – will be home to the Thirty Meter Telescope (TMT). Slated for completion by 2018, the community is divided over this project, which will be bigger than all current observatories combined. See www.kahea.org for more.

Dolphin encounters Whether in captivity or the wild, human-dolphin encounters carry potential risks for the animals. Wild dolphins may become too tired to feed, while captive 'show' dolphins can suffer from stress, infections and damaged dorsal fins. See the boxed text, p37, for more.

Sights

Hiki'au Heiau
HEIAU (TEMPLE)
(Map p198) Veer right at the base of Napo'opo'o Rd to reach public rest rooms and Hiki'au Heiau, a large platform temple. In front of the heiau, a stone beach makes a moody perch from which to observe the stunning scenery, but the surf is too rough to swim.

Captain Cook Monument
HISTORICAL SITE
(Map p198) A 27ft white obelisk marking the spot where Captain Cook was killed in 1779 (see p202), is perched just above Ka'awaloa Cove. In 1877, as an act of diplomacy, the Kingdom of Hawai'i gifted the 16 sq ft of land the monument stands on to Britain. Behind the monument are the ruins of the ancient village of Ka'awaloa.

Pali Kapu o Keoua
HISTORICAL SITE
(Map p198) The 'sacred cliffs of Keoua' were named for a chief and rival of Kamehameha I. Numerous caves in the cliffs were the burial places of Hawaiian royalty, and it's speculated that some of Captain Cook's bones were placed here as well. High, inaccessible caves probably still contain bones.

Activities

Snorkeling
At Kealakekua Bay's north end, protected Ka'awaloa Cove (Map p198) is among Hawaii's premier snorkeling spots. The fish and coral are absolutely wonderful, and those with iron stomachs can swim out 100ft to hang over the blue abyss.

The water is protected from ocean swells and is exceptionally clear. Snorkeling is limited to a narrow section along the shore, where sea stars and eels weave through coral gardens, and schools of colorful fish sweep by. Confident swimmers can seek out an underwater lava arch toward the point. If you're lucky, sea turtles and spinner dolphins might join you – but remember to keep your distance from these mammals (see p625), and avoid stepping on coral. In light of recent research revealing smaller dolphin pods and widening patches of dead coral here, we recommend considering alternative snorkel sites, such as Two-Step or Kahalu'u Bay.

There are three ways to get to Ka'awaloa Cove: rent a kayak, take a snorkeling cruise (p178) or hike the Captain Cook Monument

Trail (p288). Morning – with calm winds and reliable sunny skies – is best.

Kayaking

PERMITS

The calm waters of Kealakekua Bay make for a great paddle, even for novices. But being a premier snorkeling spot has also sparked sustained controversy over crowds and environmental impact, resulting in new regulations for kayakers. In an effort to stem degradation to fragile cultural and natural resources at Kealakekua Bay State Historical Park, permit regulations were instituted for kayakers in 2010. It's important to note that you don't need a permit to paddle in the bay or Ka'awaloa Cove, only to land your kayak. This applies to shore landings and mooring at the wharf beside the Captain Cook Monument.

Ten permits a day are issued by the **Department of Land and Natural Resources** (☑974-6200; www.hawaiistateparks.org; free). You can download an application on the 'Announcements' page of its website. Each kayaker must have a permit; permits are valid for one day only. Violators of the permit requirements will be subject to civil penalties and the kayak may be confiscated.

If you can't be bothered with a permit, you can kayak over without beaching your boat; you'll have to snorkel trailing your kayak on a leash or switch off with your paddling partner (ie one snorkels while the other remains with the boat). Another option is a guided kayak tour of the bay.

LAUNCHING

It's forbidden to launch kayaks around Hiki'au Heiau – the **Napo'opo'o Wharf** (Map p198) provides a launching point for kayakers. Locals may offer to help lift your kayak in and out of the water (a boon for solo kayakers); if you accept, a buck or two tip is expected. The paddle to Ka'awaloa Cove, typically into the wind, takes about half an hour, less returning. Arrive before 9:30am to beat the snorkel cruises; after they arrive the cove can become a zoo of bobbing, bright-colored, noodle-assisted swimmers.

RENTAL & TOURS

Outfitters along Hwy 11 rent kayaks and snorkeling kits, as do a few free agents around the parking lot. All outfitters should include paddles, life jackets, backrests and scratch-free pads for strapping the kayak to your car; make sure to get a dry bag for your things.

The only outfitters currently licensed to run guided tours in the bay are Aloha Kayak Company and Adventures in Paradise. The following outfitters all have good reputations:

TOP CHOICE Kona Boys   RENTAL, TOURS
(Map p198; ☑328-1234; www.konaboys.com; 79-7539 Hwy 11, Kealakekua; single/double kayak rental $47/67, tours $125-250; ⊙7am-5pm) This laid-back yet professional watersports outfit is the area's largest. Its kayak tours include private and group paddles to secluded Pawai Bay, sunset paddles and overnight camping.

Hawaii Pack and Paddle   RENTAL, TOURS
(☑328-8911; www.hawaiipackandpaddle.com; tours adult/child 3-12yr $120/75) Five-hour tour to Kealakekua Bay includes hiking, wildlife watching, snorkeling and a picnic lunch. Multiday tours start at $285 per person, per day. If you're after a custom or longer kayaking-hiking adventure, this is the outfitter for you.

Aloha Kayak Company   RENTAL, TOURS
(Map p198; ☑322-2868, 877-322-1444; www.alohakayak.com; Hwy 11, Honalo; single/double/triple kayak rental full day $35/60/85, ½ day $25/45/60, tours $90-130; ⊙7:30am-5pm) This popular, Hawaiian-owned outfit knows local waters, has half-day rentals (noon to 5pm) and rents glass-bottomed kayaks. Kayak tours go to Keauhou Bay and other destinations, seeking out sea caves and cliff jumping.

Adventures in Paradise   RENTAL, TOURS
(Map p198; ☑323-3005, 800-979-3370; www.bigislandkayak.com; 81-6367 Hwy 11, Kealakekua; single/double/triple kayak rental $35/60/75, tours $80; ⊙8am-4pm) Friendly and professional, this outfitter makes sure beginners know what they're doing. At the intersection of Hwy 11 and Keopuka Rd.

Diving

There are many good dive sites clustered around Kealakekua Bay, including Ka'awaloa Cove, with its exceptional diversity of coral and fish in depths from about 5ft to 120ft. Other sites near here include Hammerhead (deep dive with pelagic action), Coral Dome (a big, teeming cave with a giant skylight) and Driftwood (Map p198; featuring lava tubes and white-tip reef sharks).

In the aptly named Long Lava Tube (Map p198), an intermediate site just north of Kealakekua Bay, lava 'skylights' shoot light through the ceiling of the 70ft tube.

You may see crustaceans, morays – even Spanish dancers. Outside are countless lava formations sheltering conger eels, triton's trumpet shells and schooling squirrelfish.

For dive shops, see p176.

Other Activities

Captain Cook Monument Trail HIKING
(Map p198) To snorkel Ka'awaloa Cove without renting a kayak or taking a boat tour, hike the Captain Cook Monument Trail. The trail itself is not especially interesting – and can be hot and buggy – but it leads right to the snorkeling cove. The way down is an easy hour, but after a morning of snorkeling the uphill return seems twice as steep (in reality it's a 1300ft elevation gain in 1.8 miles); allow two hours to return.

To get to the trailhead, turn *makai* (seaward) off Hwy 11 onto Napo'opo'o Rd; within the first tenth of a mile, park along the narrow road in one of the pullouts, wherever it's safe to do so. To find the trail entrance, count four telephone poles from the start of the road, and it's *makai* across from three tall palm trees. The trail is clear and easy to follow going down; when in doubt at a confusing spur, stay to the left. The trail ends at the place where kayakers with permits pull up on the rocks. There are no facilities at the bottom; bring lots of water.

Returning uphill, stay right at the fork (back onto the lava ledge); left is a 4WD road that continues north along the coast for miles.

Kings' Trail Rides HORSEBACK RIDING
(Map p198; ☑323-2388, 345-0661; www.kona cowboy.com; 81-6420 Mamalahoa Hwy; rides $135; ◷9am-4pm Mon-Fri) Kings' leads four-hour horseback trips to the coastline just north of Kealakekua Bay. Trips include lunch and snorkeling if waters are calm. It's at the 111-mile marker.

Honaunau

POP 2800

Growing by leaps and bounds amid thick coffee and macadamia nut groves, Honaunau is fun to explore without a guidebook. The nearby 'Place of Refuge' remains the star attraction, but meander down Painted Church Rd, stopping at fruit stands and coffee shacks with sea views for another type of refuge.

◉ Sights & Activities

St Benedict's Painted Church CHURCH
(Map p198; www.thepaintedchurch.org; 84-5140 Painted Church Rd) Catholic priest John Berchmans Velghe came to Hawai'i from Belgium in 1899. Upon taking responsibility for St Benedict's church, he moved it 2 miles up from its original location on the coast near the *pu'uhonua* (place of refuge). It's not clear whether he did this as protection from tsunami or as an attempt to rise above – both literally and symbolically – what Christians considered pagan native culture.

Father John then painted the walls with a series of biblical scenes (now deteriorated) to aid in teaching the Bible. Sayings in Hawaiian (including the admonishment 'Begone Satan!' among others) are painted on columns topped with palm fronds.

Paleaku Gardens Peace Sanctuary GARDEN
(Map p198; ☑328-8084; www.paleaku.com; 83-5401 Painted Church Rd; admission $5; ◷9am-4pm Tue-Sat) Near the church on Painted Church Rd, these tranquil 7-acre gardens contain shrines to the world's religions and an intriguing 'Galaxy Garden,' in which famous space painter Jon Lomberg has created a scale model of the Milky Way – in plants. It is indeed a meditative, peaceful sanctuary. Visitors can also drop in on **yoga** ($12) and **Qijong** ($10) classes here, too.

SKEA ARTS
(Map p198; Society for Kona's Education & Art; ☑328-9392; www.skea.org; 84-5191 Mamalahoa Hwy) SKEA is a hotbed of activity, with Pilates, Polynesian dance and Japanese ink-painting classes, plus pidgin poetry readings and concerts on the lawn. Check the calendar, and look for it between the 105- and 106-mile markers.

Around the back of SKEA is the **Kona Potter's Guild** (Map p198) where you can watch potters at work and buy their unique creations.

⌚ Sleeping

TOP CHOICE **Aloha Guest House** B&B $$
(Map p198; ☑328-8955, 800-897-3188; www.aloha guesthouse.com; 84-4780 Mamalahoa Hwy; r incl breakfast $140-280; @⍦) If you're coming all the way to Hawai'i, you should have the finest digs, and damn the cost. Heady views from the lanai, guest living room and king-sized bed will make you swoon, guaranteed. The views are complemented by luxurious amenities, including organic bath products,

deliciously customized bathrooms and a hot tub. The Honu room is wheelchair accessible.

Hale Ho'ola B&B B&B $$
(off Map p198; ☑328-9117, 877-628-9117; www.hale -hoola.com; 85-4577 Mamalahoa Hwy; r incl breakfast $110-150; @☎) This friendly B&B makes for a homey, relaxed stay, with three small but comfortable rooms downstairs from the main house. Rooms have nice beds and lanai, but are packed in pretty tightly – not recommended for honeymooners or antisocial types. Best views are from the main house lanai over a big breakfast.

✖ Eating

South Kona Fruit Stand FRUIT STAND $
(Map p198; ☑328-8547; www.southkonafruitstand .com; 84-4770 Hwy 11; smoothies $5.25-6.25, sandwiches $7-8.50; ☺9am-6pm Mon-Sat, cafe 10am-4pm Mon-Sat) This chichi organic produce stand sells only the cream of the crop. The cafe whips up heavenly fruit smoothies and good sandwiches; there are nice views from the outdoor patio. The stand is between the 103- and 104-mile markers.

Bong Brothers & Sistahs TAKEOUT $
(Map p198; www.bongbrothers.com; Hwy 11; deli items $3-5; ☺9am-6pm Mon-Fri, noon-6pm Sun; ☑) Food is politics at this small organic health food store and vegetarian takeout deli in a historic 1929 building. The fresh-made curries, soups and salads are mouth-wateringly delicious, even when served with ornery aloha by unrepentant agricultural activists. There are cool gift items, too.

Pu'uhonua o Honaunau National Historical Park

This unique national park (Map p198; ☑328-2288, 328-2326; www.nps.gov/puho; 1-week pass adult/car $3/5; ☺7am-7pm, visitor center 8am-5pm) fronting Honaunau Bay provides one of the state's most evocative experiences of ancient Hawaii. The park's tongue-twister name simply means 'place of refuge at Honaunau.' In 2008 the park acquired 238 more acres, doubling its size; in 2010 all the temples and *hale* (houses) were upgraded with new roofs. Bring a picnic and snorkel at nearby Two-Step for an unforgettable visit.

History

In ancient Hawai'i the kapu (taboo) system regulated every waking moment. A com-

moner could not look at the *ali'i* or walk in their footsteps. Women couldn't cook for men, nor eat with them. Fishing, hunting and gathering timber was restricted to certain seasons. And on and on.

Violators of kapu were hunted down and killed. After all, breaking kapu infuriated the gods, according to the Hawaiian belief system. And gods wrought volcanic eruptions, tidal waves, famine and earthquakes.

There was one loophole, however. Commoners who broke a kapu could stave off death if they reached the sacred ground of a *pu'uhonua*. A *pu'uhonua* also gave sanctuary to defeated warriors and wartime 'noncombatants' (men who were too old, too young or unable to fight).

To reach this *pu'uhonua* was no small feat, though. Since royals and their warriors lived on the grounds surrounding the refuge, kapu breakers had to swim through violent, open ocean, braving currents and sharks, to safety. Once inside the sanctuary, priests performed ceremonies of absolution to placate the gods. Kapu breakers could then return home to start afresh. The *pu'uhonua* at Honaunau was used for several centuries before being abandoned around 1819.

◉ Sights & Activities

A 0.5mile **walking tour** encompasses the park's major sites – the visitor center provides a brochure map with cultural information. Avoid midday, as the park gets hot and is only partially shaded. While most of the sandy trail is accessible by wheelchair, sites near the water require traversing rough lava rock.

You enter the national park in the villagelike royal grounds, where Kona *ali'i* and their warriors lived; this area's quiet spiritual atmosphere is greatly enhanced by the gently breaking waves and wind-rustled palms. Hale o Keawe Heiau, the temple on the point of the cove, was built around 1650 and contains the bones of 23 chiefs. It was believed that the mana (spiritual essence) of the chiefs remained in their bones and bestowed sanctity on those who entered the grounds. A fishpond, lava tree molds, a hand-carved koa canoe and a few thatched huts and shelters are scattered through here. The royal canoe landing, a tongue of sand called Keone'ele Cove, is a favorite resting spot for sea turtles.

Carved wooden *ki'i* (deity images) standing up to 15ft high front an authentic-looking heiau reconstruction. Leading up to the heiau is the **Great Wall** separating the royal grounds from the *pu'uhonua*. Built around 1550, this stone wall is more than 1000ft long and 10ft high. Inside the wall are two older heiau platforms and legendary standing stones.

Just south of the park's central village area, an oceanfront palm tree grove holds one of South Kona's choicest **picnic areas**. Parking, picnic tables and BBQs face a wide slab of *pahoehoe* (smooth-flowing) lava, which is pockmarked with busy **tide pools** and littered with wave-tumbled lava rock boulders. Swimming is possible but can be dicey; judge the surf and entry for yourself. Note that it's kapu to snorkel here.

🏃 Activities

After wandering the self-guided trail, you might try some wildlife watching: humpback whales can be seen offshore in winter, plus turtles and dolphins and even hoary bats can be seen here (after sunset is best).

Two-Step
SWIMMING & SNORKELING

(Map p198) Immediately north of the park, this stellar snorkeling spot is also a popular diving, kayaking and SUP area. Leave your car in the park's lot, and hang a left outside the entrance. Alternatively, there is parking ($3) across from the snorkel entry.

There's no beach – snorkelers step off a lava ledge beside the boat ramp into about 10ft of water, which quickly drops to about 25ft. Some naturally formed steps (hence the spot's name) make entry and exit fairly easy.

Visibility is usually excellent, especially with the noon sun overhead; good-sized reef fish and a fine variety of coral are close to shore. When the tide is rising, the water is deeper and it brings in more fish. The predatory 'crown of thorns' starfish can be seen here feasting on live coral polyps. Cool, freshwater springs seep out of the ground, creating blurry patches in the water. Divers can investigate a ledge a little way out that drops off about 100ft.

1871 Trail
HIKING

(Map p198) This pretty, 2 mile round-trip hike leads to the abandoned village of Ki'ilae. The visitor center lends a trail guide describing the archaeological sites along the way. Among other things, you pass a collapsed lava tube and a tremendous, if overgrown, *holua* (sled course) that *ali'i* raced sleds down. Keep your ears peeled for feral goats in these parts.

The steep **Alahaka Ramp** once allowed riders on horseback to travel between villages; halfway up the ramp, the **Waiu o Hina lava tube** (closed for safety reasons) opens to the sea. From the top of the ramp, the incredible vista of ocean coves and ragged cliffs is a trail highlight; for confident snorkelers, some of these coves can provide water access in calm seas. Continuing on, you reach a gate that once marked the park's boundary; this is the current Ki'ilae Village site – the ruins are pretty ruined, with almost nothing to see.

Fit hikers can walk all the way to **Ho'okena Beach** on this trail (3.5 miles), though it becomes increasingly rough after the Alahaka Ramp.

✨ Festivals & Events

On the weekend closest to July 1, the park puts on a **cultural festival** (⊘9am-3pm) with traditional crafts and food, *hukilau* (net fishing), canoe rides and a 'royal court.' Park fees are waived for the festival.

Ho'okena & Around

Ho'okena is a tiny, impoverished fishing village with no businesses to speak of, but it fronts a beautiful bay with a popular charcoal-sand beach park. This is primarily a locals' spot, where large families picnic and teens hang out, blaring music from car speakers. Unlike Miloli'i, the vibe is mellow and open to outsiders and, particularly during the day, travelers should have no qualms about hanging out.

Ho'okena was once a bustling village. King Kalakaua dispatched his friend Robert Louis Stevenson here in 1889 to show him a typical Hawaiian village; Stevenson then wrote about Ho'okena in *Travels in Hawaii*. In the 1890s Chinese immigrants moved into Ho'okena, a tavern and a hotel opened, and the town got rougher and rowdier. In those days Big Island cattle were shipped from the Ho'okena landing, but when the circle-island road was built, the steamers stopped coming and people moved away. By the 1920s the town was all but deserted.

🏖 Beaches

 Ho'okena Beach Park
BEACH

The modest-sized, charcoal-colored beach here is backed by a steep green hillside. When calm, the bay's waters are good for swimming, kayaking and snorkeling (though it drops off pretty quickly). There are strong currents further out. When the winter surf is up, local kids hit the waves with bodyboards. Look for dolphins and humpback whales here (from December to April).

The beach park has a picnic pavilion, bathrooms, showers, a concession stand and drinking water. You can camp right on the sand, at the base of the cliffs. Sites are awesome and security issues have been addressed by implementing a guard patrol, and through the activism of the Friends of Ho'okena Beach Park (http://hookena.org); you can obtain the required permits and rent camping gear on their website. Permits can also be obtained from the Department of Parks & Recreation (p169). A neighborhood **potluck** is hosted Wednesday afternoons here; all are welcome.

The signed turnoff is between the 101- and 102-mile markers. A narrow road winds 2 miles down to the beach. Veer left at the bottom.

Pebble Beach   BEACH
Not quite pebbles, the smoky stones of this beach at the bottom of the Kona Paradise subdivision range from gumdrop- to palm-sized. This is a popular kayak put-in and offers a good dose of peace and quiet. Lounge for a bit, paddle a while or watch the sun go down.

The beach is 1 mile down very steep and winding Kaohe Rd, accessed between the 96- and 97-mile markers. Though Pebble Beach is reached through an ungated subdivision, there are signs saying 'private road' and 'keep out' – seek permission from locals. Also, be watchful for sneaker waves (a woman died here in 2009).

Miloli'i

Miloli'i residents highly prize the traditional lifestyle of their modest fishing village, and they are very protective of it. Compared with Ho'okena, Miloli'i feels quite prosperous, with new homes dotting the hillsides (and a 1926 lava flow), well-kept churches, and fishermen zipping around in motorized boats – along with makeshift shacks and older fishermen patiently fixing their nets by the water. Miloli'i means 'fine twist,' and historically the village was known for its skilled sennit twisters, who used bark from the *olona* (a native shrub) to make fine cord and highly valued fishnets.

WHILE YOU SNORKEL, THEY SCHEME

For many, the Big Island's remote beaches and hikes are the main event – but they also make your rental car a prime target for thieves. Follow locals' advice: leave nothing of value in your car (yes, this includes the trunk). Places to be particularly cautious include Kehena Beach and Ahalanui Beach Park (Puna), the remote Kona coast beaches and Ho'okena and Miloli'i.

Another tip is to leave your doors unlocked so would-be ne'er-do-wells know there's nothing of value in the car. This way, you can avoid a smashed window, which – if the confetti of broken glass in parking areas is any indication – occurs fairly frequently. This strategy can backfire, however: at Miloli'i, leaving the doors unlocked, we set off for Honomalino Beach. While we played, a cheeky local opened the door wide for stray cats to come in and pee.

But Miloli'i is also known for its resistance to, and lack of, tourism. Villagers prefer their isolation and are not enthusiastic about visitors. At the end of the steep, winding 5-mile road to the village is a small county beach park with bathrooms, a covered pavilion and unremarkable camping (with a county permit; see p169). It's a pretty spot with lots of tide pools, but it's also insular and intimate, and you feel a bit like a stranger crashing a family reunion. Also, its isolated locale raises concerns about personal safety for camping.

Instead of feeling like the unwanted guest you are, we suggest heading straight to Honomalino Beach, a 15-minute walk from Miloli'i. The path has improved substantially over the years: you'll find it marked and maintained just beyond the yellow church and up the rocks to the left. This beach with sand the color of all Big Island beaches crushed into one – green, gold, tawny and black – has good swimming (for kids, too) and snorkeling, plus a fair share of shade. Visitors should respect all kapu and no trespassing signs here.

The turnoff to Miloli'i is just south of the 89-mile marker.

NORTH KONA COAST

Coming from anywhere else on the lush Big Island, happening upon the sere North Kona Coast is a shock. Interminable lava fields blanket this forbidding coast, but penetrate those fields and you can snorkel with turtles, walk on black sand and experience an iconic Kona sunset. Turn inland and you'll see Mauna Kea, Mauna Loa (both snow-capped in winter) and, between the two, Mt Hualalai. North Kona technically runs 33 miles along Queen Ka'ahumanu Hwy (Hwy 19), from Kailua-Kona up the Kona Coast to Kawaihae. For Honokohau Harbor, an easy 2-mile drive from downtown Kailua, see p194.

Kaloko-Honokohau National Historical Park

Just north of Honokohau Harbor, this 1160-acre national park (☎326-9057; www.nps.gov/kaho; ☉visitor center 8:30am-4pm, park 24hr) is probably the island's most under-appreciated ancient Hawaiian site. The main draws are two ancient fishponds and a *honu-* (green sea turtle) friendly beach, but it also preserves ancient heiau and house sites (restored in 2010), burial caves, petroglyphs, *holua* and a restored 1-mile segment of the ancient King's Trail footpath. It's speculated that the bones of Kamehameha the Great were secretly buried near Kaloko.

The park takes its name from the two *ahupua'a* (ancient land divisions) it occupies. These comprise a seemingly desolate expanse of black lava, perhaps explaining the lack of visitation. If the relatively short, hot trails through this otherworldly wasteland don't appeal, you can drive and see the highlights with hardly any hiking at all. The main entrance to the park's visitor center is off Hwy 19 between the 96- and 97-mile markers.

🏖 Beaches & Sights

Kaloko Fishpond   HISTORICAL SITE
(Map p212) At the park's northern end, Kaloko is the more interesting fishpond because its massive rock retaining wall is being completely rebuilt, so it can once again be fished in the traditional way. It also provides gorgeous views. From the park's visitor center, drive north on Hwy 19 until you reach a separate gated entrance at Kaloko Rd.

'Aimakapa Fishpond   HISTORICAL SITE
(Map p212) At the southern end, 'Aimakapa is the largest fishpond on the Kona Coast. Separated from the ocean by a high berm, it resembles a rectangular lake and is home to *ae'o* (Hawaiian black-neck stilt) and *'alae kea* (Hawaiian coot), which are both endangered native waterbirds.

Honokohau Beach   BEACH
(Map p212) Adjacent to 'Aimakapa Fishpond, the salt-and-pepper Honokohau Beach is ideal for sunning, strolling and even swimming when waters are calm – it makes a nice sunset destination from the park.

Keahole Point

At Keahole Point the seafloor drops steeply just offshore, providing a continuous supply of both cold water from 2000ft depths and warm surface water. These are ideal conditions for ocean thermal-energy conversion (OTEC). These parts also provide top conditions for flower farming: turn right onto Kai'iminani Dr between the 93- and 94-mile markers and you enter Keahole Ag Park (Map p212) – a top local spot for fresh lei. Enter the first driveway on your right or left and you'll find coolers full of these flowered delights sold on the honor system.

🏖 Beaches

Wawaloli (OTEC) Beach   BEACH
(Map p212; ☉6am-8pm) The Natural Energy Laboratory of Hawaii Authority (Nelha) access road leads to Wawaloli Beach, which is perfectly positioned for sunset and contains oodles of tide pools along its rocky lava coastline. Swimming conditions are poor, but the quiet beach has bathrooms and outdoor showers. Enjoy a late-afternoon picnic as waves crash, the sun falls and the kids play in a protected *keiki* pool (best at high tide). Never mind the airplanes.

⊙ Sights & Activities

Pine Trees   SURF BREAK
(Map p212; ☉6am-8pm) Pine Trees, one of west Hawai'i's best surfing breaks, is just south of Nelha. Why Pine Trees? Early surfers spied mangrove trees near the break, which they thought were pines. No mangroves (or pines) are visible today, but the name stuck.

The break stretches along a pretty beach that is rocky enough to make swimming difficult. There is surf at a number of points depending on the tide and swell. The final bay gets the most consistent yet more forgiving waves. An incoming midtide is favorable, but as the swell picks up in winter these breaks often close out. This place attracts a crowd, so if you plan to paddle out, respect the priority of locals.

When the access road to Nelha veers to the right, look left for a rutted dirt road leading about 2 miles further south to Pine Trees. You need a high-clearance 4WD to make it, or you can walk, but it's hot. Gates close between 8pm and 6am.

Natural Energy Laboratory of Hawaii Authority
NOTABLE BUILDING

(Nelha; Map p212; www.nelha.org) That funny-looking building with the gigantic solar panels on Hwy 19 is Nelha's visitor center and crown jewel: the **Hawaii Gateway Energy Center**. This 'zero-net energy facility' was voted one of the 10 greenest buildings in the country by the American Institute of Architects in 2007. Learn about OTEC and other research and technologies at Nelha's public lectures (329-8073; adult/student & senior $8/5; 10-noon Mon-Thu). Reservations are required. The Abalone Farm Tour & Tasting (adult/student & senior $18/15) follows the lecture on Monday, Wednesday and Thursday; the Solar Thermal Plant Tour follows the lecture on Tuesday.

Today Nelha also sponsors a variety of commercial ventures, including aquaculture production of *ogo* (seaweed), algae and black pearls. One of Nelha's tenants is a Japanese company that desalinates pristine Hawaiian seawater and sells it as a tonic in Japan. Their huge ponds are hard to miss. Also here is Ocean Rider Seahorse Farm (329-6840; www.oceanrider.com; tours adult/child $35/25; Mon-Fri 10am, noon & 2pm), the only one of its kind in the country. Kids love it.

The signed turnoff to Nelha is between the 94- and 95-mile markers.

Kekaha Kai State Park

The gorgeous beaches of Kekaha Kai (9am-7pm) are all the more memorable for being tucked on the far side of a vast desert of unforgiving black lava. This nearly undeveloped 1600-acre park has four beaches, only one of which has paved access. The others are best approached with a 4WD or on foot; but if you hike, be prepared with good

BORED WAITING TO BOARD?

They were clever, whoever located the Astronaut Ellison S Onizuka Space Center (Map p212; 329-3441; adult/child under 12yr $3/1; 8:30am-4:30pm) at the Kona Airport. This little museum paying tribute to the Big Island native who perished in the 1986 *Challenger* space shuttle disaster collects celestial ephemera like moon rocks and space suits; it makes an interesting way to kill time before takeoff.

shoes, food and lots of water. It can be brutally hot, and once you reach the sand you'll want to stay till the last drop of sunlight.

Beaches

Mahai'ula Beach
BEACH

(Map p212) The park's largest, this rough, salt-and-pepper-sand beach is not great for swimming, but has good surfing during winter swells and kayaking is possible year-round. The beach has shaded picnic tables and pit toilets. Walk a few minutes north along the coast to a second, less rocky, curved tan beach with soft sand (called Magoon's) that is perfect for sunning and swimming.

Mahai'ula Beach is at the end of the park's main entrance – a ragged 1.5-mile dirt road between the 90- and 91-mile markers. A 4WD is recommended; attempting it in a 2WD is just asking for a punctured oil pan (trust us, we know). The end of this road is the junction for Makalawena and Makole'a Beaches.

Makalawena Beach
BEACH

(Map p212) Just before the parking lot for Mahai'ula, the road junction offers two choices: go south for Makole'a Beach, or go north for Makalawena Beach. If what you're after is an almost deserted, postcard-perfect scoop of pristine white-sand beach, edged by ivy-covered dunes and cupping brilliant blue-green water, head north.

The service road to Makalawena Beach is cabled off, so you have to park and walk. Either follow the service road or follow the coastline from Mahai'ula Beach (a much nicer route), and aim for the abandoned red houses; north of these, a mile-long trail continues through nasty *'a'a* (rough, jagged type of lava) to Makalawena.

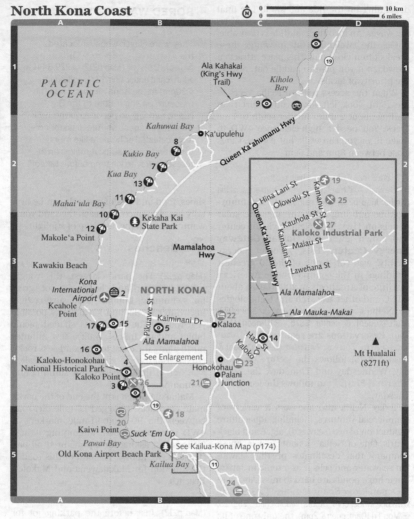

After the broiling hike, it's shocking to emerge at this series of idyllic, scalloped bays with almost-glowing velvety white sand. If it's midweek, you might be the only one here. Swimming is splendid, though the surf can get rough, and bodyboarding and snorkeling are also attractive; sea turtles seem to prefer the furthest cove. Some like to rinse off in a brackish pond behind the southernmost cove. There is no official camping, though locals sometimes do; they don't always appreciate fellow tenters.

Makole'a Beach BEACH

(Map p212) At the road junction, you can drive south to Makole'a Beach, but this section of road is definitely 4WD only; in fact, it's wise to park the 4WD after 1000yd, where coral marks the path to the ocean. You won't get lost walking: either follow the road or follow the coastline from Mahai'ula Beach and make for the lone tree.

Lacking shade and too rocky for good swimming, this black-sand beach is most popular with local fisherman, but its beauty rewards those who make the effort.

Sights

1 'Aimakapa Fishpond............................ B4
2 Astronaut Ellison S Onizuka
   Space Center.................................... B3
   Hawaii Gateway Energy Center ... (see 15)
3 Honokohau Beach B4
   Ka'upuleho Cultural Center...........(see 8)
4 Kaloko Fishpond B4
5 Keahole Ag Park................................. B4
6 Keawaiki Beach.................................. D1
7 Kikaua Beach..................................... B2
   Kona Cloud Forest Sanctuary...... (see 14)
8 Kukio Beach....................................... B2
9 Luahinewai... C1
10 Mahai'ula Beach................................. B3
11 Makalawena Beach............................. B2
12 Makole'a Beach.................................. A3
13 Manini'owali Beach............................. B2
14 Mountain Thunder Coffee
   Plantation....................................... C4
15 Natural Energy Laboratory of
   Hawaii Authority B4
   Ocean Rider Seahorse Farm........ (see 15)
16 Pine Trees A4
17 Wawaloli (OTEC) Beach...................... A4

Activities, Courses & Tours

   Captain Zodiac.................................. (see 3)
   Charter Desk.................................... (see 3)
18 Hawaii Forest & Trail..............................B5
   Kamanu Charters.......................... (see 3)
   Ocean Eco Tours............................ (see 3)
19 Plenty Pupule...D2
20 Turtle Pinnacle......................................B5

Sleeping

   Four Seasons Resort Hualalai .... (see 8)
21 Honu Kai B&B.......................................B4
22 Mango Sunset B&B................................C4
23 Nancy's Hideaway..................................C4
24 Plumeria House......................................C5

Eating

   Beach Tree Bar & Grill .... (see 8)
   Bite Me Bar & Grill .... (see 3)
25 Ceviche Dave's......................................D2
26 Harbor House Restaurant......................B4
   Hualalai Grille .... (see 8)
27 Kailua Candy Company D3
   Kona Coffee & Tea Company .... (see 18)

Manini'owali Beach (Kua Bay)   BEACH
(Map p212; ⏱9am-7pm) Welcome to another vision of paradise: a crescent-shaped white-sand beach with sparkling turquoise waters that makes for first-rate swimming and bodyboarding (especially in winter), and even decent snorkeling when waters are calm. But unlike Makalawena, a paved road leads right to it. Thus Manini'owali draws major crowds, especially on weekends; arrive late and cars will be parked a half mile up the road. That's reason aplenty for locals to continue grumbling about the easy access the paved road provides. The parking area has bathrooms and showers.

To get here, take the paved road between the 88- and 89-mile markers (north of the main Kekaha Kai entrance). Hikers will enjoy the coastal trail from here to Kukio Beach.

Ka'upulehu

Once a thriving fishing village among many dotting this lenght of coast, Ka'upulehu was wiped out by the 1946 tsunami and abandoned until the Kona Village Resort opened here in 1965 (ironically and sadly, the resort closed indefinitely following damage sustained as a result of the 2011 tsunami in Japan). The luxurious Four Seasons Hualalai – the island's poshest – followed in 1996. By law these and other resorts must provide public coastal access, meaning you can enjoy some fine beaches without the resort price tag. What you can't do is hit the links at the PGA-tour **Four Seasons Hualalai Course** (☎325-8000; www.fourseasons.com/hualalai/golf.html), designed by golfing legend Jack Nicklaus; it's for members and guests only.

 Beaches

Kikaua Beach   BEACH
(Map p212) On the south end of Kukio Bay, this beach is accessed through a private country club. Come early, as beach parking is limited to 28 stalls and can fill up. This lovely, quiet, tree-shaded beach contains a protected cove where kids can swim and snorkel in bathtub-calm water; around the kiawe-covered point, sea turtles line up to nap. Both this and Kukio Beach have bathrooms, showers and drinking water. Access is via Kuki'o Nui Rd near the 87-mile marker; request a pass at the gate.

KONA COAST FOR KIDS

» Turtle Spotting at Makalawena (p211)

» Swimming and beachcombing at Kiholo Bay (p214)

» Snorkeling in Ka'awaloa Cove (p204)

» Meeting other kids at Manini'owali Beach (p213)

Kukio Beach   BEACH

(Map p212) From Kikaua Beach, you can see (and walk to) the bay's northern Kukio Beach, which is within the grounds of the Four Seasons. This picture-perfect crescent of sand is great for swimming or lounging away an afternoon. You can follow a paved footpath north past some intriguing lava rock coastline to another beach. To drive here, turn onto the (unsigned) Ka'upulehu Rd near the 87- and 86-mile markers; go to the Four Seasons gate and request a beach pass. Public parking accommodates 50 cars and almost never fills up.

◉ Sights

Ka'upuleho Cultural Center   MUSEUM

(Map p212; ☑325-8520; Four Seasons Resort; admission free; ⊙8:30am-4pm Mon-Fri) Don't miss this often-overlooked Native Hawaiian cultural center on the grounds of the Four Seasons. Excellent displays are organized around the center's incredible collection of 11 original paintings by Herb Kawainui Kane. Each work is accompanied by a hands-on exhibit: shake an *'uli'uli* (feathered hula rattle), test the heft of a *kapa* (mulberry tree bark) beater and examine adze heads. It's run by Hawaiian cultural practitioners who actively link the present with the past. The center holds classes (usually open to resort guests only), but they'll happily refer you to *kumu* (teachers) directly. At the Four Seasons gate, tell them you're visiting the center.

🛏 Sleeping

Four Seasons Resort Hualalai   RESORT $$$

(Map p212; ☑325-8000; 800-819-5053; www.fourseasons.com/hualalai; 72-100 Ka'upulehu Dr; r $625-1095, ste from $1350; ✴@⊛⊚⊠) It's no accident that the Hualalai is the island's only five-diamond resort. Those accolades are earned through lavish attention to detail (fresh orchids in every room, crayons and

kids' robes, multimedia library) and top-flight service. The golf course, spa and lap pool are world class, plus there's a big, well-stocked snorkel tank, including manta rays. Garden units have wonderful outdoor showers. A hip, rock 'n' roll clientele adds to the cachet here; avoid rooms overlooking public areas, which lack privacy.

Kona Village Resort   RESORT $$$

(Map p212; ☑325-5555, 800-367-5290; www.konavillage.com; 1 Kahuwai Bay Dr; 1-room hale $349-$649, 2-room hale $630-1180; @⊛⊚⊠) When we went to print this resort was closed due to damage sustained by the March 2011 tsunami that devastated Japan. Plans for its reopening were unknown. Check the website for updates.

✕ Eating

Beach Tree Bar & Grill   ECLECTIC $$

(Map p212; ☑325-8000; Four Seasons Resort Hualalai; lunch mains $12-18, dinner mains $15-33; ⊙11:30am-8:30pm) The trend of New York chefs decamping to the Big Island (eg Holuakoa Café, Jackie Rey's) has reached the Beach Tree, where Nick Mastrascusa turns out tangy ceviche, thin-crust brick-oven pizzas with toothsome toppings (try the Hamakua fungi or mac nut and gorgonzola creations) and a variety of surf-and-turf delights, including a fierce paella. The beachside setting here is equal parts romantic and casual; sunset on the sofas accompanied by traditional Hawaiian music, cocktails and *pupu* is highly recommended.

Hualalai Grille   HAWAII REGIONAL $$$

(Map p212; ☑325-8525; Golf Clubhouse, Four Seasons Resort Hualalai; mains $30-56; ⊙5:30-9pm) Nicknamed the 19th Hole, the Hualalai Grille is still forging its new identity after the departure of celebrity chef Alan Wong in 2008, and was closed for renovations throughout research of this guide.

Kiholo Bay

TOP CHOICE Kiholo Bay (⊙7am-7pm), with its pristine turquoise waters and shoreline fringed with coconut trees, is yet another oasis. The shoreline and cove-like beaches here never seem to look the same twice, making it a great place to explore.

The main beach (near the parking lot) is pebbly, and swimming is fine when seas are calm. Follow a trail south over the lava to find secluded pockets of fine black sand and, further south, a coconut grove surrounding Luahinewai (Map p212), a lovely spring-fed pool. Walking north, low tide reveals tide pools that are popular feeding and napping grounds for sea turtles and offer plenty of snorkeling possibilities. Inland near the end of the gravel path is a lava tube filled with clear freshwater; adventurous swimmers can check it out. Just past this is a sandy patch with a keiki pool perfect for the little ones. You'll pass a gargantuan private estate with a yellow mansion and tennis courts and, at the northern end, you can walk across a shallow channel to a small island with white sand.

To get here, turn *makai* (seaward) on the unmarked, graded gravel road between the 82- and 83-mile markers. Follow the road for a mile, taking the left-hand fork and parking at the abandoned roundhouse. Kiholo is a popular camping spot for locals; there's no potable water.

For a little more adventure and even more solitude, check out Keawaiki Beach (Map p212) north of Kiholo Bay. This secluded black-sand strand fronts the former estate of Francis I'i Brown, an influential 20th-century Hawaiian businessman. It's fine for swimming when calm, but wear reef shoes, as sea urchins like the rocks. To get here, park between the 78- and 79-mile markers on Hwy 11; there's a small lot in front of a boulder-blocked gravel road. Walk the road to the estate's fence, then follow the trail to the right around the fence to the beach.

SOUTH KOHALA

What began in North Kona continues in South Kohala: the sometimes plumb-straight highway cuts through sweeping coastal plains; stark lava fields alternate with barren pastures, all baking under a relentless sun. Punctuating the drive, a series of sumptuous resorts have carved green oases at the water's edge on some of the island's best beaches – making their own beaches, if necessary. This region is known as the Gold Coast, but whether that's for the sun, the prevalence of yellow tang in the waters or the wealth generated by tourism, it's hard to say.

In contrast to the very modern world of the resorts, South Kohala also contains numerous ancient Hawaiian sights. Apparently, the Kohala Coast (including North Kohala)

was more populated then than now, and the region is packed with village sites, heiau, fishponds, petroglyphs and historic trails.

Waikoloa Resort Area

POP 4800

Among South Kohala's resort areas, the Waikoloa Beach Resort (www.waikoloabeachresort.com) is the most affordable and bustling. Its two mega hotels and golf courses aren't as prestigious as those further up the coast, but it does offer two shopping malls and the lion's share of events.

Note that the Waikoloa Beach Resort is not Waikoloa Village, a residential community further inland. To get to the resort area, turn *makai* (seaward) just south of the 76-mile marker. To get to the village – for general services, such as a post office – turn *mauka* (mountainward) onto Waikoloa Rd north of the 75-mile marker.

🏄 Beaches

TOP CHOICE 'Anaeho'omalu Beach Park   BEACH
(Map p216; Waikoloa Beach Dr; ⊗parking 6am-8pm) Although 'A Bay' is less famous than other Big Island beaches, its attributes are no less impressive: easy access, salt-and-pepper sand and calm waters (the only place suited to windsurfing on Hawai'i). Classically beautiful, it's backed by hundreds of palm trees and makes for fantastic sunset viewing. It's less crowded than Hapuna Beach further north.

The Waikoloa Beach Marriott fronts the beach's north end, but ancient fishponds add a buffer zone between the two. In that area, there's decent snorkeling directly in front of the sluice gate, where you'll find coral formations, a fair variety of fish and possibly sea turtles. Drinking water, showers and restrooms are available.

'Anaeho'omalu was once the site of royal fishponds, and archaeologists have found evidence of human habitation here dating back more than 1000 years. A short footpath with interpretive plaques starts near the showers and passes fishponds, caves, ancient house platforms and a shrine.

To get here, turn left off Waikoloa Beach Dr opposite the Kings' Shops.

⊙ Sights & Activities

Waikoloa Petroglyph Preserve   HISTORICAL SITE
(Map p216; Waikoloa Beach Dr; admission free) This collection of petroglyphs carved in lava

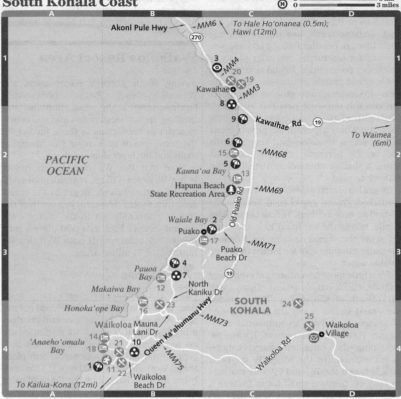

rock is so easy-access that it merits a stop, although the Puako Petroglyph Preserve further north is larger and more spectacular. Many of the petroglyphs date back to the 16th century; some are graphic (humans, birds, canoes) and others cryptic (dots, lines). Western influences appear in the form of horses and English initials.

To get here, park at the Kings' Shops mall and walk for five minutes on the signposted path. Never touch or walk on the petroglyphs. Kings' Shops offers a free, one-hour **petroglyph tour** (⊙10:30-11:30am); meet at the shopping center stage.

Ocean Sports WATERSPORTS
(Map p216; ☎886-6666; www.hawaiioceansports .com; 69-275 Waikoloa Beach Dr) Ocean Sports, established in 1981, monopolizes the ocean-activity market in South Kohala. Fortunately the company is well run, if slightly steep in its pricing. Cruises include whale watching ($93) and snorkeling tours ($132) aboard a

49-passenger catamaran. The company also offers glass-bottom boat rides ($28) and sunset dinner sails ($110). Kids between six and 12 years pay half price. Cruises depart from either 'Anaeho'omalu Bay or Kawaihae Harbor.

At Anaeho'omalu Beach Park or the Hilton Waikoloa Village, this outfit also rents beach equipment such as as bodyboards ($10 per hour), kayaks (single $14 per 30 minutes) and wacky hydrobikes ($25 per 30 minutes).

Waikoloa Beach & Kings' Courses GOLF
(Map p216; ☎886-7888; www.waikoloabeach golf.com/golf/proto/waikoloabeachgolf; Waikoloa Beach Marriott, 69-275 Waikoloa Beach Dr; guest/nonguest $135/165) The Waikoloa Beach Marriott boasts two top golf courses: the coastal Beach course is known for its par-five 12th hole; the Kings' course is more challenging and offers Scottish-style links. Tee

◎ Sights
1 'Anaeho'omalu Beach Park................A4
2 Beach 69..C3
3 Hamakua Macadamia Nut
  Company...C1
4 Holoholokai Beach Park.....................B3
  Kalahuipua'a Fishponds...............(see 16)
  Kalahuipua'a Historic Trail..........(see 16)
5 Mauna Kea Beach...............................C2
6 Mau'umae Beach.................................C2
7 Puako Petroglyph Preserve...............B3
8 Pu'ukohola Heiau National
  Historic Site....................................C1
9 Spencer Beach Park............................C2
10 Waikoloa Petroglyph
  Preserve..B4

◎ Activities, Courses & Tours
  Dolphin Quest.................................(see 14)
  Francis I'i Brown North &
    South Golf Courses ....(see 16)
  Hapuna Golf Course.......................(see 13)
  Hilton Waikoloa Village Pools.......(see 14)
  Kohala Divers ....(see 20)
  Mauna Kea Golf Course.................(see 15)
  Mauna Lani Sea Adventures ....(see 16)
  Mauna Lani Spa..............................(see 16)
11 Ocean Sports.......................................B4
  Spa Without Walls.........................(see 12)
  Star Gaze Hawaii ....(see 14)
  Star Gaze Hawaii...........................(see 13)
  Star Gaze Hawaii...........................(see 12)
  Waikoloa Beach & Kings'
    Courses ....(see 18)

◎ Sleeping
12 Fairmont Orchid.................................B3
13 Hapuna Beach Prince Hotel.................C2
14 Hilton Waikoloa Village B4
15 Mauna Kea Beach Hotel......................C2
16 Mauna Lani Bay Hotel &
  Bungalows B4

17 Puako B&B...C3
18 Waikoloa Beach Marriott.......................A4

◎ Eating
  Anuenue...(see 20)
  Blue Dragon Musiquarium............(see 19)
  Brown's Beach House.....................(see 12)
  Café Pesto......................................(see 20)
  CanoeHouse.....................................(see 16)
  Foodland Farms...............................(see 23)
  Huli Sue's..(see 16)
19 Kawaihae Harbor Grill............................C1
  Kawaihae Market & Deli ....(see 20)
  Kawaihae Seafood Bar ....(see 19)
20 Kawaihae Shopping Center C1
21 Kings' Shops..B4
  Merriman's Market Café...............(see 21)
  Monstera ....(see 23)
22 Queens' MarketPlace..........................B4
  Roy's Waikoloa Bar & Grill............(see 21)
  Sansei Seafood Restaurant &
    Sushi Bar ....(see 22)
23 Shops at Mauna Lani B4
  Waikoloa Kings' Shops Farmers
    Market..(see 21)
24 Waikoloa Village Farmers
  Market..C4
25 Waikoloa Village Market......................D4

Drinking
  Honu Bar..(see 16)
  Luana Lounge ....(see 12)

Entertainment
  Gathering of the Kings...................(see 12)
  Hilton Waikoloa Village.................(see 14)
  Kings' Shops ....(see 21)
  Legends of the Pacific ....(see 14)
  Mauna Kea Hawaiian Luau...........(see 15)
  Queens' MarketPlace....................(see 22)
  Royal Luau......................................(see 18)
  Waikoloa Beach Marriot...............(see 18)

off later and pay less (11:30am/1pm/2pm $115/105/85). Carts are mandatory.

Star Gaze Hawaii   STARGAZING
(Map p216; ☎323-3481; www.stargazehawaii.com; adult & child over 12yr/child 5-11yr $30/15; ☺Fairmont Orchid 7:30-8:30pm Fri, Hapuna Beach Prince Hotel 8-9pm Sun & Wed, Hilton Waikoloa Village 8-9pm Tue & Thu) Take advantage of Kohala's consistently clear night skies and join pro-

fessional astronomers in identifying stars using a high-powered telescope.

Dolphin Quest   DOLPHIN SWIM
(Map p216; ☎886-2875, 800-248-3316; www.dolphinquest.com; Hilton Waikoloa Village, 425 Waikoloa Beach Dr; per person from $210, group up to 6 $1350, parking self/valet per day $15/21; ☺9am-4pm; P) Minds differ on whether 'dolphin encounters' are good or bad (see p37). Judging by the popularity of this program, however,

many willingly pay big bucks to meet this adored sea creature face to face. No matter that $210 buys you but 30 minutes of dolphin time. Dolphin Quest's location at the showy, Disney-esque Hilton Waikoloa Village is somehow appropriate.

Hilton Waikoloa Village Pools   SWIMMING
(Map p216; ☎886-1234, 800-221-2424; www.hil tonwaikoloavillage.com; 425 Waikoloa Beach Dr; nonguest pool pass up to 4 people $80, parking self/ valet per day $15/21; P) Chances are, the pools at this over-the-top resort will thrill your kids. Besides the two ridiculously enormous serpentine pools (with multiple waterslides, waterfalls, hot tubs and sandy toddler areas), there's also an artificial beach on a protected lagoon (frequented by sea turtles and tropical fish) and a minigolf course. If your group numbers four, the fee might be worth a splash.

✯ Festivals & Events

TOP CHOICE A Taste of the Hawaiian Range   FOOD FESTIVAL
(www.tasteofthehawaiianrange.com; Hilton Waiko loa Village; admission advance/door $40/60) Celebrated Big Island chefs work magic with local range-fed meats (including beef, lamb, pork, mutton, sausages, poultry and goat) and local produce in late September or early October. Save room for gourmet desserts and drinks. Portions are generous and the price is right.

Moku O Keawe   HULA COMPETITION
(www.mokif.com; Waikoloa Resort Area; hula competition admission per night $6.50-30.25) Established in 2006, this early November hula competition includes *kahiko* (ancient), *'auana* (modern) and *kupuna* (elder) categories. The three-night event is logistically easy compared with the iconic, sell-out Merrie Monarch Festival (p268). Set on an outdoor lawn, the vibe is international, with troupes from Japan and the mainland.

⌂ Sleeping

TOP CHOICE Waikoloa Beach Marriott   HOTEL $$$
(Map p216; ☎886-6789, 888-924-5656; www .waikoloabeachmarriott.com; 69-275 Waikoloa Beach Dr; r $200-450; ❄@❄) The Hilton might be Waikoloa's glamour gal, but the Marriott is the solid girl next door. This airy, 555-room hotel is rather standard in design, but it fronts 'Anaeho'omalu Bay and thus boasts an awesome beach setting, plus three

oceanfront pools. Renovated around 2006, rooms feature quality beds (down comforters and 300-count linens), tastefully muted decor and the expected amenities, from cable TV to refrigerator. Internet access is wi-fi in public areas and wired in rooms. Expect a $20 'resort fee' for parking, phone, internet and other essentials. Book ahead for deep discounts.

Hilton Waikoloa Village   HOTEL $$$
(Map p216; ☎886-1234, 800-221-2424; www.hil tonwaikoloavillage.com; 425 Waikoloa Beach Dr; r $220-540, parking self/valet per day $15/21; ❄@❄) You'll either love or hate the showy, theme-park features of this 62-acre, 1240-room megahotel. There's no natural beach, so its glamour is manmade. A monorail and covered boats let you navigate the sprawling grounds without scuffing your flip-flops, while kids splash aboard kayaks in waveless artificial waterways. There's visual interest everywhere, from a giant Buddha sculpture near the lobby to interesting collections of Polynesian and Asian art pieces or replicas along sidewalks. Rooms are comfy enough, but they're standard business class, not luxury (nothing's oceanfront either) – and no additional facilities (internet access, gym, kitchen appliances) are included in the nightly rate.

✗ Eating

Increase your dining options beyond resort fare at two Waikoloa shopping malls: **Kings' Shops** (Map p216; www.kingsshops.com; 250 Waikoloa Beach Dr), with two destination restaurants, and **Queens' MarketPlace** (Map p216; www.waikoloabeachresort.com; 201 Waikoloa Beach Dr), with one big-name sushi bar, plus budget-saving food-court fare (including Subway, Dairy Queen and Arby's).

TOP CHOICE Sansei Seafood Restaurant & Sushi Bar   JAPANESE $$$
(Map p216; ☎886-6286; www.sanseihawaii.com; Queens' MarketPlace; mains $25-50, sushi $4-22; ◷5:30-10pm) Local celebrity chef DK Kodama will surprise you with innovative, fusion cuisine, from Dungeness-crab ramen in truffle broth to *panko*-crusted (with Japanese breadcrumbs) ahi (yellowfin tuna) sushi. His succulent dry-aged beef ups the ante for a great steak. There's an extensive wine list, compliments of master sommelier Chuck Furuya, and fantastic early-bird discounts: order by 6pm for 50% off food on Sunday and Monday, and 25% off during the rest of the week.

Ancient Hawaiians carved *ki'i pohaku* (stone images), called petroglyphs, into *pahoehoe* (smooth lava). These mysterious carvings are most common on the Big Island, perhaps because – as the youngest island – it has the most extensive fields of *pahoehoe*. The simple images include human figures, animals and important objects such as canoes and sails. No one can prove why the Hawaiians made *ki'i pohaku* or placed them where they did. Many petroglyph fields are found along major trails or on the boundaries of *ahupua'a* (land divisions).

In addition to the Waikoloa petroglyphs, a large field remains further north along the South Kohala coast in Puako; they're also found at Hawai'i Volcanoes National Park.

Touching the petroglyphs will damage them, so never step on or make rubbings of them. Photography is fine and best done in the early morning or late afternoon, when the sun is low.

Merriman's Market Café MEDITERRANEAN **$$**
(Map p216; ☎886-1700; www.merrimansha waii.com; Kings' Shops; dinner mains $20-30; ☺11:30am-9:30pm) Don't confuse Peter Merriman's Waikoloa outpost with his flagship in Waimea. This alfresco cafe is casual, less expensive and more touristy. Foodies from sophisticated cities might find the Mediterranean-inspired fare unremarkable, but the kitchen does feature organic island-grown produce and fresh local fish. Lunch is better value, with salads, sandwiches, pizzas and pastas from $12 to $18.

Roy's Waikoloa Bar & Grill HAWAII REGIONAL **$$$**
(Map p216; ☎886-4321; www.roysrestaurant.com; Kings' Shops; mains $30-35; ☺5:30-9:30pm) Always ridiculously bustling and noisy, Roy's will either delight or disappoint. We suggest that you focus on the food and not the atmosphere or sketchy service. The main courses, such as rack of lamb in a *liliko'i* (passion fruit) cabernet sauce or blackened *'ahi* with pickled ginger, are less than cutting-edge today, but they generally don't disappoint. For groceries, try the following:

Waikoloa Village Market GROCERY
(Map p216; ☎883-1088; Waikoloa Highlands Center, 68-3916 Paniolo Ave; ☺6am-9pm) Located *mauka* (inland) of the highway in Waikoloa Village, this branch of the excellent KTA chain is a full-service grocery store with deli, bakery and ATM.

Waikoloa Village Farmers Market MARKET
(Map p216; Waikoloa Community Church, Paniolo Ave; ☺7-10am Sat) Located on inland side of highway, in the residential Waikoloa Village community.

**Waikoloa Kings' Shops
Farmers Market** MARKET
(Map p216; Kings' Shops; ☺8:30am-1pm Wed) Opened in 2010 this market is the first set in the resort area and features 100% locally grown and produced edibles (no crafts). Come for fresh seasonal produce, honey, baked goods, coffee, tea and orchids.

☆ Entertainment

Find a wide range of free daily entertainment at the two shopping malls:

Kings' Shops MUSIC, HULA
(Map p216; www.kingsshops.com; 250 Waikoloa Beach Dr) Hawaiian music, including slack key guitarist John Keawe at 6pm Tuesday, and hula shows from 6pm to 7pm Friday.

Queens' Marketplace HULA
(Map p216; www.waikoloabeachresort.com; 201 Waikoloa Beach Dr; ☺hula shows 6-7pm Wed & 5:30-7:30pm Thu, hula lessons 5-6pm Fri) Check schedule for variety of programs, including hula shows and lessons.

For nightlife, check **Waikoloa Nights** (www.waikoloanights.com) for special events from rock concerts to hula shows. There are two ongoing luau shows in Waikoloa:

Legends of the Pacific LUAU
(Map p216; ☎886-1234; www.hiltonwaiko loavillage.com; Hilton Waikoloa Village; adult/child 5-12yr/senior & teen 13-18yr $99/51/89; ☺5:30pm Tue, Fri & Sun) The Legends of the Pacific luau show features various South Pacific dances and includes a dinner buffet and one cocktail.

Royal Luau LUAU
(Map p216; ☎886-6789, 888-924-5656; www .waikoloabeachmarriott.com; Waikoloa Beach Marriott; adult/child 5-12yr $88/40; ☺5pm Sun & Wed) This poolside luau is the typical commercial show with Hawaiian-style dinner buffet, open bar and Polynesian dances. The setting by 'Anaeho'omalu Bay is a plus.

1. Halemaʻumaʻu Crater (p283)
The most active area on Kilauea summit, Halemaʻumaʻu bubbles with molten lava.

2. Mauna Kea (p240)
A cinder cone on the top of Mauna Kea, with Mauna Loa in the background.

3. Kona Coffee Belt (p196)
South Kona is patchworked with small farms where coffee is hand-picked and processed.

4. Akaka Falls (p258)
Akaka Falls tumbles majestically down a 420ft moss- and fern-draped cliff.

GREG ELAMS / LONELY PLANET IMAGES ©

Mauna Lani Resort Area

Constructed in 1983 by a Japanese company, the Mauna Lani Resort Area resembles its neighbors, with high-end hotels, condos and golf courses. But it deserves special attention for its significant historical sites and for the Mauna Lani Bay Hotel & Bungalows' refreshingly open attitude toward nonguests who come to explore its trails and fishponds.

 Beaches

The best beaches for swimming or snorkeling are small and located around the two large hotels.

The beach fronting the Mauna Lani Bay Hotel & Bungalows is protected and relatively calm, but the water is shallow. Just 10 minutes south of the hotel by foot, in Makaiwa Bay, there's a small, calm lagoon fronting the Mauna Lani Beach Club condo. To get here, park at the hotel and walk south along the path past the fishponds.

One mile south of the hotel (at the boundary of the overall resort area), there's a small salt-and-pepper beach at Honoka'ope Bay. When seas are calm, swimming and snorkeling are fine but not fantastic. Walk here by an old coastal trail or drive toward the golf courses and turn left at Honoka'ope Pl.

Located at the Fairmont Orchid, Pauoa Bay is an excellent, little-known snorkeling spot, but nonguest access is frowned upon by the hotel.

Holoholokai Beach Park BEACH
(Map p216) Forget about sand and gentle waves here. Instead enjoy picnicking and strolling at this pleasantly uncrowded beach, blanketed by chunks of white coral and black lava. On the calmest days, the waters are fine for snorkeling. Facilities include restrooms, showers, drinking water, picnic tables and grills.

To get here, take Mauna Lani Dr and veer right at the circle; turn right on the marked road immediately before the Fairmont Orchid. The Puako petroglyphs are accessed from the park.

 Sights

TOP CHOICE Puako Petroglyph Preserve HISTORICAL SITE
(Map p216) With more than 3000 petroglyphs, this preserve is among the largest collections of ancient lava carvings in Ha-

waii. The simple pictures might not make sense to you, but viewed altogether they are fascinating and worth a visit.

The 1300yd walk from Holoholokai Beach Park to the preserve adds to the experience: take the well-marked trail at the *mauka* (inland) side of the park. The walk is easy, but wear sturdy footwear and expect blazing sun (the path is only partly shaded).

 Kalahuipua'a Historic Trail HISTORICAL SITE
(Map p216; Mauna Lani Bay Hotel & Bungalows, 68-1400 Mauna Lani Dr; admission free; P) This easy trail starts on the hotel's inland side, at a marked parking lot opposite the resort's little grocery store.

The first part of the historic trail meanders through a former Hawaiian settlement that dates from the 16th century, passing **lava tubes** once used as cave shelters and a few other archaeological and geological sites marked by interpretive plaques. Keep a watchful eye out for quail, northern and red-crested cardinals, saffron finches and Japanese white-eyes.

The trail then skirts ancient **fishponds** lined with coconut palms and continues out to the beach, where you'll find a thatched shelter with an outrigger canoe and a **historic cottage** with a few Hawaiian artifacts on display. If you continue southwest past the cottage, you can loop around the fishpond and back to your starting point (for a round-trip of about 1.5 miles).

 Kalahuipua'a Fishponds
These ancient fishponds are among the island's few remaining working fishponds and, as in ancient times, they're stocked with *awa* (Hawaiian milk fish). Water circulates from the ocean through traditional *makaha* (sluice gates), which allow small fish to enter, but keep mature, fattened catch from escaping.

To access the fishponds directly (without taking the trail), exit the hotel lobby and go south toward the beach. They lie partly under a shady grove of coconut palms and *milo* (native hardwood) trees.

 Activities

Mauna Lani Sea Adventures WATERSPORTS
(Map p216; ☑885-7883; www.hawaiiseaadventures.com; Mauna Lani Bay Hotel & Bungalows, 68-1400 Mauna Lani Dr) This outfit offers three-hour morning snorkeling cruises ($90) five morn-

ings per week; the fee applies to all, but kids (ages three to 12 years) pay half price on Sundays and Wednesdays. From mid-December to mid-April, 1½-hour whale-watching cruises (adult/child three to 12 years $75/45) run five afternoons per week.

Although Kailua-Kona is the Big Island's hub for scuba diving, the waters off Mauna Lani are perhaps even better (and also much less crowded). Mauna Lani Sea Adventures is also the main dive operator (two-tank dive $160) here. Divemasters are competent, friendly and flexible. The dive sites are close to shore, so the boat docks between dives, allowing for a snack or bathroom break. Well-regarded certification courses also offered.

Francis I'i Brown North & South Golf Courses
GOLF

(Map p216; ☑885-6655; Mauna Lani Bay Hotel & Bungalows, 68-1400 Mauna Lani Dr; guest/nonguest $160/265) The two Mauna Lani courses are among the island's top world-class golf courses. The South Course is more scenic and popular, with its signature 15th hole featuring a tee shot over crashing surf. The North Course is more challenging and interesting, however, with a par-three 17th hole within an amphitheater of black lava rock. Discounts for online bookings and twilight tee times.

Mauna Lani Spa
SPA

(Map p216; ☑881-7922; www.maunalani.com; Mauna Lani Bay Hotel & Bungalows, 68-1400 Mauna Lani Dr; massages & facials from $159; ⊘treatments 10am-4pm) A vast indoor/outdoor space landscaped with exotic tropical flora and lava-rock sauna. Treatments are pricey, perhaps overpriced; choose something Hawaiian (eg lomilomi or hot stones) for the memory.

Spa Without Walls
SPA

(Map p216; ☑887-7540; www.fairmont.com/orchid; Fairmont Orchid, 1 North Kaniku Dr; massages & facials from $159; ⊘treatments 8am-8pm) Treatments can be done in alfresco *hale,* hidden amid orchids, coconut palms, waterfalls, streams and lily ponds. Treatments feature botanicals from Kona coffee to matcha green tea. Like Mauna Lani Spa, this facility is upscale if not quite luxurious.

🛏 Sleeping

🏨 Mauna Lani Bay Hotel & Bungalows
HOTEL $$$

(Map p216; ☑885-6622, 800-367-2323; www .maunalani.com; 68-1400 Mauna Lani Dr; r $400-

950; P✻⊛🛜🏊) Among the top South Kohala resorts, the Mauna Lani offers a wonderfully Hawaiian atmosphere. The parklike grounds feature landscaped tropical gardens, hundreds of towering coconut palms and precious historic sites, and the staff is exceptionally courteous and committed to Hawaiian culture. Renovated in the mid-1990s, the 342 rooms are modern in amenities and decor; 90% are oceanfront or ocean-view. Rates include basic services (eg parking, phone, high-speed internet access), so there are no extra charges. This ecoconscious resort uses solar power for its daytime water-pumping needs, drought-resistant grass for the golf greens and recycled water for irrigation. It even raises endangered *honu* on site.

Fairmont Orchid
HOTEL $$$

(Map p216; ☑885-2000, 800-845-9905; www.fairmont.com/orchid; 1 North Kaniku Dr; r $310-700, parking per day self/valet $17/22; P✻⊛🛜🏊) Elegant and almost formal (for Hawai'i), the Orchid never lets you forget that you're at an exclusive, luxury hotel. The architecture feels more continental than overtly Hawaiian, but the meticulously maintained grounds are buoyantly tropical. The 540 rooms are quite posh, but less so than the post-renovation Mauna Lani counterparts. The Orchid's spa and restaurants are first-rate, adding to the pampering quality. Amenities, such as in-room internet access ($14.50 per day), are rather pricey.

🍴 Eating

For fine dining, the restaurants in Mauna Lani are among the island's finest and priciest.

TOP CHOICE Monstera
JAPANESE $$$

(Map p216; ☑887-2711; www.monsterasushi.com; Shops at Mauna Lani; plates $12-25, sushi rolls $9-20; ⊘11:30am-2:30pm & 5:30-10pm) Chef Norio Yamamoto left his namesake restaurant at the Fairmont Orchid to launch his own izakaya-style venue. It's a looser, cooler place, where he can offer a range of tastes, from classic nigiri sushi and seared tuna tataki to sizzling plates of kimchee stir-fried pork loin and teriyaki chicken. The fresh ingredients and friendly service often attract repeat customers.

🍴 Brown's Beach House
HAWAII REGIONAL $$$

(Map p216; ☑885-2000; Fairmont Orchid, 1 North Kaniku Dr; mains $40-56; ⊘5:30-9pm) The prices might deter you but, otherwise, this oceanfront gem is virtually faultless. The service is gracious and the menu is practically a circle-island tour of the best local ingredients. Chef de Cuisine Thepthikone 'TK' Keosavang adds Thai/Asian touches, eg Tom yum soup featuring Hawaiian ono (wahoo) and Hilo hearts of palm. Standouts include the roasted beet and heirloom tomato salad and 'Sustainable Seafood Trio,' three types of fish from the Kona coast.

CanoeHouse   HAWAII REGIONAL **$$$**
(Map p216; ☑885-6622; Mauna Lani Bay Hotel & Bungalows, 68-1400 Mauna Lani Dr; most mains $35-40; ☉6-9pm) The Mauna Lani's fanciest restaurant is lovely all round, with an oceanfront setting and a menu that highlights seafood and local ingredients. Locally raised lobster shines in a tempura appetizer or with other Kona shellfish in kaffir-lime broth, while the Ahualoa goat cheese and potato ravioli (with Hilo corn and Hamakua mushrooms) is a satisfying veg option.

Huli Sue's   ITALIAN **$$$**
(Map p216; ☑885-7777; Golf Club House, Mauna Lani Bay Hotel & Bungalows, 68-1400 Mauna Lani Dr; dinner mains $26-45; ☉11am-8pm) Overlooking the golf greens and ocean, this pleasant restaurant offers traditional Italian fare from 5pm to 8pm. Start with a Caprese salad of local tomatoes and homemade mozzarella, and continue with Florentine-style lasagna or veal osso bucco. There's a pizza combination for every craving, from seafood to a cheeseless marinara option. While dinner prices are rather steep, the all-day lunch menu offers burgers, sandwiches and salads at $12 to $16.

Foodland Farms   GROCERY
(Map p216; ☑887-6101; Shops at Mauna Lani, 68-1330 Mauna Lani Dr; ☉5am-11pm) Full-service gourmet supermarket with an impressive deli selection.

🍸 Drinking

For evening drinks (and a more affordable dinner), try an oceanfront bar:

Honu Bar   BAR
(Map p216; ☑885-6622; Mauna Lani Bay Hotel & Bungalows, 68-1400 Mauna Lani Dr; appetizers $12-18, mains $16-44; ☉5:30-11pm) Awesome bar menu (served till 9pm) ranges from roast chicken and Hamakua-mushroom pizza to Keahole lobster tail. Or just unwind with premium wines, cocktails and liqueurs.

Luana Lounge   BAR
(Map p216; ☑885-2000; Fairmont Orchid, 1 North Kaniku Dr; ☉4-11pm) This casual indoor/outdoor space lets you enjoy the sunset, drinks and *pupu,* and special exhibits of top local artists' work.

☆ Entertainment

Gathering of the Kings   LUAU
(Map p216; ☑326-4969; http://ibphawaii.com/luaus; Fairmont Orchid; adult/child 6-12yr $99/65; ☉Sat) This luau spins a thread of storytelling to highlight slightly modernized versions of Polynesian and Hawaiian dance and music; it's notable for its above average Polynesian dinner buffet and an open bar.

Puako

POP 430

Puako, a longtime beach community, is essentially a mile-long row of homes. The single road through 'town' is marked with numerous 'shoreline access' points. To get here, turn *makai* (seaward) down Puako Beach Dr between the 70- and 71-mile markers.

🏖 Beaches

The clear waters and shallow reef of Puako Bay are great for kayaking, snorkeling and diving. Rent kayaks from Plenty Pupule Adventure Sports (p195).

Beach 69   BEACH
(Map p216; Waialea Bay; ☉7am-8pm) This lovely crescent of white sand is a local favorite but remains somewhat off the tourist radar. Both family-friendly and gay-friendly, this beach is less crowded than Hapuna Beach and its calm, protected waters are ideal for morning snorkeling. Around the boundary, shady trees provide welcome relief. Restrooms and showers are available; no lifeguards. From Puako Beach Dr, take the first right turn onto Old Puako Rd. Find telephone pole No 71 to the left and park. Follow the 'road' to its end, and then tramp along the footpath that runs parallel to a wooden fence. In case you're wondering, telephone pole No 71 was once numbered No 69, which gave the beach its nickname.

⦿ Sights & Activities

Puako Tide Pools   LANDMARK
(Map p216) Puako is known for giant tide pools, set in the swirls and dips of the *pahoehoe* coastline. Some pools are deep enough

to shelter live coral and other marine life. There's no sandy beach, but a narrow strip of pulverized coral and lava covers the shore.

To get to the pools, park along the road near one of six signposted 'beach access' paths. The easiest access is the southermost path: go to the south end of the village and stop just before the 'Road Closed 500 Feet' sign. Take the short dirt road toward a small cove that's used for snorkeling and shore diving; note that the surf is generally too rough in winter. A couple of minutes' walk north brings you to a few petroglyphs, a board for *konane* (a game similar to checkers) chinked into the lava, and tide pools deep enough to cool off in.

Kohala Kayak   KAYAKING
(☑882-4678; www.kohalakayak.com; 3hr tour $60; ⊘departs 9am) Paddle to one or two snorkeling sites in Puako's pristine, less-traveled waters. Water depth is about 20ft; swim through underwater arches 10ft below. All levels are welcome; helpful guides assist newbies, discuss coral ecology and identify strange sea creatures.

🛏 Sleeping

TOP CHOICE **Puako B&B**   B&B $$
(Map p216; ☑882-1331, 800-910-1331; www.bigisland-bedbreakfast.com; 25 Puako Beach Dr; r $100-155, ste $175; 🐾) For both proximity to South Kohala beaches and a personal touch, make this inviting B&B your home base. Rooms are tastefully appointed with Hawaiian motifs, and guests are welcome to use the kitchen. The best options are the largest three, each with private sliding doors to the garden. Proprietor Paul 'Punahele' Andrade, who grew up in this very house, is a *kumu hula* who will gladly introduce you to Hawaiian and local culture. Rates include breakfast.

Hapuna Beach State Recreation Area

Hapuna Beach is world-famous for its magnificent half-mile sweep of white powder sand and crystal-clear waters. Water conditions vary depending on the season. In summer waves are calm and allow good swimming, snorkeling and diving. (Bear in mind, the fish population has woefully declined since the 1980s.) When the surf's up in winter, the bodyboarding is awesome. In general, Hapuna waters are too choppy for tots or nonswimmers. Remember that

waves over 3ft should be left for the experts; drownings are not uncommon here.

Due to its drive-up access and popularity (and the lack of state funds), the restrooms and picnic area at this state recreation area (⊘gate 7am-8pm; P) can be rather grungy. Still, facilities do include pay phones, drinking water, showers, restrooms and a picnic area. Lifeguards are on duty.

To get here, take Hapuna Beach Rd just south of the 69-mile marker. Arrive early to snag a parking space and stake out a good spot. In 2011 the state was considering charging an entry fee for nonresidents, but a decision was still pending during research for this book. Bring industrial-strength sunscreen because there's little shade.

Outdoorsy types could bunk in one of the six state-owned A-frame cabins (per night residents/nonresidents $30/50) near the beach. The awesome location is perfect for sunset and moonrise watching. While rather run-down and makeshift for the price, the cabins are decently livable and each sleeps four people on wooden platforms (bring your own beddings). There are restrooms, showers and a cooking pavilion with a stove and fridge. See p169 for information on obtaining permits.

Mauna Kea Resort Area

Celebrated for its proximity to great beaches, the Mauna Kea development began in the early 1960s when the late Laurance Rockefeller obtained a 99-year lease on the land around Kauna'oa Bay from his friend Richard Smart, owner of Parker Ranch. Five years later Rockefeller unveiled the Mauna Kea Beach Hotel, the first luxury hotel on the Neighbor Islands. 'Every great beach deserves a great hotel,' Rockefeller apparently said. Not everyone would agree, but he got his way here.

For dining options beyond hotel fare, head to Waimea, Kawaihae or the Waikoloa Resort Area for more variety.

🏃 Beaches & Activities

TOP CHOICE **Mauna Kea Beach**   BEACH
(Map p216) Rockefeller picked a winner in this picture-perfect beach, unofficially named after the hotel flanking it. Crescent-shaped Kauna'oa Bay is blanketed in powdery white sand, while the clear waters are calm and shallow (generally less than 10ft).

Snorkeling is only average near the shore; go to the north end along the rocky ledge.

Best of all, the beach is never crowded. It is open to the public, but the hotel sets aside only 40 parking spaces daily for nonguests. Arrive by 9am and obtain a parking pass at the entry booth.

Mau'umae Beach BEACH

(Map p216) This beautiful beach boasts white sand, shady trees and protected waters – and feels even more private and local than Kauna'oa Bay. Locals are proprietary about this gem (for good reason) so don't overstep your welcome.

To get here, go toward the Mauna Kea Beach Hotel, turn right on Kamahoi and cross two wooden bridges. Look for telephone pole No 22 on the left and park (you'll probably see a bunch of cars parked). Walk down the trail to the Ala Kahakai sign and turn left toward the beach. You can also get here from nearby Spencer Beach by walking 10 minutes on the Ala Kahakai Trail.

Ala Kahakai Trail WALKING

Here's another way to access Kauna'oa Bay: on foot. A 6-mile stretch of the 175-mile Ala Kahakai historical trail passes many of South Kohala's signature beaches. You'll also cover pristine shoreline and natural anchialine ponds impossible to see from the highway.

You can start at any point along the way; from the north, start at the southern end of Spencer Beach Park, where you'll pass thick kiawe groves until you reach Mau'umae Beach and eventually the Mauna Kea Resort Area, including the renowned golf course. After you navigate the Hapuna Beach Prince Hotel and then the beach, the trail continues down to Beach 69. The whole hike, especially the last leg, is scorching. Of course, you can turn back at any point. Wear strong sun protection and expect to sweat.

Mauna Kea & Hapuna Golf Courses GOLF

(Map p216; 882-5400, 880-3000; www.princere sortshawaii.com; Mauna Kea Beach Hotel, Hapuna Beach Prince Hotel; Mauna Kea course guest/non-guest $225/250, Hapuna course guest/nonguest $95/135) Golfers dream about playing the combined 36 holes of these two premier courses. The Mauna Kea course is a 72-par championship course that consistently ranks among the top courses in the USA. Designed by Robert Trent Jones Sr, it was remodeled in 2008 by his son, Rees Jones. The Hapuna course has a 700ft elevation gain and was designed by Arnold Palmer and Ed Seay.

🛏 Sleeping

Room rates significantly vary by season.

Mauna Kea Beach Hotel HOTEL $$$

(Map p216; 882-7222, 888-977-4623; www.mau nakeabeachhotel.com; 62-100 Mauna Kea Beach Dr; r $325-760, parking per day self/valet $15/20, internet per day $15; P✳✻🤖🛜) The grand dame of the Gold Coast is understated and quietly confident of its reputation. At first glance it might not wow you, but there is history here; guests are often returnees (some for decades) and staff includes many longtimers. The post-2006-earthquake renovations kept the overall design but upscaled the now-luxury 258 rooms, particularly those in the south main tower (palatial bathrooms). The hotel's crowning jewel, however, is simply its location on Kauna'oa Bay, arguably the best beach on the island.

Hapuna Beach Prince Hotel HOTEL $$

(Map p216; 880-1111, 866-774-6236; www.ha punabeachprincehotel.com; 62-100 Kauna'oa Dr; r $200-500, parking per day self/valet $15/20, internet per day $12; ✳🤖🛜) The Mauna Kea Beach Hotel's 'sister' resort, open since 1994, boasts an ideal location on Hapuna Beach and affordable rates. Depending on your taste, the architectural design is either heavy handed or striking, but all would agree that furnishings need a facelift. While the 350 rooms are clean, with large bathrooms, decor is dated and rather worn. This hotel caters to Japanese tourists and even has a bilingual concierge desk. The hotel shares amenities with the Mauna Kea, and buses transport guests between the two. Excellent value.

☆ Entertainment

Mauna Kea Hawaiian Luau LUAU

(Map p216; 882-5810; www.princeresortshawaii .com; Mauna Kea Beach Hotel; adult/child 5-12yr $96/48; ⏰5:45pm Tue) This outdoor luau show features standard entertainment (thrilling fire dance, group hula) and a gorgeous beach setting. Buffet is generous and above average; drinks are stiff but exorbitant at $15 each.

Kawaihae & Around

Kawaihae is a nondescript port town, where fuel tanks and cargo containers give it an industrial vibe. It's mainly a convenient food stop, with a family beach and historic heiau (temple) toward the south.

Offshore, Kawaihae is a relatively untrafficked spot for diving and snorkeling. For an insider's view of Kawaihae, see the **Pacific Worlds Kawaihae** (www.pacificworlds.com/kawaihae) site.

🏖 Beaches

Spencer Beach Park
BEACH

(Map p216) Shallow, sandy and gentle, this beach has a plain-Jane reputation, but it's ideal for kids (and popular with local families). Come to swim rather than to snorkel; the waters are slightly silty due to Kawaihae Harbor to the north.

Located off the Akoni Pule Hwy (Hwy 270) just north of the 2-mile marker, the park has a lifeguard, picnic tables, barbecue grills, restrooms, showers, drinking water and campsites. A footpath leads south to Mau'umae Beach.

The campsites are exposed and crowded together, but it's still the best camping beach north of Kona; a permit is required (see p169).

⊙ Sights

Pu'ukohola Heiau
National Historic Site
HISTORICAL SITE

(Map p216; ☎882-7218; admission free; ⊙7:30am-4pm) By 1790 Kamehameha the Great had conquered Maui, Lana'i and Moloka'i. But power over his home island of Hawai'i proved to be a challenge. When told by a prophet that he'd rule all the Islands if he built a heiau dedicated to his war god Kuka'ilimoku atop Pu'ukohola (Whale Hill) in Kawaihae, Kamehameha built Pu'ukohola Heiau.

It is believed that Kamehameha and his men formed a human chain 20 miles long, transporting rocks hand to hand from Pololu Valley in North Kohala. After finishing the heiau by summer 1791, Kamehameha held a dedication ceremony and invited his rival and cousin, Keoua, the chief of Ka'u. When Keoua came ashore, he was killed and taken to the *luakini* heiau (temple of human sacrifice) as the first offering to the gods. With Keoua's death, Kamehameha took sole control of the Big Island, eventually ruling all the Islands by 1810.

Back then Pu'ukohola Heiau was adorned with wooden *ki'i* and thatched structures, including an oracle tower, altar, drum house and shelter for the high priest. After Kamehameha's death in 1819, his son Liholiho and

powerful widow Ka'ahumanu destroyed the deity images and the heiau was abandoned.

Today, only the basic rock foundation remains, but it's still a massive 224ft by 100ft, with 16ft to 20ft walls. To get here, turn *makai* (seaward) off the Akoni Pule Hwy halfway between the 2- and 3-mile markers.

Hamakua Macadamia
Nut Company
FACTORY

(Map p216; ☎882-1690; www.hawnnut.com; Maluokalani St; admission free; ⊙8am-5pm) Compared with the Hershey-owned Mauna Loa macnut headquarters near Hilo, this locally owned company is tiny. But the spanking-clean factory and gift shop are staffed by multigeneration locals who give tours, answer questions and otherwise emanate much aloha spirit. An ecoconscious company, it uses ground mac-nut shells (not fossil fuels) to steam-dry its nuts. Generous free samples. To get here, turn *mauka* (inland) just north of the 4-mile marker, less than a mile from Kawaihae.

🏃 Activities

Most visitors beeline to Kailua-Kona and the Kona Coast for diving and snorkeling. But the waters off the Kohala Coast are just as pristine and teeming with marine life – and they're much less crowded. The reef here drops off more gradually than along the Kona Coast, so you'll probably see reef sharks, spinner dolphins, turtles and manta rays, but not large schools of tuna and other deepwater fish. Kohala is the oldest area of the Big Island: see lush coral growth and lots of lava tubes, arches and pinnacles. Kayaking is another activity that's awesome and relatively uncrowded in Kawaihae.

Kohala Divers
WATERSPORTS

(Map p216; ☎882-7774; www.kohaladivers.com; Kawaihae Shopping Center, Akoni Pule Hwy; dives $100-230, snorkeling $75) The best dive and snorkel outfit is conveniently located near Kawaihae Harbor and also offers intro to advanced diving courses, snorkeling and seasonal whale watching. Staff are friendly and knowledgeable, and groups small (maximum six). Also rents kayaks (single/double from $30/40 per 24 hours).

🍴 Sleeping & Eating

In this rural residential area, the only lodging options are B&Bs and vacation rentals.

Hale Ho'onanea　　　　B&B $$
(off Map p216; ☎882-1653, 877-882-1653; www
.houseofrelaxation.com; Ala Kahua Dr; ste $100-130;
☎) About 5 miles north of Kawaihae, the
price is right for these three B&B units set
on peaceful grassy knolls 900ft above sea
level. The Bamboo Suite is priciest, but the
high ceiling, hardwood floor and stunning
180-degree horizon view are worth it. The
other two get smaller and more makeshift as
the price drops, but all are clean and homey,
with kitchenette, lanai, satellite TV and wi-fi.

Café Pesto　　　　HAWAII REGIONAL $$
(Map p216; ☎882-1071; www.cafepesto.com; Kawai-
hae Shopping Center, Akoni Pule Hwy; lunch $11-14,
pizza $9-20, dinner mains $17-33; ☺11am-9pm Sun-
Thu, to 10pm Fri & Sat) This fun, stylish restaurant is a well-loved favorite, serving eclectic,
innovative cuisine you might call Mediterranean with an Asian twang, or Italian with an
island twist. Choose from curries and Greek
salads, seafood risotto and smoked salmon
alfredo, piping hot calzones and thin-crust
gourmet pizza. Walls are crowded with lively
art, and the comfy lounge is a perfect cocktail-
hour destination.

TOP
CHOICE **Blue Dragon**
Musiquarium　　　　HAWAII REGIONAL $$
(Map p216; ☎882-7771; www.bluedragonhawaii
.com; Hwy 270; mains $18-36; ☺5:30-10pm, bar
till 11pm Thu-Sun) Glowing blue, this roofless
restaurant under towering palms books live
jazz music almost nightly – as well as local
slack key favorites such as John Keawe –
creating a mood so upbeat and friendly that
(aided by potent specialty cocktails) even the
shyest couples can't resist the scallop of a
dance floor. Food is sourced locally and well
prepared into an eclectic mix of stir-fries
and curries, rib-eye steaks and teriyaki. Ser-
vice is casual (and a bit distracted). Music
ends at 10pm, but the bar goes as long as
you do.

Kawaihae Harbor Grill　　　　AMERICAN $$
(Map p216; ☎882-1368; Hwy 270; breakfast $9-16,
dinner $27-33; ☺7am-9:30pm) The Grill has
developed a loyal following for its reliably
prepared fresh seafood, pastas and steaks,
and for its family-friendly atmosphere. It
also serves a full diner-style breakfast.

Kawaihae Seafood Bar　　　　SEAFOOD $$
(Map p216; ☎880-9393; Hwy 270; pupu $9-16,
mains $15-27; ☺11am-11:30pm) Upstairs from
the Kawaihae Harbor Grill, this spot
draws a rowdier crowd for drinks, and up-
scale bar food like *poke* burger and ginger
steamed clams.

Anuenue　　　　ICE CREAM $
(Map p216; ☎882-1109; Kawaihae Shopping Cen
ter, Akoni Pule Hwy; cones from $2.50, fast food
$3.50) Excellent shave ice and premium
ice cream. The friendly owner offers flavor
samples and advice. Also serves hot dogs,
veggie burgers, chili bowls and other fast
food.

SACRED SITES

Ancient Hawaiians built a variety of heiau (temples) for different gods and different pur-
poses: healing the sick, sharing the harvest, changing the weather, offering human sacri-
fice and succeeding in warfare. Some heiau were modest thatched structures, but others
were enormous stone edifices.

Today the eroded ruins of heiau, found across the Islands, often only hint at their origi-
nal grandeur. After Kamehameha II (Liholiho) abolished the kapu (taboo) system in 1819,
many were destroyed or abandoned. But on the Big Island, two of the largest and best-
preserved heiau remain: **Pu'ukohola Heiau** (a war temple) and **Mo'okini Luakini Heiau**
(a sacrificial temple).

The war temples were typically massive platforms built with boulders, plus covered
shelters for kahuna (priests), ceremonial drums and idols of the temple's patron god.
The larger the heiau, the more threatening it appeared to enemies. Indeed, the sheer
magnitude of Pu'ukohola Heiau, built during Kamehameha the Great's rise to power,
foreshadowed his ultimate conquest of the Hawaiian Islands.

Luakini heiau (temples of human sacrifice) were always dedicated to Ku, the war god.
Only Ku deserved the greatest gift, a human life, and only the highest chiefs could order
it. But human sacrifice was not taken lightly; typically people gave offerings of food to
Ku. The actual act of killing was not a necessary ritual; an enemy slain in battle was ac-
ceptable. But the victim had to be a healthy man – never a woman, a child or an aged or
deformed man.

Kawaihae Market & Deli GROCERY
(Map p216; ☎880-1611; ☺4:30am-9pm Mon-Fri,
5:30am-8pm Sat & Sun) Standard convenience items plus locally made pasta and tofu salads.

NORTH KOHALA

Rural North Kohala has a distinct flavor all its own – a charming, successful mix of rural farmers and local artists, of Native Hawaiians and haole transplants, of tidy suburban homes, plantation-era storefronts, green valleys and ancient temples. Few visitors, and indeed few Big Island residents, make the detour off the Hawai'i Belt Rd to experience it, which irks locals, who feel North Kohala is unfairly overlooked.

Geologically the oldest part of the Big Island, the North Kohala Coast is rich in ancient history, including being the birthplace of King Kamehameha I. In modern times North Kohala was sugar country until the Kohala Sugar Company closed in 1975. Today the small historic towns of Hawi and Kapa'au contain just enough art galleries, boutiques and distinctive eateries to succeed as tourist attractions.

Rounding the peninsula's thumb on Hwy 270, you leave the Kohala Mountain's rain shadow and the land shifts steadily from bone dry to lushly tropical. By the time you reach road's end, the wet landscape has been carved into ever more dramatic contours, culminating in the Pololu Valley, the jewel of North Kohala.

Akoni Pule Highway (Hwy 270)

The land along the Akoni Pule Hwy (Hwy 270) remains largely undeveloped, affording spectacular coastal views that make Maui seem but a short swim away.

 Beaches & Sights

In order of direction, heading north toward Hawi you'll find the following:

Pua Mau Place GARDEN
(Map p231; ☎882-0888; www.puamau.org; Ala Kahua Dr; adult/child $10/8; ☺9am-4pm) Who takes 15 acres of the driest land on the island to prove it can support a flowering, 'ecofriendly' botanical garden? Octogenarian Virgil Place, that's who, and his questionable vision is marginally realized in this irrigated oasis. Expect withering heat. To get here, turn inland on Ala Kahua Dr just north of the 6-mile marker.

WILL I SEE A MANTA? 229

Whether you see one (or several) of these beauties on your night dive or snorkel depends entirely on Mother Nature. Your chances are better at the northern spot near Garden Eel Cove (aka Manta Heaven, where historical data shows an 81% chance of a sighting), and some outfitters let you repeat your cruise for free if you fail to site mantas the first go round.

Check the **Manta Pacific Research Foundation** (www.mantapacific.org) for manta sighting data and guidelines for responsible manta watching. Bring your own dive light and let them come to you!

Lapakahi State Historical Park HISTORICAL SITE
(Map p231; ☎882-6207; admission free; ☺8am-4pm, closed state holidays) This coastal park was a remote fishing village 600 years ago. Eventually some of the villagers moved to the wetter uplands and became farmers, trading their crops for fish. In the process, Lapakahi grew into an *ahupua'a*. When the freshwater table dropped in the 19th century, the village was abandoned.

An unshaded, 1-mile **loop trail** traverses the 262-acre grounds, passing the remains of stone walls, house sites, canoe sheds and fishing shrines. Visitors can try their hand at **Hawaiian games**, with game pieces and instructions laid out for 'o'o ihe (spear throwing), *konane* (checkers) and *'ulu maika* (stone bowling). Nothing is elaborately presented – so visitors need wild imaginations to appreciate the modest remains.

Lapakahi's clear waters are loaded with tropical fish and belong to a marine-life conservation district. But this is a historical, not recreational, park, with historically sacred waters. Park staff may grant permission for snorkeling, but they generally discourage it.

The park is located just south of the 14-mile marker.

Mahukona Beach Park BEACH
(Map p231) Without a sandy beach or swimmable waters, Mahukona warrants only a

brief poking around. After you turn off the Akoni Pule Hwy, the right-hand lane leads to a small pier. Once a key port for the Kohala Sugar Company, today it's a low-key fishing spot for locals.

Beyond the landing there are snorkeling and diving spots that can be explored during calm waters. Entry, via a ladder, is in about 5ft of water. Heading north it's possible to follow an anchor chain out to a submerged boiler and the remains of a ship 25ft down. Overall, however, the setting is not very inviting.

If you veer left after the turnoff, you'll reach the county park, where a shabby cluster of picnic tables and restrooms overlooks a scenic, if formidable, beach. The camping area is rather forlorn-looking.

King Kamehameha's Birthplace   HISTORICAL SITE

(Map p231) Along the coast south of Mo'okini Heiau is the supposed site of Kamehameha's birth, marked by stone-walled foundations. As the legend goes, when Kamehameha was born on a stormy winter night in 1758, his mother was told by a kahuna that her son would be a powerful ruler and conquer all the Islands. Upon hearing this, the ruling high chief of Hawai'i ordered all male newborns killed. Thus, after Kamehameha was taken to the Mo'okini Heiau for his birth rituals, he was spirited away into hiding.

To get here, turn *makai* (seaward) on the dirt road about a quarter-mile south of Mo'okini Heiau.

Mo'okini Luakini Heiau   HEIAU (TEMPLE)

(Map p231; ☎373-8000; admission free; ⊗9am-8pm, closed Wed) It's off the beaten path, but this heiau near 'Upolu Point at Hawai'i's norternmost tip is among the oldest (c AD 480) and most historically significant Hawaiian sites. Measuring about 250ft by 125ft, with walls 6ft high, the massive stone ruins sit solitary and brooding on a wind-rustled grassy plain.

According to legend, the heiau was built from 'sunrise to first light' by up to 18,000 'little people' passing water-worn basalt stones in complete silence from Pololu Valley – a distance of 14 miles – under the supervision of Kuamo'o Mo'okini. It was a 'closed' temple, reserved only for *ali'i nui* (high chiefs).

Five hundred years later Pa'ao, a priest from Samoa, raised the walls to 30ft and rebuilt the altar as his *ho'okupu* (offering) to the gods. He initiated human sacrifice,

to stem dilution of the royal bloodlines and to enforce stricter moral codes of conduct (making this the first *luakini* heiau).

In 1963 the National Park Service designated Mo'okini Heiau as Hawaii's first registered National Historic Landmark. Fifteen years later, it was deeded to the state.

The current *kahuna nui* (high priestess), Leimomi Mo'okini Lum, is the seventh high priestess of the Mo'okini bloodline serving the temple. In 1978 she lifted the kapu that restricted access to the temple, thereby opening it to visitors.

To get here take Old Coast Guard Rd, between the 18- and 19-mile markers, for just over a mile. Turn right onto a red-cinder road, blocked by a locked cattle gate. Call ahead for the gate to be unlocked; otherwise park here (without blocking the gate) and walk 15 minutes to the heiau. Alternative route if you have 4WD: drive toward 'Upolu Airport, then turn south onto the gutted coastal road, which is impassable after rains.

Hawi

POP 940

Hawi (hah-*vee*) can fit all of its businesses within two blocks, but it looms large in picturesque charm and notable restaurants. It was once a major plantation town for the Kohala Sugar Company, and many local residents are descendants of sugar workers. Mainland transplants are bringing big money to little Hawi and leading its transformation from rustic boondocks to tourist destination. But the town offers only basic services, such as a post office, grocery store and gas station.

🏃 Activities

TOP CHOICE Big Island Eco Adventures ZIPLINING
(☎889-5111; www.bigislandecoadventures.com; 55-514 Hawi Rd; 3-4hr tour $159) The forest wilderness near Pololu Valley is a perfect setting for zipping, which you do eight times on this excellent tour, which also includes hiking trails, two suspension bridges and waterfall views. Meet at Luke's Place and ride a 6WD vehicle to the course. Choose from seven daily departures between 8am and 2pm; maximum 10 guests.

Kohala Ditch Adventures KAYAKING
(☎889-6000, 888-288-7288; www.kohaladitchadventures.com; tour per adult/child under 12yr $129/65) This unique attraction (then called

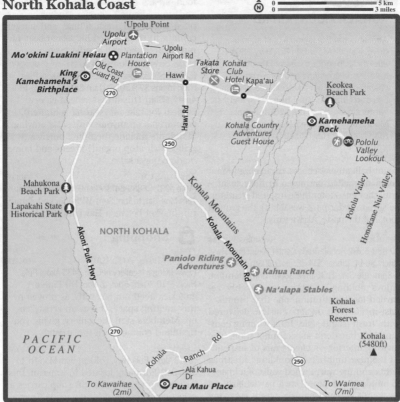

Flumin' da Ditch) closed in 2006 due to earthquake damage. It reopened in 2011 too late to review, but looks promising. In a 2.5-mile kayaking trip along historic plantation waterways, paddlers navigate through rainforest, 10 tunnels and seven flumes.

🛏 Sleeping

Kohala Village Inn   HOTEL **$**
(📞889-0404; www.kohalavillageinn.com; 55-514 Hawi Rd; r $70-80, ste $120-140; 🛜) The inn's 19 cozy rooms are much nicer than the plantation-era, motel-style building suggests. Inside each are attractive plank floors, tile baths, warm furniture, soft towels and cable TV. The free continental breakfast and convenient location (half a block from the main strip) make up for thin walls and no view.

Plantation House   COTTAGE **$$**
(Map p231; 📞889-6951; www.hawiplantationhouse.com; Akoni Pule Hwy; cottage/house/both $150/800/900; 🛜) This 340-sq-ft studio cottage makes a romantic hideaway when no one's renting the adjacent house. While it lacks a kitchen, there's a refrigerator and sofabed. For large groups, the beautifully restored plantation house offers six bedrooms and six bathrooms (sleeps 14), plus professional-caliber kitchen, laundry room, swimming pool and tennis court: a perfect setting for retreats, weddings and other events. Contact the owners for directions.

🍴 Eating & Drinking

TOP CHOICE Sushi Rock   SUSHI **$$**
(📞889-5900; www.sushirockrestaurant.net; Akoni Pule Hwy; nigiri per piece $6, sushi rolls $8-20, mains $15-28; ⏱noon-3pm & 5:30-8pm Sun-Tue & Thu, to 9pm Fri & Sat) Original sushi chef Rio Miceli has left, but this popular sushi bar has successfully continued rolling his unique (if rather offbeat), island-influenced specialties, such as the Kohala (ahi *poke*, fresh papaya and cucumber, rolled in mac nuts). Purists

DON'T MISS

KOHALA MOUNTAIN RD

Arguably the Big Island's best scenic drive, Kohala Mountain Rd (Hwy 250) affords stupendous views of the Kohala–Kona coastline and three majestic volcanic mountains: Mauna Kea, Mauna Loa and Hualalai. Start from Hawi and gently zigzag down the 3500ft Kohala Mountains to Waimea. Note that this road is called Hawi Rd close to town.

might balk at goat cheese, caramelized Maui onion or melted parmesan in their sushi – until they encounter these inspired creations. Be sure to order pure wasabi: it's the ground root, not the paste. Arrive early.

Bamboo　　　　　　　HAWAII REGIONAL **$$**
(☑889-5555; Kohala Trade Center, Akoni Pule Hwy; lunch $9-14, dinner $14-35; ☺11:30am-2:30pm & 6-8pm Tue-Sat, 11:30am-2:30pm Sun) Bamboo enjoys abiding affection as a highly regarded local institution, one that promises East-meets-West fusion cuisine delivered with 'fresh island style.' It's a winning combination, but don't expect innovation. The inviting interior – a cheery mix of suspended Balinese umbrellas, twinkling Christmas lights and the warm wood walls of a historic building – is pure Hawi, particularly on weekends when live music sweeps everyone up in a tide of aloha.

Kohala Coffee Mill　　　　　　CAFE **$**
(☑889-5577; Akoni Pule Hwy; snacks $3-5; ☺6am-6pm Mon-Fri, to 5:30pm Sat & Sun) A comfy place to hang out and treat yourself to muffins, fresh-brewed Kona coffee and heavenly Tropical Dreams ice cream. Also check out the shave ice and fudge at adjoining **Upstairs at the Mill** (☑889-5015; ☺11am-5pm; 🛜), where you can also find internet access ($5 per 30 minutes) and art displays. In the evenings, the space becomes a **kava bar** (☺4:30-9pm). Choose between traditional kava (the mildly relaxing juice of the 'awa plant) or a flavored version, such as Maya Chocolate, made with coconut milk, ginger, chocolate, cayenne and cinnamon.

Luke's Place & Tiki Lounge　　AMERICAN **$$**
(☑889-1155; www.lukeskohala.com; 55-510 Hawi Rd; sandwiches $9-13, dinner mains $12-27; ☺11am-9pm, bar to 10pm) Resembling an open-air sports bar, this friendly spot serves predictable but pleasing American standards (sea-

food, steaks and ribs), adding local flavors and ingredients. Classic sandwiches are piled high with fresh fillings and burgers contain 100% grass-fed Big Island beef. Live music on Friday and Sunday evenings.

Hula La's Mexican Kitchen　　MEXICAN **$**
(☑889-5668; Kohala Trade Center, Akoni Pule Hwy; mains $7-9.50; ☺11am-8pm Mon-Thu, to 4pm Fri-Sun) This little Mexican eatery is ideal for takeout (seating is limited), vegetarians or anyone with salsa cravings. Standouts include the filling burritos, grilled fish atop organic greens and homemade papaya salsa.

Takata Store　　　　　　　GROCERY
(Map p231; ☑889-5413; Akoni Pule Hwy; ☺8am-7pm Mon-Sat, to 1pm Sun) Well-stocked, family-run market between Hawi and Kapa'au.

 Shopping

TOP CHOICE **Living Arts Gallery**　　　GALLERY
(www.livingartsgallery.net; 55-3435 Akoni Pule Hwy; ☺10:30am-5pm, to 8pm Fri) Fine art galleries need not be stuffy, as proven by this inviting space, run as an artists' co-op. Members staff the gallery, giving you firsthand contact with the artists.

Elements　　　　　　　　　ACCESSORIES
(3413 Akoni Pule Hwy; ☺10am-6pm Mon-Fri, to 5pm Sat) Formerly located in Kapa'au, this irresistible jewelry and gift shop carries an eclectic collection of locally made finery.

L Zeidman Gallery　　　　　　GALLERY
(www.lzeidman.com; Hwy 270; ☺10am-6pm Tue-Sat, to 5pm Sun-Mon) Most people can only afford to browse the exquisitely crafted wood bowls and sculpture at this gallery, which sells museum-quality pieces by island artists.

Gallery at Bamboo　　　　　　GALLERY
(www.bamboo restaurant.info/gallery.htm; Hwy 270; ☺11:30am-8pm Tue-Sat, to 2:30pm Sun) Located in the Old General Store (together with the restaurant Bamboo), this gallery is chock-full of paintings, photos, funky art and high-end gifts. Don't miss upstairs.

Kapa'au
POP 1160

Kapa'au is another former sugar town refashioned into an attractive tourist destination, though it's not as adorably quaint as Hawi. Kapa'au is North Kohala's civic center, with a courthouse, police station, library and bank (with ATM). North Kohala was Kamehameha's childhood home, so the King Kamehameha Day festivities have extra significance here.

⭐ Beaches & Sights

FREE Kenji's House   MUSEUM
(☑884-5556; www.kohalaartists.com; Akoni Pule Hwy; ⊙11am-5pm) Nobody famous, Kapa'au native Kenji Yokoyama (1931–2004) is now known for his seashell 'art.' An avid free diver and constant recycler and repairer, he collected all the rocks, driftwood and shells that he glued together into little sculptures. While not fine art, when viewed en masse in his lifetime abode, they're original, fanciful, earnest and quite memorable. The exhibit, called **Kenji's Room: A Mini Museum**, is part of the overall Kenji's House site, which includes a **restaurant** (Pico's Bistro) and the **North Kohala Artists Cooperative Gallery**.

Kamehameha The Great Statue   MONUMENT
The statue on the front lawn of the North Kohala Civic Center has a famous twin in Honolulu, standing across from 'Iolani Palace. The Kapa'au one was the original, constructed in 1880 in Florence, Italy, by American sculptor Thomas Gould. When the ship delivering it sank off the Falkland Islands, a second statue was then cast from the original mold. The duplicate statue arrived at the Islands in 1883 and took its place in downtown Honolulu. Later the sunken statue was recovered from the ocean floor and sent here, to Kamehameha's childhood home.

Keokea Beach Park   BEACH
(off Akoni Pule Hwy; ⊙gate 7am-11pm) About 3.5 miles from Kapa'au, this beach park isn't a big draw because there's no sandy beach. But it is striking, with tall, reddish cliffs rising above a boulder bay. The surf really surges with a west swell, attracting a motley crew of experienced local surfers. Swimming is sketchy due to dangerous shore breaks and strong currents. The facilities are shoddy, but there are BBQ grills, showers, drinking water and portable toilets. The marked turnoff is about 1.5 miles before the Pololu Valley Lookout. On the way down to the beach, you'll pass an old Japanese cemetery with gravestones inscribed in *kanji* (Japanese script).

Kalahikiola Church   CHURCH
In 1855 Protestant missionaries Elias and Ellen Bond built this church on their vast estate (obviously, missionary life wasn't one

---

THE RANCH LIFE

Windswept pastureland. Grazing cattle. Cloud-dappled skies. North Kohala makes folks yearn to be a *paniolo* (cowboy), at least for a day. So head to a working ranch along the breathtaking Kohala Mountain Rd. If you're staying in Waimea, the outfits there are excellent, too.

Kahua Ranch

(Map p231; ☑882-7954; www.exploretheranch.com; Kohala Ranch Rd) Well known across Hawaii, Kahua Ranch beef and lamb are chef favorites and often highlighted on restaurant menus. Visitors can glimpse life on this 8500-acre ranch, owned by the Richards family, through the **Evening at the Ranch BBQ Dinner** (adult/child 6-11yr $95/47.50; ⊙6-9pm summer, 5:30-8:30pm winter), which includes steak and chicken dinner, beer and wine, live music, rodeo games, stargazing and a campfire. Round-trip transportation can be arranged (adult/child 6 to 11 years $119/59.50).

Na'alapa Stables

(☑889-0022; www.naalapastables.com; Kohala Ranch Rd; rides $68-88, wagon tour adult/child $36/18) Na'alapa Stables organizes rides across the pastures of the 8500-acre Kahua Ranch, affording fine views of the coast from its 3200ft elevation. Also offered is a narrated historical tour of the ranch aboard an 1860s-style farm wagon.

Paniolo Riding Adventures

(☑889-5354; www.panioloadventures.com; Hwy 250; rides $69-159) Offers short, long, picnic and sunset rides over 11,000-acre Ponoholo Ranch, a working cattle ranch. Horses are selected for the rider's experience. Boots, hats, chaps and jackets are provided free of charge.

of total deprivation). It's not a must-see, but towering banyan trees and peaceful macadamia-nut orchards surrounding the church make it a scenic detour. Large portions of three of the church's walls crumbled in the 2006 earthquake, and the congregation immediately began fundraising to rebuild.

The church is 900yd up 'Iole Rd, which is on the *mauka* (inland) side of the highway between the 23- and 24-mile markers.

Kamehameha Rock
LANDMARK

According to legend, Kamehameha carried this rock uphill from the beach to demonstrate his prodigious strength. Much later, when a road crew attempted to move it to a different location, the rock stubbornly fell off the wagon – a sign that it wanted to stay put. Not wanting to upset Kamehameha's mana, the workers left it in place. Don't blink or you'll miss it, sitting on the inland roadside about 2 miles east of Kapa'au, on a curve just past a small bridge. Also keep your eyes peeled for the facade of the Tong Building, a colorful old Chinese hall secluded in the trees above the rock.

Festivals & Events

TOP CHOICE North Kohala Kamehameha Day Celebration HISTORIC CELEBRATION

(www.kamehamehadaycelebration.org; admission free) Join thousands who flock to Hawi and Kapa'au on June 11 to honor Kamehameha the Great in his birthplace. The spectacular parade of floral-bedecked horseback riders and floats culminates in an all-day gathering with music, crafts, hula and food.

Sleeping

Kohala Club Hotel
INN $

(Map p231; 889-6793; www.kohalaclubhotel.com; 54-3793 Akoni Pule Hwy; r/ cottages $56/90) Just 0.5 miles from town, this tiny inn offers clean rooms with private bathrooms for an unbelievable price. The main house contains four small, no-frills rooms with either a queen bed or two twins, plus a TV. With two bedrooms, the cottage is perfect for families.

Kohala Country Adventures Guest House
INN $$

(Map p231; 889-5663, 866-892-2484; www.kcadventures.com; off Akoni Pule Hwy; r $85-175) If 'rustic' and 'country' appeal to you, try this relaxed, lived-in house on 10 acres of ungroomed tropical gardens, with fruit trees, livestock and coastal views. The Sundeck Suite is good for families, with kitchenette, three beds and an open loft layout. It's a comfy, not fancy, place and host Bobi Moreno, a longtime resident, puts everyone at ease.

Eating

TOP CHOICE Pico's Bistro CAFE $

(884-5555; Kenji's House, Akoni Pule Hwy; mains $8-12; ⊙11am-6:30pm) With umbrella-shaded patio seating and a teeny kitchen, Pico's resembles a beachside food stand. But the menu is all gourmet, featuring homemade pastas, quiches, chicken and lamb kebabs and classic salads – made with local, organic produce. Fresh-fruit smoothies ($5) include the eye-opening Lime Malia (homemade lime sorbet, seltzer and fresh lime juice). Biodegradable cups, cutlery and containers.

Sammy D's
DINER $

(889-5288; 54-3854 Akoni Pule Hwy; meals $7-9; ⊙11am-8pm Tue-Sat, to 4pm Sun) Fill up on burgers, sandwiches and plate lunches including mahimahi, Korean chicken and the house specialty, roast pork.

Sushi To Go
SUSHI $

(756-0132; 54-3877 Akoni Pule Hwy; rolls $6-10) Nothing fancy, just decent takeout sushi that makes a yummy lunch or snack.

Pololu Valley

With a stunning row of steep, mystical cliffs, this ancient valley is utterly memorable – and proves the diversity of the Big Island landscape. If Waipi'o Valley highlights the island's green lushness, Pololu Valley reveals its contemplative side, in twilight shades and thick mists. The Akoni Pule Hwy ends at the Pololu Valley Lookout, the endpoint and photo-op for those who cannot hike down the trail.

Pololu Valley was once abundant with wetland taro, when Pololu Stream carried water from the deep, wet interior to the valley floor. When the Kohala Ditch was built in 1906, however, it diverted much of the water and ended taro production. The valley's last residents left in the 1940s, and the area is now forest-reserve land.

For over 100 years, the ditch has been a lifeline for Kohala ranches and farms; it even became a tourist attraction with flume rides. The October 2006 earthquake wrecked the ditch and it ceased flowing for two years. Ongoing multimillion-dollar repairs are gradually restoring its condition.

🏃 Activities

TOP CHOICE **Pololu Valley Trail**   HIKING

This steep, rocky trail to the valley floor is doable for most, thanks to switchbacks and its 0.75-mile distance. Not counting scenic stops, walking time averages 20 minutes going down and perhaps 30 coming back up. But think twice about trekking down after rainfall, as the mud-slicked rocks will be precarious. Walking sticks are often left at the trailhead. There are no facilities.

At the mouth of the valley lies a gorgeous black-sand beach. The surf is rough, particularly in winter, with rip currents year-round; swimming is generally out of the question. You might see local surfers and bodyboarders testing the waves, however. Behind the beach, a hillocky ironwood forest vibrates like some Tolkien-inspired shire wood. Deeper valley explorations are blocked by a pond, beyond which cattle roam freely (an indication you shouldn't drink the water).

👉 Tours

Hawaii Forest & Trail   GUIDED HIKE

(📞331-8505, 800-464-1993; www.hawaii-forest .com; Kohala Waterfalls Tour adult/child under 13yr $159/129) This 1.5-mile loop traverses the Kohala Ditch Trail to waterfalls (swimming included); transportation from the Waikoloa Resort Area is included.

WAIMEA (KAMUELA)

POP 7030

The cool, green rolling pastureland surrounding Waimea is perhaps Hawai'i's most unexpected face. This is cattle and cowboy country, and nearly all of it, including Waimea itself, is owned, run or leased by Parker Ranch, the fifth-largest cow-calf ranch in the USA.

Waimea is full of contrasts. Weatherwise it's split into the 'dry side' and the 'wet side' and, strangely, it's a town with two names (Kamuela, used mostly by locals, is used to differentiate this Waimea from those on O'ahu and Kaua'i). From the highway all you see are bland strip malls, but closer inspection finds art galleries and gourmet restaurants. Then there are all the transplants – organic farmers, astronomers, artists – plus new money.

BEST EDIBLE EXPERIENCES   235

» *Poke* selection at Suisan Fish Market (p270)

» Taro, breadfruit and sweet potato chips by Aaron's Blue Kalo (p258 and p271)

» Wild sushi at Sushi Rock (p231)

» Turtle Cheesecake at Kailua Candy Company (p196)

» Kaleo's tempura ahi roll (p277)

» *Poha* (gooseberry), *liliko'i* (passion fruit) and other homemade preserves at Mr Ed's Bakery (p258)

For visitors, Waimea makes a good base to explore Kohala, Mauna Kea and the Hamakua Coast, since all are easily accessible. If you enjoy fine food and theater, *mo bettah,* since some of the island's best is here in cow town. Waimea has wacky weather, going from sun to rain in the swish of a horse's tail, so jeans and sweaters are definitely needed up here at 2670ft.

Orientation

The intersection of Kawaihae Rd (Hwy 19) and Mamalahoa Hwy (Hwy 190) is Waimea's town center (and near the transition between wet and dry sides).

From Hilo, Hwy 19 is commonly called the Mamalahoa Hwy, but west of Hwy 190 it becomes Kawaihae Rd, while Hwy 190 continues as the Mamalahoa Hwy. To complicate matters, there's a section of the 'Old Mamalahoa Hwy' further east that intersects and parallels Hwy 19.

◉ Sights

Until the late 2000s, Waimea's main attractions were Parker Ranch's museum and 19th-century historic homes. They're now closed permanently, but here are other worthy stops.

FREE **Isaacs Art Center**   ART GALLERY

(📞885-5884; http://isaacsartcenter.hpa.edu; 61-1268 Kawaihae Rd; ⊙10am-5pm Tue-Sat) Sometimes *where* art is shown is as moving as the art itself (eg Bilbao and the NYC Guggenheim), and that's the case at this gallery. When Building N from the Waimea school was slated for demolition, George and Shirley Isaacs and friends snapped into action to save the 1915 schoolhouse, moving it piece by piece (even the blackboards) to its present location. The result is a series of bright, spacious galleries displaying an excellent collection of local and international artwork.

As you tread the original Douglas fir floorboards, the smell of oil paint and exotic woods mingles with dreams of owning that gorgeous koa rocker ($8000) or the exquisite *milo,* tiger and *kahili* koa wood breakfront ($15,000). Some items are not for sale, including Herb Kawainui Kane's classic *The Arrival of Captain Cook at Kealakekua Bay in January 1779,* in the entryway.

Proving that art appreciation need not be a snooty, alienating experience, Director Bernard Nougés often greets visitors personally, explaining the craftsmanship behind a particular piece or the relevance of a painting's symbolism – even to trail-worn backpackers. A portion of proceeds from the center's sales goes to the Hawai'i Preparatory Academy.

Waimea Farmers Market　　MARKET
(⊘7am-noon Sat) Waimea's farmers market is an island highlight and certainly the town's most vibrant and fun community event. Locals turn out in droves to stock up on fresh produce and recent gossip. Vendors emphasize organic produce and specialty items: fresh eggs, herbs and plants, local meat and honey, beautiful flowers and plenty of cooked food. There's a smaller selection of high-quality craft stalls. The market is in front of the Hawaiian Home Lands office, near the 55-mile marker on Hwy 19.

Anna Ranch Heritage Center　HISTORICAL SITE
(☏885-4426; www.annaranch.org; 65-1480 Kawaihae Rd; tours $7; ⊘gift shop 10am-4pm) The life and times of Hawaii's 'first lady of ranching,' Anna Leialoha Lindsey Perry-Fiske, are celebrated at this 14-room historic ranch house, which contains impressive koa furniture, Anna's bountiful wardrobe and other memorabilia. Now that the Parker Ranch's historic homes are closed, this is your best bet for a look at old Hawaii. Tours must be booked in advance; it's located a mile west of the town center.

WM Keck Observatory Office　VISITOR CENTER
(☏885-7887; www.keckobservatory.org; 65-1120 Mamalahoa Hwy; ⊘10am-2pm Tue-Fri) The lobby of this working observatory is open to the public. Visitors can view models and images of the twin 10m Keck telescopes, fascinating photos and a telescope trained on Mauna Kea.

Informative volunteers talk about the latest discoveries and answer questions. It's worth visiting if you can't make it to Mauna Kea's Onizuka Center (p242).

Church Row　　　　　　　CHURCHES
In 1830 it was a grass hut. In 1838 it grew into a wooden building adorned with coral stones, carried on the backs of the parishioners. In this way, **Imiola Congregational Church** (www.imiolachurch.com; admission free; ⊘services 9:30am), Waimea's first Christian church, communed with Hawaii.

The current church, built entirely of koa, was constructed in 1857 and restored in 1976. In the churchyard is the grave of missionary Lorenzo Lyons, who arrived in 1832 and spent 54 years in Waimea. Lyons translated and wrote many hymns in Hawaiian, including the popular 'Hawai'i Aloha,' still sung here in Hawaiian the first Sunday of the month.

The green-steepled church next door is the much-photographed, all-Hawaiian **Ke Ola Mau Loa Church.** Buddhists, Baptists and Mormons also have places of worship along this curved row.

🏃 Activities

**TOP CHOICE　Dahana Ranch
Roughriders**　　　　HORSEBACK RIDING
(☏885-0057, 888-399-0057; www.dahanaranch.com; 90min ride adult/child $70/60; ⊘rides 9am, 11am, 1pm & 3pm) Hitting the trail is easy here in horse country. Located in the magnificent foothills of Mauna Kea, Dahana Ranch Roughriders is owned and operated by a Native Hawaiian family. With Hawai'i's most established horse outfit, you'll be riding American quarter horses bred, raised and trained by third- and fourth-generation *paniolo.* These are open-range rides, available to kids as young as three years. More advanced rides are also on offer. The ranch is 7.5 miles east of Waimea, off Old Mamalahoa Hwy. Reservations are essential.

**Parker Ranch Horseback
Riding Tours**　　　　HORSEBACK RIDING
(☏885-7655, 877-855-7999; www.parkerranch.com; rides $79; ⊘8:15am & 12:15pm) Two-hour rides (age seven and up) focus on ranch history and include visits to the stone corrals and the arena. To book, contact the 'Gear Up and Go' desk in the Parker Ranch store in Parker Ranch Center. Parker Ranch also offers, by reservation only, a variety of hunting trips.

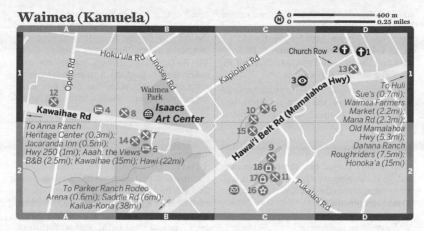

🎇 Festivals & Events

Waimea Cherry Blossom Heritage Festival *JAPANESE FESTIVAL*
(📞961-8706; Parker Ranch Center & Church Row Park; admission free) Dark pink blossoms are greeted with *taiko* drumming, *mochi* (sticky rice cake) pounding and other Japanese cultural events on the first Saturday in February.

Waimea Ukulele & Slack Key Guitar Institute Concert *MUSIC*
(📞885-6017; www.kahilutheatre.org; admission from $5) This is the go-to event at the Kahilu Theatre in mid-February, with concerts, evening *kanikapila* (open-mic jam sessions) and workshops by the giants of uke and slack key guitar, including Cyril Pahinui and Dennis Kamakahi. Private lessons are also available ($65).

Fourth of July Rodeo *RODEO*
(📞885-2303; Parker Ranch Rodeo Arena, 67-1435 Mamalahoa Hwy; admission $6) This event celebrating over 45 years of ranching has cattle roping, bull riding and other hoopla.

Old Hawaii on Horseback *CULTURAL FESTIVAL*
Traditional *pa'u* riding, in which lei-bedecked women in flowing dresses ride for show, is not to be missed, nor is the post-ride concert. Held biennially in August.

Round-Up Rodeo *RODEO*
(📞885-5669; www.parkerranch.com; Parker Ranch Rodeo Arena, 67-1435 Mamalahoa Hwy; admission $5) On the first Monday in September after the Labor Day weekend, this is another whip-cracking event.

Waimea (Kamuela)

◎ Top Sights
Isaacs Art Center B1

◎ Sights
1 Imiola Congregational Church D1
2 Ke Ola Mau Loa Church D1
3 WM Keck Observatory Office C1

🛏 Sleeping
4 Kamuela Inn A1
5 Waimea Rental Cottages B2

✗ Eating
6 Charley's Thai Cuisine C1
7 Daniel Thiebaut B2
8 Hawaiian Style Cafe B1
9 Healthways II C2
10 KTA Super Store C1
11 Lilikoi Cafe C2
Merriman's .... (see 12)
12 Pau A1
13 Tako Taco D1
14 Waimea Coffee & Co B2
15 Waimea Ranch House C2

🎭 Entertainment
16 Kahilu Theatre C2

🛍 Shopping
Gallery of Great Things .... (see 14)
17 Parker Ranch Center C2
Parker Square .... (see 14)
18 Reyn's C2
Waimea General Store .... (see 14)

Aloha Festivals Hoʻolauleʻa   CULTURAL FESTIVAL
(☎885-7786; http://alohafestivals.com/v3/pages/
events/hawaii.jsp; admission free) Statewide
Aloha festivals bring free concerts, craft
fairs and the Paniolo Parade to Waimea in
the third week of September.

Christmas parade   CHRISTMAS CELEBRATION
In early December, the town gets into the
Kalikimaka (Christmas) spirit with a block
party.

🛏 Sleeping

Waimea isn't cheap, but the rural scenery
and good sleeping weather make for a welcome change from the hot Kohala Coast, just
20 minutes downhill.

⬆TOP CHOICE Waimea Garden

Cottages   COTTAGES $$
(☎885-8550; www.waimeagardens.com; studios
$150, cottages $165-180, incl breakfast; ❀) If
you're looking for independent, comfortable
digs where you can soak in a hot tub, cook
your own dinner and take morning coffee in
a private garden, the Kohala Cottage here is
for you. The smaller Waimea Cottage is cozy
and romantic, with fireplace, kitchenette
and private garden. There's also a spacious
studio near a seasonal stream. This non-
smoking property is 2 miles west of town
(near the intersection of Kawaihae Rd and
Hwy 250); three-day minimum stay.

⬆TOP CHOICE Kamuela Inn   HOTEL $
(☎885-4243, 800-555-8968; www.hawaii-inns
.com/hi/wai/kin; 1600 Kawaihae Rd; r $60-85, ste
$90-100, incl breakfast; ❀) This motel-style
inn is awesome value. Nothing's fancy, but
everything's clean and comfy. Standard
rooms have TV and private bathroom,
while suites include kitchenette. Bed con-
figurations vary. The Mauna Kea Wing is
renovated and it shows: open-beam ceil-
ings, large windows and spruce decor. The
priciest Executive Suite ($185) is remark-
ably spiffy and includes a full kitchen. Con-
tinental breakfast includes toast, muffins,
coffee and tea.

Aaah, the Views B&B   B&B $$
(☎885-3455; www.aaahtheviews.com; 66-1773
Alaneo St; r with shared bathroom $105-135, r with
private bathroom $165-205; ❀) This B&B epito-
mizes both aloha and ʻohana (family). In
other words, it's a welcoming place, from the
lovely yard along a babbling stream to the
friendly hospitality. Whoever designed the

house had a B&B in mind, and the rooms
have ample windows (12 different kinds in
the dreamy Dream Room!) with gorgeous
mountain views. Amenities include cable
TV, DVD, phone, fridge, microwave and
coffee maker. Located 3 miles west of the
town center, this place has only one flaw:
the economy rooms share a bathroom. Rates
include breakfast.

Jacaranda Inn   INN $$$
(☎885-8813; www.jacarandainn.com; 65-1444
Kawaihae Rd; r/ste/cottage from $150/180/250;
❀) Tucked among charming gardens behind
the mansion that once hosted Kissinger and
Jackie O (not at the same time, presumably),
each of the eight rooms here are indulgent,
antique-filled visions, a mix of four-poster
beds, opulent tiled baths, carved furniture,
Jacuzzi tubs and oriental rugs over hardwood floors. No two are alike. Call ahead;
the property has long been for sale, but
promises to continue as an inn.

Waimea Rental Cottages   COTTAGE
(☎885-8533; www.waimearentalcottages.com;
PO Box 2245, Kamuela, HI 96743; studio per day/
week $125/850, 1br $135/925; ❀) Two small,
comfortable (and pricey) cottages are
conveniently located in town. The studio
has a kitchen, the one-bedroom just a
kitchenette.

✗ Eating

Merriman's   HAWAII REGIONAL $$$
(☎885-6822; www.merrimanshawaii.com; Opelo
Plaza, 65-1227 Opelo Rd; lunch $10-18, dinner $30-
55; ⊙11:30am-1:30pm Mon-Fri, 5:30-9pm daily)
An innovator of Hawaii Regional Cuisine,
chef–owner Peter Merriman created the Big
Island's first gourmet restaurant devoted to
organic, island-grown produce and meats.
He lives on Maui now, but his staff continue
his legacy: Hawaiian- and Asian-influenced
dishes like ponzu-marinated mahimahi,
wok-charred ahi and Big Island filet steak
with Hamakau mushrooms are gems. Merriman's signature coconut crème brûlée still
only wants for two spoons. Lunch is a welcome bargain.

Daniel Thiebaut   ASIAN/SEAFOOD $$$
(☎887-2200; www.danielthiebaut.com; 65-1259
Kawaihae Rd; lunch mains $11-14, dinner mains
$21-45; ⊙11am-1:30pm Mon-Fri, 10am-1:30pm
Sun, 3:30-9pm daily) Chef–owner Daniel
Thiebaut seems to remake the menu at his
namesake restaurant every other year. But

OF CATTLE AND COWBOYS

Until recently, **Parker Ranch** (www.parkerranch.com) was the nation's largest privately owned ranch, peaking at 250,000 acres. To make ends meet in today's withering market, however, the ranch has had to sell off parcels (for example, 24,000 acres to the US military in 2006). Today it's the fifth-largest cow-calf ranch in the USA, with at least 12,000 mother cows on 130,000 acres. That's 5% of the entire Big Island, producing 12 million pounds of beef annually.

The story begins in 1793, when British Captain George Vancouver gifted King Kamehameha with a herd of long-horned cattle. So the herd would grow, prescient Kamehameha made the cows kapu (taboo), off limits to the commoners. But by 1815 the burgeoning wild herd was a menace.

Enter Massachusetts mariner John Palmer Parker, who arrived on the Big Island in 1809 at age 19. Parker was so deft with a rifle, Kamehameha contracted him to control the cattle problem. With the typical pluck and determination of pioneering New Englanders, Parker cut the herd down to size, demanding elite specimens as payment.

Kamehameha rewarded Parker with quality cows, plus the hand of one of his granddaughters. With the princess and cattle came the royal chattel: a chunk of land that led to control over the entire Waikoloa *ahupua'a*, a traditional land division running from mountains to sea. Parker Ranch was born in 1847.

See www.paniolopreservationsociety.org to learn more about today's *paniolo*.

whatever he serves in the rambling, attractively restored historic building is sure to be good. Happy hour (3:30pm to 5:30pm) is a great start, with tasty *pupu* and creative cocktails. Lunch is relaxed and informal, while dinner creates a more romantic, special-occasion mood. Thiebaut has a way with seafood, which is always excellent, and the current menu adds curries, steaks, pad thai (Thai noodle stir-fry) and creative pastas.

Pau ECLECTIC $
(885-6325; www.paupizza.com; Opelo Plaza, 65-1227 Opelo Rd; salads & sandwiches $4-9; 11am-8pm Mon-Fri) Order at the counter, then sit back and enjoy the healthful salads, sandwiches, pastas and pizzas at this laid-back eatery. The varied menu includes soba noodle salad with ginger dressing, pesto island fish over pasta, and over a dozen thin-crust pizzas ($17 to $26 for a 16in pie).

Lilikoi Cafe CAFE $
(887-1400; Parker Ranch Center, 67-1185 Mamalahoa Hwy; mains $5-11.50; 7:30am-4pm Mon-Sat) You'll forget the nondescript mall location inside this sunny cafe serving healthy, innovative food such as avocado stuffed with tuna, apples, raisins and pine nuts, and beautiful artichoke and pasta salad. The fresh carrot, apple, beet and ginger 'House Cocktail' is the bomb ($5.50). No Styrofoam is used at this healthful stop.

Huli Sue's BBQ $$
(885-6268; www.hulisues.com; 64-957 Mamalahoa Hwy; mains $12-24, BBQ $15-19; 11:30am-8:30pm Mon-Sat) Huli Sue's kiawe-smoked BBQ is sweet (not hot) and can be greasy. But the sides – such as corn pudding, onion rings and garlic mashed potatoes – are rave-worthy and the salad bar is awesome. Weekly specials can see curry and other Indian food added to the menu.

Charley's Thai Cuisine THAI $$
(885-5591; Waimea Center, 65-1158 Mamalahoa Hwy; appetizers & salads $7-11.95, mains $9.50-14; 11am-3pm & 5-9pm) Great value and killer taste are a winning combination at this local hot spot. The atmosphere is Thai tourist bureau, but who cares when you're supping on a perfectly spiced dried curry with shrimp? The other curries are equally tasty and the *tom kha gai* (coconut milk, lemongrass and chicken soup) is heavenly. It's almost all good – the *pad talay* (stir-fried shrimp) with mushroom is uninspiring.

Tako Taco MEXICAN $
(887-1717; 64-1066 Mamalahoa Hwy; mains $5-12; 11am-8:30pm Mon-Sat, noon-8pm Sun) Attempting to re-create a Mexican *taqueria*, this small, colorful place serves big portions of tacos, nachos and burritos (including fish and veggie). Wash it all down with a stiff mango margarita ($6). The *'ono* (delicious) quesadilla with mushrooms, cheese and caramelized onions lives up to its name,

but the chicken taco is ho hum. With lots of Day of the Dead decorations to ogle and a *na keiki* (children's) menu, this is a great place for kids.

Hawaiian Style Cafe · LOCAL $

(☑885-4295; Hayashi Bldg, 64-1290 Kawaihae Rd; dishes $6-10; ⊘7am-1:30pm Mon-Sat, to noon Sun) The screen door, its springs shot, slams constantly as locals gather around the horseshoe-shaped counter at this favorite island-style greasy spoon. It plates generous portions of *loco moco*, pancakes, *laulau* (bundle made of pork or chicken and salted butterfish, wrapped in taro and *ti* leaves and steamed), poi, fried rice, burgers and much more. Heed the sign: 'Come early. When food is *pau*...there is no more!'

Waimea Ranch House · STEAKHOUSE $$

(☑885-2088; Waimea Center, 65-1158 Mamalahoa Hwy; mains $15-33; ⊘11am-1:30pm & 5-8:30pm Wed-Mon) When you need a flawlessly grilled rib-eye steak, come here. All the locals do. There's a down-home bar and a more formal dining room, but steak prepared without fuss and as rare as you dare is the only meal to order. Yes, it does other things, and quite well, we're told; but maybe next time.

Waimea Coffee & Co · CAFE $

(☑885-8915; www.waimeacoffeecompany.com; Parker Sq, Kawaihe Rd; sandwiches $7-8.50; ⊘7am-5:30pm Mon-Fri, 8am-4pm Sat, 10am-3pm Sun; 🖥) This upscale coffee shop has a devoted following for its espresso drinks and panini.

KTA Super Store · GROCERY

(☑885-8866; Waimea Center, 65-1158 Mamalahoa Hwy; ⊘6am-11pm) Decent takeout selection. In-store pharmacy.

Healthways II · HEALTH FOOD

(☑885-6775; Parker Ranch Center, 67-1185 Mamalahoa Hwy; ⊘9am-7pm Mon-Sat, to 5pm Sun) Everything you'd expect from a health-food store.

☆ Entertainment

Kahilu Theatre · THEATER

(☑885-6017, box office 885-6868; www.kahiluthe atre.org; Parker Ranch Center, 67-1185 Mamalahoa Hwy; admission $35-50; ⊘box office 9am-3pm Mon-Fri, show times vary) Big Islanders come from far and wide to see musicians such as Badi Assad and Hugh Masekela, plus top-flight drama (eg Elton John and Tim Rice's *Aida*) and dance (eg the Paul Taylor Dance Company) at this theater. The an-

nual Waimea Ukulele & Slack Key Guitar Institute Concert (February) is another big draw. Come early to browse the lobby **art gallery**.

🛍 Shopping

Three shopping malls line Hwy 19 through town: **Parker Ranch Center** (67-1185 Mamalahoa Hwy), where the stop signs say 'Whoa,' **Waimea Center** (65-1158 Mamalahoa Hwy) and **Parker Sq** (65-1279 Kawaihae Rd). The first two have groceries and basics, in addition to gift shops; Parker Sq aims for the more discriminating, upscale gift buyer.

Gallery of Great Things · ART GALLERY

(www.galleryofgreatthings.com; Parker Sq; ⊘9am-5:30pm Mon-Sat, 10am-4pm Sun) This stand-out gallery carries over 200 artists and is crammed with antiques, high-quality art and collectibles from Hawaii, Polynesia and Asia.

Reyn's · CLOTHING

(www.reyns.com; Parker Ranch Center; ⊘9:30am-5:30pm Mon-Sat, to 4pm Sun) If you want to dress like a local, shop at Reyn's. Its classic, understated aloha shirts (which use Hawaiian fabrics in reverse) never go out of style.

Waimea General Store · ECLECTIC

(www.waimeageneralstore.com; Parker Sq, 65-1279 Kawaihae Rd) The super-eclectic mix here is fun to peruse, from Le Creuset and Arabic compasses to soap and vintage hula-girl cards.

ℹ Information

Big Island Visitors Bureau (☑885-1655; www .bigisland.org; Suite 27B, Waimea Center, 65-1158 Mamalahoa Hwy; ⊘8am-4:30pm Mon-Fri) Though a sales office, it welcomes walk-in visitors. It's in the mall, around the corner from KTA.

North Hawaii Community Hospital (☑885-4444; 67-1125 Mamalahoa Hwy) Emergency services available 24 hours.

Post office (☑800-275-8777; 67-1197 Mamalahoa Hwy; ⊘8am-4:30pm Mon-Fri, 9am-noon Sat) Address all Waimea mail to Kamuela.

MAUNA KEA & SADDLE ROAD

Mauna Kea

At 13,796ft Mauna Kea is Hawai'i's highest peak, but measuring it from its base on the ocean floor adds more than 18,000 additional feet, making it the world's tallest mountain (just edging out Mauna Loa). Size, however, is just one measure of Mauna Kea's stature. Here, nature, spirituality and science converge and sometimes conflict in vivid ways. This dormant volcano's harsh environment once sported a glacier and is home to numerous endangered endemic species. Mauna Kea is also one of the holiest places in traditional Hawaiian spirituality, and on its most sacred spot – the summit – has gathered the greatest collection of major astronomical telescopes in the world. Plans to construct the world's 'most capable and advanced telescope' here by 2018 has advocates and opponents fighting anew for the future of the mountain (see p204).

The Hilo museum, 'Imiloa, provides a wonderful introduction to the mountain and its history, but a visit to Mauna Kea itself, particularly the summit area, is an unforgettable experience. All of Hawaii lies below as the sun sinks into an ocean of clouds – while the telescopes silently unshutter and turn their unblinking eyes to the heavens. Even though it means long pants, a thick coat (or lots of layers) and some advanced planning, you won't be sorry you left the beach to make the pilgrimage.

History & Environment

According to the Hawaiian creation narrative, every palm tree, grain of sand, volcano and valley in the Hawaiian Islands was created at Mauna Kea. This sacrosanct Mount of Wakea is home to the gods, and is the place between heaven and earth where *na kanaka maoli* (the Native Hawaiians) and their sacred taro were born. The mountain is considered the realm of the gods – where people are not meant to live. For Hawaiians, Mauna Kea was (and remains) a temple, a place of worship and a sacred burial site.

Three sister goddesses call the summit home; the most famous is the snow goddess Poli'ahu, who lives in Pu'u Poli'ahu. In legends, Poli'ahu often competes with Pele, and their snow-and-lava tussles are a metaphorically correct depiction of Mauna Kea's geology.

Between 40,000 and 13,000 years ago, ice-age glaciers covered Mauna Kea's summit, beneath which lava continued to erupt. It has since slid off the hot spot, with the last eruption occurring some 4500 years ago, rendering the mighty mount dormant.

Certain plants and animals adapted to this unique environment. Ascending the mountain, biological zones shift from rain forest to koa-and-ohia forest to open woodland to shrubs and finally (above 11,500ft) to alpine desert. Every elevation has species endemic to Hawai'i, and some found only on Mauna Kea. Plants endemic to the summit include the dramatic Mauna Kea silversword, which takes 50 years to flower, and does so only once.

Summit creatures are restricted mostly to insects. Strangest by far is the endemic *wekiu*, a bug that adapted by changing from a herbivore to a bug-eating carnivore, and by developing 'antifreeze' blood to survive the subfreezing temperatures. Further down the mountain, several of Hawai'i's endemic birds call Mauna Kea home, such as the nene, the *palia* (honeycreeper) and the endangered Hawaiian bat, the *'ope'ape'a*.

Westerners arriving here in the late 1700s introduced feral cattle, goats and sheep to Mauna Kea. By the early 20th century these animals had decimated the mountain's natural environment; animal eradication efforts, begun in the 1920s and continuing today, have helped nature to partly restore itself.

In 1960 astronomer Gerard Kuiper placed a telescope on Pu'u Poli'ahu and announced that 'the mountaintop is probably the best site in the world from which to study the moon, the planets and stars.' Kuiper turned out to be right.

In 1968, the same year the first Mauna Kea observatory was built, the University of Hawai'i (UH) was granted a 65-year lease to the summit area, now called the Mauna Kea Science Reserve. The university leases property to others, and 13 telescopes are currently in operation, which is more than on any other single mountain. They include three of the world's largest, and their combined light-gathering power is 60 times greater than the Hubble Space Telescope.

All this building on such environmentally fragile and culturally sacred land has led to heated conflicts in the past. Today concerted efforts are being made to balance the needs of all stakeholders on Mauna Kea, but plans approved in 2010 to build the Thirty Meter Telescope (TMT; www.tmt.org) here have fueled the simmering controversy. While the telescope will be the world's most accurate, multiplying by nine the collecting area of current optical telescopes, its structural footprint will be larger than all observatories currently on the summit, with all the disruption of natural and cultural resources that implies. Activists opposing the plan (for them, TMT stands for The Monster Telescope) filed court cases citing insufficient environmental impact analyses by UH and the Board of Land and Natural Resources, which manage Mauna Kea. The story continues to unfold: follow it at Kahea (http://kahea.org/issues/sacred-summits).

⊙ Sights

The Mauna Kea Access Rd is near mile marker 28 on Saddle Rd. From the Saddle Rd junction, it's paved for 6 miles to the Onizuka Visitor Information Station.

Any standard car can drive this far; it takes about 50 minutes from Hilo or Waimea and 1½ hours from Kailua-Kona. Past the visitor station, it's another 8 miles (half unpaved) and nearly 5000ft to the summit; only 4WD vehicles should be used from this point on. To visit the summit without a 4WD, you will need to join a Mauna Kea tour, hike or hitch a ride at the visitor center from someone with a 4WD (you sometimes get lucky).

Note there are no restaurants, gas stations or emergency services on Saddle Rd or the mountain. Weather conditions can change rapidly, and daytime temperatures range from 50°F to below freezing. The summit can be windy, and observatory viewing rooms are just as cold as outside. Bring warm clothing, a heavy jacket, sunglasses and sunscreen. Especially in winter, it's a good idea to check on weather and road conditions (☎935-6268; http://mkwc.ifa.hawaii.edu/current/road-conditions). Even when the fog's as thick as pea soup on Saddle Rd, it's crystal clear at the mountaintop 325 days a year.

Onizuka Visitor Information Station   VISITOR INFORMATION
(☎961-2180; www.ifa.hawaii.edu/info/vis; ☺9am-10pm) Officially the Onizuka Center for International Astronomy, the center was named for Ellison Onizuka, a Big Island native, and one of the astronauts who perished in the 1986 *Challenger* space shuttle disaster (you can learn more about him before takeoff from Kona Airport; see p211).

In itself, the one-room Onizuka Visitor Information Station is rather modest, but it's packed with information: videos on astronomy, computer feeds, virtual tours of several observatories, and exhibits on the mountain's history, ecology and geology. The rangers, interpretive guides and volunteers are extremely knowledgeable about astronomy and Mauna Kea's cultural significance, and they are eager to help with hiking and driving advice.

Also, you can purchase (and heat in a microwave) coffee, hot chocolate and instant noodles, or munch on freeze-dried astronaut food, and there are books and gifts for sale. Several hikes are possible from the visitor station, and at night the free **stargazing program** is held here.

Summit Area

If you have a 4WD, you may drive to the summit in the daytime, but you must descend from the summit 30 minutes after sunset – vehicle headlights are discouraged between sunset and sunrise because they interfere with astronomical observation. It takes about half an hour to drive the 8-mile summit road; the first 4.5 miles are gravel. Just before the pavement begins, the area on the east side of the road is dubbed **moon valley**, because it's where the Apollo astronauts rehearsed with their lunar rover before their journey to the real moonscape.

From the summit area, **sunsets** are phenomenal: look east to see 'the shadow' – the gigantic silhouette of Mauna Kea looming over Hilo. **Moonrises** can be equally as impressive: the high altitude can make the moon appear squashed and misshapen, or sometimes resemble a brushfire. See p243 for visits during special celestial events.

SUMMIT WEBCAMS

Thanks to a phalanx of webcams sweeping the summit area and night sky, you can ogle images from the mountaintop on your desktop. Check out these favorites:

Live from Mauna Kea! (http://nightskylive.net/mk/) Streams the night sky between sunset and sunrise.

Joint Astronomy Center Webcam (www.jach.hawaii.edu/weather/jac) Southwest views from the James Clerk Maxwell and UK Infrared Telescopes.

CFH Telescope Timelapse Webcam (http://cfht.hawaii.edu/webcam) Awesome views north, south, north-northwest and north-northeast are provided by this cool webcam with low-light, time lapse and movie capabilities.

Keanakako'i

Just past the 6-mile marker is a parking area; below this is the trailhead to Lake Waiau and to the ancient adze quarry Keanakako'i. Getting to both takes about an hour, depending on your rate of acclimatization.

During Mauna Kea's ice age, when molten lava erupted under the glaciers, it created an extremely hard basalt, which ancient Hawaiians chipped into sharp adzes at Keanakako'i. For 800 years, these tools were fashioned on the mountain and traded throughout the islands (you can see what they were used to create at the Pu'u Loa petroglyphs in Hawai'i Volcanoes National Park). Entering the fragile quarry is highly discouraged.

TOP CHOICE Lake Waiau
ALPINE LAKE

Nearby, sitting in Pu'u Waiau at 13,020ft, is Lake Waiau. This unique alpine lake is the third-highest in the USA and one of two lakes on the Big Island (the other, Green Lake, is in Puna). Thought by ancient Hawaiians to be bottomless, it's actually only 10ft deep and, despite desert conditions, never dry. Clay formed from ash holds the water, which is fed by melted snow, permafrost and less than 15in of rainfall annually. To Hawaiians, these sacred waters are considered the 'umbilical cord' *(piko)* connecting heaven and earth, and a traditional practice is to place a baby's umbilical cord in the water to assure good health.

Observatories
OBSERVATORIES

In the summit region are the massive dome-shaped observatories, which rise up from the stark terrain like some futuristic human colony on another planet. Unfortunately, you can't see much inside the observatories. Currently only two are open to visitors: the WM Keck Observatory visitor gallery (www.keckobservatory.org; admission free; ◷10am-4pm Mon-Fri) includes a display, a 15-minute video, public bathrooms and a plexiglass-enclosed viewing area inside the Keck I dome; tours are available to the Subaru Telescope.

True Summit
LANDMARK

The short 200yd trail to Mauna Kea's true summit begins opposite the UH telescope; it's harder than it looks, and it's not necessary to go to see the sunset nor claim you've summited Mauna Kea. The summit is marked by a US Geological Survey (USGS) summit benchmark and a Native Hawaiian

---

ⓘ STARGAZING PLANNER
243

Here are some tips from the experts about the best times – celestially-speaking – to visit Mauna Kea.

» Obviously lunar eclipses and meteor showers are special events in this rarefied air; the Leonides in November are particularly impressive; check StarDate (http://stardate.org/nightsky/meteors) for the year's meteor showers, eclipses, moon phases and more.

» The Milky Way streaks the night sky bright and white between January and March.

» Don't forget the monthly full moon; it's simply spectacular as it rises over you, seemingly close enough to touch.

---

altar. Given the biting winds, high altitude and extreme cold, most people don't linger.

🏃 Activities

Shorter Hikes
HIKING

Several short walks begin at the Onizuka Visitor Information Station. Off the parking lot is an area protecting the endemic, dramatic silversword, while across from the visitor station a 10-minute uphill hike on a well-trodden trail crests Pu'ukalepeamoa, a cinder cone that offers the best **sunset views** near the center. Several moderate hikes also begin from the summit road.

Humu'ula-Mauna Kea Summit Trail HIKING

Then there is the 6-mile Humu'ula-Mauna Kea Summit Trail, which climbs nonstop about 4600ft to the top of Mauna Kea. This is a very strenuous, all-day, high-altitude hike up such steep, barren slopes you sometimes feel you might step off the mountain into the sky. Utterly exposed to winds and the changeable weather, it makes for an eerie, primordial experience.

To do this trail, start early – by 6am if possible. It typically takes five hours to reach the summit, and half as long coming down, and you want time to explore in between. Consult with rangers for advice, and get a map and register at the center's outdoor trail kiosk before hiking.

Park at the Onizuka Center and walk 1000ft up the road; where the pavement ends, go left on the dirt road, following several Humu'ula Trail signs to the trail

Mauna Kea & Mauna Loa

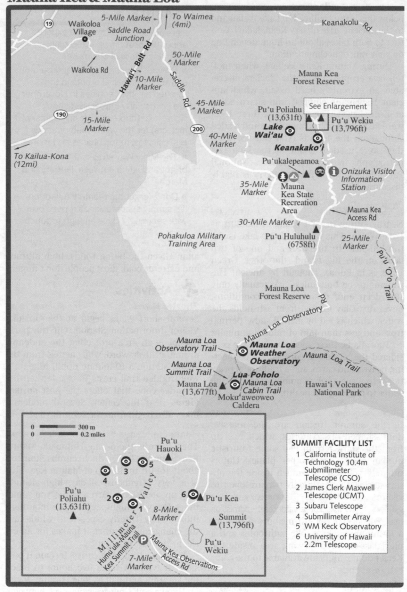

SUMMIT FACILITY LIST

1. California Institute of Technology 10.4m Submillimeter Telescope (CSO)
2. James Clerk Maxwell Telescope (JCMT)
3. Subaru Telescope
4. Submillimeter Array
5. WM Keck Observatory
6. University of Hawaii 2.2m Telescope

proper. Reflective T-posts and cairns mark the route; after about an hour the summit road comes back into view on your right, and the vegetation starts to disappear. As you weave around cinder cones and traipse over crumbled 'a'a and slippery scree, you pass various spur trails; all lead back to the access road.

Most of the way you will be passing through the Mauna Kea Ice Age Natural Area Reserve. After about three hours a sharp, short ascent leads to Keanakako'i, the

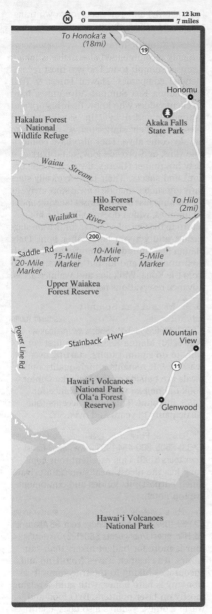

To Honoka'a
(18mi)

Honomu

Hakalau Forest
National
Wildlife Refuge

Akaka Falls
State Park

Waiau Stream

Hilo Forest
Reserve

To Hilo
(2mi)

Wailuku River

Saddle Rd
20-Mile
Marker
15-Mile
Marker
10-Mile
Marker
5-Mile
Marker

Upper Waiakea
Forest Reserve

Power Line Rd

Stainback Hwy

Mountain
View

Hawai'i Volcanoes
National Park
(Ola'a Forest
Reserve)

Glenwood

Hawai'i Volcanoes
National Park

you reach a four-way junction, where a 10-minute detour to the left brings you to Lake Waiau. Return to the four-way junction and head north (uphill) for the final push to meet the Mauna Kea Summit Rd at a parking area. Suddenly the observatories are visible on the summit, and straight ahead is Millimeter Valley, nicknamed for its three submillimeter observatories. The trail officially ends at the access road's 7-mile marker, but the true summit still snickers at you another 1.5 miles away.

For native Hawaiians, the summit is a region, a realm, not a point on a map; according to experts we talked to, you can still say you summitted if you turn back here. But if you really need to place a boot toe on Pu'u Wekiu, Mauna Kea's true summit, soldier on till you reach the UH 2.2m Telescope, where the short spur trail to the summit begins.

When descending, return along the shoulder of the access road rather than retracing the trail. Though the road is 2 miles longer, it's easier on the knees and easier to follow as sunlight fades. Also, it's common for hikers to get offered a lift downhill; sticking to the road increases your chances.

FREE Onizuka Visitor
Information Station   STARGAZING, LECTURES
The Onizuka Visitor Information Station offers a free **stargazing program** nightly from 6pm to 10pm. There are no reservations and cloudy skies only occur a couple of times a month, but call ahead if you want to double check. At 9200ft these skies are among the clearest, driest and darkest on the planet. In fact, at the station you're above the elevation of most major telescopes worldwide. This is the only place you can use telescopes on Mauna Kea; there are no public telescopes on the summit. How much you'll see depends on cloud cover and moon phase. The busiest nights are Friday and Saturday. Special scope attachments accommodate visitors in wheelchairs.

During big meteor showers, the center staffs its telescopes for **all-night star parties**; call for details. And every Saturday night at 6pm the Onizuka Center hosts a rotating series of lectures and events: The Universe Tonight is an **astronomy lecture** held on the first Saturday; on the second Saturday students from the UH Hilo Astrophysics Club assist with **stargazing**; Malalo I Ka Lani Po is a **culture lecture** on the

adze quarry, which is off to the right; look for large piles of bluish-black chips. Do not enter, or remove anything from, this protected area.

The hardest, steepest part of the trail is now behind you. After another mile third Saturday; and the fourth Saturday is a multigenre **international music night**.

Skiing & Snowboarding

For a month or two (beginning in January or February), enough snow usually falls on Mauna Kea's heights to allow for winter sports. On a nice day the 'slopes' get crowded with locals using skis, snowboards, surfboards, bodyboards, inner tubes – whatever! Activists and conservationists are concerned that increased usage during snowfall on the mountaintop, combined with the degradation caused by the monster trucks used to access the 'slopes,' is eroding habitat and culturally significant sites here. Conditions are not great and getting the gear together can be a pain; why not just make snow angels instead?

For those chasing this trophy experience, know that skiing Mauna Kea is entirely DIY (commercial ski tours are prohibited). There are no groomed trails, no lifts and no patrols; exposed rocks and ice sheets are constant dangers.

Tours

FREE **Onizuka Visitor Information Station**   SUMMIT TOURS
(☎935-6268; ⊗1pm Sat & Sun) The Onizuka Visitor Information Station offers free summit tours, but you must provide your own 4WD transportation. No reservations are needed; simply arrive at the visitor center by 1pm to join the tour. The first hour is spent watching videos about Mauna Kea as you acclimatize, then you caravan to the summit, where you hear a talk on the history and workings of the summit telescopes. The tours then visit at least one telescope, usually the WM Keck's 10m telescope. Tours depart from the summit at about 4:30pm, but most people stay for sunset and come down on their own. Pregnant women, children under 16, and those with circulatory and respiratory conditions are not allowed, and tours don't go in bad weather, so call ahead.

FREE **Subaru Telescope Tour**   OBSERVATORY TOURS
(www.naoj.org/Information/Tour/Summit; ⊗10:30am, 11:30am & 1:30pm) You can visit the world's largest single-piece mirror telescope on 40-minute summit tours offered up to 15 weekdays per month, in English and Japanese. You must make advance reservations

(online only) and you need your own transportation to the summit.

Sunset Summit Tour   SUMMIT TOURS
A highly recommended alternative is taking a sunset summit tour. The two most recommended companies, Hawaii Forest & Trail and Mauna Kea Summit Adventures, have excellent guides who know their history and astronomy; aided by 11in, satellite-guided telescopes, their stargazing sessions make the sky come alive. They also have comfortable vans, and provide gloves and parkas, a tasty hot dinner (there's always a veggie option) and snacks. Their tours typically start early afternoon, include a meal stop, arrive at the summit just before sunset (staying about 40 minutes, which doesn't allow for hiking), return to the Onizuka Center for private stargazing, and get you home after 9pm. Only Mauna Kea Summit Adventures accepts children under 16 and all but Arnott's pick up from the Kona, Waikoloa and Waimea areas. Advance reservations necessary.

TOP CHOICE **Mauna Kea Summit Adventures**   SUMMIT TOURS
(☎322-2366, 888-322-2366; www.maunakea.com; tours $200) Mauna Kea was the first company to do summit tours, starting over 20 years ago. It remains a high-quality outfit; meals are outside at the Onizuka Center. Book online two weeks in advance for a 15% discount. This outfit accepts tour participants 13 years and over.

Hawaii Forest & Trail   SUMMIT TOURS
(☎331-8505, 800-464-1993; www.hawaii-forest.com; tours $190) This excellent tour company has the nicest meal stop (at a private ranch outpost); its guides and equipment are top-notch.

Arnott's Lodge   SUMMIT TOURS
(☎969-7097; www.arnottslodge.com; 98 Apapane Rd, Hilo; guests/nonguests $80/125) Arnott's tour is more for budget hikers than stargazers. It's cheaper, leaves from Hilo and encourages hiking to the true summit; astronomy is bare bones, with guides relying mostly on laser pointers. BYO food and warm clothes. Arnott's also does a sunrise Mauna Kea tour ($300 for two people).

Sleeping

Mauna Kea State Recreation Area CABINS $
A barebones campground, with cabins (available weekends only; residents/nonresidents $50/80 per night), can be found

at the 35-mile marker. See p169 for information on obtaining permits. The site, used mainly by local hunters, is sometimes closed during droughts; get an update by contacting the Division of State Parks (☎974-6200; www.hawaii.gov/dlnr/dsp). The six-people cabins have basic kitchens and pit toilets, but no water. Nearby maneuvers at the Pohakuloa Military Training Area can be noisy.

ℹ Information

DANGERS & ANNOYANCES The Onizuka Visitor Information Station is at 9200 ft, and even here some visitors might experience shortness of breath and mild altitude sickness. At the 13,796ft summit, atmospheric pressure is 60% what it is at sea level, and altitude sickness is common. Symptoms include nausea, headaches, drowsiness, impaired reason, loss of balance, shortness of breath and dehydration. The only way to recover is to descend. Kids under 16 years, pregnant women, and those with high blood pressure or circulatory conditions should not go to the summit. Nor should you scuba dive within 24 hours of visiting Mauna Kea.

The best way to avoid altitude sickness is to ascend slowly. All hikers and travelers to the summit should stop first at the visitor station for at least 30 minutes to acclimatize before continuing.

ℹ Getting There & Around

From Kona, Saddle Rd (Hwy 200) starts just south of the 6-mile marker on Hwy 190. From Hilo, drive *mauka* (inland) on Kaumana Dr, which becomes Saddle Rd (Hwy 200). From Volcano, take Hwy 11 to Puainako which turns into Kaumana Dr. All drivers should start with a full tank of gas, as there are no gas stations on Saddle Rd.

Past the visitor center the road is suitable only for 4WD vehicles. Over half the road is gravel, sometimes at a 15% grade, and the upper road can be covered with ice. When descending, drive in low gear (or you can ruin your brakes), and pay attention for any signs of altitude sickness. Driving when the sun is low – in the hour after sunrise or before sunset – can create hazardous blinding conditions.

Saddle Road Hikes

Several exceptional hikes are possible from Saddle Rd. The most legendary and rewarding is the Mauna Loa Observatory Trail – the only way to get to the top in a single day.

Pu'u Huluhulu Trail   HIKING
The easy trail up the cinder cone **Pu'u Huluhulu** or Shaggy Hill, an ancient *kipuka*

(oasis) created more than 10,000 years ago, makes a piquant appetizer before going up Mauna Kea. The 20-minute hike climbs through secondary growth to the top of the hill, from where there are panoramic views of Mauna Kea, Mauna Loa and Hualalai. The *pahoehoe* and *'a'a* surrounding the *kipuka* are between 1500 and 3000 years old, courtesy of Mauna Kea. The trailhead is very near the turnoff to Mauna Kea, just past the 28-mile marker heading west.

Pu'u 'O'o Trail   HIKING
For a more substantial but equally peaceful ramble, try the Pu'u 'O'o Trail (also called the Power Line Rd Trail), an 8-mile loop traversing meadows, old lava flows and several pretty koa-and-ohia *kipuka* forests filled with the birdsong of Hawaiian honeycreepers. (Note this is a different trail from Hawai'i Volcanoes National Park's Pu'u 'O'o Trail.)

The signed trailhead (with a small parking area) is almost exactly halfway between the 22- and 23-mile markers on Saddle Rd. The trail is marked by *ahu* (stone cairns); it's easy to follow in good weather, less so in rain or fog. If in doubt, simply retrace your steps the way you came. Eventually the trail connects with Power Line Rd (marked with a sign), a 4WD road that can be used as the return route. Note, though, that the road returns you about a mile away from the trailhead parking area.

Mauna Loa Observatory Trail   HIKING
This trail is the most recommended way to summit Mauna Loa; those who prefer a challenge above all else might consider taking the daunting, multiday Mauna Loa Trail (see p291). However, make no mistake: the Observatory Trail is a difficult, all-day adventure, but few 13,000ft mountains exist that are so accessible to the average hiker. This is a rare and unforgettable experience.

Day hikers do not need a permit, but if you would like to overnight at Mauna Loa Cabin (p291), register the day before at the Kilauea Visitor Center in Hawai'i Volcanoes National Park (see p293).

To reach the trailhead, take the unsigned Mauna Loa Observatory Rd near the 28-mile marker on Saddle Rd; it's nearly opposite the Mauna Kea Access Rd and adjacent to Pu'u Huluhulu. The single-lane, 17.5-mile asphalt road is passable in a standard car but, except for the first 4 miles, it's in terrible condition and full of blind curves. Allow an hour; the squiggled white line is to aid drivers in the fog. The road ends at a parking area just below the weather observatory at 11,150ft. There are no visitor facilities or bathrooms. From the observatory, the Mauna Loa Observatory Trail climbs up to the mountaintop.

Begin hiking by 8am; you want to be off the mountain or descending if afternoon clouds roll in. The trail is marked by cairns, which disappear in the fog. If this happens, stop hiking; find shelter in one of several small tubes and hollows along the route until you can see again, even if this means waiting till morning.

It is nearly 4 miles to the trail junction with the Mauna Loa Trail. Allow three hours for this gradual ascent of nearly 2000ft. If it weren't for the altitude, this would be a breeze. Instead, proceed slowly but steadily, keeping breaks short. If you feel the onset of altitude sickness (p273), descend. About two hours along, you re-enter the national park, and the old lava flows appear in a rainbow of colors: sapphire, turquoise, silver, ochre, orange, gold and magenta.

Once at the trail junction, the majesty of the summit's Moku'aweoweo Caldera overwhelms the imagination. Day hikers have two choices: proceed another 2.6 miles and three hours along the Summit Trail to the tippy-top at 13,677ft (visible in the distance), or explore the caldera itself by following the 2.1-mile Mauna Loa Cabin Trail. If you can stand not summiting, the second option is extremely interesting, leading to even grander caldera views and a vertiginous peek into the awesome depths of Lua Poholo – a craterlike hole in the landscape.

Descending takes half as long as ascending; depending on how far you go, prepare for a seven- to 10-hour round-trip hike. Bring copious amounts of water, food, a flashlight and rain gear, and wear boots, a winter coat and a cap – it's cold and windy year-round.

HAMAKUA COAST

On the Big Island, where do you find that lush tropical paradise pictured on magazine covers, the one untouched by the ironic ringtones of the 21st century? Come to the Hamakua Coast. From Waipi'o Valley to Hilo, the Big Island's windward face tells a tale of rain: innumerable streams gush down the flanks of Mauna Kea, carving deep ravines and tumbling over 1000ft cliffs; farmers still work ancient taro patches; and well-preserved sugar plantation towns recall the region's economic heyday, when steam trains rumbled across the sweeping cantilevered bridges. These and other ghosts – from Kukuihaele's legendary night marchers (p253) to Laupahoehoe schoolchildren – haunt this fertile region, where along overgrown, forgotten roads it seems as if only a gauzy veil separates then from now.

Honoka'a & Around

Who would guess that Honoka'a was once the third-largest town across Hawaii, after Honolulu and Hilo? It was the hub for the powerful cattle and sugar industries, but had to reinvent itself when those industries crashed.

When the Honoka'a Sugar Company mill processed its last harvest in 1993, the agricultural town was forced to diversify its crops. Today's farms in upcountry Pa'auilo and Ahualoa produce the tomatoes, mushrooms and other goodies whipped up by gourmet chefs seeking the freshest, finest local ingredients. Indeed, organic farming – from goat cheese to green tea – is booming here and it's only a matter of time before the town reinvents itself again as the agritourism capital of the island.

For now, Honoka'a is a sweet place for browsing chockablock antique stores and lunching on a tempeh or grass-fed-beef burger before heading to Waipi'o Valley. Watching the world go by here might tempt you to stay awhile. Luckily there are some very fine places to lay your head.

⊙ Sights

All of these farms are located in Pa'auilo and Ahualoa, on the *mauka* (inland) side of the highway. Pa'auilo sits about five miles east, and Ahualoa a mile west, of Honoka'a town.

Hawaiian Vanilla Company TOP CHOICE FARM
(☑776-1771; www.hawaiianvanilla.com; Pa'auilo; tours $25, luncheon per adult/child 4-12yr $39/15) If you're a fan of this fragrant bean (and who isn't?), don't miss a chance to learn more about its cultivation, flavor and uses. This family-run farm is the first commercial vanilla operation in the USA. Tours and tastings are reasonably priced and worth your time. The Vanilla Experience Luncheon features a gourmet, vanilla-infused meal, an informative presentation and a walking tour of the Vanillery. If time is short, stop by the gift shop (☯10am-5pm) for vanilla-scented every-

thing, including coffee, tea, bath and body products and, of course, prime beans and extracts.

TOP CHOICE Volcano Island Honey Company FARM
(☏775-1000, 888-663-6639; www.volcanoisland honey.com; Ahualoa; 1½hr tour $50) In the mid-1970s, Richard Spiegel began working with bees to capture the sweet nectar of kiawe flowers. Today he runs a thriving family-run honey business that still harvests its Rare Hawaiian Organic White Honey (8oz jar $14.50 to $16) from a single forest of kiawe trees in Puako. The company promotes green policies, and beekeeping itself causes minimal environmental harm. In addition to the regular tour of the farm, you can actually don a bee suit.

Mauna Kea Tea FARM
(☏775-1171; www.maunakeatea.com; Ahualoa; tours $20-30) If you're into tea, organic farming and philosophical inquiry, arrange a tour at this small-scale, family-run plantation. Their green and oolong teas are intended to represent the inherent 'flavor' of the land, not artificial fertilizers. Check out the website for philosophical insights into tea cultivation and, really, life itself. Internship and volunteer opportunities are available here.

Long Ears Coffee FARM
(☏775-0385; www.longearscoffee.com; Ahualoa; tours $35) Prime Hawaii coffee isn't exclusive to Kona nowadays. Try the 'aged' Hamakua coffee at this family business and judge for yourself. Wendell and Irmanetta Branco process their own and other Hamakua farms' beans, creating a sustainable agricultural economy for farmers here. On the tour you'll see the entire process: growing trees, harvesting cherry, pulping, drying, husking and roasting. Plus you can talk story with the friendly owner couple.

Katsu Goto Memorial MEMORIAL
Beside the library on Mamane St, Honoka'a is a memorial to a Japanese cane-field worker who eventually opened a general store in Honoka'a. Goto was hanged by local sugar bosses and accomplices in 1889 for his attempts to improve labor conditions on Hamakua plantations. He's considered one of the first union activists.

Goto's story comes to life in *Hamakua Hero: A True Plantation Story*, a manga-

» Sunrise and sunset on Mauna Kea (p240)

» Hiking the Mulawai Trail to Waimanu Valley (p254)

» Roasting your own coffee (p193)

» Manta ray night dive (p178)

» Summiting Mauna Loa (p247)

style graphic novel by Patsy Y Iwasaki and Avery Berido.

Festivals & Events

Honoka'a Western Weekend WESTERN FESTIVAL
(Mamane St; admission free) Sleepy Mamane St startles awake with a BBQ, parade, country dance and rodeo in late May.

Hamakua Alive FOOD FESTIVAL
(www.hamakuaalive.com; Pa'ahau Plantation Park; admission free) This celebration of local agriculture is good old-fashioned fun, with a baking contest, chef and farmer pairing, a watermelon-eating contest, an egg toss and food. Typically held on the third Saturday in October.

Sleeping

Your best options for accommodation lie just outside Honoka'a town, in misty up-country Ahualoa and the Pa'auilo pasture-land toward the east. If money's no issue, consider Kukuihaele and its drop-off views of Waipi'o Valley.

TOP CHOICE Mountain Meadow Ranch VACATION RENTAL $$
(☏775-9376; www.mountainmeadowranch.com; 46-3895 Kapuna Rd, Ahualoa; cottage $150, suite incl breakfast $115) Breathe that fresh air! Green, misty Ahualoa is storybook ranchland, and you can't go wrong with either option offered here. The two-bedroom cottage sleeps four (no extra charge) and includes a full kitchen, wood stove and washer/dryer. The suite is ideal for two and, though lacking a kitchen, has a microwave, small fridge and soothing dry sauna. The hosts are accomplished equestrians and longtime residents. The only con: no wi-fi in the cottage.

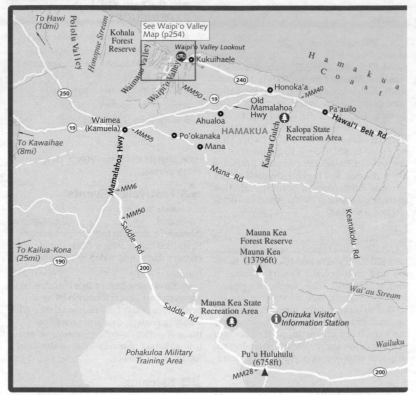

Keolamauloa   VACATION RENTAL **$$**
(☎776-1294; www.keolamauloa.com; 43-1962 Pa'auilo Mauka Rd, Pa'auilo; 2br house 2/3/4 people $100/125/150; ☎) If you're craving an earthy, back-to-nature retreat, look no further than this well-tended family farm in Pa'auilo. The comfy accommodations include full kitchen, laundry facilities and access to the grounds: towering native trees, fruit trees, vegetable patches, chickens and other livestock, plus distant ocean views. Guests enjoy fresh eggs and produce and are welcome to work and learn. Discounts for extended stays.

Waipi'o Wayside B&B   B&B **$$**
(☎775-0275, 800-833-8849; www.waipiowayside .com; Hwy 240; r incl breakfast $100-190; ☎) This attractively furnished 1932 plantation house is a classic B&B, complete with welcoming host. The five rooms differ markedly, but each enjoys designer touches, such as iron bed frames, a wooden Chinese barber chair, shower skylight and hardwood floors. Com-

mon areas include a living room with books and a large-screen TV (with DVDs), plus a spacious, secluded lanai. Full, homemade organic breakfast is included. Between the 3- and 4-mile markers on Hwy 240, about 2 miles north of Honoka'a.

Waianuhea B&B   B&B **$$$**
(☎775-1118, 888-775-2577; www.waianuhea.com; 45-3505 Kahana Dr, Ahualoa; r $210-310, ste $400; ☎) If you've got the money, honey, head straight to this exquisite place in peaceful upcountry Hamakua. Waves of relaxation will wash over you as you weigh your options from the king-sized bed: jump-start the fireplace or hit the Jacuzzi? With fine art, Tiffany lamps, fun Philippe Starck chairs, bright skylights and gleaming hardwood floors, impeccable and wonderfully unpretentious taste oozes from every cranny. Gourmet dinners (per person $48 to $58) are served with 48-hours' notice. Rates include breakfast.

See Around Hilo Map (p259)

Biodegradable takeout containers are an added bonus.

Café il Mondo   ITALIAN $$
(☎775-7711; www.cafeilmondo.com; 45-3626A Mamane St, Honoka'a; calzones $12, pizzas $12-24; ☺11am-8pm Mon-Sat) Intimate and Italian is a killer combination at this place specializing in pizzas and pastas. The calzone are huge pillows bursting with flavorful vegetables; bring your own wine to wash it down, and swoon when owner Sergio starts his guitar serenade.

Tex Drive-In   DRIVE-IN $
(☎775-0598; Hwy 19, 43-mile marker; sandwiches & plate lunches $5-9; ☺6:30am-8pm) A *malasada* is just a donut, but Tex is famous for serving them hot and fresh. They come plain (96¢) or filled ($1.31). Tex also serves an above average plate lunch, with crisp green salads; burgers on sweetbread buns are good, too.

Jolene's Kau Kau Korner   LOCAL $
(☎775-9498; 45-3625 Mamane St, Honoka'a; sandwiches & burgers $5-8, mains $10-15; ☺10:30am-3:30pm daily, to 8pm Mon & Wed) If you're not averse to meat and calories, try this casual spot where a little bit of everything (shrimp, chicken, spareribs) is served in generous portions.

Honoka'a Farmers Market   MARKET
(Mamane St, Honoka'a; ☺7:30am-noon Sat) Fresh produce directly from the farmers. Located in front of Honoka'a Trading Company.

☆ Entertainment

Honoka'a People's Theatre   THEATER
(☎775-0000; Mamane St, Honoka'a; movie tickets adult/child/senior $6/3/4) In a historic building dating from 1930, this theater shows movies and hosts special events.

🔒 Shopping

Honoka'a Trading Company   ANTIQUES
(Mamane St, Honoka'a; ☺10:30am-5pm) If a couple of Honoka'a aunties emptied their attics, basements and garages, it would look like this hangar-sized store. Weave between vintage aloha wear, antiques, used books (great Hawaiiana selection), rattan and koa furniture and hand-selected Hawaiian artifacts.

Taro Patch   SOUVENIRS
(Mamane St, Honoka'a; ☺9am-5pm) With a little of everything, this superlative shop is the place for souvenirs – from beautiful ceramic

Hotel Honoka'a Club   HOSTEL $
(☎775-0678, 800-808-0678; www.hotelhonokaa.com; Mamane St, Honoka'a Club; dm/r with shared bathroom $20/30, r $65-95, ste $130; @) Set in a historic plantation building, this hostel/hotel has character, but it's overpriced for what you get. Expect thin walls, industrial carpet and dark shower stalls. Dorm beds have linens, but no blankets. The economy rooms might be worth the savings but, for anything above $80, you can do better.

✗ Eating

TOP CHOICE Simply Natural   CAFE $
(☎775-0119; www.hawaiisimplynatural.com; 45-3625 Mamane St, Honoka'a; dishes $5-9; ☺8am-3pm Mon-Sat & 5-8pm Tue-Sat; @🕾) The bright, chipper surroundings and staff here complement the healthy food, including the yummy weekend waffles with fresh fruit. At lunchtime try the feta, asparagus and tomato melt.

i Most small working farms are closed to visitors. First priority is growing crops, not giving tours. One convenient option for a closer look at local agriculture is **Earth Bound Tours** (http://earthboundtours.com), run by Hawaiian Vanilla Company owner Jim Reddekopp. Choose from various full-day tours visiting some of the best farms across the Islands.

dishes and funky, feathery *slippahs* (flip-flops) to Waipi'o Valley mouse pads and organic soaps. The shopkeeper's organic macadamia nuts, roasted in shell and then cracked, are a must-try.

Symbiosis   APPAREL
(45-3587 Mamane St, Honoka'a; ◷10am-5pm Tue-Sat) High fashion in Honoka'a? This little boutique could hold its own in bigger cities, with hip natural-fiber tops and skirts, plus stylish baby and kid gear. Best of all, the proprietor carries as many local designers as she can.

Kukuihaele

About 7 miles north of Honoka'a, a loop road off Hwy 240 leads to sleepy Kukuihaele, a residential neighborhood with a couple of shops.

🛏 Sleeping

TOP CHOICE Hale Kukui Orchard Retreat   VACATION RENTAL $$
(☎775-1701, 800-444-7130; www.halekukui.com; 48-5460 Kukuihaele Rd; studios $160-195, 2-bedroom unit $195; 🛜) You can't go wrong with the three rentals here: each includes a full kitchen, spacious living area, private deck and outdoor hot tub, and fantastic ocean view. Orchard grounds include papaya, banana, star fruit and citrus, all for the taking. The two-bedroom unit is a real deal: four guests can stay without extra fees. Seventh night free.

Waipio Rim B&B   B&B $$
(☎775-1727; www.waipiorim.com; d $200) You won't get closer to Waipi'o Valley than this handsome B&B, gloriously perched on a cliff beyond the lookout (call ahead for directions). The upstairs studio boasts an expansive indoor–outdoor feel, with lots of windows and a private deck overlooking the entire valley. Amenities include a microwave

and refrigerator. Fifth night free. You'll get more 'house' for your money elsewhere, but this place is about the *view*.

Cliff House Hawaii   VACATION RENTAL $$
(☎775-0005, 800-492-4746; www.cliffhousehawaii.com; Hwy 240; 2-bedroom house $200, each additional person $35; @) Set on sprawling acres of pastureland, this house assures privacy and space. It's well equipped, with two bedrooms, full kitchen, comfortably sized living and dining rooms, BBQ grill, telescope, satellite TV and washer/dryer. The wraparound lanai might be the best private sunrise/whale-watching spot on Hawai'i. Set inland on the same parcel is the less dramatic but still beautifully situated **Hawaii Oceanview House** (2br house $165).

✕ Eating & Shopping

TOP CHOICE Waipi'o Valley Artworks   ART GALLERY
(Map p254; ☎775-0958, 775-7157, 800-492-4746; www.waipiovalleyartworks.com; ◷8am-5pm) This airy little shop wears many hats: stop for ice cream, muffins, sandwiches and coffee. Browse through the koa wood furniture, bowls and other crafts for gifts at all price points. Arrange overnight parking for camping in Waimanu (per day $15); call first in July and August or if you want to park before 8am.

Last Chance Store   GROCERY
(Map p254; ◷9am-3:30pm Mon-Sat) If you want snacks (or canned chili, beer, water or wine), this is your last chance before Waipi'o Valley.

Waipi'o Valley

There's something tantalizing about the end of the road. It's where adventure meets the unknown and 'what do we do now?' becomes a wonderfully enticing prospect. You'll feel it when Hwy 240 dead-ends on the cliffs overlooking Waipi'o Valley, the largest of seven spectacular amphitheater valleys on the windward side of the Kohala Mountains. Waipi'o (Curving Water) is an emerald patchwork of forest, lotus and *lo'i* (taro patches) 6 miles deep, where waterfalls plunge earthward from 2000ft vertical *pali*. Completing this natural tableau of divine proportions is the river cleaving the valley floor toward the surf-fringed, boulder-strewn, black-sand beach. Few sites in Hawaii rival sacred Waipi'o for dramatic beauty.

For 'stop and click' tourists, the scenic lookout is at the end of the road. There is a ranger-manned information booth (🕑8am-dusk) here, too.

History

Known as the Valley of the Kings, Waipi'o was the ancient breadbasket of the Big Island. Not coincidentally, it was also Hawai'i's political and religious center and home to the highest *ali'i*. 'Umi, the Big Island's ruling chief and spiritual leader in the early 16th century, was a farmer and fisherman who propagated many of Waipi'o's original *lo'i*. Some of these are still cultivated today and you may see farmers knee-deep in their patches. Waipi'o is also where Kamehameha the Great received the statue of his fearsome war god, Kukailimoku.

According to oral histories, several thousand people lived in this fertile valley before Westerners showed up. Important heiau scattered throughout Waipi'o are evidence of its status. The most sacred, Paka'alana, was a *luakini* heiau and one of the island's two major *pu'uhonua* (the other is Pu'uhonua O Honaunau National Historical Park). You won't see Paka'alana: it was destroyed in a war between Ka'eokulani of Kaua'i and Kamehameha I.

In 1823 William Ellis, the first missionary to descend into Waipi'o, guessed the population to be around 1300. In the 1880s immigrants, mainly Chinese, began to settle in the valley's green folds and taro cultivation gave way to rice, though the traditional staple was never eliminated. Over time Waipi'o couldn't compete with cheaper rice being mass produced in California, and eventually taro rebounded, with valley factories producing labor-intensive poi (steamed, mashed taro).

In 1946 Hawai'i's most-devastating tsunami slammed waves far back into the valley. Interestingly, no one in this sacred place perished during this natural disaster or the great 1979 flood. Once the waters receded, however, most people resettled 'topside,' and Waipi'o has been sparsely populated ever since.

Taro cultivation and poi production are building blocks of the Hawaiian identity that continue today in this fiercely guarded valley. The cultural resurgence of the '60s and '70s, combined with younger generations trying to retain their roots, have assured the crop's future. Other goodies produced in Waipi'o include lotus root, avocados, citrus and *pakalolo* (marijuana).

🏃 Activities

For most visitors, the short, steep road down to Waipi'o Beach is walkable in 45 minutes or by 4WD in 15 (don't even think about trying it in a regular car). There are bathrooms at the bottom, but no potable water. Only strong, prepared hikers should venture the 1.75 miles (1½ hours) further back into the valley to experience the powerful beauty of Hi'ilawe Falls – swollen streams and weather permitting. The overnight Muliwai Trail is only for experienced hikers.

Waipi'o Beach isn't swimmable, so don't expect to cool off in the ocean. You'll see truckfuls of local surfers heading down to hit Waipi'o's daunting break. But the rip currents and treacherous undertow aren't for hodads (poser surfers).

Waipi'o Valley Hike   HIKING

The short (1 mile), precipitous descent beginning from the Waipi'o Valley Lookout is slow-going due to the 25%-grade road (it takes around 30 minutes to 45 minutes). But it's paved and thus not too strenuous. There's no shade, so bring plenty of water.

At the bottom, the road left leads to where wild Waipi'o horses are usually grazing lazily along the stream; keep walking and you'll have distant views of Hi'ilawe Falls, which are the state's tallest falls (over 1400ft), with over 1000ft of free-fall, another state record. Hiking to the falls is doable but challenging – consider yourself forewarned: no trail exists for the nearly 2-mile, 4-hour round-trip hike and you'll have to crisscross the stream half a dozen times, request passage from residents and bushwhack a lot. This adventure is far too risky for children and novice hikers – and for anyone during or after rainfall. If you attempt this hike, please respect the privacy of valley residents.

Turn right at the bottom of the hill and after 10 minutes you'll reach Waipi'o Beach.

THE NIGHT MARCHERS

Kukuihaele means 'light that comes and goes' in Hawaiian, referring to the *huaka'ipo* (night marchers), the torch-bearing ghosts of Hawaiian warriors who pass through here to Waipi'o. As the legend goes, if you look at the night marchers or get in their way, you die. Survival is possible only if one of your ancestors is a marcher – or if you lie face down on the ground.

Waipiʻo Valley

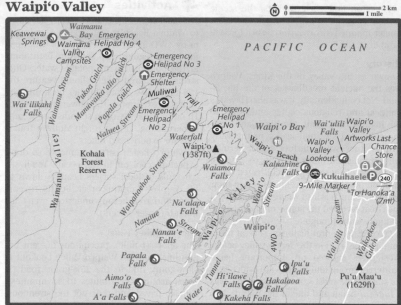

This black-sand beach is lined with graceful ironwood trees and big dark boulders, but is not swimmable. Most of the time even wading in these rough waters is a bad idea. Look for spinner dolphins and whales offshore.

Walk toward the stream mouth for a good view of Kaluahine Falls, cascading down the cliffs to the east. Getting to the falls is more challenging than it looks. High surf breaking over the uppermost rocks can be dangerous. Local lore holds that night marchers periodically descend from the upper valley to the beach and march to Lua o Milu, a hidden entrance to the netherworld.

Muliwai Trail to Waimanu Valley
HIKING, CAMPING

This 8.5 mile backcountry trail, beginning at Waipiʻo Valley Lookout, is only for strong hikers with experience on steep, slippery and potentially treacherous terrain. Don't underestimate either the difficulty or the beauty of this hike, which takes 6½ hours to eight hours and requires crossing 12 gulches – brutal to ascend and descend, but lovely green, moss-covered rock affairs with little waterfalls and icy cold pools for swimming. Note that dry weather is imperative for a safe, enjoyable experience.

Plan on at least two nights' (ideally, three or more) camping in Waimanu Valley. Hiking from the Waipiʻo lookout to Waimanu Valley takes about seven hours, while the return is easier and faster. You can park your car at the signposted 24-hour parking area or at Waipiʻo Valley Artworks in Kukuihaele.

To connect with the Muliwai trailhead from Waipiʻo Beach, ford the stream where calmest and walk toward the far end of the beach; there's a shaded path just inland that deposits you at the base of the cliffs. From here the path turns left, then veers right and ascends under thick forest cover. This ancient Hawaiian footpath rises over 1200ft in a mile of hard laboring up the steep northwest cliff face (it's nicknamed Z-Trail for the killer switchbacks). Hunters still use this trail to track feral pigs.

The hike is exposed and hot, so cover this stretch early. Eventually the trail moves into ironwood and Norfolk pine forest, and tops a little knoll before gently descending and becoming muddy and mosquito-ridden. The view of the ocean gives way to the sounds of a rushing stream.

The trail crosses a gulch and ascends past a sign for Emergency Helipad No 1. For the next few hours the trail finds a steady rhythm of gulch crossings and forest ascents. A waterfall at the third gulch is a source of fresh water; treat it before drinking. For a landmark, look for Emergency Helipad No 2 at about the halfway point from Waipi'o Beach. Beyond that, there's an open-sided emergency shelter with pit toilets and Emergency Helipad No 3.

Rest here before making the final difficult descent. Leaving the shelter, hop across three more gulches and pass Emergency Helipad No 4, from where it's less than a mile to **Waimanu Valley**. This final section of switchbacks starts out innocently enough, with some artificial and natural stone steps, but over a descent of 1200ft the trail is poorly maintained and extremely hazardous later. A glimpse of **Wai'ilikahi Falls** (accessible by a 45-minute stroll) on the far side of the valley might inspire hikers to press onward, but beware: the trail is narrow and washed out in parts, with sheer drop-offs into the ocean, and no hand holds apart from mossy rocks and spiny plants. If the descent is even slightly questionable, don't think twice: head back to the trail shelter for the night.

Waimanu Valley is a mini Waipi'o, minus the tourists. On any given day you'll bask alone amid a stunning deep valley framed by cliffs, waterfalls and a boulder-strewn beach. From the bottom of the switchbacks, Waimanu Beach is 10 minutes past the camping regulations signboard. To ford the stream to reach the **campsites** on its western side, avoid a rope strung across the water, which is deep there. Instead cross closer to the ocean entry where it is shallower.

Waimanu Valley once had a sizable settlement and contains many ruins, including house and heiau terraces, stone enclosures and old *lo'i*. In the early 19th century an estimated 200 people lived here, but the valley was abandoned by its remaining three families after the 1946 tsunami.

On the return trip, be careful to take the correct trail. Walking inland from Waimanu Beach, don't veer left on a false trail-of-use that attempts to climb a rocky streambed. Instead keep heading straight inland past the camping regulations sign to the trail to the switchbacks. It takes about two hours to get to the trail shelter, and another two to reach the waterfall gulch: refill your water here (remembering to treat before drinking). Exiting the ironwood forest soon after, the trail descends back to the floor of Waipi'o Valley.

Na'alapa Stables HORSEBACK RIDING
(☑775-0419; www.naalapastables.com; rides $88; ☺9am & 12:30pm) Visit the valley on a 2½-hour horseback ride; children eight years

and over are welcome. Tours leave from Waipi'o Valley Artworks.

Waipi'o Ridge Stables HORSEBACK RIDING
(☑775-1007, 877-757-1414; www.waipioridgestables.com; rides $85-165; ☺9am) Tour around the valley rim to the top of Hi'ilawe Falls (2½ hours) or combine with a forest trail ride (five hours), ending with a picnic and swim at a hidden waterfall. Departs Waipi'o Valley Artworks.

Waipi'o Valley Wagon Tours WAGON RIDE
(☑775-9518; www.waipiovalleywagontours.com; adult/child $55/25; ☺10:30am, 12:30pm & 2:30pm Mon-Sat) This 1½-hour jaunt in a mule-drawn wagon carts visitors around the valley floor. Tours leave from WOH Ranch, 0.5 miles beyond Hwy 240's 7-mile marker.

👉 Tours

Less-experienced hikers should consider led hikes or rides.

Hawaii Forest & Trail HIKING
(☑331-8505, 800-464-1993; www.hawaii-forest.com; Waipi'o Rim Hike Adventure adult/child under 13yr $149/119) Historic trail to rivers, taro farms, native forest, waterfalls and more.

Hawaiian Walkways HIKING
(☑775-0372, 800-457-7759; www.hawaiianwalkways.com; guided hikes adult/child $95/75) Go to waterfalls and swimming holes via a private trail.

If not by land, go by sea. Experienced sea kayakers can arrange custom tours with Plenty Pupule (p195). Kayaking from Waipi'o to Waimanu Valley is just over one

---

CARRY IN, CARRY OUT

The first rule of backpacking etiquette is to leave no trace. This is essential everywhere, but especially in pristine, sacred places like Waipi'o Valley and beyond. Campsites are only minimally maintained, so it's up to campers to remove whatever they bring. Unfortunately, some stick their garbage into crevices in the lava-rock walls surrounding the campsites; this attracts roaches, mongooses and other pests. Some also abandon unneeded gear in the valley: tents, mattress pads, beach chairs, reef shoes, rope, canned goods, you name it. The hike is easier going out than going in, so if you can carry it in, you can certainly carry it out.

mile, while hiking the switchbacks is 7.65 miles.

🛏 Sleeping

Backcountry camping in Waimanu Valley requires a state permit for a maximum of six nights (see p169 for details). There are nine campsites of your choice: recommended are No 2 (full valley views, proximity to stream, grassy spot); No 6 (view of Wai'ilikahi Falls, access to only sandy beach); and No 9 (very private at the far end of the valley, lava rock chairs and a table). Facilities include fire pits and composting outhouses.

Regarding water, there's a spring about 10 minutes behind campsite No 9 with a PVC pipe carrying water from a waterfall; all water must be treated.

❶ Dangers & Annoyances

STREAM CROSSING Hiking in and beyond the valley requires fording streams that can swell instantly during the winter rainy season. It's dangerous to try crossing streams if the water is above your knees. Such rising waters should be considered life-threatening obstacles, as flash floods are possible. Be patient – the water should subside in a few hours.

WATER Don't drink from any creeks or streams without first boiling or treating the water. Feral animals roam the area and leptospirosis is present.

PESTS There are wasps along the trail and giant centipedes that like to burrow in sleeping bags and shoes and deliver a nasty, nonlethal bite.

HELICOPTERS Expect to hear choppers from 7:30am, every two hours, until about 4:30pm. They disturb the serenity, but they also alert authorities about hurt or stranded hikers. Bring a signal device to flag one down in case of emergency.

Kalopa State Recreation Area

This 100-acre state park, with trails, camping and cabins in a quiet native forest at a cool 2000ft, is a favorite local hideaway. This is a great place to explore forests (almost) as they were when the Polynesians first arrived. There's a nature loop and hiking trail, plus large grassy expanses fringed by ironwood trees to let the kids run around on while you prep the picnic. To get here, turn *mauka* (inland) off the Hawai'i Belt Rd at the Kalopa Dr sign; follow park signs for 3 miles.

Camping is delightful in a grassy area surrounded by tall trees. Group cabins (eight people maximum) have bunk beds, linens and blankets, plus hot showers and a fully equipped kitchen. Permits ($60/90 for residents/nonresidents) are required; see p169 for more information.

An easy 1320yd **nature trail** loop begins near the cabins and passes through old ohia forest, where some of the trees measure more than 3ft in diameter. You may hear the *'elepaio,* an easily spotted brown-and-white native forest bird with a loud whistle.

A longer **hiking trail** leads into the adjoining forest reserve with old-growth forest and tremendous tree ferns. Begin along Robusta Lane, on the left between the caretaker's house and the campground. It's about 600yd to the edge of Kalopa Gulch, through a thick eucalyptus forest. The trail continues along the gulch rim for another mile, while several side trails along the way branch off and head west back into the recreation area. You can loop together over 4 miles on the spottily maintained trails.

Laupahoehoe

Another town that had its heyday when sugar was king, Laupahoehoe is now a small community with a pleasant beach park and a handful of attractions.

On April 1, 1946, tragedy hit the small plantation town when a tsunami 30ft high wiped out the schoolhouse on the point, killing 20 children and four adults. After the tsunami the whole town moved uphill.

In February, the Laupahoehoe Music Festival (admission $10; ☺9am-5pm) comes to the beach park to raise scholarship money for local students, with good eating, quality hula and tunes by the likes of Sugah Daddy and Bruddah Smitty.

Beaches & Sights

The 1.5-mile **scenic drive** to Laupahoehoe Point is a worth your while, simply to gape at the spectacular distant cliffs and dense foliage all around.

Laupahoehoe Point Beach Park   BEACH
Only real crazy *buggahs* would swim at windy, rugged Laupahoehoe, where the fierce surf sometimes crashes up over the rocks and into the parking lot. Many of the immigrant plantation laborers first set foot on the Big Island at Laupahoehoe. Now a county park, there are full facilities for **camping**.

Stop here to view the memorial for the 24 schoolchildren and teachers who died in the 1946 tsunami. The school stood around the breathtakingly huge banyan tree toward your right as you approach the park.

📷 **Laupahoehoe Train Museum**   MUSEUM
(☎962-6300; www.thetrainmuseum.com; adult/student/senior $4/2/3; ⊙9am-4:30pm Mon-Fri, 10am-2pm Sat & Sun) This unassuming little museum will fascinate history buffs. You, too, will marvel at the artifacts and archival photographs of Hawai'i's impressive plantation railroad era, so hard to imagine today. The gift shop carries a nice selection of books, including the compelling *April Fool's: The Laupahoehoe Tragedy of 1946*, an oral history of interviews with tsunami survivors. The museum is between the 25- and 26-mile markers.

✗ Eating & Sleeping

📷 **Back to the 50s Highway**
Fountain Diner   DINER $
(☎962-0808; 35-2704 Mamalahoa Hwy; burgers $4-7, plates $8-10; ⊙8am-7pm Wed & Thu, to 8pm Fri & Sat, to 3pm Sun) Nostalgia reigns in this wonderful homage to Elvis, Marilyn and the boppin' '50s. Built in a historic plantation house, the old-fashioned counter and booths set the mood for burgers (made with local beef) and shakes. The menu includes island favorites, eg fried *ono* (wahoo) filets with mashed potatoes, chili bowls and pancake and egg breakfasts. Frequented mostly by locals, it's a laid-back place to talk story and amuse the kids.

Old Jodo Temple   VACATION RENTALS $$
(☎772-3804, 650-355-5218; www.oldjodotemple.org; house per week/month $950/3500; 📶) Find peace and R&R at this historic Buddhist temple, c 1899 and wonderfully restored. Downstairs the house includes two large bedrooms (sleeps six), spacious living and dining areas, airy porches and full kitchen. Upstairs (additional fee per week/month $550/1500) the temple is now perfect for yoga retreats. Washer and dryer available. Walking distance to Laupahoehoe Point.

Hakalau & Around

It's a stretch to call this a town, but there's an active residential community, which is now a mix of old-timers and newcomers. Around New Year's Eve, hundreds flock here for the annual *mochi* pounding festival at Akiko's Buddhist B&B.

◉ Sights & Activities

Kolekole Beach Park   PARK
Beneath a highway bridge, this park sits alongside Kolekole Stream. The river-mouth break is a local surfing and bodyboarding hot spot, but ocean swimming is dangerous. There are small waterfalls and full facilities. **Camping** is allowed with a county permit (see p169), but the narrow area can get crowded and boisterous with picnicking local families.

To get here, turn inland off the Hawai'i Belt Rd at the southern end of the Kolekole Bridge, about 1300yd south of the 15-mile marker.

World Botanical Gardens   GARDENS
(☎963-5427; Hwy 19, 16-mile marker; www.wbgi.com; adult/teen 13-17yr/child 5-12yr $13/6/3; ⊙9am-5:30pm) Under development since 1995, this garden remains a work in progress. It is an admirable effort, but lacks the lushness and 'wow' of the Hawaii Tropical Botanical Garden closer to Hilo. Note that Umauma Falls are not viewable from here, although Kamae'e Falls (which are) are lovely enough. To get here from Hwy 19, turn *mauka* (inland) near the 16-mile marker, at the posted sign.

Zip Isle Zip Line Adventures   ZIPLINING
(☎963-5427, 888-947-4753; www.wbgi.com; tour $99-147; ⊙tour departures 10:30am, 1pm & 3:30pm) The affordable (relatively speaking) ziplining tours available at World Botanical Gardens are worth a stop if you're in the area. Expect seven ziplines, including a dual line, and a 150ft-long suspension bridge. A maximum 12 guests with two guides can be accommodated. Go for the 10:30am or 3:30pm tours for a discounted price of $99.

BEST HAMAKUA COAST HIGHWAY STOPS

» Waipi'o Valley Lookout (p252)
» Akaka Falls State Park (p258)
» Back to the 50s Highway Fountain Diner (p257)
» Tex Drive-In (p251)
» Laupahoehoe Train Museum (p257)

✕ Eating & Sleeping

Aaron's Blue Kalo BAKERY $
(☑963-6929; 29-2110 Hwy 19; chips per bag $5-10; ⏰9:30am-2pm Mon, Wed & Fri) Local chips aren't limited to the potato. Here, savor a colorful medley of crisp, kettle-cooked *kalo* (taro), *'ulu* (breadfruit) and purple and yellow sweet potato. Proprietors Aaron and Vinel Sumida buy their ingredients from local farmers and create gorgeous and addictively tasty chips by hand. They also bake an assortment of home-style cookies using Hawaiian root vegetables. Also sold in Hilo.

🖊 **Akiko's Buddhist Bed & Breakfast** HOSTEL $
(☑963-6422; www.alternative-hawaii.com/akiko; s/d $65/75, cottages $65-85) Appreciate the wonder of rustic simplicity at this peaceful, no-frills retreat. Rooms are simple – futons on the floor in the main house or twin beds in an adjacent house. Two off-the-grid cottages are teeny but wonderfully ensconced in tropical flora. For longer stays, ask about the artist's studio. The best part of this B&B might be Akiko herself, a *kama'aina* (born and raised in Hawaii) who farms the 2-acre grounds and invites guests to join morning meditation, coordinates a popular end-of-year **mochi pounding festival** and hosts worthy cultural events (see http://alternative-hawaii.com/akiko/calendar.htm). All rooms have shared bathroom; rates include breakfast. The B&B is in Wailea, just over 2 miles north of Honomu, on a marked turn-off from the highway.

Honomu

Honomu is a quaint old sugar town that might be forgotten if it weren't for its proximity to Akaka Falls. Life here remains rural and slow paced. Main St is lined with retro wooden buildings still lively with shops and eateries.

⦿ Sights

Akaka Falls State Park PARK
(car & admission $5, walk-in admission $1) The only way these impressive falls could be easier to reach would be to put them in the parking lot – but then you'd miss the enchanting half-mile loop trail through the rain forest, whose dense foliage includes banyan and monkeypod trees, massive philodendrons, fragrant ginger, dangling heliconia, orchids and gigantic bamboo groves. Only a tiny fraction of the park's 65 acres is open to the public.

Follow the park's advice and start by heading to the right: you come first to 100ft **Kahuna Falls**, which strikes you as the perfect Hawaiian cascade, for about as long as it takes to reach its neighbor. When you see 420ft **Akaka Falls**, you can swoon properly: the water tumbles majestically down a moss and fern-draped cliff, its spray sometimes painting a rainbow.

To get here turn onto Hwy 220 between the 13- and 14-mile markers. Drive 4 miles inland to reach the park. You can avoid the parking fee if you park outside the lot, but you must still pay the walk-in fee. Cash or credit cards accepted.

✕ Sleeping & Eating

The Palms Cliff House Inn B&B $$$
(☑963-6076; www.palmscliffhouse.com; r incl breakfast $299-449; ❄🐾) This elegant B&B fits the bill for those seeking a romantic splurge near resort-free Hilo. The eight ocean-view rooms are spacious (550 sq ft to 650 sq ft), with high-class furnishings and private entrances and verandas. Guests rave about the full hot breakfasts. One qualm: rates are steep, but you might luck out during special discounts.

Mr Ed's Bakery BAKERY $
(☑963-5000; www.mredsbakery.com; Hwy 220; ⏰6am-6pm Mon-Sat, 9am-4pm Sun) Folks drive from Hilo for the scrumptious homestyle baking found here, including old-fashioned long johns (éclair-style pastry), hearty cookies and the island's best Portuguese sweet bread. Another draw is the staggering selection of homemade preserves (jar $7.50), made with local fruit such as *poha* (gooseberry), *liliko'i*, guava and *ohelo* (native berry).

Woodshop Gallery & Café CAFE $
(☑963-6363; www.woodshopgallery.com; Hwy 220; lunch dishes $6-9; ⏰11am-5:30pm) There are several places to chow down in Honomu, including a pizza parlor and bakery, but this place is the best. Try a burger and lemonade or homemade ice cream and espresso – it's all good and served with aloha. Following lunch go on a shopping spree among the extraordinary collection of handcrafted bowls, photos and blown glass.

Onomea Bay & Around

Papaikou, Onomea and Pepe'ekeo are three more plantation villages that are now admired for their gorgeous landscape and views.

◉ Sights & Activities

Pepe'ekeo 4-Mile Scenic Drive   DRIVE

The fantastic rain forest jungle along this stretch of the Old Mamalahoa Hwy proves that all of those annoying showers are really worthwhile. Cruising along the narrow road you cross a series of one-lane bridges spanning little streams and waterfalls. In places the sun is almost blocked out by *liliko'i*, guava and tall mango and African tulip trees, which drop their orange flowers on the road.

You can begin the drive from either end, but approaching from the south (Hilo side) involves an easy right turn between the 7- and 8-mile markers on the main highway.

TOP CHOICE Hawaii Tropical Botanical Garden   GARDEN

(☑964-5233; www.hawaiigarden.com; adult/child $15/5; ☺9am-4pm) Wander leisurely along self-guided trails and see 2000 species of tropical plants set amid streams and waterfalls. The walk ends at Onomea Bay and takes an hour (assuming stops for photo-ops). Buy your ticket at the yellow building on the *mauka* (inland) side of the road. The flowers and scenery are gorgeous, rain or shine (umbrellas provided). Catch free tours (☺noon Mon, Wed & Sat) by Garden Manager Sean Callahan, who has been on staff for 20 years.

Onomea Tea Company   FARM

(www.onomeatea.com; tour/tasting/high tea $10/20/35) This 9-acre tea plantation offers garden tours, tea tastings and high tea with sandwiches and sweets at the owners' home. It's a small, personal tour, with friendly chatting about tea and its cultivation. Reservations are required; ask for directions when making reservation.

Onomea Bay Hike   HIKING

For a quick, scenic hike to the bay, take the Na Ala Hele trailhead on the *makai* (seaward) side of the road, just north of the botanical garden. After a 10-minute hike down a slippery jungle path, you'll come to a finger of lava jutting into the sea. A spur

See Hilo Map (p262)

to the right leads to a couple of small waterfalls and a cove. Continuing straight brings you to the diminutive bluffs overlooking the batik blues of Onomea Bay. Look for a rope tied to an almond tree for low-tide beach access. Hawaiian monk seals have been sighted here.

✕ Eating & Drinking

What's Shakin'   SMOOTHIES, TAKEOUT

(☑964-3080; ☺10am-5pm) At the north end of the Pepe'ekeo 4-Mile Scenic Drive, this outdoorsy spot serves luscious smoothies (all fruit, no filler) and tasty full meals.

Baker Tom's   BAKERY

(☑964-8444; 27-2111 Mamalahoa Hwy; ☺6:30am-6:30pm) On Hwy 11 in Papaikou, don't miss this roadside stand on the mauka (inland) side, between the 6- and 7-mile markers. The cookies are divine and the *malasadas* rival Tex's.

HILO

POP 41,000

If Hilo and Kona were sisters, Hilo would be the hard-working one with common sense and natural beauty. Perhaps that's because this town knows life is tough: it's been knocked down twice by tsunamis, threatened by Mauna Loa lava flows (most recently in 1984), and it gets rained on two out of three days a year (statistically speaking). Its population – a mix of Japanese, Chinese, Korean, Filipino, Portuguese, Puerto Rican and Caucasian immigrants, in addition to Native Hawaiians – is largely working or middle class. Many families came originally to work the sugar plantations, and stayed because the community became their life.

Don't let Kona's sun and sand blind you to Hilo's charms, though. The 'rainiest city in the USA' has a walkable historic downtown, interesting museums and the best in local food. Set on a calm bay and filled with lush rain forests, it makes an ideal home base, with two farmers markets, a variety of B&Bs and proximity to Hawai'i Volcanoes National Park, Mauna Kea, Puna and the Hamakua Coast.

History

Since its first Polynesian settlers farmed and fished along the Wailuku River, Hilo has been a lively port town. In the 20th century it was the trading hub for sugarcane grown in Puna and Hamakua, connected in both directions by the Hawaii Consolidated Railway's sprawling railroad.

Back then townsfolk set up homes and shops along the bay. But after being slammed by two disastrous tsunami in 1946 and 1960, no one wanted to live downtown anymore. Today you'll find parks, beaches and open space along Kamehameha Ave.

When the sugar industry folded in the 1980s and '90s, Hilo focused its economy on diversified agriculture, the university, retail and, of course, tourism. While downtown Hilo is still its charming heart, the go-to retail destinations are the big chain stores (Wal-Mart, Target, Home Depot etc) south of the airport.

🏖 Beaches

Except for Honoli'i Beach Park, Hilo's beaches are all located in the Keaukaha neighborhood.

TOP CHOICE Onekahakaha Beach Park   BEACH

(Map p262) Popular with local families, this beach has a broad, shallow, sandy-bottomed pool, protected by a boulder breakwater. The water is only 1ft to 2ft deep in spots, so toddlers can splash safely. An unprotected cove north of the protected pool is deeper but can be hazardous due to pokey *wana* (sea urchins) and rough surf; it's best to stay inside the breakwater. There are lifeguards on weekends and holidays, restrooms, showers, grassy lawns and covered pavilions.

James Kealoha Beach Park   BEACH

(Map p262) Further along the road, this county park is best for older kids and snorkelers. Locals call it Four Miles (the distance between the park and the downtown post office). For swimming and snorkeling head to the eastern side, which contains a deep, protected basin with generally calm, clear water and pockets of white sand. The park's western side is open ocean and much rougher. Locals surf here in winter or net fish. There are weekend lifeguards, restrooms, showers and covered pavilions.

Wai'olena and Wai'uli Beach Parks   BEACH

(off Map p262) Rocky and ruggedly pretty, these side-by-side beaches (commonly known by their former name, **Leleiwi Beach**) is Hilo's best shore-dive site. You might see turtles, interesting coral growth and a variety of butterfly fish. The water is freezing until you go past the reef, and the entrance is tricky; ask for advice at Nautilus Dive Center. For cultural reasons the county renamed the beaches Wai'uli (dark water) and Wai'olena (light water) in January 2008.

Richardson Ocean Park   BEACH

(off Map p262) Near the end of Kalaniana'ole Ave, this pocket of black sand is Hilo's best all-round beach. During calm surf swimming is fine, while snorkeling is good on the warmer eastern side. (Waters are cooler on the northern side due to subsurface freshwater springs.) Lava rocks create interesting nooks and crannies, and sea turtles often hang out here. High surf attracts bodyboarders. There are restrooms, showers, picnic tables and a lifeguard.

Honoli'i Beach Park   BEACH

(Map p259) Less than 2 miles north of downtown Hilo, this protected cove is Hilo's best surfing and bodyboarding spot. Don't come here to swim, as the adjacent river tends to muddy the waters. There's a pleasant grassy picnic area, restrooms, showers and a lifeguard. From Hilo take the Bayfront Hwy north; after the 4-mile marker, turn right onto Nahala St and then left onto Kahoa St. Park on the roadside and walk down to the park. On weekends cars are parked bumper to bumper.

Sights

Most sights are found in downtown Hilo, where historic early 20th–century buildings now house restaurants, stores and galleries. Outside the downtown area the main sights continue along the coast (which locals call 'bayfront'), from Hilo's landmark dock, Suisan Fish Market, to the Keaukaha beaches.

TOP CHOICE Lili'uokalani Park & Banyan Drive   PARK
(Map p262) Savor Hilo's simple pleasures with a picnic lunch amid **Japanese gardens** overlooking the bay. Named for Hawaii's last queen, the 30-acre county park has manicured lawns, shallow ponds, bamboo groves, arched bridges, pagodas and a teahouse. At sunrise or sunset join the locals and jog, stroll or just admire the Mauna Kea view.

Adjacent to the park is Banyan Dr, Hilo's mini 'hotel row', best known for the **giant banyan trees** lining the road. Royalty and celebrities planted the trees in the 1930s, and, if you look closely, you'll find plaques beneath the trees identifying Babe Ruth, Amelia Earhart and Cecil B DeMille.

Mokuola (Coconut Island)   PARK
(Map p262) Tiny Mokuola island, commonly called Coconut Island, connects to land (near Lili'uokalani Park) by a footbridge. The island is a county park with picnic tables and swimming, and it's popular with local fishermen. Definitely stop here for a fun jaunt and a spectacular view of the bay, the town and majestic Mauna Kea in the distance.

Lyman Museum & Mission House   MUSEUM
(Map p262; ☑935-5021; www.lymanmuseum.org; 276 Haili St; adult/child $10/3; ☉10am-4:30pm Mon-Sat) Compact yet comprehensive, this museum covers the basics of Hawaii's natural and cultural history. Downstairs geologic exhibits explain Hawaii's volcanic origins and include fascinating examples of lava rock, such as 'Pele's tears' (solidified drops of volcanic glass) and 'Pele's hair' (fine strands of volcanic glass), both named after the Hawaiian volcano goddess.

Upstairs, learn about ancient Hawaiian sports, religion and the kapu system, and see artifacts such as adzes, feather lei and *kapa* (cloth made by pounding paper-mulberry bark). Don't miss the fascinating, perfectly spherical stone. Other exhibits highlight the cultures of Hawaii's ethnic immigrant groups.

Catch an excellent half-hour **tour** (☉11am & 2pm) of the adjacent Mission House, built by the Reverend David Lyman and his wife, Sarah, in 1839. The minimalist house contains many original furnishings, including Sarah's melodeon, rocking chair, china and quilts, and adds a human element to the historical facts.

'Imiloa Astronomy Center of Hawai'i   MUSEUM
(Map p262; ☑969-9700; www.imiloahawaii.org; 600 'Imiloa Pl; adult/child 4-12yr $17.50/9.50; ☉9am-4pm Tue-Sun, plus Memorial Day & Labor Day) 'Imiloa, which means 'exploring new knowledge,' is a $28 million astronomy museum and planetarium complex with a twist: it showcases modern astronomy on Mauna Kea in light of ancient Hawaiian mythology and ocean voyaging.

This juxtaposition might seem incongruous, but there are parallels and continuity between ancient and modern exploration. In the Origins exhibit, attractive displays walk you through the mythical *Kumulipo* (Hawaiian creation story) and the scientific big bang theory. The Voyaging exhibit covers ancient Polynesian voyaging and today's advanced telescopes and observatories.

With many hands-on displays, a 3D theater, a **restaurant** (☉7am-4pm) and a 120-seat planetarium, 'Imiloa is a worthwhile family attraction and nicely complements a trip to the actual summit.

One planetarium show is included with admission; we suggest you go for *Maunakea: Between Earth and Sky* (check website for current show times), although the 3D space age and astronomy films are also fascinating.

TOP CHOICE Pacific Tsunami Museum   MUSEUM
(Map p266; ☑935-0926; www.tsunami.org; 130 Kamehameha Ave; adult/senior/child 6-17yr $8/7/4; ☉9am-4pm Mon-Sat) You cannot understand Hilo without knowing its history as a two-time tsunami survivor, in 1946 and 1960. This nonprofit museum might seem modest, but it's also a key education and research center – chockfull of riveting info. Allow

Hilo

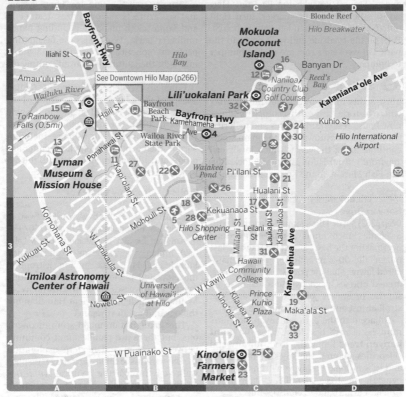

enough time to experience the multimedia exhibits, such as chilling computer simulations and filmed oral histories and documentaries, especially the heart-wrenching first-person accounts by survivors.

Hilo Farmers Market   FARMERS MARKET
(Map p266; www.hilofarmersmarket.com; cnr Mamo St & Kamehameha Ave; ⊙6am-4pm Wed & Sat) Hilo's pioneering farmers market, which opened in 1988 with four farmers selling from trucks, is one of the town's gathering places. Today the market has 200 produce and craft vendors and attracts sizeable crowds. One caveat: the produce sold here is not 100% locally grown. Most of the tropical fruit is local; enjoy delicious apple bananas, star fruit, Ka'u oranges, *liliko'i* and lychees. Papayas are always abundant, but remember that the bargain Rainbow variety is genetically modified. Machete-cut coconuts for drinking are a fun novelty. On the next block, dozens of craft and clothing stalls

entice tourists with sarongs, T-shirts and 'Hawaiian' woodcarvings and shell jewelry – occasionally real, often fake.

Wednesday and Saturday are by far the liveliest market days (and the most parking-challenged), but a few vendors also set up shop from 7am to 4pm on Monday, Tuesday, Thursday and Friday.

Kino'ole Farmers Market

FARMERS MARKET
(Map262; cnr Kino'ole St & Puainako Ave; ⊙7am-noon Sat) If the Hilo Farmers Market is a spectacle, the Kino'ole market is a community gathering. Established in 2007 and sponsored by the Hilo, Hamakua and Kohala County Farm Bureaus, this market features 100% locally grown and made products sold by the farmers themselves. The 15 to 20 vendors supply all you need – fresh produce, baked goods, taro chips, poi, plants and flowers – in clean and tidy booths, ac-

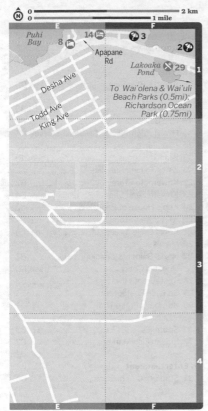

HILO SIGHTS

East Hawai'i Cultural Center ART GALLERY

(Map p266; ☑961-5711; www.ehcc.org; 141 Kalakaua St; suggested donation $2; ☉10am-4pm Mon-Sat) The best venue for local art is this downtown center, which displays primarily the work of established professionals, but also compelling school kids' and other amateurs' masterpieces. **Workshops** and **classes** on varied creative forms (eg painting, drawing, ukulele and hula) are ongoing. Check the website for special evening concerts (featuring top artists).

Rainbow Falls WATERFALL

(Map p259) A regular stop for tour buses, the lookout for this 'instant gratification' cascade is just steps from the parking lot. Depending on rainfall, the lovely 80ft waterfall can be a trickle or a torrent. Go in the morning and you'll see rainbows if the sun and mist cooperate. Waianuenue (which means 'rainbow seen in water') is the Hawaiian name for these falls. To get here, drive up Waianuenue Ave (veer right when it splits into Kaumana Dr) about 1.5 miles from downtown Hilo; follow the signage.

FREE Wailoa Center & Wailoa River State Park ART GALLERY

(Map p262; ☑933-0416; ☉8:30am-4:30pm Mon, Tue, Thu & Fri, noon-4:30pm Wed) This eclectic, state-run gallery shows the gamut of exhibits, which change monthly. You might find quilts, bonsai, Chinese watercolors or historical photos, all done by locals.

Surrounding the center is a state park, a quiet spot that's more scenery than scene. The main landmark is a 14ft, Italian-made bronze statue of Kamehameha the Great, erected in 1997 and restored with gold leaf in 2004. The Wailoa River flows through the park, ending at Waiakea Pond, a spring-fed estuarine pond with saltwater and brackishwater fish species (mostly mullet). The park features two memorials: a tsunami memorial dedicated to the 1946 and 1960 victims, and a Vietnam War memorial with an eternal flame.

FREE Mokupapapa Discovery Center MUSEUM

(Map p266; ☑933-8184; www.hawaiireef.noaa.gov/center; S Hata Bldg, 308 Kamehameha Ave; ☉9am-4pm Tue-Sat) The Hawaiian archipelago extends far beyond the eight main islands to the Northwestern Hawaiian Islands. The healthiest coral reefs in the USA are found in this long chain of uninhabited islands

companied by agricultural displays and gardening demonstrations. The low-key vibe is relaxing. No touristy doodads sold here. Parking is easy.

FREE Pana'ewa Rainforest Zoo and Gardens ZOO

(Map p259; ☑959-9233; www.hilozoo.com; ☉9am-4pm, petting zoo 1:30-2:30pm Sat) Four miles south of town, Hilo's unpretentious 12-acre zoo makes for a pleasant stroll or kiddie diversion. Find free-roaming peacocks meandering past caged monkeys, reptiles, a pygmy hippo and some of Hawaii's endangered birds. The star is a white Bengal tiger named Namaste. The zoo lives up to its rain forest moniker, with thriving tropical foliage tended by local seniors. Where else can you find all this for free?

To get here, turn *mauka* (inland) off the Volcano Hwy onto W Mamaki St, just past the 4-mile marker.

Hilo

◉ **Top Sights**
  'Imiloa Astronomy Center of
    Hawaii...A4
  Kino'ole Farmers Market......................C4
  Lili'uokalani Park...................................C1
  Lyman Museum & Mission House........A2
  Mokuola (Coconut Island).....................C1

◉ **Sights**
1 Hilo Public Library....................................A2
2 James Kealoha Beach Park....................F1
3 Onekahakaha Beach Park......................F1
4 Wailoa Center..C2

Activities, Courses & Tours
5 Balancing Monkey Yoga Center............B3
6 Ho'olulu Complex....................................C2
7 Niniloa Country Club Golf
   Course..C2

🛏 **Sleeping**
8 Arnott's Lodge..E1
9 Bay House B&B.......................................B1
10 Dolphin Bay Hotel.................................A1
11 Hilo Bay Hale...B2
12 Hilo Hawaiian Hotel..............................C1
13 Hilo Honu Inn..A2
14 Hilo Tropical Gardens Guest
    House..E1

15 Shipman House B&B..............................A2
16 Uncle Billy's Hilo Bay Hotel...................C1

⊗ **Eating**
  Aaron's Blue Kalo...........................(see 12)
17 Big Island Candies..................................C3
18 Café 100..B3
19 Hilo Bay Café...C4
  Hilo Homemade Ice Cream...........(see 14)
20 Hilo Lunch Shop....................................C2
  Island Naturals...............................(see 28)
21 Itsu's Fishing Supplies..........................C2
22 Kawamoto Store.....................................B2
23 Kawate Seed Shop.................................C4
24 Ken's House of Pancakes.......................C2
25 KTA Super Store.....................................C4
  Kuhio Grille.....................................(see 33)
26 Miyo's...C2
27 Nori's Saimin & Snacks.........................B2
  Queen's Court.................................(see 12)
28 Restaurant Miwa....................................B3
29 Seaside Restaurant................................F1
30 Sombat's Fresh Thai
    Cuisine...C2
31 Sputnik's..C3
32 Suisan Fish Market.................................C2

✪ **Entertainment**
33 Stadium Cinemas....................................C4

and atolls. Learn more about the islands' pristine ecosystems at this modest yet ambitious little center. The 2500-gallon aquarium and lots of interactive displays will catch kids' attention.

Pe'epe'e Falls & Boiling Pots   WATERFALL
(Map p259) Two miles past Rainbow Falls, find another drive-up lookout for a gorgeous series of dramatic falls cascading into swirling, bubbling pools (or 'boiling pots'). Restrooms are available here. You might be tempted to hike closer and take a plunge, but heed the warning signs; there's a drowning in this river about once a year. Currents are much stronger than they appear and pull victims downriver or underwater to their deaths.

Mauna Loa Macadamia-Nut Visitor Center   FACTORY
(Map p259; ☎966-8618, 888-628-6256; www.maunaloa.com; Macadamia Rd; ⊙8:30am-5:30pm) Hershey-owned Mauna Loa provides huge windows on its working factory, where you can watch the humble mac nut as it moves along the assembly line from cracking to roasting to chocolate dipping and packaging. The gift shop, of course, has every variation ready for purchase, with tasters. The factory is well signed about 5 miles south of Hilo; the 3-mile access road dips through acres of macadamia trees.

Hilo Public Library   LIBRARY
The Hilo Public Library is not a must-see, but if you're in the neighborhood examine the two lava stones fronting the building. The upright Pinao Stone once guarded the entrance of Pinao heiau, an ancient temple. The reclining Naha Stone, from the same heiau, is estimated at 3.5 tons; according to Hawaiian legend, anyone who had the strength to budge the stone would also have the strength to conquer and unite all the Hawaiian Islands. Kamehameha the Great reputedly met the challenge, overturning the stone in his youth.

🏃 Activities

While Hilo's coast is lined with reefs rather than sand, the gentle waters are ideal for stand up paddle (SUP) surfing, the latest craze. Rent a board and paddle, and launch from Mokuola (Coconut Island), Reed's Bay (Map p262) or Wailoa River State Park. For surfing, head to Honoli'i Beach Park.

While diving is best on the Kona side, there are decent shore-dive spots in Hilo, including Wai'uli and Wai'olena Beach Parks, with depths of 10ft to 70ft, lava arches, coral reefs, and sightings of turtles and whales in season.

The following outfits are solid and conveniently located downtown.

Sun & Sea Hawaii   WATERSPORTS
(Map p266; 934-0902; sunandseahawaii@gmail .com; 224 Kamehameha Ave; SUP package per half/full day $45/65) This friendly one-stop shop for ocean sports rents SUP packages and sells a variety of snorkeling, diving and swimming gear.

Nautilus Dive Center   DIVING
(Map p266; 935-6939; www.nautilusdivehilo .com; 382 Kamehameha Ave; scuba package per day $35; ⊙9am-5pm Tue-Sat) Hilo's go-to dive shop offers guided dives, PADI certification courses and general advice on shore diving. If you're a certified diver, rent here and head to the best East Hawai'i dive site at Pohoiki Bay in Puna.

Orchidland Surfboards   SURFING
(Map p266; 935-1533; www.orchidlandsurf.com; 262 Kamehameha Ave; ⊙9am-5pm Mon-Sat, 10am-3pm Sun) For board rentals and surf gear; Owner Stan Lawrence is an expert surfer, and he opened the Big Island's first surf shop in 1972.

TOP CHOICE Hilo Municipal Golf Course   GOLF
(Map p259; 959-7711; 340 Haihai St; greens fee Mon-Fri $29, Sat & Sun $34) Hilo's main course (the Muni) is nicely maintained and a terrific deal. Morning tee times are favored by the local contingent.

Naniloa Country Club Golf Course   GOLF
(Map p262; 120 Banyan Dr; 935-3000; greens fee $10) Most locals golf at the Muni, so this nine-hole course is uncrowded and boasts a pretty setting across from Lili'uokalani Park.

Yoga Centered   YOGA
(Map p266; 934-7233; www.yogacentered.com; 37 Waianuenue Ave; drop-in class $15; ⊙boutique 10am-5pm Mon-Thu, to 4pm Sun) Find youthful instructors, a variety of styles (mostly flow) and an attractive downtown space. Boutique items are stylish, if pricey.

Balancing Monkey Yoga Center   YOGA
(Map p262; 936-9590; www.balancingmonkey .com; 65 Mohouli St; drop-in class $14; ⊙Sun-Fri) Home studio with an indie vibe offers *vinyasa* flow classes.

Ho'olulu Complex   SWIMMING
(Map p262; 260 Kalanikoa St; 961-8698) For lap swimming, this Olympic-sized, open-air pool is generally uncrowded during the day. Call for hours.

⭐ Festivals & Events

TOP CHOICE Big Island Hawaiian
Music Festival   MUSIC FESTIVAL
(961-5711; www.ehcc.org; Hilo High School, 556 Waianuenue Ave; adult/child $10/free) A mid-July, two-day concert featuring virtuoso musicians in ukulele, steel guitar, slack key guitar and falsetto singing. The state-wide lineup has included top names such as Cyril Pahinui, Darlene Ahuna, Ozzie Kotani and Brittni Paiva.

May Day Lei Day Festival   LEI FESTIVAL
(934-7010; www.hilopalace.com; Palace Theater, 38 Haili St; admission free) Beautiful lei displays, demonstrations, live music and hula on the first Sunday in May.

King Kamehameha Day
Celebration   HISTORIC DAY
(935-9338; Mokuola; admission free) On June 11, observe the historic re-enactment of King Kamehameha's history, plus music and crafts.

Fourth of July   INDEPENDENCE DAY CELEBRATION
Entertainment and food all day at Lili'uokalani Park; fireworks display from Mokuola (Coconut Island).

International Festival of the
Pacific   JAPANESE FESTIVAL
(934-0177; Japanese Chamber of Commerce, 400 Hualani St; admission free) August celebration of the Japanese in Hawaii, featuring a lantern parade and Japanese tea ceremony at Lili'uokalani Park.

Hawai'i County Fair   FAIR
(Afook-Chinen Civic Auditorium, 799 Pi'ilani St; adult/student $3/2) Pure nostalgia comes to town in September, with carnival rides, games and cotton candy.

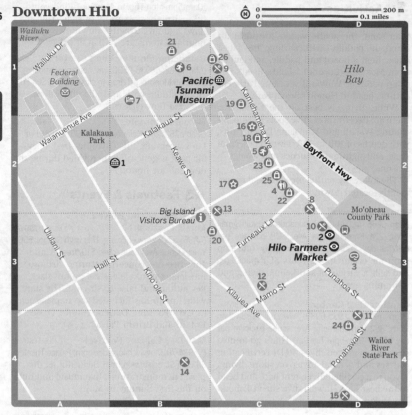

🛏 Sleeping

Hilo's 'hotel row' on Banyan Dr contains only two recommended hotels, so there's no concentration of accommodations in any one neighborhood. Instead Hilo has an excellent selection of B&Bs (at various price points) scattered across town.

For ocean views, the Banyan Dr hotels and B&Bs north of Hilo are your best bets.

Budget travelers are also in luck. Hilo boasts a surprising number of good hostels. The downtown location of Hilo Bay Hostel is ideal, but if beach proximity appeals to you, consider the other two near Onekahakaha Beach Park.

Orchid Tree B&B B&B $$
(☎961-9678; www.orchidtree.net; 6 Makakai Pl; r incl breakfast $150; ✳🤖🏊) If you want a B&B experience but value space and privacy, try this standout near Honoli'i Beach. The Koi Room is spacious (500 sq ft) and modern-

chic, with a gleaming hardwood floor and koi pond outside. The Hula Room is even bigger, containing two beds, plus a lounging area with two plump, inviting sofas. Outside you'll find a pool and 'surfer shack' patio facing the eastern horizon. The highway turn-off to this B&B is just past the 4-mile marker (but less than 2 miles from downtown Hilo) on Nahala St.

Dolphin Bay Hotel HOTEL $$
(Map p262; ☎935-1466; www.dolphinbayhotel.com; 333 Iliahi St; studios $109-119, 1 bedroom/2 bedroom $149/169; 🤖) This family-run hotel attracts many loyal, repeat guests. Since 1968 folks have appreciated the 18 spick-and-span apartment units, all with full kitchens and TV, located within a five-minute jog from downtown. The hotel owner/manager is an avid outdoorsman and he freely shares his firsthand knowledge of the volcanoes. Free coffee and locally grown fruit for breakfast.

◎ **Top Sights**
  Hilo Farmers Market.............................D3
  Pacific Tsunami Museum C1

◎ **Sights**
 1 East Hawai'i Cultural Center B2
 2 Mokupapapa Discovery Center D3

Activities, Courses & Tours
 3 Nautilus Dive Center D3
 4 Orchidland Surfboards C2
 5 Sun & Sea Hawaii...................................C2
 6 Yoga Centered B1

◉ **Sleeping**
 7 Hilo Bay Hostel.......................................B1

◉ **Eating**
 8 Abundant Life Natural Foods C3
 9 Bayfront Coffee, Kava & Tea Co C1
10 Café Pesto D3

11 Koji's Bento Korner D4
12 KTA Super Stores...................................C3
13 Ocean Sushi Deli....................................C2
14 Short N Sweet...B4
15 Two Ladies Kitchen...............................D4

◎ **Entertainment**
16 Kress Cinemas.......................................C2
17 Palace Theater.......................................C2

◎ **Shopping**
18 Alan's Art & Collectibles.......................C2
19 Basically Books...................................... C1
20 Book Gallery...C3
21 Books, Nooks, & Crannies.................... B1
22 Dragon Mama C2
23 Extreme Exposure Fine Art
   Gallery...C2
24 Hilo Guitars & Ukuleles.........................D4
25 Most Irresistible Shop...........................C2
26 Sig Zane Designs...................................C1

HILO SLEEPING

For longer stays, ask about the one-bedroom apartments in the **Annex** (per day/week/month $119/674/1400) across the street.

Hilo Bay Hale   B&B **$$**
(Map p262; ☏640-1113, 800-745-5049; www.hilobayhale.com; 301 Ponahawai St; r $139-159; ☎) You can't go wrong in this gorgeously restored 1912 plantation home, designed to be a B&B. Two upper-floor rooms feature private lanai overlooking charming koi ponds, while the spacious ground-floor room boasts a palatial garden shower and its own patch of lawn. Guests have access to the charmingly retro kitchen and open-air dining lanai. The central location lets you ditch the car for pleasant walks to the heart of downtown Hilo. For weeklong stays this place is a steal at just $99 to $119 per night!

Hilo Honu Inn   B&B **$$**
(Map p262; ☏935-4325; www.hilohonu.com; 465 Haili St; r incl breakfast $140-250; ☎) In a lovely retro home, three custom-designed guest rooms accommodate different budgets. A worthy splurge, the Samurai Suite is utterly memorable, with genuine Japanese detailing, plus tatami floor, *furo* (soaking tub), tea room and sweeping (if distant) views of Hilo Bay. The two-room Bali Hai Suite is tropical themed, with a delicious 'rainfall shower,' while the smallest, Honu's Nest, is comfy for two.

Bay House B&B   B&B **$$**
(☏961-6311, 888-235-8195; www.bayhousehawaii.com; 42 Pukihae St; r incl breakfast $150; ☎) Just across the Singing Bridge, find three immaculate guest rooms within eyeshot (and earshot) of the bay. Tastefully tropical themed, with classy hardwood and granite floors, each room includes a top-quality king bed, TV and private lanai (for that sunrise cup of coffee). The foyer contains a shared kitchenette and sitting area. Charming hosts are longtime residents who respect guests' privacy.

Hale Kai Hawaii   B&B **$$**
(Map p259; ☏935-6330; www.halekaihawaii.com; 111 Honoli'i Pl; r $150-155, suite $165; ☎⟐) Four units enjoy panoramic ocean views, including Honoli'i Beach surfing and Hilo in the distance. While all include sliding doors to the veranda, it's worth paying $5 extra for a larger room; the suite includes kitchenette. Guests rave about the breakfasts (included). Kids 13 years and older only. Located north of Hilo, off Pauka'a Dr, just south of the 5-mile marker.

Shipman House B&B   B&B **$$**
(☏934-8002, 800-627-8447; www.hilo-hawaii.com; 131 Kaiulani St; r incl breakfast $219-249; ☎) The Shipman family's grand Victorian mansion is peerless in historical significance. Queen Lili'uokalani played the grand piano; Jack

When the **Merrie Monarch Festival** (☏935-9168; www.merriemonarchfestival.org; Afook-Chinen Civic Auditorium; 2-night admission general/reserved $10/15) comes to town around Easter (late March or early April), forget about booking a last-minute room in Hilo. This three-day hula competition is a phenomenal sellout attraction that turns laid-back Hilo into the most happening place to be. Established in 1964, the festival honors King David Kalakaua (1836–91), who almost single-handedly revived Hawaiian culture and arts, including hula, which had been forbidden by missionaries for almost 70 years.

Top hula troupes from all the Islands vie in *kahiko* (ancient) and *'auana* (modern) categories. *Kahiko* performances are strong and serious, accompanied only by chanting. *'Auana* is closer to the mainstream style, with sinuous arm movements, smiling dancers and melodious accompaniment that includes string instruments. The primal chanting, meticulous choreography and traditional costumes are profoundly moving.

To guarantee a seat, order tickets by mail on December 26 (no earlier postmarks allowed); see the website for seating and payment info. The roughly 2700 tickets sell out within a month. Book your hotel room and car a year in advance.

London slept in the guest cottage. Surrounded by museum-quality antiques, the three rooms in the main house are sedate and finely (although not luxuriously) furnished. Out back in the cottage, the two rooms are more casual and airy. Welcoming hosts go the extra mile for guests; convenient location near downtown Hilo.

✏ **The Inn at Kulaniapia Falls**　　INN $$
(☏935-6789, 866-935-6789; www.waterfall.net; 1 Kulaniapia Dr; r incl breakfast $129-149, 1-bedroom house $200; ☎) To reach this grand inn you must drive four miles past acres of macadamia orchards to 850ft above sea level. Your reward? A fantastically verdant setting, complete with 120ft waterfall and swimming hole. Eight rooms (in two buildings) are exquisitely appointed with Asian antiques. The pagoda guesthouse is a worthy splurge and includes a kitchen, laundry facilities and 1.5 bathrooms. All power is hydroelectric and off the grid. The unlit 4-mile road can be tricky at night. See website for driving directions.

Holmes' Sweet Home　　B&B $
(☏961-9089; www.holmesbandb.com; 107 Koula St; r incl breakfast $80-95; ☎) In a pleasant residential neighborhood about 2.5 miles from downtown, this friendly, lived-in B&B provides comfy rooms (both wheelchair-accessible) with private entrances, plus a large common area with full-sized fridge and microwave. The $95 room, with queen and twin beds, high ceiling and double sink, is especially pleasant. It's located about 2.5 miles from downtown, heading up Kaumana Dr and onto Ainako Ave.

Old Hawaiian B&B　　B&B $
(☏961-2816; www.thebigislandvacation.com; 1492 Wailuku Dr; r incl breakfast $80-110; ☎) Perfect for discriminating budget travelers, these three pleasant rooms include private entrances and tidy furnishings. The largest (Hawaiian Room) and smallest (Bamboo Room) are the best value. All open to a backyard lanai, with dining table, microwave and refrigerator. Located about a mile above Rainbow Falls.

Hilo Hawaiian Hotel　　HOTEL $$
(Map p262; ☏935-9361, 800-367-5004; www.castleresorts.com; 71 Banyan Dr; r $155-240, ste from $315; ✳@☎) Location, location. Hilo's biggest hotel's major attribute is its prime location across from Lili'uokalani Park. It's also an apt choice for those who prefer a largish hotel feel, especially with the spiffy lobby and restaurant renovations in 2010. Rooms are standard, not plush, but oceanfront units afford fantastic bay views. No wi-fi. Book online for rooms at $105 to $135 and one-bedroom suites at $255 to $285.

Uncle Billy's Hilo Bay Hotel　　HOTEL $
(Map p262; ☏935-0861, 800-442-5841; www.unclebilly.com; 87 Banyan Dr; r $73-114; ✳☎☎) Family-owned and operated by three generations, Uncle Billy's is a bargain. It's not fancy, but the rooms overlook a central courtyard of palms, red ginger and talkative mynah birds – or the ocean (where else can you get an ocean view for just over $100?). Expect a no-frills hotel in a terrific location.

Ⓣ TOP CHOICE Hilo Bay Hostel　　HOSTEL $
(Map p266; ☏933-2771; www.hawaiihostel.net; 101 Waianuenue Ave; dm $27, r with shared/private bath-

room $67/77; 🛜) A backpacker's dream, this hostel is virtually faultless. Perfectly situated downtown (within walking distance of almost everything), it occupies an airy historic building with hardwood floors, remarkably clean restrooms and a kitchen in which you could cook Thanksgiving dinner. Staff are friendly but rule sticklers (after the 11am checkout time you must leave the premises). The crowd is older and diverse, creating a low-key, relaxed vibe.

Arnott's Lodge
HOSTEL $

(Map p262; ☎969-7097; www.arnottslodge.com; 98 Apapane Rd; dm $25, r with shared/private bathroom $60/70; 🛜) Hilo's longest-running hostel remains solid value, with a variety of lodging options. The private and semi-private rooms are ideal for groups. Now that other hostels have sprung up it's less crowded here, which might be to your advantage. Fringe benefits, such as free Sunday pizza and beer, add to the free-spirited camaraderie. Guests can book their tours (eg Mauna Kea) at a discount.

Hilo Tropical Gardens Guest House
HOSTEL $

(Map p262; ☎217-9650; www.hilogardens.com; 1477 Kalaniana'ole Ave; dm $25, d with shared bathroom $55-65; 🛜) Dorm and private rooms are tiny, but the lush garden setting is delightful. Pitch a tent (single/double $15/20) and suddenly you're camping in a jungle. Located behind Hilo Homemade Ice Cream store.

✖ Eating & Drinking

TOP
CHOICE **Miyo's**
JAPANESE $$

(Map p262; ☎935-2273; Waiakea Villas, 400 Hualani St; dinner mains $11-15; ⊙11am-2pm & 5:30-8:30pm Mon-Sat) While slightly scruffy in broad daylight, Miyo's resembles a rustic Japanese teahouse, with shoji doors opening toward Waiakea Pond. The tasty home cooking features the classics, from grilled *saba* (mackerel) to *tonkatsu* (breaded pork cutlets), with traditional sides plus fresh green salad. Especially recommended are the daily fish specials (try the locally caught whole fish).

Kuhio Grille
DINER $$

(Map p262; ☎959-2336; Suite A106, Prince Kuhio Plaza, 111 E Puainako St; mains $8.50-17; ⊙6am-10pm Sun-Thu, to midnight Fri & Sat) When in Hilo, eat as the Hiloans eat – at this unanimous-favorite, family-run diner. The fluffy

pancakes, fried-rice *loco moco* and especially the 1lb *laulau* (bundle of pork or chicken and salted butterfish, wrapped in taro and *ti* leaves and steamed) plates do lip-smacking justice to local *grinds* (food).

Café Pesto
HAWAII REGIONAL $$$

(Map p266; ☎969-6640; S Hata Bldg, 308 Kamehameha Ave; pizzas $12-20, dinner $20-30; ⊙11am-9pm Sun-Thu, to 10pm Fri & Sat) Café Pesto is a safe choice, whether for business lunches, shared pizzas or dinner with your mother-in-law. Set downtown in a lovely historic building, the versatile kitchen features local ingredients in risottos, stir-fries, pastas and salads. Its supposedly wood-fired pizzas need crust makeovers, however.

Hilo Bay Cafe
HAWAII REGIONAL $$$

(Map p262; ☎935-4939; Waiakea Center, 315 Maka'ala St; mains $15-26; ⊙11am-9pm Mon-Sat, from 5pm Sun) Foodies adore this urban-chic eatery incongruously located near a Wal-Mart. The eclectic menu features local ingredients, from organically grown produce to free-range meats. The youthful chef's creative combinations include seared macadamia-crusted scallops, blackened pork tenderloin with risotto cake, and Guinness onion rings with balsamic ketchup. Limited veggie selection.

🌿 Seaside Restaurant
SEAFOOD $$$

(Map p262; ☎935-8825; www.seasiderestaurant .com; 1790 Kalaniana'ole Ave; meals $22-33; ⊙4:30-8:30pm Tue-Thu, to 9pm Fri & Sat) Nowadays, once-lowly mullet is appearing on gourmet menus. But this family-run restaurant has raised its mullet (plus *aholehole*, rainbow trout and catfish) in Hawaiian-style fishponds since 1921. Fresh fish can't get any fresher. However, don't expect a fancy dining experience. It's a humble place with plain dinnerware and homey full meals of fish (try the *ti* leaf–wrapped steamed mullet), rice, salad, apple pie and coffee.

Restaurant Miwa
JAPANESE $$

(Map p262; ☎961-4454; Hilo Shopping Center, 1261 Kilauea Ave; sushi $5-8, meals $9-17; ⊙lunch & dinner) Tucked away in a nondescript mall, Miwa excels in Japanese classics. Generous *teishoku* (full meal) platters include miso soup, rice, tea and two mains, such as grilled *saba*, teriyaki chicken and *tonkatsu*. The setting is diner casual, but the kimono-clad servers are a nice touch. Expect no surprises here, just satisfaction.

HOME ON WHEELS: VW CAMPERS

For nostalgia or novelty, rent a VW camper and 'glamp' it. **Happy Campers Hawaii** (☑896-8777, 888-550-3918; www.happycampershawaii.com; rental per 24hr $125) rents impressively restored VW Westfalia pop-top campers that sleep up to four. At $125 per day, they're a steal, with built-in kitchenettes, sink with running water, cookware, bedding and more. Pick up and drop off in Hilo.

TOP CHOICE Suisan Fish Market   MARKET $

(Map p262; ☑935-9349; 93 Lihiwai St; poke per lb $13; ☺8am-5pm Mon-Fri, to 4pm Sat) Walk inside, take a whiff, and you know you're in a fish market here. Fortunately everything is just-caught fresh. The variety of *poke* (sold by the pound) can be overwhelming, but the *shoyu* ahi or *limu* ahi recipes are especially yummy. If you've never tried dried fish, we recommend the dried marlin, deliciously tender and flaky. On the go, a *poke* and rice bowl ($5 to $7) makes a tasty, portable meal.

Short N Sweet   BAKERY & CAFE $

(Map p266; ☑935-4446; www.shortnsweet.biz; Kino'ole St; pastries $1.50-5, sandwiches $7; ☺8am-4:30pm Mon-Fri, to 3pm Sat & Sun) Originally located in Hawi, pastry chef Maria Short now satisfies Hilo's sweet tooth. We dare you to resist her 'homemade Oreo' or anything with tart-sweet *liliko'i*! She turns out an impressive array of pastries and specialty cakes (including showstopping wedding masterpieces), plus breads, gourmet focaccia sandwiches and fresh salads. With both indoor and outdoor tables, this bakery-cafe also makes a pleasant, low-key hangout spot.

Nori's Saimin & Snacks   JAPANESE $

(Map p262; ☑935-9133; Suite 124, 688 Kino'ole St; noodle soups $4-7; ☺11:30am-3pm Mon, 10:30am-3pm & 4pm-midnight Tue-Sat, 10:30am-11pm Sun) Ignore the strip-mall setting. Focus on the Japanese noodle soups, tasty, filling and perfect for rainy days. Rippled saimin have an irresistibly chewy bite. Beware of spotty service.

Ocean Sushi Deli   SUSHI $$

(Map p266; ☑961-6625; 239 Keawe St; 6-piece rolls $3-6, meals $12-14; ☺10am-2pm & 5:30-9pm Mon-Sat) Think sushi deli, not sushi bar. This means zero decor, rushed service and cheap eats. The rolls fall short of excellent, but they're good and creative, featuring fresh fish with macadamia nuts or tropical fruit, *poke* (cubed, marinated raw fish) or even chicken *katsu* (fried cutlets) tucked inside. Service and quality can slip during rush hours.

Ken's House of Pancakes   DINER $$

(Map p262; ☑935-8711; 1730 Kamehameha Ave; meals $6-12; ☺24hr) The interior resembles any diner anywhere, but there's something comforting about a 24-hour diner with a mile-long menu. Choose from mac-nut pancakes, Spam omelettes, *kalua* (cooked in an underground pit) pig plates and steaming bowls of saimin.

Sombat's Fresh Thai Cuisine   THAI $$

(Map p262; ☑936-8849; 88 Kanoelehua Ave; dishes $8-16; ☺10:30am-2pm Mon-Fri & 5-8:30pm Mon-Sat) Eat healthy Thai classics made with local produce and fresh herbs (grown by the chef without pesticides). Sauces are never cloying, and the menu offers many veg options, such as a refreshing green-papaya salad. The location is ho-hum, in a sadly deserted commercial building. Ideal for takeout.

Sputniks   BAKERY, TAKEOUT $

(Map p262; ☑961-2066; 811 Laukapu St; doughnuts 80¢; ☺6:30am-2pm Mon-Fri) You haven't tasted buttermilk doughnuts until you've tried the rich, dense beauties from this third-generation family business. Another standout: achingly soft, moist, butter rolls. For a unique burger experience, try a memorable Sputnik burger, based on the Russian *pirozhki* (the owner wanted a name that locals could pronounce). Plate lunches are generously portioned.

Queen's Court   AMERICAN, HAWAIIAN $$$

(Map p262; ☑935-9361, 800-367-5004; www.castleresorts.com; ground fl, Hilo Hawaiian Hotel, 71 Banyan Dr; breakfast mains $8-10, dinner buffets $37.50; ☺6:30am-9:30am & 5:30-8pm daily, to 9pm Fri-Sun) Frequented by local businessfolk, retirees and big eaters, this hotel restaurant is like a familiar favorite aunt. It won't wow you with cutting-edge cuisine, but the weekend seafood or Hawaiian buffets are well prepared and all-you-can-eat (discounts for kids). The weekday prime rib and crab buffet will also satisfy.

Bayfront Coffee, Kava & Tea Co   BAR $

(Map p266; ☑935-1155; www.bayfrontkava.com; 116 Kamehameha Ave; cup $5; ☺10am-9pm Mon-Thu, to 10pm Fri & Sat) If you're curious about kava (*'awa* in Hawaiian), try a cup at this minimalist bar. Friendly bar staff serve freshly brewed, locally grown kava root in coconut shells. Get ready for tingling taste buds and a calm buzz.

Snacks

Hilo has a solution to every snack attack.

Big Island Candies CANDY
(Map p262; 935-8890, 800-935-5510; www.bigislandcandies.com; 585 Hinano St; chocolate-dipped macadamia shortbread cookies $6.75-17; 8:30am-5pm) This immaculate candy factory delights everyone, judging from the hordes of local and tourist shoppers. Taste the chocolate and macadamia confections and you'll be hooked, too.

Two Ladies Kitchen JAPANESE
(Map p266; 961-4766; 274 Kilauea Ave; 8-piece boxes $6; 10am-5pm Wed-Sat) Founded by two Hilo ladies, this hole-in-the-wall makes island-style Japanese *mochi* (sticky rice dessert). House specialty: fresh strawberries wrapped in sweet azuki-bean paste and *mochi*.

Kawate Seed Shop CRACK SEED
(Map p262; 959-8313; 1990 Kino'ole St; 9:30am-4:30pm) From sweet shredded mango to tangy lemon peel, the mouth-watering crack seed collection here can't be beat. This mom-and-pop shop also makes excellent shave ice with unique tropical syrups.

Itsu's Fishing Supplies SHAVE ICE
(Map p262; 935-8082; 810 Pi'ilani St; shave ice $1.50; 8am-5pm Mon-Fri) For generations, this family-run shop has delighted locals of all ages with soft-as-snow shave ice. The 'rainbow' (tri-flavor) is a classic.

Hilo Homemade Ice Cream ICE CREAM
(Map p262; 217-9650; 1477 Kalaniana'ole Ave; scoops $3.50; 11am-6pm) To or from the beach, stop here for creamy, dreamy flavors, including macadamia nut, Kona coffee and only-in-Hawaii *poha* berry.

Aaron's Blue Kalo CHIPS
(Map p262; 935-8085; 71 Banyan Dr; chips per bag $5-10; 9am-5:30pm Mon-Sat) Discover the yumminess of *kalo, 'ulu,* and purple and yellow sweet potato handmade chips. Cookies, too, feature island root veggies. Also sold at the Kino'ole Farmers Market.

Groceries

Besides Hilo's two farmers markets, we recommended these grocery stores:

TOP CHOICE / KTA Super Store GROCERY
Downtown (Map p266; 935-3751; 323 Keawe St; 7am-9pm Mon-Sat, to 6pm Sun); Puainako Town Center (Map p262; 959-9111; 50 E Puainako St; 5:30am-midnight) Excellent, locally owned chain carries a wide selection of mainstream groceries plus an impressive deli with fresh *poke, bento* (box meals of grilled mackerel or salmon, teriyaki beef or sushi) and other ready-to-eat items, which sell out by mid-morning.

Abundant Life Natural Foods GROCERY
(Map p266; 935-7411; 292 Kamehameha Ave; 8:30am-7pm Mon, Tue, Thu & Fri, 7am-7pm Wed & Sat, 10am-5pm Sun) Longtime downtown indie with takeout cafe (closes about 1½ hours ahead of the store) serves smoothies and wholesome sandwiches, from tamari-baked tofu to curried albacore tuna.

Island Naturals GROCERY
(Map p262; 935-5533; Hilo Shopping Center, 1221 Kilauea Ave; smoothies $3-3.75, deli dishes per lb $7; 8:30am-8pm Mon-Sat, 10am-7pm Sun) Large, well-stocked Big Island chain with a smoothie counter and gourmet deli.

☆ Entertainment

Nightlife in Hilo? Occasionally the East Hawai'i Cultural Center and Palace Theater present worthy live perfomances, but Hilo generally shuts down early.

Palace Theater THEATER
(Map p266; 934-7010, box office 934-7777; www.hilopalace.com; 38 Haili St; movie tickets $7) This resurrected, historic theater is Hilo's cultural crown jewel. Its eclectic programming includes arthouse and silent films (accompanied by the house organ), music and dance concerts, Broadway musicals and cultural festivals. On Wednesday mornings (from 11am to noon) it hosts *Hawai'iana Live* (adult/child $5/free), a touching, small-town intro to Hawaiian culture through storytelling, film, music, *oli* (chant) and hula.

For first-run movies:

Kress Cinemas CINEMA
(Map p266; 935-6777; 174 Kamehameha Ave; tickets $1.50-1.75) This awesome bargain theater is located smack downtown.

Stadium Cinemas CINEMA
(Map p262; 959-4595; Prince Kuhio Plaza, 111 E Puainako St; tickets adult/child 3-11yr/matinee $9.50/6.25/7.50) Popular with local teens and kids; typical shopping-mall cinemas.

LOCAL LUNCH FAVORITES

Okazu-ya

Pack a Hilo-style picnic with tasty bites from an *okazu-ya*, akin to a Japanese deli. These small shops are typically hole-in-the-wall family businesses selling dozens of prepared dishes, including *musubi* (rice balls), *maki* (rolled) sushi, stir-fried noodles, tofu patties, shrimp and vegetable tempura, *nishime* (root-vegetable stew), teriyaki beef, broiled mackerel, Korean or nori chicken, BBQ beef and countless other foodstuffs.

Arrive by midmorning for a decent selection; bring cash. Vegetarians won't go hungry but *okazu-ya* are geared for meat eaters.

Kawamoto Store

(Map p262; ☑935-8209; 784 Kilauea Ave; ☉6am-12:30pm Tue-Sun) Hole-in-the-wall with all the local favorites displayed in old-fashioned screened wood shelves.

Hilo Lunch Shop

(Map p262; ☑935-8273; 421 Kalanikoa St; ☉5:30am-1pm Tue-Sat) A larger operation with an excellent selection.

Loco Moco & Plate Lunches

Hearty appetites will meet their match with Hilo's famous *loco moco* (rice topped with a hamburger patty, two fried eggs and an obscene dollop of brown gravy) and plate lunches. Here are two go-to spots:

Koji's Bento Korner

(Map p266; ☑935-1417; 52 Ponahawai St; loco moco $3.25-7.50; ☉7am-2pm Mon-Fri, from 9am Sat) Also known for standout *loco moco*; the Koji *loco*, with two homemade hamburger patties, teriyaki sauce and gravy, one egg, two Portuguese sausages, macaroni salad and kimchee ($7.50) is the stuff of local cravings.

Cafe 100

(Map p262; ☑935-8683; 969 Kilauea Ave; loco moco $2-5, plate lunches $5-7; ☉6:45am-8:30pm Mon-Sat) Famous for their 20 rib-sticking varieties of *loco moco*. Thumbs up for low cost (from $2 for the original *loco*) and for fish and veggie burger options. The open-air patio, with picnic tables seating leisurely diners in T-shirts and rubbah slippahs (flip-flops), spells H-I-L-O.

🛍 Shopping

While locals flock to the chain-heavy malls south of the airport, downtown is far better for unique shops.

🖉 Sig Zane Designs   CLOTHING

(Map p266; www.sigzane.com; 122 Kamehameha Ave; ☉9:30am-5pm Mon-Fri, 9am-4pm Sat) Legendary in the hula community, Sig Zane creates iconic custom fabrics, marked by rich colors and graphic prints of Hawaiian flora. You can spot a 'Sig' a mile away. Pricey, but this is real art.

TOP CHOICE Extreme Exposure Fine Art Gallery   GALLERY

(Map p266; www.extremeexposure.com; 224 Kamehameha Ave; ☉10am-5:30pm) Sure, your pocket camera does fine, but check out this gallery for stunning shots of Hawai'i's great outdoors, notably Kilauea's spectacular lava displays. Showcasing the work of two Hilo-born photographers, the shop caters to all budgets, from framed prints to greeting cards.

Alan's Art & Collectibles   ANTIQUES

(Map p266; ☑969-1554; 202 Kamehameha Ave; ☉10am-4:30pm Mon & Wed-Fri, 1-4pm Tue, 10am-3pm Sat) Glimpse old Hawai'i in this chock-full secondhand shop: vintage glassware, household doodads, aloha shirts, vinyl LPs and scattered collectible treasures.

Dragon Mama   HOMEWARES

(Map p266; www.dragonmama.com; 266 Kamehameha Ave; ☉9am-5pm Mon-Fri, to 4pm Sat) Luscious kimonos, unique shirts and custom-made pillows from imported Japanese fabrics; also check out the gorgeous tea sets.

Hilo Guitars & Ukuleles   MUSIC STORE

(Map p266; www.hiloguitars.com; 56 Ponahawai St; ☉10am-5pm Mon-Fri, to 4pm Sat) Wide selection of ukulele, from koa or mahogany classics to far-out brass or electric creations.

Most Irresistible Shop SOUVENIRS
(Map p266; 256 Kamehameha Ave; ⊘9am-5pm Mon-Fri, to 4pm Sat) This long-running gift shop lives up to its name by offering handcrafted jewelry, kids' books, soaps and candles, koa objects, artsy greeting cards and much more.

Bookstores

When Borders closed in 2010, Hilo lost its only large bookstore, but the downtown indies are proving that size isn't everything.

[TOP CHOICE] Basically Books BOOKS
(Map p266; 160 Kamehameha Ave; ⊘9am-5pm Mon-Sat, 11am-3:30pm Sun) A browser's paradise, this shop specializes in maps, travel guides and books about Hawaii. You'll also find an irresistible gamut of gifts and toys.

Book Gallery BOOKS
(Map p266; 259 Keawe St; ⊘9:30am-5pm Mon-Fri, to 3pm Sat) Since 1968 this bookstore has stocked a wide selection of locally published history, cooking and children's titles.

Books, Nooks, & Crannies BOOKS
(Map p266; 14 Waianuenue Ave; ⊘9am-9pm Mon-Thu, to 11pm Fri & Sat, 1-7pm Sun) Find national new releases, bestsellers, history and Hawaiiana at this cozy spot, complete with coffee bar and comfy couches.

ⓘ Information

Dangers & Annoyances

COQUI FROGS This invasive species has spread across Hilo. If you are bothered by noise at night, when they are most vocal, bring earplugs. Better yet, inquire before booking accommodations whether there are coquis within earshot. See p278 for more.

Internet Access

Hilo Public Library (☎933-8888; www.librarieshawaii.org; 300 Waianuenue Ave; ⊘11am-7pm Tue & Wed, 9am-5pm Thu & Sat, 10am-5pm Fri; @) If you buy a three-month nonresident library card ($10), you can use free internet terminals and check out books.

Medical Services

Hilo Medical Center (☎974-4700, emergency room 974-6800; 1190 Waianuenue Ave; ⊘24hr emergency) Near Rainbow Falls.

KTA Super Store (☎959-9111, pharmacy 959-8700; Puainako Town Center, 50 E Puainako St; ⊘pharmacy 8am-7pm Mon-Fri, from 9am Sat) Supermarket with pharmacy.

Longs Drugs Kilauea Ave (☎935-3357, pharmacy 935-9075; 555 Kilauea Ave; ⊘pharmacy 7am-7pm Mon-Fri, to 6pm Sat, 8am-5pm Sun); Prince Kuhio Plaza (☎959-5881, pharmacy 959-4508; 111 E Puainako St; ⊘pharmacy 8am-8pm Mon-Fri, to 7pm Sat, to 5pm Sun) General store and pharmacy.

Money

All banks in Hilo have 24-hour ATMs.

Bank of Hawaii Kawili St (☎961-0681; 417 E Kawili St); Pauahi St (☎935-9701; 120 Pauahi St)

First Hawaiian Bank (☎969-2222; 120 Waianuenue Ave)

Police

Police (☎935-3311; 349 Kapi'olani St) For nonemergencies.

Post

Both post offices hold general-delivery mail, but require you to complete an application in person.

Downtown post office (Map p266; ☎933-3014; 154 Waianuenue Ave; ⊘9am-4pm Mon-Fri, 12:30-2pm Sat) Located in the Federal Building.

Main post office (Map p262; ☎933-3019; 1299 Kekuanaoa St; ⊘8am-4:30pm Mon-Fri, 9am-12:30pm Sat) Located near Hilo airport.

Tourist Information

Big Island Visitors Bureau (Map p266; ☎961-5797, 800-648-2441; www.bigisland.org; 250 Keawe St) Basic info and business brochures available. See website for events calendar.

ⓘ Getting There & Away

AIR Hilo International Airport (ITO; ☎934-5838; www.state.hi.us/dot/airports/hawaii/ito) All flights to Hilo are interisland except for two Continental Airlines routes, which fly directly from Los Angeles and from San Francisco.

BUS Hele-On Bus (www.heleonbus.org) The main Hilo station is the **Mo'oheau terminal** (Map p262; 329 Kamehameha Ave), where all intraisland buses originate. Check the website for current routes and schedules.

CAR & MOTORCYCLE The drive from Hilo to Kailua-Kona (via Waimea) is 92 miles and takes 2½ hours. See the Directory for information on car and motorcycle rentals.

If you're driving from Hilo to Mauna Kea, the fastest route is Puainako St, which leads into Saddle Rd. You'll shorten your travel time and reduce traffic on the winding, residential Kaumana Dr.

ⓘ Getting Around

TO/FROM THE AIRPORT Rental-car booths and taxis are located right outside the baggage-claim area. The approximate cab fare from the airport to downtown Hilo is $15.

BICYCLE Cycling is more recreation than transportation in Hilo.

Da Kine Bike Shop (☏934-9861; www.bicycle hawaii.com; 18 Furneaux Lane; ⊙noon-6pm Mon-Fri, 9am-3pm Sat) Reasonable rates for used bikes; call first for availability. Also runs custom cycling tours.

Mid-Pacific Wheels (☏935-6211; www.mid pacificwheels.com; 1133-C Manono St; ⊙9am-6pm Mon-Sat, 11am-5pm Sun) Large shop rents mountain bikes for $15 to $20 per day.

BUS Here are a few popular routes, but check the **Hele-On Bus** (www.heleonbus.org) website for all routes and schedules:

Bus 4 Kaumana Goes to Hilo Public Library and Hilo Medical Center.

Bus 6 Waiakea-Uka Goes to the University of Hawai'i at Hilo and Prince Kuhio Plaza.

Bus 7 Downtown Hilo Goes to Prince Kuhio Plaza.

CAR & MOTORCYCLE Free parking is generally available. Downtown street parking is free for two hours; finding a spot is easy except during Saturday and Wednesday farmers markets.

TAXI Call **Marshall's Taxi** (☏936-2654) or **Percy's Taxi** (☏969-7060).

PUNA

Smack in the path of the live lava flow and home to hippies, funky artists, alternative healers, Hawaiian sovereignty activists, *pakalolo* growers, organic farmers and off-the-grid survivalists, Puna is laid-back and cool, but it's also intense. The land vibrates with energy; emotions and creativity run high.

One settles here only by accepting wildness and impermanence as the price. Puna retains dense, unspoiled portions of sometimes hallucinatory jungle as well as long-gone neighborhoods now blanketed by a thick mass of black lava. Sultry and hang-loose Puna encourages travelers to ditch the guidebook and go with the flow.

Once the Big Island frontier, these days Puna is the fastest-growing district in the state. It has some of Hawaii's most affordable land, in subdivisions that were marked out more than 50 years ago and sparsely settled – until now. The northern half of Puna is becoming one unending suburban subdivision, with the population poised to almost

double within a decade. Most agree Puna faces an infrastructure crisis, not to mention an identity crisis. The fast food/chain store shopping mall erected at the terminus of Pahoa's historic downtown in 2010 – protested by some – is indicative of the schism.

Kea'au & Around

POP 2330

Heading down the 'hill' from Volcano towards Hilo, you whisk past blink-and-miss communities that were once sugar plantations but now are home to booming subdivisions. For travelers there are some worthy lodgings tucked away in these parts, making it an attractive base midway between Hilo, Volcano and Puna. The main town servicing these communities is Kea'au, a cluster of gas stations and stores just off Hwy 11 – provision here before heading to Volcano; the two general stores there charge an arm and a leg for a loaf of bread.

◉ Sights & Activities

FREE **Fuku-Bonsai Cultural Center** GARDEN (☏982-9880; www.fukubonsai.com; 17-856 Ola'a Rd) This working nursery cultivates the art of Japanese bonsai; tour impressive outdoor displays of these miniature trees. The specialty, dwarf schefflera, have aerial roots like handheld banyan trees; it's a kooky shift in perspective. The access road is just past the 10-mile marker on Hwy 11.

Dan DeLuz's Woods WOODWORK STUDIO (☏968-6607; www.deluzwoods.com; Hwy 11; ⊙9am-5pm) Learn as you browse at this studio and shop where master woodworker Dan takes native hardwoods such as koa, sandalwood, mango and banyan and crafts gorgeous bowls, platters and furniture.

Hilo Coffee Mill CAFE, COFFEE MILL (☏968-1333, 866-982-5551; www.hilocoffeemill .com; 17-995 Hwy 11; ⊙7am-4pm Mon-Sat; ⊛) Taste East Hawai'i coffee and take a short, free tour at this mill-cafe with a breezy lanai for enjoying tasty sandwiches and a cup of joe.

ⓖ Tours

TOP CHOICE **Harry Schick** CAVE TOURS (☏967-7208; www.fortunecity.com/oasis/ang kor/176; off Volcano Hwy, past 22-mile marker; tours from $20; ⊙by appointment) Since discovering his property lies atop the Kazumura Cave –

the world's longest lava tube – Schick has become an expert on lava caves and gives small tours (four to six people max) at low cost. On the shortest, easiest tour, participants must climb ladders and walk over rocky terrain. Check out the lava falls and maze tours. Age 10 and above.

Kilauea Caverns of Fire CAVE TOURS
(📞217-2363; www.kilaueacavernsoffire.com; 1-/3-hour tours $29/79; ⊘by appointment). A more impersonal tour through Kazumura Cave; choose from an easy one-hour walk or a three-hour scramble. Call for reservations and directions.

🛏 Sleeping

TOP CHOICE **Art & Orchids B&B** B&B $$
(📞982-8197, 877-393-1894; www.artandorchids.com; 16-1504 39th Ave; r incl breakfast $95-125; 🛜❄) This dreamy, relaxed haven set in an ohia forest is Puna at its best. Three airy (albeit frumpy) rooms here include funky mosaic-tile baths and tons of amenities. The spacious common room has a full kitchen and cozy couches, plus there's a unique lava-rock-and-mosaic-tile swimming pool with a hot tub out back. Papermaking and mosaic classes are available, and you can make your own art in the garden gazebo. The generous homemade breakfast includes hosts Markie and Jerry's eggs. This is one of the island's top 'green' properties.

Butterfly Inn INN $
(📞966-7936, 800-546-2442; www.thebutterflyinn.com; Kurtistown; s/d with shared bathroom $55/65) Since 1987 owners Kay and Patty have welcomed women to stay at their comfortable home in Kurtistown. Two tidy rooms with private entrance share an ample kitchen, living room, dining deck, bathroom and outdoor hot tub. Single female travelers will appreciate the safe, supportive environment.

Pahoa

POP 1120

If Puna is a state of mind, Pahoa is its heart – a ramshackle, ragamuffin town with raised wooden sidewalks, peeling paint and an unkempt bohemian edge. It's full of oddballs and eccentrics and gentle, genuine aloha.

👁 Sights

Maku'u Craft & Farmers Market MARKET
(www.makuufarmersassociation.org; ⊘8am-2pm Sun) Join the entire Puna 'ohana (family) at the Maku'u Craft & Farmers Market on Hwy 130 between the 7-mile and 8-mile markers. It's more like a massive village party than a market, with psychics, wood carvings, massage, old junk, surfboard repair, orchids, organic honey, sarongs and jewelry, photos of the Kalapana eruption and even fruits and vegetables. Hot food includes Hawaiian, Samoan, Mexican and Thai cuisine, and more. Morning **cultural workshops** (9am) give way to live music through the afternoon. Don't miss it.

Pahoa Museum MUSEUM
(http://pahoavillagemuseum.net; 15-2931 Pahoa Village Rd; suggested donation $3; ⊘10am-5pm) This sweet and tidy museum showcases Puna history and culture in all its splendid diversity, exhibits local artists and spearheads neighborhood involvement through projects such as the blossoming Community Garden. Donations are badly needed at this grassroots nonprofit.

🏃 Activities

Pahoa Community Aquatic Center POOL
(Kauhale St; ⊘8:30am-5:10am Mon-Fri, 9am-4:40pm Sat & Sun) For swimming, head for the gorgeous outdoor, heated Olympic-size pool behind the Pahoa Neighborhood Facility; it has nice showers and a separate kids' pool.

Jeff Hunt Surfboards SURFING
(15-2883 Pahoa Village Rd; ⊘10am-5pm Mon-Sat, 11am-3pm Sun) Jeff Hunt is one of the island's best board shapers, and at his little hut you can buy one, talk surfing and rent soft-top boards (per day $25).

TOP CHOICE **Paradissimo Tropical Spa** DAY SPA
(📞965-8883; www.spaparadissimo.com; 15-2950 Pahoa Village Rd; facials from $25) In our estimation, there's no better way to spend a rainy afternoon than getting a good pampering here. Owner Olivia is a tender soul with talented hands and the organic spa products she uses feel like a magical alchemy for the skin. Sauna and massage also available.

👉 Tours

Getting close to the lava on land or sea, birdwatching or discovering pockets of tranquility and unbridled nature along the Puna coast are highlights of guided tours in this area. Although many outfits and individuals offer cheaper outings, these are the best:

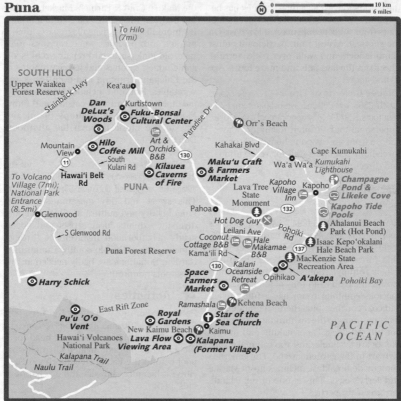

0 10 km
0 6 miles

SOUTH HILO

Upper Waiakea Forest Reserve

To Hilo (7mi)

Kea'au

Kurtistown

Dan DeLuz's Woods

Fuku-Bonsai Cultural Center

Mountain View

Hilo Coffee Mill

South Kulani Rd

Art & Orchids B&B

Orr's Beach

Kahakai Blvd

Cape Kumukahi

Kumukahi Lighthouse

To Volcano Village (7mi); National Park Entrance (8.5mi)

Hawai'i Belt Rd

Kilauea Caverns of Fire

PUNA

Maku'u Craft & Farmers Market

Wa'a Wa'a

Glenwood

Pahoa

Lava Tree State Monument

Kapoho Village Inn

Kapoho

Champagne Pond & Likeke Cove

Kapoho Tide Pools

Hot Dog Guy

S Glenwood Rd

Leilani Ave

Coconut Cottage B&B

Kama'ili Rd

Hale Makamae B&B

Pohoiki Rd

Ahalanui Beach Park (Hot Pond)

Isaac Kepo'okalani Hale Beach Park

Puna Forest Reserve

Harry Schick

Space Farmers Market

Kalani Oceanside Retreat

Opihikao

A'akepa

MacKenzie State Recreation Area

Pohoiki Bay

East Rift Zone

Ramashala

Kehena Beach

PACIFIC OCEAN

Pu'u 'O'o Vent

Royal Gardens

New Kaimu Beach

Star of the Sea Church

Kaimu

Hawai'i Volcanoes National Park

Lava Flow Viewing Area

Kalapana (Former Village)

Kalapana Trail

Naulu Trail

HAWAI'I THE BIG ISLAND PUNA

TOP CHOICE Lava Ocean Adventures   LAVA BOAT TOURS

(966-4200; www.lavaocean.com; tours adult/child 6-12yr $180/125) Getting so close to the lava ocean entry aboard the *Lava Kai* that you feel the heat and smell the sulphur is an unforgettable experience. These expertly narrated tours motor from Pohoiki Bay to the sea entry near Kalapana, where you'll see lava gushing into the ocean, boiling it on contact. For 30 minutes watch as live lava chunks explode underwater, getting churned into a water–molten rock 'smoothie' while a new black-sand beach is built – simply awesome. Go for the sunrise tour and you'll be escorted by flying fish, leaping dolphins and maybe even a rainbow.

Native Guide Hawaii   NATURE TOURS

(982-7575; www.nativeguidehawaii.com; tour incl lunch $150; ⊙by appointment) Tours with native Hawaiian and cultural practitioner

Warren Costa are different. He's trained, personal, professional and he knows his land well. All day volcano, coastal or birding tours reveal Puna mysteries you won't unravel on your own.

🛌 Sleeping

Coconut Cottage B&B   B&B $$

(965-0973, 866-204-7444; www.coconutcottage hawaii.com; 13-1139 Leilani Ave; r incl breakfast $110-140; @🔊) South of Pahoa in a trim residential neighborhood, this romantic, four-room B&B is full of sweet Balinese accents and little luxuries. The garden hot tub in a tiki hut and the breezy porch are attractive places to relax, a sensation that's cultivated by the warm, gracious hosts. Rooms are comfortably cozy; the largest is the detached bungalow with kitchenette. Breakfast is a feast.

Hale Makamae B&B   B&B $$

(965-7015; www.bnb-aloha.com; 13-3315 Maka mae St; studio incl breakfast $100, 1-/2-bedroom ste

$135/155; @ 🛜) In a clean-cut neighborhood, this B&B is immaculate, family-friendly and a bargain to boot. The suites are especially comfy, with well-equipped kitchenettes and enough space to kick back. All accommodations have separate entrance onto lush gardens. Hot breakfast is served in a breakfast room bursting with orchids. Hosts are fluent in German.

JoMamas Pahoa Town Hostel   HOSTEL $
(📋430-1573; www.jomamahawaii.com; Pahoa Village Rd; s/d $35/50; 🛜) This hostel on Pahoa's main drag makes a good crash pad. The rooms, while basic, are private, bathrooms and kitchen are shared and the gardens and lanai are spiffy. No drugs or alcohol.

Island Paradise Inn   HOTEL $
(📋990-0234; www.islandparadiseinn.com; 15-2937 Pahoa Village Rd; d $40; 🛜) Smack downtown, this inn is actually a row of former plantation-worker houses that's been converted into 20 small, clean and very affordable rooms, all with private bathroom and kitchenette. Decor varies; pleasing touches (fluffy towels, stained glass) are combined with secondhand bureaus and furniture displaying various nicks and scratches. Three-night minimum stay.

Pahoa Town House   INN $
(📋937-0588; www.kapohovillageinn.com/id69 .html; 15-2881 Pahoa Village Rd; d $60; 🛜) Recently renovated and run with the same efficiency as the Kapoho Village Inn (p278), the owners' other property.

🍴 Eating

Don't be fooled by Pahoa's Earth Mama, grow-your-own-sprouts vibe: there is some notable dining here – fine, but casual. This is a good area to try roadside *huli huli* (rotisserie) chicken or ahi jerky.

Kaleo's Bar & Grill   HAWAII REGIONAL $$
(📋965-5600; 15-2969 Pahoa Village Rd; lunch mains $9-16, dinner mains $12-25; ⊙9am-8:30pm; 🛜) Overheard in Volcano: 'Kaleo's is one of the island's best restuarants.' We might not go *that* far, but the tempura ahi roll, orzo pasta salad, and kalua pork and cabbage showcase the fresh, creative fare that's a staple here. Live music most nights.

Pahoa's Village Café   DINER $
(📋965-1133; 15-2471 Pahoa Village Rd; mains $7-13; ⊙11am-7pm Mon & Tue, 8am-midnight Wed-Sat, 7am-7pm Sun; 🛜) This attractive cafe with a central courtyard serves good-quality diner food: burgers, plate lunches, *loco moco* etc. There's a seriously cheap and fun happy

hour (free pool!) and live music Wednesday to Sunday nights.

Ning's Thai Cuisine   THAI $
(15-2955 Pahoa Village Rd; mains $10-14; ⊙noon-9pm Mon-Sat, from 5pm Sun; 🖉) Accomplished Thai is served up at this little spot; save room for the *liliko'i* or ginger ice cream.

Paolo's Bistro   ITALIAN $$
(Pahoa Village Rd; mains $13-26; ⊙5:30-9pm Tue-Sun) An intimate place serving a well-executed menu of authentic northern Italian cooking. Bring your own *vino*.

Island Naturals   HEALTH FOOD $
(15-1403 Pahoa Village Rd; ⊙7:30am-7:30pm Mon-Sat, 8am-7pm Sun; 🖉) For organic produce and picnic lunches; this place has a fresh, interesting range of sandwiches, packaged salads, baked goods and hot food.

🍷 Drinking & Entertainment

Akebono Theater   LIVE MUSIC
(📋965-9205; Pahoa Village Rd, behind Luquins; tickets $10-20) This historical theater hosts all kinds of music, from Big Island Elvis to visiting jam bands. On Sundays a small **farmers market** (⊙8am-1pm) is held in the parking lot.

Luquin's Mexican Restaurant   BAR
(📋965-9990; 15-2942 Pahoa Village Rd; mains $10-19; ⊙7am-9pm) The Mexican option, with standard plate combos. Its hopping bar does a brisk business in margaritas ($14 per pint; try the *lilko'i* number).

ℹ️ Information

Just off the main highway, north of the historic downtown, is Pahoa Marketplace – a shopping mall with a good grocery store, hardware store and fresh-fish monger (the fish and chips here are five star). Also here is **Paradise Business Center** (internet per hr $5; ⊙8:30am-5:30pm Mon-Fri, 9am-1:30pm Sat; @), with internet access, computer parts and postal services. Across the highway is a contentious new shopping center with a giant **Long's Drugs.**

Along the main street in town is a convenience store, banks, gas stations and a **post office** (15-2859 Pahoa Village Rd), as well as **Sirius Coffee** (⊙7am-6pm Mon-Fri, 7am-4pm Sat & Sun; @ 🛜) with internet access ($3 per 30 minutes), espresso coffee and baked goods ($2 to $5).

ℹ️ Getting There & Away

Hele-On Bus (www.heleonbus.org) goes from Hilo to Kea'au and Pahoa 11 times a day Monday to Friday, and four times on Saturday.

THOSE DAMN COQUI

Hawaii's most wanted alien is the Puerto Rican coqui frog, only an inch long. Why? *Da buggah* is loud! At sunset, coquis begin their nightly chirping (a two-tone 'ko-kee' call), which can register between 90 and 100 decibels from 2ft away. Even at a distance their chorus maintains 70 decibels, equivalent to a vacuum cleaner. For a demo, visit www .hear.org/AlienSpeciesInHawaii/species/frogs.

Coquis accidentally reached the Hawaiian Islands around 1988, and they've proliferated wildly on the Big Island. Around Lava Tree State Monument, densities are the highest in the state and twice that of Puerto Rico. Besides causing a nightly racket, coquis are disrupting the ecosystem by eating the bugs that feed native birds.

Some homeowners are vigilant about eliminating their habitat, spraying foliage with citric acid or hydrated lime, and searching with flashlights to nail each noisemaker within hearing range. Experts concede it's a losing battle. Light sleepers will want ear plugs.

Lava Tree State Monument

Entering this park (admission free; ☉daylight hours) beneath a tight-knit canopy of (invasive) albizia trees is an otherworldly experience. A short, easy loop **trail** passes through a tropical vision of Middle Earth, full of ferns, orchids and bamboo, and takes you past unusual 'lava trees,' which were created in 1790 when a rain forest was engulfed in *pahoehoe* from Kilauea's East Rift Zone. The lava enveloped the moisture-laden ohia trees and then receded, leaving lava molds of the destroyed trees. These mossy shells now lie scattered like dinosaur bones, adding to the park's ghostly aura. In the late afternoon the love songs of coqui reverberate among the trees. To get here follow Hwy 132 about 2.5 miles east of Hwy 130.

Kapoho

Hwy 132 goes east until it meets Red Rd at Four Corners (where four roads meet) near Kapoho. Once a small farming village, Kapoho became Pele's victim in January 1960 when a volcanic fissure let loose a half-mile-long curtain of fiery lava in a nearby sugarcane field. The main flow of *pahoehoe* ran toward the ocean, but a pokier offshoot of 'a'a crept toward the town, burying orchid farms in its path. Two weeks later the lava buried Kapoho, including nearly 100 homes and businesses.

When the lava approached the sea at Cape Kumukahi, it parted around the lighthouse which, alone, survived. Old-timers say that the lighthouse keeper offered a meal to Pele, who appeared disguised as an old woman on the eve of the disaster, and so she spared the structure.

On Hwy 132, Kapoho Village Inn (☎937-0588; www.kapohovillageinn.com; 14-4587 Kapoho-Pahoa Rd; r/ste $79/99) is an old Kapoho boardinghouse converted by an enthusiastic young couple into three attractive, breezy rooms sharing two bathrooms and a kitchen. There's also a two-bedroom suite available. All have fresh, simple decor, with bent-cane furniture, nice spreads, flatscreen TVs and screened windows. Tiled showers are sparkling clean, and there's a washer/dryer for guest use.

Red Road (Highway 137)

Scenic, winding Hwy 137 is nicknamed Red Rd because its northern portion is paved with red cinder. It's a swooping, atmospheric drive that periodically dips beneath tunnel-like canopies of milo and hala (pandanus) trees. There are many discreet paths to the shore along this road – take one for a private piece of coast.

Two side roads also make intriguing detours or shortcuts back to Pahoa: Pohoiki Rd connects Hwy 137 with Hwy 132, and is another shaded, mystical road winding through thick forest dotted with papaya orchards and wild *noni* (Indian mulberry). Further south, Kama'ili Rd connects with Hwy 130, is another pleasant country ramble. When hunger strikes, pull up to the Hot Dog Guy (intersection of Hwy 132 & Pohoiki Rd; hotdogs $5-7; ☉daily 'when it's not pouring'; 🚶) for some bison, reindeer or all-beef hotdogs grilled to order and nestled in a whole wheat bun.

KAPOHO BEACH LOTS

Top-notch **snorkeling** awaits beyond the locked gates of this seaside community perfect for a family reunion or getaway. The most celebrated spot is **Champagne Pond**, a tranquil protected area with sandy shores frequented by green turtles. To get here, follow Kapoho Beach Rd as it curves around the shore; look for the shore access sign just after 14-5027 Kapoho Beach Rd.

Another stellar snorkeling area is **Likeke Cove**, a small, crystal-clear inlet hemmed in by the walls of luxurious homes and teeming with tropical fish. To get here take Kapoho Beach Rd to Likeke St, turn left and follow the shore access sign to the right.

The **vacation rentals** here are ideal for family getaways, with many houses boasting flexible, multiroom sleeping arrangements. One terrific option is **Pualani** (805-225-1552; www.bigislandhawaiivacationhomes.com; Kapoho Beach Lots; 2-bedroom house $145; @) a modern, open-plan home with hot tub, wrap-around lanai, bikes and beach toys. Another gem is **Hale O Naia** (965-5340; www.hale-o-naia.com; Kapoho Beach Lots; r incl breakfast $90-110, ste $175), which qualifies as a Fantasy Beach House. All units feature gleaming hardwoods, ocean-view lanai, wraparound windows and use of a sauna and whirlpool tub. The sprawling Master Suite is a worthy splurge.

This stretch of coast is technically only open only to those living or renting within its gates, though you can reach Champagne Pond with a 4WD from the Kumukahi Lighthouse.

KAPOHO TIDE POOLS

The best snorkeling on the Big Island's windward side is this sprawling network of **tide pools** (7am-7pm; suggested donation $3) – officially named the Wai Opae Tide Pools Marine Life Conservation District. Here Kapoho's lava-rock coast is a mosaic of protected, shallow, interconnected pools containing a rich variety of sea life. It's easy to pool-hop for hours, tracking saddle wrasses, Moorish idols, butterfly fish, sea cucumbers and much more. For interesting coral gardens, head straight out from the blue house; sea turtles like the warm pocket a bit further south and octopuses are known to visit here.

From Hwy 137, a mile south of the lighthouse, turn onto Kapoho Kai Dr, which winds a little and dead-ends at Wai Opae; turn left and park in the lot. There are no facilities.

This area is also peppered with **vacation rentals**; see www.vrbo.com.

AHALANUI BEACH PARK

It's called 'the hot pond' because of its main attraction – a large, spring-fed **thermal pool** (admission free; 7am-7pm) that's set in lava rock and deep enough for swimming. It's a pretty sweet bathtub: water temperatures average 90°F (cooler with incoming tide), cement borders make for easy access, tropical fish abound and, though the ocean pounds the adjacent seawall, the pool is always calm. However, despite being regularly flushed by the sea, the pond contains a risk of bacterial infection (see the boxed text, p281).

The park gates are never locked – early and late soaking is the best crowd-beating strategy. The park has picnic tables, portable toilets and a lifeguard daily. Don't leave valuables in your car.

WORTH A TRIP

PUNA BACKROADS

The old lighthouse that Pele spared isn't much – just a tall piece of white-painted metal scaffolding. But it's still rewarding to head straight across Four Corners from Hwy 132 and brave the rutted, 1.5-mile dirt road to the end of **Cape Kumukahi**. This is the easternmost point in the state, and the air that blows across it is the freshest in the world (so scientists say). Even better, the lava-covered cliffs make a gorgeous perch to contemplate this meeting of sky, sea and lava. From the parking area, walk the 4WD roads that crisscross the point – all the way to Champagne Pond and other snorkeling spots, if you're up to it.

Turn left, or north, at Four Corners, and time will seem to slow to a stop as you enter a teeming, ancient, vine-draped forest pulsing with mana. The dirt road leads to **Wa'a Wa'a** and is passable for standard cars, but it's cratered, narrow and twisted. Mind the numerous 'Kapu' signs and go slow. After about 5 miles you reach boulder-strewn **Orr's beach** shaded by ironwood trees; park here and scramble along the shore to find a spot for a quiet picnic lunch.

ISAAC KEPO'OKALANI HALE BEACH PARK

Renovations in 2008 have completely changed Isaac Hale (pronounced *ha*-lay). The rocky beach along Pohoiki Bay is, of course, the same, with waves usually too rough for swimming but some of the gnarliest breaks for bodyboarding and surfing. The boat ramp area is still a popular fishing spot, and beyond that, a well-worn path still leads (past a private house) to a small natural **hot pond**. And kids and families still create a frenzy of activity on weekends – check out the **keiki pool** to the right of the boat ramp. But almost everything else is new: the parking lots, the walkways, the picnic tables, the outdoor showers and – most of all – the park across the road from the beach.

Here, the **camping** area is now a pristine lawn, trim as a putting green, with 22 sites, picnic tables, BBQs, and new bathrooms with flush toilets and drinking water. A security guard checks permits and ensures that the park's once semipermanent squatters do not return. What used to be a sketchy place best avoided is now one of Puna's best camping spots (for permit information, see p169). Lava boat tours leave from here (see p275).

MACKENZIE STATE RECREATION AREA

This grove of ironwood trees edging sheer, 40ft cliffs above a restless ocean is another of Puna's moody, mana-imbued pockets. During the day this quiet, secluded park makes an unforgettable picnic spot. Exploring the **lava tube** just back from the precipitous ledge a moment's walk from the pavilion makes a memorable post-lunch adventure. Head into the forest facing the ledge to find the entrance (requires a short, steep descent and a little boulder scrambling); after about 20 minutes walking on uneven, lava rock terrain, you'll be dumped a little ways down and across the road from the park entrance. **Camping** at MacKenzie is allowed (for permits, see p169), but not recommended due to the area's unsettling isolation, making it a site for violent crimes in the past – a long time ago, but the place retains an eerie vibe still.

About half a mile south of here is A'akepa, a hidden, other-wordly expanse of lava flats and tide pools run through with rivers of incoming surf and chartreuse ground cover. Here palm trunk bridges cross little lagoons, lichen and pine needles drip from lava boulders like glaze on a cinnamon bun and patches of white sand invite lounging. Look for the coastal path posted with a government property sign (no, you're not trespassing here).

KEHENA BEACH & AROUND

If any place captures the friendly uninhibited intensity of Puna, it's this beautiful black-sand beach at the base of rocky cliffs and shaded by coconut and ironwood trees. All types and persuasions mix easily – hippies, Hawaiians, gays, families, teens, seniors, tourists. Many come to doff their clothes but, truly, no one cares if you don't. As the drum circle plays, old guys dance with their eyes closed while parents chase their kids in the surf while others meditate, drink, swim and hang out. For a quieter experience, come early to greet the rising sun and watch the resident dolphin pod leap into the air.

The surf is powerful, even when 'calm,' so swim with caution. Deaths occur here every year, and you shouldn't venture beyond the rocky point at the southern end. Kehena is immediately south of the 19-mile marker. From the small parking lot a short, steep path leads down to the beach. Don't leave any valuables in your car.

LGBT PUNA

Along with hosting the island's biggest concentration of non-conformists, outsider artists, new agers and organic farmers, Puna is also the Big Island's gay capital. While there aren't queer bars (yet), you will find cruising and rainbow flags, plus gay-friendly places to stay, workshops and gatherings. This laid-back approach to sexual orientation is also extended to lesbians and bisexuals.

◉ Sights

Space Farmers Market FARMERS MARKET
(www.hawaiispace.com; Seaview Performing Arts Center for Education, 12-247 West Pohakupele Loop; ◷8-11:30am Sat) Closer to the 18-mile marker, the Seaview subdivision is home to this farmers market. More inventive than most, here you'll find everything from tarot readers to tie-dyes and lots of organic produce and prepared foods. To get here, turn into the subdivision, turn right on Mapuana St and left on Kehauopuna St.

Sleeping

Kalani Oceanside Retreat RETREAT $
(☑965-7828, 800-800-6886; www.kalani.com;
tents s/d $40/55, dm $75, d $115-175, treehouse
$265; @ 🛜 ⊠). For the full-on retreat experi-
ence, head north up Hwy 137 (between the
17- and 18-mile markers) to Kalani, which
occupies a 120-acre compound that hums
with activity and energy. It's a fun, communal place to stay even if you don't participate
in the daily programs, which include yoga,
meditation, dance, alternative healing and
much more. Massages ($90 to $170) are
highly recommended. Nonguests can buy
day passes (per person $20; ⊙7:30am-8pm)
for use of the facilities and grounds. An outdoor dining lanai (also open to nonguests)
serves healthy buffet-style meals (breakfast/
lunch/dinner $13/15/24), while the rooms
are all simple and breezy, with bright tropical spreads and plywood floors covered in
lauhala mats. The camping area is a great
place to park your tent. See the website
for packages and volunteer opportunities.
Weekly Ecstatic Sun-Dance (admission $15;
⊙10:30am-12:30pm Sun) gatherings here are
insanely popular; day care available ($5).

Right across the road from Kalani is the
Point – a wild spot of coast for some contemplative solitude on a rough-hewn bench
under a lone palm.

Ramashala RETREAT $$
(☑965-0068; www.ramashala.com; 12-7208 Hwy 137;
r $50-250; 🛜) Almost directly across from Ke-
hena Beach is this laid-back retreat. Among
the red-shingled Balinese buildings, the six
rooms vary wildly: from teeny rooms with a
twin bed and shared bath to spacious roosts
with full kitchens. Hardwood floors, furnish-
ings and gorgeous grounds exude a spare,
meditative elegance. There's a communal hot
tub, and two studio spaces host weekly yoga
classes. Got a group? The entire property can
be rented for $750 to $1000 per night.

KALAPANA (FORMER VILLAGE)

As with Kapoho in 1960, so it was for Kala-
pana 30 years later: in 1990 a redirection of
the ongoing eruption buried most of this vil-
lage, destroying 100 homes and obliterating
what was once Hawai'i's most famous black-
sand beach, Kaimu Beach.

Today Hwy 137 ends abruptly at the east-
ern edge of what used to be Kalapana. A few
houses here were spared and sit surrounded
by devastation. The dead-end now contains
two things: a modest complex catering to

Frolicking in tide pools and hot ponds is
tons of fun, but visitors should be aware
of health risks due to the enclosed
nature of these natural wonders –
bacteria (including staphylococcal)
has been present here in the past. To
minimize risk, locals counsel going
early in the morning when fewer people
have been in the pools; timing your
explorations for high tide; and avoiding
Mondays and other post-peak usage
times (ie after holidays). It's essential
to not enter pools with open cuts and
to shower immediately after.

tourists and an outpost of the Hawaiian
sovereignty movement. You can buy cur-
rent lava photos and gifts, an ice shave or
smoothie, and get a quite good burger or
plate lunch at Kalapana Village Cafe (mains
$8-11; ⊙8am-9pm). In the afternoon, sidle up
to Uncle's Awa Bar (⊙3-10pm), where you
can try kava, listen to live music and rub el-
bows with locals. One conversation starter
is the adjacent billboard display promoting
the establishment of the 'lawful Hawaiian
government.' The display provides a full
account of Hawaiian history, past and pres-
ent, from a native perspective. Visitors can
contract guides here for **lava walks** (flow
permitting); prices range from $25 to $50
per person.

Visitors should note that the entire lava
flow, both here and at the lava viewing area
(see p292) covers private land, and trespass-
ing is illegal. While there are no fences or
'no trespassing' signs, know that if you walk
across the flow – guided or unguided – you
do so at your own risk.

Finally, a short, public-access walk across
the lava leads to New Kaimu Beach (aka
Coconut Beach), where hundreds of baby
coconut palms surround a black comma of
sand. The water is too rough to swim (in
October 2010 a body boarder died here), but
it's a reflective spot, particularly with the fat
steam plume of a new Kalapana lava flow
rising skyward a mile or so away.

Highway 130

Red Rd intersects Hwy 130 (Old Kalapana
Rd), which leads north to Pahoa. At the

20-mile marker the 1929 Star of the Sea Church (⊙9am-4pm) is noted for the naive-style paintings that cover the walls and the *trompe l'oeil* mural behind the altar, whose illusion of depth is remarkably effective. Inside, displays recount the history of the church and of the area's missionaries, including Father (now Saint) Damien, of Moloka'i fame (see p455). The church is wheelchair accessible.

Hwy 130 ends at a public lava viewing site (see the boxed text, p292, for details), which will remain as long as the flow does. There is a large, staffed parking lot with portable toilets and vendors.

HAWAI'I VOLCANOES NATIONAL PARK & AROUND

Hawai'i Volcanoes National Park

Of all of Hawaii's marvels, none equals the elemental grandeur and raw power of the two active volcanoes contained within Hawai'i Volcanoes National Park (HAVO; www.nps.gov/havo). The entire island chain is the result of the volcanic processes on display here, which is nothing less than the ongoing birth of Hawaii.

The elder sibling is Mauna Loa, whose recumbent bulk slopes as gently as Buddha's belly, as if the earth's largest volcano (which constitutes over half of the Big Island's land mass) were nothing more than an overgrown hill. But, at 13,677ft, its navel is a frigid alpine desert that's snow-covered in winter.

The younger sibling is Kilauea – the earth's youngest and most active volcano. Since 1983 Kilauea's East Rift Zone has been erupting almost nonstop from the Pu'u 'O'o vent (southeast of the caldera), adding nearly 500 acres of new land to the island and providing residents and visitors with a front-row seat at one of the best shows on earth. In 2008 new action erupted within Kilauea Caldera, deep within Halema'uma'u Crater – Pele's home. At night the **lava lake** bubbling within this crater within a crater glows pomegranate red, drawing people from far and wide (to see lava flowing, head to Puna).

In geologic terms, Hawai'i's shield volcanoes lack the explosive gases of other volcanoes. Bomb-like explosions and geysers of lava aren't the norm: most of the time lava simply oozes and creeps along till it reaches the sea, which creates arcs of steamy fireworks. Naturally whenever Pele does send up dramatic curtains of fire people stream in from everywhere to watch.

Pele exacts a price for this entertainment. Since 1983, this side of the island has been remade. Lava blocked the coastal road to Puna in 1988, and covered the village of Kalapana in 1990. Flows then crept further west, engulfing Kamoamoa Beach in 1994, and later claiming an additional mile of road and most of Wahaula Heiau. In 2008, in addition to the Halema'uma'u eruption, a Thanksgiving Breakout vent sent lava back through Kalapana, and there is truly no telling how (or even if) lava will be flowing by the time you read this. Pele may be accommodating, but she keeps her own counsel.

However, no matter what the lava is doing, there is still plenty to see. At roughly 333,000 acres (and counting), HAVO is larger than the island of Moloka'i, and its landscape is more varied – with black-lava deserts, rain forests, grassy coastal plains, snowy summits and more. The park is Hawai'i's best place for hiking and camping, with about 140 miles of trails, but you don't *have* to break a sweat: good roads circle the caldera and take in the main highlights of what is certainly the USA's most dynamic national park.

⊙ Sights

This vast and varied park can fill as many days as you give it, particularly if you enjoy hiking. Just past the entrance, the Kilauea Visitor Center, Volcano House and Volcano Art Center are clustered together.

The park's main road is Crater Rim Dr, which circles the moonscape of Kilauea Caldera. If you only have a few hours, spend them seeing the drive-up sites on this road. The park's other scenic drive is Chain of Craters Rd, which leads south 20 miles to the coast, ending at the site of the most recent lava activity. It's a two-hour round-trip drive without stops. Note that these roads, or portions of them, may close at any time due to eruption activity (as was the case with Crater Rim Dr at time of research).

A mile from the park entrance, the village of Volcano (p294) serves visitors with a nice selection of restaurants and accommodation.

CRATER RIM DRIVE

This incredible 11-mile loop road (Map p286) starts at the Kilauea Visitor Center and skirts the rim of Kilauea Caldera. When open, it passes the visitor center, a museum, a lava tube, steam vents, rifts, hiking trails and views of the smoking crater that'll knock your socks off. Don't miss it; allow from one to three hours. Also, since it's relatively level, it's the park's best road for **cycling**. This description starts at the visitor center and goes counterclockwise.

Note that as of 2011, the portion of the road passing the Jaggar Museum and Halema'uma'u Overlook before connecting with Chain of Craters Rd was closed due to eruption activity.

Volcano Art Center   ART GALLERY

(Map p286; ☎866-967-7565; www.volcanoartcenter.org) Next door to the visitor center, inside the (original, relocated) 1877 Volcano House lodge, this gallery shop sells high-quality island pottery, paintings, woodwork, sculpture, jewelry, Hawaiian quilts and more. Browsing the stunning collection – which ranges from $8000 koa rocking chairs to $20 prints – is almost as satisfying as buying. The resident nonprofit arts organization hosts craft and cultural workshops, music concerts, plays and dance recitals, all detailed in their online events calendar.

Sulphur Banks   TRAIL

(Map p286) Near the art center, wooden boardwalks weave through steaming sulphur banks, where numerous holes and rocky vents have been stained yellow, orange and neon green by the hundreds of tons of sulfuric gases released here daily. The smoldering, foul-smelling area looks like the aftermath of a forest fire. A short, easy walk along the beautifully renovated and wheelchair-accessible **boardwalk** starts at the art center, takes in the Sulphur Banks, and crosses the road to Steaming Bluff. For a longer walk, you can connect to a variety of trails, including Crater Rim Trail.

Steam Vents & Steaming Bluff   LANDMARK

(Map p286) At the next pull-off these nonsulfurous steam vents make a good drive-up photo-op; they are the result of rainwater that percolates down and is heated into steam by hot rocks underground. Much more evocative is the short walk to the crater rim at Steaming Bluff, where the magnificent crater view feels infernolike as steam from the cliffs below pours over you. Cool early mornings or cloudy afternoons showcase the steam best.

FREE Jaggar Museum   MUSEUM

(Map p286; ⏱8:30am-8pm) The exhibits at this small museum are a nice complement to the visitor center; they introduce the museum's founder, famous volcanologist Dr Thomas A Jaggar, overview the Hawaiian pantheon, and provide a deeper understanding of volcanic geology. A bank of real-time seismographs monitor the park's daily quota of earthquakes, which number from the tens to the hundreds – kids love stomping around here to try and set the needles jumping.

When the Halema'uma'u Crater began erupting in 2008, the real show moved outside to the **viewpoint**, replete with a telescope trained 24-7 on the lava lake in the crater's center. At night oglers can run three deep. It's a thrilling vantage that also constitutes – until the eruption stops – the end of the road from this direction.

Just before you reach the museum, the **Kilauea Overlook** (Map p286) provides another pause-worthy panorama, including the **Southwest Rift** a few miles to the south. This rocky fissure is more massive and longer than it looks; it slices from the caldera summit all the way to the coast.

Halema'uma'u Overlook   SCENIC POINT

On March 18, 2008, Halema'uma'u Crater shattered a quarter-century of silence with a huge steam-driven explosion that scattered rocks and Pele's hair (strands of volcanic glass) over 75 acres. A series of explosions followed, widening a 300ft vent in the crater floor, which as of early 2011 continued to spew a muscular column of smoke, and bubble with (but not spurt) molten lava. In November 2008 this officially became the longest continuous eruption in the crater since 1924.

In 1823 missionary William Ellis first described the boiling goblet of Halema'uma'u, and this prodigious sight attracted travelers from all over the world. Looking in, some saw the fires of hell, others primeval creation, but none left unmoved. Mark Twain wrote that he witnessed:

> Circles and serpents and streaks of lightning all twined and wreathed and tied together...I have seen Vesuvius since, but it was a mere toy, a child's volcano, a soup kettle, compared to this.

Then, in 1924, the crater floor subsided rapidly, touching off a series of explosive

Hawai'i Volcanoes National Park

0 — 8 km
0 — 4 miles

PUNA

Mountain View

To Kea'au (2mi); Hilo (9mi)

Hawai'i Belt Rd

Glenwood

S Glenwood Rd

Puna Forest Reserve

Kupaianaha Vent

Pu'u 'O'o Vent

East Rift Zone

Akatsuka Orchid Gardens

2400° Fahrenheit

Old Volcano Rd

Kahaualé'a Natural Area Reserve

Napau Crater

Makaopuhi Crater

Naulu Trail

Kalapana Trail

End of the Road

Holei Sea Arch

Pu'u Loa Petroglyphs

Kealakomo

Ola'a Forest Reserve

Volcano

See Kilauea Caldera & Volcano Map (p286)

Pu'u Huluhulu

Mauna Ulu

Napau Crater Trail

Chain of Craters Rd

Kealakomo

P

'Apua Point

Puna Coast Trail

Hawai'i Volcanoes National Park

Keauhou Trail

PACIFIC OCEAN

Mauna Loa Rd

Twin Pit Crater

Kulanaokuaiki Campground

Mauna Iki Trail

Hilina Pali Rd

Halape Shelter

Keauhou Shelter

Cone Crater

Pu'u Koa'e

Mauna Iki

Hilina Pali Overlook

Ka'aha Shelter

Ka'aha Trail

Mauna Loa Observatory

Observatory Rd

To Saddle Rd (8mi)

Red Hill Cabin

Pu'u 'Ula'ula (10,035ft)

Mauna Loa Weather Observatory

Mauna Loa Trail

Mauna Loa Cabin Trail

Mauna Loa Summit Trail

Mauna Loa (13,677ft)

Mauna Loa Cabin

Moku'āweoweo Caldera

Hawai'i Volcanoes National Park

Ka'ū Desert

Hilina Pali Trail

Pepeiao Cabin

Ka'ū Desert

Southwest Rift Zone

Hawai'i Belt Rd

Kapapala Forest Reserve

KA'Ū

Wood Valley

Pahala

To South Point (Ka Lae) (30mi); Kailua-Kona (77mi)

Ka'ū Forest Reserve

Hawai'i Volcanoes National Park Kahuku Unit

eruptions. Boulders and mud rained down for days. When it was over the crater had doubled in size – to about 300ft deep and 3000ft wide. Lava activity ceased and the crust cooled.

Since then Halema'uma'u has erupted 18 times; it's the most active area on the volcano's summit. During the last eruption, on April 30, 1982, geologists only realized something was brewing that morning as their seismographs went haywire. The park service quickly cleared hikers from the crater floor, and before noon a half-mile fissure broke open and spewed 1.3 million cu yards of lava.

All of the Big Island is Pele's territory, but Halema'uma'u is her home. **Ceremonial hula** is performed in her honor on the crater rim every other month (see p292), and you'll see flower lei and other offerings to her as you venture through the park – this practice is widely frowned upon. As of early 2011, the overlook remained closed. When it's open, this is one end of the Halema'uma'u Trail (Map p286).

Devastation Trail
TRAIL

(Map p286) As of 2011 this trail was open and accessible by driving clockwise from the visitor center; although the road west of the intersection with Chain of Craters Rd was closed. You can park either at this intersection or at the trail's other end, the Pu'u Pua'i Overlook further east.

Devastation Trail is paved and passes through the fallout area of the 1959 eruption of Kilauea Iki Crater, which decimated this portion of the rain forest. This is a great trail to do on a guided ranger walk since, at first glance, it's not half as dramatic as its name. The overlook provides a fantastic vantage into the crater, and it's a quick walk to see Pu'u Pua'i, which formed during the eruption.

Thurston Lava Tube
LAVA TUBE

(Map p286) East of the intersection with Chain of Craters Rd you enter the rain forest of native tree ferns and ohia that covers Kilauea's windward slope.

Often crowded to the extreme, this lava tube is the end point of an enjoyable short walk through lovely, bird-filled ohia forest (it's a good place to spot the red-bodied 'apapane, a native honeycreeper). The lava tube itself is enormous – practically big enough for your car – and a short initial section is lit. If you've got a flashlight, exploring the tube's unlit extension (spooky!) is highly recommended.

Kilauea Iki Crater
SCENIC POINT

(Map p286) When Kilauea Iki (Little Kilauea) burst open in a fiery inferno in November 1959, the whole crater floor turned into a bubbling lake of molten lava. Its fountains reached record heights of 1900ft, lighting the evening sky with a bright orange glow for miles around. At its peak it gushed out 2 million tons of lava per hour.

An overlook provides an awesome view of the mile-wide crater, and the **hike** across its hardened surface is the park's most popular. One good strategy for visiting this often crowded, but scenic, portion of Crater Rim Drive is to park at the Kilauea Iki Overlook and walk the Crater Rim Trail to Thurston Lava Tube and back; it's about a mile all told and easy as pie.

CHAIN OF CRATERS ROAD
This scenic drive (Map p284) gets shorter all the time (most recently in 2003). It currently winds about 19 miles down the southern slopes of Kilauea Volcano, ending abruptly at the latest East Rift Zone lava flow on the Puna Coast. It's a paved but curvaceous scenic drive; allow one hour one way without stops.

For visual drama, the road is every bit the equal of Crater Rim Dr. As you descend toward the sea, panoramic coastal vistas open before you, revealing slopes covered in frozen fingers of blackened lava. Then, at the coast, you get to stare at those same flows from below, looking up to where they crested the cliffs and plunged across the land to meet the sea.

The road takes its name from a series of small, drive-up craters that lie along the first few miles. In addition, the road provides access to several trails, a campground, petroglyphs and sometimes to the active flow itself.

At one time, Chain of Craters Rd connected to Hwys 130 and 137 in Puna. Lava flows closed the road in 1969 but, slightly rerouted, it reopened in 1979. Then Kilauea cut the link again in 1988, burying a 10-mile stretch of the road. The 'Road Closed' sign here almost entirely buried in lava is a classic Big Island photo-op; before 9am or after 3pm is best for photography.

Hilina Pali Road
SCENIC DRIVE

(Map p284) The first major intersection is this 9-mile, one-lane road. Four miles along this road is the small Kulanaokuaiki Campground

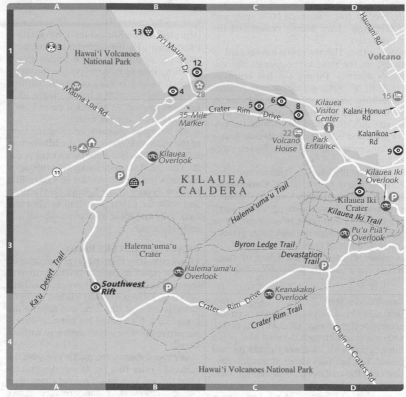

(see p293), with terrific Mauna Loa views. The road itself is nothing spectacular, and is so winding that the drive can take over 40 minutes one way. However, it ends at the Hilina Pali Overlook, a lookout of exceptional beauty. The grassy coastal plain below will beckon hikers to descend the steep Hilina Pali Trail here, but the water isn't as close as it looks and only those prepared for a backcountry trek can reach it.

Mauna Ulu LANDMARK

(Map p284) In 1969 eruptions from Kilauea's east rift began building a new **lava shield**, which eventually rose 400ft above its surroundings; it was named Mauna Ulu (Growing Mountain). By the time the flow stopped in 1974, it had covered 10,000 acres of parkland and added 200 acres of new land to the coast.

It also buried a 12-mile section of Chain of Craters Rd in lava up to 300ft deep. A half-mile portion of the old road survives,

and you can follow it to the lava flow by taking the turnoff on the left, 3.5 miles down Chain of Craters Rd. Just beyond this is Mauna Ulu itself.

The easy Pu'u Huluhulu Overlook Trail, an easy 2.5-mile round-trip hike, begins at the parking area (which is also the trailhead for Napau Crater Trail; see p290). The overlook trail ends at the top of a 150ft cinder cone, Pu'u Huluhulu, which is like a crow's nest on a clear day: the vista nets Mauna Loa, Mauna Kea, Pu'u 'O'o vent, Kilauea, the East Rift Zone and the ocean beyond. Just before you is the steamy teacup of Mauna Ulu crater. Nothing stops hikers from checking this out, but the park rangers would prefer if you didn't. The rim is fragile, and those who watched it being born feel almost parentally protective. To venture beyond the overlook and on to Napau Crater requires a free permit from the visitor center.

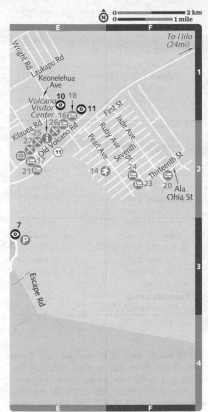

The parking area and trailhead are signed between the 16- and 17-mile markers. At the site, stay on the boardwalk at all times – not all of the petroglyphs are obvious, and you are likely to trample (and damage) some if you walk over the rocks. **Ranger-led hikes** exploring the petroglyphs beyond the boardwalk are sometimes hosted; call the visitor center to inquire.

Holei Sea Arch LANDMARK
(Map p284) Near the end of the road, across from the ranger station, is this sea arch. This rugged section of the coast has sharply eroded lava cliffs, called Holei Pali, which are constantly being pounded by the crashing surf. The high rock arch, carved out of one of the cliffs, is impressive; the wave action of Namakaokahai, goddess of the sea and sister to Pele, will one day send it crashing into the sea.

End of the Road LANDMARK
Quite. Chain of Craters Rd ends where the lava says it ends, having swamped this coastal section repeatedly over the past three decades. In years past, this was the starting point for hikes to the active flow. There's a simple information board and portable toilets here, plus a ranger outpost and snack shack that are usually only staffed when the lava is flowing nearby.

When there's no molten lava, this becomes one of the quietest, most dramatic day hikes in the park. There's no trail per se, but wander into the Mordor-like terrain until the surging, frozen, oily veins surround you, looking as if they cooled only yesterday.

MAUNA LOA ROAD
If you really want to escape the crowds, explore the 11.5-mile Mauna Loa Rd (Map p286), which begins off Hwy 11 west of the park entrance. The first turnoff leads to some neglected **lava tree molds**, deep tube-like apertures formed when a lava flow engulfed the rain forest. Then, after a mile, there is a picnic area (with toilets) and just beyond this is Kipukapuaulu, known as Bird Park. This unique 100-acre sanctuary protects an island of ancient forest containing rare endemic plants, insects and birds. About 400 years ago a major Mauna Loa lava flow buried the land here, but Pele split the flow and saved this small island of vegetation; in Hawaiian these are known as *kipuka*.

An easy 1-mile loop **trail** through the forest makes a very meditative walk, particularly in

Kealakomo SCENIC POINT
(Map p284) About halfway along the road is this coastal lookout with picnic tables and commanding views. The alternative trailhead for the Naulu Trail is across the road. After Kealakomo the road descends in long, sweeping switchbacks, some deeply cut through lava flows.

Pu'u Loa Petroglyphs HISTORICAL SITE
(Map p284) The gentle Pu'u Loa Trail leads less than a mile to the largest concentration of ancient petroglyphs in the state. Here early Hawaiians chiseled more than 23,000 drawings into *pahoehoe* lava with adze tools quarried from Keanakako'i (p243). There are abstract designs and animal and human figures, as well as thousands of dimpled depressions (or cupules) that were receptacles for umbilical cords. Placing a baby's umbilical stump inside a cupule and covering it with stones was meant to bestow health and longevity on the child.

Kilauea Caldera & Volcano

◉ **Sights**
1 Jaggar Museum B2
2 Kilauea Iki Crater D2
3 Kipukapuaulu A1
4 Lava Tree Molds.................................... B1
5 Steam Vents & Steaming Bluff............ C2
6 Sulphur Banks..................................... C2
7 Thurston Lava Tube E3
8 Volcano Art Center................................ C2
9 Volcano Art Center's Niaulani
   Campus... D2
10 Volcano Farmers Market...................... E1
11 Volcano Garden Arts.............................E1
12 Volcano Golf & Country Club B1
13 Volcano Winery B1

Activities, Courses & Tours
14 Hale Ho'loa Hawaiian Healing
   Arts Center & Spa.............................. E2

◔ **Sleeping**
15 Holo Holo In D1
16 Kilauea Lodge....................................... E2
17 Log Cabin at Hale Ohia......................... E2

18 My Island B&B E1
19 Namakanipaio Campground
   & Cabins A2
Volcano Artists Cottage .... (see 11)
20 Volcano Guest House F2
21 Volcano Hideaways...............................E2
22 Volcano House.......................................C2
23 Volcano Rainforest Retreat...................F2
24 Volcano Tree House............................... F2

⊗ **Eating**
25 Cafe Ohi'a E2
Café Ono .... (see 11)
Kiawe Kitchen ....(see 27)
26 Kilauea General Store...........................E2
Kilauea Lodge ....(see 16)
Lava Rock Café ....(see 26)
Thai Thai Restaurant ....(see 26)
Volcano House............................(see 22)
27 Volcano Store E2

✪ **Entertainment**
28 Kilauea Military Camp
   Theater B1

the morning, surrounded by birdsong. You'll see lots of koa trees and pass a lava tube where a unique species of big-eyed spider was discovered in 1973.

About 1.5 miles past Bird Park, Mauna Loa Rd passes another *kipuka* (Kipuka Ki), and 2 miles later the road narrows to one lane. Go slow; it's winding, with potholes and lots of blind curves. Along the way are several places to pull over to admire the views, and trails to explore – it's a wonderful diversion. By the end of the road, you've ascended to 6662ft; this is the start of the extremely difficult Mauna Loa Trail (p291) to the summit. Wander down the trail a few dozen yards for expansive southern vistas that include the smoking Kilauea Caldera far below.

🏃 Activities

Hiking is the park's main activity, and there are trails to suit all abilities. Some top hikes include Kilauea Iki Trail, Napau Crater Trail and the Pua Po'o Secret Lava Tube Tour (see the boxed text, p290). Note that trails may be closed due to ongoing eruptions, as were several at the time of research.

Cyclists can enjoy circumnavigating Kilauea Caldera along Crater Rim Dr, and mountain bikes are allowed on a few fire-

break roads, such as Escape Rd past Thurston Lava Tube. For guided cycles in the park and to the lava, contact **Volcano Bike Tours** (☎934-9199, 888-934-9199; www.bike volcano.com; adult $105-129, child $95-119). Helicopter tours are also popular (see p179).

Hiking

If variety is the spice of life, park trails are a feast. You can hike to secluded beaches or the snowcapped 13,677ft summit of Mauna Loa, through lush native rain forests or barren lava wastelands, across the hardened top of the world's most active volcano or, sometimes, to the glowing flow itself.

There are excellent trails of every length and level of difficulty. Plus, many trails intersect, allowing the flexibility to design your own routes. Most of the park is accessible to day hikers, while most backcountry destinations require only a single overnight. However, if you wish, you can wander backcountry trails for days. Whatever you choose, prepare for variable weather.

If you're interested in overnight backpacking, note that **backcountry camping** is limited and entirely first come, first served; backcountry trails contain hiking shelters, simple cabins or primitive campgrounds. All have pit toilets. Bring a stove, as open fires are prohibited. Almost no freshwater is available anywhere; some campgrounds have catchment water (always treat before drinking), and the visitor center posts a daily log of water levels. Overnight hikers must get a free permit (and register) at the visitor center no sooner than the day before their hike; each site has a three-day limit.

Following are some of the most popular and/or recommended day hikes, along with a few backcountry possibilities and variations. Some of the park's shortest hikes are mentioned in the descriptions of the park's main roads.

Kilauea Iki Trail   TRAIL

(Map p286) If you have time for only one hike, choose this one. It's the park's most popular trail for good reason – it captures all the summit's drama and beauty in one manageable, moderate, 4-mile, two-hour package. The trail's glossy brochure ($2) is a good investment.

The loop trail has multiple start points and trail junctions (making the hike easy to expand). Park at Kilauea Iki Overlook (avoiding the Thurston Lava Tube madness) and proceed counterclockwise along the crater rim. Passing through an ohia forest, you can admire the mile-long lava bathtub below before descending into it.

After almost a mile you descend onto Waldron Ledge; multiple trail junctions allow for quick explorations of the main caldera rim (highly recommended), or extend your loop by connecting with the Halema'uma'u and Byron Ledge Trails for an all-day adventure. Either way, once you reach the west end of the crater, descend 400ft to the crater floor.

Across the *pahoehoe* crust the trail is easy to follow, and *ahu* aid navigation. It's possible to enter the vent beneath the Pu'u Pua'i cinder cone, where ohia trees now bloom. As you continue over the surface, consider that molten magma is a mere 230ft below (less than a football field). Once you reach the crater's east end, ascend 400ft up switchbacks to the rim, and explore Thurston Lava Tube on your return to the Kilauea Iki Overlook.

Halema'uma'u Trail   TRAIL

(Map p286) Halema'uma'u Crater was closed to hikers at the time of research, though short portions of this trail along the rim were open. When open, this trail is an extremely rewarding 7-mile loop that starts near Volcano House. It quickly passes through ohia forest, and spends the bulk of its time traversing the ragged blankets of lava that cover Kilauea Caldera. You can easily add the Byron Ledge portion of the trail, a lovely forested alternative, before heading into the caldera. The trail is completely exposed; depending on the weather it'll be hot and dry or chillingly damp. Bring lots of water.

If you think lava is simply lava, this hike will change your mind. You pass numerous flows on the trail – some old (1885) and some new (1982) – and the diversity is astonishing, as is the overall effect of the otherworldly landscape. Nearly 3 miles from the start, the trail ends at the steaming (currently closed) Halema'uma'u Overlook. You return on the Byron Ledge Trail, which allows for easy peeks of, or a side trip into, Kilauea Iki Crater.

Crater Rim Trail   TRAIL

(Map p286) This 11.5-mile trek circles the summit, running roughly parallel to Crater Rim Drive; as with the road, large portions of this trail were closed at the time of research. If you do the whole thing, plan for five or six hours, but many people hike only portions. Overall the trail is mostly level. On the north side it is busiest as it skirts the crater rim, while on the south side it runs outside the paved road (and away from caldera views) and you will likely see no one. Lots of side trips are possible, and you pass through a wide variety of terrains; one of the most beautiful sections is the forested southeast portion. Note that hikers doing one-way hikes, either here or elsewhere, often hitch a ride to/from a trailhead; if you're going to do so, it's best to park at the end and hitch to the start, so you hike to your car.

Mauna Iki Trail   TRAIL

(Map p284) For solitude in a mesmerizing lava landscape, take this trail into the Ka'u Desert, but start from the north, along what is sometimes labeled the Footprints Trail. From this approach the trailhead access is easier, your initial commitment is low and variations allow great extensions of your route. This hike can be an easy 3.5-mile sampling, a moderate 7- to 8-mile afternoon or an 18-mile overnight backpack. However, the trail from the Jaggar Museum to the trailhead at Hwy 11 was closed at the time of research due to Halema'uma'u's current eruption.

DON'T MISS

SECRET LAVA TUBE TOUR

Lava tubes are formed when the outer crust of a river of lava starts to harden but the liquid lava beneath the surface continues to flow through. After the flow has drained out, the hard shell remains. Lava tubes riddle the Big Island like holes in Swiss cheese, and these remarkable caves are high-powered incubators of new species – blind spiders, wingless crickets, possibly cancer-curing bacteria, and more we don't even know about. In 1992 a pristine 500-year-old lava tube, Pua Po'o, was discovered in the national park, and it is the destination of a fascinating, free ranger-led lava tube hike (⊙12:30pm Wed).

The easy, 4-mile round-trip passes through ohia forest and involves about an hour underground exploring the cave's bizarre ecosystem. Though you learn about how Native Hawaiians used lava tubes to collect water and bury royalty, this cave holds no cultural significance. There's some entry and exit scrambling required, but inside is a giant tube with 20ft ceilings and amazing formations.

To protect the tube only 12 people are allowed once a week, and participants are asked to keep the location secret. To sign up, call the Kilauea Visitor Center (✆985-6017) the week before, on Wednesday, at exactly 7:45am; slots fill up in about 15 minutes and each caller can only reserve four spots. Children must be at least 10 years old.

On Hwy 11 between the 37- and 38-mile markers, look for the Ka'u Desert Trailhead parking area. Start early, as midday can be brutally hot and dry. Initially the trail is very clear, level and partly paved, threading through sand-covered *pahoehoe* flows. In 20 minutes you reach a structure protecting ancient footprints preserved in hardened ash; more footprints exist in the surrounding rock. As the story goes, in 1790 the army of Hawaiian chief Keoua was retreating from a battle against Kamehameha when a rare explosive eruption buried his soldiers, changing the course of island history.

Past the structure protecting the footprints, the trail is marked by easy-to-follow cairns. As you gradually ascend, views expand, with gentle giant Mauna Loa behind and the immense Ka'u Desert in front. After 1.8 miles you crest the rise at Mauna Iki (and the trail junction) and stand likely alone in the middle of a vast lava field.

From here, backpackers will turn right, following the Ka'u Desert Trail over 7 miles to Pepeiao Cabin. Day hikers can turn left, following the Ka'u Desert Trail for 1232yd to the junction with the official Mauna Iki Trail, which runs another 6.3 miles to Hilina Pali Rd (the other starting point). Hiking about halfway along the Mauna Iki Trail, to Pu'u Koa'e, makes a good end point.

The lava terrain is noticeably more intense and wild as you continue, with vivid colorful rents, collapsed tubes and splatter cones; in cracks you can find piles of golden Pele's hair. The discoveries are almost endless.

Napau Crater Trail TRAIL

(Map p284) This trail is one of the park's most varied and satisfying all-day hikes. It passes lava fields, immense craters and thick forest, and ends with distant views of Pu'u 'O'o, the source of Kilauea's ongoing eruption. For a more leisurely experience, consider backcountry camping here; the distance to the campground (the current end of the trail) is 7 miles (or 5 miles from the Kealakoma starting point), making it a 10- to 14-mile adventure (about six to eight hours roundtrip). Note that this is the only day hike that requires a permit; all hikers should register at the visitor center before heading out.

Rather than taking the Napau Crater Trail from its trailhead (the same one as for Pu'u Huluhulu Overlook Trail, p288), you'll save about 4 miles and several hours roundtrip if you begin on the Naulu Trail, which leaves from Kealakomo (p287) on Chain of Craters Rd. What you miss on this abbreviated version of the trail are the grandest Makaopuhi Crater and Mauna Loa views, plus the huffing vents and cracks peppering the active rift. The Kealakomo route is described here.

For the first hour, you hike mostly sinuous, leathery *pahoehoe* lava, following sometimes difficult-to-see cairns. Then you enter some trees and (surprise!) stumble across paved portions of the old Chain of Craters Rd, which was buried in a 1972 eruption. Follow the pavement (complete with dashed white line) past the junction with the unmaintained Kalapana Trail.

After a quick sprint across some *'a'a*, you enter moody fern-and-ohia forest; in less than a mile is the Napau Crater Trail junction – turn right.

Keep an eye on your left for openings to view the mile-wide Makaopuhi Crater. About 30 minutes later, low lava rock walls indicate the site of an old *'pulu* factory.' *Pulu* is the golden, silky 'hair' found at the base of *hapu'u* (tree fern) fiddlehead stems. Ancient Hawaiians used *pulu* to embalm their dead, and in the late 1800s *pulu* was exported as mattress and pillow stuffing, until it was discovered that it eventually turned to dust. This stretch is often festooned with cheery orchids.

You may think you're near the airport – considering the helicopter traffic – but in fact you're 10 minutes from the primitive campground (with pit toilet). Definitely take the spur to the Napau Crater overlook (to see steaming Pu'u 'O'o) – a picnic spot with a view. At the time of research, the rest of this trail was closed due to a Pu'u 'O'o vent collapse and shifts in the eruption.

When open, the trail continues through a surreal, wondrous terrain of hummocks, vents and tree molds to and through Napau Crater itself. On the other side (a longer slog than it looks), the trail continues another few miles across the shattered landscape to gaping Pu'u 'O'o. As the recent vent collapse makes clear, this is a dangerous and volatile area; respect all park signs and use common sense.

Mauna Loa Trail   TRAIL
(Map p284) If you fall within the class of extremely fit, elite hikers – for whom the easy way is no way at all – this is your trail to the 13,677ft summit (weekend hikers, however, should opt for the 6.5-mile Observatory Trail).

It begins at the end of Mauna Loa Rd, traverses 19 miles and ascends about 7000ft. While it is not technically challenging, due to the high elevation and frequent subarctic conditions it takes at least three, and usually four, days. Two simple cabins with foam pad–covered bunks, pit toilets and catchment water (which must be treated before drinking) are located on the route; the first cabin sleeps eight and the second 12, and they are available on a first-come, first-served basis. Get a free backcountry **permit**, advice and water-level updates at the Kilauea Visitor Center (p293) the day before your hike.

Typically, the first day is spent hiking 7.5 miles to Pu'u 'Ula'ula at 10,035ft, where Red Hill Cabin is located. The next day is spent hiking 9.5 miles to Moku'aweoweo Caldera, and another 2 miles to Mauna Loa Cabin at 13,250ft; from here you can admire the summit directly across the caldera. On the third day you hike nearly 5 miles around the caldera to reach the summit and return for a second night at Mauna Loa Cabin. On the fourth day you descend.

Altitude sickness is common, even expected; going slowly aids acclimatization. Nighttime temperatures are below freezing, and storms may bring snow, blizzards, whiteouts, rain and fog, all of which can obscure the *ahu* that mark the trail, making it impossible to follow. And don't forget that Mauna Loa is still active and, according to its 20-year cycle of eruptions, overdue.

Puna Coast Trails   TRAIL
(Map p284) Three main trails take hikers down to the Puna Coast: the Hilina Pali, Keauhou and Puna Coast Trails. These trails start from vastly different places, but they each eventually intersect (with each other and even more trails), and they lead to four separate **backcountry campgrounds** or shelters. Because of steep elevation changes and distance, these trails are most commonly done as overnight backpacks. This is also because once you see the grassy, wind-swept coast you won't want to leave. Talk to rangers about routes and water-catchment levels at the shelters – low water levels can close some trails to campers; such was the case of the Halape campground at the time of research. With lovely swimming and snorkeling, the Halape site is the most popular (and books up), with Keauhou a great second choice.

For day hikers, the Hilina Pali Trail looks easiest on the map (it's only 3.5 miles to snorkeling at Ka'aha), but it's actually the hardest, with a brutal initial cliff descent; the trailhead is at the end of Hilina Pali Rd. Far gentler on the knees is the 6.8-mile Keauhou Trail, which takes about four hours to the stunning coast; the trailhead is past the 6-mile marker on Chain of Craters Rd.

Guided Hikes
Not everyone grooves to guided hikes, but the geology, flora, fauna, lore and lure of this unique park pops vividly when described by the experts. In addition to daily ranger-led walks listed at the visitor center, these outfits are recommended:

GO TO THE FLOW

Lucky travelers can view **live lava** making the 64-mile journey from the Pu'u 'O'o vent to the ocean. Where the lava will be flowing when you arrive and the effort required to reach it are impossible to predict, but at the time of writing, the flow was setting trees aflame and smothering homes in the Royal Gardens subdivision in Puna. This is outside park boundaries, but a lava flow viewing area (Map p276; ⊙2-10pm, last car in 8pm) is maintained by the county at the end of Hwy 130. Visitors park and walk, less than a mile, on a narrow, paved strip and are corralled in a small area to behold the sights.

If the show is really on, there will be surface flows, lava 'skylights' and a giant smoke plume where the lava enters the ocean. Otherwise, you'll be a mile or more from the sea entry and see little more than a red glow and lots of smoke. All of this is highly changeable – staying informed about current conditions helps manage expectations (especially with kids). Call the Civil Defense hotline (☎961-8093) for the latest or visit Hawaiian Lava Daily (http://hawaiianlavadaily.blogspot.com).

When lava flows within national park boundaries, the National Park Service facilitates lava viewing (☎flow updates 967-8862; http://hvo.wr.usgs.gov). As of late 2010 it was possible to view the lava lake within Halema'uma'u Crater from the Jagger Museum. Occasionally it's possible to hike to flowing lava from the end of Chain of Craters Rd (see p287). Usually this involves a hike of one to several miles over a wracked lava landscape.

For best viewing, visit at sunset when the coast is bathed in a crepuscular glow and the lava brightens in the growing darkness. You can get closer by joining a lava walk (see p281) or jumping on a lava boat tour (p275). Hawai'i Forest & Trail (www.hawaii-forest.com) leads guided treks, as do park rangers when the flow is in park domain. However you do it, come prepared with rain gear, wear sturdy shoes, pants and a hat, and bring water and one flashlight per person.

Lava is a wonder to watch, but can also be dangerous. The explosive clash between seawater and molten 2100°F rock can spray scalding water hundreds of feet into the air and throw flaming lava chunks well inland; in 2000 two people were scalded to death here. New ledges or benches of lava can collapse without warning; in 1993 a bench collapse killed one person and seriously injured a dozen others; a 2007 bench collapse sent 58 acres into the sea (luckily injuring no one). In the excitement of the moment, don't forget to respect Pele's power. Always stay at least 500yd inland and heed all ranger warnings and advice.

Friends of Hawaii Volcanoes National Park   GUIDED HIKES
(☎985-7373; www.fhvnp.org) Leads weekend hikes and organizes volunteer activities like trail clearing and tree planting. Ask about their Institute-on-Demand customizable adventures.

Hawaii Forest & Trail   GUIDED HIKES
(☎331-8505, 800-464-1993; www.hawaii-forest .com; adult/child $180/150) Choose from day hikes and a twilight lava tour.

Hawaiian Walkways   GUIDED HIKES
(☎775-0372, 800-457-7759; www.hawaiianwalk ways.com; adult/child $170/120) Morning and afternoon departures with a Certified Volcano Guide.

☆ Entertainment

Regular park programs include After Dark in the Park (Kilauea Visitor Center Auditorium; suggested donation $2; ⊙7pm Tue), a series of free talks by experts on cultural, historic and geological matters. The Volcano Art Center hosts a full slate of events year-round, including wildly popular concert, dance and theater performances at the Kilauea Military Camp Theater (Map p286; ☎967-8333; tickets adult $25-40, student $10). For scheduling information for these events go to www.volcano artcenter.org and click on Performances.

Several times throughout the year, free hula *kahiko* performances are held as part of the **Na Mea Hawai'i Hula Kahiko Series** at the *pa hula* (stone platform) outdoors overlooking Kilauea Caldera.

✦ Festivals & Events

Kilauea Cultural Festival   NATIVE HAWAIIAN CULTURE
This annual Hawaiian cultural festival celebrating more than 30 years features native arts, crafts, music and demonstrations. Held in July.

Rain Forest Runs HALF-MARATHON

Held in early August, a popular half-marathon, 10km run and 5km run/walk passes through Volcano Village and nearby subdivisions. Kids can compete, too.

Aloha Festivals Ka Ho 'ola'ao Na Ali'i NATIVE HAWAIIAN CULTURE

(http://alohafestivals.com) Don't miss this brilliant Native Hawaiian royal court procession on the Halema'uma'u Crater rim, with ceremonial chanting and hula, during the August/September Aloha Festival.

🛏 Sleeping

Accommodation options within the national park are limited; nearby Volcano village has more choices. At the time of research, both the Namakanipaio Cabins and Volcano House (the only hotel/restaurant within park boundaries) were closed for retrofitting and renovation. The former is due to reopen in 2012; the future of Volcano House is less certain. See p169 for a rundown of camping options in the park.

The following drive-up campgrounds are first-come, first served – and fill up on busy holiday weekends. Facilities are well kept; expect nights to be crisp and cool.

FREE Kulanaokuaiki Campground CAMPGROUND

(Map p284; Hilina Pali Rd) About 4 miles along Hilina Pali Rd, this secluded, quiet, eight-site campground has pit toilets and picnic tables, but no water.

FREE Namakanipaio Campground CAMPGROUND

(Map p286) Between the 32- and 33-mile markers off Hwy 11, 3 miles west of the visitor center, this campground's two pleasant grassy meadows fill with as many tents as it will hold. It lacks privacy, but nice facilities include rest rooms, water, fireplaces, picnic tables and a covered pavilion.

🍴 Eating & Drinking

The restaurant at **Volcano House** (Map p286; www.volcanohousehotel.com), the only restaurant within park boundaries, is closed for renovations, with its expected reopening date uncertain.

❶ Information

The **park** (☑985-6000; www.nps.gov/havo; 7-day pass per car $10, per person on foot, bicycle or motorcycle $5) never closes. The toll station at the park entrance also sells two annual passes: a three-park Hawaii pass ($25, including HAVO, Pu'uhonua o Honaunau, and Haleakalā on Maui) and one for all national parks ($80).

Kilauea Visitor Center (Map p286; ☑985-6017; ☺7:45am-5pm) should be your first stop. Rangers can advise you on volcanic activity, air quality, trail conditions and the best things to see based on your time. A board lists the day's guided hikes and ranger programs (which are posted by 8:45am). A small **theater** shows free short films on Kilauea and the current eruption, with spectacular footage, on continuous rotation. Pick up free trail pamphlets, backcountry permits, and junior-ranger program activity sheets. **Wheelchairs** (free) are available for exploring the park upon request; accessible areas include Waldron Ledge, Devastation Trail, Sulphur Banks Trail, Pauahi Crater and the Volcano Art Center. The excellent bookstore has a plethora of volumes and videos on volcanoes, flora, hiking and Hawaiian culture and history. There's also an ATM, a pay phone and restrooms.

The park's **hotline** (☑985-6000; ☺24hr) provides daily recorded updates on park weather, road closures and lava-viewing conditions. The **USGS** (http://volcano.wr.usgs.gov/hvostatus .php) also has eruption updates on its website. Note that the nearest gas station is in Volcano village.

At 4000ft above sea level, the Kilauea Caldera area is generally 10°F to 15°F cooler than Hilo or Kona, but weather is unpredictable and microclimates can vary dramatically within the park. Plan and prepare for hot sun, dry wind, fog, chilly rain and soaking downpours, all in a day. At a minimum bring long pants, a jacket or sweater and a rain slicker.

Dangers & Annoyances

Active volcanoes create a few unusual hazards. Though extremely rare and highly unlikely, deaths have occurred on park visits. Statistics are in your favor (fatalities are rare), but Pele will keep you on your toes. Interestingly, molten lava is not the most threatening personal danger. Instead, deaths and injuries tend to occur when people venture too close to the active flow – and wind up on unstable 'benches' of new land that collapse, or get caught in steam explosions when lava enters the ocean.

If you plan to walk or hike about, come prepared: bring hiking shoes or sneakers, long pants, a hat, sunscreen, water (and snacks), a flashlight with extra batteries and a first aid kit.

LAVA As for less mortal dangers, remember that hardened lava is uneven and brittle; rocks can be

HAWAI'I THE BIG ISLAND HAWAI'I VOLCANOES NATIONAL PARK & AROUND

ℹ PLAN YOUR VISIT

Technology and new media helps visitors keep abreast of Pele's antics and how they may affect plans (also see the boxed text, p292) Here are some top resources:

» **Trail & road closures** www.nps.gov/havo/closed_areas.htm

» **Air quality** www.hiso2index.info

» **Kilauea status** http://volcano.wr.usgs.gov/kilaueastatus.php

» **Hawaiian Volcano Observatory Webcams** http://volcanoes.usgs.gov/hvo/cams

» **Hawai'i Volcanoes National Park iApp** www.MacroViewLabs.com

glass-sharp. Thin crusts can give way over unseen hollows and lava tubes; the edges of craters and rifts crumble easily. Deep earth cracks may be hidden by plants. When hiking, abrasions, deep cuts and broken limbs are all possible. So, it's even more important than most places to stay on marked trails and take park warning signs seriously. Blazing paths into unknown terrain can damage fragile areas, lead to injuries and leave tracks that encourage others to follow.

VOG & SULFURIC FUMES Another major, constant concern is air quality. Halema'uma'u Crater and Pu'u 'O'o vent belch thousands of tons of sulfur dioxide daily. Where lava meets the sea it also creates a 'steam plume,' which is a toxic cocktail of sulfuric and hydrochloric acid mixed with airborne silica (or glass particles). All this combines to create 'vog', which depending on the winds can settle over the park. In addition, steam vents throughout the park spew high concentrations of sulfuric fumes (which smell like rotten egg); Halema'uma'u Overlook and Sulphur Banks are prime spots. Given all this, people with respiratory and heart conditions, pregnant women, infants and young children should take special care when visiting.

DEHYDRATION Finally, vast areas of the park qualify as desert, and dehydration is common. Carrying two quarts of water per person is the standard advice, but bring more and keep a gallon in the trunk: you'll drink it.

EMERGENCIES (✆981-6170, 911)

Maps

The free color map given at the park's entrance is fine for driving around, seeing the main sights and hiking a few short and/or popular trails. The visitor center has some backcountry trail maps if you're headed into the wild blue yonder.

If you'll be backpacking or hiking extensively, consider purchasing *National Geographic's Trails Illustrated Hawaii Volcanoes National Park*. It's a comprehensive, waterproof and rip-resistant large-format topographic hiking map that identifies most terrain features, including campgrounds. For specific hikes, the USGS 1:24,000 maps *Kilauea*, *Volcano* and *Ka'u Desert* are also helpful.

ℹ Getting There & Around

The national park is 29 miles (about 40 minutes) from Hilo and 97 miles (2½ hours) from Kailua-Kona. From either direction you'll drive on Hwy 11. Volcano village is a mile east of the park entrance.

The **Hele-On bus** (www.heleonbus.org) leaves three times a day from Hilo and arrives at the park visitor center an hour later, before continuing on to Ka'u.

Volcano
POP 2600

The village of Volcano is a mystical place of giant ferns, *sugi* (Japanese evergreen), and ohia trees full of puffy red blossoms. Many artists and writers find inspiration in this small, soulful town, adding to its overall allure.

If you're in town in November, don't miss the annual **Volcano Village Artists' Hui**, an open studios extravaganza held the three days after Thanksgiving. Budding (serious) photographers might consider a customized photo tour (www.hawaiiphotoretreat.com; 1-/2-/3-day tour $275/500/725) with ace shooters Ken and Mary Goodrich, who live in Volcano.

◉ Sights & Activities

TOP CHOICE **Volcano Farmers Market**   MARKET
(Map p286; Cooper Community Center, 1000 Wright Rd; ⏰7-9am Sun) This weekly farmers market – when the whole town comes to socialize and buy local organic produce, hot food and unique crafts – is one of the warmest community events on the island. A bright play structure teems with children, and there's even a used-book store.

Volcano Garden Arts   ART GALLERY
(Map p286; www.volcanogardenarts.com; 19-3834 Old Volcano Rd; ⏰10am-4pm Tue-Sun) Artist Ira Ono and his voluptuous masks seem to be everywhere, and his garden/gallery, representing 80 artists, is central to Volcano's creative scene. Explore the gardens and sacred *sugi* grove, pet Ernest the pygmy goat or mingle at poetry readings and other events. There's a **cafe** and rental cottage (Volcano Artists Cottage) here, too.

Hale Ho'ola Hawaiian Healing Arts Center & Spa
MASSAGE

(Map p286; ☑756-2421; www.halehoola.net; 11-3913 7th St; massages 60min $65-75, 90min $100-110, 120min $140-150, treatments $45-120) After a hard day's hiking, relax with a traditional Hawaiian massage or steam bath. The extensive menu here has much more, including massages for children and elders; appointments required.

2400° Fahrenheit
ART STUDIO

(Map p284; www.2400F.com; Old Volcano Rd; ☺10am-4pm Thu-Mon) At the glass-blowing studio 2400° Fahrenheit, you can watch artists Michael and Misato Mortara create their mind-boggling glass bowls and vases. A tiny gallery displays finished pieces (here the old saying holds: 'if you need to ask how much, you probably can't afford it'). It's outside of Volcano on Hwy 11, near the 24-mile marker.

FREE Akatsuka Orchid Gardens
GARDEN

(Map p284; ☑888-967-6669; www.akatsukaorchid .com; Hwy 11; ☺8:30am-5pm) Very near the 22-mile marker, Akatsuka Orchid Gardens is famous for its unique hybrid orchids (owner Moriyasu Akatsuka, aka Mr Orchid, cultivates 50 to 70 new hybrids annually) and its warehouse stuffed with 100,000 perennially blooming plants. A visit here is an olfactory and visual delight, complemented by unsurpassed customer service. Everything sold here is ready for shipping.

Volcano Winery
WINERY

(Map p286; www.volcanowinery.com; 35 Pi'i Mauna Dr; ☺10am-5:30pm) The very attractive Volcano Winery is growing by leaps and bounds, with eight vintages available for tasting and purchase. The newest additions include a pinot noir and their award-winning Infusion Tea wine – a tasty, unusual combination of South Kona mac nut honey and black tea grown in Volcano.

Volcano Art Center's Niaulani Campus
NATURE WALKS

(Map p286; www.volcanoartcenter.org; 19-4074 Old Volcano Rd; ☺nature walks 9:30am Mon) Free half-mile nature walks through deep-green, towering native forest are offered by this extension of the park's art center. Also check the website for poetry readings, music, artist lectures and other events.

Volcano Golf & Country Club
GOLF

(Map p286; ☑967-7331; www.volcanogolfshop.com; Pi'i Mauna Dr; greens fee before/after noon $73/59) A local favorite, the 18-hole course here has majestic links with views of Mauna Kea and Mauna Loa.

🛏 Sleeping

Volcano has a preponderance of nice B&Bs and vacation homes. Volcano Gallery (☑800-908-9764; www.volcanogallery.com) is a local rental agency listing more than two dozen good properties, many in the $145 to $165 range. We've also had terrific luck with Vacation Rental by Owner (www.vrbo.com).

Almost all properties have a two-night minimum stay or a one-night surcharge.

TOP CHOICE Volcano Rainforest Retreat
COTTAGE $$

(Map p286; ☑985-8696, 800-550-8696; www .volcanoretreat.com; 11-3832 12th St at Ruby Ave; cottage d incl breakfast $125-260; @🛜) Serenity abounds within the four luxurious, individually designed cedar cottages at this meditation-minded B&B swaddled in the jungle flora that defines Volcano. Artfully positioned among giant *hapu'u*, cottages have huge windows and either outdoor hot tubs or Japanese-style soaking tubs to maximize your experience of nature. This place is off-the-chart romantic, with in-cottage massage, candlelit dinners and champagne service available.

> **WORTH A TRIP**

KIPUKA'AKIHI HIKE

Hikers alert! Hawai'i Volcanoes National Park's Kahuku Unit (Map p301; ☺9am-3pm Sat & Sun) is located four miles south of Wai'ohinu in Ka'u. Head here for a rare opportunity to explore *kipuka* (forested oases) harboring native and endangered species like the *'i'iwi* (scarlet honeycreeper).

The 1.5-mile Kipuka'akihi Hike ascends 800ft while passing through verdant old-growth forest and lava flows. You can explore solo or join a five-hour ranger-led hike (☑985-6011; www.nps .gov/havo/planyourvisit/events.htm) one weekend a month. Tours are limited to 15 and reservations are required.

TOP CHOICE **Volcano Artists Cottage** COTTAGE **$$**
(✆967-7261; www.volcanoartistcottage.com; 19-3834 Old Volcano Rd; cottage incl breakfast $130; ☎) On the grounds of Volcano Garden Arts, the caretaker's cottage of this 1908 estate has been reimagined as a tiny retreat to restore your creative muse. Somehow it holds a fully functioning kitchen, dining table, comfy chair and queen bed (with delicious spreads), as well as an inspirational stepdown, sea-green tile bathroom as big as the living area. The outdoor hot tub will probably be ready by the time you read this. Best for singles and intimate couples.

Log Cabin at Hale Ohia CABIN **$$**
(Map p286; ✆735-9191; www.crubinstein.com; Hale Ohia Rd; d $125) Step back in time to 'Old Hawaii' at this sweet log cabin built in 1906 – the only remaining authentic notched cabin in the state. The place oozes history, from the century-old *sugi* trees in the yard to the carving of Hilo's Boys School on the log wall (the first headmaster built this cabin). There are two heavenly beds in an upstairs loft, a kitchen worthy of serious cooks and a wood burning stove. This rustic accommodation isn't for everyone, but it's just right for the right people.

Volcano Hideaways VACATION RENTALS **$$**
(Map p286; ✆985-8959; www.volcanovillage.net; Hale Ohia Rd; houses $130-150; ☎) The fully renovated properties located on this quiet side street (a designated Historic District) are all spotless, expertly outfitted and tastefully decorated by hosts who put energetic care into what they do. The one-bedroom

---

and pair of three-bedroom houses here come fully equipped – from robes and quality DVDs to laundry facilities and freshly roasted coffee from the owners' Laupahoehoe farm. Rain showers, whirlpool tubs and luxurious linens are among the perks here. The one-bedroom has a hot tub and gazebo set-up.

Holo Holo In HOSTEL **$**
(Map p286; ✆967-7950; www.volcanohostel.com; 19-4036 Kalani Honua Rd; dm $25, r $64-80; @☎) Don't be put off by this small hostel's exterior. Inside, the two six-bed dorms and four private rooms are meticulously cared for, sizable and pleasant. The kitchen is nicely equipped and there's a laundry. It's a quiet, homey place tended by a gracious host.

Kilauea Lodge INN **$$**
(Map p286; ✆967-7366; www.kilauealodge.com; 19-3948 Old Volcano Rd; r $170-185, cottage d $185, 2-bedroom house $200; ☎) Volcano's biggest property is an old renovated YMCA camp that sleeps like a B&B with hotel services. The 12 rooms vary their offerings, but all embody upscale country romance with gas fireplaces, Hawaiian quilts, artistic stained glass, tall ceilings and bathroom skylights. A relaxing common room has a wood fireplace, and the manicured jungle gardens hold a gorgeous hot tub. Room 6 is wheelchair accessible. It also rents a fully equipped cottage and a house down the road. Rates include breakfast.

Volcano Guest House
(Map p286; ✆967-7775; www.volcanoguesthouse.com; 11-3733 Ala Ohia St; r $85-125, cottages $130-150; ☎) Friendly hosts, varied digs (some with kitchens) and hot tub and laundry for guests' use make this place. Rates include breakfast.

Volcano Tree House
(Map p286; www.volcanotreehouse.com; 11-3860 Eleventh St; r $170-220; ☎) For a genuine 'into the woods' experience, check out this quirky property. Set in a fern forest with raised catwalks among the trees, all three units have a kitchen and TV.

My Island B&B
(Map p286; ✆967-7216; www.myislandinnhawaii.com; 19-3896 Old Volcano Rd; s $70-105, d $85-130, house d $160; ☎) Choose from tight quarters in historic home, private studios and a three-bedroom house.

ⓘ **HOW BAD IS THE VOG?**

Volcanic smog – vog as it's known in these parts – is a toxic cocktail of sulfur dioxide and other airborne nasties, including glass particles. Since Kilauea changed its eruption pattern in 2008, vog has affected the island much more seriously; according to park rangers, Kilauea's vog output has more than doubled. When you're downwind it can be hard to breathe, especially for those with respiratory problems. A handy daily sulfur dioxide meter for the island is available at **SO2 Alert Index** (www.hiso2index.info).

✕ Eating

TOP CHOICE Thai Thai Restaurant   THAI $$
(Map p286; ☑967-7969; Old Volcano Rd; mains
$15-26; ⊘noon-9pm Thu-Tue; 🍴) The owners
get their spices directly from Thailand and
craft destination-worthy Thai cuisine here,
where satay doesn't come on a stick and the
generous-portioned, attractively presented
curries and soups arrive vibrantly flavored
with a rich tingly warmth. Avoid the tables
in the kitschy gift shop or do takeout.

Kiawe Kitchen   BISTRO $$
(Map p286; ☑967-7711; cnr Old Volcano & Haunani
Rds; pizzas $15-21, mains $20-29; ⊘11am-2:30pm
& 5:30-8:30pm) A local hot spot known as 'the
pizza place,' the thin-crust, wood-fired pies
here are tasty and the appetizers to die for
(try the haricot verts with mac nuts). Come
early for the bistro-style entrées, such as
crab-stuffed Portobello and rib-eye steak,
since they tend to run out. A front patio,
quirky art and full bar complete the welcoming atmosphere. A **takeout window** (⊘7:30-
10am Mon-Fri) does espresso and pastries.

Lava Rock Café   DINER $
(Map p286; 19-3972 Old Volcano Rd; mains $8-20;
⊘7:30am-5pm Mon, to 9pm Tue-Sat, to 4pm Sun;
@🛜👪) Behind Kilauea General Store, this basic diner is nothing special, but it's the favored spot for breakfast (try the French toast with
house specialty *liliko'i* butter) or a burger.

Kilauea Lodge   ECLECTIC $$$
(Map p286; ☑967-7366; www.kilauealodge.com;
Old Volcano Rd; breakfast $7-13, dinner mains $20-
36; ⊘7:30-10am & 5-9pm) The vaulted beamed
ceiling, historic stone fireplace and eye-
catching paintings create an upscale rus-
tic atmosphere here. The kitchen prepares
gourmet versions of mostly German comfort
food: *hasenpfeffer* (braised rabbit), venison,
sausage and sauerkraut, and Parker Ranch
steaks. Dinners come with fresh mini-loaves
of bread, the wine list is extensive and ser-
vice is attentive. Check out Sunday brunch
before your big hike. Reservations advised.
This is not a good choice for vegetarians.

🍴 **Café Ono**   VEGETARIAN $
(19-3834 Old Volcano Rd; lunch $9-12; ⊘10am-
4pm Tue-Sun; 🍴) Vegetarian cafe with killer
quiche and vegan options, plus a lovely
garden.

Café Ohi'a   CAFE $
(19-4005 Haunani Rd; soup & sandwiches $7;
⊘6am-7pm) Fresh soups, plus fabulous

sandwiches and baked goods (try the pecan
torte) – perfect for a picnic or hike. The
breakfast croissant kicks off the day right.

For groceries, try your luck at **Volcano
Store** (Upper Store; Map p286; cnr Old Volcano
& Haunani Rds; ⊘5am-6:45pm) and **Kilauea
General Store** (Lower Store; Map p286; Old
Volcano Rd; ⊘7am-7:30pm Mon-Sat, to 7pm Sun).

ℹ Information

A laundromat (open daily) and the **Volcano Visitor
Center** (Map p286; ☑985-7422; Old Volcano Rd;
⊘7am-7pm) – a teeny unstaffed hut with bro-
chures aplenty and an ATM – are located next to
Thai Thai Restaurant. Lava Rock Café has internet
and wi-fi for $10/$20 per hour/day.

The **Post office** (Map p286;19-4030 Old Volca-
no Rd) is down the street from the Volcano Store.

KA'U

Hold onto your hat! You've entered Ka'u,
a wild and windy place where Big Island
myths run thick and mysteries abound. This
makes sense, since it all began at Ka Lae
(South Point), believed to be the landing site
of the Polynesians in Hawaii. Sure, you can
spend a day at Green Sands Beach or Road
to the Sea and think there isn't much to this
arid lava land but a couple of hard-to-reach
swaths of sand. But linger in this southern-
most region of the USA and you'll see why
locals are so rabid to protect it. And protect
it they do: Ka'u folks have squashed coastal
resorts, lobbied for protected land acquisi-
tion and are pioneers of off-the-grid living.
Together, Ka'u's sights and history add in-
trigue to any itinerary.

Pahala

POP 1600

A former sugar town muddling through
hard times, Pahala hangs on via small-farm
agriculture, particularly macadamia nuts
and coffee. This quiet town's main streets
are lined with charming early-20th-century
plantation homes, but it doesn't offer much
for travelers beyond a peek at country life.

From Hwy 11 take the signed turnoff
(between the 51- and 52-mile markers) on
Kamani St; take this to Pikake St, where
you'll find Pahala's post office, bank and gas
station. Nearby is the **Ka'u Hospital** (☑928-
2050; www.kau.hhsc.org; 1 Kamani St).

Punalu'u

POP 900

Once a major Hawaiian settlement, today Punalu'u is home to a popular black-sand beach and SeaMountain, Ka'u's spooky (and controversial) condo development. Indeed, this complex has served as a bulkhead of the anti-development struggle in these parts.

TOP CHOICE Punalu'u Beach Park provides easy access to a pretty little bay with a black-sand beach famous for feeding and basking green sea turtles; snorkeling is a real treat here. Though the endangered turtles seem unfussed by gawking humans, don't harass or touch them. Punalu'u is one of the few beaches where rare hawksbill turtles lay their eggs, so be careful not to disturb their sandy nests. Responsible wildlife guidelines suggest staying at least 50 yards away from sea turtles.

The northern part of the beach is backed by a duck pond and is the best place for sunning. Most days the rough, cold waters are not good for swimming as there are forceful undertows – a lifeguard is now posted here, which is a relief. The ruins of the Pahala Sugar Company's old warehouse and pier lie slightly to the north. Follow a trail up the hill past the cement pier to find the unreconstructed ruins of Kane'ele'ele Heiau in a vast 'a'a field; the trail continues to some secluded coves.

The park has picnic pavilions, rest rooms, showers and drinking water. A concession stand is run by local aunties who happily talk story, and camping is allowed (with a county permit, see p169). Camping is only so-so, with zero privacy: the exposed area gets some heavy winds, and the parking lot can attract carousing locals at night. Come morning, the park quickly fills with picnickers and tour buses.

SeaMountain's golf course (☎928-6222; greens fee $47-50; ⊙7am-6pm) has ocean views from each of its 18 holes (many of which show signs of drought).

There are two signed turnoffs for Punalu'u between the 56- and 57-mile markers.

Whittington Beach Park & Around

This small beach park has tide pools to explore, a bird-festooned fishpond and the cement pilings of an old pier that was used for shipping sugar and hemp until the 1930s.

The ocean is usually too rough for swimming and, despite the name, there is no beach. Green sea turtles can sometimes be seen offshore. Apparently they've been frequenting these waters for some time, as the bay's name is Honu'apo (Caught Turtle).

Bathrooms with no potable water, and sheltered picnic pavilions are grouped together near a pretty, pondlike inlet. Camping on the grass is allowed with a county permit (p169).

The turnoff for the park is between the 60- and 61-mile markers. Look for it at a stop sign on the makai (seaward) side of Hwy 11, just below the rise to the Honu'apo Bay lookout.

TOP CHOICE Kawa Bay, reached via a dirt road between the 58- and 59-mile markers (stay straight rather than taking any lefts), is Ka'u's best surfable break (known locally as **Windmills**; competitions are held here occasionally). Paddle out on the northernmost end of the beach. Respect the space of locals here.

Na'alehu

POP 1070

Tiny, low-key Na'alehu is the southernmost town in the USA – a title it milks for all it's worth. The most prominent landmark is the abandoned historic theater with a giant honu painted on the roof, and movie posters announcing Citizen Kane and The African Queen. Along with its towering banyan trees and pastel plantation homes, Na'alehu has a lost-in-time rural feel.

This is Ka'u's commercial center, and it has a grocery store, laundromat, library, gas station, ATM, post office, police station and a half-dozen churches.

✕ Eating

Hana Hou Restaurant DINER $$
(☎929-9717; Spur Rd; mains $10-16; ⊙6am-7pm Sun-Thu, to 8pm Fri & Sat; 🛜🚻) A community fixture, this friendly, homespun diner offers 'the best of everything...and plenty of it.' Indeed, portions are generous and dishes, though not fancy (think stir fries and fish plates), rarely disappoint. A new 'to go' section features fresh sandwiches and wraps for picnicking, and there's live music on Friday and Saturday. Bring your own bottle. Save room for dessert.

Shaka Restaurant DINER $$
(www.shakarestaurant.com; breakfast & lunch $5-11, dinner $11-20; ⊙7am-9pm) Na'alehu's other

WORTH A TRIP

WOOD VALLEY

Near Pahala, the Tibetan Buddhist Wood Valley Temple & Retreat Center (Nechung Dorje Drayang Ling; ☑928-8539; www.nechung.org; requested donation $5; ⊙10am-5pm) makes a lovely escape. The century-old, colorful temple is wonderfully juxtaposed against the center's lush 25-acre property, where peacocks roam free. The temple's name, Nechung Dorje Drayang Ling, translates as Immutable Island of Melodious Sound, and that perfectly captures the valley's thrum of forest, wind and birdsong.

Visitors are welcome at daily chanting and meditation sittings (⊙8am & 6pm), or you can visit the temple and gift shop. In addition to a regular schedule of Buddhist teachings, Wood Valley also hosts nondenominational retreats.

For a meditative getaway, stay in the cheerfully painted guesthouse (s $65-75, d $85; 🛜). Guests have the run of the huge building, which has a full kitchen and a screened-in dining hall and lanai with lush views. The simple rooms aren't spacious, but they are clean and nicely furnished, with colorful details and new bamboo floors; bathrooms are shared. Some rooms have curtains for doors. Though rains can create dampness, there is no musty air here. There's a three-night minimum stay, or a $25 surcharge for two nights.

To get here take Maile St from Hwy 11, until it turns into Pikake St, and then Rt 151 (Wood Valley Rd); the retreat is about 4.5 miles inland. The meander up into Wood Valley is one of the island's hidden gems of a drive with farms and forest and one-lane bridges crossing babbling creeks.

---

eatery serves mainly fryer and grill fare and has a hardworking bar with *pupu* that just keep on coming. Live music most Fridays.

The well-stocked Na'alehu Market (⊙8am-7pm Mon-Sat, 9am-6pm Sun) is the best between Hilo and Captain Cook. The Punalu'u Bakeshop & Visitor Center (www.bakeshophawaii.com; Hwy 11, near Ka'alaiki Rd; sandwiches $6-8, plate lunches $8) has free samples, decent sandwiches and a picnic area in the garden out back.

A small but quality farmers market (Hwy 11; ⊙7am-noon Wed & Sat) is held in front of Ace Hardware.

Wai'ohinu & Around

Wai'ohinu has no commercial center; one sign you've reached it is when you pass the landmark Mark Twain monkeypod tree, which was planted by the author in 1866 and fell over in a 1957 hurricane. Hardy new trunks have sprung up and replaced it, and behind the tree is a macadamia-nut orchard. It's along Hwy 11, but there's no place to park.

Four miles south of Wai'ohinu is Hawai'i Volcanoes National Park's Kahuku Unit offering hikers a chance to explore ancient *kipuka* on the Kipuka'akihi Hike (p295).

🛏 Sleeping

TOP CHOICE **Margo's Corner** CAMPGROUND, COTTAGE **$$**
(☑929-9614; www.margoscorner.com; Wakea St; cottages incl breakfast $90-130; @🛜) This gay-friendly guesthouse offers two bright, pleasing cottages, plus it accommodates tent campers. The Adobe Suite has a wall of windows, double beds in *Star Trek*–like berths and a private sauna. The lavender Rainbow Cottage is smaller, and the garden setting is peaceful. Call for directions.

Macadamia Meadows B&B B&B **$$**
(☑929-8097, 888-929-8118; www.macadamiameadows.com; d incl breakfast $119-135, ste $149; 🛜🐕) Just half a mile south of town, a family of friendly macadamia-nut farmers rents rooms (one on the ground floor of their home and a couple more out back – all with private entrance). Room decor is rather chintzy, but units are spacious and clean, with lanai, cable TV and other amenities. Guests receive a free tour of the surrounding organic orchard, and there's a pool and tennis court.

South Point Banyan Tree House VACATION RENTAL **$$**
(☑217-2504; www.southpointbth.com; cnr Pinao St & Hwy 11; house $100; 🛜) Nestled high in the limbs of a huge banyan tree, this fun octagonal vacation rental offers the visually

arresting illusion of a jungle escape. Fully equipped and flooded with light, it has a great kitchen, relaxed living room (with TV) and a hot tub on a hidden deck. Honeymoon, anyone?

South Point

South Point is the southernmost point in the USA and a national historic landmark. It is widely believed this is where the first Polynesians landed. In Hawaiian it's known as **Ka Lae**, which means simply the Point, and is revered as a sacred site. You can really feel the mana here, pulsating between the windmills and grassy slopes dotted with grazing cows.

To get here take South Point Rd between the 69- and 70-mile markers. The 12-mile road is mostly one lane, so be polite, edge over to let folks pass and give a *shaka* (Hawaiian hand greeting sign). There are a couple of port-o-potties available.

For a picturesque alternative, take the backdoor route from Kama'oa Rd in Wai'ohinu to South Point Rd, an 8-mile country ramble that deposits you out just north of the wind farm.

🏖️ Beaches & Sights

Green Sands Beach (Papakolea)   BEACH
This legendary green sand beach on Mahana Bay is made of semiprecious olivine (a type of volcanic basalt), which erodes from the ancient littoral cone towering over it. The olivine sand mixes with black sand to create an unusual olive green that brightly sparkles in the sun, making this a fun, unique destination. But, as a beach, it's wanting: the tiny strand is pounded by strong waves even on calm days, making swimming dubious, and high surf can flood it completely, plus the wind howls through here something fierce. Head out before 8am for the one-hour, 2.5-mile **hike** to beat the crowds.

To get here take the road to South Point, turning left after 10 miles. Follow this road around until it dead ends at a grassy parking area; don't leave valuables in your car. Though a 4WD road continues to the beach (and locals with 4WDs sometimes wait here to sell rides), don't drive there. Braided tracks are tearing up the land, and you'll miss one of the best parts, the hike. From here, walk toward the water, past the Kaulana boat ramp, and follow the rutted dirt road left through the metal gate.

Then just keep going, enjoying the gorgeous undulating coastline and aiming for the uplifted, striated cliff-face in the distance. Once there, a slight scramble down the cliff is required to reach the beach. Bring plenty of water for this hot, unshaded hike.

Pakini Nui Wind Farm   LANDMARK
The winds are bracing here, as evidenced by tree trunks bent almost horizontal. After a few miles of scattered houses, macadamia-nut farms and grassy pastureland, you'll see the rows of high-tech windmills of this wind farm. Many are defunct leftovers from an older wind farm (Kama'oa), which was replaced in 2007 with 14 new turbines.

About 4 miles south of the wind farm are the abandoned buildings that once made up the Pacific Missile Range Station. Up until 1965 missiles shot from California to the Marshall Islands in Micronesia were tracked here.

When the road forks, veer right for Ka Lae and left for Green Sands Beach.

TOP CHOICE Ka Lae   HISTORICAL SITE
The elemental simplicity of the incessant winds, steep cliffs and endless ocean make Ka Lae feel like the edge of the earth. Even with the rushing wind filling your ears, an odd stillness and silence steals over you. From the parking area, a short walk leads down to the southernmost tip itself, where there are no markers, no souvenirs, just wave after wave rushing across the ragged lava.

Not that you will be alone, necessarily. The confluence of ocean currents here makes this one of Hawai'i's most bountiful fishing grounds, and locals fish off the craggy cliff, some bracing themselves on tiny ledges partway down. The wooden platforms built on the cliff have hoists and ladders for small boats anchored below. Locals like to cliff jump into the surging waters here, though you may want to peek over the edge and just imagine executing that heart-thumping trick. Behind the platforms, inside a large *puka* (hole), you can watch water rage up and recede with incoming waves. The only facilities are two portable toilets.

Near the parking area is **Kalalea Heiau**, classified as a *ko'a* (a small stone pen designed to encourage fish and birds to multiply). Inside is a fishing shrine where ancient Hawaiians left offerings to Ku'ula, the god of fishermen. A standing rock below the heiau has several canoe mooring holes. Ancient Hawaiians would tether their canoes

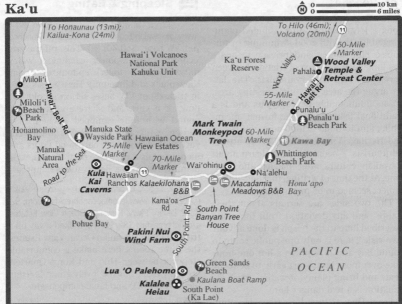

with ropes to these handles, then let the strong currents pull their canoes into the deep waters to fish.

TOP CHOICE **Lua 'O Palehomo** is about 120yd inland from the heiau, marked with a tree bent nearly horizontal from the fierce wind. A brackish watering hole (*lua* means hole in Hawaiian) that might be full enough for a refreshing dip, the views from here are breathtaking, taking in the massive flanks of Mauna Loa and everything from the southern Kona coast to Puna.

🛏 Sleeping

TOP CHOICE **Kalaekilohana B&B** B&B $$$
(☎939-8052, 888-584-7071; www.kau-hawaii .com; 94-2152 South Point Rd; r incl breakfast $249; @🛜) The *ho'okipa* (hospitality) extended by hosts Kilohana Domingo and Kenny Joyce here makes guests feel like family. Upstairs, four airy rooms feature gleaming hardwood floors, top-quality linens, open 'rainfall' showers and French doors that open to a large lanai. Downstairs, the gracious library/ music room and the wide porch invite lingering. Highly recommended are Domingo's personalized workshops on **lei making** and other native crafts. We especially love the 'community credit' initiative here, whereby

room rates are discounted for each dollar spent in Ka'u (up to $50 per day).

Ocean View

POP 2530

The largest subdivision in the USA (or the world, depending on who you ask), Ocean View is largely comprised of the *mauka* (inland) Hawaiian Ocean View Estates (HOVE) and *makai* (seaward) Hawaiian Ranchos, two huge subdivisions that were bulldozed into the desolate black lava in the 1950s. The lots were never fully settled (despite their original $1500 per acre price tag) and they remain undersettled today for a variety of reasons, including lack of jobs, blankets of vog and a reputation for substance abuse (no wonder locals call this area 'the dirty South'). Still, residents are tight-knit and proud – far preferring the rough simplicity of their independent life to the 'rat race' in Kona and Hilo, where many work.

Across the highway from each other, two shopping centers – Pohue Plaza and Ocean View Town Center – make up the commercial center of Ocean View. They contain gas stations, grocery stores, an internet cafe, ATMs and a laundromat.

Beaches

Pohue Bay
BEACH

Long a local favorite, this secluded palm-fringed beach with good swimming in turquoise blue waters and privacy to spare has long been a source of friction between developers and conservationists. The latter argue the area is a turtle nesting area, boasts innumerable **petroglyphs** and is a traditional fishing site. The former, meanwhile, aim to build a 1600-acre golf resort and Heritage Village in an effort to attract 'edutourists' – people eager to learn about Hawaiian culture after playing the back nine. At the time of writing, the long-stalled project seemed to be moving forward.

The two sides are serious about their claims, and any deviation from the route described here to the beach is done at your own risk. There is only one public route to Pohue Bay and it requires a hot one-hour hike over loose lava. Start early to beat the heat, and bring plenty of water – heat exhaustion is a real danger here.

From Hwy 11 turn into Hawaiian Ranchos at Prince Kuhio Blvd. Take your first left onto Maile St and follow that to Kama'aina Blvd. Turn left here and continue along to Poko Dr at the southern end of the subdivision. Turn left; you'll find the trail head just before the third telephone pole. Look for the white coral markers. This area is ecologically and culturally sensitive: make sure you stay on the trail, pack out what you pack in, and respect the land and community that are hosting you.

Activities

Explore a portion of the world's second-longest lava tube (with over 25 mapped miles) at Kula Kai Caverns (929-9725; www.kulakaicaverns.com; tours adult/child 6-12yr from $15/10). Evidence of ancient Hawaiians extends throughout the thousand-year-old Kanohina cave system, and tours emphasize respectful stewardship of these living museums. On the 40-minute tour you enter a short, lighted section of the cave, as expert guides present both cultural and ecological history. There's also a longer 'crawling' tour ($50) and a two-hour extended tour (adult/child $95/65). Group sizes are quite small (with two- or four- person minimums); reservations required.

Sleeping & Eating

TOP CHOICE Lova Lava Land
ECORESORT $

(www.lovalavaland.com; Hawaiian Ranchos; yurt/VW buses $60/40;) This off-the-grid 'ecoresort' (solar power, catchment water, nifty low-flush toilet) epitomizes Ocean View pluck and ingenuity. Here guests sleep in tricked-out VW buses set on an old lava flow, or a yurt, and share a central compound with fully equipped kitchen, herb garden, wi-fi and lava rock shower. The yurt, with double bed, hardwood floors and moon roof, is a cozy love nest. It's fun, well-planned DIY living. Reservations required.

Leilani Bed & Breakfast
B&B $

(929-7101; www.leilanibedandbreakfast.com; 92-8822 Leilani Pkwy, Hawaiian Ocean View Estates; s/d incl breakfast $82/93;) Tucked away on a tropical lot in Hawaiian Ocean View Estates, the three rooms here make a comfortable stopover between Hilo and Kona. Quarters are a bit tight, but the lovely grounds (complete with BBQ) and lanai compensate.

Oven Treats
BAKERY $

(Ocean View Town Center; sandwiches & meals $6-8; 6:30am-3pm Mon-Thu, to 8pm Fri & Sat, to 5pm Sun) OV's new hot spot is this bright, cozy bakery with delicious baked treats (half price after 3pm), homemade bread, sandwiches and simple meals.

Ocean View Pizzaria
PIZZA $$

(929-9677; Ocean View Town Center; pizza $13-15, sandwiches $7-12; 11am-7pm, till 8pm Fri & Sat) The submarine sandwiches are great, the pizza good and the milkshakes fine, indeed. It's a place to eat, not linger.

Road to the Sea

The Road to the Sea has a name that calls adventurers, but it's not the human-free destination it once was, despite being at the end of an extremely rugged 4WD-only road. It's a rough, windy piece of shoreline, but well worth the trip.

To get there, turn *makai* (seaward) at the row of mailboxes (near the Ka Ulu Malu Shady Grove Farm) between the 79- and 80-mile markers and set your odometer. From here you cross 6 miles over a rudimentary, seemingly never-ending lava road. The first and smaller of the two beaches is at the end of this road; it takes 45 minutes or so, depending on your comfort level driving on rough terrain.

JOHN REPLOGLE: CONSERVATION PRACTITIONER – NATURE CONSERVANCY

Job: Trail blazing and clearing, land protection advocacy, native plant conservation

Must Do

Hike to Green Sands Beach This gives you the full experience of this beautiful, windblown piece of coastline. All the 4WDs are eating away the land and accelerating erosion.

Cycle to South Point to fish and hang out.

Must See

Punalu'u's black-sand beach and turtles This place is very special. Don't miss the Kane'ele'ele Heiau here.

Hidden Gem

Lua 'O Palehemo There's a native Hawaiian saying: 'You have not seen Ka'u if you have not seen Lua 'O Palehemo.'

To reach the second beach, drive a half-mile back inland. Skip the first left fork that appears (it's a dead end) and take the second left fork. Look for arrows that are painted on the lava rock. The road heads inland before heading toward the shore again, and the course isn't always apparent. There are many places where you can lose traction or get lost. Almost a mile from the fork you'll reach a red *pu'u*. Park here and walk down to the ocean. If you decide to walk the whole distance, it's about 1.5 miles. Bring as much water as you can carry; it's hot and shadeless. These waters have excellent fishing.

Neither beach is named, but both have exquisite black-and-green sand, similar to Green Sands Beach, backed by looming cliffs. Low tide presents intriguing beach-trekking possibilities. Plan on an all-day adventure.

Manuka State Wayside Park

The facilities at this 13.5-acre state park are receiving long overdue improvements, to the tune of $1 million. You can camp with a permit (see p169), but it's isolated and there's no drinking water (only pit toilets). However, it's worth coming for the easy 2-mile **nature walk**, which provides a rare (for Ka'u) hike in the woods. A handy trail guide identifies the many native Hawaiian and introduced species you encounter, and the trail passes several ancient Hawaiian sites and ruins. The entrance is off Hwy 11, just north of the 81-mile marker.

Maui

Includes »

Lahaina 310
West Maui 322
'Iao Valley & Central
Maui 340
Kihei & South Maui . . 353
North Shore &
Upcountry 371
The Road To Hana . . . 385
Hana & East Maui . . . 392
Haleakalā National
Park 400

Best Places to Eat

» Lahaina Grill (p318)
» Mama's Fish House (p375)
» Hali'imaile General Store (p377)
» Waterfront Restaurant (p353)
» Café O'Lei (p359)

Best Places to Stay

» Ka'anapali Beach Hotel (p328)
» Pineapple Inn Maui (p358)
» Hotel Hana-Maui (p395)
» Four Seasons Maui at Wailea (p366)

Why Go?

More visitors flock to Maui than any other Neighbor Island. So many that 'Maui *no ka 'oi*' (Maui is the best) is virtually a mantra here.

It starts with the beaches, which are drop-dead gorgeous and stretch for miles. And the island boasts top-notch conditions for an oceanful of watersports. With a moonscaped national park looming from Maui's highest peak, exploring on land is stunning as well.

Maui's beachside resorts are in a class by themselves, its secluded B&Bs equally romantic. So many couples tie the knot here that 'getting Maui'd' is another bit of local lingo. Even mating humpback whales make a beeline for Maui each winter.

Have you ever stared up from the depths of a volcanic crater on a full-moon night? Kayaked past frolicking dolphins, snorkeled among sea turtles or dived into a sunken volcano? *No ka 'oi* indeed.

When to Go

Lahaina

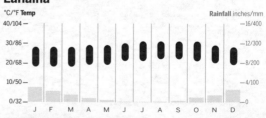

Jan–Mar Humpback whales frolic along Maui's shores during the winter months.

July Maui celebrates July 4 with a big rodeo and *paniolo* (cowboy) parade.

Oct–Nov A quiet season with good weather and lower hotel prices.

History

Maui's early history mirrors the rest of Hawaii's, with warring chiefs, periods of peace, missionaries, whalers and sugarcane. At the time of statehood in 1959, Maui's population was a mere 35,000. In 1961 Maui retained such a backwater appearance that director Mervyn LeRoy filmed his classic *The Devil at 4 O'Clock* in Lahaina, where the dirt roads and untouristed waterfront offered a perfect setting for the sleepy South Pacific isle depicted in his adventure movie. Spencer Tracy and Frank Sinatra not only shot many of their scenes at Lahaina's Pioneer Inn, but slept there too, since the inn's two dozen rickety rooms represented the bulk of Maui's hotel options.

Enter sugar giant Amfac in 1962, which sweetened its pot by transforming 600 acres of canefields in Ka'anapali into Hawaii's first resort destination outside Waikiki. Things really took off in 1974 with the first nonstop flight between the mainland USA and Kahului. Maui soon blossomed into the darling of Hawaii's tourism industry.

Its growth spurt hasn't always been pretty. In the mid-1970s the beachside village of Kihei was pounced on by developers with such intensity it became a rallying call for antidevelopment forces throughout Hawaii. Much of the last decade has been spent catching up with Kihei's rampant growth, mitigating traffic and creating plans intent on sparing the rest of Maui from willy-nilly building sprees.

Climate

Sun-worshippers will want to hightail it to Maui's west coast, which boasts dry, sunny conditions from Kapalua in the north to Makena in the south. Hana and the jungle-covered east Maui offer rain forests and gushing waterfalls. The Upcountry slopes, beneath Haleakalā, commonly have intermittent clouds, making for a cooler, greener respite and ideal conditions for land-based activities like hiking and horseback riding. For an islandwide recorded weather forecast, call ☎866-944-5025.

National, State & County Parks

The crowning glory of Maui's parks, Haleakalā National Park embraces the lofty volcanic peaks that gave rise to east Maui. The national park has two distinct faces. The main section encompasses Haleakalā's volcanic summit with its breathtaking crater-rim lookouts and lunarlike hiking trails. In the park's rain-forested Kipahulu section you're in the midst of towering waterfalls, swimming holes and ancient Hawaiian archaeological sites.

Top among the Maui's state parks is 'Iao Valley State Park, whose towering emerald pinnacle rises picture-perfect from the valley floor. For the ultimate stretch of unspoiled beach, head to Makena State Park. On the east side of Maui, Wai'anapanapa State Park sits on a sparkling black-sand beach. To explore a cool cloud forest, head Upcountry to Polipoli Spring State Recreation Area, where lightly trodden trails wind beneath lofty trees.

MAUI ITINERARIES

In Three Days

Plunge into Maui with a plunge into the sea at **Ka'anapali**, followed by a sunset cruise. On day two, stroll the historic whaling town of **Lahaina**, then treat yourself to the **Old Lahaina Luau**. Still got jet lag? Good. Set the alarm early for the drive to **Haleakalā National Park** to catch a breathtaking sunrise and hike into the crater. On the way back, stop in **Pa'ia** for Maui's hippest cafe scene and to check the surf action at **Ho'okipa Beach Park**.

In Six Days

Plan your first three days as above. Day four winds past waterfalls galore on the most legendary drive in all Hawaii, the wildly beautiful **road to Hana**. It's going to be a big day – start early, bring a bathing suit and a sense of adventure. Day five is all about those gorgeous beaches. Begin by snorkeling with turtles at **Malu'aka Beach**, followed by a picnic at magnificent **Big Beach**. In the afternoon pop by **'Iao Valley State Park** to ogle central Maui's emerald gem, and then head over to **Kanaha Beach** for the sailboarding scene. On your last day treat yourself to Maui's splashiest highlight: a **whale-watching cruise**.

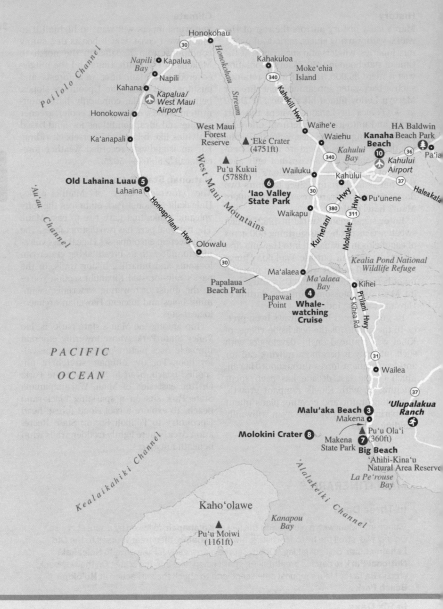

Maui Highlights

① Wind across 54 one-lane bridges on the dramatic **Road to Hana** (p385)

② Catch a soulful crater-rim sunrise at **Haleakalā National Park** (boxed text, p404)

③ Snorkel the turtle town waters of **Malu'aka Beach** (p368)

④ Sail among breaching humpbacks on a **whale-watching cruise** (p352)

⑤ Bask in the aloha at **Old Lahaina Luau** (p321)

⑥ Ogle Maui's favorite green landmark at **'Iao Valley State Park** (p350)

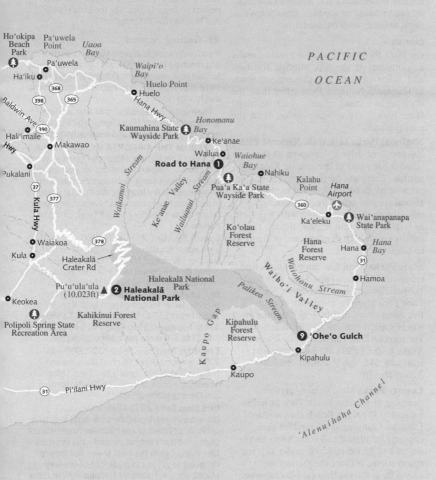

0 ——————— 12 km
0 ——————— 7 miles

PACIFIC OCEAN

Ho'okipa Beach Park
Pa'uwela Point
Uaoa Bay
Pa'uwela
Ha'iku
368
398
365
Waipi'o Bay
Huelo Point
Huelo
Hana Hwy
Baldwin Ave
390
Hali'imaile
Makawao
Hwy
Pukalani
37
377
Kula Hwy
Waiakoa
378
Kula
Haleakalā Crater Rd
Pu'u'ula'ula (10,023ft) ▲
Keokea
Polipoli Spring State Recreation Area
Kahikinui Forest Reserve
31
Pi'ilani Hwy

Kaumahina State Wayside Park
Honomanu Bay
Ke'anae
Wailua
Road to Hana ❶
Waiohue Bay
Nahiku
Pua'a Ka'a State Wayside Park
Ke'anae Valley
Wailuanui Stream
Waikamoi Stream
Ko'olau Forest Reserve
Kalahu Point
Hana Airport
360
Ka'eleku
Wai'anapanapa State Park
Hana Forest Reserve
Hana
Hana Bay
31
Hamoa
Haleakalā National Park
❷ **Haleakalā National Park**
Waihoʻi Valley
Waiohonu Stream
Palikea Stream
Kaupo Gap
Kipahulu Forest Reserve
❾ **'Ohe'o Gulch**
Kipahulu
Kaupo
'Alenuihaha Channel

❼ Watch the sunset from glorious **Big Beach** (p369)

❽ Dive the crystal-clear waters of **Molokini Crater** (boxed text, p353)

❾ Swim in the cascading pools at **'Ohe'o Gulch** (p408)

❿ Fly across the bay on a sailboard at **Kanaha Beach** (p341)

Maui's county parks center on beaches and include the windsurfing meccas of Kanaha Beach Park and Ho'okipa Beach Park. Details about county parks and beaches, including contact information and lifeguard availability, can be found on the Maui County government website: www.co.maui.hi.us.

CAMPING

On Maui there's a very clear pecking order in camping. At the top, offering the best and safest option, are the campgrounds at Haleakalā National Park. After that, the state parks – most notably Wai'anapanapa State Park – are a better option than the county parks.

National Parks Haleakalā National Park has excellent drive-up camping at the summit area and in the seaside Kipahulu section. There are no fees, reservations or permits required for drive-up camping. Haleakalā also offers free backcountry camping on the crater floor with a permit, as well as $75 cabin rentals, though the cabins are in high demand and difficult to score.

State Parks Maui has campgrounds and cabins at Wai'anapanapa State Park and Polipoli Spring State Recreation Area. Each park allows a maximum stay of five consecutive nights. Tent camping is $18 per night per site. Cabins cost $90. For reservations, contact the Division of State Parks (984-8109; www.hawaiistat eparks.org; 54 S High St, Wailuku; 8:30am-3:30pm Mon-Fri).

County Parks Maui County permits camping at Kanaha Beach Park in Kahului and at Papalaua Beach Park south of Lahaina. Camping is allowed for three consecutive nights and costs $5 to $8 per day ($2 to $3 for children under 18). For reservations, contact the Department of Parks & Recreation (270-7389; www.co.maui.hi.us; 700 Halia Nakoa St, Wailuku; 8am-1pm & 2:30-4pm Mon-Fri).

❶ Getting There & Away

AIR Most mainland flights to Maui involve at least one stopover, but direct flights to Maui are offered from some cities, including San Francisco, Los Angeles, Seattle, Dallas, Phoenix and Chicago.

Kahului International Airport (OGG; www.hawaii.gov/ogg) All transpacific flights to Maui arrive in Kahului, the island's main airport.

Kapalua Airport (JHM; www.hawaii.gov/jhm) Off Hwy 30, south of Kapalua, this regional airport has flights to other Hawaiian islands.

Hana Airport (HNM; www.hawaii.gov/hnm) This seldom-used airport in Hana sees only a few flights a week, all by prop plane.

SEA Interisland ferries connect Lahaina with its sister islands of Moloka'i and Lana'i. For information on these ferries, see the Lana'i (p415) and Moloka'i (p435) chapters.

❶ Getting Around

If you really want to explore Maui thoroughly, and reach off-the-beaten-path sights, you'll need to have your own wheels. Public transportation, while improving, is still limited to the main towns and tourist resorts.

The most comprehensive road atlas available is *Ready Mapbook of Maui County*, which shows every road on the island and is sold in bookstores.

TO/FROM THE AIRPORTS With either of the following Kahului Airport transfer services you can make advance reservations for your arrival to speed things along. Both services have courtesy phones in the baggage-claim area. Keep in mind you must reserve in advance for your *return* to the airport – and don't wait till the last minute.

Speedi Shuttle (661-6667, 800-977-2605; www.speedishuttle.com) The largest airport-transfer service on Maui. A big Speedi plus is that they've converted to bio-diesel, using recycled vegetable oil to fuel their vehicles, so if you take them you'll be traveling green-friendly. Fares for one person from Kahului Airport cost $50 to Lahaina, $54 to Ka'anapali, $74 to Kapalua, $35 to Kihei and $40 to Wailea. Add $7 to $10 more per additional person.

Executive Shuttle (669-2300, 800-833-2303; www.mauishuttle.com) More conventional vehicles, but usually has lower rates. Like Speedi, the price depends on the destination and the size of the group.

BUS Maui Bus (871-4838; www.mauicounty.gov/bus) Offers the most extensive public bus system of any Hawaiian island, except O'ahu. But don't get too excited – the buses can take you between the main towns, but they're not going to get you to prime out-of-the-way places, such as Haleakalā National Park or Hana.

The main routes run once hourly and several have schedules that dovetail with one another for convenient connections.

Routes The handiest buses for visitors are the Kahului–Lahaina, Kahului–Wailea, Kahului–Wailuku, Kahului–Pa'ia, Ma'alaea–Kihei, Lahaina–Ka'anapali and Ka'anapali–Napili routes.

Costs Fares are $1 per ride, regardless of distance. There are no transfers; if your journey requires two separate buses, you'll have to buy a new ticket when boarding the second bus. Best deal is a daily pass for just $2.

Free Routes Maui Bus also operates a couple of loop routes around Wailuku and Kahului,

ACTIVITY	BEST PLACES
Hiking	Haleakalā National Park (p400)
	Waiheʻe Ridge Trail (p340)
	Polipoli Spring State Recreation Area (p383)
Horseback Riding	Pony Express (p382)
	Maui Stables (p397)
	Piiholo Ranch (p378)
	Mendes Ranch (p339)
	Thompson Ranch (p384)
Kayaking	Makena (p369)
	Honolua-Mokuleʻia Bay Marine Life Conservation District (p334)
Kitesurfing	Kite Beach (p341)
Scuba Diving	Molokini Crater (p353)
	Makena Landing (p369)
Snorkeling	Molokini Crater (p353)
	Maluʻaka Beach (p368)
	Ulua Beach (p365)
	Kapalua Beach (p334)
	ʻAhihi-Kinaʻu Natural Area Reserve (p370)
	Puʻu Kekaʻa (Black Rock; p326)
Surfing	Lahaina (p315)
	Maʻalaea Pipeline (p352)
	Honolua Bay (p334)
Windsurfing	Kanaha Beach (p341)
	Hoʻokipa Beach (p371)
Ziplining	Piiholo Ranch Zipline (p378)
	Kapalua Adventures (p336)
	Skyline Eco-Adventures (p328)

serving major shopping centers, the hospital and government offices. These buses are geared for local shoppers, but are free to everyone – just hop on and see where it takes you!

Carry-on All buses allow you to carry on only what fits under your seat or on your lap, so forget the surfboard.

Resort Shuttles In addition to the public buses, free resort shuttles take guests between hotels and restaurants in the Kaʻanapali and Wailea areas.

CAR & MOTORCYCLE Alamo, Avis, Budget, Dollar, Enterprise, Hertz and National all have operations at Kahului Airport. Most of these rental companies also have branches in Kaʻanapali and will pick you up at the nearby Kapalua Airport. Dollar is the only rental agency serving Hana Airport. For a green option, see Bio-Beetle (p346) in Kahului.

MAUI SURF BEACHES & BREAKS

While there are hippie holdouts from the 1960s who believe the spirit of Jimi Hendrix roams the Valley Isle's mountains, today Maui's beaches are where most of the island's action is found. On the north shore, near the town of Ha'iku, is the infamous big-wave spot known as **Pe'ahi**, or **Jaws**. Determined pro surfers, such as Laird Hamilton, Dave Kalama and Derrick Doerner, have helped put the planet's largest, most perfect wave on the international map, appearing in everything from American Express commercials to mutual fund ads. Jaws' waves are so high that surfers must be towed into them by wave runners.

Not into risking your life on your vacation? No worries, there are plenty of other waves to ride. Maui's west side, especially around **Lahaina**, offers a wider variety of surf. The fun reef breaks at **Lahaina Breakwall and Harbor** cater to both beginner and intermediate surfers. To the south is **Ma'alaea Pipeline**, a fickle right-hand reef break that is often considered one of the fastest waves in the world. On the island's northwest corner is majestic **Honolua Bay**. Its right point break works best on winter swells and is considered one of the premier points not just in Hawaii, but around the world.

Gentler shorebreaks good for bodysurfing can be found around **Pa'ia**, **Kapalua** and the beaches between **Kihei** and **Makena**.

Be sure to check for any road restrictions on your vehicle rental contract. Some car rental agencies, for instance, prohibit driving on the Kahekili Hwy between Honokohau and Waihe'e and in the Kaupo district of the Pi'ilani Hwy.

The following are contacts for car rentals serving Maui.

Alamo (☎871-6235, 800-462-5266; www. alamo.com)
Avis (☎871-7575, 800-331-1212; www.avis.com)
Budget (☎871-8811, 800-527-0700; www. budget.com)
Dollar (☎877-7227, 800-800-4000; www. dollarcar.com)
Enterprise (☎877-2350, 800-261-7331; www. enterprise.com)
Hertz (☎877-5167, 800-654-3131; www.hertz. com)
National (☎871-8852, 800-227-7368; www. nationalcar.com)

Average driving times and distances from Kahului are as follows. Allow more time in the morning and late-afternoon rush hours.

DESTINATION	MILES	TIME
Haleakalā Summit	36	1½hr
Hana	51	2hr
Ka'anapali	26	50min
Kapalua	32	1hr
Kihei	12	25min
Lahaina	23	45min
Makawao	14	30min
Makena	19	40min
'Ohe'o Gulch	61	2¾hr
Pa'ia	7	15min
Wailuku	3	15min

TAXI The following taxi companies provide service throughout Maui.
Islandwide Taxi & Tours (☎874-8294)
Royal Cabs (☎875-6870)
Sunshine Cabs of Maui (☎879-2220)
TOURS A number of tour bus companies operate half-day and full-day sightseeing tours on Maui, covering the most visited island destinations. Popular routes include daylong jaunts to Hana, and Haleakalā trips that take in the major Upcountry sights.
Polynesian Adventure Tours (☎877-4242; www.polyad.com; tours $80-125) A big player among Hawaiian tour companies; offers the most variety of tours.
Roberts Hawaii (☎866-898-2591; www.rob ertshawaii.com; tours $65-120) Another biggie; more limited options but usually better prices.
Valley Isle Excursions (☎661-8687; www. tourmaui.com; tours $124) Costs a bit more but hands-down the best Road to Hana tour. Vans take just 12 passengers and guides offer more local flavor and less canned commentary.

LAHAINA

POP 10,100

Locals stop to point out rainbows in Lahaina, a one-time whaling village tucked between the West Maui Mountains and a sun-dappled sea so inviting that humpback whales return yearly to raise their young. Downtown, you can spend an afternoon browsing the art galleries, trendy shops and whaling-era sights on Front St. For a bit more excitement, stroll down to the harbor and hop aboard a catamaran for a whale-watching cruise. Hungry? After a hard day of exploring, there's no better reward than a savory meal at one of the chef-driven restaurants on the Lahaina shoreline. As for the nightlife, well, it's not exactly ripping, but it is among Maui's best, and a nightcap in a well-worn harborside pub just feels right in this history-filled town.

History

In ancient times Lahaina – known as Lele – housed a royal court for high chiefs, and its lands were the fertile breadbasket of West Maui. After Kamehameha the Great unified the islands he chose Lahaina as his base, and the capital remained there until 1845. The first Christian missionaries arrived in the 1820s and within a decade Hawaii's first stone church, first missionary school and first printing press were all in place in Lahaina.

Lahaina became the dominant port for whalers, not only in Hawaii but also for the entire Pacific. The whaling years reached a peak in the 1840s, with hundreds of ships pulling into port each year. The town took on the whalers' boisterous nature, opening dance halls, bars and brothels. The whaling industry fizzled in the 1860s, followed a decade later by the arrival of sugarcane, which remained the backbone of the economy until tourism took over in the 1960s.

Orientation

The focal point of Lahaina is its harbor and the adjacent Banyan Tree Sq. The main drag and tourist strip is Front St, which runs along the shoreline.

◉ Sights

Historic attractions in Lahaina reflect the influence of missionaries, whalers and Hawaiian royalty. Most sites are within a few blocks of the harbor. See p316 for a recommended walking tour.

FREE Old Lahaina Courthouse   MUSEUM
(☎667-9193; www.visitlahaina.com; 648 Wharf St; ⊙9am-5pm) Tucked in the shadows of a leafy banyan tree, Lahaina's 1859 courthouse is a repository of history and art. Its location beside the busy harbor was no coincidence. Smuggling was so rampant during the whaling era that officials deemed this the ideal spot for customs operations, the courthouse and the jail – all neatly wrapped into a single building. It also held the gover-

nor's office, and in 1898 the US annexation of Hawaii was formally concluded here. For gifts and a downtown map, stop by the 1st-floor **visitor center**.

The basement holds the old jail, now used as a gallery by the Lahaina Arts Society (http://lahaina-arts.com; ⊙9am-5pm), and the cells that once held drunken sailors now display artwork. The paintings, jewelry and woodwork are creations of island artists who operate the gallery as a cooperative. The entrance to the jail is outside, on the north side of the building.

On the 2nd floor, the Lahaina Heritage Museum (www.lahainarestoration.org; admission free; ⊙9am-4pm) celebrates the town's culture and history.

Banyan Tree Square   PARK
(cnr Front & Hotel Sts) Tree climbers rejoice! Lahaina's awesome banyan is the stuff of your childhood dreams. Marking the center of town, this leafy landmark sprawls across the entire square and ranks as the largest banyan tree in the USA. Planted as a seedling on April 24, 1873 to commemorate the 50th anniversary of missionaries in Lahaina, the tree has become a forest unto itself, with 16 major trunks and scores of horizontal branches reaching across the better part of an acre. On weekends, artists and craftsmen set up booths beneath the tree's shady canopy.

Wo Hing Museum   MUSEUM
(www.lahainarestoration.org/wohing.html;   858 Front St; admission $2; ⊙10am-4pm) Built in 1912 as a meeting hall for the benevolent society Chee Kung Tong, this two-story temple provided Chinese immigrants with a place to preserve their cultural identity, celebrate festivities and socialise in their native tongue. After WWII Lahaina's ethnic Chinese population spread far and wide and the temple fell into decline. Now restored and turned into a cultural museum, it houses period photos, a ceremonial dancing-lion costume and a Taoist shrine.

Be sure to stop by the tin-roof cookhouse out back. Inside is a tiny theater showing fascinating films of Hawaii shot by Thomas Edison in 1898 and 1906, soon after he invented the motion-picture camera. These grainy black-and-white shots capture poignant images of old Hawaii, with *paniolo* (cowboys) herding cattle, cane workers in the fields and everyday street scenes.

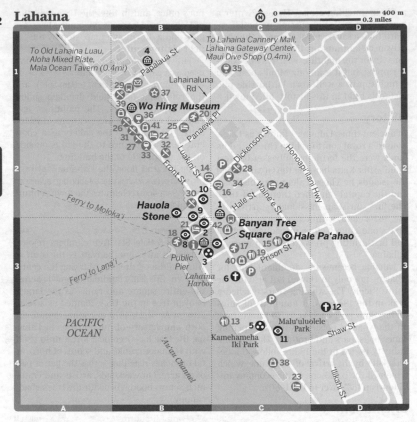

FREE Hale Pa'ahao   MUSEUM
(www.lahainarestoration.org/paahao.html; cnr Prison & Waine'e Sts; ☺10am-4pm Mon-Sat) As far as prisons go, this stone-walled calaboose doesn't look too intimidating. A remnant of the whaling era, Hale Pa'ahao (Stuck-in-Irons House) was built in 1852 by convicts who dismantled an old fort beside the harbor. The prison looks much as it did 150 years ago. One of the tiny cells displays a list of arrests in 1855. The top three offenses were drunkenness (330 arrests), 'furious riding' (89) and lascivious conduct (20).

Baldwin House   MUSEUM
(www.lahainarestoration.org/baldwin.html; 120 Dickenson St; adult/couple $3/5; ☺10am-4pm) Reverend Dwight Baldwin, a missionary doctor, built this house in 1834, making it the oldest surviving Western-style building in Lahaina. It served as both his home and the community's first medical clinic. The coral-and-lava rock walls are 24in thick, which keeps the house cool year-round. The exterior walls are now plastered over, but you can get a sense of how they originally appeared by looking at the Masters' Reading Room next door.

It took the Baldwins 161 days to get here from their native Connecticut, sailing around Cape Horn at the southern tip of South America. Dr Baldwin's passport and bible are on display as well as representative period furniture. A doctor's 'scale of fees' states that $50 was the price for treating a 'very great sickness' while a 'very small sickness' cost $10. It's only a cold, Doc, I swear.

Waine'e (Waiola) Church   CHURCH
(535 Waine'e St) The first stone church in Hawaii, Waine'e Church was built in 1832 then hit with a run of bad luck. In 1858 the belfry collapsed. In 1894 royalists, enraged that the minister supported Hawaii's annexation,

Lahaina

◎ **Top Sights**
Banyan Tree Square.............................C3
Hale Pa'ahao.......................................C3
Hauola Stone......................................B2
Wo Hing Museum................................B1

◎ **Sights**
1 Baldwin House C2
Banyan Tree Gallery.......................(see 7)
2 Brick Palace..B3
3 Fort B3
4 Hale Kahiko...B1
5 Hale Piula C4
6 Holy Innocents' Episcopal
   Church..C3
7 Lahaina Heritage Museum B3
8 Lahaina Lighthouse B3
9 Library Grounds..................................B2
10 Masters' Reading Room.......................B2
11 Moku'ula...C4
Old Lahaina Courthouse.................(see 7)
12 Waine'e Church & Cemetery................D3

Activities, Courses & Tours
Atlantis Submarine........................(see 21)
Goofy Foot Surf School.................(see 38)
13 Lahaina Breakwall...............................C4
14 Lahaina Divers.....................................B2
15 Maui Wave Riders C3
Nancy Emerson's School of
   Surfing ....(see 38)
16 Pacific Dive C2
17 Pacific Whale Foundation.....................C3
18 Reefdancer B3
19 Royal Hawaiian Surf Academy..............C3
20 Trilogy Excursions B1

◉ **Sleeping**
21 Best Western Pioneer Inn.....................B3
22 Lahaina Inn B2
23 Lahaina Shores C4
24 Outrigger Aina Nalu..............................C2

25 Plantation Inn......................................B2

◉ **Eating**
Banyan Tree Deli & Bakery ....(see 40)
Cool Cat Café ....(see 42)
Foodland..(see 37)
Gerard's...(see 25)
I'O ....(see 38)
26 Kimo's B2
Lahaina Grill...................................(see 22)
27 Ono Gelato Co......................................B2
Pacific'O...(see 38)
28 Penne Pasta Café.................................C2
29 Scoops B1
30 Sunrise Café..B2
Thai Chef ....(see 37)
31 Ululani's Hawaiian Shave Ice B2
32 Window 808..B2

◉ **Drinking**
Best Western Pioneer Inn ....(see 21)
33 Cheeseburger in Paradise.....................B2
34 Lahaina Coolers....................................C2
35 MauiGrown Coffee C1
36 Moose McGillycuddy's.......................... B1
Timba...(see 38)

◉ **Entertainment**
Feast at Lele...................................(see 38)
37 Old Lahaina Center B1
'Ulalena ....(see 37)

◉ **Shopping**
38 505 Front Street...................................C4
39 Crazy Shirts Center.............................. B1
Hale Zen Home Décor & More.....(see 28)
Lahaina Arts Society.......................(see 7)
Lahaina Printsellers.......................(see 38)
40 Maui Hands Center C3
41 Old Lahaina Book Emporium.................B2
Village Gifts & Fine Arts ....(see 10)
42 Wharf Cinema Center C3

torched the church to the ground. A second church, built to replace the original, burned in 1947, and the third blew away in a storm a few years later. One might get the impression that the old Hawaiian gods didn't take kindly to the house of this foreign deity! The fourth version, now renamed Waiola Church, has stood its ground since 1953 and still holds Sunday services.

The adjacent **cemetery** holds as much intrigue as the church. Here lie several no-

tables, including Governor Hoapili, who ordered the original church built; Reverend William Richards, Lahaina's first missionary; and Queen Ke'opuolani, wife of Kamehameha the Great and mother of kings Kamehameha II and III.

Library Grounds   PARK
(680 Wharf St) The grounds surrounding the library hold a cluster of historical sites. The yard, for example, was once a royal taro field

Volunteering on your Maui vacation couldn't be easier. In 2007 the Pacific Whale Foundation (p315 and p352), with support from the Hawaii Tourism Authority, began the **Volunteering on Vacation program** (☏808-249-8811 ext 1; www.volunteersonvacation.org) to organise voluntourism opportunities across Maui. All of the projects are free, most are at places you'd probably want to visit anyway and all of them sound cool, from removing invasive plants at Haleakalā National Park (entrance fee covered) to helping out at an organic farm or maintaining a coastal trail. And the list goes on. Since the program's inception, it has attracted 3000 volunteers who have provided 10,000 hours of service. Visit the website for a current calendar of projects. Only one or two day's notice is required for participation and most projects last about three hours.

where Kamehameha III toiled in the mud to instill in his subjects the dignity of labor.

The first Western-style building in Hawaii, the **Brick Palace**, was erected by Kamehameha I around 1800 so he could keep watch on arriving ships. Despite the name, this 'palace' was a simple two-story structure built by a pair of ex-convicts from Botany Bay. All that remains is the excavated foundation.

Walk to the northern shoreline and look down. There lies the **Hauola Stone**, a chair-shaped rock that the ancient Hawaiians believed emitted healing powers to those who sat upon it. It sits just above the water's surface, the middle of three lava stones. In the 14th and 15th centuries royal women sat here while giving birth to the next generation of chiefs and royalty.

About 100ft to the south stands the **Lahaina Lighthouse**, the site of the first lighthouse in the Pacific. It was commissioned in 1840 to aid whaling ships pulling into the harbor. The current structure dates from 1916.

FREE **Hale Kahiko**   CULTURAL PARK
(Lahaina Center, 900 Front St; ⊙9am-6pm) Yep, they paved paradise and put up a parking lot at Lahaina Center Mall. Fortunately, a patch of earth was set aside for Hale Kahiko, an authentic replication of thatched *hale* (houses) found in ancient, pre-Western Hawaiian villages.

The three houses were hand-constructed true to the period using ohia-wood posts, native *pili* grass and coconut-fiber lashings. The grounds are planted in native plants that Hawaiians relied upon for food and medicine. Each *hale* had a different function: one served as family sleeping quarters, one as a men's eating house and the third as a workshop where women made tapa (a coarse cloth made from pounded bark).

FREE **Lahaina Jodo Mission**   MISSION
(www.lahainajodomission.org; 12 Ala Moana St) A 12ft-high bronze Buddha sits serenely in the courtyard at this Buddhist mission and looks across the Pacific toward its Japanese homeland. Cast in Kyoto, the Buddha is the largest of its kind outside Japan and was installed here in 1968 to celebrate the centennial of Japanese immigration to the Hawaii islands. The mission grounds also hold a 90ft pagoda and a whopping 3.5-ton temple bell, which is rung 11 times each evening at 8pm. Inside the temple you can see priceless Buddhist paintings by Haijin Iwasaki.

Hale Pa'i   HISTORICAL SITE
(Map p324; ☏667-7040; www.lahainarestoration.org; 980 Lahainaluna Rd; donations appreciated; ⊙10am-4pm Mon-Fri) A 2-mile drive from downtown Lahaina ends at a white cottage on the grounds of Lahainaluna High School. This small building housed Hawaii's first printing press. Although its primary mission was making the bible available to Hawaiians, the press also produced, in 1834, Hawaii's first newspaper. Named *Ka Lama* (The Torch), it held the distinction of being the first newspaper west of the Rockies.

So heavily used was the original Rampage Press that it wore out in the 1850s, but several items it printed are on display. There's also an exhibit explaining the history of Hawaii's 12-letter alphabet and a reprint of an amusing 'Temperance Map' ($5), drawn by an early missionary to illustrate the perils of drunkenness. The adjacent school was founded in 1831, and students operated the press.

It's wise to call in advance. Hale Pa'i is staffed by volunteers so opening hours can be iffy.

Activities

Lahaina is not known for its beaches, which are generally shallow and rocky. For swimming and snorkeling, head up the coast to neighboring Ka'anapali (p326). For whale watching and other boat tours, see p315.

Diving & Snorkeling

Dive boats leave from Lahaina Harbor, offering dives geared for all levels. For the best snorkeling, head north to Ka'anapali or south to some of the beach parks just outside downtown. For cheap snorkel set rentals try **Snorkel Bob's** (☑661-4421; www.snorkelbob.com; 1217 Front St; ☺store 8am-5pm, office 8am-8pm), just north of downtown on Front St.

Lahaina Divers   DIVING
(☑667-7496, 800-998-3483; www.lahainadivers.com; 143 Dickenson St; 2-tank dives from $109; ☺store 8am-5pm, office 8am-8pm) Maui's first PADI five-star center offers a full range of dives, from advanced night dives to 'discover scuba' dives for newbies. The latter go to a reef thick with green sea turtles – a great intro to diving.

Maui Dive Shop   DIVING, SNORKELING
(Map p324; ☑661-5388, 800-542-3483; www.mauidiveshop.com; 315 Keawe St; 2-tank dives from $140; ☺7am-9pm) This full-service operation offers daily scuba and snorkeling trips. Everywhere we went, locals recommended the custom-built *Alii Nui*, Maui Dive's new, 65ft catamaran available for small-group scuba and sunset excursions (snorkel/sunset $129/99). Maui Dive shop has eight locations across Maui; the Lahaina branch is located in Lahaina Gateway Mall.

Stand Up Paddle Surfing

This graceful sport is easy to learn, but Maui's currents can be tricky for newcomers. Beginners should consider a lesson.

Maui Wave Riders   STAND UP PADDLE SURFING
(☑875-4761; www.mauiwaveriders.com; 133 Prison St; ☺7am-3pm) Limits class size to six students per instructor. Also offers surfing lessons.

Surfing

Never surfed before? Lahaina is a great place to learn, with first-class instructors, gentle waves and ideal conditions for beginners. The section of shoreline known as Lahaina Breakwall, north of Kamehameha Iki Park, is a favorite spot for novices. Surf-

ers also take to the waters just offshore from Launiupoko Beach Park (p323).

Several companies in Lahaina offer surfing lessons. Most guarantee you'll be able to ride a wave after a two-hour lesson or the class is free. Rates vary depending upon the number of people in the group and the length of the lesson, but for a two-hour class expect to pay about $65 in a small group or $150 for private instruction.

Goofy Foot Surf School   SURFING
(☑244-9283; www.goofyfootsurfschool.com; 505 Front St; ☺7am-9pm Mon-Sat, 8am-8pm Sun) This top surf school combines fundamentals with fun. In addition to lessons, it runs daylong surf camps and rents boards to experienced surfers.

Nancy Emerson's School of Surfing   SURFING
(☑244-7873; www.mauisurfclinics.com; 505 Front St, Suite 224B; ☺8am-8pm) The oldest surfing school on the island is owned by Nancy Emerson, who was winning international surfing contests by the time she was 14.

Tours

Lahaina Harbor abounds with catamarans and other vessels catering to the tourist trade, offering everything from whale-watching trips and glass-bottom boat tours to daylong sails to Lana'i.

Pacific Whale Foundation   ECO-TOUR
(☑667-7447, 800-942-5311; www.pacificwhale.org; 612 Front St; adult/child 7-12yr from $32/16; ☺6am-10pm; ⊕) The naturalists on this nonprofit foundation's cruises are enthusiastic, friendly and knowledgeable – and the island's best. Several types of trips, all focusing on Maui's spectacular marine environment, leave from Lahaina Harbor. Immensely popular are the whale-watching cruises, which depart several times a day in winter. In the unlikely event you don't spot whales, your next trip is free. Kids under six are always free.

TOP CHOICE Trilogy Excursions   SNORKEL TOUR
(☑874-5649, 888-225-6284; www.sailtrilogy.com; 180 Lahainaluna Rd; adult/child 3-15yr $190/95; ☺7am-7pm) This family-run operation specialises in personable eco-friendly catamaran tours that let you get your feet wet. The early (6am to 4pm) trip from Lahaina to Lana'i's Hulopo'e Beach includes a BBQ lunch and snorkeling time. Or catch the 10am boat that adds on dinner and sails back to Lahaina at sunset. In winter there's

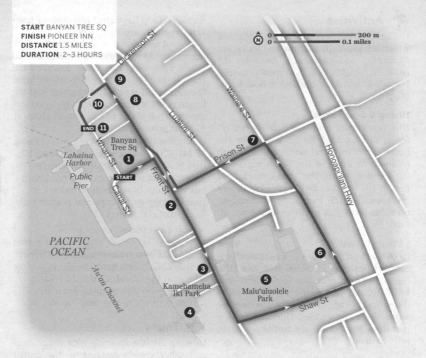

Walking Tour
Lahaina

❭ Downtown Lahaina is packed with historic sights. Swing by the visitor center (p322) for a free map of Lahaina's Historic Trail.

Begin at ❶ **Banyan Tree Sq** (p311), with its landmark banyan, the Old Lahaina Courthouse (p311) and a coral-block wall just south – ruins from an 1832 fort. Turn right on Front St to reach ❷ **Holy Innocents' Episcopal Church**, at No 561, which has a colorful interior depicting a Hawaiian Madonna, an outrigger canoe and Hawaiian farmers harvesting taro. The site was once a summer home of Hawaii's last monarch, Queen Lili'uokalani.

Just south is the foundation of ❸ **Hale Piula**, Lahaina's attempt at a royal palace. It was abandoned in mid-construction because Kamehameha III preferred sleeping in a Hawaiian-style thatched house. Fronted by ❹ **Kamehameha Iki Park**, the site is now used by local woodcarvers to build traditional outrigger canoes.

Across the street is ❺ **Malu'uluolele Park**, which once held a pond-encircled island, Moku'ula, home to ancient kings and

the site of an ornate burial chamber. In 1918 it was landfilled to make a county park.

Pivotal figures in 19th-century Maui are buried in the cemetery beside ❻ **Waine'e Church** (p312). Evocative inscriptions and photo cameos adorn many of the old tombstones. Just north, old prison cells at ❼ **Hale Pa'ahao** (p312) held drunken whalers serving time for debauchery.

Back on Front St, ❽ **Baldwin House** (p312) is the oldest surviving Western-style building on Maui, constructed around 1834. The adjacent coral-block ❾ **Masters' Reading Room** was an officers club during whaling days. It provided captains with a lookout for potential rabble-rousing in the harbor.

Returning to the harbor, stop by the ❿ **Library Grounds** (p313) for a look at the Brick Palace and Hauola Stone. End with a drink at the veranda-wrapped ⓫ **Pioneer Inn** (p320). For half a century this was Lahaina's only hotel; Jack London slept here. Despite its whaling-era atmosphere, it was actually built in 1901, after the whaling days.

whale watching along the way and you can spot spinner dolphins year-round.

Atlantis Submarine
UNDERWATER TOUR

(✆661-7827, 800-548-6262; www.atlantissubmarines.com; Pioneer Inn; adult/child under 13yr $99/45; 🚢) Visit a world usually reserved for divers aboard this 65ft sub that dives to a depth of 130ft to see coral, tropical fish and the sunken *Carthaginian,* a sailing brig that played a leading role in the 1965 movie *Hawaii.* Tours depart from 9am to 2pm from Lahaina Harbor. The reservation office is on Front St at the Pioneer Inn.

Reefdancer
GLASS-BOTTOM BOAT

(✆667-2133; Lahaina Harbor; adult/child 6-12yr per 1hr $35/19, 1½hr $45/25; ☉departures 10am-2:15pm; 🚢) A good option for younger kids, this glass-bottom boat has a submerged lower deck lined with viewing windows. The views aren't as varied as on a submarine, but the underwater scenes are still eye candy and you won't feel claustrophobic.

🎉 Festivals & Events

Lahaina's top festivals draw huge crowds, with Front St closed to traffic during these events. For updated details on Lahaina festivities, contact the **Lahaina Town Action Committee** (✆event hotline 667-9194; www.visitlahaina.com).

Ocean Arts Festival
ARTS FESTIVAL

Fete the annual humpback whale migration in mid-March at Banyan Tree Sq during this weekend-long celebration with Hawaiian music, hula, games and marine-minded art.

Banyan Tree Birthday Party
HISTORIC CELEBRATION

Branch out a bit! Lahaina's favorite tree gets a two-day birthday party, complete with a birthday cake and nature-minded art plus piñatas for the *na keiki* (children). It's held on the weekend closest to April 24.

King Kamehameha Celebration
HAWAIIAN PARADE

Traditionally dressed Hawaiian riders on horseback, marching bands and floral floats take to Front St to honor Kamehameha the Great on this public holiday in mid-June. An awards ceremony and arts festival follow at Banyan Tree Sq.

Fourth of July
FIREWORKS

Bands perform tunes on the lawn of the public library from 5pm and fireworks light up the sky over the harbor at 8pm.

Halloween in Lahaina
STREET FESTIVAL

Front St morphs into a costumed street festival on Halloween night. Forget parking; take a bus or taxi to this one.

Holiday Lighting of the Banyan Tree
CHRISTMAS CELEBRATION

Lahaina lights Hawaii's biggest tree on the first weekend in December with thousands of colorful lights, accompanied by music, carolers and a craft show. And, of course, Santa shows up for the *na keiki.*

🛌 Sleeping

Despite the throngs of tourists filling its streets, Lahaina is surprisingly sparse on places to stay. West Maui's large resort hotels are to the north, where the beaches are better, while Lahaina's accommodations tend to be small and cozy. Between Lahaina and Ma'alaea Harbor to the south are an oceanfront campground (p323) and a stylish hillside B&B (p323). See p325 for midrange B&Bs between Lahaina and Ka'anapali.

TOP CHOICE Plantation Inn
BOUTIQUE HOTEL $$$

(✆667-9225, 800-433-6815; www.theplantationinn.com; 174 Lahainaluna Rd; r incl breakfast $169-245, ste $265-290; ❋🅿🛜🏊) Alohas are warm at the 19-room Plantation Inn, a genteel oasis set back from the hustle and bustle of Lahaina's waterfront. Inside the stylish lanai (porch) rooms, flat-screen TVs and DVD players blend seamlessly with plantation-era decor. Victorian-style standard rooms come with four-poster beds. A highlight is the complimentary breakfast from Gerard's served piping-hot next to the pool. The property is not on the beach, but guest privileges are provided at sister property Ka'anapali Beach Hotel (p328).

Lahaina Inn
BOUTIQUE HOTEL $$

(✆661-0577, 800-222-5642; www.lahainainn.com; 127 Lahainaluna Rd; r $145-175, ste $195; ❋🛜) Rooms are tiny but strut their stuff like the chicest of boutique hotels. Think artsy prints, hardwood floors and a touch of greenery. And there's always the balcony if you need more space. Pastries and coffee are available in the morning in the lobby. The 12-room inn is perched above the highly recommended Lahaina Grill, and the bar is a welcoming place to enjoy a glass of wine before heading out. Per day, parking is $6 and wi-fi is $10.

LAHAINA'S BEST CHILLY TREATS

I scream, you scream, we all scream for...shave ice. And gelato. And yes, even ice cream. Downtown Lahaina whips up delectable versions of all three. For over-the-top (literally) shave ice, step up to the counter at **Ululani's Hawaiian Shave Ice** (819 Front St) and pick your tropical flavors. At **Ono Gelato Co** (815 Front St) there's always a crowd gazing at the sinful array of silky gelatos, all prepared with Maui cane sugar. **Scoops** (888 Front St) serves locally made Lappert's ice cream, but we'll make the choice easy: Kauai Pie, a luscious mix of Kona coffee ice cream, coconut, macadamia nuts and fudge.

Lahaina Shores CONDO $$$
(☎661-3339, 866-934-9176; www.lahainashores. com; 475 Front St; studio/1 bedroom from $290/355; ※◎⬚) This seven-story property is the only oceanfront condo complex in central Lahaina operated hotel-style with a front desk and full services. The adjacent beach is a good place for beginner surfers and a venue for nighttime entertainment. All the units are roomy, and even the studios have full kitchen and lanai. Parking is $8 per day, and wi-fi is $10 per day.

Best Western Pioneer Inn HOTEL $$
(☎661-3636, 800-457-5457; www.pioneerinnmaui. com; 658 Wharf St; r $150-180; ※◎⬚⬚) Between the ship figureheads and swinging saloon doors, this historic harborfront hotel packs loads of whaling-era personality. While the common space abounds in character, the rooms are disappointingly bland and lacking water views. But heck, you're in the hub of Lahaina, so who's hanging out in a room?

Also recommended:

Outrigger Aina Nalu CONDO $$
(☎667-9766, 800-688-7444; www.outrigger.com; 660 Waine'e St; studio/2 bedroom from $185/275; ※◎⬚) Tropical trees shoot through 2nd-floor walkways, giving this complex a Kipling-esque ambience. Though not on the beach, it's just one block from the Wharf Cinema Center. Hotel-style guest services available in the lobby. Wi-fi available in the pool area only.

Makai Inn CONDO $$
(☎662-3200; www.makaiinn.net; 1415 Front St; r $105-185; @◎) The furnishings could exude a bit more luster at this well-worn inn, but the vibe is welcoming and the oceanside setting shines. All units have full kitchens.

Eating

Kalua pork (cooked in an underground pit). Spicy ahi *poke* (cubed, marinated raw fish). Juicy burgers. Macadamia nut-crusted fish. Triple berry pie. Need we continue? Lahaina has the finest dining scene on Maui. But remember, fine food draws hungry hordes. Many folks staying in Ka'anapali pour into Lahaina at dinnertime and traffic jams up. Allow extra time and make reservations for the nicer restaurants.

Lahaina Grill TOP CHOICE HAWAII REGIONAL $$$
(☎667-5117; www.lahainagrill.com; 127 Lahainaluna Rd; mains $36-52; ⊙dinner) The windows at the Lahaina Grill frame a simple but captivating tableau: beautiful people enjoying beautiful food. Trust us – and the crowd gazing in from the sidewalk – there's something special about this restaurant. Once inside, expectations are confirmed by the service and the food. The menu relies on fresh local ingredients given innovative twists and presented with artistic style. Seafood standouts include the Maui onion seared ahi with vanilla-bean jasmine rice and Big Island prawns in roasted Kula corn salsa. The finishing brush stroke? Always the triple berry pie.

Aloha Mixed Plate HAWAIIAN $
(☎661-3322; www.alohamixedplate.com; 1285 Front St; mains $7-13; ⊙10:30am-10pm) This is the Hawaii you came to find: friendly, open-air and right on the beach. The food's first-rate, the prices affordably local. For a thoroughly Hawaiian experience, order the Ali'i Plate, packed with *laulau* (steamed bundle made of meat and salted butterfish, wrapped in taro and *ti* leaves), *kalua* pig, *lomilomi* salmon (minced and salted with diced tomato and green onion), poi (steamed, mashed taro) and *haupia* (coconut pudding) – and, of course, macaroni salad and rice. On your next visit tackle the awesome coconut prawns.

Mala Ocean Tavern ECLECTIC $$
(☎667-9394; www.malaoceantavern.com; 1307 Front St; mains lunch $12-24, dinner $17-19; ⊙11am-10pm Mon-Fri, 9am-10pm Sat, 9am-9pm

Sun) A favorite of Maui's smart set, Mark Ellman's stylish bistro fuses Mediterranean and Pacific influences with sophisticated flair. Recommended tapas include the kobe beef cheeseburger slathered with caramelised onions and smoked apple bacon, and the 'adult' mac & cheese with mushroom cream and three fancy fromages. For entrées, anything with fish is a sure pleaser, and everyone raves over the decadent 'caramel miranda' dessert. At sunset, tiki torches on the waterfront lanai add a romantic touch.

Kimo's   HAWAIIAN $$
(☑661-4811; www.kimosmaui.com; 845 Front St; lunch $8-16, dinner $23-36; ⊘11am-10:30pm) This is our favorite oceanfront patio on Front St. A locally beloved standby, Hawaiian-style Kimo's keeps everyone happy with reliable food, a superb water view and a family-friendly setting. Entrées include fresh fish, oversized prime rib cuts and teriyaki chicken. At lunch, if you're seeking lighter fare, don't miss the delicious Caesar salad. Mai tai are served in fun glass totems.

🍴 I'O   HAWAII REGIONAL $$$
(☑661-8422; www.iomaui.com; 505 Front St; most mains $28-39; ⊘dinner) Oceanfront I'O is the handiwork of Maui's most acclaimed chef, James McDonald. The nouveau Hawaii cuisine includes scrumptious creations such as seared, fresh catch in lobster curry and slow-braised short ribs from Maui Cattle. McDonald is so obsessed with fresh produce that he started a farm in Kula to grow his own veggies.

Cool Cat Cafe   FIFTIES DINER $$
(☑667-0908; www.coolcatcafe.com; Wharf Cinema Center, 658 Front St; mains $9-15; ⊘10:30am-10:30pm; 🍴) Burgers and sandwiches at this upbeat diner are named for 1950s icons, honoring the likes of Marilyn Monroe, Buddy Holly and Elvis Presley. The 6½-ounce burgers are made with 100% Angus beef and consistently rank as Maui's best.

Window 808   HAWAIIAN $
(www.thewindow808.com; 790 Front St; mains $3.50-8; ⊘9:30am-9:30pm) This open-air taco shack serves the best mahimahi tacos we tasted on Maui – savory bundles of fresh goodness that rise to celestial with a few drops of their potent green sauce. The *kalua* pork is also nicely seasoned. It's tucked in the courtyard just south of the intersection of Lahainaluna Rd and Front St. Cash only.

🍴 Pacific'O   HAWAII REGIONAL $$$
(☑667-4341; www.pacificomaui.com; 505 Front St; lunch $13-16, dinner $30-42; ⊘11:30am-4pm & 5:30-10pm) Contemporary cuisine with added bling jumps off the menu at this chic seaside restaurant. The food is bold and innovative – where else can you try a crispy coconut roll with seared scallops and lime pesto? Lunch is a tamer affair, with salads and sandwiches, but the same up-close ocean view.

Banyan Tree Deli & Bakery   BAKERY & DELI $
(☑662-3354; 626 Front St; mains under $10; ⊘7am-6pm) Muffins, banana bread and mango macadamia nut scones are just a few of the strumpets preening in the display case at this new pastry and sandwich shop. In the morning, return guests file in for these tasty treats, a pattern repeated at lunchtime for the top-notch pastrami sandwiches. Friendly proprietor and free wi-fi round out the appeal.

Thai Chef   THAI $$
(☑667-2814; Old Lahaina Center, 878 Front St; mains $11-18; ⊘lunch Mon-Fri, dinner Mon-Sat) In the back of an aging shopping center, this place looks like a dive, but the food's incredible. Start with the fragrant ginger coconut soup and the fresh summer rolls and then move on to savory curries that explode with flavor. It's BYOB, so pick up a bottle from the nearby Foodland.

Penne Pasta Café   ITALIAN $$
(☑661-6633; 180 Dickenson St; mains $8-18; ⊘11am-9:30pm Mon-Fri) To keep prices down, renowned chef Mark Ellman, who also operates upscale Mala, chose a side-street location and streamlined the menu to pastas, pizzas and sandwiches. That said, the food's anything but boring: garlic ahi atop a bed of pesto linguine, roasted squash with almonds, and warm focaccia.

Sunrise Café   CAFE $
(☑661-8558; 693 Front St; mains $5-11; ⊘6am-4:40pm) This hole-in-the-wall may look simple, but the breakfasts have pizzazz, from smoked salmon with eggs, Maui onions and lemon caper hollandaise to chocolate pancakes or a croissant with cheese and fresh fruit. Lunch covers the gamut of gourmet sandwiches to roast beef plates. Cash only.

Gerard's
FRENCH $$$

(☎661-8939; www.gerardsmaui.com; 174 Lahainaluna Rd; mains $33-50; ◐dinner) Chef Gerard Reversade takes fresh Lahaina-caught seafood and infuses it with flavors from the French countryside in savory dishes such as the Pacific bouillabaisse. Add a quiet candlelit porch, and it makes for a romantic evening.

Star Noodle
PAN-ASIAN $$

(☎667-5400; www.starnoodle.com; 286 Kupuohi St; lunch $9-12, dinner $9-25; ◐lunch 10:30am-3pm, dinner 5:30-10pm) Grazers can nibble from an eclectic array of Asian-fusion share plates at this sleek noodle shop. Those seeking heartier fare can dive into garlic noodles, kim chee ramen and a local saimin (noodle soup; Spam included).

For groceries, **Foodland** (☎661-0975; Old Lahaina Center, 878 Front St; ◐6am-midnight) and **Safeway** (☎667-4392; Lahaina Cannery Mall, 1221 Honoapi'ilani Hwy; ◐24hr) have everything you need for self-catering, as well as good delis.

 Drinking & Entertainment

Front St is the center of the action. Check the entertainment listings in the free weeklies *Lahaina News* and *MauiTime Weekly*, or just stroll the streets.

Bars, Nightclubs & Live Music

Aloha Mixed Plate
OPEN-AIR

(☎661-3322; 1285 Front St; ◐10:30am- 10pm) Let the sea breeze whip through your hair while lingering over a heady mai tai – come between 2pm and 6pm and they're $3. After sunset, listen to Old Lahaina Luau's music beating next door.

Best Western Pioneer Inn
PUB

(☎661-3636; 658 Wharf St; ◐7am-10pm) If Captain Ahab himself strolled through the swinging doors, no one would look up from

---

FOODLAND POKE

The ahi *poke* is served fresh, cheap and in endless combinations at the Foodland grocery store seafood counter (p381; www.foodland.com). It's one of the best deals on the island. Our favorite part? The free samples! For a to-go meal, ask for a *poke* bowl, which comes with a hefty helping of rice. The spiced ahi *poke* is outstanding.

---

their grog. With its whaling-era atmosphere and harborfront veranda, the captain would blend right in at this century-old landmark. For landlubbers, the afternoon happy hour (3pm to 6pm most days) keeps it light on the wallet.

Lahaina Coolers
CAFE

(☎661-7082; www.lahainacoolers.com; 180 Dickenson St; ◐8am-1am) This eclectic open-air cafe attracts thirtysomethings who come to mingle, munch *pupu* (snacks) and sip wine coolers. As the town's late-night bar, it's the place to head after the dance floor has emptied. Hungover? Come here in the morning for awesome *kalua* pork huevos rancheros.

Moose McGillycuddy's
FRAT PARTY

(☎667-7758; www.moosemcgillycuddys.com; 844 Front St) College kids? Bachelorettes? Dancing fools? Here's your party. This vibrant bar and restaurant attracts a convivial crowd out to party till it drops. With two dance floors, McGillycuddy's jams with live music Friday to Sunday and DJs nightly. The bar is also known for $1 drinks (cocktails and draft beers) on Tuesday and Saturday nights, with $5 cover.

Cheeseburger in Paradise
SOFT ROCK

(☎661-4855; www.cheeseburgerland.com; 811 Front St) On the corner of Front St and Lahainaluna Rd, this seaside perch is a scenic spot to watch the sunset. There's Jimmy Buffett–style music from 4:30pm to 10pm nightly.

MauiGrown Coffee
COFFEE SHOP

(☎661-2728; www.mauigrowncoffee.com; 277 Lahainaluna Rd; ◐6:30am-5pm Mon-Sat) Your view from the porch includes a sugar plantation smokestack and the cloud-capped West Maui Mountains. With 100% Maui-grown coffee, life can be good at 7am.

Timba
NIGHTCLUB

(☎661-9873; www.timbamaui.com; 505 Front St; ◐9pm-2am Thu-Sat) This sleek club above Pacific'O is as chic as it gets in Maui. Sultry lighting, posh lounges, ocean breezes, groovin' house tracks – come here to step-it-up in style. Unfortunately, style isn't free in Lahaina – there's a $10 to $15 cover on weekends. No baseball caps or MMA (mixed martial arts attire).

Hula & Luau

When it comes to hula and luau (Hawaiian feast), Lahaina offers the real deal. Catching a show is a sure vacation highlight. You can also enjoy free hula shows at Lahaina Cannery Mall (www.lahainacannery.com; 1221 Honoapi'ilani Hwy) at 7pm Tuesday and Thursday, and hula shows for the *na keiki* at 1pm Saturday and Sunday.

TOP CHOICE Old Lahaina Luau   LUAU
(☑667-1998; www.oldlahainaluau.com; 1251 Front St; adult/child 2-12yr $95/65; ⊗5:15-8:15pm Oct-Mar, 5:45-8:45pm Apr-Sep; 🚫) From the warm aloha greeting to the extravagant feast and the mesmerising hula dances, everything is first-rate. No other luau on Maui comes close to matching this one for its authenticity, presentation and all-around aloha. The feast is outstanding, with high-quality Hawaiian fare that includes *kalua* pork, ahi *poke, pulehu* (broiled) steak and an array of salads and sides. One caveat: it often sells out a month in advance, so book ahead.

🖋 Feast at Lele   LUAU
(☑667-5353; www.feastatlele.com; 505 Front St; adult/child 2-12yr $110/80; ⊗5:30-8:30pm Oct-Mar, 6-9pm Apr-Sep) Food takes center stage at this intimate Polynesian luau held on the beach in front of I'O restaurant. Dance performances in Hawaiian, Maori, Tahitian and Samoan styles are each matched to a food course. With the Hawaiian music, you're served *kalua* pork and *pohole* ferns, with the Maori, duck salad with *poha* (cape gooseberry) dressing and so on. A true gourmet feast.

'Ulalena   MODERN DANCE
(☑661-9913; www.ulalena.com; Old Lahaina Center, 878 Front St; adult $60-165, child 3-12yr $25-80; ⊗6:30-8pm Mon-Fri) This Cirque du Soleil–style extravaganza has its home at the 680-seat Maui Theatre. The theme is Hawaiian history and storytelling; the medium is modern dance, brilliant stage sets, acrobatics and elaborate costumes. All in all, an entertaining, high-energy performance.

🔒 Shopping

Classy boutiques, tacky souvenir shops and flashy art galleries run thick along Front St. You'll find lots of shops under one roof at the **Wharf Cinema Center** (☑661-8748; www.thewharfcinemacenter.com; 658 Front St) and **Lahaina Cannery Mall** (☑661-5304; www.lahainacannery.com; 1221 Honoapi'ilani Hwy).

TOP CHOICE Lahaina Arts Society   ARTS & CRAFTS
(http://lahaina-arts.com; 648 Wharf St) A nonprofit collective representing nearly 100

ART WALK

Every Friday night is 'Art Night' in Lahaina. Dozens of galleries have openings, some with entertainment, wine and hors d'oeuvres. It's an unbeatable time to stroll the Front St art scene, meet artists and nibble a little cheese. The action's from 7pm to 10pm and it's free – unless you see a treasure that catches your fancy.

island artists, this extensive gallery covers two floors in the Old Lahaina Courthouse. Works range from avant-garde paintings to traditional weavings.

Lahaina Printsellers   ART & MAPS
(www.printsellers.com; 764 Front St) Hawaii's largest purveyor of antique maps, including fascinating originals dating back to the voyages of Captain Cook. The shop also sells affordable reproductions. This location is inside Lahaina Giclee, a gallery selling a wide range of fine quality Hawaiian *giclee* (zhee-clay) digital prints.

Village Gifts & Fine Arts   CRAFTS & GIFTS
(cnr Front & Dickenson Sts) This one-room shop in the Masters' Reading Room sells prints, wooden bowls and glasswork, with a portion of the proceeds supporting the Lahaina Restoration Foundation.

Old Lahaina Book Emporium   BOOKS
(834 Front St) Maui's top independent bookstore sells new and used volumes, plus vintage Hawaiiana.

Crazy Shirts Center   CLOTHING
(www.crazyshirts.com; 865 Front St) Stylish Hawaii-motif T-shirts and hoodies for sale.

Lahaina Scrimshaw   CRAFTWORK
(845 Front St) Contemporary and antique artwork on fossil walrus teeth, mammoth ivory and bone.

Maui Hands Center   ARTS & CRAFTS
(612 Front St) Excellent selection of island-made crafts.

Hale Zen Home Décor & More   HOME DECOR
(180 Dickenson St) The zen is more Balinese than Hawaiian, but this welcoming shop is well-stocked with candles, lotions and gifts.

ⓘ Information

Emergency

Police (☎244-6400) For nonemergencies.
Police, fire and ambulance (☎911)

Medical Services

Longs Drugs (☎667-4384; www.cvs.com; Lahaina Cannery Mall, 1221 Honoapiʻilani Hwy; ☺7am-midnight) Lahaina's largest pharmacy.
Maui Medical Group (☎661-0051; 130 Prison St; ☺8am-7pm Mon-Fri, 8am-5pm Sat & Sun) This clinic handles nonemergencies.
Maui Memorial Medical Center (☎244-9056; www.mmmc.hhdc.org; 221 Mahalani St) In an emergency, this hospital in Wailuku is the nearest facility.

Money

Bank of Hawaii (www.boh.com; Old Lahaina Center, 130 Papalaua St)

Post

Downtown post office station (Old Lahaina Center, 132 Papalaua St; ☺9am-4pm Mon-Fri)

Tourist Information

Lahaina Visitor Center (☎667-9193; www.visitlahaina.com; Old Lahaina Courthouse, 648 Wharf St; ☺9am-5pm)

ⓘ Getting There & Away

The Honoapiʻilani Hwy (Hwy 30) connects Lahaina with Kaʻanapali and points north, with Maʻalaea to the south and with Wailuku to the east. Ferries to Lanaʻi and Molokaʻi dock at Lahaina Harbor.

ⓘ Getting Around

To/From the Airport

To get to Lahaina from the airport in Kahului, take Hwy 380 south to Hwy 30; the drive takes about 45 minutes. If you're not renting a car, **Executive Shuttle** (☎669-2300, 800-833-2303; www.mauishuttle.com) provides the best deal on taxi service between Lahaina and the airport, charging $43 for one person and $45 for two.

Bicycle

For bike rentals head to **West Maui Cycles** (☎661-9005; 1087 Limahana Pl; per day $15-60; ☺9am-5pm Mon-Sat, 10am-4pm Sun), which has quality hybrid and mountain bikes, as well as cheaper cruisers.

Bus

The **Maui Bus** (p322; www.mauicounty.gov) connects Kahului and Lahaina ($1, one hour) with a stop at Maʻalaea, where connections can be made to Kihei and Wailea. Another route connects Lahaina and Kaʻanapali ($1, 30 minutes). Both routes depart from the Wharf Cinema Center hourly from 6:30am to 8:30pm.

Car & Motorcycle

Most visitors rent cars upon arrival at Kahului Airport (p322)

For Harley-Davidson motorcycle rentals, try **Eagle Rider** (☎662-4877; www.eaglerider.com; 94 Kupuohi St) near the Lahaina Gateway Center. This shop rents the iconic bikes for $149 per day, helmet included.

Front St has free on-street parking, but there's always a line of cruising cars competing for spots. There's one free lot on tiny Luakini St between Lahainaluna Rd and Dickenson – but get there early, it fills fast. Your best bet is the large parking lot at the corner of Front and Prison Sts where there's free public parking with a three-hour limit. There are also several private parking lots, averaging $8 per day, with the biggest one being Republic Parking on Dickenson St. Otherwise, park at one of the shopping centers and get your parking ticket validated for free by making a purchase.

Taxi

For a taxi in Lahaina, call **Aliʻi Cab** (☎661-3688), **LA Taxi** (☎661-4545) or **Paradise Taxi** (☎661-4455). It's about $15 to $16 one-way between Lahaina and Kaʻanapali.

WEST MAUI

Simply put, West Maui is where all the action is. Whether your preference is to snorkel beside lava rocks, zipline down the mountains, thwack a golf ball, hike through the jungle or sail beneath the setting sun, West Maui has it all. The adventures are as varied as the landscape. Kaʻanapali is the splashy center of it all, a look-at-me town luring travelers with world-class golf courses, stylish resorts, oceanfront dining and a dazzling, mile-long crescent of beach.

To escape any semblance of a tourist scene, hunker down in Kahana or Napili, lovely seaside communities that are known for their condos and budget-friendly prices. Further north, Hawaiian history and swanky exclusivity have formed an intriguing, and sometimes uneasy, alliance in breezy Kapalua. And for off-the-grid excitement, there's always the wild drive around the untamed northern coast on the Kahekili Hwy.

Lahaina to Maʻalaea

The drive between Lahaina and Maʻalaea offers fine mountain scenery, but in winter everyone is craning their necks seaward to spot humpback whales cruising just offshore.

LAUNIUPOKO BEACH PARK

Beginner and intermediate surfers head to Launiupoko Beach Park, a popular surf spot 3 miles south of Lahaina. The south side of the beach has small waves ideal for beginner surfers, while the north side ratchets it up a notch for those who have honed their skills. These days, you're also likely to see paddle surfers plying through the surf. The park is ideal for families – *na keiki* have a blast wading in the large rock-enclosed shoreline pool and good picnic facilities invite you to linger. There's even a mural of young surfers hitting the waves splashed across the restroom wall. Launiupoko is at the traffic lights at the 18-mile marker.

Sleeping

For B&Bs in Maui, remember to book a room ahead of time. Showing up late at night, unannounced and without reservations, is not a good idea.

Hoʻoilo House   B&B $$$
(☑667-6669; www.hooilohouse.com; 138 Awaiku St; r $229-289; ✱@🛜🐾) One word describes this lush getaway on the slopes of the West Maui mountains: zenful. Six Asian- and Maui-themed rooms hug the A-framed center – a big-windowed community room with a grand view of Lanaʻi. Stylish furnishings differ from room to room – many contain Balinese imports – but all have a private lanai and an eclectically designed outdoor shower. Breakfast includes fresh muffins and bread, cereal, granola and fruit – often plucked from the 2-acre property's orchard (pesticide free). Proprietors Dan and Amy installed solar panels in 2011, and they anticipate that the panels will generate 90% to 95% of the house's power.

OLOWALU

The West Maui Mountains form a scenic backdrop, giving Olowalu its name, which means 'many hills.' The tiny village is marked by the Olowalu General Store and the Olowalu Juice Stand.

👁 Sights & Activities

You'll notice snorkelers taking to the water near the 14-mile marker. Don't bother. The coral reef is shallow and silty, and the 'Sharks May Be Present' signs are the real thing. There were three shark attacks off Olowalu between 1993 and 2002.

Olowalu Petroglyphs   PETROGLYPHS
A short walk behind the general store leads to these ancient Hawaiian stone carvings. Park just beyond the water tower at the back of the store and look for the signposted gate. It's a quarter-mile walk up an open road to the petroglyph site. The path is easy to follow; just keep the cinder cone straight ahead of you as you go.

As with most of Maui's petroglyphs, these figures are carved into the vertical sides of cliffs rather than on horizontal lava like on the Big Island. Most of the Olowalu figures have been damaged, but you can still make some out.

Sleeping & Eating

Camp Olowalu   CAMPING $
(☑661-4303; www.campolowalu.com; 800 Olowalu Village Rd; campsites per adult/child 6-12yr $10/5) Bordered by the ocean on one side and a dense thicket of gnarled trees on the other, the setting is pure *Survivor*. But simple amenities – cold-water showers, outhouses, picnic tables, drinking water – and a friendly caretaker kick things up a notch. A-frame cabins with six cots are also available for $20 per person.

WHALE SPOTTING

During the winter, humpback whales occasionally breach as close as 100yd from the coast. Beach parks and pull-offs along the road offer great vantages for watching the action. The best is Papawai Point, a cliffside perch jutting into the western edge of Maʻalaea Bay, and a favored humpback nursing ground (not to mention a great place to catch a sunset). During winter, the Pacific Whale Foundation posts volunteers at the parking lot to share their binoculars and point out the whales. Papawai Point is midway between the 8- and 9-mile markers. Note that the road sign reads simply 'scenic point,' not the full name, but there's a turning lane into it, so slow down and you won't miss it.

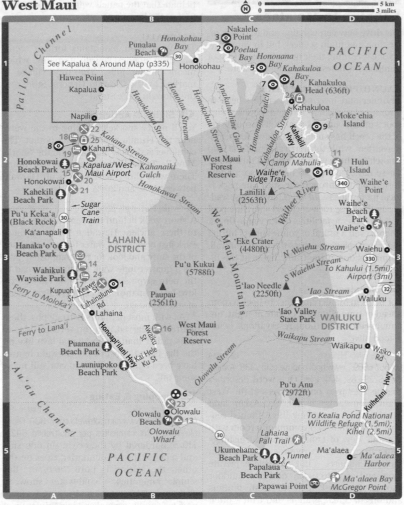

Olowalu Juice Stand　　FOOD TRUCK **$**
(Olowalu Village Rd; smoothies $5; ⊙9am-5:30pm)
Papaya. Banana. Ginger. Guava. Lime. Mango. Tangerine. And, of course, pineapple!
Smoothies made with squeezed-on-the-spot sugarcane juice are whipped up at this food truck at the north side of Olowalu General Store. Fresh fruit is also for sale.

UKUMEHAME BEACH PARK & AROUND
Midway between the 11- and 12-mile markers is Papalaua Beach Park, a lackluster county park squeezed between the road and

the ocean, though it does have firepits, toilets and tent camping under thorny kiawe trees (permit and fee required, camping not permitted on Thursdays). This place buzzes all night with traffic noise – better to skip it and head to Camp Olowalu.

At the 12-mile marker is Ukumehame Beach Park. Shaded by ironwood trees, this sandy beach is OK for a quick dip, but because of the rocky conditions most locals stick with picnicking and fishing. Dive and snorkel boats anchor offshore at **Coral Gardens**. This reef also creates Thousand

◉ **Sights**
1 Hale Pa'i B3
2 Nakalele Blowhole C1
3 Nakalele Point Light Station C1
4 Natural Ocean Baths C1
5 Ohai Viewpoint C1
6 Olowalu Petroglyphs B4
7 Pohaku Kani C1
8 Pohaku Park A2
9 Turnbull Studios & Sculpture
   Garden D2
10 Waihe'e Ridge Trailhead D2

Activities, Courses & Tours
Boss Frog .... (see 20)
Maui Dive Shop .... (see 25)
11 Mendes Ranch D2
12 Waiehu Municipal Golf Course D3

◉ **Sleeping**
13 Camp Olowalu B5
14 Guest House A3

15 Hale Kai A2
16 Ho'oilo House B4
17 House of Fountains A3
18 Kahana Village A2
19 Noelani A2

⊗ **Eating**
Farmers Market Deli .... (see 20)
20 Honokowai Okazuya A2
21 Java Jazz & Soup Nutz A2
22 Maui Tacos A2
23 Olowalu Juice Stand B5
Roy's Kahana Bar & Grill .... (see 25)
24 Star Noodle A3

Drinking
Hawaiian Village Coffee .... (see 25)
Maui Brewing Company .... (see 25)

◉ **Shopping**
25 Kahana Gateway A2
26 Kaukini Gallery & Gift Shop C1

MAUI LAHAINA TO KA'ANAPALI

Peaks toward its west end, with breaks favored by long-boarders and beginner surfers.

The pull-off for the western end of the Lahaina Pali Trail (p352) is just south of the 11-mile marker, on the inland side of the road.

Lahaina to Ka'anapali

The stretch between Lahaina and Ka'anapali offers a couple of roadside beach parks plus two good B&Bs.

WAHIKULI WAYSIDE PARK
Two miles north of Lahaina, Wahikuli Wayside Park occupies a narrow strip of beach flanked by the busy highway. Although the beach is mostly backed by a black-rock retaining wall, there's also a small sandy area. Swimming conditions are usually fine, and when the water is calm you can snorkel near the lava outcrops at the park's south end. The park also has showers and restrooms.

Sleeping
The following B&Bs are near each other in a residential neighborhood between Lahaina and Ka'anapali, inland of Hwy 30. They're not on the beach, but it's just a five-minute drive away.

Guest House B&B $$
(☑661-8085, 800-621-8942; www.mauiguesthouse.com; 1620 A'inakea Rd; s/d incl breakfast $169/189; ❋@🛜⊠) Fronted by a new saltwater pool, the welcoming Guest House provides amenities that put nearby resorts to shame. Every room has its own hot tub and 42in plasma TV. Stained-glass windows and rattan furnishings reflect a tropical motif. Free perks include beach towels and snorkel gear, a stocked community kitchen and a guest shower you can use before your midnight flight.

House of Fountains B&B $$
(☑667-2121, 800-789-6865; www.alohahouse.com; 1579 Lokia St; r incl breakfast $150-170; ❋🛜⊠) The hand-carved outrigger canoe that hangs above the common room is a showstopper, but Hawaiian flourishes don't end there. Hula rattles and warrior masks brim from every corner, and there's even a turtle painted on the bottom of the pool. The six guest rooms are nicely fitted with queen beds, refrigerators and DVD players. It's a kid-friendly place, and German is a second language here.

HANAKA'O'O BEACH PARK
This long, sandy beach, extending south from Ka'anapali Beach Resort, has a sandy bottom and water conditions that are usually safe for

swimming. However, southerly swells, which sometimes develop in summer, can create powerful waves and shorebreaks, while the occasional *kona* (leeward side) storm can kick up rough water conditions in winter. Snorkelers head down to the second clump of rocks on the south side of the park, but it really doesn't compare with sites further north. The park has full facilities and is one of only two beaches on the entire West Maui coast that has a lifeguard. Hanaka'o'o Beach is also called 'Canoe Beach,' because West Maui outrigger canoe clubs practice here in the late afternoon. A small immigrant cemetery dating from the 1850s marks the entrance.

Ka'anapali

POP 986

Ka'anapali is a place to reward yourself. Maui's flashiest resort destination boasts 3 miles of sandy beach, a dozen oceanfront hotels, two 18-hole golf courses and an ocean full of water activities. Here you can sit at a beachfront bar with a tropical drink, soak up the gorgeous views of Lana'i and Moloka'i across the channel and listen to guitarists strum their wiki-wacky-woo.

Beaches

TOP CHOICE Ka'anapali Beach   BEACH

Home to West Maui's liveliest beach scene, this gorgeous stretch of sand unfurls alongside Ka'anapali's resort hotels, linking the Hyatt Regency Maui with the Sheraton Maui 1 mile north. Dubbed 'Dig-Me Beach' for all the preening and strutting, it's a vibrant spot. Surfers, boogie boarders and parasailers rip across the water, and sailboats pull up on shore. Check with the hotel beach huts before jumping in, however, as water conditions vary seasonally and currents are sometimes strong.

For the best snorkeling, try the underwater sights off Pu'u Keka'a, also known as Black Rock. This lava promontory protects the beach in front of the Sheraton. Novices stick to the sheltered southern side of the landmark rock – where there's still a lot to see – but the shallow coral here has been stomped to death. If you're a confident swimmer, the less-frequented horseshoe cove cut into the tip of the rock is the real prize, teeming with tropical fish, colorful coral and sea turtles. There's often a current to contend with off the point, which can make getting to the horseshoe

a bit tricky, but when it's calm you can swim right in. Pu'u Keka'a is also a popular shore-dive spot; any of the beach huts can set you up.

Kahekili Beach Park   BEACH

To escape the look-at-me crowds clustered in front of the resorts, head to this idyllic golden-sand beach at Ka'anapali's less-frequented northern end. The swimming's better, the snorkeling's good and you'll find plenty of room to stretch without bumping into anyone else's beach towel. The park has everything you'll need for a day at the beach – showers, restrooms, a covered picnic pavilion and BBQ grills. Access is easy, and there's lots of free parking. Snorkelers will find plenty of coral and marine life right in front of the beach. Sea turtle sightings are common.

From the Honoapi'ilani Hwy, turn *makai* (toward the ocean) 0.2 miles north of the 25-mile marker onto Kai Ala Dr, then bear right.

Sights

TOP CHOICE Whalers Village Museum   MUSEUM

(✆661-5992; www.whalersvillage.com/museum. htm; Level 3, Whalers Village, 2435 Ka'anapali Pkwy; admission free; ☺10am-6pm) Lahaina was a popular stop for whaling ships traveling between Japan and the Arctic in the mid-1800s. This fascinating museum reveals the hardships and routines of the whaler's life. Authentic period photographs, ship logs, harpoons and intriguing interpretive plaques sound the depths of whaling history. Particularly eye-opening is the life-size forecastle displayed in back. How 20 crewmen could live for weeks in this tiny room – without coming to blows or losing their minds – is one of life's eternal mysteries. Also worth a close look is the intricate rigging between the sails on the built-to-scale replica of an 1850s-era whaling ship.

Interest piqued? Look for the full-size **sperm whale skeleton** at the front entrance to the shopping center.

Ka'anapali Beach Walk   WALKING TRAIL

Smell the salt air, take in the opulent resort sights and check out the lively beach scene along the mile-long walk between the Sheraton and Hyatt hotels. Both the Hyatt and the Westin are worth a detour for their dazzling garden statuary and landscaping replete with free-form pools, rushing waterfalls and swan ponds. A walk through the Hyatt's

Ka'anapali

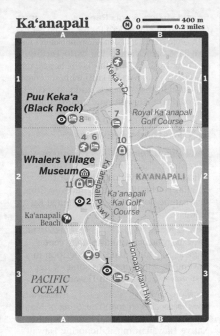

◎ Top Sights
Pu'u Keka'a (Black Rock) A1
Whalers Village Museum A2

◎ Sights
1 The Acrobats A3
2 Westin Maui Resort & Spa A2

Activities, Courses & Tours
Ka'anapali Dive Company .... (see 2)
3 Royal Lahaina Tennis Ranch B1
Skyline Eco-Adventures .... (see 10)
Teralani Sailing .... (see 11)
Tour of the Stars .... (see 5)
4 Trilogy Ocean Sports A2

◎ Sleeping
5 Hyatt Regency Maui Resort &
Spa B3
6 Ka'anapali Beach Hotel A2
7 Outrigger Maui Eldorado B1
8 Sheraton Maui A1

Eating
China Bowl .... (see 10)
CJ's Deli .... (see 10)
Hula Grill & Barefoot Bar .... (see 11)
Son'z at Swan Court .... (see 5)

◎ Drinking
Leilani's .... (see 11)
9 Longboards A3

Entertainment
Drums of the Pacific .... (see 5)
Hyatt Regency Maui Resort &
Spa .... (see 5)
Ka'anapali Beach Hotel .... (see 6)
Sheraton Maui .... (see 8)
Whalers Village .... (see 11)

◎ Shopping
10 Fairway Shops B2
11 Whalers Village A2

MAUI KA'ANAPALI

rambling lobbies is a bit like museum browsing – the walls are hung with heirloom Hawaiian quilts and meditative Buddhas. Don't miss the pampered black African penguins who love to waddle around their four-star penguin cave.

At the southern end of the walk the graceful 17ft-high bronze sculpture **The Acrobats**, by Australian John Robinson, makes a dramatic silhouette at sunset. In the early evening, you'll often be treated to entertainment from the beachside restaurants.

🏃 Activities

At Sea

Teralani Sailing   SAILING
(☑661-7245; www.teralani.net; Whalers Village, 2435 Ka'anapali Pkwy; outings $59-119; ☺hours vary) This friendly outfit offers a variety of sails on two custom-built catamarans that depart from the beach beside Whalers Village. The easygoing sunset sail is an inspiring introduction to the gorgeous West Maui coast. Snorkel sails and whale-watching outings are additional options, but no matter which you choose, you'll find a congenial crew, an open bar and decent food.

Ka'anapali Dive Company   DIVING
(☑800-897-2607; www.goscubamaui.com; Westin Maui Resort & Spa; 1-tank dives $65; ☺7am-5pm) If you've never been diving before, these are the people to see. Their introductory dive ($95) for novices starts with instruction in a pool and moves on to a guided dive from the beach. They also offer beach dives for certified divers. No rentals. Walk up, or make reservations through the 800 number, which is the American Express Tours and Activities line.

Trilogy Ocean Sports SAILING
(☑661-7789; www.sailtrilogy.com; Ka'anapali Beach Walk; ☺8am-5pm) From their beach hut in front of the Ka'anapali Beach Hotel, these folk can get you up and riding a board with a two-hour surfing lesson ($70). Snorkel sets and boogie boards rent for $15 a day.

On Land

Skyline Eco-Adventures ZIPLINING
(☑878-8400; www.zipline.com; Fairway Shops, 2580 Keka'a Dr; 4hr outing incl breakfast/lunch $150; ☺departs on the hour 7am-2pm) Got a need for speed? The Ka'anapali course takes you 2 miles up the wooded cliffsides of the West Maui mountains and sets you off on a free-glide along eight separate lines above waterfalls, stream beds and green valleys. Eco-stewardship is a mission of the company, and guides discuss local flora and fauna. If it's drizzly and breezy? Hold on tight and no cannonballs!

Ka'anapali Golf Courses GOLF
(☑661-3691; www.kaanapali-golf.com; 2290 Ka'anapali Pkwy; greens fee $195-235, after 1pm $95-120; ☺hours vary seasonally, opens about 6:45am) Of the two courses, the more demanding is the Royal Ka'anapali Golf Course, designed by Robert Trent Jones. It's tournament grade with greens that emphasise putting skills. The Ka'anapali Kai Golf Course is shorter and more of a resort course. The setting isn't as spectacular as the courses in Kapalua, but it tends to be less windy and the rates are a relative bargain.

Tour of the Stars STARGAZING
(☑667-4727; 200 Nohea Kai Dr; admission $25-30) Enjoy stellar stargazing atop the Hyatt resort. These 50-minute viewings are limited to 10 people, use a 16in-diameter telescope and are held at 8pm, 9pm and 10pm on clear nights. Romantic types should opt for the couples-only viewing at 11pm Friday and Saturday, which rolls out champagne and chocolate-covered strawberries.

Royal Lahaina Tennis Ranch TENNIS
(☑667-5200; 2780 Keka'a Dr; per person per day $10; ☺pro shop 8am-noon & 2-6pm Mon-Fri, until 5pm Sat & Sun) Named the '2010 Facility of the Year' by the USTA, this is the largest tennis complex in West Maui, with six courts lit for night play. Rackets and shoes can be rented. Private lessons and group clinics are available.

★ Festivals & Events

Maui Onion Festival FOOD FESTIVAL
(www.whalersvillage.com) Held at Whalers Village in late April or early May, this popular celebration highlights everything that can be done with Maui's famed Kula onions.

Hula O Na Keiki HULA COMPETITION
(www.kbhmaui.com) Children take center stage at this hula dance competition in November, which features some of the best *na keiki* dancers in Hawaii.

Na Mele OMaui HAWAIIAN MUSIC
(www.kaanapaliresort.com) The 'Song of Maui' features children's choral groups singing Native Hawaiian music honoring Hawaii's last monarch, Queen Lili'uokalani, who was a renowned music composer and cultural revivalist. This aloha-rich event is held in early December at the Maui Arts & Cultural Center.

🛏 Sleeping

The following accommodations are on the beach or within walking distance of it. In addition to these resorts, there are nearby B&Bs (p325) between Ka'anapali and Lahaina.

TOP CHOICE **Ka'anapali Beach Hotel** RESORT $$
(☑661-0011, 800-262-8450; www.kbhmaui.com; 2525 Ka'anapali Pkwy; r from $159; ✳@🛜🏊🐾) This welcoming property feels like summer camp – in a good way. The hotel is a little older than its neighbors and the style is far from posh, but it has its own special charms: warm staff, nightly hula shows, an

---

SPIRITS LEAP

According to traditional Hawaiian beliefs, Pu'u Keka'a (Black Rock), the westernmost point of Maui, is a place where the spirits of the dead leap into the unknown to be carried to their ancestral homeland. The rock is said to have been created during a scuffle between the demigod Maui and a commoner who questioned Maui's superiority. Maui chased the man to this point, froze his body into stone then cast his soul out to sea. Today, daring teens wait their turn to leap off the rock for a resounding splash into the cove below.

outdoor tiki bar, tidy grounds framed by palm trees and an enviable location on a gorgeous stretch of beach. Family-friendly activities, from lei-making to ukulele sing-alongs, assure that the *na keiki* will never be bored. Bring a camera and a hankie to your farewell lei ceremony. Parking is $9 per day and wi-fi $10 per day (but free in the lobby).

Outrigger Maui Eldorado
CONDO $$
(661-0021, 888-339-8585; www.outrigger.com; 2661 Keka'a Dr; studio/1 bedroom from $145/259;) How close are you to the fairways at the Maui Eldorado? One sign says it all: 'Beware of flying golf balls in the lanai areas.' And it's true, you can literally step off your lanai and onto the fairways at this quiet condo development bordering the Royal Ka'anapali Golf Course. Units are not on the beach, but the complex isn't far from the ocean, and the resort shuttle stops out front. The best rooms are the large studios which have kitchens set apart from the bedroom area. Parking is $7 per day. Wi-fi available in the lobby.

Sheraton Maui
RESORT $$$
(661-0031, 866-716-8109; www.sheraton-maui.com; 2605 Ka'anapali Pkwy; r from $525;) Hmm, darling. Shall we snorkel beside turtles? Or watch whales breach from the room? Or maybe catch the sunset cliff dive? The choices are many at this sleek hotel, which sprawls across 23 acres at the north end of the Ka'anapali Beach Walk. The beach itself bumps against Pu'u Keka'a (Black Rock), renowned for its snorkeling and silhouette. Rooms have rich wood tones and Hawaiian prints; grounds have night-lit tennis courts, a fitness center, a lava-rock swimming pool and the spa at Pu'u Keka'a. The $25 daily resort fee includes parking, local and Lahaina shuttle service and wi-fi (available in a few common areas only).

Hyatt Regency Maui Resort & Spa
RESORT $$$
(661-1234, 800-492-1234; www.maui.hyatt.com; 200 Nohea Kai Dr; r from $404;) The lobby atrium is tricked out with cockatoos in palm trees and extravagant artwork, the grounds given over to gardens and swan ponds. Kids of all ages will thrill in the water world of meandering pools, swim-through grottos and towering water slides. Angle for a room in the revamped Lahaina Tower; the furnishings were looking a bit tired in the

Napili Tower, yet to be upgraded. The $25 daily resort fee includes parking and wi-fi.

Eating

Don't limit yourself to Ka'anapali's restaurants. Many of Maui's top chefs are just a skip down the road in Lahaina.

TOP CHOICE Hula Grill & Barefoot Bar
HAWAII REGIONAL $$
(667-6636; http://hulagrillkaanapali.com; Whalers Village, 2435 Ka'anapali Pkwy; bar & grill $8-20, dinner mains $10-32; bar 11am-11pm, dining room 5-9:30pm) The Barefoot Bar is your Maui postcard: coconut-frond umbrellas, the sand beneath your sandals and the guy strumming the guitar. It's the ambience that impresses most, and there's no better place on the beach walk to sip mai tai and nibble *pupu* by the sea. The Kapulu Joe pork sandwich with mac-nut slaw – add a dash of chili water – is reliably good, and the beer-battered maui taco hits the spot too. Dinner inside at the restaurant kicks it up a notch with spicy kiawe-grilled seafood.

Son'z at Swan Court
ECLECTIC $$$
(667-4506; Hyatt Regency Maui Resort & Spa, 200 Nohea Kai Dr; most mains $32-50; dinner) Between the waterfalls, the swan pond and the tiki torches, this is Ka'anapali's most romantic night out. The award-winning cuisine includes the expected fine-dining steak and lobster entrées, but many appetisers and entrées highlight the best of Maui, from the ravioli with Surfing Dairy goat cheese to the Maui Cattle tenderloin with local coffee marinade. Incredible wine list, too.

CJ's Deli
CAFE $
(667-0968; www.cjsmaui.com; Fairway Shops, 2580 Keka'a Dr; mains $8-12; 7am-8pm) For picnics, pick up a Hana Lunch Box ($12) at this New York–style deli-cafe. It comes with a sandwich, Maui chips, a homemade Hana bar, soda and a returnable cooler. If you're dining in, salads, burgers and paninis are also on the menu, plus meatloaf and pot roast.

China Bowl
CHINESE $$
(661-0660; www.chinaboatandbowlmaui.com; Fairway Shops, 2580 Keka'a Dr; mains $9-24; 10:30am-9:30pm Mon-Sat, 11am-9:30pm Sun) This family-friendly place wok-fries authentic Szechuan dishes with fiery peppers as well as Mandarin fare for tamer palates. The kids' meal with drink is just $6.25.

🍸 Drinking & Entertainment

Most seaside bars offer live music in the evening. Luau and hula shows are also popular. Check www.mauitimes.com for performers and schedules.

Live Music

The places listed here, as well as the Hula Grill & Barefoot Bar (p329), have live music throughout the afternoon and evening. It's typically Jimmy Buffett–style guitar tunes, but is occasionally spiced up with some ukulele strumming.

Leilani's ACOUSTIC & CLASSIC ROCK
(✆661-4495; Whalers Village, 2435 Ka'anapali Pkwy) This open-air bar and restaurant beside the beach is the place to linger over a cool drink while catching a few rays. It also has a good grill and *pupu* menu. Live music Friday through Sunday.

Longboards ACOUSTIC
(✆667-8220; Marriott's Maui Ocean Club, 100 Nohea Kai Dr) Longboards has a solo guitarist from 5:30pm to 8pm Monday through Friday.

Hyatt Regency Maui Resort & Spa ACOUSTIC
(✆661-1234; 200 Nohea Kai Dr) There's live music poolside at Umalu from 6:30pm to 8:30pm nightly. Free torch lighting between 5:30pm and 6pm.

Hula, Luau & Theater

Ka'anapali Beach Hotel HULA
(✆661-0011; www.kbhmaui.com; 2525 Ka'anapali Pkwy) Maui's most Hawaiian hotel cheerfully entertains anyone who chances by between 6:30pm and 7:30pm with a free hula show. Enjoy mai tai and brews at the adjacent Tiki Bar, with music and dancing nightly in the Tiki Courtyard.

Sheraton Maui CLIFF DIVE
(✆661-0031; 2605 Ka'anapali Pkwy) Everybody swings by to watch the torch-lighting and cliff-diving ceremony from Pu'u Keka'a that takes place at sunset. There's also live music in the late afternoon at the Cliff Dive Bar.

Drums of the Pacific LUAU
(✆667-4727; Hyatt Regency Maui Resort & Spa, 200 Nohea Kai Dr; adult/teen 13-20yr/child 6-12yr $96/61/49; ☺5-8pm) Ka'anapali's best luau includes an *imu* ceremony (unearthing of a roasted pig from an underground oven), an open bar, a Hawaiian-style buffet dinner and a flashy South Pacific dance and music show.

Whalers Village HULA, DANCE
(✆661-4567; www.whalersvillage.com; 2435 Ka'anapali Pkwy) Ka'anapali's shopping center hosts free hula and Polynesian dance performances from 7pm to 8pm on Monday, Wednesday and Saturday. Check the website for a monthly calendar of all events and classes.

🛍 Shopping

You'll find more than 50 shops at the **Whalers Village** (✆661-4567; www.whalersvillage.com; 2435 Ka'anapali Pkwy; ☺9:30am-10pm) shopping center:

ABC Store SUNDRIES
(www.abcstores.com) Stop here for sunblock and great beach totes.

Honolua Surf BEACHWEAR
(www.honoluasurf.com) The place to pick up Maui-style board shorts and other casual beachwear.

Honolua Wahine WOMEN'S SWIMWEAR
(www.honoluasurf.com) Get your bikinis here.

Lahaina Printsellers ART, MAPS
(www.printsellers.com) Packable Hawaiian prints and maps.

Martin & MacArthur HAWAIIAN CRAFTS
(www.martinandmacarthur.com) Head to Martin & MacArthur for museum-quality Hawaiian-made wood carvings, paintings and other crafts.

ℹ Getting Around

The **Maui Bus** (p322; www.mauicounty.gov) connects Whalers Village Shopping Center in Ka'anapali with the Wharf Cinema Center in Lahaina hourly from 6am to 8pm, and runs north up the coast to Kahana and Napili hourly from 6am to 8pm (see the boxed text, p332).

The free Ka'anapali Trolley runs between the Ka'anapali hotels, Whalers Village and the golf courses about every 20 minutes between 10am and 10pm.

Cabs often line up beside the trolley and Maui Bus stop in front of Whalers Village on Ka'anapali Pkwy.

Ka'anapali's resort hotels offer free beach parking for nonguests, but the spaces allotted are so limited that they commonly fill up by mid-morning. Your best bet for beach parking is at the south end of the Hyatt, which has more slots on offer than the other hotels. Another option is the pay parking at Whalers Village, which costs $2 per half-hour (parking validation varies by merchant).

Honokowai

POP HONOKOWAI-NAPILI 7357

Honokowai and its condos may not have the glamour and pizzazz of pricier Ka'anapali to the south, but it has its virtues. It's convenient, affordable and low-rise, and the ocean views are as fine as in the upscale resorts. Another perk: in winter this is the best place in West Maui to spot passing whales right from your room lanai.

The main road, which bypasses the condos, is Honoapi'ilani Hwy (Hwy 30). The parallel shoreline road is Lower Honoapi'ilani Rd, which leads into Honokowai.

Beaches

Honokowai Beach Park   BEACH

The real thrills here are on land, not in the water. This family-friendly park in the center of town has cool playground facilities for kids and makes a nice spot for a picnic. Forget swimming, though. The water is shallow and the beach is lined with a submerged rock shelf. Water conditions improve at the south side of town, and you could continue walking along the shore down to lovely Kahekili Beach Park (p326) at the northern end of Ka'anapali.

Activities

Boss Frog   SNORKEL GEAR

(665-1200; www.bossfrog.com; 3636 Lower Honoapi'ilani Rd; per day from $1.50; 8am-5pm) Offers great rental prices for a mask, snorkel and fins.

Sleeping

Noelani   CONDO $$$

(669-8374, 800-367-6030; www.noelani-condo-resort.com; 4095 Lower Honoapi'ilani Rd; studios from $157, 1/2/3 bedroom from $197/290/357;) This 50-unit condo complex is so close to the water you can sit on your lanai and watch turtles swimming in the surf. The units cover a wide range, from cozy studios to three-bedroom suites, but all have ocean views. Two heated pools, a Jacuzzi, a small exercise room and concierge services are additional perks.

Hale Kai   CONDO $$

(669-6333, 800-446-7307; www.halekai.com; 3691 Lower Honoapi'ilani Rd; 1/2/3 bedroom $160/210/350;) This two-story place has plenty of Hawaiian accents, from the room decor to the lava-rock exterior. It's perched on the water's edge: step off your lanai and onto the sand. The three-bedroom corner unit has a cool loft, wraparound ocean-view windows and all the character of a Hawaiian beach house.

Eating

Farmers Market Deli   DELI $

(669-7004; 3636 Lower Honoapi'ilani Rd; sandwiches under $6; 7am-7pm;) Stop here for healthy takeout fare. The salad bar (with free samples) includes organic goodies and hot veggie dishes. The smoothies are first-rate, and Maui-made ice cream is sold by the scoop. On Monday, Wednesday and Friday mornings vendors sell locally grown produce in the parking lot.

TOP CHOICE Honokowai Okazuya   PLATE LUNCH $$

(665-0512; 3600 Lower Honoapi'ilani Rd; mains $10-18; 10am-9pm Mon-Sat) The appeal is not immediately apparent. The place is tiny, prices are high and the choices seem weird (kung pao chicken *and* spaghetti with meatballs?). But then you nibble a forkful of piping-hot Mongolian beef. Hmm, it's OK. Chomp chomp. You know, that's pretty interesting. Gulp gulp. What is that spice? Savor savor – until the whole darn container is empty. This place – primarily takeout – is all about the cooking, with plate lunch specialties taking a gourmet turn. Cash only.

Java Jazz & Soup Nutz   ECLECTIC $$

(667-0787; www.javajazz.net; Honokowai Marketplace, 3350 Lower Honoapi'ilani Rd; breakfast & lunch $6-12, dinner $10-30; 6am-10pm) With a menu as eclectic as its decor, this arty cafe never disappoints. Breakfast packs 'em in with everything from bagels to frittata; lunch revolves around Greek salads and innovative sandwiches. Dinner gets downright meaty with the tastiest flame-grilled filet mignon you'll find anywhere on Maui.

Kahana

Trendy Kahana, the village north of Honokowai, boasts million-dollar homes, upscale beachfront condominiums and Maui's only microbrewery.

Sights & Activities

The sandy beach fronting the village offers reasonable swimming. Park at seaside Pohaku Park and walk north a couple of minutes to reach the beach. Pohaku Park

ⓘ TAKE THE BUS? ARE YOU SERIOUS?

Oh yes, we are. If you're staying in Lahaina, Kahana or Napili and want to visit Ka'anapali without worrying about parking, consider the **Maui Bus** (p322; www.mauicounty.gov). Maui's buses are clean, make relatively few stops and cost only $1 per ride. In Ka'anapali, riders disembark in front of Whalers Village. The Ka'anapali Islander 25 loops between the Wharf Cinema Center in Lahaina and Whalers Village in Ka'anapali hourly between 6:30am and 8:30pm. The Napili Islander 30 runs hourly between Napili Kai and Whalers Village from 5:30am to 8:30pm.

itself has an offshore break called S-Turns that attracts surfers.

Maui Dive Shop   DIVING, SNORKELING
(☎669-3800; www.mauidiveshop.com; Kahana Gateway, 4405 Honoapi'ilani Hwy; 2-tank dives $140, snorkel set rentals per day $6; ☉8am-6pm) Come here for information about a full range of dives and to rent snorkel gear.

🛏 Sleeping

Kahana Village   CONDO $$$
(☎669-5111, 800-824-3065; www.kahanavillage. com; 4531 Lower Honoapi'ilani Rd; 2/3 bedroom from $290/445; 🛜🗐) With their A-frame ceilings, airy lofts and oceanfront views, 2nd-story units have a fun 'vacation' vibe. The breezy appeal of the interior is well-matched outside with lush tropical flora and weekly mai tai parties with live Hawaiian music. Some condos have views of Lana'i while others face Moloka'i. Every unit has a lanai, full kitchen and washer and dryer.

🍴 Eating & Drinking

Roy's Kahana Bar & Grill   HAWAII REGIONAL $$$
(☎669-6999; www.roysrestaurant.com; Kahana Gateway, 4405 Honoapi'ilani Hwy; mains $27-40; ☉dinner) From its lofty 2nd-floor perch, Chef Roy Yamaguchi's Maui flagship beckons like a guiding star, drawing gourmands to a promised land of exquisitely prepared island and regional fare. Yamaguchi runs a little empire of restaurants, and this location rakes in a crowd with savory dishes such as the sashimi-like blackened ahi with Chinese

mustard and a local rib eye with a bacon and blue cheese cream sauce. Aloha!

Maui Brewing Company   BREWPUB $$
(☎669-3474; www.mauibrewingco.com; Kahana Gateway, 4405 Honoapi'ilani Hwy; mains $12-25; ☉11am-midnight) Maui Cattle Co burgers. *Kalua* pork pizza. Mahimahi fish and chips. Pub grub takes a Hawaiian twist at this cavernous brewpub hunkered in the corner of Kahana Gateway. The company, honored as one of Hawaii's top green businesses in 2008, implements sustainable practices where it can (see the boxed text, p593). The Bikini Blonde lager, Big Swell IPA and Coconut Porter are always on tap, supplemented by a half-dozen or so seasonal brews.

Hawaiian Village Coffee   CAFE $
(www.hawaiianvillagecoffee.com; Kahana Gateway, 4405 Honoapi'ilani Hwy; snacks under $7; ☉6am-8pm Sun-Thu, until 9pm Fri & Sat; @) Off-duty surfers shoot the breeze at this low-key coffee shop. Surf the net on one of three computers in back (20 minutes for $3).

Napili

Napili is a tranquil bayside community tucked between the posh barricades of Kapalua to the north and the hustle and bustle of Kahana and Ka'anapali to the south. For an oceanfront retreat that's a bit more affordable – but not too far from the action – we highly recommend this sun-kissed center of calm.

◉ Sights

The deep golden sands and gentle curves of **Napili Beach** offer good beachcombing at any time and excellent swimming and snorkeling when it's calm. Big waves occasionally make it into the bay in winter, and when they do it's time to break out the skimboards – the steep drop at the beach provides a perfect run into the surf.

🛏 Sleeping

Napili Bay is surrounded by older condos and small, mellow resorts.

TOP CHOICE Napili Surf Beach Resort   CONDO $$
(☎669-8002, 800-541-0638; www.napilisurf.com; 50 Napili Pl; studios from $171, 1 bedroom from $260; 🛜🗐) Regulars bring their own appetizers to the Wednesday mai tai party at this friendly, well-maintained property tucked on a gentle curve of sand on Napili Bay.

One of the best deals in West Maui, a stay here includes complimentary maid service and wi-fi, not to mention the tasty free mai tai. Full kitchens are nice if you want to eat in, but the Gazebo is next door and the Sea House just a beach stroll away. Guests are welcomed with a fresh half-pineapple in the refrigerator. Cash or check only.

TOP CHOICE Hale Napili
CONDO $$

(☑669-6184, 800-245-2266; www.halenapilimaui.com; 65 Hui Dr; studios from $160, 1 bedroom $260; @🛜🏊) The aloha of the Hawaiian manager ensures lots of repeat guests at these tidy condos smack on the beach. The place is a welcome throwback to an earlier era, when everything in Maui was small and personable. The 18 neat-as-a-pin units have tropical decor, full kitchens and oceanfront lanai.

The Mauian
CONDO $$

(☑669-6205, 800-367-5034; www.mauian.com; 5441 Lower Honoapi'ilani Rd; studios with kitchens from $199, r $179; @🛜🏊) Most condos in Napili wear their age gracefully, but not the sassy Mauian, a 44-room condo/hotel hybrid kicking up her heels like a teenager. Bamboo ceilings, frond prints, crisp whites and browns, Tempur-Pedic mattresses – rooms are sharp, stylish and comfortable, and come with a lanai with big views. Units do not have TVs, phones or wi-fi, but all three are available in the common area.

Napili Kai Beach Resort
INDEPENDENT HOTEL $$$

(☑669-6271, 800-367-5030; www.napilikai.com; 5900 Lower Honoapi'ilani Rd; r/studios from $250/320; @🛜🏊) Spread across several acres at the northern end of Napili Bay, this pampering resort offers classic appeal. The units, which tastefully blend Polynesian decor with Asian touches, have oceanview lanai and, in most cases, kitchenettes. For modern style and wi-fi, reserve a room in the renovated Puna II building. Some units have air-con, so ask when booking. Wi-fi also available in the lobby.

✖️ Eating

TOP CHOICE Gazebo
CAFE $

(☑669-5621; Outrigger Napili Shores, 5315 Lower Honoapi'ilani Rd; meals $8-11.25; ⊙7:30am-2pm) Locals aren't kidding when they tell you to get here early to beat the crowds and the line. But a 7:10am arrival is worth it for this beloved open-air restaurant – literally a gazebo on the beach – with a gorgeous waterfront setting. The tiny cafe is known for its breakfasts, and sweet tooths love the white chocolate mac-nut pancakes. Meal-size salads, hearty sandwiches and the *kalua* pig plate steal the scene at lunch.

Sea House Restaurant
HAWAII REGIONAL $$

(☑669-1500; www.napilikai.com; Napili Kai Beach Resort, 5900 Lower Honoapi'ilani Rd; breakfast $9-12, lunch $9-14, dinner $25-37; ⊙breakfast, lunch & dinner) Pssst. Want a $9 meal framed by a million dollar view? Sidle up to the bar at this tiki-lit favorite, order a bowl of the smoky seafood chowder then watch as the perfectly framed sun drops below the horizon in front of you. Bravo! If you stick around, and you should, seafood and steak dishes are menu highlights.

Maui Tacos
MEXICAN $

(www.mauitacos.com; Napili Plaza, 5095 Napilihau St; mains under $10; ⊙9am-8pm) Mexican fare can be island-style healthy. The salsas and beans are prepared fresh daily, transfat-free oil replaces lard, and fresh veggies and local fish highlight the menu.

☆ Entertainment

TOP CHOICE Masters of Hawaiian Slack Key Guitar Concert Series
LIVE MUSIC

(☑669-3858; www.slackkey.com; Napili Kai Beach Resort, 5900 Lower Honoapi'ilani Rd; admission $40; ⊙7:30pm Wed) Top slack key guitarists appear regularly at this exceptional concert series, and George Kahumoku Jr, a slack key legend in his own right, is the weekly host. As much a jam session as a concert, this is a true Hawaiian cultural gem that's worth going out of your way to experience. Reservations recommended.

Kapalua & Around

POP 382

Kapalua is a posh resort sprung from the soil of a onetime pineapple plantation. Long known as a world-class golf destination, Kapalua is now making an effort to broaden its appeal. An awesome zipline takes people skyward for new thrills, trails in a once-restricted forest are open to the public and the dining scene is among the island's best. The nightlife doesn't exactly sizzle, but the beaches – all with public access – sure do.

To avoid well-manicured glitz altogether, swoop past the resort and drive the rugged northern coast. The untamed views are guaranteed to replenish your soul.

If uninterrupted sunshine is your goal, note that Kapalua can be a bit rainier and windier than points south.

🏃 Beaches & Sights

TOP CHOICE DT Fleming Beach Park   BEACH

Surrounded by ironwood trees and backed by an old one-room schoolhouse, this sandy crescent – crowned America's Best Beach by *Dr Beach* in 2006 – appears like an outpost from another era. In keeping with its Hawaiian nature, the beach is the domain of wave riders. Experienced surfers and bodysurfers find good action here, especially in winter. The shorebreaks can be brutal, however, and this beach is second only to Ho'okipa for injuries. The reef on the right is good for snorkeling in summer when it's very calm.

Fleming has restrooms, showers, grills, picnic tables and a lifeguard. The access road is off Honoapi'ilani Hwy (Hwy 30), immediately north of the 31-mile marker.

The Coastal Trail and Mahana Ridge Trail (see the boxed text, p337) connect here.

Oneloa Beach   BEACH

Also on the Coastal Trail, this white-sand jewel is worth seeking out. Fringed by low sand dunes covered in beach morning glory, it's a fine place to soak up rays. On calm days swimming is good close to shore, as is snorkeling in the protected area along the rocky point at the north side of the beach. When there's any sizable surf, strong rip currents can be present.

The half-mile strand – Oneloa means 'long sand' – is backed by gated resort condos and restricted golf greens, and beach access requires a sharp eye. Turn onto Ironwood Lane, then left into the parking lot opposite the Ironwoods gate. Arrive early or around lunchtime, when people are heading out.

Kapalua Beach   BEACH

This crescent-shaped beach, with its clear view of Moloka'i across the channel, is a sure bet for a fun day in the water. Long rocky outcrops at both ends of the bay make Kapalua Beach the safest year-round swimming spot on this coast. You'll find colorful snorkeling on the right side of the beach, with abundant tropical fish and orange slate-pencil sea urchins.

Take the drive immediately north of Napili Kai Beach Resort to get to the beach parking area, where there are restrooms and showers. A tunnel leads from the parking lot north to the beach. The beach is also a starting point for the Coastal Trail (see the boxed text, p337).

Dragon's Teeth   CULTURAL SITE

Razor-sharp spikes crown rocky Makaluapuna Point, looking uncannily like the mouth of an imaginary dragon. The 3ft-high spikes are the work of pounding winter waves that have ripped into the lava rock point, leaving the pointy 'teeth' behind.

The walk to the edge of this curious formation and back takes only 10 minutes. New signage adjacent to the point indicates that the outcropping is sacred to native Hawaiians. Visitors are strongly discouraged from walking onto the formation out of respect for native customs. The point is also potentially hazardous, subject to powerful waves and covered by uneven, sometimes sharp, rocks.

En route you'll pass the Honokahua burial site, a 13-acre native burial ground. You can skirt along the outside of this area but don't enter sites marked 'Please Kokua,' which are easily visible islets of stones bordering the Ritz's manicured golf greens.

Get here by driving north to the very end of Lower Honoapi'ilani Rd, where you'll find parking and a plaque detailing the burial site. The path to the Dragon's Teeth leads down from the plaque along the north edge of the golf course.

🏄 Slaughterhouse Beach & Honolua Bay   BEACH

This marine conservation district comes with Jekyll-and-Hyde mood swings: wild and wicked in the winter, calm and tranquil in the summer. But no matter its mood, it's always ideal for some sort of activity.

The narrow Kalaepiha Point separates Slaughterhouse Beach (Mokule'ia Bay) and Honolua Bay. Together the three form the Honolua–Mokule'ia Bay Marine Life Conservation District.

Like O'ahu's famed North Shore, Honolua Bay is a surfer's dream. It, too, faces northwest and when it catches the winter swells it has some of the gnarliest surfing anywhere in the world.

In summer, snorkeling is excellent in both bays, thanks in part to prohibitions on fishing in the preserve. Honolua Bay is the favorite, with thriving reefs and abundant coral along its rocky edges. As an added treat,

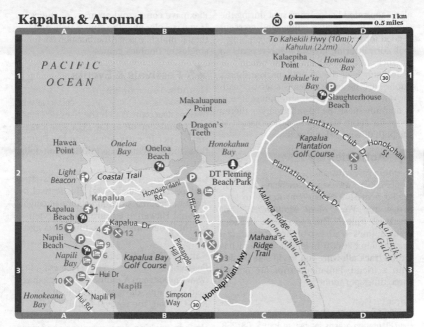

Kapalua & Around

Activities, Courses & Tours
Honolua Ridge Trail	(see 3)
Kapalua Adventures	(see 3)
1 Kapalua Dive Company	A2
2 Kapalua Golf Academy	C3
3 Kapalua Resort Center	C3
4 Kapalua Tennis Club	A3
Mahana Ridge Trail	(see 3)
Maunalei Arboretum Trail	(see 3)
Village Walking Trail	(see 3)

Sleeping
5 Hale Napili	A3
Kapalua Villas	(see 3)
6 Napili Kai Beach Resort	A3
7 Napili Surf Beach Resort	A3
8 Ritz-Carlton Kapalua	B2

9 The Mauian	A3

Eating
10 Gazebo	A3
11 Honolua Store	B3
12 Pineapple Grill	B3
13 Plantation House	D2
14 Sansei Seafood Restaurant & Sushi Bar	B3
Sea House Restaurant	(see 6)

Drinking
15 Merriman's Kapalua	A3

Entertainment
Masters of Hawaiian Slack Key Guitar Concert Series	(see 6)

spinner dolphins sometimes hang near the mouth of the bays, swimming just beyond snorkelers. When it's calm, you can snorkel around Kalaepiha Point from one bay to the other, but forget it after heavy rains: Honolua Stream empties into Honolua Bay and the runoff clouds the water.

The land fronting Honolua Bay is owned by Maui Land & Pineapple. The company allows recreational access to the bay for no fee. A few families have the right to live on this land, but they cannot charge an access fee or restrict visiting hours. Once you reach the bay, review the signage about protecting the coral, then enter via the rocky coastline. Do not enter the water via the concrete boat ramp, which is very slippery and potentially hazardous.

When the waters are calm the bays offer superb kayaking. Slaughterhouse Beach is also a top-rated bodysurfing spot during the summer. Its attractive white-sand crescent is good for sunbathing and beachcombing – look for glittering green olivine crystals in the rocks at the south end of the beach.

Just north of the 32-mile marker, there's public parking and a concrete stairway leading down the cliffs to Slaughterhouse Beach. A half-mile past the 32-mile marker there's room for about six cars to park adjacent to the path down to Honolua Bay.

🏃 Activities

Kapalua Adventures   ZIPLINING
(☎665-3753; www.kapaluaadventures.com; Office Rd; from $149; ⊙7am-7pm) Ready to soar across the West Maui Mountains – for nearly 2 miles? This adventure includes eight ziplines in all, two of them extending a breathtaking 2000ft in length. The tour has a dual track allowing you to zip side by side with a friend. Full-moon trips are offered three times per month.

Kapalua Golf   GOLF
(☎669-8044, 877-527-2582; www.kapalua.com; Bay/Plantation greens fee before 1pm $208/268, after 1pm $138/158; ⊙1st tee 6:40am) Kapalua boasts two of the island's top championship golf courses, both certified by Audubon International as sanctuaries for native plants and animals. How's that for green greens? The **Bay course** (300 Kapalua Dr) is the tropical ocean course, meandering across a lava peninsula. The challenging **Plantation course** (2000 Plantation Club Dr) sweeps over a rugged landscape of hills and deep gorges.

Kapalua Golf Academy   GOLF LESSONS
(☎665-5455; www.kapalua.com; 1000 Office Rd; 1hr private lesson $125, half-day school $195; ⊙8am-4pm) Hawaii's top golf academy is staffed by PGA pros.

Kapalua Dive Company   DIVING
(☎669-3448; www.kapaluadive.com; Kapalua Bay; dives from $85, kayak tours $85; ⊙8am-5pm) Offers a range of water activities, including kayak-snorkel tours and a full menu of dives. Rent a basic snorkel set for $15 per day. Look for its beach shack on Kapalua Beach. Will hold credit card or driver's license for rental deposit.

Kapalua Tennis Club   TENNIS
(☎665-9112; 100 Kapalua Dr; per person per day $10, racket rental $6; ⊙staffed 8am-noon & 3-6pm Mon-Fri, 8am-4pm Sat & Sun) Maui's premier full-service tennis club has 10 Plexipave courts and an array of clinics. If you're solo, give the club a ring, and they'll match you with other players for singles or doubles games.

🎆 Festivals & Events

Hyundai Tournament of
Champions   GOLF TOURNAMENT
(www.pgatour.com) Watch the likes of Tiger and friends tee off at the PGA Tour's season opener in early January at the Plantation course, vying for a multimillion-dollar purse.

Celebration of the Arts   ARTS FESTIVAL
(www.celebrationofthearts.org) This festival in April at the Ritz-Carlton celebrates traditional Hawaiian culture with storytelling, hula demonstrations, films, arts and music.

Kapalua Wine & Food
Festival   FOOD, WINE FESTIVAL
(www.kapalua.com) A culinary extravaganza held over four days in late June at the Ritz-Carlton, the festival features renowned winemakers and Hawaii's hottest chefs in cooking demonstrations and wine tastings.

🛌 Sleeping

Kapalua Villas   CONDO $$$
(☎665-9170, 800-545-0018; www.outrigger.com; 2000 Village Rd; 1/2 bedroom from $209/279; ✴@🛜⛱) These swank condos are clustered into three separate compounds. The Golf Villas line the Bay Golf Course while the Bay and Ridge Villas overlook the beach. The one-bedroom units sleep up to four; the two-bedroom units sleep six. For up-close whale watching, try the spacious Bay Villas. The $25 daily resort fee includes parking, wi-fi and use of the resort shuttle.

Ritz-Carlton Kapalua   RESORT HOTEL $$$
(☎669-6200, 800-262-8440; www.ritzcarlton.com; 1 Ritz-Carlton Dr; r from $595; ✴@🛜⛱) This luxe hotel's low-key elegance attracts the exclusive golf crowd. On a hillside fronting the greens and the sea, this hotel has a heated multilevel swimming pool shaded by palm trees, a spa and a fitness club. Rooms boast oversize marble bathrooms, goose-down pillows…you get the picture. The $25 daily resort fees covers parking, wi-fi and use of the fitness center and resort shuttle. Internet access at the business center is 75c per minute.

KAPALUA HIKING TRAILS

Whether you're after an easy coastal stroll or a hard-core trek through thick tropical flora, Kapalua (☑665-4386; www.kapalua.com/adventures) has a trail for you. The remarkable Maunalei Arboretum Trail cuts through a forest planted by DT Fleming, the arborist who developed Maui's pineapple industry. This previously inaccessible forest sits above a gated development and access is strictly via a free shuttle (☑665-9110) that departs from the Kapalua Resort Center at 9:30am, 11:30am and 2:30pm and returns from the trailhead at 9:50am, 11:50am, and 1:50pm. Reservations are required to ride the shuttle van to the trailhead. Call a day or two before your planned hike to secure a spot – the shuttle holds only 14 people.

For a fantastic one-way hike that ends at the resort, pick up the biologically diverse Honolua Ridge Trail (1.25 miles) from the Maunalei Arboretum Trail. You'll enjoy spectacular ridgeline views before dipping back into the junglelike forest for a glimpse of 5788ft Pu'u Kukui, one of the wettest spots in the world, averaging 325in annually. Pass through a stand of towering Sugi trees, then pick up the easy Mahana Ridge Trail (5.75 miles). At the golf course restrooms, the trail continues on the hill behind the restroom building. When you reach the sharp roadside bend, just after the telephone poles, turn right onto the dirt path to descend to DT Fleming Beach (look for the small sign) or follow the road left to return to the Kapalua Resort Center.

The old Village Golf Course, reincarnated as the Village Walking Trail, offers stunning scenery as it rises up the mountain slopes. For the best views, follow it all the way to the end, where there's a lake loop. The easy Coastal Trail (1.75 miles) links Kapalua Beach with Oneloa Beach then crosses below the Ritz-Carlton to end at DT Fleming Beach. During your walk, be sure to stay on the designated path to avoid disturbing nesting birds. The Coastal Trail passes ancient burial grounds and the jagged Dragon's Teeth formation, both located north of the Ritz-Carlton and the trail. These sites are of cultural significance to native Hawaiians and should not be inspected up-close. Respect the signage.

Before hiking any of the resort's trails, you must sign a release at the Kapalua Resort Center. Keep the carbon copy with you for liability and safety reasons. The release is good for one year. Free trail maps are also available at the resort center. Note that the trails can be closed at any time by the resort without notice.

✗ Eating & Drinking

TOP CHOICE Honolua Store   PLATE LUNCH $
(☑665-9105; www.kapalua.com; 502 Office Rd; most lunches $6-9; ⊙store 6am-8pm, deli until 3pm) This porch-wrapped bungalow once served as the general store for the Honolua Pineapple Plantation, and the exterior looks much as it did when it opened in 1929. Today, the store is a nod to normalcy in the midst of lavish exclusiveness. The deli is known for its reasonable prices and fantastic plate lunches. The $5.75 hobo lunch (one main and a scoop of rice) is one of Maui's best lunch deals. There's also a coffee bar with pastries.

TOP CHOICE Plantation House   HAWAII REGIONAL $$$
(☑669-6299; www.theplantationhouse.com; Plantation Golf Course clubhouse, 2000 Plantation Club Dr; breakfast & lunch $12-18, dinner $28-42; ⊙8am-3pm & 6-9pm) Breakfast at this open-air eatery is the stuff of which memories and poems are made. The crab cake Benedict? A fluffy, hollandaise-splashed affair that will have you kissing your plate and plotting your return. Adding to the allure are stellar views of the coast and Moloka'i, as well as the world-famous golf course below. For dinner, fresh fish is prepared with Mediterranean flair and a Mauian finish – think Hawaiian fish with couscous and roasted Maui onions.

Sansei Seafood Restaurant & Sushi Bar   JAPANESE $$$
(☑669-6286; www.sanseihawaii.com; 600 Office Rd; sushi $3-16, most mains $22-43; ⊙5:30-10pm) The innovative sushi menu is reason enough to dine here, but the non-sushi house specials shouldn't be overlooked. The tempura rock shrimp in garlic aioli flawlessly blends Japanese and French flavors, and the spicy

» Ulua Beach (p365) – a favorite for morning snorkeling and diving
» Ho'okipa Beach (p371) – where the pros surf and windsurf
» Ka'anapali Beach (p326) – a happening resort beach with all the amenities
» Kapalua Beach (p334) – calm-as-a-lake swimming and snorkeling
» Keawakapu Beach (p354) – the perfect place for a sunset swim
» Charley Young Beach (p354) – a hidden gem in the heart of Kihei
» Big Beach (p369) – for long strolls and bodysurfing
» Malu'aka Beach (p368) – the best place to snorkel with turtles
» Little Beach (p369) – a hangout of the clothing-optional crowd
» Pa'iloa Beach (p391) – Maui's most stunning black-sand beach

Dungeness crab ramen with truffle broth is another prize. Order before 6pm and all food is discounted by 25%. No reservation? Queue up for one of the 12 seats at the sushi bar – folks start gathering outside about 4:50pm.

Pineapple Grill   HAWAII REGIONAL **$$$**
(☑669-9600; www.pineapplekapalua.com; Kapalua Bay Golf Course clubhouse, 200 Kapalua Dr; lunch $11-17, dinner mains $26-47; ☺lunch & dinner) This beauty's got it all, from a sweeping hilltop view to a sleek exhibition kitchen that whips up creative fusion fare. Treat your taste buds with the likes of lobster-coconut bisque, wasabi-seared fish and a pork chop with a Maui Gold Pineapple glaze.

Merriman's Kapalua   HAWAII REGIONAL **$$**
(☑669-6400; www.merrimanshawaii.com; 1 Bay Club Pl; happy hour menu $9-24; ☺happy hour 3-5pm) We like Merriman's for happy hour. Perched on a scenic point between Kapalua Bay and Napili Bay, this tiki- and palm-dotted spot is a gorgeous place to unwind after braving the Kahekili Hwy.

Kahekili Highway

They call this narrow, serpentine, blind-curving thread of pavement a highway? That's some optimistic labeling, for sure. This challenging road, which hugs the rugged northern tip of Maui, charges around hairpin turns, careens over one-lane bridges and teeters beside treacherous cliffs. It's one of Maui's most adventurous drives, and undisputedly its most challenging.

Not for the faint of heart, sections slow to just 5mph as the road wraps around blind curves; a lengthy stretch around the village of Kahakuloa is a mere one lane with cliffs on one side and a sheer drop on the other – if you hit oncoming traffic here you may be doing your traveling in reverse! But heck, if you can handle that, this largely overlooked route offers all sorts of adventures, with horse and hiking trails, mighty blowholes and delicious banana bread.

Don't be fooled by car rental maps that show the road as a dotted line – it's paved and open to the public the entire way. There are no services, so gas up beforehand. Give yourself a good two hours' driving time, not counting stops.

Property between the highway and the coast is part privately and part publicly owned; trails to the shore are often uneven, rocky and slippery, and the shoreline is subject to dangerous waves. If you decide to explore, take appropriate precautions and get access permission when possible.

PUNALAU BEACH
Manicured golf courses and ritzy enclaves drop away and the scenery gets wilder as you drive toward the island's northernmost point. Ironwood-lined Punalau Beach, 0.7 miles after the 34-mile marker, makes a worthy stop if you're up for a solitary stroll. Swimming is a no-go though, as a rocky shelf creates unfavorable conditions for water activities.

NAKALELE POINT
Continuing on, the terrain is hilly, with rocky cattle pastures punctuated by tall sisal plants. At the 38-mile marker, a mile-long trail leads out to a light station at the end of windswept Nakalele Point. Here you'll find a coastline of arches and other formations worn out of the rocks by the pounding surf.

The **Nakalele Blowhole** roars when the surf is up but is a sleeper when the seas are calm. To check on its mood, park at the boulder-lined pull-off 0.6 miles beyond the 38-mile marker. Glimpse the action, if there is any, a few hundred yards beyond the parking lot.

Eight-tenths of a mile after the 40-mile marker, look for the **Ohai Viewpoint**, on the *makai* side of the road. The viewpoint won't be marked but there's a sign announcing the start of the Ohai Trail. Don't bother with the trail – it's not particularly interesting. Instead, bear left and walk out to the top of the point for a jaw-dropping coastal view that includes a glimpse of the Nakalele Blowhole. If you have kids, be careful – the crumbly cliff has a sudden drop of nearly 800ft!

OCEAN BATHS & BELLSTONE

After the 42-mile post the markers change; the next marker is 16 and the numbers go down as you continue on from here.

One-tenth of a mile before the 16-mile marker, look seaward for a large dirt pull-off and a well-beaten path that leads 15 minutes down lava cliffs to **natural ocean baths** on the ocean's edge. Cut out of slippery lava rock and encrusted with olivine minerals, these incredibly clear pools sit in the midst of roaring surf. If you're tempted to go in, size it up carefully – people unfamiliar with the water conditions here have been swept into the sea and drowned. If the rocks are covered in silt from recent storm runoffs, or the waves look high, forget about it – it's dangerous. Although the baths are on public land, state officials do not recommend accessing them due to the hazardous conditions, including slippery rocks, large and powerful surf, waves on ledges and strong currents.

That huge boulder with concave marks on the inland side of the road just before the pull-off is a bellstone, **Pohaku Kani**. If you hit it with a rock on the Kahakuloa side, where the deepest indentations are, you might get a hollow sound. It's a bit resonant if you hit it just right, though it takes some imagination to hear it ring like a bell.

KAHAKULOA

An imposing 636ft-tall volcanic dome guards the entrance to Kahakuloa Bay like a lurking, watchful dragon. They say this photogenic landmark, known as **Kahakuloa Head**, was a favorite cliff-diving spot of

Chief Kahekili. Before the road drops into the valley, there's a pull-off above town providing a bird's-eye view.

The bayside village of Kahakuloa, tucked at the bottom of a lush valley and embraced by towering sea cliffs, retains a solidly Hawaiian character. Kahakuloa's isolation (population about 100) has protected it from the rampant development found elsewhere on Maui. Farmers tend taro patches, poi dogs wander across the road, and a missionary-era **Protestant church** marks the village center. One of Hawaii's most accomplished ukulele players, Richard Ho'opi'i, is the church minister.

You won't find stores, but villagers set up hard-to-miss roadside stands selling fruit and snacks to day-trippers. For shave ice ($3), try Ululani's hot-pink stand. For free samples of *'ono* (delicious) banana bread, stop at Julia's lime-green shack (www.julias-bananabread.com) where a loaf costs $6 – and tastes fresh for days.

KAHAKULOA TO WAIHE'E

On the outskirts of Kahakuloa, near the 14-mile marker, the hilltop **Kaukini Gallery & Gift Shop** (☎244-3371; www.kaukinigallery.com; ☺10am-5pm) sells works by more than 120 island artists, with watercolors, jewelry, native-fiber baskets, pottery and more. A locator map on the front porch tells you how many more narrow miles you need to drive in either direction to reach relative safety.

Past the 10-mile marker look for **Turnbull Studios & Sculpture Garden** (☎244-9838; www.turnbullstudios.org; ☺10am-5pm Mon-Fri), where you can view Bruce Turnbull's ambitious bronze and wood creations, as well as the works of other area artists...very cool stuff.

Continuing around beep-as-you-go blind turns, the highway gradually levels out atop sea cliffs. For an Edenlike scene, stop at the pull-off 0.1 miles north of the 8-mile marker and look down into the ravine below, where you'll see a cascading **waterfall** framed by double pools.

For a real *paniolo* experience, saddle up at **Mendes Ranch** (☎871-5222; www.mendesranch.com; 3530 Kahekili Hwy; 2hr rides $110; ☺rides 8:15am & 11:30pm), a working cattle ranch near the 7-mile marker. The picture-perfect scenery on these rides includes everything from jungle valleys to lofty sea cliffs and waterfalls.

WAIHE'E RIDGE TRAIL

This fabulous trail has it all: tropical flora, breezy ridgelines, lush valley landscapes and lofty views of Maui's wild northern coast and the central valley. The best part? The well-defined trail is less than 5 miles roundtrip and only takes about three hours to complete.

The path is a bit steep, but it's a fairly steady climb and not overly strenuous. It's best to start this one before 8am in order to beat the clouds, which can obscure the view from the top later in the morning.

Starting at an elevation of 1000ft, the trail, which crosses reserve land, climbs a ridge, passing from pasture to cool forest. Guava trees and groves of rainbow eucalyptus are prominent along the way, and the pungent aroma of fallen fruit may accompany you after a rainstorm. From the 0.75-mile post, panoramic views open up, with a scene that sweeps clear down to the ocean along the Waihe'e Gorge and deep into pleated valleys.

As you continue on, you'll enter ohia forest with native birds and get distant views of waterfalls cascading down the mountains. The ridgetop views are similar to those you'd see from a helicopter, and you'll probably see a handful of them darting into the adjacent valley.

On this quiet trail, birdsong, chirping insects, a rushing stream and muffled bits of hiker conversation are the only aural interruptions. The path ends at a small clearing on the 2563ft peak of Lanilili. Here you'll find awesome views in all directions as well as a picnic table.

Solos, seniors and in-shape kids should be fine on this hike. If you have access to hiking

poles, bring them. The trail gets muddy and steep in spots.

For the trailhead, take the one-lane paved road that starts on the inland side of the highway just south of the 7-mile marker. It's almost directly across the road from the big gate at Mendes Ranch. The road (open 7am to 6pm) climbs to the Boy Scouts' Camp Mahulia and winds through open pasture, so watch for cattle. The trailhead, marked with a Na Ala Hele sign, is a mile up on the left just before the camp.

For complete details visit http://hawaiitrails.ehawaii.gov, the state's trail and access website.

WAIHE'E TO WAILUKU

Soon after the Waihe'e Ridge Trail, the Kahekili Hwy runs through the sleeper towns of Waihe'e and Waiehu before arriving in Wailuku, in Central Maui. There's not much to do here, but if you're up for a round of golf, the county-run **Waiehu Municipal Golf Course** (☏243-7400; 200 Halewaiu Rd; greens fee $55, optional cart $20) offers an affordable and easily walkable 18 holes on the coast. On-site are a small cafe, a pro shop and public restrooms.

'IAO VALLEY & CENTRAL MAUI

Let it rip! Once all but overlooked by travelers, this wind-whipped region has hit the map big time, morphing into action-central for anything with a sail. Kanaha Beach takes home gold for kitesurfing and windsurfing, bursting into color each day in a glorious mile-long sea of sails. But you don't have to get all your thrills on the water. Central Maui has exceptional green treats, most notably lush 'Iao Valley, a sight so spectacular it was once reserved for royalty; two rare waterbird sanctuaries; and the most dazzling tropical aquarium you'll ever see.

Kahului

POP 22,200

All roads lead to Kahului, the commercial heart of Maui. It's home to the island's gateway airport and cruise-ship harbor. Just about everything that enters Maui comes through this workaday town thick with warehouses and shopping centers. Hardly a vacation scene, you say. True, but if you dig a

---

ℹ SURFING ONLINE

» Art Guide Maui (www.artguidemaui.com) – for the art scene.

» Hana Hwy Surf (www.hanahwysurf.com) – for surf conditions.

» Maui News (www.mauinews.com) – for local issues.

» Maui on TV (http://hawaiiontv.com/hawaiiontv/mauiontv) – for lots of cool stuff.

» Maui Pride (www.pridemaui.com) – for the gay community.

» Sierra Club (www.hi.sierraclub.org/maui) – for the environmental scene.

little deeper you'll find more to your liking. You have to go island-style to have fun here: talk story with the locals at the Saturday swap meet, take in a concert on the lawn of the cultural center or join the wave-riding action at Kanaha Beach. There's a lot more to Kahului than first meets the eye.

Beaches

Kanaha Beach Park BEACH

When the wind picks up in the afternoon, this mile-long beach becomes surf city, with hundreds of brilliant sails whipping back and forth across the bay.

Both windsurfing and kitesurfing are so hot here that the beach is divvied up, with kitesurfers converging at the southwest ern end, known as **Kite Beach**, and windsurfers strutting their stuff at the northeastern end. It's mind-blowing to watch, and there are instructors waiting right on the beach if *you're* ready to fly.

A section in the middle of the beach is roped off for swimmers, but this place is really all about wind power. Facilities include restrooms, showers and shaded picnic tables.

Sights

Kanaha Pond Bird Sanctuary WILDLIFE PRESERVE

(Hwy 37; admission free; sunrise-sunset) This easy-access roadside sanctuary provides a haven for rare Hawaiian birds, including the *ae'o* (black-necked stilt), a wading bird with long orange legs that feeds along the pond's marshy edges. Even though there's a population of just 1500 of these elegant birds in the entire state, you can count on spotting one here.

An **observation deck** just a short walk beyond the parking lot offers the ideal lookout for seeing stilts, native coots and black-crowned night herons. Close the gate and walk into the preserve quietly; you should be able to make several sightings right along the shoreline.

Maui Nui Botanical Gardens GARDENS

(249-2798; www.mnbg.org; 150 Kanaloa Ave; admission free; 8am-4pm Mon-Sat) If you're interested in the subtle beauty of native Hawaiian plants, this garden is a gem. Come here to view rare species and to identify plants you've heard about but haven't yet seen, such as *wauke* (paper mulberry, used to make tapa), *'ulu* (breadfruit) and *'iliahi* (sandalwood). Don't expect it to be overly flowery, however. What you won't see here are the riotous colors of exotic tropicals that now dominate most Hawaiian gardens. To delve even deeper into the key role of native plants in Hawaiian culture join one of the guided tours (suggested donation $5) that are given between 10am and 11:30am on Tuesdays and Fridays.

WAVE RIDING SCOOP

Maui is known for its consistent winds. Windsurfers can find action in any month, but as a general rule the best wind is from June to September and the flattest spells are from December to February.

Get the inside scoop on kiteboarding and windsurfing from the following:

Maui Kiteboarding Association (www.mauikiteboardingassociation.com)

Maui Kitesurfing Community (www.mauikitesurf.org)

Maui Windsurfing (www.mauiwindsurfing.net)

FREE **Schaefer International Gallery** MUSEUM

(242-2787; www.mauiarts.org; 1 Cameron Way; 11am-5pm Wed-Sun) This gallery at the Maui Arts & Cultural Center features fascinating exhibits on Hawaiian culture, hula and art.

Kahului Harbor HARBOR

Kahului's large protected harbor serves many functions. It's the island's only deep-water port, so all boat traffic, from cruise ships to cargo vessels, dock here. But don't think it's all business. You'll find one of the harbor's most attractive faces at **Hoaloha Park**, where you can watch outrigger canoe clubs practice in the late afternoon.

Activities

Windsurfing

Windswept Kahului is the base for Maui's main windsurfing operations. Board-and-rig rentals cost around $50/325 per day/week. If you're new to the sport, introductory classes are readily available, last a couple of hours and cost $90. The business is competitive, so ask about discounts.

Reliable shops that rent out gear and arrange lessons:

Second Wind WINDSURFING

(877-7467; www.secondwindmaui.com; 111 Hana Hwy; 9am-6pm)

MAUI 'IAO VALLEY & CENTRAL MAUI

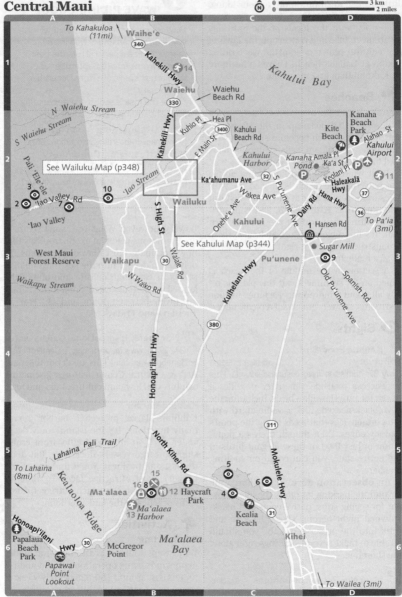

Central Maui

To Kahakuloa (11mi)

Waihe'e

340

Kahekili Hwy

14

Kahului Bay

Waiehu

330

Waiehu Beach Rd

N Waiehu Stream

S Waiehu Stream

Pali 'Ele'ele

Kuhio Pl   Hea Pl

3400

Kahului Beach Rd

See Wailuku Map (p348)

'Iao Stream

E Main St

Kahului Harbor

Kahului Airport

Kanaha Beach Park

Kite Beach

Alahao St

Kanaha Amala Pl
Pond   Ka'a St

Keolani Pl

11

3   10

2   'Iao Valley Rd   7

Ka'ahumanu Ave

32

S Pu'unene Ave

Haleakalā Hwy

37

'Iao Valley

Wailuku

Wakea Ave

Onehe'e Ave

Kahului

Dairy Rd   Hana Hwy   36

To Pa'ia (3mi)

West Maui Forest Reserve

Waikapu

30

Waiale Rd

See Kahului Map (p344)

1   Hansen Rd

Sugar Mill

9

Waikapu Stream

W Waiko Rd

Kuihelani Hwy

Pu'unene

Old Pu'unene Ave

Spanish Rd

380

Honoapi'ilani Hwy

311

Lahaina Pali Trail

North Kihei Rd

To Lahaina (8mi)

Kealaoloa Ridge

15

Mokulele Hwy

5

16 8   12 Haycraft Park

6

Ma'alaea

13 Ma'alaea Harbor

4

Kealia Beach

31

Honoapi'ilani

Papalaua Beach Park

30

McGregor Point

Ma'alaea Bay

Kihei

Papawai Point Lookout

To Wailea (3mi)

Hawaiian Island Surf & Sport WINDSURFING
(☎871-4981; www.hawaiianisland.com; 415 Dairy Rd; ⏲8:30am-6pm)

Hi-Tech Surf Sports WINDSURFING
(☎877-2111; www.htmaui.com; 425 Koloa St; ⏲9am-6pm)

Kitesurfing

Kitesurfing, also known as kiteboarding, has taken off big-time in Kahului. The action centers on Kite Beach, the southwest end of Kanaha Beach Park. If you've never tried it before, you can learn the ropes from some of

⊙ Sights

1 Alexander & Baldwin Sugar
  Museum D3
2 'Iao Valley State Park A2
3 JFK Profile... A2
4 Kealia Pond Boardwalk C5
5 Kealia Pond National Wildlife
  Refuge C5
6 Kealia Pond National Wildlife
  Refuge Visitor Center...................... C5
7 Kepaniwai Park & Heritage
  Gardens.. A2
8 Maui Ocean Center............................ B5
9 Old Pu'unene Bookstore.................... D3
10 Tropical Gardens of Maui B2

Activities, Courses & Tours

11 Kahului Heliport.................................. D2
12 Ma'alaea Pipeline B5
13 Pacific Whale Foundation.................. B6
  Quicksilver................................(see 13)
  Shark Dive Maui...........................(see 8)
14 Waiehu Municipal Golf Course B1

⊗ Eating

  Beach Bums Bar & Grill...............(see 16)
  Hula Cookies...............................(see 16)
15 Waterfront Restaurant....................... B5

⊙ Shopping

16 Harbor Shops at Ma'alaea B5

MAUI KAHULUI

the very pros who've made kitesurfing such a hot wave ride. Vans set up right at Kite Beach to offer lessons. Expect to pay about $275 for a half-day intro course. Check out the scene live at http://kitebeachcam.com.

Some recommended operators:

Kiteboarding School Maui KITESURFING
(☏873-0015; www.ksmaui.com)

Aqua Sports Maui KITESURFING
(☏242-8015; www.mauikiteboardinglessons.com)

Action Sports Maui KITESURFING
(☏871-5857; www.actionsportsmaui.com)

👉 Tours

Helicopter Rides
Several companies, including **Sunshine** (☏871-7799; www.sunshinehelicopters.com), **Blue Hawaiian** (☏871-8844; www.bluehawaiian.com) and **AlexAir** (☏871-0792; www.helitour.com) offer helicopter tours of Maui. All operate out of the **Kahului Heliport** (1 Kahului Airport Rd), at the southeast side of Kahului Airport. Thirty-minute tours of the jungly West Maui Mountains cost around $150 and one-hour circle-island tours about $275. Discounts abound. Companies advertise in the free tourist magazines, with all sorts of deals.

🎎 Festivals & Events

Ki Ho'alu Slack Key Guitar Festival MUSIC FESTIVAL
(www.mauiarts.org) Top slack key guitarists from throughout the state take the stage at this quintessentially Hawaiian festival held on the lawn of the Maui Arts & Cultural Center in June.

Maui Marathon ROAD RACE
(www.mauimarathon.com) This mid-September road race begins in Kahului and ends 26.2 miles later at Whalers Village in Ka'anapali.

Maui 'Ukulele Festival MUSIC FESTIVAL
(www.ukulelefestivalhawaii.org) A big *'ohana* (family) event, everybody from *na keiki* to elders shows up at the Maui Arts & Cultural Center on a Sunday in mid-October for this outdoor music fest showcasing uke masters from Maui and beyond.

🛏 Sleeping

Maui Seaside Hotel HOTEL $$
(☏877-3311; www.seasidehotelshawaii.com; 100 W Ka'ahumanu Ave; r from $125; ✳@🏊) If you have some dire need to spend the night in Kahului, this is the better of its two aging hotels. It's a plain Jane, but the rooms are clean.

🍴 Eating

Cynnamon's FOOD TRUCK $
(Kahului Beach Rd, at boat ramp; meals $8; ☉10am-1pm Tue-Sat) The queen of island food trucks, this family operation sells only fresh-caught fish. It's no coincidence it parks at the boat dock; the hubby reels in the fish, and Cynnamon grills it to perfection for a lunchtime crowd. Top choices include the panko-crusted mahi plate lunch and the fresh ahi *poke* made while you wait.

Campus Food Court FOOD COURT $
(www.mauiculinary-campusdining.com; Maui College, 310 W Ka'ahumanu Ave; mains $5-8; ☉11am-1:30pm Mon-Fri) With names such as Farm to

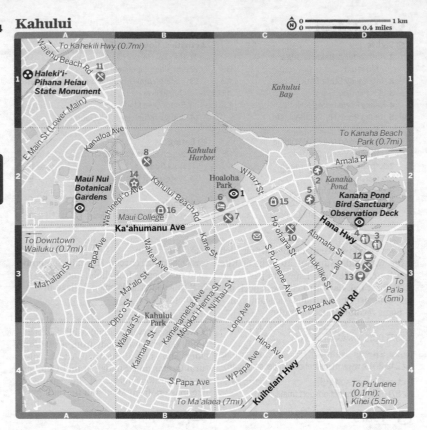

N ▲ 0 ————— 1 km
0 ————— 0.4 miles

MAUI 'IAO VALLEY & CENTRAL MAUI

Table and the Raw Fish Camp, you know this isn't your average campus fare. This food court, run by students in Maui College's acclaimed culinary arts program, is well worth a detour. You might also want to check out the **Class Act** (☎984-3280) fine dining restaurant, where students create a multicourse meal made from locally grown food.

Bistro Casanova   MEDITERRANEAN **$$**
(☎873-3650; www.casanovamaui.com; 33 Lono Ave; mains $14-32; ⊗11am-9:30pm Mon-Sat) An offshoot of the popular Italian restaurant Casanova in Makawao, this is Kahului's classiest dining option, offering a solid tapas menu, good Maui-raised steaks and plenty of organic Kula veggies. The setting is upscale and urban. Reservations are recommended at dinner, when the bistro can fill solid with a pre-theater crowd en route to a show at the MACC.

Da Kitchen   HAWAIIAN **$$**
(www.da-kitchen.com; 425 Koloa St; plate lunches $9-14; ⊗9am-9pm) Hawaiian decor and unbeatable island grinds make this a favorite meal stop. The *kalua* pork is, as they say, 'so tender it falls off da bone,' and the more expensive plate lunches are big enough to feed two. Expect a crowd at lunch but don't be deterred, as the service is quick.

Thailand Cuisine   THAI **$$**
(www.thailandcuisinemaui.com; Maui Mall, 70 E Ka'ahumanu Ave; mains $10-16; ⊗10:30am-3:30pm & 5-9:30pm; ☑) *Maui News* readers voted this family-run eatery as Maui's best ethnic restaurant. And yes, it lives up to the reputation. Start with the shrimp summer rolls, then move on to aromatic green curries or perhaps the ginger grilled mahimahi.

Piñatas   MEXICAN **$**
(395 Dairy Rd; mains $5-10; ⊗8am-8pm Mon-Sat, 11am-8pm Sun) Hey amigos, join the surfers

Kahului

◎ **Top Sights**
Haleki'i-Pihana Heiau State
Monument A1
Kanaha Pond Bird Sanctuary
Observation Deck D2
Maui Nui Botanical Gardens............... A2

◎ **Sights**
1 Hoaloha Park C2
Schaefer International Gallery.. (see 14)

Activities, Courses & Tours
2 Action Sports Maui............................. D2
Aqua Sports Maui .... (see 5)
3 Hawaiian Island Surf & Sport D3
4 Hi-Tech Surf Sports............................. D3
5 Second Wind C2

◎ **Sleeping**
6 Maui Seaside Hotel............................. C2

◎ **Eating**
7 Bistro Casanova.................................. C2
Campus Food Court .... (see 16)
8 Cynnamon's... B2
Da Kitchen .... (see 3)
9 Piñatas D3
10 Safeway... C3
Tasaka Guri-Guri......................... (see 15)
Thailand Cuisine .... (see 15)
11 Tom's Mini-Mart A1
Whole Foods .... (see 15)

◎◎ **Drinking**
12 Maui Coffee Roasters......................... D3
13 Wow-Wee Maui's Kava Bar &
Grill... D3

◎ **Entertainment**
14 Maui Arts & Cultural Center B2

◎ **Shopping**
Bounty Music .... (see 5)
15 Maui Mall C2
16 Maui Swap Meet.................................. B2

at this serape-draped cantina serving good Mexican fare at honest prices. If you're starving, order the oversized 'kitchen sink burrito,' stuffed with beef, beans, guacamole, sour cream and nearly everything else you'd find in a Mexican kitchen except the sink.

Tasaka Guri-Guri DESSERT $
(Maui Mall, 70 E Ka'ahumanu Ave; 2 scoops/quart $1.10/5; ⊙9am-6pm Mon-Sat, 10am-4pm Sun) For the coolest treat in town, queue up at

this hole-in-the-wall shop dishing up homemade pineapple sherbet. The *guri-guri,* as it's called, is so popular that locals pick up quarts on the way to the airport to take to friends on neighboring islands.

Tom's Mini-Mart SHAVE ICE $
(☑244-2323; 372 Waiehu Beach Rd; shave ice $3; ⊙7am-6pm Mon-Sat) Search out this little neighborhood shop in the middle of nowhere for supersmooth shave ice ripe with tropical fruit syrups. You gotta try the mango. To get there take E Main St northeast toward the ocean, turn left on Waiehu Beach Rd and continue north for 0.2 miles.

If you need to stock up the condo on the way in from the airport, the **Safeway** (170 E Kamehameha Ave; ⊙24hr) in the town center never closes. Like it greener? **Whole Foods** (Maui Mall, 70 E Ka'ahumanu Ave; ⊙8am-9pm) carries island-grown produce, fish and beef, and is a good place to pick up lei.

Drinking

Wow-Wee Maui's Kava Bar & Grill BAR
(www.wowweemaui.com; 333 Dairy Rd; ⊙11am-9pm Mon-Sat, 11am-6pm Sun; @) This hip cafe is *the* place to try kava served in a coconut shell. A ceremonial drink in old Hawaii, this spicy elixir made from the *Piper methysticum* plant gives a mild buzz. Wow-Wee Maui's chocolate bars, some spiked with kava, will also make you swoon. For something more conventional, staff make a killer martini.

Maui Coffee Roasters CAFE
(www.mauicoffeeroasters.com; 444 Hana Hwy; @🛜) Good vibes and good java at this coffee shop where locals linger over lattes while surfing free wi-fi. Need to jump-start your day? Step up to the bar and order a Sledge Hammer – a quadruple espresso with steamed half and half.

☆ Entertainment

Maui Arts & Cultural Center CONCERT HALL
(MACC; ☑242-7469; www.mauiarts.org; 1 Cameron Way) There's always something happening at this snazzy performance complex, which boasts two indoor theaters and an outdoor amphitheater, all with excellent acoustics. As Maui's main venue for music, theater and dance, it hosts everything from ukulele jams to touring rock bands. If you happen to be in the area on the third Thursday of the month, don't miss the exceptional Slack

MAUI KAHULUI

Key Masters show hosted by Grammy award winner George Kahumoku Jr.

Shopping

Kahului hosts Maui's big-box discount chains of the Wal-Mart and Costco variety, as well as its biggest shopping malls.

TOP CHOICE Maui Swap Meet OUTDOOR MARKET
(☑244-3100; Maui College, 310 Ka'ahumanu Ave; admission 50c; ⊘7am-1pm Sat) For a scene that glows with aloha, spend a Saturday morning chatting with local farmers and craftspeople at Maui's largest outdoor market. You'll not only find fresh organic Hana fruits, Kula veggies and homemade banana bread, but it's also a fun place to souvenir shop for everything from Hawaiian quilts to Maui-designed T-shirts. Don't be misled by the term 'swap meet' – most stands sell quality local goods and every dollar you spend here stays in the community.

Bounty Music UKULELE SHOP
(www.ukes.com; 111 Hana Hwy) Hawaiian music lovers, take note. Here you'll find all sorts of ukuleles, from inexpensive imported models to handcrafted masterpieces.

Information

Bank of Hawaii (www.boh.com; 27 S Pu'unene Ave)

Longs Drugs (☑877-0041; Maui Mall, 70 E Ka'ahumanu Ave; ⊘7am-midnight) The town's largest pharmacy.

Maui Visitors Bureau (☑872-3893; www.visit maui.com; Kahului airport; ⊘7:45am-9:45pm) This staffed booth in the airport's arrivals area has tons of tourist brochures.

Post office (www.usps.com; 138 S Pu'unene Ave)

Getting There & Around

To/From The Airport
Kahului airport is at the east side of town. Most visitors pick up rental cars at the airport. See p322 for shuttle and taxi information.

Bicycle
Island Biker (☑877-7744; www.islandbik ermaui.com; 415 Dairy Rd; per day/week $50/200; ⊘9am-5pm Mon-Fri, to 3pm Sat) Rents quality mountain bikes and road bikes well suited for touring Maui.

Bus
The Maui Bus connects Kahului with Ma'alaea, Kihei, Wailea and Lahaina; each route costs $1 and runs hourly. There are also free hourly buses that run around Kahului and connect to Wailuku.

Car
Bio-Beetle (☑873-6121; www.bio-beetle.com; 55 Amala Pl; per day/week from $50/275) Offers an eco-friendly alternative to the usual car rental scene, renting Volkswagens that run on recycled vegetable oil. It's a great option for those who want to travel green but still have their own wheels.

Haleki'i-Pihana Heiau State Monument

Overgrown and nearly forgotten, Haleki'i-Pihana Heiau (Map p344; Hea Pl; admission free; ⊘sunrise-sunset) holds the hilltop ruins of two of Maui's most important temples. The site was the royal court of Kahekili, Maui's last ruling chief, and the birthplace of Ke'opuolani, wife of Kamehameha the Great. After his victory at the battle of 'Iao in 1790, Kamehameha marched to this site to worship his war god Ku, offering the last human sacrifice on Maui.

Haleki'i, the first heiau (ancient stone temple), has stepped stone walls that tower above 'Iao Stream, the source for the stone used in its construction. The pyramid-like mound of **Pihana Heiau** is a five-minute walk beyond, but a thick overgrowth of kiawe makes it harder to discern.

Although it's all but abandoned, a certain mana (spiritual essence) still emanates from the site. To imagine it all through the eyes of the ancient Hawaiians, ignore the creeping suburbia and concentrate instead on the wild ocean and mountain vistas.

The site is about 2 miles northeast of central Wailuku. From Waiehu Beach Rd (Hwy 340), turn inland onto Kuhio Pl, then take the first left onto Hea Pl and follow it to the end.

Wailuku

POP 13,550

Unabashedly local, Wailuku is an enigma. As an ancient religious and political center, it boasts more sights on the National Register of Historic Places than any other town on Maui but sees the fewest tourists. As the county capital, its central area wears a modern facade of midrise office buildings, while its age-old backstreets hold an earthy mishmash of curio shops, galleries and mom-and-pop stores that just beg to be browsed. If you're here at lunchtime, you're

Maui's stunning scenery will entice hard-core cyclists, but casual riders hoping to use a bike as a primary source of transportation around the island may well find the island's steep topography and narrow roads daunting.

Getting around by bicycle within a small area can be a reasonable option for the average rider, however. For example, the tourist enclave of Kihei is largely level and has cycle lanes on its two main drags, S Kihei Rd and the Pi'ilani Hwy.

The full-color *Maui County Bicycle Map* ($6), available from bicycle shops, shows all the roads on Maui that have cycle lanes and gives other nitty-gritty details. Consider it essential if you intend to do your exploring by pedal power. West Maui Cycles p322 also offers the bike map online: www.westmauicycles.com/Maui-County-Bicycle-Map.html.

in luck. Thanks to a combination of low rent and hungry government employees, Wailuku dishes up tasty eats at prices that shame Maui's more touristed towns.

◉ Sights

Ready to get down to some nitty-gritty exploring? Dusty Wailuku offers a bevy of historic treasures. Hawaii's best-known architect, Maui-born CW Dickey, left his mark in this town before moving on to fame in Honolulu. The Wailuku Public Library (cnr High & Aupuni Sts), built c 1928, is a classic example of Dickey's distinctive Hawaii regional design. Another Dickey creation, the Territorial Building, lies right across the street. Within a short walk are four more buildings on the National Register of Historic Places. To discover all the gems in town, pick up a copy of the free *Wailuku Historic District* walking map at the library or the Bailey House Museum.

Bailey House Museum   MUSEUM
(📞244-3326; www.mauimuseum.org; 2375 W Main St; adult/child 7-12yr $7/2; ⊙10am-4pm Mon-Sat) This evocative museum occupies the 1833 home of Wailuku's first Christian missionary, Edward Bailey. The 2nd story, decorated with Bailey's sparse furnishings, reflects his era. But it's the Hawaiian section on the ground floor that holds the real intrigue. Check out the display of spears and shark-tooth daggers (ouch!) used in the bloody battles at nearby 'Iao Valley. There's also a notable collection of native wood bowls, stone adzes, feather lei and tapa cloth.

The link between ancient Hawaiian wave riders and modern-day surfers comes alive in a low-key exhibit adjacent to the parking lot at Bailey House Museum. There you'll find The Duke's Surfboard, a 10ft red-wood surfboard that surfing legend Duke Kahanamoku (1890–1968) rode. 'The Duke' not only won Olympian gold in swimming for the US but more importantly he revived the ancient art of surfing. A full-blooded Hawaiian, he traveled the world with his hefty surfboard in hand, introducing the sport to wannabe wave riders in Australia, Europe and the US mainland. Today, he's considered the father of modern surfing.

Ka'ahumanu Church   CHURCH
(cnr W Main & S High Sts) This handsome missionary church is named for Queen Ka'ahumanu, who cast aside the old gods and allowed Christianity to flourish. The clock in the steeple, brought around the Horn in the 19th century, still keeps accurate time. Hymns ring out in Hawaiian at Sunday morning services, but at other times it's a look-from-outside site, as the church is usually locked.

✸ Festivals & Events

E Ho'oulu Aloha   FESTIVAL
(www.mauimuseum.org) This old-Hawaii-style festival, held in November at the Bailey House Museum, features hula, ukulele masters, crafts, food and more. You won't find a friendlier community scene.

Maui County Fair   FAIR
(www.mauicountyfair.com) Get a feel for Maui's agricultural roots at this venerable fair held in late September, with farm exhibits, tasty island *grinds* and a dazzling orchid display.

Wailuku First Friday   STREET FAIR
Wailuku turns Market St into a street party complete with live music, poetry slams and a beer garden on the first Friday evening of the month.

MAUI WAILUKU

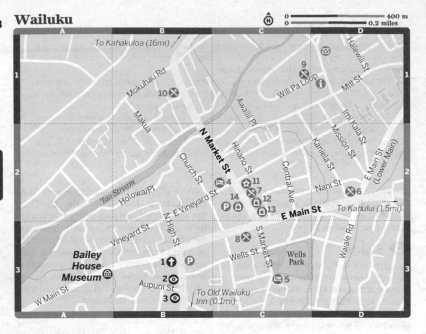

🛏 Sleeping

TOP CHOICE **Old Wailuku Inn**   B&B **$$**
(☎244-5897; www.mauiinn.com; 2199 Kaho'okele
St; r incl breakfast $165-195; ❄@) Step back into
the 1920s in this elegant period home built
by a wealthy banker. Authentically restored,
the inn retains the antique appeal of earlier
times while discreetly adding modern ame-
nities. Each room has its own personality,
but all are large and comfy with traditional
Hawaiian quilts warming the beds. The inn,
0.1 mile south of the library, is hands-down
the finest place to lay your head in Central
Maui.

Wailuku Guesthouse   GUESTHOUSE **$**
(☎986-8270; www.wailukuhouse.com; 210 S Market
St; r $79-109; ❄🛜🛜) This affordable family-
run guesthouse has simple, clean rooms,
each with its own bathroom and private
entrance. There's a refrigerator and coffee-
maker in the rooms and a park with tennis
courts across the street.

Northshore Hostel   HOSTEL **$**
(☎986-8095; www.northshorehostel.com; 2080
E Vineyard St; dm $24, s/d with shared bathroom
$55/65; ❄@🛜) The smaller and spiffier of
Wailuku's two hostels occupies an old build-
ing with a fresh coat of paint. Popular with

Wailuku

◉ Top Sights
    Bailey House Museum A3

◉ Sights
  1 Ka'ahumanu Church B3
  2 Territorial Building.................................B3
  3 Wailuku Public Library B3

🛏 Sleeping
  4 Northshore Hostel...............................C2
  5 Wailuku Guesthouse C3

✕ Eating
  6 A Saigon Café......................................D2
  7 Café O'Lei Wailuku..............................C2
  8 Main Street Bistro...............................C3
  9 Sam Sato's..C1
 10 Takamiya Market B1

✪ Entertainment
 11 'Iao Theater C2

🛍 Shopping
 12 Bird-of-Paradise Unique
     Antiques C2
 13 Brown-Kobayashi C2
 14 Native Intelligence C2

European travelers, it has separate male and female dorms as well as private rooms, a full kitchen and little perks like free international calls.

✗ Eating

TOP CHOICE A Saigon Café   VIETNAMESE $$

(☑248-9560; cnr Main & Kaniela Sts; mains $9-22; ⊘10am-9:30pm Mon-Sat, to 8:30pm Sun) The oldest and best Vietnamese restaurant on Maui is out of the way, but you'll be rewarded for your effort. Menu stars include the Buddha rolls in spicy peanut sauce and the aromatic lemongrass curries. To get there from N Market St, turn right on E Vineyard St and then right on Kaniela St.

Sam Sato's   JAPANESE $

(☑244-7124; 1750 Wili Pa Loop; mains $5-8; ⊘7am-2pm Mon-Sat) Don't even think of coming during the noon rush – islanders flock here from far and wide for Sato's steaming bowls of saimin-like dry noodles. Maui's number-one noodle house also makes amazing *manju* (Japanese cakes filled with sweet bean paste), which are sold for takeout at the counter until 4pm. To get there take E Vineyard St, go left on Central, right on Mill, left on Imi Kala and left on Wili Pa Loop.

Café O'Lei Wailuku   HAWAII REGIONAL $

(☑986-0044; 62 N Market St; mains $8-13; ⊘10:30am-3pm Mon-Fri) Sophisticated decor, waitstaff in black...Wailuku has never looked so smart. The food's on par with top-end restaurants and the average price is just $10. Don't miss the signature blackened mahimahi topped with fresh papaya salsa. The Maui onion soup, spiked with brandy and topped with Gruyère cheese, makes a fine starter.

Main Street Bistro   CAFE $$

(☑244-6816; www.msbmaui.com; 2051 Main St; mains $7-15; ⊘11am-7pm Mon-Fri) Owner Tom Selman, former top chef at the esteemed David Paul's, commandeers the exhibition kitchen here. The creative menu includes the likes of crab-cake salad and macnut smoked beef brisket, with reasonably priced wines to wash it all down.

Takamiya Market   HAWAIIAN $

(359 N Market St; meals $4-8; ⊘5:30am-6pm Mon-Sat) This oldtime grocer specialises in all things Hawaiian. Lunchtime features ahi *poke, laulau, kalua* pig and scores more – wrapped and ready to go.

☆ Entertainment

'Iao Theater   THEATER

(☑242-6969; www.mauionstage.com; 68 N Market St) Beautifully restored after years of neglect, this 1928 art-deco theater, which once hosted big names such as Frank Sinatra, is now the venue for community theater productions.

🛍 Shopping

Head to N Market St for fun browsing.

Native Intelligence   HAWAIIAN GIFTS

(www.native-intel.com; 45 N Market St) Hula instruments, koa bowls and finely handcrafted items.

Brown-Kobayashi   ANTIQUE SHOP

(38 N Market St) Museum-quality Asian antiques.

Bird-of-Paradise Unique Antiques   ANTIQUE SHOP

(56 N Market St) Stuffed to the gills with vintage Hawaiiana.

ℹ Information

First Hawaiian Bank (www.fhb.com; 27 N Market St)

Maui Memorial Medical Center (☑244-9056; www.mmmc.hhsc.org; 221 Mahalani St; ⊘24hr) The island's main hospital.

Post office (www.usps.com; 250 Imi Kala St)

Dangers & Annoyances

One caution: the town can get rough at night. The public parking lot on W Main St is an after-dark hangout rife with drug dealing and fights that gets more police calls than any other spot on Maui.

ℹ Getting There & Around

The Maui Bus runs free buses between Wailuku and Kahului hourly from 8am to 9pm. Wailuku stops include the state office building and the post office.

Wailuku to 'Iao Valley State Park

'Iao Valley is such a sumptuous sight that in ancient times it was reserved for royalty. Today much of the upper valley's natural beauty is preserved as parkland, all reached via 'Iao Valley Rd, which ends at misty 'Iao Valley State Park.

⊙ **Sights**

Tropical Gardens of Maui   GARDENS

(www.tropicalgardensofmaui.com; 200 'Iao Valley Rd; adult/child under 8yr $5/free; ☺9am-4:30pm Mon-Sat) These fragrant gardens, which straddle both sides of 'Iao Stream, showcase a superb orchid collection, endemic Hawaiian plants, brilliant bromeliads and a meditative bamboo grove with a trickling waterfall. See if you can find the world's largest orchid!

Kepaniwai Park & Heritage Gardens   PARK

(875 'Iao Valley Rd; ☺7am-7pm) Two miles west of Wailuku, this family-oriented park pays tribute to Hawaii's ethnic heritage. Sharing the grounds are a traditional Hawaiian *hale*, a New England–style missionary home, a Filipino farmer's hut, Japanese gardens and a Chinese pavilion with a statue of revolutionary hero Sun Yat-sen (who, incidentally, briefly lived on Maui). 'Iao Stream runs through the park, bordered by picnic shelters with BBQ pits. The place is cheerfully alive with families picnicking here on weekends.

JFK Profile   LANDMARK

('Iao Valley Rd) At a bend in the road a half-mile after Kepaniwai Park, you'll likely see a few cars pulled over and their occupants staring off into Pali 'Ele'ele, a gorge on the right where a rock formation has eroded into the shape of a profile. Some legends associate it with a powerful kahuna (priest) who lived here during the 1500s, but today it bears an uncanny resemblance to former US president John F Kennedy. If parking is difficult, continue on to 'Iao Valley State Park, as it's only a couple of minutes' walk from there back to the viewing site.

'Iao Valley State Park

Every Hawaiian island has a landmark scene of singular beauty that's duplicated nowhere else. On O'ahu it's Diamond Head and on Maui it's unquestionably 'Iao Needle. Rising above a mountain stream in Maui's lush interior, this sensuous rock pinnacle is the focal point of 'Iao Valley State Park (admission per car $5; ☺8:30am-5pm). The rain-forest park, which starts 3 miles west of central Wailuku, extends clear up to Pu'u Kukui (5788ft), Maui's highest and wettest point.

'Iao Needle

The velvety green pinnacle that rises straight up 2250ft takes its name from 'Iao, the daughter of Maui. 'Iao Needle is said to be 'Iao's clandestine lover, captured by an angry Maui and turned to stone. A monument to love, this is the big kahuna, the ultimate phallic symbol.

Whether you believe in legends or not, this place looks like something torn from the pages of a fairy tale. Clouds rising up the valley form an ethereal shroud around the top of 'Iao Needle. With a stream meandering beneath and the steep cliffs of the West Maui Mountains as the backdrop, it's the most photographed scene on Maui.

Just a few minutes' walk from the parking lot, you'll reach a bridge where most people shoot their photos of the needle. A better idea is to take the walkway just before the bridge that loops downhill by the stream; this leads to the nicest photo angle, one that captures the stream, bridge and 'Iao Needle together.

If the water is high you'll see local kids taking bravado jumps from the bridge to the rocky stream below. You might be tempted to join them, but expect to get the stink eye – not to mention that the rocks below are potentially spine-crushing for unfamiliar divers. Better to take your dip in the swimming holes along the streamside path instead. Even there, however, be aware of potential dangers – the rocks in the stream are slippery and there can be flash floods.

Walking Trails

After you cross the bridge you'll come to two short trails that start opposite each other. Both take just 10 minutes to walk and shouldn't be missed. The upper path leads skyward up a series of steps, ending at a sheltered lookout with a close-up view of 'Iao Needle. The lower path leads down along 'Iao Stream, skirting the rock-strewn stream-bed past native hau trees with their hibiscuslike flowers. Look around and you'll be able to spot fruiting guava trees as well. The lower path returns to the bridge by way of a garden of native Hawaiian plants, including patches of taro.

Pu'unene

Sugar's the lifeblood of Pu'unene. Endless fields of sugarcane expand out from the Hawaiian Commercial & Sugar (C&S) Company's mill, which sits smack in the center of the village. If you happen to swing by when the mill is boiling down the sugarcane, the air hangs heavy with the sweet smell of molasses.

◉ Sights

Alexander & Baldwin Sugar Museum
MUSEUM

(www.sugarmuseum.com; cnr Pu'unene Ave & Hansen Rd; adult/child 6-12yr $7/2; ⊙9:30am-4:30pm) The former home of the sugar mill's superintendent now houses this evocative museum. Exhibits, including a working scale model of a cane-crushing plant, give the skinny on the sugarcane biz. Even more interesting, however, are the images of people. The museum traces how the privileged sons of missionaries wrested control over Maui's fertile valleys and dug the amazing irrigation system that made large-scale plantations viable. Representing the other end of the scale is an early-20th-century labor contract from the Japanese Emigration Company committing laborers to work the canefields 10 hours a day, 26 days a month for a mere $15.

Old Pu'unene
HISTORICAL SITE

You could drive through Pu'unene every day without realising a little slice of a bygone plantation village lies hidden behind the sugar mill. There, a long-forgotten church lies abandoned in a field of waving cane, across from the village's old schoolhouse. Still, the place isn't a ghost town. Out back, just beyond the school, you'll find an old shack that has served as a used bookstore since 1913. It's a bit musty and dusty, but still sells books for a mere dime. To get there turn off Mokulele Hwy (Hwy 311) onto Hansen Rd and take the first right onto Old Pu'unene Ave, continuing past the old Pu'unene Meat Market building (c 1926) and the mill. Turn left after 0.6 miles, just past a little bridge. Just before the pavement ends, turn right and drive behind the old school to reach the bookstore, which is open 9am to 4pm Tuesday to Saturday.

Kealia Pond National Wildlife Refuge

A magnet for both birds and bird-watchers, this refuge (www.fws.gov/kealiapond; Mokulele Hwy; admission free; ⊙8am-4pm Mon-Fri) harbors native waterbirds year-round and mi-

gratory birds from October to April. In the rainy winter months Kealia Pond swells to 400 acres, making it one of the largest natural ponds in Hawaii. In summer it shrinks to half that size, creating the skirt of crystalline salt that gives Kealia (meaning 'salt-encrusted place') its name.

Birding is excellent from the Kealia Pond Boardwalk, as well as from the refuge's visitor center off Mokulele Hwy (Hwy 311) at the 6-mile marker. In both places, you're almost certain to spot wading Hawaiian black-necked stilts and Hawaiian coots, two endangered species that thrive in this sanctuary.

KEALIA POND BOARDWALK

You can tread gently into a fragile wildlife habitat thanks to an elevated boardwalk that's turned previously inaccessible marshland into a one-of-a-kind nature walk. The coastal marsh and dunes nestling Kealia Pond not only provide feeding grounds for native waterbirds but are also a nesting site for the endangered hawksbill sea turtle. The 2200ft boardwalk begins on N Kihei Rd just north of the 2-mile marker. Interpretive plaques and benches along the way offer opportunities to stop and enjoy the splendor, and in winter you might be able to spot passing humpback whales. You'll even find a turtle laying eggs at the end of the boardwalk. Say what? Go take a look...

Ma'alaea

POP 500

Ma'alaea literally means 'beginning of red dirt,' but once you're there you'll swear it means 'windy.' Prevailing trade winds funneling between Maui's two great rises, Haleakalā and the West Maui Mountains, whip down upon Ma'alaea. By midday you'll need to hold on to your hat. It's no coincidence that Maui's first windmill farm marches up the slopes above Ma'alaea.

🏖 Beaches

Ma'alaea Bay
BEACH

Ma'alaea Bay is fronted by a 3-mile stretch of sandy beach, running from Ma'alaea Harbor south to Kihei. It can be accessed from **Haycraft Park** at the end of Hauoli St in Ma'alaea and from several places along N Kihei Rd including **Kealia Beach** in front of the Kealia Pond Boardwalk.

SWIM WITH THE FISHES

The sharks are circling. Some 20 of them, to be exact. Blacktip reef sharks, hammerheads and, gasp, a tiger shark. And you can jump in and join them. **Shark Dive Maui** (☑270-7075; 2hr dive $199; ☻8:15am Mon, Wed & Fri) takes intrepid divers on a daredevil's plunge into Maui Ocean Center's 750,000-gallon deep-ocean tank to swim with the toothy beasts as aquarium visitors gaze on in disbelief. You do need to be a certified diver and because it's limited to four divers per outing, advance reservations are essential.

◉ Sights

TOP CHOICE **Maui Ocean Center**   AQUARIUM
(www.mauioceancenter.com; 192 Ma'alaea Rd; adult/child 3-12yr $27/19; ☻9am-5pm; ▣) The largest tropical aquarium in the USA showcases Hawaii's dazzling marine life with award-winning style. The exhibits are laid out to take you on an ocean journey, beginning with nearshore reefs teeming with colorful tropical fish and ending with deep-ocean sealife. For the spectacular grand finale, you walk along a 54ft glass tunnel right through the center of a massive tank as gliding stingrays and menacing sharks encircle you. It's as close as you'll ever get to being underwater without donning dive gear.

Kid-friendly features abound, including interactive displays on whales in the Marine Mammal Discovery Center, a cool touch pool and, best of all, *na keiki*–level viewing ports that allow the wee ones to peer into everything on their own.

🏃 Activities

Snorkel & Whale-Watching Cruises

Many of the boats going out to Molokini (see the boxed text, above) leave from Ma'alaea. Go in the morning. Afternoon trips are typically cheaper, but because that's when the wind picks up it's also rougher and murkier. Snorkel gear is included in the snorkeling cruises; bring your own towels and sunscreen.

TOP CHOICE **Pacific Whale Foundation**   CRUISES
(☑249-8811; www.pacificwhale.org; Harbor Shops at Ma'alaea; adult/child 7-12yr from $55/35; ☻7am-6pm) Led by naturalists, these Molo-

kini tours do it right, with onboard snorkeling lessons and wildlife talks. Snacks are provided and kids under six are free. Half-day tours concentrate on Molokini. Full-day tours combine snorkeling at Molokini and Lana'i. Also recommended are the whale-watching cruises (adult/child $32/16) that operate several times a day in the winter season.

Quicksilver   SNORKELING CRUISE
(☑662-0075; www.frogman-maui.com; Slip 103, Ma'alaea Harbor; cruise $95) If you want more of a party scene, hop aboard this sleek double-decker catamaran. Once you're done snorkeling, your crew cranks up Jimmy Buffett and breaks out a BBQ lunch.

Windsurfing & Surfing

Wicked winds from the north shoot straight out toward Kaho'olawe, creating some of the best windsurfing conditions on Maui. In winter, when the wind dies down elsewhere, windsurfers still fly along Ma'alaea Bay.

The bay has a couple of hot surfing spots. The **Ma'alaea Pipeline**, south of the harbor, freight-trains right and is the fastest surf break in all Hawaii. Summer's southerly swells produce huge tubes.

Hiking

Lahaina Pali Trail   HIKING
Fine hilltop views of Kaho'olawe and Lana'i are in store along this trail, which follows an ancient footpath as it zigzags steeply up through native dryland. After the first mile it passes into open, sun-baked scrub, from where you can see Haleakalā and the fertile central plains. Ironwood trees precede the crossing of Kealaloloa Ridge (1600ft), after which you descend through Ukumehame Gulch. Look for stray petroglyphs and *paniolo* graffiti. Stay on the footpath all the way down to Papalaua Beach and don't detour onto 4WD roads. The 5.5-mile trail should take about 2½ hours each way.

You can hike in either direction, but starting off early from the east side of the mountains keeps you ahead of the blistering sun. Be aware of the risk of dehydration and heatstroke on this trail – bring plenty of water and a hat that provides shade. The trailhead access road, marked by a Na Ala Hele sign, is on Hwy 30, just south of its intersection with N Kihei Rd. If you prefer to start at the west end, the trailhead is 200yd south of the 11-mile marker on Hwy 30.

✕ Eating

TOP CHOICE Waterfront Restaurant   SEAFOOD $$$
(📞244-9028; www.waterfrontrestaurant.net; Milowai Condominium, 50 Hauoli St; mains $30-42; ⏱5-10pm) Sit on the lanai, listen to the surf and order fresh-off-the-boat seafood at this harborfront restaurant. The type of fish depends on what's reeled in each day, but the preparation choice – nine tempting options – is yours. Maybe you're in a blackened Cajun mood. Perhaps Sicilian with artichoke hearts and roasted garlic. The food, service and wine selection are among Maui's best.

Beach Bums Bar & Grill   BBQ $$
(📞243-2286; Harbor Shops at Ma'alaea; mains $8-22; ⏱8am-9pm) If BBQ is your thing, you'll love this harborfront eatery, which uses a wood-burning rotisserie smoker to grill up everything from burgers and ribs to turkey and Spam. Come between 3pm and 6pm for $3 drafts of Kona-brewed Longboard Lager.

Hula Cookies   DESSERT $
(www.hulacookies.com; Harbor Shops at Ma'alaea; snacks $3-6; ⏱10am-6pm Mon-Sat, to 5pm Sun) The perfect place to take the kids for a snack after the aquarium. The fresh-baked cookies and Maui-made ice cream are chock-full of macadamia nuts, pineapple and coconut.

❶ Getting There & Away

Located at a crossroads, Ma'alaea has good connections to the rest of Maui's public bus system. The Maui Bus connects the Harbor Shops at Ma'alaea with Lahaina, Kahului and Kihei. Service depends on the route, but buses operate hourly from around 6am to 8pm.

Molokini Crater

No underwater site draws more visitors than Molokini, the volcanic crater that lies midway between the islands of Maui and Kaho'olawe. Half of the crater rim has eroded away, leaving a pretty crescent moon that rises 160ft above the ocean surface, with a mere 18 acres of rocky land high and dry. But it's what's beneath the surface that draws the crowds. Snorkelers and divers will be thrilled by steep walls, ledges, white-tipped reef sharks, manta rays, turtles and abundant fish.

The legends about Molokini are myriad. One says Molokini was a beautiful woman who was turned to stone by jealous Pele, goddess of volcanoes. Another claims one of Pele's lovers angered her by secretly marrying a *mo'o* (shape-shifting water lizard). Pele chopped the sacred lizard in half, leaving Molokini as its tail and Pu'u Ola'i in Makena as its head. Yet another tale alleges that Molokini, which means 'many ties' in Hawaiian, is the umbilical cord left over from the birth of Kaho'olawe.

The coral reef that extends outward from Molokini is extraordinary, though it has lost some of its variety over the years. Most of the black coral that was once prolific in Molokini's deeper waters made its way into Lahaina jewelry stores before the island was declared a marine conservation district in 1977. During WWII the US Navy shelled Molokini for target practice, and live bombs are still occasionally spotted on the crater floor.

Consider the following when planning your excursion to Molokini. The water is calmest and clearest in the morning. Don't fall for discounted afternoon tours – go out early for the smoothest sailing and best conditions. For snorkelers, there's simply not much to see when the water's choppy. The main departure point for outings to Molokini is Ma'alaea, but you can also get there from other ports, including Kihei.

KIHEI & SOUTH MAUI

Dubbed Haole-wood for its LA-style strip malls and white-bread resorts, South Maui *is* a bit shiny and overbuilt. But dig deeper and you'll find a mixed plate of scenery and adventure – from Kihei to Wailea, Makena and beyond – that's truly unique. You can snorkel reefs teeming with turtles, kayak to remote bays or sail in an outrigger canoe. The coral gardens are so rich you can dive from the shore. And the beaches are undeniably glorious, whether you're looking to relax beneath a resort cabana or discover your own little pocket of sand. Add reliably sunny weather and a diverse dining scene, and South Maui is a pretty irresistible place to strand yourself.

Kihei

POP 19,809

This energetic community is a good choice for short-trip vacationers who want to maximise their beach time and their budgets – and throw in an adventure or two. Yes, it's overrun with strip malls, but with 6 miles of sun-kissed beaches, loads of affordable accommodations and a variety of dining options, it offers everything you need for an enjoyable seaside vacation.

To zip from one end of Kihei to the other, take the Pi'ilani Hwy (Hwy 31). It runs parallel to and bypasses the stop-start traffic of S Kihei Rd. Well-marked crossroads connect these two routes.

Beaches

The further south you go, the better the beaches. At the northern end of Kihei, swimming is not advised, but kayaking is good in the morning and windsurfers set off in the afternoon.

TOP CHOICE Keawakapu Beach   BEACH

This sparkling stretch of sand (Map p356) is a showstopper. Extending from southern Kihei to Wailea's Mokapu Beach, it's set back from the main road and less visible than Kihei's main roadside beaches just north. Also less crowded, it's a great place to settle in and watch the sunset.

With its cushiony soft sand, Keawakapu is also a favorite for sunrise yoga and wake-up strolls and is the perfect spot for an end-of-day swim. Mornings are the best time for snorkeling: head to the rocky outcrops that form the northern and southern ends of the beach. During winter keep an eye out for humpback whales, which come remarkably close to shore here.

There are three beach access points, all with outdoor showers. To get to the southern end, go south on S Kihei Rd until it dead-ends at a beach parking lot. Near the middle of the beach, there's a parking lot at the corner of Kilohana Dr and S Kihei Rd; look for a blue shoreline access sign on the *makai* side of the street. At the northern end, beach parking can be found in a large unpaved access lot north of the Days Inn.

Kama'ole Beach Parks   BEACH

Kama'ole Beach (Map p356) is having so much fun, it just keeps rolling along. And along. And along. Divided into three sections by rocky points, these popular strands are known locally as Kam I, II and III. All three are pretty, golden-sand beaches with full facilities, lifeguards included. There's a volleyball court at Kam I and parking lots at Kam I and III.

Water conditions vary with the weather, but swimming is usually good. For the most part, these beaches have sandy bottoms with a fairly steep drop, which tends to create good conditions for bodysurfing, especially in winter.

For snorkeling, the south end of Kama'ole Beach Park III has some nearshore rocks harboring a bit of coral and a few colorful fish, though it pales in comparison to the snorkeling at beaches further south.

Charley Young Beach   BEACH

Out of sight from sightseers cruising the main drag, this side-street neighborhood beach (Map p356) is the least-touristed strand in Kihei. It's a real jewel in the rough: broad and sandy, and backed by swaying coconut palms. You're apt to find fishers casting their lines, families playing volleyball and someone strumming a guitar. It also has some of the better bodysurfing waves in Kihei. Beach parking is on the corner of S Kihei Rd and Kaia'u Pl. To get to the beach, simply walk to the end of Kaia'u Pl and follow the steps down the cliff.

Kalepolepo Beach Park   BEACH

Adjacent to the headquarters for the Humpback Whale National Marine Sanctuary, this compact park (Map opposite) is a nice spot for families with younger kids. A grassy lawn is fronted by the ancient Ko'ie'ie Fishpond (p355), whose stone walls create a shallow swimming pool with calm waters perfect for wading. There are also picnic tables and grills.

Mai Poina 'Oe Ia'u Beach Park   BEACH

This long sandy beach (Map opposite) at the northern end of Kihei is a popular morning launch for outrigger canoes and kayaks. After the wind picks up in the afternoon, it's South Maui's main venue for windsurfing.

Kalama Park   PARK

Across from the busy pub and restaurant scene at Kihei Kalama Village, this expansive park (Map p356) has ball fields, tennis and volleyball courts, a playground, picnic pavilions, restrooms and showers. There is a small beach behind a whale statue, but a runoff ditch carries wastewater here after heavy rains so best swim elsewhere.

Sights

FREE Hawaiian Islands Humpback Whale National Marine Sanctuary   MUSEUM

(Map opposite; ☎879-2818, 800-831-4888; www.hawaiihumpbackwhale.noaa.gov; 726 S Kihei Rd;

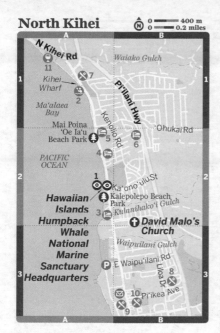

◎ **Top Sights**
David Malo's Church B2
Hawaiian Islands Humpback
   Whale National Marine
   Sanctuary Headquarters A2

◎ **Sights**
  1 Ko'ie'ie Fishpond................................A2

Activities, Courses & Tours
  2 Kihei Canoe Club................................A1

🛏 **Sleeping**
  3 Koa Lagoon.......................................A2
  4 Maui Sunseeker A2
  5 Nona Lani Cottages...........................A2
  6 Ocean Breeze Hideaway...................B2

🍴 **Eating**
  7 Kihei Farmers Market...................... A1
  8 Safeway...B3
  9 Saigon Pearl Vietnamese
    Cuisine...B3
 10 Stella Blues.....................................B3

🍷 **Drinking**
 11 Dina's Sandwitch A1

Shopping
Pi'ilani Village................................(see 8)

⊙10am-3pm Mon-Fri; 🚻) If you're curious about Maui's most famous annual visitors, stop by the marine sanctuary headquarters. The center overlooks an ancient fishpond, and its oceanfront lookout is ideal for sighting the humpback whales that frequent the bay during winter. There are even free scopes set up for viewing. Displays on whales and sea turtles provide background, and there are lots of informative brochures about Hawaiian wildlife. Swing by at 11am on Tuesday and Thursday for free '45-Ton Talks' on whales.

Ko'ie'ie Fishpond
HISTORICAL SITE
(Map above; admission free) In ancient Hawaii, coastal fishponds were built to provide a ready source of fish for royal families. The most intact fishpond remaining on Maui is the 3-acre Ko'ie'ie Fishpond, now on the National Register of Historic Places. This fascinating fishpond borders both Kalepolepo Beach Park and the Hawaiian Islands Humpback Whale National Marine Sanctuary headquarters.

David Malo's Church
CHURCH
(Map above; 100 Kulanihako'i St) Philosopher David Malo, who built this church in 1852, was the first Hawaiian ordained to the Christian ministry. He was also co-author of Hawaii's

first constitution and an early spokesperson for Hawaiian rights. While most of Malo's original church has been dismantled, a 3ft-high section of the walls still stands beside a palm grove. Pews are lined up inside the stone walls, where open-air services are held at 9am Sunday by Trinity Episcopal Church-by-the-Sea. It's really quite beautiful.

🏃 Activities

Canoeing & Kayaking

TOP CHOICE **South Pacific Kayaks & Outfitters**
KAYAKING
(📞875-4848, 800-776-2326; www.southpacifickay aks.com; 1-/2-person kayaks per day $40/50, tours $65-139; ⊙6am-9pm) This top-notch operation leads kayak-and-snorkel tours. It also rents kayaks for those who want to go off on their own, and will deliver them to Makena Landing.

Kihei Canoe Club
CANOEING
(Map left; 📞879-5505; www.kiheicanoeclub.com; Kihei Wharf; donation $25) This paddle club invites visitors to share in the mana by joining

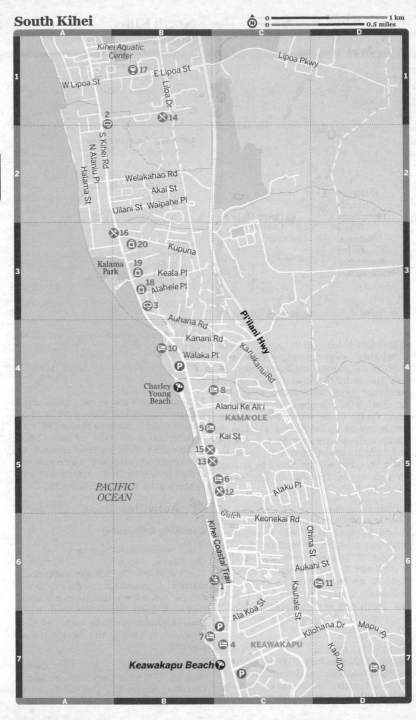

South Kihei

◎ **Top Sights**
   Keawakapu Beach C7

Activities, Courses & Tours
1 Blue Water Rafting.............................. C6
2 Maui Dive Shop A1
3 Maui Dreams Dive Company..............B3

◉ **Sleeping**
4 Days Inn Maui Oceanfront.................C7
5 Kama'ole Beach Royale B5
6 Kihei Kai Nani C5
7 Mana Kai Maui B7
8 Maui Coast Hotel C4
9 Pineapple Inn Maui D7
10 Punahoa...B4
11 Two Mermaids on Maui B&B............. D6

◉ **Eating**
   808 Bistro .... (see 12)
12 808 Deli..C5
13 Café O'Lei...B5
   Da Kitchen Express .... (see 13)
14 Eskimo Candy B1
   Fat Daddy's................................. (see 18)
   Foodland .... (see 19)
15 Hawaiian Moons Natural Food...........B5
   Joy's Place ....(see 3)
   Kihei Caffe...................................(see 18)
   Local Boys Shave Ice..................(see 18)
   Pita Paradise ....(see 18)
   Pizza Madness ....(see 2)
   Sansei Seafood Restaurant &
     Sushi Bar...................................(see 19)
16 Shaka Sandwich & Pizza.....................B3

◉ **Drinking**
   Five Palms.....................................(see 7)
17 Kiwi Roadhouse.................................... B1
   Lava Java .... (see 18)
   Oceans Beach Bar & Grill..........(see 20)
   South Shore Tiki Lounge .... (see 18)
   The Dog and Duck .... (see 18)

◉ **Shopping**
   808 Clothing Company..............(see 18)
18 Kihei Kalama Village B3
19 Kihei Town Center B3
20 Kukui Mall B3

members in paddling their outrigger canoes on Tuesday and Thursday mornings from about 7:30am to 9am. No reservations are necessary; just show up at the wharf at 7am. It's first-come, first-served, and spots fill quickly. The $25 donation helps offset the cost of maintaining the canoes.

Diving & Snorkeling

Maui Dreams Dive Company DIVING
(Map opposite; ☏874-5332; www.mauidreams diveco.com; Island Surf Bldg, 1993 S Kihei Rd; 1-/2-tank dives from $69/99; ☺7am-6pm) Maui Dreams is a first-rate, five-star PADI operation specialising in shore dives. With this family-run outfit, a dive trip is like going out with friends. Nondivers, ask about the introductory dive ($89), and to zoom around underwater, check out their scooter dive ($99 to $129).

Maui Dive Shop DIVING, SNORKELING
(Map opposite; ☏879-3388; www.mauidiveshop. com; 1455 S Kihei Rd; 2-tank dives $140-150, snorkel rentals per day $6; ☺6am-9pm) This is a good spot to rent or buy watersports gear, including boogie boards, snorkels and wetsuits.

Blue Water Rafting SNORKELING
(Map opposite; ☏879-7238; www.bluewaterraft ing.com; Kihei Boat Ramp; Molokini Express/ Kanaio Coast $50/100; ☺departure times vary) In a hurry? Try the Molokini Express trip if you want to zip out to the crater, snorkel and be back within two hours. An adventurous half-day trip heads southward on a motorised raft to snorkel among sea turtles and dolphins at remote coves along the Kanaio coast.

Stand Up Paddle Surfing

Stand-Up Paddle Surf School PADDLE SURFING
(☏579-9231; www.standuppaddlesurfschool.com; 90min lesson $159; ☺9am & 11am) This SUP school is owned by Maria Souza, a champion paddle surfer who was also the first woman surfer to tow into the monster waves at Jaws. Small classes and safety are priorities, and the paddling location is determined by water conditions. Classes fill quickly, so call a few days – or a week – ahead.

✯ Festivals & Events

Whale Day Celebration OUTDOOR FESTIVAL
(www.greatmauiwhalefestival.org; 🎪) Organised by the Pacific Whale Foundation, this family-friendly bash honors Maui's humpback whales with crafts, live music and food booths. It's held at Kalama Park, next to the big whale statue, on a Saturday in mid-February.

It's not just honeymooners that flock here – turns out humpback whales prefer Maui too. In winter they can be spotted throughout Hawaii but the waters off western Maui are the favored haunt for mating and birthing.

Fortunately, humpbacks are coast-huggers, preferring shallow waters to protect their newborn calves. This makes for terrific whale-watching opportunities whether you're on land or on water.

Whale-watching cruises are the easiest way to get close to the action, as the boats know all the best spots and offer a close-up view of humpbacks demonstrating their hulking presence in leaps and bounds. You can readily join a cruise from a green operator like Pacific Whale Foundation from either Lahaina or Ma'alaea harbor.

Not that you need a whale-watching cruise to see these 40-ton leviathans. If you're taking the Lana'i ferry in winter, a glimpse of breaching whales is a common bonus; snorkeling tours to Molokini sometimes have sightings en route; and ocean kayaking in south Maui packs good odds of seeing these colossals up close.

From the shore, whale spotting abounds – cliffside lookouts, west-facing beaches, the lanai of your oceanfront condo, most anywhere from Kapalua in the north to Makena in the south. Two particularly rewarding lookouts are Papawai Point (see the boxed text, p323), southwest of Ma'alaea on the way to Lahaina, and the Wailea Beach walk (p365) in Wailea.

Of course, binoculars will bring the action closer. If you're not carting along a pair, stop by the Hawaiian Islands Humpback Whale National Marine Sanctuary headquarters (p354) in Kihei where there's a seaside scope. While you're at it, check out the whale displays and discover the difference between a full breach, a spy hop and a peduncle slap.

Then there's the music. The Whalesong Project maintains an underwater hydrophone off Kihei – just log on at www.whalesong.net and listen to whales singing in real time. Lucky snorkelers and divers who happen to be in the water at the right time can hear them singing as well – Ulua Beach in Wailea is a top spot for eavesdropping on their haunting music. Love songs, we presume.

🛏 Sleeping

Condos are plentiful in Kihei, whereas hotels and B&Bs can be counted on one hand. Some condominium complexes maintain a front desk that handles bookings, but others are booked via rental agents. When making a reservation, be sure to ask about cleaning fees, which vary.

TOP CHOICE **Pineapple Inn Maui**   INN **$$**
(Map p356; ☎298-4403, 877-212-6284; www.pineappleinnmaui.com; 3170 Akala Dr; r $139-149, cottages $215; ✳@🛜☀) For style with a personal touch, consider this inviting boutique inn overlooking Wailea, less than a mile from the beach. Rooms, which have ocean-view lanai and private entrances, are as nice as those at the exclusive resorts, but at a fraction of the cost. You can watch the sunset from the pool. Rooms have kitchenettes, and the two-bedroom cottage comes with a full kitchen.

TOP CHOICE **Punahoa**   CONDO **$$**
(Map p356; ☎879-2720, 800-564-4380; www.punahoabeach.com; 2142 Ili'ili Rd; studios $159, 1 bedroom $244-269, 2 bedroom $274; 🛜) Sip coffee, scan for whales, savor sunsets – it's hard to leave your lanai at Punahoa, a classy boutique condo where every unit has a clear-on ocean view. Tucked on a quiet side street, this 15-unit complex offers privacy and warm alohas. It's also next to a gorgeous strand of sand, Punahoa Beach, that's a favorite of turtles and surfers alike. Penthouse units have air-conditioning.

Two Mermaids on Maui B&B   B&B **$$**
(Map p356; ☎874-8687, 800-598-9550; www.twomermaids.com; 2840 Umalu Pl; studio/1 bedroom incl breakfast $115/140; @🛜☀) I'd like to be, under the sea...yep, the happy-go-lucky Beatles tune springs to mind inside the Ocean Ohana suite, a bright space swirling with whimsical maritime imagery. The Poolside Sweet, with its sunset colors and in-room guitar, might inspire your own inner songwriter. Organic island fruit is provided for breakfast. Both units have kitchenettes, and the Ocean Ohana suite has air-con. Families are welcome.

Ocean Breeze Hideaway B&B $
(Map p355; ☎879-0657, 888-463-6687; www
.hawaiibednbreakfast.com; 435 Kalalau Pl; r incl
breakfast from $80; @🖤) Bob and Sande have
run this welcoming B&B for more than a
decade and, with their licensed activity
desk certification, the couple is a treasure
trove of insider tips. Their home has two
comfortable guest rooms, one with a queen
bed and ceiling fans, the other with a king
bed and air-con. Both have a private entrance and a refrigerator. Children 12 and
older OK.

Mana Kai Maui CONDO $$
(Map p356; ☎879-1561, 800-525-2025; www
.manakaimaui.com; 2960 S Kihei Rd; r/1 bedroom
from $190/281; 🖤@🏊) Perched on a point
overlooking Keawakapu Beach, this com-
plex offers great sunset views. You can swim
and snorkel from the beach right outside the
door. The on-site rental company manages
50 units, providing all the conveniences of a
condo as well as the pluses of a hotel, with a
front desk and a full-service restaurant. Re-
quest an upper floor for the best views.

Maui Sunseeker BOUTIQUE HOTEL $$
(Map p355; ☎879-1261, 800-532-6284; www.
mauisunseeker.com; 551 S Kihei Rd; r $105-185, ste
$125-265, studio $110-195; 🖤@🖤) No, the new
webcam doesn't sweep past the clothing-
optional rooftop deck and its hot tub, but it
does take in Mai Poina 'Oela'u Beach across
the street. Catering to gay and lesbians, this
breezy, 17-room motel consists of three adjacent properties. Opt for the one in back,
formerly the Wailana Inn; its rooms beam
with tasteful decor that outshines other
places in this price range. Amenities include
refrigerator, microwave and lanai.

Kihei Kai Nani CONDO $$
(Map p356; ☎879-9088, 800-473-1493; www.ki
heikainani.com; 2495 S Kihei Rd; 1 bedroom $168;
🖤@🏊) Rooms and decor may be a little on
the old side, but when it comes to amenities
this inviting low-rise condo is on par with
more expensive properties. On-site are a large
pool, a laundry room, shuffleboard, BBQ grills
and picnic tables – all fringed by colorful trop-
ical landscaping. Kam II is across the street.

Koa Lagoon CONDO $$
(Map p355; ☎879-3002, 800-367-8030; www
.koalagoon.com; 800 S Kihei Rd; 1/2 bedroom from
$170/200; 🖤🖤🏊) Watch the whales from
your balcony at this seaside complex with
just 42 rooms, each with a clear view of the

ocean. Other perks include a pretty backyard, a relaxing beach and a heated pool
that's seldom crowded. Comfy units – on six
floors – are fitted with king beds and everything you'd need including a washer and
dryer. A few units have wi-fi.

Nona Lani Cottages COTTAGES $$
(Map p355; ☎879-2497, 800-733-2688; www.nona
lanicottages.com; 455 S Kihei Rd; cottages from
$150; 🖤) Wooden cottages, lazy hammocks,
picnic tables, swaying palms – this place
looks like the tropical version of Camp Min-
nehaha. The eight retro cottages are com-
pact, but squeeze in a full kitchen, a private
lanai, a living room with daybed and a bed-
room with a queen bed, plus cable TV.

Kama'ole Beach Royale CONDO $$
(Map p356; ☎879-3131, 800-421-3661; www
.kbr1maui.com; 2385 S Kihei Rd; 1/2 bedroom from
$170/200; 🖤🖤🏊) Views of the ocean from
the rooftop patio on the 6th floor are superb,
and there's a grill for cooking out. Most of
the condos in the rental pool are fresh off
a renovation that has added a little pizzazz.
Some units have wi-fi.

Maui Coast Hotel HOTEL $$
(Map p356; ☎874-6284, 800-663-1144; www.
mauicoasthotel.com; 2259 S Kihei Rd; r $209, ste
$229-249; 🖤🖤🏊) We're not swooning, but
among Kihei's few hotels, this is the best.
It's clean and comfortable, and the set-back-
from-the-road location makes it quieter than
other places on the strip. The $18 daily resort
fee includes wi-fi, parking and local shuttle
service.

Days Inn Maui Oceanfront HOTEL $$
(Map p356; ☎879-7744, 800-263-3387; www.
mauioceanfrontinn.com; 2980 S Kihei Rd; r $159;
🖤@) Yeah, it's a chain, rooms are pint-sized
and the hairdryer looks like it belongs on a
1970s spaceship, but rates are the cheapest
in town, and the property borders beautiful
Keawakapu Beach.

✗ Eating

⬛TOP CHOICE Café O'Lei HAWAII REGIONAL $$
(Map p356; ☎891-1368; www.cafeoleirestaurants.
com; Rainbow Mall, 2439 S Kihei Rd; lunch $7-13, din-
ner $17-37; ⊙10:30am-3:30pm & 4:30-10pm Tue-
Sun) With its strip-mall setting, this bistro
looks ho-hum at first blush. But step inside.
The sophisticated atmosphere, innovative
Hawaii regional cuisine, honest prices and
excellent service knock Café O'Lei into the

fine-dining big leagues. For a tangy treat, order the blackened mahimahi with fresh papaya salsa. Unbeatable lunch entrées, with salads, are available for under $10. Famous martinis, too.

TOP CHOICE Da Kitchen Express
HAWAIIAN $$

(Map p356; www.da-kitchen.com; Rainbow Mall, 2439 S Kihei Rd; meals $9-16; ☺9am-9pm) Da kitchen is da bomb. Congenial service, heaping portions, loads of flavor – come here to eat like a king. Tucked in the back of anvil-shaped Rainbow Mall, this low-frills eatery is all about Hawaiian plate lunches. The local favorite is Da Lau Lau Plate (with steamed pork wrapped in taro leaves), but you won't go wrong with any choice. We particularly liked the spicy *kalua* pork.

Sansei Seafood Restaurant & Sushi Bar
JAPANESE $$

(Map p356; ☎879-0004; www.sanseihawaii.com; Kihei Town Center, 1881 S Kihei Rd; appetisers $3-15, mains $17-32; ☺5:30-10pm, until 1am Thu-Sat) The line runs out the door, but you'll be rewarded for your patience. The creative appetiser menu includes everything from traditional sashimi to lobster and blue-crab ravioli. Hot Eurasian fusion dishes include Peking duck in a foie gras demi. Between 5:30pm and 6pm all food is discounted 25%, and sushi is discounted 50% from 10pm to 1am Thursday through Saturday.

808 Bistro
ECLECTIC $$

(Map p356; ☎879-8008; www.808bistro.com; 2511 S Kihei Rd; breakfast $8-13, dinner $15-20; ☺7am-noon & 5-9pm) The creative menu at this new bistro showcases comfort foods prepared with a savory, gourmet spin – think short rib pot pie and Gorgonzola alfredo. Your diet will walk the plank at breakfast with banana bread French toast or the decadent whale pie with ham, hash browns, eggs, cheese and brown gravy. Currently BYOB, this open-air eatery is owned by the folks running the ever-popular 808 Deli.

808 Deli
CAFE $

(Map p356; ☎879-1111; www.808deli.net; 1913 S Kihei Rd; sandwiches $7-8; ☺7am-5pm) As Subway wept and Quizno's cried, 808 Deli tap-danced its way into our sandwich-loving hearts. With fresh breads, gourmet spreads and 17 different sandwiches and paninis, this tiny gourmet sandwich shop across from Kam II is the place to grab a picnic lunch. For a spicy kick, try the roast beef with wasabi aioli.

Kihei Caffe
CAFE $

(Map p356; www.kiheicaffe.com; 1945 S Kihei Rd; mains $6-11; ☺5am-3pm) Kihei Caffe newbie? Here's the deal: step to the side and review the menu before you join the queue. The cashier is chatty, but he keeps that long line moving. Next, fill your coffee cup at the inside thermos, hunt down a table on the patio, then watch the breakfast burritos, veggie scrambles and *loco mocos* flash by. And keep an eye on those sneaky birds. Solos, couples, families – everybody's here or on the way.

Joy's Place
CAFE $

(Map p356; www.joysplacemaui.com; Island Surf Bldg, 1993 S Kihei Rd; mains $9-12; ☺8am-3pm Mon-Sat; ☑) Joy takes pride in her little kitchen where the operative words are organic, free range and local harvested. The healthiest takeout salads ($9) you'll find anywhere in South Maui, wrap sandwiches made to order, overstuffed sandwiches and daily specials like fresh fish tacos on Saturdays attract a loyal following.

Stella Blues
ECLECTIC $$

(Map p355; ☎874-3779; www.stellablues.com; Azeka Mauka II, 1279 S Kihei Rd; breakfast $6-13, lunch & dinner $12-28; ☺7:30am-11pm; ☑) This Kihei favorite never skimps, and the eclectic menu offers something for every mood, from Hawaiian-style macadamia-nut pancakes to Caesar salad, pan-seared fresh fish and Maui Cattle Co burgers.

Eskimo Candy
SEAFOOD $$

(Map p356; www.eskimocandy.com; 2665 Wai Wai Pl; mains $8-17; ☺10:30am-7pm Mon-Fri) On a side street, Eskimo Candy is a fish market with a takeout counter and a few tables. Fresh-fish fanatics should zero in on the *poke,* ahi wraps and fish tacos.

Local Boys Shave Ice
SHAVE ICE $

(Map p356; Kihei Kalama Village, 1913 S Kihei Rd; shave ice $4-6; ☺10am-9pm) Local Boys dishes up soft shave ice in a dazzling rainbow of sweet syrups. Try it tropical – banana, mango and 'shark's blood' – with ice cream, *kauai* cream and azuki beans. Load up on napkins; these babies are messy!

Pizza Madness
PIZZA $$

(Map p356; ☎270-9888; 1455 S Kihei Rd; pizzas $7-20; ☺11am-9:30pm, until 9pm Sun & Mon) Picture a dark room. A small bar in back. Flickering flat-screens. And then…look, overhead. It's a giant shark! Chomping on a slice of pizza!

Madness! Weird decor or not, Pizza Madness serves Kihei's best pizza.

Saigon Pearl Vietnamese Cuisine
VIETNAMESE $$

(Map p355; ☎875-2088; Azeka Makai, 1280 S Kihei Rd; most mains $9-14; ◷10:30am-9:30pm) The curried lemongrass chicken with jasmine rice awakens the senses. Or have some fun and order *banh hoi*, a roll-your-own Vietnamese version of fajitas that come with mint leaves, assorted veggies and grilled shrimp.

Fat Daddy's
COMFORT FOOD $$

(Map p356; www.fatdaddysmaui.com; Kihei Kalama Village, 1913 S Kihei Rd; mains $8-19; ◷11:30am-10pm) Big plates of tangy barbecued ribs with all the fixings are the specialty at this smart, Texas-style smokehouse. Here, Southwest takes on a Hawaiian accent with Maui Cattle Company beef on the grill.

Pita Paradise
MEDITERRANEAN $$

(Map p356; ☎875-7679; Kihei Kalama Village, 1913 S Kihei Rd; mains $7-22; ◷11am-9:30pm) Aloha. Yassou. Dig in. Enjoy gyros and kebabs at this low-key Greek favorite in The Triangle.

Shaka Sandwich & Pizza
CHEESE STEAKS, PIZZA $$

(Map p356; ☎874-0331; 1770 S Kihei Rd; mains $7-27; ◷10:30am-9pm Sun-Thu, 10:30am-10pm Fri & Sat) Come here for the cheese steak sandwiches.

Kihei has two 24-hour supermarkets: **Foodland** (Map p356; Kihei Town Center, 1881 S Kihei Rd) and **Safeway** (Map p355; Pi'ilani Village, 277 Pi'ikea Ave). **Hawaiian Moons Natural Foods** (Map p356; http://hawaiianmoons.com; Kama'ole Beach Center, 2411 S Kihei Rd; ◷8am-9pm Mon-Fri, 9am-9pm Sat & Sun;) is a good place to pack a healthy picnic lunch. **Kihei Farmers Market** (Map p355; 61 S Kihei Rd; ◷8am-4pm Mon-Thu, to 5pm Fri) sells island-grown fruits and vegetables – a bit pricey but fresh.

Drinking & Entertainment

Most bars in Kihei are across the street from the beach and have nightly entertainment. Kihei Kalama Village, aka The Bar-muda Triangle (or just The Triangle), is crammed tight with buzzy watering holes.

South Shore Tiki Lounge
TIKI BAR

(Map p356; ☎874-6444; Kihei Kalama Village; 1913 S Kihei Rd) This cozy tropical shack has a heart as big as its lanai. Drink maestros here

regularly win annual *Maui Time Weekly* awards for best female and male bartenders. Good for dancing too.

The Dog and Duck
IRISH

(Map p356; ☎875-9669; Kihei Kalama Village, 1913 S Kihei Rd) This cheery Irish pub attracts a younger crowd – yes, they have sports TV, but it's not blaring from every corner. Decent spuds and pub grub go along with that heady Guinness draft, and there's music most nights of the week.

Oceans Beach Bar & Grill
BEACH BAR

(Map p356; ☎891-2414; Kukui Mall, 1819 S Kihei Rd) It's not on the beach, but it is open air, with surf videos and NFL games on the TV screens and dancing on the weekends.

Five Palms
COCKTAILS

(Map p356; www.fivepalmsrestaurant.com; 2960 S Kihei Rd) For sunset mai tai beside the beach, this is the place. Come early because the patio, just steps from stunning Keawakapu Beach, fills quickly.

Kiwi Roadhouse
ROADHOUSE

(Map p356; ☎874-1250; 95 E Lipoa St) Own a Hawg or a 4x4 pickup? Then rumble in and join friends at this rambunctious, freestanding roadhouse that's not at all close to the beach. Live music Wednesday to Sunday nights, from rock to blues to country.

Lava Java
COFFEE SHOP

(Map p356; www.lavajavamaui.com; Kihei Kalama Village, 1941 S Kihei Rd; ◷6am-8pm;) Counter service can be slow in the morning but that might be due to the awesome 2-for-1 drink special (6am to 9am). The super-nice owner regularly serves free samples of iced mocha. Four computers with internet access ($.20 per minute) are in the back. Scaly gekko balls are in the middle.

Dina's Sandwitch
NEIGHBORHOOD PUB

(Map p355; ☎879-3262; 145 N Kihei Rd) Old salts and young salts – but very few hot peppers – keep this divey joint loud and convivial. Stop by for a shot of local flavor and walls that are covered with one dollar bills – $17,000 worth they say.

Shopping

Pi'ilani Village
SHOPPING CENTER

(Map p355; 225 Pi'ikea Ave) Kihei's largest shopping center has scores of stores perfect for stocking up on gifts. Looking for a beach read? There's a **Borders Express** (☎875-6607) here too.

1. Tiki
Tiki (*ki'i* in Hawaiian) are wood- or stone-carved statues, usually depicting a deity.

2. Farmers Markets (p600)
For a complete list of farmers markets in Hawaii, see www.ediblehawaiianislands.com.

3. Ho'okipa Beach Park, Pa'ia (p371)
The world's premier windsurfing beach and one of Maui's prime surfing spots.

4. 'Iao Needle (p350)
This 2250ft pinnacle is the focal point of 'Iao Valley State Park.

JOHN ELK III / LONELY PLANET IMAGES ©

CUSTOMER CARDS

To save money on groceries, give the cashier at Foodland your phone number. The store saves your number and you can use it in place of a customer card for discounts on your visits. Safeway accepts customer club cards from the mainland.

Kihei Kalama Village OUTDOOR MARKET
(Map p356; ☑879-6610; 1913 S Kihei Rd) More than 40 shops and stalls cluster under one roof at this shopping arcade. Ladies, for fashionable beachwear pop into Mahina (www.mahinamaui.com). Dudes can browse 808 Clothing Company (www.the808clothingcompany.com) for T-shirts with original Maui designs.

Information

Bank of Hawaii (☑879-5844; www.boh.com; Azeka Mauka, 1279 S Kihei Rd)

Kihei Police District Station (☑244-6400; Kihei Town Center, 1881 S Kihei Rd; ☺7:45am-4:30pm Mon-Fri)

Longs Drug (☑879-2259; 1215 S Kihei Rd; ☺7am-midnight) Kihei's largest pharmacy, with one aisle stocked totally with slippers (flip flops, yo').

Post office (☑879-1987; 1254 S Kihei Rd)

Urgent Care Maui Physicians (☑879-7781; 1325 S Kihei Rd; ☺7am-9pm) This clinic accepts walk-in patients.

Getting There & Around

To/From the Airport
Almost everyone rents a car at the airport in Kahului. Otherwise, expect to pay about $31 to $37 for a shuttle service or $35 to $62 for a taxi depending on your South Maui location.

Bicycle
Bike lanes run along both the Pi'ilani Hwy and S Kihei Rd, but cyclists need to be cautious of inattentive drivers making sudden turns across the lanes.

South Maui Bicycles (☑874-0068; www.southmauibicycles.com; Island Surf Bldg, 1993 S Kihei Rd; per day $22-60, per week $99-250; ☺10am-6pm Mon-Sat) This shop rents out top-of-the-line Trek road bicycles and quality mountain bikes, as well as basic around-town bikes.

Bus
The **Maui Bus** (p322; www.mauicounty.gov) serves Kihei with two routes. One route, the Kihei Islander 10, connects Kihei with Wailea and Ma'alaea; stops include Kama'ole Beach Park III, Pi'ilani Village shopping center, and Uwapo and S Kihei Rds. From Ma'alaea you can connect with buses bound for Lahaina and Kahului. The other route, the Kihei Villager 15, primarily serves the northern half of Kihei, with a half-dozen stops along S Kihei Rd and a stop in Ma'alaea. Both routes operate hourly from around 5:30am to 7:30pm and cost $1.

Car & Motorcycle
Hula Hogs (☑875-7433, 877-464-7433; www.hulahogs.com; 1279 S Kihei Rd; per day from $120) These are the folks to see if you want to tour Maui on a Harley-Davidson Road King. Helmets are included. In the store, look for the Harley Barbie, a hoot with her leather jacket and goth lipstick.

Kihei Rent A Car (☑879-7257, 800-251-5288; www.kiheirentalcar.com; 96 Kio Loop; per day/week from $35/175) This family-owned company rents out cars and jeeps to those aged 21 and over, and includes free mileage. Provides Kahului Airport shuttle pickup for rentals over five days.

Wailea
POP 6589 (WAILEA-MAKENA)

With its tidy golf courses, protective privacy walls and discreet signage, Wailea looks like a members-only country club. Wailea is South Maui's most elite haunt, standing in sharp contrast to Kihei. Don't bother looking for gas stations or fast-food joints; this exclusive community is all about swank beachfront resorts and low-rise condo villas, with all the glitzy accessories.

One look at the beaches and it's easy to see why it has become such hot real estate. The golden-sand jewels sparkling along the Wailea coast are postcard material, offering phenomenal swimming, snorkeling and sunbathing. If you're not staying here, say a loud *mahalo* for Hawaii's beach access laws that allow you to visit anyway.

From Lahaina or Kahului, take the Pi'ilani Hwy (Hwy 31) to Wailea instead of S Kihei Rd, which is Kihei's stop-and-go main road. Once in Wailea, Wailea Alanui Dr turns into Makena Alanui Dr after Polo Beach and continues into Makena.

Beaches
Wailea's fabulous beaches begin with the southern end of Keawakapu Beach in Kihei and continue south toward Makena. All of the beaches that are backed by resorts have public access, with free parking, showers and restrooms.

Ulua & Mokapu Beaches   BEACH

You'll have to get up early to secure a parking space, but it's worth it. Ulua Beach offers Wailea's best easy-access snorkeling. Not only is it teeming with brilliant tropical fish, but it's also one of the best spots for hearing humpbacks sing as they pass offshore. Snorkelers should head straight for the coral at the rocky outcrop on the right side of Ulua Beach, which separates it from its twin to the north, Mokapu Beach. Snorkeling is best in the morning before the winds pick up and the crowds arrive. When the surf's up, forget snorkeling – go bodysurfing instead. Beach access is just north of the Wailea Marriott Resort.

Wailea Beach   BEACH

To strut your stuff celebrity-style, head to this sparkling strand, where most of Wailea's vacationers soak up the rays. The crescent-shaped beach, which fronts the Grand Wailea and The Four Seasons, offers a full menu of water activities. The beach slopes gradually, making it a good swimming spot. When it's calm, there's decent snorkeling around the rocky point on the southern end. Most afternoons there's a gentle shorebreak suitable for bodysurfing. Divers entering the water at Wailea Beach can follow an offshore reef that runs down to Polo Beach. The beach access road is between the Grand Wailea and Four Seasons resorts.

Po'olenalena Beach   BEACH

To avoid the resorts, drive south to this long and lovely crescent favored by local families on weekends. Still, it's rarely crowded, and the shallow, sandy bottom and calm waters make for excellent swimming. There's good snorkeling off both the southern and northern lava points. The parking lot is on Makena Alanui Rd.

Polo Beach   BEACH

In front of the Fairmont Kea Lani, Polo Beach is seldom crowded. When there's wave action, boogie boarders and body-surfers usually find good shorebreaks here. When calm, the rocks at the northern end of the beach provide good snorkeling. At low tide, the lava outcropping at the southern end holds tide pools harboring spiny sea urchins and small fish. To find it, turn down Kaukahi St after the Fairmont Kea Lani and look for the beach parking lot on the right.

Palauea Beach   BEACH

This untouristed sandy stretch to the south of Polo Beach attracts local surfers and boogie boarders. Kiawe trees block the view of the beach from the roadside, but you can find it easily by spotting the line of cars parked along Makena Rd.

🏃 Activities

At Sea

Hawaiian Sailing Canoe Adventures   CANOEING

(☎281-9301; www.mauisailingcanoe.com; adult/child 5-12yr $99/79; ⊙tours 8am & 10am) Learn about native traditions on two-hour sails aboard a Hawaiian-style outrigger canoe. With a max of six passengers, they're able to accommodate requests – including stopping to snorkel with turtles. Tours depart from Polo Beach.

Maui Ocean Activities   WATERSPORTS

(☎667-2001; www.mauiwatersports.com; Grand Wailea Resort, 3850 Wailea Alanui Dr; snorkel/boogie boards/kayak/stand up paddleboard rental per hr $8/8/25/40) On the beach behind the Grand Wailea, Maui Ocean rents what you need for watery fun.

On Land

Wailea Golf Club   GOLF

(☎875-7450; www.waileagolf.com; 100 Wailea Golf Club Dr; greens fee $135-179; ⊙1st tee around 7am) There are three championship courses in Wailea: the Emerald is a tropical garden that consistently ranks at the top; the rugged Gold course takes advantage of volcanic landscapes; and the Old Blue course (120 Kaukahi St) is marked by an open fairway and challenging greens. For the cheapest fees, tee off after 1pm, when 'twilight' rates are in effect.

Wailea Tennis Club   TENNIS

(☎879-1958; www.waileatennis.com; 131 Wailea Ike Pl; $15 per person; ⊙8am-noon & 3-6pm Mon-Fri, 8am-3pm Sat & Sun) Nicknamed 'Wimbledon West,' this award-winning complex has 11 Plexi-pave courts and equipment rentals. One-hour lessons are also available (clinic/private $25/95).

🎇 Festivals & Events

Maui Film Festival   FILM FESTIVAL

(www.mauifilmfestival.com) Hollywood celebs swoop in for this five-day extravaganza in mid-June. Join the stars under the stars at various Wailea locations, including the open-air 'Celestial Theater' on a nearby golf course.

Wailea & Makena

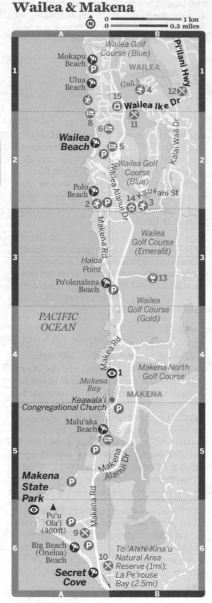

Wailea & Makena

◉ Top Sights
Makena State Park A6
Secret Cove A6
Wailea Beach A2

◉ Sights
1 Makena Landing B4

Activities, Courses & Tours
2 Hawaiian Sailing Canoe
  Adventures A2
Maui Ocean Activities ....(see 6)
3 Wailea Golf Club B2
4 Wailea Tennis Club B1

🛏 Sleeping
5 Four Seasons Maui at Wailea B2
6 Grand Wailea Resort Hotel &
  Spa A2
7 Makena Beach & Golf Resort A5
8 Wailea Beach Marriott Resort
  & Spa A2

✗ Eating
Ferraro's ....(see 5)
9 JAWZ Fish Tacos A6
Joe's Bar & Grill ....(see 4)
10 Makena Grill A6
11 Matteo's B2
12 Pita Paradise B1
Waterfront Deli ....(see 15)

🍷 Drinking
13 Red Bar at Gannon's B3

✦ Entertainment
Four Seasons Maui at Wailea ......(see 5)
14 Mulligan's on the Blue B2

🛍 Shopping
Aloha Shirt Museum &
  Boutique ....(see 15)
Blue Ginger ....(see 15)
Honolua Surf Co. ....(see 15)
Martin & MacArthur ....(see 15)
Maui Waterwear ....(see 15)
15 Shops at Wailea B1

🛏 Sleeping

TOP
CHOICE Four Seasons Maui at
Wailea   RESORT HOTEL $$$
(🕿874-8000, 888-344-6284; www.fourseasons.
com/maui; 3900 Wailea Alanui Dr; r/ste from

$465/945; ✸@🛜🏊) The Four Seasons
Wailea is a dangerous crush. She'll embrace
you with sophisticated style, offer an orange
blossom mint tea then whisper in your ear
that she has no...resort fee. Oh yes. We're
hooked. Children are welcome – there are
fun pools plus the Children for All Seasons
program – but the resort feels more low-
key than its neighbors. Standard rooms are

For the perfect sunset stroll, take the 1.3-mile shoreline path that connects Wailea's beaches and the resort hotels that front them. The undulating path winds above jagged lava points and back down to the sandy shore. In winter this is one of the best places in all of Maui for spotting humpback whales. On a good day you may be able to see more than a dozen of them frolicking offshore.

Some of the luxury hotels along the walk are worth a stroll, most notably the Grand Wailea Resort, which is adorned with $30 million worth of artwork. In front of the Wailea Point condos you'll find the foundations of three Hawaiian house sites dating to AD 1300 – it's also a fine spot to watch the sunset.

midsized and furnished with understated tropical elegance, slightly more comfy than sophisticated. Marble bathrooms have loads of counter space and a choice of piped-in music. For outlandish spa pampering, enjoy a Hawaiian hot stone massage with cocoa butter slathering in a seaside *hale*. Parking is $20 per day.

Grand Wailea Resort
Hotel & Spa   RESORT HOTEL $$$

(☑875-1234, 800-888-6100; www.grandwailea. com; 3850 Wailea Alanui Dr; r from $725; ❄@ 🛜🌊🐾) We planned to make this posh, fun-loving resort a top pick, but when Paris Hilton and Britney Spears have already given their stamp of approval, why bother? We jest, but it's OK to tease an icon you love. The Grand Wailea's unbridled extravagance, from the million-dollar artwork in the lobby to the guest rooms decked out in Italian marble, is a wonder. But it's not all highbrow. The resort, part of the Hilton's Waldorf-Astoria line, boasts the most elaborate water-world wonders in Hawaii, an awesome series of nine interconnected pools with swim-through grottos and towering water slides. The $25 resort fee includes wi-fi.

Wailea Beach Marriott
Resort & Spa   RESORT HOTEL $$$

(☑879-1922, 888-236-2427; www.waileamarriott.com; 3700 Wailea Alanui Dr; r from $395; ❄@🛜🌊) Perched between two of Wailea's loveliest beaches, this is the smallest and most Hawaiian of the Wailea resorts. Instead of over-the-top flash, you'll find warm alohas, serene koi ponds and swaying palm trees. Rooms have a fresh and modern tropical flair. The daily resort fee is $25. Wi-fi is a separate $15 per day and available only in some common areas, including the lobby.

✗ Eating

TOP CHOICE **Pita Paradise**   MEDITERRANEAN $$

(☑879-7177; www.pitaparadisehawaii.com; Wailea Gateway Center, 34 Wailea Gateway Pl; lunch $9-15, dinner $17-28; ⊘11am-9:30pm) Although this Greek taverna sits in a cookie-cutter strip mall lacking ocean views, the inviting patio, mural and tiny white lights, not to mention the succulent Mediterranean chicken pita, banish any locational regrets. Owner John Arabatzis catches his own fish, which is served in everything from pita sandwiches to grilled dinners.

Ferraro's   ITALIAN $$$

(☑874-8000; www.fourseasons.com/maui; Four Seasons Maui at Wailea, 3900 Wailea Alanui Dr; lunch $17-24, dinner $25-48; ⊘11:30am-9pm) No other place in Wailea comes close to this breezy restaurant for romantic seaside dining. Lunch strays into fun selections like *kalua* pig quesadillas with mango poi and a Maine lobster sandwich with avocado spread. Dinner gets more serious, showcasing a rustic Italian menu.

Joe's Bar & Grill   COMFORT FOOD $$$

(☑875-7767; www.bevgannonrestaurants.com/ joes; 131 Wailea Ike Pl; mains $28-40; ⊘dinner) A sister operation of the famed Hali'imaile General Store, Joe's is celebrated in its own right. Forget razzle-dazzle – the emphasis is on large portions and home-style simplicity. Think roast beef prime rib with whipped potatoes, chicken breast stuffed with herb cheese and pumpkin-seed-crusted fresh fish.

Matteo's   ITALIAN $$

(☑874-1234; www.matteosmaui.com; 100 Wailea Ike Dr; pizzas $11-25; ⊘11:30am-9pm Mon-Fri, 5-9pm Sat & Sun) Grab a spot in line and order at the counter at this Italian eatery, an open-air pizzeria and trattoria on the Old Blue golf course near the Shops at Wailea. The thin-crust pizzas are surprisingly good.

Waterfront Deli DELI $
(891-2039; Shops at Wailea, 3750 Wailea Alanui Dr; mains under $12; ⊙7am-8pm) For a quick, inexpensive meal to-go, head to this deli inside the Whalers General Store at the back of the Shops at Wailea.

⬤ Drinking & Entertainment

All of the Wailea hotels have live music, most often jazz or Hawaiian, in the evening.

Red Bar at Gannon's COCKTAILS
(www.gannonsrestaurant.com; 100 Wailea Golf Club Dr) Everyone looks sexier when they're swathed in a sultry red glow. Come to this chic spot at happy hour (3pm to 6pm) for impressive food and drink specials, as well as attentive bartenders and stellar sunsets. The bar is located inside Gannon's, Bev Gannon's new restaurant at the Gold and Emerald courses' clubhouse.

Mulligan's on the Blue IRISH
(874-1131; www.mulligansontheblue.com; 100 Kaukahi St) Rising above the golf course, Mulligan's offers entertainment nightly, anything from Irish folk music to European jazz. It's also a good place to quaff an ale while enjoying the distant ocean view – or catching a game on one of the 10 TVs.

Four Seasons Maui at Wailea HAWAIIAN
(3900 Wailea Alanui Dr) The lobby lounge has Hawaiian music and hula performances from 5:30pm to 7:30pm nightly, and jazz or slack key guitar later in the evening.

🛍 Shopping

Shops at Wailea OUTDOOR MALL
(www.shopsatwailea.com; 3750 Wailea Alanui Dr; ⊙9:30am-9pm) This outdoor mall has dozens of stores, most flashing designer labels like Prada and Louis Vuitton, but there are some solid island choices, too:

Blue Ginger WOMEN'S BOUTIQUE
(www.blueginger.com) Women's clothing in cheery colors and tropical motifs.

Honolua Surf Co BEACHWEAR
(www.honoluasurf.com) Hip surfer-motif T-shirts, board shorts and aloha shirts.

Martin & MacArthur HAWAIIAN CRAFTS
(www.martinandmacarthur.com) Museum-quality Hawaiian-made woodwork and other crafts.

Maui Waterwear SWIMWEAR
(www.mauiclothingcompany.com) Tropical swimwear you'll love to flaunt.

Aloha Shirt Museum & Boutique HAWAIIAN CLOTHING
(www.the-aloha-shirt-museum.com) Quality new and vintage aloha shirts. We like the 100% silk Elvis Aloha, aka The King's shirt, in blue ($95).

ⓘ Getting There & Around

The **Maui Bus** (www.mauicounty.gov) operates the Kihei Islander 10 between Wailea and Kahului hourly until 8:30pm. The first bus leaves the Shops at Wailea at 6:30am and runs along S Kihei Rd before heading up to the Pi'ilani Village shopping center and Ma'alaea. From Ma'alaea you can connect to buses bound for Lahaina.

Makena

POP 6589 (WAILEA-MAKENA)

Makena may be home to an oceanfront resort and a well-manicured golf course, but the region still feels wild, like a territorial outpost that hasn't been tamed. It's a perfect setting for aquatic adventurers who want to escape the crowds, offering primo snorkeling, kayaking and bodysurfing, plus pristine coral, reef sharks, dolphins and sea turtles galore.

The beaches are magnificent. The king of them all, Big Beach, is an immense sweep of glistening sand and a prime sunset-viewing locale. The secluded cove at neighboring Little Beach is Maui's most popular nude beach – you *will* see bare buns. Together these beaches form Makena State Park, but don't be misled by the term 'park,' as they remain in a natural state, with no facilities except for a couple of pit toilets and picnic tables. No one on Maui would have it otherwise.

🏊 Beaches

 Malu'aka Beach BEACH
To swim with sea turtles, make your way to this golden swath of sand in front of the Makena Beach & Golf Resort. Dubbed 'Turtle Beach,' it's popular with snorkelers and kayakers hoping to glimpse the surprisingly graceful green turtles that feed along the coral here and often swim within a few feet of snorkelers. There's terrific coral about 100yd out, and the best action is at the south end of the beach. Come on a calm day – this one kicks up with even a little wind and when it's choppy you won't see anything.

You'll find parking lots, restrooms and showers at both ends of the beach. At the

ZACH EDLAO: OCEAN SAFETY OFFICER

Best Beach for Kids in South Maui

A good one is Kama'ole Beach Park I (p354). That beach is a majority of sand except for the two ends where there's rocks. Conditions are nice, best in the morning. You're near lifeguards. The parking is right there. Showers and facilities.

Top Snorkeling Spots

There's a few on this island, but a lot of them [are] fish preserves so there's no lifeguard there. But there's Honolua Bay (p334), there's 'Ahihi-Kina'u (p370), and there's Ka'anapali's Pu'u Keka'a (Black Rock; p326). Those are the top three on the island.

Identify Dangerous Conditions

What you want to look for is the wind, and if you see whitecaps. That means there can be a surface current. Turbid water, brown water, that means there's a current in the area.

Top Ocean Safety Tips

» Make sure you talk to a lifeguard to get educated about the ocean before hopping in.

» Always swim near a lifeguard tower because if something changes, someone is there to help you and assist you in the water. And never swim alone.

» You always want to look for objects beneath the surface that are hard to see, like rocks, sticks and something you might dive into and get hurt by.

MAUI MAKENA

north side, park at the lot opposite Keawala'i Congregational Church then follow the road a short distance south. If the lot's full, take the first right after Makena Beach & Golf Resort, where there's additional parking for about 60 cars.

Makena Bay　　　BEACH
There's no better place on Maui for kayaking and, when seas are calm, snorkeling is good along the rocks at the south side of Makena Landing, the boat launch that's the center of the action. Makena Bay is also a good place for shore dives; divers should head to the north side of the bay.

Kayak-rental companies deliver kayaks to Makena Landing – you can either head off on your own or join a tour. Although the norm is to make arrangements in advance (there are no shops here), if there's an extra kayak on the trailer, you might be able to arrange something on the spot. Paddle south along the lava coastline to Malu'aka Beach, where green sea turtles abound.

TOP CHOICE Big Beach (Oneloa)　　　BEACH
The crowning glory of Makena State Park, this untouched beach is arguably the finest on Maui. In Hawaiian it's called Oneloa, literally 'Long Sand.' And indeed the golden sands stretch for the better part of a mile

and are as broad as they come. The waters are a beautiful turquoise. When they're calm you'll find kids boogie boarding here, but at other times the breaks belong to experienced bodysurfers, who get tossed wildly in the transparent waves. There is a lifeguard station here.

The turnoff to the main parking area is a mile beyond the Makena Beach & Golf Resort. A second parking area lies a quarter of a mile to the south. Thefts and broken windshields are a possibility, so don't leave valuables in your car in either lot.

Little Beach　　　BEACH
Also known as Pu'u Ola'i Beach, this cozy strand is South Maui's *au naturel* beach. Mind you, nudity is officially illegal, though enforcement is at the political whim of the day. Hidden by a rocky outcrop that juts out from Pu'u Ola'i, the cinder hill that marks the north end of Big Beach, most visitors don't even know Little Beach is there. But take the short trail over the rock that links the two beaches and bam, there it is, bare buns city. The crowd is mixed, about half gay and half straight.

Little Beach fronts a sandy cove that usually has a gentle shorebreak ideal for bodysurfing and boogie boarding. When the surf's up, you'll find plenty of local surfers here as well. When the water's calm, snorkeling is good along the rocky point.

Secret Cove   BEACH

This lovely, postcard-size swath of golden sand, with a straight-on view of Kaho'olawe, is worth a peek – although it's no longer much of a secret. The cove is a quarter-mile after the southernmost Makena State Park parking lot. The entrance is through an opening in a lava-rock wall just south of house No 6900.

🛏 Sleeping & Eating

Makena Beach & Golf
Resort   RESORT HOTEL $$$

(☎874-1111, 800-321-6284; www.makenaresortmaui.com; 5400 Makena Alanui Dr; r from $289; ❇@☻) Under new management following a foreclosure auction in 2010, this striking, fortress-like resort is having its decor revamped in all rooms. At press time, management was on a hiring spree, picking up chefs as well as golf and tennis pros from top Maui resorts. We can't vouch for any new furnishings, but we can confirm that the resort's 1800-acre perch beside Makena Beach is beautiful, not to mention a top launch pad for snorkelers and kayakers hoping to spy a sea turtle.

JAWZ Fish Tacos   FOOD TRUCK $

(Makena State Park; snacks $5.25-10; ☺10:30am-5pm) Get your beach snacks – tacos, burritos, shave ice – at this food truck beside the northernmost Big Beach parking lot. Vendors with cold coconuts, pineapples and other fruit are sometimes found along Makena Alanui Dr opposite Big Beach.

Makena Grill   ROADSIDE GRILL $

(www.makenagrill.com; Makena Alanui Dr; mains $6-10; ☺11am-4pm) This little roadside smoke grill serves up fish tacos and chicken kebabs. Hours can be irregular, but when it's open these are tasty *grinds*.

Beyond Makena

Makena Rd turns adventurous after Makena State Park, continuing for three narrow miles through the lava flows of 'Ahihi-Kina'u Natural Area Reserve before dead-ending at La Pe'rouse Bay.

'AHIHI-KINA'U NATURAL AREA RESERVE

Maui's last lava flow spilled down to the sea here in 1790 and shaped 'Ahihi Bay and Cape Kina'u. The jagged lava coastline and the pristine waters fringing it have been designated a reserve because of its unique marine habitat.

Thanks in part to the prohibition on fishing, snorkeling is incredible. Just about everyone heads to the little roadside cove 0.1 miles south of the first reserve sign – granted, it offers good snorkeling, but there are better (and less-crowded) options. Instead, drive 0.2 miles past the cove and look for a large clearing on the right. Park here and follow the coastal footpath south for five minutes to a black-sand beach with fantastic coral, clear water and few visitors. Enter the water from the left side of the beach where access is easy, snorkel in a northerly direction and you'll immediately be over coral gardens teeming with an amazing variety of fish. Huge rainbow parrotfish abound here, and it's not unusual to see turtles and the occasional reef shark.

Large sections of the preserve are closed to visitors until 2012, which will allow the Department of Land and Resource Management to protect the fragile environment from tourist wear-and-tear and to develop a long-term protection plan. Visitation in the north is still permitted between 5:30am and 7:30pm.

LA PE'ROUSE BAY

Earth and ocean merge at La Pe'rouse Bay with a raw desolate beauty that's almost eerie. The ancient Hawaiian village of Keone'o'io flourished here before the 1790 volcanic eruption. Its remains – mainly house and heiau platforms – can be seen scattered among the lava patches. From the volcanic shoreline look for pods of spinner dolphins, which commonly come into the bay during the early part of the day. The combination of strong offshore winds and rough waters rule out swimming, but it's an interesting place to explore on land.

🥾 Activities

Makena Stables   HORSEBACK RIDES

(☎879-0244; www.makenastables.com; 3hr trail rides $145-170; ☺8am-6pm) Located just before the road ends, Makena Stables offers morning and sunset horseback rides across the lava flows and up the scenic slopes of 'Ulupalakua Ranch.

Hoapili (King's Highway) Trail   HIKING

(https://hawaiitrails.ehawaii.gov/) From La Pe'rouse Bay, this trail follows an ancient path along the coastline across jagged lava flows. Be prepared: wear hiking boots, bring plenty to drink, start early and tell someone where you're going. It's a dry area with no water and little vegetation, so it can get very hot. The first part of the trail is along the sandy beach at La Pe'rouse Bay. Right after the trail emerges onto the lava fields, it's possible to take a spur trail for three-quarters of a mile down to the light beacon at the tip of Cape Hanamanioa. Alternatively, walk inland to the Na Ala Hele sign and turn right onto the King's Hwy as it climbs through 'a'a (rough, jagged lava) inland for the next 2 miles before coming back to the coast to an older lava flow at Kanaio Beach. Although the trail continues, it becomes harder to follow and Kanaio Beach is the recommended turn-around point. If you don't include the lighthouse spur, the roundtrip distance to Kanaio Beach is about 4 miles.

For complete details visit http://ha waiitrails.ehawaii.gov, the state's trail and access website.

NORTH SHORE & UPCOUNTRY

Windsurfing capital of the world and the garden belt of Maui. Local as a ton of onions on a pickup truck, a rancher on horseback, a lone surfer beating across the waves. The surf-sculpted North Shore stands in sharp contrast to the gently rolling pastures carpeting the Upcountry slopes. The towns – beachy Pa'ia, artsy Makawao and mud-on-your-boots Keokea – boast as much weathered personality as their proud residents.

Green and fragrant, the Upcountry simply begs a country drive. The possibilities for exploring are nothing short of breathtaking. Zipline over deep gorges, paraglide down the hillsides or ride a horse through a lofty cloud forest.

Everyone passes through a slice of the Upcountry on the way to Haleakalā National Park, but don't settle for a pass through. Look around the showy gardens, lightly trodden trails and rambling back roads. They alone are worth the trip.

Pa'ia

POP 2750

Home to an eclectic mix of surfers and soul seekers, Pa'ia is Maui's hippest burg. Once a thriving sugar town, a century ago Pa'ia boasted 10,000 residents living in plantation camps above the now-defunct sugar mill. During the 1950s there was an exodus to Kahului, shops were shuttered and Pa'ia began to collect cobwebs.

Attracted by low rents, hippies seeking paradise landed in Pa'ia in the 1970s. A decade later, windsurfers discovered Ho'okipa Beach, and Pa'ia broke onto the map bigtime. Its aging wooden storefronts, now splashed in sunshine yellows and sky blues, house a wild array of shops geared to visitors. And the dining scene? Any excuse to be here at mealtime will do.

Parking is notoriously tight in Pa'ia, doubly so at mealtimes. Your best bet for a vacant space is the public parking lot on the west side of town just before the Shell gas station. You'll have to walk a few minutes to the center, but you can typically find an open space. If that's full, there's a new paid parking lot behind Charley's in the town center

🏖 Beaches

Ho'okipa Beach Park　　　　BEACH

Ho'okipa is to daredevil windsurfers what Everest is to climbers. It reigns supreme as the world's premier windsurfing beach, with strong currents, dangerous shorebreaks and razor-sharp coral offering the ultimate challenge.

Ho'okipa is also one of Maui's prime surfing spots. Winter sees the biggest waves for board surfers, and summer has the most consistent winds for windsurfers. To prevent intersport beefs, surfers typically hit the waves in the morning and the windsurfers take over during the afternoon.

The action in the water is suitable for pros only. But a hilltop perch overlooking the beach offers spectators a bird's-eye view of the world's top windsurfers doing their death-defying stuff. Ho'okipa is just before the 9-mile marker; to reach the lookout above the beach take the driveway at the east side of the park.

HA Baldwin Beach Park　　　　BEACH

Bodyboarders and bodysurfers take to the waves at this palm-lined county park about a mile west of Pa'ia, at the 6-mile marker. The wide sandy beach drops off quickly, and when the shorebreak is big, unsuspecting swimmers can get slammed soundly. Calmer waters, better suited for swimming, can be found at the northeast end of the beach where there's a little cove shaded by ironwood trees. Showers, restrooms,

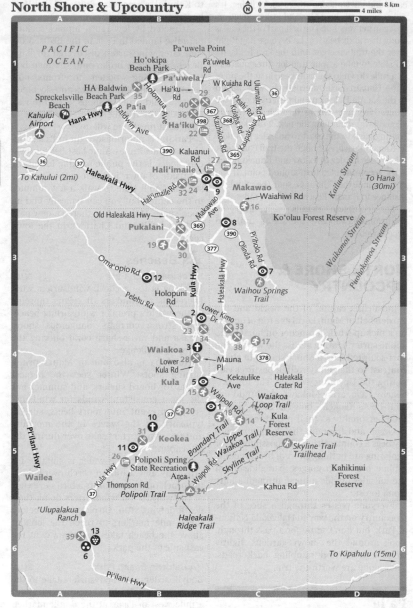

picnic tables, and a well-used baseball and soccer field round out the facilities. The park has a reputation for drunken nastiness after the sun sets, but it's fine in the daytime when there's a lifeguard on duty.

Spreckelsville Beach BEACH

Extending west from HA Baldwin Beach, this 2-mile stretch of sand punctuated by lava outcrops is a good walking beach, but its near-shore lava shelf makes it less than ideal for swimming for adults. The rocks do,

◎ Sights

1	Ali'i Kula Lavender	C5
2	Enchanting Floral Gardens	B4
3	Holy Ghost Church	B4
4	Hui No'eau Visual Arts Center	B2
5	Kula Botanical Garden	B4
6	Makee Sugar Mill Ruins	A6
7	Maui Bird Conservation Center	C3
8	Oskie Rice Arena	C3
9	Sacred Garden of Maliko	C2
10	St John's Episcopal Church	B5
11	Sun Yat-sen Park	B5
12	Surfing Goat Dairy	B3
13	Tedeschi Vineyards	A6

Activities, Courses & Tours

14	Hunter Check Station	C5
15	O'o Farm	B4
	Piiholo Ranch	(see 16)
16	Piiholo Ranch Zipline	C2
17	Pony Express	C4
18	Proflyght Paragliding	C5
19	Pukalani Country Club	B3
	Skyline Eco-Adventures	(see 17)
	Studio Maui	(see 29)
20	Thompson Ranch	B5

◎ Sleeping

21	Campground	B5
22	Haiku Cannery Inn B&B	B2
	Inn at Mama's	(see 35)
	Kula Sandalwoods Cottages	(see 33)
23	Kula View Bed & Breakfast	B4
24	Peace of Maui	B2
25	Pilialoha	C2
26	Star Lookout	B5
27	Wild Ginger Falls	C2

◎ Eating

28	Café 808	B4
29	Colleen's	B1
30	Foodland	B3
31	Grandma's Coffee House	B5
32	Hali'imaile General Store	B2
33	Kula Sandalwoods Restaurant	C4
34	La Provence	B4
35	Mama's Fish House	B1
36	NorthShore Café	B2
37	Serpico's	B3
38	Sunrise Country Market	C4
39	'Ulupalakua Ranch Store	A6
40	Veg Out	B1

however, provide protection for young kids. If you'll walk toward the center of the beach, you'll soon come to a section dubbed 'baby beach,' where local families take the little ones to splash. There are no facilities. To get there, turn toward the ocean on Nonohe Pl at the 5-mile marker, then turn left on Kealakai Pl just before the Maui Country Club.

Tavares Beach BEACH

This unmarked sandy beach is quiet during the week but livens up on weekends when local families come here toting picnics, guitars, dogs and kids. A submerged lava shelf runs parallel to the beach about 25ft from the shore and is shallow enough for swimmers to scrape over. Once you know it's there, however, the rocks are easy to avoid, so take a look before jumping in. The beach parking lot is at the first shoreline access sign on the Hana side of the 7-mile marker. There are no facilities.

🏃 Activities

Hana Hwy Surf SURFING

(☑579-8999; www.hanahwysurf.com; 149 Hana Hwy; surfboards/boogie boards per day $25/10;

⊙9am-6pm Mon-Sat, 10am-5pm Sun) At Pa'ia's surfing headquarters the staff keep their finger on the pulse of the surf scene and provide a daily recorded surf report (☑871-6258).

Simmer WINDSURFING

(☑579-8484; www.simmerhawaii.com; 137 Hana Hwy; sailboards per day $50; ⊙9am-7pm) Simmer's all about windsurfing and handles everything from repairs to top-of-the-line gear rentals.

Maui Dharma Center MEDITATION

(www.mauidharmacenter.org; 81 Baldwin Ave; ⊙6:30am-6:30pm) This Tibetan Buddhist temple shares good karma, inviting visitors to join in morning meditation. Or just swing by to take a meditative stroll around the stupa on your own.

🎊 Festivals & Events

High-Tech/Vans/Lopez Surfbash SURF MEET

(www.mauisurfohana.org) This surf contest takes place at Ho'okipa Beach on the last weekend in November or the first weekend

MAUI PA'IA

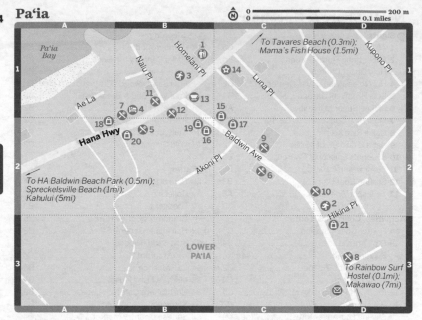

in December, with competing short-boarders, long-boarders and bodyboarders.

🛏 Sleeping

TOP CHOICE Paia Inn   INN $$
(☎579-6000; www.paiainn.com; 93 Hana Hwy; r incl breakfast $189-239; ❋@🛜) Take a classic century-old building, soundproof the walls, spruce it up with bamboo floors, travertine bathrooms and original artwork, and you've got one classy place to lay your head. This friendly boutique inn, with seven appealing rooms, offers the ultimate Pa'ia immersion. Step out the front and Pa'ia's restaurants and shops are on the doorstep; step out the back and you're on a path to the beach.

Blue Tile Beach House   B&B $$
(☎579-6446; www.beachvacationmaui.com; 459 Hana Hwy; r $110-170, ste $250) Slide into your bathing suit, step out the door of this exclusive oceanfront estate and you're literally on Tavares Beach. Sleeping options range from a small straightforward room to a spacious honeymoon suite with wraparound ocean-view windows and a four-poster bed. All six rooms share a living room and a kitchen.

Inn at Mama's   COTTAGE $$$
(☎579-9764; www.mamasfishhouse.com; 799 Poho Pl; d $175-575; ❋🛜) Maui's most famous seafood restaurant has a cluster of pretty cottages, some with ocean views, others with garden settings. Think retro Hawaiian decor, rattan and bamboo, and an airy, clean simplicity that you'd expect at a high-end operation. One caveat: there's a lot of activity nearby and Mama's is not always the quietest of places.

Rainbow Surf Hostel   HOSTEL $
(☎579-9057; www.mauirainbowsurfhostel.com; 221 Baldwin Ave; dm/r $27/75; @🛜) Within walking distance of Pa'ia center, this small hostel in a tightly packed residential neighborhood offers simple clean rooms, a guest kitchen and a TV room. It attracts mostly a surfer crowd and is well suited for early risers – quiet-time rules are strictly enforced after 10pm.

🍴 Eating

Most of Pa'ia's eateries are clustered around the intersection of Baldwin Ave and the Hana Hwy. Go poke your head in a few places and see what's cookin'. Nothing better awaits you in Hana, so grab your picnic supplies before heading onward.

Pa'ia

Activities, Courses & Tours
1 Hana Hwy Surf..................................B1
2 Maui Dharma Center.........................D2
3 Simmer..B1

😴 Sleeping
4 Paia Inn...B1

❌ Eating
5 Anthony's Coffee Company...............B2
6 Café des Amis..................................C2
Fiesta Time..................................(see 1)
7 Flatbread Company..........................B1
8 Fresh Mint.......................................D3
9 Mana Foods.....................................C2
10 Moana Bakery & Café......................D2
11 Ono Gelato.....................................B1
12 Pa'ia Fish Market Restaurant...........B1

🍷 Drinking
13 Milagros...B1

🎭 Entertainment
14 Charley's..C1

🛍 Shopping
15 Alice in Hulaland.............................C1
16 Hemp House....................................B2
17 Mandala..C2
18 Maui Crafts Guild............................A2
19 Maui Girl...B2
20 Maui Hands.....................................B2
21 Na Kani O Hula...............................D3

TOP CHOICE **Mama's Fish House** SEAFOOD $$$
(☎579-8488; www.mamasfishhouse.com; 799 Poho Pl; mains $38-50; ⏱11am-3pm & 4:30-9pm) Mama's is where you go when you want to propose or celebrate a big anniversary. Not only is the seafood as good as it gets, but when the beachside tiki torches are lit at dinnertime, the scene's achingly romantic. The island-caught fish is so fresh your server tells you who caught it, and where! Mama's is at Ku'au Cove, along the Hana Hwy, 2 miles east of Pa'ia center. Reservations are essential.

TOP CHOICE **Café des Amis** CAFE $$
(☎579-6323; 42 Baldwin Ave; mains $10-18; ⏱8:30am-8:30pm) Grab a seat in the breezy courtyard to dine on the best cafe fare in Pa'ia. It's not always fast, but it's done right. The savory options include spicy Indian curry wraps with mango chutney and mouthwatering crepes. You'll also find vegetarian

offerings, creative breakfasts and tempting drinks from fruit smoothies to fine wines. On Wednesdays, Thursdays and Saturdays there's live music in the evenings.

Pa'ia Fish Market Restaurant SEAFOOD $$
(www.paiafishmarket.com; 110 Hana Hwy; mains $10-16; ⏱11am-9:30pm) It's all about the fish: fresh, local and affordable. The local favorite is *ono* (white-fleshed wahoo) and chips, but the menu includes plenty of other tempting fish preparations, from charbroiled mahi to Cajun-style snapper. Be sure to start with the blackened ahi sashimi as an appetiser. Little wonder the tables here are packed like sardines.

Moana Bakery & Café ECLECTIC $$
(☎579-9999; www.moanacafe.com; 71 Baldwin Ave; mains $12-35; ⏱8am-8pm) The best place in town to linger over a relaxing lunch in a jazzy setting. Locals love that the chef is agreeable to any special requests. Not that you won't find what you're looking for on the varied menu – perhaps the mahi steamed in banana leaves and served with green papaya salad, or the Hana Bay crab cakes with guava puree?

Mana Foods TAKEOUT $
(www.manafoodsmaui.com; 49 Baldwin Ave; deli items $5-7; ⏱8am-8:30pm; 🅿) Dreadlocked, Birkenstocked or just needing to stock up – everyone rubs shoulders at Mana, a health food store, bakery and deli wrapped in one. Don't miss the walnut cinnamon buns made fresh every morning. Then look for the hot rosemary-grilled chicken and organic salad bar. It's gonna be a *g-o-o-d* picnic!

Flatbread Company PIZZA $$
(☎579-8989; 89 Hana Hwy; pizzas $11-20; ⏱11:30am-10pm) Wood-fired pizzas made with organic sauces, nitrate-free pepperoni, Kula onions – you'll never stop at a chain pizza house again. Lots of fun combinations, from pure vegan to *kalua* pork with Surfing Goat chèvre. Eat even greener on Tuesday night when a cut of the profits goes to a local environmental cause.

Anthony's Coffee Company COFFEE SHOP $
(☎579-8340; 90 Hana Hwy; mains $5-12; ⏱6am-2pm) The best cup of joe on this side of the island. Fresh-ground organic coffee and a delish variety of goodies from pastries to lox Benedict. Staff even pack picnic boxes for the drive to Hana. You know everything's

THE ULTIMATE WAVE

When this monster rears its powerful head, it's big, fast and mean enough to crunch bones. What is it? Jaws, Maui's famous big-wave surf spot. A few times a year, strong winter storms off the coast of Japan generate an abundance of energy that races unimpeded across the Pacific Ocean to Hawaii's shores, translating into the planet's biggest rideable waves.

News of the mammoth swells, which reach as high as a seven-story building, attracts gutsy surfers from all over the state and beyond. Unfortunately, there's no legitimate public access to the cliffs that look out toward Jaws, as getting to them requires crossing privately owned agricultural land.

When Jaws (also known locally as Pe'ahi) is up, it's impossible for surfers to paddle through the break to catch a ride. But where there's a thrill, there's a way. Tow-in surfers work in pairs, using small watercraft known as wave runners to get people and their boards beyond the break. When even a wave runner is outmatched, surfers get dropped into the ocean from a helicopter.

The equation of extreme sport says that thrill doesn't come without its share of danger. There are myriad opportunities for big-wave surfers to get hurt or killed. The insanely powerful waves can wash surfers into rocks, throw them into their wave runners, knock them against their surfboards or simply pummel them with the force of all that moving water. That said, these guys are pros and are very good at skirting the perils.

done right – you'll find the owner himself on the other side of the counter grinding away.

Ono Gelato DESSERT $
(www.onogelatocompany.com; 115 Hana Hwy; cones $5; ⏱11am-10pm) How cool is this? This little shop dishes up Maui-made organic gelato in island flavors like guava, mango and Kula strawberry. For the ultimate treat, order the *liliko'i* (passion fruit) quark, combining passion fruit and goat's cheese – it's awesome...really.

Fresh Mint VIETNAMESE $
(☏579-9144; 115 Baldwin Ave; mains $8-13; ⏱5-9pm; 🍴) Authentic Vietnamese fare but totally veg, and the chef-owner of this place takes pride in her artistically presented dishes. Even meat eaters will be amazed by how soy takes on the flavors and texture of the foods it substitutes. In doubt? Just try the spicy ginger soy beef.

Fiesta Time MEXICAN $
(☏579-8269; 149 Hana Hwy; mains $5-13; ⏱7am-8pm) Surfers line up at this hole-in-the-wall for real-deal home-cooked Mexican food that's twice as good and half the price as nearby options. Quesadillas, tostadas, hot tamales – *muy delicioso!*

🍷 Drinking & Entertainment

Charley's BAR
(www.charleysmaui.com; 142 Hana Hwy) Don't be surprised to find country-singer legend Willie Nelson at the next table. He's a part-time Pa'ia resident, and this cowboy-centric place is his favorite hang. Charley's has live music most nights – with a little luck it could even be Willie.

Milagros CAFE
(3 Baldwin Ave) *The* spot for a late-afternoon beer. The sidewalk tables are perched perfectly for watching all the action on Pa'ia's busiest corner.

🛍 Shopping

This is a fun town for browsing, with owner-run shops and boutiques selling Maui-made goodies of all sorts.

TOP CHOICE Maui Crafts Guild CRAFTS
(www.mauicraftsguild.com; 43 Hana Hwy) This longstanding collective of Maui artists and craftspeople sells everything from pottery and jewelry to handpainted silks and natural-fiber baskets at reasonable prices.

Na Kani O Hula HULA SUPPLIES
(www.nakaniohula.com; 115 Baldwin Ave) Hula *halau* (troupes) come here for *'uli'uli* (feather-decorated gourd rattles), bamboo nose flutes and other traditional dance and music crafts – any of which would make for a fascinating souvenir.

Other quirky and perky places:

Maui Hands CRAFTS
(www.mauihands.com; 84 Hana Hwy) Top-end koa bowls, pottery and Maui-themed paintings.

Hemp House   HEMP
(www.hemphousemaui.com; 16 Baldwin Ave) Sells
all things hemp – well, almost all.

Mandala   CLOTHING
(29 Baldwin Ave) Lightweight cotton and silk
clothing, Buddhas and Asian crafts.

Maui Girl   SWIMWEAR
(www.maui-girl.com; 12 Baldwin Ave) Get your
itty-bitty bikinis here.

Alice in Hulaland   GIFTS
(www.aliceinhulaland.com; 19 Baldwin Ave)
Kitschy but fun souvenirs.

ⓘ Information

Bank of Hawaii (www.boh.com; 35 Baldwin Ave)
Haz Beanz Coffeehouse (☑268-0149; 115
Baldwin Ave; ◷6am-2pm) Free wi-fi for the
price of a cup of coffee.
Post office (www.usps.com; 120 Baldwin Ave)

ⓘ Getting There & Around

Bicycle

Rent bicycles at **Maui Sunriders** (☑579-8970;
www.mauibikeride.com; 71 Baldwin Ave; per day
$30; ◷9am-4:30pm). The price includes a bike
rack, so a travel companion could drop you off at
the top of Haleakalā, or anywhere else, to cycle a
one-way route.

Bus

The Maui Bus operates between Kahului and Pa'ia
($1) every 90 minutes from 5:30am to 8:30pm.

Hali'imaile

The little pineapple town of Hali'imaile
('fragrant twining shrub') is named for
the sweet-scented maile plants used in lei-
making that covered the area before pineapple took over. The heart of town is the
old general store (c 1918), which has been
turned into Upcountry's best restaurant.
Hali'imaile Rd runs through the town, connecting Baldwin Ave (Hwy 390) with the
Haleakalā Hwy (Hwy 37).

🛏 Sleeping & Eating

TOP
CHOICE **Hali'imaile General
Store**   HAWAII REGIONAL $$$
(☑572-2666; www.bevgannonrestaurants.com;
900 Hali'imaile Rd; mains $16-40; ◷11am-2:30pm
Mon-Fri, 5:30-9:30pm daily) Chef Bev Gannon
was one of the original forces behind the
Hawaii Regional Cuisine movement and a
steady flow of in-the-know diners beats a

track to this tiny village to feast on her in-
spired creations. You can tantalise the taste
buds with fusion fare like sashimi pizza
or Asian duck tostadas. The atmospheric
plantation-era decor sets the mood.

Peace of Maui   INN $
(☑572-5045; www.peaceofmaui.com; 1290
Hali'imaile Rd; r with shared bathroom $70; @⇲)
This aptly named place in quiet Hali'imaile
is Upcountry's top budget sleep. In the
middle of nowhere yet within an hour's
drive of nearly everywhere, it would make a
good central base for exploring the whole is-
land. Rooms, spotlessly clean, are small but
comfortable, each with refrigerator and TV.
There's a guest kitchen and a hot tub. If you
need more space, there's a cottage ($140)
that's large enough to sleep a family.

Makawao
POP 6970
Paint a picture of Makawao and what you
get is a mélange of art haven and cowboy
culture, with some chic boutiques and a
dash of New Age sensibility thrown in for
good measure.

Started as a ranching town in the 1800s,
Makawao wears its *paniolo* history in the
Old West–style wooden buildings lining
Baldwin Ave. And the cattle pastures sur-
rounding town remind you it's more than
just history.

But that's only one side of Makawao.
Many of the old shops that once sold saddles
and stirrups now have artsy new tenants
who have turned Makawao into the most
happening art center on Maui. Its galleries
display the works of painters and sculptors
who have escaped frenzied scenes elsewhere
to set up shop in these inspirational hills. If
you enjoy browsing, just about every store-
front is worth poking your head into.

All of the shops and restaurants that follow
are within a few minutes' walk of Makawao's
main intersection, where Baldwin Ave (Hwy
390) meets Makawao Ave (Hwy 365).

⦿ Sights

FREE **Hui No'eau Visual Arts
Center**   ART GALLERY
(www.huinoeau.com; 2841 Baldwin Ave; ◷10am-4pm
Mon-Sat) Occupying the former estate of sugar
magnates Harry and Ethel Baldwin, the Hui
No'eau center radiates artistic creativity. The

plantation house with the main galleries was designed by famed architect CW Dickey in 1917 and showcases the Hawaiian Regional style architectural features he pioneered. The prestigious arts club founded here in the 1930s still offers classes in printmaking, pottery, woodcarving and other visual arts. You're welcome to visit the galleries, which exhibit the diverse works of island artists, and walk around the grounds, where you'll find stables converted into art studios. The gift shop sells quality ceramics, glassware and prints created on-site. Pick up a walking-tour map at the front desk. The center is just north of the 5-mile marker.

Activities

 Piiholo Ranch Zipline ZIPLINING
(572-1717; www.piiholozipline.com; Waiahiwi Rd; zip tours $140-190; 8am-3pm Mon-Sat) Maui's newest zipline is a top-rate operation that takes great care to orient zip-riders before they actually take a jump. The first zip is over a gentle sloping meadow, so you can get the butterflies out of your stomach. It gets progressively more interesting, with the last zip – Hawaii's longest – ripping an awesome 2800ft at an eagle's height of 600ft above the tree canopy. The cheaper tour bypasses the last zip, so for the ultimate rush go for it all. Dual lines let you zip side by side with a buddy. Another advantage with Piiholo – you can drive right up to the staging area for the first jump, and the need to use ATVs to get between zips is minimal.

Olinda Road SCENIC DRIVE
For the ultimate country drive head into the hills above Makawao along Olinda Rd, which picks up in town where Baldwin Ave leaves off. The scenic drive drifts up past the **Oskie Rice Arena**, where rodeos are held, and the **Maui Polo Club**, which hosts matches on Sunday afternoons in the fall. From here the winding road is little more than a path through the forest, with knotty tree roots as high as your car caressing the roadsides. The air is rich with the spicy fragrance of eucalyptus trees and occasionally there's a clearing with an ocean vista. Four miles up from town, past the 11-mile marker, is the **Maui Bird Conservation Center** (closed to the public), which breeds nene (native Hawaiian geese) and other endangered birds. To make a loop, turn left onto

Pi'iholo Rd near the top of Olinda Rd and wind back down into town.

Waihou Springs Trail HIKING
If you feel like taking some time out for a quiet walk in the woods, take this peaceful trail, which begins 4.75 miles up Olinda Rd from central Makawao. The forest is amazingly varied, having been planted by the US Forest Service in an effort to determine which trees would produce the best quality lumber in Hawaii. Thankfully, these magnificent specimens never met the woodman's ax. The trail, which begins on a soft carpet of pine needles, passes Monterey cypress and eucalyptus as well as orderly rows of pine trees. After 0.7 miles, you'll be rewarded with a view clear out to the ocean, and up to this point it is all easy going. It is also possible to continue steeply downhill for another 0.25 miles to reach Waihou Springs, but that part of the trail can be a muddy mess.

Piiholo Ranch HORSEBACK RIDES
(357-5544; www.piiholo.com; Waiahiwi Rd; 2hr ride $120; 9am-3:30pm Mon-Sat) Ride with real *paniolo* across the open range of this cattle ranch that's been worked by the same family for six generations. Mountain, valley and pasture views galore. Families can also book pony rides for children as young as three.

Festivals & Events

Upcountry Fair AGRICULTURAL FAIR
Traditional agricultural fair with a farmers market, arts and crafts, chili cook-off, *na keiki* games and good ol' country music; held on the second weekend in June at the Eddie Tam Complex.

Makawao Rodeo RODEO
Hundreds of *paniolo* show up at the Oskie Rice Arena on the weekend closest to Independence Day (July 4) for Hawaii's premier rodeo. Qualifying roping and riding events occur all day on Thursday and Friday to determine who gets to compete for the big prizes over the weekend. For thrills on Friday night, head up to the arena to see the bull-riding bash.

Paniolo Parade PARADE
Held on the Saturday morning closest to July 4, this festive parade goes right through the heart of Makawao; park at the rodeo grounds and take the free shuttle to the town center.

LABYRINTH WALKS

Up for a meditative moment? The Sacred Garden of Maliko (www.sacredgardenmaui.com; 460 Kaluanui Rd, Makawao; admission free; ⊙10am-5pm), a self-described healing sanctuary, has a pair of rock-garden labyrinth walks guaranteed to reset the harmony gauge. One's in an orchid greenhouse facing a contemplative Buddha statue; the other's in a *kukui* (candlenut trees) grove beside Maliko Stream. Take your time, feel each step on the pebbles underfoot, listen to the trickling stream, inhale the gentle scent of the garden. S-o-o-o soul soothing. To get there, turn east off Baldwin Ave onto Kaluanui Rd. After 0.8 miles you'll cross a one-lane bridge; 0.2 miles further on, look for a low stone wall – the garden is on the right just before a sharp S-curve in the road.

🛏 Sleeping

TOP CHOICE **Wild Ginger Falls** COTTAGE **$$**
(☑573-1173; www.wildgingerfalls.com; 355 Kaluanui Rd; d $155; 🐾) Fun setting! This stylish studio cottage overlooks a stone gorge and streambed that spouts a waterfall after it rains. Banana and coffee trees dot the lush garden surrounding the cottage and you can soak up the scenery from an outdoor hot tub. Owned by one of Hawaii's top contemporary ceramic artists, the cottage has an engaging retro '40s Hawaiiana decor. Breakfast items are provided for your first morning and coffee for your entire stay.

🍴 Eating

TOP CHOICE **Komoda Store & Bakery** BAKERY **$**
(3674 Baldwin Ave; ⊙7am-5pm Mon, Wed, Thu & Fri, to 2pm Sat) It's in an aging building that looks all but abandoned, but don't let that fool you. This homespun bakery, legendary for its mouth-watering cream puffs and guava-filled *malasadas* (Portuguese donut), is a must-stop. It's been a Makawao landmark since Tazeko Komoda first stoked up the oven in 1916 and his offspring, using the same time-honored recipes, have been at it ever since. Best believe they've got it down pat! Do arrive early though – they often sell out by noon.

TOP CHOICE **Casanova Restaurant** ITALIAN **$$**
(☑572-0220; www.casanovamaui.com; 1188 Makawao Ave; mains $12-32; ⊙11:30am-2pm Mon-Sat, 5:30-9pm daily) The one Makawao restaurant that lures diners up the mountain, Casanova offers reliably good Italian fare. The crispy innovative pizzas cooked in a kiawe-fired oven are as good as they get. Juicy Maui-raised steaks and classic Italian dishes like the spicy seafood *fra diavola* shore up the rest of the menu. Casanova

also has a happening dance floor and live music several nights a week.

Makawao Garden Café CAFE **$**
(3669 Baldwin Ave; mains $7-10; ⊙11am-3pm Mon-Sat) On a sunny day there's no better place in town for lunch than this outdoor cafe tucked into a courtyard at the north end of Baldwin Ave. It's strictly sandwiches and salads, but everything's fresh, generous and made to order by the owner herself. The mahimahi on homemade focaccia is killer.

Casanova Deli DELI **$**
(1188 Makawao Ave; mains $6-9; ⊙7am-5:30pm Mon-Sat, 8:30am-5:30pm Sun) Makawao's hippest haunt brews heady espressos and buzzes all day with folks munching on buttery croissants, thick Italian sandwiches and hearty Greek salads. Take it all out to the roadside deck for the town's best people-watching.

Rodeo General Store TAKEOUT **$**
(3661 Baldwin Ave; meals $5-8; ⊙6:30am-10pm) Stop here to grab a tasty takeout meal. The deli counter sells everything from fresh salads and Hawaiian *poke* to hot teriyaki chicken and plate lunches ready to go. Everything is made from scratch.

Polli's MEXICAN **$$**
(www.pollismexicanrestaurant.com; 1202 Makawao Ave; mains $8-22; ⊙11am-10pm) Locals and visitors alike flock to this old standby Tex-Mex restaurant to down a few *cervezas* (beers) while munching away on nachos, tacos and sizzling fajitas. The food's just average, but surf videos and plenty of spirited chatter keep the scene high energy.

Makawao Farmers Market PRODUCE **$**
(www.makawaofarmersmarket.com; 3654 Baldwin Ave; ⊙10am-5pm Wed) Upcountry gardeners gather to sell their homegrown veggies and

fruit once a week at this small open-air market opposite Rodeo General Store.

 Shopping

Start your exploration by wandering down Baldwin Ave, beginning at its intersection with Makawao Ave.

Hot Island Glass HANDBLOWN GLASS
(www.hotislandglass.com; 3620 Baldwin Ave) Head here to watch glassblowers spin their red-hot creations (from 10:30am to 4pm) at Maui's oldest handblown glass studio. Everything from paperweights with ocean themes to high-art decorative pieces.

Viewpoints Gallery ART GALLERY
(www.viewpointsgallery.com; 3620 Baldwin Ave) You'll feel like you're walking into a museum at this classy gallery, where a dozen of the island's finest artists hang their works.
Other recommended places:

Randy Jay Braun Gallery PHOTO GALLERY
(www.randyjaybraungallery.com; 1152 Makawao Ave) Braun's sepia hula dancers and Hawaiian cowboys are among the most recognised photo art in Hawaii today.

Aloha Cowboy SOUVENIR SHOP
(www.alohacowboy.net; 3643 Baldwin Ave) Get your cowboy-themed retro lunch pails and rhinestone-studded leather bags here.

Designing Wahine GIFT SHOP
(www.designingwahine.com; 3640 Baldwin Ave) Quality gifts, classic aloha shirts and hand-dyed Ts with *paniolo* themes.

ⓘ Information

Minit Stop (1100 Makawao Ave; ⊙5am-11:30pm) There's no bank in town, but this gas station has an ATM.
Post office (www.usps.com; 1075 Makawao Ave)

Ha'iku

POP 4500

In some ways this little town is what Pa'ia was like before the tourists arrived. Like Pa'ia, Ha'iku has its roots in sugarcane – Maui's first 12 acres of the sweet stuff were planted here in 1869, and the village once had both a sugar mill and pineapple canneries. Thanks to its affordability and proximity to Ho'okipa Beach, it's a haunt of pro surfers who have rejuvenated the town. Today the old cannery buildings are once again the heart of the community, housing a yoga stu-

dio, several surfboard shops and the kind of eateries that make a detour fun.

 Activities

Studio Maui YOGA
(☑575-9390; www.thestudiomaui.com; Ha'iku Marketplace, 810 Ha'iku Rd; classes $15-30; ⊙7:30am-10pm) Attracts a high-energy, good-karma crowd with a full schedule of yoga classes from Anusara basics to power-flow yoga, as well as ecstatic dance, New Age concerts and more.

Sleeping

TOP CHOICE **Pilialoha** COTTAGE $$
(☑572-1440; www.pilialoha.com; 2512 Kaupakalua Rd; d $145; ☎) Pilialoha blends countryside charm with all the comforts of a home away from home. The sunny split-level cottage has one pretty setting, nestled in a eucalyptus grove. Everything inside is pretty, too. But it's the warm hospitality and attention to detail – from the fresh-cut roses on the table to the Hawaiian music collection and cozy quilts on the beds – that shines brightest. Breakfast goodies for your first morning and coffee for the entire stay are provided.

Haiku Cannery Inn B&B B&B $$
(☑283-1274; www.haikucanneryinn.com; 1061 Kokomo Rd; r incl breakfast $105-125) Down a winding dirt road, surrounded by banana and breadfruit trees, this 1920s plantation house beams with character. High ceilings, hardwood floors and period decor reflect the place's century-old history. In addition to the rooms in the main house, there's a roomy two-bedroom detached cottage for $190.

 Eating

TOP CHOICE **NorthShore Café** CAFE $$
(www.northshorecafe.net; 824 Kokomo Rd; meals $5-20; ⊙7am-2pm daily, 5-9pm Tue-Sat) It's got a funky little interior with chairs that look like they were hauled out of a 1950s attic but this homespun eatery dishes up unbeatable value. Breakfast, served until 2pm, tops out at $8.08 and includes a knockout eggs Benedict. Steaks, seafood and sushi kick in at dinner. The cafe is hidden behind the power station opposite Colleen's but you'll be glad you searched it out.

Colleen's AMERICAN $$
(www.colleensinhaiku.com; Ha'iku Marketplace, 810 Ha'iku Rd; mains $8-20; ⊙6am-9pm) Surfers

get their pre-sunrise espresso jolt here and return in the evening to cap things off with a pint of Big Swell Ale. Colleen's is pure locavore. The burgers and steaks are made with hormone-free Maui cattle, the salads with organic Kula greens and the beers Colleen pours are Hawaiian microbrews.

Veg Out   VEGETARIAN $

(Ha'iku Town Center, 810 Kokomo Rd; mains $5-10; ⊘11:30am-7:30pm; 🖋) Tucked inside a former warehouse, this rasta-casual vegetarian eatery serves up a dynamite burrito loaded with beans, hot tofu and jalapenos. Also right on the mark are the taro cheeseburgers and pesto-chèvre pizza.

Pukalani & Around

POP 8150

True to its name, which means Heavenly Gate, Pukalani is the gateway to the lush Upcountry. Most visitors just drive past Pukalani on the way to Kula and Haleakalā, and unless you need to pick up supplies or gas up you won't miss much by sticking to the bypass road.

To reach the business part of town, get off Haleakalā Hwy (Hwy 37) at the Old Haleakalā Hwy exit, which becomes Pukalani's main street. There are a couple of gas stations along this street – the last gas before Haleakalā National Park.

◉ Sights & Activities

FREE Surfing Goat Dairy   FARM

(☑878-2870; www.surfinggoatdairy.com; 3651 Oma'opio Rd; tours from $7; ⊘10am-5pm Mon-Sat, 10am-2pm Sun; 🖋) 'Feta mo betta' is the motto at this 42-acre farm, the source of all that luscious chèvre adorning the menus of Maui's top restaurants. The shop here carries an amazing variety of creamy goat cheeses; for island flavor try the mango chutney. Not everything is geared to the connoisseur – your kids will love meeting the goat kids up close in a fun 20-minute dairy tour. On some of the tours they can even try their hand at milking.

Pukalani Country Club   GOLF

(☑572-1314; www.pukalanigolf.com; 360 Pukalani St; greens fee $87; ⊘7am-dusk) A mile west of Old Haleakalā Hwy, this golf course has 18 holes of smooth greens with sweeping views. Here's a bargain: come after 2:30pm

and golf the rest of the day for just $27 – cart included!

Eating

Serpico's   ITALIAN $$

(☑572-8498; www.serpicosmaui.com; cnr Aewa Pl & Old Haleakalā Hwy; mains $7-16; ⊘11am-10pm; 🖋) In the center of Pukalani, opposite McDonald's, this casual Italian eatery makes New York–style pizzas and pasta dishes, and it makes them well. If you're in a hurry, there are sandwiches and inexpensive lunch specials, as well as a $5 kids menu.

Foodland   TAKEOUT $

(cnr Old Haleakalā Hwy & Pukalani St; ⊘24hr) This always-open supermarket is a convenient stop for those heading up Haleakalā for the sunrise or coming down for supplies. There's also a Starbucks inside the store.

Kula

POP 10,720

The navel of the Upcountry, Kula is Maui's gardenland. The very name 'Kula' is synonymous with the fresh veggies on any Maui menu worth its salt. So bountiful is Kula's rich volcanic soil that it produces most of the onions, lettuce and strawberries grown in Hawaii. The key to these bountiful harvests is the elevation. At 3000ft, Kula's cool nights and sunny days are ideal for growing all sorts of crops.

Kula's farmers first gained fame during the California gold rush of the 1850s, when they shipped so many potatoes out to West Coast miners that Kula became known as 'Nu Kaleponi,' the Hawaiian pronunciation

---

MAUI FOR CHILDREN

» Getting within splashing distance of mammoth humpbacks on a whale-watching cruise (p352)

» Learning to surf (p315) on Lahaina's gentle waves

» Walking through the awesome shark tank at Maui Ocean Center (p352)

» Tramping the moonlike surface of Haleakalā (p404)

» Flying Tarzan-style on a zipline (p378)

» Letting your kids play with their kids at Surfing Goat Dairy (p381)

for New California. In the late 19th century Portuguese and Chinese immigrants who had worked off their contracts on the sugar plantations also moved up to Kula and started small farms, giving Kula the multicultural face it wears today.

◉ Sights

Stop and smell the roses...and the lavender and all those other sweet-scented blossoms. No two gardens in Kula are alike, and each has its own special charms.

TOP CHOICE Ali'i Kula Lavender   GARDEN
(☎878-8090; www.aklmaui.com; 1100 Waipoli Rd; admission free; ◉9am-4pm) Immerse yourself in a sea of purple at Ali'i Kula Lavender. Start by strolling along the garden paths where dozens of varieties of these fragrant plants blanket the hillside. Take your time, breathe deeply. Then sit for a spell on the veranda with its sweeping views and enjoy a lavender scone and perhaps a cup of lavender tea. Browse through the gift shop, sample the lavender-scented oils and lotions. If you want to really dig in, a variety of activities from garden-tea tours to wedding packages are available.

Enchanting Floral Gardens   GARDEN
(☎878-2531; www.flowersofmaui.com; 2505 Kula Hwy; adult/child 6-12yr $7.50/1; ◉9am-5pm) A labor of love, this colorful garden showcases the green thumb of master horticulturist Kazuo Takeda. Kula has microclimates that change with elevation and this garden occupies a narrow zone where tropical, temperate and desert vegetation all thrive. The sheer variety is amazing. You'll find everything from flamboyant proteas and orchids to orange trees and kava – all of it identified with Latin and common names. Your garden stroll ends with a sampling of fruits grown here.

Kula Botanical Garden   GARDEN
(☎878-1715; www.kulabotanicalgarden.com; 638 Kekaulike Ave; adult/child 6-12yr $10/3; ◉9am-4pm) Pleasantly overgrown and shady, this mature garden has walking paths that wind through acres of theme plantings, including native Hawaiian specimens and a 'taboo garden' of poisonous plants. Because a stream runs through it, the garden supports water-thirsty plants that you won't find in other Kula gardens. When the rain gods have been generous the whole place is an explosion of color.

Holy Ghost Church   CHURCH
(www.kulacatholiccommunity.org; 4300 Lower Kula Rd; ◉8am-5pm) Waiakoa's hillside landmark, the octagonal Holy Ghost Church was built in 1895 by Portuguese immigrants. The church features a beautifully ornate interior that looks like it came right out of the Old World, and indeed much of it did. The gilded altar was carved by renowned Austrian woodcarver Ferdinand Stuflesser and shipped in pieces around the Cape of Good Hope. The church is on the National Register of Historic Places.

✦ Activities

Pony Express   HORSEBACK RIDES
(☎667-2200; www.ponyexpresstours.com; Haleakalā Crater Rd; trail rides $95-185; ◉8am-5pm) A variety of horseback rides are offered, beginning with easy nose-to-tail walks across pastures and woods. But the real prize is the ride into the national park's Haleakalā crater that starts at the crater summit and leads down Sliding Sands Trail to the floor of this lunarlike wonder.

Skyline Eco-Adventures   ZIPLINING
(☎878-8400; www.skylinehawaii.com; Haleakalā Crater Rd; zip $95; ◉8:30am-4:30pm) Maui's first zipline scored a prime location on the slopes of Haleakalā. Even though the zips are relatively short compared with the new competition, there's plenty of adrenaline rush as you soar above the treetops over a series of five gulches. A half-mile hike and a suspension bridge are tossed in for good measure.

Proflyght Paragliding   PARAGLIDING
(☎874-5433; www.paraglidehawaii.com; Waipoli Rd; paraglide $79; ◉hours vary with weather) If the Skyline ziplines don't get you high enough, try surfing the sky. On this one, you strap into a tandem paraglider with a certified instructor and take a running leap off the cliffs beneath Polipoli Spring State Recreation Area for a 1000ft descent. The term 'bird's-eye view' will never be the same.

☞ Tours

TOP CHOICE O'o Farm   FARM TOUR
(☎667-4341; www.oofarm.com; Waipoli Rd; lunch tour $50; ◉10:30am-1pm Wed & Thu) Whether you're a gardener or a gourmet you're going to love a tour of famed Lahaina chef James McDonald's organic Upcountry farm. Where else can you help harvest your own meal, turn the goodies over to a gourmet chef and feast on the bounty? Bring your own wine.

🎆 Festivals & Events

Holy Ghost Feast
PORTUGUESE FESTIVAL
(www.kulacatholiccommunity.org) Enjoy the aloha of Upcountry folks at this festival celebrating Kula's Portuguese heritage. Held at the Holy Ghost Church on the fourth Saturday and Sunday in May, it's a family event with games, craft booths, a farmers market and a free Hawaiian-Portuguese lunch on Sunday.

🛏 Sleeping

Kula View Bed & Breakfast
B&B $$
(☎878-6736; www.kulaview.com; 600 Holopuni Rd; studio incl breakfast $115) With her *paniolo* roots, this host knows the Upcountry inside out. She provides everything you'll need for a good stay, including warm jackets for the Haleakalā sunrise. The studio unit sits atop her country home and offers sunset ocean views. Breakfast includes fruit from the backyard and homemade muffins.

Kula Sandalwoods Cottages
COTTAGE $$
(☎878-3523; www.kulasandalwoods.com; 15427 Haleakalā Hwy; r $130; 🐾) A half-dozen free-standing cottages dot the hillside above Kula Sandalwoods Restaurant. Think rustic – you shouldn't expect too much in terms of creature comforts, but the sweeping view from the lanai is top rate and the price is a bargain for being on the doorstep of the national park.

🍴 Eating

La Provence
CAFE $$
(☎878-1313; www.laprovencekula.com; 3158 Lower Kula Rd, Waiakoa; mains $8-15; ⊙7am-2pm Wed-Sun) One of Maui's top pastry chefs hangs his shingle here. Even if you're not hungry, just swing by to pick up a ham-and-cheese croissant or some flaky chocolate-filled pastries for that picnic further down the road. If you are hungry, the chèvre green salads are a Kula treat to savor. This place is tricky to find but worth the effort: look for the low-key sign on the Kula Hwy as you approach Waiakoa.

Café 808
LOCAL FOOD $
(☎878-6874; 4566 Lower Kula Rd, Waiakoa; mains $6-10; ⊙6am-8:30pm) Its motto, 'The Big Kahuna of Island Grinds,' says it all. This unpretentious eatery, a quarter-mile south of the Holy Ghost Church, offers a wall-size chalkboard of all things local, from banana pancakes to gravy-laden plate lunches. Serv-

---

BEST UPCOUNTRY-GROWN TREATS

» Maui Splash wine at Tedeschi Vineyards (p385)

» Chèvre at Surfing Goat Dairy (p381)

» Maui coffee at Grandma's (p385)

» Lunch tour at O'o Farm (p382)

» Lavender scones at Ali'i Kula Lavender (p382)

» Elk burgers at 'Ulupalakua Ranch Store (p385)

---

ings are hefty. Breakfast is served to 11am, making it a good choice for an inexpensive eat after sunrise on the mountain.

Kula Sandalwoods Restaurant
CAFE $$
(☎878-3523; www.kulasandalwoods.com; 15427 Haleakalā Hwy; mains $9-14; ⊙7am-3pm Mon-Fri, 7-11:30am Sat & Sun) The owner-chef earned her toque from the prestigious Culinary Institute of America. At breakfast the eggs Benedict is the favorite. Lunch features garden-fresh Kula salads and heaping chicken and beefsteak sandwiches on homemade onion rolls.

Sunrise Country Market
TAKEOUT $
(☎878-1600; Haleakalā Crater Rd; simple eats $4-8; ⊙7am-3pm) Stop at this convenient shop, a quarter-mile up from the intersection of Hwys 378 and 377, to pick up post-sunrise java, breakfast burritos and sandwiches. Then take a stroll behind the shop to enjoy the flowers in the protea garden.

Polipoli Spring State Recreation Area

Crisscrossed with hiking and mountain biking trails, this misty cloud forest on the western slope of Haleakalā takes you deep off the beaten path. The shade from tall trees and the cool moist air make for a refreshing walk in the woods. Layers of clouds drift in and out; when they lift, you'll get long vistas across green rolling hills clear out to the islands of Lana'i and Kaho'olawe.

It's not always possible to get all the way to the park without a 4WD, but it's worth driving part of the way for the view. To get there take Waipoli Rd, off Hwy 377. Waipoli Rd is a narrow, switchbacking one-lane road, but the first 6 miles are paved. After the road enters the Kula Forest Reserve, it reverts to dirt. When it's muddy, the next grinding 4 miles to the campground are not even worth trying without a 4WD.

🏃 Activities

Waiakoa Loop Trail　　　　　HIKING

The trailhead for the Waiakoa Loop Trail starts at the hunter check station 5 miles up Waipoli Rd. Walk 0.75 miles down the grassy spur road on the left to a gate marking the trail. The hike, which starts out in pine trees, makes a 3-mile loop, passing through eucalyptus stands, pine forest and scrub land scored with feral pig trails. This is a fairly gentle hike. You can also connect with the Upper Waiakoa Trail at a junction about a mile up the right side of the loop.

Upper Waiakoa Trail　　　　HIKING

The Upper Waiakoa Trail is a strenuous 7-mile trail that begins off Waiakoa Loop at an elevation of 6000ft, climbs 1800ft, switchbacks and then drops back down 1400ft. It's stony terrain, but it's high and open, with good views. Bring plenty of water.

The trail ends on Waipoli Rd between the hunter check station and the campground. If you want to start at this end of the trail, keep an eye out for the trail marker for Waohuli Trail, as the Upper Waiakoa Trail begins across the road.

Boundary Trail　　　　　　HIKING

This 4-mile trail begins about 200yd beyond the end of the paved road. Park to the right of the cattle grate that marks the boundary of the Kula Forest Reserve. It's a steep downhill walk that crosses gulches and drops deep into woods of eucalyptus, pine and cedar, as well as a bit of native forest. In the afternoon the fog generally rolls in and visibility fades.

Skyline Trail　　　　　　　HIKING

Also partially in this park is the rugged Skyline Trail, which begins near the summit of Haleakalā National Park before descending to Polipoli Spring State Recreation Area. For details of this hike, see p406.

🛏 Sleeping

To stay in Polipoli is to rough it. Tent camping is free, but requires a permit from the state. Facilities are primitive, with toilets but no showers or drinking water. Fellow campers are likely to be pig hunters. Otherwise the place can be eerily deserted, and damp. Come prepared – this is cold country, with winter temperatures frequently dropping below freezing at night.

The park also has one cabin. Unlike other state park cabins, this one has gas lanterns and a wood-burning stove but no electricity or refrigerator. See p308 for details on permits and reservations.

Keokea

Modest as it may be, Keokea is the last real town before Hana if you're swinging around the southern part of the island. The sum total of the town center consists of a coffee shop, an art gallery, a gas station and two small stores, the Ching Store and the Fong Store.

◉ Sights

Drawn by rich soil, Hakka Chinese farmers migrated to this remote corner of Kula at the turn of the 20th century. Their influence is readily visible throughout the village. Keokea's landmark St John's Episcopal Church (c 1907) still bears its name in Chinese characters. For a time Sun Yat-sen, father of the Chinese nationalist movement, lived on the outskirts of Keokea. He's honored at Sun Yat-sen Park, found along the Kula Hwy (Hwy 37) 1.7 miles beyond Grandma's Coffee House. The park has picnic tables and is a great place to soak up the broad vistas that stretch across to West Maui.

🏃 Activities

Thompson Ranch　　　HORSEBACK RIDES

(☑878-1910; www.thompsonranchmaui.com; cnr Middle & Polipoli Rds; 2hr ride $100; ⊙departs 9am) Join these folks for horseback rides across ranch land in the cool Upcountry bordering Polipoli Spring State Recreation Area. At elevations of 4000ft to 6000ft, it's a memorable ride for those who enjoy mountain scenery.

🛏 Sleeping

⌜TOP⌟ CHOICE Star Lookout　　　COTTAGE $$

(☑907-250-2364; www.starlookout.com; 622 Thompson Rd; cottage $200; 🐾) A fabulous ocean view, outdoor hot tub and grounds so quiet you can hear the flowers bloom. Half a mile up a one-lane road from Keokea center, this two-bedroom cottage with a loft could sleep four people comfortably, six in a pinch. Nice, but what makes it spectacular is the setting, which overlooks a thousand acres of green pastureland that's now owned by Oprah Winfrey and set aside for preservation.

✖ Eating

Grandma's Coffee House   CAFE **$**
(www.grandmascoffee.com; 9232 Kula Hwy; pastries $3-5, deli fare $6-10; ⊙7am-5pm) If you thought Kona was the only place with primo Hawaii-grown coffee, just check out the brew at Grandma's. This earthy cafe dishes up homemade pastries, hearty sandwiches and deli salads. Grandma's family has been growing coffee in Keokea for generations. Take your goodies out on the patio and you can eat right under their coffee trees.

'Ulupalakua Ranch

This sprawling 20,000-acre ranch was established in the mid-19th century by James Makee, a whaling captain who jumped ship and befriended Hawaiian royalty. King David Kalakaua, the 'Merrie Monarch,' became a frequent visitor who loved to indulge in late-night rounds of poker and champagne. The ranch is still worked by *paniolo,* who have been herding cattle here for generations. Some 6000 head of cattle, as well as a small herd of Rocky Mountain elk, dot the hillside pastures.

The ranch is green in more ways than one. It's staged to host Upcountry's first wind energy farm and is restoring a rare native dryland forest on the upper slopes of ranch property.

Today most people come to visit Tedeschi Vineyards, Maui's sole winery, which is on 'Ulupalakua Ranch land. After the winery, it's another 25 undulating miles to Kipahulu along the remote Pi'ilani Hwy.

◉ Sights

Tedeschi Vineyards   WINERY
(☑878-6058; www.mauiwine.com; Kula Hwy; ⊙10am-5pm, tours 10:30am & 1:30pm) Free tours and wine tastings are offered in the historic stone cottage where King David Kalakaua once slept. In the 1970s, while awaiting its first grape harvest, the owners decided to take advantage of Maui's prickly fruit – today its biggest hit is the sweet Maui Splash, a light blend of pineapple and passion fruit. Other pineapple novelties worth a taste: the dry Maui Blanc and the sparkling Hula O'Maui. This is no Napa Valley, however, and the grape

wines are less of a splash. Reservations are necessary for groups of 10 or more.

Don't miss the fascinating little **exhibit** at the side of the tasting room that features Kalakaua lore, ranch history and ecological goings-on. Opposite the winery, see the stack remains of the Makee Sugar Mill, built in 1878.

✖ Eating

'Ulupalakua Ranch Store   DELI **$**
(www.ulupalakuaranch.com; burgers $9; ⊙grill 11am-2:30pm, store 9:30am-5pm) Sidle up to the life-size wooden cowboys on the front porch and say howdy. Then pop inside and check out the cowboy hats and souvenir T-shirts. If it's lunchtime, mosey over to the grill and treat yourself to an organic ranch-raised elk burger. Can't beat that for local. The store is 5.5 miles south of Keokea, opposite the winery.

THE ROAD TO HANA

You're about to experience the most ravishingly beautiful drive in Hawaii. The serpentine Hana Hwy delivers one jaw-dropping view after the other as it winds between jungly valleys and towering cliffs. Along the way 54 one-lane bridges mark nearly as many waterfalls, some tranquil and inviting, others so sheer they kiss you with spray as you drive past. But there's a lot more to this beauty than the drive. When you're ready to get out and stretch your legs the real adventure begins: hiking trails climb into cool forests, short paths lead to Eden-like swimming holes, side roads wind down to sleepy seaside villages. If you've never tried smoked

DON'T MISS

'ULUPALAKUA SUNDAY DRIVE EVENT

Four times a year, 'Ulupalakua Ranch (www.ulupalakuaranch.com) sponsors a bash on the lawn of Tedeschi Vineyards featuring live slack key guitar music, glassblowing demonstrations and cowboy-centric food. The music's a highlight. Jeff Peterson, son of an 'Ulupalakua Ranch *paniolo* and a Grammy Award winner, performs at some of the events. The festival takes place on a Sunday in March, June, September and December.

breadfruit, taken a dip in a spring-fed cave or gazed upon an ancient Hawaiian temple, set the alarm early – you've got a big day coming up.

Twin Falls

Heading east from Pa'ia, houses give way to fields of sugarcane and the scenery gets more dramatic with each mile. After the 16-mile marker on Hwy 36 the Hana Hwy changes numbers and becomes Hwy 360 and the mile markers begin again at zero. Just after Hwy 360's 2-mile marker a wide parking area with a fruit stand marks the start of the trail to Twin Falls. Local kids and tourists flock to the pool beneath the lower falls, about a 10-minute walk in. Twin Falls gets a lot of attention as being the 'first waterfall on the road to Hana.' Truth be told, unless you're interested in taking a dip in muddy waters, this one's not worth the time. You'll find more idyllic options en route to Hana.

Huelo

With its abundant rain and fertile soil Huelo once supported more than 50,000 Hawaiians, but today it's a sleepy, scattered community of farms and enviable cliffside homes.

The double row of mailboxes and green bus shelter that come up after a blind curve 0.5 miles past the 3-mile marker marks the start of the narrow road that leads into the village. The only sight, Kaulanapueo Church, is a half-mile down.

It's tempting to continue driving past the church, but don't bother – it's not rewarding, as the road shortly turns to dirt and dead-ends at gated homes. There's no public beach access.

HANA TRIP TIPS

» Beat the crowd – get a sunrise start.

» Fill up the tank in Pa'ia; the next gas station isn't until Hana.

» Bring snacks and plenty to drink.

» Wear a bathing suit under your clothes so you're ready for impromptu swims.

» Pull over to let local drivers pass – they're moving at a different pace.

◉ Sights

Kaulanapueo Church   HISTORIC CHURCH

Constructed in 1853 of coral blocks and surrounded by a manicured green lawn, this tidy church remains the heart of the village. It's in early Hawaiian missionary style with a spare interior and a tin roof topped with a green steeple. Swaying palm trees add a tropical backdrop. There are no formal opening hours, but the church is typically unlocked during the day.

🛏 Sleeping & Eating

🍃 Tea House   COTTAGE $$

(☎572-5610; www.mauiteahouse.com; Hoolawa Rd; s/d $135/150) Built with walls recycled from a Zen temple, this one-of-a-kind cottage is so secluded it's off the grid and uses its own solar power to stoke up the lights. Yet it has everything you'll need, including a kitchen with gas burners and an open-air shower in a redwood gazebo. The grounds also contain a Tibetan-style stupa with a spectacular clifftop ocean view and a second cottage that rents by the week ($500).

TOP CHOICE Huelo Lookout   FRUIT STAND $

(www.huelolookout.coconutprotectors.com; 7600 Hana Hwy; snacks $5; ⊗7:30am-5:30pm) The fruit stand itself is tempting enough: drinking coconuts, smoothies, even French crepes...ooh la la. And everything's organic from their own 12-acre farm. But it doesn't stop there. Take your goodies down the steps, where there's a table with a wide-open panorama clear out to the coast.

Ko'olau Forest Reserve

This is where it starts to get wild! As the highway snakes along the edge of the Ko'olau Forest Reserve, the jungle takes over and one-lane bridges appear around every other bend. Ko'olau means 'windward,' and the upper slopes of these mountains squeeze passing clouds of a mighty 200in to 300in of rain annually. No surprise – that makes for awesome waterfalls as the rainwater rushes down the reserve's abundant gulches and streams.

After the 5-mile marker you'll pass through the village of Kailua. This little community of tin-roofed houses is the home base for the employees of the East Maui Irrigation (EMI) company. These workers maintain the extensive irrigation system that carries water from the rain forest to thirsty sugarcane fields in Central Maui.

After leaving the village, just past the 6-mile marker, you'll be treated to a splash of color as you pass planted groves of **painted eucalyptus** with brilliant rainbow-colored bark. Roll down the windows and inhale the sweet scent given off by these majestic trees introduced from Australia.

Waikamoi Nature Trail

Put on your walking shoes and relish the majestic sights and spicy scents along this 30-minute nature trail. A covered table at the top offers one pretty spot to break out that picnic lunch. Look for the signposted trailhead 0.5 miles past the 9-mile marker, where there's a wide dirt pull-off with space for several cars to park.

At the start of this 0.8-mile trail you're welcomed by a sign that reads 'Quiet. Trees at Work' and a strand of grand reddish *Eucalyptus robusta,* one of several types of towering eucalyptus trees that grow along the path. Once you reach the ridge at the top of the loop, you'll be treated to fine views of the winding Hana Hwy.

Waikamoi Falls

There is space for just a few cars before the bridge at the 10-mile marker, but unless it's been raining recently don't worry about missing this one. The East Maui Irrigation Company diverts water from the stream, and as a result the falls are usually just a trickle. After you drive past the bridge, bamboo grows almost horizontally out from the cliffs, creating a green canopy over the road.

Garden of Eden Arboretum

So why pay a steep $10 per person to visit an arboretum when the entire road to Hana is a garden? Well, the Garden of Eden (www.mauigardenofeden.com; 10600 Hana Hwy; admission $10; 8am-3pm) does offer a tamer version of paradise. The winding paths are neatly maintained, the flowers are identified and the hilltop picnic tables sport gorgeous views, including ones of Puohokamoa Falls and of Keopuka Rock, which was featured in the opening shot of the 1993 film *Jurassic Park.* The arboretum is 0.5 miles past the 10-mile marker.

KO'OLAU DITCH

For more than a century the Ko'olau Ditch has been carrying up to 450 million gallons of water a day through 75 miles of flumes and tunnels from Maui's rainy interior to the dry central plains. You can get a close-up look by stopping at the small pull-off just before the bridge that comes up immediately after the 8-mile marker. Just 30ft above the road you'll see water flowing through a hand-hewn stone-block section of the ditch before tunneling into the mountain. Now that you know what it looks like, keep your eye out for other sections of the ditch as you continue to Hana.

Puohokamoa Falls

Immediately after the 11-mile marker you'll pass Puohokamoa Falls. This waterfall no longer has public access, but you can get a glimpse of it from the bridge, or a bird's-eye view of the falls from the Garden of Eden Arboretum.

Haipua'ena Falls

If you're ready for a dip, Haipua'ena Falls, 0.5 miles past the 11-mile marker, provides a gentle waterfall with a zenlike pool deep enough for swimming. Since you can't see the pool from the road, few people know this one's here. Actually, it's not a bad choice if you forgot your bathing suit. There's space for just a couple of cars on the Hana side of the bridge. To reach the falls, simply walk 100yd upstream. Wild ginger grows along the path, and ferns hang from the rock wall behind the waterfall, making an idyllic setting. Be aware of slippery rocks and flash floods.

Kaumahina State Wayside Park

Clean restrooms, much appreciated right about now, and a grassy lawn with picnic tables make this roadside park a family-friendly stop. The park comes up 0.2 miles after the 12-mile marker. Be sure to take the short walk up the hill past the restrooms for an eye-popping view of the coastal scenery that awaits to the south.

ℹ TRICKLES OR TORRENTS

Take descriptions of the waterfalls on this rain-forest drive with a few grains of salt – whether you see torrents or trickles depends on recent rainfall up in the mountains. And if it really starts to pour, watch out for sudden rockslides and muddy debris on the road. For more information on flash flooding, see p633.

For the next several miles, the scenery is absolutely stunning, opening up to a new vista as you turn round each bend. If it's been raining recently, you can expect to see waterfalls galore crashing down the mountains.

Honomanu Bay

You'll get your first view of this striking stream-fed bay from the 13-mile marker, where there's a roadside pull-off that invites you to pause and take in the scene.

Its rocky black-sand beach is used mostly by local surfers and fishers. Surfable waves form during big swells, but the rocky bottom and strong rips make it dangerous if you're not familiar with the spot. Honomanu Stream, which empties into the bay, forms a pool just inland of the beach that's good for splashing in; on weekends local families take the kids here to wade in its shallow water.

Just after the 14-mile marker, an inconspicuous road plunges straight down to Honomanu Bay. But the road can be shockingly bad – if you're not in a high-clearance vehicle, send a scout before driving down.

Kalaloa Point

For a fascinating view of the coast, stop at the wide pull-off on the ocean side of the highway 0.4 miles past the 14-mile marker. From here you can look clear across Honomanu Bay and watch ant-size cars snaking down the mountain cliffs on the other side. If there's no place to park, there's another pull-off with the same view 0.2 miles further on.

Ke'anae

Congratulations – you've made it halfway to Hana. Your reward: dramatic landscapes and the friendliest seaside village on the route.

The views are sweeping. Starting way up at the Ko'olau Gap in the rim of Haleakalā Crater and stretching clear down to the coast, Ke'anae Valley radiates green, thanks to the 150in of rainfall that drenches it each year.

At the foot of the valley lies Ke'anae Peninsula, created by a late eruption of Haleakalā that sent lava gushing all the way down Ke'anae Valley and into the sea. Unlike its rugged surroundings, the volcanic peninsula is perfectly flat, like a leaf floating on the water.

You'll want to see Ke'anae up close. But keep an eye peeled, as sights come up in quick succession. After passing the YMCA camp 0.5 miles past the 16-mile marker, the arboretum pops up on the right and the road to Ke'anae Peninsula heads off to the left around the next bend.

◎ Sights & Activities

🌿 Ke'anae Arboretum   TRAILS

Up for an easy walk? Ke'anae Arboretum, 0.6 miles past the 16-mile marker, follows the Pi'ina'au Stream past an array of shady trees. Most eye-catching are the painted eucalyptus trees and the golden-stemmed bamboo, whose green stripes look like the strokes of a Japanese *shodo* (calligraphy) artist. The arboretum is divided into two sections, with exotic timber and ornamental trees in one area and Hawaiian food and medicinal plants in the upper section.

The 0.6-mile path, which starts on a paved road and then turns to dirt, takes about 30 minutes to walk. It passes ginger and other fragrant plants before ending at irrigated patches with dozens of varieties of taro. Do expect some mosquitoes on the way.

TOP CHOICE Ke'anae Peninsula   VILLAGE

A coastline pounded by relentless waves embraces a village so quiet you can hear the grass grow. This rare slice of 'Old Hawaii' is reached by taking the unmarked Ke'anae Rd on the *makai* side of the highway just beyond Ke'anae Arboretum. Here, families who have had roots to the land for generations still tend stream-fed taro patches.

Marking the heart of the village is Lanakila 'Ihi'ihi o Iehova Ona Kaua (Ke'anae Congregational Church), built in 1860. This is one church made of lava rocks and coral mortar whose exterior hasn't been covered over with layers of whitewash. It's a welcoming place with open doors and a guest book to sign. You can get a feel for the community by strolling the church cemetery, where the gravestones have cameo portraits and fresh-cut flowers.

Just past the church, **Ke'anae Beach Park** has a scenic coastline of jagged black rock and hypnotic white-capped waves. Forget swimming: not only is the water rough, but this is all sharp lava and no beach. You could drive for a couple of minutes more, but it becomes private and the scenery is no better, so be respectful and stop at the park.

The rock islets you see off the coast – **Mokuhala** and **Mokumana** – are seabird sanctuaries.

Ching's Pond   SWIMMING HOLE
Back up on the Hana Hwy, the stream that feeds Ke'anae Peninsula pauses to create a couple of tempting swimming holes just below the bridge, 0.9 miles after the 16-mile marker. You won't see anything while driving by, but there's a good-sized pull-off immediately before the bridge where you can park. Just walk over to the bridge and behold: a deep crystal-clear pool and a little waterfall. You'll often see locals swimming here, but note the 'No Trespassing' signs. Enjoy the sight, but take your dip elsewhere.

Ke'anae Peninsula Lookout   SCENIC VIEWPOINT
The paved pull-off just past the 17-mile marker on the *makai* side of the road offers a superb bird's-eye view of the lowland peninsula and village. There's no sign, but it's easy to find if you look for the yellow tsunami speaker. From here you can see how Ke'anae Peninsula was formed late in the geological game – outlined in a jet-black lava coast, it still wears its volcanic birthmark around the edges. The views of coconut palms and patchwork taro fed by Ke'anae Stream make one tasty scene. If it's been raining lately, look to the far left to spot a series of cascading waterfalls.

🛏 Sleeping & Eating

YMCA Camp Ke'anae   CABINS $
(☎248-8355; www.mauiymca.org; 13375 Hana Hwy; campsite or dm $18, cottages $150) When they're not tied up by groups, the Y's cabins, on a knoll overlooking the coast, are available to individuals as hostel-style dorms. You'll need your own sleeping bag, and cooking facilities are limited to simple outdoor grills. Another option is to pitch your tent on the grounds. The Y also has two cottages, each with full facilities, two bedrooms and a lanai with spectacular ocean views. The camp is between the 16- and 17-mile markers.

🔝 Ke'anae Landing Fruit Stand   FRUIT STAND $
(Ke'anae Peninsula; banana bread $4.95; ⊗8:30am-3pm) 'Da best' banana bread on the entire road to Hana is baked fresh every morning, and is so good you'll find as many locals as tourists pulling up here. You can also get fresh fruit and drinks at this stand in the village center just before Ke'anae Beach Park.

Wailua

After the Ke'anae Peninsula Lookout, you'll pass a couple of roadside fruit stands. A quarter-mile after the 18-mile marker, the unmarked Wailua Rd leads to the left into the village of Wailua. There's little to see other than a small church, and the village doesn't exactly welcome visitors, so you might as well stick to the highway where the real sights are.

👁 Sights

Wailua Valley State Wayside   SCENIC VIEWPOINT
Back on the Hana Hwy, just before the 19-mile marker, Wailua Valley State Wayside lookout comes up on the right, providing a broad view into verdant Ke'anae Valley, which appears to be a hundred shades of green. You can see a couple of waterfalls, and on a clear day you can steal a view of Ko'olau Gap, the break in the rim of Haleakalā Crater. If you climb up the steps to the right, you'll find a good view of Wailua Peninsula as well. Now, how's that for a package? A word of caution: the wayside is signposted but it comes up quickly after turning round a bend, so be on the lookout.

Wailua Peninsula Lookout   SCENIC VIEWPOINT
For the most spectacular view of Wailua Peninsula, stop at the large paved pull-off on the ocean side of the road 0.25 miles past the 19-mile marker. There's no sign but it's not hard to find, as two concrete picnic tables mark the spot. Grab a seat, break out your snack pack and ogle the taro fields and jungly vistas unfolding below.

Wailua to Nahiku

A magnificent run of roadside cascades pops up between the 19- and 25-mile markers as you continue down the road to Hana. Have a camera ready!

⊙ Sights

TOP CHOICE **Three Bears Falls** WATERFALL

Three Bears, 0.5 miles past the 19-mile marker, is a real beauty. It takes its name from the triple cascade that flows down a steep rockface on the inland side of the road. Catch it after a rainstorm and the cascades come together and roar as one mighty waterfall. There's a small turnout with parking for a few cars right before crossing the bridge. You can scramble down to the falls via a steep ill-defined path that begins on the Hana side of the bridge. The stones are moss-covered and slippery, so either proceed with caution or simply enjoy the view from the road.

Pua'a Ka'a State Wayside Park SWIMMING HOLE

A delightful park with an odd name, Pua'a Ka'a (Rolling Pig) rolls along both sides of the highway 0.5 miles after the 22-mile marker. Some unlucky passersby see just the restrooms on the ocean side of the road and miss the rest. But you brought your beach towel, didn't you? Cross the highway and head inland to find a pair of delicious waterfalls cascading into pools. The best for swimming is the upper pool, which is visible just beyond the picnic tables. To reach it, you'll need to cross the stream, skipping across a few rocks. (Also be aware of the possibility of falling rocks beneath the waterfall, and flash floods.) To get to the lower falls, which drop into a shallow pool, walk back to the south side of the bridge and then follow the trail upstream. And while you're at it, be sure to catch the scene from the bridge. Just don't hog the view.

Hanawi Falls WATERFALL

Another waterfall with a split personality, Hanawi sometimes flows gently into a quiet pool and sometimes gushes wildly across a broad rockface. No matter the mood, it always invites snapping a pic. The falls are 0.1 miles after the 24-mile marker. There are small pull-offs before and after the bridge.

Makapipi Falls WATERFALL

Most waterfall views look up at the cascades, but this one offers a rare chance to experience an explosive waterfall from the top. Makapipi Falls makes its sheer plunge right beneath your feet as you stand on the ocean side of the Makapipi Bridge. You don't see anything from your car so if you didn't know about it, you'd never even

imagine this one was here. It's 0.1 miles after the 25-mile marker; you'll find pull-offs before and after the bridge.

Nahiku

While the village of Nahiku is down on the coast, its tiny 'commercial' center – such as it is – is right on the Hana Hwy, just before the 29-mile marker. Here you'll find the Nahiku Marketplace, home to a little coffee shop, fruit stand and several eateries clustered together.

If you're hungry, you will want to stop. The food's tempting and this is the last place to eat between here and Hana.

✕ Eating

TOP CHOICE **Up In Smoke** HAWAIIAN $

(Nahiku Marketplace, Hana Hwy; snacks $3-6; ⊙10am-5pm Sun-Thu) Hawaiian food never tasted so good. This bustling BBQ stand is *the* place to try kiawe-smoked breadfruit and *kalua* pig tacos.

Jen's Thai Food THAI $

(Nahiku Marketplace, Hana Hwy; mains $8-10; ⊙11am-4pm) A new addition to the mix, Jen uses only fresh-caught Hana fish in her savory curries. The green papaya salad and pad Thai get raves too.

Café Romantica VEGETARIAN $

(Nahiku Marketplace, Hana Hwy; mains $5-10; ⊙noon-5pm; ✍) At this class act, a skilled chef whips up gourmet vegetarian dishes out of a vintage food truck, complete with a lighted awning and bar stools.

'Ula'ino Road

'Ula'ino Rd begins at the Hana Hwy just south of the 31-mile marker. Hana Lava Tube is half a mile from the highway and Kahanu Garden a mile further.

⊙ Sights & Activities

TOP CHOICE **Kahanu Garden** HISTORICAL SITE

(✆248-8912; www.ntbg.org; 'Ula'ino Rd; adult/child $10/free; ⊙10am-2pm Mon-Fri) This one-of-a-kind place delivers a double blast of mana. Hawaii's largest temple and one of its most important ethnobotanical gardens share the 294-acre site. The National Tropical Botanical Garden, which is dedicated to the conservation of rare and medicinal plants from the tropical Pacific, maintains Kahanu. Most interesting is the **canoe garden**, landscaped with taro and other plants brought to Hawaii by early Polynesian settlers. The scope is amazing, as the garden holds the world's largest breadfruit tree collection and a remarkable variety of coconut palms.

The garden paths also skirt Pi'ilanihale Heiau, an immense lava-stone platform reaching 450ft in length. The history of this astounding heiau is shrouded in mystery, but there's no doubt that it was an important religious site for Hawaiians. Archaeologists believe construction began as early as AD 1200 and the heiau was built in sequences. The final grand scale was the work of Pi'ilani (the heiau's name means House of Pi'ilani), the 14th-century Maui chief who is also credited with the construction of many of the coastal fishponds in the Hana area. It's a memorable place to bring the entire family and children 12 years and under are admitted free.

Visiting Kahanu Garden takes a couple of hours, so few day-trippers come this way and you may well have the place to yourself. The site, on Kalahu Point, is 1.5 miles down 'Ula'ino Rd from the Hana Hwy. The road is crossed by a streambed immediately before reaching the gardens; if it's dry you should be able to drive over it OK, but if it's been raining heavily don't even try.

While self-guided tours are limited to weekdays, the site also opens on Saturday mornings from 10am to noon, when a guided tour ($25) is offered.

Hana Lava Tube   CAVES
(www.mauicave.com; 'Ula'ino Rd; admission $12; ⊙10:30am-4pm) One of the odder sights on this otherwise lushly green drive are these mammoth caves formed by ancient lava flows. The big kahuna of lava tubes, these caves are so formidable that they once

served as a slaughterhouse – 17,000lb of cow bones had to be removed before they were opened to visitors! Winding your way through the extensive underground lava tubes, which reach heights of up to 40ft, you'll find a unique ecosystem of dripping stalactites and stalagmites. Most people take about an hour to explore it. The admission includes flashlights and hard hats. Bring a sweater – it's cool down under.

Wai'anapanapa State Park

Swim in a cave, sun on a black-sand beach, explore ancient Hawaiian sites – this is one cool park. A sunny coastal trail and a seaside campground make it a tempting place to dig in for awhile. Honokalani Rd, which leads into Wai'anapanapa State Park, is just after the 32-mile marker. The road ends overlooking the park's centerpiece, the jet-black sands at Pa'iloa Bay.

🏖 Beaches

TOP CHOICE Pa'iloa Beach   BEACH
The park's beach is a stunner – hands-down the prettiest black-sand beach on Maui. Walk on down, sunbathe, enjoy. But if you're thinking about jumping in, be cautious. It's open ocean with a bottom that drops quickly and water conditions that are challenging, even for strong swimmers. Powerful rips are the norm (Pa'iloa means 'always splashing') and there have been several drownings here.

⦿ Sights & Activities

Lava Caves   CAVES
A 10-minute loop path north from the beach parking lot leads to a pair of impressive lava-tube caves. Their gardenlike exteriors are draped with ferns and colorful impatiens,

TREAD GENTLY

Travelers wanting to explore every nook and cranny of the island sometimes come into conflict with Maui residents who feel their quality of life is being encroached upon. At no place has this come more to a head than at Blue Pool, a coastal waterfall and swimming hole off 'Ula'ino Rd. Access to this slice of paradise leads across private property and the rural landowners who cherish their privacy are increasingly at odds with day-trippers cutting across their backyards.

Gentle persuasion has come up short. A signboard posted opposite Hana Lava Tube, which explains how the Blue Pool is of spiritual significance to Native Hawaiians and encourages tourists not to visit, has been overlaid with a 'Closed to the Public. Trespassers will be Prosecuted' sign. For those who fail to heed the message, heated confrontations are common. If you don't want to chance getting bopped by a coconut, take your swim at one of the many other waterfall pools along the Hana Hwy.

RED WATERS

On certain nights of the year, the waters in Wai'anapanapa State Park's lava-tube caves take on a red hue. Legend says it's the blood of a princess and her lover who were killed in a fit of rage by the princess's jealous husband after he found them hiding together here. Less romantic types attribute the phenomenon to swarms of tiny bright-red shrimp called 'opaeula, which occasionally emerge from subterranean cracks in the lava.

while their interiors harbor deep spring-fed pools. Wai'anapanapa means 'glistening waters' and the pools' crystal-clear mineral waters reputedly rejuvenate the skin. They certainly will invigorate – these sunless pools are refreshingly brisk!

Pi'ilani Trail   HIKING

This gem of a coastal trail leads 3 miles south from the park to Kainalimu Bay, just north of Hana Bay, offering splendid views along the way. It's one of those trails that packs a lot up front, so even if you just have time to do the first mile, you won't regret it. If you plan to hike the whole trail be sure to bring water (as it's unshaded the entire way) and good hiking shoes (as it gets rougher as you go along).

The route follows an ancient footpath known as the King's Highway that was the main land route between Hana and villages to the north. Some of the worn stepping stones along the path date from the time of Pi'ilani, the king who ruled Maui in the 14th century. The trail begins along the coast just below the camping area and parallels the ocean along lava sea cliffs. Just a few minutes along you'll pass a burial ground, a natural **sea arch** and a **blowhole** that roars to life whenever there's pounding surf. This is also the area where you're most likely to see endangered Hawaiian monk seals basking onshore.

Perched above the sea at 0.7 miles are the remains of 'Ohala Heiau, a place of worship to the harvest god Lono. A **fishing shrine** ahead on the left affords a good view south of basalt cliffs lined up all the way to Hana. Hala and ironwood encroaches the shoreline past the heiau. Round stones continue to mark the way across lava and a grassy clearing, fading briefly on the way over a rugged sea cliff. A dirt road comes in from

the right as the trail arrives at **Luahaloa**, a ledge with a small fishing shack. Inland, stands of ironwood heighten the beauty of the scenic last mile of clifftop walking to Kainalimu Bay. Stepping stones hasten the approach to the bay ahead, as the trail dips down a shrubby ravine to a quiet black cobble beach. Dirt roads lead another mile from here south to Hana, but if you're up for more adventure you could continue walking along the beach all the way to Hana Bay.

🛏 Sleeping

Fall asleep to the lullaby of the surf at one of the park's campsites on a shady lawn near the beach. It's a great place to camp but there is one caveat – this is the rainy side of the island, so it can get wet at any time. Plan accordingly. The park also has a dozen cabins that are extremely popular and usually book up months in advance. See p308 for details on permits, fees and reservations.

HANA & EAST MAUI

Where do Mauians go when they want to get away? Raw and rugged East Maui, the most isolated side of the island. Instead of golf courses and beach resorts, you'll see a place that's barely changed a speck for tourism. In time-honored Hana, you'll relearn the meaning of s-l-o-w, and talk story with people who actually take the time. Beyond Hana lie fantastical waterfalls, stop-for-a-dip swimming holes and off-the-grid farms. Don't miss an adventurous romp through the cowboy village of Kaupo.

Hana

POP 1800

Hana doesn't hit you with a bam. After the spectacular drive to get here, some visitors are surprised to find the town is a bit of a sleeper. Cows graze lazily in green pastures stretching up the hillsides. Neighbors chat over plate lunches at the beach. Even at Hana's legendary hotel, the emphasis is on relaxation.

Isolated as it is by that long and winding road, Hana stands as one of the most Hawaiian communities in the state. Folks share a strong sense of 'ohana, and if you listen closely you'll hear the words 'auntie' and 'uncle' a lot. There's a timeless rural character, and though 'Old Hawaii' is an oft-used cliché elsewhere, it's hard not to think of Hana in such terms. What Hana has to offer is best appreciated by those who stop and unwind. Visitors who stay awhile will experience an authentic slice of aloha.

History

It's hard to imagine little Hana as the epicenter of Maui but this village produced many of ancient Hawaii's most influential *ali'i* (chiefs). Hana's great 14th-century chief Pi'ilani marched from here to conquer rivals in Wailuku and Lahaina, and became the first leader of unified Maui. The paths he took became such vital routes that even today half of Maui's highways bear his name.

The landscape changed dramatically in 1849 when ex-whaler George Wilfong bought 60 acres of land to plant sugarcane. Hana became a booming plantation town, complete with a narrow-gauge railroad connecting the fields to the Hana Mill. In the 1940s Hana could no longer compete with larger sugar operations in Central Maui and the mill went bust.

Enter San Francisco businessman Paul Fagan, who purchased 14,000 acres in Hana in 1943. Starting with 300 Herefords, Fagan converted the canefields to ranch land. A few years later he opened a six-room hotel as a getaway resort for well-to-do friends and brought his minor-league baseball team, the San Francisco Seals, to Hana for spring training. That's when visiting sports journalists gave the town its moniker, 'Heavenly Hana.' Today, Hana Ranch remains the backbone of Hana's economy and its hillside pastures graze some 2000 head of cattle worked by Hawaiian *paniolo*.

🏖 Beaches

Hana Beach Park   BEACH

Some towns have a central plaza. Hana's pulse beats from this bayside park. Families come here to take the kids for a splash, to picnic on the black-sand beach and to strum their ukuleles with friends.

When water conditions are very calm, snorkeling and diving are good out in the direction of the light beacon. Currents can be strong, and snorkelers shouldn't venture beyond the beacon. Surfers head to **Waikoloa Beach**, at the northern end of the bay.

Kaihalulu (Red Sand) Beach   BEACH

A favored haunt of nude sunbathers, this hidden cove on the south side of Ka'uiki Head is a beauty in contrasts, with rich red

sand set against brilliant turquoise waters. The cove is partly protected by a lava outcrop, but currents can be powerful when the surf's up (Kaihalulu means 'roaring sea'). Water drains through a break on the left side, which should be avoided. Conditions are unpredictable, so swimmers should use caution at all times; your best chance of finding calm waters is in the morning.

The path to the beach starts across the lawn at the lower side of **Hana Community Center**, and continues as a steep 10-minute trail down to the cove. The route is narrow, with a mix of crumbly volcanic cinders and slippery clay that can be treacherous, particularly when wet; wear appropriate shoes. En route you'll pass an overgrown Japanese cemetery, a remnant of the sugarcane days.

👁 Sights

Hana Cultural Center   MUSEUM

(☎248-8622; www.hanaculturalcenter.org; 4974 Uakea Rd; adult/child under 12yr $3/free; ⊙10am-4pm Mon-Thu) Soak up a little local history at this down-home museum displaying Hawaiian artifacts, woodcarvings and hand-stitched quilts.

The museum grounds harbor still more cultural gems, including four authentically reconstructed **thatched hale**, which can be admired even outside opening hours. Here, too, is a three-bench **courthouse** (c 1871). Although it looks like a museum piece, this tiny court is still used on the first Tuesday of each month when a judge shows up to hear minor cases, sparing Hana residents with traffic tickets the need to drive all the way to Wailuku.

Hasegawa General Store   HISTORIC STORE

(☎248-8231; 5165 Hana Hwy; ⊙7am-7pm Mon-Sat, 8am-6pm Sun) For a century, this tin-roofed store operated by the Hasegawa family has been Hana's sole general store, its narrow aisles jam-packed with everything from fishing poles and machetes to soda pop and bags of poi. This icon of mom-and-pop shops is always crowded with locals picking up supplies, travelers stopping for snacks and sightseers buying 'I Survived the Hana Highway' T-shirts. It's a sight in itself.

Wananalua Congregational Church   HISTORIC CHURCH

(cnr Hana Hwy & Hau'oli St) This c 1838 building, which is on the National Register of Historic Places, has such hefty walls it resembles an ancient Norman church. Also noteworthy is

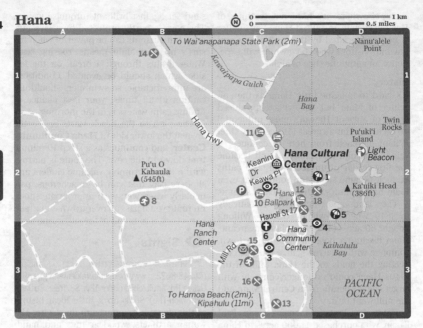

the little **cemetery** at the side, where the graves are randomly laid out rather than lined up in rows. Even at rest, Hana folks like things casual.

Hana Coast Gallery   GALLERY
(☏248-8638; 5031 Hana Hwy; ◷9am-5pm) Even if you're not shopping, visit this gallery at the north side of Hotel Hana-Maui to browse the museum-quality wooden bowls, paintings and Hawaiian featherwork.

🏃 Activities

In addition to what follows, Hotel Hana-Maui organises activities, including kayaking and snorkeling outings, for their guests.

Lyon's Hill   HIKING
Former Hana Ranch owner Paul Fagan often ended his day with a walk up Lyon's Hill to enjoy the view at sunset – and if you've got time you might want to follow in his footsteps. The big cross topping the hill, a memorial to Fagan, is Hana's most dominant landmark. The 15-minute trail up Lyon's Hill starts opposite Hotel Hana-Maui.

Hang Gliding Maui   ULTRALIGHT RIDE
(☏572-6557; www.hangglidingmaui.com; Hana Airport; 30/60min flight $150/250; ◷by appointment) For the ultimate bird's-eye view, hop

aboard a tandem ultralight aircraft with Hang Gliding Maui. Flight suits are provided; all you need is a little daring! And you actually get to fly this cool craft that looks like a motorcycle with wings – dual controls allow the passenger to take the reins once it's airborne.

Hana Ranch Stables   TRAIL RIDES
(☏270-5258; Mill Rd; 1hr ride $60) These stables, which book through Hotel Hana-Maui, give horseback riders the option to trot along Hana's black-lava coastline or head for the hills into green cattle pasture.

Honua Spa   DAY SPA
(☏270-5290; Hotel Hana-Maui, 5031 Hana Hwy; treatments $120-290) If the long drive to Hana has tightened you up, the posh Honua Spa can work off the kinks with *lomilomi* (traditional Hawaiian massage).

Luana Spa Retreat   DAY SPA
(☏248-8855; 5050 Uakea Rd; treatments $40-150) Massages and body treatments in a Hawaiian-style open-air setting.

🎉 Festivals & Events

TOP CHOICE East Maui Taro Festival   FESTIVAL
(www.tarofestival.org) Maui's most Hawaiian town throws its most Hawaiian party.

Hana

◎ **Top Sights**

Hana Cultural Center C2

◉ **Sights**

1 Hana Beach Park D2
2 Hana Coast Gallery..........................C2
3 Hasegawa General Store...................C3
4 Japanese Cemetery D3
5 Kaihalulu (Red Sand) Beach D2
6 Wananalua Congregational
   Church...C3

Activities, Courses & Tours

7 Hana Ranch Stables C3
   Honua Spa ....(see 10)
   Luana Spa Retreat.....................(see 12)
8 Lyon's Hill...B2

🛌 **Sleeping**

9 Hana Kai-Maui C2
10 Hotel Hana-Maui C2
11 Joe's Place C2
12 Luana Spa Retreat C2

🍽 **Eating**

13 Bruddah Hutt's BBQ...........................C3
14 Hana Fresh B1
15 Hana Ranch Restaurant
    Takeout...C3
16 Ono Farmers Market..........................C3
17 Pranee's Thai Food............................C2
18 Tutu's D2

Entertainment

Paniolo Bar ....(see 10)

If it's native, it's here – outrigger canoe races, a taro pancake breakfast, poi making, hula dancing and a big jamfest of top ukulele and slack key guitarists. Held on the last weekend in April, it's Hana at its finest; book accommodations well in advance.

MauiFest Hawaii　　　　FESTIVAL
(www.mauifest.net) Held on a weekend in October at Hana Bay, this big bash includes island-made films on everything from music to surfing, as well as hula dancing and big-time Hawaiian musicians like Brother Noland.

🛌 **Sleeping**

In addition to the following accommodation options, there are cabins and tent camping at Wai'anapanapa State Park, just to the north of Hana, and camping at 'Ohe'o Gulch, about 10 miles south.

TOP CHOICE **Hotel Hana-Maui**　　BOUTIQUE HOTEL **$$$**
(☎248-8211, 800-321-4262; www.hotelhanamaui.com; 5031 Hana Hwy; r from $325; @�l☑) This famed getaway hotel breathes tranquility. Everything's airy and open, rich with Hawaiian accents, from island art in the lobby to hand-stitched quilts on the beds. Rooms have a subdued elegance with bleached hardwood floors, ceiling fans and French doors opening to trellised patios. Delightfully absent are electronic gadgets – sans even alarm clocks! If that's not relaxing enough, there's complimentary yoga and a spa offering Hawaiian massage.

Luana Spa Retreat　　　　YURT **$$**
(☎248-8855; www.luanaspa.com; 5050 Uakea Rd; d $150) Just you, a yurt and a view. On a secluded hill overlooking Hana Bay, this back-to-nature charmer fuses outdoor living with indoor comforts. The yurt sports a well-equipped kitchenette and a stereo with Hawaiian music. Shower outdoors in a bamboo enclosure, enjoy spectacular stargazing over the bay – this is pure romance, Hana-style.

Hana Kai-Maui　　　　CONDO **$$**
(☎248-8426, 800-346-2772; www.hanakai.com; 1533 Uakea Rd; studio/1 bedroom from $185/210) Hana's only condo complex is just a stone's throw from Hana's hottest surfing beach. The units are nicely fitted and although the walls are thin, the sound of the surf drowns out neighboring chatter. For primo ocean views request a top-floor corner unit. Unlike most condo rentals on Maui, Hana Kai-Maui has no minimum stay.

Hana's Tradewinds Cottage　　COTTAGE **$$**
(☎248-8980; www.hanamauirentals.com; 135 Alalele Pl; d $175) In the midst of a tropical flower farm, this cozy cottage has space to accommodate a small family, though there's a $25 charge for each person beyond two. It's only a 10-minute drive to town but quiet enough to feel like you're in the boonies. Best of all, if you've been hiking all day you can come home and soak in your own private hot tub.

Joe's Place　　　　BUDGET HOTEL **$**
(☎248-7033; www.joesrentals.com; 4870 Uakea Rd; r with shared/private bathroom $50/60) Hana's only nod to the budget traveler offers a dozen basic rooms. The linoleum's worn, the decor dates back to the '60s, but there's a fresh

coat of paint on the walls and the place is kept sparkling clean. The shared facilities – a BBQ, den and kitchen – provide homey opportunities to exchange tips with fellow travelers after a day of sightseeing.

✖ Eating

Hana has just a couple of stores with limited grocery selections, so if you're staying awhile stock up in Kahului before heading down.

TOP CHOICE Bruddah Hutt's BBQ   BBQ $

(Hana Hwy; meals $8-14; ⊙10am-4pm) It's a bit like a neighborhood BBQ, with diners sitting on folding chairs under a canvas awning and an extended family cooking away over gas grills. Favorites are the barbecued chicken and the fish tacos. Expect a crowd at noon, and don't take the closing time too seriously as they shut down when the food runs out.

TOP CHOICE Pranee's Thai Food   THAI $

(✆248-8855; 5050 Uakea Rd; meals $8-10; ⊙11am-3pm Sun-Wed) Only a few lucky travelers stumble upon this hidden gem set back from the road opposite Hana Ballpark. It's just a simple outdoor cafe, but chef Pranee is famous in these parts for her fiery curries and fresh stir-fried dishes.

Hana Fresh   FARM STAND $

(www.hanafresh.org; 4590 Hana Hwy; lunch $6; ⊙8am-5:30pm Mon-Sat, 8am-2pm Sun) This roadside stand in front of the Hana Health center sells organic produce grown right on-site and healthy takeout plates featuring locally caught fish. If you happen to come by at lunchtime, it's the best deal in Hana.

Hana Ranch Restaurant Takeout   BURGER JOINT $

(✆248-8255; Hana Ranch Center, Mill Rd; meals $9-12; ⊙11am-4pm) It's just a takeout window but this is the busiest lunch spot in town. Everybody comes for the juicy burgers made of free-range Hana beef. The ocean view from the adjacent picnic tables goes down well, too.

Tutu's   SNACK BAR $

(✆248-8224; Hana Beach Park; snacks $5-10; ⊙8:30am-4pm) Hana Beach Park's fast-food grill serves the expected menu of shave ice, burgers and plate lunches. Grab a table on the beach and you've got yourself a picnic.

Ono Farmers Market   FARMERS MARKET $

(Hana Hwy; ⊙10am-6pm Sun-Thu) This is the place to pick up Kipahulu-grown coffee, jams and the most incredible array of fruit from papaya to rambutan.

Drinking & Entertainment

Paniolo Bar   BAR

(✆248-8211; Hotel Hana-Maui, 5031 Hana Hwy; ⊙11am-9pm) A classy place to enjoy a drink. This open-air bar at Hotel Hana-Maui has live Hawaiian music some evenings.

❶ Information

Hana closes up early. The sole gas station in all of East Maui is **Hana Gas** (✆248-7671; cnr Mill Rd & Hana Hwy; ⊙7am-8:30pm), so plan accordingly.

Hana Ranch Center (Mill Rd) is the commercial center of town. It has a **post office** (⊙8am-4:30pm Mon-Fri); a tiny **Bank of Hawaii** (✆248-8015; ⊙3-4:30pm Mon-Thu, to 6pm Fri) and **Hana Ranch Store** (✆248-8261; ⊙7am-7:30pm), which sells groceries and liquor. There's no ATM at the bank, but **Hasegawa General Store** (✆248-8231; 5165 Hana Hwy; ⊙7am-7pm Mon-Sat, 8am-6pm Sun) has one. For medical needs, **Hana Health** (✆248-8294; 4590 Hana Hwy; ⊙8:30am-5pm) is at the north side of town.

Hana to Kipahulu

The question on every day-tripper's mind: should we keep going beyond Hana? The answer: absolutely! The stretch ahead is arguably the most beautiful part of the entire drive. Less than an hour away lies magical 'Ohe'o Gulch, with its cascading waterfalls, swimming holes and awesome trails. Between the hairpin turns, one-lane bridges and drivers trying to take in all the sights, it's a slow-moving 10 miles, so sit back and enjoy the ride.

HANEO'O ROAD LOOP

It's well worth a detour off the highway to take this 1.5-mile loop, which skirts a scenic coastline. The turnoff onto Haneo'o Rd is just before the 50-mile marker.

At the base of a red cinder hill, less than 0.5 miles from the start of the loop, the chocolate-brown sands of Koki Beach attract local surfers. The offshore isle topped by a few coconut palms is 'Alau Island, a seabird sanctuary. Incidentally, those trees are a green refreshment stand of sorts, planted by Hana residents to provide themselves with drinking coconuts while fishing from the island.

A little further along is Hamoa Beach; its lovely gray sands are maintained by Ho-

DON'T MISS

LAULIMA FARMS

Pedal power takes on new meaning at **Laulima Farms** (snacks $3-7; ⊙10:30am-5pm; ✐), an off-the-grid fruit stand between the 40- and 41-mile markers. Here, customers take the seat on a stationary bike and rev up enough power to run the blender, juicing their own fruit smoothies. The rest of the operation is powered by solar panels and a generator using recycled vegetable oil. Everything sold here, from the hand-picked organic coffee to the GMO-free veggies, is homegrown. Refreshing in every way.

tel Hana-Maui, but it's open to all. Author James Michener once called it the only beach in the North Pacific that actually looked as if it belonged in the South Pacific. When the surf's up, surfers and boogie boarders flock to the waters, though be aware of rips. When seas are calm, swimming is good in the cove. Public access is down the steps just north of the hotel's bus-stop sign. Facilities include showers and restrooms.

WAILUA FALLS

As you continue south, you will see waterfalls cascading down the cliffs, orchids growing out of the rocks, and jungles of breadfruit and coconut trees. Hands-down the most spectacular sight along the way is Wailua Falls, which plunges a mighty 100ft just beyond the road. It appears 0.3 miles after the 45-mile marker but you won't need anyone to point this one out, as folks are always lined up along the roadside snapping photos.

'OHE'O GULCH

Fantastic falls, cool pools, paths galore. The indisputable highlight of the drive past Hana is 'Ohe'o Gulch, aka the Kipahulu section of Haleakalā National Park. Flip to the national park section (p400) for details on all the things to see and do, as well as entry fees and camping options.

Kipahulu

Less than a mile south of 'Ohe'o Gulch lies the little village of Kipahulu. It's hard to imagine, but this sedate community was once a bustling sugar-plantation town. After the mill shut down in 1922, most people left for jobs elsewhere. Today mixed among modest homes, organic farms and back-to-the-landers living off the grid are a scattering of exclusive estates, including the former home of famed aviator Charles Lindbergh.

⊙ Sights

Charles Lindbergh's Grave   GRAVESITE
Charles Lindbergh moved to remote Kipahulu in 1968. Although he relished the privacy he found here, he did occasionally emerge as a spokesperson for conservation issues. When he learned he had terminal cancer, he decided to forgo treatment on the mainland and came home to Maui to live out his final days.

Following his death in 1974, Lindbergh was buried in the graveyard of **Palapala Ho'omau Congregational Church**. The church (c 1864) is also notable for its window painting of a Polynesian Christ draped in the red-and-yellow feather capes that were reserved for Hawaii's highest chiefs.

Lindbergh's desire to be out of the public eye may still be at play; many visitors fail to find his grave. To get there, turn left at the sign for Maui Stables, which is 0.2 miles south of the 41-mile marker and then veer left after the stables. The church is 0.2 miles further. Lindbergh's grave, a simple granite slate laid upon lava stones, is in the yard behind the church. The inscription reads simply, '...If I take the wings of the morning, and dwell in the uttermost parts of the sea...C.A.L.'

Walk a minute or two past the graveyard to reach a hilltop vantage point with a fine **view** of the jagged Kipahulu coast – one look and you'll understand why Lindbergh was so taken by this area.

🏃 Activities

[TOP CHOICE] Maui Stables   HORSEBACK RIDING
(☎248-7799; www.mauistables.com; 3hr ride $150; ⊙departures 10am) Ride off into the wilderness with Maui Stables on horseback trips that mix breathtaking views with Hawaiian storytelling and chanting – a real cultural immersion experience led by Native Hawaiian cowboys. Among the sights along the way you'll see thundering waterfalls in the national park. The stable is between the 40- and 41-mile markers.

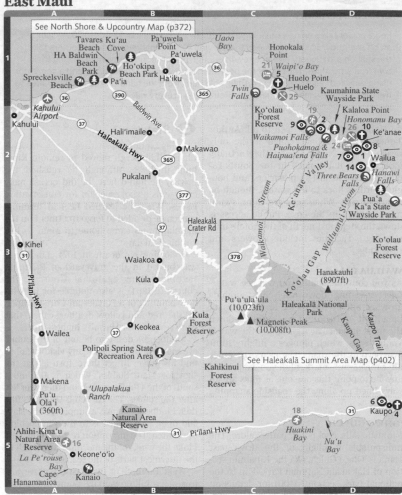

See North Shore & Upcountry Map (p372)

See Haleakalā Summit Area Map (p402)

Ono Organic Farms FARM TOUR

(☎248-7779; www.onofarms.com; 90min tours $35; ⏱1:30pm Mon-Fri) It's hard to imagine a farm as wildly exotic as Ono. The variety is amazing – scores of tropical fruits the likes of which you've never seen, spices, cocoa and coffee – all of it top rate and grown organically. The tour tops off with a generous spread of seasonal tastings. Kids under 10 are free; advance reservations required. The farm is on the inland side of the road just south of the national park.

Pi'ilani Highway

The untamed Pi'ilani Hwy travels 25 ruggedly scenic miles between Kipahulu and 'Ulupalakua Ranch as it skirts along the southern flank of Haleakalā.

Diehards will love this road, while the more timid may wonder what they've gotten themselves into in these lonesome boonies. Signs such as 'Motorists assume risk of damage due to presence of cattle' and 'Safe speed 10mph' give clues that this is not your typical highway.

The best way to approach the drive is with an early morning start, when the road is so quiet you'll feel like the last soul on earth. Pack something to eat and plenty to drink, and check your oil and spare tire before setting out. It's a long haul to civilisation if you break down – gas stations and other services are nonexistent between Hana and the Upcountry.

KAUPO

Near the 35-mile marker you'll reach Kaupo, a scattered community of *paniolo*, many of them fourth-generation ranch hands working at Kaupo Ranch. As the only lowlands on this section of coast, Kaupo was once heavily settled and is home to several ancient heiau and two 19th-century churches. However, don't expect a developed village in any sense of the word. The sole commercial venture on the entire road is **Kaupo Store** (☎248-8054; ☉10am-5pm Mon-Sat), which sells snacks and drinks and is worth popping inside just to see the vintage displays lining the shelves – it's like stepping back to your grandmother's days.

Kaupo's prettiest sight, the whitewashed **Hui Aloha Church** (1859), sits above the black-sand **Mokulau Beach**, an ancient surfing site.

KAUPO TO 'ULUPALAKUA RANCH

Past Kaupo village, you'll be rewarded with striking views of **Kaupo Gap**, the southern opening in the rim of majestic Haleakalā. Near the 31-mile marker a short 4WD road runs down to **Nu'u Bay**, favored by locals for fishing and swimming; if you're tempted to hit the water, stay close to shore, as riptides inhabit the open ocean beyond.

Just east of the 30-mile marker you'll see two gateposts that mark the path to dramatic **Huakini Bay**. Park at the side of the highway and walk down the rutted dirt drive. It takes just a couple of minutes to reach this rock-strewn beach whipped by violent surf. After the 29-mile marker, keep an eye out for a natural lava **sea arch** that's visible from the road.

At the 19-mile marker the road crosses a vast **lava flow** dating from 1790, Haleakalā's last-gasp eruption. This flow, part of the Kanaio Natural Area Reserve, is the same one that covers the La Pe'rouse Bay area. It's still black and barren all the way down to the sea.

Just offshore is Kaho'olawe and on a clear day you can even see the Big Island popping

The road winds like a drunken cowboy but most of it is paved. The trickiest section is around Kaupo, where the road is rutted. Depending on when it was last graded, you can usually make it in a regular car, though it may rattle your bones a bit. But after hard rains, streams flow over the road, making passage difficult, if not dangerous.

Flash floods occasionally wash away portions of the road, closing down the highway until it's repaired. The **Kipahulu Visitor Center** (☎248-7375) at 'Ohe'o Gulch can tell you whether or not the road is open.

◉ **Sights**
	Charles Lindbergh's Grave	(see 12)
1	Ching's Pond	D2
2	Garden of Eden Arboretum	D2
3	Hana Lava Tube	E3
4	Hui Aloha Church	D5
	Kahanu Garden	(see 13)
5	Kaulanapueo Church	C1
6	Kaupo Store	D5
7	Ke'anae Arboretum	D2
8	Ke'anae Peninsula Lookout	D2
9	Ko'olau Ditch	C2
10	Lanakila 'Ihi'ihi o Iehova Ona Kaua (Ke'anae Congregational Church)	D2
11	Ono Organic Farms	E4
12	Palapala Ho'omau Congregational Church	E4
13	Pi'ilanihale Heiau	E3
14	Wailua Valley State Wayside	D2

Activities, Courses & Tours
15	Bamboo Forest	E4
16	Makena Stables	A5
17	Maui Stables	E4
18	Sea Arch	C5
19	Waikamoi Nature Trail	D2

😴 **Sleeping**
20	Kipahulu Campground	E4
21	Tea House	C1
22	Wai'anapanapa Cabins	F3
23	Wai'anapanapa Campground	F3
24	YMCA Camp Ke'anae	D2

✖ **Eating**
	Café Romantica	(see 28)
25	Huelo Lookout	C1
	Jen's Thai Food	(see 28)
26	Ke'anae Landing Fruit Stand	D2
27	Laulima Farms	E4
28	Up In Smoke	E3

its head up above the clouds. It's such a wide-angle view that the ocean horizon is noticeably curved. You'll wonder how anyone could ever have thought the world was flat!

As you approach 'Ulupalakua Ranch, groves of fragrant eucalyptus trees replace the drier, scrubbier terrain and you find yourself back in civilisation at Tedeschi Vineyards. Cheers!

HALEAKALĀ NATIONAL PARK

With its eye-popping moonscapes, Haleakalā's like no other place in the national park system. Whether you come for sunrise, or come at the height of the day, by all means get yourself here. You simply haven't seen Maui, or at least looked into its soul, until you've made the trek up to the top of this awe-inspiring mountain. Its appeal is magnetic: ancient Hawaiians came to the summit to worship, Mark Twain praised its healing solitude, and visitors of all walks still find mystical experiences here.

Lookouts on the crater's rim provide breathtaking views of Haleakalā's volcanic surface. But there's a lot more to Haleakalā than just peering down from on high. With a pair of hiking boots you can walk down into the crater on crunchy trails that meander around cinder cones. Or saddle up and mosey down onto the crater floor on horseback. For the ultimate adventure, bring a sleeping bag and spend the night.

No food or drinks are sold anywhere in the park, though there are drinking fountains at the visitor centers. Be sure to bring something to eat if you're going up for the sunrise; you don't want a growling stomach to send you back down the mountain before you've had a chance to explore the sights.

Summit Area

Haleakalā's astonishing volcanic landscape so resembles a lunar surface that astronauts practiced mock lunar walks here before landing on the moon.

Often referred to as the world's largest dormant volcano, the floor of Haleakalā measures a colossal 7.5 miles wide, 2.5 miles long and 3000ft deep – large enough to swallow the island of Manhattan. In its prime, Haleakalā reached a height of 12,000ft before water erosion carved out two large river valleys that eventually eroded into each other to form Haleakalā crater. Technically, as geologists like to point out, it's not a true 'crater,' but to sightseers that's all nitpicking. Valley or crater, it's a phenomenal sight like no other in the US National Park system.

For a real-time view of the summit check out the crater webcam at Haleakalā Crater Live Camera (http://koa.ifa.hawaii.edu/crater).

◉ Sights

Hosmer Grove

Hosmer Grove, off a side road just after the park's entrance booth, is primarily visited by campers and picnickers, but it's well worth a stop for its half-mile loop trail (p406) that begins at the edge of the campground. The whole area is sweetened with the scent of eucalyptus and alive with the red flashes and calls of native birds. Drive slowly on the road in, as this is one of the top places to spot nene.

Waikamoi Preserve

This windswept native cloud forest supports one of the rarest ecosystems on earth. Managed by the Nature Conservancy, the 5230-acre Waikamoi Preserve provides the last stronghold for 76 species of native plants and forest birds. You're apt to spot the 'i'iwi (scarlet Hawaiian honeycreeper), the 'apapane (bright red Hawaiian honeycreeper) and the yellow-green 'amakihi (yellow-green Hawaiian honeycreeper) flying among the preserve's koa and ohia trees. You might also catch a glimpse of the yellow-green 'alauahio (Maui creeper) or the 'akohekohe (Maui parrotbill), both endangered species found nowhere else on earth.

The only way to see the preserve is to join a **guided hike**. The National Park Service offers free three-hour, 3-mile guided hikes that enter the preserve from Hosmer Grove campground at 9am on Monday and Thursday. It's best to make reservations, which you can do up to one week in advance by calling ✆572-4459. Expect wet conditions; bring rain gear. The hike is rated moderately strenuous.

Park Headquarters Visitor Center

(✆572-4400; ◷8am-4pm) This is the place to get brochures, camping permits and the skinny on ranger talks and activities being offered during your visit. And if you need to take care of earthly needs, this is a convenient stop for restrooms and one of only two places in the park where you'll find drinking fountains. If you're going hiking, make sure your water bottles are filled before leaving.

Keep an eye out for nene wandering around the grounds, as they're frequent visitors here. Also note that these endangered birds are much too friendly for their own good; do not feed them, and be careful when driving out of the parking lot – most nene deaths are the result of being hit by cars.

Leleiwi Overlook

A stop at Leleiwi Overlook (8840ft), midway between the Park Headquarters Visitor Center and the summit, offers your first look into the crater, and gives you a unique angle on the ever-changing clouds climbing up the mountain. You can literally watch the weather form at your feet. From the parking lot, it's a five-minute walk across a gravel trail to the overlook. En route you'll get a fine view of the West Maui Mountains and the isthmus connecting the two sides of Maui.

Kalahaku Overlook

Whatever you do, don't miss this one. Kalahaku Overlook (9324ft), 0.8 miles beyond Leleiwi Overlook, offers a bird's-eye view of the crater floor and the ant-size hikers on the trails snaking around the cinder cones below. The observation deck also provides an ideal angle for viewing both the Ko'olau Gap and the Kaupo Gap on Haleakalā's crater rim and on a clear day you'll be able to see the Big Island's Mauna Loa and Mauna Kea, Hawaii's highest mountaintops. It all adds up to one heck of a view.

Between May and October the 'ua'u (Hawaiian dark-rumped petrel) nests in burrows in the cliff face. Even if you don't spot the birds, you can often hear the parents and chicks making their unique clucking sounds. Of the fewer than 2000 'ua'u remaining today, most nest at Haleakalā, where they lay just one egg a year. These seabirds were thought to be extinct until re-sighted here in the 1970s.

A short **trail** below the parking lot leads to a field of native silversword ('ahinahina), ranging from seedlings to mature plants.

Haleakalā Visitor Center

(◷sunrise-3pm) Perched on the rim of the crater, at a 9745ft elevation, the visitor center is the park's main viewing spot. And what a magical sight awaits. The ever-changing interplay of sun, shadow and clouds reflecting on the crater floor creates a mesmerising dance of light and color.

The center has displays on Haleakalā's volcanic origins and details on what you're seeing on the crater floor 3000ft below. Nature talks are given, books on Hawaiian culture and the environment are for sale, and there are also drinking fountains and restrooms here.

Haleakalā Summit Area

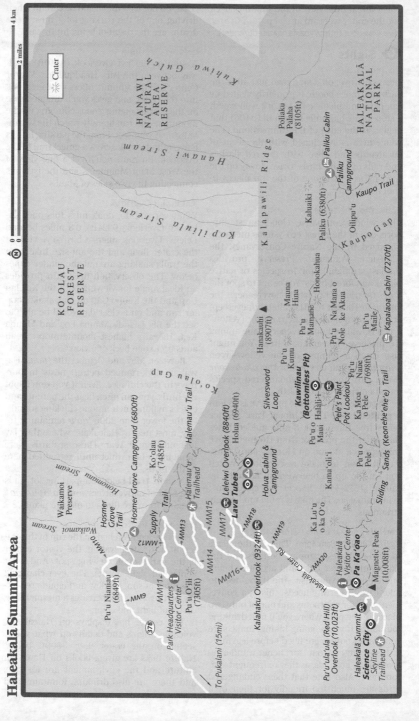

2 miles
4 km

N

Crater

HANAWI NATURAL AREA RESERVE

Kuhiwa Gulch

Hanawi Stream

Kopiliula Stream

KO'OLAU FOREST RESERVE

Kalapawili Ridge

HALEAKALĀ NATIONAL PARK

Poliaku Palaha (8105ft)

Paliku Cabin

Paliku (6380ft)

Paliku Campground

Kaupo Trail

Kaluaiki

Honokahua

Oilipu'u

Kaupo Gap

Mauna Hina

Pu'u Mamane

Pu'u Na Mana o ke Akua

Kapalaoa Cabin (7270ft)

Hanakauhi (8907ft)

Pu'u Kumu

Pu'u Maile

Ko'olau Gap

Silversword Loop

Kawilinau (Bottomless Pit)

Pele's Paint Pot Lookout

Pu'u o Maui Halali'i

Pu'u Naue (7698ft)

Ka Moa o Pele

Na Mana o ke Akua Trail (Keonehe'ehe'e)

Hosmer Grove Campground (6800ft)

Honomanu Stream

Waikamoi Preserve

Ko'olau (7485ft)

Halemau'u Trail

Halemau'u Trailhead

Leleiwi Overlook (8840ft)

Holua (6940ft)

Holua Cabin & Campground

Lava Tubes

MM18

MM19

Pu'u o Pele

Ka Lu'u o ka O'o

Kama'oli'i

Sliding Sands

Waikamoi Stream

Hosmer Grove Trail

Supply Trail

MM12

MM13

MM14

MM15

MM16

MM17

Kalahaku Overlook (9324ft)

Haleakalā Crater Rd

MM20

Haleakalā Visitor Center

Pa Ka'oao

Magnetic Peak (10,008ft)

Pu'u Nianiau (6849ft)

MM11

MM10

MM9

378

Park Headquarters Visitor Center

Pu'u O'ili (7305ft)

To Pukalani (15mi)

Pu'u'ula (Red Hill) Overlook (10,023ft)

Haleakalā Summit

Science City

Skyline Trailhead

To Pukalani

By dawn the parking lot fills with people coming to see the sunrise show (see the boxed text, p404), and it pretty much stays packed all day. Leave the crowds behind by taking the 10-minute hike up Pa Ka'oao (White Hill), which begins at the east side of the visitor center and provides stunning crater views.

Pu'u'ula'ula (Red Hill) Overlook

Congratulations! The 37-mile drive from sea level to the 10,023ft summit of Haleakalā you've just completed is the highest elevation gain in the shortest distance anywhere in the world. You've passed through as many ecological zones as you would have on a drive from central Mexico to Alaska.

Perched atop Pu'u'ula'ula, Maui's highest point, the **summit building** provides a top-of-the-world panorama from its wraparound windows. On a clear day you can see the Big Island, Lana'i, Moloka'i and even O'ahu. When the light's right, the colors of the crater from the summit are nothing short of spectacular, with an array of grays, greens, reds and browns. A **silversword garden** has been planted at the overlook, making this the best place to see these luminous silver-leafed plants in various stages of growth.

Magnetic Peak

The iron-rich cinders in this flat-top hill, which lies immediately southeast of the summit building, in the direction of the Big Island, pack enough magnetism to play havoc with your compass. Modest looking as it is, it's also – at 10,008ft – the second-highest point on Maui.

Science City

On the Big Island's Mauna Kea, scientists study the night sky. Here at Haleakalā, appropriately enough, they study the sun. Science City, just beyond the summit, is off-limits to visitors. It's under the jurisdiction of the University of Hawai'i, which owns some of the domes and leases other land for a variety of private and government research projects.

US Department of Defense–related projects here include laser technology associated with the 'Star Wars' project, satellite tracking and identification, and a deep-space surveillance system. The Air Force's Maui Space Surveillance System (MSSS), an electro-optical state-of-the-art facility used for satellite tracking, is the largest telescope anywhere in use by the Department of Defense. The system is capable of identifying a basketball-size object in space 22,000 miles away.

The Faulkes Telescope, a joint University of Hawai'i and UK operation, is dedicated to raising students' interest in astronomy, with a fully robotic telescope that can be controlled in real time via the internet from classrooms in both Britain and Hawaii.

 Activities

For information on horseback rides into the crater, see Pony Express (p382) earlier in this chapter.

Ranger Programs

Be sure to stop at the Park Headquarters Visitor Center to see what's happening. All park programs offered by the National Park Service are free. **Ranger talks** on Haleakalā's unique natural history and Hawaiian culture are given at the Haleakalā Visitor Center and the Pu'u'ula'ula (Red Hill) Overlook; the schedule varies, but they typically take place between 7am and 1pm, and there are usually half a dozen daily. On clear nights, stargazing is phenomenal on the mountain. Hour-long evening **stargazing programs** are offered between May and September at Hosmer Grove, typically on Friday and Saturday at 7pm.

Hiking

To really experience this amazing place, strap on a pair of hiking boots and step into the belly of the beast. There's something for everyone, from short nature walks ideal for families to hardy multiday treks. Those who hike the crater will discover a completely different angle on Haleakalā's lunar landscape. Instead of peering down from the rim, you'll be craning your neck skyward at the walls and towering cinder cones. It's a world away from anyplace else. The crater is remarkably still. Cinders crunching underfoot are the only sound, except for the occasional bark of an Hawaiian owl or honking of a friendly nene. Whatever trail you take, give yourself extra time to absorb the wonder of it all.

To protect Haleakalā's fragile environment, keep to established trails and don't be tempted off them, even for well-beaten shortcuts through switchbacks.

Be prepared. Hikers without proper clothing risk hypothermia. The climate changes radically as you cross the crater floor – in the 4 miles between Kapalaoa and Paliku cabins, rainfall varies from an annual average of

DON'T MISS

THE SUNRISE EXPERIENCE

'Haleakalā' means 'House of the Sun.' So it's no surprise that since the time of the first Hawaiians, people have been making pilgrimages up to Haleakalā to watch the sun rise. It's an experience that borders on the mystical. Mark Twain called it the 'sublimest spectacle' he'd ever seen.

Plan to arrive at the summit an hour before the actual sunrise; that will guarantee you a parking space and time to see the world awaken. Around that point the night sky begins to lighten and turn purple-blue, and the stars fade away. Ethereal silhouettes of the mountain ridges appear. The gentlest colors show up in the fragile moments just before dawn. The undersides of the clouds lighten first, accenting the night sky with pale silvery slivers and streaks of pink.

About 20 minutes before sunrise, the light intensifies on the horizon in bright oranges and reds. Turn around for a look at Science City, whose domes turn a blazing pink. For the grand finale, the moment when the disk of the sun appears, all of Haleakalā takes on a fiery glow. It feels like you're watching the earth awaken.

Come prepared – it's going to be c-o-l-d! Temperatures hovering around freezing and a biting wind are the norm at dawn and there's often a frosty ice on the top layer of cinders. If you don't have a winter jacket or sleeping bag to wrap yourself in, bring a warm blanket from your hotel. However many layers of clothes you can muster, it won't be too many.

The best photo opportunities occur before the sun rises. Every morning is different, but once the sun is up, the silvery lines and the subtleties disappear.

One caveat: a rained-out sunrise is an anticlimactic event after tearing yourself out of bed in the middle of the night to drive up a pitch-dark mountain. So check the **weather report** (☎866-944-5025) the night before to calculate your odds of having clear skies.

If you just can't get up that early, sunsets at Haleakalā have inspired poets as well.

12in to 300in! Take warm clothing in layers, sunscreen, rain gear, a first-aid kit and lots of water.

TOP CHOICE | **Sliding Sands**
(Keonehe'ehe'e) Trail   HIKING

Sliding Sands (Keonehe'ehe'e) Trail starts at the south side of the Haleakalā Visitor Center at 9740ft and winds down to the crater floor. If you take this hike after catching the sunrise, you'll walk directly into a gentle warmish wind and the rays of the sunshine.

Even if you're just coming to the summit for a peek at the incredible view, consider taking a short hike down Sliding Sands Trail. Just walking down 20 to 30 minutes will reward you with an into-the-crater experience and fab photo opportunities; but keep in mind that the climb out takes nearly twice as long as the walk down.

The full trail leads 9.2 miles to the Paliku cabin and Paliku campground, passing the Kapalaoa cabin at 5.6 miles after roughly four hours.

The first 6 miles of the trail follow the south wall. There are great views on the way down, but almost no vegetation. About 2 miles down, a steep spur trail leads past silversword plants to **Ka Luʻu o ka Oʻo** cinder cone, about 0.5 miles north. Four miles down, after an elevation drop of 2500ft, Sliding Sands Trail intersects with a spur trail that leads north into the cinder desert; that spur connects with the Halemauʻu Trail after 1.5 miles.

Continuing on the Sliding Sands Trail, as you head across the crater floor for 2 miles to Kapalaoa, verdant ridges rise on your right, giving way to ropy *pahoehoe* (smooth-flowing lava). From Kapalaoa cabin to Paliku, the descent is gentle and the vegetation gradually increases. Paliku (6380ft) is beneath a sheer cliff at the eastern end of the crater. In contrast to the crater's barren western end, this area receives heavy rainfall, with ohia forests climbing the slopes.

Halemauʻu Trail   HIKING

Hiking the Halemauʻu Trail down to the Holua campground and back – 7.4 miles return – can make a memorable day hike. Just be sure to start early before the afternoon clouds roll in and visibility vanishes. The first mile of this trail is fairly level and offers a fine view of the crater with Koʻolau Gap to the east. It then descends 1400ft along 2 miles of switchbacks to the crater floor and on to the Holua campground.

At 6940ft, Holua is one of the lowest areas along this trail, and you'll see impressive views of the crater walls rising a few thousand feet to the west. Large lava tubes here are worth exploring: one's up a short, steep cliff behind the Holua cabin, and another's a 15-minute detour further along the trail. According to legend, the latter tube was a spiritual place where mothers brought the *piko* (umbilical cords) of their newborns to gather mana for the child.

If you have the energy, push on another mile to reach colorful cinder cones, and make a short detour onto the Silversword Loop, where you'll see these unique plants in various stages of growth. In summer, you might even see silverswords in flower, their tall stalks ablaze with hundreds of maroon and yellow blossoms. But be careful – half of all silverswords today are trampled to death as seedlings, mostly by hikers who wander off trails and unknowingly step on their shallow roots. The trail continues another 6.3 miles to the Paliku cabin.

The trailhead to Halemau'u is 3.5 miles above the Park Headquarters Visitor Center and about 6 miles below the Haleakalā Visitor Center. There's a fair chance you'll see nene in the parking lot. If you're camping at Hosmer Grove, you can take the little-known, unexciting Supply Trail instead, joining the Halemau'u Trail at the crater rim after 2.5 miles.

Cinder Desert   HIKING

A spur trail connects Sliding Sands Trail, just west of Kapalaoa cabin, with the Halemau'u Trail, about midway between the Paliku and Holua campgrounds. This spur trail takes in many of the crater's most kaleidoscopic cinder cones, and the viewing angle changes with every step. The trail ends up on the north side of the cinder desert near Kawilinau, also known as the Bottomless Pit. Legends say the pit leads down to the sea, though the National Park Service says it's just 65ft deep. Truth be told, there's not much to see, as you can't really get a good look down the narrow shaft. The real prize is the nearby short loop trail, where you can sit for awhile in the saddle of Pele's Paint Pot Lookout, the crater's most brilliant vantage point.

Kaupo Trail   HIKING

The most extreme of Haleakalā's hikes is the Kaupo Trail, which starts at the Paliku campground and leads down to Kaupo on the southern coast. Be prepared for ankle-twisting conditions, blistered feet, intense tropical sun and torrential showers. Your knees will take a pounding as you descend more than 6100ft over 8.6 miles.

The first 3.7 miles of the trail drop 2500ft in elevation before reaching the park boundary. It's a steep rocky trail through rough lava and brushland, with short switchbacks alternating with level stretches. From here you'll be rewarded with spectacular ocean views.

The last 4.9 miles pass through Kaupo Ranch property on a rough jeep trail as it descends to the bottom of Kaupo Gap, exiting into a forest where feral pigs snuffle about. Here trail markings become vague, but once you reach the dirt road, it's another 1.5 miles to the end at the east side of the Kaupo Store.

The 'village' of Kaupo is a long way from anywhere, with light traffic. Still, what traffic there is – sightseers braving the circle-island road and locals in pickup trucks – moves slowly enough along Kaupo's rough road to start conversation, so you'll probably manage

---

HIKING BY THE CLOCK

How much time do you have? Pick the ideal day hike to suit your schedule.

Ten hours: If you're in good physical shape and can get an early start, the 11.2-mile hike that starts down Sliding Sands Trail and returns via Halemau'u Trail is the prize. Crossing the crater floor, it takes in a cinder desert and a cloud forest, showcasing the park's diversity.

Three hours: For a half-day experience that offers a generous sampling of crater sights, follow Sliding Sands Trail down to the Ka Lu'u o ka O'o cinder cone and back. The easy bit? It takes just one hour to get down. The workout? You've got yourself a 1500ft elevation rise, making the return a strenuous two-hour climb.

One hour: See Haleakalā's green side along the forested Hosmer Grove Trail.

a lift. If you have to walk the final stretch, it's 8 miles to the 'Ohe'o Gulch campground.

Because this is such a strenuous and remote trail, it's not advisable to hike it alone. No camping is allowed on Kaupo Ranch property, so most hikers spend the night at the Paliku campground and then get an early start.

TOP CHOICE Hosmer Grove Trail   HIKING

Those looking for a little greenery after hiking the crater will love this shaded woodland walk, and birders wing it here as well.

The half-mile loop trail starts at Hosmer Grove campground, 0.75 miles south of Park Headquarters Visitor Center, in a forest of lofty trees. The exotics in Hosmer Grove were introduced in 1910 in an effort to develop a lumber industry in Hawaii. Species include fragrant incense cedar, Norway spruce, Douglas fir, eucalyptus and various pines. Although the trees adapted well enough to grow, they didn't grow fast enough at these elevations to make tree harvesting practical. Thanks to this failure, today there's a park here instead.

After the forest, the trail moves into native shrubland, with 'akala (Hawaiian raspberry), kilau ferns and sandalwood. The 'ohelo, a berry sacred to the volcano goddess Pele, and the pukiawe, which has red and white berries and evergreen leaves, are favored by nene.

Listen for the calls of the native 'i'iwi and 'apapane, both sparrow-size birds with bright red feathers that are fairly common here. The 'i'iwi has a loud, squeaking call, orange legs and a curved salmon-colored bill. The 'apapane, a fast-moving bird with a black bill, black legs and a white undertail, feeds on the nectar of ohia flowers, and its wings make a distinctive whirring sound.

Skyline Trail   HIKING

This otherworldly trail, which rides the precipitous crater-dotted spine of Haleakalā, begins just beyond Haleakalā's summit at a lofty elevation of 9750ft and leads down to the campground at Polipoli Spring State Recreation Area (p383) at 6200ft. It covers a distance of 8.5 miles and takes about four hours to walk. Get an early start to enjoy the views before clouds take over.

To get to the trailhead, go past Pu'u'ula'ula (Red Hill) Overlook and take the road to the left just before Science City. The road, which passes over a cattle grate, is signposted not for public use, but continue and you'll soon find a Na Ala Hele sign marking the trailhead.

The Skyline Trail starts in barren open terrain of volcanic cinder, a moon walk that passes more than a dozen cinder cones and craters. The first mile is rough lava rock. After three crunchy miles, it reaches the tree line (8500ft) and enters native mamane forest. In winter mamane is heavy with flowers that look like yellow sweetpea blossoms. There's solitude on this walk. If the clouds treat you kindly, you'll have broad views all the way between the barren summit and the dense cloud forest. Eventually the trail meets the Polipoli access road, where you can either walk to the paved road in about 4 miles, or continue via the Haleakalā Ridge Trail and Polipoli Trail to the campground. If you prefer treads to hiking boots, the Skyline Trail is also an exhilarating adventure on a mountain bike.

Cycling & Mountain Biking

For experienced mountain bikers Haleakalā's Skyline Trail is the ultimate wild ride, plunging some 3000ft in the first 6 miles with a breathtaking 10% grade. The trail starts out looking like the moon and ends up in a cloud forest of redwood and cypress trees that resembles California's northern coast. The route follows a rough 4WD road that's used to maintain Polipoli Spring State Recreation Area. Equip yourself with full pads, use a proper downhill bike and watch that you don't run any hikers down. Crater Cycles Hawaii (☎893-2020; www.cratercycleshawaii .com; 96 Amala Pl, Kahului; downhill bikes per day $85; ◷9am-5pm Mon-Thu, 10am-5pm Sat) rents out quality full-suspension downhill bikes, complete with helmet, pads and a roof rack.

One-way downhill group cycle tours are no longer allowed to cycle within the park (see the boxed text, p408), though they do offer tours that begin pedaling just below park boundaries. A better bet is to forgo the pack and instead rent a bicycle and head here on your own. Individual cyclists are allowed to pedal their way up and down the mountain without restriction. Up is a real quad buster. If you prefer to do it just downhill, most bicycle rental companies listed in this book also rent out racks for transporting the bike.

🛏 Sleeping

To spend the night at Haleakalā is to commune with nature. The camping options are primitive: no electricity or showers.

Backcountry campgrounds have pit toilets and limited nonpotable water supplies that are shared with the crater cabins. Water needs to be filtered or chemically treated before drinking; conserve it, as water tanks occasionally run dry. Fires are allowed only in grills, and in times of drought are prohibited entirely. You must pack in all your food and supplies and pack out all your trash. Keep in mind that sleeping at an elevation of 7000ft isn't like camping on the beach. You need to be well equipped – without a waterproof tent and a winter-rated sleeping bag, forget it.

Camping

HOSMER GROVE CAMPGROUND

Hosmer Grove is the only drive-up campground in the summit area of the park. Surrounded by lofty trees and adjacent to one of Maui's best birding trails, this campground at an elevation of 6800ft tends to be cloudy but a covered picnic pavilion offers shelter if it starts to rain. Facilities include grills, toilets and running water.

Camping is free on a first-come, first-served basis. No permit is required, though there's a three-day camping limit per month. The campground is just a small field, with no individual campsites, so it can get supercrowded. It's busier in summer than in winter and is often full on holiday weekends. The campground is just after the park entrance booth. And here's a bonus: you're close to the summit, so it's a cinch getting up for the sunrise.

BACKCOUNTRY CAMPING

For hikers, two backcountry campgrounds lie on the floor of Haleakalā Crater. The easiest to reach is at Holua, 3.7 miles down the Halemau'u Trail. The other is at Paliku, below a rain-forest ridge at the end of Halemau'u Trail. Weather can be unpredictable at both. Holua is typically dry with clouds rolling in during the late afternoon. Paliku is in a grassy meadow, with skies overhead alternating between stormy and sunny. Wasps are present at both campsites, so take precautions if you're allergic to stings.

Permits (free) are required for crater camping. They're issued at the Park Headquarters Visitor Center on a first-come, first-served basis between 8am and 3pm on the day of the hike. Camping is limited to three nights in the crater each month, with no more than two consecutive nights

at either campground. Only 25 campers are allowed at each site, so permits can go quickly when large parties show up, a situation more likely to occur in summer.

Cabins

Three rustic cabins (per cabin with 1-12 people $75) dating from the 1930s lie along trails on the crater floor at Holua, Kapalaoa and Paliku. Each has a wood-burning stove, two propane burners, 12 bunks with sleeping pads (but no bedding), pit toilets, and a limited supply of water and firewood.

Hiking distances to the cabins from the crater rim range from 4 to 9 miles. The driest conditions are at Kapalaoa, in the middle of the cinder desert off Sliding Sands Trail. Those craving lush rain forest will find Paliku serene. Holua has unparalleled sunrise views. There's a three-day limit per month, with no more than two consecutive nights in any cabin. Each cabin is rented to only one group at a time.

The cabins can be reserved up to 90 days in advance, online at https://fhnp.org/wcr or by calling ☏572-4400 between 1pm and 3pm Monday to Friday.

Even those without reservations have a shot, as cancellations sometimes occur at the last minute. You can check for vacancies in person at the Park Headquarters Visitor Center between 8am and 3pm. As an added boon, if you get a vacancy within three weeks of your camping date, the cabin fee drops to $60 a day.

ℹ Information

ENTRANCE FEES & PASSES Haleakalā National Park (www.nps.gov/hale; 3-day entry pass per car $10, per person on foot, bicycle or motorcycle $5) The park never closes, and the pay booth at the park entrance opens before dawn to welcome the sunrise crowd. If you're planning several trips, or are going on to the Big Island, consider buying an annual pass ($25), which covers all of Hawaii's national parks.

DANGERS & ANNOYANCES The weather at Haleakalā can change suddenly from dry, hot conditions to cold, windswept rain. Although the general rule is sunny in the morning and cloudy in the afternoon, fog and clouds can blow in at any time, and the windchill can quickly drop below freezing. Dress in layers and bring extra clothing; don't even think of coming up without a jacket.

At 10,000ft the air is relatively thin, so expect to tire more quickly, particularly if you're hiking. The higher elevation also means that sunburn is more likely.

For years downhill bike tours were heavily promoted. A van ride to Haleakalā summit for the sunrise was followed by a bicycle cruise 38 miles down the 10,000ft mountain, snaking along winding roads clear to the coast. What a rush. And no need to be in shape, since there's no pedaling involved.

But it became *too* popular. Some mornings as many as 1000 cyclists huddled at the crater overlooks jostling for space to watch the sun rise. Then, group by group, they'd mount their bikes and take off.

Residents using Upcountry roads were forced to slow to a crawl, waiting for a gaggle of cyclists and their support van to pull over to let them pass. The narrow roads have few shoulders, so the wait was often a long one.

Then there were the accidents. Sometimes the weather was bad, with fog cutting visibility to near zero. Ambulance calls for injured cyclists became weekly occurrences. After two cyclist fatalities in 2007, Haleakalā National Park suspended all bicycle tour operations. A compromise now lets the van tours come up for the sunrise then drive back down to the park's boundary, where the trailers are unpacked and riders begin their cycle to the coast. However, another fatality in 2010 has spurred the county to consider restrictions of its own. So, for downhill bike tours, the road ahead remains a bumpy one.

MAPS National Geographic's *Haleakalā National Park Trails Illustrated Map* shows elevations and other useful features on the hiking routes. It's waterproof and can be purchased at Haleakalā Visitor Center for $12.

ⓘ Getting There & Around

Getting to Haleakalā is half the fun. Snaking up the mountain it's sometimes hard to tell if you're in an airplane or a car – all of Maui opens up below you, with sugarcane and pineapple fields creating a patchwork of green on the valley floor. The highway ribbons back and forth, and in some places as many as four or five switchbacks are in view all at once.

Haleakalā Crater Rd (Hwy 378) climbs 11 miles from Hwy 377 near Kula up to the park entrance, then another 10 miles to Haleakalā summit. It's a good paved road all the way, but it's steep and winding. You don't want to rush it, especially when it's dark or foggy. And watch out for cattle wandering across the road.

The drive to the summit takes about 1½ hours from Pa'ia or Kahului, two hours from Kihei. If you need gas, fill up the night before, as there are no services on Haleakalā Crater Rd. On your way back downhill, be sure to put your car in low gear to avoid burning out your brakes.

Kipahulu Area ('Ohe'o Gulch)

There's more to Haleakalā National Park than the cindery summit. The park extends down the southeast face of the volcano all the way to the sea. The crowning glory of its Kipahulu section is 'Ohe'o Gulch with its magnificent waterfalls and wide pools, each one tumbling into the next one below. When the sun shines, these cool glistening pools make the most inviting swimming holes on Maui.

Because there's no access between the Kipahulu section of the park and the main Haleakalā summit area, you'll be visiting the two sections of the park on different days. So hold on to your ticket – it's good for both sections of the park.

◉ Sights & Activities

Lower Pools   HIKING, POOLS
First thing on your agenda should be the Kuloa Point Trail, a half-mile loop that runs from the visitor center down to the lower pools and back. At the junction with Pipiwai Trail, go right. A few minutes down, you'll come to a broad grassy knoll with a gorgeous view of the Hana coast. On a clear day you can see the Big Island, 30 miles away across 'Alenuihaha Channel.

The large freshwater pools along the trail are terraced one atop the other and connected by gentle cascades. They're usually calm and great for swimming, their cool waters refreshingly brisk. The second big pool below the bridge is a favorite swimming hole.

However, be aware: conditions can change in a heartbeat. Heavy rains falling far away on the upper slopes can bring a sudden torrent through the pools at any time. If the water starts to rise, get out immediately; several people have been swept out to sea by flash floods. Slippery rocks and unseen submerged ledges are other potential hazards, so check carefully before jumping in. Heed all park warning signs, including temporary ones posted based on weather conditions.

Waterfall Trails
HIKING

The **Pipiwai Trail** runs up the 'Ohe'o streambed, rewarding hikers with picture-perfect views of waterfalls. The trail starts on the *mauka* side of the visitor center and leads up to Makahiku Falls (0.5 miles) and Waimoku Falls (2 miles). To see both falls, allow about two hours return. The upper section is muddy, but boardwalks cover some of the worst bits.

Along the path, you'll pass large mango trees and patches of guava before coming to an overlook after about 10 minutes. **Makahiku Falls**, a long bridal-veil waterfall that drops into a deep gorge, is just off to the right. Thick green ferns cover the sides of basalt cliffs where the fall cascades – a very rewarding scene for such a short walk.

Continuing along the main trail, you'll walk beneath old banyan trees, cross Palikea Stream (killer mosquitoes thrive here) and enter the wonderland of the **Bamboo Forest**, where thick groves of bamboo bang together musically in the wind. Beyond them is **Waimoku Falls**, a thin, lacy 400ft waterfall dropping down a sheer rock face. When you come out of the first grove, you'll see the waterfall in the distance. Forget about swimming under Waimoku Falls – its pool is shallow and there's a danger of falling rocks.

If you want to take a dip, you'll find better pools along the way. About 100yd before Waimoku Falls, you'll cross a little stream. If you go left and work your way upstream for 10 minutes, you'll come to an attractive waterfall and a little pool about neck deep. There's also an inviting pool in the stream about halfway between Makahiku and Waimoku Falls.

Tours

For fascinating insights into the area's past, join one of the ethnobotanical tours that are led by **Kipahulu 'Ohana** (☑248-8558; www.kipahulu.org), a collective of Native Hawaiian farmers who have restored ancient taro patches within the park. Tours include a two-hour morning outing ($49) that concentrates on the farm and a 3½-hour afternoon tour ($79) that adds on a hike to Waimoku Falls. Both tours leave from the Kipahulu Visitor Center; advance reservations are advised.

Sleeping

At the national park's Kipahulu Campground, there's so much mana you can almost hear the whispers of the ancient Hawaiians. The facilities are minimal: pit toilets, picnic tables, grills. But the setting – oceanside cliffs amid the stone ruins of an ancient village – is simply incredible. There's no water, so bring your own. Mosquito repellent and gear suitable for rainy conditions are also a must.

Permits aren't required. Camping is free but limited to three nights per month. In winter you'll probably have the place to yourself, and even in summer there's typically enough space for everyone who shows up.

Information

Kipahulu Visitor Center (☑248-7375; www.nps.gov/hale; 3-day pass per car $10; ☻park 24hr, visitor center 8:30am-5pm) Staffed by rangers who can give you an orientation to the park.

Getting There & Around

The Kipahulu section of Haleakalā National Park is on Hwy 31, 10 miles south of Hana. For information on the spectacular drive between Hana and Kipahulu, see p396.

DIVINE, YES. SACRED, NO

Back in the 1970s 'Ohe'o Gulch was dubbed the 'Seven Sacred Pools' as part of a tourism promotion and the term still floats around freely, much to the chagrin of park officials. It's a complete misnomer since there are 24 pools in all, extending from the ocean to Waimoku Falls, and they were never sacred – but they certainly are divine.

The waters once supported a large Hawaiian settlement that cultivated sweet potatoes and taro in terraced gardens beside the stream. Archaeologists have identified the stone remains of more than 700 ancient structures at 'Ohe'o.

One of the expressed intentions of Haleakalā National Park is to manage its Kipahulu area 'to perpetuate traditional Hawaiian farming and *ho'onanea'* – a Hawaiian word meaning to pass the time in ease, peace and pleasure. So kick back and have some fun!

KAHO'OLAWE

Seven miles southwest of Maui, the sacred but uninhabited island of Kaho'olawe has long been central to the Hawaiian-rights movement. Many consider the island a living spiritual entity, a *pu'uhonua* (refuge) and *wahi pana* (sacred place).

Yet for nearly 50 years, from WWII to 1990, the US military used Kaho'olawe as a bombing range. Beginning in the 1970s, liberating the island from the military became a rallying point for a larger resurgence of Native Hawaiian pride. Today, the bombing has stopped, the navy is gone, and healing the island is considered both a symbolic act and a concrete expression of Native Hawaiian sovereignty.

The island, 11 miles long and 6 miles wide, and its surrounding waters are now a reserve that is off-limits to the general public because of the unexploded ordnance that remains on land and in the sea.

Pathway to Tahiti

The channel between Lana'i and Kaho'olawe, as well as the westernmost point of Kaho'olawe itself, is named Kealaikahiki, meaning 'pathway to Tahiti.' When early Polynesian voyagers made the journey between Hawaii and Tahiti, they lined up their canoes at this departure point.

However, Kaho'olawe was much more than an early navigational tool. Over 540 archaeological and cultural sites have been identified. They include several heiau (stone temples) and ku'ula (fishing shrines) dedicated to the gods of fishers. Pu'umoiwi, a large cinder cone in the center of the island, contains one of Hawaii's largest ancient adze quarries.

A Penal Colony

In 1829, Ka'ahumanu, the Hawaiian prime minister, put forth an edict to ban Catholics to Kaho'olawe. Beginning in 1830, Kaulana Bay, on the island's northern side, served as a penal colony for men accused of such crimes as rebellion, theft, divorce, murder and prostitution. History does not say if Catholics were included, and the penal colony was shut down in 1853.

Into the Dust Bowl

Kaho'olawe, now nearly barren, was once a lush, forested island.

The territorial Hawaiian government leased the entire island to ranchers in 1858. None was successful, and sheep, goats and cattle were left to run wild. By the early 1900s, tens of thousands of sheep and goats had denuded most of the island, turning it into an eroded dusty wasteland (even today, Kaho'olawe looks hazy from dust when seen from Maui).

From 1918 to 1941, Angus MacPhee ran Kaho'olawe's most successful ranching operation. Granted a lease on the grounds to get rid of the goats, MacPhee rounded up and sold 13,000 goats, and then built a fence across the width of the entire island to keep the remaining goats at one end. He planted grasses and ground cover and started raising cattle. It wasn't easy, but MacPhee, unlike his predecessors, was able to turn a profit.

Target Practice

The US military had long felt that Kaho'olawe had strategic importance. In early 1941, it subleased part of the island from MacPhee for bombing practice. Following the December 7, 1941 Pearl Harbor attack, the military took control of Kaho'olawe entirely. Until the war's end, it used it to practice for invasions in the Pacific theater; in addition to ship-to-shore and aerial bombing, it tested submarine torpedoes by firing them at shoreline cliffs. It is estimated that of all the fighting that took place during WWII, Kaho'olawe was the most bombed island in the Pacific.

After the war, bombing practice continued. In 1953, President Eisenhower signed a decree giving the US navy official jurisdiction over Kaho'olawe, with the stipulation that when Kaho'olawe was no longer 'needed,' the unexploded ordnance would be removed and the island would be returned to Hawaiian control 'reasonably safe for human habitation.'

The Kahoʻolawe Movement

In the mid-1960s Hawaii politicians began petitioning the federal government to cease its military activities and return Kahoʻolawe to the state of Hawaii. In 1976, a suit was filed against the navy, and in an attempt to attract greater attention to the bombings, nine Native Hawaiian activists sailed across and occupied the island. Despite their arrests, more occupations followed.

During one of the 1977 crossings, group members George Helm and Kimo Mitchell mysteriously disappeared in the waters off Kahoʻolawe. Helm had been an inspirational Hawaiian-rights activist, and with his death the Protect Kahoʻolawe ʻOhana movement arose. Helm's vision of turning Kahoʻolawe into a sanctuary of Hawaiian culture became widespread among islanders.

In 1980, in a court-sanctioned decree, the navy reached an agreement with Protect Kahoʻolawe ʻOhana that allowed them regular access to the island. The decree restricted the navy from bombing archaeological sites. In 1981 Kahoʻolawe was added to the National Register of Historic Places as a significant archaeological area. For nearly a decade, the island had the ironic distinction of being the only such historic place being bombed by its government.

In 1982 the ʻOhana began going to Kahoʻolawe to celebrate *makahiki*, the annual observance to honor Lono, god of agriculture and peace – that same year – in what many Hawaiians felt was the ultimate insult to their heritage – the US military offered Kahoʻolawe as a bombing target to foreign nations during the biennial Pacific Rim exercises.

The exercises brought what was happening to Kahoʻolawe to worldwide attention. International protests grew, and New Zealand, Australia, Japan and the UK withdrew from the Kahoʻolawe exercises. The plan was scrapped. In the late 1980s, Hawaii's politicians became more outspoken in their demands that Kahoʻolawe be returned to Hawaii. Then in October 1990, as Hawaii's two US senators, Daniel Inouye and Daniel Akaka, were preparing a congressional bill to stop the bombing, President George Bush issued an order to immediately halt military activities.

The Navy Sets Sail

In 1994, the US navy finally agreed to clean up and return Kahoʻolawe to Hawaii. The navy promised to work until 100% of surface munitions and 30% of subsurface munitions were cleared. However, the catch was that the federally authorised cleanup would end in 10 years, regardless of the results.

Ten years later, after spending over $400 million, the navy's cleanup ended, and Kahoʻolawe was transferred to the state. The government estimated that only 70% of surface ordnance and a mere 9% of subsurface ordnance had been removed.

The same year, in 2004, Hawaii established the Kahoʻolawe Island Reserve Commission (KIRC; www.kahoolawe.hawaii.gov) to manage access and use of the island, preserve its archaeological areas and restore its habitats. KIRC's mandate calls for the island to be 'managed in trust until such time and circumstances as a sovereign Native Hawaiian entity is recognised by the federal and state governments.' No such entity is yet recognised, but KIRC works in the belief that one day a sovereign Native Hawaiian government will be, and this island will then become theirs.

Helping the ʻOhana

Working with KIRC as official stewards of Kahoʻolawe, Protect Kahoʻolawe ʻOhana (PKO; www.kahoolawe.org) conducts monthly visits to the island to pull weeds, plant native foliage, clean up historic sights and honor the spirits of the land. It welcomes respectful volunteers who are ready to work (not just sightsee). Visits last four days during or near the full moon; volunteers pay a $125 fee, which covers food and transportation to the island. You'll need to bring your own sleeping bag, tent and personal supplies. PKO's website lists full details and contact information.

Lana'i

Includes »

Lana'i City..........416
Munro Trail 422
Hulopo'e & Manele
Bays.............. 422
Keomuku Road..... 424
Road to Garden of
the Gods 425
Kaumalapa'u
Highway........... 426

Best Places to Eat

» Lana'i City Grille (p418)

» Blue Ginger Café (p418)

» Pele's Other Garden
(p418)

Best Places to Stay

» Hotel Lana'i (p417)

» Four Seasons Resort
Lana'i at Manele Bay (p424)

» Dreams Come True (p417)

Why Go?

Although Lana'i is the most central of the Hawaii islands – on a clear day you can see five islands from here – it is also the least 'Hawaiian' of the islands. Now-closed pineapple plantations are its main historic legacy, and the locals are a mix of people descended from immigrant field workers from around the world. The relatively few buildings mostly hew to a corporate plantation style and the miles of red-dirt roads see few tourists.

Its signature (imported) Norfolk Island and Cook pines give the island an other-worldly feel that could just as well come from a remote corner of the South Pacific. And therein lies the charm of Lana'i: the entire island is the ultimate off-the-beaten-path destination. Hidden beaches, archaeological sites, oddball geology and a sense of isolation are perfect for those who don't want to go far to get away from it all.

When to Go
Lana'i City

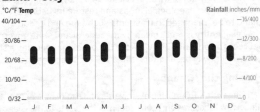

Nov–Mar Jackets needed at night in lofty, temperate Lana'i City, while the beaches stay balmy.

Apr–Aug Winter rains have stopped and the entire island enjoys breezy tropical comfort.

Sep–Oct Lana'i City stays in the sunny 70s (°F), while Hulopo'e Beach is a lovely low 80s.

History

Among its translations, Lana'i is thought to mean 'day of conquest,' and although there is debate about this, it seems appropriate. This small island (at its widest point only 18 miles across) has been affected more than anything by waves of conquest, from the first Hawaiians (who set up fishing villages around the coast) to 19th-century goats (who ate all the trees), 20th-century tycoons (who covered the place in pineapples) and modern-day visitors (looking for respite at luxury resorts).

Evil spirits were thought to be the only inhabitants of Lana'i prior to about 1400. Then a chief's son from Maui is credited with chasing off the evil-doers and making things safe for others from his home island. Little recorded history exists but there are traces of a thriving fishing culture along the coasts, especially to the north and east. Raiding parties from other islands were a frequent terror.

Colonialism largely bypassed Lana'i, although diseases brought by the odd missionary decimated the population from several thousand to 200 by the 1850s. Sporadic efforts were made at ranching and sugar growing by outsiders, but everything changed when George Gay began buying up the place in 1902. Within a few years he owned 98% of the island (a holding that has remained almost unbroken through various owners to this day). In 1922 Lana'i passed into the hands of Jim Dole, who fatefully started a pineapple plantation that was soon the world's largest.

Under Dole (and later its corporate successor, Castle & Cooke), Lana'i was not just a company town but a company island. Early managers were de facto dictators, who were known for spying on residents from their hillside mansion and ordering guards to discipline any deemed to be slackers.

In the 1980s Castle & Cooke and its hard-driving main shareholder, David Murdoch, made plans to shift Lana'i's focus from pineapples to tourists. The final harvest of the former occurred in 1992, the first resorts for the latter opened in 1990. The company continues to try to find a sustainable and profitable future for the island.

Activities

Lana'i has no national, state or county parks, but its finest beach, Hulopo'e Beach (p423), is run by Castle & Cooke as a free public park. There is good snorkeling and diving from this beach. The ridge that cuts across Lana'i's hilly interior offers good hiking opportunities with top-notch views from the Munro Trail (p422). There are also two world-class golf courses.

Guests at the island's two resorts tend to book their activities through the hotels. However, there are also excellent independent operators.

LANA'I IN...

A Day Trip

Take the early morning **ferry** from Lahaina on Maui; keep an eye out for schools of dolphins as the boat approaches **Manele Bay**. Catch the shuttle into **Lana'i City** and pour your own coffee for breakfast at **Blue Ginger Café**, before strolling the town's shops and superb **Culture & Heritage Centre**. In the afternoon, snorkel at **Hulopo'e Beach** or dive at **Manele Bay** before heading back to Maui on the sunset ferry.

Two Days

If you have an extra day, rather than heading back to Maui, wander back into town and watch the sun set over the majestic Norfolk Island pines at **Dole Park**. On the second day rent a mountain bike or put on your hiking boots and head up the **Munro Trail** for a sweeping view of everything Lana'i has to offer.

Four Days

With another couple of days, get a jeep and do some beachcombing along **Shipwreck Beach** and then explore the road to **Naha**. That night enjoy a superb meal at **Lana'i City Grille**. On day four choose from one of the old-time **eateries** on Dole Park before a day exploring the **Garden of the Gods**, the **Luahiwa Petroglyphs** and the ancient village of **Kaunolu**.

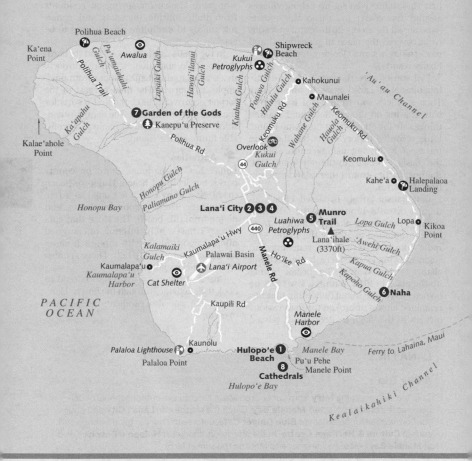

Lana'i Highlights

1 Snorkel the protected reef at the island's best beach, **Hulopo'e Beach** (p423)

2 Browse the choices, then enjoy simple but good food and drink at any of Lana'i City's many **cafes** (p418)

3 Stroll the square picking up local gossip, flavor and even artwork at **Dole Park** (p416)

4 Get into local rhythms by renting a vacation house in **Lana'i City** (p417)

5 Hike the **Munro Trail** (p422) through the island's small but lush heart, stretching just above Lana'i City

6 Get lost on the dirt track to **Naha** (p425), where ancient fishponds lie offshore

7 Count the other islands from the otherworldly heights of the **Garden of the Gods** (p426), then ponder its weird rocks

8 Explore the local diving at spectacular **Cathedrals** (p423), the best local plunge

Adventure Lana'i
OUTDOOR ACTIVITIES

(☑565-7373; www.adventurelanaiislandclub.com)
Offers a range of land and water activities
and gear rental (paddleboards, surfboards,
kayaks, bikes and more). Will meet the
Maui ferry.

Lana'i Surf Safari
SURFING

(☑306-9837; www.lanaisurfsafari.com; surf
lessons $175, board rentals from $60) Lana'i
native Nick Palumbo offers half-day surfing
lessons at secluded spots.

Trilogy Lana'i Ocean
Sports
DIVING & SNORKELING

(☑888-874-5649; www.scubalanai.com; shore/
boat dives from $120/240) Runs diving and
snorkeling trips around Manele Bay,
including to the excellent Cathedrals dive
site. It also runs diving and snorkeling
day trips (www.sailtrilogy.com; packages from
adult/child $160/80) from Maui aboard a
catamaran.

❶ Getting There & Away

AIR Lana'i airport (LNY) is about 3.5 miles
southwest of Lana'i City. There are no direct
flights to Lana'i from the mainland. Service is by
very small planes; because of weight limits for
individual bags (40lb), take a small duffel bag in
case you have to redistribute your possessions.
Island Air (☑800-652-6541; www.islandair
.com) Flies several times daily to/from Honolulu; codeshares with Hawaiian Airlines.
Mokulele Airlines (☑426-7070; www.mokule
leairlines.com) Flies several times daily to/from
Honolulu; codeshares with intra-island carrier Go!
SEA Worth it just for the ride, the **Expeditions
Maui–Lana'i Ferry** (☑661-3756, 800-695-
2624; www.go-lanai.com; adult/child one way
$30/20) links Lahaina Harbor (Maui) with
Manele Bay Harbor on Lana'i (one hour) several
times daily. In winter there's a fair chance of
seeing humpback whales; spinner dolphins are
a common sight all year, especially on morning
sails. Hulopo'e Beach is near the dock; Lana'i
tour and activity operators will meet the ferries
if you call ahead. Day-trip packages from Maui
are popular.

❶ Getting Around

Outside Lana'i City there are only three paved
roads: Keomuku Rd (Hwy 44), which extends
northeast to Shipwreck Beach; Kaumalapa'u Hwy
(Hwy 440), which extends west past the airport
to Kaumalapa'u Harbor; and Manele Rd (also Hwy
440), which flows south to Manele and Hulopo'e
Bays. To really see the island, you'll need to rent
a 4WD vehicle; Lana'i's dirt roads vary from good
to impassable, largely depending on the weather.
Rain can turn them into scarlet-hued bogs.

Outside of Lana'i City and Manele Bay
there is nowhere to buy refreshments.
So if you have a day planned on the
various rural roads to places like Naha
or the Garden of the Gods, be sure to
bring plenty of water. This is especially
important if you're embarking on hikes
such as the Munro Trail.

TO/FROM THE AIRPORT The resorts provide
a shuttle-van service that meets guests at the
airport and ferry dock. Nonguests can use the
shuttle for a fee ($5), or call a taxi ($10 per person) in advance of your arrival.
CAR The only car-rental company on the island,
Lana'i City Service (☑565-7227, 800-533-
7808; 1036 Lana'i Ave, Lana'i City; ☺7am-7pm),
is an affiliate of Dollar Rent A Car. Having a
monopoly on Lana'i translates into steep prices:
heavily used 4WD Jeep Wranglers cost from
$140 per day (the only other type of car available
is a minivan, which rent out at similar prices, but
won't give you much freedom on the bad roads).
Note that Lana'i City Service limits where you
can drive. Check in advance, as a tow from a
restricted area incurs fines, fees and possible
financial ruin.

Gas is also pricey (sold at, you guessed it,
Lana'i City Service): it can cost up to $6 per gal-
lon – a hefty charge for the gas-guzzling Jeeps.

The resorts also arrange for cars (with City
Service) and you may be able to rent from **Adventure Lana'i Ecocentre** (☑565-7373; www
.adventurelanai.com).

DRIVING DISTANCES & TIMES FROM LANA'I CITY

DESTINATION	MILES	TIME
Garden of the Gods	6	20min
Hulopo'e Beach	8	20min
Kaumalapa'u Harbor	7	20min
Keomuku	15	1hr
Lana'i Airport	3.5	10min

SHUTTLE The resorts run a shuttle that links
the Four Seasons Resort Lana'i at Manele Bay,
Hotel Lana'i and the Lodge at Koele, as well as
the airport and ferry dock. Shuttles run about
every 30 minutes throughout the day in peak
season, hourly in the slower months. The first
usually heads out about 7am, the last around
11pm. Fares may be included in the tariff for
guests; others pay from $5 (airport to Lana'i
City) to $10 (Lana'i City to Manele Bay), depend-
ing on the length of the trip.

TAXI **Rabaca's Limousine Service** (☏565-6670; rabaca@aloha.net) charges $10 per person between the airport and Lana'i City, and $10 per person between Manele Bay and Lana'i City, the latter with a two-person minimum. Island-wide custom runs are also available.

Lana'i City

POP 3000

Are you transported back in time, to another place in the Pacific, or both? Pausing to get your bearings is perfectly alright in cute little Lana'i City. In fact, you may need to pause to understand that it's really just a village, albeit one with irrepressible charm.

Lana'i City's main square, Dole Park, is surrounded by tin-roofed houses and shops, with not a chain in sight. It looks much the same as it did during its plantation days dating back to the 1920s. If you're not staying at one of the island's two resorts, you're probably staying here and that's all the better as you can wander between the surprisingly rich collection of eateries and shops, all with an authenticity not found in more touristed places. At night stroll the quiet streets and watch the moon rise through the pine trees.

History

Lana'i is the only Hawaii island where the largest town is in the highlands and not on the coast. Lana'i City is, in fact, the only town on the island – as has been the case for the last eight decades.

The village was built in the 1920s as a plantation town for the field workers and staff of Dole's Hawaiian Pineapple Company. The first planned city in Hawaii, Lana'i City was built in the midst of the pineapple fields, with shops and a theater surrounding the central park, rows of plantation houses lined up beyond that and a pineapple-processing plant on the edge of it all. Fortunately it was done with a little pizzazz. Dole hired New Zealander George Munro, a naturalist and former ranch manager, to oversee much of the work. Munro planted the now-tall Norfolk and Cook Island pines that give the town its green character and help suck some moisture from passing clouds.

⊙ Sights

Lana'i City is a charming place for a stroll. The town is laid out in a simple grid pattern, and almost all of the shops and services border Dole Park. Although threatened by 'progress' (see the boxed text, p426), it still retains the mannered order of a planned community. There's a simple dignity to the march of shops and cafes around central Dole Park. The vaguely alien-looking pine trees provide plenty of shade and you can enjoy the comings and goings of the locals. On Sunday mornings, listen for choir music spilling out of the Hawaiian church on Fraser Ave.

TOP CHOICE **Lana'i Culture & Heritage Center**

MUSEUM

(www.lanaichc.org; 111 Lana'i Ave; admission free; ⊙8:30am-3:30pm Mon-Fri, 9am-1pm Sat) Beautifully revamped, this is one of the most engaging small museums in the islands.

LANA'I SURF BEACHES & BREAKS

When it comes to surfing, Lana'i doesn't enjoy quite the bounty of waves as some of the other islands. Because rain clouds get trapped in the high peaks of Maui and Moloka'i there's very little rain on Lana'i, and therefore far fewer reef passes have been carved out by runoff.

Yet on the south shore the most consistent surf comes in around the **Manele Point** (p423) area, where the main break peels off the tip of Manele and into Hulopo'e Bay. Shallow reef and submerged rocks make this a dangerous spot at low tide or in smaller surf conditions (you're more likely to get ideal conditions on a double overhead swell, but check with locals to be safe). Not too far away from here, located in front of a deserted old Hawaiian settlement, is a spot called **Naha** (also known as Stone Shack; p425). It offers a fun two-way peak, but does close out when it gets bigger.

Across the island, the north shore's wide-open **Polihua Beach** (p426) is the longest and widest sandy beach on Lana'i. Be careful of the current here, affectionately dubbed 'the Tahitian Express.' The water flowing between Moloka'i and Lana'i in the Kalohi Channel has driven many a ship into the reef, and it could easily take you on a trip to Tahiti if you're not careful.

Displays cover the island's often mysterious history; photos show its transformation into the world's pineapple supplier. The lives of the workers are shown in detail and facts such as this jaw-dropper abound: each worker was expected to plant up to 10,000 new pineapple plants per day! Note also the shots of Lana'i City in the 1920s when it sat on bald plains before the trademark pines had taken root.

🏃 Activities

Most tourist activities take place about a mile north of Dole Park at or near the Lodge at Koele (officially the 'Four Seasons Resort at Lana'i, the Lodge at Koele').

Koloiki Ridge Trail   HIKING
This 5-mile return hike, leads up to one of the most scenic parts of the Munro Trail. It takes about three hours (return) and offers sweeping views of remote valleys (where taro was once grown), Maui and Moloka'i.

The trail begins at the rear of the Lodge at Koele on the paved path that leads to the golf clubhouse. From there, follow the signposted path uphill past Norfolk Island pines until you reach a hilltop bench with a plaque bearing the poem 'If' by Rudyard Kipling. Enjoy the view and then continue through the trees until you reach a chain-link fence. Go around the right side of the fence and continue up the hillside towards the power lines. At the top of the pass, follow the trail down through a thicket of guava trees until you reach an abandoned dirt service road, which you'll turn left on. You'll soon intersect with the Munro Trail; turn right on it and after a few minutes you'll pass Kukui Gulch, named for the candlenut trees that grow there. Continue along the trail until you reach a thicket of tall sisal plants; about 50yd after that bear right to reach Koloiki Ridge, where you'll be rewarded with panoramic views of much of the island.

Stables at Koele   HORSEBACK RIDING
(565-4424; rides from $125; ⏰7am-5pm) If you would prefer to see Lana'i from a saddle, this 25-horse operation, just west of the resort (within eyeshot), offers everything from a 1½-hour trail ride that takes in sweeping views of Maui to a four-hour private ride catered to your particular interest. Newly invigorated by some cowboy operators from Utah, there are also pony rides for kids ($25) and rides around town in carriages ($65). You can even get lessons in roping.

Experience at Koele   GOLF
(565-4653; www.golfonlanai.com; greens fee $210-225; ⏰8am-6:30pm) Curving around Four Seasons Resort Lana'i, Lodge at Koele, this Greg Norman–branded course offers world-class golfing with knockout vistas along the way. The front nine meanders through parklike settings; the signature 17th hole drops 200ft to a tree-shrouded gorge.

🎊 Festivals & Events

Lana'i's main bash, the **Pineapple Festival** (www.visitlanai.net), is held on or near July 4 and celebrates the island's pineapple past with games and live music at Dole Park (any pineapple is imported!).

🛏 Sleeping

Most people stay at the resorts or the hotel, but there are several rental houses and B&Bs right in town and an easy walk to restaurants. There are several choices at www.vrbo.com.

TOP CHOICE Hotel Lana'i   HOTEL $$
(565-7211; www.hotellanai.com; 828 Lana'i Ave; r $100-160, cottage $190) From 1923 to 1990 the Hotel Lana'i was the only hotel on the island. It seems little has changed here over the decades, other than the conversations that echo through the thin walls. The 10 immaculately renovated rooms have hardwood floors, antiques, pedestal sinks, patchwork quilts and more period pieces. Go for a room with – appropriately – a lanai (a small porch) for viewing town, or opt for privacy and quiet in the detached cottage out back.

Dreams Come True   VACATION RENTAL $$
(565-6961, 800-566-6961; www.dreamscometruelanai.com; 1168 Lana'i Ave; r $130, 4-bedroom house $520; @🛜) This spiffy plantation-style house was one of the first built in Lana'i City (1925) and has a long porch. Rooms have hardwood floors, and are furnished with a mixture of comfy antique and modern pieces. There are numerous amenities, including laundry, DVD, internet access and private marble baths. Whole house rates don't include breakfast. You can arrange vehicle rentals here through the owner.

Plantation Home   VACATION RENTAL **$$**
(☎276-1528; craige@maui.net; cnr Gay & 13th Sts; per night $135) A small, renovated two-bedroom plantation-style house, this option comes with an amazing bonus: a free Jeep (which means the house rental with the Jeep costs less than renting just a Jeep from the local monopoly). Rooms are basic in decor, but there is a long list of included sports equipment plus DVD and full kitchen and laundry.

Four Seasons Resort Lana'i, the Lodge at Koele   RESORT **$$$**
(☎565-4000, 800-321-4666; www.foursea sons.com/koele; 1 Keomuku Hwy; r from $200; ✳@🛜🐾) Pondering a sticky wicket on the croquet lawn amidst the manicured gardens, you'd be forgiven for thinking you had been transported to an English estate. But step inside the grand central building where touches such as inlaid images of pineapples in the wood flooring tell you you're in Hawaii. Guests in the 102 rooms and suites enjoy a small pool, a library, lawn bowls and misty mountain air. Activities are shared with the companion Four Seasons Resort Lana'i at Manele Bay. Outside peak season, this resort is almost somnolent and rarely busy. Find it about a half-mile north of the Dole Park on Keomuku Hwy.

✖ Eating & Drinking

The old-time feel of Lana'i City extends to eating hours: kitchens close by 8pm. Of the two main supermarkets, **Richard's Market** (434 8th St; ⊘8am-7pm Mon-Sat) has the better wine selection, so that's good enough for us. Note: if you want vittles beyond Pop-tarts and Spam, you may want to bring them with you; there is just a small convenience store for Sunday food shopping.

TOP CHOICE **Lana'i City Grille**   FUSION **$$$**
(☎565-7211; Hotel Lana'i, 828 Lana'i Ave; mains $28-40; ⊘5-9pm Wed-Sun) Famed Maui chef Bev Gannon is the brains behind the charming restaurant within the Hotel Lana'i. Sturdy 1930s schoolhouse furnishings give the wood-floored dining room a vintage air, while the menu combines fresh seafood with various meats in ways both familiar (a perfect rib-eye) and surprising (fresh local seafood with Thai spices). Specials are, well, special. The small bar pours a fine highball (often open until 11pm!) and on Friday nights there's live Hawaiian music, which draws what seems like half the island population.

Blue Ginger Café   CAFE **$**
(409 7th St; breakfast & lunch $5-8, dinner $8-15; ⊘6am-8pm) Don't worry, all the care goes into the food, not the decor at this bare-bones diner, where you can serve yourself a cup of coffee, grab a newspaper and settle back at a table outside. Muffins are some of the excellent items that arrive warm from the bakery. The long menu ranges from omelets and salads to burgers, delectable pork katsu and more. It's been run by the same family for decades.

Pele's Other Garden   ITALIAN **$$**
(cnr 8th & Houston Sts; lunch $5-9, dinner $10-20; ⊘11am-3pm & 5-8pm Mon-Sat) More bistro than deli, this restored plantation house has tables inside and out. The kitchen leans Italian and serves up classic spaghetti and meatballs, crispy thin-crust pizza and some first-rate pesto. Salads are made with organic local greens; desserts are large but not extraordinary. There's a fine beer list, although last call in the tiny bar area is 8pm.

Canoes Lana'i   HAWAIIAN **$**
(419 7th St; meals $5-12; ⊘6:30am-1pm Thu-Tue, to 8pm Fri & Sat) Breakfast is always on the menu at this old-time Hawaii cafe that is little changed since pineapple pickers filled the tables. The banana pancakes are sublime, best enjoyed at the counter. The best-seller? *Loco moco* (rice, fried egg and hamburger topped with gravy). Teriyaki figures prominently on the dinner menu.

Dining Room   ISLAND CONTEMPORARY **$$$**
(☎565-7300; www.fourseasons.com/koele; 1 Keomuku Hwy; mains $46-65; ⊘6-9:30pm Fri-Tue) Leave your sandals in the room but bring your wallet to this very high-end Lodge at Koele restaurant with a name that will remind you where you are, even after you've seen the prices. Lobster, caviar, quail and more populate a menu of expertly prepared creations presented with flawless attention to detail and service. But really, this is Lana'i and we'll take the fun and food of any of the places ringing Dole Park, first.

Coffee Works   CAFE **$**
(604 'Ilima Ave; snacks $2-4; ⊘7am-3pm Mon-Sat) Settle back on the vast deck at this long-running java-jiving caffeine house and soon most of the locals will pass by.

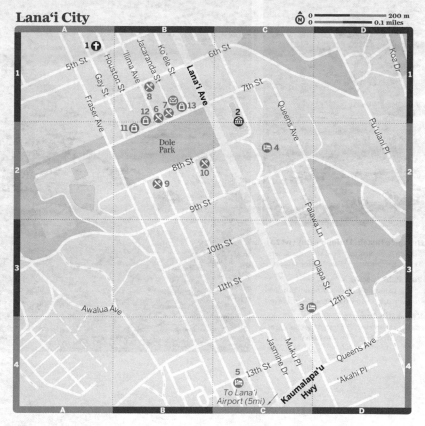

Shopping

Shops and galleries encircle Dole Park selling everything from flip-flops for locals to fine art for connoisseurs. You can spend an hour or much longer wandering.

Mike Carroll Gallery   ART GALLERY
(www.mikecarrollgallery.com; cnr 7th & Ko'ele Sts) Art lovers love Mike Carroll Gallery, where you can find the eponymous owner either creating a new masterpiece or busy displaying the work of another artist. It's also a good source for local books.

Lana'i Arts & Cultural Center   ART GALLERY
(cnr 7th & Houston Sts; ☺noon-4pm Mon-Fri plus other times) Staffed by local artist volunteers (so never assume it's closed), you can choose from works in many mediums or learn how to create your own from the artists themselves. A great place to get *very* local recommendations.

Lana'i City

◎ Sights
| 1 Hawaiian Church | A1 |
| 2 Lana'i Culture & Heritage Center | C1 |

⌖ Sleeping
3 Dreams Come True	C3
4 Hotel Lana'i	C2
5 Plantation Home	C4

⊗ Eating
6 Blue Ginger Café	B1
7 Canoes Lana'i	B1
8 Coffee Works	B1
Lana'i City Grille	(see 4)
9 Pele's Other Garden	B2
10 Richard's Market	B2

⌂ Shopping
11 Lana'i Arts & Cultural Center	B2
12 Local Gentry	B1
13 Mike Carroll Gallery	B1

1. Hulopo'e Beach, Hulopo'e Bay (p423)
This beach is manicured by the same gardeners who look after the nearby Four Seasons resort.

2. Pu'u Pehe (p423)
According to legend, Pehe was a beautiful maiden who drowned, imprisoned by her lover in a cave.

3. Kahekili's Jump (p427)
It is said that Kamehameha tested the courage of his warriors by having them leap from this cliff.

4. Lodge at Koele (p418)
Manicured gardens of one of the two Four Seasons Resorts, Lana'i.

5. Garden of the Gods (p426)
You can see up to four other islands from this volcanic landscape where the colors change with the light.

TOM TILL / ALAMY

3

4

LUAHIWA PETROGLYPHS

Lana'i's highest concentration of petroglyphs (over 400, both ancient and modern) are carved into three-dozen boulders spread over a remote slope overlooking the Palawai Basin.

To get to this seldom-visited site, head south from Lana'i City along tree-lined Manele Rd. After 2 miles, look for a cluster of six trees on the left and turn on the wide dirt road. Stay on this for 1.2 miles as you head toward the hills. When you see a house and gate, take a very sharp turn left onto a grass and dirt track for 0.3 miles. The large boulders will be on your right up the hill and there will be a turnout and small stone marker.

Many of the rock carvings are quite weathered, but you can still make out linear and triangular human figures, dogs and a canoe. Other than gusts of wind, the place is eerily quiet. You can almost feel the presence of the ancients here – honor their spirits and don't touch the fragile carvings.

Local Gentry   CLOTHING
(363 7th St) Lovers of artful clothing flock to Local Gentry, a clothing store with color and flair that caters to visitors and locals alike. There's no polyester schlock here. A top-selling T-shirt reads: 'If it happens on Lana'i, everybody knows.'

❶ Information

There's no local daily newspaper, but community notices, including rental-housing ads, are posted on bulletin boards outside the grocery stores. The monthly **Lana'i Today** (www.lanaitoday.net) is at times feisty. There is no tourist office.

Bank of Hawaii (460 8th St) Has one of the island's two 24-hour ATMs.

Lana'i Community Hospital (☎565-6411; 628 7th St) Offers 24-hour emergency medical services.

Lana'i Public Library (555 Fraser Ave; ◷10am-5pm Mon-Fri, noon-8pm Wed) Has internet access.

Post office (620 Jacaranda St)

❶ Getting There & Around

The resort shuttle (p415) stops at Hotel Lana'i, the Lodge at Koele and pretty much anywhere else you ask. Lana'i's only car-rental office is Lana'i City Service (p415; the shuttle stops there as well!).

Munro Trail

This exhilarating 12-mile adventure through verdant forest can be hiked, mountain biked or negotiated in a 4WD vehicle. For the best views, get an early start. Those hiking or biking should be prepared for steep grades and allow a whole day. If you're driving and the dirt road has been graded recently,

give yourself two to three hours. However, be aware that rains turn the dirt into a red swamp that has claimed many a 4WD. Watch out for sheer drop-offs.

To start, head north on Hwy 44 from Lana'i City. About a mile past the Lodge at Koele, turn right onto the paved road that ends in half a mile at the island's cemetery. The Munro Trail starts left of the cemetery; passing through eucalyptus groves, it climbs the ridge and the path is studded with Norfolk Island pines. These trees, a species that draws moisture from the afternoon clouds and fog, were planted in the 1920s as a watershed by naturalist George Munro, after whom the trail is named.

Before the Munro Trail was upgraded to a dirt road, it was a footpath and historically was a place of taro farms, which drew on the frequent rainfall.

The trail looks down on deep ravines cutting across the east flank of the mountain, and passes Lana'ihale (3370ft), Lana'i's highest point. On a clear day you can see all the inhabited Hawaii islands except for distant Kaua'i and Ni'ihau along the route. Stay on the main trail, which descends 6 miles to the central plateau. Keep the hills to your left and turn right at the big fork in the road. The trail ends back on Manele Rd (Hwy 440) between Lana'i City and Manele Bay.

Hulopo'e & Manele Bays

Lanai's finest beach (and one of the best in Hawaii) is the golden crescent of sand at Hulopo'e Bay. Enjoy snorkeling in a marine preserve, walking to a fabled archaeological site or just relaxing in the shade of palms. Nearby, Manele Harbor provides a protected anchorage for sailboats and other small craft, just a 10-minute walk from Hulopo'e Beach.

Manele and Hulopo'e Bays are part of a marine-life conservation district that prohibits the removal of coral and restricts many fishing activities, all of which makes for great snorkeling and diving. Spinner dolphins seem to enjoy the place as much as humans. During wintertime *kona* (leeward) storms, strong currents and swells enliven the calm and imperil swimmers.

Beaches

TOP CHOICE **Hulopo'e Beach** BEACH
One good thing about being the main beach on company-run Lana'i is that the same gardeners who manicure the Four Seasons keep things looking lovely in this free, public park. Everybody loves it – locals taking the kids for a swim, tourists on day trips from Maui and the many visitors who end up losing track of time here.

This gently curving white-sand beach is long, broad and protected by a rocky point to the south. The Four Seasons Resort Lana'i at Manele Bay sits on a low seaside terrace on the north side. But the beach is big enough that even with the hotel presence it never gets crowded. Generally, the most action occurs when the tour boats pull in from Maui at noon. Picnic tables shelter under palms and there are public restrooms with solar-heated showers.

For the best **snorkeling**, head to the left side of the bay, where there's an abundance of coral and reef fish. To the left, just beyond the sandy beach, you'll find a low lava shelf with tide pools worth exploring. Often there will be somebody renting masks and fins on the beach; if not, contact **Adventure Lana'i** (565-7373; www.adventurelanaiislandclub.com). Look for the protected shoreline splash pool, ideal for children.

Sights & Activities

Pu'u Pehe NATURAL FEATURE
From Hulopo'e Beach, a path (of around 0.75 miles) leads south to the end of **Manele Point**, which separates Hulopo'e and Manele Bays. The point is actually a volcanic cinder cone that's sharply eroded on its seaward edge. The lava has rich rust red colors with swirls of gray and black, and its texture is bubbly and brittle – so brittle that huge chunks of the point have broken off and fallen onto the coastal shelf below.

Pu'u Pehe is the name of the cove to the left of the point, as well as the rocky islet just offshore. This islet, which is also known as Sweetheart's Rock, has a tomb-like formation on top that features in the Hawaiian legend of Pehe. According to the legend, Pehe was a beautiful maiden who was stashed away in a cave by her lover, lest any other young men on Lana'i set eyes upon her. One day when her lover was up in the mountains, a storm suddenly blew in and powerful waves drowned Pehe. The grief-stricken boy carried Pehe's body to the top of Pu'u Pehe, where he erected a tomb and laid her to rest. He then jumped to his death in the surging waters.

Manele Harbor NATURAL FEATURE
During the early 20th century, cattle were herded down to Manele Bay for shipment to Honolulu. These days the herds start in Maui, traveling on day trips to Lana'i on the ferry (p415). Harbor facilities include drinking water, picnic tables, a **convenience store** (7am-6pm), restrooms and showers. If you want to do a little land exploration, you'll find the remains of a cattle chute by walking around the point at the end of the parking lot.

Cathedrals DIVING
Diving in and around the bay is excellent. Coral is abundant near the cliff sides, where the bottom quickly slopes off to about 40ft. Beyond the bay's western edge, near Pu'u Pehe rock, is Cathedrals, the island's most spectacular dive site, featuring arches and grottoes amidst a large lava tube that is 100ft in length. **Trilogy Lana'i Ocean Sports** (888-874-5649; www.scuba lanai.com) runs diving and snorkeling trips in the area.

LANA'I FOR CHILDREN

The kids will love **Hulopo'e Beach** (p422), where there are some cool tide pools filled with colorful little critters that will thrill the little ones; older kids will enjoy the great snorkeling. Other activities for children are based at the resorts; the **Stables at Koele** (p417) has pony rides open to guests and nonguests.

Challenge at Manele GOLF
(🕿565-2222; guests/nonguests $210/225; ⊘7am-
6:30pm) This Jack Nicklaus–branded course
at the Four Seasons resort offers spectacular
play along seaside cliffs. The 12th hole challenges golfers to hit across a fairway that is
really the ocean's surf.

🛏 Sleeping

Note that owners of the condos around
Manele Bay are prevented from renting out
their units to visitors.

**Four Seasons Resort Lana'i at
Manele Bay** RESORT $$$
(🕿565-2000, 800-321-4666; www.fourseasons
.com/manelebay; 1 Manele Bay Rd; r from $400;
✳@🛜🏊♿) Of the two island resorts on of-
fer, this one screams – well, stage-whispers –
Hawaii vacation! Although the decor of the
236 rooms is just slightly overstuffed and
frumpy, the views of the azure waters, the
surrounds of the vast pool and the Asian-
themed soaring public rooms are entranc-
ing. Given a choice, we'll take this resort first
as it most says 'Hawaii.'

Hulopo'e Beach Camping CAMPGROUND $
Camping is allowed on the grassy expanse
above Hulopo'e Beach. Permits are issued
by the island's owner, **Castle & Cooke**
(🕿565-3319; 111 Lana'i Ave, Lana'i City; camping
permit per night $10). Call to reserve one of
the eight spots (three-night maximum stay
during busy times, such as summer and
weekends) and make arrangements to pick
up the permit.

🍴 Eating & Drinking

The resort has many tables well-placed for
watching the orange glint of the waters at
sunset. You can get picnic supplies for the
beach at the harbor convenience store.

Hulopo'e Court AMERICAN $$$
(Four Seasons Resort Lana'i at Manele Bay; break-
fast buffet $32, dinner mains $28-40; ⊘7-11am
& 6-9:30pm) The 'casual' restaurant at the
resort has a long terrace overlooking the
ocean and pool. The buffet breakfast is
bountiful but not quite as over-the-top lavish as the prices imply. Dinner is the more
interesting choice, with an emphasis on
fresh seafood you can enjoy to the flicker
of torches and the distant rumble of surf.
The other dinner choice here is very high-
end Italian.

Keomuku Road

The best drive on Lana'i, Keomuku Rd (Hwy
44), heads north from Lana'i City into cool
upland hills, where fog drifts above grassy
pastures. Along the way, impromptu overlooks offer straight-on views of the undeveloped southeast shore of Moloka'i and its
tiny islet Mokuho'oniki, in marked contrast
to Maui's sawtooth high-rises in Ka'anapali
off to your right.

The surprisingly short 8-mile road gently
slopes down to the coast in a series of switchbacks through a mostly barren landscape
punctuated by eccentrically shaped rocks.
The paved road ends near the coast and you
are in 4WD country. To the left, a dirt road
leads to Shipwreck Beach, while turning right
onto Keomuku Rd takes the adventurous to
Keomuku Beach or all the way to Naha.

SHIPWRECK BEACH

Unlike many worldwide places named Shipwreck Beach, where the name seems fanciful at best, you can't miss the namesake
wreck here. A fairly large **WWII tanker**
sits perched atop rocks just offshore. Unlike
a metal ship (which would have dissolved
decades ago), this one was part of a series
made from concrete and later dumped here
by the Navy after the war.

Start your beach exploration by taking the
dirt road that runs 1.4 miles north from the
end of Hwy 44, past some beach shacks. Often there seems to be more sand on the road
than the beach. Park in the large clearing
overlooking a rocky cove, which is known
locally as Po'aiwa and has good **snorkeling**
among the rocks and reef, as well as protected **swimming** over the sandy bottom. The
wreck is about 440yd to the north, and you
can stroll for at least 9 miles along the shore
while looking for flotsam and taking in the
Moloka'i and Maui views. Close to the parking area is the site of a former lighthouse on
a lava-rock point, though only the cement
foundation remains.

⊙ Sights & Activities

Kukui Petroglyphs HISTORICAL SITE
From the lighthouse foundation, trail markings lead directly inland about 100yd to
the Kukui petroglyphs, a cluster of fragile
carvings marked by a sign reading 'Do Not
Deface.' The simple figures are etched onto
large boulders on the right side of the path.
Keep your eyes open here – sightings of wild

mouflon sheep on the inland hills are not uncommon. Males have curled-back horns, and dominant ones travel with a harem.

Shipwreck in Awalua   HIKING
The lighthouse site is the turn-around point for most people, but it's possible to walk another 6 miles all the way to Awalua, where there's another shipwreck, the WWII tender YO-21. The hike is windy, hot and dry (bring water); the further down the beach you go, the prettier it gets. You'll pass the remains of more than a dozen other ships along the way (timbers and machinery).

KAHOKUNUI TO NAHA
The stretch of Keomuku Rd running from Kahokunui to Naha is just the journey for those looking for real adventure on Lana'i. From the hillsides it looks barren, but once you are on it you are shaded by overhanging kiawe trees. The dirt course varies from smooth to deeply cratered (and impossibly soupy after storms). This is where your 4WD will justify its daily fee, as you explore the ruins of failed dreams and discover magical beaches. If the road is passable, driving the entire length should take about an hour. The reef-protected shore is close to the road but usually not quite visible.

◉ Sights

Maunalei   HISTORICAL SITE
Less than a mile from the end of Hwy 44 and the paving is Maunalei. An ancient heiau (stone temple) sat there until 1890, when the Maunalei Sugar Company dismantled it and used the stones to build a fence and railroad. Shortly after the temple desecration, the company was beset by misfortune, as saltwater filled the wells and disease decimated the workforce.

Keomuku   HISTORICAL SITE
Another 6 miles further along is Keomuku, the center of the short-lived sugarcane plantation. There's little left to see other than the somewhat reconstructed Ka Lanakila o Ka Malamalama Church, which was originally built in 1903. Under the dense tropical vegetation other plantation ruins can be found, including a steam locomotive and buildings, as well as clouds of mosquitoes.

Halepalaoa Landing   HISTORICAL SITE
Just under 2 miles further along the road you reach Halepalaoa Landing, which was where the sugar company planned to ship

out its product from. But little was accomplished during its short life (1899–1901), other than to shorten the lives of scores of Japanese workers, who are buried in a small cemetery. On the ocean side, you'll see the remains of Club Lana'i, a 1970s recreation spot that failed under dubious circumstances surrounding its finances. However, there's a pier here that's maintained and which provides a good stroll out from the shore. In season you may hear whales breaching just offshore.

Running southeast from the pier is the shaded Halepalaoa beach, which seems to have come from desert-island central casting and runs to Lopa. There's rarely anyone here.

Naha   HISTORICAL SITE
Another 4 miles brings you to Naha, which is both the end of the road and the site of ancient fishponds just offshore. With the wind whistling in your ears, this is a dramatic and desolate setting where the rest of Hawaii feels a thousand miles away. It's an otherworldly place that seems utterly incongruous, given the view of developed Maui just across the waters. Look for traces of a flagstone path that ran from here right up and over the hills to the Palawai Basin.

Road to Garden of the Gods

Strange rock formations, views that would overexcite a condo developer and more deserted beaches are the highlights of northwestern Lana'i.

It's all reached via the Polihua Rd, which starts near the Lodge at Koele's stables. The stretch of road leading to Kanepu'u Preserve and the Garden of the Gods is a fairly good, albeit often dusty, route that generally takes about 20 minutes from town. To travel onward to Polihua Beach, though, is another story: depending on when the road was last graded, the trip could take anywhere from 20 minutes to an hour, as you head 1800ft down to the coast in what is at times little more than a controlled skid.

Beaches & Sights

Kanepu'u Preserve   NATURE RESERVE
The 590-acre Kanepu'u Preserve is the last native dryland forest of its kind across all Hawaii. Just 5 miles northwest of Lana'i City, the forest is home to 49 species of rare native plants, including the endangered 'iliahi (Hawaiian sandalwood) and na'u

(fragrant Hawaiian gardenia). Look for the short, self-guided interpretive trail, which is inside the first of two fences protecting the preserve.

Garden Of The Gods
NATURAL FEATURE

The only fertilizer that might work in this garden is cement. All manner of volcanic rocks are strewn about this landscape of maroon- and rust-colored earth. Many have strange shapes that stand out against the seemingly Martian landscape, and you may fully expect the plucky little *Mars Explorer* probe to come buzzing past.

It's utterly silent up here and you can see up to four other islands across the white-capped waters. The colors change with the light – pastel in the early morning, rich hues in the late afternoon. Amidst the salmons and siennas, look for rocks oddly perched atop others.

Polihua Beach
BEACH

This broad, 1.5-mile-long white-sand beach at the northwestern tip of the island takes its name from the green sea turtles that nest here. Polihua means 'eggs in the bosom.' Although the beach itself is gorgeous, strong winds kicking up the sand and tiny shells often make it stingingly unpleasant; water conditions are treacherous, although serious surfers brave the waves.

Kaumalapaʻu Highway

Kaumalapaʻu Hwy (Hwy 440) connects Lanaʻi City to the airport before ending at Kaumalapaʻu Harbor, the island's deepwater barge dock. The road itself is about as exciting as a can of pineapple chunks in heavy syrup, but it runs close to Lanaʻi's best archaeological site, at Kaunolu. Just off Hwy 440 on the Kaunolu road, look for a large open-air **cat shelter**, run by local volunteers. Feral cats enjoy a life of leisure and a few even welcome your visit.

KAUNOLU

Perched on a majestic bluff at the southwestern tip of the island, the ancient fishing village of Kaunolu thrived until its abandonment in the mid-19th century after missionary-transmitted disease had decimated the island. The waters of Kaunolu Bay were so prolific that royalty came here to cast their nets.

Now overgrown and visited by few, Kaunolu boasts the largest concentration of stone ruins on Lanaʻi. A gulch separates the two sides of the bay, with remnants of former house sites on the eastern side, obscured by thorny kiawe. The stone walls of **Halulu Heiau** at the western side of the gulch still dominate the scene. The temple

---

FRUITY AFTERTASTE

Lanaʻi is defined by the pineapple, ironic given that the spiky fruit is now imported to the island's resorts and two markets. But evidence of its reign is everywhere. When you fly in, you pass over the ghostly outlines of vast fields that once produced one out of every three pineapples consumed worldwide. Much of the land – and island – now lies fallow.

Coming to terms with that past is an ongoing issue for the island today. Lanaʻi City is still very much the charming company town built by Jim Dole in the 1920s, but like the fields that were once its reason to exist, its very essence is in danger of going fallow. The stately order of vintage buildings around Dole Park is threatened by time and replacement. New buildings out of step with the old are proposed – and some are constructed (such as the current post office, which could be in Wichita). In 2006 the Historic Hawaiʻi Foundation, the leading advocate for cultural and historic preservation in the state, named the entire town as one of the most endangered places in Hawaii.

Meanwhile, the two resorts opened in 1990 are successful but haven't spawned the kind of additional development envisaged by Castle & Cooke, the corporate successor to Dole, which still controls much of the island. Condos on Manele Bay sell for $2.5 million, more than twice what Dole paid for all of Lanaʻi in 1922, but sales are slow.

'What next for Lanaʻi?' is a common question. Little of the island remains in a natural state – 10,000 goats brought by missionaries denuded much of the island in the decades before Dole even planted his first pineapple. Sheep ranches took care of the rest. Perhaps the pineapple shouldn't be relegated to just a nickname. 'Let's plant some pineapples so visitors can see how this place worked,' said one longtime resident. 'It's crazy that the pineapple at the resorts is imported. Let's at least claim that part of our history.'

once served as a *pu'uhonua* (place of refuge), where taboo-breakers fled to elude their death sentences. There are over 100 building sites here.

Northwest of the heiau, a natural stone wall runs along the perimeter of the sea cliff. Look for a break in the wall at the cliff's edge, where there's a sheer 80ft drop known as **Kahekili's Jump**. The ledge below makes diving into the ocean a death-defying thrill, but is recommended for professionals only. It's said that Kamehameha the Great would test the courage of upstart warriors by having them leap from this spot. More recently, it has been the site of world-class cliff-diving championships.

To get to Kaunolu, follow Kaumalapa'u Hwy (Hwy 440) 0.6 miles past the airport, and turn left onto a partial gravel and dirt road that runs south through abandoned pineapple fields for 2.2 miles. A carved stone marks the turn onto a much rougher but still very 4WD-capable road down to the sea. After a further 2.5 miles you'll see a sign for a short **interpretive trail**, which has well-weathered signs explaining the history of Kaunolu. Another 0.3 miles brings you to a parking area amid the ruins. One complication of a visit to this spot is that your rental firm may not allow you to drive here. Check in with them first.

Moloka'i

Includes »

Kaunakakai 435
Kamalo 443
'Ili'ili'opae Heiau . . . 444
Waialua 445
Halawa Valley 446
Pali Coast 447
Kamakou Area 448
Pala'au State Park. . 450
Ho'olehua 451
Mo'omomi Beach . . 452
Kalaupapa National
Historical Park 453
Maunaloa 457
Kaluakoi Resort Area 457
West End Beaches. . 458

Best Places to Eat

» Aunty Ruby's Cafe (p438)
» Mana'e Goods & Grindz (p445)
» Kualapu'u Cookhouse (p450)

Best Places to Stay

» Hale Lei Lani (p444)
» Aloha Beach House (p445)
» Dunbar Beachfront Cottages (p445)

Why Go?

The popular local T-shirt proclaiming 'Moloka'i time is when I want to show up' sums up this idiosyncratic island perfectly: feisty and independent while not taking life too seriously.

Moloka'i is often cited as the 'most Hawaiian' of the islands, and in terms of bloodlines this is true – more than 50% of the residents are at least part Native Hawaiian. But whether the island fits your idea of 'most Hawaiian' depends on your definition. If your idea of Hawaii includes great tourist facilities, forget it.

But if your idea of Hawaii is a place that best celebrates the island's geography and indigenous culture, then Moloka'i is for you. It regularly ranks as one of the least spoiled islands worldwide; ancient Hawaiian sites in the island's beautiful, tropical east are jealously protected and restored, and island-wide consensus eschews development of the often sacred west.

When to Go
Kaunakaka

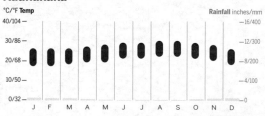

Nov–Mar Rain gear is needed in Kaunakakai and any place east, but it's otherwise balmy.

Apr–Aug Winter rains have stopped and the entire island enjoys breezy tropical comfort.

Sep–Oct Moloka'i enjoys lovely low 80s (°F) daytime temps with conditions just a tad cooler up high.

History

Moloka'i was possibly inhabited by the 7th century. Over the following years it was a vital locale within the Hawaii Islands and played a key role in local culture. It was known for its warriors, and its chiefs held great sway in the ever-shifting alliances between O'ahu and Maui. Much of the population lived in the east, where regular rainfalls, fertile soil and rich waters ensured abundant food.

Some of the most amazing historical sites in the islands can be found here, including the enormous 'Ili'ili'opae Heiau (p444) and the series of fishponds just offshore (see p443).

At first European contact in 1786, the population was about 8000, close to today's total. Missionaries turned up in the east in the 1830s. Meanwhile the possibilities of the vast western plains drew the interest of early capitalists and colonists. By the 1900s there were large plantations of sugarcane and pineapples as well as cattle ranches. All the big pineapple players – Libby, Dole and Del Monte – had operations here, but had ceased all production by 1990. Given the large local population, relatively few immigrant laborers were brought to Moloka'i, one of the reasons the island population includes such a high proportion (50%) of Native Hawaiians.

Cattle were important for all of the 20th century. The Moloka'i Ranch owns much of the western third of the island, but changing investors coupled with some unsuccessful dabbles in tourism (see the boxed text, p459) caused the ranch to shut down in 2008, throwing hundreds out of work.

Tourism plays a minor role in the local economy and, besides small-scale farming, the main employer now is Monsanto, which keeps a very low profile at its farms growing genetically modified (GM) seeds.

National, State & County Parks

The stunning Kalaupapa Peninsula, within **Kalaupapa National Historical Park**, and a tour of the leprosy settlement there are reason enough to visit Moloka'i. Verdant **Pala'au State Park** has views down to Kalaupapa and a range of attractions, from woodsy hikes to erotic rock formations.

The county's **Papohaku Beach Park**, which fronts one of Hawaii's longest and best beaches, is incentive enough to make the trek out west.

CAMPING

Moloka'i's most interesting place to camp, in terms of setting and set-up, is the county's Papohaku Beach Park (p458) on the untrammeled West End. Camping at the county's One Ali'i Beach Park is not recommended.

County permits (adult/child Monday to Thursday $5/3, Friday to Sunday $8/5) are issued by the Department of Parks & Recreation (Map p437; ☎553-3204; www. co.maui.hi.us; Mitchell Pauole Center, 90 Ainoa St, Kaunakakai; ☺8am-1pm & 2:30-4pm Mon-Fri), by phone or in person. Permits are limited to three consecutive days in one park, with a yearly maximum of 15 days.

MOLOKA'I IN...

Two Days

After checking out Kaunakakai, drive the gorgeous 27 miles east to the **Halawa Valley**, and hike out to the waterfall. Head down to Puko'o for some lunch and kicking back at **Mana'e Goods & Grindz** and a snorkel at **Twenty Mile Beach**. Wander along to **Kaunakakai** to gather vittles for a dinner under the stars at your rental pad. On your last day let the sure-footed mules give you the ride of your life to the **Kalaupapa Peninsula** and crack open some fun at **Purdy's Macadamia Nut Farm**.

Four Days

After the two days above, spend your third day in the ancient rain forests of **Kamakou Preserve**, followed by the island's best dinner at **Kualapu'u Cookhouse**. On the morning of day four, enjoy some locally grown coffee at **Coffees of Hawaii**, then head northwest to the culturally significant beaches of Mo'omomi, before finding the ultimate souvenirs at Maunaloa's **Big Wind Kite Factory**.

One Week

As above, but add in lots of time to do nothing at all. You're on Moloka'i time.

Moloka'i Highlights

1 Hear echoes of Hawaii's past while hiking in the pristine and deeply spiritual **Halawa Valley** (p446)

2 Discover underwater delights, or just laze the day away, at **Twenty Mile Beach** (p445)

3 Kick back at a picnic table with a superb plate lunch at **Puko'o** (p444)

4 Follow in the footsteps of America's first saint on the **Kalaupapa Peninsula** (p453)

5 Make friends bust a nut by sending a **Post-a-nut** (p452) from Ho'olehua

6 Kayak past the world's tallest sea cliffs on the remote **Pali Coast** (see the boxed text, p447)

7 Get your skin blasted clean on windswept and untrammeled **Papohaku Beach** (p458), on the west coast

8 Relive plantation Hawaii wandering unrefined **Kaunakakai** (p435), the intriguing main town

You can enjoy the views from Pala'au State Park (p451) and be ready for an early start on a visit to Kalaupapa from a peaceful camping area near the trailhead. For a true wilderness experience, consider the remote camping at Waikolu Lookout (p449). **State permits** (resident/non-resident $12/18 per campsite per night) are obtained from the Division of State Parks ($587-0300; www.hawaiistateparks.org) via the website. Permits cannot be obtained on Moloka'i.

None of the campgrounds listed are near sources of food or drink. If you forget a piece of camping equipment, Moloka'i Fish & Dive (p436) stocks plenty.

And if you are really ready for adventure, consider camping on private lands. You must ask for permission first, but the local spirit can respect those who care enough to learn the land. For instance, the Simms family ($336-0016) at times welcomes campers to a site surrounded by banana trees near their home in the heart of Moloka'i's lush East End. All they request is a donation.

🏃 Activities

Moloka'i has wild ocean waters, rough trails, remote rain forests and the most dramatic oceanside cliffs in Hawaii. It's a perfect destination for adventure – just don't expect to be spoon-fed.

If you're considering action at sea, note that conditions are seasonal. During the summer you'll find waters are calm on the north and west shores, and made rough by the persistent trade winds on the south shore outside of the Pala'au barrier reef. Plan on getting out early, before the winds pick up. Winter storms make waters rough all around the island (outside of the reef, which runs the length of the south side of the island) but, even so, the calm days between winter storms can be the best times to get out on the water.

Moloka'i has plenty of wind – advanced windsurfers can harness it in the Pailolo and Ka'iwi Channels; however, you'll need your own gear.

ACTIVITY	BEST PLACES
Fishing	Penguin Banks (right)
Kayaking	Northeast Coast (p446)
	South Coast (p436)
Scuba Diving	Pala'au barrier reef (p436)
Snorkeling	Dixie Maru Beach (p459)
	Kawakiu Beach (p457)
Swimming	Twenty Mile Beach (p445)
	Dixie Maru Beach (p459)
	Twenty Mile Beach (p445)
Biking	Island-wide (p436)
Golf	Ironwood Hills Golf Club (p450)
Hiking	Halawa Valley (p446)
	Kalaupapa Peninsula (p455)
	Kamakou Preserve (p449)

There are two main activities operators and outfitters who pretty much handle every activity on the island and often work together:

» Moloka'i Fish & Dive (p436), the largest of the two operators, is really the Big Kahuna of activities on the island. It operates everything from kayak to fishing trips and rents gear of all kinds. If you have a vague notion of something you'd like to do, come here and see what they advise. It has an intriguing shop in town.

» Moloka'i Outdoors (p436) does much of what its main competitor does and can custom-design adventures. It is located off the road to the main pier.

CYCLING & MOUNTAIN BIKING

There are more than 40 miles of trails on Moloka'i that are good for mountain biking: the roads of the thick Moloka'i Forest Reserve (p448) are prime, as are trails on the arid West End, many with ocean views. As for cycling, pretty much all of Moloka'i's paved highways would make for a scenic ride, especially the trip to the Halawa Valley.

Moloka'i Bicycle (p436) in Kaunakakai is the place to go for all things cycling.

FISHING

The sportfishing is excellent in the waters off Moloka'i, especially around the fish-filled Penguin Banks off the southwestern tip. Bait casting is good on the southern and western shores. Boats dock and leave from the Kaunakakai Wharf; see p453 for a list of charter boats. Rates run at about $25 per person per hour with various time and passenger minimums (eg six-person, four-hour minimum would be $600). Close to shore expect to find large fish including 'omilu, a type of trevally. Further out you'll find a'u (marlin) and the popular various species of ahi (yellowfin tuna).

KAYAKING

Moloka'i Fish & Dive runs a guided five-hour trip ($70) that paddles the south coast with the wind, finishing with a boat tow back to the dock.

Moloka'i

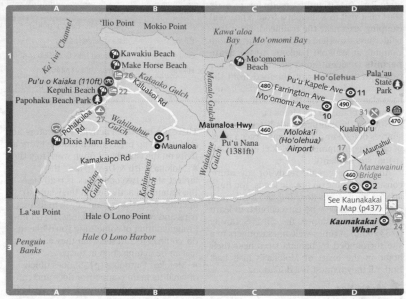

SCUBA DIVING

Moloka'i's 32-mile Pala'au barrier reef – Hawaii's longest – lies along the south side of the island, promising top-notch snorkeling and excellent diving in uncrowded waters all year long, when conditions allow. To reach the good spots, you'll need a boat.

For boat charters, see p453 or go with one of the activity operators (from $140, three to four hours).

WHALE WATCHING

Witness the sudden drama of humpback whales breaching from December to April. Moloka'i Fish & Dive, Moloka'i Outdoors and the boat charter operators (p453) all offer trips. Rates start at $70.

☞ Tours

Tours on Moloka'i mirror the island's personality. Don't expect little buses to take you around with canned commentary and a stop for souvenirs. Rather, local tours concentrate on experiences you wouldn't be able to enjoy on your own, such as a trek up the Halawa Valley (p446), Kalaupapa (p455) or the guided tours of the Nature Conservancy's Kamakou Preserve (p449) and Mo'omomi Beach (p453).

The two main activity operators offer various tours, including custom drives to pretty much any place on the island.

Much of Moloka'i's coastline is only accessible by boat. The wild beauty of the impenetrable Pali Coast (p447), home to the world's tallest sea cliffs, is unforgettable. The activity operators and boat charters (see the following list) all arrange trips that take the better part of a day, often including a stop for snorkeling, and don't run in the winter, lest storms send you to Gilligan's Island.

Boat charters generally leave from Kaunakakai Wharf and, if you're traveling in a group, can be tailored to your desires. Rates start at about $100 per hour for whole boat charters, with a four-hour minimum. Try one of these personable outfits:

Alyce C Sportfishing Charters BOAT CHARTER
(☏558-8377; www.alycecsportfishing.com) Joe Reich has over 30 years of experience and, in addition to sportfishing charters, also does whale-watching jaunts and round-island runs on his 31ft boat.

Fun Hogs Sport Fishing BOAT CHARTER
(☏567-6789; www.molokaifishing.com) Fish your heart out on the *Ahi,* a 27ft sportfishing boat. Snorkeling and whale watching are also offered. Mike Holmes is a legendary local long-distance canoeist.

Hallelujah Hou Fishing BOAT CHARTER
(☏336-1870; www.hallelujahhoufishing.com) Captain Clayton Ching runs all types of fishing

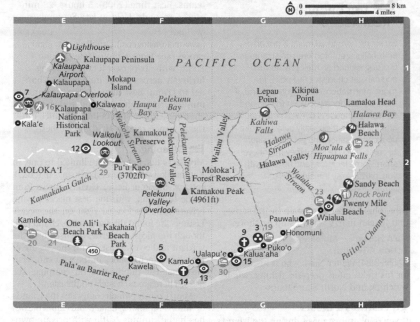

Molokaʻi

◉ Sights

1 Big Wind Kite Factory &
   Plantation Gallery B2
2 Church Row D2
3 ʻIliʻiliʻopae Heiau G3
   Ironwood Hills Golf Course .... (see 8)
4 Kahinapohaku Fishpond H2
5 Kakahaiʻa National Wildlife
   Refuge F3
   Kaluaʻaha Church .... (see 9)
6 Kapuaʻiwa Coconut Grove D2
7 Kauleonanahoa (Phallic Stone) E1
8 Molokaʻi Museum & Cultural
   Center D2
9 Our Lady of Seven Sorrows G3
10 Post-a-Nut D2
11 Purdy's Macadamia Nut Farm D1
12 Sandalwood Pit E2
13 Smith-Bronte Landing F3
14 St Joseph's Church F3
15 ʻUalapuʻe Fishpond G3
   Waialua Congregational Church .... (see 4)

Activities, Courses & Tours

16 Kalaupapa Trailhead E1
   Molokai Mule Ride .... (see 16)
17 Nature Conservancy D2

◉ Sleeping

   Aʻahi Place B&B .... (see 20)
   Aloha Beach House .... (see 23)
18 Dunbar Beachfront Cottages G3
19 Hale Lei Lani G3
   Hilltop Cottage .... (see 19)
20 Hotel Molokaʻi E3
21 Ka Hale Mala E3
22 Ke Nani Kai B1
23 Molokaʻi Beach House H2
24 Molokaʻi Shores D3
25 Palaʻau State Park Campground E1
26 Paniolo Hale B1
27 Papohaku Campground A2
28 Puʻu O Hoku Ranch H2
29 Waikolu Lookout Campground E2
30 Wavecrest Resort G3

◉ Eating

   Coffees of Hawaii .... (see 31)
   Hula Shores .... (see 20)
31 Kualapuʻu Cookhouse D2
   Manaʻe Goods & Grindz .... (see 19)
   Maunaloa General Store .... (see 1)

Drinking

   Hula Shores .... (see 20)

ⓘ UNFORGIVING TRESPASSES

Exploring unmarked roads is not advisable. Folks aren't too keen on strangers cruising around on their private turf and can get churlish. (See p636 for more information.) On the other hand, if there's a fishpond you want to see, and someone's house is between the road and the water, it's usually easy to strike up a conversation and get permission to cross. If you're lucky they might even share some local lore and history with you, particularly the old-timers.

trips, plus he's a real captain in the sense that he can marry you on ship *or* shore.

Ma'a Hawai'i – Moloka'i
Action Adventures   BOAT CHARTER
(☑558-8184) Walter Naki, who is also known for his treks, offers deep-sea fishing, whale watching and North Shore tours.

✺ Festivals & Events

If you're planning a visit during the island's culture-rich festivals, make sleeping reservations many months in advance. See www.visitmolokai.com for more details.

Ka Moloka'i Makahiki   TRADITIONAL FESTIVAL
(☑553-3673) Moloka'i is the only island still holding the ancient *makahiki* festival. It is celebrated in late January with a traditional ceremony, an Olympics-esque competition of ancient Hawaiian sports, crafts and activities.

Moloka'i Ka Hula Piko   HULA
(☑553-3673; www.molokaievents.com/ka hulapiko) As Moloka'i is known as the birthplace of hula, its hula festival in May has some profound roots. It opens with a solemn ceremony at 3am at Pu'u Nana (the site of Hawaii's first hula school), followed by a day-long festival including performance, food and crafts.

St Damien's Feast Day   RELIGIOUS EVENT
(☑553-5112) There are various events held in honor of Moloka'i's saint, including a walk between the churches in the east that he built: St Joseph's (p443) and Our Lady of Seven Sorrows (p444).

Na Wahine O Ke Kai   CANOE RACE
(www.nawahineokekai.com) Much the same as the Moloka'i Hoe, but with all-female

teams. Best time (2008): 5 hours, 22 minutes, 5 seconds. Held in late September.

Moloka'i Hoe   CANOE RACE
(www.molokaihoe.com) Grueling outrigger canoe race from remote Hale O Lono Point, with six-person teams paddling furiously across the 41-mile Ka'iwi Channel to O'ahu. Best time (2008): 4 hours, 38 minutes, 35 seconds. Considered the world championship of men's long-distance outrigger canoe racing. Held in October.

🛏 Sleeping

Moloka'i's hotel choices are limited to one, in Kaunakakai. Almost everybody stays in a B&B, cottage, condo or house. Quality ranges from rustic to swank, with the best places having private grounds located right on the ocean. Listings are found throughout this chapter, although the nicest properties are usually in the verdant and coastal east. (With the closure of Moloka'i Ranch, condos in the west can seem desolate.) For information on camping, see p429. There are no hostels on the island.

Maui County (which comprises the islands of Maui, Moloka'i, Lana'i and Kaho'olawe) has had a running battle with private owners who want to do vacation rentals. Primarily this is due to complaints on Maui and not on Moloka'i, but county rules still apply here (one of many reasons that locals feel under-represented politically). Although condos are legally in the clear, the situation is somewhat murkier for houses and B&Bs. Most owners ignore the law and a range of choices can be found on the web.

Some good sources of rental and accommodation information and reservations:

Friendly Isle Realty (Map p437; ☑553-3666, 800-600-4158; www.molokairesorts.com; 75 Ala Malama Ave, Kaunakakai) Books for more than 70 condos island-wide. Rates average $550 to $800 per week.

Moloka'i Vacation Properties (☑553-8334, 800-367-2984; www.molokai-vacation -rental.com) Well-respected local agent with houses and condos. The former cost an average of $150 to $300 per night.

Vacation Rentals By Owner (www.vrbo. com) More than 100 listings of condos and houses island-wide, from $100 to $1500 per night (average $200). An excellent source.

✕ Eating

Foodie sensations had passed by Moloka'i until recently. But there are glimmers of change here, with a few interesting options (including a great place in Kualapu'u and a fine lunch counter on the way to the Halawa Valley). But your best bet is to cook for yourself – the markets in Kaunakakai are well stocked and Moloka'i has some unique foods (see the boxed text, p442).

❶ Getting There & Away

If you have time, taking the ferry from Maui is a more sociable and scenic experience than flying – the afternoon boat catches the sunset almost year-round, and in winter breaching whales glorify the scene.

AIR Moloka'i (Ho'olehua) Airport (MKK) is small: you claim your baggage on a long bench. Single-engine planes are the norm; sit right behind the cockpit area for spectacular views forward. Because of weight limits for individual bags (40lb), pack a small duffel bag in case you have to redistribute your belongings.

The main airlines servicing Moloka'i have frequent service to Honolulu and one or two flights a day to Kahului on Maui. Unless you have a through ticket from the mainland, it's usually much cheaper to buy from the carriers listed here, rather than their larger airline partners.

Island Air (☑800-652-6541; www.islandair. com) Codeshares with Hawaiian Airlines; flies planes with two, yes two!, engines.

Mokulele Airlines (☑866-260-7070; www. mokuleleairlines.com) Partner with go! airlines.

Pacific Wings (☑888-575-4546; www.paci ficwings.com) Often the cheapest; has daily flights to Kalaupapa.

SEA Moloka'i Ferry (☑866-307-6524; www. molokaiferry.com; adult/child $70/35) runs a morning and late-afternoon ferry between Lahaina on Maui (across from the Pioneer Inn) and Moloka'i's Kaunakakai Wharf. The 90-minute crossing through the Pailolo Channel (aka Pakalolo Channel for all the pot smuggling) can get choppy; in fact, you can enjoy the thrill of a water park just by sitting on the top deck and getting drenched. Buy tickets online, by phone or on the *Moloka'i Princess* a half-hour before departure. Fares fluctuate with the price of gas.

❶ Getting Around

Renting a car is essential if you intend to fully explore the island or if you are renting a house or condo and will need to shop. All of Moloka'i's highways and primary routes are good, paved roads. The free tourist map, widely available on the island, is good; *Franko's Moloka'i Guide Map* is massively detailed and highly useful. James A Bier's *Map of Moloka'i & Lana'i* has an excellent index. Both fold up small, cost under $6 and are widely available on the island.

TO/FROM THE AIRPORT & FERRY Ask your car rental agency if they can arrange ferry pickup; all service the airport.

A taxi from the airport costs around $25 to Kaunakakai, and $30 to the West End.

One of Moloka'i's trademarks is the sign you see leaving the airport: 'Aloha. Slow down, this is Moloka'i. Mahalo.'

BICYCLE Moloka'i is a good place for cycling. The local bike shop, Molokai Bicycle in Kaunakakai, is a treasure. See p436 for details.

CAR Keep in mind that rental cars are technically not allowed on unpaved roads, and there can also be restrictions on camping. If you intend to explore remote parts of the island, such as Mo'omomi Bay, you'll at least need a vehicle with high clearance, probably a 4WD. Book well in advance, especially if planning a weekend visit. But if you're feeling lucky in low season, walk-up rates at the airport can be half that found online.

There are gas stations in Kaunakakai. Expect sticker shock at the pump.

Alamo Rental Car (www.alamo.com) The sole operator at the airport.

Island Kine Auto Rental (☑553-5242, 877-553-5242; www.molokai-car-rental.com) A local outfit, offers a full range of vehicles at good rates. Pick-ups can be arranged from anywhere, including the ferry dock and the airport.

Average driving times and distances from Kaunakakai:

DESTINATION	MILES	TIME
Halawa Valley	27	1¼hr
Ho'olehua Airport	6.5	10min
Kalaupapa Trailhead	10	20min
Maunaloa	17	30min
Papohaku Beach	21.5	45min
Puko'o	16	20min
Twenty Mile Beach	20	40min

TAXI Hele Mai Taxi (☑336-0967) Services Moloka'i.

KAUNAKAKAI

POP 2700

View a photo of Moloka'i's main town from 50 years ago and the main drag won't look much different than it does today. Worn wood-fronted buildings with tin roofs that roar in the rain seem like refugees from a Clint Eastwood Western. But there's no artifice to Kaunakakai – it's the real deal. All of the island's commercial activities are here and you'll visit often – if nothing else, for its shops and services.

Walking around the town can occupy a couple of hours if you take time to get into the rhythm of things and do a little exploring.

Another popular local T-shirt reads 'Molokaʻi Traffic Jam: Two Drivers Stopped in the Middle of the Road Talking Story.' And while there are stop signs, there are no stoplights.

If possible, stop by on Saturday morning when the street market draws much of the island.

◉ Sights

Kaunakakai is an attraction in itself. Specifically look for gems of old buildings such as the Molokaʻi Library (Map opposite; Ala Malama Ave), which dates from 1937. Kaunakakai Wharf (Map p430) is the busy commercial lifeline for Molokaʻi. OK, it's not that busy... A freight barge chugs in, skippers unload catches of mahimahi (white-fleshed fish also called 'dolphin'), and a buff gal practices for a canoe race. A roped-off area with a floating dock provides a kiddie swim area. On the west side of the wharf, near the canoe shed, are the stone foundations of oceanfront Kamehameha V house (off Map opposite), now overgrown. The house was once called 'Malama,' which today is the name of Kaunakakai's main street.

Kapuaʻiwa Coconut Grove   HISTORICAL SITE
(Map p430; Maunaloa Hwy) As Molokaʻi was the favorite island playground of King Kamehameha V, he had the royal 10-acre Kapuaʻiwa Coconut Grove planted near his sacred bathing pools in the 1860s. Standing tall, about a mile west of downtown, its name means 'mysterious taboo.' Be careful where you walk (or park) when you visit, because coconuts frequently plunge silently to the ground, landing with a deadly thump.

Church Row   HISTORICAL SITE
(Map p430; Maunaloa Hwy) Across from the coconut grove is Church Row. Any denomination that attracts a handful of members receives its own little tract of land. Religion in general is very popular on Molokaʻi; there are many churches and some denominations – such as Catholicism – have more than one.

One Aliʻi Beach Park   PARK
(Map p430; Maunaloa Hwy) Three miles east of town, One Aliʻi Beach Park is split into two parks. One side has a coconut palm–lined shore, a playing field, a picnic pavilion and bathrooms, and although not especially attractive it's very popular with local families for huge weekend BBQs. Two memorials commemorate the 19th-century immigration of Japanese citizens to Hawaii. The

other side is a greener and more attractive picnic area. The water is shallow and silty.

Pacifica Hawaiʻi   CRAFT PRODUCER
(off Map opposite; ☑553-8484; www.pacificahawaii .com; Kolapa Pl) Molokaʻi has a burgeoning foodie scene. Some noteworthy sea salt is produced close to the center in the front yard of a house belonging to well-known (among salties) salt-maker Nancy Gove. Her Pacifica Hawaiʻi salt comes in various flavors – ask for a sample of smoked salt. Tours (one hour, by appointment) reveal that there are more mysteries to making salt from ocean water than you'd imagine.

Softball & Baseball Fields   PARKS
The downtown softball and baseball fields are often the most active spot on the island. For some local flavor, go down there and cheer on the Molokaʻi Farmers as they compete against their high-school rivals, the Lanaʻi Pinelads.

🏃 Activities

While activities in Kaunakakai proper are limited, it is *the* place to rent gear or arrange tours for island activities.

There are open yoga sessions daily in town; check the *Molokai Dispatch* for locations.

Molokaʻi Fish & Dive   OUTDOOR ACTIVITIES
(Map opposite; ☑553-5926, 336-1088; www.molo kaifishanddive.com; Ala Malama Ave, Kaunakakai; ☺8am-6pm Mon-Sat, to 2pm Sun) From its interesting shop, which is crammed with sporting gear and idiosyncratic souvenirs, Molokaʻi Fish & Dive can pretty much handle any adventure request. It also rents out a full range of gear (mask and fins per day/week $10/35, fishing pole $13/35, beach chair $5/20).

Molokaʻi Outdoors   OUTDOOR ACTIVITIES
(Map opposite; ☑553-4477, 877-553-4477; www .molokai-outdoors.com; Hio Pl, Kaunakakai; ☺8:30am-4pm) Molokaʻi Outdoors can custom-design adventures, as well as doing most of what Molokaʻi Fish & Dive does. It is located off the road to the main pier.

Molokaʻi Bicycle   CYCLING & MOUNTAIN BIKING
(Map opposite; ☑553-3931, 800-709-2453; www. molokaibicycle.com; 80 Mohala St, Kaunakakai; ☺3-6pm Wed, 9am-2pm Sat) This shop's owner has a great depth of knowledge about biking across the breadth of the island. He'll do pick-ups and drop-offs outside his opening hours. As well as offering repairs, parts and sales, there is a full range of bike rentals

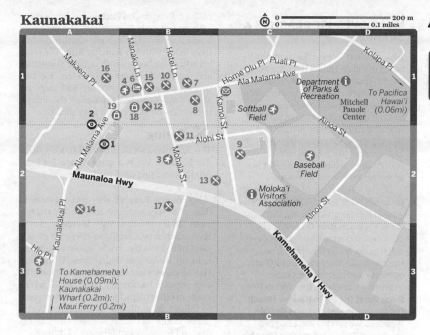

starting at $20/75 per day/week; glam models go for more. Prices include helmet, lock, pump, maps and much more.

🛏 Sleeping

Few travelers actually stay in Kaunakakai. The best places are further along the scenic east coast near the beaches and ocean. For full details on securing Moloka'i accommodations, see p437.

Hotel Moloka'i   HOTEL $$
(Map p430; ☎553-5347, 800-535-0085; www.hotelmolokai.com; Kamehameha V Hwy; r $140-250; 🛜🏊) Moloka'i's only hotel has a certain veteran feel about it, although some would say it is shell-shocked. It's not especially alluring. It has quirky rooms with a faux-native design that gives them tunnel-like qualities, and compact grounds with a small pool and hammocks along the reef-protected limpid, silty shore. Upstairs rooms are slightly larger and brighter; some units have fridges and microwaves.

Moloka'i Shores   CONDO $$
(Map p430; ☎553-5954, reservations 800-535-0085; www.castleresorts.com; Kamehameha V Hwy; 1 bedroom $125-200, 2 bedroom $150-250; 🏊) This 1970s condo development has units ranging from atrocious to charming,

Kaunakakai

◎ Sights
1 Moloka'i Acupuncture & Massage......A2
2 Moloka'i Library A1

Activities, Courses & Tours
3 Moloka'i Bicycle B2
4 Moloka'i Fish & Dive B1
5 Molokai Outdoors A3

🛏 Sleeping
6 Friendly Isle Realty B1

🍴 Eating
7 Aunty Ruby's Café B1
8 Friendly Market.................................. B1
9 Kamoi Snack-N-Go C2
10 Kanemitsu Bakery B1
11 Maka's Korner B2
12 Misaki's.. B1
13 Moloka'i Drive-Inn............................B2
14 Moloka'i Pizza Cafe A2
15 Moloka'i Wines & Spirits B1
16 Outpost Natural Foods A1
17 Paddler's Inn.....................................B2

🛍 Shopping
Kalele Bookstore.........................(see 11)
18 Moloka'i Art from the Heart B1
19 Saturday morning market.................A1

MOLOKA'I SURF BEACHES & BREAKS

What Moloka'i – one of the most breathtaking islands in Hawaii, if not the entire Pacific – possesses in beauty, it lacks in waves. Unfortunately, due to shadowing from the other islands, there just isn't much in the way of consistent surf. Yet when the surf's up, keep in mind that the Friendly Isle encompasses the ideals of 'old Hawaii' in which family remains the priority, so remember to smile a lot and let the locals have the set waves.

On the western end of Moloka'i, winter swells bring surf anywhere between 2ft and 10ft (and, very rarely, 15ft). The break known as **Hale O Lono** is one such exposed area. It comprises several fun peaks and is the starting point for the annual 32-mile Moloka'i-to-O'ahu outrigger and paddleboard races.

When it's breaking, the stretch from **Rock Point** (p445) to **Halawa Beach** (p447) on the east end, and **Kepuhi Beach** (p458) on the West End are reliable spots. Leave **Kawakiu Beach's** (p457) winter waves to the experts.

Moloka'i Fish & Dive and Moloka'i Outdoors charge from $25 to $40 per day for surfboard rentals.

depending on the whims of the individual owners. If you decide to stay here, choose your unit carefully. All have full kitchens, cable TV, lanai (veranda) and ceiling fans. The grounds are the best feature and have a large pool, shuffleboard, BBQ areas and more. Like elsewhere on this stretch of coast, the water is shallow and muddy.

A'ahi Place Bed & Breakfast COTTAGE **$**
(Map p430; ☎553-8033; www.molokai.com/aahi; main cabin from $75) This very simple, clean cedar cottage is in a small subdivision, 1 mile east of Kaunakakai. Kind of like a camp cabin (with lots of wood paneling), this place has a full kitchen, washing machine and garden lanai. More than two people will feel crowded, whether in the bare-bones 'backpackers cabin' ($35) or the somewhat more swank main cabin. Breakfast is $10.

Ka Hale Mala B&B **$**
(Map p432; ☎553-9009; www.molokai-bnb.com; apt $90, incl breakfast $100; wi-fi) Enjoy the spaciousness of a 900-sq-ft, one-bedroom apartment with a fully equipped kitchen and living room with an exposed-beam ceiling. The two-story house is secluded by lush plantings, including trees laden with low-hanging fruit. The owners add to the bounty with organic vegetables and healthy breakfasts. Rates are for two people; extras (up to two) are $20 each. It's about 5 miles east of Kaunakakai; the charming owners do airport and ferry pick-ups.

Eating

The Saturday morning market (p439) along Ala Malama Ave is a good source for local produce and prepared foods.

TOP CHOICE **Aunty Ruby's Cafe** HAWAIIAN **$$**
(Map p437; www.auntyrubys.com; Ala Malama Ave; meals $8-14; 6:30am-9pm Mon-Sat) Aunty Ruby's is run by a family as effervescent as a glass of soda water; bright smiles all around light up the simple dining area. Dishes are Hawaii classics like loco moco, roast pork, the ever-popular hamburger steak and a whole range of other treats that can trace their roots to influences as diverse as Asian and Portuguese. Soup and salad specials are mighty fine and breakfasts will do you 'til dinner.

Maka's Korner CAFE **$**
(Map p437; cnr Mohala & Alohi Sts; meals $5-8; 7am-4pm Mon-Sat) A dead-simple corner location belies the fine yet simple fare that hops hot off the grill onto your plate at Maka's. Moloka'i's best burgers come with excellent fries, although many patrons are simply addicted to the teri-beef. Pancakes are served throughout the day and many a long night has been soothed the next day with a fried-egg sandwich. Sit at the counter or at a picnic table outside.

Kanemitsu Bakery BAKERY **$**
(Map p437; Ala Malama Ave; 5:30am-6:30pm Wed-Mon) Famous throughout the islands for its Moloka'i sweet bread and lavosh crackers (the macnut ones are extraordinary). Otherwise, you'll be surprised such good stuff can come from such a drab place. Every night but Monday, slip down the alley to the bakery's back door at 10pm and buy hot loaves, sliced open and with one of five spreads, from the taciturn baker. Note: the best stuff is often gone by 1pm each day.

Moloka'i Pizza Cafe PIZZA **$$**
(Map p437; Kaunakakai Pl; meals $9-15; 10am-10pm Mon-Thu, to 11pm Fri & Sat, 11am-10pm Sun) Order at the counter or have a seat in the un-

adorned dining area at this pizza joint offering everything from salad and sub sandwiches to burgers and pasta. Divert yourself with a festival of coin-operated games with dubious 'prizes.' Lazy cooks can get their pizza half-baked (it's neither thick, thin, nor even just right) and finish cooking it in their rental unit.

Moloka'i Drive-Inn   FAST FOOD **$**
(Map p437; Kamehameha V Hwy; meals $4-7; ⊘6am-10pm) Always popular, this timeless fast-food counter is best for classic plate lunches and simple local pleasures like teri-beef sandwiches, omelettes with Spam or Vienna lunch meat, and fried saimin noodles. Serious talking story and gossip entertains while you wait.

Paddler's Inn   AMERICAN **$$**
(Map p437; 10 Mohala St; mains $8-20; ⊘7am-2am) This casual bar with a large concrete beer garden has a long menu that's served until about 9pm. There are few surprises, from the deep-fried pub grub to the burgers, steaks and simple pastas. Service is surprisingly crisp, a quality you may lack after a few runs at the vast cocktail menu.

Hula Shores   ISLAND CONTEMPORARY **$$**
(Map p430; Hotel Moloka'i, Kamehameha V Hwy; breakfasts & lunches $5-10, dinners $15-20; ⊘7-10:30am & 11am-2pm daily, 6-9pm Sat-Thu, 4-9pm Fri) You can't beat the oceanfront location but you can beat the food at Hotel Moloka'i's restaurant. Breakfasts are best; try the banana pancakes made with fruit from just up the road. Lunch and dinner is a mixed bag of sandwiches, salads and mains such as chicken with a sauce, fish with a sauce etc. The views of Lana'i, the tiki torches and the sound of the small waves divert your attention.

Kamoi Snack-N-Go   DESSERT **$**
(Map p437; Moloka'i Professional Bldg, Kamoi St; scoops $2; ⊘10am-9pm Mon-Sun) This candy store is loaded with sweets and, more importantly, Honolulu-made Dave's Hawaiian Ice Cream. The banana fudge is truly a treat.

Outpost Natural Foods   MARKET/DELI **$**
(Map p437; 70 Makaena Pl; ⊘9am-6pm Mon-Thu, to 4pm Fri, 10am-5pm Sun; ✍) Organic produce, a good selection of packaged and bulk health foods and excellent local fare. Its deli (meals $5 to $8, open 10am to 3pm weekdays) makes fresh vegetarian burritos, sandwiches, salads and smoothies.

Friendly Market   SUPERMARKET **$**
(Map p437; Ala Malama Ave; ⊘8:30am-8:30pm Mon-Fri, to 6:30pm Sat) The best selection of any supermarket on the island. In the

afternoon fresh fish from the docks often appears.

Moloka'i Wines & Spirits   MARKET **$**
(Map p437; Ala Malama Ave; ⊘9am-8pm Sun-Thu, to 9pm Fri & Sat) Has many Hawaii and mainland microbrews plus inexpensive wines and upscale cheeses and deli items. This is the place to get all you need for silly tropical drinks. Fire up the blender!

Misaki's   MARKET **$**
(Map p437; 78 Ala Malama Ave; ⊘8:30am-8:30pm Mon-Sat, 9am-noon Sun) The long hours are the key to success at this living museum of grocery retailing.

 Drinking & Entertainment

Bring board games, books and a gift for gab as nighttime fun is mostly DIY on Moloka'i.

Paddler's Inn serves booze inside and out until 2am. On Friday nights there is often a live Hawaiian band; at other times satellite sports prevails.

Hula Shores   HAWAIIAN MUSIC
(Map p432; Hotel Moloka'i, Kamehameha V Hwy; ⊘7-10:30am & 11am-2pm daily, 6-9pm Sat-Thu, 4-9pm Fri) The Hotel Moloka'i's inhouse restaurant has a simple bar and is good for a sunset drink. On many nights there is live music or, for those ready to climb every mountain, karaoke. But the real draw are the local *kapuna* (elders) who gather at a long table to play Hawaiian music on 'Aloha Fridays' from 4pm to 6pm. The music always draws a crowd; the performers range from those with some languid and traditional hula moves to jam sessions with a ukulele. It's a true community gathering with some of the people who are the heart and soul of local culture and who delight in showing off their traditional talents.

Moloka'i Mini Mart   DVD RENTALS
(Mohala St; ⊘6am-11pm) DVD rentals for your condo nights.

Shopping

Saturday morning market   MARKET
(Ala Malama Ave; ⊘8am-2pm) This weekly market at the west end of Ala Malama Ave is the place to browse local crafts, try new fruits, stock up on organic produce and pick up some flowers. You'll find much of Moloka'i here before noon.

Moloka'i Art from the Heart   ART GALLERY
(64 Ala Malama Ave; ⊘9:30am-5pm Mon-Fri, 9am-2:30pm Sat) Run by local artists, this small shop is as packed with art as a

1. St Joseph's Church, Kamalo (p443)
One of only two still standing of the four churches Father Damien built outside Kalaupapa.

2. Kalaupapa Peninsula (p453)
A mule ride is the only way down Kalaupapa's *pali* (sea cliffs), besides hiking.

3. Silversword
Silversword ('*ahinahina* in Hawaiian) takes its name from its elegant silver spiked leaves.

4. Kamakou Preserve (p449)
This preserve protects cloud forest, bogs and habitat for many endangered plants and animals.

LOCAL TREATS

Fruit trees grow in profusion in the east end of Moloka'i; if you're lucky you'll have plenty to pick from your rental. Organic farms are sprouting as well and you'll find their produce at Kaunakakai's Saturday morning market and Outpost Natural Foods. Other local foods to look for:

Purdy's macadamia nuts (p452) Probably the best you'll have anywhere

Coffees of Hawaii (p450) Grown and roasted on the island

Kumu Farms macadamia nut pesto Buy it at Kaunakakai's Friendly Market; superb and bursting with basil goodness

Kanemitsu Bakery's lavosh crackers (p438) The macadamia nut and taro varieties are crunchy and delicious

Molokai Roadside Marinade Sold at Kaunakakai's Friendly Market; turns any steak into a succulent, tangy treat

Pacifica Hawai'i sea salt (p436)

Jackson Pollock painting is packed with brushstrokes. Works in all mediums can be found here; quality ranges from the earnest to the superb. The T-shirts with local sayings are the real sleepers in the souvenir department.

Kalele Bookstore BOOKS
(64 Ala Malama Ave; ☎) New and used books, local artworks and loads of local culture and travel advice.

❶ Information

Bank of Hawai'i (Ala Malama Ave) One of many locations with ATMs.
Kalele Bookstore (☎567-9094; 64 Ala Malama Ave; ☎) A community treasure. Besides books, get free maps or enjoy a coffee and meet some locals out back on the shady terrace. Owner Teri Waros is a fount of local knowledge.
Molokai Dispatch (www.themolokaidispatch. com) Free weekly with an activist slant published each Thursday; watch the events calendar for local happenings.
Moloka'i Drugs (Moloka'i Professional Bldg, Kamoi St; ☺9am-5:45pm Mon-Fri, to 2pm Sat) Drugstore fare.
Moloka'i General Hospital (280 Puali St; ☺24hr) Emergency services.
Moloka'i Library (Ala Malama Ave; ☺9:30am-

5pm Mon-Fri, Wed noon-8pm) Buy a library card for three months ($10) or five years ($25) and enjoy internet use and library privileges here and at 50 other branches statewide.
Moloka'i Mini Mart (Mohala St; ☺6am-11pm) Convenience store with internet access (per min 8¢) plus printing, and espresso in the morning.
Moloka'i Visitor Center (www.visitmolokai .com) A website with excellent links.
Moloka'i Visitors Association (MVA; ☎553-3876, 800-800-6367; www.molokai-hawaii .com; 2 Kamoi St; ☺9am-noon Mon-Fri) This simple office can help with information about member businesses.
Post office (Ala Malama Ave) The one out west is more fun (see p452).

❶ Getting There & Around

Kaunakakai is a walking town. **Rawlin's Chevron** (cnr Hwy 460 & Ala Malama Ave; ☺6:30am-8:30pm Mon-Sat, 7am-6pm Sun) has credit card–operated pumps, making it the only round-the-clock gas station on the island.

EAST MOLOKA'I

The oft-quoted road sign 'Slow down, this is Moloka'i' really applies as you head east. Whether you are on the island for a day or a week, the 27-mile drive on Hwy 450 (aka Kamehameha V Hwy) from Kaunakakai to the Halawa Valley is simply a must.

Unlike the arid west, this is tropical Moloka'i, with palm trees arching over the road, and banana, papaya, guava and passion fruits hanging from the lush foliage, ripe for the picking. As you drive you'll catch glimpses of ancient fishponds, the neighboring islands of Lana'i and Maui, stoic old wooden churches, modest family homes, beaches and much more. But don't take your eye off the road for long or you'll run over a dog sleeping on the yellow line.

This being Moloka'i, this intoxicating drive is rarely crowded and cars tend to mosey. Of course for the final third, when the smoothly paved road narrows down to one sinuous lane, you have little choice but to slow down. But that's just as well, as each curve yields a new vista. The final climb up and over into the remote Halawa Valley is breathtaking.

On the practical side, bring gear so you can swim and snorkel at beaches that catch your fancy along the way. There's no gas east of Kaunakakai but there is an excellent small grocery and lunch counter about halfway, in Puko'o. Most of the choicest rentals are also found along this drive; see p437 for a list of agents. Mile markers simplify finding things.

Fishponds

Starting just east of Kaunakakai and continuing past the 20-mile marker are dozens of *loko i'a* (fishponds), huge circular walls of rocks that are part of one of the world's most advanced forms of aquaculture. Monumental in size, backbreaking in creation, the fishponds operate on a simple principle: little fish swim in, big fish can't swim out. Some of the ponds are obscured and overgrown by mangroves, but others have been restored by locals anxious to preserve this link to their past. The Kahinapohaku fishpond, about half a mile past the 19-mile marker, is in excellent shape and is tended to by *konohiki* (caretakers) who live simply on site. Another good one is at the 13-mile marker in 'Ualapu'e.

Kawela

Kakahaia Beach Park is a grassy strip wedged between the road and sea in Kawela, shortly before the 6-mile marker. It has a couple of picnic tables and is always popular for that high point in the locals' weekend calendar: the family picnic. This park is the only part of the Kakahai'a National Wildlife Refuge (www.fws.gov/kakahaia) that is open to the public. Most of the 20-acre refuge is inland from the road. It includes freshwater marshland, with a dense growth of bulrushes and an inland freshwater fishpond that has been expanded to provide a home for endangered birds, including the Hawaiian stilt and coot.

Kamalo

You can't help but be swept away by the quaint charm of little St Joseph's Church. It's one of only two still standing of the four island churches that missionary and saint Father Damien built outside of the Kalaupapa Peninsula. (The other, Our Lady of Seven Sorrows, is 4 miles further on; see p444.) This simple, one-room wooden church, dating from 1876, has a steeple and a bell, five rows of pews and some of the original wavy glass panes. There is also a lei-draped statue of Father Damien and a little cemetery beside the church. It is just past the 10-mile marker, where the road – like the snakes St Patrick chased out of Scotland – becomes sinuous. On St Damien's feast day, May 10, there is a procession between the two churches.

Just over three-quarters of a mile after the 11-mile marker, a small sign, on the *makai* (seaward) side of the road, notes the Smith-Bronte Landing, the site where pilot Ernest Smith and navigator Emory Bronte safely crash-landed their plane at the completion of the world's first civilian flight from the US mainland to Hawaii. The pair left California on July 14, 1927, destined for O'ahu and came down on Moloka'i 25 hours and two minutes later. A little memorial plaque is set among the kiawe trees and grasses.

'Ualapu'e

A half-mile beyond Wavecrest Resort condo development, at the 13-mile marker, you'll spot 'Ualapu'e Fishpond on the *makai* side of the road. This fishpond has been restored and restocked with mullet and milkfish, two species that were raised here in ancient times. It's a good place to ponder the labor involved in moving these thousands of large volcanic rocks.

With a striking view of green mountains rising up behind, and the ocean lapping gently out front, the Wavecrest Resort (www.wavecrestaoao.com; per day/week 1-bedroom from $100/600, 2-bedroom $150/800; ✖) is just around the bend on a small drive in from the main road. This place is as low-key as its host island. There is no beach, but the views are sweeping. Each unit is rented (and decorated) by the owner. Find links via agents and websites (see p437). All units have full kitchen, sofa bed, lanai or balcony, and use of the tennis court. Some have internet access.

Kalua'aha

The barely perceptible village of Kalua'aha is less than 2 miles past Wavecrest. The ruins of **Kalua'aha Church**, Moloka'i's first Christian church, are a bit off the road and inland but just visible, if you keep an eye peeled. It was built in 1844 by Moloka'i's first missionary, Harvey R Hitchcock. **Our Lady of Seven Sorrows** (⊙service 7:15am Sun) is found a quarter of a mile past the Kalua'aha Church site. The present Our Lady of Sorrows is a reconstruction from 1966 of the original wood-frame church, constructed in 1874 by the missionary Father Damien.

'Ili'ili'opae Heiau

Where's Unesco when you need it? 'Ili'ili'opae is Moloka'i's biggest heiau, and is thought to be the second largest in Hawaii. It also might possibly be the oldest religious site in the state. Yet this remarkable treasure is barely known, even by many locals.

The dimensions are astonishing: over 300ft long and 100ft wide, and about 22ft high on the eastern side, and 11ft high at the other end. The main platform is strikingly level. Archaeologists believe the original heiau may have been three times its current size, reaching out beyond Mapulehu Stream. Like the fishponds, this heiau represents an extraordinary amount of labor by people with no real tools at their disposal.

Once a *luakini* (temple of human sacrifice), 'Ili'ili'opae is today silent except for the singing of birds. African tulip and mango trees line the trail to the site, a peaceful place filled with mana (spiritual essence), whose stones still seem to emanate vibrations of a mystical past. Remember: it's disrespectful to walk across the top of the heiau.

Visiting this heiau is a little tricky, since it's on private property. Park on the highway (to avoid upsetting the neighbors) or, better yet, up the road near the market and walk back along the main road (about half a mile).

The trail is on the *mauka* (inland) side of the highway, just over half a mile past the 15-mile marker, immediately after Mapulehu Bridge. Look for the dirt track into the trees and a fire hydrant.

Walk up this dirt track off the main road, pass the roundabout around a patch of trees, and continue up the rocky road. Soon after, you'll see a trail on the left-hand side, opposite a house, that will take you across a streambed. Head to the steps on the northern side of the heiau.

For more info about crossing the property, call the owner **Pearl Hodgins** (☑336-0378). Alternatively, ask the owners of **Molokai Acupuncture and Massage** (Map p437; ☑553-3930; Molokai Center, 40 Ala Malama St) for permission, as they have property at the base of Heiau. Talk to either and you are good to go. They are both very nice.

Puko'o

Puko'o was once the seat of local government (complete with a courthouse, jail, wharf and post office), but the center of island life shifted to Kaunakakai when the plantation folks built that more centrally located town. Nowadays, Puko'o is a sleepy, slow-paced gathering of a few structures just sitting on a bend on the road (near 'Ili'ili'opae Heiau). But it has surprises, such as the cozy **beach** accessible just before the store, near the 16-mile marker. Take the short, curving path around the small bay, where fish leap out of the water, and you'll come to a stretch of sand with swimmable waters, backed by kiawe and ironwood trees.

🛏 Sleeping & Eating

TOP
CHOICE **Hale Lei Lani**   HOUSE **$$$**
(☑415-218-3037, 558-0808; www.tranquilmolokai.com; off Kamehameha V Hwy; from $250; ▣▩) The

---

LIVE LIKE A LOCAL

You've probably noticed that most of what there is to do on Moloka'i happens outdoors and often involves group functions. So how do you hook up with the local folks, that is, talk some story and get a feel for local culture? Start by picking up the *Molokai Dispatch* at Kalele Bookstore in Kaunakakai; it lists events of all kinds, including school benefits, church events and 4-H livestock competitions. Then go buy some crafts, get a taste of some home cooking or cheer on your favorite heifer. Other good sources in Kaunakakai are the bulletin boards outside Friendly Market, Outpost Natural Foods and the library. There are inevitably community groups selling goods to raise money along Ala Malama Ave; have a chat with these folk. Ball games at softball and baseball fields are also real community events.

Moloka'i estate you wish you had if you hadn't put all that money in Icelandic banks. Perched partway up a hill near the 16-mile marker (and more importantly, Mana'e Goods & Grindz), this contemporary home has sweeping views out to Maui and beyond. Two large bedrooms open off a great room and a kitchen that will inspire you to cook on your holiday. A walled pool is outside the door and fruit trees drop their bounty in the gardens.

Hilltop Cottage COTTAGE $$
(☑558-8161, 336-2076; www.molokaihilltopcottage.com; Kamehameha V Hwy; from $145; @) Instead of sleeping down near the water, put your head in the clouds here. The wraparound lanai is almost as big as the living space and you can savor the views of the neighbor islands by day or the millions of stars (which would be drowned out by light in cities and suburbs) by night. There's one nicely furnished bedroom, a full kitchen, laundry facilities and a two-night minimum stay.

⭐ TOP CHOICE Mana'e Goods & Grindz HAWAIIAN $
(16-mile marker, Kamehameha V Hwy; meals $5-10; ⊙8am-5pm) Even if it wasn't your only option, you'd still want to stop here. The plate lunches are something of a local legend: tender yet crispy chicken katsu (deep-fried fillets), specials such as pork and peas, and standards such as excellent teriyaki burgers. Sauces are homemade, the potato salad is superb and the mac salad is simply the island's best (it's not too gloopy). Picnic tables are shaded by trees and there's a little garden. The store manages to pack an amazing amount of groceries, goods and a few DVDs into a small space. The bit of Hwy 450 between the entrance and exit to the parking area is easily the least used stretch.

Waialua

Waialua is a little roadside community found after a few bends along the increasingly rugged coast, just past the 19-mile marker. The attractive Waialua Congregational Church was built of stone in 1855. Onward north from there, the road is waferthin, winding its way along an undulating coast that's forlorn, mysterious and fronted by white-flecked turquoise surf. The well-tended Kahinapohaku fishpond (see p443) is a half-mile past the 19-mile marker.

There are few prizes for guessing what mile marker is found at Twenty Mile Beach,

although its alias, Murphy's Beach, might keep you guessing. Well protected by a reef, the curve of fine sand fronts a large lagoon that is great for snorkeling. Near shore there are rocks and the water can be very shallow, but work your way out and you'll be rewarded with schools of fish, living sponges, octopuses and much more.

The pointy clutch of rocks sticking out, as the road swings left before the 21-mile marker, is called Rock Point (aka Pohakuloa Point). This popular surf spot is the site of local competitions and it's the place to go if you're looking for east-end breaks. The recent burst of creativity in place names extends to the fine little swimming cove about 500yd beyond the 21-mile marker: Sandy Beach. Look for a taro farm back in a verdant notch in the coast near here.

🛏 Sleeping

Some of Moloka'i's more popular rental houses are here. All offer your own little stretch of reef-protected beach, lots of privacy and nighttime views of the resorts, shops and traffic jams of Ka'anapali (Maui) flickering across the Pailolo Channel.

Aloha Beach House HOUSE $$$
(☑828-1100, 888-828-1008; www.molokaivacation.com; Kamehameha V Hwy; per day/week $290/2135; @) This modern house built in traditional plantation style has a breezeway linking the two bedrooms. The excellent kitchen flows into the living room, which flows out onto the large covered porch, which flows out onto the lawn and the beach and... There's high-speed internet and lots of beach toys. It's just past the 19-mile marker, near the church and close to Moloka'i Beach House.

Dunbar Beachfront Cottages COTTAGE $$
(☑558-8153, 800-673-0520; www.molokai-beachfront-cottages.com; Kamehameha V Hwy; 2-bedroom cottages from $180) The layout and furnishings

are tidy and functional at these two vacation cottages near the 18-mile marker. Each cottage sleeps four people and comes with a fully equipped kitchen, TV, ceiling fans, laundry, lanai and barbecue grills. The Pu'unana unit sits on stilts, while Pauwalu is more grounded. Both have good views and a three-night minimum.

Moloka'i Beach House　　　　HOUSE **$$**
(☎261-2500, 888-575-9400; www.molokaibeach house.com; Kamehameha V Hwy; per day/week $250/1600; @) Like most of the houses in the east, this simple wooden affair holds a few surprises. Rooms follow one after another until you realize you've got three bedrooms and a huge living/family room. It's not posh, but it's very relaxed. There's cable and high-speed internet, plus the usual DVD, BBQ etc. The grassy yard backs up to a narrow palm-shaded beach.

Waialua to Halawa

After the 22-mile marker the road starts to wind upwards. It's a good paved road, albeit narrow. Take it slow and watch for other cars coming around the cliff-hugging corners; there's always a place to pull over so cars can pass.

The terrain is rockier and less verdant here than over the preceding miles. The road levels out just before the 24-mile marker, where there's a view of the spiky islet of Mokuho'oniki, a seabird sanctuary and natural photo spot. If you hear a boom, it's a hapless gull setting off one of the shells left over from WWII target practice.

As you crest the hill, the fenced grassland is part of Pu'u O Hoku Ranch (☎558-8109; www.puuohoku.com; 2-bedroom cottage per day/week $140/840, 4-bedroom house $160/960; ☎), which at 14,000 acres is Moloka'i's second-largest ranch. Founded by Paul Fagan of Hana, the name means 'where hills and stars meet.' Guests who stay here enjoy views across the Pacific, and absolute isolation. A lodge that can sleep you and 21 of your closest friends is available for $1250 per night. There is a three-night minimum stay.

The ranch is also a certified **organic farm** growing tropical fruits and 'awa (kava, a native plant used to make an intoxicating drink). If you are staying in one of the east Moloka'i rentals, they will drop off a 10lb box of organic fruits and vegetables ($25) on their way to town on Thursdays; other-wise goods from the ranch can be found at Kaunakakai's Saturday morning market. A small **store** (◔9am-5pm Mon-Fri) along the road has snacks, drinks, some of the ranch's fine produce and a few locally made gifts.

A hidden grove of sacred *kukui* (candle-nut trees) on the ranch property marks the grave of the prophet Lanikaula, a revered 16th-century kahuna (priest, healer). One of the reasons the battling armies of Maui and O'ahu steered clear of Moloka'i for centuries was the powerful reputations of kahuna such as Lanikaula, who were said to have been able to pray their enemies to death. Many islanders claim to have seen the night lanterns of ghost marchers bobbing along near the grove.

Past the 25-mile marker, the jungle closes in, and the scent of eucalyptus fills the air. About 1.25 miles further on, you round a corner and the fantastic panorama of the Halawa Valley sweeps into view. Stop and enjoy the view for a bit. Depending on recent rains, the Moa'ula and Hipuapua Falls will either be thin strands or gushing white torrents back up the valley. In winter, look across the swirl of waves and volcanic sand below for the spectacle of whales breaching.

The recently paved road descends into the valley at a steep but manageable rate. Cyclists will love the entire ride, with the exception of staying alert for errant drivers in rental cars mesmerized by the views.

Halawa Valley

Halawa Valley enjoys end-of-the-road isolation, which residents guard jealously, and stunningly gorgeous scenery. It was an important settlement in pre-contact Moloka'i, with a population of more than 1000 and a complex irrigation system watering more than 700 taro patches. Little remains of its three heiau sites, two of which are thought to have been *luakini,* but you'll probably still feel the charge down here.

As late as the mid-19th century, the fertile valley still had a population of about 500 and produced most of Moloka'i's taro, as well as many of its melons, gourds and fruits. However, taro production came to an abrupt end in 1946, when a massive tsunami swept up the Halawa Valley, wiping out the farms and much of the community. A second tsunami washed the valley clean in 1957. Only a few families now remain.

◉ Sights & Activities

Sunday services are still occasionally held in Hawaiian at the saintly little 1948 green-and-white church, where visitors are welcome anytime (the door remains open). Nearby, don't be surprised if you see a bucket filled with fabulous heliconias and other stunning tropical flowers that are yours for the taking. They are grown by Kalani Pruet (☏336-1149; www.molokaiflowers.com), who runs a flower farm, offers waterfall hikes and makes a mean smoothie from fruit he gathers.

TOP CHOICE Moaʻula and Hipuapua Falls
WATERFALLS

It's possible to swim at the base of the 250ft, twin Moaʻula and Hipuapua Falls, which cascade down the back of this lush valley. They are reached via a straightforward 2-mile trail lined with historical sites. To protect these sites, and because the trail crosses private property, visiting the falls requires a hike with a local guide. The $80-per-person fee includes a wealth of cultural knowledge and walks can easily take five hours. Prepare for muddy conditions and wear stout shoes so you can navigate over river boulders.

You may be able to organize a guide with Molokaʻi Fish & Dive or the Kalele Bookstore in Kaunakakai, or Kalani Pruet. Prepare for voracious mosquitoes.

Halawa Beach
BEACH

Halawa Beach was a favored surfing spot for Molokaʻi chiefs, and remains so today for local kids, although often you won't see a soul. The beach has double coves separated by a rocky outcrop, with the north side a bit more protected than the south. When the water is calm, there's good swimming and folks launch sea kayaks here, but both coves are subject to dangerous rip currents when the surf is heavy.

Up from the beach, Halawa Beach Park has picnic pavilions, restrooms and non-drinkable running water. Throughout the valley, there's an eerie feel that you can't quite shake, as if the generations that came before aren't sure what to make of it all. Some locals aren't entirely welcoming of visitors.

Northeastern Shore Kayaking
KAYAKING

The northeastern shore, sheltered by the reef, is good for kayaking. At the very tip, Halawa Beach is a good launching point when seas are calm. In the summer, expert paddlers can venture around to the northern shore to witness the grandeur of the world's tallest sea cliffs.

Note that rental-car companies do not allow kayaks to be carried atop their vehicles and you'll have to hunt for a source of kayaks locally. Many places stopped renting them after people kept getting into trouble trying to paddle to Lanaʻi.

Pali Coast

The world's tallest sea *pali* (cliffs) rise from the Pacific along an awe-inspiring 14-mile stretch of the Molokaʻi coast from the Kalaupapa Peninsula east almost to Halawa Beach. The average drop of these sheer cliffs is 2000ft, with some reaching 3300ft. And these intimidating walls are not monolithic; vast valleys roaring with waterfalls cleave the dark rock faces. It's Molokaʻi's most dramatic sight and also the most difficult to see.

From land you can get an idea of the drama in the valleys from the remote Waikolu Lookout and the Pelekunu Valley Overlook in the Kamakou area.

But to really appreciate the cliffs, you won't want to settle for the backsides. From the Pacific you can get a full appreciation of their height. You can organize a boat trip (see p453) or really earn your adventure cred by paddling yourself here in a kayak. In summer, when conditions allow, you can leave from Halawa Beach, but this is only for expert kayakers and will require a few days plus camping on isolated stone beaches. You can get advice from Molokaʻi Fish & Dive.

A visit to Kalaupapa Peninsula also gives you an idea of the spectacle. Or you can appreciate the drama of the cliffs from the air. Many of Maui's helicopter tours (p343) include Molokaʻi's Pali Coast and some will do pick-ups on Molokaʻi. Molokaʻi Fish & Dive offers packages from $150 per person.

ⓘ WHAT FRIENDLY MEANS LOCALLY

In a cynical world, people don't realize that Molokaʻi's moniker, 'the friendly isle,' is exactly right. There are the waves you get as you explore the uncrowded corners, and the advice about which fresh fish is best when you're buying food for your holiday rental. More importantly, you'll start to slow down and understand that friendly locally means slowing waaay down and taking your sense of rhythm from others.

GETTING THE GOAT & SAVING THE REEF

Non-native feral goats, pigs and deer have run amok in the highlands of Moloka'i and are voraciously chewing their way through the foliage. This has led to deforestation and greatly increased the runoff from the frequent rains. These flows of mud slop down to the south coast along the east end of Moloka'i, choking the Pala'au barrier reef, which in parts is massively degraded. Some of the old fishponds have been filling with silt at the rate of a foot per year. Talk about Indonesian butterflies! A goat eats a shrub on a remote Moloka'i peak and coral dies off the coast.

Locals have been encouraged to hunt the critters, especially the feral pigs, which often star at family BBQs. Still, amateur efforts are not enough and the Nature Conservancy has ferried hunters by helicopter to remote parts of the mountains.

CENTRAL MOLOKA'I

Central Moloka'i is really two places. In the west there's the dry and gently rolling Ho'olehua Plains, which stretch from the remote and rare sand dunes of Mo'omomi Beach to the former plantation town and current coffee-growing center of Kualapu'u. To the east, the terrain rises sharply to the misty, ancient forests of Kamakou. Enjoy one of the island's great adventures here by going on a hike that takes you back in evolutionary time.

Moloka'i's second most popular drive (after the Halawa Valley drive in the east) runs from Kualapu'u (with its superb little cafe) up Hwy 470 to Pala'au State Park, site of the Kalaupapa Overlook, where you'll find one of the island's most captivating views.

Kamakou Area

The best reason to rent a 4WD vehicle on Moloka'i is to thrill to the views from the Waikolu Lookout before discovering the verdant mysteries of the Nature Conservancy's Kamakou Preserve, where you'll find the island's highest peaks. Exploring this secret side of Moloka'i is pure adventure. Besides gazing down into two deep valleys on the island's stunning and impenetrable north coast, you'll explore a near-pristine rain forest that is home to more than 250 native plants (more than 200 endemic) and some of Hawaii's rarest birds. Although you can't quite reach the island's highest point, Kamakou Peak (4961ft), you'll still get your head in the clouds.

Orientation

The turnoff for the Kamakou Area is between the 3- and 4-mile markers on Hwy 460, immediately south of the Manawainui Bridge. The paved turnoff is marked with a sign for the Homelani Cemetery. The pavement quickly ends, and the road deteriorates into 4WD-only conditions.

About 5.5 miles from Hwy 460 and well past the cemetery, you'll cross into the Moloka'i Forest Reserve. After a further 1.5 miles, there's an old water tank and reservoir off to the left. Another 2 miles brings you to the Sandalwood Pit, and 1 mile past that to Waikolu Lookout and the boundary of the Kamakou Preserve.

MOLOKA'I FOREST RESERVE

As you climb and enter the Moloka'i Forest Reserve, the landscape starts off shrubby and dusty but then becomes dark, fragrant woods of tall eucalyptus, with patches of cypress and Norfolk pines. Don't bother heading down the roads branching off Maunahui Rd, as the scenery will be exactly the same. Although there's no evidence of it from the road, the Kalamaula area (an old name for this general area) was once heavily settled. It was here that Kamehameha the Great (Kamehameha I) knocked out his two front teeth in grieving the death of a female high chief whom he had come to visit. Local lore says that women once traveled up here to bury their afterbirth in order to ensure that their offspring reached great heights.

⊙ **Sights**

Sandalwood Pit   HISTORICAL SITE

A grassy depression on the left side of the road marks the centuries-old Sandalwood Pit (Lua Na Moku 'Iliahi). In the early 19th century, shortly after the lucrative sandalwood trade began, the pit was hand-dug to the exact measurements of a 100ft-long, 40ft-wide and 7ft-deep ship's hold, and filled with fragrant sandalwood logs cleared from the nearby forest.

The *ali'i* (royalty) forced the *maka'ainana* (commoners) to abandon their crops and work the forest. When the pit was full, the wood was strapped onto the backs of the laborers, who hauled it down to the harbor for shipment to China. After all the mature trees were cut down, the *maka'ainana* pulled up every new sapling, sparing their children the misery of forced harvesting.

Waikolu Lookout
LOOKOUT

At 3600ft, Waikolu Lookout provides a breathtaking view into the steep Waikolu Valley and out to the ocean beyond. After rains, the white strands of numerous waterfalls accent the sheer cliffs and fill the valley with a dull roar. Morning is best for clear views, but if it's foggy, have a snack at the picnic bench and see if it clears.

The wide, grassy Waikolu Lookout campground is directly opposite the lookout. If you can bear the mist and cold winds that sometimes blow up from the canyon, this could make a base camp for hikes into the preserve. The site has a picnic pavilion. Bring water. No open fires are allowed and state camping permits are required (see p429).

KAMAKOU PRESERVE

Since 1982, the Nature Conservancy has managed the Kamakou Preserve, which includes cloud forest, bogs, shrub land and habitat for many endangered plants and animals. Its 2774 acres of native ecosystems start immediately beyond the Waikolu Lookout.

Much of the preserve is forested with *'ohi'a lehua*, a native tree with fluffy red blossoms, whose nectar is favored by native birds. It is home to the *'apapane* (bright-red Hawaiian honeycreeper), *'amakihi* (yellow-green honeyeater) and pueo (Hawaiian owl). Other treasures include tree ferns, native orchids and silvery lilies.

Sights & Activities

Pepe'opae Trail
HIKING

The hike back through three million years of evolution on the Pepe'opae Trail is the star attraction of the Kamakou area. This undisturbed Hawaiian montane bog is a miniature primeval forest of stunted trees, dwarfed plants and lichens that feels like it's the dawn of time. This bog receives about 180in of rain each year, making it one of the wettest regions in the Hawaii Islands. The trail ends at the Pelekunu Valley Overlook, where you'll enjoy a valley view of fantastic depth and, if it's not foggy, the ocean beyond. Almost the entire mile-long trail is along an extremely narrow boardwalk that feels at times like

tightrope walking. It is covered with a coarse metal grating to prevent hikers from slipping, but you should still wear shoes with a good grip.

To reach the Pepe'opae Trail from Waikolu Lookout, you can walk through the forest for about 1 mile, which takes about an hour. A 2.5-mile-long access road that was passable by 4WD was knocked out by storms in 2010, so park at the lookout and walk the rest of the way.

Visitors should sign in and out at the preserve's entrance. Look for entries from others on everything from car breakdowns to trail conditions and bird sightings. Posted notices announce if any part of the preserve is closed. Bring rain gear, as the trails in Kamakou can be wet and muddy.

☞ Tours

Excellent monthly Saturday hikes with the Nature Conservancy (☎553-5236; www.nature.org/hawaii; Moloka'i Industrial Park, 23 Pueo Pl, Kualapu'u; hike $25) explore the preserve's history and ecology. The hikes have an eight-person maximum and tend to book up several months in advance.

Walter Naki (☎558-8184) is a local who leads custom hikes in the preserve and across the island.

❶ Getting There & Away

Kamakou is protected in its wilderness state in part because the rutted dirt road leading in makes it hell to reach. A 4WD vehicle is obligatory and even then the narrow, rutted track with its sheer edges and tendency to turn into a bog after rains is a challenge. Check conditions with the Nature Conservancy (☎553-5236; www.nature.org/hawaii). The 10 miles from Hwy 460 to Waikolu Lookout takes about 45 minutes to drive.

Kualapu'u

Kualapu'u is the name of both a 1017ft hill, and a nearby village. In a fact that only a booster could love, the world's largest rubber-lined reservoir lies at the base of the hill. Its 1.4 billion gallons of water are piped in from the rain forests of eastern Moloka'i and it is the only source of water for the Ho'olehua Plains and the dry West End. Operations were threatened when its owner, the Moloka'i Ranch, ceased operations in 2008 (see the boxed text, p459).

In the 1930s the headquarters of the Del Monte pineapple plantation were located here and a company town grew. Pineapples ruled for nearly 50 years, until Del Monte pulled out of Moloka'i in 1982, and the economy crumbled.

While farm equipment rusted in overgrown pineapple fields, small-scale farming developed: watermelons, dryland taro, macadamia nuts, sweet potatoes, seed corn, string beans and onions. The soil is so rich here, some feel Moloka'i has the potential to be Hawaii's 'breadbasket.' In 1991 coffee saplings were planted on formerly fallow pineapple fields, and now cover some 600 acres.

✖ Eating & Drinking

TOP CHOICE Kualapu'u Cookhouse   HAWAIIAN **$$**
(Hwy 490; meals $5-20; ☺7am-8pm) Once called the Kamuela Cookhouse, this old roadhouse serves the island's best food. A recent revamp has put a little flair in the traditional charm, but pretension remains off the menu. When your plate lunch of the best and tenderest teriyaki beef you've ever had appears, you'll be hooked. Breakfasts are huge and feature perfect omelettes. Panko-crusted Monte Cristo sandwiches join the plate lunch brigade, while at dinner inventive fare like ahi in a lime cilantro sauce, or lusciously juicy prime rib star. At night locals sometimes serenade with Hawaiian music. Beer and wine can be purchased at the grocery across the street.

Coffees of Hawaii   CAFE, FACTORY **$**
(www.coffeesofhawaii.com; cnr Hwys 470 & 490; ☺7am-5pm Mon-Fri, 8am-8pm Sat, to 5pm Sun) Coffees of Hawaii grows and roasts its own coffee. Stop by for a tour of the plant and savor the air redolent with rich smells. There's a morning walking tour (adult/child $20/10; ☺tours 11am Mon-Fri). Ask about more strenuous guided hikes. On Sunday afternoons, the porch is the scene for the lilting tunes of Hawaiian traditional performers (see the boxed text, opposite).

Next to the grande-sized gift shop, the **Espresso Bar** (snacks $2-6) serves a range of drinks made with the house brew. There are also baked goods such as doughnuts and Danishes, sandwiches and soup. The cakes are tasty.

Kala'e

Rudolph Wilhelm Meyer, a German immigrant who had plans to make it big in the California gold rush, stopped off in Hawaii en route (he was going the long way around),

and never left. He married a member of Hawaiian royalty who had huge tracts of land on Moloka'i, and busied himself growing potatoes and cattle for export, serving as overseer of the Kalaupapa leprosy settlement and as manager of King Kamehameha V's ranch lands. In 1876, when a new treaty allowed Hawaii sugar planters to export sugar duty-free to the US, Meyer turned his lands over to sugar, and built a mill; it operated for only a decade until falling prices killed its viability.

◉ Sights & Activities

Moloka'i Museum & Cultural Center   HISTORICAL SITE
(☏567-6436; adult/concession $3.50/2; ☺10am-2pm Mon-Sat) Meyer's mill has enjoyed a series of restorations over time. It now houses a museum and cultural center, which has a small but intriguing display of Moloka'i's history with period photos, cultural relics and a 10-minute video. Features of the mill include a 100-year-old steam engine, a mule-powered cane crusher and other working artifacts. Meyer and his descendants are buried in a little family plot out back.

Ironwood Hills Golf Course   GOLF
(☏567-6000; greens fee 9/18 holes $20/26; ☺8am-5pm) The 'pro shop' in the dilapidated trailer tells you everything you need to know about this wonderfully casual nine-hole golf course, which was originally built for plantation managers in the 1920s. Electric cart rental is $8; clubs are $5.

Pala'au State Park

Thrill to views over the Kalaupapa Peninsula, listen to winds rustle through groves of ironwood and eucalyptus trees and witness sacred rocks that represent human genitals. This misty state park is at the end of Hwy 470, near the Kalaupapa trailhead. It's good for a picnic, some photos and possibly to increase your chances of falling pregnant.

◉ Sights & Activities

Kalaupapa Overlook   NATURAL ATTRACTION
The Kalaupapa Overlook provides a scenic overview of the Kalaupapa Peninsula from the edge of a 1600ft cliff. The best light for photography is usually from late morning to mid-afternoon.

It's easy to get the lay of the land from the lookout; you'll get a good feel for just how far you'll travel when you descend nearly

AUNTIE JULIA HOE

Local kupuna (elder) who sings and dances a much-lauded version of hula.

You're famous for?

I sing every Sunday at Coffees of Hawaii (opposite) with a local group of home-spun musicians, fondly known as Na Ohana Hoaloha (Family of Friends). Visitors get to realize that our entertainers are sharing just as much as performing, and this is the key to connecting with the culture of Moloka'i.

What to do first?

Visitors need to take note of the airport welcome sign that encourages them to slow down; right there they should know that they are in a special place. Then they can approach their stay here with an open heart and mind. Greet all that they meet with a smile; doesn't matter if you don't know a person, it is what you give off that is important.

On Sharing

Most locals will generously share their aloha with any who come with a true desire to understand the Hawaiian culture, to learn more about living in harmony with nature and with respect for what they find. Return the favor with a sense of gratitude and aloha. We love our island, our way of life, our Hawaiian heritage and culture and we are passionate about protecting it.

1700ft on the trail. Interpretive plaques identify significant landmarks below and explain Kalaupapa's history. The village where all of Kalaupapa's residents live is visible, but Kalawao, the original settlement and site of Father Damien's church and grave, is not.

Kalaupapa means 'flat leaf,' an accurate description of the lava-slab peninsula that was created when a low shield volcano poked up out of the sea, long after the rest of Moloka'i had been formed. The dormant Kauhako Crater, visible from the overlook, contains a little lake that's more than 800ft deep. At 400ft, the crater is the highest point on the Kalaupapa Peninsula. A lighthouse stands erect near the northern tip of land. It once boasted the most powerful beam in the Pacific, but now holds only an electric light beacon.

There's a vague trail of sorts that continues directly beyond the last plaque at the overlook. The path, on a carpet of soft ironwood needles, passes through diagonal rows of trees planted during a Civil Conservation Corps (CCC) reforestation project in the 1930s. Simply follow this trail for 20 minutes or so until it peters out.

Kauleonanahoa   CULTURAL SITE

Kauleonanahoa (the penis of Nanahoa) is Hawaii's premier phallic stone, standing proud in a little clearing inside an ironwood grove, about a five-minute walk from the parking area. The legend goes that Nanahoa hit his wife Kawahuna in a jealous rage and when they were both turned to stone, he came out looking like a dick, literally.

Reputedly, women who come here with offerings of lei and stay overnight will soon get pregnant. There's no mention of what happens to men who might try the same thing with some nearby stones that have been carved into a female counterpart to the main rock.

Before the trees were planted, the stone, which has had some plastic surgery through the years to augment its effect, was a striking pinnacle atop the ridge.

🛏 Sleeping

Camping is allowed in a peaceful grassy field a quarter of a mile before the overlook. There's a picnic pavilion and a portable toilet here (although there are good bathrooms near the main parking area). It rains a lot here and outside of the summer dry season, your tent will likely be drenched by evening showers. See p429 for permit information.

Ho'olehua

Ho'olehua is the dry plains area that separates eastern and western Moloka'i. Here, in the 1790s, Kamehameha the Great trained his warriors in a year-long preparation for the invasion of O'ahu.

Ho'olehua was settled as an agricultural community in 1924, as part of the first distribution of land under the Hawaiian Homes Commission Act, which made public lands available to Native Hawaiians. Water was scarce in this part of Moloka'i and Ho'olehua pineapple farms drew settlers as the spiky fruit required little irrigation. But the locals were soon usurped by the pineapple giants Dole, Del Monte and Libby. Most were forced to lease their lands to the plantations.

Today the plantations are gone, but locals continue to plant small crops of fruits, vegetables and herbs. And Hawaiians continue to receive land deeds in Ho'olehua in accordance with the Hawaiian Homes Commission Act.

◉ Sights

TOP CHOICE Purdy's Macadamia Nut Farm
NUT PLANTATION

(www.molokai-aloha.com/macnuts; admission free; ⊗9:30am-3:30pm Mon-Fri, 10am-2pm Sat) The nutty tour here lets you poke your pick of macadamia nuts as Tuddie Purdy takes you into his 80-year-old orchard and personally explains how the nuts grow without pesticides, herbicides or fertilizers.

Everything is done in quaint Moloka'i style: you can crack open macadamia nuts on a stone you poke with a hammer and sample macadamia blossom honey scooped up with slices of fresh coconut. Nuts (superb!) and honey are for sale. Linger and Purdy will go into full raconteur mode.

To get to the farm, turn right onto Hwy 490 from Hwy 470. After 1 mile, take a right onto Lihi Pali Ave, just before the high school. The farm is a third of a mile up, on the right.

Post-a-Nut
TOURIST ATTRACTION

Why settle for a mundane postcard or, worse, an emailed photo of you looking like a tan-lined git, when it comes to taunting folks in the cold climes you've left behind? Instead, send a coconut. Gary, the world-class postmaster of the Ho'olehua post office (Pu'u Peelua Ave), has baskets of them for free. Choose from the oodles of markers and write the address right on the husk. Add a cartoon or two. Imagine the joy when a loved one waits in a long line for a parcel and is handed a coconut! Depending on the size of your nut, postage costs $8 to $13 and takes three to six days to reach any place in the US; other countries cost more and take longer – and you may run into quarantine issues.

Mo'omomi Beach

When you think of Hawaii you think of beaches, so it is surprising that the islands have very few sand dunes. One of the few undisturbed, coastal sand-dune areas left in the state is found on remote Mo'omomi Beach. Among its native grasses and shrubs are at least four endangered plant species that exist nowhere else on earth, including a relative of the sunflower. It is one of the few places in the populated islands where green sea turtles still find suitable breeding habitat.

Managed by Hawaiian elders as well as the Nature Conservancy, Mo'omomi is not lushly beautiful, but windswept, lonely and wild. It's a classic Moloka'i sight; alluring and worth the effort to visit. Follow Farrington Ave west, past the intersection with Hwy 480, until the paved road ends. If you are in a regular car and it has been raining, your journey will end here as there is often a richly red mud swamp here.

When passable, it's 2.5 miles further along a dirt road that is in some areas quite smooth and in others deeply rutted. In places, you may have to skirt the edge of the road and straddle a small gully. It's ordinarily sort of passable in a standard car, although the higher the vehicle the better; it's definitely best to have a 4WD. If you get stuck in a car, you may gift your rental company with a windfall in fees and fines.

Look for the picnic pavilion that announces you've found Mo'omomi Bay, with a little sandy beach used at times by elders teaching the young traditional fishing techniques. The rocky eastern point, which protects the bay, provides a fishing perch, and further along the bluffs a sacred ceremony might be underway. There are toilets, but no drinking water.

There is a broad, white-sand beach (often mistakenly called Mo'omomi) at Kawa'aloa Bay, a 20-minute walk further west. The wind, which picks up steadily each afternoon, blows the dune sand into interesting ripples and waves. Like a voyeur, you're here just to look around. Swimming is dangerous.

The high hills running inland are actually massive sand dunes – part of a mile-long stretch of dunes that back this part of coast. The coastal cliffs, which have been sculptured into jagged abstract designs by wind and water, are made of sand that has petrified due to Mo'omomi's dry conditions.

Because of the fragile ecology of the dunes, visitors should stay along the beach and on trails only.

☞ Tours

Nature Conservancy   HIKE
(☎553-5236; www.nature.org/hawaii; Moloka'i Industrial Park, 23 Pueo Pl, Kualapu'u; suggested donation $25) Nature Conservancy leads excellent monthly guided hikes of Mo'omomi. Transportation is provided to and from the preserve. Reservations are required and spots fill up far in advance, so get in early.

KALAUPAPA NATIONAL HISTORICAL PARK

The spectacularly beautiful Kalaupapa Peninsula is the most remote part of Hawaii's most remote island. The only way to reach this lush green peninsula edged with long, white-sand beaches is on a twisting trail down the steep *pali,* the world's highest sea cliffs, or by plane. This remoteness is the reason it was, for more than a century, where leprosy patients were forced to isolation. From its inception until separation ended in 1969, 8000 patients were forced to come to Kalaupapa. Less than a dozen patients (respectively called 'residents') remain. They have chosen to stay in the only home they have ever known and have resisted efforts to move them away. The peninsula has been designated a national historical park and is managed by the Hawaii Department of Health and the National Park Service (www.nps.gov/kala).

State laws dating back to when the settlement was a quarantine zone require everyone who enters the settlement to have a 'permit' and to be accompanied at all times by a guide. The laws are no longer necessary for health reasons but they continue to be enforced in order to protect the privacy of the residents. You can secure a permit through Damien Tours or Molokai Mule Ride. Because the exiled patients were not allowed to keep children if they had them, the residents made a rule that no one under the age of 16 is allowed in the settlement – this is strictly enforced, as are the permit requirements. Only guests of Kalaupapa residents are allowed to stay overnight.

The guided tour is Moloka'i's most well-known attraction but, interesting as it is, the tour itself is not the highlight: this is one case where getting there truly is half the fun. Riding a mule or hiking down the steep trail, winding through lush green tropical forest, catching glimpses of the sea far below, is unforgettable.

History

Ancient Hawaiians used Kalaupapa as a refuge when caught in storms at sea. The peninsula held a large settlement at the time of early Western contact, and the area is rich in archaeological sites currently under investigation. A major discovery in 2004 indicated that Kalaupapa heiau had major ritual significance, with possible astronomical purposes.

In 1835 doctors in Hawaii diagnosed the state's first case of leprosy, one of many diseases introduced by foreigners. Before modern medicine, leprosy manifested itself in dripping, foul-smelling sores. Eventually, patients experienced loss of sensation and tissue degeneration that could lead to small extremities becoming deformed or falling off altogether. Blindness was common. Alarmed by the spread of the disease, King Kamehameha V signed into law an act that banished people with leprosy to Kalaupapa Peninsula, beginning in 1865.

Hawaiians call leprosy *mai ho'oka'awale,* which means 'separating sickness,' a disease all the more dreaded because it tore families apart. Some patients arrived at the peninsula in boats, whose captains were so terrified of the disease and the rough waters they would not land, but instead dropped patients overboard. Those who could, swam to shore; those who couldn't, perished.

Once the afflicted arrived on Kalaupapa Peninsula, there was no way out, not even in a casket. The original settlement was in Kalawao, at the wetter eastern end of the peninsula. Early conditions were unspeakably horrible, with the strong stealing rations from the weak, and women forced into prostitution or worse. Life spans were invariably short, and desperate.

Father Damien (see the boxed text, p455) arrived at Kalaupapa in 1873. He wasn't the first missionary to come, but he was the first to stay. What Damien provided, most of all, was a sense of hope and inspiration to others. Brother Joseph Dutton arrived in 1886 and stayed 44 years. In addition to his work with the sick, he was a prolific writer who kept the outside world informed about what was happening in Moloka'i. Mother Marianne Cope arrived a year before Damien died. She

ℹ️ HOLY WATER

It's hot walking down the Kalaupapa trail, but it's far hotter walking back up. Instead of lugging a lot of water both ways, or even just bringing it back up with you, take extra containers and stash them behind rocks at the numbered switchbacks on your way down. Remember the numbers and retrieve your water on the way back up.

stayed 30 years, helping to establish a girls' home and encouraging patients to live life to the fullest. She is widely considered to be the mother of the hospice movement.

The same year that Father Damien arrived, a Norwegian scientist named Dr Gerhard Hansen discovered *Mycobacterium leprae*, the bacteria that causes leprosy, thus proving that the disease was not hereditary, as was previously thought. Even in Damien's day leprosy was one of the least contagious of all communicable diseases: only 4% of human beings are even susceptible to it.

In 1909 the US Leprosy Investigation Station opened at Kalawao. However, the fancy hospital was so out of touch – requiring the patients to sign themselves in for two years, live in seclusion and give up all Hawaii-grown food – that even in the middle of a leprosy colony, it attracted only a handful of patients. It closed a few years later.

Since the 1940s sulfa antibiotics have successfully treated and controlled leprosy, but the isolation policies in Kalaupapa weren't abandoned until 1969, when there were 300 patients here. The last arrived in 1965 and today the remaining handful of residents are all in their 70s or older.

While the state of Hawaii officially uses the term 'Hansen's disease' for leprosy, many Kalaupapa residents consider that to be a euphemism that fails to reflect the stigma they have suffered, and continue to use the old term 'leprosy.' The degrading appellation 'leper,' however, is offensive to all. 'Resident' is preferred.

👁️ Sights & Activities

At the bottom of the park's near-vertical *pali* is a deserted beach with stunning views of the steep cliffs you've just come down. If you've come by mule (see p455), the ride ends here and you'll board a small bus for the tour. Remember your mule's

name so that the guides will put you back on the right one for the trip up! If you're hiking (see p455), wait for the mandatory tour here.

Leprosy Settlement   HISTORICAL SITE

The settlement is very quiet, and residents tend to stay indoors while the tour is going on. With their history of being persecuted and stigmatized, you can't blame them for avoiding curious tourists, but the guide says that residents welcome visitors because it helps prevent their story from being forgotten. Restoration of village buildings is ongoing, and the homes that have been restored are small and tidy, with covered lanai, clapboard siding and tin roofs. Other sights are mainly cemeteries, churches and memorials. Buy drinks and snacks at Fuesaina's Bar, which is run by Gloria Marks, the wife of the late Richard Marks, who was something of an ambassador for Kalaupapa for many years. A park visitor center doubles as a small museum and bookstore, with displays of items made and used by former residents ('Kalaupapa Patients Adapt & Innovate') and books and films about the settlement for sale.

Kalawao   HISTORICAL SITE

On the way to the east side of the peninsula is St Philomena Church (better known as Father Damien's Church), in Kalawao, which was built in 1872. You can see where Damien cut open holes in the floor as a way to welcome the sick, whose disease made them need to spit frequently. The graveyard at the side contains Damien's gravestone and original burial site, although his body was exhumed in 1936 and returned to Belgium. In 1995 his right hand was reinterred here. The large black cross on the revered Father's grave is adorned with shells and leis.

The tour stops for lunch at Kalawao after a short drive through lush greenery dotted with colorful lantana vines. On the way, keep your eyes open for a heiau just past the water wells; the remains of the ancient temple are on the same side as the wells.

The amazing view from Kalawao could be reason enough to visit the peninsula. It gives you a glimpse of Moloka'i's Pali Coast. This impenetrable section of the northern shore contains two majestic valleys and Kahiwa Falls, the state's longest waterfall; and is a popular film location for producers needing an almost otherworldly landscape, including the ones scouting for 'Skull Island' in the

MOLOKA'I'S SAINT

On October 11, 2009, Moloka'i (and America) got its first saint. The story of Joseph de Veuster (better known as Father Damien), the Belgian priest who sacrificed everything to care for leprosy patients, has been the subject of many books and TV movies, few of which rise above the treacly clichés inherent in such a story. And yet Father Damien's story, once learned, makes the honor of sainthood seem like the bare minimum he deserves.

In 1873 the famously strong-willed priest traveled, at age 33, to the Kalaupapa Peninsula, the leprosy settlement he'd heard called 'the living tomb.' Once on this remote place of exile he found scores of people who'd been dumped ashore by a government not quite cruel enough to simply drown them at sea. Soon he had the residents helping him construct more than 300 houses, plant trees and much more. He taught himself medicine and gave his flock the care they desperately needed. In 1888 he installed a water pipeline over to the sunny western side of the peninsula, and the settlement moved from Kalawao to where it remains today.

Father Damien contracted Hansen's disease in 1885, 12 years after he arrived, and died four years later at age 49, the only outsider ever to contract leprosy on Kalaupapa. The Vatican has recognized two miracles attributed to him. Both were people diagnosed with terminal illnesses decades after his death, who attributed their recoveries to their prayers and faith in Father Damien.

Excitement over Father Damien's sainthood was widespread on Moloka'i, although an expected immediate windfall in visitors failed to materialize. But the number of pilgrims and otherwise interested is growing slowly. His feast day, May 10, is sparking festivities, especially at the churches he built in East Moloka'i (see p434).

second – and less impressive – *King Kong*, from 1976.

Hiking

HIKING

The Kalaupapa trailhead is on the east side of Hwy 470, just north of the mule stables, and marked by the Pala'au park sign and parked Kalaupapa employee cars. The 3-mile trail has 26 switchbacks, 1400 steps and drops 1664ft in elevation from start to finish. It's best to begin hiking by 8am, before the mules start to go down, to avoid walking in fresh dung, though you have no choice on the return trip. Allow an hour and a half to descend comfortably. It can be quite an adventure after a lot of rain, though the rocks keep it from getting impossibly muddy. Many find walking sticks a huge help.

☞ Tours

Damien Tours

TOUR

(☏567-6171; tours $50; ⊘Mon-Sat) Everyone who comes to the Kalapaupa Peninsula is required to visit the settlement with this tour. Reservations must be made in advance (call between 4pm and 8pm). Tours last 3½ hours, are done by bus and are accompanied by lots of stories about life in years past. If you're not on the mule ride, bring your own lunch and a bottle of water.

Molokai Mule Ride

TOUR

(☏567-6088, 800-567-7550; www.muleride.com; rides $200; ⊘Mon-Sat) A mule ride is the only way down the *pali* besides hiking, but be prepared – this is not an easy ride. You'll be sore afterwards, even if you're an experienced rider, and it's a safe bet that you've never experienced a ride like this one. At some points the trail is only eight to 10 inches wide, nearly vertical in places, and it's simply amazing how the mules carefully pick their way down. The mule skinners happily announce on the second switchback that it's here that some people just get off and walk back to the barn, not willing to trust their lives to the sure-footed animals. So settle back and enjoy a natural thrill ride. You'll need to be quick with the camera if you want to get shots of the amazing views, because the mules don't stop for photo ops. (Hiking down would offer better chances for good pictures.) It takes about 45 minutes going down and one hour going up. The ride back is as challenging as the ride down, but it's definitely easier than hiking. Tours include a short riding lesson from real *paniolo* (Hawaiian cowboys), and lunch. Make reservations well in advance. Round-trip airport transfers are $18 per person (two-person minimum).

ℹ️ Getting There & Around

AIR The beauty of flying in on these small prop planes is the aerial view of the *pali* and towering waterfalls. Passengers need to first book a tour with Damien Tours before buying air tickets; otherwise you will be stuck at the airport. Even then you are still likely to be stuck at the airport as the flight schedules often don't mesh well with tours. The morning flight down from Ho'olehua may arrive before 7:30am and you'll have to wait at the landing strip for the tour bus at 10am. If you are coming from another island, you may need to fly to Moloka'i the night before. Return trips 'topside,' as they say locally, to Ho'olehua are more convenient and allow for easy connections to Honolulu and Maui.

Pacific Wings (☑888-575-4546; www.pacificwings.com) and its PW Express subsidiary have a range of fares and tour packages. The tour operators can also arrange charters.

LAND The mule trail down the *pali* is the only land route to the peninsula, and can be taken either on foot or by the mule rides. It is possible to combine hiking and flying. The island's activity/tour operators (see p436) and Molokai Mule Ride can organize all details of your visit.

WEST END

Seemingly deserted and just a couple of missed rainfalls from becoming a desert, Moloka'i's West End occupies a surprisingly significant place in Hawaii's history and culture. Pu'u Nana is the site of Hawaii's first-established hula school, and the Maunaloa Range was once a center of sorcery. In recent decades, much of the land has been controlled by the Moloka'i Ranch, and its fortunes – for better and more recently for much worse – have affected the entire island. Hale O Lono Harbor is the launching site for the two long-distance outrigger canoe races (p434); and the island's longest beach, Papohaku Beach, dominates the west coast.

Once you pass the airport, Hwy 460 starts to climb up through dry, grassy rangeland without a building in sight. The long mountain range that begins to form on your left past the 10-mile marker is Maunaloa, which means 'long mountain.' Its highest point, at 1381ft, is Pu'u Nana.

Given the woes of Moloka'i Ranch (see the boxed text, p459) the atmosphere out west is a bit bleak. With the exception of one superlative store, Maunaloa might as well hold tumbleweed races; while the Kaluakoi resort area is beset by financial troubles. Still, you can ignore all the earthly turmoil on one of the many fine beaches.

History

During the 1850s Kamehameha V acquired the bulk of Moloka'i's arable land and formed Moloka'i Ranch. Overgrazing eventually led to the widespread destruction of native vegetation and fishponds. Following his death, the ranch became part of the Bishop Estate (a huge estate created in 1884 by the will of Bernice Pauahi Bishop, the great-granddaughter of King Kamehameha the great), which quickly sold it off to a group of Honolulu businesspeople.

A year later, in 1898, the American Sugar Company, a division of Moloka'i Ranch, attempted to develop a major sugar plantation in central Moloka'i. The company built a railroad system to haul the cane, developed harbor facilities and installed a powerful pumping system to draw water. However, by 1901 the well water used to irrigate the fields had become so saline that the crops failed. The company then moved into honey production on such a large scale that at one point Moloka'i was the world's largest honey exporter. In the mid-1930s, however, an epidemic wiped out the hives and the industry. Strike two for the industrialists.

Meanwhile the ranch continued its efforts to find *the* crop for Moloka'i. Cotton, rice and numerous grain crops all took their turn biting Moloka'i's red dust. Finally pineapple took root as the crop most suited to the island's dry, windy conditions. Plantation-scale production began in Ho'olehua in 1920. Within 10 years Moloka'i's population tripled, as immigrants arrived to toil in the fields.

In the 1970s, overseas competition brought an end to the pineapple's reign on Moloka'i. Dole closed its operation in 1976; the other island giant, Del Monte, later followed suit. These closures brought hard times and the highest unemployment levels in the state. Cattle raising, long a mainstay industry, was the next to collapse. This was due to a controversial state decision in 1985, pursuant to which every head of cattle on Moloka'i was destroyed after an incidence of bovine tuberculosis. The majority of the 240 smaller cattle owners then called it quits. The Moloka'i Ranch still owns some 64,000 acres – about 40% of the island – and more than half of the island's privately held lands. What will happen with these fallow holdings is the question of the young century.

Maunaloa

POP 200

In the 1990s, the Moloka'i Ranch bulldozed the atmospheric old plantation town of Maunaloa, leveling all but a few buildings. New buildings mimicking old, plantation-style homes were erected. This drove up rents and forced out some small businesses, provoking the ire of island residents.

Ironically, the new development is now all but closed; the hotel, luxury beach campsite, cinema and even the local outlet of Kentucky Fried Chicken are all shuttered.

Attractions are few, unless you're an urban planner doing research. The Maunaloa General Store (⊙8am-6pm Mon-Sat, to noon Sun) is the last retail holdout, and provides the village basics. It has a limited selection of pricey groceries and alcohol, but does much to keep community spirit going. However, there is one excellent reason to visit the quiet streets, one that will literally blow you away...

TOP CHOICE Big Wind Kite Factory & Plantation Gallery   GALLERY

(☑552-2364; www.bigwindkites.com; 120 Maunaloa Hwy; ⊙8:30am-5pm Mon-Sat, 10am-2pm Sun) Big Wind custom-makes kites for high fliers of all ages. It has hundreds ready to go in stock or you can choose a design and watch production begin. Lessons are available, lest you have a Charlie Brown experience with a kite-eating tree. There are a range of other goods to browse as well, including an excellent selection of Hawaii-themed books and artworks, clothing and crafts originating from everywhere from just down the road to Bali.

Kaluakoi Resort Area

You can almost picture this place when times were good: a low-key resort fronted a perfect crescent of sand while upscale condos lined the fairways of an emerald-green championship golf course.

Well that was then (the 1980s) and the now is rather bleak. The resort was closed years ago and is in a state of advanced decay. The golf course died when Moloka'i Ranch pulled the plug in 2008. The fairways are now a sort of post-apocalyptic-desert spectacle. Meanwhile the condo complexes do their best to put a good face on the situation as the individual owners try to play up the quiet aspects of the complex in their efforts to market their vacation rentals. Surrounding house lots have

sold very slowly, although a few large mansions lurk behind walls along the beaches.

As with the rest of the west, you're best off bringing a picnic from Kaunakakai and enjoying the beautiful beaches. Everything is accessed off a good road that branches off Hwy 460 at the 15-mile marker and curves its way down to the shore.

 Beaches

Kawakiu Beach   BEACH

Kaluakoi's northernmost beach is also the best. Kawakiu Beach is a broad crescent beach of white sand and bright-turquoise waters. It's partially sheltered from the winds that can bedevil the beaches to the south and when seas are calm, usually in summer, Kawakiu is generally safe for swimming. When the surf is rough, there are still areas where you can at least get wet. On the southern side of the bay, there's a small, sandy-bottomed wading pool in the rocks; the northern side has an area of flat rocks over which water slides to fill up a shallow shoreline pool. Spindly kiawe trees provide shade. Outside of weekends, you may well have the place to yourself.

To get there, turn off Kaluakoi Rd onto the road to the Paniolo Hale condos, but instead of turning left down to the condos, continue straight toward the old golf course. Where the paved road ends there's space to pull over and park. You'll come first to a rocky point at the southern end of the bay. Before descending to the beach, scramble around up here for a scenic view of the coast, south to Papohaku Beach and north to 'Ilio Point.

Make Horse Beach   BEACH

Make Horse Beach supposedly takes its name from days past when wild horses were run off the tall, dark cliff on its northern end; *make* (mah-*kay*) means 'dead.' This pretty, tiny white-sand cove is a local favorite, and more secluded than Kepuhi further to the south. It's a sublime spot for sunbathing and sunset, but usually not for swimming as the currents are fierce. On the calmest days, daredevils leap off the giant rock ledge at the beach's southern end.

To get here, turn off Kaluakoi Rd onto the road to the Paniolo Hale condos and then turn left toward the condo complex. You can park just beyond the condos and walk, or follow the dirt road heading off to the right for a quarter of a mile to a parking area. From there, cross the golf course remains to the beach. In some of the distant reaches clothing has been deemed optional.

Kepuhi Beach   BEACH
You can see why they built the Kaluakoi Hotel here: the beach is a rocky, white-sand dream. However, swimming here can be a nightmare. Not only can there be a tough shorebreak, but strong currents can be present even on calm days. During winter, the surf breaks close to shore, crashing in sand-filled waves that can be a brutal exfoliant.

A five-minute hike up to the top of Pu'u o Kaiaka, a 110ft-high promontory at the southern end of Kepuhi Beach, is rewarded with a nice view of Papohaku Beach. At the top you'll find the remains of a pulley that was once used to carry cattle down to waiting barges for transport to O'ahu slaughterhouses. There was also a 40ft heiau on the hilltop until 1967, when the US army bulldozed it (and gave the superstitious another reason to ponder the local run of bad luck). There's plenty of parking in the resort's cracked parking lots.

🛏 Sleeping & Eating
Units in the condominium complexes are rented either directly from the owners or through various agents (see p437). All units are decorated by the owners; facilities such as internet access vary. You'll need to shop in Kaunakakai, 20 miles distant, for all but a few convenience items that you can get up the hill at the Maunaloa General Store. The closest restaurant is the splendid Kualapu'u Cookhouse, 15 miles east in Kualapu'u.

Although the two condo complexes listed here are maintaining their properties well, we need to again note that much of the rest of the area has a run-down and eerie feel. We can't recommend the Kaluakoi Resort, which has rental units in one wing of the failed resort: for one, its cooking facilities are meager and there's nowhere locally to eat.

Paniolo Hale   CONDO $$
(www.paniolohale.org; studios from $100, 1/2 bedroom from $150/180; 🖵) Separated from the environs of the failed resort by the arid expanse of the former golf course, this is an attractive option. Large trees shade this plantation-style complex, giving it a hidden, secluded air. Each unit has a long, screened-in lanai overlooking the quiet grounds; as always with condos, shop around to get one that's been recently renovated. It is a short walk to Make Horse Beach.

Ke Nani Kai   CONDO $$
(www.knkrentals.com; Kaluakoi Rd; 1/2 bedroom from $140/150; 🖵) This tidy operation shames the rest of the resort complex. The 100-plus units are large and well-maintained (though your interior-decor mileage may vary depending on the owner). The pool is big. Note that the ocean is not right outside, so the premium for 'ocean view' units is debatable. Kepuhi and Papohaku beaches are short walks away and you may have company from the local flock of wild turkeys.

West End Beaches
Windy, isolated and often untrodden, the West End beaches define moody and atmospheric. Together with the beaches in the Kaluakoi Resort area, they can easily occupy a day of beachcombing and beach-hopping.

From this stretch of coast the hazy outline of O'ahu is just 26 miles away. Diamond Head is on the left, Makapu'u Point on the right. You can, reportedly, see the famous 'green flash' (the green color results from atmospheric refraction of the setting or rising sun) during sunset here. Another flash of green worth spotting is the green sea turtles that sometimes pass by.

During the summer the West End beaches are easily accessible, magical spots for snorkeling, with clear, flat waters.

To get to the West End beaches, take the turnoff for the Kaluakoi Resort Area at the 15-mile marker. Pass the former golf course and follow Pohakuloa Rd south.

Papohaku Beach   BEACH
Straight as a toothpick, the light-hued sands of Papohaku Beach run for an astounding 2.5 miles. The sand is soft and you can often stroll from one end to another without seeing another soul.

But just when you think you may have found the ultimate strand, consider a few leveling details. That intoxicating surf is also a viper's nest of undertow and unpredictable currents. And there's no easy shade. You can bring an umbrella, but the often strong winds may send it O'ahu-bound. Those same breezes kick up the fine sand, which can sting on blustery days.

So come here for the solitude, but do so with your eyes figuratively, if not literally, wide open.

There are seven turnoffs from Kaluakoi and Pohakuloa Rds that access the beach and have parking. The first leads to Papohaku Beach Park, a grassy place with picnic facilities under gnarled ironwood and

TOO QUIET ON THE WESTERN FRONT

Even before Moloka'i Ranch began efforts to develop its lands on the West End in the 1970s, local people weren't so fond of the company. They resented the ranch for restricting access to land, which in turn restricted a number of traditional outdoor activities and visitation to sacred cultural and historical sites. And few were impressed by the Kaluakoi Hotel, which was built on Kepuhi Bay.

By 1975 feelings had mounted, and people took to the streets, marching from Mo'omomi Beach to Kawakiu Beach to demand access to private, and heretofore forbidden, beaches on the West End. The protest was successful and convinced Moloka'i Ranch to provide public access to Kawakiu. At the same time locals successfully scuttled plans to build an O'ahu suburb here that would have been linked to the neighboring island by a new airport and ferry system.

In the 1990s the ranch operated a small wildlife-safari park, where tourists snapped pictures of exotic animals, and trophy hunters paid $1500 a head to shoot African eland and blackbuck antelope. Rumors abound of how local activists, long resistant to the type of tourist-oriented development that has all but consumed neighboring Maui, made life so difficult for the ranch that the safari park was shut down.

Beginning in 2001, the current owners of Moloka'i Ranch, the Singapore-based Moloka'i Properties, began a campaign to revitalize the holdings. They developed plans to reopen the Kaluakoi Hotel (and did reopen the golf course) and transfer the title to cultural sites and recreational areas amounting to 26,000 acres to a newly created Moloka'i Land Trust, essentially turning it into public land. It would also have given up the right to develop another 24,000 acres of its own lands.

But there was one small detail...what Moloka'i Properties wanted in return: the right to develop 200 one-acre lots on pristine La'au Point into a luxury subdivision marketed to multimillionaires. Most locals had an immediate and negative reaction to this. It was the '70s all over again. Signs saying 'Save La'au Point' sprouted island-wide (and can still be seen).

Despite numerous community meetings and plans, Moloka'i Properties got nowhere, as the residents of the Hawaii island with the highest unemployment thumbed their noses at the promise of hundreds of resort and service jobs.

In 2008 Moloka'i Properties essentially took its toys and went home. It pulled the plug on all its operations, laid off dozens, closed its hotel and golf course and furthered the ghost-town feel of Maunaloa and the Kaluakoi resort area. Only a last-minute intervention by Maui County kept the water running.

With the global economy in the dumps, it's unlikely that Moloka'i Properties will be back anytime soon with new development schemes. Meanwhile, schemes to erect power-generating windmills have run afoul of Moloka'i'i's fractious politics.

kiawe trees. Bathroom and shower facilities are rugged. You can **camp** here, but be sure to read the signs that explain which areas are soaked by the automatic sprinklers on which days. See p429 for information on camping permits.

There are seldom any other campers here and the view of the stars at night and the sound of surf is mesmerizing. However, the park can be popular with rowdy folks young and old and occasionally some try to stay the night. Guards are meant to check permits but you may be happier here if you are not alone.

Dixie Maru Beach   BEACH

South of Papohaku, beach access is to small sandy coves surrounded by rocky outcrops. At the southern end of the paved road there's a parking lot with access to a small, round inlet, which the ancient Hawaiians knew as Kapukahehu. It is now called Dixie Maru, after a ship that went down in the area long ago. Dixie Maru is the most protected cove on the west shore, and the most popular **swimming** and **snorkeling** area. The waters are generally calm, except when it is stormy.

If you're up for just finding your way as you go, it's possible to **hike** south 3 miles along the coast to La'au Point, and see what all the fuss was about (see the boxed text, above). You'll pass the failed luxury camping resort and several utterly untouched beaches. So secluded is this area that the notoriously shy Hawaaiian monk seals are often found enjoying the solitude.

Nicknamed the 'Forbidden Island,' Ni'ihau remains an intriguing mystery due to its private ownership and unique isolation. Accessible only to its owners, its Native Hawaiian residents, government officials, occasional US Navy personnel and invited guests, Ni'ihau is the last bastion of traditional Native Hawaiian culture.

History

Captain Cook anchored off Ni'ihau on January 29, 1778, two weeks after 'discovering' Hawaii. Cook noted in his log that the island was lightly populated and largely barren – a description still true today. His visit was short, but it had a lasting impact. Cook introduced two things to Ni'ihau that would quickly change the face of Hawaii: he left two goats, the first of the grazing animals that would devastate the island's native flora and fauna; and his men introduced syphilis, the first of several Western diseases that would strike the Hawaiian people.

In 1864 Elizabeth Sinclair, a Scottish widow who was moving from New Zealand to Vancouver when she got sidetracked in Hawaii, bought Ni'ihau from King Kamehameha V for $10,000 in gold. He originally tried to sell her the 'swampland' of Waikiki, but she passed it up for the 'desert island.' Interestingly no two places in Hawaii could be further apart today, either culturally or in land value. Mrs Sinclair brought the first sheep to Ni'ihau from New Zealand and started the island's longstanding, but now defunct, ranching operation.

Today the island is owned by Mrs Sinclair's great-great-grandsons Keith and Bruce Robinson, brothers who also own a vast expanse of sugarcane land on Kaua'i, where they live. The Robinsons are outdoorsmen and are fluent in Native Hawaiian. Keith, who worked for years in ranching and fishing, is often found in red-dirt-covered jeans, driving a beat-up pickup or doing heavy labor to save endangered plants. Bruce, whose wife is Ni'ihauan, holds top management positions in the family businesses – while also leading hunting tours (see opposite) and efforts to safeguard Ni'ihau's monk seals.

Population & Lifestyle

Ni'ihau's population is predominantly Native Hawaiian. Over the years the population has dropped from 600 in the early 1980s, to 230 in the 1990 census, to 160 a decade later. Today Ni'ihau's population is a mere 130, and it is the only island where the primary language is still Hawaiian. Business is conducted in Hawaiian, as are Sunday church services; in its two-room schoolhouse, three teachers hold classes from kindergarten through 12th grade for the island's 40 students. Although courses are taught solely in Hawaiian up to the fourth grade, students learn English as a second language and most are bilingual.

Residents are known for being humble, generous and mellow, and most live in Pu'uwai (meaning 'heart' in Hawaiian), a settlement on the dry western coast. Their lifestyle is extremely rustic, with no sense of hurry. The island has no paved roads, no airport, no phones and no running water. Rainfall is collected in catchments, and toilets are in outhouses. While there is no island-wide electricity, homes have generators and TV. Alcohol and firearms are banned, and a code of ethics advocates monogamy. It sounds quite idyllic.

Despite the isolation, residents are not unacquainted with the outside world. Ni'ihau residents are free to go to Kaua'i or even Las Vegas to shop, drink a few beers or just hang out. While they are free to visit other islands, however, there are restrictions on Ni'ihauans bringing friends from other islands back home with them. If Ni'ihauans marry people from other islands, or if the Robinsons view particular residents as undesirable, they are rarely allowed to return.

While the Robinsons consider themselves protectors of Ni'ihau's isolation and its people, and most Ni'ihauans seem content with their lifestyle, outsiders have been critical. Some Native Hawaiians living on other islands see the Robinsons as colonialists and believe inhabitants should be granted their own land and self-determination.

Geography & Environment

Ni'ihau is the smallest of the inhabited Hawaiian Islands: 18 miles long and 6 miles at the widest point, with a total land area of almost 70 sq miles, including 45 miles of coast. The island is slightly over 17 miles southwest of Kaua'i. The climate is warm, windy and semi-arid, with a relatively extreme temperature range, from 42°F to 110°F in the shade. Ni'ihau rainfall averages a scant 12in annually because the island is in Kaua'i's rain shadow. Its highest peak, Paniau, is only 1250ft tall and cannot generate the trade wind–based precipitation that is prevalent throughout the majority of the Hawaiian Island chain, the most so on Kauai.

Ni'ihau's 865-acre Halali'i Lake is the largest in Hawaii, but even during the rainy winter season it's only a few feet deep. In summer it sometimes dries up to a mud pond.

Almost 50 endangered monk seals live on Ni'ihau, and about half of all Hawaii's endangered *'alae ke'oke'o* (coots) breed here. Introduced creatures proliferate: there are an estimated 6000 feral pigs, plus wild sheep, goats and turkeys. Ni'ihau waters have suffered depletion by outside sport and commercial fishers who sail in to fish and pick *'opihi* (an edible limpet) from the island's shorebreaks.

Economy & Politics

The island economy has long depended on Ni'ihau Ranch, the sheep and cattle business owned by the Robinsons. But it was always a marginal operation on windy Ni'ihau, with droughts devastating herds. In 1999 Ni'ihau Ranch closed, putting most of the island's inhabitants on federal welfare.

Historically the Robinsons diverted funds from their (now defunct) sugar company on Kaua'i to provide Ni'ihauans with proper shelter, food staples, medical care and higher education.

Since then, the Robinsons have focused on two income and employment sources: the military and tourism. Since 1999 military special operations forces have been leasing sites on the uninhabited southern end of the island to stage periodic training maneuvers. The operations are small scale, typically with teams of a dozen soldiers practicing mock rescue operations. The Robinsons have also pushed for Ni'ihau's participation in major Navy missile testing, which they consider less invasive and damaging (both to the physical land and to the preservation of Ni'ihau's culture and privacy) than popular tourism and overgrazing by sheep.

However, based on the minimal income actually derived from said military testing, the only other realistic option is tourism, which is why the Robinsons started offering helicopter and hunting safari tours. Neither is a booming moneymaker, probably due to the steep tour prices and the low-key Robinsons' ambivalence about opening the island to tourists. They publicize the tours mainly by word-of-mouth, with only minimal advertising.

Politically, Ni'ihau falls under the jurisdiction of Kaua'i County.

Visiting Ni'ihau

Although outsiders are not allowed to visit Ni'ihau on their own, the Robinsons offer helicopter flights and hunting excursions, and dive outfits on Kaua'i offer scuba diving tours to the waters around Ni'ihau (a typical three-tank dive costs around $265; see p534 for more information).

Ni'ihau Helicopters (☎877-441-3500; www.niihau.us; per person $325) The pilot flies over much of Ni'ihau (but avoids the population center of Pu'uwai) and lands beachside to snorkel. Tours must be arranged well in advance.

Ni'ihau Safaris (☎877-441-3500; www.niihau.us; per hunter/observer $1650/400) Provides everything you'll need (rifle, license, transportation, guide, preparation and shipping of trophies) to hunt Polynesian boar and feral sheep, mostly, but also wild eland, Barbary sheep and wild oryx. Organizers promote this as 'useful harvesting of game' (due to overpopulation and overgrazing) and obey norms of free-chase hunting.

Kaua'i

Includes »

Lihu'e 468

The Eastside 479

Wailua. 479

Kapa'a 491

Hanalei Bay & the
North Shore 499

Kilauea 499

Princeville 507

Hanalei. 513

The South Shore 526

Po'ipu 530

Waimea Canyon & the
Westside 541

Barking Sands 551

Koke'e State Park . . 554

Best Places to Eat

» Tutu's Soup Hale (p488)

» Red Hot Mama's (p522)

» Kalaheo Café & Coffee Co
(p541)

Best Places to Stay

» North Country Farms
(p501)

» Kaua'i Country Inn (p495)

» Bunk House at Rosewood
Kaua'i (p486)

Why Go?

On Kaua'i, 'aina (land) reigns supreme. While even a short stopover can offer a taste of aggressively lush landscape amongst which to 'cruise' or frolic about, an extended stay may suddenly metamorphose into a course-study of nirvana evading reality, leaving you spending your return flight home debating immediate relocation – if you go home, that is.

Or, you may just get sunburnt and have loads of fun. Redefining mellow, the pace of life on the least populated of the major Hawaiian Islands is forever in first gear, with nobody in too much of a rush to do anything. Though, if action is what's desired, rest assured that limitless potential for adventure is forever fixed into each square mile of this 5-million-year-old dormant volcano's gaping chasms, hanging valleys and velvety emerald flora. With a little willingness, thrill is just a snorkel, a pair of hiking boots, or a paddle stroke away.

When to Go
Lihu'e

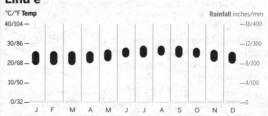

Jun–Sep Sunshine abounds, a calmer ocean, longer days and paint-splattering sunsets.

Dec–Mar Whale watching, daily rainbows and sudden rain; don't leave unattended car windows open!

Oct/Nov & Apr/May Least crowds (fall); peak ahi-eating (spring); best deals; numerous festivals.

History

Like the other Hawaiian Islands, Kaua'i saw a sea change in all aspects of life with the arrival of Captain Cook, sugar plantations, statehood and tourism. While Kaua'i developed as a sugar town through the early 1900s, it became iconic as a tropical paradise after WWII, when Hollywood glamorized Lumaha'i Beach in Mitzi Gaynor's *South Pacific* (1958) and Coco Palms Resort in Elvis Presley's *Blue Hawaii* (1961).

The 1970s saw tourism replacing sugar as the island's economic driver and while today's biggest agricultural industries are coffee and seed corn, an earnest contingent of small farmers tries to steer clear of corporate monocropping and toward locally owned and eaten crops – hence commonly seen 'No GMO Kaua'i' bumper stickers.

Hurricane 'Iniki, which hit the island in 1992 and caused destruction upwards of $1.8 billion, remains the most powerful hurricane to reach Hawaii in recorded history. See p537 for more.

The mid-2000s saw resort and luxury-end development going gangbusters, with over 5000 residential units and 6100 resort units set for development, including the massive Kukui'ula complex in Po'ipu.

Kaua'i people have always been staunch individualists. In ancient times, the locals defended themselves from King Kamehameha and spoke a distinct dialect of the Hawaiian language. Today the people continue to push back – fighting urbanization and commercialization.

Kaua'i attracts anti-urbanites, be they surfers, farmers, career-changers or nouveau hippies. Living in Honolulu guarantees access to nightlife, neurosurgeons, a university and an Apple Store. On Kaua'i, one forgoes all of that – by choice. With only one coastal highway, no town larger than 10,000 residents, no skyscrapers and a welcome lack of right angles, your attention will target what Kauaians hold sacred: the beautiful 'aina.

State & County Parks

About 30% of the island is protected by the state as parks, forest reserves and natural-area reserves. Must-see state parks include the adjacent Westside standouts, Waimea Canyon and Koke'e State Parks, for the awesome chasm, steep cliffs and native forests. Hiking trails abound, but some trailheads are accessible only by 4WD. Na Pali Coast State Park is another headliner, as the steep, slippery Kalalau Trail is now practically de rigueur. Ha'ena State Park is another favorite thanks to Ke'e Beach, a fantastic snorkeling spot. Most of Kaua'i's best and easiest-to-access beaches are designated as county parks, such as Po'ipu Beach Park, on the sunny South Shore; multiple parks at knockout gorgeous Hanalei Bay and serene 'Anini Beach Park, both on the North Shore; and family-friendly Lydgate Beach Park, on the Eastside.

KAUA'I IN...

Two Days

Immerse yourself in glorious greenery at the **National Tropical Botanical Garden**, stop at the **Koloa Fish Market** for *poke* and plate lunches then segue into a lazy afternoon at **Po'ipu Beach Park** with a South Shore sunset. Day two, head up to **Waimea Canyon** and hike at **Koke'e State Park**.

Four Days

Day three, take the road trip of your life along the epic North Shore. Test your sure-footedness on the first leg of the **Kalalau Trail**. After, meet native flora at **Limahuli Garden** and then soak up that surf-town vibe in **Hanalei**. Day four, splash yourself awake with a **surf lesson**, grab a quick snack at **Pat's Taqueria**, and end your trip with a bike ride along the **Eastside coastal path**.

A Week

Make the remaining three days count. Join **Captain Don's Sportfishing** for a half-day excursion on Kaua'i's plentiful waters, spend an afternoon as a mai tai connoisseur at **Duke's Barefoot Bar** and don your favorite aloha attire for **Kilohana Plantation's Luau Kalamaku**. Get away from it all and camp for a night at **Polihale State Park** and spend your final evening on a sunset cruise with **Captain Andy's Sailing Adventures**.

Kaua'i Highlights

1 Test your paddling strength by aqua-trekking the **Na Pali Coast** (p524)

2 Take in vistas from **Waimea Canyon** (p552) and **Koke'e State Park**

3 Lace up your boots and hike to **Hanakapi'ai Falls** (p525)

4 Hop in a kayak and meander along the **Wailua River Valley** (p481)

5 Cruise the beach or learn to surf in **Hanalei Bay** (p513)

6 Take the plunge and snorkel the **South Shore** (p526)

7 'Drink in' a sunset sail along the **Na Pali Coast** (p524)

8 Graduate an 'el naturalista' at the **National Tropical Botanical Gardens** (p531)

9 Score a bird's-eye view of the **Garden Island** (p473) on a helicopter tour

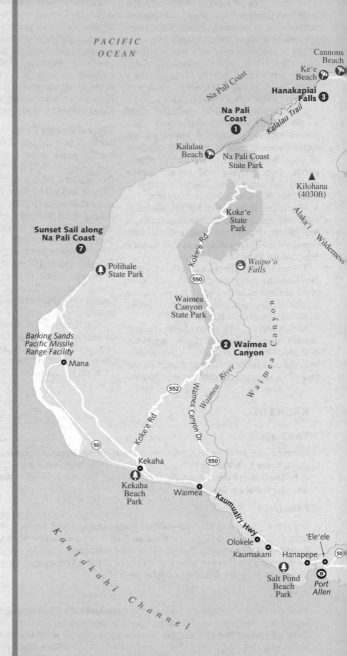

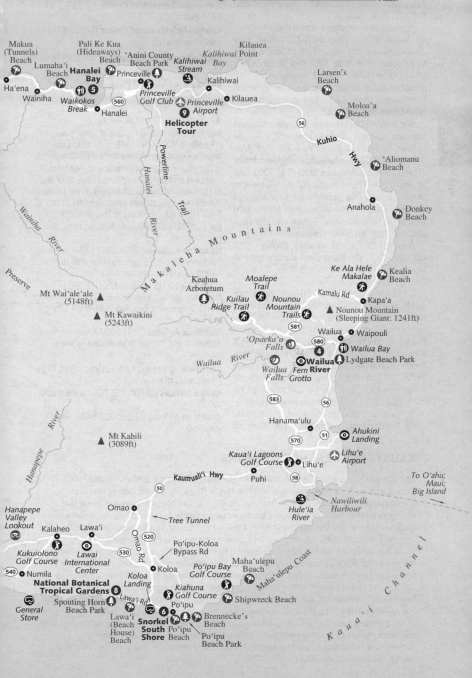

State park campgrounds can be found at Na Pali Coast State Park, Koke'e State Park and Polihale State Park.

Permits are required from the Division of State Parks (Map p472; ☑274-3444; www .hawaiistateparks.org; Department of Land & Natural Resources, State Bldg, 3060 Eiwa St, Room 306, Lihu'e, Hawaii 96766; ☺8am-3:30pm Mon-Fri), and are obtainable either in person or by mail. Fees range from $5 to $10 per night and time limits are enforced.

For remote backcountry camping around Waimea Canyon and Koke'e, there is no charge; Division of Forestry & Wildlife (Map p472; ☑274-3433; www.hawaiitrails.org; Department of Land & Natural Resources, State Bldg, 3060 Eiwa St, Room 306, Lihu'e, Hawaii 96766; ☺8am-4pm Mon-Fri) issues free permits for four sites in Waimea Canyon, two sites (Sugi Grove and Kawaikoi) in and around Koke'e and the Waialae site near the Alaka'i Wilderness Preserve.

Among the seven **county parks** with campgrounds, the most pleasant are Ha'ena Beach Park, Black Pot Beach Park (Hanalei Pier) and 'Anini Beach Park.

Camping permits cost $3 per night per adult camper (children under 18 years free) and are issued in person or by mail (at least one month in advance) at the Division of Parks & Recreation (Map p472; ☑241-4463; www.kauai.gov; Lihu'e Civic Center, Division of Parks & Recreation, 4444 Rice St, Suite 150, Lihu'e, Hawaii 96766; ☺8:15am-4pm). Requirements include a signed waiver, application and payment by cash, cashier's check or money order only.

Permits can also be obtained at four satellite locations on weekdays from 8am to noon, but only cashier's checks or money orders are accepted for payment:

Hanapepe Recreation Center (☑335-3731; 4451 Puolo Rd)

Kalaheo Neighborhood Center (☑332-9770; 4480 Papalina Rd)

Kapa'a Neighborhood Center (☑822-1931; 4491 Kou St)

Kilauea Neighborhood Center (☑828-1421; 2460 Keneke St)

ⓘ Getting There & Away

AIR All commercial flights land at Lihu'e airport (LIH; Map p468; ☑246-1448; www.hawaii.gov/dot/ airports/kauai/lih; ☺visitor hotline 6:30am-9pm).

The vast majority of incoming flights from overseas and the US mainland arrive on O'ahu at Honolulu International Airport. From there, travelers must catch an interisland flight to Kaua'i through one of these four carriers:

go! (☑888-435-9462; www.iflygo.com) Discount carrier.

Hawaiian Airlines (☑800-367-5320; www .hawaiianair.com) Biggest airline with the most flights and fares comparable to go!'s.

Island Air (☑US mainland 800-323-3345, Neighbor Islands 800-652-6541; www.islandair .com) Only one or two flights to/from Lihu'e per day.

Mokulele Airlines (☑426-7070; www.mokulele airlines.com) Partner with Alaska Airlines.

The following airlines fly directly to Lihu'e airport from the US mainland:

Alaska Airlines (☑800-252-7522; www.alaska air.com)

American Airlines (☑800-223-5436; www .aa.com)

KAUA'I SURF BEACHES & BREAKS

The Garden Isle is one of Hawaii's most challenging islands for surfers. On the North Shore, a heavy local vibe is pervasive. With the St Regis Princeville Resort overlooking the break, residents may be a bit more understanding of out-of-towners in the water at Hanalei than at other North Shore spots – but surfing with respect is a must. Between local resistance and the inaccessibility of the Na Pali Coast, not to mention a sizable tiger-shark population, you may want to pass on surfing the North Shore.

As a general rule, surf tourism is relegated to the South Shore around Po'ipu. Chances are good that you'll be staying in this popular area anyway, which is perfect, as there are some fun waves to be had here. Breaking best in the summer on south swells, spots like BK's, Acid Drop's and Center's challenge even the most experienced surfers. First-timers can get their feet wet at nearby Brennecke's. Only bodyboarding and bodysurfing are permitted here – no stand up surfing – and it's a great place to take the family.

On the Northeast Coast, Unreals breaks at Anahola Bay. It's a consistent right point that can work well on an easterly wind swell, when kona (leeward) winds are offshore.

Surfing lessons and board hire are available mainly in Hanalei and in Po'ipu. To find the swells, call the surf hotline (☑335-3720).

Delta Airlines (☏800-221-1212; www.delta.com)
United Airlines (☏800-241-6522; www.united
.com)
US Airways (☏800-428-4322; www.usair
ways.com)

BOAT The only company running interisland
cruises is **Norwegian Cruise Line** (☏800-327-
7030; www.ncl.com). Seven-day trips (starting
in Honolulu and stopping in Maui, Hawai'i Island
and Kaua'i range from about $1059 (no view)
to $1339 (balcony). The ship docks at Nawiliwili
Harbor on Thursdays for one night.

ⓘ Getting Around

TO/FROM THE AIRPORT For car rentals,
check in at the appropriate booth outside the
baggage-claim area. Vans transport you to
nearby car lots. If there's a queue, go directly to
the lot, where check-ins are quicker.
BICYCLE Bicycle-rental shops are found in
Waipouli (p490), Kapa'a (see p497) and Hanalei
(p521).
BUS The county's **Kaua'i Bus** (☏241-6410;
www.kauai.gov; 3220 Ho'olako St; adult/child
$1.50/75¢; ⊗5:15am-7:15pm Mon-Fri, reduced
schedule Sat, no service Sun) has hourly (depending on location) stops along major highway
towns. Schedules are available online.

A few caveats: drivers don't give change; no
surfboards; stops are marked but might be hard
to spot; and the schedule does not include a map.
Buses are air-conditioned and equipped with
bicycle racks and wheelchair ramps.
CAR & MOTORCYCLE Kaua'i has one belt road
running three-quarters of the way around the
island, from Ke'e Beach in the north to Polihale
in the west. The *Ready Mapbook of Kaua'i* ($11) is an
invaluable road atlas, sold online at www.ha
waiimapsource.com and at island bookstores.

Average driving distances and times from
Lihu'e follow. Allow more time during morning
and afternoon rush hours and on weekends.

DESTINATION	MILES	TIME
Anahola	14	25min
Hanalei	31	1hr
Hanapepe	16	30min
Kapa'a	8	15min
Ke'e Beach	40	1¼hr
Kilauea Lighthouse	25	40min
Po'ipu	10	20min
Port Allen	15	25min
Princeville	28	45min
Waimea	23	40min
Waimea Canyon	42	1½hr

Car-rental companies are located at Lihu'e airport.
The familiar major agencies are generally reliable:

ACTIVITY	DESTINATION
Hiking	Na Pali Coast (p524)
	Waimea Canyon (p552)
	Koke'e State Park (p554)
	Nounou Mountain Trail, aka
	Sleeping Giant (p485)
Diving	South Shore (p534)
	Ni'iahau (p493)
Kayaking	Wailua River (p484)
	Na Pali Coast (p528)
Snorkeling	Makua Beach, aka Tunnels
	(p522)
	Po'ipu Beach (p530)
Surfing	Hanalei Pier (p513)
	Po'ipu Beach (p530)
	Kalapaki Beach (p469)

Alamo (☏800-327-9633, 246-0645; www.
alamo.com)
Avis (☏800-331-1212, 245-7995; www.avis.
com)
Budget (☏800-527-0700, 245-9031; www.
budget.com)
Dollar (☏800-800-4000, 246-0622; www.
dollar.com)
Hertz (☏800-654-3011, 245-3356; www.hertz.
com)
National (☏888-868-6207, 245-5636; www.
nationalcar.com)
Thrifty (☏800-847-4389, 866-450-5101;
www.thrifty.com)
Kaua'i Harley-Davidson (☏241-7020, 877-212-
9253; www.kauaih-d.com; 3-1866 Kaumuali'i
Hwy; per day $167-188) Does brisk business
renting its 26-bike fleet, despite its going rate
of almost $200 per day plus a $1000 security
deposit.
Kauai Scooter Rental (☏245-7177; www.
kauaimo
pedrentals.com; 3371 Wilcox Rd; ⊗8am-5pm)
Rents scooters for $59 per day (from 8am to
5pm) and $75 for 24 hours. Staffers train new
moped users until they're confident enough to hit
the road – and there's no obligation if you change
your mind.
TAXI The standard flag-down fee is $3, plus 30¢
per additional 0.125 miles. Cabs line up at the airport during normal business hours, but they don't
run all night or cruise for passengers; outside the
airport, you'll need to call ahead.
Pono Taxi (☏634-4474; www.ponotaxi.com)
Akiko's Taxi (☏822-7588)
North Shore Cab (☏826-4118; www.northshore
cab.com)
Southshore Cab (☏742-1525)

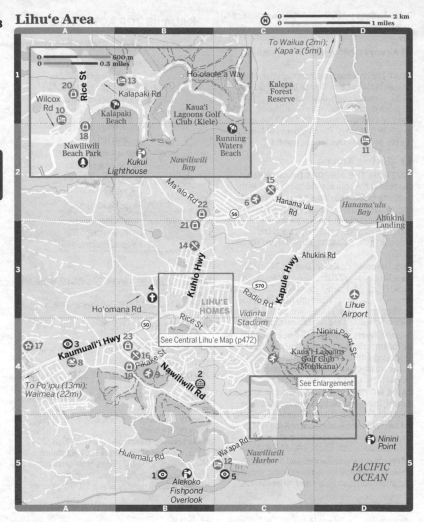

LIHU'E

POP 6101

Your first impression of Lihu'e, the island capital, will likely be lukewarm. That's because this is a drive-in, drive-out town, with no distinct center. Here, the parts are greater than the sum – and you'll find gems scattered throughout. First, there's a plethora of economical eateries and shops, including longtime family-run businesses hidden in nondescript buildings. Second, the town beach is a beauty, ideal for almost all watersports. Third, there's a down-to-earth quality

to this workaday town that's missing in the resort towns north and south. By necessity, you'll pass through Lihu'e – not a knockout but worth getting to know.

Lihu'e arose as a plantation town back when sugar was king and the massive Lihu'e Plantation sugar mill was Kaua'i's largest. The plantation closed in 2001, ending more than a century of operation. But, in Lihu'e and its vicinity, the ethnic makeup still reflects the island's plantation history, with substantial numbers of Japanese and Filipino residents, as well as Caucasians and mixed-race people.

◎ Sights
1 Alekoko (Menehune) Fishpond............ B5
2 Grove Farm Museum............................ B4
  Kauai Plantation Railway ....(see 3)
3 Kilohana Plantation A4
4 Lihuʻe Lutheran Church B3
5 Nawiliwili Small Boat Harbor............... C5

Activities, Courses & Tours
  Alexander Day Spa & Salon.......... (see 13)
  Island Adventures..........................(see 5)
6 Kauaʻi Backcountry Adventures........... C2
7 Kauaʻi Lagoons Golf Club..................... C4
8 Kauai Ohana YMCA A4
9 Puakea Golf Course............................ B4

◎ Sleeping
10 Garden Island Inn.............................. A1
11 Kauaʻi Beach Resort D2
12 Kauaʻi Inn C5
13 Kauaʻi Marriott Resort....................... B1

◎ Eating
  22° North ....(see 3)
  Café Portofino ....(see 13)
  Deli & Bread Connection ....(see 23)

  Duke's Canoe Club........................(see 13)
14 Fish Express....................................... B3
15 Hanamaʻulu Restaurant Tea
  House & Sushi Bar C2
16 Star Market B4

Drinking
  Duke's Barefoot Bar......................(see 13)

◎ Entertainment
  Café Portofino...............................(see 13)
17 Kauaʻi Community College
  Performing Arts Center...................... A4
  Kukui Grove Cinemas ....(see 23)
  Luau Kalamaku .... (see 3)
  South Pacific.................................(see 11)

◎ Shopping
18 Anchor Cove Shopping
  Centre.. A2
19 Costco.. B4
20 Harbour Mall A1
21 Kapaia Stitchery................................. B3
  Kilohana Plantation Shops............. (see 3)
22 Koa Store... B2
23 Kukui Grove Shopping Center............ B4

Now Lihuʻe's economy relies not only on tourism but on retail, which is obvious from all the big-box stores at Kukui Grove Shopping Center.

 Beaches & Sights

Kalapaki Beach   BEACH
(Map p468) This well-protected sandy beach is underrated, considering its easy-access location and remarkable versatility. The calmer waters toward the east are good for swimming, while the swells toward the west draw bodyboarders and surfers. Due to its sandy (rather than reef) bottom, waters are poor for snorkeling. Overall, it's a gem, not only for ocean sports but also for picnicking, watching the surf action, grabbing a drink at Duke's Barefoot Bar and just hanging out. It's easily overlooked because it's hidden behind a row of touristy shops and the Kauaʻi Marriott Resort.

Due to the proximity of Nawiliwili Harbor, the island's major port, you'll see ship traffic, barge containers and other industrial objects in the distance. Thus the beach is less exotic than those on the North and South Shores, but the forgiving wave ac-

tion here is a real plus. Parking close to the water is available at the hotel's north end (signs direct you to public/beach parking).

FREE **Kilohana Plantation**   HISTORICAL SITE
(Map p468; www.kilohanakauai.com; Kaumualiʻi Hwy; ⏱9:30am-9:30pm Mon-Sat, to 5pm Sun) If you're curious about how Kauaʻi's powerful sugar barons lived, visit this handsome plantation estate, which today contains a variety of classy attractions, including **22° North** (p475) and a stellar luau show (p477). The meticulously kept property feels welcoming and guests are invited to wander around.

Plantation owner Gaylord Parke Wilcox, once the head honcho of Grove Farm Homestead, built the house in 1936. The 15,000-sqft Tudor-style mansion has been painstakingly restored and its legacy as one of Kauaʻi's distinguished historic houses is unquestioned. Antique-filled rooms and Oriental carpets on hardwood floors lead you past cases of poi (fermented taro) pounders, koa bowls and other Hawaiiana to a row of gallery shops.

Our favorite attraction is the **Kauai Plantation Railway** (☎245-7245; www.kauaiplantationrailway.com; 40min ride adult/child

$18/14; ⊙departures on the hour, 10am-2pm), which features open-air replica cars and a restored historic train that passes fields of tropical crops and modest pastures with cattle and horses. The big thrill for city-slicker kids is stopping to feed an eager herd of pigs.

Kaua'i Museum
MUSEUM

(Map p472; www.kauaimuseum.org; 4428 Rice St; adult/child $10/2, 1st Sat of month free; ⊙9am-4pm Mon-Fri, 10am-4pm Sat) The island's largest museum is no bigger than the average house, but its humility is rather charming. It's worth a stop for a quick grounding in Kaua'i's history, especially if you catch a free guided tour (⊙10:30am Tue-Fri); call for reservations. Free Hawaiian quilting demonstrations and lauhala-hat weaving demonstrations are given year-round.

Wailua Falls
WATERFALL

(off Map p468) Is it worth the winding 4-mile drive to the falls made famous in the opening credits of *Fantasy Island*? The view is rather distant but to many, this gushing double waterfall (Wailua means 'Two Waters') misting the surrounding tropical foliage is a fantastic photo op, especially when the falls merge into one wide cascade after downpours. While officially listed as 80ft, the falls have been repeatedly measured at between 125ft and 175ft.

At the lookout spot, a sign reads: 'Slippery rocks at top of falls. People have been killed.' Heed it. Many have slipped while trying to scramble down the steep, untamed path.

To get here from Lihu'e, follow Kuhio Hwy north and turn left onto Ma'alo Rd (Hwy 583), which ends at the falls after 4 miles. Be sure to lock your car if venturing down the trail as recent reports of petty theft have surfaced.

Alekoko (Menehune) Fishpond
NATURE RESERVE

(Map p468) Don't expect a splash and dip – only a distant, if gorgeous, view of this tranquil 39-acre pond, an ancient *loko wai* (freshwater fishpond). According to legend, Kaua'i's *menehune* (the 'little people' who built many of Hawaii's fishponds, heiaus and other stonework, according to legend) formed the fishpond overnight when they built the 900ft stone dam across a bend in the Hule'ia River. Holes in the structure allowed young fish to enter the pond but not to escape once grown. Today you can't actually see the dam because a thick green line of mangrove trees covers it.

The pond was productive with mullet until 1824, when Kaua'i's leader Kaumuali'i died and *ali'i* (chiefs) from O'ahu and Maui ruled the island as absentee landlords. With no *ali'i* to feed and maintain the pond, it sorely declined. Later the surrounding area was planted with taro and rice. Today it is privately owned and not in use.

The US Fish & Wildlife Service owns the lands surrounding the fishpond (about 240 acres of river basin and steep forested slopes along the north side of Hule'ia River). In 1973 the area was designated the Hule'ia National Wildlife Refuge (http://pacific islands.fws.gov/wnwr/khuleianwr.html) and now provides breeding and feeding grounds for endemic water birds. The refuge is closed to the public, but kayak tours along Hule'ia River drift through it.

To get to the overlook, drive up Hulemalu Rd for 0.5 miles.

Ninini Point
LANDMARK

(Map p468) If you've seen and done everything and still want to explore, here's a modest excursion to an untouristy spot where 360-degree vistas show jets swooping in the sky above and waves crashing against the rocks below. Looking east, soaring cliffs cut off rainbows and, closer in, golfers tee off near a beckoning scoop of beach. These terrific views from Ninini Point are made more so by its 100ft **lighthouse** marking the northern entrance to Nawiliwili Bay. Here, Hawaiians still fish, pick *opihi* (edible limpet) and gather *limu* (edible seaweed).

The road to the lighthouse begins off Kapule Hwy, just over 0.5 miles south of the intersection with Ahukini Rd and marked with two concrete slabs. You'll walk for just over 2 miles, past a guard gate (usually empty) and Hole 12 of the Mokihana Golf Course, most of it rutted dirt road, before you reach the short spur to the lighthouse.

Running Waters Beach (the little slice of sand visible from Ninini Point) is not swimmable but makes a nice picnic spot. To find it, return to Hole 12 and park in the lot just before it, then follow the signs for 'Shore Access.' Turn right at Whaler's Brew Pub and descend to its parking lot, where you'll see another 'Shore Access' sign to your left. It's a steep, quick walk to the beach below.

Grove Farm Museum
MUSEUM

(Map p468; Nawiliwili Rd; 2hr tour adult/child $10/5; ⊙tours 10am & 1pm Mon, Wed & Thu;

reservations required) History buffs might enjoy this plantation museum, open only for prearranged tours, but kids might grow restless. Grove Farm was among the most productive sugar companies on Kaua'i and George Wilcox, the son of missionaries Abner and Lucy Wilcox, built this well-preserved farmhouse in 1864. It feels suspended in time, with rocking chairs sitting dormant on a covered porch and untouched books lining the shelves of the musty library.

Lihu'e Lutheran Church CHURCH
(Map p468; 4602 Ho'omana Rd; ⏱services 8am & 10:30am Sun) Hawaii's oldest Lutheran church is a quaint clapboard house, with an incongruously slanted floor that resembles a ship's deck, and a balcony akin to a captain's bridge. German immigrants built this church, styling it after their own late-19th-century boat. The building is actually a faithful 1983 reconstruction of the 1885 original, which was leveled in Hurricane 'Iwa in 1982. The church is along a curvy country lane just off Kaumuali'i Hwy (Hwy 50).

 Activities

The only way to navigate the Hule'ia River and see the Hule'ia National Wildlife Refuge is on a commercial tour.

Most fishing charters depart from Nawiliwili Small Boat Harbor (Map p468).

TOP CHOICE Just Live ZIPLINE
(☑482-1295; www.justlive.org; Kuhio Hwy; tours $79-125) Only this outfit offers canopy-based zipping, meaning you never touch ground after your first zip. The 3½-hour zip tour includes seven ziplines and five bridge crossings, 60ft to 80ft off the ground in 200ft Norfolk Island pines. Profits from commercial tours go toward community youth programs. Minimum age is nine.

Kaua'i Backcountry Adventures ZIPLINE
(Map p468; ☑888-270-0555, 245-2506; www.kauaibackcountry.com; Kuhio Hwy; tour incl lunch $130) Offers a 3½-hour zipline tour with seven lines, elevated as high as 200ft above the ground and running as far as 900ft (three football fields). Afterward, refuel on a picnic lunch at a swimming pond. Groups run as large as 11. Minimum age is 12.

Outfitters Kaua'i ZIPLINE, MULTI-ACTIVITY
(Map p532; ☑888-742-9887, 742-9667; www.outfitterskauai.com; Po'ipu Plaza, 2827A Po'ipu Rd;

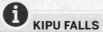

With regular injuries and even fatalities, this has become a controversial spot. Both the cliff jump and rope swing involve slippery rocks and dirty water that is likely to carry Leptospirosis. After rains the currents can be strong and access necessitates crossing private property, which is illegal. The thrill in this activity is not hard to find, but the risk is not worth the reward. People who didn't think they were going to get hurt have died here.

3hr tour adult/child $112/102, 8hr tour incl lunch $182/142) Offers two multi-activity tours at Kipu Ranch (just outside Lihu'e) that combine aspects of zipping, hiking, waterfall swimming and the ever-idealized 'rope-swinging'. Half-day tour includes five zips; full-day tour includes only one. Minimum zipping age is seven. Book in Po'ipu.

Island Adventures KAYAKING
(Map p468; ☑246-6333; www.kauaifun.com; Nawiliwili Small Boat Harbor; tour incl lunch adult/child $89/69) Offers a 4½-hour tour in the Hule'ia National Wildlife Refuge, where you'll paddle 2.5 miles into the wildlife refuge, hike to two private waterfalls, swim and picnic. If you can't hike eight to 10 flights of uneven steps, take a pass.

Kaua'i Backcountry Adventures TUBING
(Map p468; ☑245-2506, 888-270-0555; www.kauaibackcountry.com; Kuhio Hwy; 3hr tour incl lunch $102; ⏱departures 9am, 10am, 1pm & 2pm Mon-Sat, 8:30am & 12:30pm Sun) Part historical tour, part lazy-man cruise, 'tubing' means floating down former sugar-plantation irrigation ditches in old-fashioned inner tubes. This is the island's only tubing tour, and it ends with lunch at a swimming hole. Great for the whole family (including kids as young as five).

Kipu Ranch Adventures ATV
(off Map p468; ☑246-9288; www.kiputours.com; tours driver/child/adult from $125/72/100) Can driving an ATV across private, pristine ranchland really constitute an 'ecotour'? On both tours offered you do see gorgeous, otherwise inaccessible landscape, including the Ha'upu mountain range, Kipu Kai coast and Hule'ia River, plus wild pigs, pheasants, peacocks and turkeys. But gas-powered vehicles are hard to endorse.

Central Lihu'e

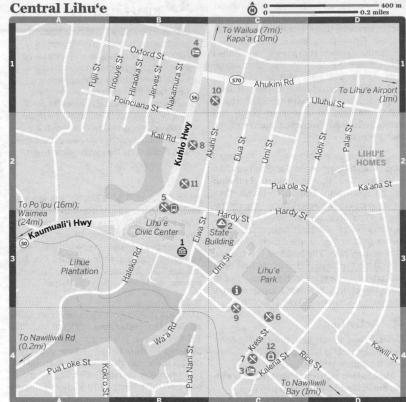

Central Lihu'e

◉ Sights

1 Kaua'i Museum...................................B3

⊜☺⛰ Sleeping

Division of Forestry & Wildlife.....(see 2)
2 Division of State Parks.........................C3
3 Kaua'i Palms Hotel..............................C4
4 Kaua'i Vacation Rentals......................B1

◉ Eating

5 Big Save..B2
6 Garden Island Barbecue &
    Chinese Restaurant..........................C4
7 Hamura Saimin....................................C4
8 Kaua'i Pasta..B2
9 Pho Kauai...C4
10 Tip Top Café & Sushi Katsu................C1
11 Vim 'n Vigor..B2

⦿ Shopping

Edith King Wilcox Gift Shop.........(see 1)
12 Flowers Forever..................................C4

For a green alternate, try Kaua'i ATV (p528).

Kaua'i Lagoons Golf Club   GOLF
(Map p468; ☎241-6000, 800-634-6400; www
.kauailagoonsgolf.com; Kaua'i Marriott, 3351
Ho'olaule'a Way; greens fee morning $135-175,
afternoon $75-99, club rental $55) The original
two Jack Nicklaus–designed 18-hole par-72
courses here were called Kiele and Mokihana. In 2008, both courses began undergoing a major renovation, also headed up by
Nicklaus. The first stage reopened in May
2011. Call to check where the renovations
are up to and what's open when you're in
the area.

Puakea Golf Course   GOLF
(Map p468; ☎866-773-5554, 245-8756; www.
puakeagolf.com; 4315 Kalepa Rd; greens fee incl cart
before 11am $99, 11am-2pm $85, after 2pm $59,
club rental $40, after 2pm $25) The lush cliffs of
Mt Ha'upu serve as a backdrop to this Robin

Nelson-designed course, which first opened in 1997 (with an odd 10 holes) and became an 18-hole course in 2003. It's near Kukui Grove Shopping Center.

Captain Don's Sportfishing FISHING
(☑639-3021; www.captaindonsfishing.com; 4hr shared charter per person $135, 4hr private charter per 6 passengers $575) Giving guests creative freedom to design their own trip (fishing, whale watching, snorkeling) on the 34ft *June Louise*, Captain Don serves with decades of experience on Kaua'i waters.

Lahela Ocean Adventures FISHING
(☑635-4020; www.sport-fishing-kauai.com; 4hr shared charter per person $219, 4hr private charter per 6 passengers $575) Captain Scott Akana is named by other fisherman as the island's 'best' and a real 'pro.' Spectators ride at half-price. Its detailed website answers all your questions and more.

Happy Hunter Sport Fishing FISHING
(☑639-4351, 634-2633; www.happyhuntersport fishing.com; 4hr private charter per 6 passengers $625) Captain Harry Shigekane has 30 years' experience and sails a fantastic 41ft Pacifica. Private charters only.

Alexander Day Spa & Salon SPA
(Map p468; ☑246-4918; www.alexanderspa.com; Kaua'i Marriottt Resort; 50min massage $115; ☺8am-7pm) This salon strives to pamper guests in the most ecofriendly way, using biodegradable water cups, recycled paper products and CFL (compact fluorescent light) bulbs.

Kauai Ohana YMCA SWIMMING
(Map p468; Kaumuali'i Hwy; day pass $10; ☺5:30am-9am & 11am-7pm Mon-Fri, 7am-7pm Sat, 10am-6pm Sun) Lap swimmers, get your fix at this open-air, Olympic-sized pool. Teach tots to swim in a nifty learning pool with 1ft–4ft steps. A weight room is also available. YMCA members from any state, show your card to pay only $5. It's across from Kilohana Plantation.

☞ Tours

Mauna Loa Helicopters HELICOPTER TOUR
(☑245-4006; www.maunaloahelicoptertours.com; 1hr tour $239) Highly qualified pilots don't skimp on full 60-minute private tours for up to three passengers. Small groups allow for more-personalized interaction between pilot and passengers. You can choose a doors-off tour for $10 to $20 more per person. Cost-wise, singles are better off with another, nonprivate tour. Also runs a flight school.

The following helicopter tours allow six passengers, which can seem crowded (if you get stuck in the middle), but they give hour-long (or close) rides and have well-qualified pilots. Go online for major discounts:

TOP CHOICE Safari Helicopters HELICOPTER TOUR
(☑246-0136, 800-326-3356; www.safarihe licopters.com; 55/90 min tours from $204/324) Besides fair prices, this outfit offers a fascinating tour that lands on a cliff overlooking Olokele Valley in Waimea. The landowner, Keith Robinson (whose family owns Ni'ihau and 2000 Kaua'i acres), chats with passengers about his conservation work with endangered species.

Island Helicopters HELICOPTER TOUR
(☑245-8588, 800-829-8588; www.islandheli copters.com; 50-55min tour $183) Long-time, small company.

Jack Harter Helicopters HELICOPTER TOUR
(☑245-3774, 888-245-2001; www.helicopters-kauai .com; 60-65min tour $229-259) You get your money's worth of air time here. Choose from standard enclosed, six-passenger AStars ($229) or doors-off, four-passenger Hughes 500s ($259). Longer 90-minute to 95-minute tours offered.

✈ Festivals & Events

E Pili Kakou I Ho'okahi Lahui HULA
(www.epilikakou-kauai.org) Annual two-day hula retreat in late February features top kumu hula (hula teachers) from across the islands. Current venue is the Hilton Kaua'i Beach Resort.

Spring Gourmet Gala FOOD
(☑245-8359) Save your appetite for the island's highest-end gourmet event ($100 per person), featuring food-and-wine pairings by famous Hawaii chefs, in early April. Funds support the Kaua'i Community College's culinary arts program. The 300 tickets sell out fast.

May Day Lei Contest & Fair LEI
(☑245-6931; www.kauaimuseum.org) Established in the early 1980s, the annual Kaua'i Museum Lei Contest on May 1 spawns legendary floral art.

Kaua'i Polynesian Festival CULTURAL
(☑335-6466; www.kauaipolynesianfestival.org) This four-day event in late May features rockin' competitions in expert Tahitian, Maori, Samoan and hula dancing, plus food booths and cultural workshops, held at various locations.

Fourth of July Concert in the Sky
CULTURAL

(☏246-2440) Enjoy island foods, entertainment and a fireworks show set to music at Vidinha Stadium, from 3pm to 9pm.

Kaua'i County Farm Bureau Fair
FAIR

(☏332-8189) Old-fashioned family fun at Vidinha Stadium in late August, with carnival rides and games, livestock show, petting zoo, hula performances and lots of local-food booths.

Aloha Festivals Ho'olaule'a & Parade
CULTURAL

(☏245-8508; www.alohafestivals.com) This statewide event in early September starts on Kaua'i with a parade from Vidinha Stadium (Map p468) to the county building lawn. The ho'olaule'a (celebration) includes an appearance by the royal court.

Kaua'i Composers Contest & Concert
MUSIC

(☏822-2166; www.mokihana.kauai.net) The signature event of the Kaua'i Mokihana Festival, this contest in mid- to late September showcases homegrown musical talent.

'Kaua'i Style' Hawaiian Slack Key Guitar Festival
MUSIC

(☏239-4336; www.slackkeyfestival.com) Held in mid-November, this opportunity to see master slack key guitarists for free is not to be missed.

Lights on Rice Parade
CULTURAL

(☏246-1004) Disney had its Main Street Electrical Parade. Kaua'i has this charming parade of illuminated floats in early December.

🛏 Sleeping

Lihu'e's sleeping options are limited mostly to a few hotels, from the high-end Marriott to no-frills motels in the nondescript town center. Unlike on the Eastside, few B&Bs and inns operate in residential neighborhoods. For vacation-rental homes, contact **Kaua'i Vacation Rentals** (Map p472;☏245-8841, 800-367-5025; www.kauaivacationrentals.com; 3-3311 Kuhio Hwy), where owner Lucy Kawaihalau is one of the island's most experienced and dedicated rental agents.

TOP CHOICE Garden Island Inn
HOTEL $$

(Map p468; ☏245-7227, 800-648-0154; www.gardenislandinn.com; 3445 Wilcox Rd; r $99-150, ste $145-180; ❈🛜❈) You won't find the Marriott's beachfront cachet and megapool here. But this two-storey inn across the street holds its own for value and friendliness. Rooms are modest but cheerful, with tropical decor, overhead fans, quality double beds and kitchenettes. The real gems are the suites on the 2nd and 3rd floors, with large ocean-view lanais.

Kaua'i Marriott Resort
RESORT $$$

(Map p468; ☏245-5050, 800-220-2925; www.marriotthotels.com; 3610 Rice St; r $239-429; ❈❈) For the complete resort experience, the Marriott won't disappoint. It's got user-friendly Kalapaki Beach, two top golf courses, the island's liveliest oceanfront restaurant and a gargantuan pool that could provide all-day entertainment. With 366 hotel rooms and 464 time-share rooms, finding your door can be a major hike. Room decor and amenities are standard and rather staid. If you can

---

LIVE & LET LIVE

Before you get too annoyed at the thousands of wild chickens on Kaua'i, try to understand their back-story. The first chickens to populate Hawaii were jungle fowl (*moa*), introduced by the first Polynesians. These vividly colored birds later cross-bred with domestic chickens brought by Westerners. During plantation days, Kaua'i's wild-chicken population was kept in check by field fires (a regular event before harvest, to allow more efficient reaping). However, when the sugar industry went bust in the 1980s, the chicken population boomed.

When Hurricane 'Iwa and Hurricane 'Iniki struck in 1982 and 1992 respectively, they obliterated the cages of Kaua'i's fighting cocks, adding even more chickens to the wild. With no mongoose or snake population to prey on fowl, wild chickens proliferated.

You'll see them perched in trees, running across fields, roaming parking lots and otherwise strutting their stuff across the island. Most locals have adopted an attitude of acceptance toward the chickens, but warn of their *lolo* (crazy) schedules: instead of crowing only at dawn, they cock-a-doodle-doo at random times and seem confused by a full moon or any late-night light. Before you book accommodations, ask whether there are chickens living within earshot. Or just wear earplugs.

afford an oceanfront unit, go for it. The view is worth it.

Kaua'i Palms Hotel
HOTEL $

(Map p472; ☑246-0908; www.kauaipalmshotel.com; 2931 Kalena St; r from $75; ☺office 7am-8pm; ☎) The island version of Motel 6, Kaua'i Palms is Lihu'e's best budget option. The 28 rooms include fridge, cable TV and windows on opposite walls to allow cooling crossbreezes. Pay more for rooms with kitchenettes and air-con. Wi-fi guaranteed only in lobby.

Kaua'i Inn
HOTEL $$

(Map p468; ☑245-9000, 800-808-2330; www.kauai-inn.com; 2430 Hulemalu Rd; r with kitchenette incl breakfast $129-149; ✸@☎☒) This large inn offers a simple home base away from traffic and crowds. While not fancy (air-con costs $10 per day), the 48 rooms include refrigerator and microwave. Ground-floor rooms have back porches, while 2nd-floor rooms are larger but sans lanai. Rooms vary in decor and bed count.

Kaua'i Beach Resort
RESORT $$

(Map p468; ☑866-536-7976; www.kauaibeachresorthawaii.com; 4331 Kaua'i Beach Dr; r $189-229; ✸☒) While it doesn't quite live up to the 'resort' in its name, it has 350-rooms newly managed by Aqua Hotel & Resorts, and equates to a decent business-class hotel. The location, north of Lihu'e, might strike you as 'middle of nowhere' because there's no beach akin to the Marriott's first-class Kalapaki Beach, but it does offer a quieter setting and lower rates. There are restaurants and a spa on-site.

✗ Eating & Drinking

Fish Express
FISH MARKET $

(Map p468; 3343 Kuhio Hwy; lunch $6-7.50; ☺10am-6pm Mon-Sat, to 5pm Sun, lunch served to 3pm daily) Fish lovers, this is a no-brainer. One day, order chilled deli items, from fresh ahi *poke* to green seaweed salad, by the pound. The next day, try a healthful plate lunch of blackened ahi with guava-basil sauce, plus rice and salad ($8.50) or a gourmet *bentō* (Japanese boxed meal). You might end up here every day.

22° North
HAWAII REGIONAL $$$

(Map p468; www.22northkauai.com; Kilohana Plantation, Kaumuali'i Hwy; lunch $8-14, dinner $20-35; ☺11am-2:30pm & 5:30-9pm Mon-Sat, brunch 9am-2:30pm Sun) As the eclectic Kaua'i-grown farmhouse menu reflects the cycle of the seasons, mains such as stuffed A'akukui Ranch veal

with island mushrooms and honey caraway carrots and pan-seared *uku* with Bhutanese red rice and avocado mayonnaise will always reflect ingredients at their flavor-peak. Chef de Cuisine Aaron Leikam's old-world Mediterranean style applied to food that essentially went through a culinary spa treatment is likely to impress even the most discerning palette.

Hamura Saimin
DINER $

(Map p472; 2956 Kress St; noodles $3.75-4.50; ☺10am-10:30pm Mon-Thu, to midnight Fri & Sat, to 9:30pm Sun) An island institution, Hamura's is a hole-in-the-wall specializing in homemade saimin (local-style noodle soup). Service can be abrupt (think Soup Nazi from *Seinfeld*) so don't hem and haw. Expect crowds at lunchtime, slurping noodles elbow-to-elbow at orange U-shaped counters. It's stifling inside with noodles boiling and no air-con, but save room for the other specialty, *liliko'i* (passion fruit) chiffon pie.

Tip Top Café & Sushi Katsu
DINER, SUSHI $

(Map p472; 3173 Akahi St; breakfast $4.50-10, lunch $5.50-11; ☺cafe 6:30am-1:45pm, Sushi Katsu 11am-1:45pm & 5:30-9pm Tue-Sun) We give this retro diner a C for atmosphere and an A for good ol' fashioned eats. The main draws are its famous pancakes and oxtail soup. Meat eaters, go local with *loco moco* (two fried eggs, hamburger patty, rice and gravy), saimin and beef stew. Sushi Katsu offers value-priced sushi and Japanese dishes.

Deli & Bread Connection
SANDWICHES $

(Map p468; Kukui Grove Shopping Center; 3-2600 Kaumuali'i Hwy; sandwiches $5-9; ☺9:30am-7pm Mon-Thu & Sat, to 9pm Fri, 10am-6pm Sun) Choose from the gamut of all-American, meal-sized sandwiches, including classics like hot tuna melts and classic clubs. Vegetarians won't starve with a nonmeat burger layered with mushrooms, pesto and melted mozzarella. Fringe benefit: it's at the mall but not a chain.

Garden Island Barbecue & Chinese Restaurant
CHINESE $

(Map p472; 4252 Rice St; plate lunches $5-6.25, mains $7-9; ☺10am-9pm) Tasty, filling, cheap Chinese food. No surprise, it's a hit. For a true local (if lowbrow) experience, try this bustling family-style eatery. The lengthy menu includes Chinese, Japanese and Hawaiian dishes, which is a red flag on the mainland but rather common in Hawaii. Try the simpler veg dishes, eg black mushrooms with Chinese broccoli.

BUY LOCAL: KAUA'I'S FARMERS MARKETS

You are what you eat. While on Kaua'i take the opportunity to let part of the Garden Island become part of you:

Monday

Po'ipu (West Kauai Agricultural Association, Poipu Rd & Cane Haul Rd; ⊙8am)

Koloa Town (Koloa Ball Park, Maluhia Rd; ⊙noon)

Lihu'e (Kukui Grove Shopping Center; ⊙3pm)

Tuesday

Hanalei (Kuhio Hwy, Waipa; ⊙2pm) Just past Hanalei.

Wailua (Wailua Homesteads Ballpark, Kamalu Rd & Malu Rd; ⊙3pm)

Kalaheo (Kalaheo Neighborhood Center, Papalina Rd & Kaumuali'i Hwy; ⊙3pm)

Wednesday

Kapa'a (Kapa'a New Town Park, Kahau Rd & Olohena Rd; ⊙2:45pm) By the bypass road.

Thursday

Hanapepe (Hanapepe Town Park; ⊙3pm) Behind the fire station.

Kilauea (Kilauea Neighborhood Center, Keneke St; ⊙4:30pm) Off Lighthouse Rd.

Friday

Lihu'e (Vidinha Stadium Parking Lot, Ho'olako St; ⊙2:45pm) Off Queen Kapule Rd.

Saturday

Hanalei (⊙9am) Next to the soccer fields.

Kekaha (Kekaha Neighborhood Center, Elepaio Rd; ⊙9am) Off Kaumualii Hwy.

Kilauea (Keneke St; ⊙1:30am) Behind the Kilauea Post Office.

Pho Kauai   VIETNAMESE $

(Map p472; Rice Shopping Center, 4303 Rice St; bowls under $8; ⊙10am-9pm Mon-Sat) Hidden in a strip mall, this no-frills eatery serves steaming bowls of well-made *pho* (Vietnamese noodle soup). Choose meat or veg toppings, such as curry chicken, grilled shrimp, snow peas or eggplant. No credit cards.

Hanama'ulu Restaurant Tea House & Sushi Bar   SUSHI $

(Map p468; 3-4291 Kuhio Hwy; mains $7-10, special platters $17-20; ⊙10am-1pm Tue-Fri, 4:30-9:30pm Tue-Sun) This fixture on the outskirts of Lihu'e stands out mainly for its historic teahouse setting. The food is good, but not great, and the menu suspiciously includes Chinese dishes, but that's the island way. It's known for crispy fried dishes, from Chinese ginger chicken to Japanese tempura and tonkatsu (breaded cutlets). Avoid the dismal front dining room; request seating in the quaint teahouse in the back.

Duke's Canoe Club   HAWAII REGIONAL $$

(Map p468; Kaua'i Marriott Resort; appetizers $8-11, mains $18-30; ⊙5-9:30pm) Even in chic Princeville and Po'ipu, you won't find an evening spot more fun and lively than Duke's, holding court on Kalapaki Beach. The steak-and-seafood menu is not very innovative, but dishes are well executed. The fresh catch baked 'Duke's style' with garlic, lemon and basil glaze is a winner. Expect a touristy crowd (matching aloha wear is not uncommon).

Café Portofino   ITALIAN $$

(Map p468; www.cafeportofino.com; Kaua'i Marriott Resort, Kalapaki Beach; appetizers $8-12, mains $16-29; ⊙5-9:30pm) A textbook example of 'romantic,' this oceanfront restaurant appeals to particular tastes. Some appreciate the white tablecloths, low lighting and solo harpist, but others find Chef Maximillian Avocadi's food overpriced and the formal atmosphere too staid. The traditional Italian menu features fine pastas and lots of veal, such as house-specialty osso bucco.

Kaua'i Pasta
ITALIAN $$

(Map p472; 4-939B Kuhio Hwy; mains $9-15; ⊙11am-2pm & 5-9pm) For a happy medium between a fast-food joint and a resort splurge, this centrally located Italian bistro is your ticket. Colorful salads meld diverse flavors, such as peppery arugula, creamy goat cheese and sweet tomatoes. Hot focaccia sandwiches, classic pasta mains and luscious tiramisu would pass muster with mainland foodies.

Duke's Barefoot Bar
BAR $$

(Map p468; Kaua'i Marriott Resort, Kalapaki Beach; tropical drinks $7.25, wine per glass $6-16; ⊙11am-11pm) For either drinks or a meal, this is a convivial, Waikiki-style tropical bar, with ringside views of Kalapaki Beach. It's a thrifty substitute for Duke's Canoe Club, with similar full-fledged menu items.

Self-Catering

Big Save
GROCERY $

(Map p472; 4444 Rice St; ⊙7am-11pm) Lihu'e's branch of this chain is decent but lacks a deli.

Star Market
GROCERY $

(Map p468; Kukui Grove Shopping Center; ⊙6am-11pm) Carries much the same stock.

Vim 'n Vigor
GROCERY $$

(Map p468; 3-3122 Kuhio Hwy; ⊙9am-7pm Mon-Fri, to 5pm Sat) Carries vitamins and supplements, health foods, organic produce and bulk staples.

☆ Entertainment

Café Portofino
BAR, CLUB

(Map p468; www.cafeportofino.com; Kaua'i Marriott Resort, Kalapaki Beach) From 10pm until late (anywhere from 2am to 4am) on Thursdays and Saturdays guest DJs spin music ranging from swing to hip-hop to salsa offering visiting night-owls and socially starved locals a chance to mingle, let loose and get their groove on.

Luau Kalamaku
SHOW

(Map p468; ☎877-622-1780; www.luaukalamaku.com; Kilohana Plantation; adult/child $99/49; ⊙luau 5:30pm Tue & Fri) Skip the same-old commercial show for mesmerizing dinner theater with a dash of Cirque du Soleil (think lithe dancers, flashy leotards and pyrotechnics) thrown in. The thrilling stage play about one family's epic voyage to Hawaii features hula and Tahitian dancing, and showstopping, nail-biting Samoan fire danc-

ing. The buffet dinner is above average, despite the audience size (typically 550, maximum 1000), and there's little cringe-worthy 'embarrass the tourist' forced dancing.

South Pacific
SHOW

(Map p468; ☎346-6500; Kaua'i Beach Resort, 4331 Kaua'i Beach Dr; adult/child $85/30; ⊙shows 5:30pm Wed) If you've never seen Rodgers and Hammerstein's *South Pacific*, it's worth your while catching this dinner-theater production directed by Brenda Turville and produced by Alain Dussaud and the Hawaii Association of Performing Arts. Line up early; seating is first-come, first-served.

Kukui Grove Cinemas
CINEMA

(Map p468; ☎245-5055; Kukui Grove Shopping Center, 3-2600 Kaumuali'i Hwy; adult/child $8/5, before 5pm $5) For mainstream first-run movies, this is your standard shopping-mall fourplex. It's also a venue for the Hawaii International Film Festival (www.hiff.org).

Kaua'i Concert Association
CONCERTS

(Map p468; ☎245-7464; www.kauai-concert.org; tickets $30-45) The Kaua'i Community College Performing Arts Center offers classical, jazz and dance concerts at 7pm. Past performers include African singer Angélique Kidjo, the Rubberbanddance Group and Alison Brown on banjo.

🛍 Shopping

Koa Store
SOUVENIRS

(Map p468; www.thekoastore.com; 3-3601 Kuhio Hwy; ⊙9am-6pm Mon-Sat, 10am-5pm Sun) Other koa galleries carry higher-end masterpieces, but here you'll find lots of affordable souvenirs, such as sleek chopsticks and desk accessories. Many items come in three grades, from the basic straight-grain koa to the rare, almost three-dimensional, premium 'curly' koa. All woodcraft are genuine koa (not the cheap fakes sold at tourist traps).

Flowers Forever
FLOWERS

(Map p472; www.flowersforeverhawaii.com; Kalena St; ⊙8am-5pm Mon-Thu, to 6pm Fri, to 4pm Sat) Voted *Best Kauai Flower Shop* eight years running, Flowers Forever offers floral arrangements, balloons, fruit and gourmet baskets, champagne and a multitude of flower and maile style ti-leaf lei. They'll ship tropical flowers, plants and lei to the mainland.

Kapaia Stitchery
SOUVENIRS, CLOTHING

(Map p468; 3-3551 Kuhio Hwy; ⊙9am-5pm Mon-Sat) A quilter's heaven, this longtime shop features countless cotton fabrics, plus island-made patterns and kits. Stop here also for handmade gifts, such as children's clothing, Japanese kimonos, potholders and an assortment of bags.

Edith King Wilcox Gift Shop SOUVENIRS
(Map p472; www.kauaimuseum.org/store; Kaua'i Museum, 4428 Rice St; ☺9am-4pm Mon-Fri, 10am-4pm Sat) Kaua'i Museum's gem of a gift shop features a variety of genuine Hawaiian crafts, such as Ni'ihau shell jewelry, koa woodwork and *lauhala* (a type of Hawaiian leaf weaving) hats, plus books on Hawaii and collectible ceramics. Enter the shop, free of charge, through the museum lobby.

Kilohana Plantation SOUVENIRS, CLOTHING
(Map p468; www.kilohanakauai.com/shopping.htm; Kaumuali'i Hwy; ☺most shops 10am-9pm Mon-Sat, to 4pm Sun) Nestled in an elegant historic manor, these classy shops will please the discriminating shopper. Find high-end jewelry, original art, woodwork, raku pottery and aloha shirts. The picturesque historic setting is reason enough to stop here.

Lihu'e's only major mall is **Kukui Grove Shopping Center** (Map p468; ☏245-7784; 3-2600 Kaumuali'i Hwy), which contains mostly chain stores such as Macy's, Sears, Longs Drugs, Kmart, Radio Shack and banks. Across the street is warehouse-sized **Costco** (Map p468; ☏241-4000; 4300 Nuhou St; ☺Mon-Fri 10am-8:30pm, Sat 9:30am-6pm, Sun 10am-6pm) carrying an abundance of everything. Near

Nawiliwili Harbor, **Anchor Cove Shopping Center** (Map p468; ☏246-0634; 3416 Rice St) and **Harbor Mall** (Map p468; ☏245-6255; 3501 Rice St) draw mainly tourists from cruise ships and the nearby Marriott. Take a pass.

ℹ Information

Bookstores
Borders (Kukui Grove Shopping Center, 4303 Nawiliwili Rd; ☺9am-9pm Mon-Thu, to 10pm Fri & Sat, to 8pm Sun) Large chain with wide range of books and CDs; good source for island maps.
Tropic Isle Music Co (www.tropicislemusic.com; Anchor Cove Shopping Center, 3416 Rice St; ☺10am-8pm) Huge selection of Hawaii-specific books, CDs and other sundry items.

Emergency
Police, Fire & Ambulance (☏911)
Police Station (☏241-1771; 3060 Umi St) For nonemergencies, incident reporting and information.
Sexual Assault Crisis Line (☏245-4144)

Internet Access
Kukui Grove Shopping Center (Kukui Grove Shopping Center, Kuhio Hwy; ☺9:30am-7pm Mon-Thu & Sat, to 9pm Fri, to 6pm Sun; 🛜) Has free wi-fi running from Sears through the food court. Free wi-fi at Starbucks Café, near the east entrance.
Cyber Connections (3366 Wa'apa Rd, behind Anchor Cove Shopping Center; per 15min $4.50; ☺10am-6pm Mon-Sat) Offers computers as well as printing capabilities.

SUPERFERRY NON GRATA

In August 2007, when the Hawaii Superferry sailed toward Nawiliwili Harbor for its first arrival, some 300 Kaua'i protesters blocked its entry. Three-dozen people even swam into the gargantuan ferry's path, shouting, 'Go home, go home!' Ultimately, service to Maui (but not to Kaua'i) was launched in December 2007, but the whole enterprise was indefinitely terminated in March 2009, when the Hawai'i Supreme Court deemed Superferry's environmental impact statement (EIS) invalid.

Why was opposition to the ferry so furious? Actually, the opponents themselves were not 'anti-ferry' but, rather, anti-Superferry. They wanted smaller, passenger-only, publicly owned and slower-moving boats. Their main concerns were nighttime collisions with whales, worsened traffic on Neighbor Islands, the spread of environmental pests and plundering of natural resources by nonresidents. Indeed, during the Superferry's brief run between O'ahu and Maui, O'ahu residents were frequently caught taking home *'opihi* (a prized edible limpet), crustaceans, algae, rocks, coral and massive quantities of reef fish.

That said, not all locals were opposed. In fact, many locals (especially O'ahu residents) viewed the Superferry as a convenient way to visit friends and family on Neighbor Islands. They also cited the need for an alternate, fuel-efficient mode of transportation between the islands (though the enormous vessels are actually gas guzzlers).

For a compelling, if overwhelmingly detailed, account, read *The Superferry Chronicles* (Koohan Paik and Jerry Mander), which also analyzes the ferry's ties to US military and commercial interests.

Medical Services

Longs Drugs (☑245-7771; Kukui Grove Shopping Center, 3-2600 Kaumuali'i Hwy; ⊘store 8am-8pm, pharmacy 8am-6pm Mon-Sat, 9am-6pm Sun)

Wilcox Memorial Hospital (Map p468; ☑245-1010, TTY 245-1133; 3420 Kuhio Hwy) Kaua'i's only major hospital. Emergency services 24 hours.

Money

Banks with 24-hour ATMs:

American Savings Bank (☑246-8844; Kukui Grove Shopping Center, 3-2600 Kaumuali'i Hwy)

Bank of Hawaii (☑245-6761; 4455 Rice St)

Post

Longs Drugs (☑245-7771; Kukui Grove Shopping Center, 3-2600 Kaumuali'i Hwy; ⊘7am-10pm Mon-Sat, 8am-8pm Sun) In-store postal center offers photocopying, FedEx and UPS, and US Postal Service.

Post office (☑800-275-8777; 4441 Rice St; ⊘8am-4:30pm Mon-Fri, 9am-1pm Sat) Main post office holds poste restante (general delivery) mail for a maximum of 30 days.

Tourist Information

Kaua'i Visitors Bureau (☑245-3971, 800-262-1400; www.kauaidiscovery.com; Suite 101, 4334 Rice St) Offers a monthly calendar of events, bus schedules and list of county-managed Sunshine Markets (farmers markets) for the sale of Kaua'i produce. Order a free 'vacation planning kit' online.

❶ Getting There & Around

Lihu'e's focal points are Nawiliwili Bay, the island's only major harbor, and Lihu'e airport, the island's only major airport. Rice St, considered the town's main drag, runs east–west and passes the government buildings and post office, while Kuhio Hwy (Hwy 56) leads to shops and restaurants toward the north, and Kukui Grove Shopping Center to the south.

BUS The Kaua'i Bus (☑241-6410; www.kauai. gov) serves Lihu'e with a shuttle that runs hourly from 6am to about 7pm, with stops at all the obvious destinations, such as Kukui Grove Shopping Center, Lihu'e airport, Vidinha Stadium, Wal-Mart, Wilcox Memorial Hospital and Big Save. In addition to this, there is a lunch shuttle that runs at 15-minute intervals within central Lihu'e.

CAR & MOTORCYCLE Kaua'i is a driving town, so most businesses have parking lots, and street parking is relatively easy to find. Metered parking in Lihu'e costs 25¢ for 30 minutes. For information about car and motorcycle rentals, see p467.

If you look past the strip malls and highway traffic, the Eastside will fascinate you on many levels. Its geography runs the gamut, from mountaintop forests and grassy pastureland to pounding surf and a majestic river. In ancient times, the Wailua River was sacred and royalty lived on its fertile banks; today, Kaua'i's population is concentrated here, creating enough critical mass for a variety of restaurants, shops, accommodations and people. From Wailua to Kapa'a, the Coconut Coast, as it is known, has a busier, more workaday vibe than the swankier resort strongholds in Po'ipu and Princeville – and that's no insult. On the northeast coast, a rustic world appears in Anahola, a residential and farming region where Native Hawaiians constitute 70% of all residents.

Wailua

POP (INCL WAILUA HOMESTEADS) 7150

Wailua makes an ideal home base for exploring this area, giving you a choice between oceanfront condos with a 24/7 soundtrack of waves, and upcountry B&Bs and vacation rentals surrounded by lush gardens and rolling hills. Other attractions include a whimsical kiddie playground, a gigantic Hindu monastery and the state's only navigable river.

◉ Beaches & Sights

See the Kaua'i Heritage Trail (http://wailua heritagetrail.org) website and map for an overview of major sights.

Lydgate Beach Park   BEACH PARK

With safe swimming, beginner snorkeling and two children's playgrounds, this popular beach park can entertain restless kids all afternoon. If you're seeking a secluded, pristine beach, Lydgate might seem too built-up. But most families will appreciate multiple diversions. Remember, the shallow seawater pool is calm thanks to the protective stone breakwater, but beware of the open ocean beyond the pool.

A volunteer group (see www.kamalani. org) in 1994 built the multifeatured **Kamalani Playground** (at the north end), a massive 16,000-sq-ft wooden castle with swings, slides, mirror mazes, a suspension bridge and other kid-pleasing contraptions. It built another wooden masterpiece, the

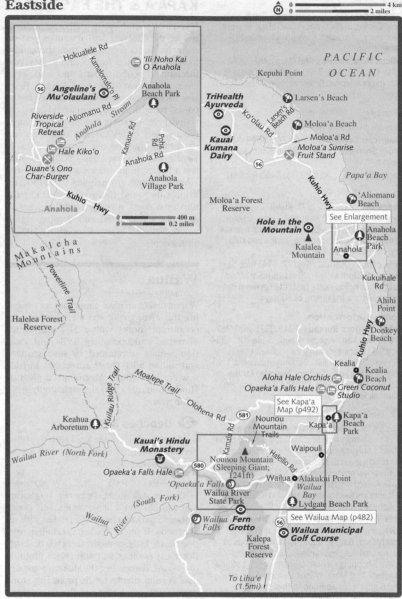

simpler, two-level **Kamalani Kai Bridge** (at the south end) in 2001. Other amenities include game-sized soccer fields, a 2.5-mile bicycle–pedestrian path, pavilions, picnic tables, restrooms, showers, drinking water, a lifeguard and ample parking.

To get here, turn *makai* (seaward) on Kuhio Hwy between the 5- and 6-mile markers.

Steelgrass Farm   FARM TOUR
(☏821-1857; www.steelgrass.org; adult/child $60/ free; ☺9am-noon Mon, Wed & Fri) Learn more about diversified agriculture and cacao

growing at this family farm, which offers a unique chocolate-farm tour. Steelgrass Farm's two other crops arc timber bamboo and vanilla, but the 8-acre farm features literally hundreds of thriving tropical species, which you'll also see on the tour. It's a fantastic introduction if you're curious to see what thrives on Kaua'i – from avocados and citrus to soursop and jaboticaba.

The farm's owners, Will and Emily Lydgate, are the great-grandchildren of Kaua'i minister and community leader John Mortimer Lydgate, the namesake of Lydgate Beach Park. The property was not an inheritance, as JM (as he was known) had no desire to acquire land or to profit from the sugar industry. Read more about the family's intriguing history on the website.

Contact the family for farm location and directions.

Smith's Tropical Paradise GARDEN
Other gardens might have fancier landscaping or loftier goals, but you can't beat Smith's for value. For $6 you can leisurely stroll a loop trail past a serene pond, grassy lawns and island-themed gardens. The setting can seem Disney-esque, with an Easter Island replica and tour trams, but it's appealingly unpretentious and large enough to accommodate all. The Smith's family-run luau (p488) is held on the garden grounds.

Kaua'i's Hindu Monastery TEMPLE
(Map p480; ☑822-3012; www.himalayanacademy.com; 107 Kaholalele Rd; ◎9am-noon) On an island virtually devoid of Hinduism, this one-of-a-kind Hindu monastery welcomes both serious pilgrims and curious sightseers. Set on 458 acres of buoyantly thriving rainforest above the Wailua River, the astoundingly green setting (enhanced by the monks' back-breaking gardening) equals that of a commercial garden. The temples, Ganesh statues and other structures are devoted to the god Shiva. While visitors can access a limited area (self-guided tour) from 9am to noon daily, we highly recommend taking a free guided tour offered once a week; call ☑888-735-1619 for tour dates and parking reservations.

Currently the temple in use is **Kadavul Temple**, where guests can see the world's largest single-pointed quartz crystal, a 50-million-year-old, six-sided wonder that weighs 700lb and stands over 3ft tall. In the temple, meditating monks have been rotating in three-hour vigils round the clock since the temple was established in 1973.

Keahua Arboretum NATURE RESERVE
Sitting pretty at the top of Kuamo'o Rd, this arboretum resembles storybook countryside, with grassy fields, gurgling stream and groves of teak, eucalyptus and other tall trees. Locals enjoy swimming or splashing in the freshwater stream and pools, but remember that the water can contain the leptospirosis bacterium. The road continues past the arboretum parking lot, but you must cross water – not recommended if you're driving a standard car, especially if it's rainy.

Kamokila Hawaiian Village MUSEUM
While not a must-see, this replicated village is a pleasant diversion, especially for kids. It's along the Wailua River and includes traditional structures, from Canoe House to Chief's Assembly House, amid thriving gardens of guava, mango and banana trees. Use your imagination! You're on your own here, but the site is modest and the simple map given is sufficient.

Kamokila also offers **outrigger canoe tours** (adult/child $30/20; ◎departures hourly 9:30am-2:30pm), which include a paddle, hike and waterfall swim. Because you start further upriver from the mouth, the trip is shorter than going by kayak, and a Hawaiian guide is guaranteed.

To get here, turn south from Kuamo'o Rd, opposite 'Opaeka'a Falls. The half-mile road leading to the village is very steep and narrow.

'Opaeka'a Falls WATERFALL
While not a showstopper, this 40ft waterfall makes an easy roadside stop, less than 2 miles up Kuamo'o Rd. For the best photographic conditions, go in the morning. Don't be tempted to try trailblazing to the base of the falls. The steep cliffs are perilous, as shown in 2006 when two tourists died after falling almost 300ft while hiking. Instead, after viewing the falls, cross the road for a fantastic photo op of the Wailua River.

 Activities

Wailua Municipal Golf Course GOLF
(Map p480; ☑241-6666; greens fee weekdays/weekends & holidays $48/60, optional cart rental $18, club rental from $32) This 18-hole, par-72 course off Kuhio Hwy north of Lihu'e is ranked among the finest municipal golf courses nationally. Plan ahead because

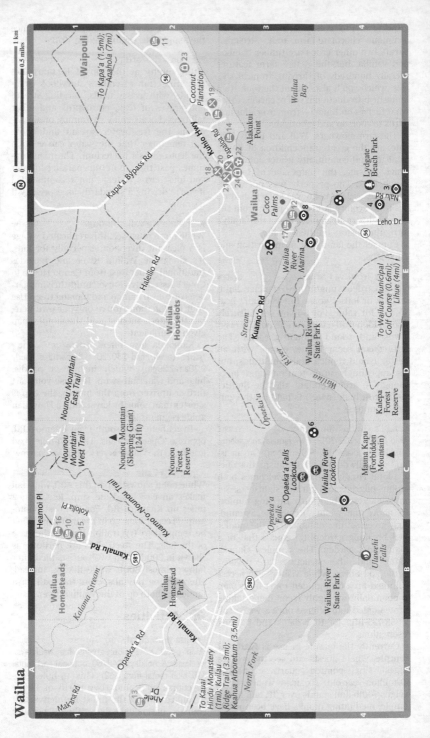

Wailua

◎ Sights

1 Hikinaakala Heiau	F4
2 Holoholoku Heiau	E3
3 Kamalani Kai Bridge	F4
4 Kamalani Playground	F4
5 Kamokila Hawaiian Village	C4
Kayak Kaua'i	(see 23)
6 Poli'ahu Heiau	C3
7 Smith's Tropical Paradise	E3
Smith's Motorboar Service	(see 7)
8 Wailua Kayak & Canoe	F3
Water Ski & Surf Company	(see 24)

🛏 Sleeping

9 Aston Islander on the Beach	G2
10 Bunk House at Rosewood Kaua'i	B1
11 Courtyard Marriott Kauai	G2
12 Fern Grotto Inn	F3
13 Garden Room	A2
14 Lae Nani	F3
15 Lani Keha	B1
16 Sleeping Giant Cottage	B1
17 Surf & Ski Cottage	E3

✖ Eating

18 Caffé Coco	F2
19 Hukilau Lanai	G2
Icing on the Cake	(see 24)
20 Kintaro	F3
21 Mema	F3
Monico's Taqueria	(see 24)
Tutu's Soup Hale	(see 24)

✖ Entertainment

Free Hula Show	(see 23)
Smith's Tropical Paradise	(see 7)
22 Trees Lounge	F3

🛍 Shopping

Bambulei	(see 18)
23 Coconut Marketplace	G2
24 Kinipopo Shopping Village	F3

WAILUA ACTIVITIES

morning tee times are sometimes reserved a week in advance at this popular course, designed by former head pro Toyo Shirai. After 2pm, the greens fee drops by half and no reservations are taken.

Water Ski & Surf Company WATERSKIING, WAKEBOARDING
(☎822-3574; www.kauaiwaterskiandsurf.com; Kinipopo Shopping Village, 4-356 Kuhio Hwy; per 30/60min $75/140; ☺9am-5pm Mon-Fri, to noon Sat) The only nonocean water skiing in the state is found here on the Wailua, only from the Wailua Bridge to the first big bend in the river. If you're up for a tow session, try waterskiing or wakeboarding. They also rent water equipment, including surfboards ($30/90 per day/week, $300 deposit), bodyboards ($5/20, $75 deposit), snorkel gear ($5/15, $75 deposit) and stand up paddle boards ($45/180, $600 deposit).

Powerline Trail MOUNTAIN BIKING
(Map p480) While this trail (which covers 13 miles between Wailua and Princeville) is used mainly by hunters, it's a decent option for die-hard mountain bikers. Hikers might find the trek rather too long, too exposed and, especially toward the north, too monotonous. The trail (a former maintenance road for electric powerlines established in the 1930s) is never crowded and it traverses an otherwise-inaccessible north–south region. Beware of steep drop-offs hidden in the dense foliage. Expect to slog through mud and puddly ruts.

The south end of the trail begins across the stream at the Keahua Arboretum (p481), at the end of Kuamo'o Rd. Consider starting from the Princeville end, where it's less messy. Just south of Princeville, look for the Princeville Ranch Stables turnoff. This is Po'oku Rd. The trail starts about 2 miles down this road, near an obvious water tank.

Smith's Motor Boat Service RIVERBOATS
(☎821-6892; www.smithskauai.com; 1½hr tour adult/child $20/10; ☺departures at 9:30am, 11am, 2pm, 3:30pm) If you're curious to see the legendary **Fern Grotto**, a boat ride is the only one way to get up close – or least as close as you can get. Since 1946 Smith's has had exclusive rights to ply the river in covered riverboats (the size of a bus) to the grotto. Bear in mind that since the heavy rains and rockslides of 2006, visitors cannot enter the grotto but must stay on the wooden platform quite a distance from the shallow cave.

The Fern Grotto, formed below an overhanging cliff at the base of **Mauna Kapu** (Forbidden Mountain), looks rather tired nowadays, having suffered from a localized drought since the 1990s, when the sugar plantations above the cliff went out of pro-

THE SACRED WAILUA RIVER

To ancient Hawaiians, the Wailua River was among the most sacred places across the islands. The river basin, near its mouth, was one of the island's two royal centers (the other was Waimea) and home to the high chiefs. Here, you can find the remains of many important heiau (religious sites), including the following places.

Hikinaakala Heiau ('rising of the sun') sits south of the Wailua River mouth, which is today the north end of Lydgate Beach Park. In its heyday, the long, narrow temple (c AD 1200) was aligned directly north to south, but only a few remaining boulders outline its original massive shape. The neighboring **Hauola Pu'uhonua** ('dew of life'; 'place of refuge') is marked by a bronze plaque. Ancient Hawaiian kapu (taboo) breakers were assured safety from persecution if they made it inside.

Believed to be the oldest *luakini* (temple dedicated to war god Ku, often a place for human sacrifice) on the island, **Holoholoku Heiau** is a quarter-mile up Kuamo'o Rd on the left. The whole area was royal property: toward the west, against the flat-backed birthstone marked by a plaque reading 'Pohaku Ho'ohanau' ('royal birthstone'), queens gave birth to future kings. Only a male child born here could become king of Kaua'i. Another stone a few yards away, marked 'Pohaku Piko,' was where the *piko* (umbilical cords) of the babies were left.

Perched high on a hill overlooking the meandering Wailua River, the well-preserved **Poli'ahu Heiau**, another *luakini,* is named after the snow goddess Poli'ahu, one of the volcano goddess Pele's sisters. Poli'ahu Heiau is immediately before the 'Opaeka'a Falls lookout, on the opposite side of the road.

Bear in mind, unmarked Hawaiian heiau might not catch your eye. Although they were originally imposing stone structures, most now lie in ruins, covered with scrub. It takes a leap of imagination for non-Hawaiians to appreciate heiau, but they are still powerful, set in places of great mana (spiritual energy).

Find an excellent brochure on the Wailua complex of heiau at www.hawaiistateparks .org/pdf/brochures/Hikinaakala.pdf. For a compelling history on the Wailua River's meaning to ancient Hawaiians, see Edward Joesting's *Kauai: The Separate Kingdom*.

duction and weren't irrigated anymore. The elongated sword ferns and delicate maidenhair seem to be struggling. If you're expecting an eye-popping emerald cascade, you might as well find old pictures.

Kayaking

Majestic and calm, the Wailua River spans 12 miles, fed by two streams originating on Mt Wai'ale'ale. It's the only navigable river across the Hawaiian Islands, and kayaking the Wailua has become a tourist must-do. Fortunately, the paddle is a doable 5 miles for all ages and fitness levels. Tours usually don't pass the Fern Grotto and instead take the river's north fork, which leads to a mile-long hike through dense forest to **Uluwehi Falls** (Secret Falls), a 130ft waterfall. The hike scrambles over rocks and roots, and if muddy it will probably cause some slippin' and slidin'. Tip: wear sturdy, washable, non-slip sandals such as Chacos.

Most tours last four to five hours and depart around 7am or noon (call for exact check-in times). The maximum group size is 12, with paddlers going out in double kay-aks. The pricier tours include lunch, but on budget tours you can store your own food in coolers and waterproof bags. Bring a hat, sunscreen and mosquito repellent.

Experienced paddlers might want to rent individual kayaks and go out on their own. Prices vary wildly. Note that not all tour companies are also licensed to rent individual kayaks.

No kayak tours or rentals are allowed on Sundays. Of course, noncommercial kayaks are always allowed on the river.

Of the following companies, Kayak Kaua'i and Outfitters Kaua'i are big and established, with many other tour offerings. But the two recommended little guys offer better value for this basic tour.

TOP CHOICE **Kayak Wailua** KAYAKING
(☎822-3388; www.kayakwailua.com; 4565 Haleilio Rd, Wailua; tour per person $40) This small, family-owned outfit specializes in Wailua River tours. It keeps boats and equipment in tip-top shape and provides dry bags for your belongings and a nylon cooler for your BYO snacks. For those who prefer to speed ahead

of the group, it's flexible enough to accommodate different abilities.

TOP CHOICE **Wailua Kayak Adventures**   KAYAKING
(☑822 5795, 639-6332; www.kauaiwailuakayak
.com; 4-1596 Kuhio Hwy, Kapaa; per day single/double kayaks $25/50, tours per couple $80; ⊙check-in 7am & 12:30pm) Go here for the cheapest individual kayak rentals. It offers three budget-friendly Wailua River tours (which include generous snacks at the waterfall). Call for times, as they vary slightly for each tour.

Wailua Kayak & Canoe   KAYAKING
(☑821-1188; Wailua River State Park; s/d kayak per 5hr $45/75, tours $55-90) Located at the boat ramp on the north bank, this outfit is very convenient for individual rentals (no need to transport the kayak). Tour quality is fine but the prices have skyrocketed in recent years.

Kayak Kaua'i   KAYAKING
(☑826-9844, 800-437-3507; www.kayakkauai
.com; Coconut Marketplace, Wailua; double kayak per person per day $27, tours adult/child $85/60; ⊙check-in 7:45am & 12:15pm) This longstanding and reputable outfit, with shop locations in Wailua and Hanalei, offers river and seakayaking tours, including the Na Pali challenge. Rates run high, but lunch is included. A good choice if you need a Japanese- or Spanish-speaking guide.

Outfitters Kaua'i   KAYAKING
(Map p532; ☑742-9667, 888-742-9887; www.outfit
terskauai.com; Po'ipu Plaza, 2827A Po'ipu Rd, Po'ipu; kayak per person per day $40, tours adult/child $98/78; ⊙check-in 7:45am) Known for its multi-adventure tours, this established outfit is good except for its steep prices.

Hiking

Most hiking on the Eastside ascends into Kaua'i's tropical-jungle interior. Expect humid air, red dirt (or mud) and slippery patches after rains. See the Eastside Trails map (p480).

Kuilau Ridge & Moalepe Trails   HIKING
The **Kuilau Ridge Trail** (Map p480; 2.1 miles; all mileage distances given are one-way) is recommended for its sheer beauty: emerald valleys, colorful birds, dewy bushes, thick ferns and glimpses of misty Mt Wai'ale'ale in the distance. After 1 mile, you'll see a grassy clearing with a picnic table; continue east in descending switchbacks until you reach the **Moalepe Trail** (Map p480; 2.25 miles). From here on, you'll see Nounou Mountain and the Makaleha Mountains.

While they are independent trails, the two are often mentioned together because they connect and can be hiked in sequence. Both are moderate hikes and among the most visually rewarding on Kaua'i. Remember, the trails don't complete a circuit so you must retrace your steps on a 9-mile out-and-back. Mountain bikers would also enjoy these forestland trails, although they're used mostly by hikers and hunters.

If you plan on doing only one trail, choose the Kuilau Ridge Trail because it takes you immediately into the forest wilderness, while the first mile of the Moalepe Trail crosses the simple, treeless pastureland of the Wailua Game Management Area. Both trails are well maintained and signposted.

The Kuilau Ridge Trail starts at a marked trailhead on the right just before Kuamo'o Rd crosses the stream at the Keahua Arboretum, 4 miles above the junction of Kuamo'o Rd and Kamalu Rd. The Moalepe Trail trailhead is at the end of Olohena Rd where it bends into Waipouli Rd.

Nounou Mountain Trails   HIKING
Climbing Nounou Mountain (Sleeping Giant), you'll ascend over 1000ft, but the views of Kaua'i's Eastside panorama are a worthy reward. You can approach the mountain from the east on the **Nounou Mountain East Trail** (Map p482; 1.75 miles), from the west on the **Nounou Mountain West Trail** (Map p482; 1.5 miles) and from the south on the **Kuamo'o-Nounou Trail** (Map p482; 2 miles). The trails meet near the center.

Visitors tend to prefer the exposed East Trail because it offers sweeping views of the ocean and distant mountains. The well-maintained trail is moderately strenuous, climbing through wild thickets of guava, liliko'i and ironwood. The trail is steep, with switchbacks almost to the ridge. At the three-way junction near the top, take the left fork, which will lead to the summit, marked by a picnic shelter. Now atop the giant's chest, only his head prevents you from a 360-degree view. Climbing further is extremely risky and not recommended.

Do this hike early in the morning, when it's relatively cool and you can witness daylight spreading across the valley. The hard-packed dirt trail is exceedingly slippery when wet; look for a walking stick, which hikers sometimes leave near the trailhead.

Translated as 'rippling water' or 'overflowing water', and with the earned nickname of The Rain Machine, Mt Wai'ale'ale averages 460–500 inches of rainfall annually, with a yearly record of 683 inches in 1982. Its steep cliffs cause moist air to rise rapidly and focus rainfall in one area. Believed by ancient Hawaiians to be occupied by the god Kane, it's located in the center of the island and is the source of the Wailua, Hanalei and Waimea Rivers, as well as the Alaka'i Wilderness Preserve and almost every visible waterfall on the island.

KAUA'I KAPA'A & THE EASTSIDE

The East Trail starts at a parking lot a mile up Haleilio Rd in the Wailua Houselots neighborhood. When the road curves left, look for telephone pole 38 with the trailhead sign.

The Nounou Mountain West Trail ascends faster but it's better if you prefer a cooler forest trail. Much of the hike is shaded by towering Norfolk Island pines and other trees. There are two ways to access the trailhead: from Kamalu Rd, near telephone pole 11, or from the end of Lokelani Rd, off Kamalu Rd. Walk through a metal gate marked as a forestry right-of-way.

The Kuamo'o-Nounou Trail runs through groves of trees planted in the 1930s by the Civilian Conservation Corps; it connects with the west trail. The trailhead is right on Kuamo'o Rd, near a grassy field between the 2- and 3-mile markers.

For guided hikes, the gold standard is geologist Chuck Blay's company, **Kaua'i Nature Tours** (☑742-8305; 888-233-8365; www.kauainaturetours.com; Nounou Mountain tour adult/child $120/75), which offers an all-day tour that includes lunch and transportation.

✹ Festivals & Events

Taste of Hawaii FOOD
(www.tasteofhawaii.com) On the first Sunday in June, the Rotary Club of Kapa'a hosts the 'Ultimate Sunday Brunch' at Smith's Tropical Paradise. For $75 to $85 per person, you can indulge in gourmet samples by 50 distinguished local chefs. With additional booths offering wines, microbrews, ice cream and desserts, you're liable to stuff yourself silly.

🛏 Sleeping

Note that many condos, B&Bs and inns require a three-night minimum and a cleaning fee. For condos, we list contact info for the agency managing the majority of units, but also check www.vrbo.com and smaller agencies. **Rosewood Kaua'i** (☑822-5216; www.rosewoodkauai.com) represents not only condos but many outstanding vacation rental homes in Wailua and Kapa'a.

TOP
CHOICE **Bunk House at Rosewood Kaua'i** HOTEL $
(☑822-5216; www.rosewoodkauai.com; 872 Kamalu Rd; r with shared bathroom $50-60; 🛜) Hostellers will be forever spoiled by these meticulously tidy bunkrooms with private entrances and kitchenettes. Expect a cleaning fee ($25). For a step up, inquire about the picturesque 'Victorian cottage' ($145) and 'thatched cottage' ($135), which are also on the storybook-pretty property, complete with white picket fence.

Opaeka'a Falls Hale B&B $$
(Map p480; ☑888-822-9956; www.opaekaafalls kauai.ws; 120 Lihau St; 1 bedroom incl breakfast $110-130; 🛋) At a whopping 1000-plus sq ft each, these immaculate B&B units are bigger than the average city apartment. The two units overlook Wailua's emerald valleys and each includes full kitchen (stocked with breakfast fixings) and private lanai, phone and washer-dryer, plus a lovely swimming pool. DSL internet access only in the upstairs unit. A cleaning fee ($50) is charged.

Lani Keha COTTAGE $
(☑822-1605; www.lanikeha.com; 848 Kamalu Rd; s/d from $55/65; 🛜) Solo travelers and sociable types will appreciate the low-key, communal atmosphere in this longtime guesthouse. Nothing fancy, the three rooms feature *lauhala*-mat flooring, king beds and well-worn but clean furnishings. Gather round the kitchen and living room.

Garden Room COTTAGE $
(☑822-5216; 6430 Ahele Dr; r $75; 🛜) Find serenity in an immaculate studio overlooking a gorgeous mini-pond with water lilies and koi (Japanese carp). The aptly named room is compact (hotel-room size) but delightful, with a private entrance, kitchenette and generous welcome basket. Recent renovations include immaculate porcelain tiling. Expect to be charmed by the host couple, longtime Kaua'i residents who make guests feel welcome.

Sleeping Giant Cottage COTTAGE $
(☑505-401-4403; www.wanek.com/sleepinggiant; 5979 Heamoi Pl; cottage $95; ☏) Be lord of the castle (no shared walls) at this airy plantation-style bungalow, pleasantly appointed with hardwood floor, kitchen, comfortably sized bedroom and living-dining room, plus a huge screened patio facing a backyard garden. Cleaning fee is $50; discounts for weekly or monthly stays.

Surf & Ski Cottage COTTAGE $
(☑822-3574; surfski@aloha.net; Ohana St; cottage $75; ☏) Suitable for solos or couples looking for a serene but convenient hideaway, this tastefully decorated studio features a more-than-functional kitchenette, a queen bed and an impressive owner-made Hawaiian palapa (open-sided dwelling with a waterproof thatched roof) ideal for a late-afternoon lounge session. Located a few steps from the Wailua River with private kayak launch.

Fern Grotto Inn INN $$
(☑821-9836; www.ferngrottoinn.com; 4561 Kuamo'o Rd; cottages $99-165, house $275; ❋☏) Charmingly retro, these remodeled, 1940s plantation-style cottages vary in size, but all feature hardwood floors, tasteful furnishings, TV and DVD, shared laundry, and kitchen or kitchenette. Rates are slightly high, but the location near the Wailua River dock reduces driving. Friendly owners go the extra mile to ensure guests' comfort.

Aston Islander on the Beach HOTEL $$
(☑822-7417, 877-997-6667; www.astonhawaii.com; 440 Aleka Pl; r $140-250; ❋☏❋) Among mid-range hotels, you can't top the Islander. It's not a resort, so don't expect frills, but the 186 rooms seem modern and upscale, with granite countertops, flat-panel TVs and stainless-steel and teak furnishings. For internet access, rooms are limited to DSL but there's free wi-fi in lobby. Deep discounts online.

Courtyard Marriot Kauai HOTEL $$
(☑822-3455, 800-760-8555; www.marriotthawaii.com; 650 Aleka Loop; r $150-380; ❋☏❋) For a presentable business-class hotel, look no further. The 300-plus-room beachside hotel has a classy, efficient feel, from the soaring lobby full of plush seating to the pleasant pool. Rooms pamper the business traveler with dark woods, black-marble counters and work desk with rolling chair. A $12 hotel fee buys you parking, local calls, internet access and daily paper. Book online. Wi-fi only in lobby.

Lae Nani CONDO $$
(☑822-4938, 800-688-7444; www.outrigger.com; 410 Papaloa Rd; 1/2 bedroom from $169/359; ❋❋) Conveniently located on Papaloa Rd, this five-building condo is particularly appealing, with a small but pretty stretch of beach (swimmable only during calm surf). Outrigger manages almost 60 of the 84 units and provides on-site support, but also check with other agents. Buildings 3 and 5 include the most oceanfront units; building 1 is far from the highway and parking lot.

✕ Eating

Without a commercial center, Wailua is not a hang-out town, but it boasts a handful of notable eateries.

COURTING HOLLYWOOD

The state woos Hollywood to shoot in Hawaii, offering a 20% tax break for production work on Neighbor Islands. In 2007, Ben Stiller filmed the $100-million *Tropic Thunder* on Kaua'i, hiring 350 local crewmembers (in a total crew of 778), plus hundreds of local extras. The cast and crew rented houses or stayed at the two Wailua hotels for some 13 weeks. They patronized local restaurants, bars and countless businesses. They filmed across the island, from Grove Farm in Lihu'e to Hanalei. Overall, the film is estimated to have contributed a whopping $60 million to the island's economy.

However, some islanders allege that the film sets caused environmental damage, such as altered streams, flattened bamboo groves, scorched 'war zones' and toxic damage from pyrotechnics. They criticize the lack of oversight by the State Department of Land & Natural Resources (or any other authority).

While the allegations remain unproven, some might conclude that Kaua'i's movie 'industry' will always entail a fine balance. Some embrace the island's long history on the silver screen. Some value the big economic boost. Some view the 'commodification' of the *'aina* (land) as never justifiable. Opinions differed over *Tropic Thunder* and will differ again the next time Hollywood comes to town.

TOP CHOICE Tutu's Soup Hale VEGETARIAN $
(Kinipopo Shopping Center, 4-356 Kuhio Hwy; breakfasts $6, lunches $8; ◷7:30am-5pm) Service spilling with *aloha* and 'comfort food' made hip but not pretentious. Breakfasts served all day include the 'Egglectic' sandwich and Dutch pancakes with coconut syrup. Lunches such as the panini caprese and the cashew and basil pâté maintain the well-established creative tone. The vibe is uberchill with a library to browse through and even a purple velvet couch to lounge on. Outside shaded seating is pleasantly cool on warmer afternoons. For meat-cravers, there are several carnivorous options.

Caffé Coco VEGETARIAN $$
(www.restauranteur.com/caffecoco; 4-369 Kuhio Hwy; salads & sandwiches $5-14.50, meals $16-21; ◷lunch Tue-Fri, dinner Tue-Sun) At this rustic little hideaway, chefs fuse Asian, Middle Eastern and other flavors into healthful dishes that would delight the *Yoga Journal* crowd. Ahi is a standout, prepared with Moroccan spices and a curried veggie samosa, or seared and rolled in black sesame with wasabi cream. If social lubrication is desired, let it be known it's BYO alcohol. Big positive: live homegrown music nightly 7pm to 9pm. Big negative: prowling mosquitoes.

Kintaro SUSHI $$
(4-370 Kuhio Hwy; appetizers $3.50-6, meals $14-20; ◷dinner Mon-Sat) Night after night, this local favorite packs 'em in. No wonder: from thick-cut slices of sashimi to a shrimp-fish-veg tempura combination, mains shine in quality and quantity. The owner is Korean, but the cuisine is authentic Japanese. A specialty is sizzling, crowd-wowing *teppanyaki*, when chefs show their stuff tableside on steel grills.

Monico's Taqueria MEXICAN $
(Kinipopo Shopping Village, 4-356 Kuhio Hwy; mains $8-14; ◷lunch & dinner Tue-Sun) Finally, 'real' Mexican food on Kaua'i. Everything tastes fresh and rings true, from the generous plates of burritos and tacos to the freshly made chips, salsa and sauces. Thumbs up for the affordable fish mains.

Mema THAI $$
(4-369 Kuhio Hwy; mains $9-18; ◷11am-2pm Mon-Fri, 5-9pm daily) While not stark-raving awesome, Mema serves decent dishes that can be tailored to your meat-philic or meat-phobic preference: you choose either tofu, chicken, pork, beef, fish or shrimp. The cozy dining room is modest but a cut above the standard local-diner setting.

Hukilau Lanai HAWAII REGIONAL $$
(www.hukilaukauai.com; Kaua'i Coast Resort at the Beachboy, 520 Aleka Loop; dinner $16-27; ◷5-9pm Tue-Sun) To ramp it up from the typical T-shirt-casual joint, we recommend this relaxed, elegant favorite. The menu features top local ingredients, from Kilauea goat cheese to Lawa'i Valley *warabi* (fiddlehead fern). Standout selections include feta-and-sweet-potato ravioli and ahi *poke* nachos. For an affordable splurge, arrive between 5pm and 6pm for the early-bird six-course, wine-paired tasting menu ($40; food-only menu $28).

Icing on the Cake BAKERY $
(www.icingonthecakekauai.com; Kinipopo Shopping Village, 4-356 Kuhio Hwy; cookies $1.25-1.75, cakes 6/9in from $25/40) Pastry chef Andrea Quinn has a knack for elegant designs and sophisticated flavors. Nothing is too cute or too sweet. While she specializes in made-to-order cakes, walk-in customers will find gourmet treats such as cocoa-nib shortbread, pecan brownies and exquisite coconut macaroons. Check the website for retail locations island wide.

☆ Entertainment

For most, the best nightlife in Wailua is curling up in bed before the roosters wake you. Or, if the price isn't a deterrent, a commercial luau might be a decent diversion.

Smith's Tropical Paradise LUAU
(www.smithskauai.com; Wailua River Marina; luau adult/child $78/30; ◷luaus 4:30pm Mon, Wed & Fri) A Kaua'i institution, Smith's Tropical Paradise launched its luau in 1985, attracting droves of tourists. It's a lively affair, run with lots of aloha spirit by four generations at the lovely 30-acre garden. The multicultural show features Hawaiian, Tahitian, Samoan, Filipino, Chinese, Japanese and New Zealand dances.

While touristy, the Coconut Marketplace's free **hula show** (☏822-3641; ◷5pm Wed) is fun and lively, featuring Leilani Rivera Bond (www.leilanirivera.com) and her *halau* (troupe). She's the daughter of famous Coco Palms entertainer Larry Rivera, who joins the show on the first Wednesday monthly.

Trees Lounge LIVE MUSIC
(☏823-0600; www.treesloungekauai.com; 440 Aleka Pl, behind Coconut Marketplace; ◷5-11pm) For those seeking a live music fix this one

of the more impressive musical venues on the island hosting nightly happy hour and headliner acts ranging from melt-your-face-off rock to mellow acoustic, jazz and traditional Hawaiian. Tuesday is open mic night, guitars are provided, but courage is not. All are welcome to perform. Do it.

🛍 Shopping

Coconut Marketplace　　　　SOUVENIRS
(www.coconutmarketplace.com; ⏱9am-9pm Mon-Sat, 10am-6pm Sun) This touristy place feels like a throwback, a once-popular venue with too many vacant spaces (too much used-to-be-thriving feeling). The survivors are a mix of midrange island attire, jewelry, T-shirt and gift stores.

Bambulei　　　　CLOTHING
(www.bambulei.com; 4-369D Kuhio Hwy; ⏱10am-6pm Mon-Fri, to 5pm Sat) This irresistible women's boutique is chock-full of feminine gear made for women who've outgrown the teenage surfer-chick look. The drapey sweaters, platform sandals and kimono-fabric accessories aren't haute couture, but they're affordable and unique. Also find vintage clothing and retro home decor.

ℹ Getting There & Away

Don't look for a town center. Most attractions are scattered along Kuhio Hwy (Hwy 56) or along Kuamo'o Rd (Hwy 580), which leads *mauka* (inland). To get to Kapa'a or beyond, take the Kapa'a Bypass Rd, which runs from Coconut Plantation to north Kapa'a.

Waipouli

Sandwiched between Wailua and Kapa'a, Waipouli is less a town than a cluster of restaurants, grocers, a drugstore and other basic businesses. You're likely to stop here to stock up.

🏃 Activities

Bear in mind that rentals are here but the actual activities are elsewhere.

Ambrose's Kapuna　　　　SURFING
(www.ambrosecurry.com; 770 Kuhio Hwy; per hr $35) Don't miss the chance to meet surf guru Ambrose Curry, who offers to 'take people surfing' (or stand up paddling), not to 'give surf lessons'. If you're baffled, then you have much to learn from this longtime surfer-philosopher, once aptly dubbed a tribal elder. Originally from California,

Curry has lived on Kaua'i since 1968 and is also an artist and board shaper.

The Yoga House　　　　YOGA
(☎823-9642; www.bikramyogakapaa.com; 4-885 Kuhio Hwy; drop-in classes $13) If your dogs face down, come get your bliss on in an obscenely warm room. Offering 12 classes weekly, there's plenty of opportunity to get centered here. If you're looking to build some serious prana, the $50 all-you-can-bend-in-a-week deal should suffice.

Spa by the Sea　　　　SPA
(☎823-1488; www.spabytheseakauai.com; Outrigger Waipouli Beach Resort & Spa, 4-820 Kuhio Hwy; 50min massage or facial $110; ⏱9am-6pm Mon-Sat, 10am-6pm Sun) Enter a world of Lomi Lomi massage, Noni Healing facial and volcanic clay body treatment and the Eastside's traffic will drift away. If you're torn between a massage and a facial, the Menehune Meditation ($115) includes 30 minutes of each.

Snorkel Bob's　　　　SNORKELING
(☎823-9433; www.snorkelbob.com; 4-734 Kuhio Hwy; basic snorkel sets per day/week $2.50/9, better sets $9/35, bodyboards $8/32; ⏱8am-5pm Mon-Sat) The cool thing about this place is that if you're island-hopping, you can rent gear on Kaua'i and return it on the Big Island, O'ahu or Maui.

BEST BEACHES

Hanalei Bay This crescent-shaped beach is ideal for a paddle, surf, swim, or leisurely meander in the sand.

Po'ipu Beach Perpetually sunny, this family-friendly beach offers good snorkeling and lounging.

Polihale State Park Isolated and ideal for camping, this is one of the state's longest stretches of sand.

Kauapea (Secrets) Beach Guarded by cliffs and exposed to the open ocean, this beach is secluded, but not so secret anymore. Best in summer months as winter swells create dangerous rip tides.

Maha'ulepu Beach The south shore's getaway, this is as rugged as it is majestic.

Ke'e Beach Prime sunset viewing and snorkeling when the swell is down. Best to look but not touch when the swell is up.

» Float along backcountry waterways on inner tubes (p471)

» Slurp up a rainbow shave ice with the works at Jo-Jo's Anuenue Shave Ice & Treats (p550)

» Feed a hungry pig herd on Kilohana Plantation's train ride (p469)

» Explore a giant beachfront playground (p479)

» Ride coaster bikes along the Eastside coastal path (p494)

» Introduce tots to the ocean at two baby beaches (p491 and p531)

» Learn to surf at Hanalei Bay (p513) or Po'ipu Beach Park (p530)

» Splash in the Grand Hyatt Kaua'i's river pools (p538)

Kauai Cycle CYCLING

(☎821-2115; www.kauaicycle.com; 4-934 Kuhio Hwy, Waipouli; per day/week cruiser $20/110, mountain or road bike $30/165, full-suspension $45/250; ☉9am-6pm Mon-Fri, to 4pm Sat) Sells, services and rents bikes maintained by experienced cyclists. Prices include helmet and lock.

🚲 Courses

FREE Kaua'i Heritage Center

(☎346-7574; www.kaieie.org; 4-831 Kuhio Hwy) The Kaua'i Heritage Center offers lectures and workshops by Kehaulani Kekua, a respected and articulate *kumu hula* (teacher of hula). The Friday lectures are free, while the hands-on Saturday workshop costs $30. Nowhere else can you find such genuine teachings on the ancient Hawaiian lunar calendar or the significance of Kaua'i's hula heiau.

🛏 Sleeping

Waipouli is sandwiched between Wailua and Kapa'a, both with plenty of options, so also check those sections.

Outrigger Waipouli Beach Resort & Spa RESORT $$$

(☎800-688-7444, 822-6000; www.outrigger waipouli.com; 4-820 Kuhio Highway; 1/2 bedroom from $225/275; ✴🛜🏊) The surrounding strip malls and traffic belie this condo's cachet as the Eastside's newest and fanciest. Units are law-firm handsome and consistently well furnished, with 37in flat-screen TVs, washer-dryers and an 'extra' bathroom per unit. There's no swimmable beach, but a saltwater 'river pool' and sand-bottom hot tubs somewhat compensate. Outrigger represents 100 of the 196 total units, but also check www.vrbo.com.

🍴 Eating & Drinking

While most restaurants have a bar-type area, the best 'nightlife' can be found at Trees Lounge (p488) in nearby Wailua.

Shivalik Indian Cuisine INDIAN $$

(www.shivalikindiancuisine.com; 4-771 Kuhio Hwy; mains $13-20, buffet $15; ☉11:30am-3pm & 5-9:30pm) Hidden in the corner of the Waipoli shopping center, its steady business is a testament to the quality of tandoori style cuisine (cooked in a cylindrical clay oven). The extensive menu covers the gamut of Indian cuisine – from lentil and lamb curry to vegetable samosas and everything in between – but the economical move may be to show up hungry and head straight to the buffet, then head back, then head back again.

Papaya's Natural Foods CAFE, GROCERY $

(Kaua'i Village, 4-831 Kuhio Hwy; dishes $5-8, salad per lb $7; ☉8am-8pm Mon-Sat, 10am-5pm Sun) At Kaua'i's biggest health-food store, you'll find the nouveau-hippie contingent, locavore-leaning mainland transplants and vegetarian-vegan types. Produce is expensive because it's either organic or local. Stock up on bulk items (including grind-your-own peanut butter), vitamins and supplements, bottled water and healthful deli fixings.

King & I THAI $

(Waipouli Plaza, 4-901 Kuhio Hwy; mains $7-11; ☉4:30-9:30pm) Ranked number one by locals, this friendly, family-run restaurant offers a lengthy menu featuring flavors such as curries popping with kaffir lime and lemongrass, as fiery (or not) as you like. Vegetarians will find loads of options, like flavorful eggplant and tofu in chili oil or a mound of traditional *pad thai* with tofu.

Kaua'i Pasta
ITALIAN $$

(4-939B Kuhio Hwy; mains $9-15; ☺11am-9pm, lounge to midnight) Tricky to find but worth the search, this is a saving grace for pasta lovers. With the list of Italian standards covered after years of perfecting the practice, they're able to focus on creative daily specials, maximizing the use of fresh local ingredients. They've recently expanded, doubling the seating capacity, opening for lunch and adding a sleek drinking lounge in the back. With steady local clientele as the strongest testament, it's a worthwhile venture.

Oasis on the Beach
PACIFIC RIM $$

(www.oasiskauai.com; Waipouli Beach Resort, 4-820 Kuhio Hwy; dishes $12-20; ☺4-9pm, Sunday brunch 10am-2pm) On the beach, like the name says, the atmosphere is unmatched, the cuisine is sophisticated and the service is spot on. Good for sharing some elegant dishes or enjoying one of the better happy hours (from 4pm to 6pm; chef's menu half-price) on the island. The Sunday brunch is a full-on affair, so come hungry.

Self-Catering

Safeway
GROCERY $

(☑822-2464; Kaua'i Village, 4-831 Kuhio Hwy; ☺24hr) Caters to mainland tourists, with familiar brands, an American-style deli and bakery.

Foodland
GROCERY $

(Waipouli Town Center; ☺6am-11pm) A slightly better option, with a decent selection of gourmet and health brands such as Kashi and Scharffen Berger. Neither stocks much local produce.

Papaya's Natural Foods
GROCERY

Foodies will prefer Papaya's for local and organic produce, plus other island specialties such as Kilauea honey and goat cheese.

Cost U Less
GROCERY

(p495) Another recommendation for local produce and national health brands; in nearby Kapa'a.

🛍 Shopping

Waipouli's two main shopping malls are Waipouli Town Center and Kaua'i Village. One notable boutique is the irresistible Marta's Boat (☑822-3926; 770 Kuhio Hwy; ☺10am-6pm Mon-Sat), which will delight 'princesses of all ages' with feminine and sexy threads from Paris, Los Angeles and New York. Distinctive lingerie and frocks shine, but locally made jewelry and excruciatingly cute little girls' outfits also enchant. Expect big-city price tags. The 'Surf for World Peace' T-shirts (hand-painted by owner Marta Curry's husband, surfer and artist Ambrose Curry (p489) make cool souvenirs.

ⓘ Information

There are ATMs inside Foodland supermarket in Waipouli Town Center and, just a minute north, inside Safeway in Kaua'i Village. Both are on the *mauka* side of Kuhio Hwy.

INTERNET ACCESS Starbucks (Kaua'i Village Shopping Center; ☺5am-8:30pm, Sun 5:30am-8pm) Offers free wi-fi.

PHARMACY Longs Drugs (☑822-4915; Kaua'i Village; ☺store 7am-9pm Mon-Sat, 8am-8pm Sun, pharmacy 8am-8pm Mon-Fri, 9am-5pm Sat & Sun) Pharmacy and general merchandise.

Kapa'a

POP 9987

The only walkable town on the Eastside, Kapa'a is a charmer. The eclectic population of old-timers, new transplants, nouveau hippies and tourists coexists smoothly. Retro diners and domestic shops mingle with live jazz, Bikram yoga and your choice of espresso drinks. A new bike- and footpath runs along the part-sandy, part-rocky coast, the island's best vantage point for sunrises. Kapa'a's downfall: it sits right along the highway. Try crossing the road during rush hour!

◉ Sights & Activities

Kapa'a Beach Park
PARK

From the highway, you'd think that Kapa'a is beachless. But along the coast is a mile-long ribbon of beach that's very low-key and local. While the whole area is officially a county park called Kapa'a Beach Park, that name is commonly used only for the northern end, where there's a grassy field, picnic tables and a public pool.

The best sandy area is at the south end, informally called **Lihi Beach**, where you'll find locals hanging out and talking story. A good starting point for the paved coastal path is the footbridge just north of the beach. To get here, turn *makai* (seaward) on Panihi Rd from the highway.

Further south is **Fuji Beach**, nicknamed **Baby Beach** because an offshore reef creates a shallow, placid pool of water that's perfect for toddlers. Located in a modest neighborhood that attracts few tourists, this

Kapa'a

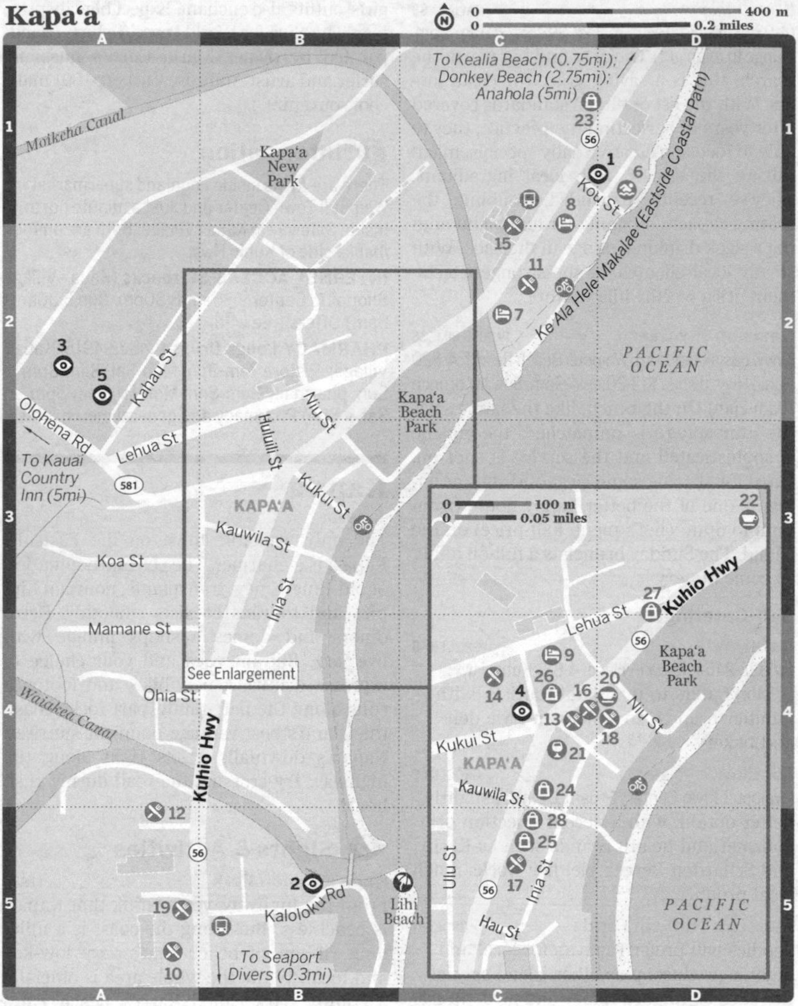

is a real locals' beach, so don't make a loud scene.

There's also a public **swimming pool** (☎822-3842; admission free; ⏰7:30am-3:45pm Tue-Fri, 10am-4:30pm Sat, noon-4:30pm Sun) here.

Studio Kauai Yoga YOGA
(☎822-5053; www.studiokauaiyoga.com; Dragon Bldg, 4504 Kukui St; drop-in classes $15, Fri by donation; ⏰Mon-Fri) Offers a weekly blend of 18 classes such as traditional hatha vinyasa, pranayama and ecstatic dance. Visit the website for a schedule of regularly occurring workshops and retreats.

Hawaiian Style Fishing FISHING
(☎635-7335; 4hr charter per person $130) Join gregarious Captain Terry on his 25ft boat. He takes four anglers at most and shares the catch. Charters depart from the small Lihi Boat Ramp at the end of Kaloloku Rd, off Kuhio Hwy. It's a good idea to book a week or more in advance.

Esprit De Corps Riding Academy HORSEBACK RIDING
(☎822-4688; www.kauaihorses.com; Kualapa Pl; tours $130-390, lessons per hr $55) Dale Rosenfeld qualifies as a 'horse whisperer' and the tours she offers are small, personalized and varied

◉ Sights
1	Coconut Coasters	D1
2	Lihi Boat Ramp	B5
3	Skateboarding Park	A2
4	Studio Kauai Yoga	C4
5	Tennis Courts	A2

Activities, Courses & Tours
6	Swimming Pool	D1

🛏 Sleeping
7	Hotel Coral Reef Resort	C2
8	Kauai Beach House Hostel	C1
9	Orchid Tree Inn	C4

✪ Eating
10	Big Save	A5
11	Coconut Cup Juice Bar & Café	C2
12	Cost U Less	A5
13	Eastside	C4
14	Hoku Foods	C4
15	Kojima Market	C1
16	Mermaids Café	C4
17	Pono Market	C5
18	Rainbow Living Foods	D4
19	Verde	A5

◎◎ Drinking
20	Java Kai	D4
21	Olympics Cafe	C4
22	Small Town Café	D3

⊕ Shopping
23	Artists of Kaua'i	C1
24	Hula Girl	C4
	Kapa'a Shopping Center	(see 10)
25	Larry's Music & Boutique	C5
26	Ship Store Galleries	C4
27	The Root	D3
28	Vicky's Fabrics	C5

KAUA'I KAPA'A

(longer tours are available for more skilled riders). Groups never exceed five people; riders must be aged 10 years and above. She also offers honeymoon rides and weddings on horseback.

Seasport Divers　　　　SNORKELING, DIVING
(☏823-9222, 800-685-5889; www.seasportdivers .com; 4-976 Kuhio Hwy; gear & lesson $155) Eastside waters are less protected by reefs and choppier due to easterly onshore winds. Therefore diving and snorkeling are very limited here. Still, this small branch of a Po'ipu-based outfit rents diving, snorkeling and other ocean gear.

Kapa'a New Park　　　　SPORTS GROUNDS
There are free **tennis courts** and a **skateboarding park**, along with a field for baseball, football and soccer in this park.

☞ Tours & Lectures

Kapa'a Town Walking Tour　　WALKING TOUR
(☏245-3373; www.kauaihistoricalsociety.org; adult/child $15/5; ☺tours 10am & 4pm Tue, Thu & Sat) Knowledgeable local guides point out landmarks, describe Kapa'a's sugar and pineapple boom days and, best of all, talk story and answer questions. Advance reservations are required.

Voyages Through Time Lecture Series　　　　HISTORY LECTURE
(☏822-4999; www.shipstoregalleries.com; Ship Store Galleries, 4-1379 Kuhio Hwy; adult/child $40/20; ☺9:30-11:30am Tue & Thu) The con-cise two-hour seminars – put on by the publishers of the *Pacific Journal* – cover eras from the Royal Hawaiian Kingdom to the reign of the sugar barons, touching on Captain Cook, Charles Darwin and Queen Emma. It's a great opportunity to learn about the path that's led to Kaua'i today and enrich your time spent on the island.

✭✭ Festivals & Events

Heiva I Kaua'i Ia Orana Tahiti　　CULTURAL
(☏822-9447) In early August, dance troupes from as far away as Tahiti, Japan and Canada join groups from Hawaii at Kapa'a Beach Park for this Tahitian dancing and drumming competition.

Coconut Festival　　　　FOOD
(☏651-3273; www.kbakauai.org) Celebrate all things coconut! Events during this free two-day festival in early October include coconut-pie-eating contests, coconut cook-off, cooking demonstrations, music, hula, crafts and food.

🛏 Sleeping

If you're seeking accommodations right in town, pickings are slim. Kapa'a has only one hotel and almost all B&Bs and inns are situated way beyond walking distance. In case you're wondering about the ideally located Pono Kai Resort, we're sorry to say that it's primarily a midrange timeshare, with a limited number of exorbitantly priced vacation rentals.

WALK THIS WAY

The Eastside's newest road is not meant for cars, but is a shared-use path reserved for pedestrians, bicyclists and other nonmotorized modes. At 10ft wide and paved in concrete, **Ke Ala Hele Makalae** (The Path that Goes by the Coast) has jump-started locals into daily fitness walking, jogging, cycling, inline skating and, perhaps, forgoing the local habit of driving everywhere.

In Kapa'a, the path currently starts at the Lihi Boat Ramp at the south end of Kapa'a Beach Park and ends just past Donkey Beach at Ahihi Point (Map p480), a 4-mile stretch. But this constitutes only a small piece of the ambitious facility, which will run over 16 miles all the way from Lihu'e to Anahola Beach Park.

Sunrise walks are brilliant but, for an added kick, rent a coaster bike! Coconut Coasters ([☎]822-7368; www.coconutcoasters.com; 4-1586 Kuhio Hwy; bike rentals per 1hr/4hr from $8.50/18; ⊙7am-6pm Tue-Sat, 9am-4pm Sun) specializes in hourly rentals for the path. Classic single-speed coasters are just right for the gentle slope north, but you can upgrade to a three-speed model ($9.75 per hour) for an extra cushy ride. Owners Melissa and Spark Costales meticulously maintain their fleet and exude aloha spirit. For daily or weekly rentals of coaster, mountain or road bikes, try Kauai Cycle (p490) at the south end of the path.

A nonprofit community group called Kaua'i Path (www.kauaipath.org) is promoting and maintaining the path; see the website for more info. Note: the path is wheelchair accessible.

That said, driving *mauka* to residential neighborhoods leads through picturesque pastures, sweeping views and excellent B&Bs and inns. Remember to ask about minimum-night requirements.

TOP CHOICE **Green Coconut Studio** INN $
(Map p480; [☎]647-0553; www.greencoconutstudio. com; 4698 Pelehu Rd; studio $98; [❄][✿]) Literally lined with windows (and a wraparound veranda), this fantastically airy studio allows spectacular coastal views and cooling cross-breezes. The layout makes great use of space, allowing a comfy satellite-TV setup and a kitchenette with full-sized fridge and the gamut of appliances. There's a $75 cleaning fee for brief stays.

Kauai Beach House Hostel HOSTEL $
([☎]822-3424; www.kauaibeachhouse.net; 4-1552 Kuhio Hwy; dm $26.50, r $65) It's unarguably the cheapest bed under a roof on the island, you can watch the sun come up over the ocean from your bed, and they run a tight ship with 9:30pm lights-out policies and airport-like security. Having said that, it is not plush. A communal kitchen and outside lounge area are the amenities while the vicinity to shops, restaurants and bus stops are bonuses.

Aloha Hale Orchids INN $
(Map p480; [☎]822-4148; www.yamadanursery.com; 5087-A Kawaihau Rd; r $55, cottage $95) Trust us, you won't top this value-priced pair of units

at a residential orchid nursery. The studio is ideal for singles and contains queen bed, mini-refrigerator and TV, while the airy one-bedroom cottage has a full kitchen, TV, windows on all walls, washer and clothesline. One drawback: no wi-fi.

Orchid Tree Inn INN $
([☎]822-5359; www.vrbo.com/118213; 4639 Lehua St; 2br s/d $85/95; [✿]) Everything's within walking distance from this rare, in-town inn. Compact, tidy units include two bedrooms, full kitchen, washer-dryer and a sofa sleeper. Ideal for sociable types who appreciate Asian philosophies (including the careful Taoist and feng shui influences on the garden). Do the proprietor a favor and hassle him about how long it's been since he surfed.

Hotel Coral Reef Resort HOTEL $$
([☎]822-4481, 800-843-4659; www.hotelcoralree fresort.com; 4-1516 Kuhio Hwy; r $110-289; [❄][✿]) Kapa'a's sole hotel has one major advantage: an oceanfront location. Otherwise it's a basic hotel, with smallish rooms and the expected amenities such as air-con and flat-screen TV. Budget rooms ($110 to $125) face the parking lot and Kuhio Hwy. Oceanfront rates vary wildly, from $149 to $289.

Dilly Dally House B&B $$
([☎]631-9186; www.dillydallyhouse.com; 6395 Waipouli Rd; r $115-165, cottage $185; [❄][✿][✿]) At this fantastic B&B, units vary in size, but

all feature modern chic furnishings such as four-post beds, finely crafted wooden dressers, tempurpedic mattresses on bedframes fit for royalty, washer-dryer, private entrance and lanai. The drive to the house might seem long and confusing at first, but the reward is panoramic mountain and ocean views. The host couple serves scrumptious home-cooked breakfasts and there's even a guest laptop.

Kaua'i Country Inn INN $$
(821-0207; www.kauaicountryinn.com; 6440 Olohena Rd; 1 & 2 bedrooms $129-179; @) With gleaming hardwood floors and upscale furnishings, this inn is one class act. The four spacious suites all include cable TV and DVD, Macintosh computers, wi-fi and kitchen or kitchenette. The inland location lends itself to serene surroundings and cooler breezy nights. Beatles fans, don't miss the chance to gawk at the owner's astounding collection of memorabilia. Can be tricky to find at first.

🍴 Eating

Roadside restaurants abound, none terrible, some terribly touristy. Here are several local-favorite picks.

TOP CHOICE Mermaids Café CAFE $
(4-1384 Kuhio Hwy; wraps & plates $9.50-11; 11am-8:45pm) This walk-up counter offers sizeable burritos, fresh organic salads and homemade entrée plates jazzed up with lemongrass and organic herbs. Get the ahi *nori* with brown rice and wasabi cream sauce and you'll return every day thereafter to repeat the experience. When you see the stand-offish local surfer 'bro' next to you drinking a creamy orange concoction go ahead and order one. It's thai tea with coconut milk, and besides coming to Kaua'i it'll be the best decision you ever make.

Rainbow Living Foods VEGAN $$
(4-1384 Kuhio Hwy; wraps $10-13; Mon-Fri 10am-7pm, Sat to 5pm) For those wanting to take their microbial bodies on vacation as well, this is the spot. Everything is gluten and dairy free, but not monetarily free. Portions can be limited for the prices they ask, but their vegan integrity – utilizing local organic farms and serving an abundance of super foods with inventive preparation – justify the expense and will have your body feeling like the first day of spring. It's cozy and simple – they let their food do the talking.

Verde MEXICAN, ECLECTIC $$
(Kapa'a Shopping Center, 4-1101 Kuhio Hwy; mains $11-14; 11am-9pm Mon & Wed-Sun) With the strongest growing reputation in town over the last couple of years serving as testimony, Chef Joshua Stevens' New Mexican–Hawaiian fusion will most likely take whatever fish tacos you've been eating and put them to shame. He is as aggressive as he is inventive with his seasonings. Be sure to save room for the sopaipilla and honey for dessert.

Coconut Cup Juice Bar & Cafe JUICE BAR, CAFE $
(4-1516 Kuhio Hwy; fruit smoothies $6-8, sandwiches $9; 9am-5pm) One part juice stand, one part legitimate health-care provider, this roadside treasure slings generously endowed sandwiches. Wash down your hulking albacore tuna or avocado veggie with a fluorescent shot of wheat grass or fresh-squeezed organic orange or carrot juice ($6 per 16oz).

Pono Market DELI $
(4-1300 Kuhio Hwy; plate lunch $6.50; 6am-6pm Mon-Fri, to 4pm Sat) Fill up on local grinds (food) at this longtime hole in the wall, now with a fully fledged espresso bar. At lunch, line up for generous plate lunches, homemade sushi rolls, fresh ahi poke and savory delicacies such as dried '*opelu* (pan-sized mackerel scad) and smoked marlin.

The Eastside HAWAII REGIONAL $$
(www.theeastsidekauai.com; 4-1380 Kuhio Hwy; lunch mains $9-13, dinner mains $19-28; 11am-2:30pm Mon-Sat & 5:30-9:30pm Tue-Sun) The only nondiner sit-down restaurant in town boasts a breezy open-air dining room, nightly live music and a brief menu of Pacific Rim cuisine such as *huli huli* chicken, hibachi ahi or luscious filet mignon. Think dressed-up versions of down-home eats. With a stellar wine selection and a tranquil atmosphere this is where you want to go to treat yourself, or to impress your date. For a quick but classy lunch sample their Baja fish or carnitas tacos.

Self-Catering

The best place for local produce is the **farmers market** (Kapa'a New Park; 3pm Wed). It's among the island's largest.

Cost U Less GROCERY $
(www.costuless.com; 4525 Akia Rd; 9am-8pm Mon-Fri, to 7pm Sat, to 6pm Sun) Find not only mainstream brands, but also local produce and meat, plus 'natural' brands, such as Kashi

and Tom's of Maine. Most items are sold in large, family size. No membership is needed.

Hoku Foods
GROCERY $

(www.hokufoods.com; 4585 Lehua St; 10am-6pm) Ideal for the cuisine conscious who seek a wide assortment of organic, gluten free (the island's largest selection) and raw foods. There's a respectable selection of local produce and those with foresight can order groceries ahead of time online, to be picked up on arrival.

Big Save
SUPERMARKET $

(822-4971; Kapa'a Shopping Center; 7am-11pm) This local chain has a deli.

Kojima Market
MARKET $

(822-5221; 4-1543 Kuhio Hwy; 8am-7pm Mon-Fri, to 6pm Sat, to 1pm Sun) Rather limited but does carry local meat and produce.

Drinking

Java Kai
CAFE

(www.javakai.com; 4-1384 Kuhio Hwy; coffee drinks $1.50-4.50; 6am-5pm Mon-Sat, 7am-1pm Sun;) Always busy, this Kaua'i-based micro-roastery is best for grabbing a cup to go. The muffins, scones and cookies are baked fresh; keep an eye out for the 'vocab word of the day' so you can *confabulate* with the always pleasant baristas about music and such.

Small Town Café
CAFE

(4-1495 Kuhio Hwy; coffee drinks $3-5; 5:30am-1pm daily, 6:30-9pm Tue-Thu;) The best day-time hangout in town, this indie coffeehouse offers plentiful indoor and outdoor seating for leisurely chats or websurfing. The organic, free-trade coffee suits the hippie-boho crowd. The food tastes like mom made it and there are perpetual good tunes playing. Too bad it closes just when you're getting comfy.

Olympic Cafe
BAR

(1354 Kuhio Hwy; happy hour drafts $3; 6-9pm) Seemingly open only to be a happy hour lo-cale, people always pack in to this spacious 2nd floor sports bar to enjoy perched views of Kapa'a's shuffle or the coconut coast's tame reefs. Good place to get things started.

Shopping

Ship Store Galleries
GALLERY

(www.shipstoregalleries.com; 4-1379 Kuhio Hwy; 10am-7pm) Browsers are welcome at this spacious showroom, where notables include maritime artist Raymond Massey (who's created an extensive, fascinating series on seafaring to the Hawaiian Islands), Lance Fairly

(who does intricate land and seascapes of Hawaiian life), Dolores 'Dee' Kirby (whose unostentatious landscapes are keepers) and Marco Cannella (whose riffs on the Old Masters' still lifes have a local twist).

Hula Girl
CLOTHING

(www.welovehulagirl.com; 4-1340 Kuhio Hwy; 9am-6pm Mon-Sat, 10am-5pm Sun) Aloha-shirt aficionados will find a wide selection of quality, name-brand shirts ($40 to $125). Feel the silky-soft Tori Richard line in cotton lawn ($70 to $75). This family-run shop is a standout for quality Hawaii souvenirs (eg clothing, jewelry, island-made ceramics, art prints, books) and simply a fun place to browse.

Vicky's Fabrics
SOUVENIRS

(www.vickysfabrics.com; 4-1326 Kuhio Hwy; 9am-5pm Mon-Sat) Established in the early 1980s, Vicky's is a gem for quilters and homemakers. Find a wide selection of Hawaiian, Japanese and batik print fabrics. Longtime owner and seamstress Vicky also offers some handmade quilts, pincushions and bags.

Artists of Kaua'i
ART

(www.artistsofkauai.ifp3.com; Kuhio Hwy; 9am-5pm Wed-Sun) Seven Kaua'i artists share a gallery to display their outstanding works in oils, pencil, watercolors and photography. Find it within Kaua'i Products Fair grounds.

The Root
CLOTHING

(4-1435 Kuhio Hwy; 9:30am-7pm Mon-Sat; noon-5pm Sun) Caters to women looking for hip contemporary fashion at affordable prices. Voted in the top-three women's clothing stores on the island – come 'get rooted' as locals say and see why.

Larry's Music & Boutique
MUSICAL INSTRUMENTS

(4-1310 Kuhio Hwy; 10am-5pm Mon-Sat) This high-quality uke-slinger offers starters from under $100 to vintage and high-end ukes from $1000 to $5000. All come with a manufacturer's warranty. Uke lessons and unique Hawaiiana jewelry are also on offer.

Information

INTERNET ACCESS Business Support Services (822-5195; fax 822-2148; 4-1191 Kuhio Hwy; per 15min $2.50; 8am-6pm) Cheap internet access, plus faxing, copies and stamps.

MEDICAL SERVICES Samuel Mahelona Memorial Hospital (Map p480; 822-4961; fax 823-4100; 4800 Kawaihau Rd) Basic emergency care. Serious cases are transferred to Lihu'e's Wilcox Memorial Hospital.

MONEY First Hawaiian Bank (☑822-4966; 4-1366 Kuhio Hwy) Has a 24-hour ATM.

ⓘ Getting There & Around

Kapaa is 8 miles north of the Lihu'e airport. Buses ($2) run from north and south through Kapa'a once an hour from 6am to 7pm. For specific bus information visit www.kauai.gov. There's also **Akiko's Taxi** (☑822-7588; fares around $12).

To avoid the paralyzing Kapa'a to Wailua crawl, take the Kapa'a Bypass Rd (Map p480). Note that except in the heart of Kapa'a, you will definitely need a car.

To be most enviro-friendly, rent a bike from **Coconut Coasters** (☑822-7368; www.coconut-coasters.com; 4-1586 Kuhio Highway; per day $20; Tue-Sat 9am 6pm, Mon & Sun 9am-4pm) and cruise at your own pace.

Kealia Beach

With easy access via car or the coastal path, beautiful sand, and a laid-back vibe Kealia fills any gaps one's Kapa'a Beach Park experience may have left unfilled. Traveling north from Kapa'a it's visible from the road at the 10-mile marker. The sandy bottom slopes offshore very gradually, making it possible to walk out far to catch long rides back. But the pounding barrels are treacherous and definitely not recommended for novices. A breakwater protects the north end, so swimming and snorkeling are occasionally possible there.

Showers, restrooms, picnic tables and ample parking – including disabled – are available; natural shade is not. Sunscreen is a must.

Anahola

POP 1930

Blink and you'll miss the predominantly Native Hawaiian village of Anahola, where there are subdivisions of Hawaiian Homestead lots at the southern and northern ends. Pineapple and sugar plantations once thrived here but today the area is mainly residential. The few who lodge here will find themselves in rural seclusion among true locals.

Grouped together at the side of Kuhio Hwy, just south of the 14-mile marker, Anahola's modest commercial center includes a post office (☉8am-4pm Mon-Fri, 9:30-11:30am Sat), burger stand and convenience store.

◉ Sights & Activities

Anahola Beach Park   BEACH
Hidden from the highway, this locals' beach makes an easy getaway – it's more secluded yet still drive-up accessible. Because this county park sits on Hawaiian Home Lands, you'll probably share the beach with Hawaiian families, especially on weekends. Remember, it's their beach: respect the locals. The wide bay, fringed with a decent swath of lovely sandy beach, is a surfers' hot spot on the choppier south end. But toward the north, waters are calm enough for swimming. There are two ways to get here: for the south end, turn off Kuhio Hwy onto Kukuihale Rd at the 13-mile marker, drive a mile down and then turn onto the dirt beach road. For the north end, take 'Aliomanu Rd at the 14-mile marker and park in the sandy lot.

'Aliomanu Beach   BEACH
Secluded 'Aliomanu Beach is another spot frequented primarily by locals, who pole- and throw-net fish and gather *limu* (seaweed). It's a mile-long stretch of beach; you can get to the prettier north end by turning onto 'Aliomanu Rd (Second), just past the 15-mile marker on Kuhio Hwy. Don't take 'Aliomanu Rd (First), a mile south, by mistake! Then, turn left onto Kalalea View Dr, go 0.5 miles and turn right at the beach access sign.

Hole in the Mountain   LANDMARK
Ever since a landslide altered this once-obvious landmark, the *puka* (hole) in **Pu'u Konanae** has been a mere sliver. From slightly north of the 15-mile marker along Hwy 56, look back at the mountain, down to the right of the tallest pinnacle: on sunny days you'll see a smile of light shining through a slit in the rock face. Legend has it that the original hole was created when a giant threw his spear through the mountain, causing the water stored within to gush forth as waterfalls.

Angeline's Mu'olaulani   SPA
(☑822-3235; www.angelineslomikauai.com; Kamalomalo'o Pl; massage treatment $150; ☉9am-3pm Mon-Fri by appointment only) Experience authentic *lomilomi* (traditional Hawaiian massage; literally 'loving hands') at this longstanding bodywork center run by the Native Hawaiian Locey family. With outdoor shower, open-air deck, massage tables separated by curtains and simple sarongs to cover up, Angeline's is a rustic contrast to plush resort spas. The signature treatment

HIGHWAY NICKNAMES

Locals call highways by nickname rather than by number. Here's a cheat sheet:

Hwy 50 Kaumuali'i Hwy

Hwy 51 Kapule Hwy

Hwy 56 Kuhio Hwy

Hwy 58 Nawiliwili Rd

Hwy 520 Maluhia Rd (Tree Tunnel) and Po'ipu Rd

Hwy 530 Koloa Rd

Hwy 540 Halewili Rd

Hwy 550 Waimea Canyon Dr

Hwy 552 Koke'e Rd

Hwy 560 Kuhio Hwy (continuation of Hwy 56)

Hwy 570 Ahukini Rd

Hwy 580 Kuamo'o Rd

Hwy 581 Kamalu Rd and Olohena Rd

Hwy 583 Ma'alo Rd

comprises a steam, vigorous salt scrub and a special four-hands *lomilomi*.

TriHealth Ayurveda SPA
(☎828-2104, 800-455-0770; www.trihealthayurvedaspa.com; Kuhio Hwy; treatments $130-315; ☻by appointment) In a simple bungalow just off the highway, you can sample traditional ayurvedic therapies, practiced by therapists trained both locally and in Kerala, India. Kudos if you can withstand a full-body (head and all) session in that intimidating horizontal steamer. Located between the 20- and 21-mile markers.

🛏 Sleeping & Eating

Hale Kiko'o INN $
(☎822-3922; 639-1734; www.halekikoo.com; 4-4382-B Kuhio Hwy; studio unit s $70-80, d $75-90; ☎) Just off the highway on an unnamed, unpaved road are two charming, modern studios, each with full kitchen. The downstairs unit is large enough for living room and features stylish slate floors, lava-rock pillars, garden patio and artsy outdoor shower. The upstairs unit is more ordinary, but brighter, with windows aplenty and a deck. Cleaning fee ($75) charged.

'Ili Noho Kai O Anahola B&B $$
(☎821-0179, 639-6317; www.kauai.net/ilinohokai; 'Aliomanu Rd; r with shared bathroom incl breakfast $100-120) This simple guesthouse fronting Anahola Beach ain't cheap, but from here you can stroll from bed to beach in a New York minute. The four compact but tidy rooms (sharing two bathrooms) surround a central lanai, where guests talk story and fill up on home-cooked breakfasts as their inner bliss is wooed out by the musical ringings of the generous hosts – Native Hawaiian activists now running a B&B on Hawaiian Home Lands for which they fought long and hard. Phone calls preferred.

Riverside Tropical Retreat INN $
(☎823-0705; www.vrbo.com/9186; 4-4382 Kuhio Hwy; ste varies seasonally $85-120; ☎) Spiritual seekers would appreciate this rustic bungalow, surrounded by green forest, river, mountains and pasture. The one-bedroom suite is well worn rather than spanking new, but includes a kitchenette and lots of louvers for ventilation, and is immaculate upon arrival. As it was in the works at time of research, inquire about the new two-bedroom unit upstairs with a loft and full kitchen (rates vary seasonally from $150 to $180). On-site ayurvedic treatments offered. Cleaning fee ($80) charged.

Duane's Ono Char-Burger FAST FOOD $
(4-4350 Kuhio Hwy; burgers $5-7; ☺10am-6pm Mon-Sat, 11am-6pm Sun) If you're a fan of In-N-Out and Dairy Queen, you'll go nuts over this indie drive-in. Try the 'old fashioned' (cheddar, onions and sprouts) or the 'local girl' (Swiss cheese, pineapple and teriyaki sauce). Add crispy thin fries and melt-in-your-mouth onion rings. See autographed photos of famous fans, from Chuck Norris to Steve Tyler.

❶ Getting There & Away

BUS The Kauai Bus stops on Kuhio Hwy across from Whalers General Store at the bottom of the hill.

Ko'olau Road

Ko'olau Rd is a peaceful, scenic loop drive through rich green pastures, dotted with soaring white egrets and bright wildflowers. It makes a nice diversion and is the way to reach untouristed Moloa'a Beach or Larsen's Beach (no facilities at either). Ko'olau Rd connects with Kuhio Hwy 0.5 miles north of the 16-mile marker and again 180yd south of the 20-mile marker.

For a quick bite, the Moloa'a Sunrise Fruit Stand (☎822-1441; cnr Kuhio Hwy &

Ko'olau Rd; juices & smoothies $3-6.25, sandwiches $5.50-7; ☺7:30am-6pm Mon-Sat, 9am-5pm Sun) offers healthful sandwiches on multigrain bread, taro burgers and brown-rice vegetarian sushi. It's past the 16-mile marker.

🏖 Beaches

Moloa'a Beach

Off the tourist path, this classically curved bay appeared in the pilot episode of *Gilligan's Island*.

To the north, there's a shallow protected swimming area good for families; to the south, the waters are rougher but there's more sand. When the surf's up, stay dry and safe – go beach walking instead. Toward the back of the beach, which is fed by Moloa'a Stream, there's plenty of shade, making for an ideal picnic or daydreaming spot.

To get here, follow Ko'olau Rd and turn onto Moloa'a Rd, which ends 0.75 miles down at a few beach houses and a little parking area.

Larsen's Beach

This long, golden-sand beach, named after L David Larsen (former manager of C Brewer's Kilauea Sugar Company), is good for solitary strolls and beachcombing.

Although shallow, snorkeling can be good when the waters are very calm, usually only in the summer. Beware of a vicious current that runs westward along the beach and out through a channel in the reef.

To get here, turn onto Ko'olau Rd from whichever end (ie where it intersects either Kuhio Hwy or Moloa'a Rd), go just over a mile then turn toward the ocean on a dirt road (easy to miss from the south: look for it just before the cemetery) and take the immediate left. It's 1 mile to the parking area and then a five-minute walk downhill to the beach.

HANALEI BAY & THE NORTH SHORE

Forget Eden. Arguably the most pristine part of the island, the North Shore's quilted green slopes and valleys are effortlessly fertile. Somewhere between Hanalei Valley and the 'end of the road,' the seemingly untouched landscape makes it easy to imagine what it must have been like for the Hawaiian gods taking in from above the sand, sea and mountains below. Savor life here: swim through the turquoise sea, bite into juicy farmers-market fruits and nap away the afternoons on warm

sugar-sand. To be sure, the sleepy little enclave that is the North Shore is an unassuming treasure; the island within the island.

Kilauea

POP 2249

Many North Shore visitors treat Kilauea as an ephemeral stop in which to gas up, grab lunch and snap a few photographs on their way north – perhaps they're a little too hasty.

The most northern point of the island offers lush vegetation, great eateries and some of the best souvenir shopping around. It's home to wine vendors, fish markets, a scenic wildlife refuge and one of the island's best fruit stands, but perhaps the fact that it has one of the most well-known (and counter intuitively named) 'secret' beaches on the island will justify you giving it a look-see.

🏖 Beaches

Kahili (Rock Quarries) Beach & Pools of Mokolea

This scenic little stretch of beach, while challenging to find, is tucked away between two densely vegetated cliffs where the Kilauea Stream meets the ocean. There's no protective barrier reef so when the surf is up waves can pound. Swimming is best kept to the middle of the beach as the west end's river flow creates a strong rip towards the open ocean. A calm summer day is most suitable for snorkeling and fishing is optimal by the river mouth, though heavy rains undoubtedly equate to murky water.

The main public access is via Wailapa Rd, which begins midway between the 21- and 22-mile markers on Kuhio Hwy. Follow Wailapa Rd north for less than 0.5 miles beyond Kuhio Hwy and then turn left on the unmarked dirt road (4WD recommended) that begins at a bright-yellow water valve. Break-ins are not an uncommon thing around here so be sure to lock your car.

Kauapea (Secrets) Beach

No, that's not Adam and Eve, it's likely a visiting couple wearing even less than fig leaves, as this is a spot renowned for (illegal) nude sunbathing. Kauapea remains reclusive, despite the fact that it's lost its virgin-quality mystique. To be sure, the oft-dubbed 'secret' beach hardly lives up to its moniker these days. If you can handle occasional nudity, this might just be the beach for you.

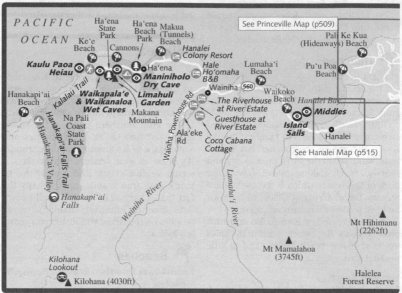

Accessing the beach requires a trek of about 15 minutes, which, during inclement weather, is dangerous. Turn right at Kalihiwai Rd (0.5 miles past the gas station) and turn at the first dirt road. Follow the trail to the bottom. If the swells are down, you can consider strolling left instead of right where the trail meets the beach. If the water is calm, continue to the lava rocks about a quarter-mile down. Be careful, as rocks can be slippery and the open ocean swells create extremely dangerous rip currents along the entirety of the beach. Be sure to lock your car.

Sights & Activities

Kilauea Point National Wildlife Refuge
NATURE RESERVE
(www.fws.gov/kilaueapoint; Lighthouse Rd; adult/child $5/free; ⊙10am-4pm, closed federal holidays) Home to some of Hawaii's endangered wildlife, this refuge also has sweeping views, as seen from the 52ft white tower of the lighthouse abutting 216ft sea cliffs. Plummeting rare birds and soaring 8ft-wingspan great frigates, along with views of breaching whales (November to March) and spinner dolphins, make this historic landmark a treasure. The list of reasons to at least stop goes on and on (it houses the world's largest clamshell lens, a beacon

up to 90 miles out to sea). You'll also see Moku'ae'ae Island, which is teeming with protected wildlife – often the endangered monk seal can be seen warming itself in the sun.

Na 'Aina Kai Botanical Gardens
GARDEN
(☎828-0525; www.naainakai.com; 4101 Wailapa Rd; tours $25-70; ⊙by reservation Tue-Fri) In a somewhat over-the-top approach, this husband-and-wife operation pays tribute to Hawaiian culture on 240 acres of botanical gardens. Also on the grounds: a beach, a bird-watching marsh and a forest of 60,000 South and East Asian hardwood trees. Turn right onto Wailapa Rd, between the 21- and 22-mile markers on Kuhio Hwy and look for their sign.

Pineapple Yoga
YOGA
(www.pineappleyoga.com; drop-in classes $20; ⊙7:30-9:30am Mon-Sat) Set out by Ashtanga Yoga Master Sri K Pattabhi Jois Institute in Mysore, this type of yoga links the breath with a series of movements and postures to create heat throughout the body and sweat (lots of sweat) that detoxifies the muscles and organs. The studio is in the parish house of the Christ Memorial Church, across the street from the Menehune Mart gas station.

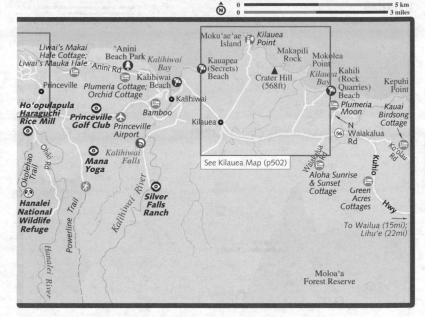

Kauai Mini Golf
MINI GOLF

(☎828-2118; www.kauaiminigolf.com; 5-2723 Kuhio Hwy; adult/child $15/10; ☺11am-10pm, last tee time 9pm) Part mini golf part botanical gardens, this environmentally educational round of putt putt may prove to be the best non-drinking nighttime activity on the North Shore. Separated into five sections (Rare Plants, Polynesian Kunu Plants, Kilauea Town Plantation Heritage, Cultural Influence and Hawaii Today), each hole gives golfers a chance to read plaques (as well as putts) and see exquisite flora firsthand. Provided booklets fill in colorful backstories and the water hazards and undulating greens make for a challenging par 47.

Kauai Kunana Dairy
TOUR

(☎651-5046; www.kauaikunanadairy.com; ☺1½hr tours by appointment only) For a snapshot of farm bliss, this microdairy offers a tour harking back to a simpler time, with fruits, vegetables and, of course, goat cheese to sample.

Christ Memorial Episcopal Church
CHURCH

(2518 Kolo Rd) This charming church is one of two of Kilauea's lava-built churches (the other is St Sylvester's Catholic Church) and boasts 11 English stained-glass windows.

🛏 Sleeping

Sleepy Kilauea has some unique B&Bs. What these lack in ocean views, they make up for with lush, tropical farm settings. With recent B&B limitations made, some gems remain well hidden. Search **Vacation Rentals by Owner** (www.vrbo.com).

North Country Farms
TOP CHOICE
COTTAGE **$$**

(☎828-1513; www.northcountryfarms.com; 4387 Kahli Makai Rd; cottages $150) Run by a couple of eco-conscious farmaholics who need to 'support their habit of farming' these cabin-like cottages pull off an alpine feel in the tropics. While Orchard's 500-sq-ft studio with a vaulted ceiling and equally large covered lanai (with outside bed) are a near indulgence, the more compact Garden's tasteful redwood layout with queen bed and a cornered couch is ideal for couples or families who get along well. Full farm-usage privileges include access to a massive garden of fresh lettuce, greens and herbs, and a copious amount of fruit. If there's a free moment in the mornings the on-campus yoga ($10) is a wise choice.

Green Acres Cottages
INN **$**

(Map p500; ☎828-0478, 866-484-6347; www.greenacrescottages.com; 5-0421C Kuhio Hwy; cottages $75; 🛜) Though the word 'cottage' is

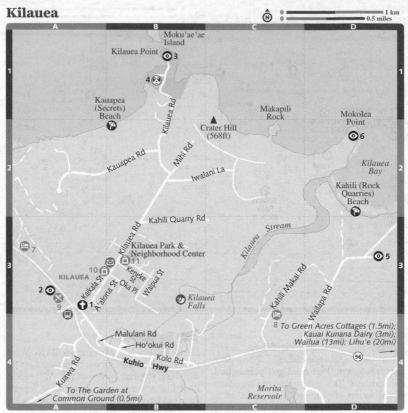

Kilauea

⊙ Sights

1 Christ Memorial Episcopal Church	A3
2 Kaua'i Mini Golf	A3
3 Kilauea Lighthouse	B1
4 Kilauea Point National Wildlife Refuge	B1
5 Na 'Aina Kai Botanical Gardens	D3
Pineapple Yoga	(see 1)
6 Pools of Mokolea	D2

⊜ Sleeping

7 Bamboo	A3
8 North Country Farms	C4

⊗ Eating

9 Banana Joe's Fruitstand	A3
Healthy Hut	(see 10)

Kilauea Bakery & Pau Hana Pizza	(see 11)
Kilauea Fish Market	(see 10)
Kilauea Town Market	(see 11)
Kilauea Video Ice Cream & Candy	(see 10)
Lighthouse Bistro	(see 11)

⊟ Shopping

Banana Patch Studio	(see 11)
Cake Nouveau	(see 11)
Island Soap & Candle Works	(see 11)
10 Kilauea Plantation Center	A3
11 Kong Lung Center	B3
Kong Lung Co	(see 11)
Oscar's K-Town Underground	(see 10)

used liberally here (essentially rooms in the back wing of someone's house), the price can't be beat in Kilauca. Each has its own private entrance, kitchenette and feels like grandma decorated it (someone's grandma probably did). Mornings spent picking fresh bananas, avocados and oranges, a communal hot tub and a charming old-school macadamia nut cracker (nuts provided) give this roadside lodging some charm.

Kauai Birdsong Cottage   COTTAGE $$
(Map p500; ☑828-6797, 652-2585; www.kauai birdsongcottage.com; 7595 Koolau Rd; cottage $150) Secluded, serene, with a hot tub and a rather large hammock under the shelter of Jamaican Lilikoi vines – this spot is worth every penny. The 650-sq-ft studio features a marble-counter-topped kitchen, stylish outdoor shower, queen bed, futon and TV-DVD-stereo set-up. Take a few steps outside and pick fresh mangoes, avocados and grapefruit from the tree. There's a $100 cleaning fee.

Aloha Sunrise & Sunset Cottages   COTTAGE $$
(☑828-1100; www.kauaisunrise.com/sunset, www.kauaisunrise.com/sunrise; Waiakalua St; cottages $185; ☎) You might forget where home is (or just not want to go back there) after a couple of days on these 7 acres of indigenous island gardens with cats, dogs and horses galloping around. The cottages are fairly new (ie very clean) with a mellow, modern feel, each with a variety of charming Hawaiian art. The Sunrise's stacked layout has an airy sky-lit bedroom–lounge upstairs while the Sunset has a more conventional design with bamboo furniture and expansive mountain views from the lanai. Low-season rates are possible.

✕ Eating

While it is charming, Kilauea is not chock-full of epic eateries. However, there are a few gems.

The Garden at Common Ground   HAWAII REGIONAL $
(www.commongroundkauai.net/thegarden; 4900 Kuawa Rd; salads/grill items $7.95/9.75; ⊙11am-3pm) Situated inland from the highway, within the sustainability-motivated Common Ground, one is engulfed by the spacious surroundings of sprouting flora. The nature-chic cafe's rotating menu utilizes seasonal crops grown on-site or by nearby local farmers and serves creative salads, wraps and grilled items. Quality outweighs quantity, but your body will thank you.

Kilauea Fish Market   FISH MARKET $
(Kilauea Plantation Center, 4270 Lighthouse Rd; plates & wraps $8-14; ⊙11am-8pm Mon-Sat) Serving healthy versions of over-the-counter plate lunches of fresh *opakapaka* or Korean BBQ chicken, *mahi mahi* tacos and aggressively large ahi burritos, consider this Hawaiian-style deli a necessity and build it into the itinerary. Service is speedy and though alcohol is not sold, bringing your own beer or wine for dinner (or lunch…no judgment) is welcomed.

Kilauea Bakery & Pau Hana Pizza BAKERY $$
(Kong Lung Center, 2484 Keneke St; pastries $4, pizza $15-33; ⊙6:30am-9pm, pizza from 10:30am) If it were ever actually cold in Hawaii, this would be a go-to comfort spot. Best for breakfast or a mid-afternoon snack as while they offer an impressive array of hearty homemade soups and baked goods, the actual meal-type food (including the pizza) may leave some satisfaction to the imagination. Great people-watching and it's the only place within 6 miles to get a latte.

Lighthouse Bistro   HAWAII REGIONAL $$
(Kong Lung Center, 2484 Keneke St; mains lunch $12-20, dinner $18-36; ⊙noon-2pm Mon-Sat & 5:30-9pm daily) The mellow-chic ambience is great at this expensive but romantic spot, though the pastas are overpriced. Live music, usually by solo artists, makes it great for a date, as does the wine list.

Banana Joe's Fruitstand   FRUIT STAND $
(www.bananajoekauai.com; 5-2719 Kuhio Hwy; smoothies $3-12; ⊙9am-6pm Mon-Sat) This low-rent-looking shack just past the 24-mile marker on the *mauka* side of the road is a smoothie-producing gem. Have you ever heard of atemoya, rambutan or mamey sapote? Don't worry, nobody else has either, but trust that when they take the shape of an icy blend they'll provide satisfaction to the point of enticing you back on a daily basis.

Kilauea Video Ice Cream & Candy   ICE CREAM $
(Kilauea Plantation Center, 4270 Lighthouse Rd; ⊙noon-9:30pm) The owner of this buzzing little shop has a lot of pride in his family, which soon becomes evident, once he starts chatting. What he exudes in gregariousness he matches in generosity; whether it's a creamy tropical ice cream or a live-culture, low-calorie Carpigiani gelato, there's no need to be shy about the samples.

1. Koke'e State Park (p554)
Hope for a clear day for ideal views into the Kalalau Valley.

2. Polihale State Park (p552)
This isolated park boasts one of Hawaii's longest stretches of sand.

3. Lihu'e (p468)
Lihu'e's town beach is ideal for almost all watersports.

4. Hanalei River (p514)
The scenic, calm Hanalei River is ideal for novice kayakers.

HOLGER LEUE / LONELY PLANET IMAGES ©

Self-Catering

Healthy Hut
GROCERY $

(Kilauea Plantation Center, 4270 Lighthouse Rd; ⊗8:30am-9pm) Has wheat-free bread, dairy-free yogurt and most all other fun-free food, and covers basic grocery needs in a high-end, healthy style.

Kilauea Town Market
GROCERY $

(Kong Lung Center, 2484 Keneke St; ⊗8am-8pm Sun-Thu, to 8:30pm Fri & Sat) Good for local fruits, herbs, stinky cheeses and a respectable selection of organic wines.

🔒 Shopping

All of the following are within eyesight of each other.

Oskar's K-Town Underground
CLOTHING

(Kilauea Plantation Center, 4270 Lighthouse Rd; www.oskarskauai.com; ⊗10am-7pm Mon-Sat, 11am-6pm Sun) A tad hodgepodge, but a great little shop if you have forgotten some necessities for baby or mom. Has some unique, albeit random, locally designed T-shirts and a great, though small, selection of gently used and recycled baby clothes.

Island Soap & Candle Works
SOUVENIRS

(www.islandsoap.com; Kong Lung Center, 2484 Keneke St; ⊗9am-9pm) Though there are several of these shops, this is the most unique on the island, as the soap is made in-house. The business also donates leftovers to local schools for crafts – a plus in our book.

Kong Lung Co
SOUVENIRS

(Kong Lung Center, 2484 Keneke St; ⊗11am-6pm) Asian-inspired art and clothing boutique with a wide array of Eastern-fusion tchotchkes as well as pricey souvenirs, reclaimed kimono quilts and kids' clothes.

Banana Patch Studio
SOUVENIRS

(Kong Lung Center, 2484 Keneke St; ⊗10am-6pm) A good place to pick up touristy, 'Hawaiian-style' souvenirs bearing local phraseology. Featured items are the ceramic knickknacks.

Cake Nouveau
CLOTHING

(Kong Lung Center, 2484 Keneke St; ⊗11am-6pm) The closest you'll come in town to an LA-inspired selection of women's boutique-style clothes. Ideal for those who have a hot date later and a pretty big budget.

ℹ Getting There & Around

The Kaua'i Bus stops hourly along the highway across from the Menehune Mart at the entrance to town. For more information, see p467.

Kalihiwai

POP 771

Sandwiched between Kilauea and 'Anini, Kalihiwai ('water's edge' in Hawaiian) is a hidden treasure that is easy to pass by. The main indication that it's on the *mauka* side is Kalihiwai Bridge, which curves dramatically after an abundance of towering albesia trees. Most venture here to discover the remote beach, which is an ideal frolicking spot for sunbathing, sandcastle building and, swells permitting, swimming, bodyboarding and surfing along the cliff on the east side. Note that this is the most localized surf spot on the island. If you paddle out and are anything but respectful and patient, plan on answering to somebody who knows more martial arts than you do. Kalihiwai Rd was at one point a road that passed through Kalihiwai Beach, connecting the highway at two points. A tidal wave in 1957 washed out the old Kalihiwai Bridge. The bridge was never rebuilt, and now there are two Kalihiwai Rds, one on each side of the river. To get here, take the first Kalihiwai Rd, 0.5 miles west of Kilauea.

For a mellow but pleasing paddle up into the lush innards of Kalihiwai Valley, your best bet is Kayak Kauai (☎826-9844, www.kayakkauai.com, s/d $29/54, ⊗8am-5:30pm, to 8pm in summer). Though they'll allow you an unsupervised rental on Kalihiwai, they do not allow renting kayaks for Wailua River, Na Pali Coast or any other open ocean.

Take in the island with a tropical jaunt on horseback at animal-friendly Silver Falls Ranch (Map p500; ☎828-6718; www.silverfallsranch.com; Kamo'okoa Rd; 1½/2/3hr ride $95/115/135). Opt for the waterfall swim and picnic lunch for the best value.

Overlooking the Kalihiwai Valley and a 10-minute walk to either 'Anini or Kalihiwai beaches, Bamboo (Map p502; ☎828-0811; 3281 Kalihiwai Rd; www.surfsideprop.com; 1br $175, per week $1100; ☎) is a charming getaway attached to a larger house inhabited by the owners. The private entrance stairs are steep to this cozy but well-appointed spot, which works well for two people.

'Anini

A popular destination for locals spending the day or weekend camping, fishing, diving or just 'beaching' it, 'Anini is unsullied, revered and golden. To get here, cross Kalihiwai

Bridge, go up the hill and turn onto (the second) Kalihiwai Rd, bearing left onto 'Anini Rd soon thereafter.

Beaches & Activities

'Anini Beach Park
BEACH PARK

One not to miss, as it wears many proverbial hats: it's an ideal windsurfing, snorkeling, camping, swimming and low-key just-cruisin' spot, plus it has some of the most reliable conditions, bubbling over a lagoon, and protected by one of the longest and widest fringing reefs in the Hawaiian Islands. At its widest point, the reef extends over 1600ft offshore. The park is unofficially divided into day-use, camping and windsurfing areas. While weekends might draw crowds, weekdays are low-key. Facilities include restrooms, showers, changing rooms, drinking water, picnic pavilions and BBQ grills.

Windsurf Kaua'i
WINDSURFING

(☑828-6838; www.windsurf-kauai.com; 3hr lesson $100, board rental per hr $25; ⊙rentals 10am-4pm, lessons 9am & 1pm Mon-Fri) Learn what it's like to glide on water with teacher Celeste Harvel, who wants nothing more than to stoke you out with her 30 years of windsurf experience. She guarantees you'll be sailing in your first lesson. Lessons by appointment only.

🛏 Sleeping

High-end vacation rentals abound in 'Anini, though they're a tad harder to find now under a new county bill that restricts vacation rentals only in specific zones on the island.

Camping at the justifiably popular 'Anini Beach Park is another option. The campground hosts a mix of frugal travelers and long-term 'residents'. It's generally very safe. Note all campers must vacate the park from Tuesday to Wednesday for regular upkeep. For information on permits, see p463.

Plumeria Cottage
COTTAGE $$

(Map p500; ☑828-0811; www.surfsideprop.com; 3585 'Anini Rd; 2½br house $225, per week $1525; ☎) A charming and unique spot that's both comfortable and chic, this child-friendly abode is worth the splurge for the location (it's a short walk to the beach). With a finely polished wood interior, sweeping views, amicable caretakers and access to any and all land and ocean toys, it is modest luxury Hawaiian-style.

Orchid Cottage
COTTAGE $$

(Map p500; ☑828-0811; www.surfsideprop.com; 3585 'Anini Rd; 1br cottage $185, per week $1250; ☎) This private, idyllic getaway is in a small-but-lovely guesthouse a minute's walk from 'Anini Beach Park. It's compact but quite charming with a cozy alcove bed, traditional but sleek design, laundry, TV and full access to any recreational equipment imaginable. Pick your own fruit and flourishing tropical surroundings.

Princeville

POP 1826

Kilauea's rich cousin, Princeville (dubbed 'Haolewood') is a methodically landscaped resort community that is about as carefully controlled – and protected – as a film set, especially when it actually is a film set. Its body is made up of high-end resorts, finely manicured golf courses and a mixture of cookie-cutter residences, vacation rentals and condominium complexes. What it may lack in personality it makes up for in convenience, as it's the most centrally located area on the North Shore. The St Regis Princeville (formerly the Princeville Resort) – an incarnation of luxury – is Princeville's Oz at the end of the road. The only major commercial area is the **Princeville Center**, with a grocery store, several restaurants and a mix of kiosks and retail stores.

Often the most referred-to spot on the North Shore by tourists (perhaps because it doesn't carry the risk of mispronunciation) it grew in population and popularity as a result of its first flagship resort in 1985.

Princeville traces its roots to Robert Wyllie, a Scottish doctor who became foreign minister to King Kamehameha IV. In the mid-19th century Wyllie established a sugar plantation in Hanalei. When Queen Emma and Kamehameha came to visit in 1860, Wyllie named his plantation and the surrounding lands Princeville to honor their two-year-old son, Prince Albert, who died only two years later. The plantation later became a cattle ranch.

🏃 Beaches

Pali Ke Kua (Hideaways) & Pu'u Poa Beaches BEACHES

Princeville is mostly cliffs overlooking the ocean, with rocky and dangerous coast at the base. There are, however, two worthwhile beaches, both of which, unfortunately, are difficult to access and require parking at the parking lot after the St Regis gatehouse. A path between two fences followed by a steep railing- and rope-assisted scramble leads you to Pali Ke Kua Beach, known locally as Hideaways, an ideal snorkel and swim spot (when it's calm) with 100yd of reef just steps off the beach. An alternative route is 0.25 miles up the road within the Pali Ke Kua condo complex, where an equally steep but paved path ends up at the east end of the beach. A path to the left of the gatehouse leads you to Pu'u Poa Beach which, although public, sits below and adjacent to the St Regis Princeville and serves as its on-campus beach.

⊙ Sights

St Regis Princeville LANDMARK

The work that's gone into this high-end resort is reason enough to get a peek. The sunset is without a doubt among the most beautiful the island has to offer at this locale, where a deck overlooks glorious views of **Makana Mountain** and the wall of the Wainiha Valley. If the hotel is too intimidating, the bluff in front offers distant vistas.

Hanalei Valley Lookout VIEWPOINT

Take in views of farmland that's been cultivated for more than 1000 years, the broad brushstroke of valley, river and taro, plus a smattering of rare wildlife. Park across from the Princeville Center (Map p509) so you don't have to cross the street, but take care to watch for other pedestrians when pulling out onto the busy highway.

🏃 Activities

Makai Golf Club at the St Regis Princeville Resort GOLF

(☎826-1912; www.makaigolf.com; 4080 Lei O Papa Rd; greens fee $200, after 1pm $135, Woods Course $50, discounts if staying in certain Princeville locations) Makai is 280 acres divided into three separate nine-hole courses designed by Robert Trent Jones Jr, each with its own distinctive personality and scenic flavor. The Ocean runs out to the magnificent coastline and offers a signature ravine-contemplating par 3 with an expansive coastal view. The Lakes winds its way around several serene lakes, culminating with a par 5 that tempts all those with valor to go for it in two. The Woods – the cheapest and gentlest of the lot – meanders through native woodlands. The Ocean and Lakes are played together as an 18-hole course.

Prince Golf Course GOLF

(☎826-5000; www.princeville.com; 5-3900 Kuhio Hwy; greens fees $200, if staying anywhere in Princeville $155) Most call it difficult; Tiger Woods is rumored to have called it 'unfair.' Regularly ranked amongst the world's best golf courses, this Robert Trent Jones Jr–designed links-style golf course is a turf and sod roller coaster that climbs slopes, careens down hills and winds its way through valleys and woods. While it's a treat to the eye, as it offers some of the most breathtaking vistas in the world, its mastery (or mere survival) demands a keen combination of creativity and discipline. It is as humbling as it can be rewarding, so players best bring their A-game to this affair, and possibly one or two extra sleeves of balls.

Tennis at the Makai Club TENNIS

(☎826-1912, 639-0638; www.makaigolf.com; 4080 Lei O Papa Rd; lessons group/private $18/65, hourly court rental per person $20) The four newly remodeled hard courts are freshly resurfaced and host lessons offered daily by pro Eric Lutz, and pick-up games and round robins. Racquets available.

Princeville Ranch Stables HORSEBACK RIDING

(☎826-6777; www.princevilleranch.com; Kuhio Hwy; tours $125, private 2hr ride $175; ⊙tours Mon-Sat) Offering a beautiful ride, even for beginners, this outfit is especially ideal for those who really care about how tour animals are treated. Newbies should wear jeans and plan for sore buttocks. Find the ranch between the 26- and 27-mile markers (across

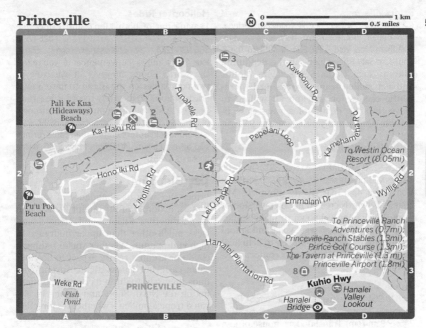

from the Prince Golf Course). The four-hour trip to Kalihiwai Falls is pleasant, and includes picnicking and a swim. Be sure to bring sunblock and insect repellent.

Powerline Trail　　　MOUNTAIN BIKING

This is a serious 11.2-mile ride that has steep climbs, deep ruts and even deeper puddles (bike-tire deep). Ample scenery makes the reward all that much sweeter along the trail, but the real reason to do this is the athletic challenge. Opt to ride in and turnaround back out, or arrange for pick-up at the **Kapa'a trailhead** or the **Opaeka'a Falls** lookout. The entire ride can be done in about four hours with a steady pace. To get there, take the road to the Princeville Ranch Stable and follow to the end to find the trailhead.

Princeville Ranch Adventures　　　MULTIACTIVITY, ZIPLINING

(☎826-7669, 888-955-7669; www.adventures kauai.com; tours $79-125) A family-friendly enterprise that can bring out your adventurous side, whether it's for a hike, kayak or a four-hour tour consisting of eight ziplines, a suspension bridge, a swimming hole and a picnic lunch. Minimum requirements are 12 years and 80lb.

Princeville

Activities, Courses & Tours

1 Makai Golf Club & Tennis Courts........B2
　 Princeville Yoga............................(see 8)

Sleeping

2 Emmalani Court.............................. B1
3 Holly's Kauai Condo C1
4 Pali Ke Kua..................................... B1
5 Sealodge.. D1
6 St Regis Princeville..........................A2

Eating

　 CJ's Steak & Seafood..................(see 8)
　 Federico's ....(see 8)
　 Foodland ....(see 8)
7 Infigo's.. B1
　 La Petite Café & Bakery...............(see 8)
　 Lappert's Ice Cream.....................(see 8)
　 North Shore Café.........................(see 8)
　 Paradise Bar & Grill ....(see 8)
　 Tamarind.....................................(see 8)

Drinking

　 Lobby Bar at St Regis Princeville..(see 6)

Shopping

8 Princeville Center..............................C3

Princeville Yoga
YOGA

(☎826-6688; www.princevilleyoga.com; Princeville Center, 5-4280 Kuhio Hwy; classes $15; ⊙9:15am Mon, Wed & Fri, 8am & 4:45pm Tue & Thu, 8am Sat) Specializing in the Beginning Bikram Yoga Hatha Series, Lynn Moffitt and her skilled team of yogis lead therapeutic classes for any and all willing to delve into the depths of a yoga class in a room that usually ranges from 95°F to 100°F.

Mana Yoga
YOGA

(☎826-9230, www.manayoga.com; 3812 Ahonui Pl; classes $20, private sessions per hr $80; ⊙8:30am Mon & Wed, 4pm Thu) It's no gimmick; Michaelle Edwards created her own version of yoga that has been known to make spines sing. Combining massage, yoga and spinal alignment, her style has proven to help heal via natural poses rather than contortionistic ones.

Halele'a Spa
SPA

(☎826-9644; www.stregisprinceville.com; St. Regis Princeville Resort, 5520 Ka Haku Rd; massages $165-245; ⊙9am-7pm) Translated as 'house of joy', this 11,000-sq-ft palatial escape offers massages, replete with couples and VIP treatment rooms. The aesthetics of the interior – use of native Hawaiian woods and natural fibers – implore sensorial consequence and the treatments are based upon a foundation of traditional Hawaiian medicine, using both botanical and ocean resources. The spa also houses a nail-and-hair salon and 24-hour fitness center.

QUEEN'S BATH

This deadly spot – formed by a sharp lava-rock shelf – has pools that provide a natural swimming hole. It's often hit by powerful waves, notorious for pulling visitors out to sea, as happens annually. Though the surf at times splashes in softly, it's the most deadly swimming hole on the island. What many people don't realize is that waves come in sets, which means a 15-to-20 minute flat period could be followed by a 10ft to 15ft wave, seemingly out of nowhere. People die here every year, most commonly by walking along the ledge used to access it. We recommend staying away.

Helicopter Rides

Leaving out of both Lihu'e and Princeville airports, Heli USA Airways (☎826-6591, 866-936-1234; www.heliusahawaii.com; 55min tour $267) offers convenience if you're on the North Shore; however, it was one of two companies on the island to have a fatal crash in 2007, so its safety record is less than perfect. Also operating out of both airports is Sunshine Helicopters (☎270-3999; www.sunshinehelicopters.com/kauai/tours/princeville_adventure.html; 40-50min tours $345, online bookings $285).

🛏 Sleeping

Princeville, with its abundance of vacation rentals, is devoid of the quaint B&Bs found in neighboring Kilauea and Hanalei and lacks much other than upper midrange to high-end options. Whether you're renting a condo or are in a resort, expect to dole out some cash, but it's worth it. Anyone who finds themselves within its central positioning on the North Shore and among its elevated tropical milieu – whether it's for a day, a week or a month – is one of the lucky ones. Having said that, with the recent economy's changing travel patterns, some real steals may be found by searching Vacation Rentals by Owners (www.vbro.com).

The following companies handle a large portion of condos, homes and resorts in Princeville:

Kauai Vacation Rentals
(☎866-922-5642; www.kauai-vacations-ahh.com)

Parrish Collection Kaua'i
(☎742-2000, 800-742-1412; www.parrishkauai.com)

Princeville Vacations
(☎800-800-3637, 828-6530; www.princeville-vacations.com; PO Box 223552)

⬛TOP CHOICE Mana Yoga Vacation Rental
VACATION RENTAL $$

(☎826-9230; www.kauainorthshorevacationrentals.com; Ahonui Pl; 2-bedroom apt $135; studio $100; 📶) Situated serenely on the private and very quiet Princeville Ranch property where the Mana Yoga Center is located, the larger apartment has all natural wood, teak cabinets and a tile floor. The lanai offers a vast 180-degree mountain view to contemplate and all the silence you could desire. Though more compact, the studio still boasts a king-size bed and a private lanai. Fresh coconuts, eggs and an orchard for the kids to run around in might just seal the deal.

A WHALE'S TALE

Every year from November to March thousands of those large loveable mammals make a 3000-mile oceanic voyage from their feeding grounds in Alaska to mate or give birth in the warm, welcoming waters of Kauai.

Holly's Kauai Condo CONDO $$
(☎826-8968; www.hollyskauaicondo.com; Ali'i Kai Resort, 3830 Edward Rd; 2br unit $150; ❋☎) Perched cliffside with nothing but water between you and Alaska, this 1200-sq-ft two-bedroom two-bath unit is a real deal. Wintertime (November to March) offers guaranteed whale sightings – basically from your bed – and the recently remodeled inside has HDTV, bamboo furnishings and new bedding and carpets.

Hanalei Bay Resort RESORT $$
(☎826-6522; www.hanaleibayresort.com; 5380 Hono'iki Rd; r from $149, 1br unit from $225; ❋☎☒) Location is the name of the game, and though some units are steeply priced, a changing economy has allowed for some real deals to pop up. New ownership has made it so only private units are rented out, which can be found at www.summitpacificinc.com or www.alohacondos.com. Units vary drastically in quality and not all carry wi-fi; be sure to inquire and request pictures.

Westin Ocean Resort RESORT $$$
(☎827-8700; www.starwoodhotels.com/westin/property/overview/index.html; 3838 Wyllie Rd; studio $225-650, 1 bedroom $300-885; ❋☎☒) Take advantage of this somewhat cheaper (though that word seems out of place) cliffside Starwood property. The views are expansive and winter (November to March) whale sightings only necessitate one to merely look out the window. Condolike 'villas' boast full kitchens, flat-screen TVs and washer-dryers while the studio units have kitchenettes. An in-house mini grocery and Starbucks are major conveniences and the poolside facilities are fanciful.

St Regis Princeville HOTEL $$$
(☎800-325-3589, 826-9644; www.stregisprinceville.com; 5520 Ka Haku Rd; r $200-3500; ❋☎☒) The aforementioned Oz at the end of the road in Princeville is what you've been dreaming of all your life. The 252 rooms terraced into the hillside overlooking Hanalei Bay range from slightly epic to 'what do I do with myself' extravagant. A 5000-sq-ft infinity pool with three hot tubs sits oceanside, with Pu'u Poa Beach just steps away. Even the 'cheapest' rooms are opulent. Decorated in a contemporary Hawaiian fashion, each has custom-designed furniture, one-way viewing glass and marble bathrooms. The higher-range options include your own round-the-clock butler service, which comes with a personal unpacker – because why not?

The following are condo complexes offering a variety of units:

Pali Ke Kua CONDO $$
(☎800-800-3637, 828-6530; www.princeville-vacations.com; 5300 Ka Haku Rd; 1 bedroom per night/weekly $140/$840, 2 bedroom $225/1350) Situated cliffside some units offer both ocean and mountain views. Easier alternative access to Pali Ke Kua (Hideaways) Beach is on property.

Sealodge CONDO $$
(☎800-800-3637, 828-6530; www.princeville-vacations.com; 3700 Kamehameha Rd; 1 bedroom per night/weekly $115/$700) Offers a swimming pool and both ocean and mountain views. Units can vary in quality, insist upon pictures.

Emmalani Court CONDO $$
(☎800-800-3637, 828-6530; www.princeville-vacations.com; 5250 Ka Haku Rd; 1 bedroom per night/week $125/$750, 2 bedroom $150/900) Adjacent to the Makai Golf Course, newly remodeled air-conditioned units are in a quieter part of town, are well kept, and have a pool; some offer ocean views.

✖ Eating

North Shore Café AMERICAN $
(Princeville Center; breakfast $2.75-5, lunch & dinner $8-22; ⊙6am-8pm Mon-Sat) For the cheapest hot breakfast in town, this gas-station watering hole offers up popular breakfast sandwiches and makes a decent pizza. The menu is one of the more creative you'll see, in a gas station. For light fair order the fresh falafel burger with tahini yogurt dressing. Or go straight to the source with one of their 'hefty burgers', which are all made with grass-fed Princeville beef. It's inside the Chevron gas station.

CJ's Steak & Seafood SEAFOOD, STEAKHOUSE $$
(Princeville Center, 5-4280 Kuhio Hwy; dinner mains $22-38; ⊙11:30am-2:30pm Mon-Fri & 6-9:30pm daily) CJ's is a Princeville standard thanks

partly to its cuisine of prime rib, lobster and fresh fish and partly to its lack of competition and ability to survive. Hearty dishes are all done up expertly, but without the frills (you won't find any wasabi marinades here). Salad-bar enthusiasts will froth over creative freedom given and the induced nostalgia for your favorite late-'70s steakhouse might even keep you coming back. Though CJ's may not dazzle, it will delight.

Nanea   HAWAII REGIONAL **$$$**
(Westin Princeville Ocean Resort Villas Clubhouse; breakfast $8-22, dinner mains $31-38; ☺6:30-10:30am & 5:30-9:30pm) With a few years to find its balance, Nanea has ironed out its kinks and proudly presents its elegant Hawaii fusion cuisine, serving dressed-down versions of gourmet dishes. Executive chef and Maui native Kahau Manzu, who cut his culinary teeth at Waikiki's renowned Moana Surfrider and at the Four Seasons Maui, craftily integrates island-grown produce, honey and Kilauea goat cheese.

Paradise Bar & Grill   AMERICAN, SEAFOOD **$$**
(Princeville Center, 5-4280 Kuhio Hwy; breakfast $8-13, lunch $10-14, dinner mains $11-22; ☺7-11am breakfast, 11am-5pm lunch, 5-10pm dinner) With a surfboard-laden ceiling, photographic testimonials on the walls and an actual surfboard-table in the bar (kids love it), there are some gems amongst its standard burger-and-fries menu. Highlights include macadamia-nut pancakes drizzled with a habit-forming homemade syrup, the island's best fresh fish sandwich or salad (get it Cajun-style) and a spot-on garlic shrimp platter. Two more words: adult milkshakes.

The Tavern at Princeville   HAWAIIAN **$$**
(☏826-8700; 5-3900 Kuhio Hwy; mains $28-36; ☺11am-4pm & 5-9:30pm) While 'tavern' might suggest some plebeian-occupied pub, this is Princeville and an offspring of revered Chef Roy Yamaguchi. Randomly situated – it occupies the bottom corner of **The Prince Clubhouse** (p508) – the atmosphere can feel hollow but the service borders on theatrically precise. Complimentary popcorn and a creative drink menu set a unique pace, which may maintain or fizzle. The menu, which at times proves inefficiently ambitious, has some gaps. We're certain the kinks at this newbie will get worked out.

Infigo's   AMERICAN, HAWAIIAN **$$**
(Pali Ke Kua Condo Complex, 5300 Ka Haku Rd; mains $18-28; ☺Mon-Wed & Fri-Sun 5:30-9:30pm) With paint still drying at the time

of research, this new venture in an old location has come hot out of the gates. Chef Nicolas Salvi churns out some inspiring dishes. Not yet with a liquor license, they welcome bottles of wine ($7 corkage fee), though two may be more appropriate as the relaxed atmosphere is most evident in the service. Live music and innovative approaches to fish, ribs, chicken and beef are quickly stimulating a reputation. Tricky to find; if you see the ocean, you just missed the turn.

Federico's   MEXICAN **$$**
(Princeville Center; tacos & burritos $12; ☺9am-8pm Mon-Sat) Serves fresh-mex-style cuisine. Keep an eye out for their daily specials and daily juice concoctions.

Tamarind   THAI **$$**
(Princeville Center; curries $12; ☺11am-8pm) Has standard curries on the sweet side and a mean Thai tea with coconut milk.

Lei Petite Cafe & Bakery   COFFEESHOP **$**
(Princeville Center, 5-4280 Kuhio Hwy; lattes $3; ☺6:30am-4pm) Princeville's premier caffeine station covers all pep-related drinks and offers bagels, muffin-tops, scones and chocolate covered strawberries.

Lappert's Ice Cream   ICE CREAM **$**
(Princeville Center, 5-4280 Kuhio Hwy; ☺10am-9pm) The sweet smell from the waffle cones beckons, and the delectable locally inspired options are sure not to disappoint. Don't miss out.

Foodland   SUPERMARKET **$**
(☏826-9880; Princeville Center, 5-4280 Kuhio Hwy; ☺6am-11pm) The biggest supermarket on the North Shore, Foodland has an abundance of fresh produce, prepared sushi, wine, beer and liquor. It has a better selection overall than Hanalei's Big Save.

🍷 Drinking & Entertainment

Lobby Bar at St Regis Princeville LIVE MUSIC
(www.princevillehotelhawaii.com; 5520 Ka Haku Rd; ☺3:30-11pm) Don't let the elegance or the enormous crystal raindrop chandelier intimidate you; the lobby bar is for any and all wanting to cruise and take a load off. The vibe is a step more welcoming than its seemingly chichi surroundings, but don't worry – most everybody else will feel as out of place as you. Relax, you made it; now enjoy the ultimate location for a sunset cocktail.

ℹ Information

Chevron Gas Station (Kuhio Hwy; ⊘6am-10pm Mon-Sat, to 9pm Sun) The last fuel option before the end of the road.

INTERNET ACCESS Princeville Mail Service Center (☑826-7331; Princeville Center, 5-4280 Kuhio Hwy; ⊘9am-5pm Mon-Fri; @) Offers FedEx, copying, computing and even dry-cleaning services.

MONEY Banks with 24-hour ATMs:

Bank of Hawaii (☑826-6551; Prineville Shopping Center; ⊘8:30am-4pm Mon-Thu, to 6pm Fri)

First Hawaiian Bank (☑826-1560; Princeville Shopping Center; ⊘8:30am-4pm Mon-Thu, to 6pm Fri)

Post Office (☑800-275-8777; Princeville Center; ⊘10:30am-3:30pm Mon-Fri, to 12:30pm Sat) In the shopping center.

ℹ Getting There & Around

Princeville is great for walking or cruising on bicycle, with one main arterial road (Ka Haku Rd) running through the middle.

Ride on Kauai (☑652-8958; rideonkauai@yahoo.com; per day/week $20/80; ⊘8am-8pm) Offers drop-off, pick-up, and repair services for its fleet of beach cruisers (soon to have mountain bikes) to the entire North Shore (Kilauea to Haena). Rental deliveries are in the morning and require 12-hour advance notice. They even have a couple of bikes with baby seats.

The Kauai Bus Stops hourly across the street from the Princeville Center on Kuhio Hwy. For more info see p467.

Hanalei Valley

There is a mist that hovers above this gem green valley, dense with deep *kalo loi* (taro fields), where fertile ground has been the lifeblood of taro for centuries. Here, expect sightings of native Hawaiian wildlife, gushing waterfalls, stubborn mountains and afternoon rainbows.

The 1912 landmark **Hanalei Bridge** (Map p509) is the first of seven bridges to cross the Hanalei River and lead you to the famed 'end of the road.' The bridge forces you to stop and appreciate the sleepiness of the North Shore. Thanks to this landmark, big trucks, buses or road-ragers can't ravage this serene little entrance to Hanalei.

Undulating, winding strips of road are canopied by mammoth trees with glimpses here and there of ocean, valley or river. The **Hanalei Valley Scenic Drive** makes driving special when heading north on 'the road' to

its end (in Ha'ena). Princeville offers some of the first famous North Shore views from its **Hanalei Valley Lookout**. To get here, turn left onto Ohiki Rd immediately after the Hanalei Bridge. You can enter the Hanalei National Wildlife Refugeon the Ho'opulapula Haraguchi Rice Mill Tour.

Hanalei

POP 514

The surfer-chic town of Hanalei has more than its fair share of adults with Peter Pan syndrome and kids with seemingly Olympian athletic prowess. A stroll down beachfront Weke Rd and you'll see men in their 60s waxing their surfboards and young 'uns carrying their 'guns' (ie big-wave surfboards) to the beach. Without a doubt, beach life is *the* life here.

☂ Beaches

Hanalei Bay   BEACH

Palisades, a crescent-shaped bay and a boatload of surfers make Hanalei Bay typify what many envision when thinking of Kaua'i. Made up of four beaches (really one beach, divided into four sections with four names), there's something for almost everyone here: sunbathing, bodyboarding and surfing. The winter months can make this stretch of water an experts-only spot, though in summer months the water is sometimes so calm it's hard to distinguish between sky and sea, but for the smattering of yachts bobbing on the horizon. Black Pot Beach Park (Hanalei Pier) and Wai'oli (Pine Trees) Beach Park offer showers, restrooms, drinking water, picnic tables and grills. Family-wise, Hanalei Beach Park Pavilion is best, with facilities and lifeguards.

Hanalei Beach Park Pavilion   BEACH PARK

With its lifeguards and sweeping views, this is a great place for a picnic, sunset or lazy day at the beach. Ideally located, its downside is the parking, which can be a challenge. Park along Weke Rd if you have to, as it can get crowded.

Black Pot Beach Park
(Hanalei Pier)   BEACH PARK

This is one of the most crowded beaches within the already-popular Hanalei Bay. Of course, its appeal is undeniable. Keep an eye out for particularly stunning views of Namolokama over the bay, when Wai'oli Falls has been rejuvenated by a previous night's rain.

Wai'oli (Pine Trees) Beach Park   BEACH PARK

A less popular but equally beautiful spot, Pine Trees beach is dominated by locals. The shorebreak is harder here than any other spot on Hanalei Bay and swimming is dangerous, except during the calmest summer surf. The park has restrooms and showers.

Waikokos   BEACH

Catch rights and lefts at Waikokos break, protected by a reef on the western bend of Hanalei Bay. To get there, park on the side of the main highway and trek a short walk near the 4- and 5-mile markers. Winter surfing is sometimes good off Makahoa Point, the western point of the bay.

Middles   BEACH

The area known as Middles (Map p500) is set in the middle of two breaks: between Waikokos and Pine Trees, outside (as in 'outside the reef') and to the left. An area on the inside of the reef going north is dubbed 'Grandpas' by surfers.

◉ Sights & Activities

Though not the largest or most sacred river in the state (the Wailua River holds that honor) the Hanalei River's 6 miles (roughly) are scenic, calm, safe and ideal for novice kayakers. And though it may be your first time, Hanalei Bay will probably be the nicest place you'll ever surf.

Wai'oli Hui'ia Church & Wai'oli Mission House   CHURCH

Built in 1912, this historic church and accompanying house (built 1936) lend some context to the picturesque, verdant green grass with Mt Namolokama as a backdrop. The church's setting and artifacts give a small glimpse of the days of missionaries on the island.

Ocean Quest Watersports   DIVING

(☑742-6991, 800-972-3078; www.fathomfive.com; ⊙dives 7am, 7:30am & 1pm Mon-Fri, North Shore dives Mar-Oct) The satellite location of the Fathom Five outfit in Koloa is geared for a North Shore dive at Tunnels. It's PADI certified. Newbies can do introductory dives with a one-hour academic lesson; one-/two-tank dives cost around $115/125. The staff will bring the gear to you.

North Shore Divers   DIVING

(☑828-1223; www.northshoredivers.com; ⊙dives 8am, 11am, 1pm Mon-Fri, North Shore dives Mar-Oct; 1st-time divers 1-/2-tank dives $109/169.) If you're certified, a one-tank dive costs $79 and a two-tank dive $119 per person at North Shore Divers. For an unforgettable experience, try night diving (summer only) for $99. An open-water certification course is $450. Meet at the beach.

Kayak Kauai   KAYAKING, STAND UP PADDLING

(☑826-9844; s/d rental per 24hr $29/54, Paddle Boards per 24hr $45; ⊙8am-5pm, to 8pm summer) Kayak Kauai offers kayaks, stand up paddle boards and a variety of outdoor gear. There's a convenient river-launch sight on the property. Find it across the street from Postcards Café.

⌐TOP⌐CHOICE Kauai Island Experience   STAND UP PADDLE SURFING

(☑346-3094; www.kauaiexperience.com; 2hr private/group lesson $125/80) Leading all the way follow into a plethora of land and sea activities, they give a pleasant introduction to this core-flexing sport.

Mitchell Alapa   STAND UP PADDLE SURFING

(☑482-0749; private lesson $75; ⊙8am-2pm) This long-time Kaua'i surfer and his wave-charging son will get you afloat in no time.

Na Pali Explorer   SNORKELING

(☑338-9999, 877-335-9909; www.napali-explorer.com; Kaumuali'i Hwy; 5hr tour adult/child $125/85) Does snorkeling trips on rigid-hull inflatable rafts (hard bottom, inflatable sides), smoother than the all-inflatable Zodiacs. Expect between 16 and 35 passengers. The 48ft raft includes a restroom and canopy for shade. Runs out of Hanalei Bay from April to October.

Na Pali Catamaran   SNORKELING CRUISE

(☑826-6853, 866-255-6853; www.napalicatamaran.com; 4hr tours adult/child $135/110; ⊙morning & afternoon May-Sep) Depending on the waves and the time of year, you might get to venture into some sea caves. Remember though, it pounds and there's no reprieve from the elements.

Captain Sundown   SNORKELING CRUISE

(☑826-5585; www.captainsundown.com; 6hr tour adult/child $162/148) Captain Sundown operates out of Lihu'e most of the year, so take advantage and use this outlet if you're here during summer. A true character, Captain Bob has more than 38 years' experience and takes a lot of pride in what he does.

Hanalei

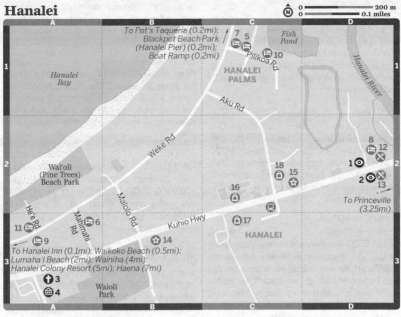

Hanalei

⊙ Sights

Hanalei Surf Company	(see 17)
Hanalei Surf Company Backdoor Store	(see 16)
1 Kayak Kaua'i	D2
2 Na Pali Kayak	D2
3 Wai'oli Hui'ia Church	A3
4 Wai'oli Mission Hall	A3
Wai'oli Mission House	(see 4)
Yoga Hanalei	(see 17)

🛏 Sleeping

5 Bed, Breakfast & Beach at Hanalei	C1
6 Blu Nui Cottage	A3
7 Hale Reed Apartment	C1
8 Hanalei Riverside Cottages	D2
9 Hanalei Surfboard House	A3
10 Ohana Hanalei	C1
11 Pine Trees Beach House	A3

✗ Eating

Big Save	(see 16)
Hanalei Coffee Roasters	(see 17)
12 Hanalei Dolphin Fish Market	D2
Hanalei Dolphin Restaurant & Sushi Lounge	(see 12)
Hanalei Pizza	(see 16)
Harvest Market	(see 17)
Neide's Salsa Samba	(see 17)
13 Postcards Cafe	D2

Drinking

Bar Acuda	(see 17)

✪ Entertainment

Hanalei Gourmet	(see 17)
14 Hawaiian Slack Key Guitar Concerts	B3
15 Tahiti Nui	C2

🛍 Shopping

aFeinPhoto Gallery	(see 18)
Backdoor	(see 16)
Bikini Room	(see 18)
16 Ching Young Village	C2
Evolve Love Gallery	(see 16)
17 Hanalei Center	C3
Hanalei Paddler	(see 17)
Hanalei Surf Company	(see 17)
18 Kauai Nut Roasters	C2
Root	(see 18)

Aloha Surf & Kitesurfing School
KITESURFING

(☑826-1517, 635-9283; 3 lessons $195) It looks hard-core fun and you want to try it. We don't blame you. The three-lesson kitesurfing package offered at this school covers basic-land to advanced-water training. Lessons by appointment only

TOP CHOICE ### Hanalei Surf Company
SURFING

(☑826-9000; www.hanaleisurf.com; Hanalei Center, 5-5161 Kuhio Hwy; 2½hr lesson $65-150, surfboards per day/week $15/65, bodyboards $5/20; ☺8am-9pm) Surf instructors Russell Lewis and Ian Vernon have an excellent reputation and are especially suited to teaching advanced surfers.

Hanalei Surf Company Backdoor Store
SURFING

(☑826-9000; www.hanaleisurf.com; Ching Young Village; 2hr group/couple lesson per person $65/75, private lesson $150, surfboards per day $20, bodyboards $6; ☺8am-9pm) This outfit rents out a selection of longboards and high-performance shortboards, as well as bodyboards. You can get insurance, too. Lessons are available by appointment.

Hawaiian School of Surfing
SURFING

(☑652-1116; 1½hr lesson $65; ☺lessons 8am, 10am & noon) Stop by or call in advance for a lesson with legendary pro big-wave surfer Titus Kinimaka or, more likely, one of his minions, who line up the boards and red rashguards daily at the pier. No more than three students per instructor.

Hawaiian Surfing Adventures
SURFING

(☑482-0749; www.hawaiiansurfingadventures.com; 2hr group/private lesson $45/95, surfboards per day/week $30/100; ☺8am-2pm) The generous lessons offered by this organization include a half-hour on land, one hour in the water and another hour of solo practice. Look for the yellow rashguards on the beach.

Kayak Kaua'i
SURFING

(Map p515; ☑826-9844; www.kayakkauai.com; Kuhio Hwy; 1hr lesson $50, surfboards/bodyboards per day $20/6; ☺10am & 2pm) If you rent gear for four days, you get an additional three days free.

Hawaiian Surfing Adventures
OUTRIGGER CANOEING

(☑482-0749; www.hawaiiansurfingadventures.com; 2hr tours per person for 1/2/3/4 people $200/100/75/45; ☺8am-2pm) A great workout and a great glimpse into this inspired Polynesian tradition; chances are you'll see marine life, too.

Island Sails
HAWAIIAN SAILING CANOE

(Map p500; ☑212-6053; http://islandsailskauai.com/home; 1½hr tours, morning snorkel trip adult/child $85/65; ☺9-10:30am, 3:30-5pm, 5:30pm-sunset) Whether snorkeling in the morning, cruising in the afternoon or taking in a sunset on the water, here's your chance to get a taste of the traditional Polynesian sailing canoe.

Yoga Hanalei
YOGA

(☑826-9642; www.yogahanalei.com; Hanalei Center, 2nd fl, 5-5161E Kuhio Hwy; classes $15) Mid-morning classes at this studio are more active, and can get pretty tight; if you're looking for something more mellow, come later in the day. The handful of teachers who take the lessons here were all one-time students of Bhavani Maki, who leads the Asthanga-based studio serving the Hanalei Valley.

BEHIND THE CURTAINS

The Okolehao Trail (Map p500) offers panoramic views of patches of Hanalei taro plots, the Kilauea Lighthouse, and the start of the Na Pali Coast. Rumored to be named for 'moonshine,' it refers to the distilled liquor made from the roots of ti plants during Prohibition.

The first half-mile is a bit of a climb which, while eliminating the possibility of trail-traffic, means a fairly quiet hike (except for your heavy breathing), and the visual spoils are worth your while. After the initial vista at the power-line tower, the 2.25-mile trail continues gradually upward, offering numerous photo opportunities and ends 1250ft above the slow shuffle of Hanalei. Bring water.

To get to the trailhead, take your first left after Hanalei's first one-way bridge heading north, along Rice Mill Rd. Go down the road about half a mile to a parking lot across from the start of the trail.

Tours

Ho'opulapula Haraguchi Rice Mill   TOUR
(Map p500; ☑651-3399; www.haraguchiricemill.
org; Kuhio Hwy; 3hr tour incl lunch per person $65;
☺tours 10am Wed) The Haraguchi family,
which also owns the Hanalei Taro & Juice
Company, offers tours (by appointment
only) of its historic rice mill and wetland
taro farm. See the otherwise inaccessible
Hanalei National Wildlife Refuge and learn
about Hawaii's immigrant history. The family helps run the biennial (even-numbered
years) **Hanalei Taro Festival**, all about
growing and cooking this surprisingly tasty
native staple.

⌂ Sleeping

Ohana Hanalei   STUDIO $$
(☑826-4116; www.hanalei-kauai.com; Pilikoa Rd;
r per day/week $115/750) It's amazing how
cheap this studio is given the location, a
mere half-block from the beach. It has its
own kitchenette, private entrance, phone,
cable TV and convenient parking. A cozy
porch table allows for pleasant (or romantic)
meals and the bikes and beach chairs have
you beach-ready from the get-go.

**Bed, Breakfast & Beach at
Hanalei**   VACATION RENTAL $$
(☑826-6111; www.bestvacationinparadise.com;
Pilikoa Rd; r $120-170; 🛜) The location is ideal,
with waves clearly audible and nearly visible. The jovial house manager is essentially an on-site tour guide–culinary executive
who daily serves a spot-on breakfast of lem-
on-coconut coffee cake or banana pancakes
with syrup. The three smallish rooms – basic with queen beds and private bathrooms
– are most suitable for couples or singles, as
the owner prefers no families for neighborhood disturbance reasons.

Pine Trees Beach House   INN $$
(☑826-9333; www.hanaleibayinn.com; 5404 Weke
Rd; r/studio/apt $69/$159/$279; 🛜) On the
frontage road of Hanalei Bay, options here
range from an embellished closet with a
twin bed and some silverware (perfect for
the low-maintenance surfer) or a cool (tem-
perature-wise) downstairs studio apart-
ment with queen bed and pull-out couch to
a 1200 -sq-ft airy upstairs space with a surf-
checking loft, Italian marble floor, snazzy
kitchen and even a stripper pole (bought
from Larry Flynt and used by Demi Moore
to train for the movie *Striptease*).

Hanalei Surfboard House   INN $$
(☑826-9825; www.hanaleisurfboardhouse.com;
5459 Weke Rd; r $175-225; ❄🛜) A work of art
and just a one-minute walk to the beach,
this uberstylish property is a surfer's haven.
Two of the 400-sq-ft rooms feature unique
vintage Hawaiiana decor, as well as a lanai
with a BBQ grill. The more spacious 'love
shack' is decked out in old-school '60s style,
and features a shower floor handcrafted
with Kaua'i sand, air-conditioning and a
surround-sound stereo. The ever-mellow
owner sets the pace for this enchanting
house.

Hanalei Riverside Cottages   COTTAGE $$
(☑826-1675; www.hanaleidolphin.com/kauai
vacationrental.html; 5-5016 Kuhio Hwy; 2 bedroom
per night/week $200/1000; 🛜) Staying here,
you can launch a canoe, kayak or stand up
paddleboard right from your backyard on
the Hanalei River. A stone's throw from the
heart of Hanalei town, each cottage is styled
in a similar fashion, with bamboo furniture,
full kitchens, outdoor (and indoor) showers,
front-of-house bedrooms and airy quasi-
lounge areas facing the river, some of which
could be used as a third bedroom.

Hale Reed Apartment   VACATION RENTAL $$
(☑826-6741; www.hanalei-vacation.com; 4441 Pi-
likoa Rd; 2 bedroom apt per week from $1200; 🛜)
Situated approximately 89 paces from the
white sand of Hanalei Bay, location is key
here. This ground floor apartment has a
full kitchen and a patio perfect for cooking
on. With one queen bed and two twins (that
could be made into a king), it can sleep up
to four people. Its semi-outdated decor is
acceptable, and more than made up for by
its exceptional location. Inquire about the
security deposit.

Hanalei Inn   INN $$
(☑826-9333; www.hanaleiinn.com; 5-5468 Kuhio
Hwy; r $139; 🛜) The four studios here –
which each have kitchen, HDTV and classic

HOMAGE TO KALO

According to Hawaiian cosmology, *Papa* (earth mother) and *Wakea* (sky father; who also gave birth to the Hawaiian Islands), gave birth to *Haloa*, a stillborn and brother to man. Haloa was planted in the earth, and from his body came taro *(kalo)*, a plant that has long sustained the Hawaiian people and been a staple for oceanic cultures.

Kalo is still considered a sacred food, full of tradition and spirituality for Native Hawaiians. The North Shore's Hanalei is home to the largest taro-producing farm in the state, where the purple, starchy potatolike plant is grown in pondfields known as *lo'i kalo* (Hawaiian wet taro fields). After crossing the first of several one-way bridges in Hanalei, you'll notice the *kalo* growing to the left.

Kalo regained the spotlight in the '70s thanks to the 'Hawaiian Renaissance,' a time during which some aspects of the Hawaiian culture enjoyed a modest, long-overdue resurgence and reclaimed practice. Though dismissed by some outsiders as little more than a glorified, garnet-colored potato, *kalo* is rich in nutrients. It is often boiled and pounded into poi, an earthy, starchy and somewhat sweet and sticky, puddinglike dish.

Families enjoy poi, defined as the 'staff of life' in the Hawaiian dictionary, a number of ways. Some prefer it fresh, while others prefer sour poi, or poi *'awa 'awa* (bitter), possibly from the method in which poi used to be served – often it sat in a bowl on the table for quite some time.

All traditional Hawaiian households show respect for taro: when the poi bowl sits on the table, one is expected to refrain from arguing or speaking in anger. That's because any bad energy is *'ino* (evil) – and can spoil the poi.

A tip: because of the spiritual relevance and cultural history of *kalo*, it's disrespectful to dismiss it as bland. If you happen upon one of many luaus on the island that include *kalo*-based poi in their smorgasbord, don't jump on the bandwagon to call it 'wallpaper paste.' It's an insult.

retro furnishings from the once famed but now dilapidated Coco Palms resort – are in an ideal locale. The on-site manager, ex-'movie-star' Bill Gaus (he was an extra in Andrew Bergman's 1992 film *Honeymoon in Vegas*), works side by side with Yin-Yang, the resident cat, to maintain a simple and serene environment. Stay for a week, pay no taxes.

Blu Nui Cottage COTTAGE **$$**
(☑800-488-3336, 826-9622; 4435 Mahimahi Rd; 2 bedroom per week $1500; 🕾) Epic mountain views are to be had from the front porch and from inside this 800-sq-ft abode, which boasts a spacious living room and a Roman-inspired wood-framed lounge chair that should come with a personal grape-feeder. There are also two bedrooms with queen beds, which share a single bathroom in the hallway. Additional features and facilities include a covered back patio with a BBQ, a kid-friendly yard with room to run around in, private parking, and Hanalei town and Hanalei Bay each an equally walkable distance in either direction.

✗ Eating

With an eating establishment every 10ft, there should be something for everyone.

 Bar Acuda Tapas & Wine TAPAS **$$$**
(Hanalei Center; tapas, $8-15; mains $22-30; 🕙6-9:30pm) A trendy wine and tapas scene presents ornately plated food that's noteworthy, but expensive. Pluses include inventive sustainability-driven uses of local products, like North Shore honeycomb, Kunana Farms goat cheese plus Mizuna greens and apples. With a 'see and be seen' atmosphere for some, service is impeccable from start to finish and musical selections perpetuate the feeling that you're in a classy movie.

Postcards Café HAWAII REGIONAL **$$**
(www.postcardscafe.com; 5-5075 Kuhio Hwy; mains $18-27; 🕙6-9pm) With a cottagelike ambience and a humble, charming innocence this vegetarian-friendly (meat is served as well) locale could just as easily be found in New England or on a French hillside. Dishes served have a sophisticated simplicity and will induce nostalgia, just

like a Robert Redford film does. The friendly family-like wait staff aims to please and group reservations are recommended.

Neide's Salsa Samba
BRAZILIAN $$

(Hanalei Center; dishes $9-17; ⊙11am-2:30pm & 5-9pm) Hidden in the back of the Hanalei Center, the food platters are abundant and the margaritas can flow too quickly. The more original items on the menu include *muqueca* (fresh fish with coconut sauce), *ensopado* (baked chicken and vegetables) and *bife acebolado* (beefsteak with onions). A rich atmosphere of Brazilian vibes helps balance out the at-times listless service.

Hanalei Dolphin Restaurant & Sushi Lounge
SEAFOOD, SUSHI $$

(www.hanaleidolphin.com; 5-5016 Kuhio Hwy; lunch/dinner mains $14/21, sushi $11-20; ⊙11:30am-3pm, 5:30-9pm) One of the oldest establishments in Hanalei (over 30 years), the 'Dolphin' is a vivacious environment where every meal feels like a celebration. The slow-roasted menu is abundant and the incisive sushi chefs will play culinary jazz with their uberfresh fish, if decision-making is not your forte. Lunch is served riverside and sushi-bar seating fills up quickly. Final tip: one dolphin ice-cream pie, two forks.

Hanalei Pizza
PIZZA $$

(Chin Young Village; slices $4-5, pies $20-30; ⊙11am-8:30pm) Tasty pizza with a mellow musically driven atmosphere. Instruments hanging on the walls beckon any takers the chance to show their chops. Traveling musicians are welcome to bargain a play-for-pie deal, but you best bring your skills. Keep an eye out for discounted closing time throwaway slices.

Harvest Market
CAFE $$

(Hanalei Center, 5-5161 Kuhio Hwy; smoothies $7, salads by weight; ⊙9am-8pm) If you like to treat your body well, there's a decent selection of organic snacks and products and with a locavore touch. Be frugal if you approach the salad bar, smoothie station or weighable-snack section (dried fruit, nuts and such), as prices can sneak up on you.

Hanalei Coffee Roasters
CAFE $

(www.hanaleicoffeeroasters.com; Hanalei Center; lattes $4.50, lunch $7.95; ⊙6:30am-6pm) The atmosphere isn't the only thing buzzing. Coffee infusions are strong, the quiche and Chef Bob's carrot cake are spot on, and the stellar social

and musical vibes will permeate your psyche. Well, that may have been the caffeine talking.

Pat's Taqueria
ISLAND CONTEMPORARY $

(parking lot, Hanalei pier; ⊙noon-3pm) If you're by the pier or prefer a more on-the-go munch, this is the place, where a couple of mahimahi tacos or a chicken or beef quesadilla will only set you back $5 to $8. Cash only.

Hanalei Dolphin Fish Market
FISH MARKET $$

(5-5016 Kuhio Hwy; ⊙10am-7pm) Possibly the quietest deal in town; they serve an aggressive $9 spicy ahi roll. There's parking around the back.

Self-Catering

Big Save
SUPERMARKET

(Ching Young Village; ⊙7am-9pm) Has an ATM and any necessary basic grocery items you might need.

 ## Drinking & Entertainment

Hawaiian Slack Key Guitar Concerts
LIVE MUSIC

(www.hawaiianslackkeyguitar.com; Hanalei Community Center; adult/child $10/8; ⊙4pm Fri & 3pm Sun) You'll find slack key guitar and ukulele concerts performed by longtime musicians Doug and Sandy McMaster year-round here, in a refreshingly informal atmosphere.

Tahiti Nui
RESTAURANT, BAR

(www.thenui.com; 5-5134 Kuhio Hwy; ⊙lunch noon-3pm, dinner 5-9pm, bar weeknights/weekends to 12:30/1:30am) The only place open past 10pm or so.

Hanalei Gourmet
RESTAURANT, BAR

(www.hanaleigourmet.com; Hanalei Center; ⊙music 8:30-10:30pm) Playful-rowdy at times but still family friendly. Nightly musical acts range from traditional Hawaiian to acoustic covers.

Bar Acuda
RESTAURANT, BAR

(Hanalei Center; www.restaurantbaracuda.com; ⊙6-10pm Tue-Sat) Has a sleek, albeit confined, bar scene offering visitors an opportunity to sport their best threads. The communal table is great for an après-meal dessert and wine.

Shopping

Ching Young Village has some great spots for outfitting yourself in some Kaua'i chic, while the Hanalei Center is where many a Kaua'i surfer girl, and most of the clothing that typifies the North Shore, can be found.

TAHITI NUI'S GLORY DAYS

The Tahiti Nui (☑826-6277; Tahiti Nui Bldg, Kuhio Hwy; ⊙2pm-2am) has changed hands and menus, and seen its fair share of dated hairdos, barflies and beer bellies. But there's a part of 'the Nui' that always seems to remain the same. It's the liveliest spot in little Hanalei, and, though certainly a dive, it remains *the* North Shore joint par excellence for regulars and visitors alike.

In 1964 a Tahitian woman named Louise Hauata and her husband Bruce Marston, founded the now iconic Tahiti Nui, a classic South Seas–style restaurant and bar. Its popularity grew and so did its draw – luring such names as Jacqueline Kennedy, who legendarily arrived unexpectedly, preceded by secret service agents. Yet despite the fact that it's seen its share of A-listers, you'd never guess it at first glance.

Bruce died in 1975, but Louise continued the spot's luau tradition, augmenting it with renditions of Tahitian songs in English, French or their original language. She was also well known for giving much aloha to her community in times of need.

Louise died in 2003, and Tahiti Nui is now run by her son Christian Marston, her nephew William Marston, and the president and CEO, John Austin, who is married to celebrated singer Amy Hanaiali'i Gilliom.

The Nui remains a lively, loud hangout long after its happy hours (from 4pm to 6pm Monday to Saturday and all day Sunday) and police regularly set up shop outside its doors around 2am to ensure no one's drinking and driving.

Though this crowded shacklike bar is divey, the staff are some of the most down-to-earth bartenders on the island.

TOP CHOICE **Kauai Nut Roasters** FOOD
(www.kauainutroasters.com; 4484 Aku Rd; packages $6-7; ⊙10am-6:30pm) Some of the most delicious treats you can find are in these unassuming little packages, bursting with sweetness. Coconut, wasabi, lavender, sesame, butterscotch or praline flavors rank tops. Be sure to wash down the free samples with the alkaline-heavy ionized water, said to have great health benefits.

Hanalei Surf Company CLOTHING, OUTDOOR GEAR
(www.hanaleisurf.com; Hanalei Center, 5-5161 Kuhio Hwy; ⊙8am-9pm) Surf, surf, surf is its MO. Surfer-girl earrings, bikinis, rashies and guys' boardshorts, slippers and all the surf gear you might need: wax, shades and even the board itself.

Backdoor CLOTHING, OUTDOOR GEAR
(Ching Young Village; 5-5190 Kuhio Hwy; ⊙9am-9pm) The same owner as Hanalei Surf Company extends the range to Los Angeles–inspired name brands and the skating lifestyle, harkening back to the days of Tony Hawk, Velcro and checker-pattern vans.

aFeinPhoto Gallery GALLERY
(4489 Aku Rd; www.afeinbergphotography.com; ☑634-5804; ⊙10:30am-7pm) Photographer Aaron Feinberg endlessly creates international award-winning fine-art landscapes of Kaua'i and beyond.

Hanalei Paddler CLOTHING
(Hanalei Center; ⊙9am-8pm) Don't miss out on the surfer-chic workout threads by Andrea Smith (www.brasilbazar.com). Paddlers and surfer girls alike show up here in droves.

Evolve Love Gallery SOUVENIRS
(Ching Young Village; ⊙10am-6pm) Chock-full of vibrant, inspired paintings, batiks and some serious sea bling. Ni'ihau shell and pearls are among the jewels adorning the work.

Bikini Room CLOTHING
(www.thebikiniroom.com; 4489 Aku Rd; ⊙10am-5pm, to 2pm Sun) They're itsy bitsy and teeny weenie, but include cheetah and a variety of wild, vibrant prints instead of the usual polka dot. Great for those blessed with a body that just won't quit.

The Root CLOTHING
(4489 Aku Rd; ⊙9:30am-7:30pm, noon-5pm Sun) This North Shore spot opted out of carrying swimwear. Instead it offers unique lingerie, sleepwear, beachwear, shoes, surfer clothes and yoga gear.

ℹ Information

Hanalei has no bank, but there is an ATM in the Ching Young Village's Big Save supermarket.
Bali Hai Photo (☑826-9181; Ching Young Village; internet per hr $9; ⊙8am-8pm Mon-Fri, 9am-5pm Sat, 10am-5pm Sun)

Post office (📞800-275-8777; 5-5226 Kuhio Hwy) On the *makai* (seaward) side of the road, just west of the Big Save shopping center.

❶ Getting There & Around

There's one road in and one road out. Parking can be a headache, and absent-minded pedestrians even more so. So do as the locals do and hop on a bike. Everything in Hanalei is walkable.

Pedal & Paddle (📞826-9069; www.pedalnpaddle.com; Ching Young Village; ⊙9am-6pm) For cruisers ($10/30 per day/week) and mountain bikes ($20/80).

Kayak Kaua'i (📞826-9844; www.kayakkauai.com; ⊙8am-5pm) Also has cruisers ($15/60 per day/week).

Ride on Kauai (rideonkauai@yaho.com; 📞652-8958; cruisers per day/week $20/80; ⊙8am-8pm) Delivers beach cruisers to the entire North Shore.

Around Hanalei

LUMAHA'I BEACH

Movie tours may claim that Lumaha'i Beach is where Burt Lancaster and Deborah Kerr kissed in *that* scene in *From Here to Eternity*, but it's not (the scene was shot at Halona Cove on O'ahu). Lumaha'i enjoys a rather more infamous status as one of the most dangerous on-island spots, as many have drowned here.

Rather than a swim, we recommend a safe-but-still-scenic stroll (which still requires being water savvy). There are two ways onto Lumaha'i Beach. The first and more scenic is a three-minute walk that begins at the parking area 0.75 miles past the 4-mile marker on the Kuhio Hwy. The trail slopes to the left at the end of the retaining wall. On the beach, the lava-rock ledges are popular for sunbathing and photo ops, but beware: bystanders have been washed away by high surf and rogue waves.

The other way to access Lumaha'i is along the road at sea level at the western end of the beach, just before crossing the Lumaha'i River Bridge. The beach at this end is lined with ironwood trees.

WAINIHA

Wainiha Valley remains as it did in the old days: a holdout for Native Hawaiians, though some vacation rentals have encroached into the area. It's not as vacation-ready as its neighboring areas east or west, and an unwelcome vibe is not uncommon. When the locals stare you down, don't take it personally.

🛏 Sleeping & Eating

The Guesthouse at River Estate   VACATION RENTAL $$$
(Map p500); 📞826-5118, 800-390-8444; www.riverestate.com; house per night/week $275/1850; ❋🛜) Airy, huge and open – it's pricey, but one look and you'll see why. It's located mid-jungle and features a master bedroom with a king bed, a second room with queen bed, a decked-out kitchen, a wraparound lanai, air-con and anything else you could possibly need.

The Riverhouse at River Estate   VACATION RENTAL $$$
(Map p500; 📞800-390-8444, 826 5118; www.riverestate.com; house per night/week $300/1925; ❋🛜) Resting on stilts 30ft above the Wainiha River, it's fit for honeymooners wanting space or a family. Brazilian hardwood floors and marble countertops ooze comfort and the screened-in lanai allows for mosquito-free BBQs or soaks in the hot tub (mini). A 10-minute drive to the Na Pali Coast to the west and Hanalei town to the east place this enchanting abode not in the middle of nowhere, but everywhere.

Coco Cabana Cottage   COTTAGE $$
(Map p500; 📞826-5141; www.kauaivacation.com/coco_cabana.htm, 4766 Ananalu Rd; per night $125; 🛜) A hot tub, chirping birds, airy ambience and nearby, swimmable Wainiha River make for a lovely secluded stay. This

SECOND SATURDAY: HANALEI

Building community through art, film, and surf, Kaua'i-filmmaker Joel Guy and a variety of the island's budding (and well-ripened) creative talents come together to put on this monthly **festival** (www.secondsaturdayhanalei.blogspot.com; Hanalei Center; ⊙4pm until dark). With musical performances, local artists' mastery on display and creative events such as health-and-wellness expos and cultural education seminars, each month promises a new variety of excitement. Kid-friendly scavenger hunts and dodge-ball games equate to a family-friendly atmosphere. The event culminates with a surf-film at dusk, ranging from Guy's latest footage of Kaua'i and beyond to popular avant-garde surf films.

cute little cottage is perfect for a couple wanting privacy and coziness, as is the two-person outdoor jungle shower.

Red Hot Mama's
TAKEOUT $
(5-6607 Kuhio Hwy; meals $8.50; ⊙11am-5pm Mon-Sat) What 'mama' slings at this roadside flavor-factory are generous Tex-Mex burritos and tacos made with heaps of TLC. It's unclear whether the establishment's name describes levels of spice in their palatable pork, chicken, beef, fresh fish or tofu products, or in their fearless hardworking leader. Consider it a must post-Na Pali hike; you earned it.

Wainiha General Store
GROCERY $
(5-6600 Kuhio Hwy; ⊙10am-dusk) If you've left Hanalei and need a few items, don't panic. Aka the 'Last Chance General Store', it offers last-minute beach necessities such as sunscreen and even snorkel gear and basic picnic snack items. If you're hiking the Na Pali, buy an extra bottle of water, it's dry out there.

Ha'ena

While the North Shore is Kaua'i's island within the island, Ha'ena is the island within the North Shore. Remote, resplendent and idyllic, it's also the site of controversy, as many of the luxury homes on the point were built on top of ancient Hawaiian burials *('iwi kupuna)*. In 2007 this topic was brought to the attention of the media, following more mobilization of the Hawaiian community, which has continued a program of peaceful civil disobedience. Aside from the squalls of social and political storm, it is the aesthetic apex of (driveable) Kaua'i, with the road gradually squeezing passersby between towering pinnacles of aggressive green growth and picture perfect coastal curvatures. Though many humbly try (cough cough), it is truly beyond verbal description.

 ## Beaches

Makua (Tunnels) Beach
BEACH
(Map p500) Another one of the North Shore's almost-too-beautiful beaches, Tunnels – named for the underwater caverns in and amongst the nearshore reef – is among the best snorkel spots on the island. The water level increases gradually for about 44yd then dramatically drops off allowing those who are adventurous to really test their comfort in the underworld. Though more suitable for the summer months, as the reef is adjacent to the beach, winter snorkeling is a possibility. Use caution and check with the lifeguards if uncertain. Beware of a regular current flowing west towards the open sea. If you can score a parking spot at one the two unmarked lots (short dirt roads), you're lucky. The next best option is parking at Ha'ena State Park and walking down.

Ha'ena Beach Park
BEACH PARK
Not necessarily good for swimming, as the winter's regularly pounding shorebreak creates a strong undertow, this beach (Map p500) is good for taking in some sun. Between October and May, ask the lifeguard about conditions before going in. To the left is **Cannons**, a particularly good wall dive in the summer months.

DRIVING WITH ALOHA

Lauded as the most scenic and breathtaking on the island, the drive to the 'end of the road' is impossibly beautiful. However, accidents have occurred from visitors pulling over for photo-ops – please avoid being 'that person.' (You'll likely see at least one other visitor pulling over.) If you're heading to the road's end (Ke'e Beach), take it slowly and enjoy the crossing of each of the seven one-lane bridges, the first of which is in Hanalei.

When crossing these bridges, do as the locals do:

» When the bridge is empty and you reach it first, you can go.

» If there's a steady stream of cars already crossing as you approach, then simply follow them.

» When you see cars approaching from the opposite direction, yield to the entire queue of approaching cars for at least five cars, if not all.

» Give the *shaka* sign ('hang loose' hand gesture, with index, middle and ring fingers downturned) as thanks to any opposite-direction drivers who have yielded.

No doubt being attacked by a *mano* (shark) could be deadly: precautions, such as not swimming in murky, post-rain waters, should be taken to avoid them. Statistically speaking, you're more likely to die from a bee sting than a shark attack, and you should be more concerned about contracting leptospirosis or staphylococcus in those infamous muddy waters than becoming a midday snack.

Rather than letting any hard-wired phobia of large predators get you down, try considering the creature from an another perspective while in Hawaii: the *mano* as sacred. For many local families, the *mano* is their 'aumakua (guardian spirit). 'Aumakua are family ancestors whose 'uhane (spirit form) lives on in the form of an animal, watching over members of their living 'ohana. Revered for their ocean skill, *mano* were also considered the 'aumakua of navigators. Even today, *mano* 'aumakua have been said to guide lost fishermen home, or toward areas of plentiful fish, to make for a bountiful sojourn.

⊙ Sights & Activities

Limahuli Garden
GARDENS
(Map p500; ☏826-1053; www.ntbg.org; self-guided/guided tour $15/20; ⊙9:30am-4pm Tue-Fri & Sun) About as beautiful as it gets for living education, this garden offers a pleasant overview of native botany and the *ahupua'a* (land division) system of management of ancient Hawai'i. The valley was gifted to the National Tropical Botanical Garden by the Wichman family, and is run by one of its descendants, Chipper Wichman, a passionate preservationist and philanthropist. Self-guided tours allow you to take in the scenery meditatively. Occasional service projects allow a glimpse into the 985-acre preserve for native ecosystem restoration.

Maniniholo Dry Cave
CAVE
(Map p500) Directly across Ha'ena Beach Park, Maniniholo Dry Cave is deep, broad and high enough to explore. A constant seep of water from the cave walls keeps the dark interior dank. Drippy and creepy, the cave is named after the head fisherman of the *menehune* who, according to legend, built ponds and other structures overnight.

Hanalei Day Spa
SPA
(☏826-6621; www.hanaleidayspa.com; Hanalei Colony Resort; massage per 60/90min $95/140; ⊙11am-7pm Mon-Sat) If you're tired or need to revitalize, this spa offers some of the islands more competitively priced massage and body treatments. It's also the Ayurveda Center of Hawaii; visit the website to view possible up-and-coming wellness retreats.

🛏 Sleeping

Ha'ena Beach Park is a popular camping spot and base for exploring the North Shore, including the Na Pali Coast. To camp,

permits are required. See p463 for county camping permit information.

There's an abundance of vacation rentals to be found, though as the county has recently formalized vacation rental permits, many have fallen between the cracks. As always, **Vacation Rentals By Owner** (www.vrbo.com) is a good source rental options, or feel free to get creative in your search.

Hale Ho'omaha B&B
B&B $$
(☏800-851-0291, 826-7083; www.aloha.net/~hoomaha; 7083 Alamihi Rd; r $150-175; @) Though the word 'communal' is applicable, don't let it turn you off. What's shared here are amenities such as an ozonated hot tub, high-end kitchen, enormous flat-screen HDTV, a guest-use computer and even an elevator. The remarkably decorated suites – each with their own lanai – boast features such as round beds and bathrooms with dual showerheads. Kirby, the spirited housemom, is the icing on the cake.

A River House & Bird's Nest
COTTAGE $$
(☏800-715-7273; www.napaliprop.com; 5121 Powerhouse Rd; house from $1610) It's got a jungle-paradise feel (because it's in a jungle), and is just a mile from glorious Makua (Tunnels) Beach and close to the Kalalau trailhead. Avocados, lychees, bananas, papayas and mountain apples (a delicacy even to locals) abound. Boasts a queen bed, full bath, refrigerator and hot plate. Also has a screened-in sleeping area called the Bird's Nest, with full bed and half bathroom. Weekly only.

Hale Oli
VACATION RENTAL $$$
(☏826-6585; www.oceanfrontrealty.com; 7097 Alimihi Rd; 2 bedroom per night/week $250/1500) Perched on stilts with nothing but heaps of greenery (and an on-site horse that likes

carrots) between the west-facing front lanai with a screened-in eating area and Haena's jaunting mountains. Inside boasts a Hawaiiana meets Zen decor, a compulsively clean bathroom and the back lanai has a spacious hot tub offering some starry and foamy nights and a sliver of an ocean view.

Hanalei Colony Resort   RESORT **$$**
(Map p500; ☑826-6235, 800-628-3004; www .hcr.com; 5-7132 Kuhio Hwy; 2 bedroom from $210; ✹@✖) The only resort west of Princeville, this series of condominiums near Makua (Tunnels) Beach is a midrange presentation in a high-end location. While the '70s decor in many of the units can seem a bit dated, the property is on the waterfront and about as reclusive as it gets. The absence of a TV or phone certainly aids locational awareness. Go to the website to arrange to have your kitchenette stocked with groceries. Stay six nights and the seventh is free.

✖ Eating & Drinking

Mediterranean Gourmet   MEDITERRANEAN **$$**
(☑826-9875; www.mediterraneangourmet.biz; Hanalei Colony Resort, 7132 Kuhio Hwy; lunch $12-17, dinner $20-35; ☉11am-9pm) A taste of the Mediterranean literally on the Pacific (if the windows weren't there you'd get ocean mist on your face), this fish out of water offers an eclectic range of dishes from rosemary rack of lamb and stuffed grape leaves to pistachio crusted ahi. Be sure to leave room for dessert: baklava, cheesecake or a cup of muddy Turkish coffee. Live music most nights and a Luau on Tuesdays.

Na Pali Art Gallery & Coffee House   COFFEE SHOP **$**
(☑826-1844; www.napaligallery.com; Hanalei Colony Resort, 5-7132 Kuhio Hwy; ☉7am-6pm Mon-Sat & 7am-3pm Sun; ☎) Order a latte or Kona coffee and peruse an assortment of local artists' paintings, scratchboards, jewelry (coveted Ni'ihau sunrise shell necklaces), and larimar (priced from $20 to $2000).

Ha'ena State Park

Wind-beaten and lava-carved, Ha'ena State Park burns with the allure, mystique and beauty usually associated with some divine tale. Pele is said to have overlooked the area as a home because of the water housed in its wet and dry caves. The 230-acre park is home to the 1280ft cliff commonly known in the tourism industry as 'Bali Hai,' its name

in the film *South Pacific*. Its real name is Makana, which means 'gift.'

🏖 Beaches & Sights

Ke'e Beach   BEACH
Perhaps the most memorable North Shore sunsets happen at this spiritual place, where the first Hawaiians came to practice hula. It offers a refreshing dip after hiking the nearby Kalalau Trail in summer months. Be aware that Ke'e Beach has appeared calm to swimmers when it's otherwise. Ke'e has a keyhole in its reef, where some have been sucked through. Summer brings car breakins in the parking lot, so leave cars (especially those that are obviously rentals, such as Mustangs, Sebrings and PT Cruisers) free from valuables. There are showers and restrooms on-site.

Wet Caves   CAVE
Two wet caves are within the boundaries of Ha'ena State Park. The first, **Waikapala'e Wet Cave** (aka the Blue Room), is just a short walk from the road opposite the visitor-parking overflow area. Formed by constant wave-pounding many years ago, this massive cavern is as enchanting as it may be spooky. Though some enter the water to experience the sunlight's blue reflection once in the deeper chamber of the cave, please note this water may have leptospirosis, the rocks are slippery, and there is nothing to hold onto once in the water. The second, **Waikanaloa Wet Cave**, is on the south side of the main road.

Kaulu Paoa Hei'au   HEIAU (TEMPLE)
The roaring surf worked as a teacher to those who first practiced the spiritual art of hula, chanting and testing their skill against nature's decibel levels. Ke'e beach is home to one of the most cherished heiau, and it's also where volcanic goddess Pele fell in love with Lohiau. Leis and other offerings for Pele can be found on the ground, and should be left as is. Enter the heiau through its entryway. Do not cross over its walls, as it is disrespectful and said to bring bad luck.

Na Pali Coast State Park

Kalalau, Honopu, 'Awa'awapuhi, Nu'alolo and Miloli'i (see Map p543) are the five major valleys on the Na Pali Coast, easily the most distinguishable example of beauty as nature on the island, if not within the entire archipelago. Don't miss seeing the

22-mile stretch by chopper, watercraft or old-school style – on foot.

History

Archaeologists maintain that the extreme, remote Nualolo Valley housed a civilization dating back more than a thousand years after ancient weapons and hunting tools were recovered from the area. Irrigation ditches and agricultural terraces suggest the Kalalau Valley was the most advanced within the island chain.

At the turn of the century, the majority of the inhabitants of the valley had moved to more centrally located spots on the island.

🏃 Hiking

For rewarding views of the Na Pali Coast, hiking along the 11-mile Kalalau coastal trail into Hanakapi'ai, Hanakoa and Kalalau Valleys is an adventure that's sure not to disappoint. Unfit for roads, the Na Pali Coast leads to the opposite side of the island, in Koke'e State Park. You won't want to miss hiking the west side of the island for those views. If you're one of those 'ultimate' fitness fanatics, perhaps the Na Pali Coast by sea on a 17-mile kayak adventure is up your alley (see p528).

Kalalau Trail   HIKING

How else could you brave the steep sea cliffs than by foot for 22 miles? Winding along the Na Pali (the cliffs) offers glimpses of some of the most pristine, extreme views from which to behold its deep, riveting pleats. This trail is without a doubt the best way to connect directly with the elements, though keep in mind that the trek, if you opt to complete the full 22-mile round-trip into the valley, is a steep, rough hike.

There are three hike options: Ke'e Beach to Hanakapi'ai Beach, Hanakapi'ai Beach to Hanakapi'ai Falls and Hanakapi'ai Beach to Kalalau Valley. There are hunters who can do the entire trail in and out in one day, but most people will either want to opt for the Hanakapi'ai Beach or Hanakapi'ai Falls hike or bring camping gear to make it to Kalalau Beach.

The state parks office in Lihu'e can provide a Kalalau Trail brochure with a map. Another good source sponsored by the county is www.kauaiexplorer.com. Keep in mind that even if you're not planning to camp, a permit is officially required to continue on the Kalalau Trail beyond Hanakapi'ai. Free day-use hiking permits are available from the Division of State Parks, which also issues the required camping permits for the Hanakapi'ai (one-night maximum) and Kalalau (five-nights maximum) Valleys. For more information on permits see p463. You'll need ample time – possibly as much as six to 12 months – in advance to get permits.

Ke'e Beach to Hanakapi'ai Beach

It shouldn't take more than two hours to complete this 4-mile (round-trip) trek – the most popular and most crowded hike. The first 2 miles of the Kalalau Trail ends at Hanakapi'ai Beach (no swimming allowed).

Hanakapi'ai Beach to Hanakapi'ai Falls

This trek begins after you've completed the 2-mile Ke'e Beach to Hanakapia'i Beach jaunt. Once you get to Hanakapi'ai Beach, crowds lessen, as the work-reward ratio compounds. The next 2 miles takes you deeper into the forest, with an increasingly sublime riverscape. Though you might be tempted to take a swim at Hanakapia'i Beach, it's best to wait until the falls for such a treat, as Hanakapi'ai Beach has notoriously dangerous waters (and the waters of Hanakapi'ai Falls are well worth waiting for).

THIS AIN'T NO DISCO

The Kalalau Trail is hella Rugged (yes, with a capital R) and therefore it's not for everyone. Being prepared is a tough call too, as you won't want to pack too much but you will need to stay hydrated, prepped for rain and you must take your trash out with you. You may see hikers with machetes, walkie-talkies, climbing rope and reef shoes; but even the trekkers with the most bad-ass gear should know not to expect a rescue by emergency responders; these precipices are to be taken seriously. Anyone with a police scanner can tell you 'plenty story' about the braggart from the mainland who was warned by friends/family/an onlooker but said something along the lines of these famous last words: 'Naw, I'm from Colorado, this is nothing.' Finally, mosquitoes here are bloodthirsty and the sun can really ravage, so always wear insect repellent and sunblock.

ℹ️ WHEN IN DOUBT, DON'T GO OUT

The waters in Hawaii are as powerful as anywhere on the planet and can catch many a toe-dipper off guard in the blink of an eye. Strong undertows have the capability of sweeping even the most experienced water-folk off their feet and out to sea in matter of seconds. Swimming with others and where lifeguards are present is always the safest way to go. Made evident by the knife-etched tally visible before hikers descend down to it, **Hanakapi'ai Beach** has ended many a vacation, and life, too soon (30 in the last 40 years). Heed the warning.

Hanakapi'ai Beach to Kalalau Valley

Past Hanakapi'ai, the real challenge begins as another 9 miles ensue. At this point, there's no turning back. The trail weaves in and out of several valleys, giving alternately shaded and sunny vistas across the Pacific. Hanakoa makes a convenient rest or camping point, as it's about halfway in. Near the end, the trail takes you across the front of Kalalau Valley, where you can feel dwarfed by 1000ft lava-rock cliffs before proceeding to the campgrounds on the beach, just west of the valley. You will need a permit (see p463).

ℹ️ Getting There & Away

The parking lot at Ke'e Beach trailhead is quite large but fills quickly during the jam-packed summer months. Break-ins are rampant; some people advise leaving cars empty and unlocked to prevent damage such as window smashing. Campers, consider parking at the campground at Ha'ena Beach Park (Map p500) or storing your belongings elsewhere and catching a cab to the trailhead; try **Kauai Taxi Company** (☑246-9554).

PO'IPU & THE SOUTH SHORE

Tourists adore Po'ipu, and it's no surprise why: sun, surf and sand. The quintessential elements of a beach vacation are guaranteed here, where the weather's less rainy and the waves less changeable than on the North Shore. Since the 1970s, huge condos and hotels have mushroomed along the shore,

spawning a critical mass of tourists that will either entertain or annoy you.

The South Shore also boasts two world-renowned botanical gardens, as well as the undeveloped Maha'ulepu Coast, where lithified sand-dune cliffs and pounding surf make for an unforgettable walk. What's missing is a town center – or any town at all. Thus, you're bound to stop in Koloa, a former plantation town that's now the South Shore's lively little commercial center.

Koloa

POP 2088

On the South Shore, all roads lead to Koloa, which was a thriving plantation town until it withered after WWII, when sugar gave way to tourism. Today its quaint 'Old West' neighborhood contains a pleasant set of affordable shops and restaurants – a welcome complement to the budget-breaking selection in Po'ipu. The adjacent residential towns of Lawa'i (population 2133) and Omao (population 1313) are low-key, neighborly and blooming with foliage.

When William Hooper, an enterprising 24-year-old Bostonian, arrived on Kaua'i in 1835, he took advantage of two historical circumstances: the Polynesians' introduction of sugarcane to the islands and Chinese immigrants' knowledge of refining sugar. With financial backing from Honolulu businesspeople, he leased land in Koloa from the king and paid island *ali'i* (chief, royalty) a stipend to release commoners from their traditional work obligations. He then hired the Hawaiians as wage laborers and Koloa became Hawaii's first plantation town.

◉ Sights

Lawai International Center HISTORICAL SITE
(☑639-4300; www.lawaicenter.org; 3381 Wawae Rd; ☺call for schedule) Magical. Enchanting. Stirring. Such words are often used to describe this quiet spiritual site in the Lawa'i Valley, northwest of Koloa and Po'ipu. Originally the site of a Hawaiian heiau, the area's strong mana (spiritual essence) attracted future generations of worshippers, including Japanese plantation families since the late 1800s.

In 1904, these immigrants placed 88 miniature Shingon Buddhist shrines (about 2ft tall) along a steep hillside path to symbolize 88 pilgrimage shrines in Shikoku, Japan. For years, island pilgrims would journey here

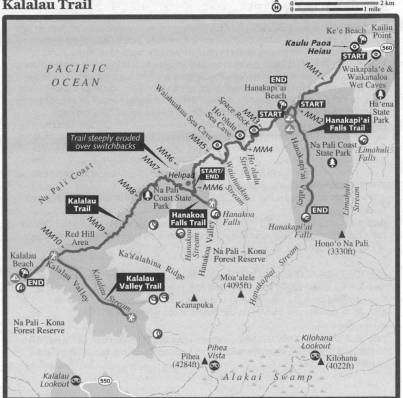

from as far as Hanalei and Kekaha. But the site was abandoned by the 1960s, and half of the shrines lay scattered in shards.

In the late 1980s, some volunteers formed a nonprofit group, acquired a 32-acre property and embarked on a backbreaking project to repair or rebuild the shrines. Today, all 88 are beautifully restored, and leisurely tours include a detailed history and trail walk. Despite the Buddhist shrines, the center is a nondenominational sanctuary for all cultures. Visits are allowed only during twice-monthly Sunday tours; call for details.

Koloa Historic Buildings TEMPLES
East of town, find the **Koloa Jodo Mission** (2480 Waikomo Rd; ☺services 6pm Mon-Fri, 9:30am Sun), which follows Pure Land Buddhism, a nonmeditating form, popular in Japan since the 12th century. The Buddhist temple on the left is the original, which dates back to 1910, while the larger temple on the right is currently used for services.

St Raphael's Catholic Church (✆742-1955; 3011 Hapa Rd), Kaua'i's oldest Catholic church, is the burial site of some of Hawaii's first Portuguese immigrants. The original church, built in 1854, was made of lava rock and coral mortar with walls 3ft thick – a type of construction visible in the ruins of the adjacent rectory. When the church was enlarged in 1936 it was plastered over, creating a more typical whitewashed appearance.

🏃 Activities

Obviously Koloa is landlocked, but it's home to two excellent ocean-sports outfits.

TOP CHOICE **Fathom Five Divers** DIVING $$
(✆742-6991, 800-972-3078; www.fathomfive.com; 3450 Po'ipu Rd; shore dives $75-140, boat dives $125-350) The island's best dive outfit is run by a husband-and-wife team, Jeannette and George Thompson. They offer the whole range, from Ni'ihau boat dives ($345) to

THE NA PALI KAYAK TREK

The Na Pali Coast has reasonable claim to offering the most spectacular scenery of all of Kaua'i. Any trip to Kaua'i without experiencing it would be incomplete; and if you're able, kayaking it arguably offers one of the most unforgettable challenges on the planet.

Kayaking the Na Pali Coast is strenuous and dangerous, and therefore not for everyone. Going with a guide helps manage the dangers, going without means you're more than just familiar with ocean (not river) kayaking. It also means you know better than to go alone. Always check several days of weather forecasting and ocean conditions before going (☑245-3564). Hanakapi'ai Beach is about a mile in. About six more miles along and you can set up camp at Kalalau. If you started very early, you can aim for setting up camp at Miloli'i, (with a permit) which is at the 11-mile point, two miles past Nu'alolo Kai. From there you have the often surfless, hot, flat stretch of Polihale, for what feels like much longer than 3 miles.

Always start on the North Shore, end on the Westside (due to currents) and never go in winter (potentially deadly swells).

If you want to do the Na Pali Kayak Trek with a guide, try the following operators:

Na Pali Kayak

(Map p515; ☑826-6900, 866-977-6900; www.napalikayak.com; Kuhio Hwy; tours $175) The Na Pali Coast trip is the only tour these folks lead and their guides have over a decade of experience paddling these waters.

Kayak Kaua'i

(Map p515; ☑826-9844, 800-437-3507; www.kayakkauai.com; Kuhio Hwy; single kayaks per day/week $28/112, double kayaks $52/208; ☺8am-5pm, to 8pm summer) Tours include a Na Pali Coast thriller for $185 from May to September, Blue Lagoon kayak and snorkel for $60, or an open-ocean paddle on the South Shore winter for $115.

Outfitters Kaua'i

(Map p532; ☑742-9667, 888-742-9887; www.outfitterskauai.com; Po'ipu Plaza, 2827A Po'ipu Rd; Na Pali Coast tour $185; ☺reservations 8am-9pm) Located in Po'ipu, but it offers tours islandwide.

night dives to certification courses. Newbies can expect reassuring hand-holding during their introductory shore dives. Groups max out at six and they avoid mixing skill levels. Call well in advance.

Snorkel Bob's
SNORKELING $

(☑742-2206; www.snorkelbob.com; 3236 Po'ipu Rd; rental mask, snorkel & fins per week $9-35; ☺8am-5pm) The king of snorkel gear rents and sells enough styles and sizes to assure a good fit. If, after renting, you want to buy an item, your rental payment deflects part of the cost.

Kaua'i ATV
ATV $$

(☑742-2734, 877-707-7088; www.kauaiatv.com; 5330 Koloa Rd; tours $125-175) This outfit commendably offers two-seater and four-seater bio-diesel vehicles for a reasonable upgrade of $10 per person. Therefore, we recommend these ATV tours only if you opt for the green machines over the gas-powered ones, which constitute most of their fleet. Riding in upcountry pastureland, you're guaranteed to

get dirty, whether merely dusty or soaked in mud. Use their loaner clothing.

★ Festivals & Events

Koloa Plantation Days Celebration
LOCAL FESTIVAL

(☑652-3217; www.koloaplantationdays.com) In July, the South Shore's biggest annual celebration spans nine days of family fun with the gamut of attractions (many free), including a parade, block party, rodeo, craft fair, canoe race, golf tournament and guided walks.

🛏 Sleeping

The following are in the Koloa, Omao and Lawa'i residential neighborhoods.

TOP CHOICE Marjorie's Kaua'i Inn
INN $$

(☑332-8838, 800-717-8838; www.marjorieskauai inn.com; Hailima St, Lawa'i; r $130-175; 🛜🌊) The magnificent vista from this classy inn perched 400ft above Lawa'i Valley will change your life, or at least your week. The rooms show off stylish furnishings and each includes a large private lanai, as well as a kitchenette. You're nowhere near the beach, but the elegant 50ft lap pool and poolside BBQ grill compensate nicely, as do breakfasts of waffles and quiche and special teas from India provided by the raw-foodist hosts.

Boulay Inn INN $
(☎742-1120, 635-5539; www.boulayinn.com; 4175 Omao Rd; 1 bedroom $85; 🖥) Your money goes far with this airy one-bedroom apartment in quiet residential Omao. The 500-sq-ft space is comfy rather than fancy, sitting atop a garage (no shared walls with the main house). Features include wraparound lanai, full kitchen, private phone line, high ceilings and free use of the washer-dryer. A cleaning fee ($50) is charged.

Cozy Kauai Cottage COTTAGE $
(☎742-1778, 877-742-1778; www.kauaivacation properties.com/cottage.htm; 3794-D Omao Rd; cottage s/d $75/100; 🖥) A pastoral retreat with modern amenities, this simple, compact cottage (best for a slim single or couple) is efficiently arranged to include a full kitchen, separate bedroom and comfy living area. The hardwood floor, granite counters and dimmer lights add style, while lots of windows let in cool breezes. Cleaning fee ($40) charged.

Hale Kipa O Koloa COTTAGE $$
(☎742-1802; 5481 Waiau Rd, Koloa; 1 bedroom cottage $125; 🖥) Great for families or groups, this plantation-style house is close to town and affords much privacy. With two bedrooms, two bathrooms, a full kitchen and washer-dryer, it's just like home. The inland location can be hot, but this cottage features high, insulated ceilings, cool tile floors and clean white walls. Additional guests cost an extra $15 per night.

Yvonne's B&B B&B $
(☎742-2418; yvonne.e.johnson@gmail.com; 3857 Omao Rd; r $79, incl breakfast $99; 🖥) Stylishly decorated with a mixture of Hawaiian artifacts and retro furnishings, this B&B is perfect for a couple wanting a gregarious and obliging host or a single traveler wanting a place to call home while on the island. Homemade breads and jams are regularly provided and the outdoor shower (there's an indoor shower, too) might have you reconsidering your previously learned hygiene habits.

✕ Eating

TOP CHOICE Koloa Fish Market TAKEOUT, SEAFOOD $
(☎742-6199; 5482 Koloa Rd; lunch $4-8; ⊙10am-6pm Mon-Fri, to 5pm Sat) Line up with locals at this hole-in-the-wall serving outstanding *poke*, Japanese-style *bentō*, sushi rolls and Hawaiian plate lunches. Don't miss the thick-sliced, perfectly seared ahi and rich slabs of homemade *haupia* (coconut pudding).

Pizzetta ITALIAN $$
(☎742-8881; 5408 Koloa Rd; pizza $17-25, pasta $11-18; ⊙11am-10pm) If this family trattoria had *any* competition, we'd be more critical, but affordable eateries are scarce around here. Choose from decent gourmet pizzas such as the El Greco (sun-dried tomatoes, artichoke hearts and feta) and filling pastas that won't ravage your wallet. Expect a mainly touristy clientele.

Koloa Mill Ice Cream & Coffee ICE CREAM, COFFEESHOP $
(6544 Koloa Rd; single-scoop ice cream $3.55; ⊙7am-9pm) Homemade cotton candy, Kauai coffee and nothing but the best Maui-born Roselani Ice Cream are always served with a smile. For those lacking decision-making abilities, start with the Pauwela Sunrise and go from there.

Self-Catering

Big Save SUPERMARKET
(cnr Waikomo Rd & Koloa Rd; ⊙6am-11pm) Has one of its best branches here. Don't miss the value-priced ahi *poke*.

Sueoka Store GROCERY
(☎742-1611; 5392 Koloa Rd; ⊙7am-9pm) Holds its own with the basics, plus packaged Japanese takeout snacks. Like all health-nut venues.

🛍 Shopping

Blue Orchid Floral Design FLOWERS
(www.blueorchidkauai.com; 5470 Koloa Rd; ⊙9am-5pm Mon-Sat) If you're in a forgotten-birthday pinch or just want to display some aloha for a loved one, they will use their combined 25 years of experience to create the ideal floral arrangement using any and all island-accessible flowers. Their vast displays of flower lei are worth a gander.

Christian Riso Fine Arts ART GALLERY
(☎742-2555; www.christianrisofineart.com; 5400 Koloa Rd; ⊙10am-9pm) Browsers are welcome at this informal gallery of paintings

and drawings by island artists, fine jewelry (including Ni'ihau shell necklaces) and fun collectibles like handpainted walking sticks. The shop specializes in custom framing using Hawaiian hardwoods such as koa and kamani.

Pohaku T's   CLOTHING
(☎742-7500; www.pohaku.com; 3430 Po'ipu Rd; ☺10am-8pm Mon-Sat, to 6pm Sun) This well-stocked shop specializes in Kaua'i-made clothing, crafts and island-themed tees and tanks. Signature shirt designs feature classic island themes (petroglyphs, *honu* and navigational maps) on stonewashed or overdyed colors. Cotton aloha shirts are locally hand-sewn yet affordable.

Island Soap & Candle Works   SOUVENIRS
(☎742-1945, 888-528-7627; www.kauaisoap.com; 5428 Koloa Rd; ☺9am-10pm) For a delicious treat with zero calories, breathe deeply inside this flowery, fruity sensation of a shop. Established in 1984 to recreate the art of soap- and candle-making, the company has grown but still makes everything by hand.

ℹ Information

Services are minimal:
First Hawaiian Bank (☎742-1642; 3506 Waikomo Rd) At the east end of town.
Post office (☎800-275-8777; 5485 Koloa Rd) Serves both Koloa and Po'ipu.

ℹ Getting There & Away

From the west, Koloa Rd (Hwy 530), which runs between Lawa'i and Koloa, is the best way in and out. From Lihu'e, take the scenic Maluhia Rd (Hwy 520) through the enchanting Tree Tunnel.

Almost all car, motorcycle and moped rental agencies are in Lihu'e, but **Kaua'i Scooter Rental** (☎245-7177; www.kauaimopedrentals. com; 3414 Po'ipu Rd; ☺8am-5pm) has a branch location in Koloa, just south of the Chevron station.

Po'ipu

POP 1156

Po'ipu (which ironically translates as 'completely overcast') is world renowned for its dependable sun and easy-access beaches. When it does rain here, you can bet it's pouring on the North Shore. Alas, no Po'ipu 'town' exists – so dining is limited and traveling by foot is challenging, except along the beaches.

The coast is already blanketed with condos, time-shares, hotels and vacation-rental homes, but a new transformation has begun with the massive luxury development, **Kukui'ula** (www.kukuiula.com). The expansion brings with it a new golf course, 1000 acres of custom homes, and Kukui'ula Village – a 90,000-sq-ft high-end shopping center built to be reminiscent of old Kaua'i, featuring authentic plantation-style architecture and lush gardens. Kukui'ula adds a new chapter to the story of Po'ipu's continual expansion.

Beaches

Po'ipu Beach Park   BEACH PARK
No monster waves or idyllic solitude here. But if you're seeking a safe, lively, family-friendly beach, this is it. Located at the end of Ho'owili Rd, it features a lifeguard station and shallow, gentle waters for swimming, snorkeling and beginner diving. The sandy beach is compact (you can see one end from the other) and is jammed on weekends, but you'll have ample elbow room on weekdays. Around the beach are grassy lawns, a children's playground, picnic pavilions and tables, restrooms and showers. What's lacking are eating options.

Check out **Nukumoi Point**, a finger of land toward the west, where you can explore tide pools and perhaps see *honu* (green sea turtles). The best snorkeling is west of the point, where you'll find swarms of curious fish.

To get here, go to the end of Ho'owili Rd. Parking is right across the street from the beach.

Brennecke's Beach   BEACH
Any time, any day, this little beach attracts a big cadre of bodyboarders, bobbing in the water, waiting for the next set. Tourists often sit on the roadside stonewall to enjoy the action. No surfboards are allowed near shore, so bodyboarders rule. If you want to join in, note that waves break dangerously close to shore. Surf is highest in summer, but the winter action is respectable, too. The beach flanks the eastern edge of Po'ipu Beach Park.

Po'ipu Beach   BEACH
Despite its nicknames of Sheraton Beach and Kiahuna Beach, this long swath of sand is not private. It merely fronts the hotel and condo, both of which scored big-time with their location along Po'ipu Beach, which

lies west of Poʻipu Beach Park. The waters here are too rough for kids, although an offshore reef tames the waves enough for strong swimmers and snorkelers.

Experienced surfers and bodyboarders can attempt the breaks near the Sheraton, but the waters are famous for sneaker sets (rogue waves that appear from nowhere) and the rocky coast makes it difficult to get offshore and back. South Shore spots tend to be fickle and highly susceptible to winds, tides and swells. **Cowshead**, the rocky outcropping at the west end of the beach, is an extremely challenging break unless you know how to approach the channel. Expert surfers can attempt offshore spots such as **First Break** in front of the Sheraton, but beginners should always remain inshore. **Waiohai**, at the east end of the beach in front of the Marriott Waiohai Beach Club time-share, also sees major swells.

To get to the beach, drive to the end of Hoʻonani Rd.

Shipwreck Beach   BEACH
Unless you're an expert surfer, bodyboarder or bodysurfer, keep your feet dry at Shipwrecks. Instead, come for an invigorating walk along the half-mile crescent of light gold sand. You'll most likely have company, as the Grand Hyatt Kauaʻi Resort & Spa overlooks much of the beach along Keoneloa Bay. Row after row of waves crashes close to the shore, giving this beach a rugged, untamed vibe. Toward the left of the bay looms **Makawehi Point**, a gigantic lithified sand dune, which you can ascend in 10 minutes.

In the movie *Six Days Seven Nights,* stunt doubles for Harrison Ford and Anne Heche leap off Makawehi Point. In real life, a few daredevils similarly dive off the rocky cliff, as shown in thrilling YouTube clips, but no one mentions the severe casualties and deaths. In a word: don't.

To get here, head toward the Grand Hyatt, turn *makai* (seaward) on Ainako St and park in the small lot at the end.

Baby Beach   BEACH
Introduce tots to the ocean at this baby beach (there's another in Kapaʻa), where the water is barely thigh-high. The sandy shore runs behind a row of beach homes on Hoʻona Rd (west of Koloa Landing), so access is easy but parking is tricky (don't block driveways). Look for the beach access sign that marks a path to the beach.

Lawaʻi (Beach House) Beach   BEACH
This tiny beach gets some major action with snorkelers and surfers. Located almost adjacent to Lawaʻi Rd (beside the iconic Beach House restaurant), it's in plain view of passersby and not especially scenic or sandy. But during calm surf, the waters are rich snorkeling turf – and crowded with a contingent of tourists from nearby time-shares and condos. There are restrooms, a shower, and a public parking across the street. On balance, however, choose this beach only if you're staying nearby.

◉ Sights

Note that you can't see any beaches from Poʻipu Rd (all you see are condos and parking lots). To reach the beaches, you must turn *makai* (seaward) on side streets, such as Hoʻowili Rd, to reach Poʻipu Beach Park and Kapili Rd for the Sheraton beach.

National Tropical Botanical Garden GARDEN
(NTBG; ☎742-2623; www.ntbg.org; 4425 Lawaʻi Rd; admission $20-60; ☺8:30am-5pm) If you're interested in plants and their preservation, a visit to these gardens is a must. The gardens are not just stunningly beautiful, but they are also sanctuaries for native plants and living laboratories for staff scientists and international experts.

Of the two Poʻipu gardens, the 80-acre **Allerton Garden** is the showy star, but it requires a pricey guided tour (adult/child $45/20). Tour guides are generally knowledgeable and enthusiastic, leisurely guiding groups (up to 20) through meticulously landscaped grounds. Highlights include otherworldly Moreton Bay fig trees (seen in *Jurassic Park*), golden bamboo groves, a pristine lagoon and valley walls blanketed with purple bougainvillea during summer. The artificial statuary and water elements somehow blend into the landscape.

The adjacent **McBryde Garden** is less manicured and fancy than Allerton Garden, showcasing palms, flowering and spice trees, orchids and rare native species, plus a pretty stream and waterfall. For budget travelers, the self-guided tour (adult/child $20/10) allows you to wander in the vast grounds without watching the clock.

FREE **Moir Gardens**   GARDEN
(☎742-6411; Kiahuna Plantation, 2253 Poʻipu Rd; ☺sunrise-sunset) If cacti are your fancy, this modest garden on the grounds of the Kiahuna Plantation condo is worth a look-see.

Po'ipu

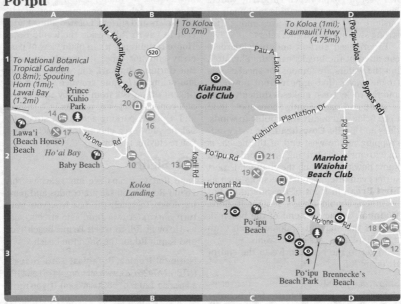

Po'ipu

⊙ Sights

Anara Spa	(see 8)
Art 103	(see 20)
1 Cowshead	D3
2 First Break	C3
Moir Gardens	(see 19)
3 Nukumoi Point	C3
4 Nukumoi Surf Company	D3
Outfitters Kaua'i	(see 6)
5 Waiohai	C3

Activities, Courses & Tours

Kaua'i Down Under Dive Team	(see 15)
6 Seasport Divers	B1

🛏 Sleeping

7 Aikane Kaua'i	D3
8 Grand Hyatt Kaua'i Resort & Spa	E2
9 Hideaway Cove Villas	D3
10 Kaua'i Cove Cottages	B2
Kiahuna Plantation	(see 19)
11 Koa Kea Hotel & Resort	C2
12 Nihi Kai Villas	D3
13 Po'ipu Kapili	B2
14 Prince Kuhio Resort	A2
15 Sheraton Kaua'i Resort	C2
16 Waikomo Stream Villas	B2

✕ Eating

17 Beach House Restaurant	A2
18 Casa di Amici	D3
Josselin's Tapas & Grill	(see 20)
Kukui'ula Store	(see 6)
Living Foods Market & Café	(see 20)
Papalani Gelato	(see 21)
19 Plantation Gardens Restaurant & Bar	C2
Roy's Po'ipu Bar & Grill	(see 21)
Savage Shrimp	(see 20)
Tidepools	(see 8)

Drinking

Seaview Terrace	(see 8)
Stevenson's Library	(see 8)
The Point Lodge	(see 15)

Entertainment

Havaiki Nui Luau	(see 8)
Surf to Sunset Luau	(see 15)

🛍 Shopping

20 Kukui'ula Village	B1
Po'ipu Plaza	(see 6)
21 Po'ipu Shopping Village	C2

KAUA'I PO'IPU & THE SOUTH SHORE

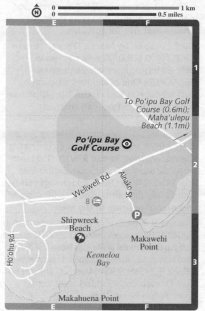

around here in 1871, is looking forlorn nowadays. The lawn is often brown and dry, and visitors rarely enter the grounds, which contain the ruins of an ancient Hawaiian heiau and fishpond. That said, no local would discount the prince's considerable contributions to Hawaii and the Hawaiian people. He was the Territory of Hawaii's first delegate to the US Congress and he spearheaded the Hawaiian Homes Commission Act, which set aside 200,000 acres of land for indigenous Hawaiians, many of whom are still waiting for it.

Koloa Landing   HISTORICAL SITE
Koloa Landing, at the mouth of Waikomo Stream, was once Kaua'i's largest port. In the 1850s farmers used it to ship Kaua'i-grown sugar, oranges and sweet potatoes, and it was the third-busiest whaling port among the Hawaiian Islands, surpassed only by Honolulu and Lahaina, Maui. The landing waned after the road system was built and it was abandoned in the 1920s. Today only a small boat ramp remains.

Underwater, it's another story: Koloa Landing is popular for snorkeling and the best shore-diving spot on the South Shore. Its protected waters reach depths of about 30ft and it's generally calm all year. See underwater tunnels, a variety of coral and fish, sea turtles and monk seals. The best sights are located toward the west.

Art 103   GALLERY
(www.art103.com; Kukui'ula Village, Ala Kalanikaumaka Rd, Suite 102/103; ⊙noon-8pm Mon-Thu, 11am-9pm Fri & Sat, noon-6pm Sun, also by appointment) For local art that goes beyond the no-brainer, easy-sell tropical motifs, visit this classy new gallery. Owner and art photographer Bruna Stude (www.brunastude.com) has assembled an impressive collection by both emerging and established names. The adjoining annex, A+, is modeled after museum shops, and offers more affordable drawings, ceramics, fiber art and other collectibles. Everything is original – no commercial giclée (ink jet) prints.

🏃 **Activities**

Diving
The Po'ipu coast offers the island's best dive sites, including **Sheraton Caverns**, a series of partially collapsed lava tubes 10ft or more in height, with shafts of glowing sunlight illuminating their dim interior; **General Store**, with sharks, octopuses, eels and the

It's a low-key, approachable collection of mature cacti and succulents, interspersed with winding paths, a lily pond and colorful shocks of orchids.

The gardens, established in the 1930s, were originally the estate of Hector Moir, manager of Koloa Sugar Plantation, and Alexandra 'Sandie' Knudsen Moir. The Moirs were avid gardeners who switched from flowering plants to drought-tolerant ones that could naturally thrive in dry Po'ipu.

A sideshow rather than a showstopper, it's worth a stroll if you're staying nearby or dining at the restaurant.

Spouting Horn Beach Park   NATURAL SITE
It resembles a geyser, but Spouting Horn is really a hole at the top of lava cave. When ocean waves pound the shore, they flood the cave and exit through the hole, erupting skyward as a fountain. The waves are unpredictable, so you might need to wait for some action. Fountains are typically under 30ft and last only seconds, but they can reach twice that height during high surf.

To get here, turn right off Po'ipu Rd onto Lawa'i Rd and continue for 1.75 miles.

Prince Kuhio Park   PARK
The simple green space honoring Kaua'i's Prince Jonah Kuhio Kalaniana'ole, born

remains of an 1892 shipwreck; and **Nuku-moi Point**, a shallow site and habitat for green sea turtles.

Dive boats and catamaran cruises usually depart from Kukui'ula Harbor, 0.5 miles east of Spouting Horn.

In addition to the dive outfits listed here, consider also nearby Fathom Five Divers (p527).

Kauai Down Under Dive Team   DIVING
(☑742-9534; www.kauaidownunderscuba.com; Sheraton Kaua'i Resort; 2440 Ho'onani Rd; ⊗8am-6pm) With one instructor per four guests, personal attention is guaranteed. They offer introductory noncertified one-tank dives ($109), two-tank scooter dives ($169) and night dives ($99) for the truly adventurous, as well as a multitude of classes including the recommended pre-arrival online academic portion of the certification for those wanting to maximize playtime while on the island.

Seasport Divers   DIVING
(☑742-9303, 800-685-5889; www.seasportdivers.com; Po'ipu Plaza, 2827 Po'ipu Rd; 2-tank dive $115-145; ⊗check-in 7:30am & 12:45pm) This outfit leads a range of dives from shore or boat, including a three-tank dive to Ni'ihau ($265), offered only in summer. All dives are guided by instructor-level divemasters; any group with noncertified divers includes an additional instructor. Groups are limited to 18 but the count is typically eight to 12.

Surfing
Po'ipu is a popular spot for surf lessons because it's got some killer breaks and year-round sun. Beware of large classes, though; four is maximum density. For lessons, we recommend the following outfits, which all meet at the beach.

[TOP CHOICE] Kaua'i Surf School   SURFING $
(☑651-6032; www.kauaisurfschool.com; 2hr lesson group/private $75/175) With 90 minutes of teaching and 30 minutes of free practice, you get your money's worth. A good outfit for children, with a special one-hour private lesson for kids aged four to 12. Also offers multiday surf clinics and surf escort services.

Garden Island Surf School   SURFING $
(☑652-4841; www.kauai-surfinglessons.com; 2hr lesson group/couple/private $75/120/150; ⊙lessons 8am, 10am, noon & 2pm) The lesson includes one hour with an instructor and

one hour of free surfing. Four students per group; minimum age is eight for groups and five for privates.

Surf Lessons by Margo Oberg   SURFING $
(☑332-6100, 639-0708; www.surfonkauai.com; 2hr lesson group/semiprivate/private $68/90/125) One of the longest-running surf schools on Kaua'i, this operation has a fine rep but classes can reach six.

Kelley's Surf School   SURFING, STAND UP PADDLE SURFING $
(☑652-9979; www.kauaisurfandsup.com; surfing 2hr lesson/private/3hr tour $75/120/150, stand up paddle boarding 2hr lesson/basic tour/elite tour $85/120/150) Offers a kids surf camp and family discounts, and has 30 years of experience to bring to the table.

Nukumoi Surf Company   SURF RENTALS
(☑742-8019; www.nukumoi.com; 2100 Ho'one Rd; soft-top board rental per hr/day/week $6/25/75, hard boards $8/30/90, bodyboards per day/week $6/20; ⊗7:45am-6:30pm Mon-Sat, 10:45am-6pm Sun) Conveniently located right across from Po'ipu Beach Park.

Progressive Expressions   SURF RENTALS
(☑742-6041; 5420 Koloa Rd, Koloa; board rental per day/week $20/100; ⊗9am-9pm) Koloa surf shop rents all types of boards, same price.

Po'ipu Surf Company   SURF RENTALS
(☑742-8797, 652-9979; Kukui'ula Village, 2829 Ala Kalanikaumaka Rd; board rental per day/week $20/95, stand up paddle board rental per day/week $40/200; ⊗9am-8pm, to 9pm Sat & Sun) Rents beginner and performance boards.

Golf
Kiahuna Golf Club   GOLF
(☑742-9595; www.kiahunagolf.com; 2545 Kiahuna Plantation Dr; greens fee incl cart before/after 3pm $103/72, club rental $52) This economical course is a relatively forgiving par-70, Robert Trent Jones Jr–designed 18 holes. Established in 1983, it's a compact, inland course using smaller targets and awkward stances to pose challenges.

Po'ipu Bay Golf Course   GOLF
(☑742-8711, 800-858-6300; www.poipubaygolf.com; 2250 Ainako St; nonguest/guest $240/160, club rental $55) The South Shore's long-standing jewel, this 18-hole, par-72 course adjacent to the Grand Hyatt Kaua'i Resort & Spa covers 210 seaside acres. Greens fees are reduced at noon (to $145) and then further reduced at 2:30pm (to $85). Greens fee includes a cart.

The windswept Maha'ulepu Coast resembles no other on Kaua'i: lithified sand-dune cliffs, pounding surf and three pristine beaches still free from mass tourism. Known as Kaua'i's last undeveloped accessible coast, it lies just east of Shipwreck Beach.

The best way to explore the coast is hiking the **Maha'ulepu Heritage Trail** (www. hikemahaulepu.org), a pleasant hike that runs for almost 4 miles from Shipwreck Beach to Ha'ula Beach (you can turn back at any point for a shorter, but still stunning, walk). To reach the trailhead, park in the Grand Hyatt lot at the end of Ainako St. From the beach, head east through the ironwood trees. Along the coast, you will pass spectacular cliffs of lithified sand dunes, tide pools in rocky coves and even the ruins of a heiau.

The Maha'ulepu Coast comprises a string of beaches – **Maha'ulepu Beach** (Gillin's Beach), **Kawailoa Bay** and **Ha'ula Beach** – from west to east. Waters are choppy and better suited to experienced swimmers than once-a-year tourists, but hiking is enticing year-round. Near Maha'ulepu Beach you'll see the sole house on the entire coast, the **Gillin Beach House** (☎742-7561; www.gillinbeachhouse.com; per week from $3090), originally built in 1946 by Elbert Gillin, a civil engineer with the Koloa Sugar Plantation.

If you must drive, go past the Grand Hyatt, proceed for 1.5 miles on the unpaved road and turn right where it dead-ends at a gate (open 7:30am to 6pm, to 7pm summer). Continue past the gatehouse until you reach the beach parking area. Access hours are strictly enforced.

Two excellent resources are the **Maha'ulepu Heritage Trail** (www.hikemahaulepu. org) website and *Kaua'i's Geologic History: A Simplified Guide* by Chuck Blay and Robert Siemers. Also see **Malama Maha'ulepu** (www.malama-mahaulepu.org), a nonprofit group working to preserve the area, which is owned by Steve Case, the co-founder of America Online.

Other Activities

Outfitters Kaua'i　　　　　KAYAKING $$
(☎742-9667, 888-742-9887; www.outfitterskauai.com; Po'ipu Plaza, 2827-A Po'ipu Rd; ☺reservations taken 8am-9pm) Offers a sea-kayaking tour (adult/child 12 years to 14 years $148/118); the eight-hour paddle makes a good training prelude to the grueling Na Pali voyage. They also offer stand up paddle tours (half-day per person $122) down a jungle stream through the Hule'ia National Wildlife Refuge.

CJM Country Stables　　　HORSEBACK RIDING
(☎742-6096; www.cjmstables.com; 2hr rides $98-125; ☺rides 9:30am & 2pm Mon-Sat) If you want a break from hoofin' it yourself, hop on a horse. The slow, nose-to-tail, follow-the-leader group rides would bore experienced riders, who can arrange private rides, instead.

Anara Spa　　　　　　　　　SPA
(☎742-1234; www.anaraspa.com; Grand Hyatt Kaua'i Resort & Spa, 1571 Po'ipu Rd; massage per hr $160-235, facials $165-250) When it was renovated in 2007, it was an extreme makeover, with the spa emerging as a 20,000-sq-ft tropical fantasyland, with gardens and waterfalls to soothe the eyes while the face and body indulges in a splurge-worthy menu of delicious

services. Access to the lap pool and fitness center is free with a 50-minute spa treatment.

Spa at Koa Kea Hotel & Resort　　SPA
(☎828-8888; www.koakea.com; 2251 Poipu Rd; massages $105-210; ☺8am-7pm) Offers five treatment rooms (including one for couples) and focuses on the use of indigenous products such as *Awapuhi* root, red Kauai clay and pineapple. Professional massage therapists are outsourced from the Po'ipu area so at least one days' notice is recommended.

☞ Tours

Unless you're as water-phobic as a cat, we recommend a snorkeling tour (see p542) and p547) to maximize your cruise experience. But if you're seeking a sunset tour, **Capt Andy's Sailing Adventures** (☎335-6833, 800-535-0830; www.napali.com; Port Allen Marina Center, Waialo Rd; adult/child $69/50) departs from Kukui'ula Harbor between 4pm and 5pm for a scenic two-hour cruise.

✸✸ Festivals & Events

Prince Kuhio Celebration of the Arts　　　　ARTS
(☎240-6369; www.princekuhio.wetpaint.com) Day-long celebration, in late March, to

honor Prince Jonah Kuhio Kalaniana'ole, who was born in 1872 on the site of Prince Kuhio Park.

Garden Isle Artisan Fair MUSIC, CRAFTS
(☑245-9021) When on Kaua'i, buy Kaua'i-made. At this triannual fair in mid-March, mid-August and mid-October, you'll find handcrafted items, Hawaiian music and local grinds. Usually located opposite Po'ipu Beach Park.

Kaua'i Mokihana Festival Hula Competition CULTURAL
(☑822-2166; www.maliefoundation.org) Three days of serious hula performances at the Grand Hyatt in late September, both *kahiko* (ancient) and *'auana* (modern). At $5 to $10, it's a must-see.

Hawaiiana Festival CULTURAL
(☑240-6369; www.alohafestivals.com) Part of the Aloha Festival, this mid-October three-day event features Hawaiian crafts, demonstrations, hula and a luau.

🛏 Sleeping

The majority of accommodations in Po'ipu are condos, which are available for all budget levels. Rates vary depending on the owner or agency renting each unit; we list typical or average rates. Vacation-rental homes can offer more privacy and drive-up access. The two major hotels are the high-end Grand Hyatt and business-class Sheraton Kaua'i.

Check out the **Po'ipu Beach Resort Association** (www.poipubeach.org) website for additional listings; note that condo links often go merely to agencies, however. If you decide on a specific condo, always check **Vacation Rentals by Owner** (www.vrbo.

com) for additional rentals; owners might offer better deals than agencies.

That said, you don't incur extra fees if you book with agencies and they can steer you to appropriate properties, especially if you're seeking a vacation-rental home.

Agencies

Parrish Collection Kaua'i CONDOS, VACATION RENTALS
(☑742-2000, 800-742-1412; www.parrishkauai. com; 3176 Po'ipu Rd, Suite 1, Koloa, Hawaii 96756) Well-established agency for condos and vacation homes. Friendly, accommodating staff. Main, on-site agency for Waikomo Stream Villas and Nihi Kai Villas.

Po'ipu Connection Realty CONDOS
(☑800-742-2260; www.poipuconnection.com; PO Box 1022, Koloa, Hawaii 96756) Condo listings only; good prices and personalized service.

Po'ipu Beach Vacation Rentals CONDOS, VACATION RENTALS
(☑742-2850, 800-684-5133; www.pbvacation rentals.com; PO Box 1258, Koloa, Hawaii 96756) Good prices; limited selection includes condos and vacation homes.

Aikane Po'ipu Beach Houses VACATION RENTALS
(☑742-1778, 877-742-1778; www.kauaivacation properties.com/poipu.htm) Choose from a choice crop of dreamy beach houses near Brennecke's Beach.

Properties

TOP CHOICE **Hideaway Cove Villas** CONDOS $$
(☑635-8785, 866-849-2426; www.hideawaycove. com; 2307 & 2315 Nalo Rd; studios $175-190, 1 bedroom $205-220, 2 bedroom $250-275; ❄🤙) Near

---

GIVE IT AWAY TO KEEP IT

While relishing all the tropical delight Kaua'i has to offer, an hour or two spent giving back may end up being your fondest memory. Here are a few welcomed volunteering opportunities. When possible, plan ahead:

Hui O Laka (☑335-9975; www.kokee.org) Hands-on work restoring forested areas impacted by overuse or invasive species.

Kauai Humane Society (☑632-0610; www.kauaihumane.org) Show up, pet a dog or cat, try not to fall in love.

Limahuli Garden (☑826-1053; www.ntbg.org) Assisting with general gardening and propagation.

National Botanical Tropical Gardens (☑332-7324; www.nbtg.org) Assisting with general gardening and propagation.

Surfrider Foundation (www.surfriderkauai.ning.com) Beach clean-ups happen regularly.

Almost two decades after the Hurricane 'Iniki blasted the island, residents can still give blow-by-blow accounts of their survival on September 11, 1992. 'Iniki blew in with sustained winds of 145mph and gusts of 165mph or more (a weather-station meter in mountainous Koke'e broke off at 227mph). It snapped trees by the thousands and totally demolished 1420 homes (and swept over 60 out to sea). Another 5000 homes were severely damaged, while thousands more sustained minor damage. Most of the island lacked electricity for over a month, and some areas were without power for up to three months. Thirty-foot waves washed away entire wings of beachfront hotels, particularly those in Po'ipu and Princeville.

During the immediate aftermath, residents were remarkably calm and law-abiding, despite the lack of power, radio or TV. Communities held parties to share and consume perishable food. Looting was rare and when grocers allowed affected residents to take what they needed, residents insisted on paying.

Miraculously, only four people died, but the total value of the damage to the island was $1.8 billion (1992 USD). The tourism industry bounced back by the late 1990s and today is thriving. While locals notice the changed landscape, newcomers would never realize the havoc wreaked 15 years ago. Unfortunately a couple of Kaua'i's native bird species have not been spotted since 'Iniki.

Because 'Iniki struck during daylight, many residents recorded the event in real time with camcorders. The best footage was compiled into an hour-long video ($24.95), which you can order at www.video-hawaii.com/iniki.html.

Po'ipu Beach Park, these impeccable, modern and professionally managed units are a cut above their peers. All feature private lanai, fine hardwood flooring, genuine art and antiques and name-brand appliances. Cleaning fees range from $95 to $145.

Po'ipu Kapili CONDOS $$
(☎742-6449, 800-443-7714; www.poipukapili.com; 2221 Kapili Rd; 1/2 bedroom from $225/340; ☒) An all-around winner, this 60-unit condo features gorgeously landscaped ground, and spacious units (1120 to 1820 sq ft) that are consistent in quality, with lots of hardwood, big plush beds, extra bathroom, quality electronics and wired internet access. The closest sandy beach, fronting the Sheraton, is within walking distance.

Prince Kuhio Resort CONDOS $
(☎888-747-2988; www.prince-kuhio.com; 5061 Lawa'i Rd; studios $50-115, 1 bedroom $90-160; ☀☒) This 90-unit condo is a budget property, so don't expect spiffy furnishings and floors. But it's great value for the location across the road from Lawa'i (Beach House) Beach. All units have full kitchens and breezy windows, while pleasantly landscaped grounds surround a decent-size pool. Units vary markedly in quality. Find low rates at Po'ipu Connection Realty, Po'ipu Beach Vacation Rentals and www.vrbo.com.

Kaua'i Cove Cottages COTTAGE $$
(☎742-2562, 800-624-9945; www.kauaicove. com; 2672 Pu'uholo Rd; studios $99-185; ☀�207) Near Koloa Landing, this trio of 'cottages' (triplex is more apt) deftly blends modern amenities into cozy tropical bungalows. Although studio size is limited, the efficient layout allows bamboo canopy beds, vaulted ceilings, fully loaded kitchenette and lots of windows. Convenient parking is right outside your doorstep. Depending on your length of stay, there's a $65 cleaning fee.

Nihi Kai Villas CONDOS $$
(☎742-2000, 800-742-1412; www.parrishkauai .com; 1870 Ho'one Rd; 1 bedroom $145-190, 2 bedroom $159-251; @�207☒) For moderate spenders who want walkable beach access, here's the ticket. Po'ipu Beach Park is just down the block, although proximity depends on unit location (ie price). Of 70 units, half are well managed by the on-site Parrish agency. At 1000 sq ft to 2000 sq ft, they're comfortable, with full kitchens, two or more private lanai and washer-dryer. Not all units have wireless.

Kiahuna Plantation CONDOS $$
(☎742-6411, 800-542-4862; www.outrigger.com; 2253 Po'ipu Rd; 1 bedroom $179-219, 2 bedroom $265-319; ☒) This aging beauty is still a hot property because it's among the rare accommodations flanking a swimmable

beach. Of course, only a few units actually sit on the beach (money talks). Units are comfy, with fully equipped kitchen, living room and large lanai, but furnishings seem worn. On-site agencies include **Outrigger and Castle Resorts** (📞742-2200; www.castleresorts.com; 1/2 bedroom from $186/390) but **Kiahuna Beachside** (📞937-6642; www.kiahuna.com; 1/2 bedroom from $365/565) manages the best beachfront properties.

Sheraton Kaua'i Resort   RESORT **$$$**
(📞800-782-9488, 742-1661; www.sheraton-kauai.com; 2440 Ho'onani Rd; garden/ocean r from $240/460; ✱☎🛜🏊) The business-class Sheraton has one enviable advantage: a prime stretch of sandy, swimmable, sunset-perfect beach. Rooms are decent, if unmemorable, and the low-end Garden View or Partial Ocean View wings are nowhere near the beach. Eco-efforts include recycling bins and free breakfast coupons for guests who forgo maid service that day.

Grand Hyatt Kaua'i
Resort & Spa   RESORT **$$$**
(📞800-554-9288, 742-1234; www.kauai.hyatt.com; 1571 Po'ipu Rd; r garden-view $280-430, deluxe ocean-view $470-720; ✱🏊) Po'ipu's glamour gal is 602-rooms strong and she loves to show off, with a soaring lobby, tropical gardens, massive spa, world-renowned golf course, oceanfront restaurants and meandering 'river pools.' Inside, the room decor is typically tropical, but obviously a class above. Recent renovations have taken *nice* rooms and put an uber in front of them, with marble countertops in the bathrooms and a splash of fresh Hawaiiana decor. What's missing is a swimmable *real* beach, not just the artificial one.

Koa Kea Hotel & Resort   RESORT **$$$**
(📞828-8888; www.koakea.com; 2251 Po'ipu Rd; r garden-view $329, partial ocean-view $349, ocean-view $449; ✱🛜🏊) With 121 rooms and a beachfront location (near Kiahuna Plantation), this high-end boutique hotel is gorgeously appointed and strives to keep a personal, family-oriented atmosphere. The Hawaiiana themed rooms are intoxicatingly decorated with koa wood, leather lounge furniture, and each boasts an unobstructed view from its private lanai.

Whalers Cove   CONDOS **$$$**
(📞742-7571, 800-225-2683; www.whalerscoveresort.com; 2640 Pu'uholo Rd; 1/2 bedroom from $349/479; ✱🛜🏊) Po'ipu's most luxurious condo suits discriminating travelers

who want luxury without a smidgen of tourist fuss. Units are palatial (1300 sq ft on average), elegant and utterly immaculate, often with gleaming marble floors, granite counters and mansion-worthy furniture. Truly gawk-worthy is the amount of prized koa wood used for doors and furnishings.

🍴 Eating

TOP CHOICE **Josselin's Tapas**
Bar & Grill   HAWAII REGIONAL **$$**
(www.josselins.com; Kukui'ula Village; tapas $9-18; ☾5-10pm) A trendy and vivacious atmosphere sets the tone for some good eats here. Heavily revered Chef Jean Marie Josselin artistically conjures daily creations of Asian fusion tapas. New to Po'ipu it has quickly nestled into its own niche among other Po'ipu big-hitters and offers a more relaxed approach to epic eats.

TOP CHOICE **Casa di Amici**   ITALIAN **$$**
(2301 Nalo Rd; dinner mains $23-29; ☾from 6pm) Often overlooked due to an obscure location, this restaurant is an unpretentious gem. The chef focuses on using the highest quality ingredients, from locally grown greens to black truffles from Italy to homemade sausage. The menu's traditional Italian pastas and meats are joined by multicultural standouts such as the grilled miso-ginger ahi and paella risotto.

Papalani Gelato   ICE CREAM **$**
(www.papalanigelato.com; Po'ipu Shopping Village, 2360 Kiahuna Plantation Dr; single scoop $3.75; ☾11:30am-9:30pm) With mouthwatering flavors (all homemade on-site), you can't go wrong with classic vanilla bean or pistachio gelato. But, for local color, try the creamy sorbetto, made with fresh, island-grown starfruit, lychee, mango, guava or avocado.

Savage Shrimp   SEAFOOD **$**
(www.savageshrimpkauai.com; Kukui'ula Village; two tacos $8.50, plates $12.50; ☾11am-9pm) Times have changed for Susan Allyn and her former roadside van serving heaping plates of Brazilian-style shrimp. Situated in the new plush Kukui'ula Village, expect a plethora of shrimp choices from fried to coconut to six varieties of scampi. Po'boys, fresh fish, and Italian salads round out the expanded menu.

Plantation Gardens
Restaurant & Bar   HAWAII REGIONAL **$$**
(www.pgrestaurant.com; Kiahuna Plantation, 2253 Po'ipu Rd; appetizers $8-12, mains $19-28; ☾5:30-9pm) Set in a historic plantation house, this

restaurant is lovely without trying too hard. The menu is mercifully concise and features locally grown ingredients, kiawe (a relative of the mesquite tree) grilling for a rich, smoky flavor and lots of fresh seafood. Lit by tiki torches at night, the setting is ideal for large gatherings.

Beach House Restaurant SEAFOOD $$$
(www.the-beach-house.com; 5022 Lawa'i Rd; dinner mains $26-40; ⊘winter 5:30-9:30pm, summer 6-10pm) It's overrated, perhaps, but the Beach House is the iconic spot for sunset dining and worth a splurge. Current chef Todd Barrett's specialties include macadamia nut-crusted mahi-mahi and watermelon salad with gorgonzola cheese and just-picked Omao greens. Book well in advance.

Tidepools HAWAII REGIONAL $$$
(Grand Hyatt Kaua'i Resort & Spa, 1571 Po'ipu Rd; mains $28-40; ⊘5:30-10pm) Surrounded by waterfalls and lagoons filled with koi, the Grand Hyatt's signature restaurant is more romantic oasis than lively nightspot. The surprisingly brief menu presents decent but derivative examples of island fusion, from grilled peppered ahi with coconut-jasmine rice to grilled chicken breast with Okinawan sweet-potato purée.

Roy's Po'ipu Bar & Grill HAWAII REGIONAL $$$
(www.roysrestaurant.com; Po'ipu Shopping Village; mains $37-47; ⊘5:30-9:30pm) Still iconic, still wildly popular, Roy's continues to please the foodies. Signature dishes include melt-in-your-mouth *misoyaki* (miso-marinated) butterfish, and pesto-steamed *'ono* (white-fleshed wahoo) sizzled in cilantro-ginger-peanut oil. Expect a shopping-mall setting and notoriously high-decibel dining room.

Self-Catering

Living Foods Market & Café MARKET, CAFE $
(www.livingfoodskauai.com; Kukui'ula Village; ⊘7am-8pm, cafe to 4pm) Gourmet groceries include cheeses, meats, wines and local produce. The cafe offers paninis, fancy pizzas and obscurely delicious items like lobster pot pie.

Kukui'ula Store MARKET $
(Po'ipu Plaza, 2827 Po'ipu Rd; ⊘8:30am-8:30pm Mon-Fri, to 6:30pm Sat & Sun) This indie supermarket resembles a bodega from the outside, but stocks a good selection of basics and wholesome foods. For more selection, go to Koloa's grocers and fish market.

TOP CHOICE **The Point Lounge** BAR
(Sheraton Kaua'i Resort; ⊘11am-midnight, closed lunch Mon & Tue) An informal hangout for sunset viewing and people-watching, this bar mixes a great mojito ($9.50 to $11.50) or pours from the tap. For lunch and dinner, cut costs by eating from the excellent menu of appetizers and sandwiches.

Stevenson's Library BAR
(Grand Hyatt Kaua'i Resort & Spa; 1571 Po'ipu Rd; ⊘6-10:30pm) Resembling a too-cool-for-you gentleman's club, this handsome lounge is rather incongruous to the island scene but serves good (if pricey) sushi, desserts and drinks. Kids are permitted until 9pm, meaning that a romper-room vibe occasionally prevails till then. Highlights include the gleaming 27ft koa-wood bar and live jazz from 8pm to 10pm.

Seaview Terrace BAR
(Grand Hyatt Kaua'i Resort & Spa; 1571 Po'ipu Rd; ⊘4:30-8:30pm) For free resort 'entertainment,' arrive before sunset on Tuesday and Saturday for a torch-lighting ceremony and either Hawaiian music or *na keiki* (children's) hula shows. Call for start time, which varies by season.

Luau

Between the two, the Sheraton's show gives you more for your money. Also consider driving to Lihu'e for Kilohana Plantation's new and different Luau Kalamaku.

TOP CHOICE **Surf to Sunset Luau** LUAU
(☎742-8205; www.sheraton-kauai.com; Sheraton Kaua'i Resort, 2440 Ho'onani Rd; adult/child $99/48; ⊘check-in 6pm Fri) We rate the Sheraton's 'Surf to Sunset' luau A (excellent) for oceanfront setting and B (good) for the food and show, which is the standard Polynesian revue. For a commercial luau, the audience size is small at 200 to 300. Beware: the humorous emcee expects lots of audience participation.

Havaiki Nui Luau LUAU
(☎240-6456; www.grandhyattkauailuau.com; Grand Hyatt Kaua'i Resort & Spa, 1571 Po'ipu Rd; adult/child $94/57; ⊘check-in 5:15pm Sun & Thu) The Havaiki Nui Luau is a well-oiled production befitting the Grand Hyatt setting, but the price is steep, especially if rain forces the show indoors.

ⓘ Information

Bank of Hawaii (☑742-6800; Po'ipu Shopping Village, 2360 Kiahuna Plantation Dr; ☺8:30am-4pm Mon-Thu, to 6pm Fri) Does not cash travelers checks.

Po'ipu Beach Resort Association (www.poipu beach.org) For general information on Po'ipu and the whole South Shore.

ⓘ Getting There & Around

To get here from Lihu'e, the quickest way is to exit on Maluhia Rd. Po'ipu, a sprawled-out town, necessitates a car to go anywhere besides the beach. Navigating is easy, with just two main roads: Po'ipu Rd along eastern Po'ipu and Lawa'i Rd along western Po'ipu.

The Kaua'i Bus (p467) runs through Koloa and into Po'ipu (Map p532). It's an option to get here from other towns but a limited in-town mode.

Kalaheo

POP 4200

From the highway, Kalaheo is a one-stoplight cluster of eateries and little else. But along the backroads, this neighborly town offers peaceful accommodations away from the tourist crowd. If you plan to hike at Waimea Canyon and Koke'e State Parks but also want easy access to Po'ipu beaches, Kalaheo's central location is ideal.

The town's post office and a handful of restaurants are clustered around the intersection of the Kaumuali'i Hwy and Papalina Rd.

◉ Sights

Kukuiolono Park   PARK

Unless you stay in Kalaheo, you would probably miss this little park (open from 6:30am to 6:30pm), which offers a nine-hole golf course, modest Japanese garden, sweeping views and grassy grounds for strolling or jogging. In 1860 King Kamehameha III leased the land to Duncan McBryde, whose son, Walter, the pineapple baron, eventually purchased the 178-acre estate. He built the public golf course in 1929 and deeded the entire site for use as a public park upon his death. Walter McBryde is buried near the eighth hole of the golf course. To get here, turn left onto Papalina Rd from Kaumuali'i Hwy (heading west).

Hanapepe Valley Lookout   VISTA

(Map p464) The scenic lookout that pops up shortly after the 14-mile marker offers a view deep into Hanapepe Valley. The red-clay walls of the cliffs are topped by a layer of green cane, like frosting on a cake. This sight is but a teaser of the dramatic vistas that await at Waimea Canyon.

While old king sugar might still dominate Hanapepe Valley, look across the highway toward the ocean to see Kaua'i's current major commercial crop, coffee.

🏃 Activities

Kukuiolono Golf Course   GOLF

(☑332-9151; Kukuiolono Park; greens fee adult/child $9/3, pull carts $6; ☺6:30am-6:30pm) Golf practically for free at Kukuiolono Golf Course, an unassuming nine-hole, par-36 golf course with spectacular ocean and valley views – and zero attitude. Grab a bucket of balls for $2 and hit the driving range – first-come, first-served.

Poise Pilates   PILATES

(☑651-5287; www.poisepilates.org; 4432 Papalina Rd; 55min private session $70, mat class $20) For an indoor workout, work with owner Theresa Ouano (the epitome of fitness) at Poise Pilates, a cheerful, well-equipped studio. Prices drop if you buy in multiples.

🛏 Sleeping

TOP CHOICE **Hale O Nanakai**   B&B $

(☑652-8071; www.nanakai.com; 3726 Nanakai Pl; r incl breakfast $75-150, 1 bedroom $150-175; ☎) Guests take first priority at this lovingly designed B&B with accommodations for every budget. Traditional rooms all feature plush carpeting, Sleep Number beds, flat-screen HDTV and generous continental breakfast. Guests share a huge deck and common area with awesome coastal views. For more privacy, choose the downstairs apartment.

Hale Ikena Nui   B&B $

(☑332-9005, 800-550-0778; www.kauaivacation home.com; 3957 Uluali'i St; r incl breakfast/1 bedroom $75/95; ☎) Located at the end of a cul de sac, this spacious in-law apartment (1000 sq ft) includes a living area with sofabed, full kitchen and washer-dryer. Singles can rent the B&B room, which is less private but includes private bathroom and use of the main house. Bonus: an irresistible dog named Bear.

Kauai Garden Cottages   COTTAGE $

(☑332-0877; www.kauaigardencottages.com; 5350 Pu'ulima Rd; studios $100; ☎) Perched high in the Kalaheo upcountry, this meticulously designed pair of studio units gleams with rich Indonesian hardwood floors under

KANE HULA

The intoxicatingly graceful movements of hula dancing have not always been practiced solely by those with two X chromosomes. Prior to Western contact, *kane* (men) performed hula, until early 19th-century Christian missionaries discouraged its practice all together. Today, a slow-growing revival of *kane hula* has taken shape, with much credit given to local *kumu* (teachers).

soaring cathedral ceilings with cheerful stained-glass accents. The rooms adjoin a vast lanai overlooking a stunningly green valley that gives new meaning to 'valley view.' Two-for-one deal: rent both rooms for only $150 nightly.

Bamboo Jungle House　　　COTTAGE $$
(332-5515, 888-332-5115; www.kauai-bedand breakfast.com; 3829 Waha Rd; r incl breakfast $130-170;) In a lovely plantation-style house, the classic B&B experience awaits: friendly hosts, home-cooked breakfasts and 8am gatherings around the morning table. The three rooms are immaculate, with snow-white walls, fluffy canopy beds and sparkling French doors. Outside, enjoy a 38ft lap pool amid jungly foliage and lava-rock waterfall. It's geared towards couples and children aren't allowed.

✕ Eating

TOP CHOICE Kalaheo Café & Coffee Co　　　CAFE, SANDWICHES $$
(www.kalaheo.com; 2-2560 Kaumuali'i Hwy; breakfast & lunch $6-10, dinner $16-26; ☺6am-2:30pm daily, 5:30-8:30pm Wed-Sat) Big thumbs up for this roadside cafe, which boasts a spacious dining room, easy parking and a satisfying menu of healthy California-style cooking. Breakfast favorites include a well-stuffed veggie wrap and build-your-own omelets, while the lunch hour brings fresh Kalaheo greens and Dagwood-sized sandwiches. The last temptation? Homemade fruit crisp.

Mark's Place　　　CAFE $
(2-3687 Kaumuali'i Hwy; plates $6-7; ☺10am-8pm Mon-Fri) If you're curious about the legendary plate lunch, skip breakfast and come here famished at noon. Classic plate lunches feature generous portions of meaty mains (from teriyaki beef to Korean chicken), plus rice and salad. Healthier gourmet options are available. Located off the highway, east of Kalaheo.

Pomodoro　　　ITALIAN $$
(Rainbow Plaza, Kaumuali'i Hwy; mains $16-27; ☺5:30-9:30pm Mon-Sat) Unless you know it's there, you'd never expect such a romantic restaurant in an unmemorable business mall. But locals always cite Pomodoro for traditional dishes such as veal parmigiana ($27) and linguini with white or red clam sauce ($22). With candlelit tables and white tablecloths, the setting is intimate yet neighborhood-casual.

Shopping

Malie Organics Boutique　　　ORGANIC BEAUTY
(866-767-5727, 332-6220; www.malie.com; 4353 Wai'alo Rd; ☺9am-4pm Mon-Fri) Partnering with sustainable farmers, Malie Organics has a claim to fame in its succulent body butters and exquisite essences. Try the Koke'e-inspired fragrance; a portion of the proceeds from that Koke'e line go specifically toward the preservation of Koke'e State Park.

WAIMEA CANYON & THE WESTSIDE

Kaua'i doesn't get more local than the Westside, where revered traditions and local-style family pride reign supreme. Here, you're more likely to hear fluent Hawaiian, spot real-life *paniolo* (cowboys) and see old-school fishermen sewing their nets from scratch than anywhere else on the island. Deep, riveting red canyons and a seemingly infinite expanse of ocean offers the widest range of atmosphere and ambience found on Kaua'i. The least touristy and the most tried and true, the Westside isn't for everyone; it's good like that.

'Ele'ele & Numila

POP 2193

You might pass by the small town of Numila and its bigger, albeit still small, neighbor, 'Ele'ele, without a second thought. However, it's a pleasant, rural area, and offers a few convenient stops at the 'Ele'ele shopping center, including a **post office** (☺8am-4pm Mon-Fri, 9-11am Sat). The most noticeable of the bunch of small shops and restaurants is

Grinds Café (Map p543; ✆335-6027; www.grinds cafe.net; 'Ele'ele Shopping Center, 4469 Waialo Rd; breakfast $5-10, lunch $5-12; ☺5:30am-6pm) – it's usually busy on weekend mornings, so your best options are to head in for a dawn-patrol espresso or Sunday-afternoon latte.

Though it lacks the cachet imparted on the reputable Kona coffee, **Kaua'i Coffee Company** (✆335-0813, 800-545-8605; www.kauai coffee.com; Halewili Rd; ☺9am-5pm) produces a sturdy cup of joe. Take the self-guided tour of the well-manicured plantation, which functions on 100% renewable energy. The drive once you're off the highway might seem long, but take in the eye candy: it's adorned with neatly placed coffee trees and ablaze with bougainvillea.

Port Allen

Though the area is being developed to take advantage of its exquisite waterfront, Port Allen remains mostly an industrial area that serves as a departure point for Na Pali tours.

The majority of Na Pali tours leave from Port Allen and, depending on the season, offer a variety of ways in which to enjoy this spectacular coastline, from snorkeling in summer to whale watching in winter.

You'll either go by Zodiac (raft) or catamaran; the former offers little respite from the waves and sun, the latter offers shaded benches, toilet and, of course, an unending supply of drinks and *pupu*. Regardless of your choice, take the information given by guides with a grain of salt – many tell tales of cannibalism and push inaccuracies about the *ali'i* in order to sensationalize the experience.

◉ Sights & Activities

Glass Beach   BEACH
Trash as art – many a visitor has pored through the colorful well-worn remnants of glass along the shoreline of the aptly named Glass Beach, east of Port Allen. Glass 'pebbles,' along with abandoned metals (some with newfound patina, some not so much), have washed up from an old dumpsite nearby, showing that decades of weather, too, can make art. To get to the little cove, take Aka'ula St, the last left before entering the Port Allen commercial harbor, go past the fuel-storage tanks and then curve to the right down a rutted dirt road that leads 100yd to the beach.

TOP CHOICE ▶ Holoholo Charters   SAILING, SNORKELING
(✆335-0815, 800-848-6130; www.holoholo charters.com; Port Allen Marina Center, Waialo Rd; adult/child $139/99; ☺6am-8pm) Among the best for delivering on its promises of sea-cave jaunts, *honu* sightings and augmented cultural lore. The two-hour sunset cruise offers the best deal, at $84. Save $10 by booking online.

Catamaran Kahanu   SAILING
(✆645-6176, 888-213-7711; www.catamaranka hanu.com; Port Allen Marina Center, Waialo Rd; 5hr tour adult/child $122/80, 3½hr tour $80/60) Another favorite that includes Hawaiian trades into its tour, thanks to basket-weaving demonstrations and making 'fishing lines' from *ti* (native plant) leaves and coconut fiber.

Capt Andy's Sailing Adventures   SAILING
(✆335-6833, 800-535-0830; www.napali.com; Port Allen Marina Center, Waialo Rd; 5hr snorkeling trip adult/child $139/99) Heads to Na Pali and prices often drop by $10 online. Plan on getting a little wet, a little cold and also a little sun along the way. The crew will be on the lookout for marine life, such as flying fish, sea turtles, dolphins and whales, depending on the time of year.

Blue Dolphin Charters   SNORKELING, DIVING
(✆335-5553, 877-511-1311; www.kauaiboats.com; Port Allen Marina Center, Waialo Rd; internet/regular booking $175/196) Offers a seven-hour snorkeling tour or five-hour Na Pali trip. For an additional $35, they'll take you on a one-tank dive – even if it's your first time.

Kaua'i Sea Tours   SAILING, SNORKELING
(✆826-7254, 800-733-7997; www.kauaiseatours. com; Aka'ula St, Port Allen) Lets you opt for summer Na Pali tour by catamaran (adult/child from $139/89) or the rougher, three-hour tour by raft (internet/regular adult from $119/129, child $69/79), or a three- to four-hour sightseeing tour of Na Pali or a five-hour dinner snorkeling tour (internet/regular from $139/148, child $99/109).

Captain Zodiac Raft Adventures   ZODIAC TOURS
(✆335-6833, 800-535-0830; www.napali.com; Port Allen Marina Center, Waialo Rd; adult/child $139/99) If a more rugged experience is your thing, then a Zodiac raft tour might be for you. Captain Andy's sister outfit offers a 5½-hour tour year-round.

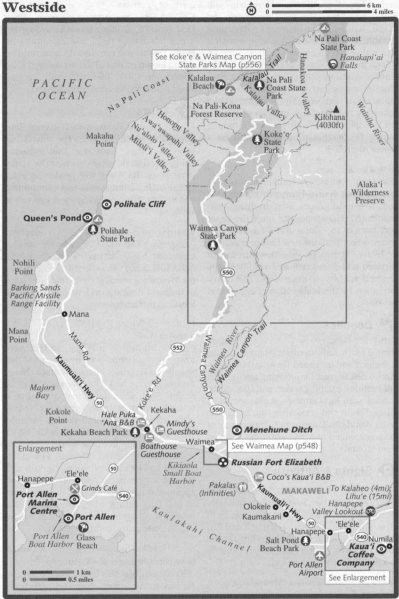

See Koke'e & Waimea Canyon State Parks Map (p556)

PACIFIC OCEAN

Na Pali Coast

Na Pali Coast State Park

Kalalau Beach

Kalalau Trail

Na Pali Coast State Park

Hanakoa Valley

Hanakapi'ai Falls

Hanapu Valley

Awa'awapuhi Valley

Nu'alolo Valley

Miloli'i Valley

Na Pali-Kona Forest Reserve

Kalalau Valley

Kilohana (4030ft)

Wainila River

Koke'e State Park

Makaha Point

Alaka'i Wilderness Preserve

Polihale Cliff

Queen's Pond

Polihale State Park

Waimea Canyon State Park

Nohili Point

Barking Sands Pacific Missile Range Facility

Mana

Mana Point

Kaumuali'i Hwy

Mana Rd

Majors Bay

Kokole Point

Koke'e Rd

552

Waimea Canyon Dr

Waimea River

Waimea Canyon Trail

550

Kekaha

Hale Puka 'Ana B&B

Kekaha Beach Park

Mindy's Guesthouse

Boathouse Guesthouse

Waimea

Menehune Ditch

See Waimea Map (p548)

Kikiaola Small Boat Harbor

Russian Fort Elizabeth

Coco's Kaua'i B&B

Pakalas (Infinities)

MAKAWELI

To Kalaheo (4mi); Lihu'e (15mi)

Hanapepe Valley Lookout

Kaua'i Coffee Company

Olokele

Kaumakani

Kaumuali'i Hwy

Hanapepe

'Ele'ele

Salt Pond Beach Park

Port Allen Airport

Numila

Kaulakahi Channel

Enlargement

Hanapepe

'Ele'ele

50

Grinds Café

540

Port Allen Marina Centre

Port Allen

Port Allen Boat Harbor

Glass Beach

0 — 1 km
0 — 0.5 miles

See Enlargement

KAUA'I HANAPEPE

🛍 Shopping

Kauai Chocolate Company FOOD
(www.kauaichocolate.us; 4341 Waialo Rd; ⊙11am-6pm Mon-Fri, to 5pm Sat, 11-3pm Sun) Prized treats include mouth-watering ganache-filled truffle, passion-fruit sugar-encrusted pastille.

Hanapepe

POP 2300

Proclaimed by its own people as 'Kaua'i's biggest little town,' Hanapepe carries a well-branded character that belies its less-than-crowded population. Here you will find some of the most local *grinds* on the island, hailing from plantation days and a tradition of home-cooking. Come with a thin wallet and an empty stomach and you will do just fine. Near Salt Pond Beach Park families continue the tradition of salt panning in basins, just as their ancestors did hundreds of years ago. The spiritual task of collecting reddish, large crystals of Hawaiian salt means the local seasoning (which cannot be purchased) continues to be a source of pride.

History

Like most river valleys Hanapepe was host to a thriving Native Hawaiian community and, like most places, that tradition was supplanted. Hanapepe was once the main port town of the island and a bustling economic center until the new harbor was built in Lihu'e. Hanapepe was downsized, but survived and found renewed vitality in the restoration of its old main street and transformation by the Friday Night Festival and Art Walk.

Beaches

Salt Pond Beach Park   BEACH
Named for its saltwater flats where seawater is drained and harvested for salt, this white-sand beach is great for lounging about, with full facilities, camping access and lifeguards. Popular with local families, it also serves as the end point and celebration site of the Expedia World Challenge, which draws some of the most skilled one-man outrigger canoers from around the globe.

◉ Sights & Activities

Kaua'i Cookie Company   FACTORY OUTLET
(1-3529 Kaumuali'I Hwy, Suite A; ⊘8am-4pm Mon-Fri, 9am-4pm Sat & Sun) If you're toting children, this island hallmark is a quick and fun stop. Kona coffee and chocolate chip are the standard faves. Find it across from Omoide Bakery & Wong's Chinese Deli.

Sparky's Peace Garden, Storybook Theatre   CHILDREN'S THEATER
(☏335-0712; 3814 Hanapepe Rd; www.storybook .org; ⊘hours vary) Though the timing might be tricky, if the stars align hours-wise with your visit, a quick stop at this multiuse theatre and interactive classroom is a fail-safe child-pleaser, offering distraction and a change of scenery. Call ahead, as hours vary.

Birds in Paradise   HANG GLIDING, FLYING
(☏822-5309; www.birdsinparadise.com; Burns Field, Puolo Rd; 30/90min lesson $150/335) For a real adrenaline rush, take an ultralight-plane lesson. You can also do a round-the-island lesson on one of these powered hang gliders for $300. Take the road for Salt Pond Beach Park to reach the airport.

Tours

Find a copy of Hanapepe's *Walking Tour Map* ($2), which describes the town's historic buildings. Look for the Swinging Bridge landmark, which crosses the Hanapepe River. Its funky old predecessor fell victim to 'Iniki, but thanks to a community-wide effort this new bridge was erected in 1996.

Inter-island Helicopters   HELICOPTER
(☏800-656-5009, 335-5009; www.interislandheli copters.com; 1-3410 Kaumuali'i Hwy; regular/waterfall flights $249/$355) Offers door-free flights over the Westside, providing views that rival some of the most rugged found; its flight record is less than perfect, however.

Hanapepe Friday Night Festival and Art Walk   ART
(⊘6-9pm Fri) Any given Friday, old Hanapepe town offers a candid peek into its art world, as galleries keep later hours, offering a chance to stroll, peruse and dine. The pace picks up around 5pm, when the former main drag is transformed by its already-heady mix of musicians, art installations and visitors. Meander through the galleries on the art walk, which house everything from the works of Sunday artists, island-inspired originals, Hawaiiana vintage and kitsch to photography, watercolors and a sampling of Asian art. Though art aficionados may snub some of the collections as less than cutting edge, remember Hanapepe is small town – and proud of it. Following are some participating galleries:

Arius Hopman Gallery   ART GALLERY
(www.hopmanart.com; 3840C Hanapepe Rd; ⊘10:30am-3:30pm Mon-Thu, to 9pm Fri) An eye for recognizing, composing and presenting nature's beauty means Hopman's photography certainly beats any postcard shot taken on the island.

Art of Marbling/Robert Bader Wood Sculpture   ART GALLERY
(3890 Hanapepe Rd; ⊘10am-5pm Sat-Thu, to 9pm Fri) Becky J Wold's work on silk and

her husband's work in wood make for unique collecting, whether it's a small paper or Cook Island Pine work.

Banana Patch Studio   ART GALLERY
(www.bananapatchstudio.com; 3865 Hanapepe Rd; ⊙10am-4:30pm Sat-Thu, to 9pm Fri) Koi pond watercolors, vibrant island art, souvenir ceramic tiles.

TOP CHOICE *Dawn Traina Gallery*   ART GALLERY
(3840B Hanapepe Rd; ⊙6-9pm Fri or by appointment) Housed in one of the more understated galleries, her detailed research of Hawaiian culture shines through in drawings, paintings and other art.

Kauai Fine Arts   ART GALLERY
(www.brunias.com; 3751 Hanapepe Rd; ⊙9:30am-4:30pm Mon-Thu & Sat, to 9pm Fri) If you're sending something home or want to get your hands on a unique map – including navigational charts – this is a great little spot to peruse. Also sells prints, Ni'ihau lei and other works.

🛏 Sleeping & Eating

Though there aren't any hotels or rentals to speak of, Salt Pond Beach Park offers convenient camping. See p463 for permit information.

TOP CHOICE Hanapepe Café & Bakery   CAFE $$
(3830 Hanapepe Rd; dinner $18-25; ⊙bakery 7am-3pm, cafe 11am-3pm, dinner 6-9pm Fri) With walls covered with the work of local artists and an air full of either the scent of freshly baked goods or the sound of live music, this quaint stop is a must. Seafood seekers and vegetarians will appreciate the menu here. Breakfasts such as frittata with red

potatoes ($8) pair well with spicy espresso, and build-your-own burgers make a great $7 lunch.

Omoide Bakery & Wong's
Chinese Deli   BAKERY, DELI $
(1-3543 Kaumuali'i Hwy; mains $7.50-9.75; ⊙9:30am-9pm Tue-Sun) This well-known establishment also serves up fresh-baked, white-flour-based comfort eats like sesame-and-black bean *manju* (Japanese cake filled with sweet bean paste) and Portuguese sweet bread (similar to what US mainlanders think of as Hawaiian or pineapple bread).

Taro Ko Chips Factory   SNACKS $
(3940 Hanapepe Rd; small bags $4; ⊙8am-5pm) This is the place to stop if you want a unique alternative to getting your French fries fix. Thinly sliced *kalo* that's seasoned, slathered with oil and tortured in a deep wok makes for some crispy, somewhat sweet but mostly salty crunching.

Bobbie's Island Restaurant HAWAII REGIONAL $
(3620 Hanapepe Rd; mains $6.95; ⊙10am-3pm Mon-Sat, 5-8:30pm Thu-Sat) With fish and chips, local-style plate lunches and a killer roast pork gravy, this is a predominantly locals' spot and boasts such comforting, high-calorie eats as *loco moco* and pork *katsu* (great for a rainy day or post-hike meal).

Da Imu Hut Café   CAFE $
(1-3959 Kaumuali'i Hwy; ⊙10am-2pm, 5-8pm Mon-Fri & 10am-1pm Sat) Specializing in local food, this is the perfect place to pick up lunch ($6.95) for a drive up to the canyon or a beach picnic.

Kaua'i Pupu Factory   TAKEOUT $
(1-3566 Kaumuali'i Hwy; plate lunch $6.25, ahi poke per lb $9; ⊙9am-5:30pm Mon-Fri, to 3pm

WHY FLY?

For many, getting a bird's-eye view of the verdant majesty of the Garden Island is a once-in-a-lifetime opportunity. As well, the chance to take a breath from above and witness aggressive earth at its finest is worth the risk of a man-made flying vessel and the dough the journey requires. But for many on the ground it's an audible thorn in their side.

The Sierra Club and other island advocacy groups have long pushed for limits on the freedom of commercial aircrafts to fly over residential neighborhoods and Federal Aviation Administraion–designated noise-abatement areas, For now it's a voluntary system, however, so the Sierra Club recommends that passengers ask pilots to avoid sensitive areas, such as the Kalalau Trail and popular beaches. Whether these recommendations are successful remains to be seen.

To stop what they call 'disrespectful air tourism,' a group called StopDAT (www.stopdat.org) is seeking to pinpoint the best and worst tour companies.

Sat) A down-home-style local. If you've got a big group, get enough for everyone, pack a cooler and head to the beach.

 Shopping

You'll find the artists who put the pep back in Hanapepe in many of the old main-street galleries.

Talk Story Bookstore   BOOKS
(www.talkstorybookstore.com; 3785 Hanapepe Rd; ⊙11am-5pm Mon-Thu, to 9pm Fri) This often stuffy (temperature, not attitude) but always intriguing 'westernmost bookstore in the United States' carries an assorted collection of both paper and hardbacks from obscure Hawaiian to a respectable 'classics' section with some real gems. The proprietors are extremely accommodating, to the point where they'll let you sample their eclectic record collection.

Puahina Moku o Kaua'i   CLOTHING
(www.warriordesignshawaii.com; 4545 Kona Rd; ⊙11am-5pm Mon-Thu, to 8pm Fri) With an eye for recognizing the need for traditional Hawaiian motifs fused with contemporary clothes, you'll find wearable keepsakes here. Originally designed shirts, skirts and tops adorning native *laua'e* and *ulu* (both symbolizing 'growth in excellence') are true keepsakes.

Amy Lauren's Gallery   GALLERY
(www.amylaurensgallery.com; 3890 Hanapepe Rd; ⊙11am-5pm Mon-Fri, to 9pm Fri) Here's a chance to buy originals instead of gicleé, though the latter are usually more affordable. This boutique-style gallery is something of a newbie, but still worth a perusal for its vibrant colors and on-site artists.

Jacqueline on Kaua'i   CLOTHING
(www.alohashirtlady.com; 3837 Hanapepe Rd; ⊙9am-9pm) Friendly and a bit eclectic, Jacqueline leaves her mark on her work in this consignment-store and boutique, where she sews the nonconsignment products herself, including Japanese-inspired silk robes and custom-made aloha shirts while you wait ($45 to $52, usually about one to two hours).

ⓘ Information

American Savings Bank (☑335-3118; 4548 Kona Rd)

Bank of Hawaii (☑335-5021; 3764 Hanapepe Rd) On the western end of Hanapepe Rd.

ⓘ Getting There & Around

Veer *mauka* onto Hanapepe Rd at the 'Kaua'i's Biggest Little Town' sign.

Waimea
POP 1924

One of several Waimeas in Hawai'i, this is not the surfing mecca nor is it the upscale cowboy town. This is the most historic Westside town, and its history can be seen from the ground up.

'Waimea' means reddish-brown water, and it refers to the river that picks up salt from the canyon and colors the ocean red. It was here that Captain Cook landed in 1778.

As is common in Hawaii, sugar played a role in the development of Waimea and the skeleton of the old Waimea mill can still be seen across the tech centers that house defense contractors working at the Pacific Missile Range Facility. The juxtaposition of what was the old economy and what some see as the economy of the future can be seen as symbolic.

As weather climates vary locationally throughout the island, so do social climates. Waimea today – an echo of its multi-generational plantation history – remains a predominantly local environment, though passersby might not notice, as the main thoroughfare moves swiftly through the quiet town, and residents of Kaua'i and Ni'ihau descent live in the above neighborhoods.

◉ Sights

West Kaua'i Technology & Visitors Center   MUSEUM
(☑338-1332; 9565 Kaumuali'i Hwy; ⊙9:30am-4pm Mon, Tue & Thu, to 12:30pm Fri) A good historical orientation point to the Westside, this two-phase complex doubles as a visitor center and offers a free, three-hour walking tour at 9:30am Mondays. Registration is required. At 9:30am on Fridays they offer a lei-making class.

Lucy Wright Park   HISTORICAL SITE
Though this park was the landing site of Captain Cook, the people chose to name it in honor of Lucy Wright, a revered schoolteacher. Here you'll find access to the river and beach, as well as camping facilities, though not much in the way of scenery. See p463 for information about camping permits.

Kiki a Ola (Menehune Ditch)   NATURAL SITE

Not much remains to be seen of this unique and still-functional ditch or aqueduct, but its archaeological significance begs repeating. It is the only example of precontact cut and dressed stonework in Hawaii, said to be the work of the *menehune*, who completed it within one night for the *ali'i*.

Russian Fort Elizabeth   HISTORICAL SITE

Russia befriended Kaua'i's King Kaumuali'i in the early 1800s; the relationship stood to help Kaumuali'i overcome King Kamehameha, and the Russians to use Hawaii as an oceangoing stop during their reign as prominent fur traders. This fort was begun in September 1816, but within a year was stopped – some say due to King Kamehameha's orders, and some to general suspicion of the Russians. Hawaiian troops used the fort until 1864. Now its remains look much like a sea-battered lava-rock wall.

Activities

There are three snorkel outfits offering Na Pali Coast snorkel tours from Kikiaola Small Boat Harbor.

 Na Pali Riders   SNORKELING

(☑742-6331; www.napaliriders.com; 9600 Kaumuali' Hwy; morning tour adult/child $109/99, afternoon tour $89/79) Tours are hosted by Captain Chris Turner, who is passionate about what he does and likes to think of his tour as being in the style of *National Geographic*. Turner offers an intimate setting, healthy snacks and a CD of photographs and footage taken on the trip, along with the feeling that you're going out with some of your favorite ragamuffin friends.

Liko Ho'okano   SNORKELING

(☑338-0333, 888-732-5456; www.liko-kauai.com; 9875 Waimea Rd; 5hr cruise adult/child $140/95) Run by a Kaua'i-born-and-raised Native Hawaiian, whose ancestors hailed from the 'forbidden island' of Ni'ihau, this outfit sails its 49ft power catamaran to the Na Pali Coast. The maximum group size is 34 and tours go as far as Ke'e Beach.

Na Pali Explorer   SNORKELING

(☑338-9999, 877-335-9909; www.napali-explorer.com; Kaumuali'i Hwy; 5hr tour adult/child $125/85) This outfit offers snorkeling trips on rigid-hull inflatable rafts – which have a hard bottom and inflatable sides, and are smoother than the all-inflatable Zodiacs. Expect between 16 and 35 passengers. The 48ft raft includes a restroom and canopy for shade. Runs out of Waimea from October to April.

Pakalas   SURFING

Between the 21- and 22-mile markers, you'll notice cars parked on the side of the highway in an area known as Makaweli. This is the access point to the fiercely defended local surf spot dubbed Pakalas, or Infinities, said to offer the 'longest lefts' anywhere on the island. It's also teeming with tiger sharks. As it's one of the few locals' breaks remaining, we'd recommend leaving it alone. Instead, try Kekaha or Polihale beach parks.

A Hideaway Spa   SPA, YOGA

(☑338-0005; www.ahideawayspa.com; Waimea Plantation Cottages, 9400 Kaumuali'i Hwy; massage $95-145, beachside extra $20, spa & skin treatments $55-130; ☺9am-6pm) The Hideaway offers a range of traditional Hawaiian massage techniques, such as *lomilomi*, and also features ayurvedic treatments, as well as oceanfront yoga classes (per person $15; ☺5pm Mon & Tue, 7am Wed & Fri, 8:30am Sat), which are ideal for newbies.

Festivals & Events

Waimea Town Celebration   CULTURAL

(☑338-1332; www.wkbpa.org) Free fun in mid-February includes rodeo, canoe race, food, crafts, and lei and hula competitions.

Waimea Lighted Christmas Parade   CHRISTMAS

(☑338-9957) Watch lighted floats through Waimea town. Parade starts at dusk, a week before Christmas.

STARRY STARRY NIGHT

With minimal city light interference the west side of Kaua'i is an ideal locale to take in the night's sky. The Kaua'i Education Association for Science & Astronomy (KEASA; ☑332-7827; www.keasa.org) holds free, monthly Starwatches on Saturdays closest to the new moon (the dark one). KEASA educators share both their gear and insights. Arrive at the Kaumakani Ball Field (between Hanapepe and Waimea) at sunset and prepare to have your mind blown. Space; it goes on forever.

Waimea

Waimea

◉ Sights

A Hideaway Spa .... (see 7)
1 Captain Cook Landing Site D4
2 Na Pali Explorer D3
3 Na Pali Riders A2
4 Russian Fort Elizabeth D4
Waimea Theater .... (see 15)
5 West Kaua'i Technology & Visitors
Center A2

🛏 Sleeping

6 Inn Waimea C3
7 Waimea Plantation Cottages A1

🍴 Eating

8 Ishihara Market C3
9 Jo-Jo's Anuenue Shave Ice &
Treats B2

10 Kaua'i Granola B2
11 Obsessions Café D3
12 Shrimp Station B2
The Grove Café .... (see 14)
13 Wrangler's Steakhouse C3

🍸 Drinking

14 Waimea Brewing
Company A1

✴ Entertainment

15 Waimea Theater B2

🛍 Shopping

16 Aunty Lilikoi Passion
Fruit Products D3
17 Red Dirt Shirts B2
18 West Kaua'i Craft Fair B2

🛏 Sleeping

TOP CHOICE Coco's Kaua'i B&B   B&B **$**

(☑338-0722; www.cocoskauai.com; btwn 21- & 22-mile markers; cottages $110, incl breakfast $130; ✱@🤶) Off the grid (call in advance) and keeping it low-key at this getaway is all part of its appeal. Owned by one of the Robinson family descendants, you're close but so far away, on the quiet side of the sugar plantation that's part of a greater 40,000 acres of agricultural land. It features a king bed, private hot tub, BBQ, air conditioning, garden, kitchenette, and sporadic cowboys riding by on horses. There's a minimum two-night stay.

Inn Waimea   INN **$$**

(☑338-0031; www.innwaimea.com; 4469 Halepule Rd; cottages $150, r from $110; @🤶) Situated in the heart of town, these suites and cottages are maintained by a self-proclaimed antique specialist, which may be evident. Features such as clawfoot tubs and classic furniture give them a certain charm. The two upstairs suites have their own lounge areas and the very reasonably priced two-bedroom cottages have a more modern decor, with bamboo furniture. ADA-certified wheelchair access available. Good for late bookings.

Waimea Plantation Cottages   COTTAGES **$$$**

(☑338-1625, 800-992-7866; www.waimea-plantation.com; 9400 Kaumuali'i Hwy; 1/2/3 bedroom from $220/275/325; 🤶🏊) These cottages are expensive, no doubt, but charming. The decor offers saliently Westside features, hailing from the tradition of plantation styles while featuring upmarket and modern Hawaiiana-inspired embellishments. The beachside campus-like property features coconut and banyon trees of freakish proportions and offers sunset views of a silhouetted Ni'ihau. The fact that it's a stone's toss from Waimea Brewing Company is a plus for those after a dose of nightlife.

West Kaua'i Vacation House   VACATION RENTAL **$$**

(☑346-5890; www.westkauaihouse.com; apt $135; ✱🤶) Just behind commercial Waimea town, this place's location allows for convenient access to all the Westside has to offer. Far from swanky, the units are fully furnished and air-conditioned. The getaway does share a wall (it's a duplex), but it also has a full kitchen and washer-dryer, as well as charcoal grill. With two bedrooms and one bathroom, it can sleep up to six people. The cleaning fee is $50.

✕ Eating

TOP CHOICE Ishihara Market   DELI **$**

(9894 Kaumuali'i Hwy; plate lunch $8.75; ⊙6am-8:30pm Mon-Fri, 7am-8:30pm Sat & Sun) It's an ad hoc lesson in local cuisine perusing this market, which is easily the island's most local eatery. Trusty lunches are the sushi *bentō*, spicy lobster salad and the archetypal spicy ahi poke. Daily specials and marinated ready-to-go meats are available for those wanting to barbecue. Parking is limited, so be patient or park on the street and walk the half-block.

Obsessions Café   BREAKFAST **$**

(9875 Waimea Rd; breakfast & lunch $6-7; ⊙6am-2pm Wed-Sun) A much-revered local-style breakfast indulgence, the *loco moco* ($6.95) is served up here the way it should be: smothered in gravy. Lighter fare includes the Chinese chicken salad ($6), but sedation-inducing sandwiches such as the Reuben – with corned beef, sauerkraut and Swiss cheese ($6.75) are the specialty. This spot is the best value on the island.

Shrimp Station   SHRIMP **$**

(9652 Kaumuali'i Hwy; dishes $8-12; ⊙11am-5pm) Quick and easy with styles such as sautéed scampi beer battered, and coconut-flaked and in taco form or ground up into a 'shrimp burger' coupled with papaya-ginger tartar sauce and fries – suffice to say it's *the* spot for shrimp. It also stocks kid-friendly ice cream and desserts such as push-up rainbow pops and Häagen-Dazs bars. A walk-up window and picnic table seating help keep this a simple operation.

Kaua'i Granola   SWEETS **$**

(9633 Kaumuali'i Hwy; www.kauaigranola.com/GranolaHome.html; granola $8; ⊙10am-5pm Mon-Sat) This former piecrust creator for Aunty Lilikoi has found her niche. And you can

KAUA'I WAIMEA

MAKE A LEI

Ever wanted to know how to make one of the most enticing and fragrant floral gestures in the world? Now's your chance. The **West Kaua'i Technology & Visitors Center** (☑338-1332; 9565 Kaumuali'i Hwy) offers free lei-making workshops for beginners every Friday from 9am to 11:30am. Bachelors, this could be quite a card to hold up your sleeve.

find sugarcane-sweetened 'sugar cane snax,' tropical trail mixes and dried fruits – ideal for when you're heading up to the canyon. Around Christmas time, don't miss out on her aloha-shirt-clad and hula-skirted gingerbread men and women – they make adorable, edible gifts. As their humility restraints them from claiming 'world's westernmost granola shop,' don't be shy, ample samples abound.

The Grove Cafe CAFE **$$**
(www.waimea-plantation.com/brew; Waimea Plantation Cottages, 9400 Kaumuali'i Hwy; mains $14; ☺6:30am-10pm) Part of the Waimea Brewery (the non-beer-making part), it'll definitely win any 'nicest place to eat in Waimea' contest. Maybe they hoped the aesthetic wow-ness would blind taste buds as the food falls a smidgen or two short of the presentation. The macadamia-nut-crusted shrimp and ale battered ahi poke roll make the grade, along with a few other randoms. Breakfast ain't too shabby and the impressive dessert selection may just win you over after all...and they serve lots and lots of beer.

Wrangler's Steakhouse STEAKHOUSE **$$**
(9852 Kaumuali'i Hwy; dinner mains $18-27; ☺11am-9pm Mon-Fri, 4-9pm Sat) Try it local style in this cowboy joint: grab a plantation lunch (which starts from $9) in a *kaukau* tin full of shrimp tempura, teriyaki and BBQ meat, along with rice and kimchi. Included in that price is soup and salad. Though they've got the 'best steaks on the Westside,' the fresh fish can leave some satisfaction to the imagination. Save room for the peach cobbler, which may beckon you back.

Jo-Jo's Anueanue Shave Ice & Treats SHAVE ICE **$**
(4491 Pokole Rd; ☺11am-5pm) As the story goes, this is the reincarnation of the 'original' Jo-Jo's (even though the other Jo-Jo's in Waimea has 'original' in the name), with Aunty Jo-Jo being the heart and soul of the operation. All syrups are homemade without additives and won't knock you out with sweetness. The superstar item is the dragon-fruit *halo halo,* nestled between Mac-nut ice cream and rich, *haupia* (coconut pudding) topping. Best to find a nice seat (possibly Waimea landing just down the street) and savor the flavor. (Hint: it's the one not on the highway.)

🍷 Drinking & Entertainment

TOP CHOICE **Waimea Brewing Company** BREWERY
(www.waimea-plantation.com/brew; Waimea Plantation Cottages, 9400 Kaumuali'i Hwy; ☺11am-10pm Sun-Thu, to 2am Fri & Sat) Tiki torches, live music and an inviting plantation-style architecture at the 'world's western most brewery' beckons, as does a long rotating list of tasty microbrews: Wai'ale'ale Golden Ale, *liliko'i* ale, Palaka Porter, Na Pali Pale Ale and Canefire Red. Try a 'sampler platter' for a 6oz taste of all drafts on hand.

Waimea Theater CINEMA
(☎338-0282; www.waimeatheater.com; 9691 Kaumuali'i Hwy; ☺7:30pm Wed-Sun) Perfect for a rainy day or early evening reprieve from the sun and sea. Kaua'i is a little behind with the new releases, but this is one of two functioning theaters on the island, so it's much appreciated. This is also a venue for the Hawaii International Film Festival (www.hiff.org).

🛍 Shopping

West Kaua'i Craft Fair GIFTS
(Kaumuali'i Hwy; ☺9am-4pm) Just near the entrance to the Old Sugar Mill you'll find Swarovski-crystal Limoges-inspired pillboxes, koa-wood bowls, Ni'ihau-shell leis, local honeys, *malasadas,* pineapples, longan, starfruit, banana, papaya and lychee. In fact, if they don't have something you want, you're too picky.

Aunty Lilikoi Passion Fruit Products GIFTS
(www.auntylilikoi.com; 9875 Waimea Rd; condiments per 10oz $5; ☺10am-5pm) In 2008 Aunty Lilikoi did it again, taking the gold medal in the Napa Valley International Mustard Competition for her *liliko'i*-wasabi mustard, making it clear that if it's a product with *liliko'i,* Aunty's got it down. Find something for almost any occasion: syrup (great for banana pancakes), massage oil (great for honeymooners) and the tasty chap stick (great for après surf), all made from, you guessed it, *liliko'i.*

Red Dirt Shirts CLOTHING
(www.dirtshirt.com; 4490 Pokole Rd; ☺11am-6pm) With chuckle-inducing sayings like 'older than dirt' and 'how's my attitude?' these born-of-necessity shirts can be very useful if you plan on hiking, as most of the dirt on the island wants to destroy your clothing. Great gifts too, it's guaranteed someone you know wants to sport a shirt that says 'life's short play dirty.'

ℹ️ Information

Aloha-N-Paradise (☑338 1522; 9905 Waimea Rd; per 30min $4; ⏰7am-5pm Mon-Fri, 8am-noon Sat; 📶) Next to the post office; offers internet access, all-day wi-fi, lattes and $1000 paintings.

Na Pali Explorer (☑877-335-9909, 338-9999; www.napali-explorer.com; Kaumuali'i Hwy; per 30min $3; ⏰7am-5pm) One-stop shop for internet, simple souvenirs, light snacks and snorkel-cruise and sportfishing bookings.

West Kauai Technology & Visitors Center (☑338-1332; 9565 Kaumuali'i Hwy; ⏰9:30am-4pm Mon, Tue & Thu, to 12:30pm Fri) Free internet access.

MEDICAL West Kauai Medical Center (☑338-9431; Waimea Canyon Dr) Emergency services 24 hours.

MONEY First Hawaiian Bank (☑338-1611; 4525 Panako Rd) On Waimea's central square.

ℹ️ Getting There & Around

Heading west from Hanapepe leads you right into town. No taxi services run out of Waimea, but if you're in a jam **Pono Taxi and Kauai Tours** (☑634-4744; www.ponotaxi.com) will service the entire island.

Kekaha

POP 3400

There's no town center in Kekaha (home to many military families), but Kekaha Beach Park offers one of the most beautiful sunsets on the island. If you're looking for a town with a scenic beach near the base of Waimea Canyon, this is nice. It is, however, off the beaten track and too remote for some.

Kaumuali'i Hwy borders the coastline while Kekaha Rd (Hwy 50), the main drag, lies parallel and a few blocks inland. All you'll find in town are a post office and a couple of stores. At its eastern end, Kekaha Rd and Kaumuali'i Hwy meet near the Kikiaola Small Boat Harbor, a state harbor with a launch ramp.

In an area known for its unrelenting sun and vast beaches, the Westside's **Kekaha Beach Park** is no exception. Just west of Kekaha town, this long beach is ideal for running, walking or beachcombing. Before jumping in, find a lifeguard station and make sure it's OK, as the sea here lacks the reef protection other beaches provide. When the surf is high, currents are extremely dangerous. Under the right conditions, it can be good for surfing and bodyboarding, but always remember to respect the locals.

🛏️ Sleeping

For more lodging listings, see Kekaha Oceanside (www.kekahaoceansidekauai.com).

Mindy's Guesthouse INN $
(Map p543; ☑337-9275; 8842 Kekaha Rd; s/d $75/85; 📶) Adorable, clean and featuring its own private deck, Mindy's is a steal for the price. A 2nd-story apartment with a full bed and large kitchen feels spacious, and will feel like home after a day or two. Though there's no air conditioning, there are ceiling fans throughout, which only add to the personable vibe. It's a perfect home base for Waimea or Polihale jaunts. The price includes fruit and coffee in the morning.

Hale Puka 'Ana B&B B&B $$
(Map p543; ☑652-6852; 8240A Elepaio Rd; www.kekahakauaisunset.com; ste $169-229; ❄@📶) The only oceanside B&B on the island offers three rooms: two with ocean view-giving private lanais; one with an obscenely big shower (honeymooners) and fine furnishings of cherrywood and bamboo; one with a private outdoor shower and entrance. An outdoor tiki-style kitchen allows evening BBQs while contemplating an ocean sunset with enigmatic Ni'ihau in the foreground. Watch whales breach (November to March) while munching a superior breakfast made by a young outdoorsy couple who may just become your new best friends. One hiccup: traffic noise.

Boathouse Guesthouse INN $
(Map p543; ☑332-9744; www.seakauai.com; 4518A Nene St; r $85) Within walking distance of Kekaha Beach, the Boathouse is much like staying in the guesthouse of your favorite (and clean) neighbors. Though a studio, it feels spacious and has its own covered lanai, kitchenette, king bed and TV. New Hawaiiana furnishings give it a welcomed burst of life. Ideal for one person or a couple, with a washer-dryer on-site.

Barking Sands

Between Kekaha Beach Park and Polihale State Park, the beach stretches for approximately 15 miles. However, since the September 11, 2001 terrorist attacks, consistent public access is no longer allowed. This is because it is home to the US navy base Barking Sands Pacific Missile Range Facility (PMRF; ☑335-4229, beach access 335-4111). The missile-range facility at Barking Sands provides the aboveground link to a sophisticated sonar network that tracks more than 1000 sq miles of the Pacific. Established during WWII, it's been developed into the world's largest (possibly excluding Blue Whales) underwater listening device.

Polihale State Park

A rugged access road and inconsistent weather have made this state park something of a headache for the Department of Land & Natural Resources in the past. For the last couple of years an ambitious and altruistic local crew has taken it upon themselves to annually repair the inevitably weather-beaten road.

Note that there aren't any car-rental vendors who offer insurance for visitors to drive the 5-mile-long dirt road that accesses the park from Mana village off Kaumuali'i Hwy, another snag in the debate over universal access rights to this surfing haven. Locals threatened to protest when a gate was put up to keep visitors out in the past few years, claiming they know the area better than nonresidents and should therefore be allowed access.

Whether you decide to drive here for a day trip or more, it's worth remembering that camping is, at times, allowed with a permit, although the entryway, toilet and shower facilities access are inconsistent – and finding a ride back should your rental transport fail is risky.

Waimea Canyon State Park

Of all Kaua'i's unique wonders, none can touch Waimea Canyon for utter grandeur. While one expects to find tropical beaches and gardens here, few expect a gargantuan chasm of ancient lava rock, 10 miles long and 2500ft deep to the riverbed (or more than 3600ft above sea level). Flowing through the canyon is the Waimea River, Kaua'i's longest, which is fed by three eastern tributaries that bring reddish-brown waters from the mountaintop bog, Alaka'i Swamp.

Waimea Canyon was formed when Kaua'i's original shield volcano, Wai'ale'ale, slumped along an ancient fault line, creating a sharp east-facing line of cliffs. Then another shield volcano, Lihu'e, developed the island's east side, producing new lava flows that ponded against the cliffs. Thus the western canyon walls are taller, thinner and more eroded – the contrast is most theatrically apparent while hiking along the canyon floor. The black and red horizontal striations along the canyon walls represent successive volcanic eruptions; the red color indicates that water seeped through the rocks, creating rust from the iron inside.

Drives on a clear day are phenomenal. But don't be disappointed by rain, as that's what makes the waterfalls gush. Sunny days following rain are ideal for prime views, though slick mud makes it a challenge.

The southern boundary of Waimea Canyon State Park is about 6 miles up the road from Waimea. You can reach the park by two roads: Waimea Canyon Dr (Hwy 550) starts in Waimea just beyond the 23-mile marker, while Koke'e Rd (Hwy 552) starts in Kekaha off Mana Rd. They merge between the 6- and 7-mile markers.

State officials generally prefer visitors to use Waimea Canyon Dr, which is 19 miles long and passes the canyon lookouts with terrific views into Kalalau Valley on the Na Pali Coast. Koke'e Rd is shorter by 3 miles and also offers scenic views, but not of the canyon.

Dangers & Annoyances

Rain creates hazardous conditions in the canyon. The red-dirt trails quickly become slick and river fords rise to impassable levels. Try hiking poles or a sturdy walking stick to ease the steep descent into the canyon.

Note the time of sunset and plan to return well before dark. The daylight will fade inside the canyon long before sunset.

While packing light is recommended, take enough water for your entire trip, especially the uphill return journey. Do not drink fresh water along the trails without treating it. Cell phones do not work here. If possible, hike with a companion or at least tell someone your expected return time.

◉ Sights & Activities

Waimea Canyon Dr   SCENIC DRIVE
Along Waimea Canyon Dr, you can see naturally growing examples of native trees, including koa and ohia, as well as invasive species such as kiawe. The valuable hardwood koa proliferates at the hunter's check station along the way. Look for the trees with narrow, crescent-shaped leaves.

Scenic Lookouts

At 0.3 miles north of the 10-mile marker, and an elevation of 3400ft, is the Waimea Canyon Lookout – the most scenic of the lookout points. Keep your eyes peeled for the canyon running in an easterly direction off Waimea, which is Koai'e Canyon. That area is accessible to backcountry hikers.

The 800ft waterscape known as Waipo'o Falls can be seen from a couple of small, unmarked lookouts before the 12-mile marker and then from a lookout opposite the picnic area shortly before the 13-mile marker. The picnic area includes BBQ pits, restrooms, drinking water, a pay phone and Camp Hale Koa, a Seventh Day Adventist camp. Pu'u Hinahina Lookout, at 3640ft, offers two lookouts near the parking lot at a marked turnoff between the 13- and 14-mile markers, while Pu'u o Kila Lookout, located past Kalalau Lookout, is the start of the Pihea Trail. Sometimes the road is closed.

At the 18-mile marker, is the view of the Kalalau Valley from Kalalau Lookout, the largest of the Na Pali. Views from the lookout change minute by minute, depending on the ever-present clouds. At 4000ft elevation, the air here is much cooler than along the coast or in the valleys – so bring a sweatshirt or jacket.

Hiking

Enjoy several rugged trails that lead deep into Waimea Canyon: keep in mind they're shared with pig and deer hunters and that it's busiest during weekends and holidays.

The **Kukui** and **Koai'e Canyon trails**, two of the steepest on Kaua'i, connect at Wiliwili Camp, 2000ft into the canyon. If the entire trek sounds too strenuous, hike just 1 mile down the Kukui Trail, as you'll reach a bench with an astounding view.

The hiking mileage given for each of the following trails is for one-way only.

Iliau Nature Loop   HIKING

This trail was named for the *iliau*, a plant endemic to Kaua'i's Westside, which grows along the route and produces stalks up to 10ft high. Canyon walls, waterfalls and bursting *iliau* are all reasons to give it a try.

The marked trailhead for the 10-minute Iliau Nature Loop comes up shortly before the 9-mile marker. Be sure to pass the bench to the left and walk about three minutes for a top-notch vista into Waimea Canyon.

WORTH A TRIP

POLIHALE: DEPARTURE POINT

A massive expanse of beach – the end of one of the longest (15 miles) and widest (300 ft) in the state – Polihale is as mystical as it is enchanting. Translated as 'home of the underworld', Hawaiian belief holds Polihale as the place where souls depart for *Po* (the underworld). The cliffs at the end of the beach are home to ancient Hawaiian ruins constructed over the ocean as the jumping-off place for spirits.

Kukui Trail   HIKING

Don't let the fact that it's only 2.5 miles in (only five miles total) fool you. The climb back out of the valley can be harrowing – it's definitely for seriously fit and agile hikers only. The narrow switchback trail covers 2000ft and doesn't offer much in the way of sweeping views, though there's a river at the canyon floor.

Keep your eyes peeled for a small sign directing hikers to turn left, and hike the steep slope down, with the hill at your back. When you hear the sound of water, you're closing in on the picnic shelter and Wiliwili Camp area, where overnight camping is allowed, but mostly hunters stay.

To get there, find the Iliau Nature Loop trailhead just before the 9-mile marker. It officially starts just beyond it at a hunter checking station on the right.

Kalalau Lookout to Pu'u 'o Kila Lookout   HIKING

This mellow, 2-mile hike offers a pleasant walk along the closed road linking two lookouts. A two-lane strip of asphalt, currently closed to traffic, connects the park's premier viewpoints of the Kalalau Valley, and in early morning and late afternoon, as the fog is wafting overhead, it is a delightful birding walk. You won't see as many species as in the forest itself, but it's worth the amble.

Koai'e Canyon Trail   HIKING

Further along, about 0.5 miles from the Kukui Trail, is the Koai'e Canyon Trail (6 miles round-trip), a moderate trail that takes you down the south side of the canyon to some swimming holes, which are best avoided after rain, because of incredibly quickly rising waters and hazardous flash floods.

The trail offers three camps. After the first, Kaluaha'ulu Camp, stay on the eastern bank of the river – do not cross it. Later you'll come upon the overgrown Na Ala Hele trailhead for the Koai'e Canyon Trail. Watch for greenery and soil that conceals drop-offs alongside the path.

Next up is Hipalau Camp. After this camp the trail can be tricky to find. Keep heading north, do not veer toward the river, but continue ascending at approximately the same point midway between the canyon walls and the river.

Growing steeper, the trail then enters Koai'e Canyon, recognizable by the red-rock walls rising to the left. The last camp is Lonomea. Find the best views at the emergency helipad, a grassy area perfect for picnicking. When ready to leave, retrace your steps.

Waimea Canyon Trail   HIKING

A difficult trail in this area is the 11.5-mile (one-way) Waimea Canyon Trail, which fords Waimea River. It starts at the bottom of Waimea Canyon at the end of Kukuio Trail and leads out to Waimea town. An entry permit is required at the self-service box at the Kukui Trail register.

You might see locals carrying inner tubes so they can exit via the river rather than hiking back out.

Cycling

Coast downhill for 13 miles, from the rim of Waimea Canyon (elevation 3500ft) to sea level with **Outfitters Kaua'i** (☑742-9667, 888-742-9887; www.outfitterskauai.com; Po'ipu Plaza, 2827A Po'ipu Rd, Po'ipu; tour adult/child $94/75; ☉check-in 6am & 2:30pm), which will supply all the necessary cruisers, helmets and snacks. Remember, you'll be a target for the setting sun during the afternoon ride.

Mountain bikers can also find miles of bumpy, 4WD hunting-area roads off Waimea Canyon Dr. Even when the yellow gates are closed on nonhunting days, cyclists are still allowed to go around and use them – except for Papa'alai Rd, which is managed by the Department of Hawaiian Home Lands and open for hunting, but not recreational use.

🛏 Sleeping

All four camps on the canyon trails are part of the forest reserve system. They have open-air picnic shelters and pit toilets, but no other facilities; all freshwater must be treated before drinking. See p463 for camping permit information.

Koke'e State Park

The expansive Koke'e State Park is a playground to those who revere the environment. Home to inspirational views, it offers an abundance of plant life and animals. You'll also enjoy some reprieve from the sun and no doubt the microclimates will leave you paying attention to the shifts in ambient air.

In ancient times, only Hawaiian birdcatchers resided up in this part of the island. The trail that once ran down the cliffs from Koke'e (ko-*keh*-eh) to Kalalau Valley on the Na Pali Coast is extraordinarily steep, and has taken the life of at least one Western trekker. Though one of the park's locally revered charms is its choppy, almost impossible 4WD roads, the state has been working (despite misgivings by many Kaua'i residents) to pave much of Koke'e. Advocates against this decision have argued it would rob the area of its reclusively rugged character.

Another potential moneymaker (of equally controversial status) is the state's plan to further modernize Koke'e by adding a helicopter landing pad, which would, in turn, increase air-tourism revenues.

This park's boundary starts beyond the Pu'u Hinahina Lookout. After the 15-mile marker, you'll pass a brief stretch of park cabins, and a restaurant, museum and campground.

Dangers & Annoyances

All of the suggestions on p552 for Waimea Canyon State Park also apply to Koke'e State Park. Further, the higher elevation produces a cooler and wetter climate, so take appropriate attire.

⊙ Sights & Activities

Koke'e Museum   MUSEUM

(☑335-9975; www.kokee.org; entry by donation $1; ☉9am-4pm) At this museum you'll find detailed topographical maps, local historical photographs and a tribute to the late photographer and educator David Boynton (and contributor to Lonely Planet guidebooks), who died in 2007 after he was hiking along a cliff trail to one of his most cherished spots on the Na Pali coastline.

You can also obtain a brochure for the short nature trail out back. It offers interpretive information corresponding to the trail's numbered plants and trees, including many native species. You'll probably notice in front an array of chickens that have, in the past decade, polluted the pristine Koke'e mornings with noise. Please don't feed them.

Kalalau Lookouts   VIEWPOINTS
Look for the 18-mile marker, where the ethereal 4000ft Kalalau Lookout stands up to the ocean, sun and winds with brave, severe beauty.

Hope for a clear day for ideal views, but know that even a rainy day can make for some settling clouds that could later disappear – followed by powerful waterfalls, and, of course, rainbows.

Though it might be hard to imagine, as the terrain is so extreme, as late as the 1920s Kalalau Valley was home to many residents – who farmed rice there, no less.

The only way into the valley nowadays is along the coastal Kalalau Trail from Ha'ena on the North Shore or by kayak (p528).

The paved road continues another mile to Pu'u o Kila Lookout, where it dead-ends at a parking lot. This road faces periodic closings.

Hiking
Generally speaking, Koke'e is unspoiled. Its sheer size might make it a bit challenging to nail down where you want to start. Know that if you want to avoid hunters (and their dogs), it's best to opt for trails like Alaka'i Swamp or the Cliff Trail to Waipo'o Falls; though those might have some other hikers on it, they're still relatively remote. Koke'e boasts 45 miles of trails that range from delving deep into the rain forest or merely skimming the perimeter, with views that can cause a vertiginous reaction in even the most avid mountain-sport enthusiasts.

Trekking around Koke'e offers a rare view at an abundance of endemic species of wildlife and plants, including the largest population of Kaua'i's native fern, the fragrant *laua'e,* alluded to in many of the island's chants and traditions. Also here you might see some of Kaua'i's rare and endangered native forest birds.

The starting point for several scenic hikes, Halemanu Rd is just north of the 14-mile marker on Waimea Canyon Dr. Whether or not the road is passable in a non-4WD vehicle depends on recent rainfall. Note that many rental-car agreements are null and void when off-roading.

During summer weekends, trained volunteers lead **Wonder Walks** (nominal donation; ☉Jun-Sep), guided hikes on various trails at Waimea Canyon and Koke'e State Parks.

Contact the **museum** (☑335-9975; www.kokee .org) for schedules and reservations.

Cliff & Canyon Trails   HIKING
The **Cliff Trail** (0.1 miles) is a perfect intro to the canyon's vast views. Being short, it's a relatively easy walk for the rewarding Waimea Canyon views it offers.

The **Canyon Trail** (1.8 miles) continues from there; you'll go down a semisteep forest trail, a grove, a lugelike tunnel that opens up to a vast, red-dirt promontory with cliffs to one side and charming logsteps to guide you further. Shortly thereafter it takes some steep finagling to get to Waipo'o Falls. If that's too much, you can always turn back around here. To get to the trailhead, walk down Halemanu Rd for just over 0.5 miles. Keeping Halemanu Stream to your left, ignore a hunting trail-of-use on the right. Then turn right onto the footpath leading to both the Cliff and Canyon Trails. At the next junction, the Cliff Trail veers right and wanders for less than 0.25 miles uphill to the Cliff Viewpoint.

For the Canyon Trail, backtrack to the previous junction. Avoid holding onto any foliage for stability. Otherwise, after hopping boulders across the stream, follow the trail to **Kumuwela Ridge** at the canyon rim. The trail ends at **Kumuwela Lookout**, where you can rest at a picnic table before backtracking to Halemanu Rd.

Black Pipe Trail
To vary your return from Canyon Trail, make a right at the intersection of Black Pipe Trail and Canyon Trail at the top of the switchback where you leave the canyon rim. The trail ends at the 4WD-only Halemanu Rd, where you walk back to the Canyon trailhead.

Halemanu-Koke'e Trail
Another trail off Halemanu Rd, which starts further down the road than the Cliff and Canyon Trails, is Halemanu-Koke'e Trail (1.25 miles). An easy recreational nature trail, it passes through a native forest of koa and ohia trees, which provide a habitat for native birds. One of the common plants found on this trail is banana poka, a member of the passion-fruit family and an invasive pest. It has pretty pink flowers, but it drapes the forest with its vines and chokes out less aggressive native plants. The trail ends near YWCA Camp Sloggett, about 0.5 miles from Koke'e Lodge.

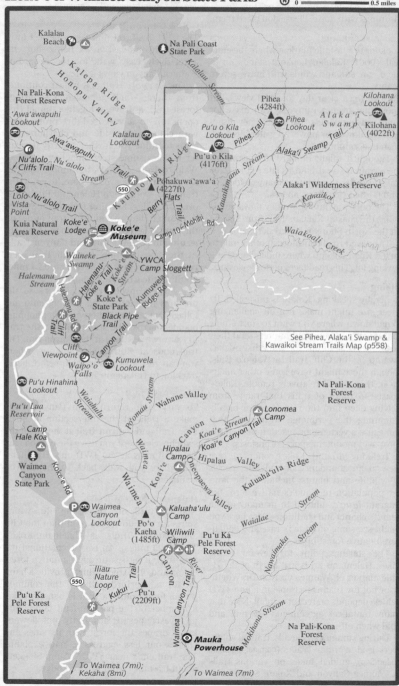

See Pihea, Alaka'i Swamp & Kawaikoi Stream Trails Map (p558)

KAUA'I WAIMEA CANYON & THE WESTSIDE

Awaʻawapuhi & Nuʻalolo Cliffs HIKING

These trails offer the best of the best. The **Awaʻawapuhi Trail** (3.25 miles) and the more challenging **Nuʻalolo Trail** (3.75 miles) afford views along 2000ft cliffs. Perhaps nowhere is more exhilarating (and vertigo-inducing) than the spot where the trails connect – the Nuʻalolo Cliffs Trail (2 miles) has points where you may feel more of an acrobat than a hiker! The **Nuʻalolo Cliffs Trail** connects to the Nuʻalolo Trail near the 3.25-mile mark and to the Awaʻawapuhi Trail just short of the 3-mile mark.

If you're undecided as to which trail to take, the Awaʻawapuhi Trail is much less technical – though there are some steep steps where you might find yourself hugging a tree. At the end you'll reach a breathtaking view of the cliffs below (much like the 'Cliffs of Insanity' featured in *The Princess Bride*).

To be sure, the Nuʻalolo Cliff Trail is steeper than Awaʻawapuhi Trail, though arguably each requires the same amount of endurance. To do this 11-mile hike as a loop, begin with the Nuʻalolo Trail (trailhead is just south of Kokeʻe Museum) and hike to the bottom of the ridge and look for a sign that says 'Nuʻalolo Cliff Trail.' Follow that right, scaling rocks and cutting through tall, eye-level grass, back up through several switchbacks, up through a ridge until it intersects with the Awaʻawapuhi Trail, another signed intersection. Make a right following the 'Awaʻawapuhi Trailhead on Kokeʻe Rd. Turn right and walk alongside of Kokeʻe Rd back to Nuʻalolo Trailhead roughly 0.75 miles.

Pihea Trail to Alakaʻi Swamp Trail HIKING

This 6-mile round-trip trek begins at Puʻu o Kila Lookout. A mere 1 mile in and you'll see the **Pihea Lookout**. Past the lookout and a short scramble downhill the boardwalk begins. After another 1.5 miles you will come to a crossing with the Alakaʻi Swamp Trail. A left at this crossing will put you on that trail to the **Kilohana Lookout**. Continuing straight on the Pihea Trail will take you to the Kawaikoi campground along the Kawaikoi stream. Most hikers start on the Pihea Trail because the trailhead is accessible by the paved road to Puʻu o Kila Lookout; however, sometimes this road is closed. For another trailhead, begin at the Alakaʻi Swamp Trail starting point. The trails are well maintained, with mile markers and signs.

Note: the stretch between Alakaʻi Crossing and Kilohana Lookout includes hundreds of steps, which can be hell on your knees.

Alakaʻi Swamp Trail HIKING

The Alakaʻi Swamp trailhead begins on a ridge above Sugi Grove on Camp 10-Mohihi Rd. While this trailhead covers less steep terrain than the beginning of the Pihea trailhead, you will need a 4WD to get there, as well as the ability to follow a map along an unmarked dirt road.

Park in the clearing at the trailhead; the trail begins as a wide grassy path for roughly 0.5 miles to where the boardwalk begins and continues through small bogs and intermittent forests until you reach the **Alakaʻi Crossing**, where the Pihea and Alakaʻi Swamp trails intersect. Continuing straight through the crossing, the boardwalk becomes a series of steep steps to the Kawaikoi Stream and a steep series of switchbacks up the other side. Past there the boardwalk is relatively flat, continuing through the almost otherworldly terrain of the Hawaiian Bogs of knee-high trees and tiny endemic carnivorous plants.

The boardwalk ends at Kilohana Lookout, where, with a little bit of luck, you will see views of Wainiha Valley, and beyond to Hanalei Bay.

Kawaikoi Stream Trail HIKING

Go to Sugi Grove by going down Camp 10 Rd (4WD only) and crossing **Kawaikoi Stream**. It's a nice little nature walk that follows the stream through the forest and rises up on a bluff at the end of the stream, then loops around back down to the stream at a cold dark swimming hole and returns you back to where you started.

✦ Festivals & Events

Eo e Emalani I Alakaʻi DANCE

(☏335-9975; www.kokee.org/details.html) Hula *halau* from all over Hawaii participate in this one-day outdoor dance festival at Kokeʻe Museum in early October that reenacts the historic 1871 journey of Queen Emma to Alakaʻi Swamp. The festival includes a royal procession, hula, music and crafts.

🛏 Sleeping & Eating

Even though it's Hawaii, don't be fooled into thinking you'll be warm all the time. Kokeʻe campgrounds are at an elevation of almost 4000ft, and nights are cold. Take a sleeping bag, waterproof jacket, change of warm clothing, extra socks and hiking shoes (instead of sneakers). See p629 for further details on the camping options.

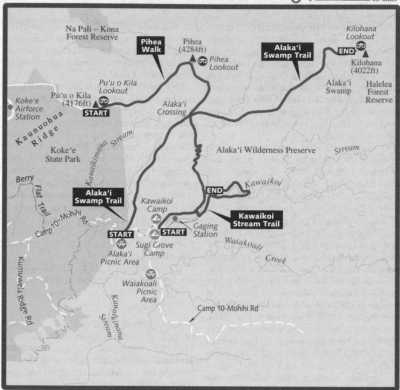

Koke'e State Park
Campground   CAMPGROUND $
The most accessible camping area is north of the meadow, just a few minutes' walk from Koke'e Lodge. The campsites sit in a grassy area beside the woods, (perfect for laying out a blanket and taking a nap) along with picnic tables, drinking water, restrooms and showers.

Kawaikoi & Sugi Grove   CAMPGROUND $
Further off the main track, these campgrounds are about 4 miles east of Koke'e Lodge, off the 4WD-only Camp 10–Mohihi Rd in the forest reserve adjacent to the state park. Each campground has pit toilets, picnic shelters and fire pits. There's no water source, so you'll need to bring your own or treat the stream water. These forest-reserve campgrounds have a three-night maximum stay and require camping permits (free) in advance from the Division of Forestry & Wildlife.

The Kawaikoi campground sits on a well-maintained 3.5-acre grassy field, and it is recommended if you are camping in a large group (ie 10 or more). The Sugi Grove site is picturesque, under sugi trees (commonly called a pine but actually a cedar), a fragrant softwood native to Japan. This site is shaded, making it ideal during hot summer months, and it is closer to Kawaikoi stream.

Koke'e State Park Cabins   CABINS $
(☎335-6061; cabins $65-90) Minimally maintained, the 12 cabins are for folks seeking a remote, rustic and somewhat grimy experience. Chalk it up to reliving dorm life (minus the phone, TV or loud music). All cabins include a double and four twin beds, a kitchen, a shower, a wood stove (your only heat source), linens and blankets. Small cleaning fee depending on length of stay.

Nothing really provides that out-of-the-ordinary experience the way a hike along the Alaka'i Swamp, a sort of soggy paradise designated a wilderness preserve in 1964, does. Almost the entire trail is linked with wood planks, to help encourage use of the approved trail and to discourage off-trail trekking. The Department of Land & Natural Resources' Forestry & Wildlife Division started laying planks around 1989 – a time-consuming (and crazy, according to some) process that was delayed when Hurricane 'Iniki hit in 1992. Today the project continues, with a plan to cover more of the Pihea Trail.

You'll traverse truly fantastic terrain on this hike – misty bogs where plants will dwarf you. On a clear day, look for outstanding views of the Wainiha Valley and whales breaching in the ocean in the distance. If it's raining, don't fret: search for rainbows, enjoy the mist and respect the area by avoiding loud talking with your fellow hikers. This is a spiritual place: Queen Emma was said to have been so moved by tales from the Alaka'i that she ventured there, only to chant in reverence during the sojourn.

The Kaua'i 'o'o, the last of four species of Hawaiian honeyeaters, was thought to be extinct until a nest with two chicks was discovered in Alaka'i Swamp in 1971. Sadly, the call of the 'o'o – that of a single male – was last heard in 1987.

YWCA Camp Sloggett   CAMPGROUND, CABINS **$**
(☑245-5959; www.campingkauai.com; campsites & dm per person $15, cabin Mon-Thu $125, Fri-Sun $155) Choose either a cabin or bunkhouse, or camp on the grass. The cabin has a king bed, full kitchen, a bathroom and a wood-burning fireplace, while the bunker has a kitchenette, two bathrooms and a fire pit. You provide the sleeping bags and towels. To tent camp, no reservations are needed.

Koke'e Lodge   SNACKS **$**
(☑335-6061; snacks $3-7; ☺9am-3:30pm) This restaurant's strong point is convenience.

Still, convenience goes a long way up in Koke'e, where you're a 30-minute drive away from other dining out options. Expect cereal, diner food and a gift shop with souvenirs and a small assortment of sundries for sale if you forgot toiletries.

❶ Information

Koke'e Museum (☑335-9975) Sells inexpensive trail maps and provides basic information on trail conditions; you can also call them for real-time mountain weather reports.

Remember, the nearest place for provisions and gas is Waimea, 15 miles away.

In 2006, the Northwestern Hawaiian Islands (NWHI) became the USA's first Marine National Monument (MNM). Encompassing almost 140,000 sq miles, it is now the largest protected marine area in the world and the USA's only Unesco World Heritage Site designated for both natural and cultural reasons.

The NWHI begin about 115 miles northwest of Kaua'i and stretch for 1200 miles. They contain the largest and healthiest coral-reef system in the US, which is home to 7000 marine species. Half of the fish species and a quarter of all species are endemic to Hawaii, and new species are discovered on every scientific voyage. NWHI is also a rare 'top predator-dominated ecosystem,' in which sharks, groupers and others make up over 54% of the biomass (which is three times greater than in the main Hawaiian islands). The islands also support around 14 million seabirds, and they are the primary breeding ground for the endangered Hawaiian monk seal and green sea turtles.

However, the islands are not absolutely pristine. Pacific Ocean currents bring over 50 tons of debris to the islands annually, and cleanups have removed over 500 tons of entangled fishing nets, plastic bottles and trash so far.

The NWHI are grouped into 10 island clusters, which contain atolls (low sandy islands formed on top of coral reefs) and some single-rock islands. From east to west, the clusters are Nihoa Island, Mokumanamana (Necker Island), French Frigate Shoals, Gardner Pinnacles, Maro Reef, Laysan Island, Lisianski Island, Pearl and Hermes Atoll, Midway Atoll and Kure Atoll.

The total land area of the Northwestern Hawaiian Islands is just under 5 sq miles. Human history on the islands extends back to the first Polynesian voyagers to arrive in Hawaii. In modern times, the most famous island has been, of course, Midway Atoll, which remains the only island open to visitors.

Today, the monument is being managed in a unique joint effort by three agencies: the National Oceanic & Atmospheric Administration (NOAA), the US Fish & Wildlife Service (USFWS), and the Hawaii Department of Land & Natural Resources (DLNR). However, the monument's 15-year management plan has raised concerns among Native Hawaiian groups and environmental groups such as the Sierra Club. The plan exempts from its regulations the US military (which conducts missile tests and Navy training within monument waters), and the plan allows for increasing visits to Midway and trips for scientific research – all of which could damage areas the monument is charged with preserving.

Nihoa & Mokumanamana

Nihoa and Mokumanamana (Necker Island), the two islands closest to Kaua'i, were home to Native Hawaiians from around AD 1000 to 1700. More than 135 archaeological sites have been identified on both islands, including temple platforms, house sites, agricultural terraces, burial caves and carved stone images. As many as 175 people may have once lived on Nihoa and traveled to the much smaller Mokumanamana for religious ceremonies.

That anyone could live at all on these rocks is remarkable. Nihoa is only 1 sq km in size, and Mokumanamana is one-sixth that size. Nihoa juts from the sea steeply, like a broken tooth, and is the tallest of the Northwestern Hawaiian Islands, with 900ft sea cliffs.

Two endemic land birds live on Nihoa. The Nihoa finch, which, like the Laysan finch, is a raider of other birds' eggs, has a population of a few thousand. The gray Nihoa millerbird, related to the Old World warbler family, numbers between 300 and 700.

French Frigate Shoals

Surrounded by over 230,000 acres of coral reef, the French Frigate Shoals contains the monument's greatest variety of coral (over 41 species). It is also where most of Hawaii's green sea turtles and Hawaiian monk seals come to nest. The 67-acre reef forms a classic comma-shaped atoll on top of an eroded volcano, in the center of which the 135ft-tall La Pérouse Pinnacle rises like a ship; this rock was named after the French explorer who was almost wrecked here in 1786. A small sand island, Tern Island is dominated by an airfield, which was built as a refueling stop during WWII. Today, Tern Island is a US Fish & Wildlife Service field station housing two full-time refuge employees and a few volunteers.

Laysan Island

Not quite 1.5 sq miles, Laysan is the second-biggest of the Northwestern Hawaiian Islands. The grassy island has the most bird species in the monument, and to see the huge flocks of Laysan albatross, shearwaters and curlews – plus the endemic Laysan duck chasing brine flies around a super-salty inland lake – you'd never know how close this island came to becoming a barren wasteland.

In the late 19th century, humans began frequenting Laysan to mine phosphate-rich guano – or bird droppings – to use as fertilizer; they also killed hundreds of thousands of albatross for their feathers (to adorn hats) and took eggs for albumen, a substance used in photo processing. Albatross lay just one egg a year, so an 'egging' sweep could destroy an entire year's hatch. Traders built structures and brought pack mules and, oddly enough, rabbits for food.

The rabbits ran loose and multiplied, and within 20 years their nibbling destroyed 22 of the island's 26 plant species. Without plants, three endemic Laysan land birds – the Laysan flightless rail, Laysan honeycreeper and Laysan millerbird – became extinct. Laysan finches and the last 11 Laysan ducks seemed doomed to follow. Then, in 1909, public outcry led President Theodore Roosevelt to create the Hawaiian Islands Bird Reservation, and the NWHI have been under some kind of protection ever since.

By 1923 every last rabbit was removed, and the rehabilitation of Laysan began. With weed-abatement assistance, native plantlife recovered, and so did the birds. The Laysan finch is again common, and the Laysan duck numbers about 600 (another small population has been established on Midway). Nearly the same sequence of events unfolded on nearby Lisianski Island and, together, these islands are a spectacular success story.

Midway Islands

The Midway Islands were an important naval air station during WWII, but they are best known as the site of a pivotal battle in June 1942, when US forces surprised an attacking Japanese fleet and defeated it. This victory is credited with turning the tide in the Pacific theater. Postwar, Midway became a staging point for Cold War air patrols.

By 1996 the military no longer needed Midway, and transferred jurisdiction to the USFWS. Before leaving, it conducted an extensive cleanup program to remove debris, environmental contaminants, rats and nonnative plants. Midway was then developed for tourism: barracks became hotel rooms, the mess hall a cafeteria. A museum and restaurant were added. A gym, theater (for movies), bowling alley and library were part of the original military facility. On Sand and Eastern Islands, various military structures (like gun emplacements) were designated a National Historical Landmark.

The prime highlight at Midway is the more than two million seabirds that nest here, including the world's largest colony of Laysan albatross, which are so thick between November and July that they virtually blanket the ground. Also, Midway's coral reefs are unusually rich and are frequented by dolphins, green sea turtles and Hawaiian monk seals.

Information

All visitors facilities on Midway Islands are managed by the US Fish & Wildlife Service (www.fws.gov/midway), which issues visitation permits to organized groups; consult the website for a current list of tour operators.

Papahanaumokuakea Marine National Monument (www.papahanaumokuakea.gov) can be visited virtually online or at the Mokupapapa Discovery Center (p263) in Hilo on Hawai'i the Big Island.

Other good websites for learning more about the monument online include Northwestern Hawaiian Islands Multi-Agency Education Project (www.hawaiianatolls.org) and Kahea (www.kahea.org/nwhi).

Waimanalo, Oʻahu (p130)
The proudly Hawaiian community of Waimanalo is nestled in a breadbasket of small family farms.

Understand
Hawaii

HAWAII TODAY **564**
Growing pains are par for the course in paradise, a Pacific cross-roads and a multicultural mosaic. Written by Michael Shapiro.

HISTORY **567**
From Polynesian wayfarers and royalty to Christian missionar-ies, sugar barons and the US military, this is Hawaii's story. Written by Michael Shapiro.

HAWAII'S PEOPLE **584**
Bust the myths and stereotypes, and experience everyday island life away from *da* mainland. Written by Michael Shapiro.

HAWAII'S CUISINE **591**
Swill tropical cocktails by the beach. Find fresh seafood shacks, mixed-plate lunch trucks and more.

HAWAIIAN ARTS & CRAFTS **603**
Discover the islands' soulful side in dramatic stories, sensuous hula dancing, creative songs and artful handicrafts.

LEI **609**
These fragrant garlands symbolize the spirit of aloha that animates the islands.

LAND & SEA **614**
Delicate coral reefs, red-hot lava flows, icy volcano summits, mist-laden cloud forests – it's Hawaii, naturally.

GREEN HAWAII **623**
Help this remote archipelago become a living laboratory for sustainability and eco-living.

Hawaii Today

The Hawaiian Renaissance

Twhough Hawaiian culture has been devastated in the 230-plus years since Western contact, it remains very much alive in more than just place names and hotel hula performances. Traditional arts like *lauhala* (pandanus leaf) weaving, *kapa* (barkcloth) making, gourd carving and tiki sculpting are all experiencing a recovery and revival. Healing arts like *lomilomi* and *la'au lapa'au* (plant medicine) are being shared with students both within and beyond the Native Hawaiian community. There are Hawaiian-language immersion programs in public schools, and Hawaiian culture-focused charter schools popping up all over the state. *Heiau* (temples) and fishponds are being restored, native forests replanted and native birds bred and released. All this is part of what's now called the Hawaiian Renaissance – one of the most exciting and dynamic cultural movements happening in Hawaii today.

In the 1970s, Hawaiian culture, battered by colonization, commodified and peddled to tourists, was ready for a revival; it just needed the spark. In 1976 a replica of the ancient Polynesian sailing canoe *Hokule'a* sailed to Tahiti using only the stars for a compass, sending a wave of cultural pride throughout Polynesia (see p571).

That same year a group of Hawaiian activists occupied Kaho'olawe (p410), aka 'Target Island,' which the US government had used for bombing practice since WWII. During a fourth occupation in 1977, two activists disappeared at sea under mysterious circumstances, becoming martyrs for the nascent Native Hawaiian rights movement.

When the state held its landmark Constitutional Convention in 1978, it passed a number of amendments, such as making Hawaiian an official

> » Population: 1.3 million
>
> » Gross state product: $63.4 billion
>
> » Median household income: $66,701
>
> » Length of coastline: 750 miles
>
> » Size: 6423 sq miles (the fourth smallest state in the US)

Top Books

The Descendants (Kaui Hart Hemmings) A novel about a missionary family struggling to preserve its legacy in modern Hawaii.

The Colony (John Tayman) Inside the leprosy colony on Moloka'i.

Shoal of Time (Gavan Daws) A general, if controversial, history of the Hawaiian Islands.

Hotel Honolulu (Paul Theroux) The quirky, weird and dissolute world of Honolulu as seen through a Waikiki hotel manager's eyes.

'Olelo Noe'au (Mary Kawena Pukui) A collection of proverbs and sayings in English and Hawaiian; almost every home in Hawaii has a copy.

belief systems
(% of population)

63 — No affiliation

28 — Christian

9 — Buddist

if Hawaii were 100 people

20 would be Caucasian
20 would be Mixed Race (excluding Hawaiian)
18 would be Japanese
24 would be Hawaiian & Part Hawaiian
18 would be Other

---

state language (along with English) and mandating that Hawaiian culture be taught in public school.

Hawaiian culture, therefore, remains an important part of the identity of the islands, reflected in ways large and small – in spontaneous hula at a concert, an *oli* (chant) sung before important occasions, the *lomilomi* treatment you receive at a spa or even a conversation conducted wholly in *'olelo Hawai'i* – the Hawaiian language.

Seeking A Sustainable Balance

At the time of Western contact, the population of Hawaii was somewhere between 200,000 and a million people – about what it is today (just shy of 1.3 million). It's incredible to think that so many people could be supported – sustainably – using ancient resource management practices and without the use of metal. Ironically, Hawaii is less stable today than it was then: it is wholly dependent on the outside world. Fully 80% of Hawaii's consumer goods, including 85% of its food, are imported. It spends nearly $5 billion a year on oil and coal, all of it imported. And in a place blessed with a wealth of natural energy sources, 95% of Hawaii's power still comes from carbon-based fuels.

As the population swells – which it did by almost 7% between 2000 and 2009 (and by 50% since 1959, the year it became a state) – new housing developments sprawl, stressing the state's water resources, transportation systems, public schools and landfills.

Hawaii's dependent on the outside world not only for its food and fuel, but for nearly its entire economy. After losing sugar and pineapple to cheap imports from the developing world, Hawaii's eggs were left in one basket: tourism. And when recession tanked the economy in 2008, tourism went with it. By year's end state revenue shortfalls soared to nearly

» Percentage of marriages that are interethnic: about 50%

» Percentage of residents who want mandatory recycling: over 80%

» Energy produced from oil: 89%

» Energy from alternative sources: 5%

Top Films & TV

Rap's Hawai'i Rap Reiplinger was a comedy icon in the '70s – the humor might seem weird to non-residents, but strikes a chord among locals.
Hawaii 5-0 Pat McGarrett redux, sans the suit and tie.

Magnum PI Dated as it is, locals still love to watch it (if only to pick out the locations).
Blue Crush A local favorite for its surf cinematography
50 First Dates Because Rob Schneider mangling a pidgin accent is not to be missed.

Top CDs

» *Facing Future*, Iz Kamakawiwo'ole
» *Masters of Hawaiian Slack Key Guitar vols 1 & 2*
» *Acoustic Soul*, John Cruz
» *Collection*, Hapa
» *On and On*, Jack Johnson

» Average number of tourists in Hawaii each day: 180,000

» Cans of Spam consumed in Hawaii annually: 7 million

» Average commute: 26 minutes

» Average price for gas 2010: $3.38 per gallon (the highest in the US)

» Seatbelt use: 95% (tied with Arizona for highest in the US)

$2 billion. Then-governor Linda Lingle imposed draconian budget cuts (including furloughs and public school closures) plus a $1.8 billion stimulus. Highways and bridges are one focus, but diversifying the economy is another. Supporting Hawaii's small farmers and encouraging consumers to 'buy local' might also mitigate Hawaii's dependency on tourism and imports. The new governor, Neil Abercrombie, intends to continue the push toward energy independence and food sovereignty.

Nevertheless, tourism will likely be Hawaii's bread and butter for the foreseeable future, but it comes at a price. It brings in about 7 million visitors annually – five times the state population – crowding roads, beaches and surf breaks and driving up the price of real estate, not to mention fueling passionate resistance to development for the resort industry. Many residents acknowledge that the current model is both unstable and unsustainable and that the islands today stand at a crossroads – Hawaii can either move toward securing a more homegrown future or it can suffer the worsening side effects of its addiction to tourism, imported goods and fossil fuel.

That future is far from decided, but there are encouraging stirrings. Hawaii is striving to become a pioneer in clean energy. In 2008 Governor Lingle signed the Hawaii Clean Energy Initiative (HCEI), which sets the goal of having a 70% clean energy economy by 2030. Hawaii's pursuing every renewable and clean energy option available – wind farms on Maui, geothermal and biomass on the Big Island, algae-based biofuels, deepwater thermal conversion for downtown Honolulu, solar farms on Lana'i, wave power, electric cars, a statewide integrated bike plan...in addition to remaking its electricity grid and embarking on its most ambitious (and controversial) new project, the construction of a $5 billion light-rail system in Honolulu. If it succeeds, Hawaii would become the first economy based primarily on clean energy.

News Sources

Honolulu Star-Advertiser (www.staradvertiser.com) Local daily newspaper. **Honolulu Weekly** (honolulu weekly.com) Alternative weekly newspaper; available every Thursday; detailed events listing.

Honolulu Magazine (www.honolulumagazine.com) Bimonthly Honolulu lifestyle and culture magazine. **Ka Wai Ola** (www.oha.org/kwo) Office of Hawaiian Affairs' paper of topics relevant to the Native Hawaiian community.

Hawaii Public Radio (www.hawaiipublicradio.org) 88.1 FM KHPR and 89.3 FM KIPO; national and local news. Live web streaming available. **OC16** (www.oc16.tv) Oceanic Cable channel 16 – 24-hour, all-local programming.

History

For the youngest body of land on the planet, Hawaii has a remarkably rich and varied history. Perhaps it was inevitable, given its remoteness and its position as a waypoint between East and West, that it would become the scene of so much uniqueness, diversity, exchange and upheaval. Its discovery and colonization is one of humanity's great epic tales: that early humans even found their way to such tiny droplets of land – the world's most isolated – in the midst of the earth's largest ocean is a testament to the skill, daring and, perhaps, luck of the voyagers who survived the journey. Of the many more who likely did not survive it, history is silent.

The early colonists brought with them everything they needed to succeed – the plants and animals they had cultivated in the islands of their origin. They arrived to a place unlike anything they'd seen: islands with varied climates and species of plants and animals found nowhere else, a land of snow-capped volcanoes, fluted cliffs, arid deserts, teeming reefs. Over the centuries they developed a highly ordered society that managed the land sustainably and produced some of Oceania's most impressive art, architecture, sport, spirituality, medicine, agriculture and oral traditions.

And then, starting on a single day in 1778, everything changed. It was the archetypal clash of civilizations: the British Empire, the most technologically advanced culture on the planet, sent an explorer on a mission, to boldly go where no (European) man had gone before. The Hawaii he stumbled upon was, to his eyes, a place inhabited by heathens stuck in prehistoric times; they had no metal, no modern technology, not even a written language. Their rigidly stratified culture, which worshipped pagan gods and engaged in human sacrifice, seemed an anathema to the Christian world view. But Hawaii's geographic position, wealth of resources and anchorage for trans-Pacific commerce meant that the islands would quickly become a target of the West's civilizing impulse, a process that in the minds of many Native Hawaiians continues today.

The ensuing two centuries saw the decline of the indigenous culture

> Native Books Na Mea Hawai'i (www.nativebook shawaii.com) is a fantastic resource for both well-known and hard-to-find books about Hawaii and Native Hawaiian culture.

NATIVE BOOKS

TIMELINE	**40–30 million BC**	**AD 300–600**	**1000–1300**
	The first Hawaiian island, Kure, rises from the sea, appearing where the Big Island is today; borne by wind, wing and wave, plants, insects and birds colonize the new land.	The first wave of Polynesians, most likely from the Marquesas Islands, voyage by canoe to the Hawaiian Islands – a half-century before Vikings leave Scandinavia to plunder Europe.	Sailing from Tahiti, a second wave of Polynesian voyagers arrives in Hawaii. Their tools are made of stone, shells and bone, and they bring taro, sweet potato, sugarcane, coconut, chickens, pigs and dogs.

ANN CECIL / LONELY PLANET IMAGES ©

'Iolani Palace, Honolulu (p62).

through displacement, disease and disenfranchisement; the rise of a plantation economy that would attract laborers from Japan, Portugal, the Philippines, China and Korea, and create a unique blend of cultures and traditions; the eventual overthrow of the Hawaiian monarchy and the Islands' inclusion into the United States; the development and marketing of one of the world's most desirable tourist destinations.

But the Hawaii of today retains features of all that's come before, all of it still alive in the folds of its landscape and the character of its cultures.

Birth of an Archipelago

The 137 islands comprising the Hawaiian chain – eight main islands and numerous islets stretching across 1500 miles of the Pacific – are all the progeny of a single volcanic hot spot. About 300 miles wide, the Hawaii hot spot has been erupting for at least 86 million years, and as the Pacific plate has drifted over it from the southeast to the northwest (at the breakneck speed of about 30 miles per million years), the vent popped up a string of islands.

1778–9	1790	1795	1810
Captain Cook, the first foreigner known to reach the islands, visits Hawaii twice. After being warmly welcomed, Cook loses his temper over a stolen boat and is killed by Hawaiians.	Kamehameha the Great invades Maui, decimating island warriors in a bloody battle at 'Iao Valley.	Kamehameha the Great unites the islands of Hawai'i, Maui, Moloka'i, Lana'i and O'ahu at the Battle of Nu'uanu.	Kamehameha negotiates peacefully to take control of Kaua'i, uniting all the islands in one kingdom for the first time.

The oldest, Kure Atoll, lies at its northwestern extreme; the youngest, the island of Hawai'i (aka the Big Island), is at the southeastern extreme. The hot spot is still adding new land to Hawai'i island, and it's a long way from being finished; a nascent new island, the Lo'ihi seamount, is forming about 22 miles southeast of Hawai'i island. But don't call your real estate agent just yet; Lo'ihi is still 3000ft underwater and won't emerge steaming from the ocean for another 10,000 to 100,000 years.

When young, all the islands looked much like Hawai'i island does today, with its characteristic gently sloping shield volcanoes. Over millions of years, through erosion, earthquakes and landslides, this smooth profile became jagged, resulting in the dramatic, fluted *pali* (cliffs) characteristic of older islands like O'ahu and Kaua'i. Eventually even the largest shield volcanoes subside and erode down to low islets and atolls before disappearing again under the sea from which they were born. Such is the eventual fate of all the Hawaiian Islands; but while they exist, these islands are home to a dynamic and fascinating geology, ecology and culture seen nowhere else on Earth.

An Explosion of Life

Isolated islands are nature's laboratories, and the mad scientist of evolution certainly went to work in Hawai'i. Over millions of years, life arrived and evolved. But only that which could make the long journey across the Pacific by wing, wind or wave could colonize the Hawaiian archipelago – at more than 2000 miles from the closest continent, Hawaii is the most isolated landmass on Earth. Before humans arrived, therefore, there were almost no mammals, reptiles or amphibians. But the lucky plants, birds and insects that survived the crossing – one species every hundred-thousand years on average – flourished and adapted in Hawai'i's varied microclimates and rich volcanic soil. In some cases, a single colonist evolved dozens, even hundreds of new species. Indeed some of the world's most astonishing examples of this process, called 'adaptive radiation,' are found in Hawaii: a single finch gave rise to over 60 new species, a lobelia plant radiated into some 125 species, a fruit fly evolved into over 600 species – and counting. By the time humans arrived, the forests of Hawai'i were utterly unique, filled with flora and fauna found nowhere else on Earth: happyface spiders, predatory caterpillars, towering *hapu'u* ferns, brilliant *'i'iwi* birds darting among red 'ohi'a blossoms.

When the first canoes arrived, bringing with them pigs, dogs, rats, mosquitoes and hungry humans, defenseless native species went into decline. Indeed, so high was the biodiversity of ancient Hawai'i and so sensitive its flora and fauna that humans were nothing short of a catastrophe. Early Polynesians pressured native species – a large flightless goose, once ubiquitous throughout the islands, was hunted to extinction – and the process

CONCISE HISTORY

Want a history of Hawaii you can finish on the flight over? Grab *A Concise History of the Hawaiian Islands* (1999), by Phil Barnes, which captures a surprising amount of nuance in 90 crisp pages.

1810	1819	1819	1820
Kamehameha the Great moves to Maui, declaring Lahaina the royal seat of the Hawaiian kingdom.	Kamehameha dies 'in the faith of his fathers.' A few months later, his son, the new king Liholiho, breaks the kapu on eating with women, repudiating the Hawaiian religion.	The first whaling ships arrive in Hawaiian waters.	The first Christian missionaries arrive in Hawaii.

accelerated dramatically after Western contact. Today the Hawaiian Islands have earned the dubious distinction as the extinction capital of the world; nearly three-quarters of all species that have become extinct in the US are native to Hawaii, and hundreds more remain endangered or threatened.

Polynesian Voyagers

Don't miss artist, historian and voyager Herb Kawainui Kane's beautiful *Voyagers* (2005). Kane's detailed and accurate paintings give a glimpse into Hawaii's mythic and historical past. Some of Kane's paintings are on display in the Ka'upulehu Cultural Center at the Four Seasons Resort Hualalai on the Big Island.

To ancient Polynesians, the Pacific Ocean was a passageway, not a barrier, and the islands it contained were connected, not isolated. Sailing double-hulled canoes fashioned without the benefit of metals, they settled an immense continent consisting largely of water. Sometime between AD 300 and 600, they made their longest journey yet and discovered the Hawaiian Islands. This would mark the northern reach of their migrations, which were so astounding that Captain Cook – the first Western explorer to take their full measure – could not conceive of how they did it, settling 'every quarter of the Pacific Ocean' and becoming 'by far the most extensive nation upon earth.' Tantalizing evidence suggests that Polynesians may even have reached the west coast of South America: the sweet potato, a staple food in Hawai'i long before Europeans arrived, comes from the Andes. While there are several theories about how the sweet potato got to Hawai'i, it's possible that skilled voyagers like the Polynesians could have made the trip to South America – and back.

Almost nothing is known about the first wave of Polynesians (likely from the Marquesas Islands) who settled Hawai'i, except that the archaeological record shows that they were here. A second wave of Polynesians from the Tahitian Islands began arriving around AD 1000, and they conquered the first peoples and obliterated nearly all traces of their history and culture. Later Hawaiian legends of the *menehune* – an ancient race of little people who mysteriously built temples and great stoneworks overnight – may refer to these original inhabitants.

For 300 years, regular voyaging occurred between Polynesia and Hawai'i, and Polynesians brought to the islands their religious beliefs, social structures and over two-dozen food plants and domestic animals. But what they didn't possess is equally remarkable: no metal, no alphabet or written language, no wheel, no clay to make pottery. In Hawai'i, the second wave of Polynesians called themselves *Kanaka Maoli,* or 'the People.' When for unknown reasons cross-Pacific voyaging stopped around 1300, a distinct Hawaiian culture began to evolve.

Ancient Hawai'i

Hawaiian society retained some of the basic features found in cultures throughout Polynesia. It was highly stratified, ruled by a chiefly class called *ali'i* whose power derived from their ancestry: they were believed to be descended from the gods. In ancient Hawai'i, clan loyalty trumped

1821	1824	1825	1826
Missionary leader Hiram Bingham opens Hawaii's first Christian church to serve as missionaries' headquarters.	Queen Kapi'olani, a devout Christian, descends into the crater of Kilauea in defiance of the fire goddess Pele.	The first sugar and coffee plantations in Hawaii are started, on O'ahu.	Missionaries formulate a 12-letter alphabet (plus glottal stop) for the Hawaiian language and set up the first printing press. It's said that Queen Ka'ahumanu learned to read in five days.

individuality, elaborate traditions of gifting and feasting conferred prestige and a pantheon of shape-shifting gods animated the natural world.

Several ranks of *ali'i* ruled each island, and life was marked by frequent warfare as they jockeyed for power. The largest geopolitical division was the *mokupuni* (island), presided over by a member of the *ali'i nui* (kingly class). Each island was further divided into *moku*, wedge-shaped areas of land running from the ridge of the mountains to the sea. Smaller, similarly wedge-shaped *ahupua'a* comprised each *moku*. The *ahupua'a* were mostly self-sustaining and had local chiefs.

Ranking just below the *ali'i*, the kahuna (experts or masters) included priests, healers and skilled craftspeople – canoe makers, navigators etc. Also beneath the chiefs were the *konohiki*, who supervised resource management within an *ahupua'a* and collected taxes from the *maka'ainana* (commoners), who did most of the physical labor. Occupying the lowest tier was a small class of outcasts or untouchables called *kaua*, who were a convenient source of *pua'a waewae loloa* – 'long-legged pigs,' a euphemism for human sacrificial victims.

VOYAGING BY THE STARS

The 62ft double-hulled canoe *Hokule'a is a* replica of a *wa'a kaulua,* an ancient Hawaiian long-distance sailing vessel. In 1976, it set off to do what no one had done in over 600 years: sail 2400 miles to Tahiti without benefit of radar, compass, satellites or sextant to prove that ancient Polynesians discovered the various islands of the Pacific in a series of intentional voyages rather than by blind luck.

Hokule'a's Micronesian navigator, Mau Piailug, was far from blind; he still knew the art of celestial navigation at a time when such knowledge had been lost to Hawaiian culture. Piailug could read currents, winds, landmarks and time in a complex system of dead reckoning to stay on course. The trick, he'd said, is to imagine the canoe as a still point in relation to the stars while the island sails toward you. In ancient times, the star leading vessels to Hawai'i was called Hokule'a, the Star of Gladness.

After 33 days at sea, *Hokule'a* reached Papeete, where it was greeted by 20,000 Tahitians. This historic achievement helped spark a revival of interest in traditional culture, today called the Hawaiian Renaissance.

Hokule'a and the Polynesian Voyaging Society (http://pvs.kcc.hawaii.edu) have been sailing by the stars ever since. They made a second Tahitian voyage in 1980 with Hawaiian navigator Nainoa Thompson; Piailug, who died in 2010, passed on his knowledge of stellar wayfinding to Thompson, who now teaches it to others. Since its 1976 voyage, the canoe has made nine more trips, sailing throughout Polynesia and to the US mainland, Canada, Micronesia and Japan. Its planned three-year voyage to circumnavigate the globe, set to begin in 2012, will visit 45 ports around the world and end in Hawaii in 2015. For more, visit www.hokuleawwv.org.

1828
Missionary Sam Ruggles introduces the first coffee tree as a garden ornamental (coffee doesn't become a commercial crop until the 1840s).

1830
To control destructive herds of feral cattle, Spanish-Mexican cowboys (dubbed *paniolo*) are recruited. They introduce Hawaiians to the guitar and 'ukulele.

» Kona coffee beans on bush.

In *Cook* (2003), Nicholas Thomas seeks the man behind the controversial legend, retelling the story of Captain Cook's Pacific voyages. For more direct sources, check out Eleanor Nordyke's *Pacific Images: Views from Captain Cook's Third Voyage* (2009), a collection of engravings by Cook's artist, plus maps and excerpts from Cook and his officers' journals.

A culture of mutuality and reciprocity infused what was essentially a feudal agricultural society: chiefs were custodians of their people, and humans custodians of nature, all of which was sacred – the living expression (or mana, spiritual essence) of the universe's immortal soul. Everyone played a part through work and ritual to maintain the health of the community and its comity with the gods; when needs and honor were satisfied, Hawaiians developed rich traditions in art, music, dance, sport and competition. And though rigidly stratified, Hawaiian society wasn't entirely autocratic; if chiefs abused their power or failed their duties, commoners were free to move to other *ahupua'a*.

Nevertheless, in practice, a very strict code – called the kapu (taboo) system – governed daily life. If a commoner dared to eat *moi*, a type of fish reserved for *ali'i*, for example, it was a violation of kapu. Penalties for such transgressions could be harsh, including death. Further, in a society based on mutual respect, slights to honor – whether of one's chief or extended family – could not be abided. As a result, ancient Hawai'i could be both a gracefully unselfish and fiercely uncompromising place.

Captain Cook & Western Contact

The great British explorer Captain James Cook spent a decade traversing the Pacific over the course of three voyages. He sought the fabled northwest passage linking the Pacific and Atlantic, but his were also voyages of discovery. He sailed with a complement of scientists and artists to document what he found. On the third voyage in 1778, and quite by accident, Cook sailed into the main Hawaiian Island chain.

His arrival ended nearly half a millennium of isolation, and it irrevocably altered the course of Hawaiian history. While Cook was already familiar with Polynesians, Hawaiians knew nothing of Europeans, nor of the metal, guns and diseases their ships carried, not to mention the world view they represented: Hawaiians lived in an island world inseparable from the spiritual realm, while Cook embodied a continental consciousness steeped in Enlightenment philosophy, in which God ruled in heaven and only men walked the earth.

In January 1778, Cook dropped anchor off O'ahu and, as he had elsewhere in the Pacific, bartered with the indigenous peoples for badly needed food and fresh water. Then he left to hunt again for the northwest passage. He returned to the islands in November, this time sighting Maui. However, he didn't land but moved on to circle the Big Island, continuing to trade for fresh supplies, until he stopped in Kealakekua Bay in January 1779.

For a fuller story of what happened next, see p202. Cook's ships were greeted by a thousand canoes, and Hawaiian chiefs and priests honored him with rituals and deference. Indeed, Cook had landed at an auspicious

1831	1846	1848	1852
Lahainaluna Seminary, the first secondary school west of the Rocky Mountains, is built in Lahaina.	At the height of the whaling era, a record 596 whaling ships stop at Honolulu and Lahaina. Ultimately, four of the Big Five sugar plantation companies get their start supplying whalers.	King Kamehameha III institutes the Great Mahele, which (along with the 1850 Kuleana Act) allows commoners and foreigners to own land in Hawaii for the first time.	The first sugar plantation contract laborers arrive from China; most are single men who upon completing their contract often stayed in Hawaii to start businesses and families.

time: during the *makahiki*, a time of festival and celebration in honor of the god Lono, and some have theorized that the Hawaiians mistook Cook for the god. The Hawaiians were so unrelentingly gracious, in fact – so agreeable in every respect, including the eagerness of Hawaiian women to have sex – that Cook and his men felt safe to move about unarmed.

Cook set sail some weeks later, but storms forced him to turn back. The mood in Kealakekua had changed, however: the *makahiki* had ended. No canoes met him, and suspicion replaced welcome. A series of small conflicts culminated when Cook led an armed party to capture the local chief, Kalaniopu'u. When the Englishmen disembarked, they were surrounded by angry Hawaiians. In an uncharacteristic fit of pique, Cook shot and killed a Hawaiian man. The Hawaiians immediately descended on Cook, killing him in return. Today a white obelisk at Kealakekua Bay marks the spot of Cook's death; it stands on a small area of lava rock, the only piece of sovereign British territory in the US.

Kamehameha the Great

In the years following Cook's death, a steady number of trading ships sought out Hawaii as a mid-Pacific supply point; with the discovery of a deepwater anchorage in Honolulu Harbor in 1794, Hawaii became the new darling of trans-Pacific commerce, first in the fur trade involving China, New England and the Pacific Northwest. The main commodity in the islands – salt – happened to be useful for curing hides. But for the indigenous chiefs, the main items of interest were firearms, which the Europeans willingly traded. Bolstered with muskets and cannons, Kamehameha, a chief from Kohala on the island of Hawai'i, began a campaign in 1790 to conquer all the Hawaiian Islands. Other chiefs had tried and failed, but Kamehameha had Western guns; not only that, he was prophesied to succeed and possessed an unyielding determination and great personal charisma. Within five years he united – bloodily – the main islands excepting Kaua'i (which eventually joined peacefully). The dramatic final skirmish in his campaign, the Battle of Nu'uanu, took place on O'ahu in 1795. Today visitors to Nu'uanu Pali State Park can stand at the edge of the 1000ft drop over which Kamehameha's advancing army drove hundreds of O'ahu's warriors.

Kamehameha was a singular figure who reigned over the most peaceful era in Hawaiian history. A shrewd politician, he configured multi-island governance to mute competition among the *ali'i*. A savvy businessman, he created a profitable monopoly on the sandalwood trade in 1810 while protecting trees from overharvesting. He personally worked taro patches as an example to his people, and his most famous decree – Kanawai Mamalahoe, or 'Law of the Splintered Paddle' – established a kapu to protect travelers from harm on the road.

In *Legends and Myths of Hawaii*, King David Kalakaua captures the shimmering nature of ancient Hawaiian storytelling by seamlessly mixing history (of Kamehameha, Captain Cook, the burning of the temples) with living mythology.

Shoal of Time, by Gavan Daws (1968), remains perhaps the most well-written account of Hawaiian history from Captain Cook's arrival to statehood in 1959.

1863	**1868**	**1873**	**1878**
Kohala Sugar Company, Hawai'i the Big Island's first sugar plantation, is established to create jobs for Hawaiians.	The first Japanese contract laborers arrive to work the sugar plantations.	A Belgian Catholic priest, Father Damien Joseph de Veuster, arrives at Moloka'i's leprosy colony. He stays for 16 years, dying of leprosy (now called Hansen's disease) himself in 1889.	The first Portuguese contract laborers arrive.

Most of all, Kamehameha absorbed growing foreign influences while fastidiously honoring indigenous religious customs. He did this despite doubts among his people about Christianity, with its foreign concepts of sin and damnation. When Kamehameha died in 1819, he left the question of how to resolve the issue to his son and heir, 22-year-old Liholiho.

Within the year, pressured by his stepmother Queen Ka'ahumanu and other leaders, Liholiho abandoned Hawaiian spirituality in one sweeping, stunning act of repudiation (see the boxed text, p575).

Missionaries & Whalers

Of Hawaii's eight ruling monarchs, only King Kamehameha I begat children who inherited the throne.

Into the midst of this upheaval, on April 19, 1820, the first group of New England missionaries arrived in Kailua, on the island of Hawai'i. Their zeal to save pagan souls was, however, matched by their disdain for Hawaiians and their culture, which they worked tirelessly to stamp out.

The missionaries arrived expecting the worst, and that's what they found: public nudity, 'lewd' hula dancing, polygamy, gambling, drunkenness, fornication with sailors. To them, all kahuna were witch doctors and Hawaiians hopelessly lazy. Because the missionaries' god, *Ke Akua* in Hawaiian, was clearly powerful, they attracted converts. But these conversions were not deeply felt; Hawaiians often abandoned the church's teachings in their everyday lives. The missionaries found one thing, however, that attracted avid, widespread interest: literacy.

The missionaries established an alphabet for the Hawaiian language, and with this tool, Hawaiians learned to read with astonishing speed. In their oral culture, Hawaiians were used to prodigious feats of memory, and *ali'i* understood that literacy was a key to accessing Western culture and power. Legend has it that Kamehameha's wife, Queen Ka'ahumanu, learned to read in five days. Within a decade, two-fifths of the population was literate, and by the mid-1850s, Hawaii had a higher literacy rate than the US and supported dozens of Hawaiian-language newspapers.

Captain William Brown of the HMS *Butterworth* was the first European to navigate the narrow entry to the harbor; he's credited with naming it 'Fair Haven,' which translates into Hawaiian roughly as 'Honolulu.'

At the same time, Pacific whaling ships found Hawaii an ideal place to provision and transfer their catch to ships heading for America. By 1824, over 100 ships were arriving annually, and this number grew for the next three decades. Once the sandalwood trade collapsed in 1830 (after profligate *ali'i* allowed the trees to be pillaged to pay off their debts), whaling became the economic backbone of the islands, especially in ports like Honolulu and Lahaina. Supplying the whalers also influenced island agriculture: sailors didn't want poi (mashed taro root) and breadfruit; they wanted beef, potatoes and green vegetables.

Additionally, sailors tended to conflict with the missionaries since they enjoyed all the pleasures the missionaries censured. Amid these influences, it became clear to Hawaiian leaders that the only way to survive in a world of more powerful nations was to adopt Western ways and styles of government.

1879	1882	1884
King Kalakaua lays the cornerstone for 'Iolani Palace, a lavish, four-story building with an ornate throne room, running water and electric lights; it costs $350,00 and is completed in 1882.	Macadamia trees are planted on Hawai'i the Big Island as an ornamental. The nuts aren't eaten till the 1920s.	The first pineapple plants are introduced.

» Pineapples.

The Great Mahele

Born and raised in Hawaii after Western contact, King Kamehameha III (Kauikeaouli) struggled to retain traditional Hawaiian society while developing a political system better suited to foreign, frequently American tastes. Hawaii's absolute monarchy denied citizens a voice in their government or the right to own land. Traditionally, no Hawaiian ever owned land, but the *ali'i* managed it in stewardship for all. However, none of this sat well with American patriots whose ancestors had a generation before fought a revolution for the right to vote and to own private property.

So, in 1840 Kauikeaouli promulgated Hawaii's first constitution, which established a constitutional monarchy with limited citizen representation. Given an inch, foreigners pressed for a mile, and in 1848

DESTRUCTION OF THE TEMPLES

One purpose of the ancient Hawaiian kapu system was to preserve mana (spiritual power). Mana could be strong or weak, won or lost; it expressed itself in one's talents and the success of a harvest or battle.

The kapu system kept *ali'i* from mingling with commoners and men from eating with women (to avoid diluting mana). It kept women from eating pork and from entering *luakini heiau* (sacrificial temples). Chiefs could declare temporary kapu, and punish by death even minor infractions, say, a commoner stepping on an *ali'i*'s shadow.

However, foreigners arriving in Hawai'i weren't accountable to the kapu system, and lesser *ali'i* saw they could possess power without following its dictates. Women saw that breaking kapu – for example, by dining with sailors – didn't incur the gods' wrath. Kamehameha the Great's powerful wife, Ka'ahumanu, chafed under the kapu, as it kept women from becoming leaders equal to men.

Eventually even Hawai'i's head priest, Hewahewa, couldn't defend the system. Upon Kamehameha's death in 1819, he and Ka'ahumanu convinced Kamehameha's heir, Liholiho, to end it. They arranged a feast where Liholiho would eat with women, thereby breaking the kapu.

This act – effectively ending Hawai'i's religion – was nearly beyond the young king. He delayed for months, and to bolster his courage on the day before, drank himself into a stupor. But to the shock of the gathered *ali'i*, Liholiho helped himself to food at the women's table. Then Hewahewa, signaling his approval, noted that the gods could not survive without kapu. 'Then let them perish with it!' Liholiho is said to have cried.

For months afterward, Ka'ahumanu and others set fire to the temples and destroyed the *ki'i*, the images of the gods. Most Hawaiians were happy to be released from kapu, but many continued to venerate the gods and secretly preserved *ki'i*.

Some openly rebelled. Hawai'i's second-highest priest, Kekuaokalani, gathered a small army to defend the gods, but Liholiho's superior forces defeated them with fusillades of musket fire.

1893	1895	1898	1900
On January 17 the Hawaiian monarchy is overthrown by a group of US businessmen supported by US marines. Queen Lili'uokalani acquiesces peacefully; not a shot is fired.	Robert Wilcox leads a failed counter-revolution to restore the monarchy. The deposed queen, charged with being a co-conspirator, is placed under house arrest.	On July 7 President McKinley signs the resolution annexing Hawaii as a US territory; this is formalized by the 1900 Organic Act establishing territorial government.	A fire set to control an outbreak of bubonic plague in Chinatown blazes out of control, burning 38 acres of Honolulu.

TRAVEL TIME

Kauikeaouli followed this with a revolutionary land reform act that was known as the Great Mahele (the Great Division).

This act divided Hawaii in three ways: into crown lands (owned by the kings and their heirs), chief lands (ali'i holdings within traditional ahupua'a) and government lands (to be held for the general public). This was followed in 1850 by the Kuleana Act, which awarded 30,000 acres of government lands to Hawaiian commoners, and it gave foreigners the right to purchase some lands.

The hope was that the Great Mahele would create a nation of small freeholder farmers, but instead it was a disaster – for Hawaiians, at least. Confusion reigned over boundaries and surveys. Unused to the concept of private land and sometimes unable to pay the tax, many Hawaiians simply failed to follow through on the paperwork to claim their titles. Many of those who did – perhaps feeling that life as a taro farmer wasn't the attraction it once was – immediately cashed out, selling their land to eager and acquisitive foreigners.

Within 30 to 40 years, despite supposed limits, foreigners owned fully three-quarters of Hawaii, and Hawaiians, who had relinquished so much of their culture so quickly, had lost their sacred connection to the land. As historian Gavan Daws wrote (in *Shoal of Time: A History of the Hawaiian Islands*), 'The great division became the great dispossession.'

King Sugar & the Plantation Era

In another fateful moment of synchronicity, 1848 was the year gold was discovered in California – spurring the gold rush, which swept west across North America and leapt to Hawaii's shores.

American entrepreneurs, increasingly landowners, discovered it was cheaper to supply California's gold miners from Hawaii than from the East Coast of the US. Foreign-controlled shipping, banking and agriculture grew, along with a struggling effort to make sugar commercially viable. These shifts accelerated in the 1860s as the whaling industry collapsed at the same time the American Civil War created a sharp demand for sugar in the north. In short order, sugar became Hawaii's white gold.

In 1860, 12 plantations exported under 1.5 million pounds of sugar; by 1866, 32 plantations were exporting nearly 18 million pounds. After the war, the demand for Hawaiian sugar dropped and the industry languished. When King Kalakaua was elected to the throne in 1874, he immediately lobbied the US for a treaty that would end import taxes on foreign sugar, thus ensuring profits for Hawaiian-grown sugar. The US agreed in 1876, and sugar production skyrocketed, rising to 58 million pounds in 1878 and 114 million pounds in 1883.

Abundant supplies of low-cost labor were also necessary to make sugar plantations profitable. The first and natural choice was Native Ha-

In 1839 New England missionaries needed five months to sail to Hawaii; later steamships took five weeks. Today airplanes cross the continent and the ocean nonstop in half a day.

1909

In Hawaii's first major labor strike, 5000 Japanese plantation workers protest low pay and harsh treatment compared to Portuguese workers. The strike fails, winning no concessions.

1912

Duke Kahanamoku wins gold and silver medals in freestyle swimming at the Stockholm Olympics; he goes on to become the ambassador of surfing around the world.

MARK NEWMAN / LONELY PLANET IMAGES ©

» Hawai'i Volcanoes National Park (p282).

waiians, but even when willing, there weren't enough left. Due primarily to introduced diseases – like typhoid, influenza, smallpox and syphilis – the Hawaiian population had steadily and precipitously declined. An estimated 800,000 people lived in the islands before Western contact, and in just two decades, by 1800, the Hawaiian population had dropped by two-thirds, to around 250,000. By 1860 there were fewer than 70,000.

Beginning in the 1850s, plantation owners encouraged a flood of immigrants from China, Japan, Portugal and the Philippines to come to Hawaii to work the cane fields. While the sugar industry is all but a memory in the islands today, its legacy remains in the plantation culture it spawned. The immigrant laborers brought to Hawaii (see the boxed text, p580) assimilated quickly and transformed it into the multicultural society it is today.

Five sugar-related holding companies, known as the Big Five, quickly rose to dominate all aspects of the industry: Castle & Cooke, Alexander & Baldwin, C Brewer & Co, American Factors, and Theo H Davies & Co. All were run by white businessmen, many the sons and grandsons of

Well designed, succinct and informative, www. hawaiihistory.org provides an interactive timeline of Hawaii's history that makes it easy to browse quickly or delve deeply into events, with lots of links.

KAPI'OLANI VERSUS PELE

With nothing to replace the kapu system when Liholiho dissolved it, many Hawaiians continued to follow the old ways. The first missionaries arriving in 1820 brought with them, however, a theology to supplant worship of the Hawaiian gods. One of Christianity's early champions was a chiefess on the Kona side of Hawai'i, Kap'iolani. But her people were less enthusiastic about worshipping the Christian god, fearing that if they failed to propitiate Pele, the volcano goddess, the consequences might be dire. This was a genuine concern for people living so close to an active volcano, many of whom had experienced its deadly 1790 eruption.

When missionaries toured Kilauea in 1823, the Hawaiians were astonished to see them flagrantly violate kapu by exploring the crater and eating 'ohelo berries (a food reserved for Pele) with impunity. This primed the ground for Kapi'olani to challenge Pele directly and prove that the Christian god was the more powerful. In 1824, the story goes, she walked about 60 miles from her home to the brink of the steaming crater and, dismissing pleas from her people and defying curses from the priests of Pele, descended into the vent at Halema'uma'u. Surrounded by roiling lava, Kapi'olani ate consecrated 'ohelo berries, read passages from the Bible and threw stones into the volcano without retribution, demonstrating thereby Pele's impotence before the god of the missionaries.

The epic scene has become legendary in modern Hawaii, and it's been the subject of artwork like Herb Kane's *Kapi'olani Defying Pele*. While the story is likely to have been embellished over the years, one can still appreciate how profound Kapi'olani's confidence in the new religion must have been to test the power of a goddess who was all too real for ancient Hawaiians.

1916	1921	1925	1927
Hawai'i National Park is established. It initially encompasses Haleakalā on Maui and Kilauea and Mauna Loa on the Big Island; these later become Haleakalā and Hawai'i Volcanoes National Parks, respectively.	The Hawaiian Homes Commission Act is passed. This sets aside 200,000 acres for homesteading by Hawaiians with 50% or more native blood, granting 99-year leases costing $1 a year.	The first flight lands in Hawaii from the mainland. Commercial flights begin 11 years later.	The $4-million, Moorish-style Royal Hawaiian Hotel, dubbed the 'Pink Palace' (for obvious reasons) opens in Waikiki, inaugurating an era of steamship tourism to the islands.

Kalo loi *(taro fields) in the Hanalei Valley (p513).*

missionaries. While their focus shifted from religion to business, they reached the same conclusion as their forebears: Hawaiians could not be trusted to govern themselves. So, behind closed doors, the Big Five developed plans to relieve Hawaiians of the job.

Overthrow & Annexation

As much as any other monarch, King Kalakaua fought to restore Hawaiian culture and native pride. He resurrected hula from near extinction – earning himself the nickname 'the Merrie Monarch' – much to the dismay of white Christians. But he cared nothing about placating the plantation oligarchy.

He spent money lavishly, piling up massive debts. Kalakaua wanted Hawaii's monarchy to equal any in the world, so he built 'Iolani Palace beginning in 1879 and held an extravagant coronation in 1883. Foreign businessmen considered these to be follies, but worse, Kalakaua was a mercurial decision-maker given to summarily replacing his entire cabinet

1941	1946	1949	1959
On December 7 Pearl Harbor is attacked by Japanese forces, catapulting the US into WWII. The sinking of the battleship USS *Arizona* kills 1177 crew; 2500 lives are lost overall.	On April 1 the most destructive tsunami in Hawaii history (generated by an earthquake in Alaska) kills 159 people across the islands, 96 of them in Hilo, and causes $10.5 million in property damage.	Dockworkers stage a 177-day strike that halts all shipping to and from the islands; this is accompanied by plantation worker strikes that win concessions from the Big Five companies.	Hawaii becomes the union's 50th state (a decision residents ratify by a margin of 17 to 1), and Hawaii's Daniel Inouye becomes the first Japanese-American elected to US Congress.

on a whim. But Kalakaua also saw Hawaii playing a role on the global stage, and in 1881 embarked on a trip to meet foreign heads of state and develop stronger ties with Japan especially. When he returned to Hawaii in November of that year, he became the first king to travel around the world.

Even so the days of the Hawaiian monarchy were numbered. The 1875 Treaty of Reciprocity, which had made Hawaii-grown sugar profitable, had expired. Kalakaua refused to renew, as the treaty now contained a provision giving the US a permanent naval base at Pearl Harbor – a provision Native Hawaiians regarded as a threat to the sovereignty of the kingdom. A secret antimonarchy group called the Hawaiian League, led by a committee of mostly American lawyers and businessmen, 'presented' Kalakaua with a new constitution in 1887. It stripped the monarchy of most of its powers, reducing Kalakaua to a figurehead, and it changed the voting laws to exclude Asians and enfranchise only those who met income and property requirements – effectively disenfranchising all but wealthy, mostly white business owners. Kalakaua signed under threat of violence, earning the 1887 constitution the moniker 'the Bayonet Constitution.' The US got its base at Pearl Harbor, and foreign businessmen consolidated their power.

When Kalakaua died in 1891, his sister and heir, Lili'uokalani, ascended the throne. The queen fought against foreign intervention and control, and she secretly drafted a new constitution to restore Hawaiian voting rights and the monarchy's powers. However, in 1893, before Lili'uokalani could present this, a hastily formed 'Committee of Safety' put in motion the Hawaiian League's long-brewed plans to overthrow the Hawaiian government.

The Committee requested support from US Minister John Stevens, who allowed 150 marines to come ashore in Honolulu Harbor 'only to protect American citizens in case of resistance.' The Committee's own 150-strong militia then surrounded 'Iolani Palace and ordered Queen Lili'uokalani to step down. With no standing army and wanting to avoid bloodshed, she acquiesced.

After the coup, the Committee of Safety formed a provisional government and requested annexation by the US. Much to their surprise, new US President Grover Cleveland refused: he condemned the coup as illegal, conducted under false pretext and against the will of the Hawaiian people, and he requested Lili'uokalani be reinstated. Miffed but unbowed, the Committee instead established their own government, the Republic of Hawaii.

For the next five years, Queen Lili'uokalani pressed her case (for a time from prison) to no avail. In 1898, spurred by new US president, William McKinley, the US annexed the Republic of Hawaii as a US territory. In part, the US justified this act of imperialism because the ongoing

Born and raised on a Kona coffee farm, Gerald Kinro brings personal insight and scholarship to *A Cup of Aloha* (2003), a wonderful portrait of the Kona coffee industry and Hawaii's agricultural life.

For a century, the trip to Moloka'i's Kalaupapa Peninsula wasn't an adventure but a death sentence. In *The Colony* (2006), John Tayman tells the story with dignity, compassion and unflinching honesty.

HISTORY OVERTHROW & ANNEXATION

1960	1961	1962	1962
A tsunami generated off South America destroys over 100 buildings and kills 61 people in Hilo.	Elvis Presley stars in *Blue Hawaii*, the first of Elvis' three Hawaii movies. Along with *Girls! Girls! Girls!* and *Paradise, Hawaiian Style*, these set the mood for Hawaii's post-statehood tourism boom.	Democrat John Burns is elected as governor, and Democrats take control of all three branches of state government (including the House and Senate), which they hold until 2002.	Hawaii's first resort destination outside of Waikiki is built at Ka'anapali Beach.

Spanish-American War had highlighted the strategic importance of the islands as a Pacific military base. Indeed, some feared that if America didn't take Hawaii, another Pacific Rim power (like Japan) just might.

White Ships & Beachboys

The years following annexation were a period of increased commerce to and from the Hawaiian Islands – sugarcane, pineapple and, most notably, tourists. WC Weedon, the owner of Waikiki's second hotel, the Moana, went on a promotional tour of San Francisco in 1901 with a stereopticon and daguerrotypes of palm-fringed beaches and smiling natives. By 1903, 2000 visitors a year were making the nearly five-day journey by

HAPA CHILDREN, PIDGIN TONGUES

Hawaii's multi-ethnic society was a side effect of 19th-century sugar plantation economics. Needing cheap labor, plantations encouraged successive waves of immigrants who, stirred together for a century in the kettle of plantation life, intermingled and intermarried, producing *hapa* ('half' or 'mixed') children; each generation inherited pidgin, a language that crossed cultural divides and that's still spoken today.

Typically plantations offered laborers two- or three-year contracts, which included monthly wages, housing and medical expenses. When their contracts expired, some workers returned home, some moved to the US mainland, but most stayed in Hawaii.

Chinese immigrants were the first to come in the 1850s, eventually reaching about 45,000 before the US 1882 Chinese Exclusion Act slowed arrivals. Each immigrant group left its cultural stamp on the islands; for the Chinese, it was the introduction of rice.

Eventually totaling about 180,000 immigrants from the late 1860s to the 20th century, Japanese would become the largest ethnic group. 'Hawaii *netsu*' (Hawaii fever) was encouraged by the Japanese government; most immigrants were single men, which led to the mail-order 'picture bride' phenomenon among those who stayed in Hawaii. The Japanese also established themselves as independent coffee farmers on Hawai'i island, and rescued the now world-renowned Kona coffee industry from near extinction.

The next major group (about 20,000) was Portuguese, who were actively recruited beginning in 1878. In part because they were Europeans, the Portuguese were treated better than Asians – they were paid more and often made *luna* (supervisors) over Asian field workers. Japanese complaints over these discrepancies led to Hawaii's first organized labor strike in 1909.

After the turn of the century, Koreans and then a huge influx of Filipinos arrived. Totaling about 100,000, Filipinos found, as others had before them, that plantation life was much harsher than promised, and they became another prominent force in Hawaii's budding labor movement.

By the 1930s, immigration slowed to a trickle, though the sugar industry would remain Hawaii's economic backbone and cultural melting pot for another 30 to 40 years.

1968	1971	1976	1978
Hawaii Five-O begins its 12-year run, becoming one of American TV's longest-running crime dramas.	The Merrie Monarch hula festival, begun in 1964, holds its first competitive hula competition; the festival, part of a Hawaiian cultural resurgence, becomes a proving ground for serious hula.	Activists illegally occupy Kaho'olawe, and *Hokule'a* – a reproduction of an ancient Polynesian voyaging canoe – sails to Tahiti. These events spur a Native Hawaiian cultural and political renaissance.	The 1978 Constitutional Convention establishes the Office of Hawaiian Affairs (OHA), which holds the Hawaiian Home Lands in trust to ensure they are used for the benefit of Native Hawaiians.

sea. Travelers departed San Francisco aboard Matson Navigation Company's white-painted steamships, inaugurating the so-called 'White Ship Era' that continued until the mid-1930s, when flying made travel by ship essentially obsolete. The Hawaii of popular imagination – lei-draped visitors mangling the hula at luau, tanned beachboys plying the surf in front of Diamond Head, the sounds of *hapa haole* music – was relentlessly commodified during this period.

It worked. Hotels sprouted along the strand at Waikiki, which had until the late 19th century been a wetland where the *ali'i* retreated for relaxation. The wetlands were drained, and the 1927 opening of the Pink Palace (the Royal Hawaiian Hotel) transformed Waikiki into a premier destination for the rich and famous, including the celebrities of the day – Groucho Marx, Shirley Temple, Bing Crosby, Clark Gable – further enhancing Hawaii's luxury destination cachet. This was the era of Duke Kahanamoku, Olympic swimmer, movie star and unofficial 'ambassador of aloha' who introduced the world beyond Hawaii's shores to the sport of surfing. Back on the mainland, an affectionate if chintzy tiki-culture craze kicked off with the 1934 opening of Don the Beachcomber's Polynesian-themed restaurant in Hollywood. By 1941, Hawaii was hosting more than 30,000 visitors a year.

Pearl Harbor & the 'Japanese Problem'

In the years leading up to WWII, the US government became obsessed with the Hawaiian territory's 'Japanese problem.' What, they wondered, were the true loyalties of 40% of Hawaii's population, the first-generation (*issei*) and second-generation (*nisei*) Japanese? During a war, would they sabotage Pearl Harbor for Japan or defend the US?

Then, on December 7, 1941, a surprise Japanese invasion consisting of 47 ships and submarines and 441 aircraft bombed and attacked military installations across O'ahu. The main target was Pearl Harbor, the most important Pacific naval base of the US: among other damage, nine battleships and other ships were sunk; seven battleships, cruisers and destroyers were damaged; and over 3000 military and civilians were killed or injured. For more on the attack, see p97.

This devastating attack instantly propelled the US into WWII. In Hawaii the army took control of the islands, martial law was declared and civil rights were suspended. Immediately following the Pearl Harbor attack, some 1500 Japanese residents were arrested and placed in internment camps.

However, a coalition of forces in Hawaii successfully resisted immense government pressure, including from President Roosevelt, to follow this with a mass internment of Japanese in the islands, similar to what was being done on the US West Coast. Ultimately some 110,000 Japanese

The popular radio program *Hawaii Calls* introduced the outside world to Island music. It ran for 40 years, from 1935 through 1975, and at its peak aired on 750 stations around the world. CD compliations are available through www.mele.com and www.hawaiian-music.com.

In 1936 designer Ellery Chun updated the 'palaka,' a solid-colored plantation worker shirt, with a tropical print and a more casual style, which he dubbed the 'aloha shirt.' The rest is history.

1983	1992	1992–96	1993
Kilauea volcano begins its current eruption cycle, now the longest in recorded history. Eruptions destroy the village of Kalapana, various subdivisions, the coastal road to Puna and other sites.	On September 11 Hurricane 'Iniki slams into Kaua'i, demolishing 1300 buildings and damaging 5000, causing a total of $1.6 billion in damage. Miraculously, only four people are killed.	The world's largest optical-infrared telescopes, Keck I and II, are installed on Mauna Kea.1993	On the 100-year anniversary of the overthrow of the Hawaiian monarchy, President Clinton signs the 'Apology Bill,' which acknowledges the US government's role in the kingdom's illegal takeover.

Most of the plantations are gone, but Moloka'i and Lana'i both have big pineapple hangovers. *Hawai'i's Pineapple Century* (2004) by Jan Ten Bruggencate is a highly readable account of how the spiky fruit changed life across Hawaii.

were interned on the US mainland, but the majority of Hawaii's 160,000 Japanese citizens were spared incarceration – though they suffered sometimes racial discrimination and suspicion about their loyalties.

In 1943, the government was persuaded to reverse itself and approve the formation of an all-Japanese combat unit, the 100th Infantry Battalion. Over 10,000 *nisei* volunteered for the 3000-soldier unit. They were sent, along with the all-Japanese 442nd Regimental Combat Team, to fight in Europe, where they became two of the most decorated units in US military history. By the war's end, Roosevelt proclaimed these soldiers were proof that 'Americanism is a matter of the mind and heart,' not 'race or ancestry.'

The 1950s would test this noble sentiment, but Hawaii's unique multi-ethnic society emerged from the war severely strained but not broken. Afterward, Japanese nisei and war veterans became some of Hawaii's most prominent politicians and businessmen, including the US senate's longest serving sitting member, Senator Daniel Inouye.

Statehood

The Territory of Hawaii had lobbied for statehood ever since it was created, but statehood bills always failed mostly because of US political reluctance to accept its multi-ethnic, Asian-majority population on equal terms. After WWII and during the Cold War, Southern Democrats in particular raised the specter that Hawaiian statehood would leave the US open not just to the 'Yellow Peril' (embodied, as they saw it, by imperialist Japan) but to Chinese and Russian communist infiltration through Hawaii's labor unions. Further, they feared that Hawaii would elect Asian politicians who would seek to end the US' then-legal segregation. Conversely, proponents of statehood increasingly saw it as a necessary civil rights step to prove that the US actually practiced 'equality for all.'

The Island Edge of America (2003), by Tom Coffman, tells the story of 20th-century Hawaii, emphasizing the impact of Japanese immigration and WWII on island politics.

In the late 1950s, both Hawaii and Alaska (which had been similarly rebuffed when seeking to join the union) were competing to be admitted as the 49th state. Alaska won, being approved in June 1958, but Hawaii was not disappointed long; eight months later, in March 1959, Congress voted again and admitted Hawaii. On August 21, President Eisenhower signed the bill that officially made Hawaii the 50th state.

A few years later, surveying Hawaii's relative ethnic harmony, President John Kennedy pronounced, 'Hawaii is what the US is striving to be.' An act that was more than optimistic symbolism, Hawaii's two new senators (along with those from Alaska) helped secure the passage of America's landmark civil rights legislation in the 1960s.

As was the hope, statehood had an immediate economic impact, and once again, Hawaii's timing was remarkably fortuitous.

The decline of sugar (and pineapple) in the 1960s – due in part to the la-

2000

Senator Daniel Akaka introduces the Native Hawaiian Government Reorganization Act (the 'Akaka Bill'), asking for federal recognition of Native Hawaiians as the islands' indigenous peoples.

2002

Linda Lingle is elected Hawaii's first Republican governor in 40 years. She is re-elected in 2006.

EMILY RIDDELL / LONELY PLANET IMAGES ©

» Merrie Monarch Festival (p268) dancers.

In February 2009, Hawaii senator Daniel Akaka reintroduced the Native Hawaiian Government Reorganization Act – aka the Akaka Bill. It seeks to establish a legal framework to form a Native Hawaiian government and gain federal recognition for Native Hawaiians. This would give Native Hawaiians similar legal status as Native American tribes.

Federal recognition of Native Hawaiians is widely supported in Hawaii, but there is controversy over what shape 'Hawaiian sovereignty' should take. The bill's sponsors emphasize that the bill doesn't establish a government (it only provides the means for doing so); it doesn't settle reparation claims; it doesn't take private land or create reservations; it doesn't authorize gambling; and it doesn't allow Hawaii to secede from the US.

Establishing a Native Hawaiian government, as Senator Akaka has said, 'is important for all people of Hawaii, so we can finally resolve the longstanding issues relating from the overthrow of the Kingdom of Hawai'i,' an act for which President Bill Clinton formally apologized in 1993, the centennial of the overthrow.

The two main frameworks for sovereignty are a 'nation-within-a-nation' model similar to that accorded Native Americans on the one hand and outright sovereignty, in which Native Hawaiians would have full autonomy over portions of land, on the other.

Both options raise thorny questions about who qualifies as 'Native Hawaiian' and what land would be used. However, there are starting points for addressing both. First, the state of Hawaii holds in trust over a million acres of 'ceded lands,' which by law are to be used for the benefit of Native Hawaiians, in addition to the island of Kaho'olawe (p410). Second, extensive Native Hawaiian genealogical databases exist – a different repatriation program, Hawaiian Home Lands, requires that applicants prove they are at least 50% Native Hawaiian.

With President Barack Obama indicating his support, hopes ran high that the bill would pass. The bill managed to pass the House in February of 2010 but died in the Senate in December 2010. Senator Akaka, however, remains committed to working toward federal recognition for Hawaii's native people.

bor concessions won by Hawaii's unions – left the state scrambling economically. Just then the advent of the jet airplane (and of disposable incomes) meant tourists could become Hawaii's next staple crop. Tourism exploded, which led to a building boom, in an ongoing cycle. In 1959, 175,000 visitors came, and by 1968, there were 1.2 million a year. By 1970, tourism was contributing $1 billion annually, four times what agriculture produced.

Ever since Mark Twain visited in the 1860s, Hawaii lived in the popular imagination as an earthly paradise, a lush, sensuous-yet-safe (and English-speaking) tropical Eden. Hawaii now gave rise to a full-blown tiki craze, in which the culture of Native Hawaiians was appropriated and commercialized to fulfill the romanticized (and media-fueled) fantasies of vacationing Westerners.

2006	**2008**	**2010**
A magnitude 6.7 earthquake wrecks the Mauna Kea Beach Hotel and key irrigation waterways in North Kohala.	Born and raised on O'ahu, Barack Obama is elected the first Hawaii-born president of the US. In the election, Obama wins 72% of the vote in Hawaii, the most of any state.	Democrat Neil Abercrombie, a former US congressman from Hawaii, is elected governor.

Hawaii's People

Everything you imagine when you hear the name Hawaii is probably true. Whatever your postcard idyll might be – a paradise of white sandy beaches, emerald cliffs, azure seas; of indolent ukulele strummers, half-naked hula dancers and sun-bronzed surfers – it exists somewhere.

But beyond the frame-edges of that postcard is another Hawaii – a place where people work and live ordinary lives, a place with shopping malls, landfills and industrial parks, a place with cookie-cutter housing developments, military bases and ramshackle small towns. In many ways, it's much like the rest of the US, and a visitor stepping off the plane expecting *Blue Hawaii* will be surprised to find a thoroughly modern place where the interstate highways, McDonald's and Pier 1s are exactly the same as they are in Tuscon or Sandusky and that no, people don't live in grass shacks (though some probably wish they did).

But underneath the veneer of the tourist industry and an imported consumer culture is a different world, a world defined by and proud of its separateness, its geographical isolation, its unique mix of Eastern, Western and Oceanic culture. And while those cultures don't always blend seamlessly, there are very few places in the world where so many different ethnicities, with no one group commanding a substantial majority, get along. Perhaps it's because they live on tiny islands in the middle of a vast ocean that residents strive to treat one another with aloha; as Native Hawaiian people often say, 'We're all in the same canoe.' And no matter their race or background, island residents share the common bond – and awareness – of living in one of the Earth's beautiful, special places.

Hawaii often feels overlooked by the other 49 states (except maybe Alaska, with which it shares the distinction of being the mainland's slightly bizarre sibling), yet it's protective of its separateness. This has both its positives and negatives; on the positive side, there's a genuine appreciation for Hawaii's uniqueness. On the negative, it reinforces an insider-outsider mentality that in its darkest moments manifests as exclusivity or blatant discrimination. Mainland transplants tend to stick out, even after they've lived in the Islands for some time. For example, as a rule loud assertiveness is discouraged. It's better to avoid confrontation and 'save face' by keeping quiet. In a stereotype that's often true, the most vocal and passionate speakers – at a community meeting, a rally – are often mainland activists who just moved in. No matter how long they live here, these folks will never be considered 'local.' Locals take justifiable umbrage at outsiders who presume to know what's good for Hawaii better than they do. To get anywhere in Hawaii, it's better to show aloha – and a bit of deference – toward people who were Island-born and raised.

Within Hawaii, there's stark contrast between life in Honolulu and on the Neighbor Islands. Honolulu is a cosmopolitan, global city – technologically savvy and fashion-conscious. It has the sports stadiums, the main university and an actual (if comparatively tame) nightlife.

FOLKTALES

Mary Kawena Pukui's *Folktales of Hawai'i* (1995), illustrated by local artist Sig Zane, is a delightful, bilingual collection of ancient teaching stories and amusing tall tales.

LEE FOSTER / LONELY PLANET IMAGES ©

Lei making is the most universally beloved Hawaiian craft

Kauaʻi, Maui, Hawaiʻi island, Lanaʻi and especially Molokaʻi are considered 'country' or 'da boonies.' (Though in a landscape as compressed as Hawaii, 'country' is relative. Rural areas tend not to be too far from the urban or suburban, and there are no vast swaths of uninterrupted wilderness in Hawaii such as there are on the mainland.) In general, Neighbor Island residents tend to dress more casually, speak more pidgin and preserve plantation-era distinctions. Status isn't measured by a Lexus but by a monster truck. *ʻOhana* (family) is important everywhere, but on islands beyond Oʻahu it's often the center of one's life. When locals first meet, they don't ask 'What do you do?' but 'Where you wen' grad?'; like ancient Hawaiians comparing genealogies, locals define themselves not by their accomplishments but by the communities to which they belong: extended family, island, town, high school. And regardless of where they're from within the state, when two locals happen to meet outside Hawaii, there's an automatic bond based on mutual affection and sometimes longing for their island home – wherever they go, they're part of the extended Hawaii *ʻohana.*

Multiculturalism

During the 2008 US presidential election, island residents were thrilled that someone from Hawaii might be president. He was embraced by locals because his calm and his respect for diversity represent Hawaii values; he can also bodysurf, and he displayed true devotion to his *ʻohana*; his grandmother, who lived in Honolulu, died days before the election, and Obama suspended his campaign to visit her before she passed. To locals, these are the things that count. What didn't matter to Hawaii is what the rest of the country seemed fixated on: his race.

That Obama is mixed race was barely worth mentioning. *Of course* he's mixed race – who in Hawaii isn't? One legacy of the plantation era is Hawaii's unselfconscious mixing of ethnicities; cultural differences are freely acknowledged, even carefully maintained, but they don't normally divide people. For residents the relaxed lifestyle and inclusive cultural values are probably the most defining, best-loved aspects of island life.

Depending on your perspective, Honolulu is either America's most Asian city or Polynesia's most American city. Hawaii is as ethnically diverse as (and more racially intermixed than) California, Texas and Florida, but it's nearly missing the African American and Latino populations that help define those states as well as most mainland multiculturalism.

Among older locals, plantation-era stereotypes still inform social hierarchies and interactions. During plantation days, whites were the wealthy plantation owners, and for years after minorities would joke about the privileges that came with being a white 'boss.' But in a growing generational divide, Hawaii's youth often dismiss these distinctions even as they continue to speak pidgin. And as different ethnicities intermarry, racial distinctions blur. It's not uncommon nowadays to meet locals who can rattle off four or five different ethnicities in their ancestry – Hawaiian, Chinese, Portuguese, Filipino and haole for example.

MAHU

To learn more about *mahu* in Polynesian culture and their experience in modern Hawaii, read Andrew Metzner's collection of spoken narratives, *'O Au No Keia* (2001).

Religion & Sexual Orientation

The values of tolerance and acceptance extend beyond race – they apply also to religion and sexual orientation. The overwhelming majority of locals are Christian, but there are substantial Buddhist communities as well as small populations of Jews, Muslims and Hindus. These different faiths conduct themselves with mutual respect and acceptance. Even among devout Christians, religion isn't a matter of rigid orthodoxy; many Native Hawaiians combine indigenous beliefs and practices with Christianity. And while for many years Hawaii was politically behind the curve in its treatment of gay, lesbian and transgendered people (in part because so many residents are Christian, and there's a powerful Mormon influence), in practice there was very little visible discrimination. In fact, in Native Hawaiian culture the *mahu*, a transgendered or cross-dressing male, is a figure of power and mystery. In February 2011 Governor Abercrombie signed a bill legalizing civil unions for same-sex couples; on New Year's Day 2012 Hawaii – already the world's premier destination for weddings and honeymoons – will become the 7th US state to legally recognize gay marriage.

WHO'S WHO

» Hawaiian – a person of Native Hawaiian ancestry. It's a faux pas to call just any Hawaii resident 'Hawaiian' (as you would a Californian or Texan), thus semantically ignoring indigenous people.

» Local – person who grew up in Hawaii. Locals who move away retain their local 'cred,' at least in part. But transplant residents (see below) never become local. To call a transplant 'almost local' is a welcome compliment, despite reiterating an insider-outsider mentality.

» *Malihini* – 'newcomer', someone who's just moved to Hawaii and intends to stay.

» Resident – a person who lives, but might not have been born and raised, in Hawaii; residents may have been here for years but still don't reflect a 'local' sensibility.

» Haole – white person (except local Portuguese); further subdivided as 'mainland' or 'local' haole.

» *Hapa* – person of mixed ancestry; *hapa* is Hawaiian for 'half.' A common racial designation is *hapa haole* (part white and part other, such as Hawaiian or Asian).

» *Kama'aina* – literally a 'child of the land.' A person who is native to a particular place, eg a Hilo native is a *kama'aina* of Hilo and not of Kona. The term connotes a deep connection to a place. In the visitor industry context, '*kama'aina* discounts' apply to any resident of Hawaii (ie anyone with a Hawaii driver's license).

If you're a visitor (particularly a white-skinned one), you might hear this said – possibly in reference to you. It's a controversial word, one that – depending upon the context – can be descriptive, warm or insulting. Originally it meant 'foreigner,' anything – person or object – exotic to the islands, but later it came to denote Caucasian people.

No one's sure why ancient Hawaiians used the word to describe Captain Cook and his crew or what they meant by it. A popular explanation is that the British explorer didn't *honi* (share breath) with the natives. In ancient Hawai'i and still today Hawaiians often greet one another by touching foreheads and breathing together. Breath (*ha* in Hawaiian) is considered an expression of life force, and exchanging it is a gesture of respect and welcome. Instead the British kept their distance, shaking hands; thus it's reasoned the Hawaiians called them 'haole,' meaning 'without breath' – something of an insult. Another explanation is that after praying, the British would speak, saying 'amen,' rather than breathing three times after *pule* (prayers), as the Hawaiians would.

Others challenge these explanations on linguistic grounds. In the Hawaiian language, glottal stops and long vowels are critical to a word's meaning. The word for 'without breath' is 'ha'ole,' not 'haole.' Transcriptions of ancient chants indicate that 'haole' meant 'foreign,' and that it was used before the English arrived.

Regardless of how it happened, today the word means 'white person,' particularly one of European descent (excluding local Portuguese). If you're called haole, don't automatically let your lily-white skin turn red with anger; in many cases, it's a completely neutral descriptive term, as in 'See that haole guy over there?' Sometimes it's playful, as in 'Howzit haole boy/girl!' Some local white people will describe themselves as haole, often with self-deprecating humor.

At other times, it's clearly a racial slur. If someone calls you a 'stupid haole,' you can be reasonably sure they meant to insult both your intelligence and your race.

Hovering somewhere between is the phrase to 'act haole.' This describes people of any color who are condescending, presumptuous or demanding – deriving from islanders' experiences with pushy visitors and transplants. If someone tells you to 'stop acting haole,' better dial it down a notch.

Ethnic Tension

Tensions among ethnicities, while they exist, are quite benign and rarely violent compared with racial strife on the mainland. Among locals, island stereotypes are the subject of affectionate humor, eg talkative Portuguese, stingy Chinese, goody-goody Japanese and know-it-all haoles. Hawaii's comedians of the 1970s and 1980s – Andy Bumatai, Frank DeLima and Rap Reiplinger – used such stereotypes to hilarious comic effect. When racial conflict occurs, it's usually incidental to some other beef – if a white surfer cuts off a Hawaiian on a wave, the Hawaiian might curse the 'f'n haole.' But rarely is anyone insulted or attacked merely *because* of their race.

Things shift when nonlocals enter the picture, since they aren't always sensitive to Hawaii's colonial history and don't always appreciate island ways. For instance, while the legitimacy of pidgin as a language has many challengers, the loudest critics are often mainlanders who don't speak it. In general, tourists and transplants are welcomed but have to earn trust by being *pono* – righteous, respectful and proper.

What does it mean to be Hawaiian today? Read sharp-eyed journalist Sally-Jo Bowman's *The Heart of Being Hawaiian* (2008), a moving collection of articles and interviews that circle this question with unsentimental tenderness.

Island Style

'On the islands, we do it island style,' sings local musician John Cruz in 'Island Style,' his slack key guitar anthem to life in Hawaii. While he doesn't say explicitly what 'island style' means, he doesn't have to; every local understands. Island style is easygoing, low-key, casual; even guitar strings are more relaxed. Islanders take pride in being laid back –

What makes Hawaii *no ka 'oi*, or 'the best?' Hawaii residents have the longest life expectancy in the US: 81 years, compared with the US average of 78.

that everything happens on 'Hawaii time' (ie about an hour late), that aloha shirts are preferred over suits, that an auntie will hold up a line to chat with the checkout person at Long's (and no one waiting seems to mind). 'Slow Down! *This ain't the mainland!*' reads one popular bumper sticker. Even in urban Honolulu, the 43rd largest city in the US with a population of about 375,000, there's something of a small-town vibe.

Shave ice, surfing, 'talking story,' ukulele, hula, baby lu'au, pidgin, broken-down rubber slippers and particularly *'ohana* – these are the touchstones of everyday life, which is relatively simple and often family-oriented. School sports events are packed with eager parents, plus the gamut of aunties and uncles (whether actual relatives or not). Working overtime is the exception, not the rule; weekends are for play and pot-lucks at the beach. Locals are of course not inured to Hawaii's natural beauty and the opportunities it offers: life is lived outdoors, and golfing, hiking, camping, fishing and surfing rule.

Social Statistics

By most social indicators, life is good. Hawaii has been ranked the second-healthiest state in the nation, with a low uninsured population. Almost 85% of residents graduated from high school, and nearly 30% have a bachelor's degree or higher (both above the national average). At 6.5% in November 2010, unemployment was lower than the national average of 9.1%. Violent crime is typically about half what it is on the mainland. Despite the mass quantities of Spam consumed in the islands, Hawaii had the fifth lowest obesity rate in the US in 2009. In 2008 Hawaii's median household income ($66,701) ranked seventh, and its poverty rate (8%) was third lowest among US states.

Hawaii leads the nation in shared housing: 6.6% live with parents or relatives, compared with 2.6% nationally.

That last percentage, however, glosses over glaring inequity in the distribution of wealth; while there are a large number of wealthy transplants with magnificent estates and vacation homes skewing the average, there's a much larger number of locals, particularly Pacific Islanders, struggling with poverty and all the social ills that come with it. The state is currently trying to control one of the highest rates of ice (crystal methamphetamine) abuse in the US, a problem that leads to a significant percentage of the robberies and violent crimes that do occur. Homelessness remains another serious concern – on average, 12,000 to 15,000 people are homeless statewide per year. Most telling about the cost of living in Hawaii, however, is this statistic: up to 42% of homeless people are employed full time. Sprawling tent communities develop at beach parks and other public areas; every now and then police disperse them, but the problem is never solved – only moved.

In *Folks You Meet in Longs* (2005), local newspaper columnist and playwright Lee Cataluna captures the flavor and the voice of working-class Hawaii in these painfully funny, exquisitely real monologues.

Cost of Living

Whether rich or poor, residents spend their income quickly. Honolulu has the second-highest cost of living among US cities (behind the New York metro area). Utility bills average three times higher than those on the mainland and grocery bills are exorbitant (since more than 85% of all food is imported). Limited land area (especially in a place where 20% of the land is controlled by the US military) leads to sky-high real-estate prices; many locals are unable to buy a home. Though home prices have fallen as they have in the rest of the US, they haven't slid nearly as far. The median price of a home on O'ahu in 2009 was $525,000. One study found that nearly 50% of renters and homeowners spent 30% or more of their income on housing. Most affordable housing isn't close to the majority of jobs (near resort areas), resulting in long commutes and nightmarish traffic jams. Honolulu is currently debating – hotly – whether to build a multibillion-dollar

» Don't try to speak pidgin – unless you're *really* good at it.

» Do liberally dispense *shakas* (Hawaiian hand greeting sign; keep your wrist loose, look the receiver in the eye and smile).

» Do take off your shoes when entering a home (most residents wear 'rubbah slip-pahs' partly for that reason – easy to slip on and off, no socks required).

» Don't overdress. The nattiest locals you'll see are wearing Tommy Bahama aloha shirts and slacks.

» Don't say, 'When I get back to the States...' or ask whether businesses take American money. Hawaii, despite some evidence to the contrary, is part of the US.

» Do ask permission before you pick fruit or flowers from trees on private property.

» Don't be pushy. You'll get what you want (this time), but you'll get no aloha with it.

» Do drive slowly. Locals rarely have far to go, and they drive that way. In fact, do everything slowly.

» Unless you're about to hit someone, don't honk your car horn. That's a sure way to attract 'stinkeye.'

» Don't refer to Maui, Kaua'i, Moloka'i, Lana'i and Hawai'i island as 'outer islands.' This is considered 'O'ahu-centric.' A preferred term is 'Neighbor Islands,' which indicates the islands other than the one you're on.

» Do try to correctly pronounce Hawaiian place names and words. Even if you fail, the attempt is appreciated. If you aren't sure how to say it, ask. Even long names aren't that hard with a little practice.

» Don't grumble about shelling out more for everything. You're (probably) not being gouged by the business owner: eighty-percent of Hawaii's consumer goods must be shipped in, which adds significantly to the cost. If you're miffed about paying $8 for a gallon of milk, think about how residents feel.

» Do visit a farmers market; it's an excellent way to interact with locals and to get less expensive, delicious local produce – some of which might be new to you.

» Don't freak out at every gecko and cockroach you see. It's the tropics. There are critters.

» Don't collect (or even move) stones at sacred sites. Hawaiian culture follows protocols for disturbing stones and other elements of nature. If you're not sure whether something's sacred, consider that in Hawaiian thinking, *everything* is sacred.

» Don't stack rocks or wrap them in *ti* leaves as gifts to the spirits of waterfalls, streams or other sites. This is a bastardization of the Hawaiian practice of leaving *ho'okupu* (offerings) at sacred sites. If you must offer something, offer your appreciation.

» When you're leaving the islands, it's tradition to cast a lei into the ocean; if it returns to the beach, it's said, you will one day return to Hawaii. But don't throw your lei into the water without first removing the string and the bow.

light-rail system to relieve the congestion, which is only likely to get worse as affordable housing developments grow on the outskirts of town. The new governor, Neil Abercrombie, has asserted his commitment to seeing the controversial project through.

Marginalization of Native Hawaiians

Native Hawaiians are still struggling with the colonial legacy that has marginalized them in their own homeland. Hawaiians constitute a disproportionate number of those homeless (about a third) and impoverished. Native Hawaiian schoolchildren, on average, lag behind state averages in reading and math and are more likely to drop out of school. Hawaiian charter schools were created to address this problem, and

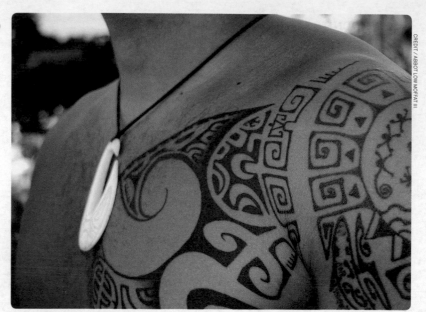

Island identity and culture takes many forms.

they have demonstrated some remarkable success using alternative, culturally relevant approaches. However, many Native Hawaiians feel that some form of sovereignty is necessary to correct these deeply entrenched inequities (see p583).

These stresses – along with having to deal with a constant flow of travelers purchasing temporary paradise in resorts that many locals could never themselves afford – can sap the aloha of residents. 'The beaches they sell to build their hotels, my father and I once knew,' sang Gabby Pahinui in 'Waimanalo Blues,' a very different anthem of island life. For many locals and Native Hawaiians in particular, tourism is a Faustian bargain at best; with it comes jobs and economic stability, but many question whether it's worth the cost. In recent years, there's a hard-to-quantify feeling that life isn't as good as it once was, which is partly why the state is so focused on developing a sustainability plan (see the boxed text, p625).

And yet, whatever difficulties arise, finding someone who'd prefer to live somewhere else is hardest of all. No matter what comes, locals say, 'lucky you live Hawaii.'

Hawaii's Cuisine

The word 'cuisine' sounds too formal for Hawaii. It suggests a need for categories and rules, for a regimented approach to food that doesn't quite work for the Islands. In Hawaii, the culinary tradition is one of inclusiveness, where foreign flavors and cooking styles are incorporated and shared – usually in heaping, savory portions. This no-worries embrace of international flavors is reflected in the state's most iconic dishes: the plate lunch; the *loco moco* (dish of rice, fried egg and hamburger patty topped with gravy or other condiments); the mighty Spam *musubi* – a rice ball topped with sautéed Spam and wrapped with sushi nori (dried seaweed). It's a fun, but tasty, insouciance that flouts any formal rules.

To best understand Hawaii's gastronomic style, it's helpful to consider the state's multicultural background. Before human contact, the only indigenous edibles were ferns and *ohelo* berries. The Polynesians brought *kalo* (taro), *'ulu* (breadfruit), *'uala* (sweet potato), *mai'a* (banana), *ko* (sugarcane) and *niu* (coconut), plus chickens, pigs and dogs for meat – and they enjoyed an abundance of seafood.

Westerners brought cattle and horses, salted salmon and fruits such as pineapple and guava that now connote Hawaii. When the sugar industry rose to its peak in the late 1800s – bringing waves of immigrants from China, Japan, Portugal, Puerto Rico, Korea and the Philippines – Hawaii's cuisine developed an identity all its own. It took the plantation-era ethnic ingredients (including rice, soy sauce, ginger and chili pepper) but never abandoned Native Hawaiian *kalua* pork (rich and smoky, traditionally roasted underground) and *poke* (marinated chunks of raw fish).

What does this mean for travelers? It's simple, really: sample the unknown, take another bite and travel the world on a single plate. And always remember one thing: Hawaii isn't a place to diet. It's the *broke da mout* (delicious) reward.

Island Diet

Sticky white rice is more than a side dish in Hawaii. It's a culinary building block, an integral partner in everyday meals. Without rice, Spam *musubi* would just be a slice of canned meat. The *loco moco* would be nothing more than an egg-covered hamburger. And without two-scoop rice, the plate lunch would be a ho-hum conversation between meat and macaroni rather than a multicultural party.

And just so you know, sticky white rice means sticky white rice. While you might find couscous or mashed potatoes at fancy restaurants, day-to-day meals require sticky white rice. Not flaky rice. Not wild rice. Not flavored rice. And *definitely* not instant. Locals can devour mounds of the stuff and it typically comes as two scoops.

The top condiment is soy sauce, known by its Japanese name *shōyu*, which combines well with sharp Asian flavors like ginger, green onion and garlic.

There are food bloggers galore covering Honolulu. Get started with restaurant blurbs, foodie posts and plenty of links at http://eatizenjane.com and http://tastyislandhawaii.com/blog/.

FOOD BLOGS

Ahi (tuna) poke with limu *(seaweed), green onion, chili pepper and* shoyu *(soy sauce)*

Did you know? *Manapua*, the local term for Chinese *bao* (steamed filled bun), derives from either of two Hawaiian phrases: *mea 'ono pua'a* ('good pork thing') or *mauna pua'a* ('mountain of pork').

MANAPUA

Meat, chicken or fish are often key components. For quick, cheap eating, locals devour anything tasty, from Portuguese sausage to hamburger steak to corned beef. But the dinner-table highlight is always seafood, especially fresh-caught fish.

One word of caution: Maui's attempts at nonlocal classics like pizza, bagels, croissants and southern BBQ are typically disappointing. Stick with *local* local food.

Although food in Hawaii resists strict categorization, it can be helpful to consider most distinctive dishes within the context of three separate but overlapping food groups: Local, Native Hawaiian and Hawaii Regional.

Local Food

Day-to-day eats reflect the state's multicultural heritage, with Chinese, Japanese, Portuguese and Native Hawaiian influences the most evident. Cheap, fattening and tasty, local food is the stuff of cravings and comfort.

The classic example of local food is the ubiquitous plate lunch. Chunky layers of tender *kalua* pork, a dollop of smooth and creamy macaroni and two hearty scoops of white rice. Yum, right? The pork can be swapped for other proteins like fried mahimahi and teriyaki chicken. Served almost like street food, the plate lunch is often eaten with chopsticks on disposable plates. A favorite breakfast combo includes fried egg and spicy Portuguese sausage (or bacon, ham, Spam etc) and, always, two scoops of rice.

Pupu is the local term used for all kinds of munchies or 'grazing' foods. Much more than just cheese and crackers, *pupu* represent the ethnic diversity of the Islands and might include boiled peanuts in the shell, edamame (boiled fresh soybeans in the pod) and universal items like fried shrimp.

Not to be missed is *poke,* which is raw fish marinated in soy sauce, oil, chili peppers, green onions and seaweed. It comes in many varieties – sesame ahi (yellowfin tuna) is particularly delicious and goes well with beer.

ANN CECIL / LONELY PLANET IMAGES ©

Another local 'delicacy' is Spam *musubi*. Locals of all stripes enjoy this only-in-Hawaii creation.

Nowadays kids veer toward mainstream candy and gum, but the traditional local treat is mouth-watering Chinese crack seed – preserved fruit (typically plum, cherry, mango or lemon) that, like Coca-Cola or curry, is impossible to describe. It can be sweet, sour, salty or licorice-spicy. Sold prepackaged at grocers or by the pound at specialty shops, crack seed is mouthwatering and addictive.

And finally, there's shave ice. Don't believe those joyless cynics who'll tell you that shave ice is nothing more than a snow cone. Shave ice is *not* just a snow cone. It's a 21-gun tropical salute – the most spectacular snow cone on earth. The specifics? The ice is shaved as fine as powdery snow, packed into a paper cone and drenched with sweet fruit-flavored syrups in dazzling hues. For added decadence, add a scoop of ice cream on the bottom.

Native Hawaiian Food

With its earthy flavors and traditional ingredients, Hawaiian food is like no other, and a native Hawaiian meal will likely be one of your fondest memories after a visit to the islands. The best venues for good, authentic Hawaiian food are plate-lunch shops, diners, fish markets and supermarket delis. Commercial luau buffets include all the notable dishes, but the quality can be mediocre or haole-fied (watered down for Caucasians).

Kalua pig is traditionally roasted whole underground in an *imu,* a sealed pit of red-hot stones. Cooked this way, the pork is smoky, salty and succulent. Nowadays *kalua* pork is typically oven-roasted and seasoned with salt and liquid smoke. At commercial luau, a pig placed in an *imu* is only for show (and it couldn't feed 300-plus guests anyway).

Perhaps the most famous (or infamous) Hawaiian dish is poi, steamed and mashed wetland taro, which was sacred to Hawaiians. Locals savor the bland-to-mildly-tart flavor as a starchy palate cleanser, but its slightly sticky and pasty consistency can be off-putting to nonlocals. Taro is highly nutritious, low in calories, easily digestible and versatile to prepare. Locals typically eat poi as a counterpoint to strongly flavored fish dishes such as *lomilomi* salmon (minced salted salmon tossed with diced tomato and green onion) and *poke*. In case you're wondering, salmon is an import, first introduced to Hawaiians by whaling ships.

A common main dish is *laulau,* a bundle of pork or chicken and salted butterfish wrapped in a taro leaf that's steamed until it has a soft spinach-like texture. Other Hawaiian foods include baked *'ulu* (breadfruit), which

Shave Ice
» Itsu's Fishing Supplies (Hilo, Hawai'i the Big Island)
» Jo-Jo's Anuenue Shave Ice & Treats (Waimea, Kaua'i)
» Tom's Mini-Mart (Wailuku, Maui)
» Matsumoto's (Hale'iwa, O'ahu)

CUISINE SCENE: WHAT'S HAPPENING NOW

Food Trucks O'ahu is embracing the mainland's food-truck trend with global flair – look for vendors serving up Korean tacos, pad thai and more.

Ecofarm tours Agrotourism is booming, with new excursions on the Big Island (coffee, tea, vanilla, honey), Maui (organic tropical fruit), Kaua'i (chocolate, coffee, taro) and O'ahu (coffee, chocolate, aquaculture farms, organic produce).

Green Beer Hawaii's microbreweries are going green, producing solar-brewed suds and implementing ecofriendly business practices.

Evolved plate lunches With two scoops of *brown* rice, and steamed veggies or tossed greens instead of mayo-laden macaroni salad, the popular mixed plate gets a healthy makeover.

Big-name chefs DK Kodama and Peter Merriman continue to expand their empires to Neighbor Islands.

Eco-minded packaging Single-use plastic bags have been banned on Maui and Kaua'i, and sustainable carry-out containers are filling the bagging void.

has a texture similar to a potato, and *haupia*, a delicious pudding made of coconut cream thickened with cornstarch or arrowroot. *Haupia* ice cream offers a nice cross between traditional and modern.

Hawaii Regional Cuisine

Twenty years ago, Hawaii was a culinary backwater. Sure, you could slum it on local *grinds* (food) and get by on the slew of midrange Asian eateries, but fine dining was typically a European-style meal that ignored locally grown fare and the unique flavors of the islands.

In the early '90s a handful of island chefs created a new cuisine, borrowing liberally from Hawaii's various ethnic influences. They partnered with farmers, ranchers and fishers to highlight fresh local fare, and transformed childhood favorites into gourmet masterpieces. Suddenly macadamia-crusted mahimahi, seared ahi, miso glaze and *liliko'i* (passion fruit) anything were all the rage.

The movement was dubbed 'Hawaii Regional Cuisine' and the pioneering chefs became celebrities. Back then HRC was rather exclusive, found at destination restaurants and created by celebrity chefs. Its hallmark was elaborate fusion preparation. By the 2000s the focus began shifting toward the ingredients, which ideally are locally grown, organic, seasonal and handpicked. Today, individual farms are lauded like designer brands.

So HRC is now more encompassing. The top restaurants are still its mainstay, but that little bistro or even plate-lunch stand might fall under the HRC umbrella if it satisfies locavore requirements.

When deciding on a main course, remember that almost all meats, poultry and shellfish are imported. If they're local, they'll probably be labeled as such. To experience the core of Hawaii's finest cuisine, you should partake in ingredients that start and end here.

Hawaii's Locavore Movement

A whopping 85% to 90% of Hawaii's food is imported, despite its natural biodiversity. Now, a growing contingent of small-scale farmers is trying to shift the agriculture industry away from the model of corporate-scale, industrialized monocropping (eg sugar and pineapple) enabled by chemical fertilizers, pesticides and herbicides. Instead, family farms are growing diverse crops for the table or for sale locally.

A 2007 study by the Rocky Mountain Institute suggests, unsurprisingly, that an increase in production and consumption of locally grown food will benefit Hawaii in four areas: food security, the regional economy, the

---

Best Regional Cuisine

» Roy's Waikiki Beach (Waikiki, O'ahu)

» Alan Wong's (Honolulu, O'ahu)

» Town (Honolulu, O'ahu)

» Bar Acuda Tapas & Wine (Hanalei, Kaua'i)

» Lana'i City Grill (Lana'i City, Lana'i)

» Hali'imaile General Store (Hali'imaile, Maui)

» I'O (Lahaina, Maui)

» Kualapu'u Cookhouse (Kualapu'u, Molokai)

SPAMTASTIC

Hawaii may be the only place in the US where you can eat Hormel's iconic canned ham with pride. Here in the nation's Spam capital, locals consume almost seven million cans per year!

Of course, Spam looks and tastes different in Hawaii. It is always eaten cooked (typically sautéed to a light crispiness in sweetened *shōyu*), not straight from the can, and served as a tasty meat dish – Spam and eggs, Spam and rice, Spam and vegetables.

Spam was first canned in 1937 and introduced to Hawaii during WWII, when the Hawaiian Islands were considered a war zone. During that period fresh meat imports were replaced by this standard GI ration. By the time the war ended, Hawaiians had developed an affinity for the fatty canned stuff.

The most common preparation is Spam *musubi*: a block of rice with a slice of fried Spam on top (or in the middle), wrapped with a strip of black sushi nori (Japanese seaweed). Created in the 1960s, it has become a classic, and thousands of *musubi* are sold daily at grocers, lunch counters and convenience stores.

For Spam trivia, recipes, games and more, go to www.spam.com. You could also check out Waikiki's Spam Jam festival.

vitality of the land and community pride. On the Big Island, diversified agriculture is booming, not just with its signature coffee and macadamia nuts, but also a range of edibles from mushrooms to shellfish.

Local milk is also making a comeback. Until 1980, 100% of the state's milk was produced by local dairies. High feed prices, including shipping costs, forced eight dairy closures by 1999. Today about 80% of the state's milk is imported from the mainland. Two dairies on the Big Island – Island Dairy and Cloverleaf Dairy – are working to reduce this percentage; a third dairy hopes to open its doors on Hawai'i soon.

Even with local bounty, building a solid consumer market isn't easy. Locals tend to buy whatever's cheapest and often balk at paying for fruit they see falling off neighborhood trees. Safeway and island-based supermarket chains typically prefer the blemish-free consistency of Sunkist oranges and California grapes. An exception is KTA Super Stores on the Big Island. This mini-chain carries 240 products – including milk, produce and beef – from more than 50 local vendors under its Mountain Apple Brand.

As for imported staples such as wheat and other grains, some ask if they're needed. Why not substitute native starches such as breadfruit, taro and sweet potato? Well, rice is king among local staples and can single-handedly keep Matson and Young Brothers (shipping barges) in business.

Bottom line: the only way that small-scale farmers can thrive is to sell their products. Buy local!

Fish

Locals eat twice as much seafood as the per-capita US national average. Ahi is the local favorite for eating raw, but mahimahi and *ono* are also popular for cooking.

The Hawai'i Seafood Buyers' Guide (www.hawaii-seafood.org) is a fascinating one-stop resource (whether you're interested in the catching, the selecting or, of course, the eating of island fish). Got an iPhone? Download the FishPhone app from the Blue Ocean Institute (www.blueocean.org). It provides information about ocean-friendly seafood, including sustainability specifics of various fish, as well as their average mercury levels.

The species most commonly eaten in Hawaii:

» ahi – yellowfin or bigeye tuna, red flesh, excellent raw or rare
» aku – skipjack tuna, red flesh, strong flavor; *katsuo* in Japanese
» 'ama'ama – mullet, delicate white flesh
» awa – milkfish, tender white flesh
» kajiki – Pacific blue marlin; *a'u* in Hawaiian
» mahimahi – dolphin fish or dorado, firm pink flesh, popular cooked
» moi – threadfish, flaky white flesh, rich flavor; reserved for royalty in ancient times
» monchong – pomfret, mild flavor, firm pinkish-white flesh
» nairage – striped marlin; *a'u* in Hawaiian
» 'o'io – bonefish
» *onaga* – red snapper, soft and moist; *'ula'ula* in Hawaiian
» ono – wahoo, white-fleshed and flaky
» opah – moonfish, firm and rich
» 'opakapaka – pink snapper, delicate flavor, premium quality
» 'opelu – mackerel scad, pan-sized, delicious fried
» papio – jack fish; also called ulua
» shutome – swordfish, succulent and meaty
» *tako* – octopus, chewy texture; *he'e* in Hawaiian
» tombo – albacore tuna, light flesh, mild flavor, silky texture

Pick up a free copy of *Edible Hawaiian Islands* (www.edibleha waiianislands .com), a colorful quarterly magazine focusing on Hawaii's locavore movement and other foodie trends.

QUARTERLY

An abundance of fruit trees means fruit juice and tropical cocktails are ubiquitous in Hawaii

Drinks

Fruit trees thrive in Hawaii, so you'd expect to find fresh juices everywhere. Alas, most supermarket cartons contain imported purees or sugary 'juice drinks.' You can find real, freshly squeezed or blended juices at fruit stands, health food stores, farmers markets and specialty bars. Don't assume that the fruit is local. Also bear in mind that the ancients never tasted that succulent mango or tangy pineapple. Juice-bar standouts include Lanikai Juice (Kailua, O'ahu, p137) and the Oloawalu Juice Stand (Olowalu, Maui).

Hawaii's original intoxicants were fruit juices: *'awa* (kava), a mild sedative, and *noni* (Indian mulberry), which some consider a cure-all. Both fruits are pungent, if not repulsive, in smell and taste, so they are typically mixed with other juices.

Coffee

World-renowned Kona coffee wins raves for its mellow flavor that has no bitter aftertaste. The upland slopes of Mauna Loa and Hualalai in the Big Island's Kona district offer the ideal climate (sunny mornings and rainy afternoons) for coffee cultivation. While Kona coffee has the most cachet, recent crops from Ka'u (the southernmost district on Hawai'i) have won accolades and Ka'anapali Estate's MauiGrown Coffee (Lahaina, Maui) has impressed many aficionados.

Cafe culture has taken root, with baristas brewing espresso at deli counters, indie hangouts and, of course, Starbucks.

Beer

Beer is cheap and widely available. National brands are popular, but once-novel microbreweries are now firmly established across the islands. Brewmasters claim that the high mineral content and purity of Hawaii's water makes for excellent-tasting beer. Another hallmark of local microbeer is the addition of a tropical hint, such as Kona coffee, honey or *liliko'i*.

The biggest companies also run lively brewpubs, where you should try the following picks: Pipeline Porter by Kona Brewing Company (p183) on the Big Island, Bikini Blonde by Maui Brewing Company (Kahana, Maui), Kaka'ako Cream Ale by Sam Choy's Big Aloha Brewery (Honolulu, O'ahu) and Liliko'i Ale by Waimea Brewing Company (Waimea, Kaua'i).

Wine

Hawaii isn't known for its wineries and vineyards, and mai tais and Blue Hawaiians dominate most drink menus. But wine enthusiasts need not despair. Fine dining establishments like the Lahaina Grill in Lahaina (Maui) cater to grape connoisseurs looking to complement their meals with the right varietal. Locally, wine-tasting parties and clubs are proliferating, wine sales have skyrocketed and wine bars have opened in Honolulu.

As for locally made wine, head to Maui for pineapple wine at Tedeschi Vineyards (p385) and to the Big Island for the imaginative guava or macadamia-honey concoctions of Volcano Winery (p295).

Celebrations

Whether it's a 300-guest wedding or an intimate birthday party, a massive spread is mandatory. If not, why bother? Most gatherings are informal, held at parks, beaches or homes, featuring a potluck buffet of homemade dishes. On major American holidays, mainstream foods appear (eg Easter eggs and Thanksgiving turkey) alongside local fare such as rice (instead of mashed potatoes), sweet-potato tempura (instead of yams) and hibachi-grilled teriyaki beef (instead of roast beef).

Luau

In ancient Hawaii, a luau commemorated auspicious occasions, such as births, war victories or successful harvests. In modern times, the 'commercial luau' arose in the 1970s and '80s on the four largest islands. Today, only such commercial shows (at $78 to $110 per person) offer the elaborate Hawaiian feast and Polynesian dancing that folks expect. Bear

ISLAND BOUNTY

Bananas, bell peppers, cabbage, tomatoes, avocados and other locally grown basics are found across the islands. But each island has its star crops (and, often, brand names that you might notice on menus). There are too many notables to name, but here's a starting point:

» Hawai'i – mushrooms from Hamakua Mushrooms; tomatoes and salad greens from Hamakua Springs Country Farms; vanilla from Hawaiian Vanilla Company; Ka'u oranges; *kampachi* (yellowtail) from Kona Blue Water Farms; lobster from Kona Cold Lobster; abalone from Big Island Abalone; Kona or Ka'u coffee; yellow-flesh Solo papayas

» Kaua'i – goat cheese from Kaua'i Kunana Dairy; beef from Medeiros Farm; ginger from Kolo Kai Organic Farm; Kilauea honey; Hanalei-grown taro; red-flesh Sunrise papayas

» Maui – grass-fed beef from Maui Cattle Co; lavender from Ali'i Kula Lavender; goat cheese from Surfing Goat Dairy; elk from 'Ulupalakua Ranch; strawberries from Kula Country Farms; sugar from Maui Brand Hawaiian Raw Sugar

» Moloka'i – coffee from Coffees of Hawai'i; sea salt from Pacifica Hawai'i; macadamia nuts from Purdy's

» O'ahu – salad greens from Nalo Farms; beef from North Shore Cattle Co; tomatoes from North Shore Farms; 'Ewa-grown melons; supersweet corn from Kahuku

HAWAII'S CUISINE CELEBRATIONS

ANN CECIL / LONELY PLANET IMAGES ©

Saimin is a local-style noodle soup

in mind, the all-you-can-eat buffet of luau standards is toned down for the Western palate, eg poi, *kalua* pig, steamed mahimahi, teriyaki chicken and *haupia* (coconut custard).

Most commercial luau are overpriced and overly touristy, but two stand out: the Old Lahaina Luau (Lahaina, Maui) and the Kona Village Resort luau (Ka'upulehu, Hawai'i the Big Island). On Kaua'i, try Kilohana Plantation's theatrical Luau Kalamaku (in Lihu'e), or for nostalgia's sake, the show at Smith's Tropical Paradise (in Wailua).

Private luau celebrations, typically for weddings or first birthdays, are often large banquet-hall gatherings. The menu might be more daring – and include raw *'a'ama* (black crab) and *'opihi* (limpet) – and the entertainment more low-key (no fire eaters).

Festivals & Events

Food festivals often showcase island crops, such as the Kona Coffee Cultural Festival (Kailua-Kona, Hawaii the Big Island), East Maui Taro Festival (Hana, Maui), Maui Onion Festival (Ka'anapali, Maui), Wahiawa Pineapple Festival (www.hawaiipineapplefestival.com) and the biennial (even-numbered years) Hanalei Taro Festival (Hanalei, Kaua'i). Beer drinkers should mark their calendars for the Kona Brewers Festival (Kailua-Kona, Hawai'i the Big Island). Only in Hawaii will you find the Waikiki Spam Jam (Waikiki, O'ahu).

Gourmet culinary events are all the rage across the islands; they vary in price and formality. On O'ahu, Restaurant Week Hawaii (Honolulu) is a great chance to check out the gamut of venues offering special menus and deals. Maui hosts the Kapalua Wine & Food Festival (Kapalua). Kaua'i's Spring Gourmet Gala (Lihu'e) and Taste of Hawaii (Wailua) bring top chefs to the island, while the Big Island's A Taste of the Hawaiian Range (Waikoloa Resort Area) is an affordable treat for the carnivorous. Search for others at www.gohawaii.com/event.

For a Sunset Cocktail

» Huggo's on the Rocks (Kailua-Kona, Hawai'i the Big Island)

» The patio of the Lobby Bar at St Regis Princeville (Princeville, Kaua'i)

» Kimo's (Lahaina, Maui)

» Merriman's Kapalua (Kapalua, Maui)

» Five Palms (Kihei, Maui)

» House Without a Key (Waikiki, O'ahu)

Where To Eat & Drink

The dining scene in Honolulu, with its variety and quantity, is much different than the dining scene on the Neighbor Islands. On Kaua'i, we can count the number of established Japanese restaurants on one hand, while O'ahu's selection will number in the hundreds, from impeccable sushi bars to noodle shops to trendy *izakaya* (Japanese pubs serving tapas-style food, which by and large have not reached the Neighbor Islands yet). That said, the Big Island and especially Maui are closer to O'ahu as trendsetters, whether they be boutique farms or four-star dining rooms.

Still, across the islands, you'll find similar types of restaurants. For sit-down meals, there is a big divide between highbrow restaurants that could rival mainland counterparts and lowbrow diner-type, family restaurants that serve classic, plantation-style cookery, loved for familiar flavors and generous portions. If you want to splurge on a meal, pick the foodie darlings rather than any oceanfront resort restaurant (where you're paying mainly for the view).

You'll find fantastic prices on fresh fish at indie fish markets, which typically sell *poke*, seared ahi and fish plates. If calories are no concern, go for true local *grinds* at '70s-style drive-ins (for plate lunches and *loco moco*). Ideal for picnics are *okazu-ya* (Japanese takeout) lunch shops, mainly in Hilo and Honolulu.

While all-night eateries are readily found in Honolulu, Neighbor Island restaurants typically open and close (by 10pm) early. For late-night dining, you'll have to seek out bars or the rare 24-hour coffee shop. In general, locals tip slightly less than mainlanders do, but still up to 20% for good service and at least 15% for the basics.

Local produce is surprisingly pricey and hard to find except at farmers markets, fruit stands and some locally owned supermarkets (see the boxed text, p600). Both residents and tourists cannot resist the deals at Costco (which actually has an impressive deli serving *poke* that garners raves from locals).

In this guide, a restaurant is considered a budget ($) option if most of its menu items cost less than $12. Typical budget choices are bakeries, breakfast joints and sandwich and taco shops. Midrange restaurants ($$), serving pizza, gourmet sandwiches, plate lunches, Chinese, Thai and no-frills seafood, cost between $12 and $30. Top-end dining establishments ($$$) are typically found on prime oceanfront perches as well as in resorts and golf-course clubhouses. Entrées cost more than $30 per person. To sample top cuisine at a good price, visit during happy hour when prices for appetizers are often reduced.

Plate Lunch

» Big Island Grill (Kailua-Kona, Hawai'i the Big Island)

» Koloa Fish Market (Koloa, Kaua'i)

» Blue Ginger Cafe (Lana'i City, Lana'i)

» Ted's Bakery (Waimea, O'ahu)

» Da Kitchen Express (Kihei, Maui)

» Aloha Mixed Plate (Lahaina, Maui)

» Manae Goods & Grindz (Puko'o, Moloka'i)

GREEN BEER

The beer served at Maui Brewing Co and Kona Brewing Co isn't really *green*, but the folks who brew these local suds are implementing eco-minded business practices. At Maui Brewing (Kahana, Maui), vegetable oil used in the brewpub is converted to diesel fuel, which powers the cars of owners Garrett and Melanie Marrero as well as the delivery truck. Spent grain is given to local ranchers for composting, and the brewery's retail beers are sold in recyclable cans. Cans over glass? Yep, cans aren't breakable, so they're less of a threat on the beach. Cans are also lighter than glass, leaving a smaller footprint. Kona Brewing (p183) hopped on the green bandwagon in 2010 with its solar-brewed Suncharged Pale Ale as well as the state's first and only certified green beer, the Oceanic Organic Saison. Cheers for green beers!

Habits & Customs

At home, locals rarely serve formal sit-down meals with individual courses. Even when entertaining, meals are typically served potluck style with a spread of flavorful dishes that to the unfamiliar palate will seem ridiculously clashing. Locals may be laid-back, but they're punctual when it comes to meals. If you're invited to a local home, show up on time, bring dessert and remove your shoes at the door. Locals are generous with leftovers and might insist that you take a plate (along with homegrown fruits) with you.

Top-end restaurants are relatively casual (called 'island casual' here), with no jackets or ties required. Tourists can even get away with neat khaki shorts and an aloha shirt at resorts. In general, service at fancy restaurants might seem a tad unpolished (although polite) to those harking from big cities.

Meals are early and on the dot in Hawaii: typically 6am breakfast, noon lunch and 6pm dinner. Restaurants are jammed around the habitual mealtime, but they clear out an hour or two later, as locals are not lingerers.

Locals tend to consider quantity as important as quality, and portion sizes reflect this attitude, especially at plate-lunch places. If you're a light eater feel free to split a meal or take home the leftovers.

Vegetarians & Vegans

Top-end restaurants almost always include meatless selections, including grilled vegetables, garden pastas and creative uses of tofu. The multitude of Asian eateries ensures vegetable and tofu options, even in rural towns, while healthy versions of traditional local fare are now available, especially at establishments run by mainlanders influenced by 'California cuisine.' Popular offerings include tofu (or fresh ahi for fish-only eaters) wraps, meal-sized salads and grilled-vegetable sandwiches or plates, often with whole-wheat bread or brown rice.

That said, finding an exclusively vegetarian restaurant isn't easy. Vegans, especially, must seek out the few eateries that use no animal products.

AGTOURISM

Learn more about local agriculture, farm tours and farmers markets at www.hiagtour ism.org. It's not exhaustive, but it's a good start.

PRODUCE MARKETS

Here's a list of recommended farmers markets, produce stands and grocers that stock a lot of locally grown produce. Beware of markets selling imported produce, flowers and man-made junk. For a complete list of farmers markets, see www.ediblehawaiianislands.com.

Hawai'i the Big Island
» Waimea Farmers Market (Waimea)
» South Kona Green Market (Captain Cook)
» Maku'u Craft & Farmers Market (Pahoa)

Kaua'i
» Vidinha Stadium Parking Lot (p476)

Maui
» Maui Swap Meet (Kahului)
» Huelo Lookout (Huelo)

Moloka'i
» Kaunakakai Saturday morning market (Kaunakakai)

O'ahu
» Saturday Farmers Market at KCC (Diamond Head and Kahala)

ONLY IN HAWAII: MUST-TRY TASTES

» Mr Ed's Bakery: *poha* (gooseberry), *liliko'i* (passion fruit) and other homemade preserves (Honomu, Hawai'i the Big Island)

» Cafe 100: 20 varieties of *loco moco*, including fish and veggie (Hilo, Hawai'i the Big Island)

» Puna's roadside *grinds* (food) including ahi jerky and hulihuli chicken (rotisserie-cooked chicken; Hawai'i the Big Island)

» Kanaka Kava: fresh ahi with island-grown taro and thirst-quenching kava juice (Kailua-Kona, Hawai'i the Big Island)

» Kailua Candy Company: turtle cheesecake, *a'a* bark (flat piece of chocolate with coconut and macadamia nuts; Honokohau Harbor, Hawai'i the Big Island)

» Fish Express: *poke* – raw fish marinated in soy sauce, oil, chili peppers, green onions and seaweed (Lihu'e, Kaua'i)

» Sam Sato's: *manju* – Japanese cake filled with sweet bean paste (Wailuku, Maui)

» Surfing Goat Dairy: chevre cheese (Pukalani, Maui)

» Julia's Banana Bread (Kahakuloa, Maui)

» Leonard's: *malasadas* – Portuguese fried dough, served warm and sugar-coated (Waikiki, O'ahu)

When ordering at restaurants, ask whether a dish is indeed meatless; soups and sauces often contain meat, chicken or fish broth.

The most economical way to ensure no meat or animal ingredients: forage at farmers markets and health food stores.

Eat Your Words

FOOD GLOSSARY

Hawaii cuisine is multiethnic and so is the lingo. (See also a list of commonly eaten fish on p595)

adobo	Filipino chicken or pork cooked in vinegar, *shōyu*, garlic and spices
'awa	kava, a native plant used to make an intoxicating drink
bentō	Japanese-style box lunch
broke da mout	delicious; literally 'broke the mouth'
char siu	Chinese barbecued pork
chazuke	Japanese tea-soaked rice porridge
crack seed	Chinese-style preserved fruit; a salty, sweet and/or sour snack
donburi	meal-sized bowl of rice and main dish
furikake	a catch-all Japanese seasoning or condiment, usually dry and sprinkled atop rice; in Hawaii, sometimes used for *poke*
grind	to eat
grinds	food; see *'ono kine grinds*
guava	fruit with green or yellow rind, moist pink flesh and lots of edible seeds
hamachi	yellowtail
haupia	coconut-cream dessert
hulihuli chicken	rotisserie-cooked chicken
imu	underground earthen oven used to cook *kalua* pig and other luau food
izakaya	a Japanese pub serving tapas-style dishes
kalo	Hawaiian word for taro
kalua	Hawaiian method of cooking pork and other luau food in an *imu*
kare-kare	Filipino oxtail stew
katsu	Japanese deep-fried cutlets, usually pork or chicken; see *tonkatsu*

Hawaiian Cookbooks

» *Roy's Feasts From Hawaii* by Roy Yamaguchi

» *The Hali'imaile General Store Cookbook* by Beverly Gannon

» *What Hawaii Likes to Eat* by Muriel Miura, Betty Shimabukuro

» *Hawaii Cooks With Taro* by Marcia Zina Mager and Muriel Miura

Chocolate Farms & Factories

» Original Hawaiian Chocolate Factory (Keauhou Resort Area, The Big Island)

» Waialua Estate (www .waialuaestate. com), O'ahu

» Steelgrass Farm (Waialua, Kaua'i)

kaukau	food
laulau	bundle of pork or chicken and salted butterfish, wrapped in taro and *ti* leaves and steamed
li hing mui	sweet-salty preserved plum; type of crack seed; also refers to the flavor powder
liliko'i	passion fruit
loco moco	dish of rice, fried egg and hamburger patty topped with gravy or other condiments
lomilomi salmon	minced, salted salmon, diced tomato and green onion
luau	Hawaiian feast
mai tai	'tiki bar' drink typically containing rum, grenadine, and lemon and pineapple juices
malasada	Portuguese fried doughnut, sugar-coated, no hole
manapua	Chinese steamed or baked bun filled with *char siu*
manju	Japanese steamed or baked cake, often filled with sweet bean paste
mochi	Japanese sticky-rice cake
natto	fermented soybeans
nishime	Japanese stew of root vegetables and seaweed
noni	type of mulberry with smelly yellow fruit, used medicinally
nori	Japanese seaweed, usually dried
ogo	crunchy seaweed, often added to *poke; limu* in Hawaiian
ohelo	shrub with edible red berries similar in tartness and size to cranberries; a berry sacred to the volcano goddess Pele
'ono	delicious
'ono kine grinds	good food
pani popo	Samoan coconut buns
pho	Vietnamese soup, typically beef broth, noodles and fresh herbs
pipi kaula	beef jerky
poha	gooseberry
poi	staple Hawaiian starch made of steamed, mashed taro
poke	cubed, marinated raw fish
pulehu	broiled
pupu	snacks or appetizers
ropa vieja	Chinese shredded beef in tomato sauce
saimin	local-style noodle soup
shave ice	cup of finely shaved ice sweetened with colorful syrups
shōyu	soy sauce
soba	thin Japanese buckwheat-flour noodles
star fruit	translucent green-yellow fruit with five ribs like the points of a star, and sweet, juicy pulp
taro	plant with edible corm used to make poi and with edible leaves eaten in *laulau; kalo* in Hawaiian
teishoku	Japanese set meal
teppanyaki	Japanese style of cooking with an iron grill
tonkatsu	Japanese breaded and fried pork cutlets, also prepared as chicken katsu

Hawaiian Arts & Crafts

Contemporary Hawaii is a garden of different cultural traditions, with the state capital of Honolulu a fertile crossroads between East and West. Underneath it all beats a Hawaiian heart, evidenced by an ongoing revival of Hawaii's indigenous language, artisan crafts, music and the hula. *E koko mai* (welcome) to the islands.

Hula

Ancient Stories

In ancient Hawaii, sometimes hula was solemn ritual, in which *mele* (songs, chants) were an offering to the gods or celebrated the accomplishments of *ali'i* (chiefs). At other times hula was lighthearted entertainment, in which chief and commoner danced together. Hula embodied the community – telling stories of and celebrating itself.

Dancers trained rigorously in *halau* (schools) under *kumu hula* (hula teachers), so their hand gestures, expressions and rhythms were exact. In a culture without written language, chants were equally important, giving meaning to the movements. Songs often contained *kanoa* (hidden meanings), which could be spiritual, but also amorous or sexual.

Modern Revival

One can only imagine how hard Christian missionaries blushed at the hula, which they disapproved of as licentious. Missionary efforts to suppress hula were aided by Christian convert Queen Ka'ahumanu, who banned public hula dancing in 1830.

In the 1880s, King Kalakaua revived the traditional dances, saying famously, 'Hula is the language of the heart and therefore the heartbeat of the Hawaiian people.' But after the 'Merrie Monarch' died, the monarchy was soon overthrown, and hula faded again, until a 1960s Hawaiian cultural renaissance brought it back for good.

Today, *hula halau* run by revered *kumu hula* are thriving, as hula competitions blossom and some islanders adopt hula as a life practice.

Celebrating Hula

In hula competitions today, dancers vie in *kahiko* (ancient) and *'auana* (modern) categories.

Kahiko performances are raw and primordial, accompanied only by chanting and thunderous gourd drums; costumes are traditional, with *ti*-leaf leis, primary colors and sometimes lots of skin.

Western contemporary influences – English singing, stringed instruments, pop culture jokes, innovative costumes, sinuous arm movements

Hawaiian Folktales, Proverbs & Poetry

» *Folktales of Hawai'i* (Bishop Museum Press, 1995), illustrated by Sig Zane

» *'Olelo No'eau* (Bishop Museum Press, 1997), illustrated by Dietrich Varez

» *Obake Files* (Chicken Skin Series, Mutual Publishing, 2000) by Glen Grant

ANN CECIL / LONELY PLANET IMAGES ©

The ukulele (Hawaiian for 'jumping flea') is named for the way players' fingers deftly jump around the strings.

and smiling faces – may appear in *'auana* dances. Some hula troupes even flirt with postmodern dance styles.

Hawaii's own Olympics of hula is the Big Island's Merrie Monarch Festival (p268). But hula competitions and celebrations fill island calendars year-round; for the biggest, see p23.

Island Music

The traditional Hawaiian musical sound incorporates *ha'i* (falsetto singing) and often features three instrument styles: steel guitar, slack key guitar and ukulele. If you tune your rental-car radio to today's island stations, you'll hear everything from island rock, hip-hop and country to reggae-inspired 'Jawaiian' sounds. Some Hawaii-born singer-songwriters, such as Jack Johnson, have even made an international name for themselves.

Cowboy Heritage

Spanish-speaking cowboys first introduced the guitar to Hawaiians in the 1830s. Fifty years later, O'ahu-born high school boy Joseph Kekuku started experimenting with playing a guitar flat on his lap while sliding a pocket knife or comb across the strings. He invented the Hawaiian steel guitar *(kika kila)*, which lifts the strings off the fretboard using a movable steel slide, creating a signature smooth sound.

During the early 20th century, Kekuku and other Hawaiians introduced the islands' steel guitar sounds to the world. The steel guitar later inspired the creation of resonator guitars such as the Dobro, now integral to bluegrass, blues and other genres, and country-and-western music's lap and pedal steel guitar. Today Hawaii's most influential steel guitarists include Alan Akaka, Bobby Ingano and Gregory Sardinha.

The Jumping Flea

Universally beloved is the ukulele, derived from the *braguinha*, a Portuguese stringed instrument introduced to Hawaii in the late 19th century.

Ukulele means 'jumping flea' in Hawaiian, referring to the way players' deft fingers swiftly 'jump' around the strings. The ukulele is enjoying a revival as a young generation of virtuosos such as David Kamakahi and genre-bending rockers led by Jake Shimabukuro emerges.

Both the ukulele and the steel guitar contributed to the lighthearted *hapa haole* (Hawaiian music with predominantly English lyrics) songs popularized in Hawaii after the 1930s, of which *My Little Grass Shack* and *Lovely Hula Hands* are classic examples. Thanks to *Hawaii Calls* radio show, broadcast worldwide over four decades from Waikiki, *hapa haole* music became instantly recognizable as Hawaiian.

Slackin' Sounds

Since the mid-20th century, the Hawaiian steel guitar has usually been played with slack key *(ki ho'alu)* tunings, in which the thumb plays the bass and rhythm chords, while the fingers play the melody and improvisations, in a picked style. Traditionally, slack key tunings were closely guarded secrets among *'ohana* (family and friends).

The legendary guitarist Gabby Pahinui launched the modern slack key era with his first recording of 'Hi'ilawe' in 1946. In the 1970s, Gabby and his legendary band the Sons of Hawai'i embraced the traditional Hawaiian sound. Along with other influential slack key guitarists such as Sonny Chillingsworth, they spurred a renaissance in Hawaiian music that continues to this day. The list of contemporary slack key masters is long and ever growing, including Keola Beamer, Ledward Ka'apana, Martin and Cyril Pahinui and Ozzie Kotani.

To learn more about slack key guitar, visit George Winston's Dancing Cat music label website (www.dancingcat.com) to listen to sound clips, browse bios of celebrated island guitarists and download a free e-book.

MODERN MELE

Ideally, this guidebook would come bundled with a CD and ukulele. Instead, here's a list of essential Hawaiian music albums, past and present:

» Genoa Keawe, *Party Hulas* – 'Aunty Genoa' and her signature falsetto epitomized old-school Hawaiian hula music, and this sets the standard.

» Raiatea Helm, *Hawaiian Blossom* – *Village Voice* compared young Helm to Diana Krall with a ukulele, and her soaring falsetto is Aunty Genoa reborn.

» Gabby Pahinui, *Gabby* – No self-respecting slack key music collection is complete without this seminal album.

» Dennis and David Kamakahi, *'Ohana* – Father Dennis and son David are two of Hawaii's best musicians, here combining their talents on slack key guitar and ukulele, respectively.

» Israel Kamakawiwo'ole, *Facing Future* – 'Braddah Iz' touched Hawaii's soul with songs like 'Hawai'i '78,' while his version of 'Somewhere Over the Rainbow' is now world-famous. When Braddah Iz died in 1997, his body lay in state at the Capitol in Honolulu, an honor never before bestowed on a musician.

» Jake Shimabukuro, *Walking Down Rainhill* – Check out Jake's ukulele cover of 'While My Guitar Gently Weeps' on YouTube, then buy this.

» Keali'i Reichel, *Kawaipunahele* – Charismatic vocalist and *kumu hula* (hula teacher), Reichel combines ancient chanting and soulful ballads.

» HAPA, *In the Name of Love* – Cross a New Jersey slack key guitarist and a Hawaiian vocalist, and you get HAPA's contemporary yet traditional, pop-flavored fusion.

» John Cruz, *One of these Days* – Cruz is a classic singer-songwriter crafting modern, blues-tinged Hawaiian-style songs.

Traditional Crafts

In the 1970s, the Hawaiian renaissance sparked interest in traditional artisan crafts. Perhaps the most universally beloved craft is lei-making, stringing garlands of flowers, leaves, berries and nuts. For all about Hawaii's lei traditions, see p609.

Woodworking

Ancient Hawaiians were expert woodworkers, carving canoes out of logs and hand-turning lustrous bowls from a variety of beautifully grained tropical hardwoods, such as koa, kou, milo and mango. *Ipu* (gourds) were also dried and used as containers and as drums for hula. Contemporary woodworkers now take native woods to craft traditional bowls, exquisite furniture, jewelry and free-form sculptures. Hawaiian bowls are not decorated or ornate, but are shaped to bring out the natural beauty of the wood. The thinner and lighter the bowl, the finer the artistry and greater the value.

Fabric Arts

The making of *kapa* (pounded-bark cloth) for clothing and artworks and *lauhala* weaving are two other traditional Hawaiian crafts. Weaving the *lau* (leaves) of the *hala* (pandanus) tree is the easier part, while preparing the leaves, which have razor-sharp spines, is messy work. Traditionally *lauhala* served as floor mats, canoe sails, protective capes and more. Today, the most common *lauhala* items are hats, placemats and baskets. Most are mass-produced; for handmade beauties, look for specialty shops like the Big Island's Kimura Lauhala (in Holualoa).

Island Writings

From Outside & Inside

Until the late 1970s, Hawaii literature was dominated by nonlocal Western writers observing Hawaii's exotic-seeming world from the outside; favorites are James Michener's saga *Hawaii* and Paul Theroux's caustically humorous *Hotel Honolulu*.

Since then, contemporary locally born writers have created an authentic literature of Hawaii that evokes island life from the inside. Leading this has been Bamboo Ridge Press (www.bambooridge.com), which for over 30 years has published contemporary local fiction and poetry in an annual journal and launched the careers of many Hawaii writers.

The 'ohana (extended family) of one of the most highly regarded traditional Hawaiian quilters, Althea Poakalani Serrao, runs an encyclopedic website (www.poakalani. net) that has everything about Hawaiian quilting: classes, shops, patterns, history and more.

QUILTING

QUILTING A HAWAIIAN STORY *LISA DUNSFORD*

With vibrant colors and graphic patterns, the appeal of Hawaiian appliqué quilting is easy to see. But look more closely and you'll discover the story behind the beauty.

Protestant missionaries introduced quilting to Hawaii in the early 19th century, but the craft has evolved since then. Traditional quilts typically have a solid color fabric, which is folded into fourths or eighths, cut into a repeating pattern derived from nature (remember making snowflakes in school?), and then appliquéd onto neutral foundation cloth.

If the quilt's center, or *piko* (navel), is open, it's said to be a gateway between the spiritual and physical worlds; a solid core embodies the strength of family. Fruits and plants have symbolic meaning, too: *ulu* (breadfruit) represents prosperity and is traditionally the first quilt made, a pineapple signifies hospitality, taro equates to strength, a mango embodies wishes granted...

Don't look for human figures on a traditional quilt, though; they might come alive at night. Each original design is thought to contain the very spirit of the crafter. To prevent their souls from wandering, early Hawaiian quilts were buried with their makers.

WAYNE LEVIN / ALAMY

Sewing a vibrant Hawaiian quilt.

The University of Hawai'i Press (www.uhpress.hawaii.edu) and Bishop Museum Press (www.bishopmuseum.org/press) have also made space for local writers to have their voices heard, especially insightful nonfiction writings about Hawaiian culture, history, nature and art.

Pidgin Beyond Plantations

In 1975, *All I Asking for Is My Body*, by Milton Murayama, vividly captured sugar plantation life for Japanese nisei (second-generation immigrants) around WWII. Murayama's use of pidgin opened the door to an explosion of vernacular literature, particularly since the 1990s. Lois-Ann Yamanaka has won widespread acclaim for her poetry (*Saturday Night at the Pahala Theatre*, 1993) and novels (*Wild Meat and the Bully Burgers*, 1996), in which pidgin embodies her characters like a second skin.

Indeed, redeeming pidgin – long dismissed by academics and disparaged by the upper class – has been a cultural and political cause for some. The hilarious stories (*Da Word*, 2001) and essays (*Living Pidgin*, 2002) of Lee Tonouchi, a prolific writer and playwright, argue that pidgin is not only essential to understanding local culture, but also a legitimate language. Another great introduction to pidgin is *Growing Up Local* (1998), an anthology of poetry and prose published by Bamboo Ridge Press.

New Voices

Other influential Hawaii writers who found their voices toward the end of the 20th century include Nora Okja Keller, whose first novel, *Comfort Woman*, won the 1998 American Book Award, and Kiana Davenport, whose *Shark Dialogues* (1994) is a sweeping multigenerational family saga entwined with Hawaii's own history.

Contemporary Hawaii women writers abound. Some, like Mia King (*Sweet Life*, 2008), eschew purely ethnic or Hawaii-centered narratives, while others – like short-story writers Kaui Hart Hemmings (*House of Thieves*, 2005) and Marie Hara (*An Offering of Rice*, 2007) – continue to

PIDGIN

More than a pidgin dictionary, *Pidgin to Da Max*, by Douglas Simonson (aka Peppo), Pat Sasaki and Ken Sakata, is a side-splitting primer on local life that's knocked around forever because it (and its sequels) are so damn funny.

VISUAL ARTS

explode the 'paradise myth' as they explore real Hawaii. Hemmings' first novel, *The Descendants* (2007), has a dissolute, sickly-sweet Southern Gothic air, as the children of haole plantation owners and a Hawaiian princess lose their inheritance and their way in a crumbling paradise.

Hawaii has been home to many lauded modern painters, including Herb Kane and Madge Tennent. Scores of visual artists also draw inspiration from the islands' rich cultural heritage.

Hawaii On Screen

Nothing cemented the fantasy of Edenic Hawaii in the popular imagination as firmly as Hollywood. Today, the 'dream factory' continues to peddle variations on a 'South Seas' genre that first swept movie theaters in the 1930s. Whether the mood is silly or serious, whether Hawaii is used as a setting or a stand-in for someplace else, the story's familiar tropes hardly change, updating the original tropical Garden of Eden soap opera and providing a romantic gloss to the real history of colonization.

Hollywood first arrived in 1913, and Hawaii has been catnip ever since. By 1939, over 60 movies had been shot here, including musical comedies like *Waikiki Wedding* (1937), in which Bing Crosby crooned the Oscar-winning song 'Sweet Leilani.' Later favorites include the WWII–themed *From Here to Eternity* (1953) and *South Pacific* (1958), and Elvis Presley's goofy postwar *Blue Hawaii* (1961).

Today, Hawaii actively encourages and supports the lucrative film industry by maintaining state-of-the-art production facilities and providing tax incentives. Hundreds of feature films have been shot in the state, including box-office hits like *Raiders of the Lost Ark* (1981), *Jurassic Park* (1993), *Pearl Harbor* (2001) and *Pirates of the Caribbean: On Stranger Tides* (2011). Kaua'i is the most prolific island 'set' and has appeared in over 70 films. Today, avid fans can tour movie sites on Kaua'i and O'ahu (Kualoa Ranch; p142).

Hawaii has hosted dozens of TV series since 1968. The most famous and perhaps least sentimental was *Hawaii Five-O,* an edgy cop drama featuring Honolulu's gritty side. In 2010 *Hawaii Five-O* was reincarnated as a prime-time drama, filmed on O'ahu. O'ahu also served as the location for the hit series *Lost,* which, like *Gilligan's Island* (the pilot of which was filmed on Kaua'i), is about a group of island castaways trying to get home. To find *Lost* locations, visit www.lostvirtualtour.com.

For a complete Hawaii filmography and a list of hundreds of TV episodes filmed here, including what's currently being shot around the islands, visit the Hawaii Film Office online (www.hawaiifilmoffice.com).

Lei

Greeting. Honor. Respect. Peace. Love. Celebration. Spirituality. Good luck. Farewell. A Hawaiian lei – a fresh garland handcrafted from the islands' rainbow myriad of flora – can signify all of these meanings, and more.

The Art of the Lei

Lei-making may be Hawaii's most sensuous – and also transitory – art form. Fragrant and ephemeral, lei embody the beauty of nature and the embrace of the community, freely given and freely shared.

In choosing their materials, lei makers tell a story – since flowers and plants embody place and myth – and express emotions. Lei makers may use feathers, nuts, shells, seeds, seaweed, vines, leaves and fruit, in addition to more familiar fragrant tropical flowers. The most commons methods of making lei were by knotting, braiding, winding, stringing or sewing the raw natural materials together.

Worn daily, lei were integral to ancient Hawaiian society. In the islands' Polynesian past, lei were made part of sacred hula dances and given as special gifts to loved ones, healing medicine to the sick and offerings to the gods, all practices that continue in Hawaii today. So powerful a symbol were they that on ancient Hawaii's battlefields, the right lei could bring peace to warring armies.

Today, locals continue to wear lei for special events, such as weddings, birthdays, anniversaries, graduations and public ceremonies. In general, it's no longer common to make one's own lei, unless you're a devoted member of a *hula halau* (hula school). For ceremonial hula (as opposed to popular competitions or shows for entertainment), performers are often required to make their own lei, even gathering the raw materials by hand.

Modern Celebrations

For visitors to Hawaii, the tradition of giving and receiving lei dates back to the 19th-century steamships that first brought tourists to the islands. In the early 20th century, the heyday of cruise-ship tourism, disembarking passengers were greeted by local vendors who would toss garlands around the necks of *malihini* (newcomers or foreigners).

The tradition of giving a kiss with a lei began during WWII, allegedly when a hula dancer at a USO club was dared by her friends to give a military serviceman a peck on the cheek when she placed a flower lei over his head.

In 1927, the poet Don Blanding and Honolulu journalist Grace Tower Warren called for making May 1 a holiday to celebrate lei. The next year, Leonard and Ruth Hawk composed the popular tune 'May Day is Lei Day in Hawaii,' a song that later became a hula *mele* (song). Today,

An artful, beautiful blend of botany and culture, *Na Lei Makamae: The Treasured Lei* (University of Hawai'i Press, 2003), by Marie McDonald and Paul Weissich, surveys Hawaiian flowers traditionally used in leis and their meaning and mythology.

Ka Lei: The Leis of Hawaii (Ku Pa'a Publishing, 1995), by Marie McDonald, a recognized *kapuna* (elder), is an in-depth look at the art of Hawaiian lei making before Western contact and during contemporary times.

Lei Day is celebrated across the islands with Hawaiian music, hula dancing, parades, lei-making workshops and contests, and more fun.

Lei: Dos & Don'ts

» Do not wear a lei hanging directly down around your neck. Instead, drape a closed (circular) lei over your shoulders, making sure that equal lengths are hanging over your front and back.

» When traditionally presenting a lei, bow your head slightly and raise the lei above your heart. Do not drape it with your own hands over the head of the recipient, as this isn't respectful; let them do it themselves.

» Don't give a closed lei to a pregnant woman, as it may bring bad luck to the unborn child; choose an open (untied) lei or *haku* (head) lei instead.

» Resist the temptation to wear a lei intended for someone else. It's bad luck.

» Never refuse a lei, and do not take one off in the presence of the giver.

» When you stop wearing your lei, don't throw it in the trash. Untie the string and return the lei's natural elements to the earth (eg scatter flowers in the sea, bury seeds or nuts) instead.

On O'ahu, it's believed that if passengers throw their lei into the sea as their departing ship passes Diamond Head, and the flowers of their lei float back toward the beach, they'll be guaranteed to return to Hawaii someday.

Shopping for Lei

A typical Hawaiian lei costs anywhere from $10 for a single strand of orchids or plumeria to thousands of dollars for a 100% genuine Niihau shell lei necklace. Beware that some *kukui* (candelnut) and *puka* shell lei are just cheap (even plastic) imports.

When shopping for a lei, ask the florist or shopkeeper for advice about what the most appropriate lei for the occasion is (eg for a bride, pick a string of pearl-like *pikake* jasmine flowers), and indicate if you're giving the lei to a man or a woman. Of course, it's okay to buy a lei for yourself anytime!

On O'ahu buy freshly made flower lei in Chinatown at Cindy's Lei Shoppe (Honolulu). For intricately crafted feather lei, visit Waikiki's Na Lima Mili Hulu No'eau workshop.

WHAT'S IN A LEI?

Lei are a universal language in Hawaii, but some special lei evoke a particular island.

O'ahu The yellow-orange *'ilima* is the island's official flower, and a symbol of Laka, the Hawaiian goddess of hula dancing. Once favored by royalty, an *'ilima* lei may be made of up to a thousand small blossoms strung together.

Hawai'i the Big Island Lei made from *lehua*, the pom-pom flowers of the *'ohia* plant, are most often colored red or pink. According to Hawaiian legend, the very first lei was made of *lehua* and given by Hi'iaka, goddess of healing, to her sister Pele, goddess of fire and volcanoes.

Maui The *lokelani* (pink damask rose, or 'rose of heaven') is a soft, velvety and aromatic flower. It was first planted on the island by early-19th-century Christian missionaries in the gardens of Lahaina. Today it's Maui's official flower, the only exotic species of flora to be so recognized in Hawaii.

Lana'i A yellowish-orange vine, *kaunaoa* is traditionally gathered from the island's windward shores, then twisted into a lei. One traditional Hawaiian chant sings of this plant growing on Lana'i like a feathered cape lying on the shoulders of a celebrated chief.

Moloka'i *Kukui* lei are either made from the laboriously polished, dark-brown nuts of Hawaii's state tree (in which case, they're usually worn by men) or the tree's white blossoms, which are Moloka'i's official flower.

Kaua'i On the 'Garden Island,' leathery *mokihana* berries that faintly smell of licorice are often woven with strands of glossy, green maile vines. *Mokihana* trees grow in the rain-soaked forests on the western slopes of mighty Mt Wai'ale'ale.

On Hawai'i the Big Island, roadside stands and farms sell affordable, fresh, high-quality lei on the honor payment system, including at Keahole Ag Park (p210) and on Lower Napo'opo'o Rd (p201). Also try the aunties at Kona's Kailua Village Farmers Market (Kailua-Kona). Otherwise, KTA supermarkets are a convenient local alternative to airport lei stands.

On Maui you can pick up lei at the gift shop at Kahului's airport, but a better stop is at Whole Foods (Kahului, just a mile from the airport), which sells fresh lei made at Paradise Flower Farms in Kula.

On Kaua'i choose from over 30 kinds of flower lei at Blue Orchid Floral Design (Koloa). For handcrafted maile (a native plant with twining habit and fragrant leaves), *ti*-leaf, flower, nut and seed lei, visit Flowers Forever (Lihu'e).

Does an airport lei greeting to surprise your *ipo* (sweetheart) sound like fun? Several companies in Hawaii offer this service, including Greeters of Hawaii (www.greeter sofhawaii.com), which has been in the business of giving aloha since 1957.

LEI

1. Stringing a lei
The most common methods of making lei are knotting, braiding, winding, stringing or sewing.

2. Girls wearing lei
Lei were integral to ancient Hawaiian society and were worn daily.

3. 'Ilima
Once favored in royal lei, the *'ilima (Sida fallax)* is a symbol of Laka, the Hawaiian goddess of hula dancing.

4. Lei and lauhala hats
Traditional arts such as *lauhala* (pandanus leaves) weaving are experiencing a revival in Hawaii.

Land & Sea

Many people think of the Hawaiian Islands as tiny rafts of white sand and tiki bars sailing westward inch-by-inch to Japan. In fact, these islands are the palm-fringed tops of the planet's largest mountain range, something whales may appreciate more than we do.

For 80 million years, a 'hot spot' beneath the earth's mantle has operated like a volcanic conveyor belt, manufacturing a 1500-mile string of shield volcanoes that bubble out of the sea in the most geographically isolated spot on the planet, almost 2000 miles from the closest continent. This profound isolation has created a living textbook of evolution, with a spectacular diversity of wildlife.

It has been said that if Darwin had arrived in Hawaii first, he would have developed his theory of evolution in a period of weeks instead of years. On the other hand, few places have felt humanity's heavy footprint as deeply as Hawaii, which today holds the ignominious title of being the 'endangered species capital of the world' while facing other critical environmental issues, too.

Volcanoes & Hot Spots

The Hawaiian archipelago embraces over 50 volcanoes (and 137 islands and atolls), part of the larger, mostly submerged Hawaiian-Emperor Seamount chain that extends 3600 miles across the ocean. Hawaii's volcanoes are created by a rising column of molten rock – a 'hot spot' – under the Pacific Plate. As the plate moves westward a few inches each year, magma pierces upward through the crust, creating volcanoes.

Each new volcano slowly creeps northward past the hot spot that created it. As each volcanic island moves off the hot spot, it stops erupting and instead of adding more new land, it starts eroding. Wind, rain and waves add geologic character to the newly emerged islands, cutting deep valleys, creating sandy beaches and turning a mound of lava into a tropical paradise.

At the far northwestern end of the chain, the Hawaiian Islands have receded below the ocean surface to become seamounts. Moving eastward from Kure Atoll, the islands get progressively taller and younger until you reach the Big Island of Hawai'i, the still-growing, 500,000-year-old child of the Hawaiian group.

Straddling the hot spot today, the Big Island's Kilauea is the world's most active volcano. All Hawaiian volcanoes are shield volcanoes that erupt with effusive lava to create gentle dome-shaped mountains, but they can also have a more explosive side, as Kilauea dramatically reminded onlookers and scientists in 2008.

Under the sea about 20 miles east of the Big Island, a new undersea volcano is erupting – Lo'ihi Seamount. Although you can't see it today, stick around: in 10,000 years or so, it will emerge from the water to become the newest island in the Hawaiian Islands chain.

The ongoing Kilauea eruption, which began in 1983, is the most voluminous outpouring of lava on the east rift zone in 500 years. It has added well over 500 acres of new land to the Big Island – so far.

KILAUEA

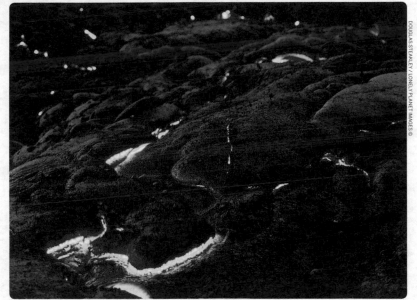

Pahoehoe *(quick and smooth-flowing lava) from Kilauea Volcano, Hawai'i Volcanoes National Park (p292).*

Wildlife

In the Beginning

Born of barren lava flows, the Hawaiian Islands were originally populated only by plants and animals that could traverse the Pacific – for example, seeds clinging to a bird's feather or fern spores that drifted thousands of miles through the air. Most species that landed here didn't survive. Scientists estimate that successful species were established maybe once every 70,000 years – and these included no amphibians, no browsing animals, no mosquitoes and only two mammals: a bat and a seal.

However, the flora and fauna that did succeed thrived on an unusually rich, diverse land, containing nearly every ecological or life zone. Without predators or much competition, new species dropped their defensive protections: thorns, poisons and strong odors disappeared. This process accounts for why over 90% of native Hawaiian species are endemic, or unique to the islands, and why they fare so poorly against modern invaders and artificial environmental changes.

Hawaii is the northernmost point of the triangle of Pacific islands known as Polynesia ('many islands'); the other points are New Zealand and Rapa Nui (Easter Island).

HAWAII BY THE NUMBERS

» Hawaii comprises 6423 sq miles of total land area, less than 1% of the total US landmass.

» In the state of Hawaii, there are eight main islands, but only seven are populated.

» West of Kaua'i, the minuscule Northwestern Hawaiian Islands stretch for 1200 miles.

» On the Big Island, Ka Lae (South Point) is the USA's southernmost point, 18°55′N of the equator.

HOARY BAT

The endangered 'ope'ape'a (Hawaiian hoary bat), one of Hawaii's two endemic mammals, has reddish-brown, white-tinged fur, making it appear 'hoary' (grayed by age). With a foot-wide wingspan, these tree-dwellers exist predominantly around forests on the leeward sides of the Big Island, Maui and Kaua'i.

Humans Invade

When Polynesians arrived, they introduced new animals and plants, including pigs, chickens, rats, coconuts, bananas, taro and about two-dozen other plants, not to mention people. These 'Polynesian introductions' caused the first wave of species extinctions, including an estimated 50-plus birds that had disappeared by the time Captain Cook dropped off goats and melon, pumpkin and onion seeds in 1778. Later European, Asian and American immigrants introduced more exotic (or 'alien') species, like cattle that foraged at will, invasive ground covers and ornamental plants.

Today, Hawaii is the 'extinction capital of the USA,' accounting for 75% of the nation's documented extinctions. Over two-thirds of Hawaii's known birds, over half of known snails and about 10% of endemic plant species are already extinct. But the islands have also become a unique laboratory in the global scientific effort to discover sustainable methods of conservation – preserving the diversity of wildlife, and by extension our own skins.

Animals

In modern times, nearly every animal introduced to the islands – whether rabbits, goats, sheep, pigs or horses – has led to devastating environmental damage. Some, like Maui's axis deer and the Big Island's cattle, were 'gifts' to Hawaiian kings that spun off out-of-control feral populations. The ubiquitous mongoose was originally introduced to control sugarcane rats, but has become a worse plague than the rats. Today, feral animals are the most destructive force in Hawaii, and getting rid of them is central to re-establishing native landscapes and saving many endangered species.

Feathered Friends

Many of Hawaii's birds are spectacular examples of adaptive radiation. For instance, all 53 species of endemic Hawaiian honeycreepers most likely evolved from a single finch ancestor. Today, over half of those bright-colored honeycreepers – along with two-thirds of all native birds – are extinct, the victims of more aggressive, nonnative birds, predatory feral

ANGRY BIRDS

How delicately interdependent are Hawaiian ecosystems? Consider how pigs are driving Hawaiian birds to extinction. Not directly, of course, but the chain of cause and effect is undeniable.

Feral pigs, most likely the descendants of domestic pigs brought by early Europeans, have caused widespread devastation to the islands' native wet forests. At Hawaii's national parks, pigs are considered public enemy number one, with federally sponsored eradication and fencing programs. Outside of federal lands, eradication efforts are few, and one estimate is that there may be as many as one feral pig for every 33 state residents.

Pigs trample and kill native fauna, destroy the forest understory and spread far and wide the seeds of invasive plants. Pigs love native tree-fern stems, knocking them over and eating the plants' tender insides, while the bowl-like cavities left behind catch rainwater and create ideal breeding pools for mosquitoes.

Common mosquitoes – presumed to have arrived in Hawaii in water casks aboard whaling ships in 1826 – pick up avian malaria and avian pox (also introduced from the European continent) and spread it to native birds, particularly honeycreepers, who have lost their natural immunity to these diseases.

It's a simple equation: no feral pigs, far fewer mosquitoes, far less avian malaria and far more honeycreepers. What's not so simple is how to make it a reality statewide.

animals (like mongooses) and infectious avian diseases against which they have no natural immunity.

The endangered nene, Hawaii's state bird, is a long-lost cousin of the Canada goose. Nene usually nest in sparse vegetation on rugged lava flows, to which their feet adapted by losing most of their webbing. While seven or eight other species of Hawaiian geese (now extinct) became flightless, nene remain strong flyers. There were once as many as 25,000 nene on all islands, but by the 1950s there were only 30 left. Intensive breeding programs have raised their numbers to around 1300 on Hawai'i, Maui, Kaua'i and Moloka'i.

The only hawk native to Hawaii, the 'io was a symbol of royalty and often an 'aumakua (protective deity). They breed only on the Big Island; their numbers have held steady at over 3000 for the last decade, and in 2008 the 'io was proposed for delisting from the endangered species list, but a decision is still pending.

Marine Superstars

Up to 10,000 migrating North Pacific humpback whales come to Hawaiian waters for calving each winter, and whale watching (p40) is a major highlight. The world's fifth-largest whale, the endangered humpback can reach lengths of 45ft and weigh up to 50 tons. Other whales (such as rarely seen blue and fin whales) migrate through, and Hawaii is home to a number of dolphins, the most notable of which is the spinner dolphin, named for its acrobatic leaps from the water.

One of the Pacific's most endangered marine creatures is the Hawaiian monk seal, named both for the monastic cowl-like fold of skin at its neck and for its solitary habits. The Hawaiian name for the animal is 'ilio holo kai, meaning 'the dog that runs in the sea.' Adults are over 7ft and 500lb of tough, some with the scars to prove they can withstand shark attacks. Once nearly driven to extinction, their population today numbers around 1300. Although monk seals breed primarily in the remote Northwestern Hawaiian Islands, recently they have begun hauling out on beaches on O'ahu and the Big Island.

Fish

Hawaii's coral reefs constitute 84% of all US reefs, and they are home to over 500 fish species, of which 25% are endemic. Protected main-island coral reefs teem with vast numbers of tropical fish: bright yellow tangs, striped butterflyfish and Moorish Idols, silver needlefish, and gape-mouthed moray eels. Neon-colored wrasse, which have more species than any other Hawaiian reef fish, mate daily and change sex (and color) as they mature.

The contrast between the variety and numbers of fish in the main islands and the protected Northwestern Hawaiian Islands is stunning. For instance, the weight of fish per acre in the Northwestern Hawaiian Islands is 2000lb, but it's 600lb in the main islands, and only 250lb on O'ahu; meanwhile, predators like sharks and jacks are 15 times as numerous in the Northwestern Hawaiian Islands' shallow reefs.

Plants

Mile for mile, Hawaii has the highest concentration of climate or ecological zones on earth. Whether you're in tropical rain forests or dry forests, high-altitude alpine deserts or coastal dunes, wetland marshes or grassy plains, extravagantly diverse flora occupies every island niche.

Of course, what we see today is not what the first Polynesians saw. Most 'Hawaiian' agricultural products were originally exotic imports – papayas, pineapples, mangoes, bananas, macadamia nuts, coffee. Also, over half of Hawaii's native forest is now gone due to logging, conversion to

---

LAND & SEA WILDLIFE

Hawaii for the Bird(er)s
» James Campbell National Wildlife Refuge, O'ahu
» Kealia Pond National Wildlife Refuge, Maui
» Haleakalā National Park, Maui
» Koke'e State Park, Kaua'i
» Papahanaumokuakea Marine National Monument

Having migrated to the islands over 10 million years ago, the Hawaiian monk seal has evolved into a unique species that has been called a 'living fossil.'

MONK SEALS

SABRINA DALBESIO / LONELY PLANET IMAGES ©

Protea flowers, Kula Botanical Garden (p382).

agriculture, invasive species and so on. Another sobering fact: of Hawaii's 1300 endemic plant species, nearly 100 are already extinct and almost 300 remain endangered or threatened.

Exotic Beauties

The classic hibiscus is native to Hawaii, but many varieties have also been introduced, so that now hundreds of varieties grow on the islands. However, it's perhaps fitting that Hawaii's state flower, the *pua aloalo* (yellow hibiscus), was added to the endangered species list in 1994. The *kokiʻo keʻokeʻo*, a native white shrub or small tree that grows up to 30ft high, is the only Hawaiian hibiscus with a fragrance.

Strangely enough, while Hawaii's climate is ideal for growing orchids, there are only three native species. In the 1800s Chinese immigrants

SACRED HONU

Native Hawaiians traditionally revere the green sea turtle, which they call *honu*. Often considered a personal *ʻaumakua* (protective deity), *honu*'s image frequently appears in petroglyphs (and today in tattoos). For ancient Hawaiians, sea turtles were a delicious and prized source of food, but their capture and consumption were typically governed by strict religious and traditional codes.

As with Hawaii's other two native species of sea turtles – the hawksbill and the leather-back – *honu* are endangered and protected by federal law. Adults can grow over 3ft long and weigh more than 200lb. Young turtles are omnivorous, but adults (unique among sea turtles) become strict vegetarians. This turns their fat green – hence their name.

Green sea turtles can be seen throughout the Hawaiian Islands, often while feeding in shallow lagoons, bays and estuaries. However, their main nesting site is French Frigate Shoals in the Northwestern Hawaiian Islands. There, up to 700 female turtles (90% of the total population) come to lay their eggs each year.

began importing them, and today they're a thriving industry. Hawaii is also abloom with scores of introduced ornamental and exotic tropical flowers, including blood-red anthurium with heart-shaped leaves, brilliant orange-and-blue bird-of-paradise and myriad heliconia.

Notable exotic trees include ironwood, a nonnative conifer with drooping needles, which acts as a natural windbreak and prevents erosion from beaches; majestic banyan trees, which have a canopy of hanging aerial roots with trunks large enough to swallow small children; and towering monkeypods, a common shade tree that has dark glossy green leaves, puffy pink flowers and longish seed pods.

Going Native

Perhaps the most bewitching of native Hawaiian trees is the koa, growing over 50ft high and nowadays found only at higher elevations. Traditionally, this rich hardwood has been used to make canoes, surfboards and even ukuleles. The endemic *wiliwili* is a lightweight wood also popular for surfboards and canoes. Hawaii was once rich in fragrant *'iliahi* (sandalwood) forests, but these were almost entirely sold off to foreign traders by the mid-19th century.

The widespread and versatile ohia is one of the first plants to colonize lava flows. Its distinctive tufted flowers (lehua) consist of petalless groups of red, orange, yellow, pink and white stamens; the flowers are considered sacred to Pele. Native forests of ohia and *hapu'u* (tree ferns) are vital, endangered habitats. Brought by early Polynesian settlers, the *kukui* (candlenut tree) has light silver-tinged foliage that stands out brightly in the forest; the oily nuts from Hawaii's state tree can be burned like candles and are used for making leis and lotions.

Flowering native coastal plants include *pohuehue* (beach morning-glory), with its glossy green leaves and pink flowers, found just above the wrack line along the coast; beach *naupaka,* a shrub with oval green leaves and small pinkish-white, five-petaled flowers that look as if they've been torn in half; and the low-growing *'ilima,* its delicate yellow-orange blossoms popularly strung into leis.

Ancient Hawaiians didn't have metals and never developed pottery, so plants fulfilled most of their needs. Ethnobotanist Beatrice Krauss delves into this fascinating history in *Plants in Hawaiian Culture* and *Plants in Hawaiian Medicine.*

Hawaii's Parks & Preserves

Hawaii has two national parks (www.nps.gov/state/HI/): Haleakalā National Park on Maui and Hawai'i Volcanoes National Park on the Big Island. Both have volcanoes as centerpieces, contain an astonishing range of environments and provide some of the best hiking in the islands. The latter, named a Unesco World Heritage Site in 1987, welcomes 1.2 million visitors a year, making it Hawaii's most popular attraction.

In addition, the islands have five national historical parks, sites and memorials, most helping to preserve traditional Hawaiian culture. Three are on the Big Island, notably Pu'uhonua o Honaunau (Place of Refuge) National Historical Park. Another is on Moloka'i, Kalaupapa National Historical Park, a living history interpretive site. O'ahu claims the famed USS *Arizona* Memorial at Pearl Harbor, part of the larger WWII Valor in the Pacific National Monument. Hawaii also has nine national wildlife refuges (NWR; www.fws.gov/pacific/refuges) on the five biggest main islands; their primary focus is preserving endangered plants and waterbirds, making them a delight for birders.

Incredibly, Hawaii has over 50 state parks, monuments and recreational areas (www.hawaiistateparks.org). These diverse natural and historic areas include stunners like Waimea Canyon on Kaua'i and Diamond Head on O'ahu. Each island also has county-managed beach parks and natural areas, as well as privately run botanical gardens, zoos, aquariums and more.

Hawaii Books for Nature Lovers

» *A World Between Waves,* edited by Frank Stewart

» *Hawaii: The Islands of Life* by the Nature Conservancy, with text by Gavan Daws

HAWAII'S TOP 15 NATURAL AREAS

PROTECTED AREA	FEATURES	ACTIVITIES	BEST TIME TO VISIT
O'ahu			
Hanauma Bay Nature Preserve	enormous coral reef in volcanic ring	snorkeling, swimming	year-round
Malaekahana State Recreation Area	sandy beach, Moku'auia (Goat Island) bird sanctuary	swimming, snorkeling, camping, birding	May-Oct
Big Island			
Hawai'i Volcanoes National Park	lava fields, craters, fern forests, petroglyphs	hiking, camping	year-round
Kealakekua Bay State Historical Park	calm waters, coral reefs, sea caves	snorkeling, diving, kayaking	year-round
Mauna Kea	Hawaii's highest peak	hiking, stargazing, ancient Hawaiian sites	year-round
Maui			
Haleakalā National Park (Kipahulu area)	bamboo forest, waterfalls, cascading pools, ancient Hawaiian sites	hiking, swimming	year-round
Haleakalā National Park (summit area)	cloud forest, eroded volcanic summit basin	hiking, camping, birding	year-round
Makena State Park	unspoiled, expansive sandy beaches	swimming, sunset-watching	year-round
Lana'i			
Hulopo'e Beach	pristine bay, white-sand beach, dolphins	swimming, snorkeling	year-round
Moloka'i			
Kalaupapa National Historical Park	remote peninsula, steep sea cliffs, historic Hansen's disease colony	hiking, mule riding, touring	year-round
Kamakou Preserve	rain forest, striking valley vistas, waterfalls, montane bog	hiking, bird-watching	May-Oct
Kaua'i			
Koke'e State Park	clifftop lookouts, waterfalls, rain forest, 4WD roads	hiking, birding	year-round
Na Pali Coast State Park	beaches, waterfalls, classic 11-mile backpack trek	hiking, camping, swimming, snorkeling	May-Sep
Waimea Canyon State Park	unbeatable views of 'Grand Canyon of the Pacific'	scenic lookouts, hiking, cycling, mountain biking	Apr-Oct
Northwestern Hawaiian Islands			
Midway Islands	Laysan albatross colony, epic coral reef, WWII history	birding, touring, snorkeling, hiking	Nov-Jul

SABRINA DALBESIO / LONELY PLANET IMAGES ©

It's the tropics; you're sure to see critters like this gecko.

Environmental Report Card

Wild Hawaii

Two of the most dire environment problems facing Hawaii are feral exotic animals and the continuous introduction and uncontrolled proliferation of invasive, habitat-modifying plants. Even in Hawaii's most protected areas (national parks and state reserves) inadequate budgets and funding cuts continue to hamper eradication and rehabilitation efforts.

Wildlife conservation reports can be depressing reading, but success stories do happen, proving that with enough effort and the right conditions, nature can rehabilitate itself. The Nature Conservancy (www.nature.org/hawaii), a nonprofit organization that purchases land to protect rare ecosystems, is very involved in Hawaii, and it has published its own biodiversity conservation assessment and plan (visit www.hawaiiecoregionplan.info).

Land Development

Until the recent economic recession hit, Hawaii's rising population and real-estate profits had spurred a building boom, some of it by off-island speculators with little concern for environmental impacts. Sprawling subdivisions and resorts have put even more pressure on a limited watershed and nearly full landfills. Meanwhile, construction often uncovers and disturbs archaeological and ancient Hawaiian cultural sites like heiau (temples), petroglyphs and burial mounds. Protecting sites and repatriating remains is a contentious issue that can delay road building and construction for years. Some former agricultural and industrial land has been successfully placed under conservation easement protections for future generations, however.

Future development of Mauna Kea's summit is another hot-button topic. Many environmental and Native Hawaiian groups adamantly

Natural Disasters

» Hurricanes, tsunamis and earthquakes occur in Hawaii, sometimes to devastating effect. In 2006 the Big Island was shaken by a 6.7 earthquake that caused $200 million in damage, but no deaths. In 1992 Hurricane 'Iniki wrecked large swathes of Kaua'i (see p537), and in 1946 the largest tsunami in Hawaii's history killed 159 people and caused enormous damage.

oppose building any new astronomical observatories on the peak. In 2006, a proposal to build six new telescopes around the Keck observatories was abandoned after a judge ruled that nothing new could be built without first developing a comprehensive summit management plan and environmental impact statement (EIS). In 2010, Mauna Kea's final EIS paved the way for building a new Thirty Meter Telescope – the world's largest – right on the sacred summit.

Military & Farm Cleanup

Long-standing friction over Hawaii's military presence continues, especially on O'ahu. The military has not always complied with environmental regulations, and its training maneuvers frequently impact Native Hawaiian cultural sights and local communities.

Consider the following examples:

» In 2002 it was discovered that the army dumped tons of conventional weapons off the Wai'anae Coast in western O'ahu, likely during WWII. Underwater robots are being tested as a way to clean up the 'Ordnance Reef,' littered with military munitions. At the time of writing, cleanup efforts are still ongoing.

» In 2006 and 2007, after years of denial, the army admitted to having used depleted uranium (banned under the Geneva Convention) at O'ahu's Schofield Barracks and the Big Island's Pohakuloa Training Area. Public calls for independent monitoring and cleanup have been deemed unnecessary by the military.

» In 2008, conflicts over the military's planned expansions to conduct maneuvers with Stryker combat vehicles (for use in Iraq) on O'ahu and the Big Island were settled by lawsuit. The military was allowed to move ahead by agreeing to let Native Hawaiians survey proposed training areas for cultural sites.

Corporate agribusiness in Hawaii has also been guilty of violating Environmental Protection Agency (EPA) guidelines regarding soil and groundwater contamination on the islands. In 2010 – almost 15 years after being added to the EPA's Superfund national priority list – O'ahu's Del Monte Foods plantation was finally cleaned up. Other environmental issues include water pollution caused by agricultural runoff and debates over whether GMOs (genetically modified organisms) should be outlawed.

By the Sea

In contrast to the land, Hawaii's coral reefs are comparatively healthy. Overfishing is a major concern. Three-quarters of Hawaii's reef fish have been depleted during the last century; not surprisingly, the species most in danger are those fish popular for aquariums or eating. Fair Catch (www.faircatchhawaii.org) is leading the effort for a statewide ban on laying gill nets while encouraging sustainable fishing practices.

Hawaii's shorelines are still in danger, however. The threat of rising seas due to global warming and persistent beach erosion are raising alarm bells. Scientific studies have found that 25% of O'ahu and Maui beaches have been lost in the last 50 years; meanwhile, if tides rise a foot by the end of this century (as some predict they will), half of Waikiki's hotels would then be standing in ocean water.

For the latest environmental issues facing the islands, check out the investigative journal *Environment Hawaii* (www.environment-hawaii.org), or browse its free online archives.

KAHEA

The Native Hawaiian, grassroots activist organization Kahea (www.kahea.org) tackles a wide range of environmental, developmental and cultural rights issues, including those surrounding Mauna Kea and the Northwestern Hawaiian Islands.

Green Hawaii

Hawaii is a Polynesian paradise possessing one of the most astoundingly varied natural environments on the planet. It's also a high-profile test case of whether humans can achieve a sustainable relationship with nature. With rising ecotourism and a renaissance of Hawaiian traditions, both environmentally and culturally responsible businesses are sprouting up around the islands. Conservation efforts, both state-funded and grassroots, are gaining strength. From marine biologists and wildlife conservationists to Hawaiian artists and land-loving locals, *aloha 'aina* (respect for the land) runs strong.

The Islands Go Green

Hawaii breathes green. From volcano summits to verdant cloud forests to the ocean depths where great whales gather, the natural beauty of this place swallows you up. Green is also a way of thinking and living on these islands, where residents spend many of their waking hours outdoors, communing with each other and with nature. It's fair to say that nearly everyone who lives here feels a close connection to the land and the sea (see p614).

Environmental concerns are entangled in just about every major issue facing Hawaii, too. Islanders of all backgrounds have become activists – from Native Hawaiians restoring ancient fishponds to scientists fighting to keep invasive plants at bay. Hawaii residents are also showing their support for 'green' initiatives at the ballot box; in recent years, they've repeatedly voted in favor of light-rail transit and renewable energy initiatives.

Development is a particularly contentious issue in the islands, partly due to the mixed impact that tourism, the military and agribusiness have had on Hawaii's land and traditional culture. While Hawaii's economy would not survive without these industries, particularly tourism, some residents are asking what kind of jobs they really bring, and at what cost? Unemployment has soared recently, and many of the jobs still available are in the lower-paid service sector. How to achieve a more diversified economy is a question on everyone's minds.

Tourism is another thorny issue. Over 6.5 million visitors land on these shores every year – outnumbering residents five to one – and tourism, either directly or indirectly, provides one out of every three jobs in Hawaii. Pressures from tourism can be intense, as corporations seek to build more condos and hotels, to irrigate golf courses and to, well, sprawl. Multi-million-dollar vacation homes for wealthy off-islanders have made housing unaffordable for some locals. Homelessness is on the rise, especially on O'ahu (see p164).

Of course, even without tourism, the state's growing population has created its own pressure cooker. Finding ways to let the steam escape – while balancing environmental protection, Native Hawaiian rights and sustainable economic interests – has become critical for the islands' survival. Making Hawaii energy independent through wind and solar power; reducing landfill waste by using biodegradable products; and starting

Curious about Hawaii's environmental health? Get the lowdown from Environment Hawai'i (www.environment-hawaii.org), a watchdog group that publishes a wide-ranging monthly newsletter, and Hawaii Ecosystems at Risk (www.hear.org), whose website focuses on invasive species and eradication efforts.

Focused on Hawaii's natural and cultural beauty, the website Alternative Hawaii (www.alternative-hawaii.com) offers hundreds of ecofriendly tourism listings, from accommodations and restaurants to tours and events.

Wind power will contribute to energy independence for Hawaii.

Hawaiian language and cultural immersion charter schools are just a few of the ways that Hawaii is working to ensure a more sustainable future.

For a more in-depth look at the environmental issues facing Hawaii today, see our 'Environmental Report Card,' p621.

Choosing Sustainability

'Sustainability' is a buzzword in Hawaii today, particularly with regard to tourism. Green travel and ecotourism are booming, and every visitor to Hawaii can help do their part.

Consume Green

» Everything not grown or raised in Hawaii has to be shipped to the islands by boat or plane, which increases greenhouse emissions.

» When shopping in grocery stores and choosing restaurants, look for places that feature locally grown produce and sustainably caught seafood.

» For more about Hawaii's locavore movement, see p594. For ecoconscious microbreweries, see p593.

» Takeout food containers are a nightmare for Hawaii's limited landfills. Patronize places that use biodegradable takeout-ware, even if it costs you a bit extra.

» Bottled water may be convenient, but tap water is perfectly fine to drink, so bring along a refillable container.

Stay Green

» Many hotels have not jumped on the environmental bandwagon. Even such simple eco-initiatives as switching to bulk soap dispensers are rare.

» Ask about a hotel's 'green' policies before booking your stay. Turn off all lights and electronics whenever you leave your hotel room.

» Consider camping or staying at an ecofriendly, locally owned B&B or guesthouse. Renting a condo with a kitchen can also reduce your environmental impact.

GREEN BUSINESS

The Hawaii Ecotourism Association (www.hawaiiecotourism.org) keeps a directory of 'green' businesses – particularly hotels and tour operators. Because members are self-selecting and don't have to meet any general sustainability criteria, do your own research, too.

Recycle & Reuse

» Recycling bins are not common at hotels or on the street, but you'll find them at beaches, public parks and some museums and tourist attractions.

» Momentum is growing to ban plastic bags statewide. Cut down on landfill waste by reusing your own cloth bags.

On the Road

» Avoid driving if you can walk, cycle or take public transportation (the latter is limited on all islands except O'ahu).

» If you're renting a vehicle, choose the most fuel-efficient option; ask the rental agency if hybrid, electric or bio-fueled vehicles are available.

Tread Lightly

So many travelers come to enjoy Hawaii's legendary scenery and wild-life that only strict protections keep certain extremely popular, beautiful places – like O'ahu's Hanauma Bay – from being loved to death. But many equally scenic and fragile areas have fewer regulations, or little oversight, and the question becomes: just because you can do something, should you? What are the impacts, and what are the best ways to experience nature without harming it in the process?

For many activities, there isn't a single definitive answer, but here are a few universal guidelines and impacts to consider:

» **Coral-reef etiquette** When snorkeling or diving, never touch the coral reef. It's that simple. Coral polyps are living organisms, so oil from fingers and broken pieces create wounds and openings for infection and disease. Watch your fins; avoid stirring up clouds of sand, which can settle on and damage reef organisms. Don't feed fish.

» **Dive etiquette** Practice proper buoyancy control to avoid hitting the reef. Don't use reef anchors or ground boats over coral. Limit time in caves, as air bubbles can collect on roofs and leave organisms high and dry.

For more easy ideas about how to make your trip more sustainable and ecofriendly, pick up 50 Simple Things You Can Do to Save Hawai'i by environmental studies professor Gail Grabowsky.

GREEN HAWAII TREAD LIGHTLY

HAWAII IN 2050

Dubbed 'the people's plan,' the Hawai'i 2050 Sustainability Plan (www.hawaii2050.org) is the first statewide planning effort since the 1978 Constitutional Convention. As the plan itself states: this 'is not an academic or political exercise; it is a matter of the survival of Hawai'i as we know it.'

The first task was defining 'sustainability' in Hawaii-specific terms. What came out of conversations with 10,000 island residents was a 'triple bottom line' that recognized the interdependence of Hawaii's economic, cultural and environmental health. This is expressed in five goals. To quote from the plan:

» 1. Living sustainably is part of our daily practice in Hawai'i.

» 2. Our diversified and globally competitive economy enables us to meaningfully live, work and play in Hawai'i.

» 3. Our natural resources are responsibly and respectfully used, replenished and preserved for future generations.

» 4. Our community is strong, healthy, vibrant and nurturing, providing safety nets for those in need.

» 5. Our Kanaka Maoli [Native Hawaiian] and island cultures and values are thriving and perpetuated.

The plan laid out nine urgent priorities for 2020 (covering affordable housing, education, energy, the environment), establishing benchmarks for progress and 55 indicators to measure Hawaii's health.

Although Hawaii's state legislature has not yet enacted the report's recommendations (which were updated by UH Manoa's Public Policy Center in 2010), Hawai'i 2050's goal to plant a sustainability ethic within residents islandwide is already bearing fruit.

» **Encountering wild turtles and marine mammals** Federal and state laws protect all wild ocean mammals and turtles from 'harassment.' Legally, this means approaching them closer than 50yd or doing anything that disrupts their behavior. If these animals approach you, simply admire them. The most important actions to avoid are pursuing wild dolphins to get close to them, and disturbing seals or turtles resting on beaches.

» **Dolphin swims** Boat tours promising swims with wild dolphins are notorious for ignoring both federal law and dolphin welfare. What about swimming with captive dolphins? Some scientists and environmental activists believe that captivity itself is too harmful to justify. For more on the controversy, see p37.

» **Hiking** Scrub the soles of your shoes and wipe down any gear before arrival to avoid importing any invasive species via stray seeds. Prevent erosion by staying on marked trails. Respect 'No Trespassing – Kapu' and 'Private Property' signs, unless a trustworthy local resident says it's actually OK. See the boxed text, p636.

» **Helicopter rides** Some places you can't reach except by air. However, as air tours increase, aircraft noise disturbs visitors and island residents on the ground (see p545), and it may stress bird populations. If you do fly, pick the most fuel-efficient helicopter possible, and consider carbon offsetting.

» **4WDs & ATVs** Always stay on the road, track or pre-established trail. Off-roading, even on private land, can cause scars that take decades to heal. Better yet, consider mountain biking or hiking as alternative low-impact transportation.

Get Involved

Volunteering provides an experience you'll never get by just passing through a place. More people than ever before are raising environmental alarms and working toward green solutions for everyday island living. There's always something to get involved in – even if it's for just an afternoon.

The best central place to find out about volunteer opportunities is Malama Hawaii (www.malamahawaii.org), a partnership network of community and nonprofit organizations. It posts a wide-ranging calendar that also includes fund-raising concerts, educational events and cultural workshops.

Some organizations that run volunteer projects:

» GrowFood (www.growfood.org)
» Habitat for Humanity (www.habitat.org)
» Hawaii Food Bank (www.hawaiifoodbank.com)
» Hawaii Nature Center (www.hawaiinaturecenter.org) On O'ahu and Maui.
» Hawaii State Parks (www.hawaiistateparks.org/partners)
» Hawai'i Wildlife Fund (http://wildhawaii.org)
» Koke'e Resource Conservation Program (www.krcp.org) On Kaua'i.
» O'ahu Invasive Species Committee (www.hawaiiinvasivespecies.org/iscs/oisc/)
» Pacific Whale Foundation (www.volunteersonvacation.org) On Maui.
» Protect Kaho'olawe 'Ohana (www.kahoolawe.org) On Kaho'olawe.

For more volunteer opportunities, check alternative local newspapers such as Honolulu Weekly (www.honoluluweekly.com/calendar) and online classified ads at Craigslist (http://honolulu.craigslist.org/vol/).

AGRITOURISM

Agricultural tourism in Hawaii is growing along with the increasing number of small organic farms. The Hawai'i Agritourism Association (www.hiagtourism.org) facilitates farm visits and maintains a clickable online map of farmers markets statewide.

SUSTAINABLE ICON

It seems like everyone's going green these days, but how can you know which Hawaii businesses are actually ecofriendly and which are simply jumping on the sustainable bandwagon? Throughout this book, just look for our sustainable icon (⬛). Some of our authors' sustainable picks are involved in environmental conservation and/or education, while others support and preserve Hawaiian identity and culture, and many are owned by local operators.

Survival Guide

DIRECTORY A–Z 628

Accommodations 628
Business Hours 630
Courses 630
Customs Regulations . . . 630
Discount Cards 630
Electricity 631
Gay & Lesbian Travelers . . 631
Insurance 631
Internet Access 631
Legal Matters 632
Maps 632
Money 632
Public Holidays 633
Safe Travel 633
Shopping 633
International Visitors 634
Telephone 635
Time 635
Tourist Information 635
Travelers with
Disabilities 635
Hazards & Trespassing . . 636
Work 636

TRANSPORTATION . . 637

Getting There & Away . . . 637
Air 637
Sea 638
Getting Around 638
Air 638
Bicycle 638
Boat 639
Bus 639
Car 639
Hitchhiking 641
Moped & Motorcycle 641
Taxi 641
Tours 641

HEALTH 642

Before You Go 642
In Hawaii 642
Infectious Diseases 642
Environmental Hazards . . 643

GLOSSARY 644

Directory A–Z

Accommodations

Rates

In this guide, unless otherwise stated our reviews indicate high-season rates for a double-occupancy room:

» $ under $100
» $$ $100 to $250
» $$$ over $250

Quoted rates generally don't include taxes of almost 14%. Unless noted, breakfast is not included and bathrooms are private.

Reservations

A reservation guarantees your room, but most reservations require a deposit, after which, if you change your mind, the establishment may not refund your money. Note cancellation policies and other restrictions before making a deposit.

Peak vs Off-Peak Times

» During high season – mid-December through March or April, and June through August – lodgings are more expensive and in demand.

» Certain holidays and major events command premium prices, and for these, lodgings can book up a year ahead.

» In low or shoulder seasons expect discounts and easier booking.

» Unless otherwise noted, all lodgings listed in this book are open year-round.

Amenities

» Accommodations offering online computer terminals for guests are designated with the internet icon (@). A fee may apply (eg at hotel business centers).

» In-room internet access at Hawaii hotels is often wired (not wireless) and a daily fee may apply.

» When wireless internet access is offered, the wi-fi icon (🛜) appears. Look for free wi-fi hot spots in common areas (eg hotel lobby, poolside).

» Where an indoor or outdoor pool is available, the swimming icon (🏊) appears with the review.

» Air-conditioning (❄) is a standard amenity at most chain hotels and resorts. At some independent properties, only fans may be provided.

» For more icons and abbreviations used with reviews in this book, see Quick Reference inside the front cover.

B&Bs & Vacation Rentals

B&B accommodations vary from spare bedrooms in family households to historic homes to pull-out-the-stops romantic hideaways. Mostly family-run operations, B&Bs can provide more personal experiences than hotels, but offer fewer services.

True to their name, most B&Bs offer breakfast or provide food for guests to cook on their own. Ask what kind of breakfast is served; most B&Bs do not have state-approved restaurant kitchens, and they can be fined if caught making hot meals for guests.

Because B&Bs discourage unannounced drop-ins, they sometimes do not appear on maps in this book. Hosts are often out during the day, so same-day reservations are hard to get – always try to book B&Bs in advance (especially because they tend to fill up ahead of time). Many B&Bs have two- and three-night minimum-stay requirements, though some will waive this if you pay a higher one-night rate.

Typically, a vacation rental means renting an entire house (with no on-site manager and no breakfast provided), but many B&Bs also rent stand-alone cottages, and often all these kinds of properties are handled by the same rental agencies. Ask about cleaning fee surcharges, especially for stays of less than five nights.

BOOK YOUR STAY ONLINE

For more reviews by Lonely Planet authors, check out hotels.lonelyplanet.com/Hawaii. You'll find independent reviews, as well as recommendations on the best places to stay. Best of all, you can book online.

PRACTICALITIES

» **Electricity**
110/120V, 50/60Hz

» **Newspapers** *Honolulu Star-Advertiser* (www.staradvertiser.com) is Hawaii's major daily

» **Radio** Hawaii has about 50 radio stations; National Public Radio (NPR) at lower end of the FM dial

» **TV** All major US TV networks and cable channels available

» **Video Systems** NTSC standard (incompatible with PAL or SECAM systems); DVDs coded region 1 (US and Canada only)

» **Weights & Measures** Imperial

Some islands have their own B&B associations, which are listed in individual island chapters. For B&B and vacation rental listings statewide, try the following:

Affordable Paradise Bed & Breakfast (www.affordable-paradise.com)

Bed & Breakfast Hawaii (www.bandb-hawaii.com)

Purple Roofs (www.purpleroofs.com) LGBTQ-friendly accommodations.

Vacation Rental by Owner (www.vrbo.com)

Camping & Cabins

Hawaii has almost no full-service private campgrounds. The best public camping facilities are in national parks, next best are state parks and typically the least well cared-for are county parks. Campgrounds are less busy during the week than on weekends.

NATIONAL PARKS
Hawaii's two national parks – Maui's Haleakalā National Park and the Big Island's Hawai'i Volcanoes National Park – have free drive-up campgrounds that are first-come, first-served; these may be just grassy dispersed areas without many amenities. Permits required for backcountry campsites and usually available same-day for walk-up visitors. Advance reservations are strongly recommended for all cabin rentals.

STATE PARKS
» The five largest Hawaiian Islands offer camping ($12 to $30 per site per night) at state parks.

» State park campgrounds usually have picnic tables, BBQ grills, drinking water, toilets and showers.

» Some state parks also rent basic housekeeping cabins ($30 to $90 per night).

» Obtain camping and cabin permits in person from any **Division of State Parks** (www.hawaiistateparks.org) office or book ahead online up to 30 days in advance.

» On Oahu, the **Department of State Parks (DSP) Headquarters** (☏587-0300; www.hawaiistateparks.org; Room 310, 1151 Punchbowl St, Honolulu; ☺8am-3:15pm Mon-Fri) handles camping reservations for all islands.

COUNTY PARKS
Some county parks are wonderful, with white-sand beaches and good facilities, while others are terribly run-down. Keep in mind that just because you *can* camp somewhere doesn't necessarily mean you'll *want* to. Check out the campground in person or ask around before committing yourself.

For county-park camping reservations, permit requirements and fees, see individual island chapters.

Condominiums

Typically more spacious than hotel rooms, condos are individually owned apartments furnished with everything a visitor needs, including a kitchen(ette). They're often cheaper than all but the cheapest hotel rooms, especially if you're traveling with a group.

» Most condo units have a multiday minimum stay, especially in high season.

» The weekly rental rate is often six times the daily rate, and the monthly rate three times the weekly.

» Ask about cleaning fees, a one-time charge that depends on the length of stay.

» To save money, try booking condos directly first, then go through island rental agencies.

» Do your own internet search for online condo-rental classifieds at **Vacation Rentals by Owner** (www.vrbo.comor) and **Craigslist** (www.craigslist.org).

Hostels

Hawaii has only two hostels associated with **Hostelling International USA** (www.hiusa.org), both of which are in Honolulu. However, all of the main islands have a small selection of private hostels, usually in larger towns. A few are appealing, friendly and well kept, but

---

SAFE CAMPING

For safety reasons, a few county and state parks are not recommended because they either are very isolated or are regular late-night carousing spots. Theft and violence aimed at campers is uncommon, but you should still choose your campgrounds carefully. See recommendations at the start of every island chapter, and ask locals and park staff for advice.

the majority are aimed at backpackers or seasonal surfers, and are essentially worn-out crash pads. Most are spartan, offer a common kitchen, internet access and have bulletin boards and lockers. Dorm beds average $20 to $30 nightly.

Hotels

It is common for hotels, particularly chains, to discount their published rack rates, typically by offering advance-purchase internet booking discounts. Other hotels may discount by the season, week or day depending on demand. Ask about special promotions and vacation packages before booking. The main thing that influences room rates is the view and which floor it is on; an ocean view can easily cost 50% to 100% more than a parking-lot view (which is sometimes euphemistically called a 'garden view'). Be aware that descriptors such as 'oceanfront' and 'oceanview' are liberally used, even where you may require a periscope to spot the surf.

Resorts

Hawaii resorts do not mess around: they are pleasure palaces designed to anticipate your every need and provide 'the best' of everything (to keep you on the property every minute of the day). Beach resorts provide myriad dining options, multiple swimming pools, children's programs, nightly entertainment and fitness centers. Mandatory daily resort fees may be charged; inquire when booking.

Business Hours

Unless there are variations of more than a half-hour in either direction, the following opening hours apply for all entries and reviews in this book:

Banks	8:30am-4pm Mon-Fri; some open to 6pm Fri and 9am-noon or 1pm Sat
Bars	noon-midnight daily; some open to 2am Thu-Sat
Businesses	8:30am-4:30pm Mon-Fri; some post offices open 9am-noon Sat
Restaurants	breakfast 6-10am, lunch 11:30am-2pm, dinner 5-9:30pm
Shops	9am-5pm Mon-Sat, some also open noon-5pm Sun; major shopping areas & malls keep extended hours

Courses

Some resorts and shopping centers offer free or low-cost classes and workshops in hula, traditional Hawaiian arts and the like. Since many schedules are unpredictable, you should keep your eyes and ears open, and ask your hotel concierge about what's on while you're in town. See also the individual island chapters for more opportunities.

For Road Scholar learning vacations for adults aged 50 and older, see p641.

Customs Regulations

Currently, each international visitor is allowed to bring into the USA duty-free:
» 1L of liquor (if you're over 21 years old)
» 200 cigarettes (1 carton) or 50 (non-Cuban) cigars (if you're over 18)
Amounts higher than $10,000 in cash, traveler's checks, money orders and other cash equivalents must be declared. Don't even think about bringing in illegal drugs.

For more complete, up-to-date information, check with **US Customs and Border Protection** (www.cbp.gov).

Most fresh fruits and plants are restricted from entry into Hawaii (to prevent the spread of invasive species), and customs officials are militant in enforcing this. Similarly, because Hawaii is a rabies-free state, the pet quarantine laws are draconian. For details, contact the **Hawaiian Department of Agriculture** (http://hawaii.gov/hdoa).

Discount Cards

Free tourist magazines packed with discount coupons are widely available at airports and tourist hot spots. However, for activities and tours, usually the best deals are offered by booking directly in advance online.

Children, students, seniors and military personnel usually receive discounts at museums and other sights; all but children need to present valid ID confirming their status.

American Association of Retired Persons (AARP; www.aarp.org) This advocacy group for Americans aged 50 years and older offers member discounts (usually 10%) on hotels, car rentals and more.

American Automobile Association (AAA; www.aaa.com) Members of AAA and its foreign affiliates (eg CAA) qualify for small discounts (usually 10%) on car rentals, hotels and attractions.

Student Advantage Card (www.studentadvantage.com) For international and US students, one of these cards will give you offers discounts of 10% to 20% on airfares, hotels and shopping.

Electricity

120V/60Hz

120V/60Hz

Gay & Lesbian Travelers

Hawaii has a heritage of Polynesian tolerance that extends to gays and lesbians. The state has strong minority protections and a constitutional guarantee of privacy that extends to sexual behavior between consenting adults.

Same-sex couples have the right to civil unions, granting equality with heterosexual married couples.

Locals also tend to be very private about their personal lives in general, so you will not see much public hand-holding or open displays of affection. Even in Waikiki, which is without question the epicenter of Hawaii's gay scene (see the boxed text, p118), the laid-back 'scene' is muted by US mainland standards. Everyday queer life is low-key – it's more about picnics and pot-lucks, not nightclubs.

That said, Hawaii remains a very popular destination for LGBTQ travelers, who are served by a network of B&Bs, resorts and tours. The monthly magazine *Odyssey* (www.odysseyhawaii.com), free at gay-friendly businesses throughout Hawaii, covers the islandwide scene, as does *eXpression!* magazine (www.expression808.com).

For more information on LGBTQ Hawaii, including recommended places to stay, gay beaches, events and more, surf these community websites:

Gay Hawaii (www.gayhawaii .com)

Lesbian and Gay Businesses of Hawaii (www .lgbhawaii.com)

Out in Hawaii (www.outin hawaii.com)

Out Traveler (www.out -traveler.com)

Out Traveler: Hawai'i (www.rainbowhandbook.com)

Pacific Ocean Holidays (www.gayhawaiivacations.com)

Purple Roofs (www.purple roofs.com)

Insurance

For car-rental insurance, see p639.

Getting travel insurance to cover theft, loss and medical problems is highly recommended. Some policies do not cover 'risky' activities such as scuba diving, motor-

cycling and skiing, so read the fine print. Make sure your policy at least covers hospital stays and an emergency flight home.

Paying for your airline ticket or rental car with a credit card may provide limited travel accident insurance. If you already have private US health insurance or a homeowners or renters policy, find out what those policies cover and only get supplemental insurance. If you have prepaid a large portion of your vacation, trip cancellation insurance may be a worthwhile expense.

Worldwide travel insurance is available at www. lonelyplanet.com/travel_ser vices. You can buy, extend and claim online any time – even if you're already on the road.

Internet Access

» In this book, the @ symbol indicates an internet terminal is available, while the 🛜 symbol indicates a wi-fi hot spot; either may be free or fee-based.

» Most hotels and resorts, and many restaurants, coffee shops and other businesses, now offer high-speed internet access. In-room internet access is usually wired.

» Cities and larger towns usually have cybercafés and business centers offering pay-as-you-go internet terminals, averaging $6 to $12 per hour, and sometimes wi-fi.

» Hawaii's **public libraries** (www.librarieshawaii.org) provide free internet access via PC computer terminals if you get a temporary non-resident library card ($10). A few library branches now offer free wi-fi, too (no card required).

» To find wi-fi hot spots in Hawaii, try **Jiwire** (www.jiwire .com) and **Wi-Fi Free Spot** (www.wififreespot.com).

Legal Matters

You have the right to an attorney from the moment you are arrested. If you can't afford one, the state must provide one free of charge. The **Hawaii State Bar Association** (☎537-9140; www.hawaiilawyer referral.com) makes attorney referrals. Foreign visitors may want to call their consulate for advice; police will provide the telephone number upon request.

MINIMUM LEGAL AGE TO...	
Drink alcohol	21
Drive a car	16
Smoke tobacco	18
Vote in an election	18

Driving

» If you are stopped by the police while driving, be courteous. Don't get out of the car unless asked.

» In Hawaii, anyone driving with a blood alcohol level of 0.08% or higher is guilty of driving 'under the influence' (DUI), which carries severe penalties.

» Police can give roadside sobriety checks to assess if you've been drinking or using drugs. Refusing to be tested is legally considered the same as if you had taken and failed the test.

» It's illegal to carry open containers of alcohol inside a vehicle, even if they're empty. Store them inside the trunk.

» For more road rules, see p640.

Alcohol & Drugs

» Bars, clubs and liquor stores may require photo ID to prove you're of legal age to buy alcohol.

» Consuming alcohol anywhere other than at a private residence or licensed premises is a no-no, which puts parks and beaches off-limits.

» As with most places in the USA, the possession of marijuana and narcotics is illegal in Hawaii. Foreigners convicted of a drug offense face deportation.

Smoking

» Smoking is generally prohibited inside all public buildings, including airports, shopping malls, bars and nightclubs.

» There is no smoking allowed at restaurants, even on outdoor patios or at sidewalk tables.

» At hotels, you must specifically request a smoking room. Note that some properties are entirely nonsmoking by law, with high penalty fees for noncompliance.

Other Laws

» Public nudity (as at beaches) and hitchhiking are illegal, but rarely enforced.

» Due to security concerns about terrorism, never leave your bags unattended, especially at airports or bus stations.

Maps

By far the most detailed street maps are found in the **Ready Mapbook** series. These atlas-style books cover virtually every paved and unpaved road on the main islands. They're sold at bookshops and convenience stores.

Map geeks and backcountry hikers wanting topo maps can buy them at bigger bookstores and at national park visitor centers. Or download and print topo maps for free online from the **US Geological Survey** (www.usgs.gov).

Franko's Maps (www .frankosmaps.com) offers a range of colorful, laminated and waterproof ocean sports and island sightseeing maps, including *Obama's O'ahu* and *Pearl Harbor: Then and Now Historical Guide*. They're sold at bookstores and outdoor outfitters.

Money

ATMs

» ATMs are available 24/7 at most banks, shopping malls, airports and grocery and convenience stores.

» Expect a minimum surcharge of $2 per transaction, in addition to any fees charged by your home bank.

» Most ATMs are connected to international networks (Plus and Cirrus are the most common) and offer decent exchange rates.

Credit Cards

» Major credit cards are widely accepted (except occasionally by B&Bs).

» Credit cards are typically required for car rentals, hotel reservations, etc.

» Visa, MasterCard and American Express are the most commonly accepted credit cards.

Moneychangers

» Exchange foreign currency at the Honolulu International Airport or larger Hawaii banks, like **Bank of Hawaii** (www.boh.com) and **First Hawaiian Bank** (www.fhb.com).

» Outside of cities and larger towns, exchanging money may be impossible, so make sure you carry enough cash and/or a credit card.

Tipping

» In the USA, tipping is *not* optional. Only withhold tips in cases of outrageously bad service.

Airport and hotel porters $2 per bag, min per cart $5

Bartenders 10% to 15% per round, minimum $1 per drink

Concierges Nothing for simple information, up to $20 for securing last-minute restaurant reservations, etc

Housekeeping staff $2 to $4 daily, left under the card provided; more if you're messy

Parking valets At least $2 when your keys are returned

Restaurant servers and room service 15% to 20%, unless a gratuity is already charged

Taxi drivers 10% to 15% of metered fare, rounded up to the next dollar

Traveler's Checks

» Traveler's checks in US$ are accepted like cash at many midrange and top-end businesses (but rarely at budget places, such as supermarkets or fast-food chains).

Public Holidays

On the following national holidays, banks, schools and government offices (including post offices) close, and transportation, museums and other services operate on a Sunday schedule. Holidays falling on a weekend are usually observed the following Monday.

New Year's Day January 1

Martin Luther King Jr Day Third Monday in January

Presidents Day Third Monday in February

Easter March or April

Memorial Day Last Monday in May

King Kamehameha Day June 11

Independence Day July 4

Statehood Day Third Friday in August

Labor Day First Monday in September

Columbus Day Second Monday in October

Election Day Second Tuesday in November

Veterans Day November 11

Thanksgiving Fourth Thursday in November

Christmas Day December 25
For a major events calendar, see p23.

Safe Travel

In general, Hawaii is a safe place to visit. Because tourism is so important, state officials have established the

Visitor Aloha Society of Hawaii (VASH; ☎808-926-8274; www.visitoraloha societyofhawaii.org), which provides aid to visitors who become the victims of accidents or crimes while vacationing in Hawaii.

For common health concerns, see p642.

Flash Floods

No matter how dry a streambed looks, or how sunny the sky above is, a sudden rainstorm miles away can cause a flash flood in minutes, sending down a huge surge of debris-filled water that sweeps away everything in its path. Always check the weather report before setting out on a hike; this is crucial if you're planning on hiking through any narrow canyons or swimming in waterfalls or natural pools.

Tell-tale signs of an impending flash flood include sudden changes in water clarity (eg the stream turns muddy), rising water levels and/or floating debris, and a rush of wind, the sound of thunder or a low, rumbling roar. If you notice any of these signs, immediately get to higher ground (even a few feet could save your life). Do not run downstream or down canyon – you can't beat a flash flood.

Scams

The main scams directed toward visitors in Hawaii involve fake activity-operator booths and timeshare booths. Salespeople at the latter will offer you all sorts of deals, from free luaus to sunset cruises, if you'll just come to hear their 'no obligation' pitch. *Caveat emptor.*

Theft

The islands are notorious for rip-offs from parked cars, especially rentals. It can happen within seconds, whether at a remote trailhead parking area or a crowded beach or hotel parking lot. As much as possible, do not leave anything

valuable in your car, ever. If you must do so, pack all valuables out of sight *before* arriving at your destination, where thieves may be hanging out and waiting to see what you put in the trunk. Some locals leave their car doors unlocked with the windows rolled down to discourage break-ins and avoid costly damages.

Tsunami

On average, tsunami (incorrectly called tidal waves – the Japanese term *tsunami* means 'harbor wave') occur about once a decade in Hawaii and have killed more people statewide than all other natural disasters combined. The tsunami warning system is tested on the first working day of each month at 11:45am for less than one minute, using the yellow speakers mounted on telephone poles around the islands.

It's highly unlikely that a natural disaster will occur while you're here, but earthquakes as far away as Japan, New Zealand or Chile can send tsunami racing across the Pacific Ocean toward Hawaii. If you hear tsunami warning sirens, head for higher ground immediately. The front sections of telephone books have maps of tsunami safety evacuation zones. Turn on the radio or TV for news bulletins. For more information, visit the websites of the **Pacific Disaster Center** (www.pdc.org) and **Hawaii State Civil Defense** (www.scd.hawaii.gov).

Shopping

If you're looking for high-quality handmade Hawaiian art and crafts (see p603), prepare for high prices – the real stuff ain't cheap. The best way to ensure that what you buy is authentic Hawaiiana is to shop at well-respected art galleries and artists cooperatives. Farmers markets are great places for well-priced crafts, often sold by the artist,

INTERNATIONAL VISITORS

Entering Hawaii

» Depending on your country of origin, the rules for entering the country keep changing. Double-check current visa and passport requirements *before* coming to the USA.

» For up-to-date information about entry requirements and eligibility, check the visa section of the **US Department of State website** (http://travel.state.gov) and the travel section of the **US Customs & Border Protection website** (www.cbp.gov).

» Upon arrival in the US, most foreign visitors (excluding for now, many Canadian citizens) must register with the **US-Visit program** (www.dhs.gov/us-visit), which entails having electronic (inkless) fingerprints and a digital photo taken; the process usually takes less than a minute.

PASSPORTS

» A **machine-readable passport (MRP)** is required for all foreign citizens to enter Hawaii.

» Your passport must be valid for six months beyond your expected dates of stay in the USA.

» If your passport was issued/renewed after October 26, 2006, you need an 'e-passport' with a digital photo and an integrated chip containing biometric data.

VISAS

» Currently, under the US **Visa Waiver Program (VWP)**, visas are not required for citizens of 36 countries for stays up to 90 days (no extensions).

» Under the VWP program you must have a return ticket (or onward ticket to any foreign destination) that is nonrefundable in the USA.

» All VWP travelers must register online at least 72 hours before arrival with the **Electronic System for Travel Authorization** (https://esta.cbp.dhs.gov), which currently costs $14. Once approved, registration is valid for two years.

» Foreign travelers who don't qualify for the VWP must apply for a tourist visa. The process is not free, involves a personal interview and can take several weeks, so apply early.

» The website www.usembassy.gov has links for all US embassies abroad. You're better off applying for a visa in your home country rather than while on the road.

Embassies & Consulates

Hawaii has no foreign embassies. O'ahu has a few consulates in O'ahu, including the following:

» **Australia** (☎529-8100; Penthouse, 1000 Bishop St)

» **Japan** (☎543-3111; 1742 Nu'uanu Ave)

» **Korea** (☎595-6109; 2756 Pali Hwy)

» **Netherlands** (☎531-6897; Suite 702, 745 Fort St Mall)

» **New Zealand** (☎595-2200; 3929 Old Pali Rd)

Money

For US dollar exchange rates, see p18.

Post

» The **US Postal Service** (USPS; ☎800-275-8777; www.usps.com) is inexpensive and reliable.

» Mail delivery to/from Hawaii usually takes slightly longer than on the US mainland.

» To send urgent or important letters and packages, **Federal Express** (FedEx; ☎800-463-3339; www.fedex.com) and **United Parcel Service** (UPS; ☎800-782-7892; www.ups.com) offer door-to-door delivery.

but sometimes it can be hard to distinguish cheap imports from locally made articles.

Specialty food items are a classic Hawaii gift, but make sure that any fresh food or produce has been commercially packaged and approved for travel (or you'll be forced to surrender your pineapples at the airport). The same holds for flowers: make sure any orchids, anthuriums or proteas are inspected and approved for travel by the US Department of Agriculture. International visitors should check with their airline about agricultural restrictions in their home country.

Telephone
Cell Phones
Check with your service provider about using your phone in Hawaii. In terms of US providers, Verizon has the most extensive network, but AT&T, Cingular and Sprint are decent. Cellular coverage is best on O'ahu, more spotty on Neighbor Islands and nonexistent in many remote areas.

International travelers need a multiband GSM phone in order to make calls in the USA. With an unlocked multiband phone, popping in a US prepaid rechargeable SIM card is usually cheaper than using your own network. SIM cards are available at any major telecommunications or electronics store. If your phone doesn't work in the USA, these stores also sell inexpensive prepaid phones, including some airtime.

Dialing Codes
» All Hawaii phone numbers consist of a three-digit area code (☎808) followed by a seven-digit local number.
» To call long-distance from one Hawaiian Island to another, dial ☎1-808 + local number.
» Always dial ☎1 before toll-free numbers (☎800, 888, etc). Some toll-free numbers only work within Hawaii or

from the US mainland (and possibly Canada).
» To make international calls from Hawaii, dial ☎011 + country code + area code + local number.
» To call Hawaii from abroad, the international country code for the USA is ☎1.

Useful Numbers
» Emergency (police, fire, ambulance) ☎911
» Local directory assistance ☎411
» Long-distance directory assistance ☎1-(area code)-555-1212
» Toll-free directory assistance ☎1-800-555-1212
» Operator ☎0

Payphones & Phonecards
» Pay phones are a dying breed, usually found in shopping centers, hotels and public places.
» Some payphones are coin-operated (local calls usually cost 50¢), while others only accept credit cards or phonecards.
» Private prepaid phone cards are available from convenience stores, newsstands, supermarkets and pharmacies.

Time
» Hawaii-Aleutian Standard Time (HST) is GMT minus 10 hours.
» Hawaii doesn't observe Daylight Saving Time (DST).
» When it's noon in Honolulu, it's 2pm in Los Angeles (3pm during DST), 10pm in London (11pm during DST) and 8am the next day in Sydney (9am during DST).

Tourist Information
The most convenient place to pick up information is at the airport. In the arrivals areas there are staffed tourist-information desks, and while

you're waiting for your bags to appear on the carousel, you can peruse racks of free tourist brochures and magazines, such as **101 Things to Do** (www.101thingstodo.com) and **This Week** (www.thisweek.com).

For pre-trip planning, call or consult the information-packed website of the **Hawaii Visitors & Convention Bureau** (☎800-464-2924; www.gohawaii.com). Local tourist information centers and visitor bureaus throughout Hawaii are listed in the individual island chapters.

Travelers with Disabilities
» Major hotels and resorts in Hawaii have elevators, TDD-capable phones and wheelchair-accessible rooms (reserve these in advance).
» Telephone companies provide relay operators (dial ☎711) for the hearing impaired.
» Many banks provide ATM instructions in Braille.
» City intersections have dropped curbs and sometimes audible crossing signals.
» Guide and service dogs are not subject to the same quarantine requirements as other pets; contact the Department of Agriculture's **Animal Quarantine Station** (☎808-483-7151; http://hawaii.gov/hdoa/ai/aqs/guidedog) for details.

Transportation
» Where available on the islands, public transportation is wheelchair-accessible.
» Some major car-rental agencies (p640) offer hand-controlled vehicles and vans with wheelchair lifts, but you'll need to reserve these well in advance.
» If you have a disability parking placard from home, bring it with you and display it inside your rental vehicle when using designated disabled-parking spaces.

Flash floods, rock falls, tsunami, earthquakes, volcanic eruptions, shark attacks, jellyfish stings and, yes, even possibly getting brained by a falling coconut — the potential dangers of traveling in Hawaii might seem alarming at first. But like the old saying goes, statistically you're more likely to get hurt crossing the street at home.

Of course, that's not to say that you shouldn't be careful. It's best to educate yourself first about potential risks to your health and safety. This advice becomes even more important when you're engaged in outdoor activities in a new and unfamiliar natural environment, whether that's an island snorkeling spot, a jungle waterfall, a high-altitude mountain or an active (and thus unpredictable) volcanic eruption zone.

Wherever you choose to explore on the islands, remember to mind your manners and watch your step. Hawaii has strict laws about trespassing on both private land and government land not intended for public use. Trespassing is always illegal, no matter how many other people you see doing it. As a visitor to the islands, it's important to respect all 'Kapu' or 'No Trespassing' signs. Always seek explicit permission from the land owner or local officials before venturing onto private or public land that is closed to the public, regardless of whether it is fenced or signposted as such. Doing so not only respects the *kuleana* (rights) of local residents and the sacredness of the land, but also helps to ensure your own safety.

For ecotravel tips on how to tread lightly on Hawaii's land and conserve its sea life, see p625. For tips on dealing with some common travelers' health concerns, from animal bites and infections to heat exhaustion and vog, turn to p642.

Helpful Resources

Access Aloha Travel (☎545-1143, 800-480-1143; www.accessalohatravel.com) Established local travel agency can help book wheelchair-accessible accommodations, rental vans and sightseeing tours and cruises.

Disability & Communication Access Board (☎586-8121; www.hawaii.gov/health/dcab/travel; Room 101, 919 Ala Moana Blvd, Honolulu) Online 'Traveler Tips' brochures provide information about airports, accessible transportation, sightseeing, and medical and other support services on the main islands only.

MossRehab Resource Net (www.mossresourcenet .org/travel.htm) Useful links and general information for enabling accessible travel.

Wheelchair Getaways (☎800-638-1912; www.wheel chairgetaways.com) Rents wheelchair-accessible vans on Hawai'i the Big Island, Maui and Kaua'i.

Work

US citizens can pursue work in Hawaii as they would in any other state – the problem is finding a job. Foreign visitors in the USA on tourist visas are not legally allowed to take employment. To work legally, foreigners must secure sponsorship from an employer or international work-exchange program and apply for a visa before leaving home.

Finding serious 'professional' employment is difficult because Hawaii has a tight labor market. The biggest exceptions are for teachers and medical professionals. Those in the latter category can browse classified ads online at **Hawaii-Jobs** (http://jobshawaii.com).

Otherwise, joining the waitstaff of tourist-area restaurants and bars is the most likely employment opportunity. Folks with foreign-language, scuba, fishing or guiding skills might investigate employment with resorts. Most housekeeping or groundskeeping jobs at hotels and resorts go to locals.

In addition to notice boards in hostels, coffeeshops and natural-foods stores, check the classified ads in the **Honolulu Star-Advertiser** (www.staradvertiser.com) daily newspaper and at **Craigslist** (www.craigslist.org) online. Continue surfing at **HireNet Hawaii** (www.hirenethawaii .com), run by Hawaii's **Department of Labor & Industrial Relations** (☎586-8700; http://hawaii.gov/labor; 830 Punchbowl St, Honolulu).

Transportation

GETTING THERE & AWAY

Roughly 99% of visitors to Hawaii arrive by air, and the majority of flights – both international and domestic – arrive at Honolulu International Airport on O'ahu. Nonstop and direct flights to the Neighbor Islands are increasingly available (and costly). Flights and tours can be booked online at www.lonelyplanet.com/bookings.

Air

Airports

The majority of incoming flights from overseas and the US mainland arrive at **Honolulu International Airport** (HNL; http://hawaii.gov/hnl) on O'ahu.

Following are the main Neighbor Island airports:

Big Island East Hawaii **Hilo International Airport** (ITO; http://hawaii.gov/ito) West Hawaii **Kona International Airport at Keahole** (KOA; http://hawaii.gov/koa)

Maui Kahului airport (OGG; http://hawaii.gov/ogg)

Lana'i Lana'i airport (LNY; http://hawaii.gov/lny)

Moloka'i Moloka'i airport (MKK; http://hawaii.gov/mkk)

Kaua'i Lihu'e airport (LIH; http://hawaii.gov/lih)

Note that flights to Lana'i and Moloka'i originate from either Honolulu or Maui. For more information on flights to individual islands, see p638.

Tickets

Hawaii is a competitive market for US domestic and international airfares, which vary tremendously by season, demand, number of stopovers etc.

Competition is highest among airlines flying to Honolulu from major US mainland cities, and the 'lowest fare' fluctuates constantly. In general, return fares from the US mainland to Hawaii cost $350 (in low season from the West Coast) to $800-plus (in high season from the East Coast).

AirTech (☎212-219-7000; www.airtech.com) has cheap flights between the West Coast and Hawaii. However, you must be flexible: AirTech sells last-minute seats and doesn't guarantee a specific flight. Flights currently depart from San Francisco and Los Angeles to Honolulu and Maui year-round, and seasonally to Hawai'i the Big Island.

Vacation Packages

Vacation packages offered by major airlines and travel booking websites sometimes are the cheapest option. Basic packages cover airfare and accommodations, while deluxe ones include car rental, activities and even island hopping. **Pleasant Holidays** (☎800-742-9244; www.pleasantholidays.com) offers competitive vacation packages from the US mainland.

CLIMATE CHANGE & TRAVEL

Every form of transport that relies on carbon-based fuel generates CO_2, the main cause of human-induced climate change. Modern travel is dependent on aeroplanes, which might use less fuel per kilometer per person than most cars but travel much greater distances. The altitude at which aircraft emit gases (including CO_2) and particles also contributes to their climate change impact. Many websites offer 'carbon calculators' that allow people to estimate the carbon emissions generated by their journey and, for those who wish to do so, to offset the impact of the greenhouse gases emitted with contributions to portfolios of climate-friendly initiatives throughout the world. Lonely Planet offsets the carbon footprint of all staff and author travel.

Sea

Most cruises to Hawaii include stopovers in Honolulu and on Maui, Kaua'i and the Big Island. Cruises usually last two weeks, with fares starting around $100 per person per day, based on double occupancy; airfare to/from the departure point costs extra.

Popular cruise lines visiting Hawaii:

Holland America (☎877-932-4259; www.holland america.com) Departures from San Diego, Seattle and Vancouver.

Princess (☎800-774-6237; www.princess.com) Departures mainly from Los Angeles.

Royal Caribbean (☎866-562-7625; www.royalcaribbean .com) Typically departs from Vancouver, but some cruises start in Honolulu and finish in Vancouver.

For interisland cruises that start and end in Hawaii, see p639.

GETTING AROUND

Most interisland travel is by plane, but a limited number of ferries connect a few islands. Renting a car is usually necessary if you want to explore, although public transportation exists on the bigger islands, notably O'ahu.

Air

Hawaii's major airports handling most interisland traffic are Honolulu (O'ahu), Kahului (Maui), Kailua-Kona and Hilo (Hawai'i the Big Island), and Lihu'e (Kaua'i). See p637 for these airports' codes and websites.

Airlines in Hawaii

Two major interisland carriers – reliable Hawaiian Airlines and upstart go! (operated by Mesa Airlines) – offer frequent scheduled flights in jet planes between Honolulu and the main Neighbor Islands (Maui, Kaua'i and Hawai'i the Big Island).

Two smaller, commuter-oriented airlines – Island Air and Mokulele Airlines – provide scheduled service in both prop and jet planes to the main islands, as well as to Moloka'i and Lana'i.

These commuter airlines and a few other tiny airlines – like Pacific Wings – are the only ones that fly to secondary airports, such as Hana on Maui and Waimea-Kohala on the Big Island. Many of these smaller airlines also offer charters. Flights in small turboprop planes fly so low they almost double as sightseeing excursions – fun!

Expect further schedule changes and possible shake-ups in the interisland biz. When this book went to press, the main interisland air carriers were the following:

go! (☎888-435-9462; www. iflygo.com) Flies frequently from its Honolulu hub to Kaua'i, Maui and the Big Island.

Hawaiian Airlines (☎800-367-5320; www.hawaiianair .com) Flies nearly 200 daily routes on 717s and 767s between Honolulu, Kaua'i, Maui and the Big Island, with code-share flights to Moloka'i and Lana'i.

Island Air (☎800-388-1105; www.islandair.com) Flies 37 passenger turboprop jet planes from hubs in Honolulu (to all Neighbor Islands except the Big Island) and Maui (to all but Lana'i).

Mokulele Airlines (☎866-260-7070; www.mokuleleair lines.com) Scheduled service to all six islands, in both prop and small jet aircraft; partners with go! airlines.

Pacific Wings (☎888-575-4546; www.pacificwings.com) Charter single-engine Cessnas between all the islands except for Kaua'i.

For more information on flights to/from individual islands, also see the Getting There & Away sections near the start of the island chapters.

Tickets & Reservations

Given the intense competition between airlines, interisland airfares vary wildly. Expect to pay around $60 to $180 one way. Flights to islands with less frequent service, or which are furthest from each other, are more expensive. Round-trip fares are usually double the one-way fares without any additional discounts. It's usually best to buy tickets via the airlines' websites, which post internet-only fares and other promotions.

While it's often possible to walk up and get on a flight among the four main islands (particularly to/from Honolulu), advance reservations are recommended, especially for peak hours (and to secure the cheapest fares). Airline regulations concerning surfboards and oversize equipment vary and can be restrictive – ask before booking.

Bicycle

Cycling around the islands is a great, nonpolluting way to travel, but as a primary mode of transportation can be challenging. All islands have narrow highways, dangerous traffic and changeable weather. Long-distance cycling is best done with a tour group, but if you're adventurous and in good shape, it can be done on your own. Some islands are better for this than others; see the Getting Around sections at the start of the island chapters for specifics.

Rental

» Usually only resort areas and specialty bicycle shops rent beach cruisers, hybrids and road or mountain bikes.

» Rental rates average $15 to $35 per day (more for high-tech bikes); multiday and weekly discounts may be available.

» Some B&Bs, guesthouses and hostels rent or loan bicycles to guests.

Road Rules

» Generally, bicycles are required to follow the same laws and rules of the road as cars. Bicycles are prohibited on freeways and sidewalks.

» State law requires all cyclists under the age of 16 to wear helmets.

» For more bicycling information, as well as maps of current and proposed bike lanes by island, check the **Department of Transportation website** (http://hawaii.gov/dot/highways/Bike/bikeplan/index.htm).

» For recommended cycling and mountain-biking routes, turn to p41.

Transporting Bicycles

» Bringing your own bike to Hawaii costs $100 (or more) on flights from the US mainland, while interisland flights charge $35 (or more) to transport your bike.

» Check your bicycle at the airline counter, the same as any baggage, but it will need to be boxed or prepared by wrapping the handlebars and pedals in foam, or fixing the handlebars to the side and removing the pedals.

» Some local buses are equipped with front-loading bicycle racks (a small surcharge may apply).

Boat

Interisland ferry service is surprisingly limited in Hawaii. Currently, only Moloka'i (p435) and Lana'i (p415) have regular, passenger-only public ferry service to/from Lahaina, Maui.

Norwegian Cruise Line (☎866-234-7350; www.ncl.com) is the only company offering cruises that both start and end in Hawaii. Seven-day interisland cruises make round-trips from Honolulu and visit the four main islands (from $999 per person).

For cruises to the Hawaiian Islands, see p638.

Bus

O'ahu's islandwide public transportation system, called **TheBus**, makes O'ahu the easiest island to get around without a car. Schedules are frequent, service is reliable and fares are inexpensive. That said, TheBus doesn't go everywhere – for example, to most hiking trailheads.

Public bus systems on the Neighbor Islands are more geared toward resident commuters; service is infrequent and limited to bigger towns, sometimes bypassing tourist destinations entirely.

» After O'ahu, the next best system is **Maui Bus** but it doesn't reach Hana or Haleakalā National Park.

» The Big Island's **Hele-On Bus** will get you around to most island towns (and includes Hawai'i Volcanoes National Park), but schedules are too limited for sightseeing.

» **Kaua'i Bus** can take visitors between the major island towns and as far north as Hanalei, but doesn't reach Waimea Canyon.

Car

Most visitors to Hawaii rent their own vehicles, particularly on Neighbor Islands. If you're just visiting Honolulu and Waikiki, a car may be more of a hindrance than a help.

Automobile Associations

AAA has reciprocal agreements with automobile associations in other countries, but be sure to bring your membership card from home. **American Automobile Association** (AAA; ☎593-2221, 800-736-2886 from Neighbor Islands; www.hawaii.aaa.com; 1130 N Nimitz Hwy, Honolulu; ☺9am-5pm Mon-Fri, 9am-2pm Sat) On O'ahu, AAA's only Hawaii office provides members with free maps

and travel information. AAA members also enjoy discounts on select car rentals, air tickets, hotels and sightseeing attractions. For emergency roadside service and towing, members should call ☎800-222-4357.

Driver's License

» The minimum age for driving in Hawaii is 18 years.

» International visitors can legally drive in Hawaii with a valid driver's license issued by their home country.

» Car-rental companies will generally accept foreign driver's licenses, but only if they're written in English.

» If your foreign driver's license isn't in English, be prepared to present an International Driving Permit (IDP), obtainable in your home country.

Fuel

» Gasoline (petrol) is readily available everywhere on the islands except along a few remote roads (eg Saddle Rd on the Big Island, the Road to Hana on Maui).

» Gas prices in Hawaii currently average $3.85 to $4.35 per US gallon. As a rule of thumb, expect to pay at least 50¢ more per gallon than on the US mainland.

Insurance

» Legally required by the state of Hawaii, liability insurance covers any people or property that you might hit.

» For damage to the actual rental vehicle, a collision damage waiver (CDW) is available for an extra $15 to $20 a day.

» If you decline a CDW, you will be held liable for any damages up to the full value of the car.

» Even with a CDW, you may be required to pay the first $100 to $500 for repairs; some agencies will also charge you for the rental cost of the car during the entire time it takes to be repaired.

» If you have collision coverage on your vehicle at home, it might cover damages to car rentals; ask your insurance agent in advance of your trip.

» Some credit cards offer reimbursement coverage for collision damages if you rent the car with that credit card; again, check this before you leave home.

» Most credit-card coverage isn't valid for rentals over 15 days or for 'exotic' models (eg convertibles, 4WD Jeeps).

Rental

AGENCIES

» Most rental companies require that you be at least 25 years old, possess a valid driver's license and have a major credit card, not a debit or check card.

» A few major companies will rent to drivers between the ages of 21 and 24, typically for a surcharge of around $25 per day; call ahead to check.

» Without a credit card, many agencies simply won't rent you a vehicle, while others require prepayment by cash or traveler's checks, a deposit of $200 per week, proof of return airfare and more.

» When picking up your vehicle, most agencies will request the name and phone number of the place where you're staying.

» Some agencies are reluctant to rent to visitors who list a campground as their address, and a few specifically add 'No Camping Permitted' to rental contracts. Major car-rental agencies in Hawaii, some of which may offer 'green' hybrid models and carbon offsetting:

Advantage (☎800-777-5500; www.advantage.com) O'ahu and Maui only.

Alamo (☎877-222-9075; www.alamo.com)

Avis (☎800-331-1212; www.avis.com)

Budget (☎800-527-0700; www.budget.com)

Dollar (☎800-800-3665; www.dollar.com)

Enterprise (☎800-261-7331; www.enterprise.com)

Hertz (☎800-654-3131; www.hertz.com)

National (☎877-222-9058; www.nationalcar.com)

Thrifty (☎800-847-4389; www.thrifty.com)

Most islands also have one or two independent car-rental agencies, and these are worth checking out – on Maui, it's the only way to rent a biofuel car (p322), and on the Big Island, it's the only way to rent a 4WD that's allowed on Mauna Kea's summit road (p171). Independent agencies are also more likely to rent to drivers under 25 and/or offer deals on one-day rentals, especially 4WD vehicles.

RATES

» The daily rate for renting a small car usually ranges from $35 to $75, while typical weekly rates are $150 to $300.

» When getting quotes, always ask for the full rate including taxes, fees and surcharges, which can easily add more than $5 a day to any rental.

» Rental rates usually include unlimited mileage, though if you drop off the car at a different location than where you picked it up, expect a hefty surcharge.

RESERVATIONS

Always make reservations in advance. With most car-rental companies there's little or no cancellation penalty if you change your mind before arrival. Walking up to the counter without a reservation will subject you to higher rates, and during busy periods it's not uncommon for all cars to be rented out, even in Honolulu. Reservations are always essential on Lana'i and Moloka'i. For child safety seats rentals ($10 per day, maximum $50), reserve them when booking your car.

Road Conditions & Hazards

» The main hazards are usually narrow, winding or steep roads that wash out after heavy rains. Every island has several, as noted in each island chapter.

» Drunk drivers can also be a hazard; in some rural areas, so can livestock on the road.

» On unpaved or potholed roads, locals may hog the middle stripe until an oncoming car approaches.

» Don't drive your standard car on 4WD roads, which is usually prohibited by rental companies and will void damage-insurance coverage. Always ask when booking about the company's road restrictions for its vehicles.

» If you get into trouble with your car, towing is mighty expensive in Hawaii – avoid it at all costs.

Road Rules

Slow, courteous driving is the rule in Hawaii, not the exception. Locals don't honk (unless they're about to crash), they don't follow close and they let people pass. Do the same, and you may get an appreciative *shaka* (Hawaiian hand greeting sign) from other drivers.

» As on the US mainland, drive on the right-hand side of the road.

» Speed limits are posted and enforced. If you're stopped for speeding, expect a ticket, as police rarely just give warnings.

» Turning right on red is allowed (unless a sign prohibits it), but island drivers usually wait for the green light.

» At four-way stop signs, cars proceed in order of arrival. If two cars arrive simultaneously, the one on the right has the right of way. When in doubt, politely wave the other driver ahead.

LOST?

Street addresses on some Hawaiian highways may seem random, but there's a pattern. For hyphenated numbers, such as 4-736 Kuhio Hwy, the first part of the number identifies the post office district and the second part identifies the street address. Thus, it's possible for 4-736 to be followed by 5-002; you've just entered a new district, that's all.

» For one-lane-bridge crossings, one direction of traffic usually has the right of way while the other must obey the posted yield sign.

» Downhill traffic must yield to uphill traffic where there is no sign.

» Diamond-marked carpool lanes are reserved for high-occupancy vehicles during morning and afternoon rush hours.

» When emergency vehicles (ie police, fire or ambulance) approach from either direction, carefully pull over to the side of the road.

Safety Laws

» Talking or texting on a cell phone or mobile device while driving is illegal.

» Driving under the influence (DUI) of alcohol or drugs is a serious criminal offense (see p632).

» The use of seat belts is required for the driver, front-seat passengers and all children under age 18.

» Child safety seats are mandatory for children aged three and younger; children aged four to seven who are under 4ft 9in tall must ride in a booster seat or be secured by a lap-only belt in the back seat.

Hitchhiking

Hitchhiking is illegal statewide.

Moped & Motorcycle

Moped and motorcycle rentals are not common in Hawaii, but are available in some resort areas. Surprisingly, they can be more expensive to rent than cars. Rental mopeds cost from $35/175 per day/week, while motorcycles start around $100/500 per day/week, depending on the make and model.

Road Rules

» You can legally drive a moped in Hawaii with a valid driver's license issued by your home state or country. Motorcyclists will need to have a specially endorsed motorcycle license.

» The minimum age for renting a moped is 16; for a motorcycle it's 21.

» State law requires mopeds to be ridden by one person only and prohibits their use on sidewalks and freeways.

» Mopeds must always be driven in single file and may not be driven at speeds in excess of 30mph.

Safety Tips

» Helmets are not required in the state of Hawaii, but moped and motorcycle rental agencies often provide free helmets – use 'em.

» Riding on the windward sides of the islands may require foul-weather gear, as it rains often.

Taxi

» All the main islands have taxis, with metered fares based on mileage, although a few drivers may offer flat rates.

» Taxi rates vary, as they're set by each county, but average $3.25 at flagfall, then $3 or more per additional mile.

» Since taxis are often station wagons or minivans, they're good value for groups (maximum number of passengers is usually four).

» Outside of Honolulu and Waikiki, and at most hotels and resorts, travelers will have to call ahead for a taxi.

» Taxi pick ups from remote locations (such as after a long one-way hike) sometimes can be arranged in advance.

Tours

For cruises around the Hawaiian Islands, see p639.

Popular land, air and sea-based tour companies operating on the main islands include the following:

Road Scholar (☎800-454-5768; www.roadscholar.org) Formerly Elderhostel, Road Scholar offers educational programs for those aged 50 or older. Many focus on Hawaii's people and culture, while others explore the natural environment.

Roberts Hawaii (☎on O'ahu 954-8652, from the Neighbor Islands & US mainland 866-898-2519; www.robertshawaii. com) If you want to visit another island while you're in Hawaii but only have a day or two to spare, consider an island-hopping tour to the Neighbor Islands.

Many local companies also operate half- and full-day sightseeing bus tours on each island. Specialized adventure tours, such as whale-watching cruises and snorkeling trips, are available on all the main islands. Helicopter tours are offered mostly on Hawai'i the Big Island, Maui and Kaua'i. For chartered sightseeing flights, contact the airlines listed on p638. All of these tours can be booked after arrival in Hawaii, but if your schedule is tight or you're visiting during peak times, reserve ahead.

Health

BEFORE YOU GO

» If your policy from home won't cover you in Hawaii, purchase travel health insurance (p631).

» Bring any medications you may need in their original containers, clearly labeled.

» Carry a signed, dated letter from your doctor describing all medical conditions and medications (including generic names).

IN HAWAII

» For immediate medical assistance anywhere in Hawaii, call ☑911.

» If you have a medical emergency, go to the emergency room (ER) of the nearest hospital.

» If the nearest hospital is not close by, your best choice may be an expensive stand-alone, for-profit, urgent-care center.

» If the medical problem isn't urgent, phone around to find a local physician who will accept your insurance.

» Some insurance policies require you to get pre-authorization for medical treatment from a call center before seeking help. Keep all medical receipts and documentation.

Infectious Diseases

Dengue Fever

» In Hawaii the last dengue fever outbreak was in 2002; for updates, consult the **Hawaii State Department of Health website** (www.state.hi.us/doh).

» Dengue is transmitted by aedes mosquitoes, which bite preferentially during the daytime and breed primarily in artificial water containers (like barrels, plastic containers and discarded tires).

» Dengue usually causes flulike symptoms, including fever, muscle aches, joint pains, severe headaches, nausea and vomiting, often followed by a rash.

» If you suspect you've been infected, see a doctor to be diagnosed and monitored; severe cases may require hospitalization.

» Do not take aspirin or NSAIDs (eg ibuprofen), which can cause hemorrhaging.

Giardiasis

» Symptoms of this parasitic infection of the small intestine include nausea, bloating, cramps and diarrhea, and may last for weeks.

» To protect yourself, don't drink from waterfalls, ponds, streams and rivers, which may be contaminated by animal or human feces.

» Giardiasis is diagnosed by a stool test and treated with antibiotics.

Leptospirosis

» Leptospirosis is acquired by exposure to water contaminated by the urine of infected animals, especially rodents.

» Outbreaks often occur after flooding, when overflow contaminates water sources downstream from livestock or wild animal habitats.

» Initial symptoms, which resemble a mild flu, usually subside uneventfully in a few days, but a minority of cases involve potentially fatal complications.

» Diagnosis is through blood and/or urine tests and treatment is with antibiotics.

» Minimize your risk by staying out of bodies of freshwater (eg pools, streams, waterfalls); avoid these entirely if you have open cuts or sores.

» Take trailhead warning signs about leptospirosis seriously. If you're camping, water purification and good hygiene are essential.

Staphylococcus

» Hawaii leads the nation in staphylococcus infections, having over twice the rate of infection as on the US mainland.

» Staph infections are caused by bacteria that enter the body through an open wound.

» To prevent infection, practice good hygiene (eg wash your hands frequently, shower or bathe daily, wear clean, dry clothing) and stay out of recreational water with any open cuts or sores.

» If a wound becomes painful, looks red, inflamed or swollen or leaks pus, seek medical help. Some types of staph infection are now antibiotic-resistant.

Environmental Hazards

Altitude Sickness

» Acute Mountain Sickness (AMS), aka altitude sickness, may develop at elevations greater than 8000ft.

» Being physically fit offers no protection; the risk increases with faster ascents, higher altitudes and greater exertion.

» When traveling to high altitudes, avoid overexertion, eat light meals and abstain from alcohol.

» Initial symptoms of AMS may include headaches, nausea, vomiting, dizziness, malaise, insomnia and loss of appetite.

» The best treatment for AMS is descent. If you are exhibiting symptoms, stop ascending. If symptoms are severe or persistent, descend immediately.

» If symptoms are more than mild or don't resolve promptly, see a doctor, as altitude sickness can be life-threatening when severe.

Bites & Stings

Any animal bite or scratch – including from unknown dogs, feral pigs, etc – should be promptly and thoroughly cleansed with soap and water, followed by application of an antiseptic (eg iodine, alcohol) to prevent wounds from becoming infected.

Hawaii is currently rabies-free. The state has no established wild snake population, but snakes are occasionally seen, especially in sugarcane fields.

INSECTS

» The most effective protections against insect bites are common-sense behavior and clothing: wear long sleeves and pants, a hat and shoes.

» Where mosquitoes are active, apply a good insect repellent, preferably one containing DEET (but not for children under two years old).

» Some spider bites (eg from black widows or brown recluses) contain toxic venom, which children are more vulnerable to, for anyone who is bitten, apply ice or cool water to the affected area, then seek medical help.

» Centipedes also give painful bites; they can infiltrate buildings, so check sheets and shoes.

» Leeches found in humid rainforest areas do not transmit any disease but their bites can be intensely itchy, even for weeks afterward.

MARINE ANIMALS

Marine spikes, such as those found on sea urchins, scorpion fish and Hawaiian lionfish, can cause severe local pain. If this occurs, immediately immerse the affected area in hot water (as hot as can be tolerated). Keep topping up with hot water until the pain subsides and medical care can be reached. The same advice applies if you are stung by a cone shell.

Stings from jellyfish and Portuguese man-of-war (aka bluebottles) also occur in Hawaii's tropical waters (for more information, visit www.808jellyfish.com). Even touching a bluebottle hours after it's washed up onshore can result in burning stings. Jellyfish are often seen eight to 10 days after a full moon, when they float into shallow near-shore waters. If you are stung, rinse (or carefully peel) off the tentacles, then immerse the affected area in hot water (see above), followed by rapid transfer to a hospital; antivenins are available.

Heat

When it's hot:

» Drink plenty of fluids (minimum one gallon per day) to prevent dehydration.

» Eat enough salty foods – when you sweat, you lose electrolytes, too.

» Avoid strenuous exercise (eg hiking across lava or at high altitudes).

» Apply sunscreen (SPF 30 or higher) regularly, even on cloudy days.

» Wear a hat, preferably one with a wide brim.

HEAT EXHAUSTION

» Symptoms include feeling weak; headache; irritability; nausea or vomiting; dizziness; muscle cramps; heavy sweating and/or cool, clammy skin; a fast, weak pulse; and a normal or slightly elevated body temperature.

» Treatment involves getting out of the heat and/or sun to rest, removing clothing that retains heat (cotton is OK), cooling skin with a wet cloth and fanning continuously, and rehydrating with water.

» Recovery is usually rapid, though you may feel weak for days afterwards.

HEATSTROKE

» Heatstroke is a serious medical emergency that can be fatal.

» Symptoms come on suddenly and include weakness; nausea; hot, flushed and dry skin (sweating stops); elevated body temperature; dizziness; confusion; headaches; hyperventilation; loss of coordination; and eventually seizures, collapse and loss of consciousness.

» Seek medical help and rapidly commence cooling by getting the person out of the heat; removing clothes and covering them with a wet cloth or towel; fanning them vigorously; and applying ice or cold packs to the neck, armpits and groin.

Vog

» Vog, a visible haze or smog caused by volcanic emissions on the Big Island, is usually dispersed by trade winds.

» Short-term exposure is not generally hazardous, however, high sulfur-dioxide levels can create breathing problems for some.

» For more about vog, see p296.

Glossary

For food terms, see p601

'a'a – type of lava that is rough and jagged

ae'o – Hawaiian black-necked stilt

'ahinahina – silversword plant with pointed silver leaves

ahu – stone cairns used to mark a trail; an altar or shrine

ahupua'a – traditional land division, usually in a wedge shape that extends from the mountains to the sea (smaller than a *moku*)

'aina – land

'akala – Hawaiian raspberry; also called a thimbleberry

'akohekohe – Maui parrotbill

'alae ke'oke'o – endangered Hawaiian coot

'alae 'ula – Hawaiian moorhen

'alauahio – Maui creeper

ali'i – chief, royalty

ali'i nui – high chiefs

aloha – the traditional greeting meaning love, welcome, good-bye

aloha 'aina – love of the land

'amakihi – small, yellow-green honeycreeper; one of the more common native birds

anchialine pool – contains a mixture of seawater and freshwater

'apapane – bright red native Hawaiian honeycreeper

a'u – marlin

'aumakua – protective deity or guardian spirit, deified ancestor or trustworthy person

'awa – see *kava*

'awa 'awa – bitter

azuki bean – often served as a sweetened paste, eg as a topping for shave ice

braguinha – a Portuguese stringed instrument introduced to Hawaii in the late 19th century from which the ukulele is derived

e koko mai – welcome

'elepaio – Hawaiian monarch flycatcher; a brownish native bird with a white rump, common to O'ahu forests

ha – breath

ha'i – high falsetto

haku – head

hala – pandanus tree; the leaves (*lau*) are used in weaving mats and baskets

hale – house

Haloa – the stillborn son of Papa and Wakea, brother to man

haole – Caucasian; literally, 'without breath'

hapa – portion or fragment; person of mixed blood

hapa haole – Hawaiian music with predominantly English lyrics

hapu'u – tree fern

hau – indigenous lowland hibiscus tree whose wood is often used for making canoe outriggers (stabilizing arms that jut out from the hull)

he'e nalu – wave sliding, or surfing

heiau – ancient stone temple; a place of worship in Hawaii

holua – sled or sled course

honi – to share breath

honu – turtle

ho'okipa – hospitality

ho'okupu – offering

ho'olaule'a – celebration, party

ho'onanea – to pass the time in ease, peace and pleasure

hukilau – fishing with a *seine*, involving a group of people who pull in the net

hula – Hawaiian dance form, either traditional or modern

hula 'auana – modern hula, developed after the introduction of Western music

hula halau – hula school or troupe

hula kahiko – traditional hula

'i'iwi – scarlet Hawaiian honeycreeper with a curved, salmon-colored beak

'iliahi – Hawaiian sandalwood

'ilima – native plant, a ground cover with delicate yellow-orange flowers; O'ahu's official flower

'ilio holo kai – 'the dog that runs in the sea'; Hawaiian monk seal

'io – Hawaiian hawk

ipo – sweetheart

ipu – spherical, narrow-necked gourd used as a hula implement

issei – first-generation Japanese immigrants; born in Japan

kahili – a feathered standard, used as a symbol of royalty

kahuna – knowledgable person in any field; commonly a priest, healer or sorcerer

kahuna lapa'au – healer

kahuna nui – high priest(ess)

kalo lo'i – taro fields

kama'aina – person born and raised, or a longtime resident, in Hawaii; literally, 'child of the land'

kanaka – man, human being, person; also Native Hawaiian

kane/Kane – man; if capitalized, the name of one of four main Hawaiian gods

kanikapila – open-mic jam sessions

kanoa – hidden meaning

kapa – see *tapa*

kapu – taboo, part of strict ancient Hawaiian social and religious system

kapuna – elders

kaua – ancient Hawaiian lower class, outcasts

kaunaoa – a yellowish-orange vine used in Lana'i lei

kava – a mildly narcotic drink ('*awa* in Hawaiian) made from the roots of *Piper methysticum,* a pepper shrub

keiki – child

ki – see *ti*

ki ho'alu – slack key

kiawe – a relative of the mesquite tree introduced to Hawaii in the 1820s, now very common; its branches are covered with sharp thorns

kika kila – Hawaiian steel guitar

ki'i – see *tiki*

ki'i akua – temple images

kilau – a stiff, weedy fern

kipuka – an area of land spared when lava flows around it; an oasis

ko – sugarcane

koa – native hardwood tree often used in making native crafts and canoes

koki'o ke'oke'o – native Hawaiian white hibiscus tree

kokua – help, cooperation

koloa maoli – Hawaiian duck

kona – leeward side; a leeward wind

konane – a strategy game similar to checkers

konohiki – caretakers

ko'olau – windward side

Ku – Polynesian god of many manifestations, including god of war, farming and fishing (husband of Hina)

kukui – candlenut tree; the official state tree; its oily nuts were once burned in lamps

kuleana – rights

kumu hula – hula teacher

Kumulipo – Native Hawaiian creation story or chant

kupuna – grandparent, elder

ku'ula/Ku'ula – a stone idol placed at fishing sites, believed to attract fish; if capitalized, the god of fishermen

la'au lapa'au – plant medicine

lanai – veranda; balcony

lau – leaf

lauhala – leaves of the *hala* plant, used in weaving

lei – garland, usually of flowers, but also of leaves or shells

leptospirosis – a disease acquired by exposure to water contaminated by the urine of infected animals, especially rodents

limu – seaweed

lokelani – pink damask rose, or 'rose of heaven'; Maui's official flower

loko i'a – fishpond

loko wai – freshwater fishpond

lolo – stupid, feeble-minded, crazy

lomi – to rub or soften

lomilomi – traditional Hawaiian massage; known as 'loving touch'

Lono – Polynesian god of harvest, agriculture, fertility and peace

loulu – native fan palms

luakini – a type of *heiau* dedicated to the war god Ku and used for human sacrifices

luau – traditional Hawaiian feast

luna – supervisor

mahalo – thank you

mahele – to divide; usually refers to the sugar industry–initiated land divisions of 1848

mahu – a transgendered or cross-dressing male

mai ho'oka'awale – leprosy (Hansen's disease); literally, 'the separating sickness'

mai'a – banana

maile – native plant with twining habit and fragrant leaves; often used for lei

maka'ainana – commoners; literally, 'people who tend the land'

makaha – a sluice gate, used to regulate the level of water in a fishpond

makahiki – traditional annual wet-season winter festival dedicated to the agricultural god Lono

makai – toward the sea; seaward

make – dead

malihini – newcomer, visitor

mamane – a native tree with bright yellow flowers; used to make lei

mamo – a yellow-feathered bird, now extinct

mana – spiritual power

mauka – toward the mountains; inland

mele – song, chant

menehune – 'little people' who, according to legend, built many of Hawaii's fishponds, heiau and other stonework

milo – a native shade tree with beautiful hardwood

moa – jungle fowl

mokihana – a tree with leathery berries that faintly smell of licorice, used in Kaua'i lei

moku – wedge-shaped areas of land running from the ridge of the mountains to the sea

mokupuni – island

mo'i – king

mo'o – water spirit, water lizard or dragon

muumuu – a long, loose-fitting dress introduced by the missionaries

na keiki – children

na'u – fragrant Hawaiian gardenia

naupaka – a native shrub with delicate white flowers

Neighbor Islands – the term used to refer to the main Hawaiian Islands outside of O'ahu

nene – a native goose; Hawaii's state bird

nisei – second-generation Japanese immigrants

niu – coconut palm

no ka 'oi – the best

'ohana – family, extended family; close-knit group

'ohi'a lehua – native Hawaiian tree with tufted, feathery, pom-pom-like flowers

'olelo Hawai'i – the Hawaiian language

oli – chant

olona – a native shrub

'omilu – a type of trevally

'o'o ihe – spear throwing

'ope'ape'a – Hawaiian hoary bat

'opihi – an edible limpet

pahoehoe – type of lava that is quick and smooth-flowing

pakalolo – marijuana; literally, 'crazy smoke'

palaka – Hawaiian-style plaid shirt made from sturdy cotton

pali – cliff

paniolo – cowboy

Papa – earth mother

pau – finished, no more

pa'u – traditional riding, in which lei-bedecked women in flowing dresses ride for show

pau hana – happy hour

Pele – goddess of fire and volcanoes; her home is in Kilauea Caldera

pidgin – distinct local language and dialect, influenced by its multiethnic immigrants

pikake – jasmine flowers

piko – navel, umbilical cord

pili – a bunchgrass, commonly used for thatching houses

pohaku – rock

pohuehue – beach morning glory (a flowering plant)

pono – righteous, respectful and proper

pua aloalo – yellow hibiscus

pua'a waewae loloa – 'long-legged pigs,' an ancient Hawaiian euphemism for human sacrificial victims

pueo – Hawaiian owl

puka – any kind of hole or opening; puka shells are those that are small, white and strung into necklaces

pukiawe – native plant with red and white berries and evergreen leaves

pule – prayers

pulu – the silken clusters encasing the stems of *hapu'u* ferns

pupu – snack or appetizer; also a type of cowry shell

pu'u – hill, cinder cone

pu'uhonua – place of refuge

raku – a style of Japanese pottery characterized by a rough, handmade appearance

rubbah slippah – rubber flip-flops

sansei – third-generation Japanese immigrants

seine – a large net used for fishing

shaka – hand gesture used in Hawaii as a greeting or sign of local pride

shōji – translucent paper-covered wooden sliding doors

stink-eye – dirty look

taiko – Japanese drumming

talk story – to strike up a conversation, make small talk

tapa – cloth made by pounding the bark of paper mulberry, used for early Hawaiian clothing (*kapa* in Hawaiian)

ti – common native plant; its long shiny leaves are used for wrapping food and making hula skirts (*ki* in Hawaiian)

tiki – wood- or stone-carved statue, usually depicting a deity (*ki'i* in Hawaiian)

tutu – grandmother or grandfather; also term of respect for any member of that generation

'ua'u – dark-rumped petrel

ukulele – a stringed musical instrument derived from the *braguinha*, which was introduced to Hawaii in the 1800s by Portuguese immigrants

'uli'uli – gourd rattle containing seeds and decorated with feathers, used as a hula implement

'ulu – breadfruit

'ulu maika – ancient Hawaiian stone bowling game

wa'a kaulua – an ancient Hawaiian long-distance sailing vessel

wahi pana – sacred place

Wakea – sky father

warabi – fiddlehead fern

wauke – paper mulberry, used to make *tapa*

wiliwili – the lightest of the native woods

zendo – communal Zen meditation hall

behind the scenes

SEND US YOUR FEEDBACK

We love to hear from travelers – your comments keep us on our toes and help make our books better. Our well-traveled team reads every word on what you loved or loathed about this book. Although we cannot reply individually to postal submissions, we always guarantee that your feedback goes straight to the appropriate authors, in time for the next edition. Each person who sends us information is thanked in the next edition – and the most useful submissions are rewarded with a free book.

Visit **lonelyplanet.com/contact** to submit your updates and suggestions or to ask for help. Our award-winning website also features inspirational travel stories, news and discussions.

Note: We may edit, reproduce and incorporate your comments in Lonely Planet products such as guidebooks, websites and digital products, so let us know if you don't want your comments reproduced or your name acknowledged. For a copy of our privacy policy visit lonelyplanet.com/privacy.

OUR READERS

Many thanks to the travelers who used the last edition and wrote to us with helpful hints, useful advice and interesting anecdotes:

Meg Barlow, Benjamin Blaise, Lori Chesney, Stuart and Pamela Davis, Lisa Duncan, Hans Eckert, Helary Guillaume, Laurie Joyce, Peter Kawohl, Tanja Muecke, Sian Olsen, Raphael Richards, Jessica Schoeller, Prashant Sharan, Ronald Wolff, Beth and Greg Stehulak.

AUTHOR THANKS

Sara Benson

Thanks to Margo Vitarelli for the hidden heiau tour in Manoa Valley and to Jan Pickett for helpful Kailua and Lanikai tips. Without Emily Wolman, Jennye Garibaldi, Suki Gear, Sasha Baskett, Alison Lyall and my coauthors Luci Yamamoto, Conner Gorry, Ned Friary, Glenda Bendure, Amy Balfour, Clark Carroll and Ryan Ver Berkmoes, this book wouldn't have been such smooth sailing. Big thanks to Michael Connolly Jr for driving around O'ahu like, a hundred times.

Amy C Balfour

Mahalo to Emily Wolman for entrusting me with this fantastic assignment, and Jennye Garibaldi, who took the helm with finesse. Thanks also to style-maestro Sasha Baskett, hiking expert and CA extraordinaire Sam Benson, and to fab Maui cowriters Ned and Glenda. Kudos to my Maui experts: Jay and Erin Habel, Beckee Morrison and Kihei's Na'auso Book Club, plus Libby Fulton, Gary Hogan, John Christopher, Judy Heilman, Tim Schools, Sheila Gallien, Collin Chang, Brayzlee Ilikea Dutro, Keoki Benjamin and Zach Edlao.

E Clark Carroll

All gracious Kaua'i *hoaloha*; especially Rosewood Rosemary, Mini Golf Mike, Surfboard House Simon and Farmaholic Lee. Also, Cath Lanigan for warm correspondence, Emily Wolman, Sam Benson and the entire Hawaii team for guidance, Brandon Presser for gravity, Maria not Maria for *aloha*, Bill W for the road, Barclay for the email, Emma for the walks, Trey for the music, Reed for the phone conversation, Kat for the lobster risotto. Mom and Dad, without y'all this would not be.

Ned Friary & Glenda Bendure

We'd like to especially thank Allen Tom of the Hawaiian Islands Humpback Whale National Marine Sanctuary, Jeff Bagshaw of Haleakalā National Park, Glynnis Nakai of the Kealia Pond National Wildlife Refuge, and slack key guitarist extraordinaire George Kahumoku Jr.

And a big *mahalo nui loa* to the ace team that captained this ship: Emily K Wolman, Sasha Baskett, Jennye Garibaldi and Sam Benson.

Conner Gorry

Many folks helped keep me sane and happy through this guide's crafting, including island girls Carla, Marri and Cristina, and old friends Erva and Mike of Puna. *Mahalos* to my local knowledge crew and Luci Yamamoto, the consummate pro. Ditto coordinating author Sam Benson. Thanks also to Cynthia Rubenstein, Kim Grant and Catherine Direen. Anitra Pickett, and Arne and Ase Borg epitomize *aloha*: one day I hope to repay the favor. And to JSR for all these years.

Ryan Ver Berkmoes

Teri Waros on Moloka'i was infectious with her enthusiasm. And then there are all the people I spoke with at one point or another, whose faces lit up as they shared their thoughts and knowledge of the islands they love. And thanks to the rain gods who flooded out Hwy 450 on Moloka'i causing me to stop and smell the wet fruit, as well. And to Erin who means the heart of the Friendly Isle to me.

Luci Yamamoto

Mahalo to my Big Island insiders, including Danny Akaka, David Bock, Derek Kurisu, Stan Lawrence, Akiko Masuda and Wayne Subica, all of whom gave me invaluable food for thought. I owe much to Jeff Campbell, whose work on prior Big Island chapters informed mine; and to the LP team, especially coordinating author Sam Benson, ever impressive, and my inimitable coauthor, Conner Gorry. Special thanks to MJP, friends and family, especially my parents, who make Hilo remain 'home' to me. *Aloha.*

ACKNOWLEDGMENTS

Climate map data adapted from Peel MC, Finlayson BL & McMahon TA (2007) 'Updated World Map of the Köppen-Geiger Climate Classification', *Hydrology and Earth System Sciences*, 11, 163344.

Cover photograph: Kalalau Valley from a lookout in Koke'e State Park (p555), Ann Cecil. Many of the images in this guide are available for licensing from Lonely Planet Images: www.lonelyplanetimages.com.

This Book

This 10th edition of *Hawaii* was written by Sara Benson, Amy C Balfour, Glenda Bendure, E Clark Carroll, Ned Friary, Conner Gorry, Ryan Ver Berkmoes and Luci Yamamoto, with contributions by Michael Shapiro. The previous edition was written by Jeff Campbell, Glenda Bendure, Sara Benson, Ned Friary, Amanda C Gregg, Scott Kennedy, Ryan Ver Berkmoes and Luci Yamamoto. This guidebook was commissioned in Lonely Planet's Oakland office, and produced by the following:

Commissioning Editors Emily K Wolman, Jennye Garibaldi
Coordinating Editor Angela Tinson
Coordinating Cartographer Diana Duggan
Coordinating Layout Designer Mazzy Prinsep
Managing Editors Sasha Baskett, Kirsten Rawlings
Managing Cartographers Alison Lyall, Amanda Sierp
Managing Layout Designers Chris Girdler, Jane Hart
Assisting Editors Susie Ashworth, Peter Cruttenden, Pat Kinsella, Anne Mulvaney, Charlotte Orr, Helen Yeates
Assisting Cartographers Julie Dodkins, Mick Garrett, Jennifer Johnston, Marc Milinkovic
Assisting Layout Designers Nicholas Colicchia, Jessica Rose, Kerrianne Southway
Cover Research Naomi Parker
Internal Image Research Sabrina Dalbesio
Thanks to Heather Dickson, Ryan Evans, Lisa Knights, Suyin Ng, Raphael Richards, Gabrielle Stefanos, Simon Tillema, Gerard Walker

index

A

accommodations 628-30, *see also individual locations*
activities 34-45, *see also individual activities*
  Hawai'i the Big Island 170
  Kaua'i 467
  Lana'i 413, 415
  Maui 309
  Moloka'i 431-2
  O'ahu 59
agritourism 626
'Ahihi-Kina'u Natural Area Reserve 370
Ahupua'a o Kahana State Park 143
air travel 637, 638
airports 637
  Hawai'i the Big Island 170
  Kaua'i 466
  Lana'i 415
  Maui 308
  Moloka'i 435
  O'ahu 58
Akaka Falls State Park 258, **191**
Akoni Pule Highway 229-30
Alaka'i Swamp 559, **558**
aloha 12
Aloha festivals 25, 108
aloha shirts 581
altitude sickness 643
Anahola 497-8
animals 569-70, 616-17
  coqui frogs 278
  feral animals 448, 474, 621
  Laysan Albatross 85, **85**
  manta rays 14, 229, **14**
  monk seals 617
  turtles 368, 426, 452, 626
'Anini 506-7
annexation 578-80

aquariums

  Maui Ocean Center 352
  Sea Life Park 129
  Waikiki Aquarium 105
area codes 635

art museums & galleries

  Art 103 533
  Chinatown 71
  Contemporary Museum 71
  Contemporary Museum at First Hawaiian Center 67
  Donkey Mill Art Center 192
  East Hawai'i Cultural Center 263
  Hanapepe 544
  Hawai'i State Art Museum 63
  Honolulu Academy of Arts 69
  Hui No'eau Visual Arts Center 377
  Isaacs Art Center 235-6
  Lahaina Arts Society 311
  SKEA 206
  Turnbull Studios & Sculpture Garden 339
  Volcano Art Center 283
  Volcano Garden Arts 294
  Wailoa Center 263
arts 603-8
astronomy 15, 45, 217, 242, 243, 245, 328, 547
ATMs 632

B

backpacking, *see* hiking
Barking Sands 551-2
bats 616
Battle of Nu'uanu 132

beach parks

  Ala Moana Beach Park 62
  'Anaeho'omalu Beach Park 215
  Anahola Beach Park 497
  'Anini Beach Park 507
  Bellows Field Beach Park 132
  Disappearing Sands 172
  Ha'ena Beach Park 522
  Hana Beach Park 393
  Hanaka'o'o Beach Park 325
  Hau'ula Beach Park 144
  Holoholokai Beach Park 222
  Honokowai Beach Park 331
  Ho'okipa Beach Park 8, 371, **363**
  Hulopo'e Beach 13, 423, 620, **13, 420**
  Kahana Bay 143
  Kahe Point Beach Park 160
  Kaiaka Bay Beach Park 152
  Kaihalulu Beach 147
  Kalama Beach Park 134
  Kalepolepo Beach Park 354
  Kama'ole Beach Parks 354
  Kapa'a Beach Park 491
  Kapi'olani Beach Park 101
  Kehena Beach 280
  Keokea Beach Park 233
  Kolekole Beach Park 257
  Kualoa Regional Park 141
  Kuilima Cove 147
  Lanikai Beach 134
  Lydgate Beach Park 479
  Magic Sands 172
  Mai Poina 'Oe Ia'u Beach Park 354
  Makapu'u Beach Park 129, **127**
  Manini Beach 203
  Mokule'ia Beach Park 156
  Old Quarry 150
  One Ali'i Beach Park 436
  Papalaua Beach Park 324
  Papohaku Beach Park 458
  Po'ipu Beach Park 530
  Punalu'u Beach Park 298
  Pupukea Beach Park 149-50
  Salt Pond Beach Park 544
  Sandy Beach Park 128
  Ukumehame Beach Park 324
  Wahikuli Wayside Park 325
  Wai'alae Beach Park 122
  Wai'olena & Wai'uli Beach Parks 260
  Wawaloli (OTEC) Beach 210
  White Sands Beach Park 172, 173
  Whittington Beach Park 298
beaches 20, 34-5, *see also* beach parks, nudist beaches, surf beaches & breaks, swimming beaches
  Baby Beach 531
  Brennecke's Beach 530
  Glass Beach 542
  Halona Blowhole & Cove 128
  Hanalei 513-14
  Hawai'i the Big Island 172
  Kaua'i 489
  Kealia Beach 497
  Kepuhi Beach 458
  Larsen's Beach 499
  Lumaha'i Beach 521
  Make Horse Beach 457
  Maui 338
  Mo'omomi Beach 452-3
  O'ahu 101
  Papohaku Beach 458
  Pu'u Poa Beach 508
  Shipwreck Beach 531
beer 176, 596, 599
bicycle travel 41, 638-9, *see also* mountain biking

650

bicycle travel *continued*
 Hawai'i the Big Island 171
 Kaua'i 467
 Maui 347, 406
 Moloka'i 431, 435
 O'ahu 59, 79
Big Beach (Oneloa) 369
bird refuges & sanctuaries
 James Campbell National Wildlife
  Refuge 147
 Kanaha Pond Bird Sanctuary
  341
 Kaohikaipu Island 129
 Kealia Pond National Wildlife
  Refuge 351
 Manana Island 129
 Moku'auia (Goat Island) 145
 Mokuho'oniki 446
bird watching 617
birds 616
Bishop Museum 73-5
boat travel 638, 639
bodysurfing & bodyboarding 35
books 564, *see also* literature
 culture 584, 586, 587, 588
 food 601
 history 567, 569, 572, 573, 579,
  582
 nature 619
breweries 176
Bronte, Emory 443
budget 18
bus travel 639
 Hawai'i the Big Island 171
 Kaua'i 467
 Maui 308, 332
 O'ahu 59-60
business hours 630

C
campervans 270
camping 629
 Hawai'i the Big Island 169
 Kaua'i 466
 Maui 308
 Moloka'i 429-31
 O'ahu 58
canoeing 40, 108, 178, *see also*
 kayaking
Cape Kumukahi 279
Captain Cook (town) 201-3, *see also*
 Cook, Captain James
car travel 19, 522, 626, 632, 639, *see*
 also scenic drives
 Hawai'i the Big Island 171

000 Map pages
000 Photo pages

Kaua'i 467
Lana'i 415
Maui 309
Moloka'i 435
O'ahu 60
caves & lava tubes, *see also* caving
 Blue Room 524
 Hana Lava Tube 391
 Kaneana Cave 163
 Kanohina cave system 302
 Kazumura Cave 274
 Kula Kai Caverns 302
 Maniniholo Dry Cave 523
 Pua Po'o 290
 Wai'anapanapa State Park 391
 Waikanaloa Wet Cave 524
 Waikapala'e Wet Cave 524
caving 41, 170, 275, 286, 303
cell phones 19, 635
Chain of Craters Road 285-7, **191**
cheese 318, 501
chickens 474
children, travel with 46-9
 Hawai'i the Big Island 192, 214
 Kaua'i 490
 Lana'i 423
 Maui 381
 Moloka'i 445
 O'ahu 80, 83
Chinaman's Hat 141
Chinatown 68-9, 71, **64-5**
 food 86-7
 walking tours 81
Chinese medicine 69
chocolate 602
 Kona Chocolate Festival 188
 Original Hawaiian Chocolate
  Factory 188
 Steelgrass Farm 480
churches
 Christ Memorial Episcopal Church
  501
 David Malo's Church 355
 Father Damien's Church 454
 Holy Ghost Church 382
 Imiola Congregational Church
  236
 Ka'ahumanu Church 347
 Kalahikiola Church 233
 Kalua'aha Church 444
 Kaulanapueo Church 386
 Kaunakakai 436
 Kawaiaha'o Church 67
 Ke Ola Mau Loa Church 236
 Lanakila 'Ihi'ihi o Iehova Ona
  Kaua 388
 Lihu'e Lutheran Church 471
 Moku'aikaua Church 176
 Our Lady of Seven Sorrows 444

St Andrew's Cathedral 68
St Benedict's Painted Church
 206
St Joseph's Church 443, **440**
St Peter's Church 187
St Philomena Church 454
Star of the Sea Church 282
Waialua Congregational Church
 445
Waine'e (Waiola) Church 312
Wai'oli Hui'ia Church & Wai'oli
 Mission House 514
Wananalua Congregational Church
 393
cinemas 93, 271, 477
climate 18, *see also individual regions*
climate change 637
coffee 193, 570, 596, **570**
coffee farms & factories
 Coffees of Hawaii 450
 Greenwell Farms 197
 Holualoa Kona Coffee Company
  193
 Hula Daddy Kona Coffee 193
 Kaua'i Coffee Company 542
 Kona Blue Sky Coffee 193
 Kona Coffee Living History Farm
  197
 Long Ears Coffee 249
 Mountain Thunder Coffee
  Plantation 193
consulates 634
Cook, Captain James 202, 204, 546,
 572-3
coqui frogs 278
courses 79-80, 108, 630
crafts 603-8
credit cards 632
cruises 638
culture 564-5, 584-90
 books 584, 586, 587, 588
 etiquette 589
currency 18, 19
customs regulations 630
cycling, *see* bicycle travel

D
dangers, *see* safety
dengue fever 642
Diamond Head State Monument
 121-3, **127**
disabilities, travelers with 635-6
discount cards 631
dive sites
 Cathedrals 423
 Coral Gardens 324
 Kaiwi Point 194
 Molokini Crater 7, 353, **7**
 Shark's Cove 150, **36**

Suck 'Em Up 194
Three Tables 150
Turtle Pinnacle 194
diving 35-7, 229
Hawai'i the Big Island 170, 176, 205-6
Kaua'i 467, 533-4
Maui 309, 315, 327, 355
Moloka'i 432
O'ahu 59, 107, 135-6, 153
Dole Plantation 158
dolphin encounters 37, 204, 217, 626
drinks 596-7, see also beer, coffee, tea, wine
driving, see car travel, scenic drives
DT Fleming Beach Park 334
Duke, Doris 123
DVDs 629

E
economy 164, 565-6, 588
electricity 629, 631
'Ele'ele 541-2
embassies 634
emergencies 19
End of the Road 287
environmental issues 204, 621-2, 623-6
climate change 637
dolphin encounters 204, 626
feral animals 448, 474, 621
helicopter rides 545, 626
sustainability 565-6, 623-5
etiquette 589
events, see festivals & events
exchange rates 19

F
farmers markets, see markets
farms 252, see also chocolate, coffee farms & factories
Hawaiian Vanilla Company 248
Kauai Kunana Dairy 501
Mauna Kea Tea 249
Onomea Tea Company 259
O'o Farm 382
Purdy's Macadamia Nut Farm 452
Surfing Goat Dairy 381
Volcano Island Honey Company 249
Father Damien 443, 453-4, 455
Fern Grotto 483
ferry travel 478, 639
festivals & events 23-6, see also hula festivals

film 26, 82
food 188, 598
Hawai'i the Big Island 180
Ironman Triathlon World Championship 26, 180, 183
Kaua'i 473, 486, 493, 535-6
Maui 317, 328, 336, 347, 357
Merrie Monarch Festival 24, 268, **582**
Moloka'i 434
O'ahu 80-2, 108
Triple Crown of Surfing 26, 152, 153, **126**
film 565, 608, see also movie & TV sites
film festivals 26, 82
fish 617
fishing 37-8, 622
Hawai'i the Big Island 170, 177, 183, 188
Kaua'i 473
Moloka'i 431
fishponds
'Aimakapa Fishpond 210
'Ai'opio fishtrap 194
Alekoko (Menehune) Fishpond 470
He'eia Fishpond 140
Huilua Fishpond 143
Kahinapohaku fishpond 443, 445
Kalahuipua'a Fishponds 222
Kaloko Fishpond 210
Ko'ie'ie Fishpond 355
Moli'i Fishpond 141
Moloka'i 443
Naha 425
'Ualapu'e Fishpond 443
flash floods 633
food 8, 591-602
cheese 318, 501
chocolate 188, 480, 602
festivals & events 598
fish 595
honey 249
kalo 518
kalua pork 593
macadamia nuts 227, 452
markets 600
pineapples 159, 574, 580, 582
plate lunches 593, 599
poi 518, 593
poke 592, **592**
pupu 592
shave ice 156, 318, 593, **85**
shrimp trucks 146, **126**

Spam 594
taro 518
vanilla 248
French Frigate Shoals 560

G
Garden of the Gods 426, **420**
gardens, see parks & gardens
gay marriage 586
gay travelers 280, 631
geology 568-9, 614
geography 568-9
giardiasis 642
Gilligan's Island 140, 499
gliding 157
global warming 622
golf 41
Ala Wai Golf Course 107
Challenge at Manele 424
Experience at Koele 417
Francis I'i Brown North & South Golf Courses 223
Hawai'i Kai Golf Course 123
Hawai'i the Big Island 170, 223, 226, 266
Hilo Municipal Golf Course 265
Ironwood Hills Golf Course 450
Ka'anapali Golf Courses 328
Kapalua Golf 336
Kaua'i Lagoons Golf Club 472
Kiahuna Golf Club 534
Ko Olina Golf Club 160
Ko'olau Golf Club 140
Kukuiolono Golf Course 540
Makaha Resort & Golf Club 162
Makai Club at the St Regis Princeville Resort 508
Mauna Kea & Hapuna Golf Courses 226
Moanalua Golf Club 79
Naniloa Country Club Golf Course 265
O'ahu 59, 127, 135, 142, 155
Olomana Golf Links 132
Pali Golf Course 140
Po'ipu Bay Golf Course 534
Prince Golf Course 508
Puakea Golf Course 472
Pukalani Country Club 381
SeaMountain 298
Turtle Bay Resort 147
Volcano Golf & Country Club 295
Waiehu Municipal Golf Course 340
Waikoloa Beach & Kings' Courses 216
Wailua Municipal Golf Course 481
Goto, Katsu 249
Green Sands Beach (Papakolea) 300

H

Ha'ena 522-4
Ha'ena State Park 524
Ha'iku 380-1
Hakalau 257-8
Halawa Valley 11, 446-7, **11**
Haleakalā National Park 6, 10, 400-9, 620, **402, 6, 42**
  accommodations 409
  camping 407
  cycling 406, 408
  hiking 403-6, 408-9
Hale'iwa 152-5
Haleki'i-Pihana Heiau State Monument 346
Halema'uma'u Crater 283, **220**
Halepalaoa Landing 425
Hali'imaile 377
Hamakua Coast 248-59, **250-1**
Hamakua Macadamia Nut Company 227
Hana 392-6, **394**
Hanalei 13, 513-21, **515, 13**
Hanalei Bay 13, 513, **13**
Hanalei Valley 513, **578**
Hanapepe 543-6
Hanauma Bay Nature Preserve 124-8, 620
Haneo'o Road Loop 396
hang gliding 43, 59, 382
Hansen's disease 453-4
haole 587
Hapuna Beach State Recreation Area 225
Hauola Pu'uhonua 484
Hau'ula 144
Hawaii Calls 581
Hawaii International Film Festival 26
Hawai'i Kai 123-4
Hawaii Superferry 478
Hawai'i the Big Island 50, 165-303, **166-7**
  accommodations 165
  activities 170
  beaches 172
  camping 169
  children, travel with 192, 214
  climate 165
  festivals & events 180
  food 165, 183, 235
  highlights 166
  itineraries 28, 33, 168
  national, state & county parks 168-71
  planning information 165
  safety 209
  surfing 173
  tours 172, 179, 180
  transportation 170-2, 186, 200
  travel seasons 165
Hawai'i Volcanoes National Park 4, 282-94, 620, **4, 190, 576**
Hawaiian Vanilla Company 248
Hawaii's Plantation Village 159
Hawi 230-2
health 281, 642-3
heatstroke 643
he'e nalu 43
heiau (temples) 228
  Ahu'ena Heiau 175
  Haleki'i-Pihana Heiau State Monument 346
  Halulu Heiau 426
  Hapaiali'i Heiau 187
  Hiki'au Heiau 204
  Hikinaakala Heiau 484
  Holoholoku Heiau 484
  'Ili'ili'opae Heiau 444
  Kalalea Heiau 300
  Kane'aki Heiau 162
  Kane'ele'ele Heiau 298
  Kapuanoni 187
  Kaulu Paoa Hei'au 524
  Kea'iwa Heiau 98
  Ke'eku Heiau 187
  Ku'ilioloa Heiau 161
  Manoa Heritage Center 71
  Mo'okini Luakini Heiau 228, 230
  Pi'ilanihale Heiau 391
  Poli'ahu Heiau 484
  Pu'u o Mahuka Heiau State Monument 150-1
  Pu'ukohola Heiau National Historic Site 227, 228
  Ulupo Heiau State Monument 135
helicopter tours 43, 47, 545, 626
  Hawai'i the Big Island 179
  Kaua'i 473, 544
  Maui 343
herbalists 69
hiking 20, 43-4, 255, 626
  Diamond Head State Monument 122, **127**
  Hau'ula Loop Trail 144
  Hawai'i the Big Island 170, 195, 206, 208, 235
  Hawai'i Volcanoes National Park 288-91, 295
  Ka'ena Point Satellite Tracking Station 163
  Ka'ena Point Trail 164
  Kapa'ele'ele Trail 143
  Kaua'i 467, 485-6, 524, 525-6, 551, 553-4, 555-7
  Kaunala Loop Trail 151
  Kealia Trail 157
  Kuaokala Trail 157
  Kuli'ou'ou Ridge Trail 124
  Likeke Falls Trail 141
  Maui 309, 337, 340, 384, 397, 403-6
  Mauna Kea 243-4, **221**
  Maunawili Falls 132
  Maunawili Trail System 132, **133**
  Nakoa Trail 143
  O'ahu 59, 76-9, 94, 119, 158
  Saddle Road 247-8
  Waihe'e Ridge Trail 340
  Waipi'o Valley 253-5
Hilo 260-74, **262-3, 266**
  accommodations 266-9
  activities 265
  beaches 260-1
  food 269-71, 272
  shopping 272-3
  sights 261-4
historical buildings & sites
  Ali'iolani Hale 67
  Brick Palace 314
  Captain Cook Monument 204
  Hulihe'e Palace 173
  'Iolani Palace 62, **126, 568**
  Kaneana Cave 163
  Moana Surfrider 106
  Pali Kapu o Keoua 204
  Pink Palace 106, **84**
  Queen Emma Summer Palace 75
  Royal Hawaiian 106, **84**
  Washington Place 68
history 567-83
  annexation 578-80
  books 567, 569, 572, 573, 579, 582
  Cook, Captain James 202, 204, 546, 572-3
  creation 568-9
  Great Mahale 575-6
  internet resources 577
  Kamehameha the Great 230, 233, 234, 573-4
  missionaries 574
  Pearl Harbor 7, 96-9, 581-2, **63**
  Polynesian arrivals 570
  sovereignty 583
  statehood 582-3
  sugar & plantation era 576-8
  trading ships 573
  whaling 574
  WWII 97, 581-2

hitchhiking 632, 641
Hokule'a 571
holidays 633
holua 43
Holualoa 192-4
Honalo 196-7
Honaunau 206-7
honey 249
Honoka'a 248-52
Honokohau Harbor 194-6
Honokowai 331
Honolua-Mokule'ia Bay Marine Life Conservation District 334
Honolulu 61-96, **63**, **64-5**
  accommodations 82
  activities 76-9
  Ala Moana 69 70, 87 8, **72-3**
  bars & clubs 91
  beaches 62
  cafes 90
  Chinatown 68-9, 71, 86-7, **64-5**
  courses 79-80
  Downtown 62-8, 83, **64-5**
  festivals & events 80-2
  food 83-90
  Greater Honolulu 73-5, 89-90, **63**
  live music 92
  Makiki Heights 70-3, **76-7**
  performing arts 92-3
  shopping 93-5
  sights 62-75
  tours 80
  transportation 95-6
  University Area 70, 88-9, **72-3**
  Upper Manoa Valley 70-3, **76-7**
  walking tours 81
Honomanu Bay 388
Honomu 258
Honouliuli Forest Reserve 159
Ho'okena 208-9
Ho'okipa Beach Park 8, 371, **363**
Ho'olehua 451-2
horseback riding 44, 47
  Hawai'i the Big Island 206, 236, 255
  Maui 309, 337, 375, 379, 381, 395
  O'ahu 59, 136, 142, 147
Huakini Bay 399
Huelo 386
hula 116-8, 320-3, 330, 541, 603-4
hula festivals 80, 82, 108
  E Pili Kakou I Ho'okahi Lahui 473
  Merrie Monarch Festival 268
  Moku O Keawe 218
Hulopo'e Bay 422-4
Hulopo'e Beach 13, 423, 620, **13**, **420**
Hurricane 'Iniki 537

I
'Iao Valley State Park 350, **363**
immigration 580
insurance
  car 639-40
  health 642
  travel 631
internet access 631
internet resources 294
  air tickets 637
  children, travel with 48
  environmental issues 622, 623
  health 642
  history 577
  news 566
  planning 19
  stargazing 242
  surfing 340
'Iolani Palace 62, **126**, **568**
Ironman Triathlon World Championship 26, 180, 183
itineraries 27-33
  Hawai'i the Big Island 28, 33, 168
  Kaua'i 31, 33, 463
  Lana'i 32, 413
  Maui 30, 32, 305
  Moloka'i 32, 429
  O'ahu 27, 33, 55

J
James Campbell National Wildlife Refuge 147
Jaws 376
JFK Profile 350
Jurassic Park 142

K
Ka Lae 300-1
Ka'a'awa 142
Ka'anapali 326-30, **327**
Ka'awaloa Cove 204
Ka'ena Point 157
Ka'ena Point State Park 163-4
Kahakuloa 339
Kahakuloa Head 339
Kahala 121-3
Kahana 331-2
Kahana Valley 142-3
Kahanamoku, Duke 106
Kahe Point 160-1
Kahekili Highway 338-40
Kahekili's Jump 427, **421**
Kaho'olawe 410-11
Kahuku 146
Kahului 340-6, **344**
Kahulu'u Beach Park 173, 187, **29**
Kailua (Maui) 386

Kailua (O'ahu) 6, 133-9, **134**, **6**
Kailua-Kona 172-87, **174**
  accommodations 180-2
  activities 176-80
  bars 184
  beaches 172-3
  festivals & events 180
  food 182-4
  shopping 185-7
  sights 173-6
  tours 180
  transportation 186-7
Kainaliu 197
Kalaheo 540-1
Kalahuipua'a Historic Trail 222
Kalakaua, King 576, 578-9
Kalaloa Point 388
Kalapana 281
Kalaupapa National Historical Park 453-6, 620, **441**
Kalaupapa Peninsula 10, 453-6, **10**, **441**
Kalawao 454
Kalihiwai 506
Kaloko-Honokohau National Historical Park 210
Kalopa State Recreation Area 256
Kalua'aha 444
Kaluakoi Resort Area 457-8
Kamakou Preserve 448-9, 620, **441**
Kamalo 443
Kamehameha III 575
Kamehameha the Great 230, 233, 234, 573-4
Kaneana Cave 163
Kane'ohe 139-40
Kanepu'u Preserve 425
Kaohikaipu Island 129
kapa 606
Kapa'a 491-7, **492**
Kapa'au 232-4
Kapalua 333-8, **335**
Kap'iolani 577
Kapoho 278
kapu 575
Ka'u 297-303, **300**
Kaua'i 51, 462-561, **464-5**
  accommodations 462
  activities 467
  beaches 489
  camping 466
  children, travel with 490
  climate 462
  festivals & events 473, 486, 493, 535-6
  food 462
  highlights 464
  highways 498

Kaua'i continued
itineraries 31, 33, 463
planning information 462
state & county parks 463-6
surfing 466
tours 473, 544
transportation 466-7, 494
travel seasons 462
Kauikeaouli 575-6
Kaumahina State Wayside Park 387-8
Kaunakakai 435-42, **437**
accommodations 437-8
activities 436-7
food 438-9
shopping 439-42
sights 436
transportation 442
Kauna'oa Bay 225
Kaunolu 426-7
Kaupo 399
Ka'upulehu 213-14
Kawa Bay 173
Kawa'aloa Bay 452
Kawaihae 226-9
Kawaihae Harbor 173
Kawela 443
Kawela (Turtle) Bay 147
kayak fishing 188
kayaking 38, 205, see also canoeing
Hawai'i the Big Island 170, 195
Kaua'i 467, 484, 528
Maui 309
Moloka'i 431
O'ahu 59, 135
Kazumura Cave 274
Kea'au 274-5
Keahole Point 210-11
Keahua Arboretum 481
Kealakekua 197-201
Kealakekua Bay State Historical Park
9, 173, 203-6, 620, **9**
Kealia Beach 497
Kealia Pond National Wildlife Refuge
351
Ke'anae 388-9
Keauhou Bay 188
Keauhou Resort Area 187-92
Kekaha 551
Kekaha Kai State Park 173, 211-13
Keokea 384-5
Keomuku 425
Keomuku Road (Hwy 44) 424-5
Kihei 353-64, **355**, **356**
accommodations 358-9

activities 355-7
bars & pubs 361
beaches 354
food 359-61
festivals & events 357
shopping 361-4
sights 354-5
transportation 364
Kiholo Bay 214-15
Kilauea 499-506, 614, **502**, **615**
King Kalakaua 576, 578-9
Kipahulu 397-8
Kipahulu Area ('Ohe'o Gulch) 408-9
kitesurfing 38
Maui 309, 342
O'ahu 59
Ko Olina Resort 160
Kohala 215-35, **216**, **231**
Kohala Mountain Road 232
Koke'e State Park 554-61, 620,
556, **504**
Koko Crater 128
Koko Head Regional Park 128
Kolekole Pass 158-9
Koloa 526-30
Kona Chocolate Festival 188
Kona Cloud Forest Sanctuary 195
Kona Coast 196-214, **198**, **212**
Ko'olau Ditch 387
Ko'olau Forest Reserve 386
Ko'olau Road 498-9
Kualapu'u 449-50
Kualoa 141-2
Kualoa Ranch 142
Kukuihaele 252
Kula 381-3

L
La Pe'rouse Bay 370
Lahaina 310-22, **312**
accommodations 317-18
activities 315
bars & pubs 320
festivals & events 317
food 318-20
shopping 321
sights 311-14
tours 315-17
transportation 322
walking tours 316
La'ie 144-5
Lana'i 51, 412-27, **414**
accommodations 412, 417-22, 424
activities 413-15
children, travel with 423
climate 412
food 412
highlights 414

itineraries 32, 413
planning information 412
surfing 416
transportation 415
travel seasons 412
Lana'i City 416-22, **419**
land rights & ownership 142
language 19
language courses 80, 108
Launiupoko Beach Park 323
Laupahoehoe 256-7
Lava Tree State Monument 278
lava tubes, see caves & lava tubes
Lawai International Center 526
Laysan albatross 85, **85**
Laysan Island 561
legal matters 632
lei 609-11, **22**, **585**, **612**, **613**
leprosy 453-4
leptospirosis 642
lesbian travelers 280, 631
Liholiho 575
Lihu'e 468-79, **468**, **472**, **505**
accommodations 474-5
activities 471-3
beaches 469
festivals & events 473-4
food 475-7
nightlife 477
shopping 477-8
sights 469-71
tours 473
transportation 479
Lindbergh, Charles 397
literature 606-8, see also books
Lo'ihi Seamount 614
lookouts, see viewpoints
Lost 142, 157
luau 14, 597-8
Hawai'i the Big Island 184-5,
224, 226
Kaua'i 488
Maui 320-3, 330
O'ahu 118-19
Old Lahaina Luau 14, 321, **14**

M
Ma'alaea 323-5, 351-3
macadamia nuts 277, 452
magazines 566
Magnetic Peak 403
Maha'ulepu Coast 535
mahu 586
Ma'ili 161
Makaha 162
Makapu'u Point 129
Makawao 377-80
Makena 368-70, **366**

Makena Bay 369
Makena State Park 368-9, 620
Makole'a Beach 212
Makua Valley 162-3
Malaekahana State Recreation Area
    145-6, 620
Manana Island 129
Manele Harbor 423-4
manta rays 14, 229, **14**
Manuka State Wayside Park 303
maps 632
marathons 26, 44, 82, 343
marine reserves & refuges
    'Ahihi-Kina'u Natural Area Reserve
        370
    Hawaiian Islands Humpback Whale
        National Marine Sanctuary 354
    Honolua-Mokule'ia Bay Marine Life
        Conservation District 334
    Papahanaumokuakea Marine
        National Monument 560-1
markets 11, 600
    Chinatown Markets 68
    Hilo Farmers Market 262
    Kaua'i 476
    Kaunakakai 439
    Keauhou Farmers Market 188
    Kino'ole Farmers Market 262
    Maku'u Craft & Farmers Market
        275
    Na'alehu Market 299
    Saturday Farmers Market at
        KCC 123
    Space Farmers Market 280
    Volcano Farmers Market 294
    Waialua Farmers Market 156
    Waimea Farmers Market 236
Matsumoto's 156
Maui 51, 304-411, **306-7**, **324**
    accommodations 304
    activities 309
    beaches 338
    camping 308
    children, travel with 381
    climate 304, 305
    festivals & events 317, 328, 336,
        347
    food 304, 383
    highlights 306
    itineraries 30, 32, 305
    national, state & county parks
        305, 308
    planning information 304
    surfing 310, 340, 376
    tours 310, 315-17, 343
    transportation 308, 332, 347
    travel seasons 304
Mauna Kea 15, 240-7, 620, **244-5**,
    15, **221**

Mauna Kea Resort Area 225-6
Mauna Lani Resort Area 222-4
Maunalei 425
Maunaloa 457
measures 629
medical services 642
Merrie Monarch Festival 24, 268, **582**
Meyer, Rudolph Wilhelm 450
Midway Islands 561, 620
military presence 622
Miloli'i 209
minigolf 501
missionaries 66-7, 574
mobile phones 19, 635
Mokoli'i 141
Moku o Lo'e 140
Mokuho'oniki 446
Mokule'ia 156-7
Mokule'ia Army Beach 156
Mokumanamana 560
Moloka'i 51, 428-61, **430**, **432-3**
    accommodations 428, 434
    activities 431-2
    beaches 438
    camping 429-31
    children, travel with 445
    climate 428
    festivals & events 434
    food 428, 434-5, 442
    highlights 430
    itineraries 32, 429
    national, state & county parks
        429, 431
    planning information 428
    tours 432-4
    transportation 435
    travel seasons 428
Moloka'i Forest Reserve 448
Molokai Mule Ride 10, 455, **10**
Moloka'i Ranch 456, 459
Molokini Crater 7, 353, **7**
money 19, 630, 632-3
monk seals 617
Mo'okini Luakini Heiau 228, 230
Mo'omomi Beach 452-3
motorcycle travel 641, see also
    scenic drives
    Hawai'i the Big Island 171
    Kaua'i 467
    Lana'i 415
    Maui 309
    Moloka'i 435
    O'ahu 60
mountain biking, see also bicycle
    travel
    Ka'ena Point Trail 164
    Kaunala Loop Trail 151
    Moloka'i 431

O'ahu 59
movie & TV sites
    Gilligan's Island 140, 499
    Jurassic Park 142
    Kualoa Ranch 142
    Lost 142, 157
    Six Days Seven Nights
        531
    Tora! Tora! Tora! 159
    Tropic Thunder 487
Mt Wai'ale'ale 486
mule rides 10, 455, **10**
multiculturalism 585-7
Munro Trail 11, 422, **11**
museums, see also art museums &
    galleries
    Alexander & Baldwin Sugar
        Museum 351
    Anna Ranch Heritage Center
        236
    Astronaut Ellison S Onizuka Space
        Center 211
    Bailey House Museum 347
    Baldwin House 312
    Bishop Museum 73-5
    Grove Farm Museum 470
    Hale Pa'ahao 312
    Hale Pa'i 314
    Hana Cultural Center 393
    Hawai'i Army Museum 106
    Hawaii Children's Discovery
        Center 80
    Hawai'i Heritage Center 69
    Hawai'i Maritime Center 67
    Hawaiian Islands HumpbackWhale
        National Marine Sanctuary
        354
    HN Greenwell Store Museum
        198
    'Imiloa Astronomy Center of
        Hawai'i 261
    Jaggar Museum 283
    Kamokila Hawaiian Village 481
    Kaua'i Museum 470
    Ka'upuleho Cultural Center 214
    Kenji's House 233
    Lahaina Heritage Museum 311
    Lana'i Culture & Heritage Center
        416
    Lyman Museum & Mission
        House 261
    Mission Houses Museum 66-7
    Mokupapapa Discovery Center
        263
    Moloka'i Museum & Cultural
        Center 450
    North Shore Surf & Cultural
        Museum 153
    Old Lahaina Courthouse 311
    Pacific Tsunami Museum 261

656

museums *continued*
Pahoa Museum 275
Schaefer International Gallery
341
West Kaua'i Technology & Visitors
Center 546
Whalers Village Museum
326
Wo Hing Museum 311
music 116, 565, 604-5
myths & legends
'Iao Needle 350, **363**
Kalo 518
Maui 328
night marchers 253
Pele 43, 577
Polihale 553
Pu'u Pehe 423, **420**
Red Waters 392

N
Na Pali Coast State Park 5, 524-6,
620, **5**
Na'alehu 298-9
Naha 425
Nahiku 390
Nakalele Point 338
Nanakuli 161
Napili 332-3
national, state & county parks 619-20,
see also marine reserves &
refuges, wildlife refuges &
sanctuaries
Ahupua'a o Kahana State Park
143
Akaka Falls State Park 258, **191**
Ha'ena State Park 524
Haleakalā National Park 6, 10,
400-9, 620, **402, 6, 42**
Hanauma Bay Nature Preserve
124-8, 620
Hapuna Beach State Recreation
Area 225
Hawai'i the Big Island 168-71
Hawai'i Volcanoes National Park 4,
282-94, 620, **4, 190, 576**
He'eia State Park 140
'Iao Valley State Park 350, **363**
Ka'ena Point State Park 163-4
Kalaupapa National Historical Park
453-6, 620, **441**
Kaloko-Honokohau National
Historical Park 210
Kalopa State Recreation Area 256
Kaua'i 463-6

000 Map pages
000 Photo pages

Kaumahina State Wayside Park
387-8
Kea'iwa Heiau State Recreation
Area 98
Kealakekua Bay State Historical
Park 9, 173, 203-6, 620, **9**
Kekaha Kai State Park 173, 211-13
Koke'e State Park 554-61, 620,
556, 504
Lai'e Point State Wayside 145
Lapakahi State Historical Park 229
Lava Tree State Monument 278
MacKenzie State Recreation
Area 280
Makena State Park 368-9, 620
Malaekahana State Recreation
Area 145-6, 620
Manuka State Wayside Park 303
Maui 305, 308
Moloka'i 429, 431
Na Pali Coast State Park 5, 524-6,
620, **5**
O'ahu 55-8
Old Kona Airport State Recreation
Area 172
Pala'au State Park 450-1
Polihale State Park 552, **505**
Polipoli Spring State Recreation
Area 383-4
Pu'uhonua o Honaunau National
Historical Park 207-8
Wai'anapanapa State Park 391-2
Waimea Canyon State Park 12,
552-4, 620, **556, 12**
Natural Energy Laboratory of Hawaii
Authority 211
natural formations
bellstone 339
Dragon's Teeth 334
Garden of the Gods 426, **420**
'Iao Needle 350, **363**
JFK Profile 350
Kauleonanahoa 451
phallic stone 451
Pohaku Kani 339
Pu'u Konanae 497
Pu'u o Kaiaka 458
Pu'u Pehe 423, **420**
Spouting Horn Beach Park 533
Necker Island 560
newspapers 566, 629
Nihoa 560
Ni'ihau 460-1
Northwestern Hawaiian Islands
560-1
nudist beaches
Kaihalulu (Red Sand) Beach 393
Kauapea (Secrets) Beach 499
Pu'u Ola'i Beach 369
nudity 632

Numila 541-2
Nu'u Bay 399

O
O'ahu 50, 54-164, **56-7**
accommodations 54, 137
activities 59
camping 58
climate 54
food 54, 89, 115
highlights 56-7
itineraries 27, 33, 55
national, state & county parks
55, 58
planning 54
transportation 58, 99
travel seasons 54
Obama, President Barack 78, 585
observatories, *see also* planetariums
Science City 403
WM Keck Observatory Office
236
WM Keck Observatory visitor
gallery 243
Ocean Rider Seahorse Farm 211
Ocean View 301-2
'Ohe'o Gulch 397, 408-9
Okolehao Trail 516
Old Lahaina Luau 14, 321, **14**
Olowalu 323
Onizuka Visitor Information
Station 245
Onomea 259
opening hours 630
Original Hawaiian Chocolate Factory
188
outrigger canoeing, *see* canoeing

P
Pahala 297
Pahoa 275-7
Pa'ia 8, 371-7, **374**
Pala'au State Park 450-1
Pali Coast 447-8
Pali Hwy 129-30
Pali Kapu o Keoua 204
Papahanaumokuakea Marine National
Monument 560-1
Papaikou 259
paragliding 43, 59, 382
parks & gardens, *see also* national,
state & county parks
Akatsuka Orchid Gardens 295
Ali'i Kula Lavender 382
Amy BH Greenwell Ethnobotanical
Garden 200
Banyan Tree Square 311
Enchanting Floral Gardens 382

Foster Botanical Garden 69
Fuku-Bonsai Cultural Center 274
Garden of Eden Arboretum 387
Hale Kahiko 314
Hawaii Tropical Botanical
    Garden 259
Ho'omaluhia Botanical Garden 139
Kahanu Garden 390
Kalama Park 354
Kapi'olani Park 106
Keahua Arboretum 481
Kea'iwa Heiau State Recreation
    Area 98
Kepaniwai Park & Heritage
    Gardens 350
Koko Crater 128
Kukuiolono Park 540
Kula Botanical Garden 382
Lili'uokalani Park 261
Limahuli Garden 523
Lucy Wright Park 546
Lyon Arboretum 70-1
Maui Nui Botanical Gardens
    341
Moir Gardens 531
Mokuola (Coconut Island) 261
Na 'Aina Kai Botanical Gardens
    500
National Tropical Botanical
    Garden 531
Paleaku Gardens Peace
    Sanctuary 206
Prince Kuhio Park 533
Pua Mau Place 229
Sacred Garden of Maliko 379
Senator Fong's Plantation &
    Gardens 140
Smith's Tropical Paradise 481
Tropical Gardens of Maui 350
Wahiawa Botanical Garden 158
Waimea Valley 150
World Botanical Gardens 257
passports 634
Pearl Harbor 7, 96-9, 581-2, **63**
Pele 43, 577
Pepe'ekeo 259
petroglyphs 219
    Kukui Petroglyphs 424
    Luahiwa Petroglyphs 422
    Olowalu Petroglyphs 323
    Pohue Bay 302
    Puako Petroglyph Preserve
        222
    Pu'u Loa Petroglyphs 287
    Waikoloa Petroglyph Preserve
        215
phonecards 635
Pi'ilani Highway 398-400
pineapples 159, 574, 580, 582
planetariums 75

planning, *see also individual regions*
    activities 34-45
    budgeting 18
    calendar of events
        23-6
    children 46-9
    Hawaii basics 18-19
    Hawaii's regions 50-1
    internet resources 19
    itineraries 27-33
    travel seasons 18, 23-6
plants 617-19
    banyans 261
    hapu'u 619
    hibiscus 618
    'Ilima 613, **613**
    koa 619
    ohia 619
    pineapples 159, 574, 580, 5
        82
    proteas **618**
    silversword 441, **441**
Pohaku Kani 339
Pohoiki Bay 173
Po'ipu 530-40, **532-3**
Polihale 553
Polihale State Park 552, **505**
Polihua Beach 426
Polipoli Spring State Recreation
    Area 383-4
Pololu Valley 234-5
Polynesia 615
Polynesian Cultural Center
    144
population 564, 585-7
Port Allen 542-3
postal services 634
Post-a-Nut 452
Princeville 507-13, **509**
private land 434
Puako 224-5
public holidays 633
Pukalani 381
Puko'o 444-5
Puna 274-82, **276**
Punalau Beach 338
Punalu'u 143-4, 298
Pu'u Keka'a 328
Pu'u Pehe 423, **420**
Pu'uhonua o Honaunau National
    Historical Park 207-8
Pu'unene 350-1

Q
Queen Lili'uokalani
    579-80
Queen's Bath 510
quilting 606, **607**

R
radio 566, 581, 629
ranches
    Kahua Ranch 233
    Kualoa Ranch 142
    Moloka'i Ranch 456, 459
    Na'alapa Stables 233
    Parker Ranch 239
    Ponoholo Ranch 233
    Pu'u O Hoku Ranch 446
    Thompson Ranch 384
    'Ulupalakua Ranch 385-6
recycling 507, 625
Red Road 278-81
religion 565, 574, 575, 586, *see also*
    myths & legends
retreats
    Kalani Oceanside Retreat 281
    Ramashala 281
road rules 19
Road to Hana 5, 385-92, **5**, **21**
Road to the Sea 302-3
Royal Gardens 292
running 26, 44, 82, 343
Russian Fort Elizabeth 547

S
Saddle Road 247-8, **29**
safety 636
    water 35, 526, 633
    hitchhiking 632, 641
    road rules 641
sailing 38, 107, 327
scams 633
scenic drives 21
    Chain of Craters Road 285-7, **191**
    Haneo'o Road Loop 396
    Keomuku Road (Hwy 44) 424-5
    Pepe'ekeo 4-Mile Scenic Drive 259
    Pi'ilani Highway 398-400
    Road to Hana 5, 385-92, **5**, **21**
    Tantalus-Round Top Scenic Drive 72
    Waimea Canyon Dr 552
Schofield Barracks Military
    Reservation 158
Science City 403
Sea Life Park 129
seahorses 211
Secret Cove 370
senior travelers 631
Shangri La 123
shark diving 352
sharks 523
Shark's Cove **36**
shave ice 156, 318, 593, **85**
shopping 633, 635
Six Days Seven Nights 531
skiing 246

skydiving 59, 157
slack key guitar 605
small towns 21
Smith, Ernest 443
smoking 632
snorkeling 38-9, 229
  Garden Eel Cove 173
  Hawai'i the Big Island 170, 178, 187, 204, 208, 280
  Kaua'i 467, 521, 530
  Maui 309, 315, 324, 333, 351, 361, 365, 366
  O'ahu 59, 107, 121, 142, 144, 145, 147, 153
  Pu'u Keka'a 326
  Shark's Cove 150
  Three Tables 150
  Two-Step 208
snowboarding 246
South Point 300-1
sovereignty 583
spas 44
  A Hideaway Spa 547
  Alexander Day Spa & Salon 473
  Anara Spa 535
  Angeline's Mu'olaulani 497
  Hale Ho'ola Hawaiian Healing Arts Center & Spa 295
  Halele'a Spa 510
  Hanalei Day Spa 523
  Ihilani Spa 160
  Mamalahoa Hot Tubs & Massage 200
  Mauna Lani Spa 223
  Paradissimo Tropical Spa 275
  Spa at Koa Kea Hotel & Resort 535
  Spa by the Sea 489
  Spa Without Walls 223
  TriHealth Ayurveda 498
  Waikiki 109
Spirits Leap 328
Spreckelsville Beach 372
St Damien 443, 453-4, 455
stand up paddle boarding 39-40, 170, 178
staphylococcus 642
stargazing 15, 45, 217, 242, 243, 245, 328, 547
State Capitol 68
student cards 631
sugar 469, 570, 572, 576-8
Superferry 478
surf beaches & breaks
  Backyards 149

Banyans 173
Banzai Pipeline 149
Cowshead 531
Diamond Head Beach Park 121-2
DT Fleming Beach Park 334
'Ehukai Beach Park 149
First Break 531
Fort DeRussy Beach 101
Halawa Beach 447
Hale'iwa Ali'i Beach Park 152
Hanalei Bay 513
Hawaiian Electric Beach 161
Honoli'i Beach Park 260
Honolua Bay 334-6
Honomanu Bay 388
Isaac Kepo'okalani Hale Beach Park 280
Jaws 376, **7**
Kahalu'u Beach Park 173, 187, **29**
Kanaha Beach Park 341
Kawa Bay 298
Ke'ei Bay 203
Kuilei Cliffs Beach Park 121
Launiupoko Beach Park 323
Lawa'i (Beach House) Beach 531
Mahai'ula Beach 211
Makaha Beach Park 162
Makua Beach 163
Middles 514
Pakalas 547
Palauea Beach 365
Pine Trees 173, 210
Pipeline 149
Po'ipu Beach 530
Publics 104
Razors 122
Richardson Ocean Park 173
Rock Point 445
Sunset Beach Park 149
Thousand Peaks 324
Waikokos 514
Waimanalo Bay Beach Park 132
Waimea Bay Beach Park 150
Waiohai 531
Yokohama Bay 164
surfboards 517
surfing 7, 39-40, 43, 47
  Hawai'i the Big Island 173, 179, 195
  internet resources 340
  Kaua'i 466, 467, 534
  Lana'i 416
  Maui 309, 310, 315, 376
  Moloka'i 438
  O'ahu 59, 61, 79, 107, 135
  Triple Crown of Surfing 26, 152, 153, **126**
sustainability 623-6
swimming 35

swimming beaches
  Ahalanui Beach Park 279
  Beach 69 224
  Central Waikiki Beach 101
  Charley Young Beach 354
  Dixie Maru Beach 459
  Fort DeRussy Beach 101
  Gray's Beach 101
  HA Baldwin Beach Park 371
  Hale'iwa Beach Park 152
  Hamoa Beach 396
  Hapuna Beach 225
  Hawaiian Electric Beach 161
  Honokohau Beach 194, 210
  Ho'okena Beach Park 208-9
  Hukilau Beach 144
  James Kealoha Beach Park 260
  Ka'anapali Beach 326
  Kahanamoku Beach 100
  Kahekili Beach Park 326
  Kahili (Rock Quarries) Beach & Pools of Mokolea 499
  Kailua Beach Park 134
  Kaimana Beach 104
  Kamakahonu Beach 176
  Kapalua Beach 334
  Kawakiu Beach 457
  Kawela Bay 147
  Keawaiki Beach 215
  Keawakapu Beach 354
  Ke'e Beach 524
  Kikaua Beach 213
  Kuhio Beach Park 101
  Kukio Beach 214
  Lai'e Beach Park 144
  Magoon's 211
  Ma'ili Beach Park 161
  Makalawena Beach 211
  Makua (Tunnels) Beach 522
  Malu'aka Beach 368
  Manini'owali Beach (Kua Bay) 213
  Mauna Kea Beach 225
  Mau'umae Beach 226
  Mokapu Beach 365
  Moloa'a Beach 499
  Nanakuli Beach Park 161
  Onekahakaha Beach Park 260
  Oneloa Beach 334
  Pali Ke Kua Beach 508
  Pebble Beach 209
  Pohue Bay 302
  Poka'i Bay Beach Park 161
  Polo Beach 365
  Po'olenalena Beach 365
  Punalu'u Beach Park 143
  Queen's Surf Beach 101
  Richardson Ocean Park 260

000 Map pages
000 Photo pages

Sans Souci Beach Park 104
Shipwreck Beach 424
Slaughterhouse Beach 334-6
Spencer Beach Park 227
Ulua & Mokapu Beaches 365
Wailea Beach 365
Waimanalo Beach Park 131
swimming holes, see waterfalls & swimming holes

T

Tahiti Nui 520
Tavares Beach 373
taxis 171, 641
tea
Mauna Kea Tea 249
Onomea Tea Company 259
telephone services 19, 635
temples, see also heiau (temples)
Byōdō-In 139
Daifukuji Soto Mission 196
Izumo Taisha 69
Kaua'i's Hindu Monastery 481
Koloa Historic Buildings 527
Kuan Yin Temple 69
Lahaina Jodo Mission 314
Lai'e Temple 145
Taoist Temple 69
Wood Valley Temple & Retreat Center 299
tennis 44, 147
textiles 606
theaters
Hawaii Theatre 92
Palace Theater 271
theft 633
theme parks
Dole Plantation 158
Hawaii's Plantation Village 159
Polynesian Cultural Center 144
Three Bears Falls 390, **5**
Three Ring Ranch Exotic Animal Sanctuary 177
tiki 362, **191**, **363**
time 635
tipping 632-3
Tora! Tora! Tora! 159
tourism 566, 623
tourist information 635
tours 641, see also helicopter tours
farms 252
Hawai'i the Big Island 172, 179, 180
Kaua'i 473, 544
Maui 310, 315-17, 343
Moloka'i 432-4
O'ahu 80
transportation 19, 637-41, see also air

travel, bicycle travel, bus travel, car travel, ferries, motorcycle travel
travel within
Hawaii 638-41
Hawai'i the Big Island 170-2, 186
Kaua'i 467
Lana'i 415
Maui 308, 332
Moloka'i 435
O'ahu 58
travel to/from
Hawaii 637-8
Hawai'i the Big Island 170
Kaua'i 466
Lana'i 415
Maui 308
Moloka'i 435
O'ahu 58
traveler's checks 633
trekking, see hiking
trespassing 434, 636
Triple Crown of Surfing 26, 152, 153, **126**
Tropic Thunder 487
tsunami 633
turtles 368, 426, 452, 626
TV 565, 629, see also movie & TV sites

U

'Ualapu'e 443
ukulele 604-5, **604**
'Ula'ino Road 390-1
'Ulupalakua Ranch 385-6
University of Hawai'i at Manoa 70
USS Arizona Memorial 7, 96, **7**

V

vacations 633
Valley of the Temples 139
vanilla 248
vegetarian travelers 600
Veuster, Joseph de, see Father Damien
video systems 629
viewpoints
Hanalei Valley Lookout 508
Hanapepe Valley Lookout 540
Kalahaku Overlook 401
Kalaloa Point 388
Kalaupapa Overlook 450
Ke'anae Peninsula Lookout 389
Lana'i Lookout 128
Leleiwi Overlook 401
Ninini Point 470
Nu'uanu Valley Lookout 77
Ohai Viewpoint 339
Pelekunu Valley Overlook 449
Pololu Valley Lookout 234
Pu'u 'Ualaka'a State Wayside 73

Pu'u'ula'ula (Red Hill) Overlook 403
Waikolu Lookout 449
Wailau Peninsula Lookout 389
Wailua Valley State Wayside 389
Waimea Canyon 553
visas 19, 634
vog 296, 643
Volcano (village) 294-7
volcanoes 292, 614
Haleakalā National Park 6, 10, 400-9, 620, **402**, **6**, **42**
Hawai'i Volcanoes National Park 4, 282-94, 620, **4**, **190**, **576**
volunteering 314, 536, 626

W

Wa'a Wa'a 279
Wahiawa 158
Waiahole 140-1
Waialua 155-6, 445-6
Wai'anae 161-2
Wai'anapanapa State Park 391-2
Waikamoi Nature Trail 387
Waikamoi Preserve 401
Waikiki 5, 99-121, **102-3**, **5**, **16**, **85**
accommodations 108-12
activities 106-7
bars & cafes 116-17
beaches 100-4
courses 108
festivals & events 108
food 112-16
gay & lesbian travelers 118
live music & hula 116, 117-18
luau 118-19
nightclubs 118
shopping 119-20
sights 105-6
transportation 120-1
Waikoloa Beach Resort 215-19
Waikoloa Village 215
Wailea 364-8, **366**
Wailua 389, 479-89, **482**
accommodations 486-7
activities 481-6
beaches 479
entertainment 488
festivals & events 486
food 487-8
shopping 489
sights 480-1
transportation 489
Wailua River 484

Wailuku 346-9, **348**

Waimanalo 130-3, **562**

Waimea (Kamuela, Hawai'i the Big Island) 235-40, **237**

Waimea (Kaua'i) 546-51, **548**

Waimea (O'ahu) 148-52

Waimea Canyon State Park 12, 552-4, 620, **556**, **12**

Wainiha Valley 521

Wai'ohinu 299-300

Waipi'o Bay 173

Waipi'o Valley 9, 252-6, **254**, **9**

Waipouli 489-91

walking, see hiking

walking tours
  Chinatown 81
  Honolulu 81
  Lahaina 316

war memorials & monuments
  Battleship *Missouri* Memorial 97
  National Memorial Cemetery of the Pacific 75
  Pacific Aviation Museum 97
  Pearl Harbor 96-9
  USS *Arizona* Memorial 96-7
  USS *Bowfin* Submarine Museum & Park 97

water safety 35, 526, 633

waterfalls & swimming holes 20, 388
  Akaka Falls 258, **221**
  Blue Pool 391
  Haipua'ena Falls 387
  Hanawi Falls 390
  Hi'ilawe Falls 253
  Hipuapua Falls 447

Kahuna Falls 258

Kaluahine Falls 254

Kipu Falls 471

Likeke Falls 141

Makapipi Falls 390

Manoa Falls 77

Maunawili Falls 132

Moa'ula Falls 447

'Opaeka'a Falls 481

Pe'epe'e Falls 264

Puohokamoa Falls 387

Rainbow Falls 263

Three Bears Falls 390, **5**

Twin Falls 386

Uluwehi Falls 484

Waikamoi Falls 387

Wailua Falls 397, 470

watersports 34-41, see also individual activities

weather 18, see also individual regions

weights 629

whale watching 40
  Hawai'i the Big Island 179
  Kaua'i 542
  Maui 323, 352, 354, 358
  Moloka'i 432
  O'ahu 153

whales 511, 617

whaling 572, 574

Whittington Beach Park 298

wi-fi 631

wildlife 615-19, see also animals, plants, individual animals

wildlife refuges & sanctuaries, see also bird refuges & sanctuaries, marine reserves & refuges
  James Campbell National Wildlife

Refuge 147

Kakahai'a National Wildlife Refuge 443

Kealia Pond National Wildlife Refuge 351

Kilauea Point National Wildlife Refuge 500

Three Ring Ranch Exotic Animal Sanctuary 177

windsurfing 8, 40, 41
  Maui 309, 341, 352, 371
  O'ahu 59

wine 295, 597

Wood Valley Temple & Retreat Center 299

woodwork 606

work 636

WWII 97, 581-2, see also war memorials & monuments

Y

yoga 44-5, 79
  Hawai'i the Big Island 179, 200, 265
  Kaua'i 489, 500, 510, 516, 547
  Moloka'i 443
  Maui 380
  O'ahu 136

Z

ziplining 45, 47, **42**
  Hawai'i the Big Island 170, 230, 257
  Kaua'i 471, 509
  Maui 309, 328, 336, 382

zoos
  Honolulu Zoo 106
  Pana'ewa Rainforest Zoo and Gardens 263

000 Map pages
000 Photo pages

how to use this book

These symbols will help you find the listings you want:

- ◉ Sights
- 🏊 Beaches
- 🏃 Activities
- 🔄 Courses
- ☞ Tours
- 🎎 Festivals & Events
- 📋 Sleeping
- ✕ Eating
- 🍷 Drinking
- ☆ Entertainment
- 🛍 Shopping
- ℹ Information/Transport

These symbols give you the vital information for each listing:

- 📞 Telephone Numbers
- ⊙ Opening Hours
- P Parking
- ⊖ Nonsmoking
- ✳ Air-Conditioning
- @ Internet Access
- 🛜 Wi-Fi Access
- 🏊 Swimming Pool
- 🥗 Vegetarian Selection
- 📖 English-Language Menu
- 👪 Family-Friendly
- 🐾 Pet-Friendly
- 🚌 Bus
- ⛴ Ferry
- Ⓜ Metro
- Ⓢ Subway
- ⊖ London Tube
- 🚋 Tram
- 🚆 Train

Reviews are organised by author preference.

Look out for these icons:

- TOP CHOICE — Our author's recommendation
- FREE — No payment required
- 🌱 — A green or sustainable option

Our authors have nominated these places as demonstrating a strong commitment to sustainability – for example by supporting local communities and producers, operating in an environmentally friendly way, or supporting conservation projects.

Map Legend

Sights
- 🏊 Beach
- ▲ Buddhist
- 🏰 Castle
- ✝ Christian
- 🕉 Hindu
- ☪ Islamic
- ✡ Jewish
- 🏛 Monument
- 🏛 Museum/Gallery
- ⊗ Ruin
- 🍷 Winery/Vineyard
- 🦁 Zoo
- ◉ Other Sight

Activities, Courses & Tours
- 🤿 Diving/Snorkelling
- 🛶 Canoeing/Kayaking
- ⛷ Skiing
- 🏄 Surfing
- 🏊 Swimming/Pool
- 🚶 Walking
- 🏄 Windsurfing
- ◎ Other Activity/Course/Tour

Sleeping
- 🛏 Sleeping
- ⛺ Camping

Eating
- ✕ Eating

Drinking
- 🍷 Drinking
- ☕ Cafe

Entertainment
- ✪ Entertainment

Shopping
- 🛍 Shopping

Information
- ✉ Post Office
- ℹ Tourist Information

Transport
- ✈ Airport
- ⊗ Border Crossing
- 🚌 Bus
- 🚡 Cable Car/Funicular
- 🚲 Cycling
- ⛴ Ferry
- Ⓜ Metro
- 🚝 Monorail
- P Parking
- Ⓢ S-Bahn
- 🚕 Taxi
- 🚉 Train/Railway
- 🚋 Tram
- ⊖ Tube Station
- Ⓤ U-Bahn
- • Other Transport

Routes
- Tollway
- Freeway
- Primary
- Secondary
- Tertiary
- Lane
- Unsealed Road
- Plaza/Mall
- Steps
-)=(Tunnel
-)-(Pedestrian Overpass
- Walking Tour
- Walking Tour Detour
- Path

Boundaries
- --- International
- ---- State/Province
- -- Disputed
- Regional/Suburb
- Marine Park
- Cliff
- Wall

Population
- ✪ Capital (National)
- ◉ Capital (State/Province)
- ● City/Large Town
- ● Town/Village

Geographic
- 🏠 Hut/Shelter
- ⚐ Lighthouse
- 👁 Lookout
- ▲ Mountain/Volcano
- 🌴 Oasis
- 🌳 Park
-)(Pass
- 🌳 Picnic Area
- 🏞 Waterfall

Hydrography
- River/Creek
- Intermittent River
- Swamp/Mangrove
- Reef
- Canal
- Water
- Dry/Salt/Intermittent Lake
- Glacier

Areas
- Beach/Desert
- Cemetery (Christian)
- Cemetery (Other)
- Park/Forest
- Sportsground
- Sight (Building)
- Top Sight (Building)